An Introduction to the

NEW TESTAMENT

CONTEXTS, METHODS
& MINISTRY FORMATION

DAVID A. deSILVA

ivp

InterVarsity Press
Downers Grove, Illinois

Apollos
Leicester, England

InterVarsity Press
P.O. Box 1400, Downers Grove, IL 60515-1426
World Wide Web: www.ivpress.com
E-mail: mail@ivpress.com

APOLLOS (an imprint of Inter-Varsity Press, England)
38 DeMontfort Street, Leicester LE1 7GP, England
Website: www.ivpbooks.com
E-mail: ivp@uccf.org.uk

InterVarsity Press® is the book-publishing division of InterVarsity Christian Fellowship/USA®, a student movement active on campus at hundreds of universities, colleges and schools of nursing in the United States of America, and a member movement of the International Fellowship of Evangelical Students. For information about local and regional activities, write Public Relations Dept., InterVarsity Christian Fellowship/USA, 6400 Schroeder Rd., P.O. Box 7895, Madison, WI 53707-7895, or visit the IVCF website at <www.intervarsity.org>.

Design: Cindy Kiple

Cover images: Jerusalem coins: Sandy Brenner

> *Cameo with portrait of Augustus: Italy, Roman, reign of Tiberius, A.D. 14-36. Travertine, H.4.6 cm; W.6.4 cm © The Cleveland Museum of Art. The John L. Severance Fund, 1991.154.*
> *Papyrus of New Testament: Papyrology Collection, University of Michigan*

USA ISBN 0-8308-2746-3

UK ISBN 1-84474-023-4

Printed in the United States of America ∞

Library of Congress Cataloging-in-Publication Data

deSilva, David Arthur.
  An introduction to the New Testament: contexts, methods and
  ministry
formation / David A. deSilva.
     p. cm.
Includes bibliographical references and index.
  ISBN 0-8308-2746-3 (alk. paper)
  1. Bible. N.T.—Introductions. I. Title.
  BS2330.3.D47 2004
  225.6'1—dc22

                                                                                             2003023200

British Library Cataloguing in Publication Data

A catalogue record for this book is available from the British Library.

| **P** | 21 | 20 | 19 | 18 | 17 | 16 | 15 | 14 | 13 | 12 | 11 | 10 | 9 | 8 | 7 | 6 | 5 | 4 | 3 | 2 | 1 |
| **Y** | 21 | 20 | 19 | 18 | 17 | 16 | 15 | 14 | 13 | 12 | 11 | 10 | 09 | 08 | 07 | 06 | 05 | 04 | | | |

In honor of my father,

J. Arthur F. de Silva,

on his seventieth birthday,

and in loving memory of my grandfather,

Stephen Frederick de Silva

(1902-1981)

When the father dies he will not seem to be dead,
for he has left behind him one like himself,
whom in his life he looked upon with joy
and at death, without grief.
He has left behind him an avenger against his enemies,
and one to repay the kindness of his friends.

BEN SIRA 30:4-6

CONTENTS

MAPS

Abbreviations

Dead Sea Scrolls

1QS	*Rule of the Community, Manual of Discipline*
11QT	*Temple Scroll* (11Q19)
4QMMT	*Miqsat Maʿasʾeh ha-Torah* (4Q394-399)
4Q521	*Messianic Apocalypse*
CD	Cairo (Genizah text of the) *Damascus Document/Rule*

Apocrypha and Pseudepigrapha

Jub.	*Jubilees*
1-2-3-4 Macc	1-2-3-4 Maccabees
Sir	Sirach (Ben Sira)
Wis	Wisdom

Ancient Authors and Sources

Aristotle
Eth. Nic.	*Ethica Nicomachea*
Rhet.	*Rhetorica*

Augustine
Quaest. Evan.	*Quaestiones Evangeliorum*

Cicero
De Offic.	*De Officiis*

Dio Chrysostom
Or.	*Orationes*

Diodorus of Sicily
Bib. Hist.	*Bibliotheca Historica*

Epictetus
Diss.	*Dissertationes*
Ench.	*Enchiridion*

Eusebius
Hist. Eccl.	*Historia Ecclesiastica*

Ignatius
Ign. Smyrn.	*Letter to the Smyrneans*

Irenaeus
Haer.	*Adversus Haereses*

Isocrates
Dem.	*Ad Demonicum*

Josephus
Ant.	*Antiquities of the Jews*
Ag. Ap.	*Against Apion*

Life	*Life*
War	*Jewish Wars*
Juvenal	
Sat.	*Satirae*
Philo	
Conf. Ling.	*De Confusione Linguarum*
Fug.	*De Fuga et Inventione*
Leg. All.	*Legum Allegoriae*
Migr. Abr.	*De Migratione Abrahami*
Quaest. in Gen.	*Quaestiones in Genesin*
Quaest. in Ex.	*Quaestiones in Exodum*
Spec. Leg.	*De Specialibus Legibus*
Vit. Mos.	*De Vita Mosis*
Plato	
Cri.	*Crito*
Gorg.	*Gorgias*
Pliny the Younger	
Ep.	*Epistolae*
Plutarch	
Mor.	*Moralia*
Self-Praise	*On Inoffensive Self-Praise*
Polycarp	
Phil.	*Letter to the Philippians*
Pseudo-Aristotle	
Rhet. ad Alex.	*Rhetorica ad Alexandrum*
Pseudo-Cicero	
Rhet. ad Her.	*Rhetorica ad Herennium*
Quintillian	
Inst. Orat.	*Institutio Oratoria*
Seneca	
Ben.	*On Benefits*
Constant.	*De Constantia Sapientis*
Prov.	*De Providentia*
Ep. Mor.	*Epistulae Morales*
Sophocles	
Oed. Col.	*Oedipus at Colonus*
Oed. Tyr.	*Oedipus Tyrannus*
Strabo	
Geog.	*Geographica*
Tacitus	
Ann.	*Annales ab Excessu Divi Augusti*
Hist.	*Historiae*
Thucydides	
Hist.	*History of the Peloponnesian War*

Periodicals and Series

AB	Anchor Bible
ANTC	Abingdon New Testament Commentary
AUSS	*Andrews University Seminary Studies*
BBR	*Bulletin for Biblical Research*
BECNT	Baker Exegetical Commentary on the New Testament
BNTC	Black's New Testament Commentary
BTB	*Biblical Theology Bulletin*
CBQ	*Catholic Biblical Quarterly*
CBQMS	Catholic Biblical Quarterly Monograph Series
CGTC	*Cambridge Greek Testament Commentary*
CTJ	*Calvin Theological Journal*
EvQ	*Evangelical Quarterly*
GBSNTS	Guides to Biblical Scholarship, New Testament Series
HTR	*Harvard Theological Review*
ICC	International Critical Commentary
IVPNTC	IVP New Testament Commentary
JAAR	*Journal of the American Academy of Religion*
JBL	*Journal of Biblical Literature*
JETS	*Journal of the Evangelical Theological Society*
JSNT	*Journal for the Study of the New Testament*
JSNTSup	Journal for the Study of the New Testament Supplement Series
JTS	*Journal of Theological Studies*
LCL	Loeb Classical Library
LEC	Library of Early Christianity
NABPRSS	National Association of Baptist Professors of Religion Special Studies
NCB	New Century Bible
NICNT	New International Commentary on the New Testament
NIGTC	New International Greek Testament Commentary
NovT	*Novum Testamentum*
NTS	*New Testament Studies*
SBLDS	SBL Dissertation Series
SBLSBS	SBL Sources for Biblical Study
SEG	*Supplementum Epigraphicum Graecum*
SIG	*Sylloge Inscriptionum Graecarum*
SJT	*Scottish Journal of Theology*
SNTSMS	Society for New Testaments Studies Monograph Series
TD	*Theology Digest*
TNTC	Tyndale New Testament Commentary
TynB	*Tyndale Bulletin*
WBC	Word Biblical Commentary
WUNT	Wissenschaftliche Untersuchungen zum Neuen Testament

LIST OF TABLES

PREFACE

The Perspective of This Introduction

In our current environment I find two rather different ways of reading and searching the Scriptures. With a devotional reading of Scripture, hearing from God is the focus. The academic study of Scripture focuses on understanding the text in relation to its historical context.[1]

These two approaches and their results are often posed antagonistically against one another. There are critical scholars who devalue the devotional reading of Scripture and the quest to hear the voice of the living God in it. There are others who dismiss the academic study of these texts as inconsequential, since the Spirit is "all they need" to interpret the Scriptures. The former reduce the witness of Scripture to a basic, workable, rational morality that does not interfere with the modern agenda. The latter privilege their potentially idiosyncratic and erroneous readings and applications with divine authority.[2] As the reader will quickly discern, I find neither position and neither result acceptable.

Both kinds of inquiry can and should work together in the community of faith. The academic study of the Scriptures can be used by people of faith as a means to allow the text to speak its own word on its own terms. But this avenue of inquiry is also best pursued prayerfully and in connection with the God who continues to speak through these texts. With these spiritual disciplines, the fruits of academic study are brought back into the conversation with God and with other Christians about what God would say to God's people today through these texts. The critical study of the New Testament acknowledges the distance between the modern reader—in his or her cultural, political, theological and economic setting—from the author and immediate readers of a New Testament text. The devotional use of the New Testament presumes the imme-

---

[1]As J. J. Griesbach, one of the leading figures in nineteenth-century Gospel studies put it, "the New Testament must be explained as every ancient book is explained" (quoted in William Baird, *A History of New Testament Research*, vol. 1, *From Deism to Tübingen* [Minneapolis: Fortress, 1992], p. 139).

[2]David L. Dungan has written a bold analysis of the ways in which the historical-critical study of the Bible arose as part of a movement to delegitimate the power of king and priest and to end religious interference in secular affairs. Historical criticism, he avers, served to reduce Scripture to a book that taught private morality, of no consequence to the political and economic spheres, which were now made safe for capitalism, democracy and rationalism. Reflecting on his own work as a biblical scholar, he writes, "I never knew that I was a foot soldier in a great crusade to eviscerate the Bible's core theology, smother its moral standards under an avalanche of hostile historical questions, and, at the end, shove it aside so that the new bourgeois could get on with the business at hand" (*A History of the Synoptic Problem* [New York: Doubleday, 1999], p. 148). His book serves as a reminder that there are no neutral readings of Scripture and that every reading—whether devotional or critical—grows out of an agenda, legitimates real-life arrangements in this world, and is made possible only by a host of presuppositions about the way things "really" are.

diacy and accessibility of the Word for the worshiper. Pursuing both avenues of inquiry, allowing neither to overwhelm the other, bringing the results of each into vigorous interaction with the other, puts the Christian leader on the surest ground, enjoying the riches of both while being less liable to the limitations of either.

This introduction to the New Testament seeks to nurture this kind of integrated approach to Scripture, attending both to the methods and results of academic and critical study of the New Testament as well as to the ways that these texts continue to speak a word from the Lord about discipleship, community and ministry. My objectives in writing this book are to prepare Christian leaders to (1) more fully engage the critical and prayerful study of the New Testament, and (2) more reliably discern the direction the Spirit would give through these texts for nurturing disciples and building communities of faith that reflect the heart and character of their Lord. These objectives have shaped this introduction in a number of ways.

First, I take a text-centered as opposed to phenomenon-centered approach. My focus remains on the texts that make up the New Testament (and, of course, on the situations envisioned by each text) rather than the broader phenomena behind the New Testament that belong properly to "early church history" and "Christian origins." I am interested primarily in the context, production and message of each text, in the pastoral challenges each addresses and in the way each author brings the revelation of God in Christ to bear on those challenges. There is thus no attempt to reconstruct the Jesus of history, though I do, of course, introduce the working principles of that important scholarly pursuit. There is no discussion of the history of the expansion of the church from the "Q community" to Rome, except insofar as such topics have bearing on reading and understanding particular New Testament texts.

Second, I give a great deal of attention (probably a full tenth of the book) to a wide range of interpretative strategies that represent the major trends in scholarly study of the New Testament and that remain available and accessible for every student's exploration of the text. These "Exegetical Skill" sections appear in every chapter on a New Testament text (twice in some chapters). I usually include an extensive example of the exegetical strategy at work in a particular passage and offer suggestions for further exercises and study. It is my hope that these sections will not only open up new strategies for reading but also enable readers to interact more critically with commentaries and other literature written about the text (including devotional literature *and* sectarian propaganda). The student is urged to employ a variety of these avenues of exploration when studying any particular passage in the New Testament. Each interpretative strategy is designed to answer particular questions or bring into focus certain kinds of data: only in conjunction with one another do they provide a meaningful basis for interpretation.

Third, my discussion of the message of each text, and more particularly my reflections on how the text contributes to ministry formation, gives this textbook a distinctive focus on the church (from the local congregation to the global family of God) and the work of ministry (from the general ministry of all Christians to a variety of professional ministries). These texts are formative and transformative, a facet that often goes unexplored in New Testament introductions. If academic study of these texts is to inform their prayerful and practical application, a New Testament introduction is precisely the place to begin forging that connection. Since I believe that hearing the text in its original pastoral context leads directly to the most fruitful explorations of how the text invites Christian leaders and workers in our age to enflesh its ideals anew, I close each chapter with a section on ministry formation. These sections are intended

1. to keep the reader mindful of the ways that careful study can connect with careful application (to close the gap between the two ends of the typical seminary curriculum, namely, biblical studies and practical theology)

2. to stimulate thought and discussion about what I take to be the primary value and purpose of these texts—shaping faithful disciples, supportive communities of faith and ministry to the world.

In the process of writing this introduction I have been continually reminded and often daunted by the fact that the study of the New Testament is a broad field with many questions and problems that despite centuries of critical study remain unanswered. I do not, therefore, pretend to write as an expert on every topic. Some chapters and sections will reflect years of careful study, reflection and prior writing on my part. Some sections reflect my own initial efforts to wrestle with issues I have encountered but only begun to engage seriously in the preparation and writing of this volume. The reader is therefore invited not to learn from a master but to wrestle alongside a fellow learner with these magnificent texts that have opened up hearts to God, nourished faith and shaped lives for two millennia.

While the footnotes and bibliographies show those older and wiser students to whom an author is indebted for intellectual support, it is the custom of authors to use a preface to acknowledge the many other people whose support, influence, insight and love contribute equally, if not more, to the book. Dr. Dan Reid of InterVarsity Press, who kindly received my proposal for this textbook, offered many helpful suggestions for making the book more useful for the audience it seeks to serve and showed a great measure of patience with this laborer as I took a full year longer to complete the book than we had originally agreed. Several readers made helpful comments after reading portions of the draft of this book, but pride of place must go to Dr. Paul N. Anderson of George Fox University for his generosity in providing many specific, detailed suggestions that have made this textbook stronger.

The majority of illustrations in this book were selected from the more-than-five thousand pictures in the *Pictorial Library of Bible Lands,* a digital collection maintained by Mr. Todd Bolen. This book would have been so much less without the glimpses of important sites and artifacts from the Mediterranean made available by him. I am also grateful to Dr. Michael Bennett and Dr. Rachel Rozenzweig of the Cleveland Art Museum for providing me with images of three important pieces from their collection of Roman Art; Dr. Trainos Gagos, archivist of papyrology and associate professor of papyrology and Greek at the University of Michigan, for permission to use an image of the vitally important manuscript P[46] in his care; and Mr. Ben Primer of Princeton University for permission to reproduce a picture of the fragment of the epistle of James. An important body of illustrative materials is ancient coinage, and I am grateful to Mr. Wayne Pratali of Superior Galleries (Beverly Hills, Calif.); Mr. Victor England and Mr. Brad Nelson of Classical Numismatic Group, Inc. (Lancaster, Penn.); Mr. Edward Waddell Jr. (Edward J. Waddell Ltd., Frederick, Md.); Mr. Edgar L. Owen (Edgar L. Owen, Ltd., Lake Hepatcong, N.J.); and Mr. Sandy Brenner of JerusalemCoins.com for providing images of museum-quality coins from their catalogs and archives. A number of illustrations come from the Flora Archaeological Center at Ashland Theological Seminary, and I thank Mr. Sam Renfroe, our university photographer, and Dr. Kenneth Walther, my colleague in New Testament and curator of the collection, for their assistance. I also wish to thank Mr. Bruce Ferrini for his assistance in acquiring several illustrations, and my graduate assistant Rev. Joseph Burkhardt for compiling the index of ancient citations.

As in all such endeavors, I am grateful to Dr. Frederick J. Finks, president of Ashland Theological Seminary, and the administration and faculty for their ongoing encouragement and support of my research and writing. My wife, Donna Jean, and my sons, James Adrian, John Austin and Justin Alexander, deserve my heartfelt thanks for their support during these difficult two years. They were witnesses to the many struggles I faced as well as to the breakthroughs that make writing, in the end, worthwhile. I thank Donna Jean also for compiling the index of modern authors and for helping compile the subject index for this volume.

Finally, I wish to thank my parents but, in this volume, especially my father, Dr. J. A. F. deSilva. He always pursued excellence in his intellect and in his professional achievements and set a fine example in this regard for me to follow. In my youth he always took the time to take me to the park on weekends and taught me the importance of always finding time to play with my own sons. He taught me that there are two sides to every argument, and he perhaps contributed more than anyone else to my awareness of ideology and rhetorical strategy in people, no less than in texts. It is with gratitude, respect and love that I dedicate this book to him.

David A. deSilva

USING THE
"EXEGETICAL SKILL"
SECTIONS

A primary goal of most courses in New Testament introduction is to cultivate facility in exegetical method. This book seeks to do the same by introducing the reader to a broad, representative sample of the skills that open up a rich, full exegesis of biblical texts. Most often the procedures and results of each skill are discussed not merely in theory but in connection with a specific New Testament passage, along with suggested exercises for developing the particular skill. In this way, the reader can learn about the method, see it in action and apply it.

Exegesis is not fully engaged simply by performing one or two of these methods; rather, the fruits of the application of a good number of these skills must be combined and integrated before the interpreter can truly claim to have mined the text and unearthed its message and significance. Interpreters therefore need a master plan for exegesis that will lead them to engage the text from a wide variety of angles and lenses. This is the goal of many books on exegetical method, the most popular of which, however, seem to me to be far too restrictive in their scope. That is, they tend to focus the interpreter on questions of historical setting, literary genre, grammar and the meaning of words. All of these are important, to be sure, but they do not provide a multidimensional appreciation for the richness of the text.

The paradigm that I employ here is based on a master plan for exegesis called "socio-rhetorical interpretation," a model developed by Vernon K. Robbins.[3] I have found this to be an especially appropriate approach to exegesis for people involved in Christian ministry, since the goal of socio-rhetorical interpretation is to enter as fully as possible into how a text works to persuade its hearers at every level, using a great variety of resources, and to nurture and sustain Christian community in the face of the exigencies of a particular situation. It connects us with the ancient texts precisely in the manner in which modern Christian leaders, again in the face of the exigencies of particular situations, hear, interpret and apply these texts to persuade others to deeper discipleship, and to nurture and sustain meaningful and supportive relationships throughout the global Christian community.

Socio-rhetorical interpretation is not so much a new method (although the less familiar name might suggest this) but rather a model for analysis that encourages interpreters to make use of

---

[3]Vernon K. Robbins, *The Tapestry of Early Christian Discourse: Rhetoric, Society and Ideology* (London: Routledge, 1996); and *Exploring the Texture of Texts: A Guide to Socio-Rhetorical Interpretation* (Valley Forge, Penn.: Trinity Press, 1996).

the full spectrum of established exegetical skill, and to do so in a way that puts the results of each discrete avenue of investigation in conversation with the results of all the other methods. It is a model that invites careful study of the text at a number of levels: the interpreter (1) engages the text itself in detailed analysis, (2) examines the ways the text converses with other "texts" in its environment, (3) investigates the world that produced the text, and (4) analyzes how the text affects that very world. The language Robbins uses is that of a tapestry—many threads are interwoven together in a text to produce multiple textures that together provide us with a rich, three-dimensional understanding of the meaning and impact of the text we are studying.

As we give close attention to the words on a page, we explore "inner texture," the threads that the author has woven together to make a meaningful text. At this level we want to be sure we are as close as possible to the author's original wording (textual criticism) and understand the meanings and connotations of the words that we are reading (word studies, or lexical analysis, and grammatical analysis). We pay careful attention to the way in which the passage derives meaning and significance from its relationship to the whole work of which it is a part, especially from neighboring passages and thematically connected passages (literary context). We examine the ways in which the repetition of words and phrases helps the hearer identify themes, make correlations and the like (repetitive texture). At this stage we also give careful attention to the way in which a text persuades its readers or hearers to accept the values, behaviors or decisions it promotes (rhetorical criticism). We also reflect on the way the text communicates and creates meaning as literature (narrative criticism), and consider ways other genre-specific signals can help us "hear" the text more authentically (interpreting parables; epistolary analysis).

A second level of analysis calls us to examine the conversations the author is creating with other texts, a phenomenon called "intertexture." New Testament authors very often quote verses or incorporate lines from the Hebrew Scriptures; they even more often allude to events, echo phrases and reconfigure the pattern of familiar stories from the Old Testament and intertestamental literature in the new texts they create. Early Christians also drank deeply from the streams of the Greco-Roman and Hellenistic Jewish traditions. What resources, then, does an author use? How does he incorporate, reshape and reapply them? When the audience hears the older texts woven into the new text, what impact will the text have that the passage might not otherwise have made? How does an author's perspective and purpose emerge through the study of changes made to a literary source (redaction analysis)? The fruitfulness of such investigations will be explored as we consider the use of comparative materials in New Testament exegesis and the analysis of intertexture at a variety of levels.

New Testament texts are not merely about words and conversations between texts, but they also enflesh the Word in very real, three-dimensional social and cultural contexts. A third arena for exegesis, then, is social and cultural texture, which moves from the world of the text to the world of the author and audience. Every passage we study speaks out of and to a real historical situation that we must seek to recover, and it represents that situation in a strategically shaped manner (discerning the situation behind a text). The text also has meaning for its hearers because the author shares and communicates within the same social and cultural matrix, which we must fully enter into if we want hear the text as they did. Readers are therefore given a thorough introduction to cultural-anthropological analysis of New Testament texts, first through explicit treatments of the cultural and social environment of the first-century, and then through applications of these insights to the reading of specific texts. The practice and potential fruitfulness of each is highlighted in the context of a discussion of a particular Gospel (honor discourse in Mt, purity and pollution in Mk, patronage and reciprocity in Lk, and kinship in Jn), emerging again in discussions of other texts as appropriate.

Most New Testament texts, like modern sermons based on them, seek to influence history and social relationships as well. We will therefore explore how a passage orients its audience to the world of everyday life and how it seeks to shape their relationships and interactions with one another (social-scientific analysis). What kind of community does a text seek to nurture? What role do rituals and religious symbols play in shaping relationships within the group, and relationships with (or boundaries against) those outside? What is the relationship between the symbols invoked in a text and the real-life behaviors an author wishes to promote?

Finally, we have to consider "ideological texture," which recognizes that a text is not just a vehicle for ideas but rather a vehicle by which the author hopes to achieve a certain goal. What goal or goals drive the author? How does the author use the text to achieve this goal? This may involve changing the audience's perception of their situation, alerting them to dangers that are going unperceived or drawing stark alternatives in order to move the audience to more readily choose the author's favored alternative. Successful analysis of the author's ideological strategy requires the integration of insights gleaned from exploring the other textures. Repetition of words and phrases, rhetorical analysis, use of other texts (intertexture), use of cultural and social scripts, and the rest have the potential of advancing the author's agenda for the hearers in their situation. In this way we will unearth the ideology within the text.

As we probe ideological texture, however, we also need to look honestly and critically at the interests and agendas that have guided the interpretation of the text by scholars and lay leaders alike, as well as our own interaction with the text. Cultural studies, postcolonial criticism and feminist criticism have been of great value in raising our awareness of how biblical interpretation is a political and ideological act. As we explore our own ideology and biases more openly, we are freed to pursue self-critical interpretations, encounters with the text in which we step outside of our own ideology and allow it to be critiqued by other interpreters and by the text itself. It is at this point that we are most powerfully confronted with the text as Word of God, interpreting *us* rather than the other way around.

An interpreter will not always use all the resources of socio-rhetorical interpretation when studying every passage; some skills are more suited to one kind of text than to another. However, a full exegesis requires that we engage each of the four textures when studying a text and to reflect on the interplay between these areas of investigation. How does repetition of words and phrases contribute to the persuasive strategy and advance the ideology of the author? What are the rhetorical contributions of the author's invocation of other texts (like the Hebrew Scriptures)? How do the results of historical reconstruction of the situation and social-scientific analysis mutually inform one another and in turn inform rhetorical and ideological analysis?

By pursuing such a thorough and integrated investigation of the text, our understanding of a passage of Scripture will be enriched by the full range of interpretive strategies. Our awareness of the richly textured manner in which the text spoke within and to its original context will provide a much more reliable and creative basis for hearing and proclaiming the word afresh—in a rich, multidimensional way—in a new context.

INDEX OF EXEGETICAL SKILLS

In Order of Appearance

By Area of Focus

1

THE NEW TESTAMENT AS PASTORAL RESPONSE

How did we get this collection of texts called the New Testament? The answer moves through two stages: first, the composition of *each* of the texts now included in the New Testament; second, the selection by the church of this *group* of texts to stand in a position of central importance, reference and authority within the church. Both stages can be understood in terms of pastoral response. These texts would never have been written in the first place were it not for the kinds of concerns and challenges that early Christians faced. Each text was written to serve some specific pastoral needs and answer a range of important questions arising out of the life of the church. Because these texts answered those perennial questions so well, they continued to provide the basic point of reference for each successive generation of Christians in ever-widening circles from the texts' places of origin. Faced with the same or new challenges, Christians kept turning to *these* texts to find guidance from the apostolic witness and, ultimately, from their Lord himself. Canonization was a long, natural and consensual process by which the churches in every place throughout the Greco-Roman world came to recognize the indispensable value of *these* texts for their continuing life, nurture and direction.

ISSUES IN THE FIRST-CENTURY CHURCH

A bishop sent a vibrant, innovative minister to a dwindling United Methodist congregation in a big city in the hope that she would build up the congregation. One of the less conventional moves she made was to rent ad space on buses. The side of a bus featured her likeness, adorned in liturgical garb, with a Bible tucked prominently under her arm and a caption that read: "When our new minister came, she brought the manual." The Scriptures of the Old and New Testaments function very much as the church's "manual" or "handbook" (*manual* is derived from the Latin *manus,* meaning "hand"). These are the resources that give us our identity, vision, mission and hope, and that orient us to our past, to the world around us and to our future.

The early Christians, however, did not have access to such a manual. From the parent religion, they inherited the Jewish Scriptures (the Old Testament), which were foundational to the forging of the new group's identity, but not in nearly the same way that they were for the synagogue. Gentile Christians were connected to these texts only on account of their connection with Jesus. Jewish Christians were wholly reoriented to their Scriptures by the same. Both were called together into one new community by the preaching of the apostolic witnesses to what God was doing in Jesus. Access to the traditions about and sayings of Jesus—together with the direction and guidance of reliable apostolic voices—was therefore of critical (and one dare say primary) importance to the early church. These voices played the central role in shaping early Christian identity, community life and response to the world, with the Hebrew Scriptures providing legitimation and grounding. This access and guidance came firsthand through leaders like Paul, James, Peter and John, and through those directly trained by them; only after letters and then Gospels began to be written were *texts* available to fulfill the same purpose.

What kinds of questions and challenges would confront the people who joined the early Christian community? First, they would naturally want to learn more about the identity and focus of the movement, the teachings of the one they had come to call "Lord" and the manner in which they should live out their lives as a community. They would be asking

- Who is this Jesus whose identity is to shape ours? What is his significance, and why does he deserve my complete loyalty and obedience?
- What does it mean to follow Jesus? How should calling him "Lord" affect the way I live, the things I do or don't do, the ambitions I pursue or don't pursue, the way I use the things of the world and so forth?
- How is the scandal of the Messiah's disgraceful execution to be understood and made into something positive, purposeful and beneficial? What does the mystery of this crucified, risen and returning Messiah tell us about our relationship with God and place in this world?
- How can we be sure that we are indeed the heirs of God's promises and a legitimate phenomenon in the history of God's dealings with humanity?
- How are we to live together as this new "people of God"? What codes of conduct and values are to guide our interactions with one another? What qualities should be apparent in and what characteristics banished from this new community? (As might be expected, a great deal of the texts that

would compose the New Testament addresses these questions.)

- What should our worship look like? What are the distinctive rituals that set us apart and give us identity? How should they be performed, and what is their significance? How are we to regulate the life of the community?
- When will our labors have their reward (that is, when will Christ return)?
- How are we to keep our hearts focused on God's reward, and not be distracted by the temporal ambitions which marked our pre-Christian lives and still mark the lives of our peers?
- How can we discern the true prophet or reliable teacher from the deceiver? Where are the boundaries of this new faith?

Forming a new community, the early Christians would need to come to terms with their relationship with other communities. A number of particularly pressing questions would center on the relationship of this new people of God to the historic people of God, the Jews. These questions would be made more pressing by challenges from and actions performed by some Jews and Jewish Christians, as well as by the fact that the Christian group claimed the Jewish Scriptures as its own. This would raise several prominent issues discussed at length in the early church:

- What is the role of Torah—the law of God and the covenant it regulates—in the new people of God?
- What is the place of Gentiles in the people of God? Must they become Jews first and enter by means of the signs and statutes of the Mosaic covenant?
- If Jesus is the Messiah promised to the Jewish people and prophesied in their Scriptures, why have they responded so poorly?
- What is the church's relationship to the Jewish Scriptures and to the promises made to the particular nation Israel? Does the church exhibit continuity or discontinuity

with Israel and the revealed plan of God?

Christians had to come to terms not only with questions of how to relate to the Jewish people and their heritage but also to non-Christian Gentile society (the Greco-Roman society). This would be especially pressing for Gentile converts to Christianity, whose way of life would have radically changed simply by the move from a polytheistic, pluralistic approach to religion to the strict monotheism enjoined by the preachers of the Gospel. Pious expressions of devotion to the gods cradled all kinds of social gatherings, from the household to the business guild, from the private dinner to the civic festival. Refusing to join such rites would be regarded with puzzlement, suspicion and eventually hostility. Moreover, the provinces were generally thriving under Roman imperial rule, and the continued stability of the empire and the order it ensured were highly desirable. Small wonder then that a growing movement that encouraged "impiety" (the avoidance of idolatry) and spoke of an imminent overthrow of the present order (the coming of the kingdom of God) should meet with resistance. Again, this led to a barrage of questions asked by Christians throughout the Roman world:

- How do we make sense of the world's hostility toward the work of God, the alleged good news and the people of God?

- If we are God's children, why do we face shame and marginalization? How are we to maintain self-respect in the face of dishonor?

- When do we "live at peace with all people," and when does accommodation become apostasy?

- How should we relate to non-Christian family members? What effect does our commitment to obey Jesus have on our roles in the household?

- How should we interpret what we see going on around us every day—our neighbors' continued devotion to the traditional religions, Roman imperial presence and propaganda, the economics of empire and province—so we won't be drawn back into the life we left behind?

Of course, other kinds of questions would arise as well. The list could be multiplied. Every New Testament text—whether Gospel or history, epistle or apocalypse—emerged as a response to one or more such pastoral concerns, whether for the nurture of disciples in the faith, the putting out of "fires" in various congregations, the encouragement of faithful witness in the face of hostility, whatever the challenges happened to be. The epistles and Revelation help us become aware of the range of concerns and issues which were being raised within the early church, but these reflect the very same concerns and issues that, in a different way, the Gospels also address. This awareness should help us read the Gospels not only at their face value (i.e., "lives" of Jesus) but also as texts that serve pastoral needs, showing the ways Jesus traditions were applied in the early church to real questions, debates and issues. Moreover, as we become more aware of the kinds of questions these texts were written to answer, we also become more adept at discerning how their answers can address questions that still (or newly) challenge communities of disciples.

FORMATION OF A "NEW" TESTAMENT

Early Christians came to speak of the new covenant (in Greek, this would be indistinguishable from the phrase "new testament") quite early. The concept was made available by Jeremiah, who prophesied concerning a time when God would establish a new covenant unlike the old covenant made at Sinai (Jer 31:31-34). This new covenant would succeed where the old covenant had failed, namely, enabling people to be obedient to God from the heart so that the divine-human relationship would rest secure. The author of Hebrews seizes on this image to explain the significance of Jesus' death and ascension into heaven (Heb

8:1—10:18) as the ratification of this new covenant. The traditions about the Last Supper of Jesus with his disciples, recorded as early as Paul's first letter to the Corinthians (1 Cor 11:25; see also Mt 26:28; Mk 14:24; Lk 22:20), also connects Jesus' death with the inauguration of the new covenant.

Just as the Jewish Scriptures contained the texts that bore witness to the formation and living out of the first covenant at Sinai, so early Christians began to gather and collect the texts that bore witness to the new covenant in Christ, all the more as the living voice of the apostolic witnesses became less accessible. It was only natural that the books that preserved this apostolic witness and that spoke to the Christian community's central questions and concerns as it dedicated itself to the promises and obligations of this new covenant would rise to a position of authority and centrality in that community.

The process of selection was self-evident in many cases. Writings of the apostles who had founded the congregations with their preaching and nurture together with the Gospels that meaningfully brought together large amounts of the traditions about Jesus and sayings of the Lord would naturally continue to be valued and consulted regularly as touchstones for identity and direction. These were the texts into which early Christians could look and remember who they were, texts that accurately reflected the Christians' understanding of who they were. It was equally evident in many cases when a text reflected not the self-understanding and vision of the "Great Church" (that which would emerge as the orthodox church as opposed to heretical movements) but rather the identity and vision of a select few within the church (for example, the reflections of the Gnostic vision in *Gospel of Thomas* or the radical advocacy of celibacy, and thus renunciation of the social and domestic order, in *Acts of Paul and Thecla*).

Although written to specific churches, Paul's letters appear to have enjoyed a wider readership rather early. For example, Paul himself recommends that the Colossians and Laodiceans read one another's letters from himself (Col 4:16), and the reference to "all" of Paul's letters in 2 Peter 3:15-16 suggests that a collection of Pauline letters was already known to the author of 2 Peter. If *any* of the major theories of the composition of the Gospels is correct, then at least the earliest Gospel enjoyed a sufficiently wide and early circulation to have become a source for other Evangelists. A papyrus fragment of the Gospel of John (P^{52}) found in Egypt bears witness that John, probably written in Asia Minor, was read and copied in Egypt by the early second century. Tatian, a student of Justin Martyr, conflated all four Gospels into a single, continuous narrative called the *Diatessaron* in the mid- to late-second century, providing further evidence for the circulation of all four Gospels by the middle of the second century.[1]

The postapostolic fathers (church leaders flourishing between 95 and 150 C.E.) quote many of the texts that would become part of the New Testament, though only in the rarest occasions referring to them as "scripture." Even where direct quotations are not made, these authors show themselves to be deeply informed by and familiar with these texts, their writings very frequently resonating with identifiable passages in the Gospels and epistles.[2] When Justin Martyr, writing in the middle of the second century, speaks of the public reading of the "memoirs of the apostles" in the church alongside the Old Testament, he gives

---

[1]Arthur G. Patzia, *The Making of the New Testament* (Downers Grove, Ill.: InterVarsity Press, 1995), p. 64; Eduard Lohse, *The Formation of the New Testament* (Nashville: Abingdon, 1981), p. 19.

[2]See the fuller discussion in Bruce M. Metzger, *The Canon of the New Testament* (Oxford: Clarendon, 1987), pp. 39-73.

a clear sign of the growing authority of the written Gospels at that time.

As these texts circulated more widely and began to be set apart as a standard collection of witnesses to Jesus and the apostolic voice, other developments contributed in unforeseen ways to the urgency of defining the boundaries of this collection. First, there was the specific challenge of Gnosticism in the second century, one of the more popular innovations on the apostolic witness. Marcion, an influential proponent of Gnosticism in the West, drew up a list of authoritative apostolic documents that included only the Gospel of Luke (purged of its Jewish connections) and ten letters of Paul (the Pastoral Epistles are omitted). Second, there was a proliferation of spin-off texts patterned after the genres of the literature received by the church as a whole. Many new gospels (such as the *Gospel of Peter*, the *Gospel of Thomas* and the *Infancy Gospel of Thomas*), further "Acts" of various apostles (the *Acts of Andrew*, the *Acts of Paul and Thecla*), a few epistles attributed to one or another apostle, and several apocalypses (of which the most widely read was the *Apocalypse of Peter*) began to circulate. The majority of these clearly promoted a different understanding of Jesus and his significance as well as a different vision for discipleship and the church than what had previously been received as "apostolic."[3]

It became increasingly important, then, for church leaders both to promote all those books that had been widely used and accepted by the churches (against the shorter list of Marcion) as well as establish the limits of this authoritative collection (against the proliferation of texts written in the names of apostles). Against the claim that there should be only a single Gospel in witness to Jesus, we hear the late-second-century Irenaeus, bishop of Lyons, theologizing about the fourfold Gospel as a reflection of the four winds, the four elements and the four faces of the living creatures that surround God's throne (Rev 4:6-8; cf. Ezek 1:5-14). We find Irenaeus, Tertullian and Clement quoting the majority of texts that would be called the New Testament as possessing the authority of the Spirit and of God.

An early and important monument to this process is the Muratorian Canon, a fragmentary discussion of the canon dating from the end of the second century.[4] This catalog of texts sought to provide a comprehensive list of the church's Scripture and mark the boundaries by discussing several kinds of excluded texts. The beginning of the discussion is lost, picking up at the close of the discussion of Mark's Gospel. The catalog goes on to discuss the church's acceptance of the Gospels of Luke and John, the Acts of the Apostles, all thirteen letters ascribed to Paul, Jude, 1 and 2 John, and Revelation (probably the text intended by "Apocalypse of John"). It also specifically mentions the Wisdom of Solomon (usually thought of as being included in the Old Testament)[5] and the *Apocalypse of Peter* among the received books, although the author acknowledges that the public reading of the latter in church is a matter of dispute. It commends the *Shepherd of Hermas* as edifying reading, but denies it the status of the others since it was written after the time of the apostles. The writings of various Gnostic sects and specifically the "forged" *Letter to the Laodiceans* and *Letter to the Alexandrians* are rejected from the reading list, saying "it is not fitting for gall to be mixed with honey."

---

[3]See further, ibid., pp. 75-106; F. F. Bruce, *The Canon of Scripture* (Downers Grove, Ill.: InterVarsity Press, 1988), pp. 134-57.

[4]Bruce, *Canon of Scripture,* pp. 158-69; Metzger, *Canon of the New Testament,* pp. 191-201. The second-century date, however, is vigorously debated by A. C. Sundberg Jr., "Canon Muratori: A Fourth-Century List," *HTR* 66 (1973): 1-41.

[5]Protestant Christians would, of course, later separate this text out as apocryphal, including it in the Old Testament Apocrypha.

A number of important observations can be made from this text. First, the author is concerned to provide a list of what texts are, by consensus, received and read by the churches he is familiar with, but not unilaterally impose a standard list on his readers. The honest mention of dispute concerning *The Apocalypse of Peter,* without attempting to force a judgment, reveals this. The list bears witness to a basic consensus regarding the Gospels and Paul, but a certain fluidity in usage as far as the General Epistles are concerned. Hebrews, 1 and 2 Peter, and 3 John do not appear on the list at all, for example. It also bears witness to the increasing importance of apostolicity as a criterion of value. For all its devotional worth, *Shepherd of Hermas* cannot claim to have been written by an apostle or at an apostle's direction, so it remains at a second tier of importance for the churches. Despite their claims to apostolic authorship, the *Letter to the Laodiceans* and *Letter to the Alexandrians* are examined and rejected as spurious on the basis of their content, which witnesses not to the Pauline gospel but to Marcion's innovations thereof.

Origen, a third-century Alexandrian church father, and Eusebius, a well-known Christian scholar flourishing in the early fourth century, also discuss the state of "consensus" among the churches regarding the Christian Scriptures. These authors use the categories of "acknowledged" and "disputed," with the Gospels and Pauline corpus well established among the former and Hebrews, James, 2 Peter, 2 and 3 John, Jude, and Revelation tending to fall among the latter. Hebrews, for example, is by this point well established in the East, being read as Pauline, but not in the West, where its apostolic origin is (rightly) disputed. Revelation is firmly established in the West, though not in the East. Origen and Eusebius also take note of those books that were explicitly rejected from standing as part of this central core. Some of these rejected books were still highly regarded as edifying, like the *Shepherd of Hermas* or the letters of Ignatius, Polycarp and Clement. While these texts clearly reflected the church's sense of its authentic identity, their distance from and dependence on "apostolic" writings and witness made their authors stand more "with us" (the readers) than at the church's roots and foundation. Rejection for others, however, like the *Gospel of Thomas,* meant their disdainful dismissal as heretical.[6]

It was not until the middle of the fourth century, with the "Easter Letter" written by Bishop Athanasius in 367 C.E. and disseminated throughout the churches, that we can begin to speak of an endpoint to this process of striving after consensus. His listing of the twenty-seven books of the New Testament as we now know it shows that by this point even the collection of the General Epistles had advanced far toward a point of agreement between the churches, an agreement that was ratified at the Council of Carthage in 397 C.E. These acts by bishops, however, merely represent the formalization of what the church universal, with a very few exceptions, already knew; it was an attempt to make public throughout the churches the standard collection that the church universal (that is, the apostolic church) had selected as the authentic witnesses to the apostolic gospel.[7]

---

[6]See Lohse, *Formation of the New Testament,* pp. 23-24; Metzger, *Canon of the New Testament,* pp. 135-41, 201-7; Bruce, *Canon of Scripture,* pp. 192-95, 197-207.

[7]The process of the formation of the New Testament was somewhat different in the Syrian churches. First, Tatian's *Diatessaron,* the conflated harmony of the Gospels, was widely used in place of the four separate accounts until the fifth century C.E. Second, a number of the General Epistles took much longer to gain acceptance (and in some small circles of the Syrian church still do not have acceptance as canonical). See, further, Lohse, *Formation of the New Testament,* pp. 24-25; Metzger, *Canon of the New Testament,* pp. 218-23; Patzia, *Making of the New Testament,* p. 100.

The endpoint of a process of consensus, however, is rarely so cleanly achieved. The fourth-century Codex Sinaiticus and the sixth-century Codex Claromontanus, two important manuscripts of the Christian Bible (including both the Old and New Testaments), continue to include the *Epistle of Barnabas* and *Shepherd of Hermas,* and the latter also includes the *Acts of Paul* and the *Apocalypse of Peter* while omitting Hebrews. The fifth-century Codex Alexandrinus includes two letters attributed to Clement of Rome (the first, authentic letter would have been written about 95-100 C.E.). Whether these were attempts to save these texts from oblivion by continuing to copy them (to provide a Christian community with easy access to these texts) or to make statements about the authority of these texts for the community that produced them is difficult to assess with certainty, but the likelihood of the second of these possibilities remains quite strong.

Despite such ongoing debates in some circles, the limits of the New Testament observed by the fourth-century bishops came to define the second Testament for the Christian church as a whole. As we examine this process, we can begin to recognize criteria of canonicity. It would be misleading, however, to think of councils of bishops voting on each book of the New Testament with a checklist of criteria in hand, although a number of these criteria became important where a book was disputed. It is more to the point that these criteria appear to have been at work at the grassroots level as Christian communities elevated certain texts as having lasting and central value. These include

- apostolicity: first, in the sense of agreement with the faith, ethos and practice learned from the apostles and received throughout the church;[8] second, in the sense of being authored by, or at least authorized by, an apostolic witness
- antiquity: thus Ignatius, Polycarp and Hermas, though orthodox, do not become standard texts
- catholicity: both in the sense of the applicability of these texts to the church in every place and in the sense of the widespread use of and reverence for these texts in churches throughout the Mediterranean basin

Although *inspiration* would later become linked with *canonicity,* the early church did not equate the two. Everything in the New Testament was deemed to be inspired, but everything inspired would not be found in the New Testament. The churches of the first two centuries were very much aware of the activity of the Spirit and the prophetic word in the congregation and among church leaders. Many noncanonical authors considered their works inspired (e.g., Ignatius, Clement of Rome), and the writings of Gregory the Great and Basil of Nyssa could be lauded as inspired by others.[9] The attempt to define a standard collection of inspired texts was not an attempt to distinguish between words that God had inspired and words that God had not inspired, but rather an attempt to gather together the resources that would continually and reliably point the churches back to the apostolic witness. The canon acted as an anchor to keep the church moored in the harbor of orthodoxy and a fountain that would continue to refresh them with the voice of the apostles and the voice of Jesus as they continued to wrestle with endless permutations of the same questions and challenges that had called those texts into being in the first place.

---

[8]This first aspect of apostolicity is sometimes treated separately under the heading of "orthodoxy," as in H. Y. Gamble, *The New Testament Canon* (Philadelphia: Fortress, 1985), pp. 69-70.

[9]Patzia, *Making of the New Testament,* p. 106; Metzger, *Canon of the New Testament,* p. 256.

For Further Reading

Bruce, F. F. *The Canon of Scripture.* Downers Grove, Ill.: InterVarsity Press, 1988.

Gamble, H. Y. *The New Testament Canon: Its Making and Meaning.* Philadelphia: Fortress, 1985.

Lohse, Eduard. *The Formation of the New Testament.* Nashville: Abingdon, 1981.

Metzger, Bruce M. *The Canon of the New Testament: Its Origin, Development, and Significance.* Oxford: Clarendon, 1987.

Patzia, Arthur G. *The Making of the New Testament: Origin, Collection, Text and Canon.* Downers Grove, Ill.: InterVarsity Press, 1995.

Westcott, Brooke F. *A General Survey of the History of the Canon of the New Testament.* 7th ed. London: Macmillan, 1896.

2

THE ENVIRONMENT OF EARLY CHRISTIANITY

Essential Landmarks

When the Word became flesh, it did so within a rich matrix of social, cultural, political, economic and religious realities. We are accustomed to thinking about how the Word speaks to us in our situation (or to "me" in "my" situation), but we often do so without considering how the Word spoke within the setting of its incarnation. The word that Jesus brought was a "word on target" for Jews in early-first-century Israel. The challenges that Christ-followers faced as they sought to respond to the gospel were challenges posed by the conflict between the call of God and the demands (and opportunities) of the society and culture around them (and inside them!). The apostles' visions for their congregations took shape with reference to and in response to the local settings in which Christians were called to witness to the one God and his Christ.

Entering as fully as possible into the world of those who wrote and received the stories of Jesus and the world of the early church throughout the Mediterranean brings us a richer and deeper understanding of the New Testament texts that spoke within and to that world. The more we immerse ourselves into that world and hear how the word called forth a faithful response within that world, the better equipped we will be to proclaim that word reliably and incisively in our setting. In this chapter we will begin a journey that will continue throughout this book. We will explore information about the political and cultural environment of the New Testament to illumine the individual texts and the situations within which they spoke and sought to achieve particular effects.

PROLOGUE: IMPORTANT DEVELOPMENTS IN THE INTERTESTAMENTAL PERIOD

Since in its earliest decades the Jesus movement took shape within Judaism, we will also begin our overview by looking at the development of several "programs" within Palestinian Judaism by which Jews sought to secure Israel's future, and a few key events that had a lasting impact on Jewish consciousness. This approach does not seek to minimize in any way the influence of Greco-Roman culture on the emerging church. Indeed, we will find that Greek culture was already interacting in important ways with Jewish culture centuries before Jesus was born, with the result that the church's Jewish roots already drew the nutrients of Greek culture into the sapling Christian communities in Palestine and throughout the Diaspora. We only need to look at the writings of Josephus (a Palestinian Jew) and Philo (an Alexandrian Jew) to see how fully enculturated into Hellenism Jews could be—both in the ancestral land of Israel and in the lands of "exile."

Focusing on the ways different groups of Jews conceived of Israel's hope and the strategies they pursued to secure its well being will help us understand that the various movements around Jesus were not merely driven by beliefs or traditions but also by a cause. More was at stake in the conflicts between Jesus and the Pharisees or between Pauline Christianity and non-Christian Judaism (and significant circles of Jewish Christianity!) than matters of doctrine and practice. The well-being of the Jewish people, the preservation of their place in God's covenant and the attainment of their hope were all involved as well. This will also help us understand that the Pharisees were not just narrow-minded grouches, nor the Zealots wide-eyed fanatics. Each group had firm convictions, rooted in centuries of experience, about how God would bring God's faithful ones to the good things God had promised for them.

Jews in the intertestamental period, especially in Palestine, conceived of their hope as being attainable by three basic strategies. The first strategy involves assimilation to the Gentile world in varying degrees. Prosperity and secure employment will come to the individual Jew or even the nation as a whole as a result of blending in with the dominant, Greek culture. A second strategy focused on political independence and autonomy for the Jewish people. This included visions of the conquering Messiah, the son of David who will restore the kingdom and the power to Israel, although the figure of a Messiah was not essential to this hope. A third strategy centered on spiritual renewal and purification. Under this heading fall attempts to restore or renew covenant loyalty through Torah, visions of priestly messiahs, promises of the breaking in of the Spirit of God to renew all things and apocalyptic expectations (which are not apolitical, sometimes promoting a nonmilitaristic watching for divine intervention, sometimes promoting armed revolution).

In the practice and ideology of actual groups, several of these strategies could be combined. For example, the Hasmonean family (see pp. 47-50) combined significant assimilation to Greek culture (at least, after their rise to power) with political independence as the strategies to bring good to the nation. The sectarian community at Qumran combined spiritual renewal with readiness for armed resistance. In their day-to-day lives they devoted themselves to scrupulous observance of Torah and purity; their intense apocalyptic expectations, however, included their own readiness to participate in the end-time battle, when they would be at the head of the army of God, cleansing Israel of the unrighteous. Zealots combined the quest for political independence through armed revolution with devotion to God and often exceptional piety.

Israel: from independent monarchy to peripheral client state. The foundational stories that shaped Jewish identity involved God's choice of a particular kinship group, the descendants of Abraham through Isaac and Jacob, and fashioning a choice destiny for this group. When oppressed by Egypt, God visited judgment on that Gentile nation and led God's chosen race to take possession of the land of Canaan. Dispossessing the native Canaanites, God established the descendants of Jacob in the "land of promise," ultimately making of them a great nation state under the kingship of David and Solomon. This ideology of election by God, possession of a particular homeland and political independence was shaken by events that followed not long after Israel had reached its zenith.

In 721 B.C.E. Sargon II, king of Assyria, conquered the northern kingdom of Israel, deporting many Israelites to Assyria and Media and resettling foreigners (probably military retainers and veterans of his campaigns) among the remaining Israelites (2 Kings 17). In 597 B.C.E. Nebuchadnezzar made the southern kingdom of Judah a province of his expanding empire. Ten years later, as a result of revolutionary stirrings in Judah, Nebuchadnezzar made another punitive expedition to Judah, destroying Jerusalem and its temple and deporting its elites (2 Kings 24—25; Jer 52). The destruction of the temple, the end of Jewish independence and the exile from the land of promise became occasions for reexamining and reshaping Jewish identity and hope. Since departure from the covenant was deemed to be the cause of these misfortunes, careful observance of the Torah came to be viewed as the path to recovery. This also became the means by which Jews maintained their distinctive identity as a group both in the lands of exile and in the Gentile-dominated land of promise.

In 539 B.C.E. Cyrus of Persia conquered Babylon and became heir to its empire. He allowed those Jews who so wished to return to Judea and rebuild their temple and capital city. While cultic worship then resumed, disillusionment with the second temple and with continued Gentile domination also set in. Some Jews would question more and more whether the "restoration" achieved during this time really corresponded to the idealistic visions set forward in Isaiah and elsewhere, or whether they should look forward to new interventions of God. Dissatisfaction with the present gave rise to new hopes for the future, often referred to as apocalyptic eschatology. The restored temple would also come to stand at the center not only of Jewish unity but Jewish disunity as well, as questions arose concerning what families had the qualifications to administer the temple cultus (e.g., Zadokites versus Hasmoneans), what calendar should be followed in calculating sabbaths or festivals (a solar or lunar calendar, a point at which the Qumran community disagreed sharply with the Hasmonean administration of the temple) and other such questions.

During this period the Jewish people also began to wrestle with questions of definition: Who was the genuine Jew? There were significant tensions between those who returned from exile in Babylon, who had kept their genealogies and bloodlines pure (Ezra 9—10; Neh 13:23-27), and those who had remained in the land of Israel, who considered themselves fully Jewish but whose pedigree was suspect in the eyes of the returnees. Sectarianism was born as the "congregation of the exile" distinguished itself from the "people of the land," and as criteria for belonging to the people of the covenant were weighed. Would belonging to the covenant be a matter of religious observance or genealogy or both? As Ezra and Nehemiah enforced endogamy within the "congregation of the exile," making the returnees put away foreign wives and disown their children by these women, questions were being raised concerning how and how far Jews can relate to their non-Jewish (or questionably Jewish) neighbors.

The challenge of Hellenization and the strategy of becoming "like the nations." A new phase in world history begins with the rise of Philip II of Macedon, who united the city-states of Greece and Macedonia into a force capable of competing with the Persian Empire. It fell to his son, Alexander III ("the Great"), to use this force to unite Egypt, Palestine, Syria, Asia Minor, Greece and the lands that had belonged to the Persian Empire as far as the Indus River into a single empire. This empire would be administered according to the principles of the Greek *polis* (city-state), with Alexander founding new cities or reshaping existing capital cities, across this broad expanse after the model of the Athenian constitution. Within each of these cities the organs for propagating and maintaining Greek culture among the dominant elites were to be found: the gymnasium and lyceum, where youth would be trained in Greek language and literature, athletics and culture; theaters, stadia and hippodromes, for the enjoyment of Greek forms of entertainment (the first of which, incidentally, would be an important venue for Greek thought, poetry and music); temples, for Greek forms of worship. Through his efforts the influence of Greek culture could be felt in cities throughout the known world.

After Alexander's death in 323 B.C.E. at the age of thirty-three, his empire was divided among his generals, the Diadochoi or "successors." These generals would go on to form dynasties of their own and would be in frequent conflict with one another as each strove to increase his share of Alexander's legacy. However, they would be united in continuing to nurture an environment in which Greek culture encountered indigenous cultures. This process is known as Hellenization, a vitally important and potent process in the formation of the world into which the church was born.

Hellenization did not mean the eradication of native languages or cultures but rather the coexistence and, to a large extent, the blending of Greek culture with native cultures. The most basic level of Hellenization involved learning the Greek language, the pathway to power and influence for native elites. Since politics and diplomacy were conducted in the language of the conquerors, learning this language would be necessary if one wished to have a place in the hegemony of the dominant culture.[1] Merchants and artisans would have also been interested in learning at least enough Greek to facilitate doing business. The majority of an indigenous population—those who were tied to the land—would have had little occasion or need to learn Greek. Perhaps as an ancillary trend, native elites, especially, took Greek names for themselves and gave Greek names to their children. This may stem from an interest on the part of natives to present themselves more as an open and adaptable

part of the dominant culture than part of a subjugated, barbaric people.

Travel was greatly facilitated during the Hellenistic period, with the result that many people migrated, taking their ideas and their cultures along with them. Again, native cultures were not lost,[2] but the degree to which a people gained exposure to other cultures increased. People of one region were more apt to be exposed to elements of the philosophies, religions, traditions and stories that would constitute "cultural literacy" for Greeks and other people groups united within the Hellenistic kingdoms. Jewish authors came more and more to use the literary genres and topics of Greek and other non-Jewish cultures during this period. This process would be much more rapid in the Diaspora than in Palestine, but by 75 C.E. a Palestinian Jew named Josephus composed a history of the Jewish Wars after the pattern of Greek historiography, complete with speeches displaying facility in Greek rhetoric, and incidentally introducing Jewish sects in terms of their resemblances to Greek philosophical schools. A full generation prior to this Philo and the anonymous author of 4 Maccabees interpreted the observance of Jewish laws in terms that would have been intelligible to any Greek philosopher or moralist as the means by which reason may rule over the passions (the emotions, desires and physical sensations that subvert virtue). Aside from the possibilities for dialogue that this opens up between Jews and Gentiles, the very fact of Jews rethinking and reevaluating their ancestral ways in terms of Greek standards of morality and ethical achievement is an astounding witness to the far-reaching effects of Hellenization on people of a non-Greek culture.

The lasting results of Hellenization in Palestine were far-reaching. We can no longer maintain the idealized and highly ideological

---

[1]Martin Hengel, *Jews, Greeks, Barbarians* (Philadelphia: Fortress, 1980), p. 62.
[2]L. L. Grabbe, *Judaism from Cyrus to Hadrian* (Minneapolis: Fortress, 1992), 1:170.

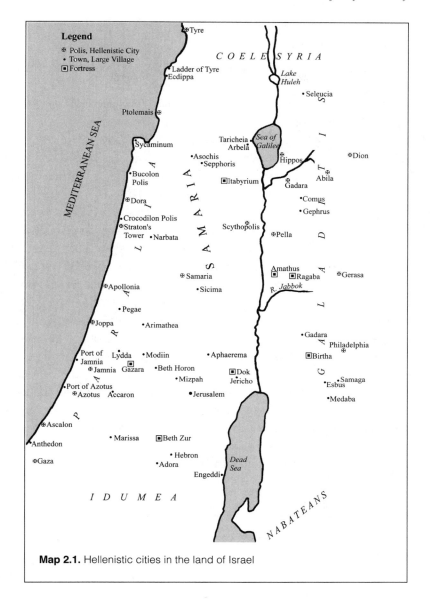

Map 2.1. Hellenistic cities in the land of Israel

picture of a Judaism untainted by Greek culture thriving in Palestine, contrasted with a highly acculturated Judaism in the Diaspora. Rather, by the Roman period especially, we find a wide range of degrees of Hellenization in both Palestine and the Diaspora. Within the borders of the ancestral land of Israel itself, we find Gentile populations well represented. Galilee was home to many Gentiles, including a noted Stoic philosopher. The region called

the Decapolis was a federation of Greek cities. Herod's Caesarea Maritima was constructed as a seaside resort city for Greeks and Romans, and became the headquarters of the Roman governor.

Hellenization was not in and of itself incompatible with remaining a faithful Jew. On the contrary, some of the most Hellenized Jewish authors also show themselves the most zealous advocates for and strictest followers of

The Septuagint

The Septuagint is a monument to the Hellenization of Jews in the Diaspora, particularly in Egypt, by the late third century B.C.E. According to the *Letter of Aristeas,* Ptolemy II commissioned a translation of the Jewish Torah into Greek for the Library of Alexandria. More probably, the translation was necessitated by the fact that Jews living in Egypt had become alienated from their native tongue and required their Scriptures to be available in Greek. Over the course of the next century the prophetic books and the writings would also be translated into Greek and would become the Scriptures for many Diaspora Jews and for the early Christian churches throughout the Mediterranean.

Those responsible for translating the different books worked with divergent philosophies of translation. Some books follow the Hebrew text closely and woodenly. Other books are more like paraphrases of the Hebrew than translations. The grandson of Yeshua Ben Sira, a Jerusalem sage flourishing in the late-third to early-second century B.C.E., observed concerning the translation of Hebrew into Greek that "what was originally expressed in Hebrew does not exactly have the same sense when translated into another language. Not only this book [referring to his own translation of his grandfather's wisdom sayings], but even the Law itself, the Prophecies, and the rest of the books differ not a little when read in the original" (prologue to Ben Sira). The act of translating the Hebrew Scriptures into Greek greatly facilitated the interplay of Greek thought and philosophy with Jewish interpretation of its own tradition, since topics of Jewish faith were now brought fully into the linguistic framework of Greek thought.

The leaders of the emerging rabbinic movement would not regard the Septuagint so kindly. Perhaps because it lent itself so well to Christian claims about Jesus, perhaps because it lent itself so well to a highly Hellenized Judaism, they likened the translation of the Hebrew Scriptures into Greek to a second golden-calf incident and opposed its continued use in synagogues. It came to be supplanted by authorized translations, far more literal and wooden.[a]

---

[a]For more information, see the excellent and innovative introduction to Septuagint studies provided by Karen Jobes and Moisés Silva in their *Invitation to the Septuagint* (Grand Rapids: Baker, 2000).

the Jewish way of life. There were, however, lines that pious Jews could not cross but which their leaders and Gentile authorities might try to push them across. It was at these points that adopting the "Greek way of life" would be deemed unacceptable, and not at the level of speaking Greek or expressing one's commitment to God in terms of Greek philosophy and ethics. When we come at last to the Maccabean Revolt, we should not confuse its attempt to preserve the Jewish way of life with a cultural war against the influence of Helle-nism. It was rather a reinforcing of those lines that simply could not be crossed.

The successors to Alexander of immediate interest to the Jews were Seleucus I, whose armies secured Syria, Asia Minor and Babylonia, and Ptolemy I, whose forces held Egypt. Palestine stood as a buffer zone between these powerful warlords, belonging at first to the Ptolemies from 323 to 198 B.C.E. The Ptolemaic kings allowed the Jews to govern themselves and observe their law and customs, being satisfied with taxes and a loyal buffer. In

198 B.C.E. Antiochus III, the great-great-grandson of Seleucus I, wrested Palestine from Ptolemaic control. He continued the Ptolemies' policy of toleration, confirming the Jews' right to self-regulation under the Torah (see Josephus, *Antiquities* 12.3.3-4 §138-146). The accession in 175 B.C.E. of his second son, Antiochus IV "Epiphanes" ("the manifest god"), brings us to the beginning of the most significant and well-documented crisis of Second Temple Judaism before Pompey's invasion and the advent of Roman power (see figure 2.2).

Prior to Antiochus IV's accession Judea was governed by Onias III, a rather conservative high priest. Onias's more progressive brother, Yeshua (who took the name of Jason), raised an enormous sum of money as a gift to Antiochus IV, seeking the privilege of being named

high priest in his brother's place and of refounding Jerusalem as a Greek city. Jason established a list of citizens, no doubt including mainly those who supported his political renovations. He established a gymnasium with a list of young men enrolled to take part. This would become the educational and cultural center of the new Jerusalem.

Jason's policy of voluntary Hellenization had a lot of support, especially among the upper classes. Only if this were the case could Jason have promised such an extensive annual "gift" to Antiochus. All our sources agree that a group of renegade Jews sought the Hellenization of Judea and secured the right to become a Greek city from the Syrian king at their own initiative, and that many in Jerusalem enthusiastically took part in the Greek institutions (see

Figure 2.1. A well-preserved codex leaf from the Septuagint translation of Exodus, written on papyrus and bearing a resemblance to the Alexandrian textual tradition of Exodus. The page would have been folded in half as part of a bound volume, with the right page coming first. The right page contains most of Exodus 26:22-25; the left page contains Exodus 30:19-21. (Courtesy of a private collector)

1 Macc 1:11-13; 2 Macc 4:13-15). What kind of Jews were these? Josephus tells of a certain Joseph ben Tobias who, during Ptolemaic rule of Palestine, attained great wealth for himself and brought economic benefit to his country by being willing to adapt himself to Gentile customs and expectations.[3] In a letter to an official, Joseph writes "many thanks be to your gods," a striking concession. He also appears to have sold a Jewish girl slave to a Gentile, and to have kept some male slaves uncircumcised, two practices forbidden in Torah. Joseph maintains good relations with Samaritans, who help

bring Israel into the international arena, making it a player in international politics and economics. Such a policy brought untold opportunities for the elite to enhance their wealth, prestige and influence. Such a policy also meant, however, that Torah had been replaced as the foundation of government by a Greek constitution (this is reflected, somewhat exaggeratedly, in 2 Macc 4:10-11).

A few years later, however, a rival faction in Jerusalem made a bid to Antiochus IV with a substantially bigger bribe and replaced Jason with Menelaus (notably, another Greek-named

Figure 2.2. A silver tetradrachm of Antiochus IV. The image on the obverse bears a portrait of the king; the reverse bears an image of Zeus, seated with "Victory" standing in his hand. The inscription reads "of King Antiochus, God Manifest, Bringer of Victory." (Photos courtesy of Sandy Brenner, www.JerusalemCoins.com)

finance his first visits to Alexandria, despite the tendency of his fellow Jews to avoid dealings with Samaritans. Nevertheless, he never appears to regard himself as apostate in any way. Rather, he represents the kind of non-exclusivist behavior typical of many Jewish elites and certainly those who would have supported Jason and his reforms. Jason and his supporters saw themselves as national reformers and benefactors, not renegades. They sought to

Jew). While the population of Judea was no doubt appalled by Jason's purchase of the most sacred office, at least he was a suitable incumbent, being a descendent of Zadok. Menelaus, however, had no such credentials. At this point people remembered as "Hasideans" (perhaps from *Hasidim,* "faithful ones") broke with the temple and became a potential force for rebellion. Jason, moreover, retained his supporters and watched for an opportune time to re-

---

[3]The story of Joseph ben Tobias is recorded in Josephus *Antiquities* 12.4.1-11 §157-236; see Grabbe, *Judaism from Cyrus to Hadrian,* 1:192-98 for a critical discussion of this source.

Table 2.1. Alexander and His More Significant Successors

Alexander the Great (336-323 B.C.E.)

Ptolemy I, general and successor to Alexander in Egypt (king over Egypt and Palestine from 305-283 B.C.E.)

Ptolemy II Philadelphus (282-246 B.C.E.), the hero of *Letter of Aristeas*

Ptolemy VI Philometor (180-145 B.C.E.), the Ptolemy against whom Antiochus IV campaigned

Cleopatra VII Philopator (51-30 B.C.E.), wife of Marc Antony

Seleucus I, general and successor to Alexander in Babylonia, Armenia, and Syria (king from 305-281 B.C.E.)

Antiochus III ("the Great," 223-187 B.C.E.), who wrested Palestine from Ptolemaic control

Seleucus IV (187-175 B.C.E.), son of Antiochus III

Antiochus IV "Theos Epiphanes" ("the god revealed," 175-164), the antagonist in 1 and 2 Maccabees, supporter of the radical Hellenization of Jerusalem

gain his position—another source of volatility in an unstable situation.

The stage was set for radical action. While Antiochus IV was pressing his attack on Egypt, a false rumor spread that he had been killed in battle. Jason seized the opportunity to rally his supporters and drive Menelaus into the citadel of Jerusalem. The local population, however, also seems to have used this occasion to rid themselves of both problems—driving Jason out of Jerusalem and keeping Menelaus, who had made himself utterly abominable by raiding the temple treasury to pay the promised bribes to Antiochus, besieged in the citadel.[4] Menelaus got word to Antiochus IV, who treated Jerusalem as a city in revolt against his own rule, brutally slaughtering thousands. Continual resistance finally led Antiochus, perhaps under the advice of Menelaus himself, to attack the people's adherence to their ancestral customs (the Torah) as the root of their rebelliousness.

In 167 B.C.E. Jews in Jerusalem were forbidden to circumcise their young or to possess copies of the Torah. Those who persisted in practicing Torah observance met with fearful penalties. Foreign mercenary soldiers were brought in to maintain order; the temple was made the common property of the Jews and Gentiles in Jerusalem and the worship altered to accommodate the practices of the foreigners. This change in cult practice would be remembered in the sources as the "abomination of desolation" (1 Macc 1:54; Dan 9:27). At this point the process of Hellenization had overstepped the limits of the people's tolerance, and a revolution against Menelaus's priesthood and Syrian rule ensued.

These events made a long-lasting impression on Jews—so much so that apocalypticists tended to use these events as a prototype of the final woes or persecution of the righteous. The persecutions themselves came to be interpreted as divine punishment for the nation's

---

[4]Jason appears to have fled Jerusalem before Antiochus's armies had arrived, leading Victor Tcherikover (*Hellenistic Civilization and the Jews* [reprint; Peabody, Mass.: Hendrickson, 1999], p. 188) to posit an intermediate revolt, in which some conservative party ousted Jason shortly after Jason ousted Menelaus.

leaders' willingness to set aside the Torah and thus a warning about the dangers of Hellenization, which far outweighed its promise. Significant segments of Judaism would come to view with suspicion any impetus to loosen the observance of Torah. If Jews followed some figure who taught the setting aside of Torah, it might endanger the whole nation, bringing down another chastisement from God. Reactions to Jesus and Stephen, for example, may be understood in part as responses against their questionable regard for Torah and temple, the two pillars of assuring divine favor. The motivation of Saul (Paul) and the other Jewish persecutors of the early Christian movement may be seen more clearly in light of this shadow as zeal for the Torah and the safety of Israel, lest this newest movement lead to God's wrath on the nation which was slow to declare its absolute allegiance to Torah. Attempts to pursue the "hope of Israel" through assimilation, therefore, would encounter greater resistance hereafter from those who had become even more certain that the "hope of Israel" lay in fidelity to the distinctive way of life set out for her by God.

The saviors of Israel: Political independence and Israel's hope. The attempt to suppress observance of the covenant, and the intolerable situation in Jerusalem and Judea led to the revolt of a priest named Mattathias and his five sons. A Syrian official came to Mattathias's village of Modein calling for an idolatrous offering as a sign of allegiance to the new policy. Mattathias reenacted the zeal of Phineas the son of Aaron by killing this official and the first Israelite who stepped forward to comply. Mattathias and his sons rallied a guerilla army, including at first the enigmatic Hasideans, and began to purge Judea by attacking Jews who had abandoned observance of the boundary-keeping commands of Torah. Boys left uncircumcised were forcibly circumcised; Jews who had accommodated too far were left to fear for their lives (1 Macc 2:44-48; 3:5-6). The threat

was not taken sufficiently seriously by the Greco-Syrian government, with the result that insufficient forces were dispatched at first to crush the revolution. This resulted in some early victories that fueled the fire of resistance and demoralized the Syrian occupying forces, more or less setting the tone for the campaigns that followed.

The momentum of the revolution outpaced Antiochus IV's increased commitment of his forces to pacifying Judea, with the result that Antiochus IV finally revoked the prohibitions against Torah observance. Judas Maccabaeus (the "Hammer"), the military leader among the five brothers, and his revolutionaries recaptured the temple itself and purged it of its pagan trappings, rededicating it to the Torah-regulated service of God. The movement that had begun as an attempt to restore religious freedom to Judea pressed forward until nothing short of political independence had been gained for the nation by the surviving brothers of Judas, who were themselves established at the head of the new nation state successively as its high priests. As this office passed on to the sons of the last surviving brother, Simon, the Hasmonean dynasty was born. The title of high priest, and from 104 B.C.E. on the title of king, remained in this family until 63 B.C.E.

Mattathias, Judas and his brothers were remembered as nothing less than messianic. Judas was praised as "a lion in his deeds," words used in Hosea 5:14 to speak of God's appointed agent (1 Macc 3:4), and as the "savior of Israel" (1 Macc 9:21), the one through whom God brought deliverance to God's people. Simon's reign is described in 1 Maccabees 14 in explicitly messianic terms: the prophetic visions of old men sitting at leisure in the streets and of people sowing in peace while the vine yielded its fruit and the ground its harvest (Zech 8:4, 12; Ezek 34:27; Mic 4:4) are woven into a poem showing how these promises of a messianic kingdom were fulfilled in Simon's time (1 Macc 14:8-9). Judas

Table 2.2. The Hasmonean Dynasty

Mattathias (d. 165 B.C.E.), father of Judas and his brothers, first leader of the Maccabean revolt (against Seleucid king Antiochus IV)

Judas "Maccabaeus" (165-160 B.C.E.), third son of Mattathias, second leader of the revolt

Jonathan (160-142 B.C.E.), fifth son of Mattathias, third leader of the revolt; named high priest by Alexander Balas, son of Antiochus IV)

Simon (142-135 B.C.E.), second son of Mattathias; named "high priest, commander and leader" of the Judeans (1 Macc 13:42; 14:35, 41)

John Hyrcanus I (135-104 B.C.E.), son of Simon; leader and high priest

Judas Aristobulus I (104-103 B.C.E.), oldest son of John Hyrcanus I

Alexander Jannaeus (103-76 B.C.E.), youngest son of John Hyrcanus I

Salome Alexandra (76-67 B.C.E.), wife of Alexander Jannaeus

Aristobulus II (67-63), older son of Alexander Jannaeus

Hyrcanus II (63-43), younger son of Alexander Jannaeus

[Parthian invasion and interregnum]

Antigonus (40-37 B.C.E..), son of Aristobulus II

Herod the Great (37-4 B.C.E.), the "legitimate" successor to the dynasty through marriage to Mariamne I, granddaughter of both Aristobulus II and Hyrcanus II (her parents were first cousins).

and his brothers became the pattern for the military, political messiah. They renewed the vision of the hope of Israel as a political hope, securing religious, cultural and ethnic identity through power, a vision that would become important again with the advent of Roman rule. The image of the earthly, military Messiah figure has its real roots here. We should also pause to observe that the "zeal for the Torah" associated with Mattathias and his sons (see 1 Macc 2:27), by which Judas "turned away wrath from Israel" (1 Macc 3:8), involved forcing apostate Jews to return to the covenant. This again remains an important feature for the development of the early church. Non-Christian Jewish persecutors have been informed by this tradition of how to enact zeal for Torah, a connection Paul will make explicitly in Philippians 3:6: "as to zeal, a persecutor of the church" (NRSV).

The Hasmonean dynasty degenerated into a series of kings who resembled more the Gentile Seleucids than the dream of a new Davidic monarchy. Even from its inception some Jews criticized the family for not giving the high priesthood back to the Zadokite line. One important point of contention between the Qumran community (the sect with which the Dead Sea Scrolls are most commonly connected) and the Hasmonean leadership concerned precisely this "usurpation" of the high priesthood. Although the descendants of Simon would push the borders of the newly independent Judea to regain the dimensions of the Solomonic kingdom, acts of brutality against Judean opponents, questions about the dynasty's legitimacy and internecine rivalries weakened the family's position. The dynasty

The Old Testament Apocrypha

The term *Apocrypha* refers to a collection of Jewish writings contained in the Old Testament canon of the Roman Catholic and Eastern Orthodox churches, but excluded from the Bible of Protestants and Jews. These texts were written between 250 B.C.E. and 100 C.E. by pious Jews seeking to make sense of their experiences and to discover how to remain faithful to God in a changing world. Some originated in the land of Israel (written either in Hebrew or Greek); many were written by Jews living outside of Israel in what is called the Diaspora (written mainly in Greek, some in Aramaic).

Many of these books stand firmly in the tradition of the Old Testament writings. Historical books like 1 and 2 Maccabees continue the story of God's dealings with his covenant people such as is read in 1 and 2 Samuel, 1 and 2 Kings. The Wisdom of Ben Sira and Wisdom of Solomon stand in the tradition of Proverbs, Job and Ecclesiastes. Some of the Apocrypha arose as Old Testament books were rewritten or expanded, such as 1 Esdras (a version of Ezra-Nehemiah), the Greek versions of Esther and Daniel (both of which contain substantial additions) and the Prayer of Manasseh and Letter of Jeremiah (inspired by events and situations narrated in the Old Testament). There are a number of stories written both to entertain and to re-inforce important values, like Tobit and Judith, as well as prayers and psalms, a "prophetic" book (Baruch), an apocalypse (2 Esdras, itself a composite work), and an essay on the way strict obedience to the Jewish Torah better trains a person in all the virtues prized by the Greek world than any Greek philosophy (4 Maccabees).

Catholic and Orthodox churches stand in a long tradition of the Christian use of and respect for these texts as reliable resources, a tradition that extends all the way back to the early church. We notice a growing willingness to speak of these texts as Scripture during the second and third Christian centuries and the inclusion of most or all of these books in the Bibles of the fourth and fifth century church. These books make a great contribution both to the New Testament and to the development of Christian theology during these early centuries. The Roman Catholic and Eastern Orthodox churches stand in this tradition.

Protestants, on the other hand, continue the tradition of the vocal minority in the early church that questioned whether these books should be regarded as of equal value to the other canonical books or relegated to a second tier. Jerome, a fourth-century priest and scholar, argued forcefully that since the Jewish rabbis did not acknowledge them as Scripture, neither should the church that inherited its Old Testament from the synagogue. The Protestant policy of "Scripture alone" as a guide to theology made it important to establish the boundaries of Scripture, all the more as the more objectionable doctrines like the idea that we can make atonement on behalf of the dead and free them from punishment after death were based on an Apocryphal text (2 Macc 12:39-45). This stood behind masses celebrated for the dead and the selling of indulgences, in short, many of those practices that Luther explicitly attacked. By taking up the old critique of Jerome and arguing that the Apocrypha should not be considered Scripture, Protestants were able to undercut support for this major issue.

There is a tendency among Protestants to undervalue these writings, even to regard them as dangerous (why else would they be "removed" from the canon?). The Reformation heritage, however, commends these texts as resources to be read and valued (just not to be used as an independent source for theology and points of doctrine). Luther took pains to translate the Apocrypha and include them in his German Bible, separated out between the Testaments. The Church of England recommended them as edifying devotional literature and as useful for teaching ethics. As publishers began to publish Bibles without the Apocrypha (which made books cheaper to produce and easier to sell), setting a new standard for Protestant Bibles, unfamiliarity led to prejudice and contempt, which led to a harmful avoidance of this literature.

The Apocrypha provide us with essential information about the history of the period between the Testaments; the theological developments during the period; the ways Old Testament traditions were selected, remembered and expanded; the piety and ethics of the Jewish people at the turn of the era; and the religious, cultural, social and political challenges they faced. Moreover, the influence of the books of the Apocrypha on New Testament voices and authors is unmistakable, as will be pointed out throughout this book. If the early church found these books such valuable resources (independent of the questions of inspiration or canonicity), it would be a shame for the modern church to neglect them.

These books, however, are not merely of academic interest. The Apocrypha are also of lasting value as devotional reading, bearing witness to the faith and piety of the Jewish people in the centuries around the turn of the era, and to the way many met the challenges to their calling to be a holy people with covenant loyalty. These books teach a zeal to walk faithfully before God in the face of adversity, encourage a commitment to choose obedience to God over succumbing to the passions or the weaknesses of the flesh, and to witness to the experience of God's forgiveness and the hope of God's deliverance—all of which cannot fail to strengthen the faith both of Jews and of Christians.

FOR FURTHER READING

deSilva, David A. *Introducing the Apocrypha: Message, Context, and Significance.* Grand Rapids: Baker, 2002.

Harrington, D. J. *An Invitation to the Apocrypha.* Grand Rapids: Eerdmans, 1999.

Metzger, Bruce M. *An Introduction to the Apocrypha.* New York: Oxford University Press, 1957.

---

ended in civil strife, with two brothers involved in a feud for the title of high priest and king. One side appealed to Rome to settle the issue, which was all the opening Pompey the Great needed to begin to bring Judea under Roman administration—first by awarding the title "high priest" to one of the brothers, but denying the title "king" to either.

Despite the family's fall from grace in the popular eye, Judas and his brothers left an enduring legacy—a renewed zeal for the restoration and secure establishment of the kingdom of Israel. Even though Jews would no longer view the Hasmonean kings as worthy or faithful leaders, they would continue to hope for a worthy king in the future who would take the best achievements of the Hasmoneans and combine them with the perfect embodiment of traditional Jewish virtues. Thus messianism and the fostering of hopes for God's perfect restoration of Israel (seen in shadowy form in the Hasmonean restoration) also flourished during this period. Of course, the advent of a new Gentile empire on the Judean scene—the Roman Republic—renewed all the old questions and concerns about how to live securely as Jews under the domination of non-Jews.

The renewal of Israel through fidelity to God. For some, the hope of Israel lay in the hands of God alone. During the Hellenization crisis it appeared to some that only God's direct intervention could restore Israel. God would bring God's promises to pass; the role of the community was simply to keep faith with this God through diligent observance of God's law. This conviction was not the sole property of any one group but rather pervaded many circles within Judaism.

One manifestation of this conviction was apocalypticism. Apocalypticists looked to the larger contexts in which they lived, beyond the present to the distant past and forthcoming future, beyond the visible to the unseen activity in the realms above and below. Looking to conflicts in the past explained tensions experienced in the present. Looking to God's forthcoming interventions made continued fidelity to God's commands advantageous. Looking beyond the visible world gave a behind-the-scenes perspective on the realities encountered and experienced by the audience of the apocalyptic message. In the heavenly realm God's rule is already manifest—the whole cosmos is not out of order, only the earth. The inhabitants of heaven are subservient to God's will, and only the inhabitants of

the earth and the demonic powers fail to recognize God's authority.[5] Placing everyday life within these broader contexts changes how aspects of the everyday world are understood, interpreted and even valued.

Apocalypticism essentially arose in response to the apparent failure of the Deuteronomistic view of history. Deuteronomy declares that those who are faithful to Torah prosper while those who violate it are punished. The history of the twin kingdoms of Israel and Judah written in the books of Samuel and Kings sought to demonstrate the truth of this claim by explaining the fall of both kingdoms as the result of their departure from Torah. The experience of Hellenistic era Jews radically challenged this premise, since the apostate was more likely to enjoy prosperity in this life than the faithful Jew, who from time to time was actually endangered by and sometimes violently executed for his or her commitment to God's law. Thus the doctrine of two ages came into being—this temporary, present age, when wicked people have the upper hand, and the age to come, when God's rewards and punishments will be meted out and the faithful will enjoy the blessings that God's justice guarantees them. Apocalypticism was also fueled by the apparent failure of other promises of God, for example, the promise made to David to establish his line forever. The conviction that the God of Israel was absolutely faithful, however, led to the positing of a future time when all these promises would be fulfilled, when the prophets' visions of Israel's prosperity and glory would all seem like understatement.

Dualism is a prominent characteristic of apocalypticism. This dualism manifests itself

---

[5]Apocalypticism thus gives strong impetus to the development of angelology and demonology; the stories of the inhabitants of these unseen realms are given more specificity. God is surrounded by distinct orders of angels, many of whom are now known by name. The story of the angels who left heaven to mate with human females (Gen 6:1-4) becomes the canonical anchor for extravagant epics concerning the fall and rebellion of these angels, the forbidden lore they brought to humankind to lead them astray, the birth and death of the giants, whose souls became the evil spirits that afflict humankind, and the like (see 1 Enoch 6—36; the story is known to the authors of 2 Peter and Jude).

temporally, distinguishing between the present age, which is hopelessly corrupt, and the coming age, the reign of God and God's servants. It manifests itself socially, as humanity is divided up into the children of darkness, who are lost together with this age, and children of light, who are God's favored elect. Many apocalyptic circles no longer defined Israel in terms of ethnicity but rather in terms of a shared spiritual commitment. With this the concept of an elect remnant of faithful ones as the "true" Israel comes into view. The dualistic thinking promotes a marked pessimism with regard to the majority of humanity and the possibility of justice and peace in this age. There is a strong preference for grounding the message in the world beyond experience and beyond disconfirmation. Visions and revelations from God or an angel are the preferred media of communication, creating a sense of proximity to that heavenly, otherworldly realm.

Apocalypticism proved to be a flexible and powerful ideological strategy by which to maintain commitment to a particular group and to the "hope of Israel" more generally. It rescued the tenability of the Deuteronomistic worldview—rewards and punishments are no longer expected to be meted out in this life. Making the realm beyond experience more real for the audiences through visions and revelation, direct communications between angels and visionaries, helped them to invest themselves more fully and freely into otherworldly rewards, even when the cost was great in temporal losses. Apocalypticism also enhances group solidarity and group boundaries, articulating the privileges of the group as the elect and the immense disadvantages facing the outsiders, who are damned. Maintaining allegiance to the group, showing solidarity until the end and being "found faithful" emerge as primary strategies for attaining the apocalyptic hope. Finally, apocalypticism is especially suited to enabling resistance to the dominant culture by promoting the view that while

outsiders might seem to be a powerful majority in the present age, in a short time the group members will be shown to have chosen the right side and to have the hosts of heaven in their party. Apocalyptic thought and forms of expression emerge in almost every book of the New Testament as well as in Jewish responses to the fall of Jerusalem in 70 C.E. (e.g., *4 Ezra* and *2 Baruch*).

Many Jews regarded the intensification of attention to the doing of Torah and bringing every aspect of their lives into line with the law of God as the paramount strategy to attaining the well-being of the nation and of individuals. The Hasidims, Essenes and the more familiar Sadducees and Pharisees, who emerge during the Hasmonean period as powerful coalitions within Judea, embodied this response in their belief that loyalty to the covenant is the path to Israel's prosperity and security under God's favor. Only by returning with a whole heart to Torah, the covenant, can Israel enjoy a future of blessing and peace. Opportunities for division, or sectarianism, arose within this general consensus, chiefly in connection with how the Torah was to be interpreted and applied beyond the rather limited cases actually covered within the Pentateuch. Disagreements between Pharisees, Sadducees and Essenes (including the Qumran community) often revolve around minute points of how the law is to be performed correctly. Pharisees and the Qumran covenanters, in their different ways, exemplify how the concept of an elect within Israel worked. The Pharisees and the inhabitants at Qumran both viewed themselves as the sole group that paid proper attention to the covenant and fulfilled its stipulations and requirements correctly. They were the faithful, and nonmembers were following Torah imperfectly at best. Behind these debates, we must always remember, stands not a petty-minded legalism but the conviction that the nation's faithful response to God and enjoyment of God's promised blessings are at issue. Many of the conflicts between Jesus and representatives of these groups can be seen to fall within these lines as well.

Strict observance of Torah as a strategy to experience God's blessings might be combined with apocalypticism or with political messianism or both. Early Judaism was capable of great variety and recombination. It was also combined with an intense interest in and commitment to the Jerusalem temple. Indeed, the functioning of the temple could emerge for some Jews as the cornerstone of Israel's hope. As long as the temple was functioning, and thus the means of reconciliation to the patron deity kept readily at hand, Israel's hope was secure. There was no division of the Torah into moral and cultic laws: both were bound together, supported one another and assumed the functioning of the other. Some Jews would prove far more resilient, however, in the wake of the removal of the temple from the scene by the Roman legions in 70 C.E.

The advent of Rome and a new impetus to assimilate. In the wake of the failure of any of Alexander's successors to revive his empire, the balance of power in the Mediterranean gradually shifted westward as one central power, guided from one central city, emerged as the true successor to Alexander. Both the Roman Republic and the Roman Empire continued and expanded Alexander's ideology of world domination, promoting the unification of all people in a Helleno-Roman culture, administration and shared religious pantheon (ever expanding to accommodate new conquered peoples). Under its emperors, Rome fulfilled this ideal better than any predecessor: culture remained thoroughly Greek, with the distinctive Roman flavoring of central administration, the glorification of power and the promise of peace through unopposable force.

The power of the Roman Republic began to be felt in the eastern Mediterranean during the time of the Ptolemies and the Seleucids. When Antiochus III attempted to annex the coastal lands of Asia Minor, a representative of Rome halted Antiochus's advance and imposed a heavy tribute on him. When Antiochus IV invaded Egypt, a Roman consul prevented him from taking control of Egypt, warning him against attempting such an enterprise again. Already, then, Rome was policing the affairs of otherwise sovereign kingdoms, using its role as "peacekeeper" as a prelude to more direct control.

Because Rome's power rested on its armies, it was essential to provide for the armies' rapid deployment throughout the territory controlled by Rome. Roman engineers built upon and vastly improved existing road systems and trade routes, incidentally facilitating travel between cities for all merchants, travelers and preachers of one philosophy or another. The missionary endeavors of Paul and other evangelists, the relentless movements of other Christian teachers and emissaries of various churches, and the ongoing and regular contact between Christians of different communities would profit greatly from the Roman road network.

Roman rule came to Judea after Pompey the Great, a leading general and later a triumvir of the Roman Republic, intervened in the feud between Hyrcanus II and Aristobulus II. In the interests of more effective government of the peoples in Palestine, Pompey assigned large parts of the former Hasmonean state to the Roman governor of Syria and, after conferring only the title of high priest on Hyrcanus, appointed an Idumean named Antipater and his sons, Phasael and Herod, as governors of Judea and Galilee.

There was a strong impetus to accept Roman power as the hope of Israel, just as so many other peoples and nations had embraced Rome as their own salvation. This need not have meant participation in idolatrous cults, for Rome was exceptionally tolerant of Judaism. It was enough to cooperate, to facilitate Roman administration, to drink in the benefits of the *pax Romana,* the peace provided by Roman power. The priestly aristocracy, the Herodian family and its administration, and many enterprising Jews had nothing to gain from antagonizing Rome and everything to gain from promoting submission to the Roman yoke.

The new political messianism. Not all Jews were content to leave Israel under the governance of a Gentile power. Indeed, Pompey's entry into Jerusalem stirred up tremendous anti-Roman animosity. After defeating Aristobulus, Pompey personally inspected the interior of the temple, desiring to see its treasury and its holy of holies, thus desecrating it in the opinion of Jews. Pompey meant no harm; he took no souvenirs. Nevertheless, it was a traumatic reminder of what foreign domination had always meant: not even the temple, the place where God's favor could be secured for Israel, was secure. It also fueled anti-Gentile stereotypes that spoke of the arrogance and godless character of non-Jews, especially non-Jews in positions of power.

This gave new impetus to expressing the hope of Israel in terms of military deliverance and political power. The *Psalms of Solomon* responded directly to the advent of Pompey. The author laments the wickedness of the later Hasmonean dynasty and calls down divine judgment on the Gentile who trampled the holy place with his boots. In two of these Psalms (*Pss. Sol.* 17 and 18), the author cries out to God to send his anointed One to drive out the wicked Gentiles and to overturn the native rule of the Hasmoneans, and establish the kingdom of David once more. This is not an otherworldly hope. It is the cry for a very tangible, this-worldly kingdom ushered in by a powerful general-king whom God selects, the cry for the fulfillment of the promises made to David that one of his line would sit on the very real throne of the very real nation of Israel.

Throughout the period of Roman domination, Jewish resistance movements continued (sporadically) to emerge, rallying together supporters with promises of God's miracu-

Figure 2.3. Silver Tetradrachm (called a *sela*) from the second year of the Bar Kochba Revolt (133/4 C.E.). The obverse shows the face of the Jerusalem temple with the Ark of the Covenant visible within, and bears the inscription "Shimon," for the leader of the revolt. The reverse features a lulav and an etrog, symbols of the feast of Sukkot (Booths), and bears the revolutionary inscription "Year Two of the freedom of Israel." (Photo courtesy of Superior Galleries, Beverly Hills)

lous deliverance of Israel through the hand of the latest would-be "anointed." These movements would become especially numerous in the years leading up to the First Jewish Revolt of 66-70 C.E. For example, Theudas (perhaps the one mentioned anachronistically in Acts 5:36) staged an unsuccessful revolt, promising to part the Jordan and reenact Joshua's conquest of the land. The sons of Judas the Galilean (who had himself been executed for sedition in 6 C.E.) were captured and executed by the governor Tiberius Julius Alexander. The unnamed Egyptian for whom Paul was mistaken in Acts 21:38 had gathered together a large crowd on the Mount of Olives, promising to ride in and take the city, only to have his followers dispersed or slaughtered by Felix.

The hope for political independence and restoration of Israel through armed revolt took on something of an organized shape with the rise of the Zealot movement, which was fueled ideologically by the examples of Phinehas and Mattathias but was not limited to members of a terrorist party. It was a widely shared hope for Israel, such that Jesus' own disciples are shown continually slipping into this mode of thinking about Jesus' mission, even after Jesus' resurrection (Acts 1:6). Jesus may himself have countered such expectations for a messianic "Son of David" who will restore the glory of the Davidic monarchy to Israel in his question to the scribes (Mt 22:41-46).

It is nearly certain that the Jewish leaders (see Jn 11:45-50) and Roman authorities (see the questions posed and inscription written in Mk 15:2, 9, 12, 26) interpreted Jesus' actions according to this model as well, leading to his execution as a leader of sedition.

This vision of and strategy for attaining the hope of Israel culminates in the two disastrous revolts against Rome, the first in 66-70 C.E. and the second in 132-135 C.E., the revolt of Bar Kosebah, whom Rabbi Akiba hailed as Bar Kokhba, "son of a star," the Messiah (and after the defeat, Bar Koziba, "son of a lie"). (See figure 2.3.)

Continued commitment to Torah. Alongside these developments many Jews persisted in their belief that God's good promises would come to Israel in good time and that faithfulness to God's law was the only agenda that needed to be pursued. The Pharisees, for example, continued to derive guidance from Torah for new situations. Their goal was to make applicable for a more centralized and urban culture the divine laws which had been given to a very decentralized, agrarian culture. Loyalty to the one God and the belief that obedience from the heart meant blessing and divine favor were the driving forces of their endeavor. Similarly, the community at Qumran (which persisted from about 160 B.C.E. to 68 C.E.), sought to enact the law in "perfection of way" as God's elect within Israel, through whose purity all Israel would benefit in God's new order.

During this period a number of authors, perhaps representing a sizable number of Jews, no longer concerned themselves with the hope of Israel per se, but rather took a more individualistic approach to the problem. The Wisdom of Solomon, a work of Diaspora Judaism, probably from Alexandria, speaks much of God's election of and deliverance of Israel in the past, but the real hope for the future is the immortality in God's presence granted to those individual Jews who remain faithful to God's Torah amidst the pressures to assimilate. Fourth Maccabees, written by a Jewish author perhaps in Antioch, similarly speaks not of the hope of a nation but of the hope of individuals as they continue steadfast in the ways of Torah. Although these are both Diaspora writings, the fluid connections between Diaspora and Palestinian Jews (through the pilgrimage of the former to the temple or through connections forged by family or commercial ties) would suggest that such thought would also be found among Palestinian Jews.[6]

Summary. We see in the period prior to and during the ministry of Jesus and the composition of the Gospels a number of different avenues for hope, some of which are directly opposed and some that merely sit side by side. What will provide for the well-being of myself, my family, my nation? What will make for a world where all is in order with God, where promises do not go unfulfilled and where virtue does not go unrewarded? What will make life meaningful? Some sought the answers to these questions in some measure of accommodation to the Gentile culture; some sought the just kingdom of David through political and military hopes; some set their hearts on the covenant, on the hidden kingdom or on the future kingdom of God's own founding. This is not only a world of divergent hopes but a world where people react strongly against what they perceive to be a threat to their hope and thus their well-being. When Christians appeared to challenge—even to reject or subvert—the hope held out by Roman power, those who set their hope and security in Roman power (the majority of the Gentile Mediterranean world together with many Jewish elites) responded actively to protect their hope and their interests. Seen from this light, the central landmarks of the "world behind the Gospels" in this way (Hellenization, the Hellenization crisis, the Maccabean Revolt, the rise of Rome, Roman imperial ideology and so forth) emerge not merely as dry facts but as lasting influences that motivate real behavior and real responses to new situations. Keeping these backgrounds in mind will also help us understand why some opposed, some misunderstood and some warmly welcomed Jesus and the movement that spread in his name,

proclaiming Jesus as a very distinctive embodiment of hope.

KEY PLAYERS AND PLOTS IN THE WORLD OF THE GOSPELS AND THEIR READERS

Luke begins his account of the story of Jesus' birth and public appearance with two passages connecting Jesus' story with the story of the Roman Empire.

> In those days a decree went out from Emperor Augustus that all the world should be registered. This was the first registration and was taken while Quirinius was governor of Syria. (Lk 2:1-2 NRSV)

> In the fifteenth year of the reign of Emperor Tiberius, when Pontius Pilate was governor of Judea, and Herod was ruler of Galilee, and his brother Philip ruler of the region of Ituraea and Trachonitis, and Lysanias ruler of Abilene, during the high priesthood of Annas and Caiaphas, the word of God came to John son of Zechariah in the wilderness. (Lk 3:1-2 NRSV)

Even though Jesus' story will outlast the story of the Roman Empire, Luke does not let us forget that those stories are intertwined. Indeed, the narratives of all four Gospels and Acts are populated with emperors, proconsuls, prefects or procurators, Herods, high priests and rabbis as well as a number of special-interest groups within Judaism such as the Pharisees, Sadducees, scribes and revolutionary activists. Some acquaintance with these figures, families and groups is required for a fuller appreciation of the Gospels and of the place of the Jesus movement within Judaism. I have

---

[6]Second Maccabees bears eloquent witness to the way in which a Jew would be able to keep both the hope of the righteous individual (e.g., in the promise of immortality articulated by the martyrs in chaps. 6 and 7) *and* the hope of the nation (e.g., in the conviction that keeping Torah would lead to national peace and prosperity; 2 Macc 3:1; 4:13-17; 6:12-17; 7:37-38) in view.

tried to limit this introduction as much as possible to those details of the first-century landscape that are important to reading the Gospels and, to a lesser extent, to appreciating the circumstances of the first readers of the Gospels. Once again, these pages are intended merely to provide a *beginning* for the reader, who is urged to delve more deeply into each topic treated here using the resources listed at the end of the chapter.

The Roman Empire and its emperors. The Roman Republic operated on the basis of shared power among the senatorial class (Roman males with an annual income of one million sesterces or more, mainly from their immense farmlands). Ambition and competition were central Roman values, but those who held on to more power than was their due or for longer than proper for one man were opposed. Thus the norm was for two senators to hold the office of consul each year, and for many senators to have the opportunity to hold this office. Toward the end of the Republic personalities emerged that sought to dominate the whole, each backed by a substantial faction. Julius Caesar, Sextus Pompeius and Marcus Licinius Crassus were three such persons who settled on an uneasy compromise—the first triumvirate ("rule of three men"). Not satisfied with sharing the imperium, these three leaders led the Roman Republic and its provinces into a bloody civil war, which ended in 46 B.C.E.

Julius Caesar emerged as the supreme commander, but his lack of sensitivity to Rome's hatred of anything approaching monarchy led to his assassination in 44 B.C.E. This led to a second civil war waged by Caesar's supporters, Octavian and Marc Antony, against Caesar's assassins, Brutus and Cassius, and all their allies.

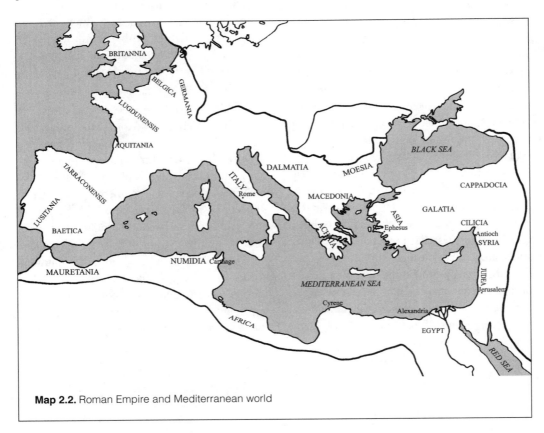

Map 2.2. Roman Empire and Mediterranean world

Figure 2.4. Cameo portrait of Augustus Caesar. (Photo courtesy of the Cleveland Museum of Art)

After the defeat of the assassins, a second triumvirate was formed between Octavian, Marc Antony and Marcus Lepidus. Once more, shared rule was impossible. Lepidus retired peacefully, but Octavian and Antony were embroiled in a vicious civil war. These civil wars, the result of factionalism within the empire, ravaged the resources of the whole Mediterranean world from Italy to Egypt. People lived with insecurity. The internal divisions meant increased threat from outside as well as pillaging and destruction inside.

Then in 31 B.C.E. it was all over. Marc Antony, painted as the betrayer of Rome who sought to establish a monarchical rule over the Mediterranean with his illicit lover, Cleopatra of Egypt, was defeated at the battle of Actium by Octavian and his forces. Octavian had personally indebted large segments of the population to himself as his clients—even the veterans of the Antony's army. In gratitude and in the hope that complete allegiance to Octavian would forestall any future civil wars and the incredible loss of property, security and life which accompanied them, the Senate and people of Rome gave Octavian the imperium, the right to command the legions of the empire[7] and made him perpetual consul. Octavian thus concentrated all power in his hands through constitutional, "Roman" means, unlike his adoptive father Julius Caesar. He was given the title Augustus, which denoted him both as "pious" and as "worthy of reverence," and named him *Pontifex Maximus,* the high priest of the official religious life of the Greco-Roman world (see figure 2.4).

The provinces were glad to accept Augustus's imperium. He brought security and stability to their agrarian and urban lives—for many, for the first time in their lives! What the Mediterranean needed and wanted was a strong ruler and a clear line of succession. Poets lauded Augustus as the bringer of salvation and good news. (Luke will use the same terms to speak of the significance of Jesus' birth.) Virgil hymned the birth of an heir apparent as the coming of a Golden Age. This was the atmosphere in which the Roman Empire began (although, constitutionally, it had not ceased to be a republic). While court poets and propagandists did their part to stir up these emotions, we must remember that they were only reinforcing what the people, local elites and senate had already decided—the strong, unchallenged power of Augustus was the future of the people of the Mediterranean.

Since the rise of Augustus to this position of supreme leadership brought peace, security and prosperity to the provinces again, he was hailed in the provinces as nothing less than a god. As one ancient author put it, "since he provided gifts worthy of the gods, he was deemed worthy of the honor due the gods."[8] The line between human beings and deities was not impossible to cross, especially for people in the eastern half of the Mediterranean. Heracles and Asclepius both became divine by

virtue of their benefactions toward humanity. If virtue or skill or prowess could lead to deification, what less was deserved by the bringer of world peace and order? Emperor worship was proposed and promoted by people in the provinces of the empire, who responded to Augustus as to a benefactor. The gifts of lasting peace and a return to security were so great, however, that only the honor due a god could be deemed ample return.

Roman imperial ideology centered not only on the person of the emperor, but also on the city of Rome, which was worshiped alongside the emperor as *Roma Aeterna.* Rome was the city destined by the gods to bring their order to the world and rule forever. She was the bringer of peace and wealth, the security of the world. The emperor was the patron of the whole world, whose favor meant well-being for an entire province. To participate in the cults of Rome and the emperors was to show loyalty to the agents of the gods and gratitude to the givers of good. Wherever one traveled in the eastern Mediterranean (outside of Judea), one would find plentiful local manifestations of this ideology in temples, festivals and coins, all promoted by provincial officials or assemblies and their activities. We will also find resistance to this ideology within the New Testament in varying degrees, from Paul, who is willing to see Rome as a temporary expedient for the spread of the gospel, to John, who sees Rome as the arrogant enemy of God. Both, however, see Rome as temporary, and that was enough of a political statement to make the Christians' neighbors uncomfortable.

Augustus organized the provinces of the Roman Empire into two different classes: senatorial and imperial. The peaceful, stable provinces threatened neither from barbarians without nor rebellion within were placed under

---

[7]It is from the Latin *imperator,* "commander of the legions," that we derive the English title for Augustus and his successors, "emperor."

[8]Nicolaus of Damascus *Life of Augustus* 1.

direct senatorial administration, with a proconsul being appointed by the Senate (with the emperor's approval) for a short term. More difficult provinces were placed under imperial administration, and in these were stationed the legions of the Roman army. In this way Augustus (and his successors) would maintain direct control of the army, preventing some ambitious senator from stirring up another civil uprising. Imperial provinces were also governed by members of the senatorial class directly answerable to Augustus, but Judea and Egypt employed prefects or procurators drawn from the second tier of Roman society (the "equestrians" rather than the senators) for the administration of the imperial affairs. The Judean prefect worked under the imperial legate of Syria, who often had to help with military support. The Egyptian prefect was directly answerable to the emperor, who kept Egypt pretty much as a personal territory. As the supplier of grain to most of the Western provinces, Egypt was the most strategic holding: in the emperor's hands, it again strengthened his position. Not all territories within the Roman Empire were made into provinces governed by Romans. Many smaller kingdoms had willingly entered into an uneven partnership with Rome, making themselves clients and allies. These retained their native monarchies, as long as there were no signs of uprising. Judea began as such a client kingdom under the last Hasmoneans and later under Herod and his family.

Augustus held the reins of empire from 31 B.C.E. to 14 C.E. The heir was neither a child nor grandchild of his blood, and his personal family story is really quite tragic. The elder son of Augustus's wife Livia, Tiberius, succeeded to the cluster of offices and powers that distinguished Augustus as constitutional emperor. Tiberius continued to exercise an effective rule until about 29 C.E., when he moved from Rome to Capri. His prefect of Rome, Sejanus, an ambitious equestrian, became Tiberius's only link to the affairs of state, and Sejanus used this position to destroy his personal enemies, stock key positions with his friends and prepare to seize the imperium. The plot was discovered, and Sejanus was beheaded. He had been the personal patron of Pontius Pilate, prefect of Judea.

Tiberius left the imperium to his nephew Caligula in 37 C.E. Caligula seems to have started out well, but after a severe fever he took on the behaviors for which he is remembered today, including excessive depravity, capricious cruelty and extravagant promotion of his own worship, even in Rome (where living emperors were not worshiped). His importance for students of the New Testament comes mainly from his attempt to install a cult statue of himself in the Jerusalem temple, as he had in many other temples around the world, as a "favor" to the Jewish people (putting a face on their unseen God). Faced with the ultimate desecration of their holy place with the erection of a graven image of a false god, the Jews made it clear to the governor of Syria that they would rather be slaughtered en masse than tolerate this sacrilege. Only the governor's cautious delays and Caligula's timely assassination prevented disaster. Caligula's encouragement of emperor worship also provided anti-Jewish Gentiles in Egypt with an opportunity to violate the synagogues of the Alexandrian Jews with busts of the emperor. Those who removed the statues could then be prosecuted for sacrilege (attacking the sacred image of the emperor). This was but the prelude to the tumultuous anti-Jewish riots that broke out late in Caligula's reign in both Alexandria and Caesarea.

Caligula had become too unstable a center for the empire and was assassinated by members of the elite Praetorian Guard in 41 C.E. His uncle Claudius was conscripted to be the next emperor by the Praetorians, the emperor's personal bodyguard of four hundred soldiers, who did not want to go back to field duty in

Figure 2.5. Three coins minted to commemorate the Flavian dynasty's pacification of the Jewish Revolt of 66-70 C.E. The first coin is a bronze sesterce of Vespasian, the reverse of which shows Judea (or perhaps a Jewess) mourning beneath a palm tree with a Roman soldier looking on. The inscription reads, "Judea Taken" or "Judea Secured." (Photo courtesy of Classical Numismatic Group, Inc., www.CNGcoins.com) The second is a gold aureus of Vespasian, also with Judea (or a Jewess) bound and sitting under a palm tree. The third is an aureus of Titus, with a reverse featuring a Roman trophy monument showing the helmet, cuirass, swords and shield of the Roman legionnaire. A male captive is bound and kneeling at the base. (Photos courtesy of Superior Galleries, Beverly Hills)

the disease-infested marshes of Germany or the parched camps of Syria. Claudius restored some measure of security to the beleaguered Jewish populations in Egypt and Caesarea. He also intersects with the New Testament story in his expulsion of many Jews from Rome in 49 C.E. on account of a riot stirred up by one "Chrestus." Many scholars believe that the Roman historian Suetonius, who records this act, mistook the common name "Chrestus" (often, but not always, a slave name) for the messianic title "Christus," and that we see here a glimpse of a violent disturbance within the Roman Jewish community over Jesus. It was this exile that caused Prisca and Aquila to relocate to Corinth shortly before Paul's arrival in 50 C.E. (see Acts 18:1-2).

Claudius named Nero, the son of his second wife Agrippina by her former husband, his successor. Nero's rule was quite stable from 54 to 61 C.E., when he lived under the guidance of his tutors. After Burrhus's death and Seneca's forced suicide, however, his true character emerged. His behaviors scandalized the senatorial families, particularly his penchant for singing and acting on stage (which was a low-class profession then). His desire to refashion Rome after his own tastes led him, it is believed, to burn down most of the old city to make way for his new Rome. He found a convenient group of scapegoats in the Roman Christians. This was the first time that Christians are hunted and executed simply for being Christians: it was a local persecution and did not become an official policy of the empire until the late-second and early-third centuries C.E. The barbaric and burlesque nature of the executions, of course, made an impression on Christians worldwide, disclosing a new and demonic side to the imperial rule and changing the way the emperor was viewed in many Christian circles (most dramatically seen in Revelation). This incident also revealed the marginal status of Christians in an urban center. If they could be singled out and scapegoated without even the semblance of due process, they did not have many friends and supporters among their neighbors. Already they must have come to be seen as a potentially subversive group, and indeed their proclamation of the eternal kingdom of God supplanting the kingdoms of the world may have very easily fed into the charge of hastening

that coming through arson. That Christians could have been believed capable of burning the capital of the empire is itself a significant indicator of popular sentiments toward them.

Nero's leadership was finally rejected, and he committed suicide to avoid a more degrading exit from the world, leaving no successor. The year 68-69 C.E. marked the return of chaos to the Roman world. Another series of civil wars erupted as four different emperors were named in different quadrants of the Mediterranean. All eyes were on Rome, waiting to see the outcome. The Spanish legions declared Galba, their general, emperor in 68 C.E. He marched on Rome with his legionaries and ruled for six months before being murdered by the supporters of the senator Otho, who had been a friend to Nero. While Otho was being confirmed as emperor by the Senate, the legions in Germany declared their general, Vitellius, emperor and proceeded to march on Rome. Otho resisted with the legions at his disposal but lost to Vitellius's superior generalship. At the same time the Syrian and Alexandrian legions declared their general, Vespasian, emperor. Vespasian had been engaged in suppressing the Jewish Revolt that broke out in 66 C.E. Leaving his son, Titus, to finish up in Judea, he too marched on Rome with a significant portion of his army. Vespasian emerged victorious from this turmoil, and the deadly wound which threatened the very life of the empire was healed after only one year.

After Rome and the provinces had been reminded of the ills of civil war, they were quite ready to support Vespasian wholeheartedly, all the more because the general had two strong sons, already adult and proven, to succeed him. Thus began the Flavian dynasty, hailed as the family that restored Rome after its near-fatal wound. Vespasian was succeeded first by his older son Titus (79-81 C.E.), who personally oversaw the siege of Jerusalem and destruction of the its temple in 70 C.E., and then by his younger son, Domitian (81-96 C.E.), whose policies are important as a background for the revelation to John (see figure 2.6).

Assessment of Domitian is very difficult, for the major sources for his rule (Tacitus, Suetonius, Pliny the Younger) were clients of the new dynasty of Nerva (96-98 C.E.) and his adopted son Trajan (98-117 C.E.). These authors used Domitian as a foil for the glorious rule of Trajan. Domitian appears to have made himself very unpopular with the senatorial class, but this might speak very well of him if we consider, for example, how he curtailed their privileges for the sake of the prosperity of provincials. The provinces appear to have benefited from his policies, and the marked increase in imperial cult activity (especially in Asia Minor, in the very cities to which John the Seer ministered) is the result of local appreciation of Domitian rather than the enforcing of self-deifying policies from the emperor himself. There is also no solid evidence of an empire-wide persecution of Christians under Domitian. Quite the opposite: even the most

anti-imperial author, John, can only point to one martyr by name from his period. This does not mean that Christians had it easy during his reign. Local people still stirred up trouble, and the imperial cult was a growing affront to Christian sensitivities about the lordship of Christ. However, Domitian was probably not personally responsible for these developments.

Domitian was murdered by conspirators and left no heir. An old senator, Nerva, acceded to the imperium and adopted as his son a strong general from Spain named Trajan, under whom the empire reached its greatest size and under whom Christians were for the first time legally persecuted. An especially poignant testimony to these proceedings is to be found in the correspondence of Pliny the Younger (*Ep.* 10.96), senatorial governor of Bithynia and Pontus in or around 110-112 C.E., and in the terse response of Trajan (*Ep.* 10.97), which set policy for the second century.

Judea under Roman rule. *The Herodian family.* The Herodian family emerged from ob-

Figure 2.6. A bronze *as* coin minted under Domitian. The obverse bears his image and titles. The reverse features the goddess Fortuna and bears the inscription "To the fortune of the Augustus." (Photo courtesy of Edward Waddell, www.coin.com)

Table 2.3. Roman Emperors During the First Century C.E.

Name	Relationship to Previous Emperor	Dates
Augustus (Octavian)	adopted heir of Julius Caesar	31 B.C.E.-14 C.E.
Tiberius	Stepson and adopted heir	14-37
Caligula	nephew and adopted heir	37-41
Claudius	uncle	41-54
Nero	stepson and adopted heir	54-68
Galba	usurper	68-69
Otho	adopted heir	69
Vitellius	usurper	69
Vespasian	usurper	69-79
Titus	son	79-81
Domitian	brother	81-96
Nerva	legal successor	96-98
Trajan	adopted heir	98-117

scurity as the Hasmonean dynasty came to an end. Because of the civil unrest fomented by Hasmonean rivals, Antipater the Idumean, a proven administrator, was made procurator of Judea and Idumea. After his death his sons Herod and Phasael became joint "tetrarchs," rulers of parts rather than the whole of a province or ethnic group. Phasael was killed when the last Hasmonean, Antigonus, the son of Aristobulus II and nephew of Hyrcanus II, gained the support of the Parthians to the east and invaded Judea. Clipping his uncle's ears to disqualify him from ever holding high priestly office again, Antigonus established himself in that position and attempted to take back the secular power that had been stripped from his uncle by Pompey. Herod fled to Rome for help. Faced with the choice between a loyal vassal in charge of Judea and a Parthian presence at their eastern border, the Roman consuls Octavian and Marc Antony appointed Herod "King of the Judeans," and supported his recapture of Jerusalem. Thus Herod became the king of the Jews, and held sway from 37-34 B.C.E.

Herod's most celebrated achievements were architectural. He constructed entire cities, with the most astounding being Caesarea Maritima ("Caesarea by the Sea") with its human-made harbor, a tremendous feat of engineering. He is also known for promoting Hellenistic culture throughout his realm with the construction of stadia, theaters and hippodromes, typical venues for Greek forms of entertainment, even in Jerusalem.[9] Herod's most famous building project, of course, involved the expansion and beautification of the second temple. Begun under his direction, this project was not to be completed until 63 C.E. (see Jn 2:20), a few years before it would be destroyed.

Herod did much to bring order to the province and wiped out many bands of brigands.

---

[9]See Josephus *Ant.* 15.8.1 for a splendid testimony to this phenomenon.

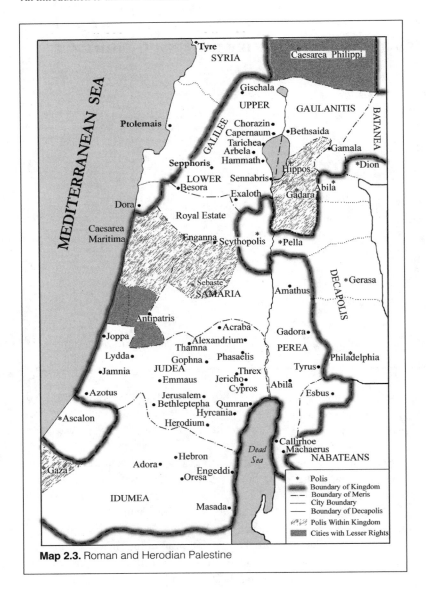

Map 2.3. Roman and Herodian Palestine

For all his accomplishments, however, he was viewed rather negatively by his subjects. First, he was by descent an Idumean—an Edomite—and the scriptural tradition bears witness to a long and bitter rivalry between Judeans and Edomites going back to Jacob and Esau themselves. Second, he took his kingdom by force of arms, even attacking Jerusalem itself. Third, he was insufferably generous to Gentile subjects as well as Jewish ones.

While he spent vast sums of money on the Jerusalem temple, he also erected temples to pagan gods in his predominantly Gentile cities. (For example, he erected a temple to Augustus in Samaria.) He also underwrote the cost for constructing pagan temples or offering lavish sacrifices to the Greek gods in the Gentile cities in Syria and Greece. For Herod, these were acts that established diplomatic relations and made Judea less of a second-class player in the Roman Empire. For his subjects, however, these were acts of idolatry and sacrilege.

The last few years of Herod's thirty-three-year reign were plagued by suspicion and intrigue among his successive wives and their several sons. During his last years he executed three of his own sons on suspicion of conspiracy and reduced another (Herod Philip, Herodias's first husband) to private life. Someone who would thus ravage his own house would have no scruples about killing a few dozen children in Bethlehem if he suspected a pretender to the throne (Mt 2:16-18).

In 4 B.C.E. Herod died, and his kingdom was divided between three surviving sons. Although the Judeans petitioned Rome to restore the temple hierocracy (that is, internal rule by the high priest rather than the family of Herod) Augustus essentially upheld Herod's will. Archelaus became ethnarch of Judea, Samaria and Idumea (4 B.C.E.-6 C.E.); Herod Antipas became tetrarch of Galilee and Perea

(4 B.C.E.-39 C.E.); and Philip became tetrarch of Iturea and Trachonitis (4 B.C.E.-34 C.E.). Archelaus was a brutal ruler (see the comment about Archelaus's jurisdiction in Mt 2:22), quelling disturbances with excessive violence. His policy only exacerbated unrest, culminating in a joint delegation of Judeans and Samaritans to Rome to request his removal. Augustus deposed Archelaus and exiled him to Gaul (modern France). Judea and Samaria became a Roman province administered by prefects until the outbreak of the Jewish Revolt in 66 C.E. (with a brief return to a Jewish king from 41-44 C.E.).

Philip ruled a territory that was primarily Gentile (Greek and Syrian), located mainly to the north and west of the Decapolis, which also supported a large Gentile population (hence the presence of the herds of swine made available for the Gadarene demoniac's many guests in Mt 8:28—9:1; Mk 5:1-20; Lk 8:26-39). The Decapolis actually remained un-

Figure 2.7. Herod's Palace and, in the open courtyard to the right of the city wall, the Jerusalem agora, as reconstructed in the Holy Land Hotel model of ancient Jerusalem. (Photo courtesy of the Holy Land Hotel and Todd Bolen [BiblePlaces.com])

der the direct administration of the Roman governor of Syria. Philip renovated and expanded Bethsaida and Caesarea Philippi, two cities that figure at a prominent juncture in the story of Jesus (see, e.g., Mk 8:22-30).

Herod Antipas is the most important member of the family for the Gospel narratives. He served Roman interests well and remained a patron for both Jews and Gentiles in his territory. Like his father and brother Philip, Antipas also gave much attention to building projects. Sepphoris, just a few miles from Nazareth, and Tiberias are two cities especially indebted to him for their growth. The latter was a full-fledged Greek city with a Greek constitution.[10] He divorced the daughter of King Aretas of the Nabateans in favor of Herodias, the former wife of Herod Philip (not the tetrarch in the North but the private citizen in the family). This was a flagrant offense to Jewish law and was openly denounced as such by John the Baptist. Antipas finally imprisoned and executed John for this attack since it provided a potentially hazardous focal point for rallying his enemies. It is possible that Jesus' pronouncement on adultery was heard as an implicit criticism of both Herodias and Antipas for their dissolutions of their first marriages (Mk 10:11-12). Antipas plays a large part in the Lucan passion narrative, where Pilate uses Jesus as an opportunity to show deference to Antipas and so repair their poor relationship (both had offered each other affronts in the past).

Antipas maintained a peaceful province for over forty years. When Herodias's brother Agrippa I, who had been educated at Rome and had come to be a close friend of Caligula and Claudius, was installed in 37 C.E. as Philip's successor with the title "king" instead of tetrarch, Herodias persuaded Antipas to seek a similar elevation of title for himself. His appeal was not without justification, for he had served Augustus and Tiberius with complete loyalty. Agrippa I, however, made Antipas look like a potential revolutionary, informing Gaius of Antipas's fortifications and large stores in the armories. Gaius sentenced Antipas to exile in Gaul. Herodias, as Agrippa's sister, was offered amnesty but chose exile with her husband instead.

Herod Agrippa I obtained the territories of the exiled Antipas. His friendship with Caligula proved providential in averting Caligula's plan to provide the Jewish temple with a statue of himself. We can only imagine how this episode impressed itself into the minds of Jews (both non-Christian and Christian). It evoked all the associations of Antiochus IV's desecration of the temple by instituting pagan rites, defiling the place where God promised to meet Israel and accept her sacrifices. Jesus' apocalyptic discourse (Mk 13) might well have come to mind during this crisis, with the possibility of a new "desolating sacrilege" imposing itself "where it ought not to stand" (Mk 13:14). When Claudius received the imperial office, he added Judea and Samaria to Agrippa I's kingdom, making him "King of the Judeans" after thirty-five years of Roman prefects. He governed a kingdom the size of Herod the Great's. He catered to the sensibilities of his Judean subjects, refusing, for example, the regal privilege of sitting down while he read the Torah selection at the Feast of Tabernacles. Outside Jewish areas, he continued the policy of Herod the Great and Antipas, being a Gentile to Gentiles as well as a Jew to Jews. He appears only once in the New Testament, where he is credited with executing James the son of Zebedee and imprisoning Peter for later execution (Acts 12:1-4). Luke ascribes this to a desire to "please the Judeans," who may have thus come to regard him as a protector of the Torah (which the Christian movement had begun to violate in its actions

---

[10]H. W. Hoehner, *Herod Antipas*, SNTSMS 17 (Cambridge, U.K.: Cambridge University Press, 1972).

Table 2.4. Herod and His Major Heirs

- Antipater (d. 43 B.C.E.), father of Herod the Great
- Herod the Great (king of Judea, 37-4 B.C.E.)
- Archelaus (ethnarch of Judea, 4 B.C.E.-6 C.E.), son of Herod the Great by Malthace
- Herod Antipas (tetrarch of Galilee and Perea, 4 B.C.E.-39 C.E.), son of Herod the Great by Malthace and second husband of Herodias
- Philip (tetrarch of Ituraea and Trachonitis, 4 B.C.E.-33 C.E.), son of Herod the Great by Cleopatra
- Herod Philip (private citizen), son of Herod the Great by Mariamne II, half-brother to Herod Antipas, Herodias's first husband, father of Salome
- Herod Agrippa I (king of Judea, 41-44), grandson of Herod the Great through Mariamne I (brother-in-law to Herod Antipas through his sister, Herodias)
- Herod Agrippa II (ethnarch of Chalcis and various regions north of Judea after 50 C.E.), son of Agrippa I, husband to Berenice (Acts 25:13)

---

toward Gentiles). According both to Luke and Josephus, Agrippa I died a horrible death after failing to refuse acclamation as a god by his Gentile subjects in Phoenicia (Acts 12:20-23; Josephus *Ant.* 19.8.2).

Agrippa II, the young son of Agrippa I, did not succeed at once to his father's kingdom. Judea was given back to procurators and remained so perpetually. Agrippa received the small kingdom of Chalcis after the death of his uncle, Herod of Chalcis, and finally the more Gentile portions of Agrippa I's kingdom. He became important to Roman administration of Judea and Samaria as an adviser in Jewish affairs (as in his appearance at Paul's trial in Acts 26) and enjoyed the oversight of the temple worship. He is remembered in Josephus's account of the Jewish War for valiantly trying to dissuade Jerusalem from revolution against Rome (*War* 2.16.2-5). He finally died in 92 C.E., and his territories were incorporated into the Roman province of Syria.

The high priestly office and its incumbents. During the period after the return from exile the high priest was the head of Israel. While there was a governor appointed to ensure that the interests of the foreign, dominating power were served, the high priest was the chief authority for internal affairs. He presided over the Sanhedrin, or council. He also performed the most important of the priestly duties, including leading the sacrifices on the high festal days and performing the rites for the Day of Atonement, for which he was uniquely qualified (see Lev 16). The office of the high priesthood suffered during the radical Hellenization of Jerusalem in 175-164 B.C.E. The high priesthood was basically auctioned off to the person with the most affluent supporters (including Menelaus, who had no pedigree for the office), and the office itself was used to diminish, not promote, Torah observance. Members of the Hasmonean family filled the office from 161 B.C.E. until 37 B.C.E., when Herod executed the last Hasmonean incumbent of the priesthood. The Hasmonean family had provided stability for the office but also provoked critique. In response to Hasmonean control of the office, for example, the Teacher of Righteousness moved to the community of Qumran and gave it its distinctive shape and hopes. The Pharisees, too, from time to time

Figure 2.8. The minting of native coinage signaled Judea's intention to regain its political independence. This half-shekel was minted in the first year of the Jewish Revolt (66 C.E.). The obverse depicts a chalice with the inscription "Shekel of Israel" (the date is above the cup). The reverse shows three pomegranates surrounded by the inscription "Jerusalem Is Holy," showing the connection between "holiness," "belonging to God" and the ideology of revolt. (Photo courtesy of Superior Galleries, Beverly Hills)

expressed displeasure at the arrangement. The *Psalms of Solomon* show disgust with the Jewish corrupters of the temple.

Herod received, with his kingship, the right to appoint the high priest. This was always done with an eye toward political concerns. For example, Herod wanted to marry a certain Mariamne, but could not marry the daughter of a rather insignificant noble, so he made her father the high priest. After Herod, Archelaus received the authority to confer the office. On Archelaus's removal Quirinius, the legate of Syria, appointed Annas ben-Seth to the high priesthood. Annas's family was to dominate the high priesthood during the period of Jesus' life and of the early church. Annas himself served from 6-15 C.E., and his son-in-law Joseph Caiaphas served from 18-36 C.E. As head of the family Annas continued to exercise much influence after his official term in office was ended (thus explaining the otherwise impossible "high priesthood of Annas and Caiaphas" in Lk 3:2). Their names are familiar to

all who have read the passion narratives. From 6 to 66 C.E. the high priesthood was passed between four or five of the wealthiest families whose members followed the Sadducean interpretation of the faith and were distinctly pro-Roman. Where a number of high priests follow in rapid succession, we may suspect bribery of the appointing governor. The last high priest was a commoner appointed by the rebels in Jerusalem during the Great Revolt (see figure 2.8).

Roman procurators. Roman rule was in principle tolerant of native customs and to a large extent the rights of local government to regulate internal affairs. This principle is seen at work in the Sanhedrin's arrest, trial and condemnation of Jesus (an act of self-governance). Indeed, in the Fourth Gospel the high priest and his council closely regulate internal affairs and forestall disturbances of the peace so Roman authorities would not take matters in their own hands, with more disastrous consequences (Jn 11:48-50). Their limits are also seen in that this judicial body must receive confirmation of the sentence from the Roman prefect, since the right to execute capital punishment was reserved for Roman authorities.

Both Julius Caesar and Augustus had confirmed the rights of Jews throughout the empire to observe their ancestral laws without hindrance. Unlike their neighbors to the north and south, Jews were not expected to participate in the imperial cult; emperors were satisfied with sacrifices on behalf of the emperor rather than to the emperor as a sign of the nation's good will and loyalty. The Roman governors of Judea were not to interfere in the religious life of that region (although the Romans' "safe-keeping" of the high priestly vestments when they were not in use was a potent reminder of the dependence of that freedom of religion on Roman good will).

As an imperial province Roman legions were stationed in Judea. It is quite natural then that soldiers and their officers would be encountered in the Gospels and Acts (e.g., the centurions in Lk 7:1-10 and Acts 10:1-48) and regarded as suitably well-known realities for use as teaching illustrations (as in Mt 5:41). On rare occasions Roman soldiers would be openly antagonistic of Judeans; more often they were just an unwelcome reminder of foreign domination and the might of Rome. Rome relied heavily on collaborators—from the local indigenous elites who correctly understood that the best way to remain in power was to defer to Roman power to non-elites (e.g., tax-farmers) who found in the Roman administration opportunities for advancement they did not find in other occupations.

Judea was not considered a pacified province. There were several rebellions against Roman rule during this period, always put down with ruthless efficiency. Varus, for example, executed over two thousand revolutionaries by crucifixion shortly after Herod's death. The ethos of Roman government placed a high value on maintaining order and promoting the value of submissiveness to authority (the statements in Rom 13:1-7 and 1 Pet 2:13-17 would have met with approval), and consequently Roman authorities showed a distinct impatience with resistance and insurgents. Crucifixion proved a valuable and much-used tool to communicate these values to the Judean population. Rome's contributions to Judean society would be extolled by some Jews, whereas those who focused on the heavy-handed administration of justice, the burden of taxation and the occasional indiscretions by governors or their soldiers rejected the legitimacy of Roman rule.

The first twenty years of the direct government of prefects appear to have passed without incident and without the prefects causing offense to their Jewish subjects. The prefecture of Pontius Pilate, governor from 26 to 36 C.E., marks a turn for the worse. His administration began inauspiciously, as he twice affronted Jewish sensibilities. Seeking to honor Emperor Tiberius in typically Roman ways, he twice managed to violate the sanctity of Jerusalem. First, he brought the imperial standards, bearing the image of Tiberius, into the city under cover of night. A riot ensued the next day, and he was forced to remove them. On another occasion he set up dedicatory shields to Tiberius in Herod's palace (the governor's residence in Jerusalem) bearing no image but an inscription saying who had dedicated them and to whom they were dedicated. This second part of the inscription no doubt included the divine titles (found, for example, on imperial coinage) which would have been offensive to most Jews, particularly when set within the city devoted to the exclusive worship of the one God. Once more, he was forced (this time by Tiberius himself) to remove them.

Three other incidents involving Pilate deserve to be mentioned. Seeking to make a positive contribution to the life of Jerusalem, especially its temple, Pilate set out to construct an aqueduct. To accomplish his goal, however, he appropriated funds from the temple treasury, thus violating the sanctity of the temple and the funds dedicated to it. Protesters were beaten and dispersed by Pilate's soldiers. Luke tells of another occasion when Pilate slaughtered a number of Galilean pilgrims within the temple precincts, mingling "their blood with their sacrifices" (Lk 13:1). Perhaps these Galileans became a focus for unrest in the city and posed a threat to order. Pilate's measures, however, are in line with his heavy-handedness and his disregard for the temple. The final straw came when Pilate intervened in a movement that was growing in Samaria. A self-styled prophet gathered a large following, promising to reveal where the sacred vessels of the Mosaic tabernacle were hidden and thus show himself to be the "prophet like Moses" promised in Deuteronomy 18, a pattern of messianic expectation that enjoyed special currency among the Samaritans but also the early church (see Acts 3:22-26, as well as Matthew's presentation of Jesus as the authoritative interpreter of the Mosaic law). Pilate dispersed the gathering with a detachment of cavalry, killing many. The Samaritans filed a complaint with the legate of Syria, who sent Pilate back to Rome to answer for his actions.

From 37-41 C.E. Roman prefects continued to be appointed, followed by the return of a Jewish monarch, Agrippa I, in 41-44 C.E. The relative peace under these local rulers was upset only by Gaius Caligula's attempt to install his statue in the Jerusalem temple. After the death of Agrippa I the administration of Judea was handed back to procurators. Under these procurators, we observe a distinct rise in "military messianism" and armed opposition to Roman rule. Two of these procurators are known from the pages of Acts: Antonius Felix (52-59/60 C.E.) and Porcius Festus (59/60-62 C.E.). Felix crucified so many brigands and sus-

pected revolutionaries that he stirred up widespread resentment and a new wave of terrorist resistance activity—the *sicarii* or "daggermen," who struck their targets (usually collaborators) and then faded into the crowd. Festus also had to suppress a revolutionary movement in the wilderness. All this activity points to the extremely volatile nature of Judea during this period. Roman rule was viewed increasingly as unacceptable and incompatible with allegiance to God. Also noteworthy is the intentional imitation of biblical patterns by the would-be messiah-kings. The Jewish tradition itself, it seemed, cried out to many people for a rejection of the Roman yoke.

In addition to overly harsh and repressive measures against potential dissidents, several other incidents contributed much to anti-Roman sentiment. During the procuratorship of Cumanus (48-52 C.E.), Samaritans had killed a number of Jewish pilgrims from Galilee. Cumanus dismissed the Jews' petition for justice, with the result that a band of Zealots tried to take matters into their own hands. Cumanus violently suppressed them, further alienating the Judean populace. Eventually the matter came before Claudius, who recognized that Cumanus's negligence resulted in the multiplication of lost lives and removed him.

A more serious situation erupted in Caesarea. The Jewish and Greek citizens of this city disputed the civic rights of the former, and rioting ensued. Felix intervened, siding hard with the Greeks. When the matter was referred to Nero, he too ruled in favor of the Greeks, denying the Jewish claim to be equal citizens. After this ruling the Greek citizens took every opportunity to insult and cajole the Jewish population of Caesarea, going so far as to desecrate a synagogue by sacrificing birds outside the door to purify the place of the Jewish plague, as it were. The Jews sought redress from Gessius Florus, procurator from 64-67 C.E., who, even after accepting a large

Table 2.5. Noteworthy Roman Governors During the First Century C.E.

Pontius Pilate	26-36
Cuspius Fadus	44-46
Tiberius Julius Alexander	46-48
Ventidius Cumanus	48-52
Antonius Felix	52-60
Porcius Festus	60-62
Lucius Albinus	62-64
Gessius Florus	64-66
Flavius Silva	73-??

bribe from the Jewish elders, disregarded their petition. Further, he raided the temple treasury on the charge that Judea was in arrears in their taxes, thus committing sacrilege against the temple. Josephus accuses him of trying to provoke a Jewish revolt as a means of covering the tracks of his own crimes. When moving from Caesarea to Jerusalem he instructed his soldiers to return no Jew's salutations when they arrived at Jerusalem. The Jews, finding their salutations scorned, began to accuse Florus. The soldiers responded to these words by slaughtering any Jews they could reach. In response to this final straw not a Zealot but the captain of the temple declared war by suspending the sacrifices offered on behalf of the emperor.

The Jewish Revolt and its aftermath: Judaism without a temple. The Zealots emerge as leaders during this time, stirring up the population of Judea into a full-scale revolution against Roman rule in a futile fight for independence. The Jewish heritage spoke at numerous points about how God could give victory to a faithful army, no matter how small it was and no matter how vast the enemy hosts (1 Sam 14:6; 1 Macc 3:18-22; 4:6-11). The

Zealots rallied the people with an ideology of "no king but God" and with a messianic fervor for the restoration of the Jewish state. Despite the Jews' preparations and dedication, however, the legions of Vespasian quickly regained control of Galilee and most of Judea. After Nero's suicide Vespasian withdrew in order to wait for confirmation of his orders from the new emperor—and eventually he became the new emperor after the civil wars of 68-69 C.E. This delay gave the factions in Jerusalem time to lose sight of their common enemy and to begin to make war on each other. Vespasian dispatched his son Titus to finish the retaking of Jerusalem. The city made preparations for the siege but was divided into three factions, each preying on the others as the siege was pressed and famine set in. Starvation and pestilence did most of Titus's work for him. In 70 C.E. he took the city, destroyed its walls and razed its temple. Titus returned to Rome in victory, leaving his general Flavius Silva to clean up the last pockets of resistance, the most famous being the fortress of Masada (see figures 2.9 and 2.10).

The destruction of the temple had a devastating impact on the Jewish people and posed a formidable challenge to the Jewish religion, which had now, for the second time, lost its center. Except for three years, the second temple had functioned as the place where God met Israel and the divine-human relationship could be repaired and enacted for almost six hundred years. So momentous were these events that Luke regarded them as the fulfillment of Jesus' predictions concerning the woes that would precede his return (compare Lk 21:20-24 with Mt 24:15-18 and Mk 13:14-23).

Two apocalypses—*4 Ezra* (= 2 Esdras 3-14) and *2 Baruch*—attest to the theological and pastoral challenges posed by Rome's destruction of Jerusalem. *4 Ezra* wrestles with the fact that an idolatrous and impious nation would be allowed to destroy God's holy place, and go unpunished itself. What will give meaning and hope to life as a Jew in these sadly changed circumstances? Both apocalypses look to the keeping of the covenant, the Torah, as the way forward. Finally,

the definition of Israel's hope as dedication to walking in line with the Torah and thus keeping faith with God would emerge as the winning answer to the ongoing question. Even though Jewish sages (rabbis) would move away from apocalypticism, the direction they were going was finding enormous support among apocalypticists.

Under the leadership of Yohanan ben-Zakkai and the rabbis that met in Jamnia, Judaism began to take the shape familiar to us today—a Judaism without sacrifices. There was ample theological preparation for this in the Psalms, which had already begun to speak of acts of contrition as more valuable than sin offerings, prayers as the equivalent of the offering of incense and acts of praise as an appropriate for of a thanksgiving offering (e.g., Ps 50:23; 51:16-17; 141:2). The sect at Qumran, alienated from the temple during the Hasmonean and Roman periods on account of their perception that it was being run counter to God's

Figure 2.9. The fortress of Masada, another of Herod's places of refuge. Well fortified and armed, well stocked with food and water, Judean revolutionaries held out here for three full years after the fall of Jerusalem in 70 C.E. (Photo courtesy of Todd Bolen [BiblePlaces.com])

Figure 2.10. The mountain fortress of Masada. The Roman army, along with many slaves, laboriously constructed a ramp against the side of the mountain so that it could bring its siege ladders and battering ram against the walled palisades at the top. (Photo courtesy of Kim Guess [Bible-Places.com])

appointed calendar and practices, had already adopted this as a working principle: the people of the covenant at Qumran would "atone for the guilty rebellion and for sins of unfaithfulness . . . without the flesh of holocausts and the fat of sacrifice. Prayer rightly offered shall be as an acceptable fragrance of righteousness, and perfection of way as a delectable free-will offering" (1QS 9.4-6).

The keeping of Torah thus became the center of Judaism. Repentance, prayer, acts of charity and study of the Torah took the place of the temple sacrifices. The synagogue, already a well-established institution throughout Judea and the Diaspora, became the sacred space in which to meet God. After the destruction of the temple the Pharisaic party gained the ascendancy. Their vision of the covenant, as developed by generations of rabbis, became for the first time normative for Judaism. Consequently, for the first time one could speak of "heretical" Judaism. The new

form of Judaism could not be as tolerant of diversity as its pre-70 C.E. forebear, and for the first time we find discussion of grounds for the expulsion of heretics from the synagogues. As a result of Judaism's need to consolidate and reformulate its essence, the churches found their tethers to the synagogue severed. What were once two movements within the larger whole of Judaism gradually became two independent entities, moving in their own directions.

TORAH, TEMPLE AND TRADITION: THE COMMON FOCAL POINTS OF JEWS

The way of Torah: One holy people for one holy God. First-century Judaism was a highly diverse and variegated phenomenon. The basic, unifying principle that held the different expressions of Judaism together was commitment to the one God through the keeping of the Torah, the covenant made with God at Si-

The Shema

Hear, O Israel: The LORD our God is one LORD; and you shall love the LORD your God with all your heart, and with all your soul, and with all your might. And these words which I command you this day shall be upon your heart; and you shall teach them diligently to your children, and shall talk of them when you sit in your house, and when you walk by the way, and when you lie down, and when you rise. And you shall bind them as a sign upon your hand, and they shall be as frontlets between your eyes. And you shall write them on the doorposts of your house and on your gates. (Deut 6:4-9 RSV)

And if you will obey my commandments which I command you this day, to love the LORD your God, and to serve him with all your heart and with all your soul, he will give the rain for your land in its season, . . . that you may gather in your grain and your wine and your oil. And he will give grass in your fields for your cattle, and you shall eat and be full. Take heed lest your heart be deceived, and you turn aside and serve other gods and worship them, and the anger of the LORD be kindled against you, and he shut up the heavens, so that there be no rain, and the land yield no fruit, and you perish quickly off the good land which the LORD gives you. (Deut 11:13-17 RSV)

Make tassels on the corners of their garments throughout their generations, and . . . put upon the tassel of each corner a cord of blue; and it shall be to you a tassel to look upon and remember all the commandments of the LORD, to do them, not to follow after your own heart and your own eyes, which you are inclined to go after wantonly. So you shall remember and do all my commandments, and be holy to your God. I am the LORD your God, who brought you out of the land of Egypt, to be your God: I am the LORD your God. (Num 15:38-41 RSV)

nai and mediated through Moses.[11] At the same time this shared principle became a point of division as soon as the questions "How should we keep the Torah?" or "What does it mean to keep this particular commandment?" arose. Issues concerning the application of Torah distinguished Sadducees from Pharisees, the inhabitants of Qumran from the followers of Jesus, and even followers of Jesus from one another (for example, in the situa-

tion that emerges behind the writing of Galatians). All agreed that Torah was to be fulfilled; there were many disagreements over how it was to be fulfilled in daily, community life.

The importance of keeping Torah as the fundamental expression of Judaism cannot be overestimated. During the Hellenization crisis Jews accepted torture and execution rather than acquiesce to eat foods like pork, proscribed by Torah, or fail to inscribe their chil-

---

[11]This is not meant to be taken as a statement about the authorship of the Pentateuch, nor an ascription of all the legal material in the Pentateuch to Moses himself. One noteworthy development concerning the traditions of the giving of the Torah involved the emergence of angelology. Most Jews appear to have held to the belief that the holy God dealt with the impure, unholy world through intermediaries—superhuman spiritual beings that served God (or in the case of demons and Satan, opposed God). Torah itself was believed to have been given by God *through* angels (*Jub.* 1.27-2.1 and following; Gal 3:19-20; Heb 2:1-4). For New Testament authors this became a useful way to set God's intention in Torah over against God's intention in his direct, unmediated oath (whether to Abraham, as in Galatians, or to and through Christ as "priest for ever" in Hebrews).

dren into the covenant through circumcision. The way of Torah was the way to walk in God's favor, bringing blessing for both individual and nation. Transgression of the covenant meant provocation of God's honor by those who should most uphold that honor and thus danger for the individual and the nation. The way of Torah was the way of devotion to the one God and the way of survival under the watchful eyes of the God who blesses the loyal and chastises the disloyal.

The centrality of Torah and its relationship to walking with the one God is best expressed in the *Shema,* the closest thing to a creed in early Judaism. Taken from Scripture (Deut 6:4-9; 11:13-21; Num 15:38-41), this liturgical piece was recited twice daily by most Jews, keeping forever in the forefront of their minds the one God and God's prescribed way.

The *Shema* places the doing of the Torah at the center of the life of the individual, the family and the community. It gives specific directions for mnemonic devices that would help the Jew to keep the obligation to follow Torah ever in the center of his or her identity. The garments of the males were indeed fringed with tassels, whose sole purpose was to remind the wearer and the onlooker of the distinctive way of life that set the Jew apart from all other peoples. Males would also wear the phylactery, a small box containing a tiny parchment on which the *Shema* was written, bound to the right forearm or forehead. Several of these parchments have been found at Qumran, written in an astoundingly small print (a sample specimen measures only two inches square). These reminded the wearer that every intention or ambition and every action in which the wearer used his hand must be in line with the commandments of God. The mezuzah was an ornament on the doorpost of a Jewish home, consisting of a piece of decorative enamel containing or covering a small parchment with the *Shema* written on it. This was yet another visible reminder that the home was to be a place where the law of God was observed and taught.

The temple and its sacrifices. During most of the first century the temple was the focal point of Jews throughout the world. This was the place where God promised to meet Israel, to hear its prayers and accept its sacrifices. Many Jews would make pilgrimages to the temple from their homes throughout the Diaspora and throughout Palestine on occasions of high festivals. The temple provided not only a symbol of the connection of all Jews with their ancestral land but also an occasion for renewing those connections. As long as the temple cult ran smoothly, according to God's directions, a ready means of access to God (however limited) was at hand. The well-being of the people could be secured and transgressions against God's law covered so they would not jeopardize the covenantal relationship between a sinful people and its holy God. Thus Torah and temple were not separated in the minds of most Jews—even where a Jewish group was highly critical of the temple, like the Qumran community, it still could not envision a covenant without a temple. Rather, the two were inseparably linked. The Torah prescribed and regulated the temple; the temple provided for the interaction between the people and their covenant God.

The temple the New Testament authors refer to is the Herodian temple, the glorious result of Herod the Great's renovations and expansions on the second temple, built to replace the Solomonic temple after the exile. The temple complex sits on an elevated area. The temple proper was surrounded by a large enclosure, the Court of the Gentiles, which was itself enclosed by vast stretches of columned porches where teachers and students would gather in the shadow of the temple to study the Torah. Inside the Court of the Gentiles was to be found the Court of Women, into which all Israelites could come. It was forbidden for non-Jews to cross from the Court of the Gentiles into the interior courts. Inscriptions over the gate to the Court of Women prescribed the death penalty for desecration by a Gentile. Still closer to the temple itself was the Court of Israelites, where males of thirteen years or more alone could enter. Beyond this place only the priests could move. In the Court of the Priests were found the altar and, finally, the massive temple building, a visually striking monument to the greatness of Israel and the one God. Its marble exterior and gold plate decorations made it glorious to behold and visible from afar. Within this building were two chambers, the "holy place" and the "holy of holies," into which only the high priest could enter, and that only once a year on the Day of Atonement. Even though the Jew knew God to be everywhere, God was specially present in the holy of holies.

The temple was administered and maintained by a cadre of priests and Levites. The priests would attend to the sacrifices (animal sacrifices which were constant; offering of incense at the times of prayer, such as we find Zechariah doing at the opening of Luke's Gospel; the grain and cereal offerings; and the like). The Levites provided support services from the singing of the psalms to the provision of wood for the altar. The expenses of the temple and the livelihood of the priests came from the portions allotted them from the sacrifices, freewill offerings, the half-shekel temple tax from Jews around the world, the monetary redemption of the firstborn and the offerings of the first fruits. The general tithe supported the Levites, who in turn gave a tenth to the priests.

For both Jews and Gentiles in the ancient world, sacrifice was the primary vehicle for communication with deity, and it was believed to be an effective means of doing business, as it were, with the patrons above. In Israel there were several kinds of occasional offerings—sacrifices made as the need arises. These include "thank offerings," which represent the appropriate display of gratitude to God for a specific gift; "sin offerings," which represent the appropriate restitution to God's provoked honor, acknowledging the offense and making it good; and "votive offerings," sacrifices promised to God for desired benefits. Certain sacrifices were also offered on a regular basis. Of note is the daily offering, the *tamid*: one lamb in the morning and a second in the midafternoon. Both were accompanied by an offering of incense, grain and wine, choral singing, and a prayer service for the people who assembled. This continual burned offering represented the nation's unswerving loyalty to God, their divine patron, a continual acknowledgment of dependence on God. The daily sacrifice was doubled on sabbaths and multiplied on new moons and festivals. Another regular sacrifice since the accession of Augustus was the daily offering on behalf of the emperor, which was offered by the Jerusalem leadership as a sign of loyalty in lieu of the more usual provincial demonstrations through the imperial cult.

A constant fact throughout Jewish history is the vulnerability of the temple. First destroyed by Nebuchadnezzar in 587 B.C.E., the temple was rebuilt between 538 and 515 B.C.E., only to be subjected to further desecration by Antiochus IV (167-166 B.C.E.), Pompey the Great (63 B.C.E.), and nearly by Caligula (40 C.E.), and finally destroyed by the legions of Rome under the command of Titus (70 C.E.). Its impressive appearance, being fashioned from enormous blocks of stone and towering over its surroundings, could not help but inspire awe (e.g., among the disciples in Mk 13:1). Jesus would have to remind them, however, of the lessons of history that were destined to repeat themselves (Mk 13:2). Ultimately, Judaism would have to understand how the covenant with God could continue to function without the temple: the Christian movement and the rabbinic movement were the two principal forms in which this survival became possible (see figure 2.11).

The liturgical year: The rhythm of life. The

Figure 2.11. The Arch of Titus, a monument erected in Rome to celebrate the achievements of Vespasian's oldest son, emperor 79-81 C.E. Prominent among the decorations is a relief sculpture of the treasures of the Jerusalem Temple being carried away by Roman soldiers, with Jewish captives in their train. (Photos courtesy of Todd Bolen [BiblePlaces.com])

Jewish year was given a rhythm and sense of sacredness from the close observance of the fasts and festivals that made up their liturgical year. Many of these observances are specifically prescribed in Torah. Others, like Purim, Hanukkah and the Fast for the Destruction of the Temple, were added to the calendar to commemorate newer developments. We will look at these festivals in their order of occurrence. As we contemplate these celebrations that divide the Jewish year, we are also invited into the traditions of the Hebrew Scriptures and Jewish history that were kept foremost in Jewish consciousness by means of this annual cycle. These traditions are of central importance for understanding the New Testament as well, whose authors assume a high level of familiarity with them and develop Christian identity and theology in constant relation to them.

The most basic and regular observance was the sabbath. Hallowing the sabbath brought to remembrance two essential aspects of the Jewish tradition. First, the sabbath calls to mind God's creation of the heavens and the earth, after which God rested—hence the observance of the seventh day of the week as a day of rest and appreciation for what God has done (Gen 2:1-3; Ex 20:8-11). This was also a reminder of the uniqueness of the God of Israel, the true Creator God who stands apart from the false gods of the nations. Second, the sabbath provided a reminder of the rest that God gave to the descendants of Jacob when God delivered them from slavery in Egypt and brought them into a land of their own (Deut 5:12-15). The Jews' obligation to rest on the sabbath was a perpetual reminder of God's gift of rest, a privilege that had not been theirs in Egypt.

In a world without weekends a day of rest was a practice distinctive to the Jews. It was one of their hallmarks in the eyes of outsiders and often occasioned sharp criticism. Jews might choose to die rather than defend themselves when attacked on the sabbath (where military action would be regarded as work and thus a violation of the sabbath; see 1 Macc 2:29-38). For the Jew this is an expression of piety; for the Greek author Plutarch it is disdained as cowardice and laziness. Different groups might argue about how the sabbath was to be kept. Pharisees actually sought to relax the rules somewhat, while the people of Qumran were much more rigid. For the majority of Jews the sabbath was chiefly a day of joy—a time to celebrate God and Torah at the synagogue, and to enjoy family and friends around the best meal of the week.

The three cardinal festival days, days on which all male Israelites were to appear in Jerusalem, were linked to the agricultural cycle (see the discussion of these festivals in Lev 23). The Feast of Passover (*Pesach*) marked the beginning of the wheat and barley harvest. The feast of Pentecost, fifty days later (hence the name, derived from the Greek word for fifty), celebrated the grain harvest. The feast of Tabernacles in the early fall marked the end of the olive and grape harvest. By the first century the religious significance of these festivals dominated their celebration, particularly as Jews in Judea and the Diaspora came to inhabit an increasingly urbanized, less agrarian, environment.

Passover celebrated the foundational event in the story of Israel—the deliverance of the Hebrews from bondage in Egypt. This was the beginning of their story as a nation and the central redemptive act of God on their behalf in which God also committed God's self to them: "out of Egypt have I brought my son" (Hos 11:1). Bound up with Passover are the themes of God's election of Israel as God's special possession and God's commitment to deliver Israel from all its oppressors. The God who once delivered Israel from Egypt and who repeated that liberation by making a way in the wilderness for the returnees from the Babylonian exile, would again bring deliverance to Israel from Gentile domination. The Exodus story was often reenacted by would-be messiahs who called their followers out into the wilderness and promised a new parting of the Jordan or new conquest of their ancestral land, and Passover was often an occasion for the stirring of nationalistic zeal and the hopes for revolution.

Pentecost was associated with the giving of the law on Mt. Sinai "on the third new moon after the people had gone forth from Egypt" (Ex 19:1). While the timing is not exact, the agricultural festival of Shavuot, or Pentecost, was close and available for this religious overlay. The giving of the Spirit on the festival of Pentecost in Acts 2 thus carries a spiritual message for the reader familiar with the associations of the festival.

The Jewish New Year, *Rosh ha-Shanah,* occurs prior to Succoth in the fall, with the end of the dry season and the coming of the first rains. This marks the time for ploughing and seeding, and thus the start of another agricultural cycle. *Yom Kippur,* the Day of Atonement, fell nine days after the New Year. Until 70 C.E. it was celebrated with the ritual prescribed in Leviticus 16 (a ritual that becomes an important resource for interpreting the significance of Jesus' death and ascension in Heb 7:1—10:18). It is a day of fasting and repentance, the day when the high priest enters the holy of holies to offer the blood from the sin offering in God's very presence. It is an essential day in the life of Israel, the day on which the covenant is repaired from all breaches, individual and collective, and God's holiness "covered" and contained anew by the blood, and thus prevented from breaking out to consume sinners.

The festival of Booths, or *Succoth,* came to be associated with the traditions of Israel wandering the wilderness and celebrating God's provision for them there. A harvest festival was a natural setting to remember not only God's annual provision but also God's special provisions for Israel as the Hebrews traveled from Egypt to the Promised Land. Just as the Exodus and Sinai traditions were memorialized in Passover and Pentecost, the wilderness and conquest traditions were enshrined in the autumn harvest festival. This autumn festival retained much of its agricultural significance. While it came to celebrate the period of wandering in the wilderness, when both God and Israel dwelled in tents, it was also the festival at which the people sought God's gift of rain for the coming season. The Day of Atonement was strategically placed just a few days before this festival so the people could approach God with confidence that their sins would not provoke God's anger and prevent the coming of the necessary rains. The *Shema* itself twice daily reminded Jews that even the gift of rain, grain and thus daily bread depended on fidelity to the covenant.

As an example of how knowledge of the festival can enhance the reader's appreciation of the significance of the gospel proclamation, we may consider Succoth as the backdrop for John 7:2, 37-39. On the first seven days of this festival the priest pours out a libation of water, symbolizing the people's dependence on God for the rains and thus for life itself. On the eighth day, the climax of the festival on which no libation was performed, Jesus is portrayed as standing up and shouting to the masses assembled in the temple: "If anyone thirsts, let whoever believes in me come to me and drink. As the Scripture says, 'out of that one's heart shall flow rivers of water'" (Jn 7:37-39). Jesus is thus presented as the answer to the petitions of the previous seven days' libations, indeed as an eschatological fulfillment since the water is not merely the annual rain but the life-giving Spirit.

Hanukkah, called the Feast of Dedication in John's Gospel, celebrated the reconsecration of the temple and its altar on the twenty-fifth of Chislev, 164 B.C.E., when Judas and his brothers put an end to the pagan rituals in Jerusalem, purified the temple, rebuilt the altar and restored the proper sacrifices. The miracle of the single flask of oil lasting eight days is a rather minor thing compared to the miracle of Judas's little army driving out the Seleucid forces. The festival appears to have taken hold during the early years of the Hasmonean dynasty (who, of course, would avidly promote a festival that reminded all their subjects of the ruling family's benefits) and is commended to Jews in the Diaspora by the letters prefacing 2 Maccabees (see 2 Macc 1:1—2:18). This festival kept in remembrance the dangers of foreign domination, the heroism of the martyrs who died rather than sacrifice fidelity to the covenant with God, and the remarkable successes of the Jewish revolutionaries who routed superior Gentile forces. It also spoke eloquently of God's continuing fidelity to God's holy place.

Purim was a downright rowdy festival celebrating the deliverance of the Jews by God through Esther and Mordecai. The book of Esther was read in its entirety, a good time was generally had by all, so much so that a later rabbinic *halakha* states that the Jew is to drink until he can no longer distinguish between the sentences "Blessed be Mordecai" and "Cursed be Haman" (*b. Megillah* 7b). The feast, particularly through the annual reading of Esther, would be an occasion to remember the tensions that existed between Gentiles and Jews, the vulnerable position of Jews living under foreign rule and subject to anti-Jewish manipulation of the system, but also God's providential care for God's people and even the triumph of the latter over their (Gentile) enemies.

The sabbaths and cycles of festivals kept Jews keenly aware of their identity, their heritage and their hopes. Together with a commitment to follow the way of Torah and to participate in the temple service (in person where practicable but always at least through contributions for the sacrifices performed on behalf of all Israel), these provided a foundational body of traditions that bound Israelites together. Teachers like Jesus, James and Paul were able to build on these traditions as they gave expression to the new invasions of God's benevolence in human history.

The synagogue. While the temple served as the formal and symbolic center for Jewish religious life, going to the temple was in fact a

The "Eighteen" Benedictions

Blessed are You, O Lord, our God and God of our fathers, God of Abraham, God of Isaac and God of Jacob, the great, mighty and revered God, God Most High, the creator of heaven and earth, our Shield and the Shield of our fathers, our confidence from generation to generation. Blessed are you, O Lord, the Shield of Abraham!

You are mighty, bringing low the proud; strong, judging the unmerciful; eternal, raising the dead, making the wind to blow and sending down rain. You sustain the living and give life to the dead; in the twinkling of an eye you make salvation to spring forth for us. Blessed are you, O Lord, who gives life to the dead!

Forgive us, our Father, for we have sinned against you; blot out and cause our transgressions to pass from your sight, for great is your mercy. Blessed are you, O Lord, who forgives abundantly!

Heal us, O Lord our God, from the pain of our heart; make weariness and sighing to pass away from us; cause healing for our wounds to rise up. Blessed are you, O Lord, who heal the sick among your people Israel!

Bless for us, O Lord, this year for our welfare, with every kind of produce, and bring near speedily the year of the end of our redemption; give dew and rain upon the face of the earth and satisfy the world from the treasuries of your goodness, and give a blessing upon the work of your hands. Blessed are you, O Lord, who bless the years!

Blow the great horn for our liberation and lift a banner to gather our exiles. Blessed are you, O Lord, who gathers the dispersed of your people Israel!

Restore our judges as at the first and our counselors as at the beginning, and reign over us— you alone! Blessed are you, O Lord, who loves justice!

Be merciful, O Lord our God, in your great mercy toward your people Israel, and toward your city Jerusalem, and toward Zion, the place where your glory abides, and toward your glory, and toward your temple and your habitation, and toward the kingdom of the house of David, your righteous anointed one. Blessed are you, O God, God of David, the Builder of Jerusalem!

Hear, O Lord our God, the sound of our prayer and have mercy on us, for you are a gracious and merciful God. Blessed are you, O Lord, who hears prayer!

Accept us, O Lord our God, and dwell in Zion; and may your servants serve you in Jerusalem. Blessed are you, O Lord, whom we serve in reverent fear!

We give thanks to you, the Lord our God and God of our fathers, for all the good things, the lovingkindness and the mercy which you have wrought and done with us and with our fathers before us: and if we said, "Our feet slip," your lovingkindness, O Lord, held us upright. Blessed are you, O Lord, unto whom it is good to give thanks![a]

[a]Everett Ferguson, *Backgrounds of Early Christianity,* 2nd ed. (Grand Rapids: Eerdmans, 1993), pp. 543-44.

rare privilege for the majority of Jews. When Diaspora became a reality for significant Jewish populations, Jews began to meet together on the sabbath in order to enjoy regular interaction around their sacred Scriptures. The place in which they met came to be known as a "prayer house" (*proseuchē*) or "assembly" (*synagōgē*). The synagogue functioned also as a sort of local court, regulating internal Jewish affairs. The synagogue rose to a place of importance within Palestine as well, every village having a designated place for prayer and for the reading and study of Scripture, since even in Palestine Jews would rarely be able to travel to the temple more frequently than the three prescribed feasts.

The synagogue service began with an invocation, a recitation of Psalm 95 or some other invitation to attend to God. It continued with the recitation of the *Shema* and the reading of the Decalogue (the Ten Commandments), thus contributing to keeping the commandments in the forefront of the communal consciousness. It also included prayer in the form of the *Shemoneh Esre',* the "Eighteen Benedictions," so called because each petition ended with a benediction ("Blessed are You, O God") celebrating some facet of God's character or activity, making these prayers incidentally a window looking directly into Jewish theology. The enumeration of eighteen benedictions represents the expanded form as it existed during the second century. Their form at the turn of the era is believed to have included eleven petitions, and these give us an important taste of Jewish weekly prayer from the time of Jesus. These prayers cultivate an awareness that God is merciful toward his people's iniquities (pardoning them) and infirmities (healing them). God also provides for them in life (through the provision of food and safety) and in death (through the hope of the resurrection). The prayers also reinforce the conviction that the God of the universe is also in some special sense the God of Abraham, Isaac and Jacob, and the defender of their descendants, Israel. The prayers orient the worshipers' hopes in a decidedly nationalistic direction, nurturing a longing for the land of Israel, the glorification of Jerusalem, the restoration of theocracy and indigenous leadership (as opposed to foreign domination), and the gathering of the Jews living outside of Palestine.

The service continued with the reading of a portion of Torah (the whole Pentateuch being covered in sequence in one year in some lectionaries, in three years in others), a reading from the Prophets or Writings based on thematic connection with the reading from Torah, and a "word of exhortation" interpreting and applying the readings. The service concluded with a benediction of the people. The singing of selected psalms could be expected to have been a part of the service.

The synagogue attracted a number of Gentiles, some merely curious, others committed to join in the worship of the one God and, perhaps, some basic requirements (the so-called Noachic laws imposed by God on all humanity generally, requiring abstinence from idolatry, murder, fornication, consumption of blood and the like), still others becoming proselytes, taking on the whole yoke of Torah (the laws specially imposed by God on Israel). It was particularly among the second group that Jewish-Christian missionaries had marked success, offering full connection with the people of God without the burdens of circumcision and dietary laws. The synagogue also provided a pattern for the organization of the Christian "assembly" (*ekklēsia*), although the Greco-Roman voluntary organizations known as *collegia* also exercised an important influence in this regard. The synagogue's contribution to its members of a sense of connectedness with one another, with other synagogues and with the mother community in Judea is also reflected in the early church's sense of the same.

Personal prayer. We do not have access to the personal prayers of the average Jewish person. Prayer at morning and evening appears to have been the norm. Just how closely this was followed we can only guess, but Jews of all social levels appear to have been closely attached to their distinctive faith and disposed to its practice. The recitation of the *Shema* was part of this prayer, and eventually the "Eighteen Benedictions" came to be a daily prayer (though this is more likely a second-century development). We may assume that other formal prayers like the Psalms were used by individuals to express their longings and praises to God. The Psalms bear eloquent witness to what was expected of both a faithful God and the faithful petitioner, nurturing the individual Jew's expectations for his or her interaction with God and how God could be asked to intervene in certain situations. They also provided models for fresh, ad hoc prayers as well.

New prayers were composed and committed to writing by a number of Jews whose works have survived. For example, the Prayer of Manasseh is a beautiful penitential psalm providing a vehicle for sorrow at one's sins and for the affirmation of God's forgiving character and determination to manifest God's mercy through the forgiveness even of blatant and extreme sinners. The additions to Daniel, the book of Baruch and several additional psalms (such as were found at Qumran and also in the Syriac version of the Scriptures) bear witness to the liturgical creativity of pious Jews. The ad hoc prayers preserved in larger narratives like Tobit, the four books of the Maccabees, Judith and the Greek additions to Esther presuppose that Jews were accustomed to praying as the need arose, offering spontaneous (if somewhat formulaic) prayers from the heart for guidance, deliverance or forgiveness. Matthew's Jesus attributes "vain repetition" to Gentile, never Jewish, prayers.

Thus while God was to be found in the temple in a special way, Jews around the Mediterranean also knew God to be close at hand wherever God's people were, ready to hear their petitions and to deliver them from every danger.

THE DIVERSITY WITHIN JUDAISM

If there was agreement concerning the essential foci of the Jewish way of life, there were also certainly differences—even debates and divisions—concerning the proper expression of one's commitment to those essentials. It must also be remembered that before 70 C.E. and the rise of so-called Rabbinic Judaism, this was a debate without a real referee. Only after the rise of the second Sanhedrin at Jamnia in the last decades of the first century could there be some decisive determination of what was "normative" and what was "heretical."

Pharisees. Among the "sects" within first-century Judaism the Pharisees emerge as the most prominent in the New Testament (not only in the Gospels but, indirectly, in the letters of Paul the Pharisee) and in the reformulation of Judaism after the destruction of the temple. Rabbinic literature tends to uphold Pharisaic positions with regard to the application of Torah and overturn Sadducean positions, suggesting that they saw themselves as basically the students and heirs of the former rather than the latter.

The Pharisees sought ways of adapting the old commandments of Torah, fitted for an agrarian economy and concerns, to an ever-changing world. Drawn mainly (though not exclusively) from laypeople, the Pharisees were driven by a vision for the whole people of Israel as a "kingdom of priests" for God, just as Exodus 19:5-6 declared Israel should be. They thus sought to apply the whole law to all of life, including priestly codes. This led them to take great care for ritual purity, the washing of hands and vessels, the tithing of all the produce of the land, and keeping the sabbath according to their interpretations of what constituted work. Many of these details emerge in the Gospels as points of conflict between the Pharisees and other Jewish teachers, including Jesus (e.g., Mt 23; Mk 7:1-23). For them, this was the way to live before God, fulfilling the requirements of the daily call to every Jew, the *Shema*.

The Pharisees considered the traditional interpretation and application of Torah to hold equal authority with the written Torah itself. In other words, former judgments concerning how to apply Torah in given situations came to have the force of Torah itself. For this reason the "traditions of the elders" were extremely important in their understanding of walking in line with God's law (Mk 7:3-5; Gal 1:14; Josephus *Ant.* 13.10.6). This was a point of conflict with Jesus, who found that the clear teaching of the written Torah could be contravened by appealing to a tradition about Torah's application (e.g., in Mk 7:8-13). For Jesus, the divine law could never be circumvented or subordinated on the basis of a teaching developed by human beings.

The Pharisees' distinctive (and rather far-reaching) manner of obeying the Torah led to the erection of social boundaries and distinctions between themselves and other Jews. If they were committed to eating only produce that had been properly tithed (no cutting corners even on mint, cummin and dill; Mt 23:23), they could not eat with just anybody, lest they partake of food that had not been properly tithed (thus consuming God's portion and violating the Torah). If they were to maintain ritual purity, they could not eat in a house whose members did not observe the same purity rules for handling foods and dishes. They thus had table fellowship only with those of like mind, regarding the "people of the land" (the masses) as sinners (cf. Jn 7:49: "this crowd, which does not know the law, is accursed"). At the same time, they were known for having great authority among the people, assiduously teaching their neighbors a better way to keep the covenant and striving to increase holiness throughout the land.

Pharisees believed in the resurrection of the dead and eternal rewards and punishment (Josephus *War* 2.8.14; *Ant.* 18.1.3), and appear to have been comfortable with the developments in beliefs about angels and spiritual beings that had developed during the intertestamental period. This gave them common ground with the early Jewish Christians over against, say, the Sadducees (something Paul could exploit to his advantage; see Acts 23:6-10). They also held to a high view of divine providence. God's will and purpose guide the course of history. At the same time, they allowed for human freedom in response to God (see Josephus *War* 2.8.14). As one rabbi put it, "all is foreseen in heaven except the fear of heaven." Modern scholars rightly caution us to beware of painting the Pharisees as hypocrites, concerned only with appearances, or as legalists who replace devotion to God with minute rules. Both Jesus and Pharisaic sages criticize those who pursue religion for the sake of appearances or who lose sight of the one legitimate reason to keep Torah, namely the love of God.

Ancient sources also mention scribes, often in connection with the Pharisees. Scribes were trained interpreters of Torah, akin to jurists and lawyers who devote themselves to understanding the law and the principles for determining lawful and unlawful actions in innumerable circumstances based on a limited body of legislation. The scribes might belong to one party or another, or to none, but in practice it would appear that many were deeply influenced by the Pharisaic principles of interpretation, such that Matthew's Jesus can virtually equate the two (Mt 23).

Sadducees. The Sadducees have left no known firsthand sources for their own beliefs and hopes. Instead, our sources are written mainly by those who disagreed with them (e.g., the Pharisees and the early Christians), so that we know more about what they did *not* stand for than what they embraced. Sadducees appear to have occupied the upper levels of the aristocracy or to have concerned themselves mainly with influencing the Jewish ruling classes (see Josephus *Ant.* 13.10.6). The high-priestly family of Annas was Sadducean in its orientation. They looked to the Torah as authoritative and all other texts (whether the Prophets and Writings or the traditions of legal interpretation) as commentary rather than as possessing the same authority as the Torah. As might be expected they are remembered in rabbinic literature to have debated with the Pharisees on many fine points of Torah's application; for example, certain causes of impurity, the limits of the sabbath and the conduct of the temple service.

The Sadducees are most celebrated for their rejection of the hope of the resurrection from the dead, the survival of the soul and rewards and punishments beyond this life (see Josephus *War* 2.8.14; *Ant.* 18.1.4). In addition to this they appear to have rejected the extravagant developments in angelology and demonology that marked the intertestamental period, perhaps in keeping with their view that God has left moral determination to a person's free will (thus not to the coercive power of a holy spirit or an evil spirit). Their beliefs correlate well with an empowered group that regards itself as the master of its own fortune and has no need of postmortem compensators for inequities during this life. The Sadducees, whose power base was the temple cult, do not survive as a viable current within Judaism after 70 C.E.

Essenes, Qumran and the Dead Sea Scrolls. A wealth of sources attest to the beliefs and practices of the Essenes, though these sources often conflict in some details. To the classical sources (see Josephus *War* 2.8.2-13; *Ant.* 18.1.2, 5; Philo *Hypothetica* 11.1-18; *Every Good Person is Free* 12-13 [§75-91]) the extensive literature called the Dead Sea Scrolls (found near the community at Qumran) can now be added. The majority of scholars acknowledge that this community has some relationship with the Essene movement and many would openly identify it as an Essene center.

The vision of the Qumran community was "perfection of way," walking fully and completely in line with the covenant stipulations laid out by God. The sect arrived at the right understanding of the Torah through the "Teacher of Righteousness," a mysterious figure who emerged after the community occupied the site but before it found its direction.

Figure 2.12. Among the Dead Sea Scrolls were many previously unknown manuscripts of biblical books that have been of enormous importance for the textual criticism of the Hebrew Bible. The Isaiah Scroll, a nearly complete manuscript of Isaiah that predated the then best known manuscript by one thousand years, was among the first texts to be discovered in 1947. This small fragment is from another Qumran manuscript of Isaiah. (Courtesy of a private collector)

The Teacher appears to have been a Zadokite priest who clashed with an early Hasmonean high priest (called the Wicked Priest throughout the Dead Sea Scrolls) and who therefore left Jerusalem. The Teacher settled in Qumran and began to prepare for God's intervention by ordering the community after God's law, correctly interpreted. The community was to "prepare the way of the Lord in the wilderness and make straight in the desert a path for our God," and the "path" was the correct and meticulous observance of Torah and the community rule (1QS 8:14-16).

The sect was highly apocalyptic, deterministic and sectarian. It was sectarian in that its members alone joined themselves to the "covenant," while the rest of Israel floundered in error of way. The secrets of the sect, including the correct way of doing Torah, were carefully reserved for the fully initiated, and it was part of the member's duty to keep this knowledge from the outsider. The sect was deterministic in that the lot of every human being was held to have been determined by God long ago. God destined some to be "children of light," giving them the "spirit of truth," and others to be "children of darkness," giving them over to the "spirit of error" or "deceit." This corresponds to the classical sources' description of the Essenes as given to a high view of providence, with little or no room for human freedom. (At the same time, however, the member of the sect is enjoined to strive against the spirit of error and to follow the spirit of truth within.) There is a correspondingly strong doctrine of election as well, which results in a surprising combination of an awareness of God's unmerited favor and a commitment to a highly legalistic expression of piety. Determinism and stark dualism (dividing humanity into children of light and of darkness) are already features of apocalypticism. The sect also shares in apocalyptic Judaism's interest in the activities of the angels around God's throne, who impinge on community life, and in the expec-

tation of God's imminent intervention in human affairs, resulting in the casting down of the "lawless" and the elevation of the members of the sect to leadership over Israel.

There appear to have been two kinds of commitment to the Essene way of life. Some members of the group continued to live in towns and even raise families. Others withdrew into a sort of protomonastery, holding all property in common and maintaining a celibate lifestyle. The Essenes pursued simplicity of life in terms of food and clothing, and held to an extremely rigorous application of Torah. For example, when Jesus asked, "which of you, having a sheep which fell into a pit, would not lift it out on the sabbath," any Essene in the audience would have ruined his point by saying "I wouldn't!" (see CD 11:13). The lifestyle of those at Qumran was especially rigorous. They lived as if they were in a perpetual state of readiness for holy war, with God present among them in the camp, as it were. The purity codes for the camp of Israel during holy war, therefore, are followed at Qumran. For example, Deuteronomy prescribes that in times of war when God moves with the encamped army of Israel, the men will go outside the camp, dig a hole for themselves before they defecate and then fill the hole with the dirt (Deut 23:12-14). This practice was followed at Qumran.

Their observance of the law was so strict that the sect member did not even defecate on the sabbath, since digging the required hole would constitute work. They would probably not have agreed with Jesus' statement that "the sabbath was made for people, not people for the sabbath" (Mk 2:27). They also pursued a high degree of ritual purity, performing ritual purifications before prayer and before the daily community meal. The Qumran facility is equipped with several *mikvoth* for these purificatory immersions. The community's diligence in observing Torah was believed to atone for the sins of Israel, and to be counted as sacrificial offerings in God's sight (1QS 9:4-6).

The Dead Sea Scrolls

In 1947 a cache of texts stored in clay jars was discovered in an elevated cave near the Dead Sea. In the years that followed, texts and artifacts were found in ten other caves in this region, while archaeological interest in the nearby settlement at Qumran, a long-neglected site, was renewed. Many of the Dead Sea Scrolls originated at Qumran; at least some of them were brought to the community for safe-keeping and, eventually, hiding at the time of the Jewish Revolt. Some were found in an excellent state of preservation; many were found in such fragmentary condition and so thoroughly mixed up with other fragments of other texts that it took decades to fit the puzzles together. The sect that produced and preserved these scrolls was devoted to the study of Torah, the searching out of the wisdom of the ancients, the preservation of learning and the production of new expressions of piety and wisdom.

The Qumran literature falls into three categories. The first class includes the many manuscripts of the Hebrew Scriptures recovered. Fragments of every book of the Hebrew Bible except Esther and Nehemiah were found among the caves; many of these scrolls preserve substantially complete books of the Bible. Together they provide the earliest manuscript evidence for the Old Testament, antedating other manuscripts by more than a thousand years. These discoveries have given new life to textual criticism of the Hebrew Scriptures. In a few places textual critics have determined that the reading preserved in the Qumran manuscripts is the more original (see, for example, the newly inserted paragraph after 1 Sam 10:27 in the NRSV). In other places the discoveries have not changed the determination of the original text but have given increased weight to previously known variants. For example, the Septuagint version of Jeremiah 10:1-10 does not include Jeremiah 10:6-8, 10. A manuscript of Jeremiah from Qumran agrees with the Septuagint in these omissions over against the Masoretic Text.

The Qumran scrolls have reopened the question of the boundaries of the canon during the later intertestamental period. Was the number of psalms fixed at 150? The inclusion of several additional psalms in the Psalms Scrolls provides possible evidence to the contrary. Did all Jews agree on the number of books that were canonical? The Qumran community regarded *Jubilees,* an expansive paraphrase of Genesis 1 through Exodus 14, as an authoritative text and used it alongside the Pentateuch itself. *Jubilees* was especially important as support for the community's practice of calculating sabbaths and festivals according to the solar calendar, as opposed to the lunar calendar followed in the Jerusalem temple (see *Jub.* 6.32-38). Similarly, the community preserved a text called the *Temple Scroll,* a reinterpretation and systematization of the Pentateuchal law code. They may have regarded this scroll as authoritative and binding alongside the Pentateuch, perhaps in a manner similar to the Pharisaic regard for the "traditions of the elders."

The second category includes books that were not included by most Jews in the Bible, but also were not the peculiar products and property of the Qumran sect. Several apocryphal and pseudepigraphic works were found among the scrolls, including Tobit, Ben Sira, the Letter of Jeremiah (all of which are found in the Roman Catholic and Greek Orthodox canons), *1 Enoch, Genesis Apocryphon, Aramaic Testament of Levi* and the apocryphal Psalms. Many of these works had been known prior to the discovery of the scrolls.

The third and most celebrated category includes the scrolls that represent the literary compositions of the sect itself and in some cases of its eminent leader, the "Teacher of Righteousness." Distinctive among these are the *Rules,* books outlining topics that would come to be associated with church discipline: the procedures for conversion to the sect, the duties of various officials and the members of the sect in general, disciplinary actions to be taken on certain violations as well as summaries of the history and the teaching of the sect. The two main rules, the *Community Rule* (1QS) and the *Damascus Document* (CD), differ in a number of respects and may represent the community's practice at different stages in its history or reflect the differences in practice between the mother group at Qumran and the members of the community that continued to live in the villages and cities of Judea.

Another distinctive genre is the commentary, or *pesher* (plural, *pesharim*). The interpreter provides a brief excerpt from the biblical text, then segues into a discussion of the meaning of that passage with the phrase "its interpretation is" *(peshro).* The members of the sect read the Hebrew prophets (among which the Psalms were included) as predictions of what would transpire in the life of the founder of the sect (the Teacher of Righteousness) or in the history of the sect. This hermeneutic shares much in common with the early Christian interpretation of the Old Testament.

The sect also produced a great variety of liturgical material, attesting to the major role assigned to worship within the community. *Thanksgiving Hymns* speak of the blessings God has given in allowing the worshiper to know the right way to walk in God's commandments and to be joined to the community of God's holy ones. *Songs for the Sabbath Sacrifice* speak of the mystical communion of the earthly sectarians with the angelic hosts as they all gather together before the throne of God to worship.

Finally, the sect produced texts that bore witness to its expectations for the future and especially for the way in which God would bring the world back into its proper order. The *War Scroll* is a blueprint for the end-time conflict between the children of light and the armies of darkness. The *Messianic Rule* is a community rule for the restored Israel, in which the Messiah of Israel (a kingly figure) and the Messiah of Aaron (a priestly figure) would preside over the community.

The Qumran community, as the classical sources will also say of the Essenes, had extensive and formal procedures for receiving new members. Those contemplating joining the group went through a one-year novice period, then after making an initial commitment they underwent a further two-year probationary period before taking the binding oath

> that he will practice piety towards God, observe justice towards other people; do wrong to none whether on his own initiative or another person's orders; hate evildoers and help the just; keep faith with all people, especially authorities (since no one achieves dominion except by the will of God); not to abuse any authority conferred on him, nor outshine his subjects by dress or decoration; always to love the truth and expose liars; to keep his hands free from theft and his soul pure from impious gain; to conceal nothing from his fellow-Essenes, but to reveal their secrets

Figure 2.13. The remains of the scriptorium at Qumran, where texts were painstakingly copied and preserved. (Photo courtesy of Daniel Gebhardt [BiblePlaces.com])

to none, even though he be tortured to death; to transmit their rules exactly as he received them, and to preserve the books of the sect and the names of the angels. (Josephus *War* 2.8.7)

Such an oath shows not only sectarian concerns but also the broad commitment to the moral and righteous life among this sect. The group held property in common, with the possible exception of a few personal items.[12] They pursued a self-sufficient lifestyle through tending their own crops and herds, producing their own utensils, clothing and tents.

The community was rigidly structured. There was a body of priests, Levites and many gradations of members below them, with each member sitting in his proper place and deferring to those of more advanced standing than himself. To say that communal meals and assemblies proceeded "decently and in order" would be a gross understatement. Discipline within the community was strict. Speaking out of turn, spitting in the assembly and so forth met with reduced rations for a period of time. More serious offenses could mean banishment from the group for a set period and might easily result in starvation unless the group took the member back in time (after all, how could they violate their oath and eat with the impure?).

The discovery and study of the scrolls has encouraged much study of the connections between the Qumran community and the early church. Earlier overstatements of these connections, such as the fantasy that the Dead Sea Scrolls actually told the story of conflicts within the early church, have (largely) given way to more sober and conservative judgments. In Qumran, as in the early church, we have the opportunity to observe how a Jewish sect distinguished itself from the rest of Israel, crafted rites of passage into the community, organized into a community that could sustain itself and provide for the relief of all its members, theorized about the struggles of attaining virtue and pleasing God in this life, drew inspiration from a variety of texts (not all of which would be considered Scripture by outsiders), and read their own story through the lens of sacred Scripture (or vice versa).

Samaritans. Ancient prejudices against the Samaritans run deep and have colored the picture of the inhabitants of the region recorded in the Hebrew Scriptures. It is often said that relatives fight worst of all, and this is certainly the case here. Samaritans are descendants of the people of the northern kingdom, the nine-and-a-half tribes that split from Judah and

---

[12]Philo says even those Essenes living in towns are to consider all property held by individuals as property held in common and to freely support those of their own in need (see *Every Good Person Is Free*, pp. 85-87).

Benjamin after Solomon's death. There are indications early on of a rival sanctuary in Bethel, and a number of patriarchal stories support the sanctity of this site. This is a trend actively opposed by the Deuteronomistic editors of the Hebrew Scriptures, who balance these stories with affirmations of God's exclusive choice of Mount Zion in Jerusalem for cultic encounter with the deity. These prejudices are made worse after the return of the Judean exiles from Babylonia, who regard the Samaritans as a half-breed race, neither truly Jew nor Gentile. Near the end of his compilation of his life's teaching of wisdom, Yeshua Ben Sira adds an almost random attack on Judea's neighbors: "Two nations my soul detests, and the third is not even a people: Those who live in Seir, and the Philistines, and the foolish people that live in Shechem" (Sir 50:25-26). The Samaritans fare worse in Ben Sira's estimation than Israel's longstanding foes, the Philistines and the Edomites.

By the time of Alexander the Great the Samaritans have certainly established a rival temple on Mount Gerizim. Relations with Judea could not have been improved when the Samaritans voluntarily renamed their sanctuary for "Zeus the friend of strangers," completely avoiding any trouble under Antiochus IV (see 2 Macc 6:2). During the Hasmonean period John Hyrcanus actually attacked and destroyed Samaria and its temple, a campaign that brought him popularity in Judea but that no doubt renewed anti-Judean sentiments among the Samaritans. It is therefore not surprising that Samaritans are portrayed consistently as a marginal group in the Gospels, and that "Jews have no dealings with Samaritans," as the author of the Fourth Gospel comments (Jn 4:9 RSV).

The Samaritans had their own version of the Pentateuch, the sum total of their Scriptures. In some cases the Samaritan text of the Pentateuch may represent a more original reading; in some places it has been altered to prescribe more explicitly that true worship happens on Gerizim. Worship at Gerizim rather than Jerusalem was a major point of contention between Judeans and Samaritans (see Jn 4:20). Samaritans offered the sacrifices prescribed by Moses at their temple. (They survive as a religious entity in that region to this day.) Not only does Jesus encounter Samaritans throughout his ministry (with both positive and negative results), but Samaria is a region of very early Christian missionary work and success. Their distinctive beliefs (particularly their expectation of a "prophet like Moses" as their messianic figure, based on Deut 18:18) were in a good place to contribute to the shaping of early Christian theology (see, for example, the use of this motif in Peter's sermon in Acts 3:22-26). Unfortunately, the lack of first-century Samaritan texts makes the study of this influence difficult.

Other Jewish movements. Josephus mentions a "fourth sect of the Jewish philosophy," one that we have already encountered in earlier discussions of Jews who sought to secure Israel's fortunes by throwing off the yoke of the foreign power through violent revolution. This tendency culminates in the formation of the Zealot party shortly before the Revolt but is an important strain even before the formal organization of this party. The label "Zealot" has come to be applied more loosely to all the attempts to recover the hope of Israel by force of arms, and need not be exclusive of other groups—both individual Pharisees and an Essene are named by Josephus as prominent revolutionaries of the period. Zealots (both in the broad sense and specialized sense) were not merely freedom fighters. They were Jews expressing their religious convictions: "No lord but God" (Josephus *Ant.* 18.1.6). The Jewish tradition was rich with models for their activity: Phineas expressing zeal for God by killing the accommodating Israelite and his Gentile concubine; Joshua driving the Gentiles out of the land God promised to Israel; Mattathias killing the apostate Israelite and the Syrian officer who invited the pagan sacrifice; Judas and his brothers driving out the overwhelming Seleucid forces, since God fought with them.

Most of the movements that aimed at overthrowing Roman power in Palestine consciously reenacted scriptural patterns, affirming that God was again, by means of a new leader whom God raised up, delivering Israel from bondage or renewing their complete possession of the promised land. In 45-46 C.E. Theudas gathered a crowd and led them to the Jordan River, where he promised to lead them across after he divided the river by his command. The parallel with Joshua's crossing of the Jordan and the revolutionary implications of bringing in a mob of Israelites for a new (re)conquest of Judea were probably not lost on the procurator Cuspius Fadus, who met the crowd at the river with his troops and slew many, including Theudas.[13] During the procuratorship of Felix an Egyptian Jew gathered a large following on the Mount of Olives and promised they would see the walls of Jerusalem fall, after which he would lead them in a march on Jerusalem to take the city. Felix, of course, attacked the crowd with his troops, killing several hundred (though not capturing the leader; see Acts 21:38).[14] Small wonder, then, that when Jesus had done the same thing a decade or so before and occupied the court of the temple for several days with a large crowd of adherents, authorities began to fear a coup under this messiah figure.

Other short-lived movements arose throughout the first centuries B.C.E. and C.E. John the Baptist provides an example of a spontaneous, nonviolent religious movement that could arise within Judaism around a central figure and that Judaism as such could tolerate. John, like leaders with more military and political aspirations, enacted scriptural paradigms. He centered his movement on the banks of the Jordan and made the wilderness his field of ministry. The wilderness represented the place for meeting God and recalled the time of Israel's formation as a people following God out of Egypt. Overtones of deliverance and conquest were strong, making the wilderness a common launching place for revolutionary movements as well. John's goal, though, was repentance for violations of God's law and renewal of commitment to walking in justice. He gained a sufficient following to be noticed by Josephus (see *Antiquities* 18.5.2).[15] According to Josephus it was his influence with the people that led Antipas to remove him before John could lead an insurrection. Antipas read John as a potential revolutionary, and John's sharp criticism of Antipas's own violation of Torah (marrying his sister-in-law, Herodias) may have been seen by Antipas as a prelude to rallying the people to revolt. So popular was John that when Antipas's army was destroyed in an ill-advised war seven years later, people interpreted this as God's punishment for the execution of the righteous prophet.

GRECO-ROMAN RELIGION

In the ancient world, religion was not just one compartmentalized part of life alongside and separable from other parts of life like family, business, civic life and diplomacy. Rather, religion enveloped and embraced all other aspects of life. Traditional Greek and Roman religion sought the preservation of the status quo in the family, city and state, or if the situation was unstable, a return to stability. Participation in the

---

[13]See Josephus *Ant.* 20.5.1. This may be the same Theudas referred to in Acts 5:36.

[14]See ibid., 20.8.6.

[15]While Josephus's paragraph on Jesus (*Ant.* 18.3.3) shows strong signs of later Christian editing, his account of John the Baptist does not and may be taken as an independent witness.

rituals that surrounded family meals, social gatherings, civic festivals and agricultural rites showed a person's solidarity with the larger society, symbolizing willingness to do his or her part to secure social and civic harmony, agricultural productivity, and political stability. These were cultic expressions of loyalty and commitment to ever-widening social units: family, city, province, empire.[16] It was therefore impossible to be religiously deviant without this having political and social ramifications. The deviant would not be the person who added mystery cults to participation in traditional religion but rather the person who shied away from participation in traditional forms of religion in favor of exclusive participation elsewhere.

Forms of traditional religious expression centered on sacrifices of various kinds. Public sacrifices were first and foremost an inducement to the gods to continue to provide their benefactions of peace, stability and agricultural prosperity. The way people related to those in power in the human sphere was transferred to the way they related to the divinities, the ultimate powers. Thus the gods were revered as the ultimate patrons, often approached through the priests who acted as brokers or mediators.[17] The people therefore sought to show themselves as faithful and worthy recipients of favors, both by acknowledging former benefits with gratitude and by courting the continued favor of the gods. Sacrifices were only secondarily acts of appeasement for offenses.

Figure 2.14. A pool and colonnaded walkway from the Asculapium in Pergamum, a kind of ancient health resort where the sick or infirm sought healing from the god Asclepius with the help of the staff at the sacred site. Aelius Aristides, an author from the second century C.E., has left a first-hand testimony to his stay at this facility. (Photo courtesy of Todd Bolen [BiblePlaces.com])

[16]The phenomenon of imperial cult—the worship of the emperors and the goddess Roma Aeterna—has already been discussed. This was a prominent feature of public religious life in the eastern Mediterranean and one closely connected with the veneration of traditional deities.

[17]The Latin word for priest—*pontifex*, or "bridge builder"—is telling in this regard.

Gnosticism, the Nag Hammadi Library and the Hermetica

Gnosticism refers broadly to a variety of religious traditions that held to some common core beliefs. The essence of a person (the soul, as it were) comes from the divine realm but has fallen from the perfect, immaterial realm through the levels of the material creation, becoming enmeshed and trapped in matter (the body). By means of correct knowledge *(gnōsis)* about their nature as spiritual beings and about the process by which the soul would ascend through the heavenly spheres, humans can be freed from the prison house of the body and of material creation, and ascend again to join with the deity. The Gnostic's goal was personal liberation and reunion with the deity. Associated with some Gnostic groups is the belief that the material world was not created by the supreme God but by a lesser divinity called the "Demiurge." This figure is responsible for the evils that beset humankind, having brought the material creation with its lures and entrapments into being.

The problem with reconstructing Gnosticism is that the forms in which it is best and most distinctively known postdate the rise of Christianity, only coming to flourish in the second and third centuries C.E. Even non-Christian Gnostic texts quite often show the strong influence of Jewish thought (for example, dependence on the creation and fall stories of Genesis 1—3). Scholars therefore take different views on the development of Gnosticism. Some assert that a pagan Gnosticism flourished during the first century and later was combined first with Jewish and then Christian elements. Others suggest that proto-Gnostic (often merely Platonic) motifs were common in the first century (e.g., the belief in the soul's heavenly origin and return, the devaluing of the material world as corruptible and transitory), but that Gnosticism really only took root in history as heretical forms of Judaism and Christianity. It is certainly possible that Paul and other New Testament authors had to counter at least the beginning tendencies in this direction, although we must always be wary of reading second- and third-century Gnostic systems of belief back into the minds of the first century deviants these authors combat.

The study of Gnosticism takes us to two bodies of literature. The first corpus is the Nag Hammadi Library, a collection of fifty-two texts on twelve scrolls discovered in Egypt (the most celebrated of which is the *Gospel of Thomas,* which has played an important role in many recent quests for the historical Jesus). The collectors of these texts were Christian, and the majority of the texts reflect a variant form of second-century Christianity (or, less kindly, a Christian heresy) rather than an independent religious movement. Another collection of literature often associated with Gnosticism is the *Hermetica,* so named because it relates the revelations of Hermes Trismegistus ("thrice great"), a Greek name for the Egyptian god Thoth.

A particularly important text within this corpus is the *Poimandres,* a discourse of self-disclosure by the heavenly Mind, who shows the way human beings may ascend again to God. This text is a Gnostic exposition of the creation and fall stories in Genesis; it offers many parallels with the presentation of Jesus in the Fourth Gospel. In both, a heavenly being reveals himself to a human disciple, teaches the disciple about human beings' fallen state, the "life" and "light" that come from God, the way the souls that can be saved share the essential nature of God, and the way to restoration. The heavenly revealer figure finally commissions the disciple to proclaim the message to others, some of whom will hear and follow, but others will scoff. The revealer also speaks in lengthy discourses, while the role of the disciple is merely to ask questions, a form reminiscent of Johannine style (but also of other self-disclosure statements by divinities across the Mediterranean).

Which way does the influence go? Did John's Gospel influence the author of *Poimandres* or the reverse? There may also be no direct influence, with both John and *Poimandres* offering parallel but independent concepts, for the differences between the two texts are just as striking. In the person of Jesus, divine *logos* or reason has actually became flesh, shared earthly life with humanity for a considerable amount of time and even experienced death before returning to the Father. The early church would struggle to preserve the reality of the incarnation and passion of Jesus against docetic and Gnostic tendencies to deny that the revealer actually took on corrupt flesh or experienced suffering.

The *Poimandres* suggests ways that Gnosticism could connect with ethics. First, the revealer says that he remains "far removed from the person who is foolish, evil, deceptive, full of envy and covetousness, murderous and impious," turning such people over to the avenging daemon that drives the person further and further into the delusions of the sense world, and thus to greater punishment. With such statements the Gnostic teacher promotes virtue and dissuades from vice. Similarly, the revealer discusses the postmortem stages the soul passes through and what the soul sheds at each stage: in the first sphere, mutability; in the second, evil scheming; in the third, lust and its deceitfulness; in the fourth, arrogance; in the fifth, overreaching and rashness; in the sixth, covetousness and injustice; in the seventh, falsehood. Such an itinerary might lead the Gnostic to divest him- or herself of these things even while alive so he or she might be the better equipped to journey to the heavens after death, or even enjoy mystical union with the divine during life. On the other hand, the belief that the soul would be divested of such things after death was also taken by some Gnostics as a license for self-indulgence in this present life.

Acts provides us with several opportunities to see the piety of the Greco-Roman world—and the importance of the gods for civic life. For example, Paul in Athens is shown to describe the city as full of temples and sacred shrines. So pious are the Athenians that they even erected an altar to "an unknown god" (Acts 17:22-23), perhaps to acknowledge benefits received from a deity whose priests had not claimed credit for the timely favors on the god's behalf (hence the source remained unknown) or, more probably, to acknowledge any favors that had been granted from one or more deities not revealed in Greek tradition. In Ephesus, Paul's success among the Ephesians is seen to detract from the worship of Ephesus's patron deity, Artemis (transformed in the East into a mother goddess and goddess of fertility). The city's pride and reputation as well as the economic interests of the silversmith's guild that flourished making sacred souvenirs of the place are all drawn up into what a modern person might regard as an essentially religious conflict (Acts 19:23-41). This episode shows us, rather, the embeddedness of economics and civics in religion in the ancient world.

Families and individuals could also interact with the divine through sacrifice. The libations and offerings of incense and produce made within the home represented the family's connections with the gods of hearth and home (and, in Italy, with the protective spirits of the ancestral heads of the family), and continual courting of their favor. Votive offerings were also common in Greco-Roman religion (as also in ancient Israelite religion). Individuals promised a particular sacrifice or gift in return for some favor sought from a god; paying the vow then became a witness to the benevolence of the deity.

Other religious practices bear witness to the beliefs and attitudes of this period. The fate of individuals and nations was believed to be written in the stars, with the result that astrology was an important facet of religion. The underlying conviction of determinism also stands behind the reading of omens, divination and the consultation of oracles—at both levels of state inquiries about auspicious times for beginning a war and levels of individual inquiries about conception, business ventures or marriage. At the same time the widespread use of magic suggests that divine forces could be manipulated to do one's own will (rather than always the reverse). Incantations, amulets and spells were frequently used to catch the affections of another person, harm a rival or gain vengeance on an offender.

Domestic and traditional forms of religious expression did not satisfy all inhabitants of the Greco-Roman world. Many sought a more personal connection with a divinity. Many longed for some assurance of deliverance from the powers of fate and of death. Many desired religious experiences that would involve their minds, imaginations and emotions far more fully than the pious rites of the civic temples. These perceived needs made it possible for more exotic and experiential cults to take deep root in Asia Minor, Greece and Rome. Most of these fall under the category of "mystery religions." Some of these were built around myths indigenous to these regions, for example, the cult of Attis and Cybele (Asia Minor) or the Or-

phic, Dionysian and Eleusinian mysteries (formed around traditional Greek divinities and their stories). The cult of Isis (Egypt) and Mithras (Persia), however, also gained immense popularity in the Greek and Roman world.

Common to most of these mystery religions was the promise of sharing in the eternal life of the deity. It is not surprising that a myth of dying and rising again stands at the core of many of these mysteries, nor that several of the myths originally had their home in fertility cults (e.g., the myth of Demeter and Kore in the Eleusinian mysteries, or Attis and Cybele in the Asian mysteries). The annual cycle of growth, harvest, death and replanting mirrored in many ways the individual's cycle of birth, growth, death and hope for a renewal of life beyond death. A person would be initiated into a mystery cult through an elaborate ritual, sometimes through several stages of induction. At each stage the officiants would reveal to the initiate more of the cult myth and its significance for the eternal destiny of the individual. In most cults some ritual was provided so the initiate could identify with or participate in the dying and rebirth of the central figure of the myth (e.g., Attis or Osiris). The most famous of these rites belonged to the cult of Mithras, identified with the sun god Helios (the rhythm of its setting and rising again cannot make this choice accidental), and was called the *taurobolium*. The initiate entered a pit over which was placed a slatted roof. A bull was slaughtered on the roof, and the initiate was ritually purified by the blood, partaking of the bull's strength and vitality. It is easy to see how the gospel of the crucified and resurrected Jesus would appeal to people familiar with such mystery cults, and how baptism could develop far beyond a rite of purification to a dying with Christ in the hope of rising with Christ for eternity.

Greco-Roman religion was, on account of its polytheistic nature, tolerant of foreign divinities. Attempts were made to correlate

Figure 2.15. A Coptic gnostic text. The discovery of the library of Nag Hammadi vastly increased our knowledge of Gnosticism and related movements in second- to fourth-century Egypt. Our understanding of this ancient religious movement is still being refined as many early gnostic texts, like the one pictured here, still wait to be translated and studied. (Courtesy of a private collector)

Egyptian, Greek and Roman deities so that the gods of non-Greek peoples could be identified with known Greek and Roman gods and incorporated into the pantheon. A person could call on whatever god he or she wished as long as a place was made for the other gods. To deny the gods, however, whether in favor of none (like the Epicureans) or in favor of one's own ancestral/tribal divinity (like the Jews) was to deny the order of society, or to assert that society's order was somehow perverse (for

example, in the charge that it goes after false gods). Such an attitude toward the traditional deities was labeled "atheism" (*atheotēs*) by Greek and Roman authorities and supporters of traditional religion. So seriously did the society view this as a dangerous attitude that it was often punishable with death. In 95 C.E. near the end of his reign, the emperor Domitian executed several high ranking Roman citizens on this charge. Dio Cassius connects their fate to their taking up of Jewish practices and beliefs (*Roman History* 67.14.2).

The Christian gospel, therefore, was also very much a political proclamation, an aberration, a dissenting voice. Even though it generally called for obedience to political authorities, it nevertheless threatened the socio-political order by calling its religious foundations into question as well as by calling it a temporary arrangement awaiting replacement by the order (kingdom) of the one God. The Christian gospel thus presented a grave affront to Roma Aeterna and to all who found security and peace under her wings. By withdrawing from all settings where another god would be venerated, the Christians appeared antisocial. They neither participated (any longer) in the festivals nor came out for supper to their non-Christian friends' homes or accepted invitations to parties at the idol's table. This led to suspicion and antipathy on the part of those whose company was spurned.

Religious activity was not the vehicle for moral education in the Greco-Roman world (as it is so prominently in the modern world). There were a number of pollution taboos connected with entering sacred shrines, for example, the avoidance of murder or incest prior to entering the sanctuary. These fell far short, however, of connecting personal morality with religious behavior. Moreover, these pollution taboos included many morally neutral acts (e.g., childbirth, contact with a corpse). One telling example of the lack of concern with personal morality is the prohibition of intercourse with one's spouse for one day before coming to the temple, or intercourse with someone other than one's spouse for three days. The latter is seen as more polluting, but the concern of the taboo is not to reinforce sexual morality generally—such as a general prohibition of extramarital intercourse would. Sexual morality and other areas of conduct

were mandated not by religion but by practical and social deterrence.[18] The sad fact of infanticide in the Greco-Roman world—exposing or even killing unwanted children—attests to the absence of a strong basis for morality, such as the inviolable sanctity of human life that the Judeo-Christian tradition would bring to the Greco-Roman world and eventually to Roman legislation after Constantine.

GRECO-ROMAN PHILOSOPHICAL SCHOOLS

It was left to philosophers and families to draw out the implications of the will of the gods for personal morality, and to inculcate moral behavior. The philosophers would often seek to derive moral principles from the gods, urging people to imitate the gods, but in doing so they had to be selective in the points of imitation. Seneca, for example, frequently urged those who would give benefactions to others to imitate the gods, who give good gifts to the good and the bad because it is in their nature to be generous, not because they are looking for a return on their investment.[19] However, it would not do to imitate the gods in the sexual exploits told about them in Homer and in ancient myth. For such stories philosophers invented the allegorical method of interpretation, turning a story of a god's descent to have illicit intercourse with a mortal, for example, into a story about the superior faculty of reason mastering the inferior drives of the body (or sometimes a paradigm of the dangers of the reverse, when the passions overcome the mind, with monstrous consequences).

Greco-Roman philosophy should not, therefore, be viewed as distinct from religion; most often it takes religion as the starting point for (or at least reinforcement of) the way of life promoted by the philosopher. Greco-Roman philosophy combined a concern for

---

[18]A. A. Bell Jr. *Exploring the New Testament World* (Nashville: Thomas Nelson, 1998), pp. 222-23.
[19]See Seneca *Ben.* 1.1.9; 3.15.4; 4.26.1; 4.28.1.

metaphysics and physics (inquiries into the ultimate nature of the reality humans inhabit) with a concern for ethics (the proper manner in which to live in this reality). The latter especially takes us into points of contact with the early Christian movement, whose leaders employed many topics, argumentative strategies and forms found in Greco-Roman ethics to promote the distinctive way of life of the Christian "philosophy."

Platonism. Plato, a disciple of Socrates, left a strong mark on the ancient world with his teaching about the true nature of reality. He held that all visible, material objects were the shadows and copies of pure, invisible, ideal forms. For example, there is an endless variety of tables, but all are recognized as tables because there exists the ideal form of "table," which the mind apprehends apart from the senses. For Plato it was the ideal form that was truly real and eternal. Plato's thought exercised a strong influence on Jewish thought as the latter came into increasing contact with the Greek world in the process of Hellenization. The writings of Philo provide perhaps the high water mark of this tide of influence, but the influence is apparent also in the Wisdom of Solomon and the concept of a heavenly temple, the ideal form that provided the model for the earthly temple (Wis 9:8; see Heb 8:1-5).

In Jewish thinking Plato's essentially timeless view of reality is combined with a spatial and historical view. The visible, earthly realm is viewed as temporary; the invisible, heavenly realm is eternal. The author of 4 Maccabees, Paul and the author of Hebrews share this mindset, allowing them both to draw the conclusion that only the invisible is worth striving for, worth any price in terms of temporary, visible realities.[20]

Plato's works also contribute greatly to the formation of ethics, as do the works of Plato's most celebrated student, Aristotle. It is in this literature that the cardinal virtues of the Greek world are discussed, refined and promoted. Basic Platonic definitions of virtues, such as justice entailing giving to each what is due him or her and piety entailing justice toward the gods, have shaped Greek culture to such a degree that their imprint can be seen across a wide spectrum of literature from all Hellenized cultures, including the texts of the New Testament (Mk 12:17; Rom 13:7). Platonic commonplaces like the superiority of suffering unjustly (suffering even though one has not committed some crime to deserve it) to suffering justly, or the idea that those who injure the innocent really harm themselves, also emerge in Jewish and Christian literature (see, for example, 4 Macc 9:7-9; 1 Pet 3:17; 4:14-16). The definition of courage as the endurance of hardship in the quest for a greater good becomes a staple of minority cultural literature, where persevering in the group's way of life often involves hardship (see 2 Cor 4:16-18; Heb 12:2).

Stoicism. The Stoics were especially concerned with discovering the means to live a meaningful, virtuous life. Stoicism appears to have developed in response to an awareness of human powerlessness in the face of history, death and the slings and arrows of fate and other people. The Stoic way of life sought to attain, therefore, (1) self-sufficiency (*autarkeia*), such that contentment was found mainly in a person's moral character, (2) freedom, such that one's moral faculty could operate without constraint and knowledge of what was virtuous or advantageous was not tainted by popular fallacies about the same, and (3) apathy, in the sense of being undisturbed and unmoved by the violent movements of the lower nature (emotions, desires and inclinations).

Stoics divided experience into two categories. "Some things are under our control," like desire or moral virtue, while "other things are not under our control," like reputation,

---

[20]See 4 Macc 15:2-3, 8, 26-28; 2 Cor 4:16-18; Heb 8:1-5; 11:16; 13:14.

wealth, physical well-being (Epictetus *Ench.* 1). The wise person (the ideal Stoic) placed no value on the things not under his or her control and sought the good solely in cultivating the things properly his or her own—the things that nothing external could affect. This was the essential path to freedom and self-sufficiency. Paul has drunk deeply of this ethos, with a Christian twist: whatever condition befell his body or reputation, all that really mattered to him was gaining Christ and being faithful to God. This enabled Paul, however, to remain essentially free, as the Stoic would define freedom. No external necessity or compulsion could deter him from acting in accordance with his own moral purpose.

A common topic for Stoics was the proper hierarchy within the human being, such that the person was led by reason and not directed (really, thrown off the moral course) by the pull of the passions. The passions are all those forces that can pervert or derail a person's commitment to virtue (e.g., fear, lust, pleasure and pain). They thus included emotions, desires and physical sensations. Where the passions exercised influence, virtue and the self-respect that accompanies it are threatened. The Stoics therefore aimed at the eradication of the passions, although a few more moderate voices would call only for the mastery or moderation of the passions. It was in this form that the topic entered the Jewish thought world, since God had planted the passions and inclinations within the human being. What was desired, then, was the proper subordination of the passions to reason, a goal effected for the Jewish philosopher through diligent following of Torah (see 4 Macc 1:1—3:18; *Letter of Aristeas* 221-227; Philo *Leg. All.* 3.116-117). This in turn becomes an important background to Paul and other early Christian leaders for whom the mastery of "the passions and desires of the flesh" remains an essential goal (see Gal 5:16-25; Tit 2:12; 3:3; Jas 1:14-15; 1 Pet 2:11; 4:1-3). For Paul, however, this goal

is achieved by following neither the moral faculty nor the Jewish law, but the Spirit.

The Stoics sought to do all things "according to Nature," meaning, according to the purpose and goal for which something exists. Humans, as creatures gifted with reason, are meant to live as reason dictates, not as their baser passions dictate. Cooperation among human beings is more natural and beneficial than hindering one another. The unity of humanity is more natural and beneficial than divisions according to nationality or ethnicity. Just as God permeates the universe with order, so the life of the individual is to be permeated with rational order. There is a transformation of this in Paul's appeal to the Corinthians to abstain from fornication because "the body is not meant for immorality, but for the Lord" (1 Cor 6:13 RSV). Sin is against the nature of things in that it violates the purpose and goal of human life, which is properly directed to the Lord, holiness and divine service.

This perception of the "law of nature" led to a critique of ethnic laws, customs and the unwritten laws of public opinion. For Stoics all that was required was to live according to reason and to pursue virtue. It was a form of slavery to be concerned with the latest fashion trends. It was another form of slavery to be overly concerned with traditions and rules that did not proceed from reason but held force only through long use among a given people. This was an unnecessary burden and a dangerous distraction from the real business of being human. Again, Paul drinks deep from this well. The law of God and the law of Moses are no longer the same: circumcision and dietary rules can be ignored, even rejected, for the universal law of God speaks to Gentiles and Jews alike without giving privilege to one ethnic group. Once again, that law bears fruit in human lives by means of submission to the Spirit of God.

Cynics. The Cynics, whose origins are to be traced to Diogenes of Sinope (a contemporary of Plato), were an intentionally odd lot. They sought freedom both from convention and compulsion. They often deliberately violated the norms of decent people, showing by their lives that the codes and norms that regulated every action and pursuit of the majority of people were not absolutes; they were not even necessary and were the equivalent of slavery. Cynics were known for complete openness of speech, even an obnoxious style of reviling people for their dependence on reputation, property or their slavery to human conventions. Cynics were especially desirous of achieving freedom from the bondage of public opinion, often pursuing a shameless way of life as an antidote to that poison.

In pure Cynic teaching simplicity of life was the goal: to be dependent on as few things as possible. Thus many Cynics were homeless, without goods except perhaps a cloak, a walking stick and a small sack for the absolute bare minimum of essentials (a cup, a knife, the food for the day). For them nothing natural was shameful. They were known, for example, for copulating, defecating or urinating in quite public places. Like the Stoics they also believed that virtue was the only prerequisite for true happiness and that happiness which depended on external circumstances was an insecure state indeed. The Cynic lifestyle attracted many would-be philosophers—people bored with life and seeking the name of a philosopher without the discipline required. It was easy to don the right outfit, to revile people in the marketplace and to flout customs honored by others. Such characters were satirized, for example, by Lucian as people who just couldn't make an honest living and so turned to pseudo-philosophy, set themselves up as teachers and fed on the gullible masses. It was important to Paul that he not be seen as such a huckster (2 Cor 2:17). Jesus appears to have instructed his disciples to avoid the classic Cynic garb of a double tunic, staff and knapsack, and to wear sandals where the Cynics tended to go barefoot (Mk 6:7-9).

Epicureans. Stoics and Epicureans appear together as part of Paul's audience in the Areopagus of Athens in Acts 17:18. The Epicurean school exercised a palpable influence on the first century world and was often viewed by the dominant culture in the same way as Christians. That two so very different groups could achieve the same reputation is instructive, for it highlights even more clearly the boundaries of what was acceptable in the Greco-Roman world and how Christians stepped over the line.

Epicurus taught, in complete opposition to Plato, that reality is completely material. The gods may indeed exist, but in a state of absolute imperturbability (*ataraxia,* the Epicurean ideal). Therefore, the gods take no thought for human activity, neither rewarding nor punishing, for they are completely untroubled by the activity of mortals. Death is merely the dissolution of the atoms (Epicurus's term) that constitute our whole being. No part of a human being survives death, and therefore there is no need to be anxious about the other side of death. Epicurus sought to free people, as he saw it, from fear of the gods and death, focusing them on what was truly their concern—a pleasant life in this world, free from pain, anxiety and frustration.

Epicurus sought to help people experience pleasure and to facilitate their endurance of necessary pain. Pleasure is not to be understood hedonistically here, for Epicurus himself taught that a person cannot live pleasantly without also being committed to just, prudent and honorable actions. Overindulgence in any pleasure inevitably led to pain, and so moderation was the mark of the wise person. Mental pleasure was superior to physical pleasure, and the highest pleasure of all was friendship. In order to secure and perpetuate this highest pleasure Epicureans often withdrew from public life (the source of much perturbation) and lived a communal existence, even holding all property in common. They lived out in practice the idea of friendship commended by Aristotle. A catchy little quatrain encapsulates the distinctive Epicurean ethos:

Nothing to fear in God,
Nothing to feel in death;
Good is easily enjoyed,
Pain is easily endured.[21]

Outsiders reacted with suspicion to Epicureans.[22] Their view of the gods made prayer and sacrifice meaningless activities, and so this philosophy was tantamount to atheism. Gods who did not care were as good as gods who were not there. The tendency to withdraw from public life and form tight-knit, exclusive communities appeared to be a betrayal of civic unity and a renunciation of civic duty. Thus they generally were not looked well upon for the same two reasons that Christians and Jews became the brunt of popular hatred: denial of the gods and withdrawal from investment in the welfare of the whole community. Fortunately for the Epicureans they tended to be wealthy and well-connected, and so did not come under fire as did their less well-connected counterparts.

JEWS IN THE GRECO-ROMAN WORLD

By the first century C.E. many more Jews lived outside of Palestine than within its borders. This phenomenon, known as the Diaspora, traces its roots back in large measure to the conquest of Israel's northern kingdom by the Assyrians in 721 B.C.E. and of Judea by the Babylonians, culminating in the destruction of the temple, in 587 B.C.E. Massive, forced relocations of the Jewish population accompanied these conquests. In connection with the Babylonian advance on Judea, moreover, a large

number of Jews voluntarily relocated to Egypt in order to flee the impending disaster. While some of the Jews opted to return to their homeland when it became safe and advantageous to do so, many more chose to remain in the land of their "exile," where they had put down roots. The Jewish communities in Babylon and Egypt remained the strongest and most populous Diaspora communities through the first century C.E.

Further actions of Gentile leaders in Palestine resulted in more deportations. When Ptolemy I gained control of Palestine, he took many Jews to Egypt as slaves or conscripts for his armies. Freed by Ptolemy's son, most of the Jewish deportees nevertheless continued to live in Egypt as soldiers or farmers. After Antiochus III wrested control of Palestine from the Ptolemies in 198 B.C.E., he conscripted thousands of Jews to serve as soldiers in Syria and Asia Minor. Pompey the Great took thousands of Jews back to Rome as captives in 63 B.C.E., augmenting an already significant Jewish presence in Rome. During these centuries many Jews also migrated voluntarily, seeking the opportunities afforded by the great cities of the Hellenistic world, or working as merchants and seafarers along the trade routes that connected Palestine to the rest of the world. Alexandria in Egypt, Antioch in Syria and Rome itself became major centers of the Diaspora.

Jews, especially those in the Diaspora, were faced with many challenges. They lived as a minority group in the midst of and daily proximity to a dominant, Gentile culture—one that frequently made the Jew who remained aloof from the dominant culture feel inferior or unwelcome. How could a Jew both thrive in a Gentile's world *and* remain faithful to his or her Jewish heritage and identity? When these goals came into conflict, which

---

[21]Gilbert Murray, *Five Stages of Greek Religion* (New York: Doubleday, 1955), pp. 204-5.
[22]See especially the attacks of Plutarch on Epicureanism in, for example, the essays "That Epicurus makes a pleasant life impossible" and "Reply to Colotes."

would he or she choose? Individual Jews worked out an astounding variety of responses to these challenges.

Some Jews restricted their social life to the Jewish community, avoiding traffic with non-Jews as far as possible. Others, however, enjoyed daily interactions with non-Jews through commerce and even entertainment (e.g., through attending the theaters and games). Still others sought to participate fully in the Gentile community, seeking a gymnasium education and even abandoning their distinctive way of life, eliminating all that separated them from their non-Jewish neighbors. Again, some Jews did not even learn the Greek language. More often Jews ably conversed in Greek and were acquainted with the basics of Greco-Roman culture; many took Greek (or Latin) names and showed signs of being influenced by Greco-Roman culture in their own artistic and literary expression. For example, one of the Jewish catacombs in Rome is decorated with not only symbols from the Jerusalem cultic festivals but also human and animal figures from Greek mythology. Still other Jews attained a high level of facility in Greek composition, literature, philosophy, rhetoric and ethics. Jews like Philo of Alexandria, the author of Wisdom of Solomon and Josephus show an astounding degree of Hellenization in terms of their linguistic and cultural fluency. Once again we see that Hellenization was not simply an antithetical alternative to remaining a Jew. Rather, Jews became Hellenized in a variety of ways, to a variety of degrees, to a variety of ends.[23]

Diaspora Jews committed to preserving their distinctive identity and way of life had several supports for their efforts. To a large extent these supports (both social and ideological) provided ample reinforcement for the minority group, helping millions of Jews resist the centrifugal force of assimilation. The synagogue, the regular gathering of Jews for worship around the reading of their sacred Scriptures according to their ancestral customs, allowed Jews to renew their bonds as a community and remain in touch with the essential elements of their heritage. The rational worship of the one God in the synagogue served not only to help Jews remain Jews but also attracted their Gentile neighbors to this oriental cult much as other Gentiles were attracted to the worship of the Egyptian Isis or Persian Mithras. The bond of kinship, reinforced wherever Jews were reminded of their common descent from Abraham, Isaac, Jacob and the twelve patriarchs, helped to foster a sense of solidarity and mutual support in the midst of other peoples (Gentiles) who were not kin. The observance of Torah was a cornerstone for preserving Jewish identity, and a better code for maintaining distinctiveness could not have been devised. Torah's promotion of distinctive practices like sabbath observance and circumcision set the Jews apart from other people quite visibly and physically. The prohibition against all participation in idolatry kept observant Jews from many places and settings where Gentiles were most at home. The regulations concerning foods and purity, moreover, pushed Jews toward forming their own markets and eating within their own communities. So effective were these practices in the maintenance of Jewish distinctiveness that every Gentile author indulging in anti-Jewish slander mentions these in particular.

Gentile responses to Jews. Gentiles had ample opportunity to observe Jewish behavior, whether in connection with some Gentile ruler's initiatives in Palestine or in their own cities most anywhere in the Mediterranean. Positively, there were some Gentiles who admired the Jewish way of life. Jewish commit-

---

[23]For a fuller discussion, see J. M. G. Barclay, *Jews in the Mediterranean Diaspora from Alexander to Trajan* (Edinburgh: T & T Clark, 1996), pp. 92-101.

ment to monotheism seemed to have much in common with the rational teachings of many philosophical schools concerning the oneness of God. Jewish dietary practices and sexual ethics could be viewed as a form of asceticism, aimed at bringing the passions of the body under the control of reason and developing the virtue of temperance. In many ways, then, Judaism could be seen as another school of philosophy. Some Gentiles were attracted enough to this way of life to attend synagogue worship and become patrons of the Jewish community through their support of this institution. Some (more often women, who would not need to submit to surgical modifications of their anatomy, that is, circumcision) even went so far as to proselytize completely. This phenomenon would also contribute, however, to the more general animosity felt toward Jews: under the influence of the Jewish philosophy, good Gentiles who *had* honored the traditional gods and had participated fully in society began to act impiously toward the gods and avoid many of their former associations.

Negatively, we find many literary monuments to ancient anti-Judaism, usually posed as criticism of Jewish behavior as irreligious or anti-social. These two charges were often connected. Linking the Jews' social behavior with their theology, the rhetorician Apollonius Molon of Rhodes (early first century B.C.E.) wrote that "the Jews do not accept people who have other views about God" (quoted in Josephus *Contra Apionem* 2.258). Ironically, Jews were often regarded as atheists on account of their denial of the existence of all gods save one. Greeks and Romans understood piety toward the gods as a reflection of loyalty to the city and a marker of reliability. The person who knew how to pay proper respect to the gods would know his or her duty in a civic crisis, would be a reliable partner in business and would not foment division in the city. The Jews did not participate in the worship of these gods and were thus never free from sus-

picion and slander. Their devotion to the one God allegedly reflected their concern for the one people, the Jews, and their lack of concern for the public welfare (cf. 3 Macc 3:3-7; Esther 13:4-5 LXX). The connection between acceptance of a city's divinities and participation in civic life emerges rather strikingly in the tense and tumultuous circumstances surrounding the attempts of Jews to gain the right of "equal citizenship" (*isopoliteia*) with the Greek citizens of Alexandria, Caesarea and other Hellenistic *poleis*. In Alexandria, Antioch and the cities of Ionia the cry of the Greek citizens was "If they are citizens, why do they not worship the same gods as us?" (see Josephus *Ant.* 12.3.1 §121-23; 12.3.2 §125-26).

The other word that surfaces again and again in anti-Jewish polemics is *misoxenia,* or "hatred of foreigners." The dietary laws and restrictions on social intercourse practiced by Jews loyal to Torah, while an effective means of maintaining group boundaries and cohesion, gave rise to anti-Jewish slander from outsiders. Correctly observing how Jews' dedication to their ancestral customs kept them visibly distinct and separate from other people groups, Hecataeus interpreted these customs and restrictions as misanthropic. Their desire to preserve ethnic identity and solidarity could be seen from the outside as xenophobic and therefore "barbaric," a backwards resistance to the universalizing and unifying ideals of Hellenism. Diodorus of Sicily (*Bib. Hist.* 34.1-4; 40.3.4), Tacitus (*Hist.* 5.5), Juvenal (*Sat.* 14.100-104), and Apion (Josephus *Ag. Ap.* 2.121) all accuse the Jewish people of supporting their fellow Jews but showing no good will to those who are not of their race. The Jews' loyalty and solidarity was often perceived to be not with the larger *polis* but rather with the Jewish community within the city. This was not without exception, and we find evidence in Rome, for example, of Jews who were patrons of civic life and fully part of their city. More often, however, they were viewed by non-Jews in the cities as people with no sense of civic unity (cf. 3 Macc 3:4, 7).

While usually enjoying official grants of toleration, Jews were nevertheless frequently the objects of the dominant culture's hostility on account of these threatening differences. This could take the form of ridicule and denigration of the Jews' ancestral way of life. It was slandered as a "foolish superstition" rather than an honorable philosophy. Plutarch, for example, criticizes the strict observance of the sabbath that led Jews to refuse to defend themselves on that day as a "cowardly excuse," the result of being "fast bound in the toils of superstition as in one great net" (*Superstition* 8 [*Mor.* 169C]). Jewish abstinence from pork (the "most proper type of meat," according to Plutarch) is the frequent target of contempt, ridicule and misunderstanding.[24] The Jewish author of the *Letter of Aristeas* also notes the "curiosity" that Gentiles have toward the Jewish law's distinctions between clean and unclean foods, despite the fact of "creation being one" (*Ep. Aristeas* 128ff.). While the ethnic, human law of the Jews regards eating pork as a "shameful" thing, nature passes no such judgment on the flesh of this animal. In observing his or her customs the Jew could be charged with injustice against nature, showing ingratitude by spurning its gifts (see 4 Macc 5:8-9).

Anti-Jewish sentiments did not result merely in such philosophical critique or popular ridicule. When authorities were willing to look the other way or were temporarily removed from their jurisdiction, hostility against Jews could break out in more violent forms. A particularly ghastly episode took place in Alexandria during the rule of Caligula, with anti-Jewish riots resulting in the dispossession of a large percentage of the population, physical assaults on Jews of all ages, genders and social ranks, and even the brutal lynching of a great many Jews (the story is recounted in Philo *Against Flaccus*).

Jewish responses to Gentile critique and hostility. Some Jews responded to their Gentile neighbors' disdain by dissociating themselves from their Jewish heritage and customs. Wishing to be honored by the Gentile world, and perhaps to achieve prominence in the Roman administration, some Jews went so far as to adopt the Greek way of life and put the Torah aside completely. Caught between the values they inherited from their ancestral tradition and the values they learned from their new environment, these Jews came to evaluate their own cultural heritage and social location in terms of the standards of their Gentile neighbors. Philo's own nephew, Tiberius Julius Alexander, apostatized and actually enjoyed a distinguished career in Roman public service as governor of Alexandria and, eventually, procurator of Judea. Such Jews may well have been persuaded by the Stoic critique of ethnic legal codes like the Torah, namely, that it was the Torah of Moses, a human law like those given by Lycurgus or Zarathustra, and not the divine and absolute law, which was not to be found in any such civil code.[25] Apostates might thus have drawn on this Stoic concept of the law of nature as the one true law and all particular civil or ethnic codes as imperfect, burdensome shadows of it. Traces of this argument appear in the defense against it in 4 Maccabees 5:18; Philo *Vit. Mos.* 1.31; *Conf. ling.* 2.

The majority of Jews, however, remained steadfast to their way of life. Their fidelity was facilitated by the work of Jewish apologists who, far from being convinced by the critics, put their facility in Greek language and culture to use explaining and defending the reasonableness of the Jewish law and way of life. Some Jewish apologists sought to minimize

---

[24]Plutarch *Table-Talk* 5.1 (*Mor.* 669E-F); Tacitus *Hist.* 5.4.3; Juvenal *Sat.* 14.98-99; Josephus *Ag. Ap.* 2.137.

[25]E. Bickermann, "The Maccabean Uprising: An Interpretation," in *The Jewish Expression,* ed. Judah Goldin (New Haven, Conn.: Yale University Press, 1976), pp. 66-86.

the difference between the Jewish philosophy and Greek philosophy, presenting the Jewish tradition as essentially the same as the dominant culture. Others, however, asserted the supreme value of the Jewish way of life as the path to virtue, promoting it as far superior to any Gentile way of life. The works of Philo, the *Letter of Aristeas* and 4 Maccabees all fall under this heading of apologetic, with 4 Maccabees being the most aggressive in its claims for the superiority of the Jewish "philosophy."

The purpose of apologetics is often assumed to be to convince outsiders of the value of the beliefs and practices of a religion or way of life. This may be an occasional side effect, but it cannot be the primary function. Rather, works of apologetics are really written for insiders. The arguments in such books may find their way into discussions between adherents and outsiders, but the primary audience is the believing audience. Apologetic writings sustain the insider's commitment in the face of critique, ridicule or contradiction from outside (and from questions and doubts inside).

Philo, 4 Maccabees and *Letter of Aristeas* reinterpret the keeping of the Jewish Torah as the pursuit of virtue. Judaism becomes a philosophy that can hold its ground alongside the Greco-Roman philosophies. Judaism is shown to be the way—indeed, the best and surest way—to fulfill even the dominant cultural ideal of the virtuous person. Greeks organized their ethics around the four cardinal virtues of justice, temperance, courage and wisdom. Jewish apologists would frequently turn to these topics to show that "one who lives subject to [the Torah] will rule a kingdom that is temperate, just, good, and courageous" (4 Macc 2:23 NRSV). In the face of Gentile ridicule the Jewish philosopher retorts: "You scoff at our philosophy as though living by it were irrational, but it teaches us self-control, so that

we master all pleasures and desires, and it also trains us in courage, so that we endure any suffering willingly; it instructs us in justice, so that in all our dealings we act impartially, and it teaches us piety, so that with proper reverence we worship the only living God" (4 Macc 5:22-24 NRSV). Such words address Jews who have absorbed the ethos of Hellenistic culture and need to be assured that their ancient ways are valuable in terms of that ethos. A Jew in Antioch, Alexandria, Rome or Caesarea could take such words to heart and know that the opinion so many Gentiles had of him or her was ill-founded. Apologetic literature thus enables the Jew to maintain commitment to his or her ancestral ways and remain faithful to God through keeping of Torah. It is not, after all, a barbaric superstition but rather a divinely given philosophy that trains its disciples in every virtue.

Apologists also help to translate Judaism into terms that outsiders can begin to appreciate more and more as they engage in discussion or debate with their Jewish neighbors. Indeed, the philosophers Epictetus and Galen appear to have had respect for the Jewish way of life. While they might still find it irrational, they could at least begin to appreciate that the Jew's goal was not so dissimilar from the goals of other philosophical schools.[26] To engage in apologetic thus indicates (1) the insider group has embraced the fundamental values of the society and must now demonstrate that its way of life measures up, and (2) the insider group believes that outsiders may be open to dialogue and that misunderstanding rather than malice lies at the root of Jew-Gentile tensions.

Another available response, however, reflects a more negative view of outsiders. This could take the more constructive form of launching a countercritique of Gentile religion and wisdom, as in the Wisdom of Solomon or

---

[26]See Epictetus *Diss.* 1.22.4; Louis H. Feldman and Meyer Reinhold, eds., *Jewish Life and Thought Among Greeks and Romans* (Minneapolis: Fortress, 1996), p. 376.

Letter of Jeremiah, insulating Jews against attraction to the practices they saw around them by pointing out the folly of idolatry or its very human origins. At the extreme we find indications of Jews completely rejecting and condemning non-Jews. A kind of "anti-Gentilism" emerges in certain texts as an equally effective insulation against the Gentiles' censure of the Jewish way of life. For example, the author of 3 Maccabees frequently speaks of Gentiles as godless and depraved in their thinking (3 Macc 4:16; 5:12; 6:4-5, 9, 11). Apocalypses like 4 Ezra also often take this approach. Gentiles are irredeemable. Their values and their opinions should not matter at all to the Jew since God will destroy them all anyway. This became a more prominent option after the destruction of the temple in 70 C.E., the suppression of Jewish rebellions in the Diaspora in 115-117 C.E. and the final de-Judaizing of Jerusalem after the suppression of the Bar-Kosebah revolt of 132-135 C.E.[27]

CHRISTIANS IN THE GRECO-ROMAN WORLD

If Jews faced significant pressure from their Gentile neighbors, Christians faced pressure on two fronts. First, the sources record that the Jesus movement stood in tension with the parent body, the Jewish subculture, from the outset. Not only was Jesus' own ministry marked by conflict with other Jewish groups and the eventual and successful termination of his life by the Jewish leaders in conjunction with the Roman authorities, but his Jewish Christian followers remained vulnerable to the discipline of the synagogue in the Diaspora and the Judean authorities in Palestine (see Mt 10:16-39; Jn 15:18-20; 16:1-2; Acts 1—8). Paul is a noteworthy example both of the persecutor of the "deviant" Jews who followed Jesus and of the recipient of community discipline at the hands of synagogue leaders after his encounter with the risen Jesus.[28] Paul accuses his rivals who are preaching circumcision in Galatia of being motivated by a desire to escape persecution (disciplinary measures) by the non-Christian Jewish community (Gal 6:12-13). The Christian proclamation about Jesus (which involved the deabsolutizing of the temple and Torah) and, more and more, the tendency for Jewish Christians to loosen their observance of certain regulations for the sake of having table fellowship and worshiping with Gentile Christians, led to strong attempts on the part of non-Christian Jews to "correct" the threatening behavior of their deviant sisters and brothers.

Matters were no better for Gentile Christians. Christianity's commitment to the one God and rejection of all other deities led serious Christians to withdraw from participation in the cultic ceremonies that were a part of most political, business and social enterprises in the Greco-Roman world (see 1 Cor 10:14-22; 2 Cor 6:14—7:1; 1 Thess 1:9). As a result Christianity inherited much of the suspicion and prejudice that arose against Jews in a world where loyalty to the gods was intimately connected with loyalty to ruler, city, authorities, friends, family and associates. Along with this suspicion came reproach, rumor and slander, which together made it disgraceful and often dangerous to be associated with the name "Christian." The sources bear ample witness to the ways unofficial persecution and other attempts at deviancy control were used in an attempt to "rehabilitate" Christians (see 1 Thess 1:6; 2:14—3:5; 1 Pet 4:12-19).

Like Jews, Christians were prey to the charge of atheism and the censure of their religion. Tacitus speaks of Christianity as a

---

[27]See, further, David A. deSilva, *Introducing the Apocrypha* (Grand Rapids: Baker, 2002), pp. 123-25, 142-48, 217-20, 238-42, 315-20, 359-69.

[28]For the former, see Acts 7:54—8:3; 9:1-2; 1 Cor 15:9; Gal 1:13, 23; Phil 3:6; for the latter, see 2 Cor 11:24; Gal 5:11.

"deadly superstition" (*Ann.* 15.44). Pliny the Younger calls Christian beliefs a "depraved and fanciful superstition" (*Ep.* 10.96). Christianity was regarded as a cult of foreign origin that did not support traditional values and social bonds, promoting rather the decay of society and erosion of its central values. The emergence of the group in Rome is regarded by Tacitus as one more example of "things horrible or shameful" from around the world breaking out in the imperial capital.

Since avoiding all participation in idolatry meant the withdrawal from many domestic, private and public activities, Christians also inherited the charge of "misanthropy," of despising their fellow-citizens and their former friends and associates. Because of the economic and political disadvantages of such withdrawal, not to mention the suspicion and dislike it aroused, some Christians sought to rationalize continued participation in idolatry, which would allow them to maintain strategic relationships with important non-Christians. Christian leaders consistently countered this tendency, seeking to preserve the distinctive character and witness of the group. The Christians' withdrawal from Greco-Roman religious and social life aroused suspicion and prejudice, often resulting in ridicule, insult and prejudice, and sometimes going considerably further—toward physical and economic sanctions. Writing about the one confirmed imperially sanctioned persecution of Christians in Rome under Nero, Tacitus attributes the real cause for hounding out and punishing the Christians not to the genuine suspicion of arson but to *odium humani generis,* "the hatred of the human race." The celebrated Latin phrase contains an ambiguity: did the human race hate the Christians, or were the Christians seen to hate the human race? It must be both at once. The tendency of Christian Gentiles, formerly seen to be loyal, pious members of the empire, to withdraw from associating with outsiders and their idols fueled the outsiders' tendency to despise the Christians in return.

The Christians were further stigmatized as immoral criminals given to barbarous atrocities. Tacitus speaks of the Christians as a class of people "loathed for their vices," as if these were well and widely known. Pliny the Younger, in his famous letter to Emperor Trajan concerning the legal handling of those denounced as "Christians" (110-111 C.E.), shows surprise that no evidence can be found for the crimes of which Christians were commonly accused. Suspicion of subversive activity in general led to suspicion of specific abominations. In the writings of second-century detractors Christian rituals were associated with infanticide, orgies, cannibalism and oaths committing the members to political subversion.

While Christianity was recognized as a form of Judaism, its novelty (and therefore dubiousness) is also readily apparent to outsiders. Tacitus knows that it started rather recently and that its founder was executed by the Roman governor. The fact that Christianity's leader was shamefully executed as a criminal under a duly appointed Roman governor became well known, and Christians had to answer this readily available disqualification of their message. Christians thus inherited the basic prejudices and criticisms leveled at Jews by the less-enlightened majority of the Greco-Roman world, with one important distinction. Jews had always been given, as it were, to anti-Roman values, but their way of life was ancient and enjoyed the official protection of imperial policy. Christianity, however, made formerly reliable Gentiles unreliable and subversive: it eroded the constituency of traditional Greco-Roman cults and created a new, exclusivist group. Toward the end of the first century it became increasingly apparent that the Jewish people did not claim this offshoot as their own. This made the legal status of Christians shaky as they entered the second century.

Such a dominantly negative view from outside was calculated to turn deviant Christians back to their proper place in the society, to shame them into returning to the values of piety, loyalty and civic unity they had abandoned. Christian communities had to respond in a variety of ways. First, we find in the pages of the New Testament a great deal of attention being given to making the *ekklēsia*, the assembly of believers, a resource for strong, positive reinforcement of the individual's attachment to the group and commitment to the new way of life. If the individual lost his or her roots in the Gentile society, those roots would be recovered in the family of God; if the individual lost honor and "place" in the Gentile society, these would be recovered in the esteem bestowed by the Christian community and the love and support experienced therein.

Second, Christian leaders sustained the commitment of believers by explaining the nature of the dishonor they now experience as a small price for the greater honor they have before God, the honor that will be manifested on the day of Christ's return. The pattern of Christ's own life became increasingly important for this task, as portrayed in the Gospels and texts like the epistle to the Hebrews. Third, Christian leaders sought increasingly to demonstrate that commitment to Christ did not mean subversion of the Roman order. Obedience to authorities (see Rom 13:1-7) and the careful avoidance of any crime (see 1 Pet 4:14-16) would, it was hoped, show the outsiders that their suspicion and fear were unfounded. An alternative response, however, was to launch a counterattack such as we find in Revelation. In the Christian apocalypse Greco-Roman religions (both traditional cults and the imperial cult) are denounced as partnership with the primal source of chaos (Satan) and the Greco-Roman political and economic system is symbolized as a whore, certainly not the divine Roma Aeterna. The constant was the need to maintain Christian identity and commitment in an unsupportive society; the variable was whether this would be done in a spirit of apologetics or polemics.

FOR FURTHER READING

Students desiring to grow in their appreciation of the message of the New Testament will intentionally read more comprehensive treatments of the first-century environment and will also read broadly in Greco-Roman and Hellenistic Jewish literature. The following are three excellent resources for the next leg of the journey.

Evans, Craig A., and Stanley E. Porter, eds. *Dictionary of New Testament Background.* Downers Grove, Ill.: InterVarsity Press, 2000. This 1300-page resource contains approximately 300 articles contributed by more than 150 scholars on the history, politics, religion, philosophy, literature (especially valuable are the articles on individual texts), economics, social institutions and cultural environment of Judaism and the Greco-Roman world, each with an up-to-date and thorough bibliography for further study. No more complete single-volume guide to early Christian backgrounds exists.

Ferguson, Everett. *Backgrounds of Early Christianity.* 2nd ed. Grand Rapids: Eerdmans, 1993. This thorough and well-illustrated volume is the standard textbook on the subject and is written by an acknowledged authority. Every section concludes with a helpful bibliography of both primary (i.e., ancient) and secondary (i.e., scholarly) texts for more in-depth investigation.

Bell, Albert A., Jr. *Exploring the New Testament World.* Nashville: Thomas Nelson, 1998. Smaller than the others, this book provides a very readable and reliable guide to the same body of material. The topical bibliographies at the end of each chapter are extensive and invaluable.

Because of the comprehensive bibliographies in each of these three resources, the following list is merely a representative sample of other works students may find helpful to consult on particular aspects of the environment of early Christianity:

Bruce, F. F. *New Testament History.* New York: Doubleday, 1971.

Cohen, Shaye. *From the Maccabees to the Mishnah.* Philadelphia: Westminster Press, 1987.

deSilva, David A. *Honor, Patronage, Kinship and Purity: Unlocking New Testament Culture.* Downers Grove, Ill.: InterVarsity Press, 2000.

————. *Introducing the Apocrypha: Its Message, Context, and Significance.* Grand Rapids: Baker, 2002.

Grabbe, Lester L. *Judaism from Cyrus to Hadrian.* 2 vols. Minneapolis: Fortress, 1992.

Keener, Craig. *The IVP Bible Background Commentary: New Testament.* Downers Grove, Ill.: InterVarsity Press, 1993.

Newsome, James D. *Greeks, Romans, Jews: Currents of Culture and Belief in the New Testament World.* Philadelphia: Trinity, 1992.

Nickelsburg, George W. E. *Jewish Literature Between the Bible and the Mishnah.* Philadelphia: Fortress, 1981.

Perkins, Pheme. *Gnosticism and the New Testament.* Minneapolis: Fortress, 1993.

Sanders, Ed P. *Judaism: Practice and Belief 63 B.C.E.-66 C.E.* Philadelphia: Trinity Press, 1992.

Schiffman, Lawrence H. *Reclaiming the Dead Sea Scrolls.* ABRL. New York: Doubleday, 1995.

Scott, Julius J. *Customs and Controversies: Intertestamental Jewish Backgrounds of the New Testament.* Grand Rapids: Baker, 1995.

Stone, Michael E., ed. *Jewish Writings of the Second Temple Period.* Philadelphia: Fortress, 1984.

VanderKam, James C. *The Dead Sea Scrolls Today.* Grand Rapids: Eerdmans, 1994.

Vermes, Geza. *The Complete Dead Sea Scrolls in English.* London: Penguin, 1997.

Wilken, Robert. *The Christians as the Romans Saw Them.* New Haven, Conn.: Yale University Press, 1984.

One of the best ways to enter into the world of the New Testament is to read other texts written from that period and before. There are many voices that still speak to us from the Greek and Roman periods, affording us important first-hand information about the ancient world. I usually direct my own students who want further exposure to the history, philosophy, ethics and piety of the intertestamental and New Testament periods first to the following:

GREEK AND LATIN AUTHORS

1. Aristotle *Nicomachean Ethics.* London: Penguin, 1955. This is a foundational book on the Greco-Roman conception of virtue and vice, especially as conceived within specific relationships (e.g., family, friendship, civic relationships).

2. (Pseudo-)Isocrates *Ad Demonicum* and *Ad Nicoclem.* LCL. Cambridge, Mass.: Harvard University Press, 1928. This is a collection of short pieces of advice, providing a very pleasant introduction to the aims, ambitions, values and practices of a Greek citizen.

3. Virgil *Aeneid.* Available in numerous prose and poetic translations. This is the foundational myth of the Augustan Age and an excellent sourcebook in Roman imperial ideology and the Roman ethos.

4. Tacitus *The Annals of Imperial Rome* and *The Histories.* London: Penguin, 1971, 1986. Tacitus is the primary source for historical information for the reigns of Augustus through the accession of Vespasian.

5. Suetonius *The Twelve Caesars*. Harmondsworth, U.K.: Penguin, 1957. Though regarded as less reliable than Tacitus, Suetonius remains a crucial source for the history of the Roman Empire from Julius Caesar to Domitian.

6. Pliny the Younger *Letters* 10.95-96. 2 vols. LCL. Cambridge, Mass.: Harvard University Press. Pliny's collection of letters gives us a firsthand witness into the life of a successful Roman senator and the kinds of domestic and public situations and issues a Roman would face. The two letters highlighted here contain the most important early evidence for how imperial Rome viewed and persecuted Christians at the start of the second century.

7. Seneca *Moral Essays*. 3 vols. LCL. Cambridge, Mass.: Harvard University Press, 1928-1935.

8. Epictetus *Discourses and Enchiridion*. 2 vols. LCL. Cambridge, Mass.: Harvard University Press, 1925, 1928.

9. Diogenes Laertius, *Lives of the Eminent Philosophers*. 2 vols. LCL. Cambridge, Mass.: Harvard University Press, 1925.

10. Plutarch *Moralia*. 15 vols. LCL. Cambridge, Mass.: Harvard University Press, 1927-1976. Selected essays are also available. See Plutarch, *Essays* (London: Penguin, 1992); and Plutarch, *Selected Essays and Dialogues* (Oxford: Oxford University, 1993).

These last four authors provide important witnesses to the philosophical tradition of the classical, Hellenistic and Roman periods, offering many points of contact with, and greatly illumining, early Christian "philosophy" and "ethics." Plutarch, in addition, writes across a broad range of topics. His essay "On Inoffensive Self-Praise" is essential reading for understanding how and why Paul writes about himself so much; his essay "On Fraternal Affection" expounds the ethics of brotherhood and sisterhood, illumining what early Christian leaders were striving for as they applied these labels to Christians; his essay "On the Destiny of Rome" is a classic source on Roman imperial ideology; the list could be multiplied endlessly.

JEWISH AUTHORS

1. The Old Testament Apocrypha (RSV and NRSV translations are readily available as part of study Bibles or ecumenical Bibles). Arguably the most important collection of texts to read after the Hebrew Bible and New Testament. See the "Old Testament Apocrypha" on pp. 48-49.

2. Select Old Testament pseudepigrapha (*1 Enoch, Jubilees, Epistle of Aristeas, Testaments of the Twelve Patriarchs, Psalms of Solomon, 2 Baruch*), available in *The Old Testament Pseudepigrapha,* ed. J. H. Charlesworth, 2 vols. (New York: Doubleday, 1983, 1985), and H. F. D. Sparks, ed., *The Apocryphal Old Testament* (Oxford: Clarendon, 1984). Each of these texts has something of great value to offer in terms of the development of Old Testament traditions in the intertestamental period (developments picked up by New Testament authors), reflections on ethics prior to the time of Jesus, tensions within Israel and between Israel and foreign powers, the way Hellenistic Jews made sense of their peculiar laws in terms of Greek philosophical and ethical values, and so forth.

3. Select Dead Sea Scrolls (*The Community Rule, The Damascus Document, The Thanksgiving Scroll* and the commentaries on Habakkuk, Nahum and the Psalms), available in Vermes, *The Complete Dead Sea Scrolls*. This is literature arising within and providing firsthand evidence about an important early Jewish sect. The combination of an awareness of grace and election with an absolute diligence in regard to doing the works of the law seen in these texts has provided a stunning counterpoint in Pauline studies; they are also important witnesses

to apocalypticism, biblical interpretation and a host of other topics ancillary to Bible study. (See "The Dead Sea Scrolls" on pp. 86-87.)

4. Qumran biblical manuscripts, available in translation in M. Abegg Jr., P. Flint and E. Ulrich, *The Dead Sea Scrolls Bible* (San Francisco: HarperSanFrancisco, 1999). An excellent translated collection of actual biblical manuscripts as they existed in 68 C.E. and before, often very instructive to compare with Old Testament and apocryphal texts as we have them today in our modern translations.

5. Josephus *Antiquities of the Jews.* 6 vols. LCL (Cambridge, Mass.: Harvard University Press, 1926-1965), especially books 12-20. Written at the end of the first century, this remains an important history of the intertestamental and New Testament periods (up to the first Jewish Revolt). The earlier books are largely a retelling of the biblical narrative from Genesis through 2 Kings, but with some interesting additions and divergences that provide windows into how the biblical stories were being expanded and shaped by the first century (see also *Jubilees, Testaments of the Twelve Patriarchs, Apocalypse of Abraham* and other pseudepigrapha for more examples of the "rewritten Bible").

6. Josephus *The Jewish War.* London: Penguin, 1970. The firsthand history of the Jewish Revolt of 66-70 C.E., its antecedents (going back to the reign of Herod) and its aftermath (through the stunning story of Masada, captured in 73 C.E.).

7. Josephus *Against Apion.* LCL. Cambridge, Mass.: Harvard University Press, 1926. A work of apologetics showing what kind of prejudice existed against Jews in the Second Temple Period and how these prejudices and calumnies were answered.

8. Philo *In Flaccam* ("Against Flaccus") and *Quod Omnis Prober Liber Sit* ("That Every Good Person Is Free"), in *The Works of Philo,* ed. C. D. Yonge (Peabody, Mass.: Hendrickson, 1993). Philo is a testimony to how Greek philosophy, rhetoric and hermeneutics could be put in the service of the Jewish way of life. "Against Flaccus" is a stirring account of the kind of unofficial, local pogrom that could flare up against the Jewish people; in "Every Good Person Is Free" we find a definition of true slavery and freedom in philosophical terms (vice and virtue).

9. *Pirke Aboth* ("Sayings of the Fathers"), available in *The Apocrypha and Pseudepigrapha of the Old Testament,* ed. R. H. Charles (Oxford: Clarendon, 1913). The most accessible tractate of the Mishnah, this collection of sayings gives a fine introduction to the values and ethos of early rabbinic Judaism.

Also helpful are the collections and selections from primary sources gathered in the following books:

Barrett, C. K. *The New Testament Background: Selected Documents.* New York: Harper & Row, 1961.

Feldman, Louis H., and Meyer Reinhold, eds. *Jewish Life and Thought Among Greeks and Romans.* Minneapolis: Fortress, 1996.

3

THE CULTURAL AND SOCIAL WORLD OF THE EARLY CHURCH

Purity, Honor, Patronage and Kinship

In order to hear the New Testament as its authors intended and as its first audiences did, we need to explore these texts not only in their historical or literary or social contexts, but also in their cultural contexts. By *culture* I mean the set of values, ways of relating and ways of looking at the world shared by members of a particular group or region, and providing the framework for meaningful communication. The early Christians shared certain social values (such as honor), ways of forming and maintaining relationships (such as patronage and kinship) and ways of ordering the world (such as the pure and the polluted). Recognizing the cultural cues that an author has woven into the text's strategy and instructions helps us discern more closely what gives the text its persuasive power, or what contributions to the formation of Christian culture a text is making as the meaning of honor, the definition of kinship, the lines of purity and the direction of favor are redrawn. We begin to see how the New Testament texts use deep-rooted values and codes to uphold a faithful and obedient response to God, and to sustain the new community in its quest to be conformed to the image of Christ and no longer to the society from which it had separated itself.

As a means of demonstrating how knowledge of the cultural and social environment of the early church can help open up new readings of and insights into the New Testament texts, the chapters on each of the four Gospels will include a section dedicated to viewing that Gospel through the lens of one of these four areas—purity in Mark, honor in Matthew, reciprocity in Luke and kinship in John. Insights from the analysis of how other New Testament authors invoke these topics will be further integrated into the discussion of Acts through Revelation. By the time you finish reading this book, you will be equipped to incorporate the insights to be gained from "cultural-anthropological analysis" into your own practice of the art of biblical interpretation.[1]

PURITY AND POLLUTION

Purity and pollution are prominent concepts throughout the literature of Israel and the early church. We frequently encounter words like *holy, clean, pure, undefiled, unblemished, sanctified, saints, unholy, unclean, defiled, common* and the like. Modern, Western Christians tend not to have a natural sympathy for purity and pollution language and the symbolic codes and social dynamics they represent. Af-

---

[1]This chapter is a "digest" of my *Honor, Patronage, Kinship and Purity: Unlocking New Testament Culture* (Downers Grove, Ill.: InterVarsity Press, 2000). Please refer to that volume for fully developed introductions to each of these cultural and social topics, and the ways attention to them illumines the New Testament.

ter the great drama of Genesis and Exodus, it is hard for many to stomach Leviticus, with its lengthy discussions of how purity is lost and how purity is to be regained. Two theological convictions stand behind this distaste. First, the ritual law of the Old Testament is regarded as part of an externalistic religion that was fulfilled and rendered obsolete by the work of Jesus (an enduring legacy of the epistle to the Hebrews), and so the relevance of purity and pollution codes is obscured. Second, access to God has been largely deregulated and stripped of its purification requirements, especially among Protestant Christians. The idea that anyone in any state can come before the "throne of grace" (Heb 4:16) and seek an audience with God is antithetical to the notions of graded access to God and the need for special rites of purification and abstinence from defiling activities before entering the holy precincts in ancient Israel and early Judaism.

This poses a serious stumbling block, however, to understanding Jesus' interaction with the purity codes of first-century Judaism. We need to gain a sympathetic understanding concerning why purity would be worthwhile or important to people. When we do we will no longer dismiss Jesus' opponents as incomprehensible, shallow or legalistic. We also need an insider's perspective on the dynamics of purity and pollution language to appreciate the power of New Testament appeals to these codes and the ways they continued to be vital forces guiding, shaping and providing boundaries for the early Christians. These concepts are essential to understanding the world they lived in. Such an insider's understanding, moreover, will allow us to integrate those texts more fully and powerfully into our discipleship and ministry.

Modern purity codes and purification rites. Reflecting on our own purity codes and rituals is a first step on this journey toward a sympathetic appreciation for Jewish purity codes. Being located in the United States, I will speak about American purity codes. That which is in its proper place at the proper time is "pure" or "clean"; that which is "out of place" is a polluting presence.[2] Attention is given in households to keeping things "in their proper place" and to restoring things or conditions that are "out of place" back to a proper state. We may have an aversion to soil, sand, grass clippings and the like being scattered across the kitchen floor. These things are proper to the outside world and are "clean" there, but inside our house they become "dirt," and we tend to move quickly to "purify" the inside spaces by removing such pollutants. Food spread across the kitchen counter during meal preparation is in its proper place, "clean." Food served on a plate remains "clean." When it falls to the floor or is spread across the hallway stairs, it is out of place, both "polluting" the hallway or floor and being itself "polluted," to be thrown into the trash. We tend to regard the bodily fluids of others with the same suspicion, and we avoid them with the same energy and passion as the author of Leviticus, some people going even so far as to use paper towels to turn on faucets and open doors in rest rooms, for example.

The fact that these codes differ from region to region and family to family is also very important for our investigation. People raised in a family with rather rigid purity codes might be uncomfortable in the home of a family with noticeably looser purity codes—where fallen food is placed back on the plate, or where residents do not wash their hands after using the bathroom. Those of us with more rigid codes might cease to visit the houses of people (or restaurants) who were found to pay little attention to the requirements of purity we hold dear, in fact

---

[2]Mary Douglas, *Purity and Danger* (London: Routledge & Kegan Paul, 1966), p. 35.

Figure 3.1. The exterior of a multilevel house at Qatzrin in Galilee. This type of house was fairly typical of houses in Palestine during the time of Jesus. (Photo courtesy of Qatzrin Park and Todd Bolen [BiblePlaces.com])

inviolable. Legitimations of this separation would begin to emerge, and almost invariably a labeling of the "less pure" as somehow inferior social beings. The aversion of many people toward the homeless in their midst appears to be an extreme example of purity codes and regulations at work. The homeless are "out of place," since people live in private houses and not the common, public spaces. They also have no "place" in the internal structure of our society but are off the map (the corporate ladder, if you will) entirely. Lacking homes, they tend to be viewed as lacking the means for "cleansing" and for maintaining the standards required of "polite company," and so tend to suffer extreme social marginalization, even at the hands of those who bear Christ's name.

Even our very modern society, then, has distinctive purity codes and ways of dealing with pollution, ways of explaining and legiti-mating those codes and processes, and a reluctance to part with them even when explanations are weak or lacking. As you explore the ways purity and pollution act as forces in the way you order your own life, you will become more in touch with the power and self-evident quality of the purity codes of early Judaism—at least for those raised in that environment.

Purity and holiness. People of a particular culture create a system that defines what is proper and improper to specific places, times, and people. This is part of a natural social process of creating order within the particular social entity and defining and defending the boundaries of that social entity. Purity is concerned with the proper ordering of the world and making sense of everyday experiences in light of that order. Purity codes regulate "what and who belong when and where"[3] and thus enable people in the

---

[3]Jerome H. Neyrey, "The Idea of Purity in Mark's Gospel," *Semeia* 35 (1986): p. 93.

society to know when order is being maintained and when something is out of place and requires attention.

A closely related concept, which governed and necessitated considerations of purity and pollution in Israel, is "holiness." Something "holy" is beyond the sphere of the ordinary; it is whole, complete, and perfect,[4] and therefore stands out as something "other" and awe-inspiring. The "holy" is invested with power for either blessing or destruction. Both the Jew and the Gentile understand that the "holy" can only be approached with care on the part of the members of the society, often only by certain members of society (hence the introduction of the distinctions between priests and laity, and the creation of internal hierarchy in the group), and always by those who have undergone purifications for the removal of that which is unclean or defiling—such things as must never come into contact with holiness. Most sources of defilement or pollution observed in Leviticus, moreover, stem from some condition that betrays the lack of wholeness of a person or creature (skin diseases, bodily discharges, corpses), and it is essential to contain and eliminate pollution before entering the presence of the divine. The message is that those who would encounter the holy/whole God must themselves be holy/whole and must offer that which is holy/whole.

Pollution and defilement are undesirable, first, because they disqualify persons from entering the presence and fellowship of God (threatening destruction should someone be foolish enough to enter God's presence anyway). If passed on, they may prevent others from securing the needed favor of God and might even provoke the holy God to "break out" against the whole people. Cultures like ancient Israel, then, drew extensive lines of purity, of clean and unclean, in an attempt to create a model of God's cosmic order and help people locate their place in that order so that they may know when pollution has been contracted and what needs to be done to dispel it. Thus, access to the holy God and his benefits will remain open.

These lines and concern with remaining pure, or returning to a state of purity with regard to these lines, serve central social functions for the maintenance of a culture. Purity issues undergird morality and the ethos of a group, identify the boundaries of the group and protect the social group from erosion from without, and create internal lines within the group, giving structure and hierarchy to the group. The significance of these social effects must never be forgotten, even as we ponder the theological or ideological rationales for the regulations.

Purity and pollution in the Greco-Roman world. Before looking more closely at purity and pollution in early Judaism, we need to understand that Greek culture was also pervaded with pollution taboos. Purity language would be meaningful to Christians *whatever* their ethnic background. Gentile Christians might need to be educated in the particulars of Jewish purity regulations and restrictions (if only for the sake of understanding the boundaries that Christ overcame on behalf of the disciple, or the significance of his death and ascension), but the meaning and significance of *pure* versus *defiled*, of *sanctified* versus *profane*, would already be deeply inscribed in his or her mind. While the New Testament authors are predominantly dealing with the reworking of Jewish purity codes, we can be sure that the significance of their discussions would not be lost on Gentile Christians.

Entrance into a sacred space required the worshiper to be free from pollution contracted by childbirth, contact with the dead, recent

---

[4]Douglas, *Purity and Danger,* p. 54.

Purity and Pollution in the Oedipus Plays of Sophocles

The dynamics of murder pollution and its purification drive what is perhaps the most famous Greek tragedy, Sophocles' *Oedipus the King.* [a] The city of Thebes is suffering plague because it has been "polluted" by the presence of a murderer who has gone unpunished (*Oed. Tyr.* 95-101). Expelling the polluting presence either by execution or exile will cleanse the city and end the plague. The opening scenes of the drama thus attest to the use of purity and pollution language to uphold justice and morality as well as to the great danger to the common good (and the individual good, since the defiled one must be eliminated) inherent in pollution. King Oedipus makes it his own mission to "drive pollution from the land" (*Oed. Tyr.* 136), and, of course, the prophet Teiresias must reveal to him: "you are the land's pollution" (*Oed. Tyr.* 353). As the drama unfolds Teiresias's words are proven true, leading to Oedipus' self-blinding. He laments that he was allowed to survive infancy, to become "a child of impurity" (*Oed. Tyr.* 1360); finally, Creon tells him to go inside the palace, away from the public eye—if not out of "shame before the face of men" then at least out of "reverence" for the Sun: "do not show unveiled to him pollution that neither land nor holy rain nor light of day can welcome" (*Oed. Tyr.* 1423-29). From here the terminology can be applied as a sanction promoting or prohibiting a wide variety of behaviors, as in the sequel drama *Oedipus at Colonus* 280-84. Oedipus labels the citizens' intent to cast him out after promising him hospitality "unholy," a "blot" or "stain" on their city's reputation if they carry it out.

The second play in the Oedipus trilogy provides an excellent example of Greek sensitivity to the requirements of entering sacred spaces and preserving the holiness of such spaces. At a pause in his endless wandering (now as a blinded beggar), Oedipus sits down to rest in a sacred grove. When a stranger encounters him, the stranger's first words are:

First move from where you sit; the place is holy;
It is forbidden to walk upon that ground.
It is not to be touched, no one may live upon it;
Most dreadful are its divinities, most feared. (*Oed. Col.* 36-40)

The "chorus" of citizens of Colonus arrives, censures Oedipus for "profaning" the sacred grove, and then explains the elaborate rite of expiation for the profanation of the sacred grove, making amends to the Eumenides with ritual libations and prayers (*Oed. Col.* 466-90).

[a]Quotations are taken from Sophocles *Oedipus* and *Oedipus at Colonus*, in *Sophocles I*, ed. David Greene and Richmond Lattimore (New York: Pocket Books, 1967).

sexual activity, murder, sacrilege and madness.[5] As in Israelite codes of purity we find that both natural events in the life cycle and morally reprehensible acts incur pollution without distinction. In Greco-Roman literature, such as the Oedipus trilogy and other literary

[5]Robert C. T. Parker, "Pollution, the Greek Concept of," in *The Oxford Companion to Classical Civilization,* ed. Simon Hornblower and Antony Spawforth (Oxford: Oxford University Press, 1998), p. 553. Friedrich Hauck gathers references to pregnancy, childbirth, menstruation, corpses, tombs and, for the Pythagoreans, eating of animals (because the meat is dead flesh) as pollutants in various sectors of the Greco-Roman world ("μιαίνω, etc.," *Theological Dictionary of the New Testament* [hereafter TDNT], ed. Gerhard Kittel and Gerhard Friedrich [Grand Rapids: Eerdmans, 1964], 4:645).

artifacts such as questions asked of oracles, pollution taboos frequently reinforce ethics at important junctures. Unless murder or sacrilege or another glaring offense was prosecuted and put right, whole families—even cities—stood under the threat of the avenging gods.[6] Greek and Latin ethical philosophers take up the language of pollution to dissuade people from vice, as when Epictetus urges his students not to defile the indwelling deity "with unclean thoughts and filthy actions" (*Diss.* 2.8.13).[7]

In addition to a wide range of pollution taboos covering both natural and ethical phenomena, the Greek society also observed distinctions between sacred space and common space, the former being highly restricted because the designated space was the special ground of a particular deity, the latter being ordinary space accessible to mortals. While the map of sacred space promoted by the canonical traditions of Judaism centers on a single sacred site, namely, the temple in Jerusalem, Greek and Roman purity maps had sanctuaries and holy places throughout the land, much as the Canaanite religion had the "high places."[8] Nevertheless, both cultures understood the danger of "encroachment," that is, unauthorized people trespassing into sacred spaces. Once again, this kind of transgression

of a taboo placed not only the offender but also the surrounding area under the threat of divine vengeance unless reparations were successfully made.

Entrance to sacred shrines required that the visitor obey the purification requirements specific to the shrine. Without a centralized cult these tended to vary considerably. Giving birth, sexual intercourse and contact with a corpse rendered a person impure. Persons with pollutions of such kinds might be instructed to wait a full day or two before entering the sacred precincts, and all might be required to perform certain ritual washings of their hands, feet or whole bodies.[9] Some shrines might even prescribe clothing and the way hair was to be worn.[10] Not all such purity requirements were external. A law in Lindos stipulates moral purity for those who would enter a temple: "It is of primary importance that those who enter be pure and sound in hands and mind and have no guilt on their conscience."[11] Those who functioned as priests—that is, the mediators between gods and people—had more intense rules governing the purity they were to maintain for their service in sacred places.

Greeks and Romans had fully developed sacrificial systems. Individuals might bring an

---

[6]Parker, "Pollution," p. 554. Parker gives as an example a question posed to an oracle at Dodona: "is it because of a mortal's pollution that we are suffering the storm?" (*SEG* 19.427), as well as a reference to the classical Greek orator Antiphon: "According to Antiphon's *Tetralogies,* for instance, murder pollution threatens the victim's kin until they seek vengeance or prosecute, the jurors until they convict. Thus the threat of pollution encourages action to put right the disorder"; see also Douglas, *Purity and Danger,* p. 133.

[7]Reference given in Friedrich Hauck, "μολύνω, μολυσμός," *TDNT,* 4:736-37.

[8]These were a persistent problem throughout the period of Israel's monarchy—local sacred sites die hard!

[9]Parker, "Pollution," p. 553. Everett Ferguson gives an example of such an inscription at the temple of Athena in Pergamum: "whoever wishes to visit the temple of the goddess . . . must refrain from intercourse with his wife (or husband) that day, from intercourse with another than his wife (or husband) for the preceding two days, and must complete the required lustrations. The same prohibition applies to contact with the dead and with the delivery of a woman in childbirth" (*Backgrounds of Early Christianity,* 2nd ed. [Grand Rapids: Eerdmans, 1993], pp. 174-75).

[10]According to Ferguson a woman's hair might be required to be worn loose and a man's head to be uncovered (ibid., p. 175).

[11]From an inscription (*SIG* 983.4-7) cited in F. W. Danker, *Benefactor: Epigraphic Study of a Graeco-Roman and New Testament Semantic Field* (St. Louis, Mo.: Clayton, 1982), p. 356. We might compare this with the emphasis in the letter to the Hebrews on the importance of cleansing the "conscience" (the same noun is used) as a prerequisite for entering God's presence.

animal to a deity's temple for sacrifice, perhaps to show gratitude for a favor received, perhaps as an inducement to the divinity to grant a petition that would be uttered during the sacrifice.[12] There were also public sacrifices performed on behalf of the whole city or even province, which were frequently occasions of civic celebration and public feasting. The sacrifice began with the participants purifying their hands while hair was cut from the animal and burned on an altar (see figure 3.2). At this point the officiant would offer a prayer, specifying the favor that was requested or expressing the cause of the sacrificial act (thanksgiving, for example). The animal was then killed and its entrails examined (which revealed whether or not it was accepted). Finally, the meat was divided: the gods' portion was burned (and thus transferred to the divine realm); the priests received a portion (which they might sell in the market); the worshipers shared the rest either in a banquet at the temple or at home.[13] Sacrifice in Rome and its colonies followed a similar practice. The Roman rites appear particularly to have affirmed the gods' superiority to human beings in a number of ways. First, the gods' portion was consumed first (by fire) before any mortal took a share of the animal; second, the portions reserved for the gods and the offering of incense and pure

Figure 3.2. A sacrificial altar from the theater at Priene. Religious ceremonies surrounded and supported nearly every aspect of Greek and Roman life. (Photo courtesy of Todd Bolen [BiblePlaces.com])

[12]Robert C. T. Parker, "Sacrifice, Greek," in Simon Hornblower and Anthony Spawforth, *The Oxford Companion to Classical Civilization* (Oxford: Oxford University Press, 1998), p. 628; Ferguson, *Backgrounds of Early Christianity,* p. 179. This last aspect is emphasized in Plato *Euthyphro* 14C-E, where Socrates sums up Euthyphro's view of piety: "To sacrifice is to make a gift to the gods, whereas to pray is to beg from the gods. . . . It would follow from this view that piety would be a knowledge of how to give to, and beg from, the gods, . . . a sort of trading skill between gods and men."
[13]Parker, "Sacrifice," p. 628. He refers the reader to the lengthy description of a sacrifice in Homer *Odyssey* 3.430-63. As one of the foundational texts for Greek religion and culture, this passage might be expected to reflect the practice followed in Greek rites.

wine with the meat spoke to the gods' privilege above mortals.[14]

Purity lines in Israel and early Judaism. God commanded Aaron to "distinguish between the holy and the common, and between the unclean and the clean," and to teach the people how to do the same (Lev 10:10 NRSV). This verse introduces the two main pairs of terms used within Israel to construct its purity maps. Each pair has a neutral term and a more loaded term. *Common* (or *profane*) is a neutral term, referring to the ordinary spaces and things of the world that are accessible to human beings. *Holy* is the corresponding loaded term, referring to special spaces or things that have been "set apart" from the ordinary (common) as belonging in some special way to God. *Clean* is a neutral term, referring generally to a person or thing in its normal, proper state.[15] *Unclean* is the corresponding loaded term, denoting that something has crossed the line from the normal state into a dangerous state of pollution.[16] Breaches of boundaries rendered something unclean, as when a person had a discharge or a torn surface (leprosy, for example), or when an animal combined characteristics thought to be proper to different environments (like lobsters, who lived in the sea but walked on legs).

One would use a category from each pair to describe any single object or person at a given time. The typical lay Israelite would be clean and common most of the time. If a woman suffered a bloody discharge, for example, she would become unclean and common. The tithes collected for the priests were clean and holy, while food sold in the market was (supposed to be) clean and common. The former were thus to be eaten only by the holy priests in a state of cleanness, and if the common lay Israelite ate them, he or she would profane what was holy and risk divine wrath. A graveyard was unclean and common, while the temple precincts were clean and holy. The one combination that would be problematic is unclean and holy, which were held to be an incompatible and dangerous combination (except in special circumstances, like the ashes of the red heifer in Numbers 19).[17] It was the duty of Israel to preserve the holy from being profaned and used as common or from being brought into contact with the impure (the unclean), so that the source of holiness, God, would continue to show favor toward Israel and would not be provoked either to withdraw from the people or consume them.

Israel believed that the one holy God lived in the midst of his special people, God's special possession (Deut 4:20; 7:6). God's presence gave Israel access to great benefits as God protected and prospered God's people (see Lev 26:3-12) as long as the people maintained the purity of the land so that God could continue to remain there. But there was also danger—affronting the holy God with defilements and uncleanness, which would result in disasters for Israel (Lev 26:14-33), just as it had for the former inhabitants of the Holy Land (Lev 18:24-25, 27; 20:22-23). These latter texts are especially instructive, for they show that for the Jew there is no distinction between moral and ritual law. Idolatry, sexual perversity and failure to keep the dietary laws are all pollution for which the land would vomit forth its inhabitants.

Purity codes draw important lines around

---

[14]John Scheid, "Sacrifice, Roman," in Simon Hornblower and Anthony Spawforth, *The Oxford Companion to Classical Civilization* (Oxford: Oxford University Press, 1998), p. 631.

[15]Richard P. Nelson, *Raising Up a Faithful Priest: Community and Priesthood in Biblical Theology* (Louisville, Ky.: Westminster John Knox, 1993), p. 21.

[16]David P. Wright, "Holiness (OT)," in *Anchor Bible Dictionary*, ed. David N. Freedman (Garden City, N.Y.: Doubleday, 1992), 3:246-47.

[17]Nelson, *Raising Up a Faithful Priest,* p. 33.

and within the social body. The Israelites are "a holy people" (Wis 10:15), in contrast to the Gentile nations who are unclean by definition. There is thus an important, boldface line drawn around Israel, circumscribing it from association with the practitioners of abomination. Circumcision—a religious rather than a medical procedure—inscribes on the body of the male Jew this distinctiveness from the Gentiles. Gentiles are not excluded from the people of God, but they must enter it not only by putting away their idols but also by accepting circumcision. Within Israel an internal hierarchy was created on the basis of access to the holy God in his holy temple, a hierarchy that is reflected in the sacred precincts of the temple itself and the limits on how far a particular person could move toward the holy of holies.

At the top of this hierarchy stood the high priest, then the priests and, third, the Levites. Along with the privilege of being, in effect, the elite of Israel on account of brokering access to the divine came the added risks and responsibilities of remaining clean and holy for contact with God. The lay Israelites, though "holy to the Lord," were not as holy as the priests; Israelite women are unclean one quarter of their adult lives on account of menstruation, with the result that their access to the holy places is even more limited. Those whose lineage could not be verified and those (males) whose reproductive organs were damaged were in the outer margins of Israel's purity map.[18] Those "born of an illicit union" (Deut 23:2 NRSV) and their descendants to the tenth generation were barred from the congregation. Since the race was holy, those whose place in that race was questionable (or who were unable to generate themselves) were pushed to the outermost fringes.

Just as Israel was holy to God, so was the land it inhabited. Moreover, Jerusalem was the holy city, of greater sanctity than the rest of Israel, since it contained the temple, the place where the sphere of human action intersects with the sphere of God's realm: the holy places are a sort of overlapping area where these two spheres coexist and thus where transactions (such as sacrifices) between the two spheres become possible. The division of the temple into a series of courts, a holy place and a holiest place reflects the increasing sanctity of spaces as one approached the very presence of holy God. As might be expected, increasingly stricter purity requirements and pollution taboos regulated access to the inner courts and holy places.

Times and seasons are also divided into sacred and common. The sabbath, or seventh day of the week, was set apart as a holy day. It was not to be profaned (treated as common or ordinary) by working on that day, that is, by bringing the activity of the other six days into the sacred time of the seventh day. The severe penalties for profaning the sabbath (nothing short of death; see Ex 31:12-17) shows the importance of this sacred time as a marker of the social identity of the Jewish people. Indeed, it was one of the marks of the Jew that outsiders knew about, together with circumcision and avoidance of pork, hence it clearly functioned to set apart the people of Israel from the nations around them. New moons and other sacred days like Passover, the week-long Festival of Booths, the Day of Atonement and *Rosh ha-Shanah* were also observed in special ways, but the sabbath was by far the most important sacred time, the most visible sign of the Jews' distinctiveness, and therefore not surprisingly a frequent point of contention between Jews (like Jesus and the Pharisees).

Foods were also classified according to the categories of clean (i.e., proper for a Jew to ingest) and unclean (not proper for a Jew but fine for Gentiles, who are themselves unclean). Since food was encountered daily, this became

---

[18]Neyrey, "Idea of Purity," pp. 95-96.

one of the more important reminders of the Jews' distinctiveness and set-apartness for God that was built into the purity system of Torah. Animal blood, which contained the "life," belonged to God alone and was never to be ingested (Lev 17:10-14; Deut 12:16). The Jews regarded this prohibition as binding on all humanity, with the result that the Gentiles' lack of concern to drain the blood from their meat was regarded as one of the abominations committed by them. Jewish meat was limited to grasshopper family. Whether an animal was clean or unclean depended on how it was equipped to move in its environment (Lev 11:3, 9, 12, 20-21) and on its diet. Scavengers are thus unclean, as are sea creatures that move on legs (proper for the land) rather than by fins (proper to the sea).

Like the observance of the sabbath and circumcision, dietary laws also reinforced Jewish identity and group boundaries in some very

Figure 3.3. An olive press from Chorazin. Olive oil was considered "clean" by Jews and was used not only in the preparation of food but also in lamps around the Mediterranean. (Photo courtesy of Todd Bolen [Bible-Places.com])

mitted by them. Jewish meat was limited to land mammals that both ruminated (chewed the cud) and had a split hoof (rather than a paw, like the weasel, or a single hoof, like the horse). It was essential that the animal should have both features. Their seafood was limited to fish with both fins and scales. Birds could be eaten as long as they were not birds of prey (that is, feeding on other animals or carcasses). Insects were unclean, save for the locust and practical ways. The fact that Jews studiously avoided certain foods was well known to the Gentiles in whose midst they lived, particularly their avoidance of pork. The Jews' cuisine, therefore, became another essential point at which the lines between insider (Jew) and outsider (Gentile) were drawn. Jews had to be sure that the source of their food was clean—that is, that an animal had been properly killed (all the blood was drained rather than left to settle in the meat) and had no connection with the polluting idols of the world around them. This would not have been so great a concern in Judea but would have occupied the Jews' attention in the Diaspora. The result is that Jews tended to develop their own markets for food, and they gathered their communities around these markets, showing how remarkably effective dietary restrictions can be for reinforcing social grouping.

The assigning of specific portions of sacrifices to God, priests and, in the case of "well-being sacrifices," lay persons added another dimension to the social function of purity laws concerning food. God's portion was too holy for any human to ingest, and the priests' portions were too holy for the lay people to ingest (Lev 22:10). While distinguishing between clean and unclean animals is common to all Israelites as a sign of Israel's separation from the nations, there is another dimension to food (seen especially in tithes, reserved for priests alone, and well-being offerings, divided between God, priests and worshipers) that reinforces the social structures within the group.

Finally, Jewish purity codes were concerned with the boundaries of individual Jewish bodies. Mary Douglas's extensive study of modern tribal cultures as well as ancient Israelite culture leads her to the insight that "the body is a model which can stand for any bounded system."[19] Many purity codes display a strong interest in the wholeness of the surfaces of the human body, which in turn reflects the interest in the wholeness of the boundaries of the social body (the firm, fixed definition of who belongs to the group and who does not). Concern over what enters and exits a body also correlates with the larger concern over what enters and exits the social body and the desire for regulating that flow. Given this analysis it comes as no surprise, then, that so much discussion of pollution with regard to the human body focuses on surfaces (clothing and the skin), on fluids that cross through the "gates" of the body and on bodies that have crossed the boundary between life and death.[20]

The death of a community member evokes powerful feelings and a sense that something numinous and threatening has broken into normal life. Dead bodies, therefore, and the houses they lie in are sources of pollution. The rotting appearance of the skin associated with a variety of disorders lumped together under the heading of "leprosy" is another potent source of uncleanness. This condition is closely connected with death (see Num 12:12, which compares Miriam's leprosy with the flesh of a stillborn child), and the focus for its diagnosis is the erosion of the surface and the loss of integrity to the body's outer boundary. The result is a state of uncleanness and communicable defilement, with the result that the leper is excluded from the general population as long as the outbreak lasts (Lev 13:45-46). While sweating, crying, urinating, defecating or even bleeding from a cut are not regarded as polluting, all discharges related to the sexual apertures and reproductive processes are, again, no doubt, because the processes of birth and death are seen as charged with sacral power and danger.

In addition to substances that passed out of the sexual orifices, pollution could come through what passed into the mouth. Here the dietary regulations concerning what is "abominable" to eat (like blood), and what is clean or unclean for the Jew, come into play. Eating unclean food is a different class of pollution from suffering a discharge or touching someone who has a discharge. Leviticus specifies what is to be done *when* discharge pollution occurs, but it does not envision the possibility of purifications after eating pork. Pollution could at-

---

[19]Douglas, *Purity and Danger,* p. 115.
[20]Neyrey, "Idea of Purity," pp. 102-3.

tack the Israelite through his or her food from a number of indirect sources as well. Unclean swarming creatures like lizards and rodents would defile clay, wood, cloth or animal-skin utensils and containers; open containers of liquids and wet foods and seeds were liable to contract pollution (e.g., Lev 11:37-38), whether from corpse contamination or the carcasses of swarming creatures. Israelites were especially careful to protect the food set apart for the priests in Jerusalem from such contamination, for unclean food could pollute the temple and defile its personnel!

Many boundaries within the system are inevitably crossed in the course of everyday life, and for these there exists a complex system of rituals that allow the polluted person to be integrated back into a state of cleanness (or purity), or for ordinary objects and persons to pass into the realm of the holy. Ultimately, the Day of Atonement rituals were meant to cleanse the sanctuary itself from the accumulated defilements of a year's worth of pollution and sins, known and unknown. The removal of pollution from the presence of a holy God was essential if God was to continue to live in the midst of Israel without either withdrawing (thus making his favors unavailable) or consuming the people.

Remember, the pious Jew observed no distinction between moral law and cultic law. The fact that both eating unclean food and committing incest brought about pollution shows the essential integration of the Torah as a single code. Holiness is enacted through the avoidance of defiling foods (Lev 11), but also through the pursuit of fairness, honesty and justice in all dealings with other people (Lev 19). Distinguishing between virtue and vice, justice and injustice, was every bit as important as distinguishing between clean and un-

clean foods. The system of sacrifices also shows the essential unity of what we now call the moral law and the ritual law: the "sin offering," which is better called a "purification offering,"[21] is offered both for certain moral offenses and for the pollution incurred without any moral failure (like childbirth). Both were equally deviations from the norm requiring purgation of the pollution.[22] Both *ethical* transgressions like fraud with regard to business and capital and the unnoticed contraction of *ritual* uncleanness from contact with an unclean person or animal require a kind of guilt offering (Lev 5:2-7; 6:2-7).

The Torah, received as the divinely given revelation of the divine order, does not merely lay out purity laws and purification regulations: it also explains their meaningfulness. One strong motivator for maintaining the purity system was national security. The decision of the holy God to associate himself with Israel and dwell in its midst requires that the people be holy as well so that the relationship will be beneficial and not destructive. Moreover, the holy land that Israel inhabits calls for its inhabitants to be holy, lest they be "vomited forth" by the land like the defiled and defiling Canaanites before them (Lev 18:24-30).

A more theological principle behind these codes and rites is the imitation of God's holiness as God's holy people: "You shall be holy, for I am holy" (Lev 11:44-45; 19:2 NRSV). The Israelites reflect God's holiness, or otherness, by remaining different and distinct from the peoples around them.[23] Because God made a distinction between Israel and the rest of the peoples of the earth, selecting Israel for himself and for a special destiny, Israel is to imitate God's action by observing distinctions between clean and unclean and holy and com-

---

[21]See Jacob Milgrom, *Leviticus 1-16*, AB (New York: Doubleday, 1991), p. 253; E. P. Sanders, *Judaism: Practice and Belief 63 B.C.E-66 C.E.* (Philadelphia: Trinity Press, 1992), p. 108.

[22]Thus Sanders, *Judaism*, p. 108.

[23]Baruch Levine, *Leviticus* (Philadelphia: Jewish Publication Society, 1989), p. 256.

mon (see Lev 20:22-26, with particular reference to the dietary laws). Observing purity codes allowed the Jew to move in step, as it were, with God. Setting apart the sabbath from other days as holy time and abstaining from work, which defiles or profanes the sabbath, was a means to reflect God's rhythms in creation and to bear witness to God (Ex 31:12-17). Carefully selecting clean animals for food (like cows, fish and certain birds) and avoiding unclean animals (like pigs and shellfish, which were permissible for Gentiles but not for Jews) mirrored God's careful selection of Israel as clean and proper for God among the many unclean nations (Lev 20:22-26).

Israel's purity codes were not only rich with meaning for the practicing Jew, they also gave form and boundaries to Israel's national identity. In the practical working out of these rules, purity concerns achieved the social-engineering goal of keeping observant Jews close together and making high boundaries between the congregation of observant Jews and the world of Gentiles. Acts shows us this principle at work: Peter says as he enters the house of the Gentile Cornelius, "You yourselves know that it is unlawful for a Jew to associate with or to visit a Gentile" (Acts 10:28 NRSV). A book called *Jubilees* (written about 160 B.C.E.) also stresses the importance of this separation: "Separate yourselves from the nations, and eat not with them, and do not do according to their works, and become not their associate. For all their works are unclean, and all their ways are a pollution and an abomination and uncleanness" (*Jub.* 22:16). This is of great importance. If contact between the two groups was limited, and if the Jews at least were aware of the necessity of keeping the boundary high and well-defined, Jewish identity would not be swallowed up into Hellenism. Israel (defined ethnically, not geographically) would not become "like the nations" and lose its cove-

nant relationship with God.

The purity codes were also given an added dimension of meaning by means of their ethical interpretation. The *Letter of Aristeas,* for example, explains the dietary laws that are incomprehensible to Gentiles in terms of the moral instructions they encode. Animals that chew the cud and part the hoof represent the importance of meditating on virtue and discerning between right and wrong (*Aristeas* 150), while forbidden animals represent various vices associated popularly with the animal in question (like sexual looseness with the weasel or violence with the birds of prey; *Aristeas* 144-148). Observing these dietary laws exercised a person in virtue.

Different groups manifested different levels of concern with maintaining purity and avoiding pollution. Interest and care was, understandably, highest in the temple (where the presence of the holy God resided) and in groups that regarded themselves as some kind of alternative gateway to God's court (like the Qumran Essenes). Strong taboos warned against defiling the sacred precincts; thus Israelites would take great care to approach the temple safely—in a state of cleanness.[24] Even away from the temple, however, many Israelites were concerned not to allow the multiplication of pollution in the land, which might result in national disaster. This did not make for a paranoid avoidance of pollution but called rather for an awareness for how and when an individual contracted pollution so that he or she could observe the proper purification in connection with unavoidable pollution (such as childbirth, contact with a corpse, an irregular or menstrual discharge, contact with a person with such a discharge, sexual intercourse and the like). As long as the proper purifications were performed, no danger would ensue.

To be avoided by all Jews, however, were the prohibited pollutions. These included the

---

[24]Sanders, *Judaism*, p. 71.

intentional (or neglectful) delay of purifications for permitted pollution (which constituted a willful transgression and polluted the holy places; see Lev 17:15-16; Num 19:12), corpse pollution for priests (save for the priest's closest of relatives), sexual pollutions (incest, intercourse with a menstruating woman, bestiality and homosexuality; Lev 18:6-30; 20:10-21), defilement by association with idols and idol worship (e.g., Lev 20:2-5), murder (see Num 35:33-34), neglect of circumcision (Gen 17:14),[25] and defilement of the sacred (e.g., entering the temple while unclean or breaking the sabbath).

One important variable in observance of purity laws became an occasion for some degrees of segregation within Israel. The majority of the people were not, it appears, concerned with "secondary pollution," that is, the pollution caused by touching something touched by a person or thing that was in a state of uncleanness. Pharisees were concerned with this level of contamination, with the result that the stricter Jews were wary about how close their association should be with less strict Jews. Essenes (including the men who inhabited the Qumran settlement) were the most strict about the avoidance of pollution and the safeguarding of their "priestly" purity. They went to the extremes of segregation from the rest of the holy people of God. Purity regulations designed to bind Israel together in solidarity in the midst of the nations thus also contained the seeds for sectarianism within Israel.

Purity codes and reading the New Testament. Becoming aware of the meaningfulness of Jewish purity codes in itself is a great aid to reading both the Hebrew Bible and the New Testament. Avoiding certain foods, observing the sanctity of the sabbath, continuing to participate in God's setting the Israelites apart for himself in a myriad of observances—these were all deeply meaningful manifestations of Jewish identity and sense of belonging to God, not mere externalistic and legalistic rules. Only from such a vantage point can we understand why many Jews, including Christian Jews, would consider them indispensable, inviolable and worth fighting for.

As we read through the New Testament, we will want to note where early Christians are reaffirming, pushing against, arguing about or redrawing the purity maps inherited from the Hebrew Scriptures and their Jewish heritage, and we need to remember what is at stake in these debates and activities so that we can hear them "from inside" rather than regard them as remote and arcane. What is Jesus, Paul, the pharisaic Christians of Acts 15 or the Judaizing missionaries of the Galatian crisis saying about purity and pollution in regard to food, people (especially Gentiles), times and seasons, and spaces? Why are there heated debates about such matters—pressing even to the point of hostile opposition? What new "purity maps" emerge from Pauline Christianity and other voices within the early church? How are these different from the maps drawn in the Hebrew Scriptures and their ongoing interpretation by other Jewish groups? How are these differences justified within the Christian group? What significance do they have?

It is not as though early Christian leaders simply threw off purity codes and pollution taboos, however. On the contrary, they continue to use the language of purity and defilement, and to harness the persuasive power of such language for a variety of community-shaping tasks. The community is still holy, and the people are called to maintain their holiness in terms of observing certain boundaries and distinctions between themselves and non-Christians. New Testament authors often use the concept of holiness to develop the ethics of the Christian group in contrast to the behaviors found outside the holy community. Purifica-

---

[25]Milgrom, *Numbers,* JPS Torah Commentary (Philadelphia: Jewish Publication Society, 1989), p. 406.

tion and purity also play an important role as early Christian leaders develop the significance of boundary-making rituals like baptism, discuss the meaning and significance of Jesus' death and ascension into the heavenly sanctuary, and caution disciples about eating the holy meal of the community in a state of defilement (e.g., bringing divisions and shaming of fellow Christians into the celebration of the Lord's Supper in 1 Corinthians 11).

HONOR AND SHAME

Honor and group values. The social values of honor and dishonor were foundational to first-century culture, whether Roman, Greek, Egyptian or Jewish.[26] A person born into that culture was led from childhood to seek honor and to avoid disgrace. Honor comes from the affirmation of a person's worth by peers and society, awarded on the basis of the individual's ability to embody the virtues and attributes his or her society values. Some of these attributes are ascribed and are frequently beyond the individual's control. For example, birth into a powerful or wealthy family gives a person a certain honor by virtue of that origin; birth into a particular *ethnos* (e.g., Roman or Jewish) means a share in the honor (or dishonor, in some eyes) that attaches generally to that whole people. Other qualities or virtues, such as piety, courage and reliability, are accessible to all, and individuals will strive to achieve honor by pursuing behaviors that are generally held to embody these virtues.[27] The definitions of honorable and disgraceful behaviors vary between cultures and over time, but honor remains an abiding concern. Male honor and female honor tend to be defined differently according to the double standards of antiquity.

Female honor was associated primarily with modesty and chastity (cf. Sir 26:10-16; 42:9-12; 4 Macc 18:6-8; Thucydides *Hist.* 2.45.2; Plutarch *Advice on Marriage* 9, 31-32).

Since people are raised in a world where honor is of great importance to an individual's sense of worth, the social group is in a strong position to motivate conformity among its individual members. A group can uphold those values deemed essential for the group's continued existence by rewarding with greater honor those who embody, and by censuring or showing contempt toward those who fail to live in conformity with, those values. The threat of dishonor supports a society's prohibitions of socially disruptive behavior. For example, adultery—the violation of the sanctity and peace of a bond foundational to society—often carries the threat of disgrace (cf. Prov 6:32-33). Agreement and unity, essential values for the orderly life of a city, are lauded as honorable, while dissensions and strife bring the threat of disgrace for the city (cf. Dio *Or.* 48.5-6; Phil 1:27—2:4). Similarly, courage in battle, necessary for a city's survival, wins honor and lasting remembrance (cf. Thucydides *Hist.* 2.35-42). In a society that has as its basic building block the patron-client relationship, the demonstration of gratitude to one's patron is supported by the threat of irrevocable dishonor and therefore exclusion from future patronage (Dio *Or.* 31; Heb 6:4-8; 10:26-31).

Greco-Roman manuals on rhetoric attest to the importance of honor and to the way an orator would play on the audience's desire for honor in order to achieve persuasion. Those seeking to win assent to a certain course of action (including the authors of the New Testament) would do so by showing that it leads to

---

[26]For detailed demonstration of this premise from ancient sources, see deSilva, *Honor, Patronage, Kinship and Purity*, chap. 1; *Despising Shame: Honor Discourse and Community Maintenance in the Epistle to the Hebrews*, SBLDS 152 (Atlanta: Scholars Press, 1995), esp. chaps. 2 and 3.

[27]On "ascribed" and "achieved" honor, see further Bruce J. Malina and Jerome H. Neyrey, "Honor and Shame in Luke-Acts: Pivotal Values of the Mediterranean World," in *The Social World of Luke-Acts: Models for Interpretation*, ed. Jerome H. Neyrey (Peabody, Mass.: Hendrickson, 1991), esp. pp. 28-29.

greater honor than some alternative course of action (see Aristotle *Rhet.* 1.9.35-36; *Eth. Nic.* 2.3.7; Quintilian *Inst. Orat.* 3.7.28; 3.8.1; Ps-Cicero *Rhet. ad Her.* 3.2.3). Conversely, showing how a certain course of action would result in dishonor created a strong deterrent. Additionally, praising or censuring people (whether living persons or examples from the past) would motivate the hearers to take up the qualities or actions that led to the praise or abandon the behaviors or attitudes that led to the censure. Observing these topics at work in the New Testament takes us deep into the pastoral and rhetorical strategy of its authors.

Honor in a multicultural arena. One of the particular challenges of life in the Roman Empire (as well as its predecessors in the Mediterranean) was that not all the people in a given region agreed on what was honorable behavior and what was dishonorable. The first-century Mediterranean world was far from monolithic. Within a dominant, Romanized, Hellenistic

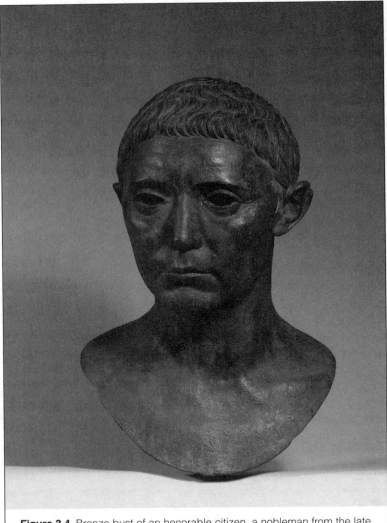

Figure 3.4. Bronze bust of an honorable citizen, a nobleman from the late Roman Republic. (Photo courtesy of the Cleveland Museum of Art)

Figure 3.5. A silver denarius from the earlier years of Augustus's principate. The reverse shows the facade of the temple erected in Rome to the Divine Julius Caesar, the birth, in effect, of the deification and worship of the emperors. (Photo courtesy of Edward Waddell, www.coin.com)

culture, the ethnic subculture of Judaism, philosophical schools and the Christian minority culture (among others) could be found. All of these groups defined the honorable and dishonorable in different ways. Even if groups agreed that piety was an essential virtue and component of honor, for example, different groups defined piety quite differently. Among Greeks and Romans piety entailed respect for the traditional gods and the emperor (see figure 3.5); for the Jews piety demanded sole worship of the God of Israel through observance of Torah and complete separation from idolatrous cults; for Christians piety entailed the worship of the God of both Jews and Gentiles through obedience to Jesus. Even within groups there would be differences (for example, in Paul's conflicts in Antioch and Galatia with Christian Judaizers). To the Romans, then, the Jews were atheists—their neglect of the gods was impious and therefore dishonorable. To the Jews, the Greeks and Romans with

their idol worship were acting dishonorably, failing to give honor to the only God, as were the Christians, who, though they worshiped the God of Israel, nevertheless did so in flagrant disregard for many of the commandments of Torah. A powerful tension could exist between self-respect—a person's awareness of embodying the criteria that should lead to honor—and actual honor in the eyes of the many people encountered in the course of life.

In such an environment it was essential to define very carefully who constituted an individual's group of "significant others"—those people whose approval or disapproval mattered—and to insulate group members from concern about the honor or dishonor they received from people outside the group.[28] A person who seeks status in the eyes of the larger society will maintain the values and fulfill the expectations of the dominant (pagan) culture. If a person has been brought into a minority culture (e.g., a philosophical school or a vol-

---

[28]See Halvor Moxnes, "Honor and Shame," *BTB* 23 (1993): 167-76.

untary association like the early Christian community) or has been born into an ethnic subculture (such a Judaism), then adherence to the group's values and ideals will only remain strong if that person redefines his or her circle of significant others. The "court of reputation" must be limited to group members who will support the group values in their grants of honor and censure (this is a common topic among philosophers, as in Plato *Cri.* 46C-47D; Seneca *Constant.* 13.2, 5; Epictetus *Ench.* 24.1). Groups in the minority could offset their obvious minority status by claiming that God or reason or nature shared the evaluations of the honorable and dishonorable held by the group. The opinion of an individual's fellow group members is thus fortified by and anchored in a higher court of reputation whose judgments are of greater importance and more lasting consequence than the opinion of the disapproving majority or the dominant culture. Both Greco-Roman philosophers and Jewish authors routinely point to the opinion of God as a support for the minority culture's values: both admonish group members to remain committed to the group's values because that is what God looks for and honors in a person.[29]

Where the values and commitments of a minority culture differ from those of a dominant (or other alternative) culture, members of that minority culture must be moved to disregard the opinion of nonmembers about their behavior (Seneca *Constant.* 11.2-12.1; Epictetus *Diss.* 1.29.50-54). All groups use honor and disgrace to enforce the values of their particular culture, so each group must insulate its members from the pull of the opinion of nonmembers. Those who do not hold to a particular group's values and worldview will be written off by that group as shameless or errant. Approval or disapproval in their eyes should

therefore mean nothing since it rests on error, and the representative of the minority culture can look forward to the vindication of his or her honor when the extent of that error is revealed (e.g., at the Last Judgment). The group members' experience of dishonor or degradation at the hands of outsiders may even be reinterpreted and transformed into a badge of honor within the group. Athletic (insult and abuse become a competition in which the minority culture's members must endure unto victory), military and educational imagery are frequently employed to this end.

Relationships within the group—the sense of connectedness and belonging so essential to the social being—must offset the sense of disconnectedness and alienation from the larger society through frequent and meaningful interaction. Encouragement to pursue what group members know to be truly honorable must outweigh the discouragement coming from outside the group. Those who begin to show signs of slackening in their commitment to the group out of a growing regard for outsiders must be made to feel ashamed and thus pulled back from assimilation.

Honor, shame and reading the New Testament. Reflection on the importance of honor and shame (and the connection between group values and the ascribing of honor and shame) opens us up to the experiences of, challenges facing and deliberations of the early Christians. On the one hand they had to confront the obvious fact of a degraded, executed Messiah, coping with ongoing challenges to the honor of (the memory of) Jesus, their leader. Therefore, we often find early Christian leaders engaged in discussing Jesus' ascribed and achieved honor (as in the Gospel narratives that speak of his descent, his confirmation by God, his noble deeds) and interpreting Jesus' crucifixion as a noble death—a volun-

---

[29]See, for example, Plato *Gorg.* 526D-527A; Epictetus *Diss.* 1.30.1; Sir 2:15-17; 23:18-19; Wis 2:12—3:5; 4:16—5:8; 4 Macc 13:3, 17; 17:5.

tary act undertaken to bring benefit to others at great cost to oneself, and accepted as the outcome of obedience to virtue (here, obedience to the will of God).

Christians also faced frequent challenges to their own honor as their non-Christian kin and neighbors (both Jewish and Gentile) exercised a range of deviancy-control techniques—from mild scorn to physical assaults—intended to make the believers feel ashamed of their association with Jesus and his followers. Early Christian leaders frequently needed to counter this pressure, this erosion of commitment, through a variety of shaming tactics. We are in touch with "honor discourse" first whenever we encounter statements that try to define and delimit whose opinion counts as far as the honor and dishonor of the Christians is concerned. Christian leaders often explicitly name those persons for whose opinion and approval the disciple should have regard (e.g., God, Christ, the angels, Christian leaders, one another within the community, the community of saints) and censure outsiders as unreliable guides to conduct (whether they are shameless, dishonorable, given over to vice or ignorance—in short, influences that ultimately would lead the disciples astray). They often emphasize the differences between disciples and outsiders in terms of the access to knowledge that the former have and the latter lack, the essential nature and origin of the former (as "children of light" or "children of God") as opposed to the latter (people in "darkness," children of the devil, etc.), and the virtuous conduct of the former as opposed to the vice of the latter.

We are also in touch with honor discourse when we read statements that seek to affirm the honor of Christians in the eyes of this alternate court of reputation by

- describing the honor the disciples now possess as a result of their belonging to the group (e.g., adoption into the family of God)
- praising the group for its adherence to the values prized within the early church and

showing how their honor and reputation has thus been enhanced within the larger community of faith (e.g., "the church of God in every place," the supratemporal minority culture; e.g., the ancestors in the faith, the court of God and the myriads of God's angels)

- reinterpreting the disciples' experience of dishonor or disapproval at the hands of outsiders in ways that are now seen as honorable from the vantage point of the group (e.g., a noble contest, the proving of the worth of their faith, the means by which God shapes them for an eternal inheritance and the like), thus undermining the society's deviancy-control techniques and even turning them to advantage vis-à-vis group honor and commitment
- promising future honor and vindication for the Christians and dishonor for the disciples' opponents, and advising individuals to follow the course that will promote the survival of the church and the preservation of its distinctive values and witness as the path to their own honor and security

Growing in sensitivity to honor and shame language in the New Testament serves two important ends. First, it opens up what was for the first hearers an important part of what made the texts persuasive. It helps us enter into a flesh-and-blood community struggling with issues of how to keep their self-respect, how to remain faithful to their newfound faith and hope in the midst of real social pressures. Second, as we become more sensitive to the social agendas of the authors, who were engaged in forming communities based on values and an ideology wholly other from that of the society, we are equipped to look more incisively into our social setting. We are better equipped to help those struggling to live out their faith in a world that does not agree with the values and ideology of the gospel. We are better equipped to create effective, energizing congregations and support groups that enable individuals to remain faithful to the life and witness to which God has called them. And we are better equipped to defuse the messages they receive from other members of society that dissuade them from wholehearted commitment to this outdated religion and seduce them into caring first for the things of this life.

PATRONAGE AND RECIPROCITY

Luke 22:25 records that in the Gentile world, "those in authority over them are called benefactors," (NRSV) attesting to the appropriateness of describing the ancient Mediterranean world as a patronal society, where the giving and receiving of benefactions was "the practice that constitutes the chief bond of human society" (Seneca *Ben.* 1.4.2).[30] It is a description that continues to be applied to the Mediterranean societies of today, a testimony to the depth to which this practice was infused into those cultures. The Greco-Roman world was a patronal society, supported by an infrastructure of networks of favor and loyalty. Such bonds existed between social equals who called each other "friends" and for whom the dictum "friends possess all things in common" held true. Partners in such relationships exchanged favors as needed, with neither party being in an inferior, dependent role.[31] Such bonds were also forged between social unequals, in which one party was clearly the patron of the other. These relationships might still employ the language of friendship out of

sensitivity to the person in the inferior role (for example, when Pilate is called "Caesar's friend," Jn 19:12). The system did not lend itself to precise evaluations of favors, such that mutual commitment tended to be long-term.[32] That is to say, the point of the institution was not even exchange but ongoing exchange. Mutual bonds of favor and the accompanying bonds of indebtedness provided the glue that maintained social cohesion. In such a society gratitude becomes an essential virtue, and ingratitude the "cardinal social and political sin" (Seneca *Ben.* 7.31.1).

In a world where wealth and property were concentrated in the hands of a very small percentage of the population, the majority of people often found themselves in need of assistance in one form or another; therefore they had to seek the patronage of someone who was better placed in the world than themselves. Patrons might be asked to provide money, grain, employment or land. The better connected persons were sought out for the opportunities they would give for professional or social advancement (see Seneca *Ben.* 1.2.4). A person who received such a benefit became a client to the patron, accepting the obligation to publicize the favor and his or her gratitude for it, thus contributing to the patron's reputation. The client also accepted the obligation of loyalty to a patron and could be called on to perform services for the patron, thus contributing to the patron's power. The reception of a gift and the acceptance of the obligation of gratitude are inseparable.[33]

---

[30]Some very helpful and penetrating primary texts attesting to the ethos of reciprocity and the nature of giving and receiving gifts include Aristotle *Eth. Nic.*, bks. 8 and 9; Demosthenes *On the Crown* (*De corona*); Seneca *On Benefits* (*Ben.*); Dio Chrysostom *Orations* (*Or.*) 31 (To the Rhodian Assembly).

[31]R. P. Saller, *Personal Patronage Under the Early Empire* (Cambridge: Cambridge University Press, 1982), pp. 8-11.

[32]Hence, contractual relationships where the obligations of both parties are spelled out in advance need to be distinguished from relationships of patronage and friendship.

[33]A distinction must be made between public benefaction and personal patronage. The wealthy people in a city would often provide public entertainments, food distributions and public improvements. Through such benevolence their own local reputation would be enhanced but no personal ties between giver and recipients were formed. Usually, the response of a grateful public would be the public proclamation of the benefactor's virtue and generosity, whether at an event, in an inscription or, in exceptional cases, with a statue, as well as renewed signs of respect as a benefactor passed by in public. On public benefaction see Seneca *Ben.* 4.28.5; 6.19.2-5.

Figure 3.6. A denarius of the emperor Trajan (98-117 C.E.). The inscriptions on both sides display his titles and offices: "Emperor Caesar Nerva Traianos, the highest prince, the Augustus, conqueror of the Germans, conqueror of the Dacians (over); Chief Priest, holder of the tribune's power, Consul for the 6th time, Father of the fatherland." The figure on the reverse represents "Providence of the Augusti," standing beside a pillar (a symbol of firmness) with the world at her feet, giving visual expression to the conviction that divine Providence was working out its irresistible will for the world through the rule of the emperors. (Photo courtesy of www.CNGcoins.com)

A third figure in this network of patronage has been called the "broker"[34] or mediator. This mediator acts as a patron, but his or her primary gift to the client is access to a more suitable or powerful patron. This second patron was a "friend" (in the technical sense) of the broker, a member of the broker's family or the broker's own patron. Sophocles provides an early literary example of this in Creon's defense against Oedipus's charge of conspiracy to usurp the kingship:

I am welcome everywhere; every man salutes me,

And those who want your favor seek my ear,

Since I know how to manage what they ask. (*Oed. Tyr.* 771-774)

Creon enjoys the salutation of a patron, but his chief benefaction is access to Oedipus and favor from the king.

Brokerage was exceedingly common and personal in the ancient world. The letters of Pliny the Younger, Cicero and Fronto are filled with these authors' attempts to connect a client with one of their friends or patrons.[35] Pliny's letters to Trajan (see figure 3.6), for example, document Pliny's attempts to gain imperial *beneficia* (benefits) for Pliny's own friends and clients. In *Epistle* 10.4, Pliny asks Trajan to grant a senatorial office to Voconius Romanus. He addresses Trajan clearly as a client addressing his patron and proceeds to ask a favor for Romanus. Pliny offers his own character as a guarantee of his client's character, and Trajan's assessment of the second-hand client is inseparable from his assessment of Pliny—indeed, Trajan's favorable judgment of Pliny (not Ro-

---

[34]J. Boissevain, *Friends of Friends: Networks, Manipulators and Coalitions* (New York: St. Martin's Press, 1974), p. 148.

[35]See the discussion of these in G. E. M. de Ste. Croix, "Suffragium: From Vote to Patronage," *British Journal of Sociology* 5 (1954): 33-48.

manus) is the basis for Trajan's granting of this favor. Such considerations in the patron-client exchange have an obvious corollary in the church's Christology and soteriology, wherein God, the Patron, accepts Christ's clients (i.e., the Christians) on the basis of the mediator's merit. Pliny's repeated attempts (*Ep.* 10.5-7, 10) to gain from Trajan a grant of Roman citizenship for his masseur, Harpocras, outlines a similar structure of relationships, wherein Pliny affords Harpocras access to the emperor, the fount of patronage, which he would never have enjoyed otherwise.

Within these webs of patronage, indebtedness remains within each patron-client (or "friend-to-friend") relationship. Voconius Romanus will be indebted to Pliny as well as Trajan, and Pliny will be indebted further to Trajan. The broker, or mediator, at the same time incurs a debt and increases his own honor through the indebtedness of his or her client.[36] Brokerage occurs also between friends and associates in private life. A familiar example appears in Paul's letter to Philemon, in which Paul approaches his "friend" Philemon on behalf of Paul's new client, Onesimus: "if you consider me your partner, welcome him as you would welcome me" (Philem 17 NRSV).

A term of central importance for discourse about patronage is *charis*, frequently translated "grace." Classical and Hellenistic Greek authors use this word primarily as an expression of the dynamics within the patron-client relationship. Within this social context *charis* has three distinct meanings. Aristotle, for example, defines *charis* as the disposition of a benefactor, "the feeling in accordance with which one who has it is said to render a service to one who needs it, not in return for something nor in the interest of him who renders it, but in that of the recipient" (*Rhet.* 2.7.1- 2). The first meaning of *charis*, then, is the benefactor's favorable disposition toward the petitioner. In its second sense the term can be used to refer to the actual gift or benefit conferred, as in 2 Corinthians 8:19 where Paul speaks of the "generous gift" he is administering (i.e., the collection for the church in Jerusalem).[37] The third meaning is the reciprocal of the first, namely, the response of the client, the necessary and appropriate return for favor shown. In this sense the term is best translated as "gratitude."[38]

According to ancient ethicists writing about giving, benefactors were to give without calculation of reward. Giving was to have in view the interest of the recipient, not the self-interest of the giver.[39] When forming personal ties of patronage, however, patrons were cautioned to select their beneficiaries well, which meant selecting people who had a reputation for honoring the giver with gratitude.[40] In exceptional circumstances, however, a patron could be exhorted to give even to a known ingrate, thus imitating the generosity of the gods (Seneca *Ben.* 1.1.9; 4.26. 1-4.28.1) and possibly arousing a grateful response with a second gift, like a farmer working and reworking hardened soil (Seneca *Ben.* 7.31-32).

A person who received "grace" (a patron's favor) knew also that "grace" (gratitude) must be returned.[41] Greco-Roman mythology included the "three Graces" (*Charites*), who were depicted as dancing hand-in-hand in an unbroken circle. Seneca explains this image thus: a benefit "passing from hand to hand

---

[36]R. P. Saller, *Personal Patronage*, p. 75 n. 194.

[37]This meaning is frequently attested in honorary inscriptions, especially in the plural form. See F. W. Danker, *Benefactor.*

[38]As in Demosthenes *On the Crown* 131; Rom 6:17; 7:25; Heb 12:28.

[39]See Aristotle *Rhet.* 2.7.1; Seneca *Ben.* 1.2.3; 3.15.4; Sir 20:13-16.

[40]See Isocrates *Dem.* 29; Sir 12.1; Cicero *De Offic.* 2.62; Seneca *Ben.* 4.10.4.

[41]See Aristotle *Eth. Nic.* 1163b12-15; Cicero *De Offic.* 1.47-48; Seneca *Ben.* 2.25.3.

nevertheless returns to the giver; the beauty of the whole is destroyed if the course is anywhere broken" (Seneca *Ben.* 1.3.3-4). Gratitude was a sacred obligation, and the client who failed to show gratitude appropriately was considered ignoble and even sacrilegious (Dio Chrysostom *Or.* 31.37; Seneca *Ben.* 1.4.4). The best credit rating one could have in the ancient world was a reputation for knowing how to show gratitude: such a person would not fail to find help when needed in the future.[42] Those who fail to respond with gratitude, however, or who have insulted a benefactor "will not be thought worthy of a favor by anyone" (Dio Chrysostom *Or.* 31.36, 65) and thus are in a very vulnerable position.

The greater the benefit bestowed, the greater should be the response of gratitude. In the ancient world gratitude involved first the demonstration of respect for the benefactor (Aristotle *Eth. Nic.* 1163b1-5)[43], acting in such a way as to enhance his or her honor and certainly avoiding any course of action that would bring him or her into dishonor. A client who showed disregard for a patron would exchange favor for wrath (Aristotle *Rhet.* 2.2.8). The client would return this gift of honor not only in his or her own demeanor and actions but in public testimony to the benefactor:

> The greater the favour, the more earnestly must we express ourselves, resorting to such compliments as: . . . "I shall never be able to repay you my gratitude, but, at any rate, I shall not cease from declaring everywhere that I am unable to repay it." (Seneca *Ben.* 2.24.2)

Let us show how grateful we are for the blessing that has come to us by pouring forth our feelings, and let us bear witness to them [*testemur*], not merely in the hearing of the giver, but everywhere. (Seneca *Ben.* 2.22.1; see also Ps 116:12; Tob 12:6-7)

Gratitude also involves intense personal loyalty to the patron, even if that loyalty should lead the client to lose his or her physical well-being, wealth, reputation or homeland (Seneca *Ep. Mor.* 81.27). This is the level of gratitude and loyalty the New Testament authors claim should be given to Jesus and, through him, to God. "Grace," therefore, has very specific meanings for the authors and readers of the New Testament, who are themselves part of a world in which patronage and reciprocity form primary social bonds.

While not as dominant as *charis* ("favor, gratitude") in discussions of patronage, *pistis* (usually translated as "faith") and its related words also receive specific meanings in the context of the patron-client relationship.[44] To place *pistis* in a patron is to trust him or her to be able and willing to provide what he or she promised. It means, in effect, to entrust one's cause or future to a patron (cf. 4 Macc 8:5-7), to give oneself over into his or her care. *Pistis* also represents the response of loyalty on the part of the client. Having received benefits from a patron, the client must demonstrate *pistis,* "loyalty," toward the patron.[45] In this context, then, *pistis* speaks to the firmness, reliability and faithfulness of both parties in the patron-client relationship or the relationship of "friends."

The opposite of *pistis* ("trust," "loyalty") is

---

[42]Sir 3:31; see also Cicero *De Offic.* 2.70 and five inscriptions that explicitly present the act of showing gratitude to a present benefactor as a pledge to future benefactors that they will meet with appropriate gratitude as well; Danker, *Benefactor,* pp. 57, 77-79, 89-91, 152-53, 283-85.

[43]See also the evidence of the honorary inscriptions studied by Danker, *Benefactor.*

[44]Again, see the analysis of the semantic range of this term in the inscriptions studied by Danker, *Benefactor.*

[45]This is reflected in the English *fidelity,* derived from the Latin word for faith, *fides;* see also 4 Macc 7:19; 15:24; 16:18-22; 17:2-3; Seneca *Ben.* 3.14.2.

apistia. This refers in one sense to "distrust" toward a patron or client. It would entail a negative evaluation of the character and reliability of the other person and could be insulting in the extreme. However, it was also recognized that a person had to be prudent concerning the placement of trust (cf. Dio Chrysostom *Or.* 74, "Concerning Distrust"), just as a patron would need to weigh carefully whether or not to accept the responsibility of a client's "trust" (Seneca *Ben.* 1.1.2; 4.8.2; Dio Chrysostom *Or.* 73, "Concerning Trust"). The term may also refer, in its second sense, to "disloyalty" or "unfaithfulness," as when clients fail to remain steadfast in their commitment to their patron or prove untrustworthy in their service.

Reciprocity relationships could take a variety of forms. The stereotyped Roman model, where the clients turn out at the patron's doorstep every morning to greet him, should not be read into every such relationship. Patronage could be personal, the formation of a lasting reciprocal bond between individuals; it could be general, taking the form of public benefactions (like the laying of a public road, the provision of public entertainments, liberation of a city from a siege or an act of famine relief), in which the beneficiaries do not become clients of the benefactor in any personal sense. In both cases, however, the dynamics of grace and gratitude would be at work. Personal patronage and benefaction are at home not only in Rome and Roman colonies but are also well attested in Greek city-states and in the Hellenized and Romanized provinces (including Palestine). Patronage, friendship and reciprocal obligations were a matter not only for the power-climbing elites but were also known among small landholders and farmers in the villages.[46] "Grace" represents, then, a set of social roles and codes of behavior that would be familiar, pervasive and compelling throughout the world of the first-century church.

Patronage, reciprocity and reading the New Testament. As we turn to the New Testament, we find not only examples of friendship relations (e.g. Paul and Philemon, Paul and the Philippian Christians, Herod and Pilate after the trial of Jesus), patron-client relationships (like, most probably, Theophilus and Luke) and public beneficence (like the centurion who showed uncommon generosity toward the local Jewish population in Lk 7:2-10) among people, for which the foregoing discussion is immediately relevant. We also find New Testament authors—like Jewish and Greco-Roman authors—using the language of patronage and reciprocity to give expression to supernatural or unseen realities, especially our relationship with God and God's Messiah. Even their use of family imagery (e.g., calling God "father" and speaking of the "household of God") connects with the image of the patron who brings a host of clients into the "household," although now with the special status of adopted daughters and sons.

The Hebrew Scriptures speak of God as the Patron of Israel, who protects and provides for the people with whom God has formed this special relationship of favor. When Israel does not make the proper response (i.e., by failing to return honor, exclusive loyalty and service in the form of obedience to Torah), God responds by punishing them. What is remarkable is God's loyalty to the relationship: though breached on one side, God never abandons the nation utterly despite its ingratitude. Both the Jewish and Greco-Roman backgrounds lead the early church to view God in a similar fashion. God is the Patron of all, since God has given to all the matchless gift of existence and sustenance (Rev 4:11). God will be the benefactor of all who seek and trust God's

---

[46]See deSilva, *Honor, Patronage, Kinship and Purity,* pp. 95-121 for a discussion of patronage, reciprocity and the necessary nuances.

favor (Heb 11:6). God is celebrated as the Patron whose favor and benefits are sought in prayer and whose favorable response to prayer is assured (Heb 4:14-16).

God's favor is surprising not in that God gives freely or uncoerced. Every benefactor, in theory at least, gave freely. Rather, God astonishes humanity in God's determination to benefit those who have insulted and alienated God in the extreme. The high-water mark for generous giving in the ancient world was to consider giving to the ungrateful—if a patron had enough to spare after giving to the worthy beneficiaries. Providing some modest assistance to someone who had failed to be grateful in the past would be counted a proof of a noble spirit. God, however, exceeds all expectation when God gives the most costly gift, the life of God's own Son, to benefit those who have not merely been ungrateful but have been openly hostile to God and God's law.

A second distinctive aspect of God's favor is God's determination to take the initiative in seeking reconciliation with those who had affronted God. Rather than wait for the offenders to make overtures of repentance and other conciliatory gestures, God sets aside God's anger and sets forth Jesus, providing humanity with an opportunity to return to favor and escape the consequences of having previously acted as God's enemies. The provision of "deliverance" (*sōtēria*, commonly translated as "salvation") thus becomes a dominant image of God's gift.

Not all, however, honor God as the Patron merits (cf. Rom 1:18-25; Rev 9:20-21; 14:9-11). Even the covenant people brought God's name into dishonor on account of disloyalty and disobedience (Rom 2:17-24). Nevertheless, God remains faithful to those whom God has benefited in the past, continuing to offer favor (even the gift of adoption into God's household) for those who return to God in trust and gratitude.

Jesus is presented likewise as a patron of the Christian community. The author of Hebrews, for example, presents Jesus as one who "helps the descendants of Abraham" (Heb 2:16) and comes "to the aid of those who are tempted" (Heb 2:18). He supplies for the Christians what is wanting in their own resources. Jesus' patronage may be more precisely defined, however, as brokerage. He is the mediator (Heb 8:6; 9:15; 12:24) who secures favor from God on behalf of those who have committed themselves to Jesus as client dependents. As God's Son, who is placed closest to the head of the household, Jesus' successful mediation is assured. Jesus' gift of access to God (Heb 4:14-16; cf. Heb 10:19-22) gives the community access to resources for endurance in faith in the present world so that they may receive the benefactions promised for the future, awarded before God's court at the end of the age. The believers may draw near to God and expect to "receive mercy and find favor"—that is, the disposition of God to give assistance—"for timely help" (Heb 4:16). Christians, indeed, have been brought into God's household (Heb 3:6) through their clientage to the Son; thus they are under God's protection and provision.

Other New Testament authors share the conviction that Jesus is the one who mediates the favor of God. We gain access to God only through the Son, and apart from Jesus there is none who can secure for us God's favor (Lk 9:48; 10:22; Jn 13:20; 14:6). Paul, in his formulation of "salvation by grace," uses this background to articulate the gospel. Being saved by grace points to God's uncoerced initiative in reaching out to form a people from all nations through God's anointed agent, Jesus. The role of "faith" in this process is, on the one hand, Jesus' reliability as broker of God's favor, and, on the other hand, our trust in and loyalty toward Jesus. Paul reacts so strongly against requiring circumcision and observance of dietary laws for Gentile converts because this displaces the favor of God (Gal

135

2:21), evidenced in the benefaction of the Holy Spirit (Gal 3:1-5), which Jesus, has gained for his faithful clients (Gal 2:21; 5:2-4). It casts doubt on Jesus' ability to secure God's favor by his own mediation and thus shows distrust toward Jesus.

The proper response toward a patron is gratitude: offering honor, loyalty, testimony and service to the patron. Reciprocity is such a part of this relationship, that failure to return grace (gratitude) for grace (favor) results in a breach of the patron-client relationship. God's favor seeks a response of faithfulness (*pistis*) and service from God's clients. Paul speaks, for example, of the "obedience of faith" (Rom 1:5; 16:26) as the goal of his mission, calling forth the proper response of those who have benefited from God's gift. The recipients of God's favor are called to offer up their whole selves to God's service, to do what is righteous in God's sight (Rom 6:1-14; 12:1). This response centers not only on honoring God but on love, generosity and loyal service toward fellow believers (Rom 13:9-10; Gal 5:13-14; 6:2).

The author of Hebrews also calls Christians to remain firm in their trust and loyalty (Heb 10:35-39; chap. 11), to take great care not to dishonor the Giver nor show contempt for the gift won at such cost to the Broker (Heb 10:26-31) through apostasy, to avoid distrust (Heb 3:19—4:2), and to show gratitude (Heb 12:28) to God by continuing to bear witness to their Benefactor in a hostile world (Heb 13:15), and by assisting one another through love and service, encouraging and supporting one another in the face of an unsupportive society (Heb 6:10; 13:1-3, 16). While God's favor remains free and uncoerced, the first-century hearer knows that to accept a gift also meant accepting the obligation to respond properly.

The Christian mission depended on the financial support of its richer converts. Individuals might provide aid for the community and so be remembered honorably (cf. Acts 4:34-36; Philem 7). Householders within the movement would host the meetings of the group (Rom 16:23; 1 Cor 16:19; Philem 2) and provide hospitality for missionaries and teachers (Philem 22; 3 Jn 5-8, 10). Paul sought to develop relationships of reciprocity between churches so that beneficence between Christians might span the Mediterranean. The collection of relief funds for the churches in Judea is presented as an act of reciprocity for the "spiritual benefits" the Gentiles received from those Judean churches (Rom 15:25-29); similarly, Paul assures the Achaian churches that their contributions to other churches will establish ties of reciprocity for the future (2 Cor 8:13-14). Churches are to act, in essence, as collectives of "friends" who share all things in common. Paul presents himself frequently as a partner or friend who brings spiritual benefits and receives material support (Phil 1:5-7; 4:15; Philem 17), but he is also conscious of his role as patron or "father" (1 Cor 4:15) to the converts since he has provided the gift of access to Jesus, which has saved them from God's wrath (Philem 19).

Patronage within the church is not, however, meant to be pursued as a means of advancing one's own honor or power within the group. Acts of love and service toward fellow believers was the service placed on the clients by the divine Patron. Giving to fellow believers is presented as a reflection of Christ's own act on our behalf (2 Cor 8:9-14), and Paul presents giving as itself a spiritual gift (Rom 12:8). Patrons within the church are acting as stewards of God's gifts (2 Cor 9:8-10), so that the concept of stewardship (and also the sharing of goods among "kin") replaces notions of patronage and beneficence (with the potentially divisive claims to power and loyalty that accompany them) in the earliest churches. Christians are also urged to extend their own beneficence to the outside world (Rom 13:3-4; 1 Thess 5:15; 1 Pet 2:15-17), not only as a reflection of the generosity of God but also as a sign that Christians too were honorable people who contributed to the welfare of all.[47]

Knowledge of the social codes of patronage and reciprocity, then, will be of great value to our appreciation of early Christian theology. We will read about the ways God's favor has always been and continues to be known (e.g., in creation, the preservation of life and the like) and the new ways God's favor flows into the human situation through the person of Jesus, the gift of the Holy Spirit, and the promises of deliverance and an eternal inheritance for those who approach God through Jesus. We will be alert to the ways early Christians are urged to make a suitable response to the favor of God and of Jesus or warned against responding in a dis-graceful manner. We be will attuned as well to why this logic is compelling. Additionally, we will be equipped to understand many of the relationships between the people presented in the pages of the New Testament—reciprocity relationships that are sometimes merely noted or affirmed, sometimes reshaped and redirected (e.g., patronage of the community by the richer Christians being transformed into stewardship), and sometimes opposed (e.g., importing the worldly dynamics of using generosity to gain power and advance personal interests).

THE SHAPE AND SIGNIFICANCE OF "FAMILY" IN THE ANCIENT WORLD

The experience of family is a universal, human phenomenon, for without some kind of social group committed to its survival a human child dies. What did family mean for the first readers of the New Testament? What were the assumptions, roles and values associated with family or household for them, and how did the authors of the New Testament build on or reshape these basic assumptions?[48]

A person's family of origin established his or her "place" in the world, both in terms of self-perception and the perception of others. Family reputation was the starting point for an individual's own reputation. Israelites gave careful attention to preserving lineage because without a solid pedigree a person's place and privileges within Israel were in jeopardy. Both testaments record important genealogical information about particular individuals. Genealogies can be used to establish the legitimacy of claims made about or by a person (as in the genealogy in Matthew, which establishes Jesus' status as heir of the promises given to David and to Abraham), display the collective honor embodied in the present generation or establish relationships between people or nations.

Orators would begin their praise of an individual by praising his or her illustrious ancestors and immediate forebears. The reputation of the family of origin sets up the expectations for what the progeny will be like, whether noble or shameful, virtuous and reliable, or base and unreliable.

The father's reputation becomes the starting place for the reputation of the children. If they come from a good, reliable father, it is a given that they will be good and reliable unless they prove otherwise. Conversely, a father in disgrace is a hard legacy to overcome (see Sir 41:7). Insults (then as now) often involve a suggestion that one is an illegitimate child, the son of something unflattering (like "offspring of vipers" in Mt 3:7; 12:34; 23:33) or the descendent of scurrilous people (like "murderers" in Mt 23:31-32) who will act out the same vices as their forebears.

---

[47]On this last point see Bruce Winter, *Seek the Welfare of the City: Christians as Benefactors and Citizens* (Grand Rapids: Eerdmans, 1994).

[48]Important ancient witnesses to family and kinship in the Greco-Roman world include Aristotle *Eth. Nic.* bks. 8 and 9; Plutarch "On Affection for Offspring," "On Fraternal Affection," and "Advice on Marriage"; Xenophon *Oeconomicus*.

If someone acted in ways that were considered incompatible with the reputation and social location of his or her family of origin, the broader public might react negatively. In the Gospels, Jesus' natural kinship group is often seen to contradict any possible claim that he is the Messiah. The fact that he is the son of a carpenter whose family is all well-embedded in the life of a small village seems to belie any claim he might make to being a teacher, let alone the anointed one of God (Mk 6:3). The way he is "located" in Judean culture becomes problematic for the acceptance of his message.

membrance of kinship. All Jews are ultimately brothers and sisters (Tob 2:2; 2 Macc 1:1). This is especially the case in the Diaspora, where Jews were more fully aware of their minority status and their vulnerability, but also in Palestine when their nation or religious ideology was threatened or challenged. Within the local community, however, there were tribes or clans or even households competing rather than cooperating. Where kinship is invoked or established between two people, however, competition and distrust can quickly give way to cooperation and trust. Jesus and John the Baptist

Figure 3.7. The courtyard of a simple house at Qatzrin in Galilee. (Photo courtesy of Qatzrin Park and Todd Bolen [BiblePlaces.com])

People who were kin thought of themselves as also being "kind" in the sense of "being of the same sort" or "being like," as in a "kindred spirit." These close bonds of connectedness were established by nature itself. Where they drew the line between kin and nonkin, between the "us" who are alike and the "them" that are not like us, could vary from situation to situation. Jews drew on their kinship as an entire ethnic body, the collective family of Abraham, Isaac and Jacob, and derived great solidarity from that re-

clearly tried to recover among Palestinian Jews a larger sense of kin and cooperation on the basis of shared lineage with Abraham (see, e.g., Lk 13:16; 19:7-9).

How do kin behave? Greco-Roman ethicists and Jewish moralists alike held to and promoted clear standards for how kin should behave toward one another. This remains quite relevant for the Christian who considers herself or himself part of the family of God, for the New Testament authors promote within the church precisely this same ethic.

First, kin (especially siblings) should show solidarity and cooperate toward the attainment of goals and goods that promote the advancement of each sibling individually and the family as a whole. Though a person competes mightily for those goods against people outside of the extended household, there is no room for competition or division within the family, for such behavior would erode the family's strength, unity and viability. We speak freely of sibling rivalry as a natural phenomenon, but such rivalry was seen as a great evil in the classical world, to be guarded against completely or defused as soon as possible.[49]

Second, there is a high measure of trust between members of a kinship group, but people outside the kinship group are distrusted unless circumstances proved otherwise through long trial of their character. This is directly linked to the ethic of cooperation among kin but competition outside the kinship group.[50]

Third, kinship relations should be characterized by harmony, agreement and unity, a state that would manifest itself in common commitment to the same ideals, the sharing of a common religion and the sharing of resources. The unity of kin came to fullest expression in their attitudes toward their wealth. Since friends were held to "own all things in common" (Aristotle *Eth. Nic.* 1159b31-32), the same was all the more to be expected of close kin. Money could be a powerful, divisive force in a family, and the family that would be strong and unified had to guard against any sense of "mine" over against "ours."

Fourth, when things go wrong between family members, there is a tendency for family to hide any disgrace or dishonor that kin might have incurred rather than parade the failings of their family members in "public" view. (Sometimes, however, this is impossible, and the family can only preserve its collective honor by disowning an errant member.) Ancient moralists stressed the importance of practicing forgiveness within the kinship group, of bearing patiently with one another, and seeking reconciliation wherever a breach occurs. An erring family member is to be rebuked with gentleness, and restored with all speed. The family member who feels injured is to confront the alleged offender with gentleness and extend forgiveness quickly; the member who has injured another is to seek reconciliation with all speed.

The instructions of Jesus, Paul and the other New Testament voices concerning how believers (the family united by Christ's blood) are to act toward one another thus parallels most fully the ancient ethic of kinship.

The ancient household. While family or kin encompasses far more than the people living in the same dwelling, the "household" itself is an important and basic kinship unit in the ancient world. The household would include a husband and wife and their children, and very often slaves. The "household codes" in the New Testament (Eph 5:21—6:9 being the fullest example) reflect precisely this set of household relationships. We also might find grandparents, unmarried sisters or aunts and other blood relatives living within the household. Simon Bar-Jonah's living situation may not have been atypical: he lived with his mother-in-law (Mt 8:14) and his (unmarried?) brother (Mk 1:29); probably his wife, though unmentioned, is alive as well; also he may very well have children by her.

---

[49]See especially Plutarch "On Fraternal Affection" for an excellent primary source on how family should behave toward one another. Plutarch spends the greater part of this essay giving advice concerning how to avoid competition and envy between brothers and engender a spirit of cooperation and unity. The advice resonates clearly with the kind of behavior Paul seeks to inculcate among the Christians in Corinth, who were acting as rivals rather than sisters and brothers in Christ.

[50]See, for example, how Tobit comes to extend trust to Azariah in Tobit 5:8-14.

Jesus certainly assumes that some of his disciples have left behind wives and children as well as parents and siblings (Mt 19:27, 29). Guests and clients would also be considered part of the household, even though the latter would not necessarily ever live under the same roof. Clients were, nevertheless, conceptually under the same roof, even as they maintained their own households.

The ancient household tended to be a producing unit as well as a consuming unit. The members of a household would work together in some trade or craft for the purpose of income.[51] This could be as simple as selling surplus crop production as grain in the market, or it might involve a trade like leather-working, pottery, or even surgery. For the purpose of the trade a room of a house in a city or village would be allowed to open onto the street and serve as a shop. For upper class families, a person's home and the homes of others were places for networking with friends and supporters. The household for people of the upper strata of the Greco-Roman world embraced the staff of agricultural estates as well as a mansion in the city.[52]

The purpose of marriage was chiefly provision for the future, both in terms of offspring and inheritance. It was not the result of a process of dating, falling in love or talking about compatibilities, but was arranged by parents (or by bride's parents and groom) with a view to the future of their families and their honor. Marriage was not a provision for the fleshly desires. Unrestrained lust in marriage was considered dishonorable to such an extent that it might be considered a sign of honoring the marriage bed for a husband to seek debauchery elsewhere.

Jews tended to marry within their kinship group, often seeking to marry close kin without getting so close as to violate incest laws. This strategy is called "endogamy." This was certainly the pattern of ancient Israel, adopted so that tribal inheritances would remain intact. At the very least Jews were expected to marry Jews: intermarriage with Gentiles tended to be regarded as the path to apostasy. The "holy race" was thus preserved from mixing with the nations (see Ezra 9—10, especially 9:2). Jewish marriages were preceded by a lengthy betrothal, which itself could only be broken by divorce.

Roman marriage practice was exogamous, marrying outside of one's kinship group, and was based more on interest in creating strategic alliances between different families. Women remained under the guardianship of a male, whether the father (which could persist through marriage) or the husband. Slaves had no legal basis for marriage, yet raised families anyway (despite the fact that no inheritance could be left to children and that owners could break up families by sale).[53]

If a couple divorced, the woman would return to her father's family (or a brother's house if her father was dead), along with her dowry. Greek and Roman law allowed either partner to initiate divorce; among Jews only the husband had this prerogative. Divorce was a common recourse for infertility (particularly if a woman had not borne sons) and for adultery, but divorce would also be initiated for much less substantial reasons as well.

A household was ultimately under the management of the male who, as husband, father and master, was the "hub" or "head" of the household. This male acted on behalf of

---

[51]See Carolyn Osiek and David L. Balch, *Families in the New Testament World* (Louisville, Ky.: Westminster John Knox, 1997), p. 54; Halvor Moxnes, *Constructing Early Christian Families* (London: Routledge, 1997), p. 23.

[52]Such estates might be leased out to tenant farmers for rent or a percentage of the harvest. Such a scenario is envisioned in Mk 12:1-12.

[53]See Osiek and Balch, *Families in the New Testament World*, p. 62. This sad reality figures in one of Jesus' parables; see Mt 18:23-35.

the household and represented it to the outside world. He was not to rule as a tyrant, however, or exploit his position. While the father's rule over children and slaves was absolute, like a monarch's power, his authority over the wife was compared to "constitutional rule": the two were equal as persons but one was accorded the authority over the other (an inequality in terms of role).[54] Although women were treated like property in many ways, it is not clear that they were regarded as property. The hierarchical arrangements may not have been as devaluing or depersonalizing of women as we might assume from our modern viewpoint. With his rule came heavy moral responsibility for the welfare and guidance of the whole household. Only those who managed their households well were deemed worthy of authority in the public sphere.

Jewish and Greco-Roman authors agreed to an astonishing extent on the ideal they held up for women to emulate—an ideal that clearly served the interests of its male proponents. In a nutshell it combined submission to the authority of the male head of the household (which included adopting his religion), a love for remaining in the private sphere of the household, silence in public places (speaking "through her husband"), modesty and chastity.

As recipients of the gift of life, children had incurred a debt to their parents that they could never repay. So the virtuous person would honor the parents and "return the favors" bestowed by the parents throughout childhood and for the remainder of the parents' lives (see Aristotle *Nic. Eth.* 8.14 1163b14-27). Children were to honor their parents in word and deed, and especially to be loyal and serviceable to them in the parents' old age. Children were never to despise the old age and feebleness of their parents but

to continue to honor and serve them at that stage in life when they most needed their children. It was the mark of piety to use that stage of life as an opportunity most fervently to repay the favors of early childhood nurture.

Our expression "like father, like son" stands in line with the ancient tradition of stressing the likeness between parents and their children, a likeness that extended past physical features to character, values, emotions and predispositions. This led to the common belief that a person's behavior reflects on his or her parentage, a topic that can be used to praise or insult (as in Jn 8:31-45).

Most children tended to be educated in the home. Education was mainly geared toward the practical (participation in a trade, learning how to deal successfully with others, the family's religious traditions and so on). Mothers had primary care during the first few years; after the children were five or six years old, the father would take a more active role in their education. During the early years of a child's education, people of means would employ a pedagogue, a combination of a disciplinarian and elementary educator.[55] Mothers would continue to teach their daughters the skills necessary for managing a household, preparing them to be marriageable. Schools existed in both Greek and Jewish contexts to provide advanced education for the aristocratic families, training the next generation of statesmen and leaders of the community. Rhetoric, philosophy, ethics and religion were essential parts of the curriculum.

About one in four people in the Roman Empire was a slave. Slavery was not predicated on race, as in the Western experience of the sixteenth- through nineteenth-centuries. People became slaves through military conquest, defaulting on debts, criminal activity and, of

---

[54]Jewish authors, however, tended to be more sweeping in their claims about the husband's primacy.
[55]The pedagogue plays an important role in the metaphor Paul uses for salvation history itself in Gal 3:23-25, suggesting that his readers would have widespread familiarity if not direct experience with such a figure.

course, birth to a slave. Moreover, slaves were occupied with a great variety of duties, from imperial slaves serving as high-level administrators to domestic stewards to those assigned menial duties in home and field to the slaves in galleys or mines.

Aristotle defined a slave as a "living tool" (*Politics* 1.4 1253b27-33); he defended the institution based on nature. Masters were to exercise their authority, however, judiciously and virtuously, mindful that the slave is an extension of him- or herself. In practice, however, punishment of slaves could be quite severe and harsh.[56] The conditions of slavery were wholly dependent on the virtue or lack of virtue of the master. Jewish, Christian and Gentile philosophers and ethicists sought to foster a benevolent relationship between masters and slaves, advising masters to take an interest in the training of their slaves in virtue as well as duty, and to be anxious for their well-being as members of the household. A slave's family life was precarious and completely under the master's control. Slave marriages were not recognized legally, and children born to slaves were the property of the master. It was always a possibility that a slave family would be broken up if the master decided to give away or sell any of them. This lack of autonomy and security made slavery an evil for those unfortunate enough to be born or fall into it. Slaves of private individuals, however, did have the hope of purchasing their freedom or being freed by the master in his or her will as a gift for decades of faithful service.

Fictive kinship. The nature of kinship—that is, what really constitutes kinship—was a frequent topic of debate in the Hellenistic and Roman periods. Natural kinship (kinship by blood or marriage) might not be considered an ultimate or unbreakable bond if important components of what made people kin were missing, such as commitment to the same values and way of life. Christian wives, young adults and slaves could face severe pressure from their families if the head of the household was an unbeliever. In some cases kinship ties were broken—the deviant family member was cut off from the family—to preserve its reputation in the eyes of the wider public.

On the other hand many philosophers (Jew and Gentile) were willing to regard common devotion to a particular set of ideals and way of life as sufficient basis to make people kin. Non-Jews, for example, who left behind "their country, their kinsfolk and their friends for the sake of virtue and religion" were welcomed into a new family, namely, the Jewish community (Philo *Spec. Leg.* 1.52). Philo's words are stunningly close to Jesus' thought on the subject, down to the promise of a replacement "family" for those whose natural ties are severed (see Mt 12:46-50; 19:27-29). In such cases natural kinship ties are less defining for the family than commitment to a shared way of life.

Because family relations and the bonds of kin were so powerful and pervasive, these aspects of life provided a potent set of metaphors for binding people who were not related by blood together in new configuration, and cultivating an ethos of support and appropriate ways of relating. The application of the roles and ethos of family to people who are not related is called "fictive kinship." This was prominently at work, for example, in Roman imperial ideology, according to which the whole empire was a household with the emperor as the *pater patriae,* the "father of the country," the head of a vastly extended family. It is also very prominent in the early Christian movement, wherein members are joined to one another as brothers and sisters by virtue of the fact that they are all born into one family under one Father, namely, God.

The most well-known passage in this re-

---

[56]See Osiek and Balch, *Families in the New Testament World,* pp. 79-80.

gard is Matthew 12:46-50 (see parallel passages Mk 3:31-35; Lk 8:19-21), in which Jesus redefines his own kin not as those born into his father Joseph's household but rather as "whoever does the will of my Father in heaven," that is, whoever is born into his heavenly Father's household. Many of his first disciples did, in fact, leave their natural families behind. Jesus replies to their perceived loss by assuring them that "everyone who has left houses or brothers or sisters or father or mother or children or fields, for my name's sake, will receive a hundredfold, and will inherit eternal life" (Mt 19:29 NRSV). The emerging community of disciples becomes this hundredfold family, a body of people united by devotion to Jesus and his teaching, committed to love, support and help one another as completely as any natural family.

Ideals of kinship and reading the New Testament. There are many ways that the experience of the early church intersects with the social institutions of kinship and the household, and the ethos that is to characterize family. Most obvious is the experience of strangers (across the Mediterranean!) being brought together into a new family—God's family—by virtue of their trust in Jesus, their reception of the Holy Spirit, their being "born from above" or "adopted" by God the Father. Early Christian leaders like Paul, John and the author of 1 Peter spend a great deal of space talking about the way this new family is formed, tracing the new lines of descent that Christians claim (for example, retracing descent from Abraham through Christ the "seed," making Christians the heirs of the promises in Galatians) and drawing out in a great variety of situations the implications of being kin for interaction between Christians. Indeed, nothing seems to drive New Testament ethics quite so much as kinship topics, from showing oneself a true child of God by embodying the characteristics of God and of Christ (the motif of "like parent, like child") to reinforcing the ethos of siblings among the sisters and brothers in the household of faith, and barring the way to unfamilial behaviors like competitiveness, divisiveness, vying for precedence and the like.

Another important avenue of reflection concerns the interface between the household of faith and natural households. The church grew as a household movement: frequently, early Christian missionaries gathered a church around a converted householder and his family (like Stephanus, Gaius and Chloe in Corinth, or Lydia and the jailer in Philippi, or Philemon in Colossae). Christians gathered to worship, pray, hear teaching and break bread in the house of one of their members. Missionaries and teachers traveled from house to house as they carried on their work in the cities of the empire. Wives, children and slaves in non-Christian households also found themselves converted to the new faith, and had to negotiate the tensions of fidelity to the one God and the expectations of their non-Christian husbands, parents and masters. Thus we also find a corresponding interest in the natural household across the New Testament texts, from prescribing codes of conduct for behavior in Christian and non-Christian households (see Eph 5:21—6:9; Col 3:18—4:1; 1 Pet 2:18—3:7) to preparing believers for the inevitable tensions that will exist between them and their unbelieving families and households.

FOR FURTHER READING

Bell, Albert A., Jr. *Exploring the New Testament World.* Nashville: Thomas Nelson, 1998.

Danker, Frederick W. *Benefactor: Epigraphic Study of a Graeco-Roman and New Testament Semantic Field.* St. Louis, Mo.: Clayton, 1982.

deSilva, David A. "Exchanging Favor for Wrath: Apostasy in Hebrews and Patron-Client Relationships." *Journal of Biblical Literature* 115 (1996).

————. *Honor, Patronage, Kinship and Purity: Unlocking New Testament Culture*. Downers Grove, Ill.: InterVarsity Press, 2000.

————. *The Hope of Glory: Honor Discourse and New Testament Interpretation*. Collegeville, Minn.: Liturgical Press, 1999.

Douglas, Mary. *Purity and Danger*. London: Routledge & Kegan Paul, 1966. This is the bedrock study of the meaning of purity laws and the danger perceived in pollution.

Elliott, John H. *A Home for the Homeless: A Sociological Exegesis of I Peter, Its Situation and Strategy*. Philadelphia: Fortress, 1981.

————. "Patronage and Clientism in Early Christian Society." *Forum* 3 (1987): 39-48.

Malina, Bruce J. *The New Testament World: Insights from Cultural Anthropology*. 2nd ed. Louisville, Ky.: Westminster John Knox, 1993.

Malina, Bruce J., and Jerome H. Neyrey. "Honor and Shame in Luke-Acts: Pivotal Values of the Mediterranean World," pp. 25-66. In *The Social World of Luke-Acts: Models for Interpretation*. Edited by Jerome H. Neyrey. Peabody, Mass.: Hendrickson, 1991.

————. "Conflict in Luke-Acts: Labelling and Deviance Theory," pp. 97-124. In *The Social World of Luke-Acts: Models for Interpretation*. Edited by Jerome H. Neyrey. Peabody, Mass.: Hendrickson, 1991.

Milgrom, Jacob. *Leviticus 1-16*. Anchor Bible. New York: Doubleday, 1991. The introduction and the comment sections provide a wealth of information about purity regulations, the meaning of purity and pollution, and the role of purification and defilement in the temple cult.

Moxnes, Halvor, ed. *Constructing Early Christian Families: Family as Social Reality and Metaphor*. London: Routledge, 1997.

————. "Honor and Shame." *Biblical Theology Bulletin* 23 (1993): 167-76.

————. "Honor, Shame, and the Outside World in Paul's Letter to the Romans," pp. 207-18. In *The Social World of Formative Christianity and Judaism*. Edited by J. Neusner et al. Philadelphia: Fortress, 1988.

————. "Honour and Righteousness in Romans." *Journal for the Study of the New Testament* 32 (1988): 61-77.

Nelson, Richard P. *Raising Up a Faithful Priest: Community and Priesthood in a Biblical Theology*. Louisville, Ky.: Westminster John Knox, 1993.

Neusner, Jacob. "The Idea of Purity in Ancient Judaism." *Journal of the American Academy of Religion* 43 (1975): 15-26.

Neyrey, Jerome H. "Body Language in 1 Corinthians: The Use of Anthropological Models for Understanding Paul and His Opponents." *Semeia* 35 (1986): 129-70.

————. "The Idea of Purity in Mark's Gospel." *Semeia* 35 (1986): 91-128.

Osiek, Carolyn, and David L. Balch. *Families in the New Testament World: Households and House Churches*. Louisville, Ky.: Westminster John Knox, 1997.

Pilch, John J. "Biblical Leprosy and Body Symbolism." *Biblical Theology Bulletin* 11 (1981): 108-13.

Riches, John K., ed. *Jesus and the Transformation of Judaism*. New York: Seabury Press, 1982. See especially his chapter "Jesus and the Law of Purity."

Saller, Richard P. *Personal Patronage Under the Early Empire*. Cambridge: Cambridge University Press, 1982.

Stambaugh, John E., and David L. Balch. *The New Testament in Its Social Environment*. Philadelphia: Westminster Press, 1987.

Wallace-Hadrill, Andrew, ed. *Patronage in Ancient Society*. London: Routledge, 1989.

4

THE FOUR GOSPELS AND THE ONE JESUS

Critical Issues in the Study of the Gospels

Before exploring the message of each Gospel and the contribution each made to the formation of Christian identity and ethos, it is important to wrestle with the question of what kind of literature the Gospels are, and to inquire more closely into the stages by which the Jesus traditions came down to the Evangelists and then, ultimately, on to successive generations of readers.

In this chapter we will look first at the question of the genre of the Gospel. The answer to this question can guide our interpretation of these texts and help us form appropriate expectations for what these texts will and will not tell us about Jesus. Then we will investigate the currents by which Jesus' sayings and stories about Jesus flowed through the decades after his earthly ministry down to the pools from which the Evangelists drew their living waters. This will take us into the period of oral tradition and into the exegetical skill of form criticism, the means by which that period has been investigated. Following this we will examine the literary relationships between the Gospels and the explanations for their composition that have emerged from the discipline of source criticism. The story of the Gospels does not end with their composition, however. We will also give attention to the church's selection of *these* four Gospels from a larger pool of literature about Jesus, and the

ongoing development of the Gospel texts after they left the hands of the Evangelists and were passed down through generations of scribes and copyists. Finally, we will review a topic that perhaps more than any other in New Testament studies has gripped the popular imagination and polarized scholarship—the quest for the historical Jesus.

WHAT IS A GOSPEL?

Recognizing a text's genre and understanding the conventions and expectations that belong to that genre is of great importance for reliably and meaningfully reading that text. We regularly use identification of literary genre as a guide to interpretation, and most often this identification happens intuitively. Consider the different ways you read (or hear) an advertisement, a legal contract, a devotional book, a novel, a personal letter and a form letter. Consider how watching a movie differs from watching a video clip on the news. The reader (or hearer) comes to these texts with different expectations and goals, depending on the kind of text he or she is reading (or hearing). The author, similarly, chooses to write or speak within the framework of a certain genre based on the purpose for communicating. Identifying the genre is a key to identifying a work's purpose and becoming alert to the conventions it uses to convey content and achieve its purpose.

If an ancient person wanted to read a copy of the Gospels at an ancient library, to what section would the librarian direct her?[1] How would the first-century person have classified the Gospels? Mark labels his work "gospel," but a gospel was not its own literary genre. If it had no connection with existing genres in the ancient world, its audience would not know how to interpret it, being without the necessary cues and clues that knowledge of genre provides. The readers of the Gospels would have sought to determine, again intuitively (as we do), what kind of literature it was most like so they would have a starting point for reading and interpreting these texts.

Justin Martyr (d. 164 C.E.) called the Gospels "memorabilia" (apomnēmoneumata), the "memoirs of the apostles," recalling Xenophon's Memorabilia, a kind of biography of Socrates.[2] Ancient biography differs markedly from modern biography, with the latter's interest in chronological presentation, development of personality and thought, inner motivations, and the like. Xenophon's Memorabilia focuses both on the deeds and sayings of Socrates in order to capture the significance of the man and the way of life he embodied. Xenophon's purpose, as a disciple of Socrates, was to persuade readers of the praiseworthy character of Socrates and to demonstrate that the way of life he followed and proclaimed was worthy of imitation.

If we look more widely at the surviving works of the classical period, we find many such biographies, which usually go by the title of "Lives" (Latin vita, Greek bios).[3] Many of these "lives" construct a basic chronological framework for the life of the subject of the narrative. But they set within that framework illuminating anecdotes and stories that show more of the character of the subject, and often the "philosophy of life" or teaching of the subject without claims to strict, chronological order (especially in the case of philosophers as opposed to figures of public life).[4] Often a more topical arrangement characterizes the ordering of this material: stories linked by a common setting or theme are narrated in a group, even if they were separated by years. The author often gives detailed attention to how the subject approached and faced death, since this was the ultimate proof of his or her character and way of life.[5]

Plutarch wrote the largest and most famous collection of Lives, comparing the various figures with one another in an attempt to discern who was more virtuous and significant.[6] Diogenes Laertius composed a series of Lives of Eminent Philosophers in which he gives prominence to the sayings and teachings of the leading figures in Stoicism, Platonism and other schools. Philostratus's Life of Apollonius of Tyana comes very close to our Gospels in its record of the marvelous deeds as well as the teachings of a charismatic philosopher of the later first century C.E., exemplifying the interest in the lives of holy men in later antiquity.[7]

---

[1]Thanks to G. N. Stanton for this fine image (Gospel Truth? [Valley Forge, Penn.: Trinity Press, 1995], p. 136).

[2]G. N. Stanton, A Gospel for a New People (Louisville, Ky.: Westminster John Knox, 1993), p. 63.

[3]See R. A. Burridge, What Are the Gospels? SNTSMS 70 (Cambridge: Cambridge University Press, 1992), pp. 109-239; David E. Aune, The New Testament in Its Literary Environment (Philadelphia: Westminster Press, 1987), pp. 27-36 and the bibliography on pp. 43-44.

[4]R. A. Burridge, "About People, by People, for People: Gospel Genre and Audiences," in The Gospels for All Christians, ed. Richard Bauckham (Grand Rapids: Eerdmans, 1998), p. 122; Warren Carter, Matthew (Peabody, Mass.: Hendrickson, 1996), p. 47.

[5]Burridge, "About People," p. 122.

[6]Despite Plutarch's interest in character and manner of life, developing a series of models for contemporary statesmen and others involved in public life, these Lives are still of great value to the historian of ancient Greece and Rome. The two interests are not mutually exclusive; it is merely a matter of which interest is primary.

[7]Aune, New Testament in Its Literary Environment, p. 34.

Philo, the Alexandrian Jewish author, writes a "Life of Abraham," a "Life of Joseph" and a "Life of Moses," all of which set forth not only the greatness of the person but the nobility of his way of life, thus encouraging continued commitment to Judaism and seeking to elevate the reputation of the Jewish "philosophy." The ancient biography, the *bios,* had thus a deeply moral and exemplary character.[8]

An author would write a "life," or *bios,* for one or more of a number of reasons. He or she might focus on an illustrious historical figure as a paradigm to promote a way of life or set of values, or critique an alternative group's or culture's set of values. The *bios* could be used to provide a pattern for imitation for all who aspire to the virtues or ideals represented by the person, to dispel false images of who that person was and what he or she stood for (e.g., to counter views promoted by rivals or other hostile voices), to preserve information about and sayings of the person, simply to entertain readers, and to arouse admiration for the figure.[9] The ancient biography can be seen to have developed out of the funeral oration, with which it shares many goals and characteristics, especially its moral interest in using reflection on a particular life (and the enviable honor accorded that life) to arouse commitment to certain values and virtues, making the audience better, more virtuous, and more fruitful citizens of the Greco-Roman world. Plutarch cites this explicitly as his motive in writing the numerous *Lives* of noble Greeks and Romans (*Pericles* 3), just as this arousal of imitation was made an explicit part of numerous surviving eulogies.[10]

The ancient librarian, then, would probably have shelved the Gospels among the *Lives,* that larger family of literature which focused on the deeds and sayings of illustrious persons. The ancient reader would have come to the Gospels expecting them to articulate and defend the significance of Jesus, and to legitimate the value system embodied by the figure of Jesus.[11] The reader would expect to go away renewed in his or her commitment that Jesus is worthy of being heard—indeed, that Jesus is *the* authoritative teacher and revealer of the way—and that Jesus' life is worthy of emulation. He or she would not expect strict chronological order but rather would look for the contents to be arranged in the best way to bring out the character, message and significance of Jesus within the general chronological framework of his birth, career and death. Indeed, the focus on Jesus' death in the Gospels would also be entirely in keeping with the *bios,* the death of the subject receiving similar attention across a wide sampling of *bioi.*[12]

The reader would also be prepared to expect the Gospels to differ from other *Lives.* One expects divergence within a genre. Many differences can be noted between the *bioi* written by Philo and those written by Plutarch. It is no surprise, then, that the Gospels have distinctive features as well. "Adaptation of a literary genre is more common than its close imitation."[13] The attention given to the interpretation of Old Testament prophesy, for example, would be a distinctive feature of these *bioi,* but still quite in keeping with the general aims of the "life," for example, highlighting the significance of the subject.

---

[8]Ibid., p. 33.

[9]Burridge, *What Are the Gospels?* pp. 149-52, 214-17; "About People," pp. 134-37; Aune, *New Testament in Its Literary Environment,* pp. 35-36.

[10]On this point, see David A. deSilva, *Despising Shame: Honor Discourse and Community Maintenance in the Epistle to the Hebrews,* SBLDS 152 (Atlanta: Scholars Press, 1995), pp. 47-50.

[11]Stanton, *Gospel for a New People,* pp. 69-70.

[12]Burridge, "About People," p. 122.

[13]Stanton, *Gospel for a New People,* p. 66; Aune, *New Testament in Its Literary Environment,* p. 46.

Strictly speaking the purpose of the Gospels, therefore, is not historical. That would be a rather shallow assessment of their goal. They seek rather to present the person of Jesus to those who have committed themselves already to follow him (or at least are provisionally interested, as perhaps in the case of Luke's broader audience), to renew commitment to Jesus' authority, to determine how the believers will live their lives, and to promote Jesus' example as the pattern for imitation. In short, they seek to make a contribution to how the communities of believers would live out their Christian commitment.

This brings us to the major difference between the Gospels and other ancient *vitae* that sought to promote a way of life. The subject of the biography is not dead but is still very much available to the community through the Holy Spirit to give support, direction and help. The figure of Jesus is not, therefore, merely a figure for imitation but a living person whose voice still speaks to the churches with the authority of the Son of God, the eschatological Judge, the anointed One. The Evangelists can therefore shape their presentation of Jesus to address his words to the specific needs and questions of their communities. The community can be expected to respond to the powerful and compelling figure presented in the narrative, knowing that the subject of the biography remains the Lord of the church.

FOR FURTHER READING

Aune, David E. *The New Testament in Its Literary Environment*, pp. 17-76. Philadelphia: Westminster Press, 1987.

Burridge, Richard A. *What Are the Gospels? A Comparison with Graeco-Roman Biography.* SNTSMS 70. Cambridge: Cambridge University Press, 1992.

————. "About People, by People, for People: Gospel Genre and Audiences." In *The Gospels for All Christians: Rethinking the Gospel Audiences.* Edited by Richard Bauckham, pp. 113-46. Grand Rapids: Eerdmans, 1998.

Carter, Warren. *Matthew: Storyteller, Interpreter, Evangelist*, pp. 35-53. Peabody, Mass.: Hendrickson, 1996.

Stanton, Graham N. *A Gospel for a New People: Studies in Matthew*, pp. 59-71. Louisville, Ky.: Westminster John Knox, 1993.

FROM THE HISTORICAL JESUS TO THE CANONICAL GOSPELS

There are Medieval paintings and illuminations of the four Evangelists writing in seclusion (like the monks who drew them), often shown looking up away from their paper, listening to some otherworldly being as they write. Similarly, many people today believe the Evangelists took divine dictation: they were merely stenographers, the secretaries of the Holy Spirit. Close study and comparison of the Gospels themselves suggests that this model of inspiration is not very helpful, and is certainly not a complete picture of how the Evangelists worked to produce these Gospels. Luke's depiction of his own task is rather mundane—comparing written works about the ministry and teaching of Jesus, examining other sources, and setting out to do a better job for the sake of instructing Theophilus and others like him (Lk 1:1-4).[14] His prologue suggests that we must take seriously the Evangelists' role as authors and compilers, and not picture them either as mere recorders of what

---

[14]David L. Dungan, *A History of the Synoptic Problem* (New York: Doubleday, 1999), p. 16.

the Spirit spoke or as individuals writing their private memoirs of their time with Jesus.

A side-by-side reading of the Gospels raises many questions, and these questions have led to centuries of concerted efforts to investigate the manner and purpose of their composition:

- Why do Matthew, Mark and Luke, on the one hand, tell many of the same stories in almost the same ways but then display puzzling lacks of overlap with regard to other aspects of their Gospels?
- Why are the sayings of Jesus grouped differently in different Gospels?
- Why does the same saying or parable appear in different contexts in Matthew and Luke?
- Why are some sayings and parables unique to certain Gospels?
- Why does John share so little sayings material in common with the other three?
- Why does John arrange the story so differently, including events that have no parallel in the other Gospels and leaving out so many events from the other Gospels?
- Why do only two Evangelists include infancy narratives, and why does each share so little material with the other in this area?
- Why are the stories and order of postresurrection appearances so different?

These and similar questions have led to alternative models to the "divine dictation" model promoted in Medieval art.

After Jesus' ascension his disciples, whom Luke describes as "eyewitnesses and servants of the word" (Lk 1:2 NRSV) and who were clearly not limited to the twelve (see Acts 1:15, 21-23), proclaimed his death and resurrection, and sought to make disciples through passing on Jesus' teachings and example. Sayings of Jesus, parables, stories of his confrontation with members of various groups all served this catechetical purpose (that is, the task of instructing and shaping disciples and communities of disciples). Stories about Jesus' acts of healing and miracles both enhanced the community's appreciation of Jesus' authority to prescribe a way of life and opened them up to the possibilities of God's power in their midst to heal and deliver. The passion narrative (Jesus' trial, death and burial) was a natural follow-up for those who heard the briefer proclamation of his death and resurrection. It was no doubt relevant at celebrations of the Lord's Supper, a Christian ritual attested as early as Paul's first letter to Corinth (1 Cor 11:17-34), and was also instrumental in arming the followers of Jesus with a positive interpretation of what outsiders viewed as a shameful execution.

This period is called the "oral tradition" stage, a stage that did not end with the writing of Mark or Matthew, although as these Gospels circulated in written form, the public reading in Christian worship would have gradually replaced recitation from memory. The sayings, parables and stories all served the goals of edification, instructing disciples, sustaining the life of the church and answering the criticisms of outsiders. Those sayings and stories that were not relevant to this ongoing use were for the most part forgotten, no matter how wonderful the stories may have been (see the hyperbolic claim in Jn 21:25). Moreover, the traditions were not uniformly distributed throughout the early Christian movement. This would explain, for example, why we find sayings in Matthew that are not also found in either John, Mark or Luke. Similarly, some of the now best-known parables of Jesus (the good Samaritan, the prodigal son) are found only in Luke's Gospel, probably reflecting Jesus traditions known only in particular regions, which became available to the whole Mediterranean Christian community only as Luke's Gospel was copied and spread.

When the earliest Evangelist sat down to write, then, he had at hand a host of traditional materials that had been used, shaped and shared (if unevenly) by the early Christian communities. The Evangelist did not create the stories anew but rather worked with sayings and parables of Jesus and stories about Jesus that had been used in preaching and teaching for at least three decades, and that had become the common property of believers. The Evangelists are doing something distinctly new in the church—putting together the whole story, a life or *bios* of Jesus—but they are not doing it in a vacuum or as personal memoirs and reminiscences. They are using catechetical material for the sake of carrying on the same goals, like teaching about discipleship, sustaining the life of the church, answering the church's critics, demonstrating Jesus' authority and so forth by constructing a "Life of Jesus" in the ancient sense. Moreover, scholars regard it as likely that one or more of the Evangelists had access to the work of another Evangelist (most commonly, that Matthew and Luke both had access to Mark; less commonly, that Luke and Mark had access to Matthew; least commonly, that Mark had access to Matthew and Luke). Luke himself points in this direction; he refers to his own familiarity with and use of previous attempts to write a "Life of Jesus" (Lk 1:1-4). The composition of several of the Gospels, then, may involve an Evangelist's use of oral tradition, a written predecessor as well as other sources of Jesus traditions.

These Evangelists shaped their *Lives* of Jesus as a means of responding to the concerns, questions and challenges faced by the Christian community. Like the other *Lives* discussed above, these Gospels defend the subject from misunderstanding and criticism, demonstrate the virtue of his way of life, promote the imitation of his example, preserve the Jesus traditions in a meaningful and usable arrangement, and answer some of the more specific concerns of the early Christians (see chapter one). The choice of the genre allows the Evangelists to speak more "universally" to

the early Christian community as a whole than the more particularistic genre of the letter, written to one community or to one person.[15] If theories of literary composition are correct, the Gospels reflect the gathering of material from a variety of sources, not merely the inbred traditions of a single community. But the Evangelists were not merely collectors of tradition; they were pastors and preachers of the living Christ. The early church expected the risen Lord to continue to speak to the churches. Acts 9 attests to this as it portrays Jesus speaking to Paul and Ananias, giving each specific instructions. The Revelation to John shows this process at work as John reports words given to him from Jesus addressing the particular challenges facing seven different Christian communities in Asia Minor (Rev 2:1—3:22). The Evangelists shaped and molded the traditions in an environment in which Christ and the Spirit were known to be actively guiding the community of disciples "into all truth" (Jn 16:12-14). This environment nurtured the conviction that the Gospels were written under the guidance of the Spirit, who was revealing more of the truth and applicability of the teachings of Jesus, providing richer answers to questions old and new.

Perhaps it would be more precise to speak about the inspiration of the Evangelists in terms of the way they have presented Jesus to the church, the new meanings and relevance they give to Jesus' sayings by reshaping or recontextualizing them, and the claims that Jesus makes on early Christian communities (and, indeed, the church throughout the millennia) through their writings. They could have addressed the short-term needs of Christians through a letter, as most early Christian leaders did. They preferred, however, to help their readers meet these challenges by bringing them in contact with the living Jesus, and to let him challenge and encourage them, reas-

---

[15]Burridge, "About People," pp. 123-34.

sure and provoke them, reminding them of who he is and what he seeks in his followers. In so doing they bring something new to the oral traditions and pass along more fully developed narrative interpretations of Jesus to the church of each succeeding generation.

We will now turn with greater detail to each step in this process of the transmission of the Jesus traditions, first by examining the oral tradition stage (and "form criticism," the primary exegetical tool used to uncover this stage), then by examining the literary composition of the Gospels (and "source criticism," the essential tool for that task).

THE BUILDING BLOCKS BEHIND THE GOSPELS: ORAL TRADITION

Jesus was a teacher and was seen as such by friends and competitors alike (see, e.g., Mt 8:19; 9:11; 12:38; 17:24; 19:16; 22:16, 24, 36; 26:18). Matthew presents him quite explicitly as a teacher of wisdom and the correct living of the law (Mt 5:17-48; 11:28-30; compare the latter with the invitation of another wisdom teacher in Sira 51:23-28). His sayings and parables, once spoken, would be remembered, quite probably memorized, and used by his disciples to speak to the church and to outsiders of Jesus' message and its implications for Christian identity. Stories about Jesus will be remembered and passed on for similar purposes. These traditions would have become part of a great pool of resources which Christian leaders could draw on for the daily work of evangelism, the defense and confir-

mation of the gospel (i.e., the proclamation about Jesus' work and significance), ordering the Christian community and instructing the church. For the three decades between Jesus' resurrection and the writing of the first Gospel, this is how Jesus' teachings and the stories about Jesus were made available to the community and the world.[16]

There are signs within the Gospels of "oral transmission." The placement of the same sayings in different settings and contexts suggests that the saying was part of the available tradition, while the placement of that saying, where it would best serve his pastoral intent when composing the Gospel, was left to the Evangelist. Sayings often appear to be disconnected or only loosely connected in many contexts. Luke 16 provides a case in point. We can study the logic of the compilation of these sayings into what now appears to be a single speech, but only as Luke's compilation and not as a single speech as uttered by Jesus. In Luke 16 we find two independent parables (Lk 16:1-9, 19-31) serving as an interpretative frame for several other independent sayings of Jesus (Lk 16:10-12, 13, 14-17, 18).[17] They are brought together by Luke in such a way that each becomes the new interpretive context for the other sayings. In the Gospels, the similarity of the "form" of miracle stories or of conflict stories has been seen as an indication of the regularization of how these stories were told over the decades of oral transmission (very similar to the formulaic patterns of folk tales).

More impressive are the signs of oral trans-

---

[16]If the hypothesis of the sayings collection Q is correct, of course, we would have to add that written collections of these sayings of Jesus were introduced into the resource pool of at least some communities and their leaders during this time.

[17]Luke 16:10-12 seems to flow from the parable of the dishonest steward, until we recognizes that, in fact, the point of Luke 16:10-12 (in which dishonesty in little leads not to commendation but condemnation) runs contrary to the point of Luke 16:1-9, where a dishonest steward is the hero of a parable. Luke 16:13, of course, is recognizable as a discrete saying that Matthew places in the context of the saying about treasures in heaven in the Sermon on the Mount. The sayings in Luke 16:14-18 are tied to the topic of money only by Luke's introduction of the Pharisees as lovers of money but can be used here by Luke as part of his demonstration that the proper use of money for the relief of those in need is central to the doing of the "law and the prophets," a point dramatically reinforced by the parable of the rich man and Lazarus.

mission outside the Gospels, especially the sayings of Jesus preserved outside the Gospels. For example, Acts 20:35 preserves the saying, "It is more blessed to give than to receive." Only Paul connects the instruction "Do this, as often as you drink it, in remembrance of me" (1 Cor 11:25 NRSV).[18] Paul also refers to a saying of Jesus to the effect that "those who preach the gospel should make their living by the gospel" (1 Cor 9:14). The textual history of the Gospels is replete with instances of scribes inserting sayings of Jesus and stories about Jesus into the written Gospels. What continued to be passed on and valued in oral tradition was in danger of being forgotten, and copyists eagerly sought out room in the Gospels for pieces of oral tradition not taken up by the Evangelists.[19] The most famous example is the story of the woman caught in adultery (presently found in Jn 7:53—8:11).[20] The testimony of Papias that Mark wrote down the stories he heard Peter using in his preaching also documents the relationship of the written Gospels to the oral tradition.

Form criticism. In the early part of the twentieth century a number of scholars sought to penetrate the veil of the Gospels to get back to the oral tradition phase of these Jesus traditions, ultimately attempting to discern what kernel of which traditions might go back to Jesus himself. Studying the development of the Gospel traditions was, in large measure, a handmaiden to recovering the "historical Jesus" behind the accretions of the decades. To facilitate this task these scholars adapted the discipline of "form criticism," prominent in Old Testament studies since the mid-nineteenth century. Form critics see the Gospels as collections of units of tradition (the sayings material and the stories about Jesus). These units can be studied independently of their literary context in the Gospels (once freed of the redactional modifications of the Evangelists) as windows into the life of the early churches that preserved these traditions.[21] Ultimately, the goal is to theorize about the development of a particular tradition in order to recover its earliest form, which will also be the most historically reliable and useful form.

Form criticism works with several cardinal presuppositions:[22]

1. The Gospel traditions (with the exception of the lengthy passion narrative) originally circulated as short, independent sayings and stories that were used as needed for specific occasions and purposes. We have already seen that this principle is reasonable enough and well supported by evidence both within and outside the Gospels themselves.

2. These traditions can be classified accord-

---

[18]Matthew and Mark say nothing about remembrance; Luke only connects the topic of remembrance with the bread (Lk 22:19).

[19]See William Morrice, *Hidden Sayings of Jesus* (Peabody, Mass.: Hendrickson, 1997), pp. 33-36 for a few examples.

[20]The third- and fourth-century manuscripts of John's Gospel lack this story, which finds its way into the tradition only in later manuscripts and, tellingly, in a number of places before taking lasting and unquestioned root after John 7:52. This story was such an important testimony to the character of Jesus and the restorative nature of his mission, and thus of the mission the church was to continue, that early Christians would not consign it to oblivion. Instead, they found places in the canonical Gospels to insert the story so that it would remain a permanent part of the church's Scripture and memory (some here, after Jn 7:52; others add the story after Jn 7:36; 21:25; Lk 21:38; and Lk 24:53). This does not make the story any less true or significant. If anything, it makes it more significant, since so many Christians felt strongly enough about the story's value to weave it into the Gospel story somewhere. It also helps us understand better the nature of the "pieces" all four Evangelists worked with.

[21]Admittedly, form criticism has been much more successfully applied to the Synoptic Gospels than to the Gospel of John, since the materials included in the Fourth Gospel had a very different history of development.

[22]See, further, E. Basil Redlich, *Form Criticism* (London: Duckworth, 1939), pp. 34-74; Robert H. Stein, *Studying the Synoptic Gospels*, 2nd ed. (Grand Rapids: Baker, 2001), pp. 174-94.

ing to their literary form. Major kinds of "forms" include

- Independent *logia,* or sayings, of Jesus. These can be further classified as wisdom sayings, prophetic or apocalyptic sayings, church rules (sentences of "holy law") and "I" sayings. One of the sayings forms that has received the most attention is the parable, the memorable analogy or fable told by Jesus. The parable is further subdivided into the similitude (using generalities or typical phenomena as points of comparison, like the mustard seed or leaven), the parable proper (creating a particular story to communicate a point, like the sower), the example story (like the good Samaritan, the rich man and Lazarus) and the allegory (like the wicked tenants).[23]

- Short narratives about Jesus. These narratives are of several types: First, we find *pronouncement stories* that center on some pithy statement or ruling given by Jesus and by necessity also include the discussion or event that gave rise to that pronouncement. These are often conflict stories, as in the cleansing of the temple in Mark and John or the controversy over eating with sinners (which climaxes in the saying "I have come not to call the righteous, but sinners to repentance"). These conflict stories are remembered and used because they are perceived by early Christians to speak to conflicts also experienced in the life of the early church. Some pronouncement stories involve a more neutral inquiry that Jesus answers or a story that elicits a remark by Jesus. Second, we find *miracle stories,* including healing narratives, exorcisms and nature miracles. These often had the function of eliciting praise or speaking about Jesus' identity and significance.

- "Myths," the label attached to stories about the interaction of supernatural beings with human characters. The baptism, temptation and transfiguration fall under this category. For scholars with a naturalistic worldview, such stories would obviously lack any historical basis (the choice of label can hardly be said to be value free).

- Passion narrative, a narrative development of the basic proclamation that Jesus was arrested, tried, crucified, died and buried. The passion narratives are distinct from the shorter stories in that they exhibit a certain unity of composition. They are not easily divided into stories that would have been used independently of one another. The passion narratives are not without theological interest. This comes through in the centurion's pronouncement (which correctly identifies Jesus and his innocence), the taunt of the chief priests (which reminds the reader of Psalm 22, showing even the mockery and scorn to be part of the divinely ordained plan rather than an accurate reflection of Jesus' low honor, and which also sets up the interpretation of the resurrection as God's deliverance and approval of Jesus), and the rending of the veil (which says something significant about the temple cult and where God's favor may be attained). The Evangelists weave the Hebrew Scriptures into the tapestry of the narrative, interpreting the meaning of Jesus' death as an event that occurs "according to the Scriptures." It is not the death of a law-breaker but the working out of the plan of God.

3. Each kind of "form" functioned within and was further stylized by its repeated use within a typical kind of "life situation" (*Sitz im Leben*) in the early church. Controversy stories (a subcategory of pronouncement stories) are thought to be linked with apologetics, the de-

---

[23]Aune, *New Testament in Its Literary Environment,* p. 51; K. F. Nickle, *The Synoptic Gospels,* 2nd ed. (Louisville, Ky.: Westminster John Knox, 2001), pp. 33-34.

fense of the Christian group's practices in the face of criticism from (especially) non-Christian Jewish leaders. Miracle stories are thought to be used especially in evangelism, setting out the greatness and power of Jesus. Each form may also have had a "life situation" in the ministry of Jesus, although individual traditions need to be weighed and sifted for their authenticity.

4. The preservation of these traditions in these particular forms was determined by the practical needs of early Christian communities and their leaders. Not every saying of Jesus was remembered through the decades; not every story continued to be told. John 21:25 attests to the fact that not every saying of or story about Jesus was preserved in the memory of the church.[24] John 20:30-31, moreover, shows how a pastoral interest determines why these stories are retold and guides the selection of particular stories. Papias again reflects the connection between pastoral utility or need and continued use of a tradition when he says that Peter "adapted his teaching to the needs of his hearers" and "used to give his teachings as demanded by necessity."[25]

5. The Evangelists were primarily collectors of oral tradition, not authors. This disabuses us of the image of the Evangelists composing lives of Jesus freehand, spinning a narrative out of their heads, as it were. Rather than writing their personal memoirs, they were putting together material that had long been the property of the church's teaching and the apostles' preaching. However, the principle is unhelpful where it devalues the contribution the Evangelists did make to the material, either by purposeful arrangement (with the interpretative guidance this gives to the individual traditions) or by editorial crafting.

6. The earliest form of a particular tradition can be recovered by understanding the rules for the development of oral traditions (learned, for example, through the study of folklore). For example, it was commonly assumed by form critics that traditions tended to expand with time, with the result that the simplest version of a tradition is the oldest; similarly, traditions tended to become more detailed; variations of a tradition tended to become conflated; an early Christian tradition tended to lose Semitic features as time passed (i.e., as Christianity became further removed from its Palestinian beginnings). The validity of these rules, however, has been subjected to rigorous criticism. E. P. Sanders, for example, gathered decisive evidence that shows traditions developing from longer to shorter, more detailed to less detailed, and so forth—in short, in ways contrary to the alleged "rules."[26]

Form criticism and its results contributed in many ways to the study of Jesus and the Gospels. Some of these contributions (and the presuppositions they rest on) require careful scrutiny and sharp critique. Others, resting on firmer evidence, continue to be of great help to students of the Gospels.

The most problematic claim of form critics concerns the reliability of the Gospel tradition. Many form critics claim that in many of the units of Gospel tradition we don't have a window into the life of Jesus but only (or chiefly) a window into the life of the church. The practical result of this conviction is the elimination of a great number of Gospel traditions from historical Jesus research and, in addition, the modification of a great many more

---

[24]Stein, *Studying the Synoptic Gospels*, p. 184.

[25]Papias, quoted in Eusebius *Ecclesiastical History* 3.39.15; Dungan, *History of the Synoptic Problem*, p. 20.

[26]E. P. Sander, *The Tendencies of the Synoptic Tradition*, SNTSMS 9 (Cambridge: Cambridge University Press, 1969).

to arrive at the "original" or "pure" form of the tradition.[27] Such a view of the tradition rests on presuppositions about how the disciples and other early Christian leaders handled the Jesus traditions. The disciples are seen to keep the gist of Jesus' words in mind, while freely reinventing the actual wording as the situation merited. They are also seen to invent sayings and stories out of whole cloth, creating traditions where needed.

Therefore form critics tend not to place great confidence in the church's *memory*. Birger Gerhardsson, however, after a comprehensive study of the transmission of tradition in rabbinic circles, has argued strongly in favor of the disciples' commitment to the accurate preservation and transmission of their master's sayings:

> The words and works of Jesus were stamped on the memories of these disciples. Remembering the attitude of Jewish disciples to their master, it is unrealistic to suppose that forgetfulness and the exercise of a pious imagination had too much hand in transforming authentic memories beyond all recognition in the course of a few short decades.[28]

Whether Jesus' disciples followed the pattern of rabbis' disciples committing their teacher's word to memory or the pattern of a sage's students doing the same, it is quite plausible that they gave his words the same attention, all the more as they regarded him as *the* authoritative teacher of the way to please God. Some scholars have also suggested that the disciples and other eyewitnesses may have taken notes of what they learned from Jesus, keeping collections of sayings on hand as a resource.[29]

Form critics also tend to assume a high degree of creativity on the part of early Christian leaders. Did the early church invent traditions as issues needed to be addressed, or did it usually or even exclusively use and adapt authentic traditions? It is more plausible that the traditions about Jesus gave rise to the kinds of issues and questions faced by the church than the reverse,[30] all the more with the absence of Jesus traditions addressing lively and burning issues like circumcision or the regulation of spiritual gifts. Moreover, form critics have tended to neglect or downplay the role of eyewitnesses to the ministry of Jesus in the generation between Jesus' death and resurrection and the first written Gospel. Stein finds in Luke 1:2 a connection between being an eyewitness and a transmitter and preacher of the Jesus tradition, suggesting that form critics have far overstated the gulf between Jesus and the church's traditions about Jesus.[31] Appealing to eyewit-

---

[27]Many questions have been raised about the actual practice of form criticism in this regard, namely, how it peels back the layers of tradition to arrive at the older, more reliable core. For example, when should two similar stories be taken as double developments of a single tradition or event, and when should they be taken as witnesses to two different events or traditions? This would be a pertinent question to bring to the traditions about Jesus being anointed by a woman, where we must negotiate between three disparate traditions and decide whether they go back to a single event, two events or (as Origen resolved it) anointings of Jesus on three different occasions. Another methodological question asks how much the identification of a form should influence judgments about authenticity. S. H. Travis gives an excellent example with regard to Mark 2:18-20 ("Form Criticism," in *New Testament Interpretation,* ed. I. Howard Marshall [Grand Rapids: Eerdmans, 1977], p. 159). Mark 2:18-19a would make a textbook example of a pronouncement story (indeed, a "chreia" or "apophthegm"). This has been used as evidence that Mark 2:19b-20 is a secondary addition to the tradition. Should the heuristic device of the "form" be more definitive for determining authenticity than independent examination of the content? Can authentic traditions be preserved in some mixed form or in some other way that violates the principles of the definition of forms?

[28]Birger Gerhardsson, *Memory and Manuscript* (Uppsala: Gleerup, 1961), p. 329.

[29]Travis, "Form Criticism," p. 160; H. Schürmann, "Die vorösterlichen Anfänge der Logienstradition," in *Der historische Jesus und der kerygmatische Christus,* ed. H. Ristow and K. Matthiae (Berlin: Evangelische Verlagsanstalt, 1960), pp. 342-70.

[30]Stein, *Studying the Synoptic Gospels,* p. 187.

[31]Ibid., pp. 200-202.

nesses does not mean that every tradition is authentic and an accurate reminiscence. Eyewitnesses do not always see things correctly, interpret what they see accurately or remember them without embellishment. Nevertheless, their presence, availability and active role in proclaiming Jesus suggest more continuity between Jesus' ministry and the Gospel traditions than many form critics (and "Historical Jesus" researchers) tend to assume or allow.[32]

A more balanced assessment, then, might be that the units of Gospel tradition are not simply transparent windows into the life of Jesus but have been given certain tints and etchings by the early church as these units were applied and reapplied to the life of the Christian community. The stories of conflict between Jesus and Pharisees or scribes, for example, point not only to an aspect of Jesus' ministry (i.e., conflict with other groups within Judaism) but also reveal the interests of the early church as they are remembered and passed on. What is our relationship now to Torah's purity or sabbath regulations? What is our purpose as an organ of God's will—to build boundaries to protect holiness or to enact holiness by extending God's gift? The traditions are remembered and pointed to answer such questions, but it is still the desire of the early Christian leader to bring an authentic tradition of Jesus to bear on those questions.

Having said this, form criticism raises important questions about recovering the *ipsissima verba* (the very words) of Jesus. Do we affirm that all forms of a parable or saying are exact quotes from separate occasions? Do we choose between two forms of a saying? Do we reconstruct a third, supposedly more original form from the two or three forms that have survived? Or do we rather just accept that our access to Jesus' words is thoroughly mediated through the memory of the church and the re-

daction of the Evangelists (Augustine had recognized this problem and found this last position a sensible solution), and authoritative in that form?

A second, more positive area in which form critics have made a helpful contribution concerns the connection between these Jesus traditions and the practical needs of the early Christian communities, particularly in the preaching in the early church. The importance of sharing the good news about Jesus rather than keeping silent out of fear of ostracism could be supported with pronouncements of Jesus ("A light is not lit to be put under a bushel"). A message on the problem of including Gentiles in the church could appeal to Jesus' calling sinners to repentance or by his free association with those who were not careful Torah-observant Jews. The stories about and sayings of Jesus were never disconnected from the ongoing life of the community of his followers. Form critics have helped us to recover a sense of these traditions as pastoral resources rather than personal reminiscences. That is to say, the Gospel traditions were preserved not to speak primarily to the biographical or historical questions about who Jesus was but to the church about what it means to be a community of followers of this Jesus.

Third, form critics have contributed greatly to our understanding of the role of the Evangelists in composing the Gospels. Given the basic independence of the units of tradition, we are alerted to the fact that the grouping and arrangement of sayings may largely reflect the work of the Evangelists (or in some cases the emerging tradition behind the Evangelist in his community). Sayings of Jesus originally independent of any traditional context are given a context, to be interpreted within that context. Our exploration of the ways the Evangelists have arranged, grouped and contextualized sayings and stories will help us grasp the

---

[32]See the finely nuanced discussion of this topic in Stanton, *Gospel Truth?* pp. 52-56.

particularities of their portrait of Jesus and their understanding of the significance of his teachings and deeds.

For example, in Mark 2 and 3 we find a series of five pronouncement stories that reflect challenges to Jesus' way of following God. This series does not mean that Jesus just had a really bad week early in his ministry. Rather, it is a means Mark used to provide a picture of Jesus' relationship to other Jewish groups and the implications this would have for followers of Jesus. Again, Mark places the transfiguration story immediately after a series of sayings on discipleship, which culminate in "Truly I say to you, there are some standing here today who will not taste death until they see the kingdom of God coming in power" (Mk 9:1). The placement of the transfiguration story by this saying interprets the saying. The results of form criticism strengthen the observations made on the basis of genre that the Gospels are not chronological biographies of Jesus but interpretative proclamations of the meaning and significance of Jesus, his work and his message.

Fourth, study of the various forms and the thrust of each can be a valuable aid to exegesis. A spate of books on the parables approached through form-critical analysis has shown how helpful it can be to recognize the purpose behind a parable and to interpret the text in line with that purpose. For example, recognizing that the parable of the good Samaritan is an exemplification story directs us to focus on the Samaritan in the parable as the paradigm for fulfilling the command to love our neighbor as ourselves, preventing us from losing sight of Jesus' point (and the Evangelist's point as well) for the parable in an extravagant allegorical reading.[33] It also cautions the

interpreter against making too much out of metaphorical language or details in parables, such as developing a doctrine and geography of the afterlife from the parable of the rich man and Lazarus.

Finally, form critics, by noting the original independence of these units, open up the possibility of exploring a saying's meaning apart from the interpretative context and shape given to it by an Evangelist. The discipline invites us to inquire into the setting of a saying or story in the life of Jesus and the program he was announcing in Palestine, as well as the setting of that saying or story in the ongoing life and formation of the early Christian communities. Source and redaction criticism (the latter will be introduced at length in the chapter on Matthew), with their focus on the finished texts of the Gospels, let us look at the application of that saying or story by one particular early Christian preacher, the Evangelist.

For example, let's look at the parable of the wicked tenants (Mt 21:33-44; Mk 12:1-12; Lk 20:9-19). Within the ministry of Jesus this parable probably served as a prophetic denunciation of the leadership of the temple. Jesus is declaring that the leaders of the Jewish people have always and continue to oppose God's spokespersons. They have consistently put their own interests ahead of the righteous demands of the covenant, for which the prophets, John the Baptist and now Jesus call. God will therefore remove them from leadership, since they have proven faithless, and raise up leaders who will be faithful to God and to their calling. Thus the parable can be understood as an example of the prophetic woe oracle that predicts God's judgment on the unjust leaders.

The content of the parable is very close in

---

[33]Augustine's interpretation of this parable is notorious: the traveler is Adam, the thieves the devil and his minions who rob him of eternal life (he is "half dead"—alive as a mortal but not for eternity). The priests and the Levite represent the Old Testament law and sacrifices, which do nothing to help his condition. The Samaritan is, of course, Jesus, who dresses Adam's wounds and hands him over to the care of the inn (the church), and especially the innkeeper (the apostle Paul), to cure him. However sound Augustine's theology may be, as a reading of the parable's meaning for Jesus' audience or the Evangelist's audience this is quite a misstep.

all three Synoptic Gospels, but Mark and Luke appear to preserve Jesus' original point and an interpretation of the parable that would be very much at home in the ministry of Jesus. The parable is used in other ways, with other meanings, however, in the early church. Matthew's Gospel has preserved this later application and extension of the parable, chiefly in the modest alteration of "others" (Mk 12:9; Lk 20:16) to "a nation [ethnei] producing the fruits of it" (RSV). The parable thus becomes an explanation and legitimation of the church's predominantly Gentile constituency and of the Jewish people's rejection of their Messiah. It also becomes in Matthew, at least, a challenge to the "nation" (Christians) that has inherited the vineyard (now spiritualized to mean "God's promises" rather than the governance of the land of Israel) to offer those timely fruits.

Similarly, in the context of Jesus' ministry the argument concerning true defilement (Mt 15:1-20; Mk 7:1-23) was Jesus' defense of his disciples' practice and a critique of Pharisees' emphasis on ritual purity. Mark gives a clear indication, however, of how Jesus' ruling (pronouncement)—it is not what enters the mouth but what comes out of a person that defiles him or her—was applied in the early church. This becomes, for Christians struggling with whether or not to follow the *kashrut* regulations of Torah (also a part of the church's Scriptures), an argument against their ongoing validity. The Marcan gloss, "Thus he declared all foods clean," brings the parable into the orbit of a very real concern of early Christians in the post-Easter period. The mixed church of Jews and Gentiles is thereby focused on pursuing ethical "purity" instead, a goal that can be shared by Jews and Gentiles in the one church without calling attention to racial or ethnic differences. The controversy, in which Jesus so clearly bests his critics, also continues to function as assurance to the Christians in the face of criticisms from Jewish detractors, throwing the accusation back at them.

Form criticism thus stimulates our thinking about how Jesus traditions were used in the early church, pushing us beyond the question of biographical interests to the interests of community formation, moving us from regarding the Gospel traditions in terms of historical questions and the agenda of historical criticism on to studying them as pastoral resource and proclamation about Jesus' significance for the church and the world.

THE COMPOSITION AND RELATIONSHIP OF THE GOSPELS

Why write a Gospel? If the independent units of tradition had sufficed for the church for three decades, why even write a Gospel? Shouldn't the concerns and needs of the Evangelists' communities be addressed by a letter or sermon, with some supporting references to Jesus traditions, as in so many other situations in the early church?

Only two of the four Gospels offer any explicit indication of the Evangelist's purpose. Luke's prologue (Lk 1:1-4) suggests on the one hand that a number of such accounts already existed at the time of Luke's writing and that he is adding his efforts to this endeavor. Why? He seeks to confirm the "catechesis," or instruction, that his reader received. Theophilus, whether an actual person (the name would be quite in keeping with Greek practices of naming children) or a sort of representative for any reader (any "friend of God"), has been instructed already in the Christian faith. Luke intends for his work (Luke-Acts) to confirm Theophilus in his new way of life as a follower of the Way. A narrative tapestry of Jesus traditions and sayings presents to Theophilus a picture of the Jesus he has believed in. The church's claims about Jesus are confirmed as Theophilus reads or hears about the preparation for Jesus' coming, ministry, and death and resurrection "according to the Scriptures," and, indeed, about the ongoing work of the Holy Spirit through the community of Jesus' followers, again "according to Scripture." Theophilus is confirmed in the community's way of life, values and goals as the narrative demonstration proceeds.

The Fourth Gospel includes the brief notice near the end that while many other signs of Jesus could be recounted, "these are written so that you [the reader] may come to believe that Jesus is the Messiah, the Son of God, and that through believing you may have life in his name" (Jn 20:31 NRSV). While this could be regarded as an evangelistic purpose, it might also be read as an indication that the fourth Evangelist wrote to confirm Christians in a particular interpretation of the significance of Jesus (i.e., as "Son of God") that is life-giving, thus shaping and solidifying the Christian faith they already had.

Other possible aims exist, but in the absence of other explicit statements by Evangelists we can only theorize. One possible reason for composition would be to undermine Christologies and views of discipleship that were not consonant with the apostolic teaching. The *Gospel of Thomas,* though probably a second-century composition and not a text directly addressed by an Evangelist, at least shows us the possible emergence of a "Gospel" that took Jesus in a different direction (in particular, a Gnostic direction). We see glimpses of another Christology behind the opponents in 1 John and quite possibly behind 2 Corinthians. Discrete sayings or stories could be insufficient for refutation. What was required was context, a story line that showed Jesus' path of messiahship to glory *through the cross,* which remained the part of discipleship most eagerly avoided.

Another purpose might include providing a resource for training new believers. Matthew's Gospel was used in catechesis very early, and there is no reason to suppose that it was not so used from the first. Oral tradition served this function, and teaching new disciples would continue to be relational. Now, however, the oral traditions were fixed in writing and set within the Evangelist's framework of interpretation as an aid to the catechist and as a safeguard for the continuity of the community's understanding of those traditions.

A final observation rests on the determination of the genre of the Gospels. In the ancient world a way of life might best be demonstrated and recommended through the portrait of its best (or first) representative or proponent. Equally effective as a letter or hortatory speech for motivating behavior, the "life" (*bios, vita*) presented a pattern for living to its readers. Example and authoritative teaching (and not only argument, as in epistolary literature) would have a profound influence on the hearers and readers. We saw earlier how the Gospels resemble other *Lives* in the ancient world that have aims beyond the mere recounting of facts. Like many of these *Lives* the Gospels were written to recommend the way of life exemplified by Jesus as well as to preserve his memory and defend against alternative presentations of Jesus (e.g., executed revolutionary; sorcerer and deceiver). The depiction of Jesus' character and teaching becomes a model for imitation and an articulation of the ethos of the communities addressed. Gradually four Gospels came to be held together by the church as the witness to Jesus and, even more to the point, the witness to the church's ethos, vision and way of life as the community formed by and obedient to this Jesus.

Literary relationships between the Gospels. The widespread rejection among scholars of the model that places each Evangelist in his private cell taking dictation from the Spirit is not to be dismissed as an attack on scriptural authority. Rather, it is often the result of taking careful and intentional note of the similarities and differences between the four Gospels and asking what would most plausibly account for them. This process is not a product of the modern era but goes back at least sixteen centuries to Eusebius and to Augustine. Eusebius of Caesarea, most famous for his *Ecclesiastical History,* noted and drew detailed attention to the parallel material in the four Gospels. In a sense he created the first synopsis of the Gospels. Numbering each paragraph in each Gospel, Eusebius created tables (called "canons") showing all the parallel paragraphs in all *four* Gospels, then in material common to *three* of the Gospels (one list for Matthew, Mark and Luke, another for Mark, Luke and John, and a third for Matthew, Luke and John), then in material common to any *two* Gospels, and then finally the material special to each one.[34] Augustine addressed not merely the question of the order of the composition of the four Gospels (which had been taken up in the second century) but also their interdependence. It has evolved from there into the discipline of source criticism.

When you place Matthew, Mark and Luke side by side (such is conveniently done using a synopsis of the Gospels), you will be struck by similarities in wording, content (even parenthetical remarks like "let the reader understand" in Mt 24:15; Mk 13:14) and order.[35] At the same time you will note divergences in exact wording, content and arrangement in the same passages. You will also notice blocks of material present in one or two Gospels but not present in the other(s) (e.g., the Sermon on the Mount in Matthew is paralleled in large measure by the Sermon on the Plain in Luke but is completely absent from Mark). If you map out the content of all three Gospels, you will notice that the content and order of Mark is almost completely preserved in both Matthew and Luke (to a greater extent in the former), that about half or more of the teachings of Jesus in Matthew (beyond what can be found in Mark) have a parallel in Luke, and that both Matthew and Luke have a noticeable amount of important Jesus traditions particular to each.

Such observations beg for explanation, which has most commonly been sought in the notion that one or more of the Gospel writers knew and used the work of the other(s). This is especially the case where Matthew and Mark are concerned. Anyone who reads Matthew and Mark in succession will spend the better part of the time reading Mark in a state of déjà vu. Indeed, Mark reads like Matthew with all the long sermons cut out. An early solution promoted by Augustine was to read Mark as an abridgement of Matthew (the "abridger and lackey of Matthew"). There are, however, considerable problems with this view. First, Mark has a message and purpose that go beyond mere abridgement. With his emphasis on the cruciform shape of messiahship and discipleship, it is clear that Mark is preaching through his Gospel, not merely abridging someone else's Gospel. Mark's Gospel, moreover, includes much more detail in his narratives. If he were an abridger, why should he have so little interest in Jesus' discourses, removing such priceless teaching as the Sermon on the Mount, and yet spend more space than his source filling in added details?

Mark and Luke also appear to stand in some kind of literary relationship to one another as well. The two follow the same order of events and even include many of the same details in their narratives. It is especially significant that these are details that are found only in Mark, and not in Matthew. This suggests a relationship between Luke and Mark specifically. Even the fact that Luke does not provide any parallel to the material found in Mark

---

[34]This set of tables and the cover letter to Carpian is still printed in the Nestle-Aland and United Bible Societies editions of the Greek New Testament.

[35]Since they seem to be telling the same story and drawing on the same pool of traditions, they are referred to as the Synoptic Gospels.

6:45—8:26 (i.e., all together in one large block rather than scattered, smaller omissions) becomes a significant clue that Luke is working with Mark as a resource and passes over this block of material for his own reasons.

The large body of shared Jesus sayings in Matthew and Luke raises the question of literary dependence of one on the other or both on a common resource for these teachings of Jesus. The Greek wording is often too similar to be explained as coincidental or as shared knowledge of Aramaic oral traditions. At the same time the order and placement of these sayings varies greatly between Matthew and Luke, each giving the individual sayings a different nuance or application in the way he arranges their context and setting. How can we explain both the similarities and the divergences?

Questions multiply when the Fourth Gospel is brought alongside the other three. What relationship (if any) exists between John and the Synoptic Gospels? There is very little overlap in terms of the selection and order of events narrated. The chronology is quite different in John, who places the cleansing of the temple at the beginning of Jesus' public ministry and distributes that ministry between three Passover festivals. Very little sayings material is shared by John and the Synoptics, and the style of speech is vastly different. In the Synoptics, discourses, where they exist, are made up of collected sayings related by theme. In John, discourses exist as whole entities that are not made up of shorter, discrete (independent) sayings. The style of Jesus' speech in John is further distanced from his speech in the Synoptics by the "revealer" or "self-disclosure" form ("I am the light of world"; "I am the way, the truth, and the life"; and so forth).

Source criticism and the "Synoptic problem." Such observations of the similarities and differences between the Gospels in terms of wording, content and order gave rise to the discipline of source criticism. As its name suggests, source criticism inquires into the ways the author of a particular text may have used other available texts as resources for the new composition. A working premise is that ancient authors frequently relied heavily on written and oral sources and incorporated them, often wholesale, into the new work. Source criticism has been most prominently employed in the study of the literary relationship of the Gospels: holding up the texts of the three Synoptic Gospels and deriving some explanation of the literary relationship that best explains the present form of each text.

The enterprise is not a foreign and modern imposition on the texts. Reflecting on his own experience of composing a Gospel, Luke writes:

> Since many have undertaken to set down an orderly account of the events that have been fulfilled among us, just as they were handed on to us by those who from the beginning were eyewitnesses and servants of the word, I too decided, after investigating everything carefully from the very first, to write an orderly account for you, most excellent Theophilus. (Lk 1:1-3 NRSV)

The opening verse of Luke attests to the existence of written lives of Jesus known to Luke prior to his composition of a new and carefully researched account, as well as the relationship of these written lives to the oral tradition passed on by eyewitnesses of Jesus' ministry, who were also ministers of the Word. As a careful researcher Luke would be expected to have read these lives and to have used what he deemed the most reliable as a literary source for his "orderly account," in addition to weaving in material he found from other sources (written and oral) and deemed authentic and salient to the presentation of Jesus' message and significance.

Source analysis can proceed with greater confidence when comparing two or more texts thought to stand in some kind of literary relationship. Therefore the Synoptic Gospels have been the primary field for such explorations. These texts can be compared side by side for agreement and disagreement in wording, order of material, content, style, topics and theological perspective. All these observations will contribute in some way to a hypothesis concerning which Gospel served as a resource for which, and even for the reconstruction of sources no longer available in their original form.

When studying a single document in search of possible incorporated sources (e.g., John; Acts), the student must proceed more tentatively since there are no obvious source documents available for comparison and confirmation. Here, source analysts look for signals within the single text that one work has been incorporated into another. Important signals include breaks or dislocations in the sequence (including redundancy), stylistic inconsistency within the text, theological inconsistencies (thus reflecting the perspective of two different sources or the Evangelist and one other source) and historical inconsistencies.[36]

What have source critics been able to contribute to the investigation of the literary relationships between the Gospels and our understanding of how the Gospels (particularly here the Synoptic Gospels) came to be composed? This question takes us to the heart of the "Synoptic problem," namely, how to make sense out of both the similarities *and* differences between Matthew, Mark and Luke.

The earliest solution, which still finds proponents today, is that one or more Evangelists used the work of the other Evangelists. Augustine pioneered this view when, in his *On the Harmony of the Gospels*, he suggested that Mark abridged Matthew: "for Matthew is understood to have taken it in hand to construct the record

of the incarnation of the Lord according to the royal lineage, and to give an account of most part of His deeds and words as they stood in relation to this present life of men. Mark follows him closely, and looks like his attendant and epitomizer [abridger]" (*De consensu* 1.2.4).

Toward the end of "On the Harmony of the Gospels" Augustine observes more sharply the Synoptic problem, namely, the concord of Mark with Matthew, on the one hand, and also with Luke, on the other: "Mark . . . holds a course in conjunction with both [the other Synoptists]. For although he is at one with Matthew in the larger number of passages, he is nevertheless at one rather with Luke in some others. And this very fact shows him to stand related at once to the lion [Matthew] and to the steer [Luke]" (*De consensu* 4.10.11). Similar observations would lead J. J. Griesbach in the late eighteenth century to propose that this phenomenon would be best explained if Mark had composed his Gospel by conflating Matthew and Luke. The similarities between Luke and Matthew, in turn, suggested to him that Luke had composed his Gospel using Matthew as a resource.

These theories have the advantage of relying only on documents that we actually have at hand today (that is, they do not rely on hypothetical documents like "Q"), but there are significant problems with either solution.

We have already touched on some of the problems with the idea that Mark used Matthew. How do we reconcile the theory of abridgement with the addition of so many details that do not address the concerns of any community except the desire to be entertained? To do this, especially at the cost of excising whole discourses or poignant episodes,

---

[36]David Wenham, "Source Criticism," in *New Testament Interpretation,* ed. I. H. Marshall (Grand Rapids: Eerdmans, 1977), pp. 144-45. With regard to John, for example, the enumeration of the first two signs and the purpose statement in Jn 20:30-31 about the purpose of recounting "signs" has been taken as a signal that the Fourth Evangelist used a "signs source," a text recounting selected miracles of Jesus, interpreted as signs of who he was. The farewell discourse of Jn 13—17 has been thought to incorporate two Johannine traditions concerning Jesus' final teaching to his disciples, since chapters 15-16 cover much of the same topics as chapter 14, only in expanded form.

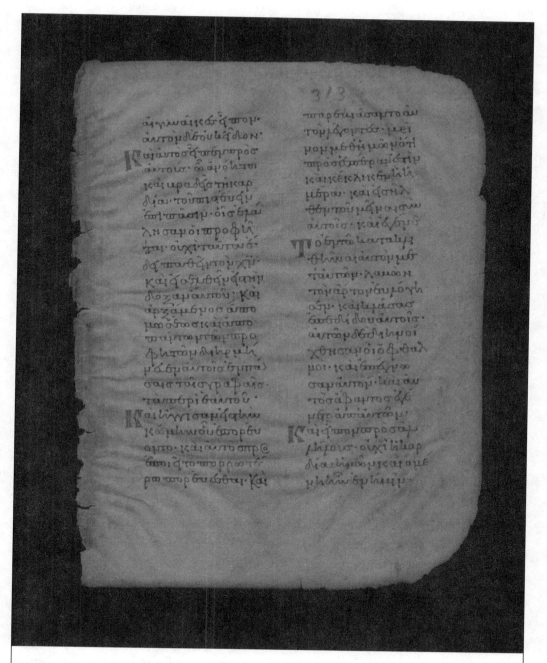

Figure 4.1. A page from a sixth-century New Testament codex written in cursive script rather than the printed capitals of the major uncial codices. This page and its reverse (not shown) features the story of the walk to Emmaus from Luke 24. (Courtesy of Ashland Theological Seminary)

nativity narratives and links with Jewish Scriptures—all of which would have been relevant material for the faith and edification of the audiences—is difficult to explain. Additionally, there are several points where a difference between Matthew and Mark is more readily explained by positing that Matthew has corrected or clarified Mark. For example, Mark incorrectly lumps two quotations together as quotations from Isaiah (Mk 1:2-3), where one of the two quotations is really from Malachi. Matthew smoothes this over by omitting the quotation from Malachi so that only Isaiah is quoted (Mt 3:3). It is thus a more reasonable explanation that Matthew used Mark, cutting out details and making more room for the inclusion of large amounts of Jesus' teachings, correcting a few problems in Mark along the way, than that Mark used Matthew and threw in some errors and difficulties. Finally, a plausible purpose for an abridged Gospel has not been proposed. For example, the idea of Mark as a missionary tract falters on the fact that Jesus' ethical teachings (i.e., most of the material that Mark would have been supposed to omit) would have been of first value in winning admiration for Jesus among outsiders and arousing their interest in this figure.

There are also several difficulties affirming that Luke used Matthew:[37]

1. Luke's handling of Matthew's discourse material is especially difficult to explain. Why would Luke take Matthew's mission discourse (Mt 10:5-42) and scatter its contents in five different places (Lk 9:1-6; 21:12-17; 12:2-7, 51-52; 14:26-27)? Why would Luke break up Matthew's elegant "Sermon on the Mount" to create an abridged "Sermon on the Plain" with a very different set of Beatitudes (now with Woes) and a very different Lord's Prayer, scattering the remainder of the material throughout the Gospel? Why does Luke separate Matthew's fifth discourse on "the end" into two separate discourses on the end (Lk 17 and 21)? Can we believe that Luke separated out Mark's version from Matthew's version and placed the two in different contexts rather than simply preserving Matthew's version? These questions especially lead many to favor the hypothesis that both Luke and Matthew are using a sayings collection, each arranging them independently of the other.

2. In the triple tradition Luke rarely includes any of the details or phrases that Matthew has added to Mark (the exceptions being details in the baptism account, the temptation story, the Beelzebul controversy, the commissioning speech and the parable of the mustard seed).[38] Why would Luke, who seems to like detail, carefully and intentionally avoid so many of Matthew's expansions on Mark if he had Matthew on hand? Luke would also have had to treat the two sources very differently, respecting Mark's order and content while approaching Matthew's order and content much more freely, now abridging sayings and discourses, now rearranging, now omitting.

3. Is there a coherent explanation for Luke's decision to omit the Jesus traditions that have come to be known as Matthew's "special material"? Did he have no use for the infancy narratives, a score of parables (e.g., the wheat and the tares, the merchant buying pearls, the dragnet full of good and bad fish, the laborers in the vineyard, and the unforgiving servant), the posting of a guard at the

---

[37]See Scot McKnight, "Source Criticism," in *New Testament Criticism and Interpretation*, ed. D. A. Black and David S. Dockery (Grand Rapids: Zondervan, 1991), pp. 151-55; Stein, *Studying the Synoptic Gospels*, pp. 99-112.

[38]Stein, *Studying the Synoptic Gospels*, pp. 99-104.

tomb or Matthew's resurrection narratives?[39]

4. Is there a coherent explanation for Luke's decision almost always to change the setting and context Matthew gave to the majority of the sayings of Jesus they do share, while at the same time honoring Mark's order of material and Marcan contexts for sayings and the like?

5. If Luke relied on Matthew for this collection of Jesus sayings, we would expect the tradition in Luke to be as theologically developed, or even more so, than the tradition in Matthew. However, very often Jesus' sayings show less signs of development in Luke than in Matthew.

Finally, there are also problems affirming that Mark conflated Matthew and Luke (in addition to the problems with postulating that Mark used Matthew). Ancient editorial practice appears to have been to select one principal source and work in material from other sources as appropriate and necessary, and, moreover, to conflate large blocks of material. Mark is envisioned, however, as moving line by line through two sources, choosing a word or phrase from one, then moving to the other for a word or phrase, weaving them together at such a close and confined level as no other ancient author/editor is seen to have worked.[40]

Because of these objections at every step of the hypothesis, the Griesbach hypothesis remains the minority report among Gospel scholars.[41] Two rather neglected options also merit our consideration, if only as a safeguard against the two-source hypothesis (Matthew and Luke's use of Mark and Q) becoming too assured a dogma. Martin Hengel has drawn attention to the fact that, while Luke's use of Matthew remains problematic in the extreme, the possibility that Matthew has used Mark and Luke has not been given adequate attention and may prove, in the end, the most elegant solution (requiring no formulation of a hypothetical sayings source like Q; see pp. 167-74).[42] Matthew's systematization and rearrangement of Luke's material would certainly be easier to explain than the reverse. J. W. Wenham argues that Matthew and Luke were composed independently of one another, and although both used Mark, they did not use a shared sayings source. Rather, Luke relies on independent traditions for the sayings of Jesus, perhaps coming to him from one of the "seventy" (one of the eyewitnesses he refers to in his preface, Lk 1:1-4). This would also account for the framework of the journey to Jerusalem. Wenham relies on the presupposition (which is plausible enough) that Jesus would have repeated his teachings on numerous occasions, in varying contexts and order.[43] In his view oral tradition (and the variety of channels it could pass through to an Evangelist like Luke) has not been given sufficient weight in solving the Synoptic problem.

---

[39]This kind of question, which also arises as an objection to Lucan priority and Marcan priority, loses a good deal of its force if we posit that the later Evangelists wrote not to *replace* the earlier available Gospels but to supplement them. On the former model we must explain why material is regarded as insufficiently valuable to be retained; on the latter model the later Evangelist would presume that any material not included by him would still be available to the Christian communities in the other Gospel(s).

[40]F. G. Downing, "Compositional Conventions and the Synoptic Problem," *JBL* 107 (1988): 69-85. T. Longstaff, however, has argued that there are other signs in Mark that it is a conflated document (*Evidence of Conflation in Mark? A Study in the Synoptic Problem* [Missoula, Mont.: Scholars, 1977]). This only demonstrates, however, that Mark used sources, not that Mark used Matthew and Luke as his sources in particular.

[41]See the works of William Farmer and David Dungan (in "For Further Reading"), some of its more avid and persistent supporters.

[42]Martin Hengel, *The Four Gospels and the One Gospel of Jesus Christ* (Harrisburg, Penn.: Trinity Press, 2000), pp. 169-207, 303-23.

[43]J. W. Wenham, "Synoptic Independence and the Origin of Luke's Travel Narrative," *NTS* 27 (1981): 507-15.

B. H. Streeter's Solution to the Synoptic Problem

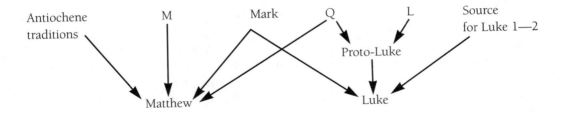

Taken from *The Four Gospels* (New York: MacMillan, 1925), p. 150.

Of all the options the two-source hypothesis has been greeted by the most scholars as the cleanest solution to the question of the literary interdependence of the Gospels. This hypothesis also meets with objections, but not nearly so many and so difficult. It is important always to remember, however, that it remains a theory, not a given. According to this hypothesis Matthew and Luke each used Mark as a source, together with a sayings collection (labeled "Q," an abbreviation of the German *Quelle,* or "source"). Matthew and Luke, however, each drew on their own special traditions as well (often referred to by the symbols "M" and "L"). About one-quarter of Matthew and one-third of Luke represents traditions not shared by the other Evangelists, and gives each Gospel even more of a distinctive character. These latter components make the label, "two-source hypothesis," something of a misnomer.

The lynchpin of the two-source hypothesis is Marcan priority, the availability of Mark's Gospel as a resource for Matthew and Luke. Supporting arguments have included the following:[44]

1. Given the close correspondence between Matthew and Mark, and objections against the view that Mark abridged Matthew, the reverse (Matthew's use of Mark) becomes the more likely explanation.

2. Unusual or rough expressions in Mark are given a smoother, more refined expression in the Matthean and Lucan parallels. David Aune refers to this as the process of "literaturization,"[45] referring not only to the improvement of Mark's style by Luke and Matthew but also to the overall improvement of Mark's life (*bios*) of Jesus. The addition of stories that address the topic of the origin and birth of the subject of the *bios,* a frequent component of ancient "lives," enhances the presentation of Jesus' significance. The improvement of the narrative of the death of the subject and its aftermath (in this case, Jesus' resurrection and ascension) also brings Mark's Gospel more in line with the expected topics of the "Life."

3. Material that might be theologically problematic in Mark tends to be resolved in

---

[44]See, further, Stein, *Studying the Synoptic Gospels,* pp. 49-96.
[45]Aune, *New Testament and Its Literary Environment,* p. 65.

the Matthean and Lucan parallels (e.g., Jesus' *inability to do* miracles in Nazareth in Mk 6:5-6 simply becomes the fact that Jesus *did not do* many miracles there in Mt 13:58).[46] Mistakes in Mark are also omitted or corrected in Matthew and Luke.

4. Observations from redaction analysis tend to strengthen this theory. For example, the appearance of the term "righteousness" seven times in Matthew is not paralleled in Mark or Luke. Is it more likely that Matthew added this word to Marcan material to introduce and underscore this theological concept, or that both Mark and Luke wished to eliminate a theme that otherwise represents a central Christian value?[47] Conversely, stylistic features of Mark appear in the parallel sections of Matthew *more often* than in Matthean material not shared with Mark.[48] This also suggests that Mark was available for Matthew to use as a source rather than the reverse.

As the second source for Matthew and Luke this hypothesis postulates an early collection of Jesus' sayings, "Q." B. H. Streeter, who gave the hypothesis its classic form, understood Q to have been composed not after the pattern of the *bios* but rather after the pattern of the Old Testament prophetic book, narrating the baptism and temptation as a counterpart to the "call" to the messianic office and then focusing on sayings (comparable to oracles of the prophet) with the "occasional narrative to explain some piece of teaching."[49] This collection, if it existed in written form,

might have predated Mark as well.

Aware of the vulnerability of proposing a hypothetical document to solve the mystery of the relationship of the Synoptic Gospels, scholars advance the following arguments in favor of Q:

1. The existence of a sayings collection is in itself quite plausible, given the widespread composition of works of this kind[50] and the appropriateness of such a collection (or collections) being made about Jesus. The discovery of the *Gospel of Thomas* confirms early Christian interest in collecting the sayings of Jesus apart from a narrative framework.

2. In the likely event that Luke did not use Matthew (or vice versa), the large body of shared tradition and the often very close verbal similarity between Matthew and Luke in reproducing these Jesus sayings and traditions needs to be explained somehow. An early, written sayings source would provide this explanation.

3. A good number of these roughly 230 sayings follow a shared order in Matthew and Luke (compare, for example, the order of topics in the Sermon on the Mount and the Sermon on the Plain), allowing for the fact that Matthew has pursued an editorial policy of grouping these sayings (together with his distinctive materials) into five major discourses, which would naturally preclude wider agreement in order between the two Gospels.[51] It must be admitted that Matthew's rearrange-

---

[46]McKnight, "Source Criticism," p. 150.

[47]Ibid., pp. 150-51.

[48]The words "more often" need to be stressed, for features that are more prominent characteristics of Matthean style also appear in Mark and Luke; see Lamar Cope, *Matthew: A Scribe Trained for the Kingdom of Heaven*, CBQMS 5 (Washington: Catholic Biblical Association, 1976).

[49]B. H. Streeter, *The Four Gospels* (New York: Macmillan, 1925), p. 291.

[50]See J. S. Kloppenborg, *The Formation of Q* (Philadelphia: Fortress, 1989), pp. 263-325, 329-41, for an extensive catalog and discussion of this literary form. One need think only of wisdom collections in Israel and the ancient Near East for one important body of similar literature (the collection and preservation of the words of the sages).

[51]See C. M. Tuckett, *Studies on Q* (Edinburgh: T & T Clark, 1996), pp. 34-38.

The Contents of Q

Q represents the large body of sayings shared by Matthew and Luke. The precise delineation of the contents of Q remains a matter of debate and uncertainty. For example, some allowance may need to be made for the possibility that Matthew included some sayings from Q that Luke found uncongenial to his purposes (like Mt 10:5b-6, 23), and that Luke included some sayings that Matthew would have omitted. The following list of shared material between Luke and Matthew may be taken as a representative sample of what this early sayings collection might have contained.[a] Reading these passages will give the reader a flavor of what the Q source, on its own, might have sounded like. The reconstruction of the precise wording of Q is a specialized discipline, often moving scholars to parallels in the *Gospel of Thomas* as well. As a general rule of thumb the Lucan wording and order tends to be preferred as a closer guide to Q.

John the Baptist's preaching (Lk 3:7-9//Mt 3:7-10)

The temptation story (Lk 4:1-13//Mt 4:1-11)

Beatitudes (Lk 6:20-23//Mt 5:3-12)

Meeting evil with good (Lk 6:27-36//Mt 5:39-48; 7:12)

Judging others (Lk 6:37-42//Mt 7:1-5; 10:24; 15:14)

Trees and their fruit (Lk 6:43-45//Mt 7:15-20)

Building on sand and on rock (Lk 6:47-49//Mt 7:24-27)

Healing the centurion's servant (Lk 7:1-10//Mt 8:5-10, 13)

John the Baptist's inquiry (Lk 7:18-35//Mt 11:2-19)

Excuses delaying discipleship (Lk 9:57-60//Mt 8:19-22)

The mission of Jesus' disciples; woes upon Galilean cities (Lk 10:2-16//Mt 9:37-38; 10:9-15; 11:21-23)

Jesus' thanksgiving; all things given to the Son (Lk 10:21-24//Mt 11:25-27; 13:16-17)

The Lord's Prayer (Lk 11:2-4//Mt 6:9-13)

Ask, seek, knock (Lk 11:9-13//Mt 7:7-11)

Jesus and Beelzebul (Lk 11:14-23//Mt 12:22-32)

The return of the unclean spirit (Lk 11:24-26//Mt 12:43-45)

Jonah and the Queen of the South (Lk 11:29-32//Mt 12:38-42)

The eye is the light of the body (Lk 11:33-36//Mt 5:15; 6:22-23)

Woes upon the scribes and Pharisees (Lk 11:37-52//Mt 23:4-7, 13-16)

Exhortation to bold witness (Lk 12:2-12//Mt 10:19, 26-33; 12:32)

---

[a]As compiled by M. A. Powell, *Jesus as a Figure in History* (Louisville, Ky.: Westminster John Knox, 1998), pp. 39-40. John S. Kloppenborg, a Q scholar of international renown, delineates Q's "probable" contents thus: Lk 3:3, 7b-9, 16b-17; 4:1-13; 4:16a; 6:20-33; Mt 5:41; Lk 6:34-49; 7:1b-2, 6b-10, 18-19, 22-35; 9:57-62; 10:2-16, 21-22, 23b-24; 11:2-4, 9-36, 39-44, 46-52; 12:2-21, 22b-31, 33-34, 39-40, 42b-46, 49, 51-56, 58-59; 13:18-21, 24-30, 34-35; 14:11 [18:14], 16-24, 26-27 [17:33], 34-35; 15:4-10; 16:13, 16-16; 17:1b-2, 3b-4, 6b, 20-21, 23-24, 37b, 26-30, 34-35; 19:12-13, 15b-26; 22:28-30. Doubtful possibilities include Lk 3:21-22; Mt 10:5b-6, 23; Lk 10:25-28; 11:5-8; 12:35-38; 14:5; 17:7-10 (J. S. Kloppenborg Verbin, *Excavating Q: The History and Setting of the Sayings Gospel* [Minneapolis: Fortress, 2000], p. 100).

Against being anxious for food and clothing (Lk 12:22-34//Mt 6:19-21, 25-33)

The thief; the watchful servant (Lk 12:39-46//Mt 24:43-51)

Jesus brings division (Lk 12:51-53//Mt 10:34-36)

Discerning the weather forecast, but not the times (Lk 12:54-56//Mt 16:2-3)

Make peace with your adversary (Lk 12:57-59//Mt 5:25-26)

The narrow and wide gates; knocking at the door of the kingdom (Lk 13:23-30//Mt 7:13-14, 22-23; 8:11-12)

Parables of the mustard seed and the yeast (Lk 13:18-21//Mt 13:31-35)

Lament over Jerusalem (Lk 13:34-35//Mt 23:37-39)

Parable of the Banquet (Lk 14:15-24//Mt 22:1-14)

The cost of discipleship (Lk 14:26-27//Mt 10:37-38)

The lost sheep (Lk 15:1-7//Mt 18:12-14)

Two masters (Lk 16:13//Mt 6:24)

John as the turning point in history (Lk 16:16-17//Mt 5:18; 11:13)

Causing sin; restoring the sinner; faith as a mustard seed (Lk 17:1-6//Mt 18:6-7, 15, 20-22)

The sudden appearance of the Son of Man (Lk 17:23-27, 33-37//Mt 24:17-18, 26-28, 37-41)

The parable of the talents (Lk 19:11-27//Mt 25:14-30)

---

ment of the materials makes this one of the less persuasive arguments.

4. The presence of doublets in Matthew and in Luke suggests that each Evangelist was working with two shared sources. For example, Matthew and Luke both incorporate Mark's sayings on discipleship—"If any would come after me, let them deny themselves and take up their cross daily and follow me. Those who seek to save their lives will lose it; whoever loses it for my sake will save it" (Mk 8:34-35)—at the appropriate place in their parallel narratives (i.e., after Peter's confession; see Mt 16:24 and Lk 9:23). Matthew and Luke, however, each incorporate a very similar saying at a different point in their Gospels (Mt 10:38-39; Lk 14:27 and 17:33). This suggests that Matthew and Luke have incorporated both Mark's version of this saying and a second tradition of the same saying (i.e., the tradition learned from Q).

The two-source hypothesis has also met with objections, though these are fewer and more readily answered than those addressed to the Griesbach hypothesis. The first question concerns agreements in wording between Matthew and Luke *against* Mark.[52] Where there is a triple tradition (a narrative or saying preserved in all three Synoptics), given the two-source hypothesis, we would expect agreement of Matthew and/or Luke with Mark, or the divergence of Matthew *or* Luke against Mark, but not agreement of Matthew and Luke against their reputed source. Is this not rather a sign that Luke used Matthew (or vice versa)?

Many of these agreements can be attributed to stylistic tendencies on the part of Matthew and Luke. For example, Matthew and Luke both tend to prefer coordinating clauses with the conjunction *de* rather than *kai*, Mark's preference (both are functionally the equivalent of the English *and*). Another example is

---

[52]See, further, Stein, *Studying the Synoptic Gospels,* pp. 125-42; Streeter, *Four Gospels,* pp. 295-331.

Matthew and Luke's replacement of present tense verbs in Mark with past tense verbs. Thus many can reasonably be attributed to Matthew and Luke sharing similar editorial policies. Since both Matthew and Luke seek to improve Mark grammatically and stylistically, and do so at so many points, it is not unreasonable that they would have made identical improvements independently some of the time, and thus look like they "agree" against Mark. The tendency of Christian copyists to harmonize Luke's Gospel to Matthew's text, or the possibility of an early scribal "corruption" of Mark's text (such that Mark, Matthew and Luke would have originally agreed, but Mark's text got changed in the process of being copied again and again), could explain a number of these agreements.

The most impressive agreements of Matthew and Luke against Mark can be explained by a mere six places of overlap between Mark and the Q material. This would require Q to have a version of the temptation story, the Beelzebul controversy, the parable of the mustard seed, the mission charge to the Twelve, the request for a sign and parts of the eschatological discourse.[53] There is no reason that Mark and Q, as independent collections of Jesus traditions, should not overlap at several points and perhaps even beyond these. They could also be explained by the influence of oral tradition at these points, with both Matthew and Luke knowing the same, more compelling version of the tradition than Mark's in current use, and conforming Mark's version to that oral version.

The other major objections to the two-source hypothesis center on lingering doubts about Q, the more speculative theories about its stages of development, community and distinctive Christology perhaps discrediting the more reasonable aspects of the hypothesis. This stumbling block will not be removed unless a future archaeological dig should turn up a manuscript of Q. If one retains a flexible conception of Q (probably a written collection, but still quite possibly a cipher for shared oral tradition), the two-source hypothesis remains the most viable explanation advanced to date, and our discussion of the Synoptic Gospels will proceed on this basis. According to this view, then, both Matthew and Luke respect Mark's achievement, and both build on his foundation. Mark's vision of Jesus' messiahship and the nature of discipleship, for example, is fully taken up by Matthew and Luke. Each wants, however, to add a number of dimensions to the presentation of Jesus to the church. This purpose is reflected in the actual differences, the ways in which Matthew and Luke have used Mark, contextualized material from Q and incorporated still other traditions special to each.

FOR FURTHER READING

Bock, Darrell L. "Form Criticism," pp. 175-96. In *New Testament Criticism and Interpretation*. Edited by David A. Black and David S. Dockery. Grand Rapids: Zondervan, 1991.

Catchpole, David R. "Tradition History," pp. 165-80. In *New Testament Interpretation: Essays on Principles and Methods*. Edited by I. Howard Marshall. Grand Rapids: Eerdmans, 1977.

Conzelmann, Hans, and Andreas Lindemann. *Interpreting the New Testament*, pp. 45-87. Peabody, Mass.: Hendrickson, 1988.

Dungan, David L. *A History of the Synoptic Problem: The Canon, the Text, the Composition, and the Interpretation of the Gospels*. New York: Doubleday, 1999.

---

[53]Tuckett, *Studies on Q*, p. 31. A critic of the two-source hypothesis has referred to this derisively as the "blessed overlap" but the defense requires only a very small blessing! (See David L. Dungan, "Mark—the Abridgement of Matthew and Luke," in *Jesus and Man's Hope* [Pittsburgh: Pittsburgh Theological Seminary Press, 1970], p. 73.)

Farmer, William R. *The Synoptic Problem: A Critical Analysis.* 2nd ed. Dillsboro: Western North Carolina, 1976.

―――――. *The Gospel of Jesus: The Pastoral Relevance of the Synoptic Problem.* Louisville, Ky.: Westminster John Knox, 1994.

McKnight, Edgar V. *What Is Form Criticism?* Philadelphia: Fortress, 1969.

McKnight, Scot. "Source Criticism," pp. 137-72. In *New Testament Criticism and Interpretation.* Edited by David A. Black and David S. Dockery. Grand Rapids: Zondervan, 1991.

Nickle, Keith F. *The Synoptic Gospels: An Introduction.* 2nd ed. Louisville, Ky.: Westminster John Knox, 2001.

Patzia, Arthur G. *The Making of the New Testament,* pp. 40-60. Downers Grove, Ill.: InterVarsity Press, 1995.

Stanton, Graham N. *Gospel Truth? New Light on Jesus and the Gospels,* pp. 49-76. Valley Forge, Penn.: Trinity Press, 1995.

―――――. *A Gospel for a New People,* pp. 23-84. Grand Rapids: Eerdmans, 1993.

Stein, Robert H. *Studying the Synoptic Gospels: Origin and Interpretation.* 2nd ed. Grand Rapids: Baker, 2001.

Streeter, B. H. *The Four Gospels: A Study of Origins.* New York: Macmillan, 1925.

Taylor, Vincent. *The Formation of the Gospel Tradition.* London: Macmillan, 1935.

Travis, Stephen H. "Form Criticism," pp. 153-64. In *New Testament Interpretation: Essays on Principles and Methods.* Edited by I. Howard Marshall. Grand Rapids: Eerdmans, 1977.

Tuckett, Christopher M. *The Revival of the Griesbach Hypothesis.* SNTSMS 44. Cambridge: Cambridge University Press, 1982.

Wenham, David. "Source Criticism," pp. 139-52. In *New Testament Interpretation: Essays on Principles and Methods.* Edited by I. Howard Marshall. Grand Rapids: Eerdmans, 1977.

Witherington, Ben, III. "Principles for Interpreting the Gospels and Acts." *Ashland Theological Journal* 19 (1997): 35-70.

Is Q the lost Gospel of a forgotten Christianity? Although the *probability* that a sayings source (Q) existed in written form and was used by both Matthew and Luke is very high (but only if the two-source hypothesis is espoused), many scholars are seeking more from Q than can be reasonably expected from a hypothetical document. Within the parameters of the two-source hypothesis the contents of Q can be tentatively reconstructed from the material common to Matthew and Luke but absent from Mark (with just a few, plausible exceptions of overlap with Mark). But there are a number of obstacles that should never erase the description "tentative" from our minds.[54]

• The wording of Q has to be reconstructed by picking and choosing from the wording of the parallel sayings in Matthew and Luke or positing a third alternative that would plausibly have been developed two ways into a Matthean and Lucan form. The editorial tendencies of the Evangelists often help the scholar decide which Evangelist is more likely to have altered the Q material, but this criterion is not always helpful (and it assumes that neither Evangelist *learned dis-*

---

[54]Reconstructing Q from Matthew and Luke would be akin to trying to reconstruct Mark from Matthew and Luke if we did not have Mark. How close would such a hypothetical reconstruction of Mark come to the actual Mark we are fortunate enough to have available (see Wenham, "Synoptic Independence and the Origin of Luke's Travel Narrative," p. 514 n. 3). Kloppenborg, to be sure, shows an awareness of all these issues and the fact that Q scholars should temper their methodologies and findings accordingly (*Excavating Q,* pp. 91-111).

tinctive emphases from Q). It also assumes that the text of Q was fairly well fixed at the time of its use by the Evangelists.

- The contents of Q are impossible to fix with precision. Q might have been much fuller than the traditions that comprise the intersection of Matthew and Luke (against Mark), including sayings that neither Evangelist desired to include as well as material that only one of the Evangelists desired to include (i.e., some of the material designated as "M" or "L"—the material peculiar to Matthew or Luke). A version of Q might even have been the source for Luke's distinctive passion narrative, which, if true, would radically change evaluations of Q and "Q Christianity."[55]

- It is still unclear that Q must represent a *single* written source rather than several shorter collections.

Nevertheless, confidence in the Two-Source Hypothesis and in the existence of Q has inevitably led to confident reconstructions of Q. This process has culminated in the publication, in one of the most prestigious commentary series, of a critical edition of Q showing the relationship of the reconstruction to parallels from canonical and noncanonical Gospels.[56] Some of these display truly impressive scholarly rigor and discipline, and become mines of information about the formation of the Synoptic tradi-

tion and the use of Jesus traditions before the Gospels, whether or not we make Q our principal focus.[57]

Once Q was given substance as a real text, however, it also became the subject of literary criticism, theological study and redaction criticism. The most controverted result of the latter (especially) is the reconstruction of the stages in the formation of Q. John S. Kloppenborg and Burton Mack have each presented a history of the formation of Q, moving from a stage when Q mainly consisted of wisdom sayings of Jesus, through a stage when prophetic and apocalyptic sayings were added that were critical of Israel. In the third stage the temptation narrative and some sayings about the Torah are added, reflecting a move from the instruction genre to a proto-biography. This reconstruction of the history of Q, then, facilitates the reconstruction of the history of the "community" that compiled, preserved and looked to Q for its inspiration.[58] The assumptions behind such an enterprise are obvious. First, each assumes that only one kind of material originally stood together in this "lost Gospel," namely, the wisdom material. Jesus emerges here as a kind of Jewish or Cynic sage. There is no reason, however, why this should be separated from or conceived as prior to the prophetic and apocalyptic material.[59] The greater assumption, however, is that

---

[55]Streeter proposed that the third Evangelist used Mark and proto-Luke as his source, proto-Luke having already been formed by the combination of Q and L, and complete with the distinctive passion narrative (*Four Gospels*, pp. 199-222). The third Evangelist, then, made proto-Luke his primary authority (hence retaining its passion narrative). But even this does not prove the matter of which source originally contained that Lucan passion narrative. Matthew's nonuse of this tradition does not prove it had been part of L rather than Q, but need only indicate that he chose Mark as his primary authority for the passion narrative. Kloppenborg attempts to dismiss the possibility, and while I concur that a passion narrative would be out of place in what seems to be a sayings collection (but *not* as a Gospel, pace Kloppenborg), it simply remains another unknown about this hypothetical document (see Kloppenborg, *Formation of Q*, pp. 85-87).

[56]J. M. Robinson, P. Hoffman and J. S. Kloppenborg, *Critical Edition of Q*, Hermeneia (Minneapolis: Fortress, 2000).

[57]Especially worth consultation are Kloppenborg, *Formation of Q*; C. M. Tuckett, *Q and the History of Early Christianity* (Edinburgh: T & T Clark, 1996); and E. P. Meadors, *Jesus the Messianic Herald of Salvation* (Tübingen: J. C. B. Mohr/ Paul Siebeck, 1995).

[58]See Kloppenborg Verbin, *Excavating Q*, pp. 166-213.

[59]Indeed, the opposite development—from prophetic and apocalyptic material to a stage where wisdom material comes to be included—has been defended by Siegfried Schulz, *Q—Die Spruchquelle der Evangelisten* (Zurich: Theologischer Verlag, 1972).

the history of redaction of a hypothetical document can be recovered at all—or be a historically meaningful datum if it is! At each stage in this progression of Q research, the results become increasingly tenuous, like the upper stories of a house of cards on a breezy day.[60]

One additional step in this scholarly odyssey requires attention: the proposition that Q provides an alternative and more appropriate basis for shaping Christian faith for the twentieth and twenty-first centuries than the canonical Gospels.[61] Q, especially in its most primitive layer (according to Mack), puts us in touch with the moral teaching of Jesus in a way that is freed from traditional claims about the saving efficacy of Jesus' death, about his vindication in resurrection and about his coming again in judgment—the three tenets of the "mystery of faith" that some scholars and bishops find distasteful.[62]

The reader of such discussions will need to sharpen his or her critical faculties in order to consider the merits of other explanations that a scholar might not present (at least not as persuasively as the explanation she or he advocates). Does the existence of a sayings collection like Q necessarily—or even probably—signify a lack of interest in or conviction about Jesus' death and resurrection on the part of those who preserved these sayings? Or was this sayings collection preserved, read and proclaimed by Christians in the context of their understanding of Jesus' death as a death "for them," of their belief in Jesus' resurrection, and of their conviction that he would indeed return as Judge?[63] Would Matthew and Luke have found the collection so congenial to their faith in a dying, risen and returning Christ, and incorporated it wholesale into their Gospels as a valuable and viable source, had it reflected a radically different Christianity? Even if many manuscripts of Q in each of the various recensions proposed should be discovered, the answer would still elude us. An artifact like Q does not tell us the limits of the beliefs of those who wrote, read and used it. Those are details to be filled in as each scholar decides and desires, usually according to his or her own convictions. The interest in Q as a representative of the "difference and diversity" within early Christianity can easily be seen to serve the interests of legitimating one emerging stream in the diverse landscape of modern Christianity.[64]

There are many documents known to have existed in antiquity that survive only as a name in a list of writings or a fleeting reference in some other author's work. So the fact that no manuscript of Q has surfaced is a poor ar-

---

[60]N. T. Wright remarks: "The blithe 'reconstruction' not only of Q, not only of its different stages of composition, but even of complete communities whose beliefs are accurately reflected in these different stages, betokens a naive willingness to believe in anything as long as it is nothing like Mark (let alone Paul)" (*Jesus and the Victory of God* [Minneapolis: Fortress, 1996], p. 81). It is ironic that the flight from Christianity as represented by Mark's Gospel and Pauline Christianity, which were deemed too far removed from the historical realities and too much given to ideological and theological overlay (i.e., too hard to believe), should result in so many taking refuge in the hypothetical shelter of the Q community!

[61]Adolf Harnack originally proposed this in *The Sayings of Jesus* (London: Williams and Norgate, 1908); the proposal has been given new life by Burton Mack and, indirectly, in the work of the Jesus Seminar that has found the majority of its authentic sayings in the Q material. See Mack's *The Lost Gospel* (San Francisco: Harper, 1993).

[62] We will return to this particular move when we consider the Quest for the Historical Jesus.

[63]Streeter himself had suggested that Q was a supplement to the readily available oral tradition about the "passion and its redemptive significance" (*Four Gospels*, p. 292), and that the latter would be the assumed context for hearing and using Q. I cannot help but think of the various kinds of collections of Jesus' sayings that circulate in popular religious bookstores, like *What Jesus Said About It* (New York: New American Library, 1970). The material in such books contains nothing about the preexistence of the Son or Jesus' birth, death, resurrection or coming again. Rather, they are compendia of Jesus' ethical teachings. But they are written (for the most part) and read (for the most part) by people who adhere to the traditional Christian faith. The silence is a function of the genre, not of the theology of the "community" that writes and preserves such documents.

[64]The phrase comes from Kloppenborg Verbin, *Excavating Q*, p. 408.

gument against its plausibility. At the same time some New Testament scholars have not been examples of moderation and judicious judgment in the claims that have been made about and on the basis of a completely hypothetical construct.

FOR FURTHER READING ON THE Q SOURCE

Attridge, Harold W. "Reflections on Research into Q." *Semeia* 55 (1992): 222-34.

Catchpole, David R. *The Quest for Q.* Edinburgh: T & T Clark, 1993.

Goodacre, Mark. *The Case Against Q.* Harrisburg, Penn.: Trinity Press, 2002.

Kloppenborg Verbin, John S. *Excavating Q: The History and Setting of the Sayings Gospel.* Minneapolis: Fortress, 2000.

————. *The Formation of Q: Trajectories in Ancient Wisdom Collections.* Philadelphia: Fortress, 1989.

Mack, Burton L. *The Lost Gospel: The Book of Q and Christian Origins.* San Francisco: Harper, 1993.

Meadors, Edward P. *Jesus the Messianic Herald of Salvation.* Tübingen: J. C. B. Mohr/Paul Siebeck, 1995.

Robinson, James M., Paul Hoffman and John S. Kloppenborg. *The Critical Edition of Q.* Hermeneia. Minneapolis: Fortress, 2000.

Stanton, Graham N. *Gospel Truth? New Light on Jesus and the Gospels,* pp. 63-76. Valley Forge, Penn.: Trinity Press, 1995.

Tuckett, Christopher M. *Q and the History of Early Christianity.* Edinburgh: T & T Clark, 1996.

Vaage, L. E. *Galilean Upstarts: Jesus' First Followers According to Q.* Valley Forge, Penn.: Trinity Press, 1994.

THE FOURFOLD GOSPEL COLLECTION

Matthew, Mark, Luke and John were not the only attempts at presenting a narrative interpretation of Jesus. Indeed, the essence of a Gospel as an interpretation of Jesus and the promotion of a corresponding way of life becomes ever clearer when these four are set alongside the "other" Gospels. The Jesus Seminar brought a great deal of attention to the *Gospel of Thomas,* a Gnostic Gospel written in Coptic (an Egyptian dialect) in the second century. It was discovered among the Nag Hammadi Library, a cache of literature discovered in Egypt in 1947. *Thomas* is a collection of sayings attributed to Jesus, similar in form to Q (although Q is said to have contained at least three narratives: the baptism of Jesus, temptation in the wilderness and the healing of the centurion's servant), and also to dozens of pure sayings collections associated with wisdom circles. About one half of its sayings have parallels in the canonical Gospels; the rest belong to another tradition entirely.

Thomas, as we have it, promotes a Gnostic Jesus for Gnostic Christians. Its tendency and ideology are immediately apparent. While some scholars have dubbed this the "fifth Gospel," bearing independent witness to Jesus, most are much more skeptical about its value. The early church gave no thought at all to its preservation and promotion. Only one complete manuscript and two or three fragments have been found, which means it wasn't considered sufficiently valuable to be copied often, distributed widely and preserved. Even its strongest advocates admit that at most it gives us five new authentic sayings of Jesus, but even its usefulness as parallel material is questionable because it may be directly dependent on the canonical Gospels. As it stands the *Gospel of Thomas* bears witness to what the early church considered "another Jesus, a different Gospel."

Three other fragments of ancient Gospels have also received considerable attention in connection with the quest for the historical Jesus, namely, the *Gospel of Peter,* the *Secret Gospel of Mark* and the fragments of the Egerton Gospel. Despite the opposition of some (like John Dominic Crossan, who favors the *Gospel of Peter*), generally these Gospels are viewed as dependent on the canonical Gospels, but they reshaped the material for a purpose that was not consonant with the universally received witness of the apostles. The early church fathers also preserved within their writings fragments of three Jewish Christian Gospels: the *Gospel of the Ebionites,* the *Gospel of the Hebrews* and the *Gospel of the Nazoreans.* These reflect the interests of believers who wished to maintain their Jewish identity together with their Christian confession, a concern reflected in many places in the early church (see Galatians and Acts 15, for example). Since they did not reflect the larger church's understanding of Jesus' significance for bringing together a new humanity, these also never enjoyed a wide following.

That the "Great Church" (the streams of Christianity that would eventually emerge as "orthodox" Christianity) never gave a special place to *Thomas, Peter, Secret Gospel of Mark* or the Jewish Christian Gospels is not much of a surprise. They were written for small circles within the church that wanted to take Jesus in a new direction, often esoteric groups that proved to be sectarian. It is, however, rather remarkable that the churches continued to use side by side the four Gospels we now hold as canonical. This was not an automatic or obvious choice but rather an intentional decision made in the wake of many challenges.

Some Christians living in the early second century, like Papias of Hierapolis, could speak of preferring the oral tradition, to hear the "living word" about Jesus from the mouths of those who saw him. Indeed, oral tradition continued long after the Gospels were committed to writing. Its influence is apparent in the development of the longer ending to Mark's Gospel (Mk 16:9-20) and the introduction of the story of the woman caught in the act of adultery, an originally independent tradition, into the Gospel of John (Jn 7:53—8:11).[65] The decreasing pool of witnesses bearing the "living voice," and the usefulness of the four Gospels for the life and nurture of the church, made the written word the new standard. Toward the middle of the second century Justin Martyr notes that the words of the Evangelists and apostles were being set alongside the Jewish Scriptures.

Some, however, fought the tendency to accept a multiplicity of Gospels. Marcion, the famous proto-Gnostic of the mid-second century, sought to promote a single Gospel as the authoritative witness. He selected Luke (after it was purged by Marcion of Jewish sentiments) as the most congenial to his understanding of Christianity. The multiplicity of Gospels—and especially their "irreconcilable differences"—often played into the hand of Christianity's critics. Celsus, for example, accused the Christians of changing the text of their sacred writings (referring to the Gospels) whenever they encounter criticism, so they could deny the difficulties.[66] In the last third of the third century Porphyry used the discrepancies in the crucifixion accounts of the Gospels to demonstrate the unreliability of these texts.[67] In 172 Tatian presented his solution to the problem of four Gospels by weav-

---

[65]These texts will be discussed in the chapter on Mark ("The Ending of Mark" and the "Exegetical Skill: Textual Criticism" section).

[66]Dungan, *History of the Synoptic Problem,* p. 63.

[67]Ibid., pp. 94-95

ing the four into one harmonized account called the *Diatessaron* ("through four"). Tatian was disturbed by attacks on the credibility of the Christian faith made by outsiders on the basis of the discrepancies in the Gospels. His teacher, Justin Martyr, tended to deal with these criticisms by harmonizing the Synoptic Gospel accounts when he quoted the Gospel tradition.[68] Tatian took the next step by composing a single, continuous narrative out of the four Gospels. This appealed to many early believers, and harmonies of the Gospels still capture attention today. Many churches in Syria continued to use this version into the fifth century. Indeed, we do not need to go so far as to reorganize and rewrite the four Gospels to follow Tatian's lead: we often speak as if the four Gospels can and should be harmonized into a sort of "Life of Christ" or "Greatest Story Ever Told," and modern movies about the life of Jesus certainly have assisted this tendency.

The majority of Christians, however, eventually opted for accepting the four Gospels in all their individuality and particularity. Irenaeus of Lyons (late second century) strongly advocated the acceptance of four Gospels over one harmonized Gospel, using the four living creatures of Revelation 4 as a divine legitimation of the four pictures of Jesus: (1) the servant-Messiah, the ox of Mark; (2) the lion of the tribe of Judah, the lion of Matthew; (3) the Davidic king, the humanoid creature of Luke; and (4) the one who brought revelation from heaven, the eagle of John. While Irenaeus intends this as an affirmation of the fourfold canon of Gospels, it also attests to the fact that each portrait is distinctive, having its own special character and thus contributing something valuable to the church by virtue of not being blended in with the other three Gospels.[69]

By the end of the second century, the four Gospels were all fairly well established and widely received. Matthew's Gospel received the widest and earliest approval in the Christian community. It is already quoted as Scripture by Clement of Rome (late first century) and Ignatius of Antioch (early second century). Mark and Luke also gained wide recognition early in the process. John's Gospel had a more difficult time gaining acceptance in the wider church beyond Asia Minor, partially on account of the fact that Gnostic Christians found it as conducive to promoting their own system as did orthodox Christians. Second-century church fathers invested a great deal of energy claiming its witness for the apostolic faith, however.

The readers of these four Gospels perceived that these writings gave authentic expression to the readers' own faith. This is an important consideration. As we encountered in the general introduction, canonization was neither a process imposed from above nor a mandate of fourth-century church leaders. The Gospels were, in effect, self-authenticating because their testimony agreed with the inner witness of the majority of believers throughout the Mediterranean world. When a writing bore witness to "a different Jesus, a different gospel," it did not receive a wide reading or acceptance and fell by the wayside or became the peculiar property of some sectarian group. The people knew which writings accorded with the "rule of faith," the central creed or kerygma of the apostolic witnesses. The central pattern found as early as the "Christ hymn" in Philippians 2:5-11 remains the spine of each Evangelist's portrait of Jesus and, tellingly, remains missing in several of the Gospels rejected by the church as a whole. The Gospels

---

[68]Ibid., p. 39.

[69]The discipline of redaction criticism (see the chapter on Matthew) is dedicated to uncovering the distinctive portrait of Jesus in each Gospel while also acknowledging what is the same in all four presentations of Jesus.

that spoke of him who came in self-giving love in obedience to God and calls us to have that same mind, very naturally became authoritative and nurturing texts across the network of churches.

Having embraced a fourfold Gospel collection, leading figures in the early church sought some other solution to the problems of their differences than the paths taken by Marcion or Tatian. Origen (an early third-century Christian teacher), for example, often sought to resolve the discrepancies by careful reasoning. Studying the similarities and differences between the stories in the Gospels about the woman anointing Jesus, he concluded that three different women anointed Jesus on three different occasions.[70] However, sometimes the difficulties could neither be resolved by harmonization or by suggesting that the Gospels describe different events—the discrepancies just could not be resolved at the literal level. This led him to conclude that the Gospels communicate truth not only and always at the level of the literal text, and that difficulties in the text are meant to goad us on to seek the spiritual or symbolic message.[71] While he may have gone too far in his allegorizing approach, he nevertheless correctly perceived that "Gospel truth" was more than "historical reconstruction." Indeed, Origen concluded that the spiritual truth communicated by the Gospels was harmonious and true, and that God preferred to sacrifice the harmony at the literal level so that this greater truth could be adequately and accurately communicated to the Evangelists.[72]

Augustine laid heavier stress on the harmony of the Gospels, but he also acknowledged the differences between them. Not overly concerned with disagreement about exact wording (e.g., the exact words the disciples cried out to Jesus in the boat as the storm swept over them), Augustine was more concerned to display harmony of the sense (e.g., the disciples called out for help).[73] He affirmed that the Holy Spirit stood behind every word written by each Evangelist, even if the accounts seemed contradictory. These difficulties invited the faithful to inquire more deeply into the text, always to seek an explanation that would accord with the "rule of faith," namely, the orthodox creeds of Christianity.

The early Christians' decision to cling to four Gospels meant that they would have to live with the historical complications that ensued. They were convinced, however, that "the historical difficulties did not undermine the one Gospel of Jesus Christ, inspired by the one Spirit."[74] The famous Muratorian Fragment (about 200 C.E.) deals with the problem of the differing and multiform witness of the four Evangelists thus: "Though different beginnings are taught in the various Gospel books, yet that makes no difference to the faith of believers, since by the one primary Spirit, everything is declared in all [the Gospels] concerning Christ's nativity, his passion, his resurrection, his life with his disciples, and concerning his two comings, the first in humility when he was despised, which is past, the second, glorious in royal power, which is still in the future." This basic creed, this "rule of faith" or summation of the kerygma, holds together the four different witnesses so readers may appreciate their multifaceted presentation of the person of Jesus and the meaning of discipleship without fearing for the basic truth of the gospel.

---

[70]Dungan, *History of the Synoptic Problem*, p. 76.

[71]Ibid., pp. 77, 81.

[72]Ibid., p. 85.

[73]Ibid., p. 137.

[74]Stanton, *Gospel Truth?* p. 110.

FROM THE EVANGELISTS TO US: HANDING DOWN THE GOSPEL TEXTS

Up to this point we have focused on the process that preserved the words and deeds of Jesus, and disseminated them throughout the early church. These came to be "inscripturated" as Gospels by the four Evangelists. Another important process, but one frequently dropped from sight, is the transmission of the Gospels from the original authors to us, the modern readers. We will look more closely into this side of the process in the "Textual Criticism" section in the chapter on Mark, but it is worth bearing in mind at this stage a few ways in which the Gospels continue to develop after their composition.

The Gospels, like all ancient books, were reproduced manually. For every church that wanted to have access to the Gospel of Luke, there was a copyist at work (whether a skilled believer or a professional copyist) reproducing a manuscript word by word. Copyists were not afraid to "improve" the text if they encountered a problem, whether a grammatical mistake, a stylistic infelicity or a concept or reference requiring a brief explanation. We often find, not surprisingly, scribal attempts at harmonization—assimilating one Evangelist's version of a saying to the version familiar to the scribe. This is nowhere more obvious than in the attempts by many scribes to bring Luke's version of the Lord's Prayer in line with Matthew's version, the form the prayer was known and said in the churches (also preserved in the *Didache,* a late-first-century or early-second-century church manual).[75] Resistance to difference and internal contradiction runs deep. A copyist familiar with the Septuagint, the Greek translation of the Jewish Scriptures, might also tend to "correct" quotations of Scripture as he copied a Gospel to make the quotation conform to the Old Testament more closely or attempt to make better sense out of the text.

Since oral traditions about Jesus and sayings attributed to Jesus continued to be preserved and used in the early church, it occasionally happened that these affected the text of the Gospels as scribes sought to include—to preserve from oblivion—a discrete saying of Jesus or even an entire episode not previously incorporated into the written text but still circulating in oral tradition. A single codex from the fifth century introduced an independent saying of Jesus into the story of the controversy over rubbing the heads of wheat on the sabbath (Lk 6:1-5): "in the same day, seeing a man working on the sabbath, he said to him, 'Man, if you understand what you are doing, you are favored; but if you do not understand, you are cursed and a violator of the Law." Clearly, this saying has no claim to have been in Luke's original. Rather, a scribe has seen fit to incorporate a saying he learned from oral tradition and believed to be indeed authentic into an appropriate place in a Gospel narrative to preserve it.

Much more dramatic evidence for this continuing, modest modification of the Gospel tradition appears in the textual evidence for the ending of Mark's Gospel and the story of the woman taken in the act of adultery. The original ending of Mark was either Mark 16:8, or it was lost early in the life of that book (e.g., through damage to the original before suffi-

---

[75]A fruitful exercise would be the following: compare the Lord's Prayer in Luke 11:2-4 and Matthew 6:9-13 using the KJV, and then compare the same two passages using the NRSV. The KJV, translated in 1611, was based on the manuscript evidence available at that time, which did not include any of the third-century papyrus manuscripts or the great fourth- and fifth-century codices. The NRSV, on the other hand, is based on a Greek text that has taken all this earlier manuscript evidence into consideration. The difference between the Lucan Lord's Prayer in the NRSV and the KJV, then, shows the reader how much scribal harmonization took place between the third century, when the Lord's Prayer in Luke was still considerably different, and the manuscripts of the late Medieval period, when it had been almost completely harmonized with Matthew's form.

cient copies were made). Ending a Gospel with women saying nothing about the resurrection out of fear, however, was far from satisfactory, so a new ending was shaped using other oral traditions about Jesus' postresurrection appearances and instructions.

The famous story of the woman taken in adultery (Jn 7:53—8:11) does not appear in the third- or fourth-century manuscripts of John. It first appears in a fifth-century manuscript, but it is also occasionally inserted into the Gospel tradition at Luke 21:25, 21:38 or 24:53. This suggests that although not originally included by either Luke or John, the story remained an important part of the oral tradition about Jesus. Indeed, it pointed so dramatically to a vital dimension of Jesus' purpose and mission that scribes were unwilling for it to be lost to posterity and so sought to find a place for it in the written record.

The oral traditions about Jesus and the composition of the Gospels thus continued to intersect after the Evangelists finished their work, in several instances preserving for the whole church in every age very important and formative traditions about Jesus' character, mission and triumph.

FOR FURTHER READING

Patzia, Arthur G. *The Making of the New Testament.* Downers Grove, Ill.: InterVarsity Press, 1995.

Stanton, Graham N. *Gospel Truth? New Light on Jesus and the Gospels.* Valley Forge, Penn.: Trinity Press, 1995.

SEARCHING FOR THE JESUS OF HISTORY

Why this quest? Perhaps on seeing the subhead "Searching for the Jesus of History" you wondered, *How did Jesus get lost in the first place? What is so hard about finding the historical Jesus?* The nature of the Gospels themselves poses some challenges to pure, historical inquiry. There are notable differences in order, detail and outline, and some are frankly irreconcilable. These differences appear at all levels, whether at the microlevel of the order of the temptations posed by Satan (Mt 4:1-11; Lk 4:1-13) or the median level of the resurrection appearances and accounts of what transpired that Sunday morning or the macrolevel of whether the cleansing of the temple occurred at the beginning of Jesus' ministry (as in Jn 2) or near its close (as in Mk 11 and its parallels in Mt 21 and Lk 19). How significant are these differences? They are significant enough to suggest that we cannot simply harmonize or collate the order of events and visits to the tomb after the crucifixion, but the accounts at least agree on the major points of the facts of resurrection and the witnesses to the empty tomb and risen Jesus.

Nevertheless, the differences between the Gospels—not to mention the purposes of the Evangelists, which are not, strictly speaking, historical purposes—raise the question of the history of Jesus' life and ministry. The Evangelists were people with convictions about Jesus and a message to proclaim about Jesus and his significance. Their work is therefore not a mere repository of facts like an almanac. Historical research seeks to get behind the sources and their interpretations or reconstructions to the "actual" events and persons, although scholars are increasingly aware that there is no "history" without bias and interpretation. "Tradition history" is the discipline that, combined with redaction criticism and form criticism, seeks to move back further and further to authentic sayings of Jesus and authentic traditions about him, past the redactional crafting of these materials by the Evangelists, past the shaping of these materials by the early church,

Figure 4.2. According to the Gospels, Jesus' body was laid in a rock-hewn tomb similar to this one found near Megiddo. (Photo courtesy of Todd Bolen [BiblePlaces.com])

to their most original form in the life of the historical Jesus.

Other factors also motivate this quest. Historical investigation of Jesus is a product of the Enlightenment worldview that became increasingly closed to the possibility of the supernatural or its interventions in the fabric of nature and history. The stories of miracles, angelic interventions, the virgin birth and the resurrection were stumbling blocks to the naturalistic worldview and its adherents.[76] "Scientific" research into the life of Jesus, operating by its own rules that systematically exclude the unobservable or unrepeatable (hence, the supernatural or the miraculous), worked inexorably and predictably to create a nonsupernaturalistic explanation of the offending events and a historical recreation of Jesus' life. Disappointment with or alienation from the Jesus of the traditional Christian creeds has also driven several contributions to this quest. Several scholars have been quite outspoken concerning what they perceive to be the inadequacies of the historic Christian confession and the shape of traditional Christianity. Recovering the "historical" Jesus provides a way forward to a new Christianity free from dogma and free to follow the preacher from Nazareth.

[76]On the problem of worldview and New Testament studies, see David A. deSilva, "The Meaning of the New Testament and the *Skandalon* of World Constructions," *EvQ* 64 (1992): 3-21. See also Marcus Borg, *Jesus: A New Vision* (San Francisco: HarperSanFrancisco, 1987), p. 33: "The reality of the other world deserves to be taken seriously. Intellectually and experientially, there is much to commend it. The primary intellectual objection to it flows from a rigid application of the modern worldview's definition of reality. Yet the modern view is but one of a large number of humanly constructed maps of reality."

For others, however, the quest for the historical Jesus is motivated by the fact that the Christian confession is rooted in history, an absolute consequence of the incarnation. If God is revealed most fully in the person Jesus the Messiah, Christians are thereby driven to keep looking toward a historical person to discover more of God's character and will.

The history of the Quest. The quest for the "historical Jesus" could be seen to proceed from the conviction that the Christian should follow Christ as closely as possible. Those who follow Jesus, therefore, should inquire as closely as possible into who he was, what his mission was about and what his vision was for human response to God. The "First Quest" of the eighteenth and nineteenth centuries, however, was birthed by the conviction that the Jesus of the Gospels and of Christian tradition was not the *real* Jesus.[77] The modern worldview made nonsense of the virgin birth, the working of miracles, the resurrection and an apocalyptic second coming. The christological discussions of the third and fourth centuries concerning the divine and human natures of Christ, the embeddedness of Jesus in the Godhead, and the atoning significance of Jesus' death seemed only to obscure the man Jesus and his message with a lot of superstitious mumbo jumbo. An Enlightened Christianity required a Jesus freed from the baggage of an outdated worldview and the wild theological accretions of his followers.

Albert Schweitzer reviewed the results of this quest in a 1906 publication, concluding that historical research only served to create a Jesus in the researcher's own image.[78] Jesus could not be credibly wrenched from his first-century context or from the worldview in which he lived, moved and had his being. In particular the attempt to reconstruct a "moral Jesus," who would be congenial to the nineteenth-century worldview and ethos, divorced from the eschatological prophet whose words about the kingdom of God and imminent end would never be welcome in a post-Enlightenment parlor, failed miserably since Jesus was both. Schweitzer believed historical research was possible, just not that Jesus could be domesticated to suit nineteenth-century expectations.

Schweitzer's critical history of the quest effectively discouraged further investigation, and biblical scholarship turned to other considerations for half a century (including, notably, the history of the Synoptic tradition with the energetic application of form criticism to the Gospels). A "New Quest" (sometimes called the "Second Quest") was initiated in 1953 by Ernst Käsemann.[79] Käsemann reacted against the early twentieth-century tendency to divorce the Christ of faith entirely from the Jesus of history, making of Christianity a kind of existential mystery religion centered on a Christ myth. The dangers of divorcing Jesus from his Jewish context, moreover, had made themselves grossly apparent to Käsemann during the Nazi regime. The scholars involved in this Second Quest understood that Christianity remained a historical religion, that its connection to a real person who acted in history—and, in particular, its rootedness in the alleged historicity of certain events like the death and resurrection of the man Jesus—was central to its self-understanding. Not surprisingly, however, the historical Jesus once again ended up looking a lot like his scholarly biog-

---

[77]Indeed, its inception in the work of Reimarus (1694-1768) was explicitly "anti-theological, anti-Christian, anti-dogmatic" (Wright, *Jesus and the Victory of God,* pp. 16-17).

[78]Albert Schweitzer, *The Quest of the Historical Jesus: A Critical Study of Its Progress from Reimarus to Wrede,* trans. William Montgomery (German original 1906; New York: Macmillan, 1964).

[79]Ernst Käsemann, "The Problem of the Historical Jesus," reprinted in his *Essays on New Testament Themes* (London: SCM Press, 1964), pp. 15-47. The first bloom of the Second Quest is surveyed in J. M. Robinson, *A New Quest of the Historical Jesus* (Naperville, Ill.: A. R. Allenson, 1959).

raphers, this time as an existential philosopher strangely divorced from his first-century, Jewish milieu.

Since the early 1980s there has been no end to scholarly research into the life of Jesus and a spate of books attempting to present the historical Jesus.[80] Many of these continue to work from the basic starting points of the older quests, for example viewing the Gospels as basically "theological fiction" with little historical fact behind them and striving to detach Jesus from the unfashionable baggage of Jewish apocalypticism.[81] But alongside this line of research a "Third Quest" has also emerged. The Third Quest marks a return to the close study of Jesus in his first-century, Palestinian Jewish context—indeed, the study of the Jewishness of Jesus and his message, and how Jesus might have been intelligible to Jews living in Israel during the first part of the first century. Of course, apocalyptic eschatology plays a large part in this landscape, and so it cannot be excluded from Jesus' message a priori. The Third Quest seeks to understand Jesus' own aims and self-understanding, discerned through a careful reading of his actions as well as his words within the social, political, theological and economic realities of first-century Israel. It also shows an interest in understanding Jesus as a credible hinge between the Judaism of which he was a part and the Jewish-Christian and then Jewish-and-Gentile Christian community that grew around the proclamation of Jesus as Messiah.[82]

In many of the books that have come from the ongoing Quest(s), one can see the best of the scholarly tradition at work: researchers patiently sifting through data, weighing these data according in light of reasonable criteria, making modest claims about the findings, questioning their own assumptions and the role their worldview and interests have played in their work. In some cases—generally those that draw the most public attention—one finds what can only be described as the attempt to create a Jesus that will serve as an ally and promoter of the scholar's own cause. A very visible figure in the continued Quest has said that "It is impossible to avoid the suspicion that historical Jesus research is a very safe place to do theology and call it history, to do autobiography and call it biography."[83] Time and again that proves true. A pioneering feminist scholar finds in Jesus the advocate of egalitarianism and the worship of God as "Wisdom," *Sophia*. The scholar who is profoundly antagonistic toward traditional religion discovers an iconoclastic Jesus who debunks contemporary religious practices. Or Jesus emerges as an itinerant Cynic sage, a first-century cultural critic quite congenial to the twentieth-century academic that sculpted him. Even after the observation had been made about the first and second quests, the portrait of a Jesus continues frequently to reflect the social location and interests of the researcher to a remarkable degree. It remains to be seen if self-critical and sound historical research will ever be able to overcome this cycle.

The methods and resources for the Quest.
A great deal of historical Jesus research during the 1980s and 1990s has focused on sifting

---

[80]Excellent introductions to the modern landscape of the quest can be found in Ben Witherington III, *The Jesus Quest* (Downers Grove, Ill.: InterVarsity Press, 1996); Powell, *Jesus as a Figure in History*; Wright, *Jesus and the Victory of God*, pp. 3-124. Wright includes an insightful survey of the quest from its beginnings in the eighteenth century.

[81]An important insight developed by Wright (*Jesus and the Victory of God*, pp. 28-89) is that the "three quests" are not strictly divided chronologically but that each quest has continued, in some sense, to be pursued in each generation. Thus the methods and presuppositions of the earlier quests continue to drive much Jesus research, including, Wright argues, the Jesus Seminar, while a third quest with different methods and presuppositions has arisen alongside the "renewed New Quest."

[82]Wright, *Jesus and the Victory of God*, pp. 85-86, 123.

[83]John Dominic Crossan, *The Historical Jesus* (San Francisco: HarperSanFrancisco, 1991), p. xxviii.

through the ancient sources about Jesus and deciding rather atomistically about which pieces of data can be used in the reconstruction of a credible portrait of Jesus. What presuppositions, sources and criteria have, in general, characterized this line of research?

One important principle of the quest is that Jesus is to be investigated like any other person in history—like Socrates or Alexander or Siddhartha—and not as the object of faith. Pious presuppositions about Jesus of Nazareth are not to contaminate the results of pure, scientific research into the facts of history. In practice this principle also means that the post-Enlightenment, antisupernaturalistic worldview is assumed, so that any report of a "violation of natural law" or the like is automatically deemed inauthentic and impossible.[84] Just as the historian would not deem as historical facts the miracles reported to have been performed by Apollonius of Tyana or Emperor Vespasian, so it should be with the investigation of the life of Jesus.

A second principle addresses the issue of the sources for this quest. The Synoptic Gospels are elevated above John's Gospel as more reliable sources. Although all four Gospels have overlaid the Jesus of history with the claims of faith and retell the story through the lens of faith, John does this to such an extent that his Gospel remains even more opaque to objective research. Furthermore, the two-source hypothesis is generally regarded as a reliable explanation of the composition of the first three Gospels, with the result that Mark and Q provide access to the earliest and most reliable traditions about Jesus—although these too need to be carefully sifted.[85]

The Jesus Seminar—the most visible though hardly most representative voice in this quest—included other operating principles as well. These presuppositions (like the aforementioned) have directly influenced the results of the study. First, it is taken for granted that Jesus' message is non-eschatological (something that links them a priori with the older quests). The thing to be demonstrated is already stated as a presupposition, and one that is very questionable, given the eschatological orientation of Jesus' forerunner (John the Baptist) and Jesus' disciples in the early church. Luke Timothy Johnson has suggested that this presupposition derives from the fact that the seminar's members (and particularly its founders) have no room for eschatology and myths of cosmogony.[86] When we consider that several prominent scholars believe Jesus' eschatological orientation to be an irrefutable fact of history, this presupposition emerges as all the more surprising.[87] Another presupposition is that in oral cultures only short sayings can be remembered. This is a problematic assumption about oral cultures and the ability of people raised in such cultures to remember much longer blocks of material. It is also a presupposition that automatically weighs the evidence in favor of Jesus as a teacher of wisdom, since the shorter sayings tend to belong to this stream of tradition. Another important principle for the Jesus Seminar is that the burden of proof falls on the side of demonstrating the authenticity of a saying, thus assuring that the picture of Jesus will be a minimalist one.

The historian has a number of sources at his or her disposal in the study of Jesus. The place of the canonical Gospels in this quest has already been discussed. Other streams of tradition within the New Testament also provide evidence about Jesus, his life and teachings, most notably the Pauline letters, which occasionally

---

[84]Powell, *Jesus as a Figure in History,* p. 50.

[85]Dungan has correctly observed that the Synoptic problem is not just about how the Gospels were written but is also driven by the desire to find reliable information about Jesus (*History of the Synoptic Problem,* p. 346).

[86]Luke Timothy Johnson, *The Real Jesus* (San Francisco: HarperSanFrancisco, 1996), p. 8.

[87]See Witherington (*Jesus Quest,* pp. 116-36) on the work of E. P. Sanders and Maurice Casey.

provide evidence of Jesus sayings as well as traditions about his passion and postresurrection appearances. The historian also looks beyond the canonical sources to extracanonical Gospels like *Gospel of Thomas, Gospel of Peter* and *Secret Gospel of Mark* and, as mentioned above, reconstructed sources such as Q.[88] The usefulness of these sources (particularly the first three) depends on the individual scholar's estimation of the source's date and relationship to the canonical Gospels. *The Gospel of Thomas,* undoubtedly the most celebrated of the extracanonical Gospels, has played a very important role in the work of the Jesus Seminar, even being presented as the fifth of *The Five Gospels*.[89] The members of the Jesus Seminar consider *Thomas* to represent Jesus traditions independent of the Synoptics that were composed rather early (during the second half of the first century). Scholars who regard *Thomas* as a second-century composition that is itself dependent on one or more of the Synoptic Gospels give it far less weight in Jesus research.

Historians also turn to non-Christian literature. Ancient historians like Josephus and Tacitus refer briefly to Jesus, and rabbinic texts also contain references to Jesus (e.g., as a sorcerer and deceiver). Beyond literary texts historians also make use of archaeological and geographical information to construct a fuller picture of Galilee and Judea in the early first century.[90] This work is of great importance in establishing the broader parameters of Jesus' world: what would be appropriate to expect

him to have encountered, been influenced by, responded to and the like.

All of the literary sources have points of convergence and divergence; all of them are laden with some kind of ideology about Jesus and an agenda into which Jesus traditions are made to fit. How then do historians sift through the sources to find reliable data? A sophisticated catalog of criteria for evaluating the authenticity of a Jesus saying or tradition has emerged from the last century of Jesus research.[91]

Multiple attestation. A tradition appearing in multiple, independent streams of tradition is more likely to be authentic. If all three Synoptic Gospels (Mark, Matthew and Luke) share a particular saying or tradition, this would tend to count as one stream of tradition (whether one ascribes to the two-source, Griesbach or Augustinian hypothesis). A saying or tradition that appears in both Mark and Q or in Mark, Q and *Thomas*, for example, would score really high by this criterion, since it was preserved by what are deemed by at least some to be independent streams of tradition. This criterion becomes problematic when used in reverse: a saying or story appearing in only one stream of tradition is not thereby deemed inauthentic.[92]

Multiple forms. A topic that is enshrined both in sayings and narratives (e.g., Jesus' mission to call the marginal, the outcast, the "lost"—a theme appearing both in sayings of Jesus and in stories about Jesus' interactions with such people) is more likely to be authentic.

Dissimilarity. If a saying or deed attributed to

---

[88]See the convenient collections of such Jesus sayings in Morrice, *Hidden Sayings of Jesus,* and W. D. Stroker, *Extracanonical Sayings of Jesus* (Atlanta: Scholars Press, 1989). For a brief introduction to four extracanonical Gospels, see Stanton, *Gospel Truth?* pp. 77-95.

[89]Robert W. Funk and R. W. Hoover, eds., *The Five Gospels: The Search for the Authentic Words of Jesus* (New York: Macmillan, 1993).

[90]See further Stanton, *Gospel Truth?* pp. 111-34; R. A. Horsley and John S. Hanson, *Bandits, Prophets, and Messiahs: Popular Movements of the Time of Jesus* (Minneapolis: Winston, 1985); John Dominic Crossan and J. L. Reed, *Excavating Jesus: Beneath the Stones, Behind the Texts* (San Francisco: HarperSanFrancisco, 2001).

[91]For further study of these criteria see especially the bibliography compiled on each in C. A. Evans, *Jesus,* IBR Bibliographies 5 (Grand Rapids: Baker, 1992), pp. 52-67. Also quite useful is an article by M. E. Boring, "Criteria of Authenticity: The Lucan Beatitudes as a Test Case," *Forum* 1, no. 4 (1985): 3-38.

[92]Powell, *Jesus as a Figure in History,* p. 47.

Jesus has no parallel in early Jewish literature and at the same time differs from early Christian teaching and practice, the tradition has a very high probability of being authentic. This is a strong and valuable criterion for demonstrating authenticity. If there is no likely source for a Jesus tradition in early Judaism, and if there is no evidence that early Christians would have invented the tradition (since it does not reflect early Christian liturgy, ideology or practice), it must indeed be an authentic saying of Jesus. Where else could it come from?

This criterion is misused, however, when it is made a *necessary* criterion for authenticity: we construct a Jesus who neither learned anything from his Jewish environment and heritage nor had any real influence on the movement that bears his name. The misuse of this criterion as a *negative* criterion also tends to guarantee the outcome in many respects, such as the emergence of a non-eschatological Jesus (eschatology being prominent in early Judaism, the preaching of John and the early church).

N. T. Wright insists that the use of this criterion should be balanced by the use of a criterion of "double similarity." When an act or saying of Jesus "can be seen to be credible (though perhaps deeply subversive) within first-century Judaism, *and* credible as the implied starting point (though not the exact replica) of something in later Christianity," then it is probable that the tradition is an accurate reflection of what Jesus did or said.[93] A very similar suggestion comes from Gerd Theissen and Dagmar Winter, who would prefer the criterion of "historical plausibility" over the criterion of "dissimilarity."[94] A tradition that can be understood

plausibly within the context of first-century Judaism *and* explain developments in the early church would stand a good chance of being authentic. In reaction against approaches to the "historical Jesus" that result in a "Jesus" that is completely removed from the causal nexus by which Christianity emerges from Judaism, these scholars seek to understand Jesus as the "hinge" between early Judaism and the emerging church. The criterion of dissimilarity and its critics reflect the larger debate about how much continuity or discontinuity to assume between the Jesus of history and the early Christian movement that flourished after his death.

Simplest form of a tradition. If a tradition is attested in several different versions, the simplest form (sometimes involving the removal of editorial accretions from even the shortest attested form) is most likely to be authentic. This criterion seems logical enough, but it is often belied by the actual development of traditions as far as this can be determined. Sometimes a tradition will develop from longer to shorter![95]

Embarrassment. A tradition that the early church might have wished to suppress if it could but had to admit and explain instead, is very likely to be authentic. Examples of this include traditions (1) of Jesus' submitting to baptism by John the Baptist, (2) that Jesus was connected with Nazareth as a place of origin when Bethlehem, the "city of David," was the preferred location for the Messiah's emergence, and (3) of Jesus' sense of an exclusive mission to Israel during his lifetime.[96]

Disagreement with the tendencies of recording Evangelist. Here the results of redaction criti-

---

[93]Wright, *Jesus and the Victory of God*, p. 132.

[94]Gerd Theissen and Dagmar Winter, *The Quest for the Plausible Jesus* (Louisville, Ky.: Westminster John Knox, 2002).

[95]E. P. Sanders, *The Tendencies of the Synoptic Tradition*, SNTSMS 9 (Cambridge: Cambridge University Press, 1969).

[96]At this point a word should be said about the early church's respect for the tradition as well. Sayings were not ignored simply because they were problematic, but rather they were interpreted within the larger framework of traditions. The church did not discard sayings by Jesus about his mission being limited to Israel (cf. Mt 10:5-6 and 15:24) once it decided to move fully in the direction of a universal mission (cf. Mt 8:11-12; 12:17-21; 28:19-20). In the context of Matthew these sayings can exist alongside one another, affirming that Jesus' ministry was understood as limited to Israel— but *not* the church's ministry nor, indeed, the plan of God itself.

Criteria of Authenticity: A Summary

- multiple attestation
- multiple forms
- dissimilarity (alternatively, double attestation)
- simplest form of a tradition
- embarrassment
- disagreement with tendencies of recording Evangelist
- anachronism
- coherence
- memorable form (maxims, parables, brief stories) or content (surprising, humorous)

cism are brought to bear on the quest for the historical Jesus. If a Jesus tradition within Matthew, for example, actually runs counter to Matthew's own pastoral and theological interests, that tradition is likely to be authentic.

Anachronism. Something that would be inappropriate, out of place or irrelevant for an early first-century Palestinian setting is likely to have originated in the early church, not with the Jesus of history. For example, extending the declaration of Mark 10:11-12—that a husband commits adultery by divorcing his wife and marrying another—to cover also the case of a woman "if she divorces her husband" has frequently been seen as an anachronism, since Jewish women in Palestine did not initiate divorce, whereas in Rome, either the wife or the husband could initiate divorce. This added clause then would seem to reflect circumstances outside of Palestine and be out of place within Palestine, hence it could reflect an inauthentic addition.[97]

Coherence. A saying or tradition that coheres with other traditions already established as authentic by other criteria is also likely to be authentic.

Memorable form (maxims, parables, brief stories) or content (surprising, humorous). While again this criterion has the force of logic behind it (more pithy or remarkable sayings or stories are more likely to be remembered and passed on accurately), its users sometimes run into difficulty by underestimating the ancient person's capacity to memorize, which is by all accounts greater than our own.

The application of these criteria, particularly to the sayings material in the Gospels, produces widely varying results. For the Jesus Seminar the burden of proof fell on the side of demonstrating authenticity—a minimalist approach, by definition—with the result that about 18 percent of the words attributed to Jesus in the canonical Gospels plus the *Gospel of Thomas* emerged as authentic.[98] Where the

---

[97]Powell, *Jesus as a Figure in History*, p. 49. In this particular example, however, Jesus might have been making a passing reference to Herodias's divorce of Herod Philip in order to marry Herod Antipas (Ben Witherington III, "Herodias," *Anchor Bible Dictionary*, ed. David N. Freedman [Garden City, N.Y.: Doubleday, 1992], 3.174-76). Given Jesus' connections with John the Baptist and the fate of the latter at the hands of Antipas and Herodias, it is not out of the question and so could be an authentic form of the tradition.

[98]Funk and Hoover, *Five Gospels*. A more positive approach would take these results as indicating that *at least* 18 percent goes back assuredly to the historical Jesus, but it is far more often approached in a way that limits research into the historical Jesus to this small body of material (Marcus Borg, "The Jesus Seminar from the Inside," *Quaker Religious Thought* 30 [2002]: 21-27).

criterion of dissimilarity is not applied to exclude sayings, where a researcher displays greater confidence in the ancient memory and especially where the criteria of historical plausibility and explanation are applied, the results tilt more in favor of affirming a greater proportion of the Jesus traditions to be authentic in some form. It must be remembered that most of these criteria are devised to provide *positive* evidence to support authenticity and are not designed to function as *negative* criteria (with the exception of the criterion of anachronism or incongruence with first-century Palestine). They are made to serve the latter task functionally when only the demonstrably authentic sayings are used to create a picture alleged to represent the "whole" of the Jesus of history.

Behind many of these criteria stand assumptions about the reliability of the Gospel tradition and the degree of continuity or discontinuity we should posit between the disciples' pre-Easter experiences with Jesus and their post-Easter claims about Jesus. How innovative were Christian teachers in their shaping of the tradition to meet the needs and answer the dilemmas of their congregations? It is useful to remember that several important controversies emerged in the early church, such as the debate over whether or not Gentiles need to be circumcised, for which no Jesus sayings were invented, however helpful they would have been.[99] Neither Paul nor any other advocate of Gentile inclusion ever tried to place words on Jesus' lips to the effect that "neither circumcision nor uncircumcision counts for anything" (Gal 5:6 NRSV). On the other hand, the traditions that had been preserved, though not addressing this issue in anything like a direct way, may have been sufficient to provide some guidance. In these traditions Jesus himself moved toward acceptance of the marginal, putting people and their restoration ahead of purity lines. Scholars tend to agree that these traditions, moreover, are among the authentic ones.

Graham Stanton believes that the discontinuity between Jesus' ministry and teachings and the life of the early church has been overemphasized. The above represents a perfect example of currents in Jesus' life and ministry that provide a plausible backdrop for developments within the early church without being crassly reworked to address contemporary needs directly. This kind of continuity has been overlooked. Nothing comes about ex nihilo.[100] The trend among scholars of the First and Second (New) Quests has been to regard the worship of Jesus in the early church as a radically discontinuous development from the Jesus of history. But, Stanton asks, why would Jesus be worshiped in the early church if there was nothing about his pre-Easter life that suggested a special relationship with God or a unique role in God's interventions in the human story? The subtle ways Jesus refers to himself as the "son" in parables like the "wicked tenants" combined with the way that both the Gospels and rabbinic sources testify to open debates concerning the source of Jesus' power (whether God or Beelzebul), suggest that the Jesus of history not only taught wisdom and preached a prophetic word but also that the topic of his relationship with God was also addressed during his lifetime.[101] Such critiques of the application of criteria of authenticity are important indeed if our historical reconstructions are not to be unduly skewed by our presuppositions about who Jesus should be or by an agenda to rescue Jesus from the christological claims of the church.

---

[99]Stanton, *Gospel Truth?* p. 148.
[100]Ibid., pp. 145, 189-90.
[101]Ibid., pp. 154-63, 190.

Just the Facts

What can a historian discover about Jesus? A number of historians[a] would answer the quest with a short list of "facts" that can be recovered as "highly probable" data for the life of Jesus (together with the criteria that help establish the "fact"):

- Jesus came from Nazareth (embarrassment, multiple attestation).
- Jesus began his public life as a disciple of John (criteria of embarrassment and multiple attestation).
- Jesus was a teacher and healer/exorcist (multiple attestation; criterion of embarrassment applied to rabbinic sources: It would have been more convenient for non-Christian Jews to dismiss Jesus' miracles, but since they could not, they explained them away as works of Satan instead).
- Jesus had a group of followers, with twelve being of central importance (multiple attestation, multiple forms).
- Jesus focused his mission on Israel (criterion of embarrassment).
- Jesus preached the coming of the "kingdom of God" (multiple attestation, multiple forms).
- Jesus clashed with Jerusalem authorities concerning the temple (multiple attestation).
- Jesus was crucified as a Messianic pretender (a claimant to the throne of David) by the Romans on the authority of Pontius Pilate (multiple attestation, multiple forms, embarrassment).
- Jesus' followers believed they encountered him after his death (multiple attestation).
- Jesus' followers formed a movement, awaiting his return, winning new adherents (multiple attestation).

What *can* be established on historical-critical grounds is not inconsistent with the proclamations about Jesus made by the four Evangelists (Stanton, *Gospel Truth,* p. 192). Neither can it be said to provide sufficient ground for all the claims made by them and by other early Christian teachers about Jesus. The difficulty lies in the limitations of the historical method and the fact that the bulk of a person's words, acts and experiences lie beyond the scope of historians to recover.

The result is that a significant distance exists between any historical reconstruction and the real, historic person. The great fallacy of several modern researchers is that the Jesus reconstructed by such limiting and tendentious methods can in any way reflect the whole, real person of Jesus any better than the Gospels written within a lifetime after his death and resurrection. But as Witherington (*The Jesus Quest,* p. 12) correctly observes, "what is true about the historical Jesus and what the *historical method* can demonstrate are not one and the same. The latter will always be at best a truncated version of the former." The "Jesus of history" denotes the man Jesus, who lived and walked in Judea and Galilee, and all he did and said. The "historical Jesus" denotes the scholarly construct of what can be determined with a high degree of probability about the Jesus of history by historical-critical methods. The latter is but a partial and pale shadow of the former.

---

[a]Johnson, *Real Jesus,* pp. 105-40; Stanton, *Gospel Truth?* pp. 146, 145-93; Witherington, *Jesus Quest,* pp. 119-20; E. P. Sanders, *Jesus and Judaism* (Philadelphia: Fortress, 1985), p. 11; *The Historical Figure of Jesus* (London: Penguin, 1993), pp. 10-11.

The historical Jesus and Christian faith.
Despite the limitations of historical research, an emerging trend among scholars is to suggest that "true Christianity" must be based on reconstructions of Jesus derived from historical research, the "historical Jesus."[102] Real Christians, they assert, will follow a Jesus who has been "freed" from the accretions of his followers. In so doing they re-embody the truth observed by Albert Schweitzer, namely, that "the historical investigation of the life of Jesus did not take its rise from a purely historical interest; it turned to the Jesus of history as an ally in the struggle against the tyranny of dogma."[103] The reconstructed sayings collection Q (or a partial selection of sayings and deeds from the canonical and extracanonical Gospels) displaces the canonical Gospels (not to mention the reflection on Jesus' significance throughout the rest of the New Testament) as the basis for knowing who Jesus "really" was, and thus as the basis for "genuine" Christian faith.

A major challenge posed by such scholars, then, is whether or not historical research fundamentally alters the basis for Christian faith and should result in a wholesale reformulation of Christianity. Since historical research operates by its own rules and laws, excluding by necessity great amounts of the Jesus traditions, the Jesus that emerges will be radically different from the Jesus of the Gospels and of Christian tradition. Because so much of who Jesus really was lies beyond the ability of historical investigation to recover by its own rules, historical research with its minimalist approach does no better bringing us to the real Jesus who walked throughout Galilee and Judea than the maximalist approach of reading the four Gospels in their entirety as reflections of this Jesus. But unlike pure historical research

(which most Jesus research never remains since there is almost always an agenda for change in the present world behind it), the four Gospels approach Jesus from the perspective of Christian faith. The Evangelists ask and answer questions about who this Jesus really is, what his significance is and what it means to follow him faithfully. They were among the first interpreters of Jesus and the meaning of his teachings and life. They continue to have the stronger claim to provide the basis for Christian faith, for that is the purpose to which they are best suited, whereas historical research is not.

Several scholars have tried to replace the four Evangelists in this role, with the difference being that "scientific research" now legitimates their program. Because historical research is bound by and committed to an antisupernaturalistic worldview (which has radical consequences for traditional Christian theology), the attempt to promote a new "Christianity" on the basis of such research must be named for what it is: a domestication of the Gospels and the Christian faith that works within rather than challenges that worldview. There is a great deal of impetus to reinvent Jesus apart from the tradition of the church, but for the person of faith it is equally if not more reasonable to understand Jesus through the tradition of the church, the community of those who throughout the centuries have encountered Jesus and sought the way of discipleship. According to this tradition Christian faith is based not on reconstructions of the historical Jesus but on an encounter with the living Jesus. As Albert Schweitzer observed, "The abiding and eternal in Jesus is absolutely independent of historical knowledge and can only be understood by contact with

---

[102]This position goes back to the early period of the historical-critical method. J. J. Griesbach, for example, declared that "theology must be based on the results of sound historical research" (quoted in William Baird, *A History of New Testament Research*, vol. 1, *From Deism to Tübingen* [Minneapolis: Fortress, 1992], p. 139).

[103]Schweitzer, *Quest of the Historical Jesus*, p. 4. See, as an example of this principle in action, Robert W. Funk, *Honest to Jesus: Jesus for a New Millennium* (San Francisco: HarperSanFrancisco, 1996).

His spirit which is still at work in the world. In proportion as we have the Spirit of Jesus we have the true knowledge of Jesus."[104]

Some lessons from the Quest. The fact that so many gifted and intelligent biblical scholars have, in essence, fallen into the trap of recreating Jesus in their own image—finding a "lord" who will promote their own agendas—must serve as a warning to all Christians not to do the same. Members of the Jesus Seminar were supposed to be guided by the warning, "Beware of finding a Jesus entirely congenial to yourself." It remains good advice. Dietrich Bonhoeffer wrote concerning discipleship: "When Christ calls a person, he bids that person come and die." Such a lord does not allow us to remain in our comfort zones for long, and we must never so domesticate Jesus that he ceases to challenge us or challenges us only in comfortable ways.

Looking at the wealth of perspectives on Jesus' mission can help us avoid that trap. Surveying the vast field of modern Jesus research, Witherington observes that "any one model for characterizing Jesus is likely to be inadequate."[105] Just as the early church treasured four different Gospels as means of preserving the many-faceted character of Jesus and the manifold appreciation of his mission and significance, so the readers of Jesus research do well to hold together the varying elements of Jesus' life and mission that emerge, rather than opting for one "part" of the picture as the "whole."

This requires us to be critical readers of scholarship, but we still can benefit from the vast amount of probing into Jesus' life that has taken place over the last decade or two. Where a scholar claims to have found the "historical Jesus," we may find that he or she has perhaps captured *one* facet of Jesus' work and significance. The Jesus presented in any one scholarly reconstruction is bound to be a partial picture, and often an exaggerated one, but taken together they highlight important aspects of Jesus' life and ministry. Consider, for example, the following sample pictures of Jesus that have emerged:

- *Jesus the practitioner of open table fellowship, who broke with traditional purity codes (sanctioned by centuries of religious tradition!) in order to extend the kingdom of God to those who were marginalized.*[106] When we forget this aspect of Jesus' mission, we might not break bread with those who live far away from the "religious" gatherings of our communities, whether they be the homeless, the "rough crowd" that gathers in bars late into the night or the dancers in the strip club outside of town. We might forget to show these fellow human beings God's love and extend the possibility of belonging to the family of those who follow Jesus. We might forget that we are not to avoid the divorced person or the unmarried mother or the disabled as "unclean," but rather make it our special aim to make them at home in God's redeemed and redeeming family.
- *Jesus the social reformer.* Richard Horsley and R. David Kaylor emphasize the challenges Jesus posed to the social and economic systems of his day, calling for radical reforms that would bring them closer to a system that would please God (i.e., one in which the poor were not victimized to keep a small elite in power and luxury).[107] Were we to neglect this aspect of Jesus' mission, we

---

[104]Schweitzer, *Quest of the Historical Jesus,* p. 401.

[105]Witherington, *Jesus Quest,* p. 100.

[106]John Dominic Crossan, *The Historical Jesus: The Life of a Mediterranean Jewish Peasant* (San Francisco: HarperSanFrancisco, 1991).

[107]Horsley and Hanson, *Bandits, Prophets, and Messiahs*; R. David Kaylor, *Jesus the Prophet: His Vision of the Kingdom on Earth* (Louisville, Ky.: Westminster John Knox, 1994); Witherington, *Jesus Quest,* 160.

might allow racial prejudice or class divisions to be perpetuated in our congregations. We might forget that Jesus calls us to invest not in our excess but in meeting the needs of our poorer brothers and sisters worldwide. We might forget that we too are called to denounce injustice and oppression rather than focus our ministries entirely on the redemption of the soul apart from the proclamation of justice for the whole person.

• *Jesus the opponent of patriarchy.* Elisabeth Schüssler Fiorenza may overstate her case by not allowing Jesus to call God "Father," insisting that he proclaimed God as the feminine "Sophia," yet her investigation does call us to reexamine Jesus' attitude toward women—especially as this clashed with the expectations of the men and women around him. We see a man who welcomed women among his disciples, who allowed (indeed encouraged) them to step out of "female" spaces and enter "male" spaces in order to sit at his feet, who encouraged and affirmed their expressions of piety and love even as males criticized them. When we forget this aspect of Jesus' ministry, we perpetuate the errors of his disciples, or of Martha, and fail to permit women to take their place as gifted disciples in a community of equals.

The list of examples could be extended considerably. The point is that critical inquiry into the life and ministry of Jesus has much to teach the present-day disciple who can sift through the exaggerated claims or pretensions of "historical Jesus" researchers.

Although historical research can establish the probability of several key facts about the life of Jesus and its aftermath, it does not ultimately present us with the real Jesus.[108] The Gospels' primary purpose is to facilitate our encounter with the real Jesus, but not by asking us to find him on the field of historical reconstruction. Some err by trying to get behind the presentation of Jesus in the Gospels to a purer version of Jesus, which then becomes a new norm for faith. Others (notably, more conservative scholars), also proceed as if the church's faith in Jesus should be established on historical reconstruction. They too err by insisting on the Gospels' accuracy in every detail, with the result that the four Gospels are harmonized and their distinctive images of Jesus lost in other equally invalid reconstructions.

Christian faith is founded, however, not on historical investigations of the Jesus of history but on an encounter with the risen, living Lord. The Gospels seek to facilitate the latter, to bring people closer to the living Jesus, to allow him to shape and challenge our lives. Their real value is in their witness to Jesus' significance, his purpose for our lives and his authority and ability to bring about that purpose. Because we need to be continually challenged and surprised by the many facets that become visible, probing the Gospels concerning the "facts" of Jesus' mission and career will always be valuable. However, the Gospels are better equipped to answer the key question: How would Jesus shape our lives together as a community of his followers?

FOR FURTHER READING ON THE HISTORICAL JESUS

Borg, Marcus. *Jesus: A New Vision: Spirit, Culture, and the Life of Discipleship.* San Francisco: Harper & Row, 1987.

Boring, M. Eugene. "Criteria of Authenticity: The Lucan Beatitudes as a Test Case." *Forum* 1, no. 4 (1985): 3-38.

Brown, Colin. "Historical Jesus, Quest of," pp. 326-41. In *Dictionary of Jesus and the Gospels.* Ed-

---

[108]See Johnson, *The Real Jesus,* pp. 141-66.

ited by Joel B. Green and Scot McKnight. Downers Grove, Ill. InterVarsity Press, 1992.

Crossan, John Dominic. *The Historical Jesus: The Life of a Mediterranean Jewish Peasant.* San Francisco: HarperSanFrancisco, 1991.

Evans, Craig A. *Jesus.* BBR Bibliographies 5. Grand Rapids: Baker, 1992.

Funk, Robert W., R. W. Hoover and the Jesus Seminar. *The Five Gospels: The Search for the Authentic Words of Jesus.* New York: Polebridge, 1993.

Funk, Robert W., and the Jesus Seminar. *The Acts of Jesus: The Search for the Authentic Deeds of Jesus.* San Francisco: HarperSanFrancisco, 1998.

Gerhardsson, Birger. *The Reliability of the Gospel Tradition.* Peabody, Mass.: Hendrickson, 2001.

Johnson, Luke Timothy. *The Real Jesus: The Misguided Quest for the Historical Jesus and the Truth of the Traditional Gospels.* San Francisco: HarperSanFrancisco, 1996.

McDonald, Lee M., and Stanley E. Porter. *Early Christianity and its Sacred Literature,* pp. 100-224. Peabody, Mass.: Hendrickson, 2000.

Morrice, William. *Hidden Sayings of Jesus: Words Attributed to Jesus Outside the Four Canonical Gospels.* Peabody, Mass.: Hendrickson, 1997.

Powell, Mark A. *Jesus as a Figure in History: How Modern Historians View the Man from Galilee.* Louisville, Ky.: Westminster John Knox, 1998.

Sanders, E. P. *The Historical Figure of Jesus.* London: Penguin, 1993.

Schüssler Fiorenza, Elisabeth. *In Memory of Her.* New York: Crossroad, 1983.

Schweitzer, Albert. *The Quest of the Historical Jesus: A Critical Study of Its Progress from Reimarus to Wrede.* 1906. Translated by William Montgomery. New York: Macmillan, 1964.

Stanton, Graham N. *Gospel Truth? New Light on Jesus and the Gospels.* Valley Forge, Penn.: Trinity Press, 1995.

Stroker, William D. *Extracanonical Sayings of Jesus.* Atlanta: Scholars Press, 1989.

Theissen, Gerd, and Dagmar Winter. *The Quest for the Plausible Jesus: The Question of Criteria.* Louisville, Ky.: Westminster John Knox, 2002.

Witherington, Ben, III. *The Jesus Quest.* Downers Grove, Ill.: InterVarsity Press, 1996.

Wright, N. T. *Jesus and the Victory of God.* Minneapolis: Fortress, 1996.

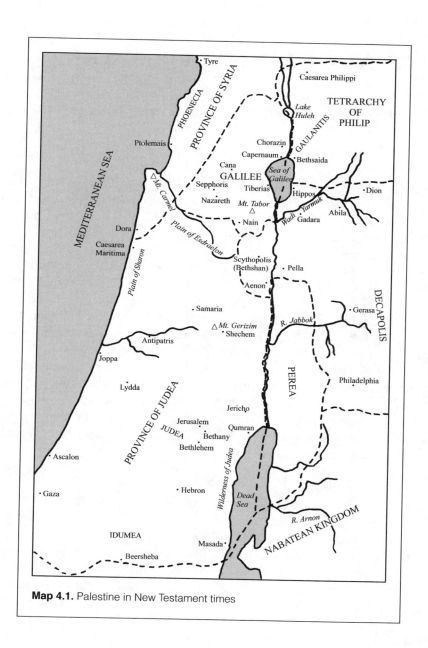

Map 4.1. Palestine in New Testament times

5

THE GOSPEL
ACCORDING TO MARK

Following in the Way of the Cross

Mark's Gospel stands second in the New Testament canon as a result of the overwhelming influence and importance of Matthew in the early church. In fact, Augustine considered Mark an abridgement of Matthew and all but ignored it on that account. Nevertheless, it now appears to most scholars that Mark was the earliest written Gospel to have survived. As such, the Evangelist made an important contribution to the church, bringing together diverse strands of Jesus sayings and traditions into a coherent narrative that is more than the sum of its parts. While regarded as a mere compiler of traditions for the first eighteen centuries of church history, Mark's theological and pastoral genius is now broadly recognized. He preached the gospel of the suffering, self-giving Messiah, and demanded that all the traditions about Jesus as a wonder-worker be read in that light. He also called the churches to the radical, self-sacrificing discipleship that matched the pattern of the Messiah the church claimed. After a brief survey of the historical questions surrounding the composition of this Gospel, we will focus on these and other contributions of Mark to early Christian belief and discipleship.

THE HISTORICAL AND PASTORAL CONTEXT OF MARK'S GOSPEL

Authorship. Assessing traditions of the Gospels' authorship is notoriously difficult. There are no internal claims to authorship, unlike the literature in the second half of the New Testament. The Gospels' titles are not original to the authors—they were just "Gospels" and only became Gospels "according to Mark" and so forth as the churches began to use multiple Gospels side by side, requiring a clearer identification of each one. This identification was based on early church traditions about each Gospel's development rather than on internal evidence.

These church traditions are early and quite possibly accurate, but many scholars through the centuries have found occasion to doubt their reliability. The traditions, moreover, did not emerge in a completely neutral setting. Where they are preserved in writing (e.g., the Muratorian Canon or the fragments of the writings of Papias, a Christian leader in the first third of the second century), they are actually recommending certain texts and employing apostolic connections as part of the basis for the recommendation. The attributions of authorship thus serve to legitimate and promote the continued use of certain Gospels that have spoken to the needs of the early churches, and frequently in opposition to the use of other Gospels that were in circulation at the time (e.g., the *Gospel of Thomas,* the *Gospel of Peter* and the *Gospel of the Nazoreans*). Since a particular Gospel communicated what the church recognized as an accurate reflection of the apostolic witness, traditions began to emerge attributing the authorship of the Gospel to a leading, historic apostolic figure in their church's history. These traditions express the community's endorsement of the work and their witness to its value. Such attribution later became essential for formal adoption by the universal (i.e., supralocal) church. Thus, for example, when apostolicity became important as an expression of the reliability of Gospel writings, an early tradition that a particular Gospel took shape in a community guided by Matthew might be transformed into a claim that Matthew directly authored the Gospel.

Concerning the authorship of Mark we have the following testimony from Papias, preserved as a fragment quoted in Eusebius:

> The elder also used to say: "Mark, who had been Peter's interpreter, wrote down carefully, but not in order, all that he remembered of the Lord's sayings and doings. For he had not heard the Lord or been one of his followers, but later, as I said, one of Peter's. Peter used to adapt his teaching to the occasion, without making a systematic arrangement of the Lord's sayings, so that Mark was quite justified in writing down some things just as he remembered them. For he had one purpose only—to leave out nothing that he had heard, and to make no misstatement about it." (*History of the Church* 3.39.15)

What questions was Papias trying to answer here? His testimony looks like an attempt to justify the form of Mark's Gospel when set alongside Matthew and Luke. Matthew's Gospel contains a systematic arrangement of Jesus' sayings, and Mark lacks this. Luke claims to have set everything down "in order," making necessary some explanation for the places where Mark's order departs from Luke's (as in the visit to Jesus' home synagogue). Furthermore, this statement concerning Mark's "one purpose" seems rather shallow when set against the actual achievement of his Gospel. This early view that Mark was merely a compiler of traditions persisted into the nineteenth century, but it has since been abandoned in light of observations concerning the careful structuring of his Gospel and the interpretative guidance Mark provides by juxtaposing, intercalating and grouping certain stories and sayings.

Papias's testimony about the authorship of the Second Gospel, however, was universally accepted among early church leaders (see, for example, Irenaeus *Against Heresies* 3.1.1). Thus the Gospel's place in the canon was secured by linking it with the prince of apostles, Peter. Given inaccuracies in Papias's testimony concerning Matthew's Gospel (see the following chapter),[1] many scholars are justifiably reluctant to affirm his explanation of the origin of Mark's Gospel too quickly, but it is also impossible to say definitively that the attribution is wrong.[2] What the testimony does tell us, however, is that the early church gave its unreserved stamp of approval to this text that, while not written as an eyewitness account, nevertheless provided an authoritative and accurate representation of the Jesus tradition as mediated and shaped by apostolic preaching.

---

[1] Paul Achtemeier, "Mark, Gospel of," in *The Anchor Bible Dictionary*, ed. D. N. Freedman (Garden City, N.Y.: Doubleday, 1992), 4:542.

[2] Indeed, as Paul Anderson pointed out to me in personal correspondence (2003), Papias's modest claims for the Gospel of Mark could be taken as a sign of the credibility and accuracy of his testimony. "If Papias (or Irenaeus) were wanting to bolster Mark's contents uncritically, why mention that they were *not* preserved in order? Also, why mention that Mark had *not* heard the Lord? If this was fabricated, why not locate Mark close to Jesus as an eyewitness? I think the Petrine references are therefore modest and not overstated." In other words, a fabrication invented to legitimate Mark's Gospel would have been likely to make more extravagant claims about its author and apostolicity.

This harmony with the apostolic witness is, as Lane has correctly observed, the "central question" in discussions about authorship.[3]

What is certain is that resolving the matter of authorship does not enhance our reading of the Gospel, and leaving the matter open does not detract from it. These four Gospels remain the Word of God and the churches' witness to the person of Christ and pattern of discipleship irrespective of claims about authorship. The texts, not the titles, are "word of God" to the churches.

Circumstances and purposes of composition. Early church tradition locates this Gospel's composition in Rome, either shortly before or after Peter's execution. Nineteenth- and twentieth-century scholarship, moreover, has largely embraced this tradition and sought to read Mark specifically as a "word on target" to the Roman churches in conjunction with the situation of persecution under Nero. There is some internal evidence to confirm a setting in Rome (or at least in the western part of the empire). First, while several of the Latinisms (Latin loan words or technical terms borrowed by another language) present in Mark are common to texts around the Mediterranean (even appearing in rabbinic writings emerging from Palestine), at two places Mark specifically explains a Greek term with a Latin one. These strongly suggest an audience that was more familiar with Roman currency (the *quadrans*, Mk 12:42) and administrative terms (the *praetorium*, Mk 15:16) than the eastern equivalents, hence a western audience.[4] Aramaisms, on the other hand, can be explained by the ultimate Palestinian provenance of the Jesus traditions and their apostolic carriers themselves (and perhaps to a Jewish Christian author), and not to

the composition of the Second Gospel in Palestine or Syria.

While the tradition that locates the origins of this Gospel in Rome may be accurate, the most we can say with certainty is that Mark was written outside of Palestine to an audience unfamiliar with Aramaic and many Jewish customs. Hence Mark found it necessary to translate Aramaic words or proper names (Mk 3:17; 5:41; 7:11, 34; 10:46; 14:36; 15:22, 34) and explain Jewish customs (e.g., purificatory washing at Mk 7:3-4). This audience was also assumed by the author to be familiar with the Old Testament, as well as to have previously been socialized into the Christian community (since the reader is presumed to be familiar with the majority of characters encountered in the Gospel narrative). Wherever its precise place of origin, Mark's Gospel soon enjoyed widespread circulation—both Matthew and Luke show specific knowledge of Mark and use it as a written source.

With regard to date, a time before 70 C.E. is quite likely. The author does not attempt to bring Jesus' prediction of the fall of Jerusalem and the temple into closer conformity with the events of 70 C.E. (as Luke does).[5] The primary reason many scholars tend to date Mark's Gospel after 70 C.E. is the presupposition that Jesus could not foresee the destruction of Jerusalem—an ideological conviction clearly not shared by all. Locating Mark in pre-70 C.E. Rome leads naturally to the conclusion that its composition was spurred on by and sought primarily to address the needs of Christians facing or recovering from the persecution in Rome under Nero.[6] One major emphasis of Mark is indeed that the shape of discipleship must necessarily follow the pattern of the rejected and executed Messiah, but this should

---

[3]William L. Lane, *The Gospel of Mark,* NICNT (Grand Rapids: Eerdmans, 1974), p. 7.
[4]Ibid., p. 24; Bas M. F. van Iersel, *Mark,* JSNTSup 1644 (Sheffield, U.K.: Sheffield Academic Press, 1998), p. 34.
[5]Luke Timothy Johnson, *The Writings of the New Testament: An Interpretation,* 2nd ed. (Minneapolis: Fortress, 1996), p. xxx.
[6]Thus Lane, *Mark,* pp. 12-13; van Iersel, *Mark,* pp. 39-41.

Who Was the Evangelist's Audience?

Scholars in the nineteenth and twentieth centuries have tended to read Gospels rather like Paul's Epistles. In the commendable quest for historical contextualization of a Gospel, they have adopted the model that a Gospel, like an epistle, is addressed to the specific needs of a particular Christian community, be it Rome (Mark), Antioch (a frequent choice for Matthew and Luke) or Ephesus (John). The Gospel then becomes a window into the history of that particular community. Unlike epistles, however, Gospels give us little information about the circumstances of composition or about any alleged community to which it is addressed or from which it emerges. Thus we can speak at length about the circumstances surrounding Paul's responses to the Galatian or Corinthian churches, but we are not on the same secure ground when we try to reconstruct the circumstances of the composition of Mark's Gospel. An extreme example of such an endeavor is Raymond Brown's reconstruction of the history of the "Johannine community" on the basis of discerning five stages in the composition of John's Gospel. If John was composed in five stages over a period of time, what is to prevent it from having been shaped by several different communities as its primary author moved from place to place in an itinerant ministry?

Another problem with the current majority view is the Evangelists' choice of narrative as a means of expression. While an epistle or letter tends to be addressed to a particular individual or group at a particular time, a Gospel is more akin to the genre of the *Vita,* or "Life," a narrative of sayings and deeds that would be profitably read by people in many different communities. If Mark's Gospel was composed at Rome, then, did he frame it only with the needs of the Roman Christian community in mind, or did he expect his Gospel to speak to all the churches in the circum-Mediterranean? A collection of essays edited by Richard Bauckham advances impressive arguments concerning the scholarly dogma of the "evangelist's community,"[a] and rather than perpetuate that dogma in yet another introduction, this volume will seek to forge a mediating path. On the one hand, the question of the Evangelist's historical context is vitally important, since this will often shape the emphases prominent in a particular Gospel. On the other hand, the Gospels were quickly embraced by a wide readership throughout the Mediterranean churches and therefore may be assumed to have spoken not merely to the needs of the church in a particular locale, but to the needs of the Christian movement as a whole. Paying attention to the former allows us to be more historically rooted in our interpretation of the Gospels. Paying attention to the latter—to the broader set of questions and concerns raised by Christians throughout the second half of the first century (evidenced in the Epistles, extrabiblical sources and internal evidence in the Gospels) and addressed by the Gospels—assists us in the ongoing task of connecting the Gospels with their vastly extended audience.

---

[a]Richard Bauckham, ed., *The Gospels for All Christians* (Grand Rapids: Eerdmans, 1998). See especially the introductory essay by Bauckham (pp. 9-48). These authors build on earlier caveats against reading the Gospels too closely or too exclusively as mirrors of the communities that allegedly produced them. See, e.g., A. J. Malherbe, *Social Aspects of Early Christianity,* 2nd ed. (Philadelphia: Fortress, 1983), p. 13; B. Holmberg, *Sociology and the New Testament: An Appraisal* (Minneapolis: Fortress, 1990), p. 125.

not be allowed to overshadow or minimize other interests that drive Mark as well.

Mark is straightforward about the cost of discipleship. But does he write to comfort persecuted Christians or to challenge Christians who might be reserved about their witness to Jesus, their loyalty to the one God and solidarity with one another in the face of possible rejection by their society? He certainly addresses the question of the relationship of believers to society, transforming the experience of rejection, misunderstanding and hostility for the sake of the Name into a meaningful, even honorable, sharing in the way of the Lord. He also calls for a reexamination of the meaning of the confession "you are the Christ" within the community, opening up the possibility that this has been misunderstood. Mark recognized that both the independently circulating oral traditions about and the sayings collections of Jesus fail to safeguard against misunderstanding Jesus' significance and character. Stories about Jesus' healings and nature miracles could lead to interpreting and following Jesus as another magician or wonderworker. On their own the sayings might lead to interpreting and following Jesus as the founder of a wisdom or philosophical school.[7] Only by anchoring miracle discourse and wisdom discourse in suffering-death discourse could the Evangelist create a statement about Jesus that preserved the correct picture of his significance *and* the significance of following this Jesus. To accomplish this Mark composed a narrative that weaved together and correctly interrelated the various strands of the Jesus tradition.

This is not just a doctrinal interest; it has very practical ramifications. Discipleship itself depends on a right understanding of Jesus' messiahship. Mark's presentation of the disciples' failures in both regards leads the readers or hearers to reconsider their own discipleship and seek any necessary correctives so they will be true followers of Jesus, prepared for the Master's return. Mark is also quite interested in redefining the believers' relationship to Jewish Scriptures, Torah, temple and Jewish piety, seeking in Jesus' sayings and deeds the guidelines for how the Christian community is to connect with the ancient tradition. Mark also seeks to nourish the spirituality and the ethos of the believing community, giving Christians a stronger sense of their values and focus (e.g., on the return of Christ and being prepared for that day) together with reminders of the resources that will enable them to achieve their goal.

Structure. The overall structure of Mark's Gospel follows the outline of early Christian preaching as found in the sermons of Acts 10:36-41[8] or Acts 13:24-31. The author begins with the preaching of John the Baptist, follows Jesus through his period of ministry, telling "how God anointed Jesus of Nazareth with the Holy Spirit and with power; how he went about doing good and healing all who were oppressed by the devil, for God was with him," and finally relating the trial, crucifixion, and resurrection. It is thus a narrative amplification of the basic, apostolic message about Jesus.

Outlines of Mark abound, and commentators tend to devise outlines that highlight what each desires to underscore. Donald Guthrie, for example, privileges geography in his outline: Galilee (Mk 1:14—5:43); further journeys in Galilee (Mk 6:1—9:50); the Judean period (10:1—13:37); passion and resurrection (14:1—16:20).[9] Movement is certainly important in Mark's Gospel, and such an outline is one way this can be emphasized. Others see the recognition of Jesus as the Messiah as the driving pulse of the book. So they create an outline

---

[7]Achtemeier, "Mark," p. 544.
[8]Lane, *Mark,* pp. 10-11.
[9]Donald Guthrie, *New Testament Introduction* (Downers Grove, Ill.: InterVarsity Press, 1970), pp. 86-87.

Figure 5.1. The Jordan River, south of the Sea of Galilee. At such a place as this John, and then Jesus and his disciples, baptized their followers. (Photo courtesy of Todd Bolen [BiblePlaces.com])

that points up the confession of Peter (Mk 8:29) and the confession of the centurion (Mk 15:39) as the two climaxes of the narrative.[10]

Mark gives one important clue to the outline of his narrative. Mark 8:22—10:52 is a very tightly interconnected segment structured by three passion predictions and teachings on discipleship framed by an *inclusio* of stories of healing blind men.[11] The *inclusio* is a common structuring device in ancient literature, particularly appropriate for an oral culture. An author would reintroduce at the end of a section the words, themes or stories that opened that section of discourse. This would be received as a signal of that section's close. This, then, is the center of Mark's

Gospel, the turning point of the whole as Jesus reveals to his disciples the true meaning of the confession of his messiahship as well as the true meaning of following him as Lord. The opening chapters (Mk 1:1—8:21) are a period of growing awareness of Jesus' anointing and attraction to following him, but this awareness remains incomplete. The chapters that follow (Mk 11:1—16:8) show the unfolding of Jesus' messiahship, from the triumphal entry (which is still surrounded with mistaken understandings of what that entry into Jerusalem means) to the cross (where Jesus' identity is finally seen with utmost clarity by the centurion in charge of the execution; Mk 15:39).

---

[10]For example, Lane, *Mark*, pp. 1, 30.

[11]This grouping is also noted by Norman Perrin and Dennis Duling (*The New Testament: An Introduction*, 2nd ed. [New York: Harcourt, Brace, Jovanovich, 1982], p. 239) and Iersel (*Mark*, p. 70). Some, like Robert Guelich ("Mark, Gospel of," in *Dictionary of Jesus and the Gospels*, ed. Joel B. Green, Scot McKnight and I. H. Marshall, [Downers Grove, Ill.: InterVarsity, 1992], p. 516) and Raymond Brown (*Introduction to the New Testament* [Garden City, N.Y.: Doubleday, 1997], pp. 135-36) regard the first healing of a blind man to close the first major section of the Gospel, but this slightly misconstrues the structuring function of the *inclusio*.

An Outline of Mark's Gospel

Opening: Mk 1:1—8:21

    The initiation of Jesus' ministry: 1:1-15

    Jesus' authority demonstrated in teaching, healing and exorcism: 1:16-45

    Challenges and opposition: 2:1—3:6

    Stories about creating an alternate family/kinship group: 3:7-35

    Parables separating insiders from outsiders: 4:1-34

    The failure of miracles to awaken true faith: 4:35—8:21

        Rejection of Jesus and John the Baptist: 6:1-29

        Challenge over purity regulations: 7:1-23

        Three miracles and a dispute with the Pharisees over a "sign": 7:24—8:21

Middle: Mk 8:22—10:52

    Healing of a blind man: 8:22-26

    First teaching on Messiahship (passion prediction) and discipleship: 8:27—9:1

    Transfiguration and the suffering forerunner: 9:2-13

    An exorcism: 9:14-29

    Second teaching on messiahship (passion prediction) and discipleship: 9:30-50

    Challenge concerning divorce: 10:1-12

    Children and the kingdom: 10:13-16

    Possessions and the kingdom (cost and rewards of discipleship): 10:17-31

    Third teaching on messiahship (passion prediction) and discipleship: 10:32-45

    Healing of a blind man: 10:46-52

Closing: Mk 11:1—16:8

    The Messiah rides into Jerusalem: 11:1-11

    Indictment of the temple and its replacement: 11:12-26

    Challenges and opposition: 11:27—12:44

    The apocalyptic discourse (cost and rewards of discipleship): 13:1-37

    Fulfillment of the passion predictions: 14:1—16:8

The literary character of Mark's Gospel. Mark is known as the Gospel of action. The terse style of his opening chapter plunges the readers into the drama of Jesus' ministry. The frequent use of "immediately" *(euthys)* and the stringing together of briefly narrated episodes create a phrenetic pace as Jesus sweeps across the Galilean stage, healing, casting out demons and growing in fame. The Greek style of Mark is less refined, giving the narrative a more straightforward and forceful tone than the more ornate Luke. Mark also provides a more human portrait of Jesus than the other Evangelists, presenting him now as tired, then angry, now compassionate, then reflective.

Mark achieves his goals through narrative artistry. As the one who first brought diverse and discrete stories about Jesus into a unified whole, Mark is able to (1) guide the audience's interpretation of each tradition by arranging their sequence, intercalation and juxtaposition, or (2) intensify the effects of individual units of tradition by grouping together stories of similar theme. The pace of Jesus' ministry at once captures the attentiveness of the hearers. Mark embroils the audience in conflict early in the Gospel (Mk 2:1—3:6), beginning to introduce the tension that builds throughout the narrative and leads ultimately to Jesus' rejection, suffering and crucifixion. It is this, in fact, that gives the plot of Mark the necessary unity.

Perhaps it is the mysterious, shadowy dimension of Mark that accounts for its ongoing appeal. A clear, plain presentation of Jesus' significance is replaced with the motif of secrecy; thus the reader must take the journey along with the disciples to discover deeper dimensions of what it means to call Jesus "the Christ, the Son of God" (Mk 1:1). Jesus' failure to be understood by those closest to him heightens the sense of mystery, the awesomeness and otherness of divine revelation. The dark, strenuous and demanding presentation of messiahship and discipleship gives the Gospel a tragic dimension, in the most stately sense of the word—a tragedy that becomes good news. This good news is found in the redemptive purposes of God for a new people through Jesus' death and in God's final word of vindication, both on behalf of Jesus in his resurrection and on behalf of Jesus' disciples at the coming of the Son of Man on the clouds of heaven.

MARK'S MESSAGE

The confession of Jesus as Christ and the meaning of discipleship. One of the first aspects of Mark that caught the eye of researchers and alerted them to Mark's role as a theologian rather than a mere compiler of Jesus traditions is the "messianic secret" theme.[12] While Jesus exercises great power and authority, he repeatedly gives orders to conceal this power. Whenever Jesus' identity is correctly perceived, he gives orders to not make it known. This continues throughout the first half of the Gospel, appearing last at Mark 9:9 (after the transfiguration). Why does Jesus prohibit the demons from making his divine connection known (Mk 1:24-25, 34; 3:11-12)? Why does he prohibit his disciples from spreading the claim that he is the Christ (Mk 8:29-30) or from reporting the revelation of his divine glory (Mk 9:9)? Why does he command many who are healed or who witness his power not to tell anyone about what he has done (Mk 1:44; 5:43; 7:36; 8:26)? Why does he even go so far as to tell the mourners at Jairus's house that the child is not dead, but only sleeping, thus attempting himself to defuse reports that he raised the dead girl (Mk 5:39)?

Wilhelm Wrede, who first drew attention to the messianic secret, theorized that these passages were a literary invention by Mark attempting to explain why the church made messianic claims for a man who had not made any claims to messiahship himself during his lifetime. The invention of these commands not to reveal Jesus' messiahship suggested to Wrede that, in fact, Mark and his audiences had no knowledge of any Jesus sayings in which Jesus declared himself the Christ. This explanation, however, fails to account for some striking contradictions to the messianic-secret theme. For example, Jesus commands the man delivered from a host of demons ("Legion," Mk 5:1-20) to tell those in his home country about what happened to him, thus at least to bear witness to Jesus' agency in effecting deliverance. Moreover, Jesus himself shatters the secret at his trial before the high priest. Another explanation for this "secret" must be sought.

---

[12]William Wrede, *The Messianic Secret,* trans. J. C. G. Greig (Cambridge: J. Clarke, 1971); German original: *Das Messiasgeheimnis in den Evangelien: zugleich ein Beitrag zum Verständnis des Markusevangeliums* (Göttingen: Vandenhoeck & Ruprecht, 1913). This has been the subject of considerable investigation. A helpful collection of essays representing the spectrum of inquiry is C. M. Tuckett, ed., *The Messianic Secret* (Philadelphia: Fortress, 1983). See also D. E. Aune, "The Problem of the Messianic Secret," *NovT* 11 (1969): 1-31.

A better explanation for Jesus' reluctance to have reports of his miracles and identity spread is found in Mark's conviction that Jesus' messiahship cannot be understood apart from his passion, and thus discipleship itself cannot be properly lived until the confession "Jesus is the Christ" is stripped of its misunderstandings and seen in light of the passion. Jesus' prohibitions to demons, to those who are healed and to those who guess correctly concerning his identity reveal Jesus' desire to guide the revelation of his own messiahship, to forestall premature declarations of his messiahship that will only be misunderstood before he faces the cross. There were, indeed, many models of messianic expectation in first century Judaism. A number of these focused on a divinely anointed military leader and king who would restore independent rule to Israel and raise his supporters to positions of power and influence. Even his inner circle of disciples were not immune to ambitions of this kind.

Premature confessions that Jesus was the Messiah would be meaningless, for the term *messiah* would be filled with a content and set of expectations not corresponding to his mission. Thus following Jesus would be an error, for it would be for the wrong reasons, with the wrong hopes and with misguided expectations. A careful definition of his own messiahship was essential for awakening true faith in human beings, delivering them from bondage to the world's wisdom and raising up disciples who could be fully committed to walk "the way of the Lord." In a modern context Mark might have to use this technique to show Christians that the gospel of Jesus Christ is not about having God's help in achieving materialistic goals or a trouble-free, pain-free life.

How does Mark present Jesus so that the readers release inadequate understandings of their confession of Jesus as the Messiah and move toward a fuller understanding of who he is? How does this reevaluation of "who Jesus is" lead to a reevaluation of what it means to be a follower of Jesus? Mark presents the story as "the good news of Jesus, the Messiah, the

Figure 5.2. Mt. Tabor, the site of the transfiguration. (Photo courtesy of Todd Bolen [BiblePlaces.com])

Figure 5.3. The theater of Gerasa, seen here from the less expensive seating. The *scena frons* is still intact, appearing much as it did when the Greek tragedies and comedies were performed here. Gerasa is thought by some to be the region in which Jesus cast out "Legion." (Photo courtesy of Todd Bolen [BiblePlaces.com])

Son of God" (Mk 1:1). For the readers there is no secret about Jesus' identity or the titles that belong to him. Demons, however, can make this confession but remain fundamentally opposed to the reign of God, and Peter can make this confession but remain ignorant of its meaning. The readers, too, must allow Mark to guide them in reconsidering the meaning of the confession so their faith is not as hollow as Peter's before the resurrection, nor as ineffective as the demons' confession.

At the outset of his ministry Jesus is certified by God: "You are my beloved Son, in whom I am well pleased" (Mk 1:11). This alerts the reader that Jesus shows the way of God and that his actions are all validated by God, whatever the temporal religious and political authorities may think of him. The way Jesus opens up for the disciples is also validated from the outset. This is the "way of the Lord," the highway from exile to the kingdom

of God promised by Isaiah (Mk 1:2-3). Just as the Lord led Israel from Egypt to Canaan and then from exile in Babylon to Judah, so Jesus leads the new people of God out of exile into the place of God's promise.

Jesus teaches with authority and charisma. The impression he makes on the people in general is strong and favorable. Crowds respond with astonishment to Jesus' teaching, acts of healing and exorcisms. His reputation grows and attracts followers from ever-wider circles of Palestine: by Mark 3:8 there are representatives from every corner of Israel among the crowd. The only people who remain unimpressed are those who stand to lose by his growing popularity, namely, the scribes and Pharisees who sought to broaden support for their understanding of following the way of God. Otherworldly beings (demons) recognize him as the "Holy One of God" or the "Son of the living God," but they are not allowed to make him known. Jesus works frequent miracles of healing and exorcism, which more than anything else seem to draw the attention of the crowd. Debates arise concerning the source of his power: is it the devil, as the scribes allege (Mk 3:22), or God, as the crowds assume as they glorify God in response to Jesus' works (Mk 2:12; 7:37)?

Jesus claims more for himself than his opponents believe right. When he forgives the sins of the paralyzed man in Mark 2:5, the scribes respond that only God has authority to forgive sins (Mk 2:7). The scribes are correct, but Jesus offers them a physical proof of his spiritual authority, healing the paralytic as a demonstration of his authority to forgive sins. Just as God alone is able to heal the paralyzed, so God alone does forgive the paralytic's sins. The scribes, however, are unable to grasp the point of Jesus' demonstration—that God is powerfully at work in Jesus—and so continue to oppose Jesus. A similar moment of revelation is offered to the disciples in the strange story of the stilling of the storm. They do not yet understand Jesus' identity. Interestingly, they do not say, "Save us, Lord, for we are perishing," but "don't you care that we [inclusive] are about to go under?" Do they expect Jesus to bail them out, as it were, or just meet the danger and death with eyes open? They clearly were not expecting Jesus to still the winds and the waves, for this act produces awe and fear. The disciples' question, "who is this, that even the winds and the sea obey him," has an implicit answer for any reader familiar with the Scriptures. Only One "makes the winds his messengers" (Ps 104:4) and says to the sea "here shall your proud waves be stopped" (Job 38:8-11 NRSV), namely, God.

The disciples, however, are having great difficulty putting this all together. Even after more healings, exorcisms, the spectacular raising of a dead girl and the provision of bread in the wilderness (an echo of God's earlier provision of manna in the wilderness), they still

cannot figure out who it is they are following. At the end of this first section Mark leaves the disciples in confusion. The disciples and Jesus embark on a boat having only one loaf of bread with them. Jesus says, "Beware of the leaven of the Pharisees and the leaven of Herod," and the disciples think he's talking about their failure to make adequate provisions for their evening meal. Jesus now applies to the disciples the same text from Isaiah that he had applied to the uncomprehending outsiders (Is 6:9-10; Mk 4:10-12): "Do you have eyes, and fail to see? Do you have ears, and fail to hear?" (Mk 8:18 NRSV). He rehearses with them the outcomes of the two miraculous feedings of the crowds and asks them "Do you not yet understand?" There is no response to this. The disciples don't understand, and in fact the reader is hard pressed to understand. This is a moment where Matthew added another verse to show that the disciples got the point ("Then they understood that he was speaking about the teaching of the Pharisees"), but Mark simply leaves us with the question.

The literary stage is set: Mark now reveals the true understanding of Jesus' messiahship. While the disciples themselves fail to understand until after the resurrection, they must return to these teachings in order to come to a correct assessment of Jesus' messiahship. Indeed, they should not be blamed for their lack of comprehension throughout the Gospel, nor judged too harshly for denying and forsaking Jesus at the threshold of his passion, for they could not come to a true faith in—or an informed loyalty to—Jesus until after his resurrection from the dead. Mark 8:22—10:52 is framed by two stories of the healing of blind men. In the first story the healing takes place in stages: the darkness over his sight leaves only by increments. In the second story the healing takes place at once, and the healed man immediately follows Jesus "on the way." This contrast in healing stories suggests that the intervening material also is concerned with removing blindness and allowing clear sight, not of the eyes but of spiritual insight into Jesus and the "way of the Lord" the disciples are called to follow.

Peter's confession (Mk 8:29) is not the climax of the Gospel, but only the first stage in a process of healing spiritual blindness. He has made a correct confession, but, together with the other disciples, must learn what it means that Jesus is the anointed agent of God's coming kingdom. Jesus immediately begins to teach them in the first of three passion predictions: "The Son of Man must undergo great suffering, and be rejected by the elders, the chief priests, and the scribes, and be killed, and after three days rise again" (Mk 8:31). Peter at once reveals his lack of insight into the very confession he has made, for he takes Jesus aside and seeks to correct Jesus' presentation of his own mission. Jesus returns the rebuke in front of the other disciples, thus letting them all know that "the things of God" are not in line with human expectations and preferences.

The first clear teaching on messiahship becomes then the occasion for the first clear teaching on what it means to follow this Messiah, namely, denying oneself, taking up the cross and following Jesus. It is a summons to pour out and give away one's life, and to stand boldly alongside the Messiah, who is degraded by this world but glorified by God (Mk 8:34-38). The shape of Jesus' messiahship is also the pattern of discipleship: bearing a cross, losing our life, despising the opinion of worldly people so that we may remain loyal to the One whose testimony to our worth alone counts.

This first teaching, however, fails to have an impact. Jesus offers a second prediction of his passion in Mark 9:31, which is met not with resistance but quiet incomprehension. Like so many students, "they did not understand what he was saying and were afraid to ask him" (Mk 9:32 NRSV). Their failure to understand Jesus'

mission, however, goes hand in hand with their failure to understand their own calling. Rather than inquire into Jesus' words about his messiahship, they indulge in an argument concerning who was the preeminent disciple. Status and honor were very important to the people of the ancient Mediterranean: for the Twelve, following Jesus meant a rise in status, for they became the gatekeepers to the favor of a great and powerful figure. Which of them was the leader, Jesus' right-hand person? Once more, a teaching on discipleship follows hard upon a teaching on messiahship: "Whoever wants to be first must be last of all and servant of all" (Mk 9:35 NRSV). Following Jesus was incompatible with seeking status and honor above fellow disciples. Rather, discipleship is about welcoming the little one, the weak, the child (Mk 9:36-37). The disciples were not the gatekeepers of Jesus' healing gifts and power but were to welcome the little ones, the ungreat, as those who themselves mediated God's presence. God's favor could not be controlled, channeled through the right people to make those people great and honored. Instead, God's presence is only known as the blessings of God's reign are extended to others. It is possessed only in the giving. In short, discipleship consists of serving others, not measuring rank.

The second teaching also fails to have an impact. This is made immediately clear by the narrative that follows: "John said to him, 'Teacher, we saw someone casting out demons in your name, and we tried to stop him, because he was not following us.' But Jesus said, 'Do not stop him; for no one who does a deed of power in my name will be able soon afterward to speak evil of me'" (Mk 9:38-39 NRSV). Someone who was not in the inner circle was intruding on the turf of the twelve, stealing the limelight. Jesus again had to remind the disciples that they could not be protective of exclusive rights to channel God's power. A little later, completely contrary to Jesus' second teaching on discipleship, the disciples try to send away people who brought their little children for Jesus to touch and bless (Mk 10:13-16). Once more they were trying to act as brokers of Jesus' power, trying to be judicious gatekeepers of the kingdom of heaven. This elicits Jesus' rebuke, and he provides an object lesson in the new order of the kingdom, where the little, powerless, unprofitable ones are welcomed guests.

Finally, leading them "on the way" to Jerusalem, Jesus speaks for a third time about passion, in greater detail now than before (Mk 10:32-34). Once again the disciples fail to understand. John and James come to Jesus and ask him for the preeminent places in the new order he will establish. Jesus cryptically points them to his passion, namely, the "baptism" he will receive and the "cup" he will drink. Indeed, the placement at the right and left hand has already been prepared for two criminals who will not share in Jesus' glory but in his suffering and humiliation. This final passion prediction and failure to understand gives rise to a third teaching on discipleship. Here Jesus explicitly contrasts the world's way of evaluating greatness, which has dominated the disciples' vision of Jesus and their own calling, and the way God measures greatness (see Mk 10:42-45). In the world greatness is preeminence, power and recognition. It includes being honored and being served by others. In God's sight greatness consists in serving others and pouring oneself out for them, even as Jesus himself came "not to be served but to serve, and to give his life as a ransom for many." Here Mark forges the closest link between Jesus' messiahship and true discipleship. Both are explicitly countercultural, and as long as a person remains blinded by the world's values he or she cannot see clearly to follow Jesus "on the way," as Bartimaeus does in the episode that closes this section of the Gospel (Mk 10:46-52).

After this point Jesus becomes quite open about his messiahship. He enacts a clear messianic paradigm as he enters Jerusalem, riding into the city as the king promised in Zechariah 9:9 (Mk 11:1-11). He openly affirms that he is "the Messiah, the Son of the Blessed One" in his trial before the Sanhedrin (Mk 14:61-62

Figure 5.4. Capernaum, on the shore of the Sea of Galilee, as seen from the air. Capernaum was the center of much of Jesus' ministry in Galilee. (Photo courtesy of Todd Bolen [BiblePlaces.com])

John the Baptist

The Gospel of Mark opens not with the sweet stories of a newborn baby and his virgin mother but with the hoarse shouting of a desert prophet, the one raised up by God at the appointed time to "prepare the way of the Lord" (Mk 1:3). The public ministry of Jesus is closely linked in all four Gospels to the public ministry of John the Baptist, and not all followers of the latter appear to have recognized that he was but the "forerunner" of Jesus (see Acts 19:1-5).

What was the significance of John's ministry? How would he have been understood by those who were immersed by him in the waters of the Jordan? Purifications in water were an important part of the everyday life of those Jews living in the community at Qumran, and at least a regular part of the lives of the more strictly observant Jews throughout Judea. Many homes have been found to contain a *mikveh,* a small stone pool hewn into the ground. A person would descend into the *mikveh,* be immersed in the water and emerge "clean." Similarly, the temple precincts were equipped with pools of water for the purification of those entering the sacred spaces.

In the context of the proclamation of the coming of God's holy, end-time agent, however, John's baptism may well have taken on the connotations of a ritual preparation for a theophany (an appearance of the Divine, as in Ex 19:9-15). The daily ritual purifications undertaken at Qumran, while regular as opposed to a single, decisive act, also were done with a view to entering into company of the holy One and his angels in the communal worship of the group. The letter to the Hebrews speaks of Christian baptism as purifying both the conscience *and the body* for an

Figure 5.5. A *mikveh* found in Jericho. Such pools for ritual purification were an important part of maintaining and recovering purity in Israel. (Photo courtesy of Todd Bolen [Bible-Places.com])

encounter with the holy God (Heb 10:19-22). Combined with repentance and confession of sin in preparation for the "more powerful one," John's baptism probably was regarded as a call to prepare oneself inside and out for encountering God on the near horizon. Thus John's ritual use of water was probably something of a transition between such precedents and the initiatory rite of baptism that would come to be a defining mark of the early Christian community.

John himself is regarded as the "forerunner" in Christian tradition (Mk 1:2-4). In Mark, John's message has to do wholly with this role (contrast Mt 3:7-12 and Lk 3:7-17, which develop at greater length John's call for repentance and a new ethic of sharing possessions). He is said to fulfill the expectation that Elijah, the prophet who was taken into heaven alive, would return at the appointed time to prepare Israel to encounter God favorably (see Mk 9:11-13). This expectation is introduced in Malachi 4:5-6, which Mark reads as an amplification and explanation of Malachi 3:1 (recited at Mk 1:2-3 in combination with Is 40:3). Ben Sira (see Sir 48:10), a wisdom teacher from about 180 B.C.E., also bears witness to this expectation. John the Baptist dresses in a manner reminiscent of Elijah (Mk 1:6; see 2 Kings 1:8) and encounters his death in a story that recalls the stories of Elijah, Ahab and Jezebel. In both, a king's wife, a flagrant transgressor of Torah, is responsible for the persecution of the prophets of the God of Israel.

Mark recounts the death of John the Baptist in detail, almost giving him a passion narrative of his own (Mk 6:14-29). The suggestion that Jesus is John raised from the dead and the fact that mortal opposition against Jesus already exists by Mark 3:6 begins to link the fate of these two emissaries of God. The interpretation of John's ministry and end in Mark 9:11-13 further suggests that the fate of the forerunner foreshadows the destiny of the Messiah as well. Just as Elijah returned and was treated shamefully at the hands of human beings, so the Son of Man, the "more powerful one," would also suffer and die. Mark offers the controversy story in Mark 11:27-33 as the final link between forerunner and Messiah. The scribes' and authorities' ambiguity about John the Baptist's authority mirrors their ambiguity about Jesus: both are regarded as God's spokespersons by the masses, but both will be opposed and executed by the leaders who fear their influence with the masses.

NRSV). As the passion approaches and becomes inevitable, his messiahship is increasingly in less danger of being misunderstood, so Jesus can abandon all the "secrecy." The disciples do not arrive at a true understanding within the space of the narrative, but the reader knows that when the risen Lord does encounter them in Galilee (Mk 16:7), their eyes will indeed be opened. The disciples who are Mark's audience, however, can come to that understanding as they read or hear read the Gospel itself, for they already know that Jesus is risen, that God has placed his eternal seal of approval on Jesus by raising him from the dead.

What does Mark wish to say to his readers? Jesus' messiahship is not present in his power only but also in his suffering and death. His lordship is not merely in his exaltation to the right hand of God but in his service to others to the point of being lifted up on a cross. Indeed, his subsequent exaltation shows that Jesus' way is the way of true greatness and honor in the sight of God. God's ways are *not* human ways. The world has it all wrong, and the disciples must unlearn what they have been taught by the world before they can be-

come true disciples. Honor and greatness cannot be found in achieving power over or greater prestige than others, but only in serving, in extending God's favor freely to others. It is found not in protecting one's status and power but in voluntarily giving up all such claims in order freely to serve the other. The "way of the Lord," prepared for by John the Baptist and pioneered by Jesus, will run counter to society's values and will provoke contempt, even hostility. Nevertheless, it is the way *of the Lord*, the path that stands approved by God, who will vindicate all who remain loyal to Jesus, who pioneered that way.

In sum, Jesus' messiahship is misunderstood when seen only in his working of miracles and compelling teaching. People can admire those aspects of Jesus without being transformed in their thinking. They can even want to be close to those aspects of Jesus, so that they may enjoy the prestige and power of being the brokers of such charisma ("may we sit at your right and left hand?"). Only after the contempt and the cross can Jesus' messiahship be understood, for only then do we understand God's will, God's values, God's way and signs of God's approval and anointing apart from worldly notions of success and greatness. Jesus' teachings concerning his mission and the true way of discipleship were nothing short of scandalous. He turned the world and its values upside down and still must today. Faith lives as if Jesus is right about the world's values being upside-down.

The relationship of Jesus and his followers to the Torah, temple and Judaism. Mark preserves many traditions that deal with conflicts between Jesus and representatives of other religious groups of the period, particularly Pharisees, scribes (which might be Pharisaic, Sadducean or nonpartisan) and Sadducees. These stories were of interest to the early church, in part, because they preserved the triumphs of Jesus in debate. These stories enhanced Jesus' honor, showed his quick thinking and demonstrated his superior grasp of the essence of the revelation of the Jewish Scriptures and the meaning of keeping God's Torah.

It is precisely here, however, that these stories would have become even more valuable to the early Christian communities. The Christians themselves took as their Scriptures the same books used by the synagogue. These books imparted God's revelation, to which the Christians looked for guidance and for legitimation for their faith and practice. The meaning of these Scriptures, however, was much debated within Judaism, and the interpretation given to the Scriptures by Christians was particularly suspect to most observant Jews. First,

Figure 5.6. The Second Temple, as reconstructed in the Holy Land Hotel model of ancient Jerusalem. The large outer court is the Court of the Gentiles, where Jesus' indictment of the temple occurred. (Photo courtesy of the Holyland Hotel and Todd Bolen [BiblePlaces.com])

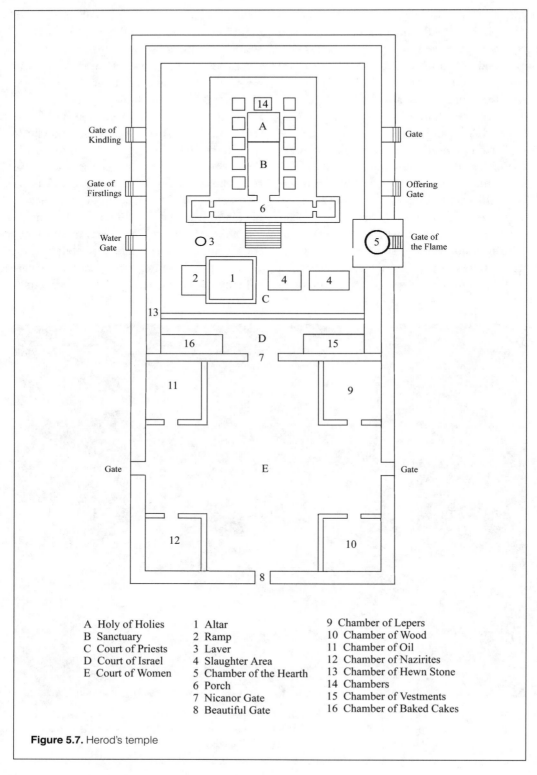

A Holy of Holies
B Sanctuary
C Court of Priests
D Court of Israel
E Court of Women

1 Altar
2 Ramp
3 Laver
4 Slaughter Area
5 Chamber of the Hearth
6 Porch
7 Nicanor Gate
8 Beautiful Gate

9 Chamber of Lepers
10 Chamber of Wood
11 Chamber of Oil
12 Chamber of Nazirites
13 Chamber of Hewn Stone
14 Chambers
15 Chamber of Vestments
16 Chamber of Baked Cakes

Figure 5.7. Herod's temple

the Christian's Messiah was markedly different. While Jesus fulfilled the "works of the Messiah" by healing the blind and the lame and giving life to the dead (an expectation shared by the people of Qumran, as seen in 4Q521), he also died a shameful death, which was part of no early Jewish messianic model. Second, the Christian way of keeping Torah (in seeming contempt for dietary rules, purity regulations and the like) struck at the heart of mainstream Jewish observance. Mark's attention to Old Testament Scriptures, to Jewish practices and to the central pillars of Jewish religion (i.e., Torah and temple) did far more than celebrate Jesus' triumphs in debate. It also helped strengthen Christian readers in their particular orientation to the Jewish Scriptures and to the law of God. It confirmed the believers' reading to be correct and their practice to be acceptable to God, even though the majority of Jews—the people most obviously addressed by the Jewish Scriptures—did not agree.

Old Testament citations. While Matthew does much more in terms of presenting Jesus' story as the fulfillment of Old Testament expectations, Mark already points the way to a Christian rereading of the Jewish Scriptures. Mark, indeed, opens his Gospel with quotations from Malachi and Isaiah. In Mark's reading of these texts (and we do not need to assume this is original to him), John the Baptist is the promised messenger, the herald of the Lord's coming. Unlike Malachi, the "Lord" in mind is not simply the visitation of the divine presence but the incarnation, the coming of Jesus who is the Lord. God is not coming, moreover, to purify the temple so that its sacrifices may again be acceptable (the broader context of Mal 3:1-4), but the Lord is coming to indict the temple for its failure and to replace it with the establishment of the Christian community as the place of God's favor. Isaiah declares that God will soon lead God's people on the way back from exile. The "way of the Lord" is the highway God has prepared back from Babylon to

Judah. Now, however, the "way of the Lord" is read as Jesus' way, the way of the cross, the way of discipleship. Mark also shows the disciples alluding to the wider expectation, drawn from Malachi 4:5, that Elijah would first return before the restoration (Mk 9:11). Again, this is interpreted as fulfilled in the ministry of John the Baptist, who suffered the fate of all prophets.

Mark also introduces a quotation from Isaiah 6:9-10 ("they may indeed look, but not perceive, and may listen, but not understand; so that they may not turn again and be forgiven") as part of an explanation of Jesus' teaching in parables. Jesus' own ministry reenacts Isaiah's ministry of stretching forth his hands to a rebellious people who would not receive his divinely appointed message. The parables become the vehicle that separates insiders from outsiders. Mark begins here to point to Scriptures which explain the rejection of Jesus by his own people and perhaps even the continued rejection of the Christian interpretation of the promises to Israel among Jews. Another Scripture that functions in a similar way is Psalm 118:22, "The stone that the builders rejected has become the cornerstone," used as the conclusion to the parable of the wicked tenants. This rather obscure passage takes on an important role for Christians, showing that God's written oracles themselves point to the rejection of the One who would become the cornerstone of the new temple of God, the Christian community.

Mark also affirms that the Jewish Scriptures attest to the strange and unexpected form of messiahship embodied by Jesus, showing that this was in fact the form of messiahship promised by God. No other set of messianic expectations within first-century Judaism includes a suffering and dying Messiah. While in some eschatological schemes the Messiah may be mortal and die, he never dies on behalf of others as a disgraced and executed criminal. The death and resurrection of Jesus sent early

Christians back to the Old Testament to read it in a new light. Their experience of the risen Lord convinced them that Jesus was indeed the Messiah, and this conviction made new texts jump out at them—texts that supported the paradigm discovered retrospectively in Jesus' ministry, passion and resurrection.

The disciples' reluctance to understand the concept of a suffering Messiah is not surprising. It was a new concept, completely at odds with the models of messiahship available to first-century Jews. Indeed, Mark's presentation of the disciples' difficulty with the concept also helps the readers understand why more Jews did not become a part of the early Christian movement. Mark begins to anchor this pattern in Scripture in a general way. For example, Mark depicts Jesus as asking his disciples: "How then *is it written* about the Son of Man, that he is to go through many sufferings and be treated with contempt" (Mk 9:12 NRSV). During the Last Supper, Jesus announces that "the Son of Man goes *as it is written of him*" (Mk 14:21 NRSV). After his prayer in the garden of Gethsemane, Jesus accepts his arrest with the words "let the scriptures be fulfilled" (Mk 14:49). In none of these, however, are specific texts invoked. Instead, a general claim is made that the Old Testament Scriptures do talk about a suffering and dying Messiah.

Mark also records specific Scriptures he regards as fulfilled in Jesus' passion and death. First, the desertion of the disciples is presented as the fulfillment of Zechariah 13:7: "I will strike the shepherd, and the sheep will be scattered" (Mk 14:27). The crucifixion narrative is filled with echoes of Old Testament Scriptures, especially Psalm 22, which is reconfigured in the passion narrative. Jesus explicitly quotes the first verse of this psalm—the only words he speaks from the cross in Mark: "My God, my God, why have you forsaken me" (Mk 15:34). While many have seen in this an expression of Jesus' utter abandonment, or have deduced doctrines to the effect

that God had to withdraw God's presence from Jesus so that Jesus could die, Mark's purpose is much more straightforward, namely, to point the reader to a rich scriptural oracle in which the sufferings of the Messiah are prefigured. The casting of lots for Jesus' garment and the mocking of the passersby also resonate with this psalm. Psalm 22, moreover, ends on a note of promise, that God will indeed deliver the righteous afflicted one, pointing suggestively ahead to the resurrection of Jesus.

The use of Scripture to interpret Jesus' ministry does not, however, stop at the passion and resurrection. It is also present in the depiction of his future actions on behalf of his people. Old Testament depictions of the end of the ages, when God would decisively intervene in human history, reappear in Mark 13:24-25, but with the new conviction that God's end-time agent is in fact Jesus himself. Mark weaves Daniel 7:13 into Mark 13:26 and 14:62, presenting Jesus as that "Son of Man" who will come in the clouds of heaven to usher in God's final rule. In Mark 14:62—Jesus' confession before the high priest and the Sanhedrin—this apocalyptic text is joined with Psalm 110:1, an otherwise very important text for relating the Scriptures to Jesus' person and ministry: "The LORD said to my Lord, 'Sit at my right hand, until I make your enemies a footstool for your feet'." This text establishes Jesus' present place in the cosmos, seated at God's right hand, awaiting the subjection of all who oppose his rule. Mark's incorporation of these texts would no doubt provide strong incentive to remain loyal to Jesus and to strain forward to the day when Jesus' rule would indeed be absolute.

Mark thus shares with the early church a strong commitment to the Jewish Scriptures but also to a specific reading of those Scriptures that highlights the pattern of the suffering and rising Messiah. The repeated appeal to Scripture, and the almost refrain-like claim that "the Son of Man does as it is written concerning him," reminds the community that Jesus was the end-time agent promised by God to effect salvation, and that in following him they are in the center of God's will.

Halakha and Torah's applicability. Jesus said, "Whoever does the will of God is my brother and sister and mother" (Mk 3:35 NRSV), but the prevailing view within Judaism was that the will of God is revealed in Torah. Were the Christians rightly interpreting the Torah? Was their way of walking in the commandments acceptable in God's sight? There were rival opinions within the ancient church concerning how God's law is to be kept (for example, the controversies regarding circumcision in Acts 15 and Galatians), and there were certainly many differences between the way Christians observed Torah and the way most Jewish groups observed Torah, to the extent that many Jews questioned whether or not Christians were keeping God's law at all.

Controversies between Jesus and Pharisees are remembered and retold in order to assure Christians that they are indeed fulfilling Torah the way God wants it to be fulfilled. In the context of an argument over the keeping of purity laws, Mark portrays Jesus quoting Isaiah's lament (Is 29:13; Mk 7:6-7 NRSV) that "this people honors me with their lips, but their hearts are far from me" as an indictment of the Pharisaic development of Torah, an increasingly influential stream of thought in first-century Judaism. This assures Mark's readers that their own *halakha* (their way of "walking" in line with God's law, a Hebrew word derived from *halak*, "to walk") and not the *halakha* of the Pharisees is the way to walk in order to please God. They are not outside of God's will because they have departed from the interpretation of Torah followed by other Jewish groups, but rather are affirmed in their following of Jesus' *halakha*. What Jesus has to

Table 5.1 "Prophecy and Fulfillment" in Mark's Gospel

OT passage	Marcan text	Topic	Kind of Reference
Is 40:3; Mal 3:1	Mk 1:2-3	John the Baptist's ministry	recitation
Mal 4:5	Mk 9:11	John the Baptist's ministry	reference
Is 6:9-10	Mk 4:12	rejection of Jesus	recitation
Is 29:13	Mk 7:6-7	Jesus' rivals	recitation
unspecified	Mk 9:12	Jesus' suffering	general reference
Ps 118:26	Mk 12:10-11	rejection of Jesus	recitation
Dan 7:13	Mk 13:26; 14:62	Jesus' return	recontextualizations
Unspecified	Mk 14:21	Jesus' suffering	general reference
Zech 13:7	Mk 14:27	disciples scattered	recitation
"the Scriptures"	Mk 14:49	Jesus' suffering	general reference
Ps 110:1	Mk 14:62 (12:36)	Jesus' exaltation	recontextualization (recitation)
Ps 22	Mk 15:23-36	Jesus' crucifixion	echoes
Ps 22:1	Mk 15:34	Jesus' crucifixion	recitation

say about Torah and how to live out obedience to God will be of great importance for his followers.

First, Jesus affirms much of Torah. When asked about the greatest commandment, he replies by quoting the opening of the *Shema* (Deut 6:4) together with a commandment from Leviticus 19:18: "'Hear, O Israel: The Lord our God, the Lord is one; you shall love the Lord your God with all your heart, and with all your soul, and with all your mind, and with all your strength.' The second is this, 'You shall love your neighbor as yourself.' There is no other commandment greater than these" (Mk 12:29-31 NRSV). Commitment to the one God revealed in Torah, to the exclusion of all other "gods," was one tenet Christians and Jews could agree on. When the rich young man approaches Jesus seeking the way to inherit eternal life, Jesus again affirms several of the commandments: "You know the commandments: 'You shall not murder; You shall not commit adultery; You shall not steal; You shall not bear false witness; You shall not defraud; Honor your father and mother'" (Mk 10:19 NRSV). The story of the rich young man, however, also shows that keeping the commandments is insufficient: we must also follow Jesus in order to be walking correctly before God.

In Mark, Jesus does not arbitrarily set aside Torah. Indeed, in a number of places Jesus is shown attacking the Pharisees for not obeying God's Torah well enough! For example, the Pharisees developed the principle of "Corban," whereby some portion or all of a person's belongings are dedicated as an offering to God, although the person retained the use of them during his or her life. If such a vow was undertaken, the person's goods were considered sacred, as if already deposited in the temple, so that person might justly refuse aid to his or her parents. Jesus condemned this development as an offense to the fifth commandment of the Decalogue.

Jesus was, however, not only critical of developments of later Jewish law which contravened Torah, but he was also critical of Torah itself where it contravened the clear purpose of God. This comes out clearly in the argument concerning divorce. Divorce was an acceptable practice according to the Torah itself, for "Moses allowed a man to write a certificate of dismissal and to divorce her" (Mk 10:4 NRSV). Jesus, however, opposes the practice based on God's purposes revealed in creation (Mk 10:6-9). Torah's allowance is a concession to "hardness of heart" (Mk 10:5). This is an important principle for the early church's handling of Torah—not as it pertained merely to divorce but as a rule of broader application. God's earlier purposes and designs are not limited or set aside by the Torah, which begins increasingly to appear as a mixture of God's will for people, God's concessions to fallen people and God's temporary provisions for a particular people "until the fullness of time." For example, Paul used a very similar argument in Galatians, when he points out that God's will was to bless all nations in Abraham, not privilege just one nation. The Torah, "added 430 years later, does not nullify a testament previously ratified by God, so as to make the promise void" (Gal 3:17-18).

While Jesus affirms the aspects of Torah that have universal applicability and enhance the fulfillment of the promise to Abraham, he is also portrayed as setting aside or violating the commandments that promote boundaries between observant and nonobservant Jews. This becomes an important precedent for the later question of whether or not to maintain those aspects of Torah that preserve the barrier between Jew and Gentile.

First, Pharisees would call Jesus remiss in his observation of purity rules. Very early in the story (Mk 1:40-45) he touches a leper, a ritually unclean and marginalized Jew. As the story unfolds however, the contact does not defile Jesus but rather results in the leper's being made clean. He is told to go to the priests in Jerusalem to offer the sacrifice that will witness to this cleansing. In the second of a series of five controversy stories (Mk 2:1—3:6), some Pharisees question Jesus' practice of eating with tax collectors and sinners—those Jews who were not careful about keeping Torah to the same degree and in the same way as the Pharisees. In the Pharisees' eyes Jesus' act was incomprehensible, for he was opening himself up to being defiled by having table fellowship with the defiled. Jesus responds not in terms of purity but in terms of mission. He is appointed by God as a physician to the sick. He walks among the unrighteous in order to call them to righteousness, and he does not avoid his mission out of fear that his own purity will be compromised.

The third episode centering on Jesus' relationship to purity is the most well-developed and the most important for defining Jesus' *halakha* for his disciples. The Pharisees challenge Jesus because his disciples do not perform a ritual purification of the hands before eating, a safeguard against defilement (Mk 7:1-5). The Pharisees seek to fulfill Torah—particularly the commandments about keeping pure from defilement—according to the *halakha* developed by their teachers. So they question why Jesus' disciples disregard such concerns. In response Jesus proclaims an entirely new definition of what constitutes purity and what defiles a person in God's sight: "Hear me, all of you, and understand: there is nothing outside a person which by going into that person can defile him or her; but the things which come out of a person are what defile" (Mk 7:14-15). This is such a radical teaching concerning purity regulations that his own disciples ask for further clarification. Jesus explains that "whatever goes into a person from outside cannot defile a person, since it enters not the heart but the stomach and so passes on?" (Mk 7:18-19). Instead, Jesus points to "what comes out of a person," namely, "evil thoughts, fornication, theft, murder, adultery, coveting, wicked-

ness, deceit, licentiousness, envy, slander, pride, foolishness," as the things that actually "defile a person" (Mk 7:20-23).

These words were no doubt of particular importance to early Christians, providing authoritative guidance concerning the observance of the purity regulations of Torah (and its later developments). Observing the form of the commandment, which had the practical effect of keeping the observant separate from the sinners, is replaced by a concern for moral purity and moral defilement, in effect keeping the follower of Jesus separate from sin within and from the sin that poisons human relationships. The language of purity and defilement remains meaningful, but the way of remaining pure has received a new definition. We can observe that Mark (or an early copyist) also draws his own conclusion with regard to Jesus' statements: "Thus he declared all foods clean" (Mk 7:19). This shows that early Christians were engaged in a similar process as the Pharisees themselves, namely, taking the commandments of God (or, for Christians, of Jesus), which do not cover every possible circumstance of life, and extending them to cover more and more ground. Jesus' words about purity have obvious implications also concerning the dietary laws of Torah: there is no longer any distinction between clean and unclean food, and therefore no barrier to Jewish followers of Jesus eating with Gentile followers of Jesus.

Jesus also engages the Pharisees concerning the keeping of the sabbath. Jesus does not explicitly affirm the sabbath commandment when he cites summaries of the law, but he does not appear to have disregarded it entirely. On the first occasion (Mk 2:23-28) Jesus' disciples were rubbing heads of grain, foraging for their lunch as it were, on a sabbath. The Pharisees ask Jesus to account for his disciples' action, which was clearly in breach of sabbath-keeping as envisioned by the Torah. The observance of the sabbath was a very visible sign of Jewishness, particularly in the Diaspora. Even if a Gentile knew little else about Jews, he or she knew that they took one day off every week. Sabbath-keeping was an important identity-marker for Jews. Jesus' appeal to Scripture and his declaration that "the sabbath was made for people, not people for the sabbath," place human need above religious observance. Similarly, he contends in the next episode (Mk 3:1-6) that healing (or doing good in general) is permissible on the sabbath, for doing good, releasing the captives and healing the sick is never displeasing in God's sight. Indeed, to withhold good for the sake of rigid observance of the prohibition of working on the sabbath would be the true violation of God's law, according to which mercy and compassion are never out of season.

What gives Jesus the authority to teach how Torah is to be observed, indeed, to set aside the literal observance of Torah altogether in many respects? To the non-Christian, Jesus died as a sinner, a transgressor of Torah (not only a blasphemer but a breaker of the sabbath, of purity laws and so forth). The Christian proclamation that God raised this Jesus from the dead was absurd. Why would God vindicate a sinner, a law-breaker? For those who believed that God raised Jesus from the dead, however, this very vindication by God means that Jesus was *not* a sinner but that he taught "the way of God in accordance with truth" (Mk 12:14 NRSV). God's raising of Jesus shows him to be righteous in God's sight, vindicates Jesus' way of observing Torah and commends that way to Jesus' disciples as the way of obedience that pleases God.

Temple. Together with Torah the Jerusalem temple formed the center of Jewish identity and piety. Jesus' actions with regard to the temple would remain important for early Christians, since the Scriptures taken over by the Christian church from the synagogue speak of the temple as the place where God meets God's people, where sacrifices for sin are offered, where forgiveness is obtained, and where God will hear the prayers of God's people. The structure of the temple precincts, however, mapped out the distance between Gentiles, including Gentile Christians, and this holy God. Gentiles were permitted only to enter the Court of the Gentiles, the outermost court in the temple complex. Though they could bring sacrifices, which would be taken by priests from the Court of the Gentiles into the inner courts and finally to the altar, the exclusion of the worshipers themselves from the inner courts (the Court of Women and the Court of Israelites [males only]) conveyed a very different message from the Christian proclamation of adoption as God's daughters and sons to the Gentiles. Which message accurately represented the Gentile Christians' place in God's house? Jesus' disruption of the activity in the temple's Court of the Gentiles, together with the declaration that the inner curtain of the temple was rent at Jesus' death, would have been of crucial significance in clarifying the ongoing role of the temple in mediating God's favor and presence for Jesus' followers.

Unlike Matthew and Luke, Mark places the story of Jesus' cleansing of the temple within the story of the cursing of the fig tree (see Mk 11:12-25). This context gives Jesus' action in the temple a much sharper edge in Mark's version of the story. Jesus comes to the temple looking for fruit, just as he went to the fig tree looking for fruit. Both have the appearance of flourishing, but both are found to be barren. Jesus does not exactly "cleanse" the temple, as if he is purifying it so that its sacrifices may be again acceptable. Rather, he indicts the temple's administrators for not fulfilling God's purpose for the temple, namely, making it a "house of prayer for all nations" (Is 56:7). Instead, the Court of the Gentiles is so empty and irrelevant to their concern that it serves as a convenient place for the moneychangers and vendors of animals for sacrifice. Mark understands this visit to the temple to be a rejection of the temple as the place of mediating God's favor and forgiveness. Just as the fig tree withers after it was found not to have lived up to its promise, so the temple will wither for failing to raise up a godly crop from all nations to serve the one God (Mk 13:1-2). The promises entrusted to Israel for the blessing of the nations now find fruition in a new place of mediation, namely, the cross of Jesus Messiah. As Jesus' sacrifice of himself is consummated, the veil that preserved the sanctity of the holy of

Israel. Mark speaks, finally, to the question of the believers' relationship to historic Israel, the ethnically defined nation. In the second series of controversy stories (Mk 11:27—12:37), Mark recounts Jesus' parable of the wicked tenants. This begins with familiar imagery from Isaiah 5:1-7, where God plants a vineyard, Israel, and comes looking for grapes. There is an important difference in Jesus' version of this ancient parable: the focus is now on the "tenants," those who are given the vineyard for a term but are not

Figure 5.8. The Western Wall is perhaps the most significant surviving part of the Second Temple enclosure. The stones whose size had so impressed the disciples (Mk 13:1-2) are clearly visible. (Photo courtesy of Todd Bolen [BiblePlaces.com])

holies is (quite probably figuratively) ripped by unseen hands.

Where can a person now meet God, receive forgiveness and petition the divine Patron for help? In Mark 11:22-25, Jesus teaches his followers not to rely on assembling in a sacred space for their prayers, but by praying and practicing mutual forgiveness to make the place of their assembly sacred. Jesus assures them of the efficacy of their prayers offered in trust and of God's forgiveness of those who themselves forgive their neighbors.

themselves the vineyard. As the parable unfolds, the vineyard's yield is much more bitter than the wild grapes of Isaiah. The tenants abuse and murder those whom the owner sends to them, an allusion to God's prophetic messengers sent to call Israel back to bearing the fruits of righteousness. At the end of the parable the wicked tenants are cut off, and the vineyard is given to others.

By focusing on the tenants who have custodial charge over the vineyard, Jesus focused his indictment on Israel's leaders (as they apparently understood; Mk 12:12). Jesus' opponents would no longer enjoy the privilege of overseeing the people of God, which passes instead to Jesus' followers. For Mark and his readers, however, this revision of Isaiah's parable does not narrowly identify the vineyard of God with the ethnic people of Israel. Under the leadership of the disciples of Jesus, the vineyard, the new people of God, now includes both Jews and Gentiles who have committed themselves to following God's Son. The vineyard is no longer defined by ethnicity but by obedience to the Son's call to bring forth the fruit God desires.

Mark as an "apology for the cross." Scholars have often viewed Mark's Gospel as a corrective for a "theology of glory," a view of Christ that took too little account of the significance of his suffering and death. According to this "theology of glory," following Christ meant the experience of God's power, being endowed with the Holy Spirit and the supernatural gifts, and possessing a quality of life above and beyond what could be enjoyed otherwise. We find evidence for such a view in the Corinthian churches, for example, where Christ and his true apostles are regarded as figures of power and impressiveness: the "power of God" manifested in powerful personages. Just as Paul had to correct that view with his emphasis on being conformed to Christ's death as a necessary prerequisite for sharing in Christ's glory, so Mark may be shaping his Gospel toward the passion so his readers may finally grasp "the power of God perfected in weakness." There is much to commend this view, since foreshadowings of the passion fill the first half of Mark's narrative. As early as Mark 2:20, Jesus points to the time when "the bridegroom will be taken away."

Robert Gundry highlights another side to this discussion. He reads Mark not as a presentation of suffering as a counterbalance to

glory, but as a presentation of Christ's glory as a counterbalance to his sufferings.[13] Gundry correctly notes that death on a cross was an astounding affront to ancient sensibilities. Mark may take his place alongside many other early Christian writers who attempt to deal with the scandal of the cross. Both sides of the debate are correct. On the one hand, Mark does seem clearly interested in locating the correct interpretation of Jesus' messiahship and therefore Christian discipleship in the passion of Jesus (see pp. 204-6). Christianity is not about enjoying the power of God except as this power leads us to self-giving service to others and wholehearted obedience to God, whatever that might entail. However, Mark also affirms that Jesus was an honorable figure, that the crucifixion is not a reflection on Jesus' lack of honor and therefore that any diminishing of status Christians might suffer here on account of loyalty to Jesus is no reflection on their true honor as children of God. Thus while the stories of divine power are not correctly seen except in light of the passion, the passion is also not correctly seen except in light of God's presence and power at work in Jesus.

From an outsider's perspective Jesus' execution could appear to have been that of a troublemaker. After all, Jesus rode into the capital city in a manner that suggested kingly (and thus revolutionary) aspirations, and he was accompanied by a crowd that could make that revolution happen in the volatile setting of Roman Judea. He staged a demonstration in the temple itself, something that would be recognized as a revolutionary disturbance by both Judean and Roman officials, and he was tried and executed accordingly.

Mark's presentation of Jesus, however, makes it clear that his execution was not the deserved end of a criminal and deviant. Jesus is affirmed by God as God's own beloved Son, whose life pleases God, who shows the way to

---

[13]Robert H. Gundry, *Mark: A Commentary on His Apology for the Cross* (Grand Rapids: Eerdmans, 1993).

EXEGETICAL SKILL
Examining Literary Context

In many liturgical traditions a worship service includes the reading of anywhere from one to four short selections from the Bible, one or more of these being the basis of the pastor's sermon. This practice does not encourage the parishioner to think of a passage of Scripture as part of a single, integrated, literary whole, but rather as an isolated incident in the life of Jesus or a brief meditation by the apostle Paul. Every paragraph of Scripture, however, is part of a larger text, and was composed to be heard in the context of that larger text. Thus 1 Corinthians 13, often excerpted and read at wedding services, is not merely a poem on love but an integral part of that sustained attempt at reshaping the attitudes and ethos of Christians churches. In order to understand Paul's word to the churches in 1 Corinthians 13, it is imperative to consider how that chapter fits into the overall case that Paul is making.

When the biblical interpreter studies the literary context of a passage, he or she seeks to understand how it is informed by and how it informs the larger text it is a component of. Can we identify other passages that resonate with themes of the passage under investigation? How does the larger conversation about that theme within the book affect the way the particular passage is read? Where does the passage stand within the flow of the book? Does it prepare for what comes later in the book? Does it clarify, provide more information concerning or fulfill something that comes before? Does it provide an argument or an example that will be built on later? Or does it draw conclusions or frame exhortations based on preceding arguments? It is important also to consider the immediate literary context: is there some sense in which the passages immediately before and after guide or affect the way the passage under investigation is read? Do they amplify its impact or perhaps form intentional contrasts?

In the discussion of messiahship and discipleship in the central section of Mark's Gospel, we saw how the investigation of literary context enlightens and enlivens the study of a particular passage of Scripture. Mark did not intend for the teaching about discipleship in Mark 10:35-45, for example, to instruct Christians on its own but rather as part of a carefully structured and programmed whole. The person who would hear and help others hear Mark 10:35-45 as its author intended, then, would do well to attend to the following as part of his or her preparation and presentation.

First, how does this passage build on or advance material that has preceded it in Mark? This third teaching on discipleship clarifies the first two in the series of instructions on discipleship (Mk 8:34-37; 9:33-37). Mark 10:35-45 clarifies what "taking up a cross" or "losing one's life" actually looks like and provides this information more fully than even Mark 9:33-35; those vague yet powerful and pervasive images of discipleship that ring out from the first teaching on discipleship are made real.

Second, how is this teaching on discipleship illumined by its immediately preceding context, namely, the third passion prediction that precedes it (Mk 10:32-34)? Since each instruction on discipleship is preceded by such a prediction, Mark clearly is trying to impress Christians with the fact that claiming *this* Jesus as Lord and Messiah entails walking as he walked. They must be attentive to the ways God will call each of them to lay down their lives in service to others rather than using religion as a means to self-satisfaction or self-aggrandizement. The ways Mark 10:35-45 foreshadows Jesus' passion (the "cup" and "baptism" images, the connection between James's and John's request to "sit at the right and the left hand" and the crucifixion of the thieves to the right and left of Jesus, and Jesus' claim to give his life "as a ransom for many") also reinforce this message.

Third, how does the sequel to this passage, Jesus' healing of the blind Bar-Timaeus, enhance the reading of the passage and grasp of its meaning? This invites reflection on Mark's larger framing technique, which places healings of blind persons on either side of this middle section on seeing Jesus' messiahship and our discipleship more clearly. More specifically, this next episode provides a concrete demonstration of Jesus' servanthood—and the servanthood Jesus expects from his disciples—as he stops the grand procession to Jerusalem in order to help this poor, powerless beggar.

Fourth, how does this passage prepare for episodes yet to come in the narrative? Mark 10:45 continues Mark's preparation for the passion narrative. Just as the passion predictions throughout the middle section of Mark underscore the voluntary nature of Jesus' death and the assurance of God's vindication of Jesus, Mark 10:45 underscores the advantage that this death will bring to others, using the language of dying on behalf of others. Together, this contributes to the perception of the passion as a noble death, quite contrary to the usual response to reflecting on a crucifixion.

As a second example of exploring a passage in its literary context (as well as the importance and fruitfulness of doing so) we may consider the episode in the temple (Mk 11:15-19). This episode can be viewed in one of two ways. Traditionally, it is called "The Cleansing of the Temple," a title that suggests Jesus is acting as one who restores the temple to its proper function. An alternative view would call it "The Indictment of the Temple," regarding Jesus' actions in the temple as a performative act signaling the temple's failure to achieve God's purposes for it and its forthcoming destruction under divine judgment.

How does Mark understand this episode? Thinking about the passage in its literary context may provide some important clues. First, Mark has embedded the temple episode in between the initial cursing of the fig tree and the disciples' next-day observation of the tree's death (Mk 11:12-14, 20-26). This use of the fig tree episode as the literary frame for the temple episode is unique to Mark, and represents a conscious choice (one that

Matthew and Luke will undo) that leads the reader to interpret the temple episode in light of the fig tree episode. Just as Jesus came to the fig tree, which gave signs of bearing fruit even though the visitation was "out of season," and cursed it for its deceptive appearance, so Mark understands Jesus' visit to the temple to be a visit at an unexpected season resulting in a curse for its failure to bear the appropriate fruit. The Evangelist's interpretation may be at variance with the traditional understanding of Jesus' act, and the detail retained by Mark that Jesus actively preserved the sanctity of the temple for a short while by not allowing through traffic (Mk 11:16) may suggest more of a restorative hue. Mark's frame, however, suggests judgment and replacement, particularly Mark 11:20-26. There, Jesus speaks of faith, prayer and mutual forgiveness as all the resources the disciples need for ongoing access to God's favor (the basic role of the temple) in the aftermath of the indictment of the temple's failure as a "house of prayer" (Mk 11:17).

Looking to the broader literary context, we find that the passage prepares for subsequent passages concerning the temple, namely, the prophecy of the temple's eventual destruction (Mk 13:1-2) that sets the stage for the "Apocalyptic Discourse," and the rending of the veil of the temple at the crucifixion (Mk 15:38). The indictment of the temple is thus the first of three crucial references to the temple; the second clarifies the significance of Jesus' action in the temple (plainly prophesying its destruction); and the third points to the replacement of the temple with the cross of Jesus as the place for atonement and securing God's favor. The passage also gives added poignancy to the instructions to the disciples to "watch" carefully for Christ's future coming at an unexpected time (or out of season; Mk 13:32-37). The discerning hearer might recall the temple episode with its framing narrative about the fig tree when Jesus warns: "from the fig tree learn its lesson" (Mk 13:28), even though a second fig tree example follows. The fate of the first fig tree and that of the temple would also be their own, should they fail to "watch" and produce the sort of fruits for which Jesus looks.

Finally, the passage stands at an important juncture in the narrative development of Mark, for whom conflict and opposition have been important themes from the outset. The passage builds on Jesus' critique of contemporary Jewish religion and religious symbolism (sabbath, purity and now temple) in light of God's purpose for Israel and the law. This conflict and critique continues into Mark 12. The action in the temple prepares for the arrest and trial of Jesus before the Sanhedrin; it arouses the hostile intent of the chief priests (Mk 11:18). Charges concerning Jesus' attitude toward the temple reemerge at his trial (Mk 14:58), where his action in the temple is interpreted (correctly?) as a threat to the temple's existence.

One of the most basic exegetical skills to apply, then, is reading a passage in its literary context. Whether working with narrative (as in the Gospels and Acts) or discourse (as in the Epistles) or apocalypse (Revelation), every paragraph in a given book is interconnected with, builds on and clarifies, and prepares for and is further clarified by other paragraphs in that book. Asking the kinds of questions of a passage posed above will assure that you hear—and help others hear—the meaning of the passage as it is informed by and informs that larger whole of which it is a part.

You may wish to explore this skill using one or more of the following passages: Mark 3:1-6; Matthew 21:33-44; Luke 4:16-20; 1 Corinthians 13; Galatians 5:1-11; Hebrews 2:1-4. Read the passage itself, then look at the pericopes and even the whole chapter before and after the passage, and finally read through the entire text in which the passage appears, noting possible connections and interrelations at each phase. Then pose the questions listed in the second paragraph of this section to each text that you have chosen. How has attention to the literary context of a particular passage enriched your understanding of what that passage means, how it functions within and what it contributes to the whole book of which it is a part?

please God: "This is my Son, the Beloved; *listen to him*" (Mk 9:7 NRSV). Jesus, moreover, moves throughout the Gospel as a mediator of divine favor, a savior and benefactor who gives sight to the blind, restores the paralytic, opens the ears of the deaf, gives life to the dead, and drives out unclean spirits that torment people and destroy their lives. The verdict of public opinion is that "he has done all things nobly" (Mk 7:37). The proper response to one who provides gifts of such magnitude is gratitude, loyalty and service.

Why then does Jesus come to trial and execution? Jesus' teaching concerning how to do the will of God departs radically from the way many other Jews understand their covenant obligations. His opponents do not accept that Jesus has been divinely appointed as the teacher of how to truly fulfill the covenant and perform God's will. To the scribes, Pharisees and priests, he appears rather as an enemy of the law. Mark suggests, however, that the motives of Jesus' opponents were not pure. First-

century Judaism contained many diverse interpretations of how to follow Torah, how to please God. The environment was competitive, seen for example in the successful attempts of one party—the Sadducees—to retain control of the temple, or the increasingly successful attempts of another party—the Pharisees—to gain support for their interpretation of Torah among the non-elites. Jesus, Mark suggests, was a threat to the success of such parties. When Jesus comes to trial, the Sanhedrin is not seeking an explanation but a conviction. When Jesus stands before Pilate, even this dull governor recognizes that Jesus' accusers are acting out of "envy" (Mk 15:10). Envy was considered a base passion in the ancient world. Unlike emulation, which is spurred on to more virtuous and energetic enterprises by the success of another, envy is destructive, seeking to deprive a virtuous person of the rewards he or she has justly achieved.[14]

What then is the impact of Mark's presentation of Jesus' trial and execution? Far from

[14]See Aristotle *Rhet.* 2.11 (1388a 33-36) on the distinction between emulation and envy.

rousing disgust at Jesus as a shameful deviant, Mark rouses indignation at Jesus' crucifixion. For Mark's audience Jesus has clearly done nothing to deserve death, but rather he deserves honor and obedience. The same indignation appears when we hear the parable of the wicked tenants; indeed it motivates the householder to destroy the wicked tenants and give the vineyard to others. Christians will also realize that just as the verdict of condemnation, the mocking, beating, and shameful death of Jesus were no true reflection of Jesus' honor and character, so the Christians' experience of society's suspicion, hostility or rejection is no true reflection of their honor and virtue. If society forms a low opinion of Christians, it is not because the Christians merit this low rating. Christians are loyal and obedient to the One whose walk and character God approved, and so they can be assured of their virtue and honor. They are freed from the social pressure to conform to their former non-Christian ways by the assurance that in God's sight they have made the right commitment. Just as God vindicated Jesus by raising him from the dead, so God will approve the Christians at the judgment, vindicating them in the sight of their detractors.

Mark's presentation of Jesus' teachings about his own messiahship and true discipleship causes readers to be sure they understand that if they continue to think according to the world's values and definitions of greatness, they will miss Jesus' message and fail to respond. However, Mark also assures them that the way of Jesus, while it moves them away from "glory" as the world recognizes it, will lead to true honor and lasting approval before the One whose opinion alone counts eternally.

Mark goes even further than this: having shown that Jesus' death was not the deserved execution of a criminal, he goes on to show that it was not merely an unfortunate injustice either. Jesus' death is an act that will benefit many. It is the outworking of the will of God (Mk 14:36), foreordained by God as announced in sacred oracles (Mk 12:10-11; 14:49). It is an experience that Jesus undergoes voluntarily and intentionally. The predictions of the passion show that Jesus was not caught

Figure 5.9. Three crosses erected at Tantur, showing a rough-hewn crossbar, such as would have been carried by the criminal to the place of execution, affixed to the stumps of large trees. (Photo courtesy of Todd Bolen [BiblePlaces.com])

off guard but rather knew that his suffering and death was forthcoming, and that he embraced it freely. The prayer in the garden shows that it was not an easy act by any means; this makes it all the more generous and astounding. Jesus offered his death on behalf of others, rendering it noble no matter what form it took. "The Son of Man came not to be served but to serve, and to give his life a ransom for many"; "This is my blood of the covenant, which is poured out for many" (Mk 10:45; 14:24 NRSV). Jesus presents his death in terms similar to those used by the martyrs during the Hellenization crisis, who endured a disgraceful death rather than disobey God's Torah (see 4 Macc 6:27-29; 17:20-22). They prayed that God would accept their deaths in obedience to God's will on behalf of the rest of their nation, and that God would therefore turn again in mercy toward the people. In a similar manner Jesus' death is presented as that self-giving sacrifice which secures God's favor for all who follow in Jesus' way. This is a theme that is much more fully developed in Paul and Hebrews, for example, but that is not absent from Mark's presentation of the significance of Jesus' death on the cross. When his sacrifice is completed, God rips the veil of the temple—an image expressing the conviction that access to the holy God is no longer limited and regulated by the Levitical cult, but enjoyed openly in Jesus.

The ending of Mark's Gospel. The ending of Mark's Gospel poses a special problem. The majority of later manuscripts include a number of resurrection appearances and a commissioning speech (Mk 16:9-20, the "longer ending"), although not all witnesses agree on the extent of this longer ending. One manuscript includes within the longer ending a very interesting conversation between the disciples and Jesus; the disciples seek to excuse their slowness of faith by pointing to Satan's influence over this present age. Jesus responds that his death makes provision for sinners to return to the truth and inherit the next age. A number

of manuscripts that include the longer ending also mark it as potentially spurious. A single manuscript closes Mark with a "shorter ending" (included in brackets in the NRSV), while a number of manuscripts incorporate both the longer and the shorter ending. The most ancient manuscripts, however, end Mark's Gospel abruptly at Mark 16:8.

How can we account for this textual chaos? Are either the shorter or longer endings original to Mark? This is unlikely for a number of reasons. The shorter ending blatantly contradicts Mark 16:8. While Mark leaves the first witnesses mute ("they said nothing to anyone, for they were afraid"), the shorter ending adds that "all that had been commanded them they told briefly to those around Peter" (NRSV). If Mark had provided this shorter ending himself, he would have contradicted himself: did the women tell no one, or did they tell the disciples briefly? A more reasonable explanation is that a later copyist, sensing that something was missing after Mark 16:8, added a notice that the women did indeed tell the disciples about the resurrection. The copyist, aware of the tension of Mark's silent witnesses and the tradition of the women telling the disciples what they found, sought to resolve the tension by having them tell the disciples, but only "briefly."

The longer ending is the more revered and widely used of the two, preserving an early Christian tradition whose status as canonical Scripture is beyond question. Nevertheless it does not appear to have been part of the original form of Mark's Gospel. If it were, there would have been no explanation for many early manuscripts omitting it, while it is easy to see why later copyists and readers would want to bring closure to a narrative that ended so anticlimactically as Mark 16:8. Indeed, it is easy to see how a scribe constructed this ending out of traditions present in the other three Gospels, Acts and the letter to the Hebrews. This provided Mark with an ending consonant with the other canonical books. An indirect piece of evidence for Mark 16:9-20 being unoriginal is the fact that Matthew, who follows Mark so very closely everywhere else, departs from Mark's narrative precisely at Mark 16:8a and following. Both external evidence (the manuscript tradition) and internal evidence (Synoptic comparison as well as style: Mk 16:9-20 uses Greek participles very frequently and in a very sophisticated manner) point to the longer ending being a secondary addition attached to Mark.

If neither of the two endings provided by later scribes is original, did the Gospel really end at Mark 16:8, or was an original ending lost very early in transmission?[15] Some have argued that the Gospel *could not* have ended at 16:8 because the last word in the Greek is a conjunction. This claim is misleading, however, since the Greek conjunction *gar* ("for") never stands at the beginning of a clause, so it is unlike its English equivalent, "for." In a two-word clause such as the second part of Mark 16:8, the rules of Greek grammar place the conjunction *gar* in the second position, hence at the end. It would thus be grammatically correct for Mark to end a sentence, a paragraph or even a book with this word. While many authors end sentences and even paragraphs with *gar,* however, Mark would be the *only* known instance of ending a book (or even a speech) with this word.[16] The grammatical argument is therefore false, but the stylistic argument is weighted in the direction of a lost ending.

Clayton Croy argues that Mark has created the expectation of resurrection appearances and a rendezvous in Galilee, expectations that must be fulfilled within the narrative. Closure and fulfillment of narrative expectations was very important to the ancient reader, who was not as disposed to approve a cliffhanger ending or the loose end that leaves open the possibility of a sequel so common in modern novels and movies.[17] Moreover, the Christian proclamation itself made the framework of death, burial and resurrection appearances part of the expectation of the Christian readers. For Mark to have ended intentionally at 16:8 would have been a uniquely bold and suspiciously modern move for a first-century author.[18] Those early, creative scribes who appended the shorter and longer endings to Mark 16:8 bear witness to the poor reception an ending like 16:8 would have had among Greco-Roman (Christian) readers. One should note, however, that Mark, like Matthew and Luke, does create other expectations that are not fulfilled, namely, the predictions of Jesus' return and the preaching of the gospel to all nations. There can be no narrative fulfillment of these expectations, since the community of readers themselves are still looking forward to the fulfillment of these hopes. The argument is again inconclusive but again weighted in favor of supposing a lost original ending.

It remains quite possible then that Mark's original and intended ending was lost at some early point in the manuscript tradition. This strong possibility must temper any judgments made about Mark's own view of the disciples (generally negative throughout), since we do not know whether Mark included a scene restoring and authorizing the disciples such as we find in the other Gospels. We must not be quick to speak of Mark as a Gospel that places all the emphasis on the cross and avoids the

---

[15]This has been a matter of great debate and inquiry during the past two centuries. For an excellent, recent treatment of the question and a comprehensive bibliography on the investigation, see N. Clayton Croy, *The Mutilation of Mark's Gospel* (Nashville: Abingdon, 2003).

[16]See C. H. Kraeling, "A Philological Note on Mark 16:8," *JBL* 44 (1925): 357-58; R. O. Klein, "The Lost Ending of the Gospel According to Mark," *JBL* 45 (1926): 81-103; P. W. van der Horst, "Can a Book End with *Gar*? A Note on Mark XVI.8," *JTS* 23 n.s. (1972): 121-24; Croy, *Mutilation,* pp. 47-50, 180-85.

[17]Croy, *Mutilation,* pp. 57-63. See also the literature therein reviewed.

[18]See, further, ibid., pp. 28, 33-44, 89-96, 104-7, 171.

resurrection and the empty tomb (or worse, as evidence that "empty tomb" traditions did not exist at the time Mark wrote his Gospel), since again we may indeed not possess Mark's ending (not to mention the fact that Mark does include the sayings of Jesus pointing ahead to his resurrection on the third day, as in Mark 8:31; 9:31; 10:34.[19]

We are left to reckon, however, with the fact that *our* text of Mark ends at Mark 16:8. While the longer ending has value as an ancient and early Christian witness to the resurrection and Jesus' postresurrection activity, it does not complete *Mark's* vision for this Gospel (a fact that should caution us against supplying "endings" of our own to Mark's work). Reading Mark 16:8a as an ending resonates with the generally darker, shadowy dimension of Mark's Gospel, as well as with Mark's generally rigorous depiction of discipleship as demanding commitment and deferring rewards. In its own right it orients readers to the world in a distinctive way. First, we are left with the expectation that Jesus is to be met "out there," not in the end of the story but in the ongoing life of the church and its mission to the world. Just as the disciples are left to look for Jesus in Galilee after his resurrection, so we are left to watch for Jesus' appearing to us. This is precisely the posture of expectant watching Jesus calls his followers to in the "Apocalyptic Discourse" of Mark 13. We are left to look for Jesus' coming, to live out our lives waiting for Jesus' return and thus to engage in activities we want to be found doing when the master of the house returns. Jesus' last words of instruction in Mark are "Watch therefore—for you do not know when the master of the house will come. . . . What I say to you I say to all: Watch" (Mk 13:35, 37 RSV). Reading Mark as ending at 16:8a, we are left in this same posture, watching for our own encounter with the risen Lord and moving out to engage the world in the hope of the second coming.

Second, just as the silence and fear of the women was necessarily broken at some point, so too we cannot keep silent about the word we have received because of fear. The women felt fear in the face of the awesome implications of this message, a fear no doubt replicated among Mark's original readers. In their world the Gospel would not be an entirely welcome message, for it declared that the Roman order was not a reflection of God's order and that God would break in dramatically to establish a truly eternal rule. Once it was proclaimed the words could not be retracted. To proclaim it the believers would have to give up their place in that Roman order, giving up their attachment to its benefits—not because they would be immediately hounded out and persecuted but because they would have to accept the truth that they would not have the Roman order to fall back on. Their security would have to rest entirely on hope in God, not in the good things of life they could take for granted as long as the Roman order remained intact. Nevertheless, they were compelled to proclaim God's coming reign in Christ and to proclaim the transitoriness of the Roman order—not only to those outside but also to themselves, for now they would have to renounce their own embeddedness in that order.

In a similar fashion Mark 16:8a challenges us to faith in the face of fear, to announce the news and live out our witness to Jesus as Lord. The open ending may in fact motivate this much better in the postmodern age than any commissioning speech, for the story of Jesus itself cannot be completed until the church in every age proclaims the resurrection, God's approval of Jesus' life and way. We are left then with a challenge in place of an ending: will *you* watch for Jesus' appearing? will *you* proclaim his resurrection and accept its implications for our life in this society and this world?

---

[19]Ibid., pp. 167-70.

CULTURAL AWARENESS
Jewish Purity Codes and Mark's Gospel

Throughout the Gospel of Mark, Jesus' conduct frequently moves him to cross lines that many of his contemporaries, concerned to guard against defilement where possible, would not cross. He also frequently engages in conflict with his contemporaries, such as the Pharisees, who were deeply concerned about being holy according to the Levitical codes concerning the purity maps of Israel, purifications and the proper mirroring of God's holiness in the world.

First, Jesus touches the people he ought not to touch, failing to guard against defilement by direct contact. He voluntarily touches a leper (Mk 1:40-45); he is touched by a woman with a flow of blood (Mk 5:25-40); he touches the corpse of the dead daughter of Jairus (Mk 5:41). Second, he does not guard against the defilement that pollutes by entering the mouth. He eats with sinners and tax collectors, whose observance of purity codes may be quite loose (Mk 2:15); not all his disciples perform a ritual washing of their hands before eating, suggesting that Jesus did not teach or enforce this observance (Mk 7:1-2); Jesus shares a meal with crowds of five thousand and four thousand people, never raising the question of their suitability for table fellowship (Mk 6:37-44; 8:1-9). Third, Jesus does not observe the sacredness of times to the satisfaction of certain other Jews, performing (or allowing his disciples to perform) activities not deemed "proper" to the sabbath by his contemporaries. Jesus heals on a sabbath (Mk 3:1-6), thus polluting the day of rest with a creative work (the ends do not justify the means for his critics); his disciples pluck heads of wheat in order to satisfy their hunger on a sabbath (Mk 2:23-24). Finally, Jesus appears to have challenged the most holy of places, charging that it was a place of defilement—a "den of thieves"—rather than a sacred house (Mk 11:17-18).

Was Jesus unconcerned about purity? Was he a threat to the purity of Israel, both violating purity regulations (thus violating the Torah and spreading uncleanness) and teaching his disciples to do so as well? While Mark suggests that the Pharisees understood Jesus in this way, he does not suggest that Jesus was in fact unconcerned about purity. Rather, Jesus is very much interested in remaining "holy to the Lord God" and teaching holiness to others. Why then is Jesus so casual about matters of great concern to his peers?

The explanation lies not in Jesus' neglect for purity but in his redefinition of purity. Mark presents Jesus as one who has the authority to define what is clean and unclean. First, and perhaps most important, Jesus receives God's Holy Spirit at the outset of this Gospel. Jesus is clean indeed, since the Spirit of holiness dwells in him in bodily form as it were. This holiness, this cleanness, however, is not something that must be protected. Rather, it is something that spreads beyond existing boundaries in order to extend holiness, to make the unclean clean and the impure pure once more. As Jesus receives the Holy Spirit, he also receives God's explicit approval and legitimation: "You are my Son, the Beloved; with you I am well pleased" (Mk 1:11 NRSV). There is no uncleanness or defilement in Jesus that would provoke God's displeasure. Even the demons can bear witness: "I know who you are, the Holy One of God." (Mk 1:24 NRSV). The second time God bears witness to Jesus, the testimony becomes an imperative: "This is my Son, the Beloved; listen to him" (Mk 9:7 NRSV). God's voice thus explicitly legitimates Jesus as the one who has the authority and knowledge to show the way that pleases God, to reflect God's holiness in the world.

Jesus is not capable of being defiled by the unclean. Their uncleanness does not touch him, but rather he removes their uncleanness by the power of his holiness. Touching the leper does not defile Jesus but heals (hence, cleanses) the leper. The woman with an issue of blood does not defile Jesus, but she goes away from the encounter restored (again, cleansed). The corpse does not defile Jesus, but Jesus' touch restores life to the dead body. Jesus drives out the unclean spirits, restoring the formerly possessed to their proper place in society. While eating with the ritually unclean (the tax collectors and sinners), Jesus likens himself to a physician—one specially appointed to walk among the sick for the sake of healing them.

Just as Jesus is the bearer of wholeness and cleanness to the unwhole and unclean, just as Jesus is able to cross the boundaries of pure and impure without fear of defilement, so Jesus is also able to redefine those boundaries. Mark preserves many controversies between Jesus and the Pharisees or other groups within Judaism, many of which are precisely about redrawing purity lines and redefining what constitutes defilement. We have looked into a number of these above, and so I will only rehearse some of the highlights here. First, in the midst of a controversy about ritual purity and purification (Mk 7:1-23), Jesus declares that the current manner of observing the call to be holy as God is holy is far from God's desire for God's people: "This people honors me with their lips, but their hearts are far from me" (Mk 7:6-7 NRSV). Jesus teaches that true purity is a matter of the heart—guarding not what enters the heart from outside but what defiles it from within. Building on the ethical reinterpretation of purity codes within early Judaism, Jesus points to the second half of the Ten Commandments, saying that violation of those principles is what constitutes defilement. Remaining pure from vices and sins of that kind makes a person clean in God's sight.

Jesus' actions in his ministry make a deep impression on his followers. Jesus' disregard for many boundaries, and his commitment to crossing those boundaries for the sake of bringing God's mercy to others, led the church to understand that the crucial boundary of Jew and Gentile was no longer to be observed. The period after Jesus' ministry is no longer the time for protecting personal purity by avoiding contact with defiling persons, but a time for pursuing an open strategy of entering into unclean places to proclaim God's cleansing. The experience of the Holy Spirit became a sign to the church that God had accepted and cleansed both Jew and Gentile in the new people of God, a proof Paul points to in Galatians 3:1-5; 4:6-7 (see also Acts 10:44-48; 11:15-18). It is the "fullness of time," the time for the bringing in of the Gentiles to worship the one God, the time when "all flesh shall see the salvation of God."

Even as old purity lines break down, however, new purity lines are being formed. Throughout the letters of the New Testament, the Christians are referred to as "saints," that is as "holy ones," set apart for the Lord. They have been "sanctified," that is, "made holy," and set apart for God from the profane activity and associations that characterized their life as Gentiles before receiving the Holy Spirit. For this reason, associating with idols or prostitutes is forbidden. (It defiles what has been set apart for God; it crosses a boundary.) Being set apart for God leads to the working out of a code of conduct that seeks to maintain this holiness and avoid defilement. We will frequently encounter language of purity and pollution in early Christian literature as a way of specifying what behaviors and attitudes are proper for Christians, and what behaviors are defiling or "out of place" among the believers (cf. 1 Cor 6:15-20; 2 Cor 6:14—7:1; Phil 2:14-15; 1 Pet 1:2, 13-16; 2:9-11). The definitions are new, but they are still based on, motivated by and conceived in terms of the cultural value of purity and the fear of pollution.[a]

---

[a]On purity in relation to Mark's Gospel and more broadly to the New Testament, see David deSilva, *Honor, Patronage, Kinship and Purity* (Downers Grove, Ill.: InterVarsity Press, 2000), chaps. 7 and 8; Jerome H. Neyrey, "The Idea of Purity in Mark's Gospel," *Semeia* 35 (1986): 91-128; J. K. Riches, "Jesus and the Law of Purity," in *Jesus and the Transformation of Judaism* (New York: Seabury, 1982), pp. 112-44.

MARK AND MINISTRY FORMATION

Perhaps the most important lesson Mark teaches those who minister in Christ's name is that Jesus embodied servant-shaped leadership and his representatives are to embody the same. The Christian leader must model servanthood for those in his or her care, just as Jesus modeled it for his followers. This does not mean self-neglect or self-abuse, but it does mean approaching ministry with the attitude of serving and facilitating. Christian leaders must strive to help parishioners grow in their spiritual life, discover the spiritual gifts God gives them and find suitable areas of ministry. They depart from Jesus' model if they seek to protect their position "over" their charges, or feel threatened as the disciples under their care grow to spiritual maturity or develop ministries that may outshine the leaders' own. Rather, such growth is to be encouraged. The pastor as a servant-leader will raise up servant-leaders.

Jesus teaches the importance of giving up attempts to have power over others, to control other people, to gain power and preeminence over them. The desire to control poisons and perverts relationships, and results generally in inauthentic living. We cannot be fully ourselves with others. For example, an insecure woman may try to control her husband and children by developing strategies for making them dance to her tune. This prevents both the woman and the members of her family from living authentically, creating a web of power plays rather than loving and nurturing relationships. Or a man can be so intent on managing the perception other people have of him that he invests himself more fully in his image than in authentic personhood. Jesus' words about relinquishing the quest for power and becoming truly other-centered is a call to healing. A word of caution, however, is merited. We need to apply this medicine of servanthood and other-centeredness wisely. We could do great harm by encouraging people in dysfunctional relationships to be more submissive, thus making the Gospel play into the hands of the domineering family member who holds him or her in personal bondage.

A second contribution pertains to Mark's directions for rethinking purity codes in the church. Mark's Jesus is an encouragement to the "defiled." Jesus is a model of openness to all people. No one is too marginal or too unclean to receive his care. No one in need is invisible, but each person is the object of God's purpose and desire. Jesus would rather endure criticism from other religious leaders than withhold help and his healing touch. This is not to say that Jesus does not discern good from evil or that he accepts people's sins, but rather that Jesus does not turn away from a sinner, a broken person, a polluted person. As such, Mark's Jesus poses a strong challenge to churches to seek out the expression of holiness, not through remaining separate from the "defiled" but through reaching out across our assumed boundaries to the "defiled" or "unclean" or "untouchable" in our contexts, offering them the gift of cleansing and healing in Jesus' name.

Rather than striving to be separate from "those people," whoever we would so name, we are challenged by Jesus to face what truly pollutes and to seek purification from those defilements. Jesus understands the true source of pollution to be sin (Mk 7:14-23), whether it expresses itself in the idolatrous pursuit of things, the misuse and abuse of other human beings or self-aggrandizing self-centeredness. We can neither move to wholeness nor assist others on the road to wholeness without confronting the sin within and being cleansed of these defilements. This is not meant to provoke guilt trips, but part of the art of pastoral care is knowing when and how to help a person face his or her own sin, and how to facilitate the release of the weight of these sins.

A third, closely related contribution Mark makes to Christian ministry is to help us remember the authority of Jesus over all sources of unwholeness. Jesus moves powerfully across the landscape of this Gospel, releasing people from sin (as Mark instructs us concerning the importance of accepting forgiveness if we hope for wholeness and freedom from the debilitating effects of guilt on our psyche) and taking authority over Satan and his legions. This same Jesus would be expected, therefore, to possess authority over modern demons as well, including unhealthy family and social systems beyond the power of the individual.

Mark instructs us concerning the importance also of forgiving (Mk 11:25-26). While disciples need to accept forgiveness rather than live under the weight of guilt, they must also be brought to the place where they can forgive those who have brought them pain. Unforgiveness is a powerful enemy to our own psychological health: it drains the life of individuals and perverts their very character. Ultimately, our own experience of forgiveness is interdependent with our experience of forgiving: both burdens are released or retained together.

A fourth area in which Mark's Gospel has the potential to shape ministry is in its emphasis on prayer. A deep prayer life is the prerequisite for ministries of healing, and Mark's Jesus is a fine model of this as he seeks solitude and refreshment in quiet and prayer. How much more should those who minister in his name avail themselves of times of refreshment, quiet and rest, allowing God to fill them again and empower their ministries! Jesus did not insist that his times of rest be undisturbed, nor did he turn away those who sought him in those quiet places—but he did make sure that he found refreshment as needed, even avoiding the public eye for a whole leg of his journey toward Jerusalem (Mk 9:30). Sometimes the needs of those we care for will invade our private time. We can be flexible, but we also need to acknowledge the importance of getting the refreshment we need. The disciples must linger in prayer if they hope to cast out the really tenacious demons, just as they must also linger in prayer to remain strong themselves in the face of testing (Mk 9:29; 14:38). The ultimate foundation of all Christian ministry is not your mind, your skills or your strength, but God's mind, God's direction and God's enabling. The more finely tuned your ear for God's leading, the more effective will your ministry be.

Fifth, Mark addresses a number of the tensions that we might face in ministry and discipleship, and he provides resources to cope with those tensions or threatening obstacles. The story of Jesus' conflict with his own family and his declaration of kinship with all who do the will of God (Mk 3:21, 31-35) encourages those whose religious commitments—or whose commitment to grow in faith—have cut them off from their own family networks. Jesus assures that those who left family members for the sake of the gospel would receive a family network one hundred times as extensive (Mk 10:28-30). Acceptance into this larger family of God could be an important assurance, particularly in cases where the disciple's earthly family is not a stable base of support for healing and growth (or is the root of the problem). Mark challenges us to train Christian communities to be this family for one another so that Jesus' words have some counterpart in real life. The early church was such a powerfully growing entity, in part, because of the intense commitment each member had toward the other members.

The parable of the soils (Mk 4:3-20) explores another set of obstacles to growth in discipleship, namely, forgetfulness of the liberating word, external hostility and too great an involvement in the affairs of the world. The latter two continue to be explored throughout the Gospel (e.g., Mk 8:34-38; 10:17-31, 38-39; 13:9-13; 14:66-72). The principles of this parable have far-reaching implications for all forms of ministry, and not just for evangelism (the initial sowing of the word). In pastoral counseling, for example, the counselee receives insights about him- or herself that must be guarded, nourished and applied. It is easy for the client to go back into daily life and lose the precious word that was so welcome and valuable in the session. He or she may not simply forget the insight on account of the "cares of the world" but may actually suffer trial on account of the new insights he or she has into how the larger family relates, controls, manipulates. As soon as one member starts to grow, change is forced on the larger family, which may react quite negatively to the healing process. As Christian ministers we need to assist our charges in guarding the insights, applying the discoveries made while in the office, classroom or sanctuary, and supporting their growth in the face of opposition. Then the work may indeed bear abundant fruit in their lives.

Where failure arises, however, Mark's Gospel offers hope. In this regard the disciples' slowness to understand and Peter's own trial and failure take on a special significance. Weakness, misunderstanding and failure are all granted a place in Christian discipleship. The disciples' own failures give room for the next generation of disciples to fail and stand up again, to grow through and past their misunderstandings. Mark may be addressing a community that has had to deal with failure in the faith. The failure and restoration of the original disciples—the very pillars of the church—would help later believers put old failures behind them and confront new trials with greater firmness. The second-century Acts of Peter makes such an impact explicit. In chapter seven of that text Peter uses his own example as a testimony to Jesus' mercy and commitment to restore the fallen, encouraging those who were straying that a return was indeed possible.

Finally, Mark places all our ministry, all our attempts to bring wholeness to people, families and our world, against an eschatological horizon that we dare not ignore. There is a certain therapy in acknowledging the limitations on wholeness in this world and looking ahead with confidence in God's renewal of all things. There is also a misuse of the eschatological in pastoral ministry, such as the advice to "stay in the abusive relationship now, and God will reward your faithfulness when Jesus returns." Apocalypticism rose as a form of protest against injustice and the failure of human society to reflect God's virtues. It would be perverse now to use it to maintain injustice and godlessness. There are, however, times when brokenness is so great that only the hope of the new beginning, the coming of God's kingdom, can give a person the strength to survive and continue to face life. For example, when a child is senselessly murdered, what could a minister possibly offer except the empathy of a whole creation that groans along with the mourning parent, aware of the power of sin and injustice in this present age, longing for the time when God will set things right? The martyrs' therapy is to cry out "How long, O Lord," and to receive the assurance "yet a little while, and I will shake the heavens and the earth." Such a perspective empowers us for prophetic critique of this world's systems, to work for greater justice in society (without falling into the positivistic pride of thinking that we can create a just society, such as befell Marx and Lenin with disastrous results). This perspective emboldens us to acknowledge the extent and the depth of the depravity of human beings and their systems, since it also proclaims the power of the One who comes to usher in the kingdom of God.

FOR FURTHER READING

Evans, Craig A. *Mark 8:27—16:8*. WBC. Waco, Tex.: Word, 2000.

Guelich, Robert. *Mark 1:1—8:26*. WBC. Waco, Tex.: Word, 1993.

Gundry, Robert. *Mark: A Commentary on His Apology for the Cross*. Grand Rapids: Eerdmans, 1993.

Hengel, Martin. *Studies in the Gospel of Mark*. London: SCM Press, 1985.

Hooker, Morna D. *The Gospel According to St. Mark*. Peabody, Mass.: Hendrickson, 1991.

Iersel, Bas M. F. van. *Mark: A Reader-Response Commentary*. JSNTSup 164. Sheffield, U.K.: Sheffield Academic Press, 1998.

Lane, William. *Commentary on the Gospel of Mark*. NICNT. Grand Rapids: Eerdmans, 1974.

Mann, Christopher S. *Mark*. AB. New York: Doubleday, 1986.

Myers, Ched. *Binding the Strong Man: A Political Reading of Mark's Story of Jesus*. Maryknoll: Orbis, 1988.

Robbins, Vernon K. *Jesus the Teacher: A Socio-Rhetorical Interpretation of Mark*. Minneapolis: Fortress, 1992.

Witherington, Ben, III. *The Gospel of Mark: A Socio-Rhetorical Commentary*. Grand Rapids: Eerdmans, 2000.

6

THE GOSPEL
ACCORDING TO MATTHEW

Following the Words of the Messiah

Matthew retains most of Mark's traditions about Jesus but presents a very different picture of Jesus. Jesus is still a wonderworker, healer and exorcist, but all of this is overshadowed by Jesus the interpreter of Torah, Jesus the teacher of the way that pleases God. Disciples are still called to walk in the way of the Messiah, but Matthew provides much more guidance than Mark concerning *how* to walk, namely, committing oneself to follow the words of Jesus, to live in line with his teaching. It is no doubt the abundance of relevant and authoritative sayings material that Matthew preserves—organized so helpfully in five thematic discourses—that led the church to gravitate toward this Gospel as a primary handbook on discipleship and church life.

THE HISTORICAL AND PASTORAL CONTEXT OF MATTHEW'S GOSPEL

Authorship. This Gospel has traditionally been ascribed to Matthew, one of the twelve apostles. Once again this ascription is based on early Christian traditions about the origins of the Gospels, not on claims made in the text itself. Internal evidence for authorship is indeed tenuous. Some authors defend Matthean authorship on the basis of the greater degree of specificity used with regard to Roman and Judean coinage in this Gospel. The reference to Matthew as "the tax collector" in Matthew 10:3 (rather than merely "Matthew" as in Mk 3:18) has led some to believe that the apostle himself is thus reminding his readers of his sinful past. Neither of these carries significant weight. You could probably write in detail about your country's coinage, but that would not prove that you were a banker, and the presence of other people in the early church by the name of Matthew or a close equivalent (e.g., Judas's replacement in Acts 1:23) would explain why this Evangelist would specify the "tax collector."

One frequent objection to authorship by Matthew brought from internal evidence is the author's use of Mark's Gospel. Why would an eyewitness rely so heavily on the work of someone who was not an eyewitness?[1] Ancient historians prized the testimony of eyewitnesses, and those historians who were eyewitnesses to the history they recorded (like Xenophon, Thucydides and Josephus) made that fact evident in their writing. Matthew's failure to claim eyewitness status, then, when even the author of John's Gospel does so explicitly (Jn 19:35; 21:24, although the third-person references to the eyewitness there command attention), is indeed surprising.

---

[1]Donald Senior, *What Are They Saying About Matthew?* (Ramsey, N.J.: Paulist, 1983), p. 14; Raymond Brown, *Introduction to the New Testament* (Garden City, N.Y.: Doubleday, 1997), pp. 210-11.

This objection, however, does not eliminate the possibility that Matthew, the eyewitness, used Mark, especially since the Evangelist's aim was not historiography but community formation and maintenance. The primary aim of Matthew is to instruct the church and to address concerns the author believes to be important for faithful perseverance and growth in Jesus Christ. Mark's collection and arrangement of the Jesus traditions was widely known to the churches. It was representative of genuine apostolic traditions about Jesus (including those that Matthew himself would have recognized) and already widely accepted by the churches as an authentic statement of those traditions. Therefore to use Mark as a starting point would not be so implausible in light of those aims. Matthew, in this hypothesis, would not try to reinvent that part of the wheel that worked for him, giving his attention rather to combining Mark's building blocks with his own enormous collection of Jesus' teachings to present his distinctive understanding of Jesus and his significance for the Christian communities.

The external evidence commands more attention. Papias says that Matthew "collected the sayings (*logia*) of the Lord in Aramaic, and everyone translated these as best as they could" (Eusebius *Hist. Eccl.* 3. 39.16). Papias reports a tradition that goes uncontested in the early church (as far as our sources allow us to say), and it becomes the standard view.[2] His testimony, however, raises two problems. First, the word *logia* generally refers to sayings or oracles in biblical and extrabiblical Greek, so its application to stories as well as sayings would be unusual. The fact that many of the narratives in the Gospels enshrine pronounce-

ments or other words of Jesus might account for Papias's use of the term (much as form critics highlight the "saying" when they label a narrative a "pronouncement story") and soften, if not solve, the problem. Second, the Gospel of Matthew that we read was composed in Greek and gives little evidence of being a translation from an Aramaic or Hebrew original, semiticisms notwithstanding (since these are frequently present in original Greek compositions by Jewish authors). The so-called *Hebrew Gospel of Matthew* represents a reconstruction from a Medieval Jewish source that was based on Greek Matthew. What then did Papias have in mind when he spoke of an Aramaic collection of *logia*? Is it possible that Papias preserves an accurate tradition about a Matthean writing that came to be identified with the First Gospel but was not identical to it, such as an Aramaic or Hebrew collection of Jesus' teachings?[3]

We need, therefore, an explanation that accounts for the early church's awareness that Matthew was somehow intimately connected with the production of this Gospel and for the problems raised both in the examination of the external and internal evidence. Both may be honored and yet not stretched beyond their bounds by positing that Matthew did compile an Aramaic sayings source, recording what Jesus taught in the course of his own apostolic ministry. This became the possession of the communities that Matthew founded and nurtured. A disciple of Matthew took his teacher's materials, other Jesus sayings familiar to the community and the Mark's Gospel, and fashioned a presentation of Jesus' life and instruction more complete than any of the sources on their own. Because Matthew stood behind one of these sources, indeed the source that made

---

[2] See Irenaeus *Haer.* 3.1.1; Pantaenus's opinion, cited in Eusebius *Hist. Eccl.* 5.10l; Origen's opinion, cited in Eusebius *Hist. Eccl.* 6.25.

[3] See Paul Achtemeier, "Mark, Gospel of," in *Anchor Bible Dictionary,* ed. D. N. Freedman, (Garden City, N.Y.: Doubleday, 1992), 4:542.

this Gospel distinctive, it would be quite natural for his name to continue to stand behind the finished product as author and, more importantly for the early church, authenticator of that tradition.[4]

Circumstances and pastoral purposes. Matthew became the most influential Gospel in the early churches, being read and appreciated by Christians in many regions from all races. However, Matthew's emphases seem to address very directly and successfully a rather well-defined set of problems that would have been most meaningful in areas where Jewish Christians were a prominent part of the audience, *and* where Christians had maintained a closer connection with the synagogues and non-Christian Jews (with the result that legitimating the separation would be more of an issue) than seems to be the case for Pauline churches in Asia Minor, Macedonia and Greece.[5] We will therefore think first about how these emphases served the communities that may have been the ideal or primary "target" audience.[6] We will also analyze how they addressed the ideological and pastoral needs of the broader church audiences with whom the Gospel was soon shared.

D. A. Hagner identifies a number of particular pastoral concerns that Matthew keeps in the foreground and on that basis theorizes about Matthew's likely target audience. Hagner observes the noteworthy tension within the Gospel between an exclusive mission to Israel (Mt 10:5-6, 23; 15:24) and a strong emphasis on Gentile inclusion (Mt 1:5; 2:1-12; 8:5-13; 12:21; 13:38; 15:21-28; 21:33-43; 22:1-10; 24:14; 27:54; 28:19-20), the tension between the very Jewish tone of the Gospel and the strong polemic against the representatives of the parent body of Judaism (Mt 11:20-24; 22:8; 23:1-39; 27:25), and the "us" versus "them" mentality throughout the Gospel (reflected, for example, in the distinction between *"their* synagogues" and "the church" (Mt 4:23; 7:29; 9:35; 10:17; 12:9; 13:54; 23:34; 28:15).[7] Hagner seeks a reading of the Gospel and its intended pastoral effects that renders both sides of these tensions meaningful, rather than devaluing one side of the tension in favor of the other. For example, while it may be convenient to claim that Jesus' sayings about his exclusive mission to Israel are merely fossilized parts of the tradition, it does not really do them justice, nor account for Matthew's retention of these sayings.

Matthew clearly assumes that Jewish Christians will be prominent among the readership of this Gospel. Several Jewish customs are mentioned without explanation (such as the wearing of phylacteries and fringes in Mt 23:5), and Marcan explanations of Jewish practices are omitted (Mt 15:1-2 omits the explanation of the custom of washing hands and vessels given in Mk 7:1-5). The reader is assumed to know that both the gnat and the camel are unclean animals (Mt 23:24). Matthew's emphasis on the ongoing validity of Torah would be much more at home among Jew-

---

[4]Donald Guthrie assumes that the distinction between Matthew as author of a sayings source and as author of a finished Gospel would have had to be "forgotten" long before Papias for this hypothesis to work, but this assumes a very modern, individualistic notion of authorship (*New Testament Introduction* [Downers Grove, Ill.: InterVarsity Press, 1970], p. 43).

[5]This view comes very close to a scholarly consensus: see Brown, *Introduction,* pp. 212-16; Senior, *What Are They Saying About Matthew?* pp. 6-10; Craig S. Keener, *A Commentary on the Gospel of Matthew* (Grand Rapids: Eerdmans, 1999), pp. 45-51; and the literature cited in these discussions.

[6]Keener helpfully introduces this distinction to mediate between the traditional scholarly quest for the Gospel audiences and the emerging critique of that quest as too narrow for texts in the genre of *bios* and in the well-traveled network of Christian communities (*Commentary on Matthew,* p. 45).

[7]D. A. Hagner, "The *Sitz im Leben* of the Gospel of Matthew," *Treasures New and Old: Recent Contributions to Matthean Studies,* ed. D. R. Bauer and M. A. Powell (Atlanta: Scholars Press, 1996), pp. 27-62, 29-32; see also G. N. Stanton, *A Gospel for a New People: Studies in Matthew* (Louisville, Ky.: Westminster John Knox, 1993), pp. 146-68.

Figure 6.1. The remains of the first-century synagogue at Masada. (Photo courtesy of Todd Bolen [BiblePlaces.com])

ish Christians than, for example, among Paul's predominantly Gentile converts in Galatia. This does not rule out, however, the probability of a mixed audience of Jewish and Gentile Christians from the beginning of the Gospel's reception. One issue on which scholarship is divided concerns the connection of Matthew's Christian audience with the Jewish synagogue. Were these Christians still trying to maintain relations with and a place in the local synagogue? Weighty arguments have been offered in favor and against this possibility,[8] and a definitive solution seems elusive. The importance of the audience's connection with the Jewish *heritage*, however, is beyond dispute, and it is precisely this connection that is at issue in some form throughout the early church.

Matthew's Gospel offers a defense against the kinds of criticisms and arguments that would be directed mainly at Jewish Christians by non-Christian Jews. This defense, however, is for the benefit of the Christian readers of the Gospel (rather than the non-Christian critics),

who need assurance that they stand in continuity with the revelation of God and God's will to and through the people of Israel. Matthew achieves this primarily by portraying Jesus as the fulfillment of scriptural paradigms and by presenting his teaching as the true way of keeping Torah. Matthew also deflects the labels leveled by non-Christian Jews at Jesus, such as the charges that he was a "deceiver" and "sorcerer." He affirms believers' conviction that Jesus was the true teacher of the way to do God's will as revealed in Torah; thus he also affirms that the community stands approved in God's sight as they follow Jesus. Thus Matthew's Gospel was vitally concerned with insulating the Jewish Christian from the rejection and hostility of his or her non-Christian family, friends and neighbors.[9] Matthew also helps address the relationship of Jewish and Gentile Christianity, both with regard to the plan of God and the ongoing importance of Torah in an increasingly Gentile movement. Far from suggesting discontinuity with historic Israel,

---

[8]See Senior, *What Are They Saying About Matthew?* pp. 8-10; Keener, *Commentary on Matthew,* pp. 48-50.
[9]Hagner, *"Sitz im Leben,"* pp. 46-47.

Matthew rather assures the audience that the growing Gentile majority in the *ekklēsia* proves that God's purposes from of old are being fulfilled in the church.[10]

But Matthew's message also is a word on target to Gentile Christians, who may fail to value the Jewishness of Jewish Christians, pressuring them to minimize all those Jewish practices that were a threat to the Gentile believer's sense of "equality" within the body. This is a known problem in the early church. Paul's letter to the Christians in Rome reflects a situation where both Jews and Gentiles needed to be reminded of each other's importance and equality in the plan of God. Jewish ethnic privilege, on the one hand, could not be countenanced, but the holiness of the root and natural branches could not be ignored either, and the essential fulfillment of God's law remains a lasting goal and value. Moreover, it was vitally important for Gentile Christians to know that they were joining themselves to the legitimate heirs of the promises of God revealed in the revered Scriptures of Israel. The Galatian controversy amply attests to the importance Gentile Christians attached to being "heirs of Abraham" alongside their Jewish Christian sisters and brothers.

Location and date. Several scholars locate Matthew's composition in Syrian Antioch.[11] The history of the church in that city admirably fits with the kinds of issues addressed by Matthew. The Antioch church began as a Jewish Christian movement that pioneered a Gentile mission. In light of Paul's confrontation with Peter and the "people from James" recounted in Galatians 2:1-11, it seems that the Jewish Christians there were persuaded to take a more conservative stance vis-à-vis the ongoing validity of dietary laws in the church (but not circumcision). At the same time as the church was becoming increasingly Gentile, the hostility of non-Christian Jews toward their Jewish Christian neighbors was increasing, particularly after the Jewish Revolt (of which Jewish Christians were conspicuously unsupportive).[12] Antioch, however, may be taken as somewhat representative of a variety of churches in Syria and even North Palestine, and many scholars remain content with the designation of this general region as Matthew's first sphere (but not exclusive sphere) of concern.[13]

Dating a Gospel is a tenuous enterprise, since so much depends on the relative dating of Matthew or Luke to Mark, which itself *could* have been written between 50 and 70 C.E. (or even outside that range).[14] Nevertheless, if Mark's Gospel is placed near the end of the 60s, then Matthew would need to be dated after that. The peculiarly harsh nature of the polemic against the Pharisees and scribes best accords with a post-70 situation, the time when Judaism gradually became less tolerant of the diversity in its midst. But it *could* in theory reflect an earlier period, since hostility between non-Christian Jews and Jewish Christians is attributed to the period immediately following Jesus' ascension, to Paul's missionary journeys and the like (see the early testimony of 1 Thess 2:13-16). Matthew seems to make veiled references to Jerusalem's destruction (e.g., Mt 22:7; 23:38), which tend to point to a post-70 date, although this is not a completely firm case.

---

[10]Ibid., pp. 48-49.

[11]See the magisterial treatment of the history of the Antioch church and its suitability as the target audience of Matthew in Raymond E. Brown and J. P. Meier, *Antioch and Rome* (New York: Paulist, 1983), pp. 15-27, 45-72. This position is also followed, for example, in W. D. Davies and D. C. Allison Jr., *A Critical and Exegetical Commentary on the Gospel According to Saint Matthew*, ICC (Edinburgh: T & T Clark, 1988, 1991, 1996), 1:138-47.

[12]Brown, *Introduction to the New Testament*, pp. 213-14.

[13]See, for example, Keener, *Commentary on Matthew*, p. 42.

[14]R. T. France, *Matthew*, TNTC (Grand Rapids: Eerdmans, 1985), p. 30.

An Outline of Matthew's Gospel

Prologue: infancy narratives (Mt 1:1—2:23)

Part 1: Mt 3:1—7:29

    Narrative: Mt 3:1—4:25

    Discourse (Sermon on the Mount): Mt 5:1—7:27

    Concluding/transitional formula: Mt 7:28-29

Part 2: Mt 8:1—11:1

    Narrative: Mt 8:1—9:35

    Discourse (missionary discourse): Mt 9:36—10:42

    Concluding/transitional formula: Mt 11:1

Part 3: Mt 11:2—13:53

    Narrative: Mt 11:2—12:50

    Discourse (parables of the kingdom): Mt 13:1-52

    Concluding/transitional formula: Mt 13:53

Part 4: Mt 13:54—19:1

    Narrative: Mt 13:54—17:27

    Discourse (regulations for church life): Mt 18:1-35

    Concluding/transitional formula: Mt 19:1

Part 5: Mt 19:2—26:2

    Narrative: Mt 19:2—22:46

    Discourse (denunciation of Pharisees/apocalyptic discourse): Mt 23:1—25:46

    Concluding/transitional formula: Mt 26:1-2

Mt 26:3—28:20 passion, resurrection and commissioning narrative

Attempts to be more specific often involve assumptions about the nature and influence of the work of Jewish sages at Jamnia (beginning between 85 and 90 C.E.) and the introduction of the *birkhat ha-minim,* the "benediction against heretics," into the synagogue liturgies around the Mediterranean. There are a number of problems with these arguments, however, since (1) the actual wording of this prayer to God to extirpate the "Nazarenes and heretics" and blot out their names from the book of life varies from text to text, (2) dating its introduction into the synagogues in Palestine, Syria and beyond is quite speculative, (3) the formulation of such a prayer merely reflects the hostilities of non-Christian Jews toward Jewish Christians that had been present for decades (from the beginning, according to Acts 3—7).

Structure. Matthew sends mixed messages with regard to the structure of his Gospel, allowing readers to discern different outlines, depending on which cues they underscore. Matthew himself did not follow all of Mark's cues concerning the structure of his earlier Gospel. Matthew, for example, breaks up what Mark had joined together so artfully in Mark 8:22—10:52. The frame Mark provided by presenting two healing stories about blind persons is obliterated as Matthew removes the first healing story to a much earlier point in his Gospel (where it becomes a healing of two blind men). The perfect parallels between the three passion predictions followed by three teachings on discipleship are also broken up somewhat, the second passion prediction being followed by a controversy concerning the temple tax rather than the corresponding teaching on discipleship (who is the greatest in the kingdom).

In lieu of Mark's structuring devices, Matthew offers his own. The most obvious cues center on the five discourses, all of which conclude with a brief narrative introduced each time by the phrase "when Jesus had finished [all] these sayings" (these could also be viewed as transitional narratives).[15]

According to this outline Matthew's structure highlights the presentation of Jesus as the authoritative teacher of God's way, as well as the teachings to the community themselves. This is certainly in keeping with Matthew's redactional interests, namely, abbreviating Mark's narratives in order to make room for a rich array of Jesus sayings, organized into thematic discourses. Bacon regarded the fact that there are five major discourses as an indication that Matthew sought to provide a new Pentateuch composed of Jesus' teachings. Such a statement would have to be refined in light of the importance for Matthew of the continuity between Jesus' teachings and the Torah. Jesus' discourses would not represent a "replacement" for the Pentateuch so much as its "re-embodiment" of it as taught and extended by Jesus and followed in the churches.

Another set of cues, however, is given in Matthew 1:1, 4:17 and 16:21, which can also be taken as introductions to major sections.[16] The first speaks of the beginning of Jesus' ministry. The second and third both open with the same formula ("From that time, Jesus began to . . ."), introducing first a section of Jesus' teaching on the kingdom of God and his powerful works confirming the breaking in of the kingdom (Mt 4:17—16:20) and then a section dealing with Jesus' redemptive work and his teachings to the church, preparing it for life in the interim between his first and second comings (Mt 16:21—28:20). Either scheme may be adopted, and there is really no bar to viewing the two structures as active at the same time.

We should also pay attention to the ways Matthew structures smaller units within his Gospel. Repetition is one technique employed to achieve this end. Thus the form of the Beatitude gives structure to Matthew 5:1-12; the refrain contrasting what was said "of old" and what Jesus now teaches (5:21, 27, 31, 33, 38, 43) gives structure to 5:21-48; the introductions to the parables in Matthew 13:24, 31, 33, and Matthew 21:33 and 22:1 provide indications of the structure and grouping of those materials.[17] A second technique, sometimes overlapping with the first, is Matthew's tendency to order stories or blocks of teaching in groups of three. This can be seen, for example, in Matthew 6:1-18, where a general instruction (Mt 6:1) is explained by three specific examples, each introduced by a repetitive formula ("whenever you give alms," Mt 6:2; "whenever you pray," Mt 6:5; "whenever you fast," Mt 6:16).[18] Careful structuring both at the macro- and microlevel once again gives strong evidence for the Evangelists' redactional and authorial activity. They are not mere collectors of tradition but careful arrangers, editors and interpreters of the tradition.

---

[15]This was first suggested by B. W. Bacon, "The 'Five Books' of Matthew Against the Jews," *Expositor* 15 (1918): 56-66; *Studies in Matthew* (London: Constable, 1930).

[16]J. D. Kingsbury, "The Structure of Matthew's Gospel and His Concept of Salvation-History," *CBQ* 35 (1973): 451-74; *Matthew: Structure, Christology, Kingdom* (Philadelphia: Fortress, 1975).

[17]See Davies and Allison, *Saint Matthew,* 1:88-92 for a more complete listing.

[18]See ibid., pp. 65-72 for a thorough analysis of triads in Matthew.

MATTHEW'S USE OF OTHER EARLY CHRISTIAN RESOURCES

According to the working hypothesis that dominates scholarly study of the Gospels, Matthew's primary sources were Mark's Gospel, a sayings source that focused on Jesus' teachings (Q), and a body of traditions that appear in Matthew but nowhere else (e.g., the infancy narratives in Mt 1:18—2:23, the parable of the unforgiving servant in Mt 18:23-35 or the parable of the laborers in the vineyard in Mt 20:1-16).[19] Since Mark's Gospel is available for comparison, while Q and M exist only as reconstructions, we are on the surest ground when discussing how Matthew has used this source.[20]

Matthew uses about 90 percent of Mark's stories and sayings, although often in abridged form. Although Augustine thought Mark was the abridger of Matthew, it appears rather that the reverse is the case: Matthew has abridged Mark's narratives with a view to making room, as it were, for the vast amount of teaching material Matthew wanted to include.

By this virtual absorption of Mark, Matthew shows himself to be in substantial agreement with Mark's main emphases. Mark's paradigm of Jesus as the Messiah who comes to serve rather than to be served, and who teaches his disciples to pour out their lives in service to one another as the path to true fulfillment of God's will, remains intact. Indeed, Matthew expands this emphasis by adding a number of additional sayings that reinforce this posture of discipleship (Mt 10:24-25; 18:4; 23:8-12). Matthew also retains and promotes the conviction that Jesus' life, ministry, death and resurrection reflect the working out of the pro-

phetic oracles of God in the Old Testament. Matthew retains all of Mark's contributions in this area and greatly expands them both in explicit citation of Old Testament texts (see p. 247) and in shaping details to reflect other Old Testament texts (e.g., Matthew's passion narrative has more numerous and explicit echoes of Psalm 22 than Mark's).

Matthew has modified Mark in several significant ways beyond abbreviation, however. First, Mark depicted Jesus as forbidding most everyone healed by him to spread the report of his miraculous activity. This messianic-secret motif was part of Mark's attempt to focus attention on the passion as the heart of Jesus' ministry. In Matthew, however, this motif is greatly reduced and, where it occurs, is now reinterpreted as fulfillment of Isaiah 42 (notably, one of Isaiah's servant songs). Matthew thus subdues this emphasis and subordinates it to his emphasis on Jesus' actualization of scriptural paradigms (see Mt 12:15-21).

Moreover, Matthew has significantly modified the presentation of the disciples. Although they still abandon and deny Jesus at the end (the facts of the story cannot change), they are consistently presented as more intelligent and comprehending throughout the Gospel. When Jesus walks on the water, the disciples respond in Matthew with an insightful confession: "And those in the boat worshiped him, saying, 'Truly you are the Son of God' " (Mt 14:33 NRSV) (see figure 6.2). In Mark the disciples had responded to this same event quite differently: "And they were utterly astounded, for they did not understand about the loaves, but their hearts were hardened" (Mk 6:51-52 NRSV). Matthew tells us that after Jesus had connected

---

[19]Of course, the Old Testament is a major formative influence on Matthew's Gospel, as the Evangelist greatly expands the number of explicit quotations and readily discernable allusions to the sacred Scriptures of Israel, but we will treat this subject in detail further on.

[20]Q has been painstakingly reconstructed from the materials shared by Matthew and Luke, and Matthew's use of Q could also be investigated by comparing the Matthean versions of the Q materials with the reconstructed Q materials. The enterprise, however, would have to be far more tentative than an investigation of Matthew's use of a source (like Mark) that does not have to be reconstructed.

his warning to beware of the leaven of the Pharisees with the results of the miraculous feedings, "then they understood that he had not told them to beware of the yeast of bread, but of the teaching of the Pharisees and Sadducees" (Mt 16:12 NRSV). Mark, however, had closed this episode with Jesus' rather incredulous question, "Do you not yet understand?!" (Mk 8:21 NRSV). After Jesus' second passion prediction in Matthew, the disciples are "greatly distressed," suggesting that they do indeed comprehend the ramifications of what Jesus has told them (Mt 17:23). In Mark we are told explicitly that "they did not understand what he was saying and were afraid to ask him" (Mk 9:32 NRSV). Matthew distances the disciples from embarrassing bickering over status and preeminence: after the second passion prediction in Mark, the disciples are caught arguing about which of them is the greatest (Mk 9:33-37), but in Matthew there is no parallel to this sorry argument (Mt 17:22-23). Matthew also distances John and James in Matthew 20:20

from the request to enjoy preeminence over the other disciples: now it is the mother of John and James who instigates the unseemly request. Finally, the disciples are blamed not for faithlessness, as in Mark 4:40, but for too little faith (*oligopistoi;* see Mt 8:26; 14:31; 16:8). Scholars offer a number of explanations for these modifications, but perhaps the most likely is Matthew's concern to show the twelve disciples as reliable, intelligent mediators of Jesus' teachings and interpretation of the law. In a setting where the community's *halakha* (its way of applying God's commandments to everyday life) is contested by members of the parent body (the Jewish synagogues), it would not help to think of or to portray the community leaders as dull of comprehension.

A number of omissions on the part of Matthew suggest editorial intent as well. First, Matthew omits several blocks of material (Mk 1:23-28, 35-38; 4:26-29; 7:31-37; 8:22-26; 9:38-40; 12:41-44; 14:51-52). Three of these are miracle stories, and Matthew may have felt

Figure 6.2. A mosaic from Magdala showing a simple boat such as would have been used for fishing and industry on the Sea of Galilee. (Photo courtesy of Todd Bolen [BiblePlaces.com])

Matthew's Special Material (M)

Although Matthew shares a great amount of Jesus sayings and traditions with Mark and Luke, this Gospel also contains a notable body of traditions unique to it among the Gospels. These include the following passages:

- infancy narratives (Mt 1:18—2:23)
- several of the Beatitudes (Mt 5:5, 7-10)
- fulfilling the law and the "greater righteousness" (Mt 5:17-20)
- Jesus' application of the "Old Law" (Mt 5:21-24, 27-30, 33-38, 41)
- instructions on charity, prayer and fasting (Mt 6:1-8, 16-18)
- caution against benefiting the unworthy (Mt 7:6)
- instructions on mission (Mt 10:5-6)
- invitation to take Jesus' yoke (Mt 11:28-30)
- parable of the weeds (Mt 13:24-30, 36-43)
- parable of the hidden treasure and the pearl of great price (Mt 13:44-46)
- parable of the good and bad fish (Mt 13:47-50)
- the temple tax (Mt 17:24-27)
- instructions on community discipline (Mt 18:10, 15-17, 19-20)
- parable of the unforgiving servant (Mt 18:23-35)
- eunuchs for the sake of the kingdom of God (Mt 19:10-12)
- parable of the laborers in the vineyard (Mt 20:1-15)
- parable of the ten bridesmaids (Mt 25:1-13)
- description of the last judgment (Mt 25:31-46)
- stationing the guard at the tomb (Mt 27:62-66)
- the bribing of the guard (Mt 28:11-15)
- the Great Commission (Mt 28:16-20)

In addition Matthew contains numerous brief sayings and descriptions not found in his Synoptic counterparts (for example, the earthquake and the angel rolling away the stone in Mt 28:2-4). Several of the places where Matthew and Luke overlap may in fact represent separate traditions. For example, the parable of the wedding feast in Matthew 22:1-14 is significantly different from the parable of the banquet in Luke 14:15-24, particularly with Matthew's addition of the second scene in the parable (Mt 22:11-14). This parable might also be conceptualized better as a part of Matthew's distinctive material (with a similar, but not identical, parable appearing in Luke's special material) rather than as a common dependence of Matthew and Luke on the same parable in Q.

that this aspect of Jesus' ministry was already adequately represented. The omission of the other traditions is more difficult to account for (although the possibility always exists that they were not present in the copy of Mark used by Matthew). Matthew, like Luke, also omits several of Mark's attributions of powerful emotions to Jesus (compare Mk 3:5 with Mt 12:12; Mk 8:12 with Mt 12:39) as well as a number of other troubling details, such as Jesus' *inabil-*

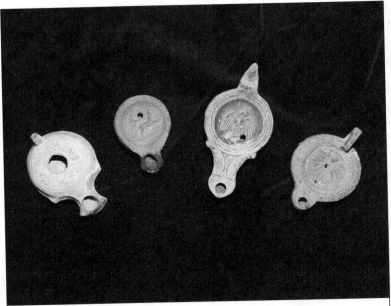

Figure 6.3. These single-wick, earthenware lamps from the Roman period feature decorative details: grape clusters on the vine, a chariot with rider, a Roman eagle, a sunburst. We may imagine these lamps in the hands of the bridesmaids of Jesus' parable in Matthew 25:1-13. (Photo: Sam Renfroe; courtesy of Ashland Theological Seminary)

ity to do miracles at Nazareth (compare Mk 6:5 with Mt 13:58).[21]

But Marcan material accounts for only about half of Matthew, who brings in extensive blocks of sayings material and parables from the sayings source Q, from his own storehouse of Jesus traditions (M), and explicit references to the Old Testament (notably in the LXX reading in a number of cases) being fulfilled in particular episodes or groups of episodes. These additions speak to the concerns of Matthew and his community, and to the universal church. We should remember that Matthew's Gospel enjoyed the widest appeal and acceptance, so well did he address issues of great importance for the whole church. Rather than reduplicate those aspects of Matthew's message

that were already covered in Mark, his primary source, our discussion of Matthew will focus on the contributions of the traditions that are woven into the Marcan narrative.

THE MESSAGE OF MATTHEW

It would be impossible to do justice to all of Matthew's contributions to the nurture of early Christian communities, but two major contributions involve the demonstration of the church's relationship to the sacred tradition of Israel and the nurturing of a particular ethos within the Christian communities. The first focuses on a wide array of traditions that Matthew has assembled (such as the controversies between Jesus and rival religious teachers) or contributed himself (such as the

---

[21]For a fuller discussion of this topic, see Warren Carter, *Mathew: Storyteller, Interpreter, Evangelist* (Peabody, Mass.: Hendrickson, 1996), pp. 56-60.

Matthew as the Manifesto of a Jewish Messianic Sect

Graham Stanton has correctly observed that Matthew and the communities shaped by his Gospel relate to late first-century Judaism much as a sect relates to its parent body, the group from which it has severed itself or been severed.[a] The tensions between Christians (especially Jewish Christians) and non-Christian Jews results from their being so closely related to one another—an intrafamily fight, as it were. The traditions about Jesus and the sayings of Jesus assembled by Matthew bear witness to disputes over mutually accepted values (such as the correct application of Torah or interpretation of shared Scriptures). Jesus accepts standard Jewish expressions of piety (prayer, fasting and almsgiving) but teaches a distinctive way of putting these into practice (see Mt 6:1-18), thus differentiating his followers (at least ideologically) from other Jewish groups. He employs distinctive terminology to distinguish an "us" from a "them." Other Jewish groups have "their synagogues," but the followers of Jesus form an "assembly" *(ekklēsia);* other groups have "rabbis" but the followers of Jesus are not to use this title for their leaders. Certain sayings also make clear distinctions between believers and "the Gentiles" (i.e., non-Christian Gentiles; see Mt 6:7-8, 32-33; 20:25-26), thus defining the Christian group against a second, alternative body (the dominant culture). Matthew's Gospel also evidences a strong hostility toward the parent religion (seen most clearly in chap. 23), which also provides a means to solidify the group's boundaries and identity. Sharp criticism of the parent body, an awareness of potential or actual persecution at the hands of the parent body, and the promise of judgment on the parent body and vindication of the sectarian group all contribute to the distancing process between sect and parent religion.

Matthew has a strong interest in the legitimation of the existence, conduct and beliefs of the new group. First, he answers criticisms brought by the parent body against the sect. In Matthew the explanations concerning why the "Jews to this present day" are wrong about the resurrection of Jesus is one such example (Mt 28:11-15). Second, he explains why the separation happened, and why the separation is a legitimate state of affairs in the eyes of God. In Matthew, texts from the shared sacred texts are used to point out the inevitable rejection of the "true" way by the "faithless" parent body ("They shall see, but not perceive" and "This people honors me with their lips"; Mt 13:14-15; 15:8-9). Additionally, historical precedents are invoked. Just as the parent body has always rejected God's prophets, so now they have rejected God's ultimate messenger (Mt 21:33-44; 23:34-39). Third, he demonstrates that the sect is not an innovation, not a deviation, not a perversion of the shared tradition, but rather it is a true fulfillment, while denouncing the parent body for having departed from the way. Matthew accomplishes this through increased attention to the fulfillment of sacred oracles in the life and work of Jesus and those surrounding him, together with the claim that the shared ancestral law (Torah) is only rightly fulfilled as taught by this Jesus.

---

[a]See Stanton, *Gospel for a New People,* chap. 4

considerable multiplication of Old Testament testimonies to Jesus' life, ministry and significance). The second Matthean contribution emerges as a result of careful selection and placement of the vast amount of Jesus sayings included in this Gospel. The organization of these sayings into five significant discourses makes Matthew a kind of handbook of instruction on being the church, the community of those who follow Jesus.

THE CONTINUITY OF THE *EKKLĒSIA* AND THE HERITAGE OF GOD'S PEOPLE

A prominent interest of Matthew's Gospel is to demonstrate the connectedness of the new body, the "church," with the historic people of God through whom God spoke, which received and kept God's oracles, and which was to be the vehicle of promise. Non-Christian Jews, no doubt, stressed the discontinuity between Christian Jews and their heritage: the latter are charged with leaving the congregation of Israel and "joining with the nations around them" while at the same time following the teachings of a lawbreaker and blasphemer. The claim of Gentiles to have joined the heritage of Israel by joining the Christian sect would have been rejected outright by non-Christian Jews. Matthew therefore seeks to demonstrate the complete continuity between the *ekklēsia* and the Jewish religious heritage, assuring the Christian communities that, far from being deviants or heretics, they are the legitimate heirs of that heritage and stand at the center of God's plan of salvation.

Jesus as the focus and culmination of the Jewish scriptural hope. Against any claims to the contrary from outsiders, Matthew assures his Christian readers that they read the Scriptures correctly when they read them in light of Jesus' life and teaching: "Blessed are your eyes, for they see, and your ears, for they hear. Truly I tell you, many prophets and righteous people longed to see what you see, but did not see it, and to hear what you hear, but did not hear it"

(Mt 13:16-17 NRSV). In looking to Jesus the Christians have seen what all the Old Testament seers and kings had longed to see, and what non-Christian Jews now refused to see. To press this conviction further home, Matthew builds several stories on the foundation laid by Mark concerning Jesus as the realization of the hope of Israel and the embodiment of the scriptural heritage. Matthew's pastoral goal is to confirm that, far from being a departure from God's will for Israel and from the history of God's revelation to Israel, Jesus and the community formed in his name are the realization of that will and the culmination of that revelation.

Why don't all who share the same Scriptures realize this? The Jesus tradition provides an answer: their eyes have been blinded, their hearts hardened (Mt 13:14-15). That is, they have not, Matthew alleges, read their Scriptures correctly. Thus when the scribes take offense at the cries of "Hosanna to the Son of David" on the lips of the children in the streets, it is because they failed to discern the present realization of the Scripture in the scene around them: "have you never read, 'Out of the mouth of babes and sucklings thou hast brought perfect praise'?" (Mt 21:16, quoting Ps 8:2 in the Septuagint tradition). Jesus' followers may now do what Jesus did to point out his opponents' blindness to the work of God. Matthew has given them a sort of textbook which assures them that in Jesus the scriptural revelation is being worked out and perfected. And from this they can, if they dare or care, counter their detractors in the synagogue.

It is important to realize, however, that the ministry of Jesus matched none of the many varieties of messianic expectation embraced by various Jewish groups. The majority of Jews agreed that God was going to do something wonderful and extremely beneficial for God's faithful people at some point in the future through an heir to the promises of David. However, no one expected a Messiah who would come in humility to suffer and die

Table 6.1. "Prophecy and Fulfillment" in Matthew's Gospel

OT passage	Matthean text	Topic	Kind of reference
Is 7:14	Mt 1:23	Jesus' birth	recitation
Mic 5:2	Mt 2:5-6	Jesus' birth in Bethlehem	recitation
Hos 11:1	Mt 2:15	flight to Egypt	recitation
Jer 31:15	Mt 2:18	slaughter of the innocents	recitation
uncertain	Mt 2:23	Jesus in Nazareth	recitation
Is 40:3	Mt 3:3	John the Baptist's ministry	recitation
Is 9:1-2	Mt 4:14-16	Jesus' ministry in Galilee	recitation
Is 53:4	Mt 8:17	Jesus' healing ministry	recitation
Mic 7:6	Mt 10:35-36	strife over Jesus	recontextualization
Is 29:18-19; 35:5-6; 61:1	Mt 11:2-6	Jesus' ministry	recontextualization, reference
Mal 3:1	Mt 11:10	John the Baptist	recitation
Is 42:1-4	Mt 12:17-21	Jesus' ministry	recitation
Is 6:9-10	Mt 13:14-15	rejection of Jesus	recitation
Ps 78:2	Mt 13:15	Jesus' use of parables	recitation
"many prophets"	Mt 13:17	Jesus' ministry	general reference
Is 29:13	Mt 15:8-9	Jesus' rivals	recitation
Mal 4:5-6	Mt 17:10-11	John the Baptist	reference
Is 62:11; Zech 9:9	Mt 21:5	Jesus' triumphal entry	recitation
Ps 118:25-26	Mt 21:9	Jesus' triumphal entry	recontextualization
Ps 118:22-23	Mt 21:42	rejection of Jesus	recitation
Zech 12:10, 14	Mt 24:30	Jesus' second coming	recontextualization
Dan 7:13-14	Mt 24:30; 26:64	Jesus' second coming	recontextualization
Zech 13:7	Mt 26:31	disciples scattered	recitation
unspecified	Mt 26:24, 54	Jesus' arrest and death	general reference
Ps 110:1	Mt 26:64	Jesus' exaltation	recontextualization
Zech 11:12-13	Mt 27:8-10	Judas' wages	recitation
Jer 32:6-9	Mt 27:8-10	purchase of a field	recitation
Ps 69:21	Mt 27:34	wine "mixed with gall"	echo
Ps 22:18	Mt 27:35	soldiers cast lots	echo
Ps 22:7	Mt 27:39	passersby "wag their heads"	echo
Ps 22:8	Mt 27:43	taunt of the victim	recontextualization
Ps 22:1	Mt 27:46	Jesus' cry from the cross	recitation

a shameful death. More popular was the expectation of a military hero who would usher in God's kingdom, replacing the kingdoms of the world with the rule of God (see, for example, the messianic visions of *Psalms of Solomon* 17 and 18). This expectation fueled many abortive revolutions in Palestine. The early church was creatively engaged from its earliest days (even during the ministry of Jesus) in discovering a new messianic paradigm from the Scriptures that would match the facts of Jesus' life, driven by the believers' conviction that God raised up Jesus as God's anointed one. Christians started speaking of two comings of the Messiah rather than just one. It was easy to demonstrate from Scripture a final, end-time coming when the kingdoms of the world would yield to the reign of God. It was much more difficult to show the scriptural viability of an earlier coming, a first coming "in meekness." This is, however, precisely what Mark, and to a greater extent Matthew, achieved.

The birth narrative. Matthew begins to respond to these challenges by going back to the birth of Jesus, a step that Mark did not deem necessary or helpful. Luke would also take this step, but Luke shares very little material in common with Matthew, save for an announcement of Jesus' importance in God's plan (given different nuances) and a recounting of the birth itself. What do Matthew's first two chapters contribute to the ongoing life of early Christians and their understanding of Jesus? How, in particular, do these chapters address the concerns of a still young movement trying to define itself and maintain its legitimacy over against its parent religion?

Matthew begins his Gospel very much like Mark: Mark's "The beginning of the good news of Jesus Messiah, the Son of God" (Mk 1:1) is closely reflected in Matthew's "The book of the origin of Jesus the Messiah, the son of David, the son of Abraham" (Mt 1:1). Matthew, however, does not launch immediately into the thick of the drama. Rather, he begins with a lengthy genealogy, tracing Jesus' roots back to Abraham the patriarch. While this gives Matthew a slow start in the eyes of modern readers, this genealogy makes an important contribution to the church's faith. It supports the claim made in the first verse, showing that Jesus was indeed the descendant of David and Abraham. Jesus is therefore eligible to be the promised descendant who would be the seed through whom the promises of Abraham would bear fruit and would receive the throne of David. Jesus as "son of David" would be the one who inherited the promise of divine sonship and an eternal throne (2 Sam 7:12-16). As "son of Abraham," Jesus would be the one through whom "all nations shall be blessed" (Gen 12:3).

Moreover, Matthew lays out his genealogy in a perfectly structured sequence. There are fourteen generations between Abraham and David, between David and the exile to Babylon, and between the exile to Babylon and the birth of the Messiah. The choice of "fourteen" generations is also far from random. In Hebrew the letters in David's name (*dwd*) add up to fourteen. This ordered genealogy expresses the conviction that God's plan, conceived from the beginning, was working itself out in perfect fashion as it culminated in the birth of Jesus. The divine determination of history and the organization of history into numerically balanced and orderly periods are an important facet of the apocalyptic worldview. It expresses the conviction that God is in control and that God is working out God's purposes in an inexorable and measured fashion. The most significant points in Israel's history are presented as perfectly spaced: the conception of the people in God's choice of Abraham; the pinnacle of the people's strength in David; the nadir of the people's history in the deportation to Babylon, the sign of the broken covenant; the birth and ministry of Jesus the Messiah, who would fulfill the promises made to both David and Abraham, whose houses lay desolate for so long. Matthew looks beyond Jesus' human lineage, however, to establish his significance. Jesus is Joseph's son by adoption—he is thus legally the "son of David" and "son of Abraham," but his actual parentage is divine. This concept is brought to the foreground again late in the story when Jesus asks in light of Psalm 110:1: "If David thus calls him Lord, how can he be his son?" (see Mt 22:45 NRSV).

These opening chapters begin to set forth the significance of Jesus. As the Messiah, the son of David and son of Abraham, Jesus is the one through whom the promises to these great figures of Israel's heritage come to fulfillment. The very name of Jesus, however, takes on significance in Matthew. *Y'shua* was, of course, a rather common name, Joshua being a prominent hero of Israel's history. It was even shared by Jesus Barabbas. This name, however, was not selected by his parents—it was the name appointed for the child by God, the name delivered through an angel, the name that would encapsulate the meaning of his life and work: "he will save his people from their sins" (Mt 1:21 NRSV). The passion is already foreshadowed in the infancy narrative, for it is through the voluntary death of the righteous one that the sinners are spared.

It is also at this moment of naming that Matthew introduces his first formulaic citation of Old Testament Scriptures: "this took place to fulfill what had been spoken by the Lord through the prophet" (Mt 1:22 NRSV). These references to the Jewish Scriptures are a very important part of Matthew's Gospel for the Christian readers, demonstrating to them that despite the claims of their opponents the Christian community is in true continuity with the ancient revelations of God to God's people, and so constitute that holy people. The first fulfillment of an Old Testament oracle occurs as the angel gives the child his name and as Mary conceives without sexual intercourse: "'Behold, a virgin shall conceive and bear a son, and his name shall be called Emmanuel'

(which means, God with us)" (Mt 1:23 RSV). This verse from Isaiah gives Jesus, in effect, a second name—Emmanuel, "God with us." Jesus' actual name is not the subject of the Isaianic text, but his significance as encapsulated by the name certainly is. Jesus is now the one who mediates God's presence to God's people, a theme that will be sounded throughout the Gospel (see Mt 10:40; 11:27; 28:20). This assures the early Christian readers that far from being cut off from God by following a deceiver, they rather enjoy access to and knowledge of the one whose presence in their midst is the very presence of God.

The events that follow—Jesus' birth in Bethlehem, the flight into Egypt, the slaughter of the innocents and the settling of Joseph's family in Nazareth—are all tied to specific Old Testament texts, being presented in relation to them as fulfillment to prediction (see the use of Mic 5:2 in Mt 2:5-6 and Hos 11:1 in Mt 2:13-15). While in its original context Hosea 11:1, for example, speaks of God's deliverance of Israel from bondage in Egypt, the text is now applied to Jesus' return from Egypt after Herod's death. On the one hand, by the canons of historical criticism Matthew is surely stretching the text at this point. On the other hand, there is something profound in Matthew's claim that Hosea 11:1 pertains to Jesus, for it identifies Jesus as God's Son and with the collective body of Israel, which was also God's son. Just as Israel experienced an exodus from Egypt, now Jesus experiences an exodus from Egypt. Indeed, this identification with Hosea shows us how Matthew also comes to bridge the collective reading of the servant songs of Isaiah to the messianic readings of the same: Jesus redefines Israel itself. He becomes, in effect, the repository of Israel's heritage and its future. He is the faithful son of God, and he embodies the character of righteous Israel. What Israel as a collective entity did not do, Jesus as a righteous individual representative of the larger body now does. Henceforth, whoever is joined with Christ is joined with the people of God. A similar principle is at work in the next Old Testament reference, linking the slaughter of the male infants in Bethlehem with the lamentation of Jeremiah 31:15: "A voice was heard in Ramah, wailing and loud lamentation, Rachel weeping for her children; she refused to be consoled, because they were no more." Judah's experience of desolation and exile is captured, or reenacted, in the early history of its Messiah.

The last Old Testament reference in these opening chapters is astoundingly vague. Joseph settles his family in Nazareth, "that what was spoken by the prophets might be fulfilled, 'He shall be called a Nazarene' " (Mt 2:23 RSV). This does not correspond to any single text in our Hebrew Bible, either in the Masoretic or Septuagint text traditions, and can only be constructed from several passages with much ingenuity and creativity. It does, however, point us to another concern that Matthew has been addressing throughout these infancy chapters. How does it happen that "Jesus of Nazareth" is the promised Messiah, when Bethlehem, the city of David, is known to be the place for any Davidic Messiah's birth? "What good can come out of Nazareth?" asks Nathanael in John 1:46, and perhaps some critics of the church were asking the same thing. Three of the four Evangelists are at pains to answer this question: Matthew and Luke explain how Jesus was really born in Bethlehem, while John explains that he comes from no earthly village but from the side of the Father to whom he has also returned.

Old Testament formula quotations. Matthew continues to saturate his narration of events of Jesus' ministry with references to the Jewish Scriptures. Jesus' relocation from Nazareth to Capernaum is read as a realization of Isaiah 9:1-2: "The land of Zebulun, land of Naphtali, on the road by the sea, across the Jordan, Galilee of the Gentiles—

the people who sat in darkness have seen a great light, and for those who sat in the region and shadow of death light has dawned" (Mt 4:14-16). This is a rather sophisticated appeal to an Old Testament Scripture. The Isaiah passage speaks of the land formerly possessed by three of the tribes of Israel that was annexed by Assyria and made a Gentile region since it was under their direct rule. Isaiah promises the people of this land that a king is coming who will deliver them from Gentile rule. He goes on to speak of the coming king in words which Handel made famous: "For unto us a child is born, unto us a son is given, and the government shall be upon his shoulder, and his name shall be called 'Wonderful Counselor, the Mighty God, the Everlasting Father, the Prince of Peace'" (Is 9:6). Jesus' proclamation of the kingdom of God is identified by Matthew as God's fulfillment of this hope for those regions, a token of God's faithfulness to the house of Israel.

Matthew interprets Jesus' ministry of healing in light of the famous servant song of Isaiah 53: "He took our infirmities and bore our diseases" (Mt 8:17 NRSV). We have already noted a connection made between Jesus and an earlier servant passage in Matthew 12:17-21 (cf. Is 42:1-4). Reading Jesus' story in light of the servant passages of Isaiah contributes significantly to early reflection on the significance of Jesus' work, especially foundational to understanding Jesus' death as a sacrifice that brings healing to others and effects the restoration of humanity's relationship with God. Matthew even understands Jesus' style of preaching—the use of parables—as a fulfillment of an Old Testament pattern: "I will open my mouth in parables, I will utter what has been hidden since the foundation of the world" (Mt 13:35; cf. Ps 78:2). Jesus' triumphal entry into Jerusalem is presented as a fulfillment of Zechariah 9:9 (modified slightly in light of Is 62:11):

Tell the daughter of Zion,
Look, your king is coming to you,
  humble, and mounted on a donkey,
    and on a colt, the foal of a donkey.
(Mt 21:5 NRSV)

Scriptural precedent and fulfilling event are so mutually informing for Matthew that, unlike Mark, he places Jesus on two animals (a donkey *and* a colt) based on his reading of the Zechariah passage. Such a historically implausible detail serves to underscore Matthew's

Jesus is itself the fulfillment of scriptural paradigms. Matthew gives a much more extensive and accurate citation of Isaiah 6:9-10 than Mark does, using the prophetic depiction of Isaiah's impossible task to explain Jewish resistance to Jesus' message (Mt 13:14-15). The response of the Jews to Jesus is for him just another example of their resistance to God's messengers throughout the history of God's relationship with Israel. This offers an antidote to the pressure Christians (especially Jewish Christians) faced from the synagogue

Figure 6.4. A street in Jerusalem, in the Old City. (Photo courtesy of Todd Bolen [BiblePlaces.com])

overriding purpose, namely, to demonstrate the thoroughgoing connection between the oracles of God and the ministry of Jesus.

Not only is Jesus' life itself a fulfillment of Scripture, but people and events around him also enact scriptural paradigms. Matthew therefore retains the two texts used by Mark to speak of John the Baptist (Mt 3:3-4 quotes Is 40:3; Mt 11:10 quotes Mal 3:1). Judas's treachery is foreseen in Scripture, down to the very wages he received (see Mt 27:8-10). Moreover, the Jewish people's rejection of

to rethink their commitment to this Jesus. Matthew wants the Christian communities to understand that pressure, that very resistance, as just another in a long series of rebellions against God. The community of Christians may thus be assured that they have made the correct response to God's initiative.

Matthew also forges stronger links between the passion of Jesus and the oracles of the Jewish Scriptures. It was especially important to place Jesus' death in the context of the divine purpose. His death was the most scandalous aspect of Jesus' ministry, the confirmation for outsiders of his distinct lack of a place in the divine plan for Israel. Matthew affirms that far from being a derailment of his messianic career, Jesus' death is the culmination of that career, fulfilling the very purpose inherent in his name: *Y'shua*—"he will save." To Mark's achievement in this arena (all of which Matthew retains), Matthew adds details to the narrative, such as the exact sum of money Judas received for his part in the conspiracy (Mt 26:14-15), which then went toward buying the "field of blood":

> Then was fulfilled what had been spoken through the prophet Jeremiah [well, Zechariah mostly], "And they took the thirty pieces of silver, the price of the one on whom a price had been set, on whom some of the people of Israel had set a price, and they gave them for the potter's field, as the Lord commanded me." (Mt 27:9-10 NRSV)

How does Matthew know the wages Judas received? His conviction that the Scriptures themselves speak concerning the life and work of the Messiah Jesus allow him to look to Zechariah 11:12 for the answer!

Matthew adds an additional general reference to the fulfillment of the Scriptures through Jesus' arrest, trial and passion (Mt 26:54), and continues to shape the passion narrative toward clearer resonances with particular texts. Rather than offering Jesus wine mixed with myrrh, as in Mark, Matthew gives the recipe as "wine mixed with gall" (Mt 27:34), bringing in an echo of Psalm 69:21. Mark's Gospel committed to writing the link between Psalm 22 and Jesus' cross and resurrection: Jesus' cry from the cross is a quotation of Psalm 22:1; the soldiers cast lots for Jesus' clothing (cf. Ps 22:18); the passersby "wag their heads" (Ps 22:7). Matthew now adds the words of Ps 22:8 to their taunt: "He trusted in God; let God deliver him, if God desires him,

for he said 'I am God's Son' " (Mt 27:43). The last phrase, which is not part of the psalm, may show Matthew's acquaintance with Wisdom of Solomon 1:16—2:20, adding a single detail to the taunt reflecting that first-century B.C.E. text. Wisdom of Solomon speaks of the apostates persecuting the righteous person, testing him with insult, torture and a shameful death:

> [the righteous man] is inconvenient to us and opposes our actions; he reproaches us for sins against the law, and accuses us of sins against our training. He professes to have knowledge of God, and *calls himself a child of the Lord*. . . . We are considered by him as something base, and he avoids our ways as unclean; he calls the last end of the righteous happy, and *boasts that God is his father*. Let us see if his words are true, and let us test what will happen at the end of his life; for *if the righteous man is God's son, he will help him*, and will deliver him from the hand of his adversaries. (Wis 2:12-13, 16-18 RSV)

This passage becomes a very useful text in the early church for speaking about opposition to Jesus, and is often brought into sermons on the passion. Matthew himself may have been among the first to lead in this direction. Wisdom of Solomon goes on to say that the righteous do indeed fall victim to the unrighteous in this life, but that vindication comes when all stand before God's judgment seat. It also was well known in the early church that the plans of Jesus' enemies succeeded, but God vindicated his son by raising him from the dead, and will vindicate him before the eyes of all at his second coming.

Another important facet of Matthew's demonstration of Jesus' continuity with God's revelation to Israel and, specifically, his messianic role within that history of revelation is provided by the paradigm of the "works of the

Figure 6.5. The "Seat of Moses" from the synagogue at Chorazin, a symbol of the teaching authority of the synagogue leaders and the rabbis (see Mt 23:1-3). (Photo courtesy of Todd Bolen [BiblePlaces.com])

Messiah." When the imprisoned John the Baptist sent his disciples to Jesus to ask whether Jesus was indeed the coming one, Jesus offered his works—healing the blind, the lame, the deaf and the lepers; raising up the dead; and proclaiming God's kingdom and justice to the poor—as the most conclusive demonstration of his identity (Mt 11:2-6). Here Matthew brings together passages from Isaiah 29:18-19, 35:5-6 and 61:1. The last two of these passages, in their historical context, look forward to the time of God's deliverance of the people from exile in Babylon; in the first century they become portraits of God's activity in the end time. Among the documents found at Qumran is a text (4Q521) that bears witness to a messianic reading of these Isaiah passages from the first century B.C.E.[22] This allows us to see the significance of Jesus' miracles and preaching for Matthew's readers: these are the very activi-

ties expected in the messianic age.

Jesus as a reliable teacher of the Law. A third component of Matthew's demonstration that the followers of Jesus are actually standing closest to the scriptural tradition and to the will of God is his portrayal of Jesus as the reliable teacher and perfecter of that tradition, particularly of Torah. He must assure his readers that Jesus was no innovator, no heretic who perverted the tradition. Jesus' continuity with the tradition, with Torah and with God's will assures his followers that they too are firmly fixed in the center of God's will and are walking in God's ways.

The two moments when God speaks in the narrative continue to fulfill for Matthew the function they served in Mark. God explicitly approves Jesus as "pleasing" and affirms Jesus as the one who shows the way that is pleasing to God, directing those who are able to hear the

---

[22]For a fine discussion of this text and its significance, see J. J. Collins, *The Scepter and the Star: The Messiahs of the Dead Sea Scrolls and Other Ancient Literature* (New York: Doubleday, 1995), pp. 117-22.

voice of God to learn from and obey Jesus' teachings ("listen to him," Mt 17:5; see also Mt 3:17). Where Mark merely mentions the temptation of Jesus by Satan, Matthew provides the details of this encounter, probably learned from the Q tradition. The audience learns from this how the enemy of God was unable to sway Jesus from doing God's will. Indeed, Jesus' deep rootedness in the Jewish Scriptures and his commitment to walk in the way of God's revelation (seen in the three quotations from Deuteronomy that guide Jesus' responses) allows him to defeat the adversary and remain steadfast.

The passage that speaks most strongly and directly to this concern is Matthew 5:17-20, one of the more problematic texts in Matthew for generations of Christians raised on Romans and Galatians:

> Do not think that I have come to abolish the law or the prophets; I have come not to abolish but to fulfill. . . . Therefore, whoever breaks one of the least of these commandments, and teaches others to do the same, will be called least in the kingdom of heaven; but whoever does them and teaches them will be called great in the kingdom of heaven. (vv. 17, 19 NRSV)

Who thinks that Jesus has come to abolish the Law and the Prophets? In the first century this probably represents the position of critics from the synagogue who speak of Jesus as a lawbreaker and his followers as walking no longer in the ways that please God. Matthew 5:17-20 assures the believers, however, that Jesus' mission, far from overthrowing Torah or departing from Torah, was fulfilling Torah. Not only that, but those who pass down Jesus' teachings are likewise not annulling Torah but showing the way to keep the full Law, from the greatest to the least of the commandments. Those who follow Jesus, therefore, have not departed from the sacred tradition but fulfill it in a way that pleases God more than the way taught by non-Christian Jews. In a less direct way, Matthew 7:21 also speaks to this concern: "Not every one who says to me, 'Lord, Lord,' will enter the kingdom of heaven, but only the one who does the will of my Father in heaven." Following Jesus means that one is doing the will of God, not departing from it as the church's critics claim.

Rabbinic materials provide only scant witness to the life of Jesus, but they still play a supplementary role in the quests for the "historical Jesus"—particularly as they speak of Jesus as a deceiver and sorcerer, as one who led Israel astray and who engaged in the demonic arts to effect his wonders.[23] It appears that these alternative interpretations of Jesus were available early on, because Matthew already bears witness and responds to them at some length in his Gospel. Indeed, the charges may in fact go all the way back to Jesus' earthly ministry.

First, Jesus is spoken of by his adversaries as a "deceiver" and his life is summed up for them in the word "deception":

> Sir, we remember how that deceiver said, while he was still alive, "After three days I will rise again." Therefore order the sepulcher to be made secure until the third day, lest his disciples go and steal him away, and tell the people, "He has risen from the dead," and the last deception will be worse than the first. (Mt 27:63-64)

Against this view of Jesus, Matthew affirms Jesus as a true and faithful teacher of God's way. His miracles confirm his authority to teach (cf. Mt 9:6-8), and Matthew shows at numerous points that Jesus' teaching is in accord with Scripture. Again God explicitly endorses Jesus' teaching as showing the path to please God: "This is my Son, the Beloved; . . .

---

[23]Luke Timothy Johnson, *The Real Jesus* (San Francisco: HarperSanFrancisco, 1996), pp. 114-15.

listen to him" (Mt 17:5 NRSV). Indeed, it is the Pharisees (and their descendants) who are leading Israel astray and departing from following Torah. Matthew brings this out by showing Jesus at work correcting their reading of the Law (Mt 9:13; 12:7-8), pointing out the lack of consistency in their teaching (Mt 12:9-12) and condemning their setting aside of the commandments of God in order to establish certain traditions (Mt 15:2-9).

Second, Jesus' adversaries attribute his healings, exorcisms and miracles to the power of Satan. That is, they allege that he works wonders through sorcery and magic rather than through divine anointing (Mt 9:34; 10:25; 12:24). Against this charge Matthew, as Mark before him, emphasizes Jesus' anointing with the Holy Spirit and the power of God (cf. Mt 3:17; 12:25-32), his war against the forces of Satan (e.g., Mt 4:1-11; 8:16, 28-34) and his continual approval in God's sight (Mt 17:5), which precludes any cooperation with God's enemies. At this point we begin to get a sense of the importance of the stories of Jesus' baptism and transfiguration: possibly the most significant aspect of each is the divine pronouncement that forms the climax of each episode, God's own legitimation of Jesus as God's representative.

The role of the exclusive mission to Israel in Jesus' ministry. Some of the more difficult passages in Matthew are the sayings concerning Jesus' exclusive ministry to the Jewish people. "Go nowhere among the Gentiles, and enter no town of the Samaritans, but go rather to the lost sheep of the house of Israel" (Mt 10:5-6 NRSV); "I was sent only to the lost sheep of the house of Israel" (Mt 15:24 NRSV). These sayings have suggested to some scholars that Jesus himself only intended a renewal of Israel and never wanted to launch a movement that would quickly move to include Gentiles, let alone become a Gentile-dominated offshoot of Judaism. Why did Matthew retain the sayings about Jesus' exclusive mission to the house of Israel in an age when the Gentile mission was already a reality and a Gentile constituency in the church strongly established? Are these mere relics of the Jesus tradition, or would they have some ongoing significance for Matthew's audience?

It is instructive that both Paul and the author of Luke-Acts also preserve the tradition that Jesus (and then his disciples) went to the Jews first and then the Gentiles with the proclamation of God's kingdom. Two texts are especially important in this regard. First, Romans 15:8-12 weaves together a tapestry of Scriptures Paul regards as being fulfilled in the Gentile mission. The most salient point for this discussion is Rom 15:8: "Christ has become a servant of the circumcised on behalf of the truth of God in order that he might confirm the promises given to the patriarchs, and in order that the Gentiles might glorify God for his mercy" (NRSV). Jesus' mission to Israel was a demonstration of God's faithfulness to the promises given to the patriarchs, an act of God's mercy. It was an initial step toward the fulfillment of other eschatological hopes, namely, bringing all the nations into the people of God and to the worship of the one God. Acts 15:16-17 refers to a string of Old Testament texts (Amos 9:11-12; Is 45:21), giving expression to the same pattern:

> After this I will return,
> and I will rebuild the dwelling of David,
>> which has fallen;
>> from its ruins I will rebuild it,
>> and I will set it up,
> so that all other peoples may seek the Lord—
>> even all the Gentiles over whom
>> my name has been called,
>> thus says the Lord. (v. 16 NRSV)

Jesus' mission to Israel, and the mission in Judea that follows his ascension, represents the fulfillment of God's promise to "rebuild the fallen house of David," which becomes that nucleus of the Christian community, the Jewish converts. Into this newly constituted people of God, this new house of David, come the Gentiles who are called in their turn.

By remembering Jesus' mission to the house of Israel, Matthew reminds the Jewish Christian believers that they, even though now perhaps a minority in the church, are not in any way an embarrassment or a quaint remainder. Rather, they are the core of the newly constituted people of God. Where Gentile believers might wish to minimize the importance of the Jewishness of these Jewish Christians (as perhaps in the Roman churches addressed by Paul), Matthew affirms the value of their Jewishness. They represent God's faithfulness to God's historic people, and in effect their presence in the new body connects the whole body of Christian Jews and Gentiles to the historic people that received God's promises, and provides the continuity in salvation history itself (Paul addresses similar concerns in Rom 11:1-24). Jesus' words to Peter after Peter's confession also support and affirm the significance of Jewish Christians in the new community: "I tell you, you are Peter, and on this rock I will build my church, and the gates of Hades will not prevail against it" (Mt 16:18 NRSV). Peter, who came to be identified with the Jewish Christian mission (see Gal 2:7-9), is named by Jesus as the solid foundation of the church Jesus would build. In a first-century setting this spoke of the core of believing Jews, with Peter as their hero and representative, as the foundation of the new people of God, onto which living stones from every nation would be fitted. They are the remnant, the kernel of the people of Israel, to which the Gentiles are joined as God's purposes are fulfilled.

Matthew also takes pains to record the failure of Jesus' mission to Israel. Jesus gives instructions to his disciples concerning the towns within Israel that do not receive them or their message: "shake off the dust from your feet as you leave that house or town. Truly, I tell you, it will be more tolerable for the land of Sodom and Gomorrah on the day of judgment than for that town" (Mt 10:14-15 NRSV). This is echoed in the next chapter as Jesus pronounces woes on the towns that did not respond to him (Mt 11:21-24). Pagan, Gentile cities would fare better at the last judgment than these towns in Israel, for they would have responded to Jesus' message. Just as Tyre and Sidon will be privileged over Capernaum and Bethsaida at the day of judgment, so also Gentiles will rise up as prosecutors on that day to condemn the people of Israel who reject Jesus (Mt 12:41-42). Nevertheless, it was necessary first for Jesus and his disciples to proclaim their message to the house of Israel, for the sake of God's faithfulness to God's promises.

Perhaps the passage that speaks most directly and sharply to Israel's rejection of Jesus and his message is Matthew 21:33—22:14, the parables of the wicked tenants and the wedding feast (see further discussion in "Exegetical Skill: Redaction Criticism"). In both parables the figure who represents God is faithful in his commitment to his clients, whether the tenants of the vineyard or the invited guests. Their refusal to respond in kind, and their continuing rejection of God's invitation to respond, result in their rejection and the possibility of opening up the kingdom to "a people that produces the fruits of the kingdom" (Mt 21:43). Indeed, the first parable sets the majority Jewish response to Jesus within the context of the people's ongoing rejection of God's prophets and messengers—a point strongly reinforced by Jesus' words in Matthew 23:34-38. Jesus' exclusive mission to Israel thus becomes a sort of hinge: it establishes the continuity of his movement with historical Israel but also becomes the point of transition to the mission to the Gentiles after Israel as a whole rejects Jesus.

It is worth noting, however, that Matthew does not substitute one doctrine of "election" for another: just as Israel was called to bear fruit and found itself excluded when it failed to do so, so the new invitees, the new tenants of the vineyard, also must "produce the fruits of the kingdom," and must put on the wedding garment of righteousness and of doing the will of the Father in heaven. There is no triumphalism in Matthew, for the new community of Jews and Gentiles who have responded to Jesus are called not to rejoice in the misfortune of Israel nor preen themselves on their new status, but only to "do the will of my father in heaven."

Finally, Israel remains an important symbol for the future hope. The new people of God in the *palingenesia,* the "new genesis," is modeled after the historic people of God: "Truly I tell you, at the renewal of all things, when the Son of Man is seated on the throne of his glory, you who have followed me will also sit on twelve thrones, judging the twelve tribes of Israel" (Mt 19:28 NRSV). The continuity between church and Israel, in effect, endures into the new creation.

Gentiles in the body: Deviation from or realization of the divine will? Just as it is important for Matthew to demonstrate God's faithfulness to Israel and speak to the importance of the Jewish Christian constituency, so also he affirms throughout the Gospel that the inclusion of the Gentiles was not an afterthought, a mere "plan B" in the will of God in case of Israel's rejection. This is important not only for the Gentile Christians in the congregations that read Matthew's Gospel, but also for the Jewish Christians, who needed to understand that the Gentile majority in the churches does not signal the church's separation from the people of God. Rather, the presence of so many Gentiles in the new people of God signals the fulfillment of longstanding promises and revelations of God's will for all people. Thus Matthew begins his Gospel by connecting Jesus not only to David, the Jewish monarch par excellence, but also to Abraham, the Gentile convert who received the promise that "in you all the nations of the world will find blessing" (Gen 12:3).

First, as Matthew crafts Jesus' genealogy, he mentions a number of women. He is under no compulsion to do so, so his choice here is all the more important. The stories of Tamar, Ruth and Bathsheba have in common some irregularity in the acquisition of a mate and offspring, which might prepare for the grand irregularity in Mary's case. It is more likely, however, that all four women were regarded in Jewish lore as converts to Judaism (although the Old Testament does not specify the foreign origin of Tamar and Bathsheba).[24] The stories about these women circulating by Matthew's time present them as Gentiles who were included into the people of God, and thus for Matthew they represent a foreshadowing of what would be achieved through Jesus. More directly, Matthew recites an Old Testament text that looks forward to the Gentiles' coming to faith and the true worship of God:

> Here is my servant, whom I have chosen,
> my beloved, with whom my soul is
>   well pleased.[25]
> I will put my Spirit upon him,
> and he will proclaim justice to the
>   Gentiles. . . .
> And in his name the Gentiles will
>   hope. (Mt 12:18, 21 NRSV, reciting
>   Is 42:1-4)

God's purpose from of old has been to bring all nations to the true worship of the one God through God's chosen people, and Matthew claims that it is Jesus and the Jewish Christians who have accomplished this purpose by gathering so many Gentiles into the "assembly," the new congregation of the people of God.

---

[24]See Davies and Allison, *Saint Matthew,* 1:171-72.

[25]Note here how God's pronouncements over Jesus at his baptism and transfiguration echo this Scripture and may have suggested it to Matthew.

EXEGETICAL SKILL
Redaction Critism

Redaction criticism is an essential tool for discovering the distinctive interests of the Evangelists and the way they interpreted and shaped the Jesus traditions to address the needs, concerns and questions of the church. By setting parallel passages in the three Synoptic Gospels side by side,[a] the ways the Evangelists have shaped the tradition become apparent. (Or at least the distinctive emphases of a particular Gospel's presentation of the material become evident.) The exercise presupposes that the differences are not random but, at some level, significant. They are signs of how an early Christian leader was "preaching" and "applying" the Jesus traditions for the ongoing life of the churches.

In simplified form, redaction analysis constitutes the search for the distinctive message of a particular Gospel by means of close study of (1) the distinctive wording of material found in the particular Gospel (whether the distinctiveness is a result of the Evangelist's alteration of Jesus traditions or the Evangelist received the tradition in a distinctive form—the differences are easy to spot, but proving editorial alteration is sometimes more difficult) and (2) the distinctive placement of the tradition in the larger context of the Gospel (since arrangement is also a matter of the Evangelist's intentional design). Redaction analysis places value on the differences, whereas a harmonizing approach finds the differences troublesome and tends to smooth them out or disregard them.

One brief example will provide some beginning direction for your own application of this technique of exegesis, teasing out the pastoral message and distinctive contribution of a particular Evangelist's work. Compare Matthew 7:11 and Luke 11:13:

If you, although you are wicked, know to give good gifts to your children, how much more will your Father in heaven give good things to those who seek him? (Mt 7:11)

If you, although you are wicked, know to give good gifts to your children, how much more will the Father from heaven give the Holy Spirit to those who ask him? (Lk 11:13)

There are two significant differences—the identification of God and the specification of the gift. Matthew frequently refers to God as "your father in heaven," while Luke does not. Luke's text is particularly troublesome at this point in the manuscript tradition. Quite a few scribes tried to assimilate Luke's version to Matthew's, making Luke read "your heavenly father." It appears, however, that Luke did not use that designation for God here, but the more

---

[a]John's Gospel would be included, of course, for those few passages where it overlaps with the Synoptic Gospels.

simply "Father" ("from heaven" refers to the origin of the gift in a number of witnesses and the location of the Father in others, so this remains unclear).

The more striking difference, however, is the description of the gift. Matthew leaves this quite general: God knows how to give good gifts to those who ask him. Luke's version of the saying, however, focuses the reader's attention specifically on the one gift of central value to discipleship (at least as Luke-Acts develops it), namely, "the Holy Spirit" (Lk 11:13). Some redaction critics would be most interested in discerning which version of the saying represents Jesus' actual words (or at least the earlier stream of tradition). This is, however, a problematic process and ultimately bears little pastoral fruit. We may never be able to decide with certainty whether Luke made specific what Jesus left general or Matthew generalized what Jesus made specific. We can, however, observe how the form of this saying in Luke contributes to the distinctive focus of this Gospel (and Acts) on the role of the Holy Spirit in the life of the believer and believing community.

As we work through the more extended examples of Matthew's redaction of the parable of the wicked tenants (Mt 21:33-44; Mk 12:1-12; Lk 20:9-19) and the parable of the wedding feast (Mt 22:1-14; Lk 14:16-24), we will see more fully how looking at the differences within the passage *and* at the way the passage has been situated within the whole Gospel (and resonates with its broader context) contribute to redaction criticism. The skill of "reading in literary context" is a prerequisite to redaction criticism. We must look not only beyond the passage to its immediate literary context but also test our hypotheses about Matthean emphases (for example) displayed in a particular passage. This is done by rereading the whole of Matthew to discover if that emphasis is borne out elsewhere in the Gospel. The distinctives of the Evangelist's presentation of the passage often connect directly with the themes or topics that are of greatest interest to the Evangelist, and so these two skills are highly complementary.

Read the parable of the wicked tenants in all three Synoptic Gospels and list the differences that you observe, bearing in mind that Matthew, rather than Mark or Luke, is our focus. You probably noticed some if not all of the following distinctive features of Matthew's version:

1. Matthew alone explicitly places this parable as the second in a series of three parables offered by Jesus in response to the Pharisees' challenging of Jesus' authority (Mt 21:23-27). Matthew's placement of the parable shows that the reader is being led to interpret it in light of the parable of the two sons, which speaks to the issue of who is truly obedient to God's commands. This is no doubt significant for the conflict between the Pharisees' disciples (the post-70 C.E. synagogues) and Jesus' disciples (the post-70 C.E. churches). Matthew is intent on shoring up the commitment and confidence of the latter that *they* are the obedient children of God.

2. Matthew reverses the details concerning the demise of the son from

their order in Mark. The son is first cast out of the vineyard and then killed, bringing the details of the parable closer in line with the execution of Jesus, the Son.[b]

3. Matthew allows the Pharisees to answer the question about the fate of the tenants so Jesus can use the Psalm quotation to convict them by their own words. This makes the drama and Jesus' victory in the scene more apparent. Moreover, the repetition of having first the chief priests and Pharisees state the outcome and then Jesus applying their own words to their own future in God's vineyard (in a manner reminiscent of Nathan's entrapment of David) stresses the transfer of the vineyard to others.

4. The interpretation of the parable in Matthew 21:43 highlights the motif of the transference of the kingdom from the ethnic body of Israel to a "race/nation that performs the kingdom's fruits." This raises the stakes considerably from the Marcan form of the parable, where the religious leaders were the main target and their position in Israel was in jeopardy. Now, Matthew uses the parable to legitimate the separation of the church (the new "race/nation") from the parent body (the Jewish people).

These suggestions about Matthew's interpretation and use of the parable of the wicked tenants may be confirmed by examining the third parable in the series, the parable of the wedding banquet. Read this parable in both versions (Mt 22:1-14; Lk 14:16-24), and list the differences you observe. Again you may have discovered the following:

1. Matthew sets the banquet at a more specific occasion—the marriage feast of the king's son, giving the parable a frame that suggests a messianic and eschatological context.

2. In Matthew the messengers are not only scorned but also seized, beaten and killed. There is thus a heightening of hostility between the messengers (perhaps not indeed the Hebrew prophets but the Jewish Christian missionaries to other Jews) and the original invited guests. Correspondingly, the king takes time out from the wedding preparations to raise an army, slaughter those originally invited who abused his messengers, and destroy their city. Matthew's version of this parable is much more violent than Luke's version, the escalated hostility perhaps reflecting a situation of higher tension between Christians and non-Christian Jews.

---

[b]Craig Blomberg objects that Matthew (and Luke) cannot be changing this order intentionally to reflect the death of Jesus, since the "vineyard" is Israel and not Jerusalem (*Interpreting the Parables* [Downers Grove, Ill.: InterVarsity Press, 1990], p. 123). The change must therefore be a mere matter of style without significance. Blomberg, in my opinion, is here showing an uncharacteristic rigidity in his allegorical reading of the parable. If the Son is meant to "stand for" Jesus anyway, and the order of events ("cast him outside," "killed him") recalls the procession "outside" the city and the crucifixion—irrespective of the alleged geographical limits of the vineyard when the image first appears—I would not find it problematic at all to ascribe this change to the Evangelists' desire to make the resonances between the parable and the history of Jesus louder and more evident.

4. Matthew alone has the second scene of the parable, where the new body of guests fall under the king's scrutiny. This connects with Matthew's pervasive interest that disciples respond to Jesus not only with their lips but in their lives, and resonates with the scenes of judgment where those brought into the kingdom are sorted out (e.g., the net full of good and bad fish, and the field with both wheat and tares; notice the detail in Mt 22:10 that the slaves gathered into the wedding hall are "both good and bad").

5. The placement of this parable together with the parable of the wicked tenants is also a redactional choice. The juxtaposition of these two parables affects the reading of the second.

While Luke therefore has used this parable as an illustration of his theme that those who seek to build up wealth are distracted from seeking God's kingdom, while those who lack wealth are more free to respond to God's invitation, Matthew has used the parable as a means of underscoring both the salvation-historical message already promoted in the parable of the wicked tenants and the necessity of the new people of God bearing the fruit God seeks. Our investigation would need to proceed from here to a review of the whole Gospel, of which these two parables form a part in a sequentially ordered whole. We need to ask: What distinctive emphases from among those we have identified stand out elsewhere in the Gospel? Which do not emerge elsewhere, suggesting perhaps that we should not overly stress their importance in the passages under scrutiny?

In order to apply redaction analysis in a more nuanced manner, there are a number of additional premises that we should remember.[c] First, the distinctive features of a particular Evangelist's version may not *all* be the work of the Evangelist himself (and, indeed, we should be surprised if they were). Each Evangelist is located within a community and its traditions about Jesus. In many instances the Evangelist simply may be incorporating the form of a saying as it was remembered in his community.[d] Second, Mark may have undergone some developments after Matthew and Luke used it. The oral traditions and the texts of the Gospels themselves continued to develop. We cannot be entirely certain, therefore, whether every divergence noted in our texts is the result of a change made by Matthew or Luke to Mark. Third, Matthew and Luke may also have undergone some redaction after they left the hands of the Evangelist. Fourth, an Evangelist's "theology" is not to be reconstructed solely on the basis of the differences

---

[c]See Stanton, *Gospel for a New People*, pp. 36-40.

[d]It is even possible in some cases that Jesus himself was responsible for two forms of a similar statement (such as the parable of the banquet discussed above), which he used in different contexts to different ends (see Blomberg, *Parables,* p. 118). In such a case all the observations about the different nuances brought out in the different Gospels remain valid: the different emphases of the different forms of the parable still contribute to the distinctiveness of each Evangelist's proclamation of the Gospel even if the Evangelist was not personally responsible for their alteration.

but also in the similarities with his sources. Matthew and Luke incorporate so much of Mark because they agree to a remarkable extent with Mark's Christology, picture of discipleship and the like. Finally, the comparison of texts is fruitful even where there are no theories of literary dependence. When we set John's Gospel next to the (admittedly few) parallels in the other three Gospels, John's interests and manner of operating become more apparent. Additionally, the fruitfulness of redaction criticism is not ultimately dependent on the two-source hypothesis. Even if Matthew should be shown to be the source for Mark and Luke or if the complete independence of the three Synoptic Gospels should be demonstrated some day, redaction criticism (perhaps then better styled "Synoptic comparison") would still bring to the fore the distinctive facets of each Gospel, and thus help us hear each Evangelist's distinct voice and message.

You may wish to practice this exegetical skill further on one of more of the following passages, comparing it with its parallels in Mark or Luke: Matthew 3:1-17; 6:9-15; 15:21-28; 16:13-20; 21:1-11.

FOR FURTHER READING

Perrin, Norman. *What Is Redaction Criticism*. GBSNTS. Philadelphia: Fortress, 1969.

Stanton, Graham. *A Gospel for a New People: Studies in Matthew*, chap. 2. *Louisville, Ky.: Westminster John Knox, 1993.*

Chapters on redaction criticism in the following:

Black, David A., and David S. Dockery, eds. *New Testament Criticism and Interpretation*. Grand Rapids: Zondervan, 1991.

Hayes, John H., and Carl R. Holladay. *Biblical Exegesis: A Beginner's Handbook*. Atlanta: John Knox Press, 1982.

Haynes, Stephen R., and Steven L. McKenzie. *To Each Its Own Meaning: An Introduction to Biblical Criticism*. Louisville, Ky.: Westminster John Knox, 1993.

Marshall, I. Howard, ed. *New Testament Interpretation: Essays on Principles and Methods*. Grand Rapids: Eerdmans, 1977.

The Gentile mission also has important roots in Jesus' ministry—a second stage, perhaps, but not an afterthought, not a deviation from the divine plan. Foreshadowing of this appears in the infancy narratives (Mt 1—2). Gentiles are the first to greet and worship God's Messiah; the Jews, represented by Herod and all Jerusalem, resist his coming. In the next scene John the Baptist warns against relying on descent from Abraham for one's standing before God, for "God is able from these stones to raise up children to Abraham" (Mt 3:9 NRSV). This relativizing of ethnic privilege opens up the way for God to raise up Gentiles as children for Abraham. While Jesus goes "only to the lost sheep of the house of Israel," a

Gentile's faith in Jesus twice intrudes on this exclusive mission and he briefly turns aside to respond to their trust (Mt 8:5-13; 15:21-28). In response to the Gentile centurion's faith, Jesus predicts "many will come from east and west and eat with Abraham and Isaac and Jacob in the kingdom of heaven, while the heirs of the kingdom will be thrown into the outer darkness, where there will be weeping and gnashing of teeth" (Mt 8:11-12 NRSV). As Jesus' parables of the wicked tenants and the wedding guests look forward to the inclusion of others (Mt 21:41-43; 22:1-14), so Jesus' final commission to his disciples set in motion the mission that makes this a reality: "Go therefore and make disciples of all nations, baptizing them in the name of the Father and of the Son and of the Holy Spirit, and teaching them to obey everything that I have commanded you" (Mt 28:19-20 NRSV). Both in the plan of God and the ministry of Jesus, then, the gathering in of the Gentiles is not an afterthought or a deviation, but rather the fulfillment of God's just design for all people. The Jewish Christians may be assured that far from being cut off from the true Israel on account of the large numbers of Gentiles in their body, they show themselves to be the true Israel precisely because within their body the purpose of God for all nations is being accomplished.

The church and the Torah. Matthew makes the strongest statements in the New Testament concerning the ongoing validity of the Torah. On the one hand, the Torah represents a point of connectedness with the Jewish Christians' heritage, and Matthew refuses to relinquish the centrality of doing Torah as the means of doing God's will. On the other hand, Matthew is committed to a very specific interpretation of what it means to fulfill Torah, or to do the will of God. That is, Torah is truly fulfilled only in the light of Jesus' authoritative teaching on doing God's will. The connection with Torah is important because both the Jewish Christians and the non-Christian Jews are con-

vinced that Torah shows the way of God and that to depart from Torah is to depart from obedience to the covenant. Matthew reaffirms for the Christian communities that following Jesus is entirely consonant with doing the will of God as revealed in Torah. Along the way he also goes further than any other New Testament author in showing why the alternative way of doing Torah, namely, the Pharisaic-rabbinic *halakha* (the way of "walking" in line with the Law), is not the fulfillment of Torah.

Jesus presents his own teaching not as a replacement for Torah but as a guide to its fulfillment (again see Mt 5:17-20). When approached by the rich young man, Jesus points to God's commandments as the way to life: "If you wish to enter into life, keep the commandments" (Mt 19:17 NRSV). The way to enter life, however, is really to follow Jesus as a disciple and learn from him how to walk in line with Torah. Indeed, Jesus' own words have a lasting validity that even outstrips that of Torah: the Law endures only until heaven and earth pass away, but "my words will not pass away" (Mt 24:35). In Matthew 5:21-48, Jesus gives some very specific instructions concerning how Torah is truly fulfilled and how our righteousness can exceed that of the scribes and Pharisees. As Jesus' expansions of the prohibitions against murder and adultery show, following Jesus' teachings means that Torah becomes a matter not only of action but of thought, word and deed. The person who follows Jesus' *halakha* will "become obedient from the heart" (Rom 6:17 NRSV). Moreover, concessions in Torah made to human weakness are set aside. Oaths are prescribed to enforce truthfulness and reliability in certain situations, but the true doer of God's will would always speak the truth and be reliable. The oath, in effect, countenances lying and deceit where oaths are not taken, and so is set aside in Jesus' *halakha*. Similarly, divorce, while provided for by Torah, is set aside in Jesus' *halakha* as conflicting with God's original intentions for man and woman (with the interesting exception that appears only in Matthew, "except for the cause of unchastity," perhaps because such an act has already initiated the dissolution of the marriage, which a divorce would merely formalize).

The essence of Torah, seen near the end of Matthew 5 and elsewhere, is to love and to do the things love requires. The Pharisees (and their late-first-century descendants) are faulted in their application of Torah because they have chosen the wrong hermeneutical key. They focus on holiness as "separateness," whereas God calls for holiness as "mercy and love." Ultimately, our understanding of the requirements of Torah (as "separateness" or "holiness as love and generosity") reflects our understanding of God's character. In Jesus' *halakha* the latter is emphasized and rooted directly in the character of God: "Love your enemies and pray for those who persecute you, so that you may be children of your Father in heaven; for he makes his sun rise on the evil and on the good, and sends rain on the righteous and on the unrighteous" (Mt 5:44-45 NRSV).

Twice Jesus is shown taking the Pharisees to task for missing this hermeneutical key: "Go and learn what this means, 'I desire mercy, not sacrifice.' For I have come not to call the righteous but sinners" (Mt 9:13 NRSV); "if you had known what this means, 'I desire mercy, not sacrifice,' you would not have condemned the guiltless" (Mt 12:7 NRSV, quoting Hos 6:6). The latter charge is made during a conflict over Jesus' healing on a sabbath, in which Jesus proves that mercy is more in line with God's intent for the sabbath than refraining from mercy out of a desire to keep the sabbath (see Mt 12:7-12). How does a person keep the commandments concerning the sabbath? Not by rigidly separating times of rest and work if this intrudes on the witness to God's character as merciful, generous and caring! How does a person keep the commandments concerning purity and dietary regulations? Not by rigidly

separating from less observant Jews (or Gentiles!) if God's purposes of calling the sinner back from death to life will go unfulfilled!

In several other places Matthew preserves Jesus' emphasis on love and mercy as the heart of Torah. Jesus twice summarizes the Law (as did many rabbis) by focusing on compassion and love: "in everything do to others as you would have them do to you; for this is the law and the prophets" (Mt 7:12 NRSV); " 'Teacher, which commandment in the law is the greatest?' [Jesus] said to him, 'You shall love the Lord your God with all your heart, and with all your soul, and with all your mind. This is the greatest and first commandment. And a second is like it, You shall love your neighbor as yourself. On these two commandments hang all the law and the prophets' " (Mt 22:36-40 NRSV). It is significant that in both of these statements (as well as in the thematic statement of Mt 5:17-20), Matthew has pointed to "the prophets" in addition to "the law." Jesus indicates that the will of God is not merely found in the first five books of the Jewish Scriptures but is also revealed in the words of the prophets, which were also to be received as the Word of God. The prophetic literature has much to say about how to keep Torah. One especially prominent strain of thought is that the offering of sacrifices, the observance of holy days and the like paled in importance when set alongside deeds of love, mercy, compassion and relief for the poor, and the like. Jesus clearly stands in this tradition and criticizes the Pharisees from within this tradition (as noted above, he cites Hosea and Isaiah against the Pharisaic-rabbinic way of keeping Torah).

As a sort of capstone to this emphasis on mercy and love as the way to fulfill God's desires for God's people revealed in Torah, Matthew provides the vision of the Judge separating people from all nations (no ethnic privilege for Jews) based on their performance of deeds of mercy and compassion (see Mt 25:31-46).

Does Matthew take a more conservative

stand than Mark with regard to Torah? For example, when retelling the tradition about the controversy over defilement (Mt 15:1-20; Mk 7:1-23), Matthew does not explicitly draw the inference that in light of Jesus' teaching concerning true purity, all foods are now declared clean (Mk 7:19). Did Matthew believe Christians (or at least Jewish Christians) should continue to follow the dietary laws of Leviticus? Did he require circumcision and other such works of Torah? How open would Matthew have been to Paul's position concerning the Torah? It is not possible to be certain, but in light of Jesus' attitude toward outsiders (as preserved in Matthew), reaching out to the sinner with the same generosity seen in God would mean that Torah was actually fulfilled when Jews and Gentiles ate at the same table—when Gentiles were accepted on the basis of their new commitment to live out the love and mercy of Jesus rather than on the basis of circumcision or taking on of the yoke of Torah in terms of dietary prescriptions and the like. The new community takes on the yoke of Torah only as it is fashioned by Jesus: "Come to me, all you that are weary and are carrying heavy burdens, and I will give you rest. Take my yoke upon you, and learn from me; for I am gentle and humble in heart, and you will find rest for your souls. For my yoke is easy, and my burden is light" (Mt 11:28-30 NRSV).

Jesus' words here bear a striking resemblance to the invitation Ben Sira gives to prospective students at the end of his collection of wisdom sayings:

> Draw near to me, you who are
>   untaught, . . .
> Put your neck under the yoke,
>   and let your souls receive
>   instruction; . . .
> See with your eyes that I have
>   labored little
>   and found myself much rest"
> (Sir 51:23, 26-27 RSV).

Like Ben Sira, Jesus is inviting the addressees to learn from him about keeping Torah, the way to fulfill God's commands, promising that it is a rest-giving rather than a wearying way. Jesus' yoke is a light burden in sharp contrast to the yoke of Torah as designed by the Pharisaic-rabbinic school: "They tie up heavy burdens, hard to bear, and lay them on the shoulders of others; but they themselves are unwilling to lift a finger to move them" (Mt 23:4 NRSV). Just as Jesus is the point of continuity between God's revelation in the past and purpose in the future, so Jesus' teachings are the lens that refracts God's Torah into a prism of righteousness. Those who hold fast to Jesus have found the One in whom Old Testament revelation finds fulfillment. Those who take up the yoke of his teachings and follow in his way are assured that they are doing the will of God as revealed in "the law and the prophets."

Matthew's polemic with the parent body, non-Christian Judaism. Matthew engages non-Christian Judaism, whether directly or indirectly, in a debate over the correct reading of Scripture. We have seen how Matthew presents Jesus' life and ministry (and future work) as the correct key to unlocking the significance of the oracles of God preserved in the Hebrew Scriptures. The synagogue's resistance to the confession of Jesus as the Messiah is ultimately a result of its failure to perceive how God was at work in Jesus fulfilling the promises of old. This is encapsulated in Jesus' disagreement with the priests at his entry into Jerusalem:

> When the chief priests and the scribes saw the amazing things that he did, and heard the children crying out in the temple, "Hosanna to the Son of David," they became angry and said to him, "Do you hear what these are saying?" Jesus said to them, "Yes; have you never read, 'Out of the mouths of infants and nursing babies you have prepared praise for yourself?'" (Mt 21:15-16 NRSV)

265

Non-Christian Jews, Matthew avers, respond to Jesus and to the church out of a lack of understanding of their shared scriptural heritage. Matthew preserves sayings of Jesus that answer the church's critics on its behalf:

You are wrong, because you know neither the scriptures nor the power of God. (Mt 22:29)

"What do you think of the Messiah? Whose son is he?" They said to him, "The son of David." He said to them, "How is it then that David by the Spirit calls him Lord, saying, 'The Lord said to my Lord, "Sit at my right hand, until I put your enemies under your feet"?' If David thus calls him Lord, how is he his son?" No one was able to give him an answer. (Mt 22:42-46 NRSV)

These serve as important reinforcements for the Christian communities. As they look out and see the synagogue pursuing an entirely different reading of the Scriptures and rejecting, even censuring, the churches' reading of those texts, they can be assured that these differences actually point to the synagogue's departure from God's revelation, not to the Christian assembly's alienation from the truth.

The second aspect of this polemic is Matthew's debate over the correct interpretation and performance of Torah. We have already addressed this at length above when we looked at Jesus' criticisms of the Pharisees' application of Torah. The hermeneutical key of mercy and love, provided by the prophets and underscored by Jesus, was missing (it is alleged) in the Pharisaic-rabbinic *halakha*. Indeed, that *halakha* is set aside in Matthew, as in Mark, as a collection of "human precepts" that have replaced and subverted God's commandments (Mt 15:7-9). Matthew has sharpened Mark's presentation of Jesus' indictment: "Then Pharisees and scribes came to Jesus from Jerusalem and said, 'Why do your disci-

ples transgress the tradition of the elders? For they do not wash their hands before they eat.' He answered them, 'And why do you break the commandment of God for the sake of your tradition?' " (Mt 15:1-3). Matthew also includes a lengthy denunciation of the scribes and Pharisees in Matthew 23:1-36, attacking the *halakha*—the way of keeping Torah—of these rival teachers. Matthew probably includes this lengthy polemic because it also served his own need and the perceived needs of the Christian communities for clarification concerning why the church was correct in its Torah-keeping and why the synagogue (those Jews who followed the scribes, Pharisees and their rabbinic descendants) was off the mark.

If the leaders of the synagogue, those non-Christian Jewish interpreters of the Law, are not to be followed in their *halakha,* who is? For Matthew, of course, it is Jesus, whose teaching provides the solid rock on which to build one's house. Jesus' words anchor us firmly in the will and pleasure of God (Mt 7:24-27). Jesus teaches with God-given authority, an authority superior to that of "their scribes" (Mt 7:29). Perhaps the most striking passage addressing this question is Matthew 9:36-38: "When he saw the crowds, he had compassion for them, because they were harassed and helpless, like sheep without a shepherd. Then he said to his disciples, "The harvest is plentiful, but the laborers are few; therefore ask the Lord of the harvest to send out laborers into his harvest" (NRSV). This was a biting critique of religious leadership in Judah, asserting that there was no adequate leadership for the sheep of God's pasture. Who fills in this crying need? In Matthew's presentation the commissioning and sending out of the twelve immediate follows this prayer to God to supply the lack of solid religious leaders (Mt 10:1-15). The apostles are God's provision for God's people in the face of a leadership (i.e., the Pharisees and their heirs) that does not lead the people as true shepherds. The Christian missionaries have gone out as God's shepherds to raise up flocks of righteousness who will fulfill God's Torah in the way that reflects God's character of love, mercy and generosity.

MATTHEW'S FORMATION OF THE CHURCH'S ETHOS AND DISCIPLINE

Matthew was widely received by the churches so early because it contained so much that was of direct relevance to believers' life together as a church, both in terms of what it meant to be the church and what it meant to be Christians in the church. It was an exceptional textbook for doing the very thing Jesus commissions at the end of the Gospel: making disciples (not just converts) by teaching them to live as Jesus instructed.

Matthew is, in fact, the only Gospel to use the term *ekklēsia,* the Greek word often translated "church" (Mt 16:18; 18:17). A number of scholars have suggested that the use of this term is anachronistic: it is out of place to have Jesus talking about the "church," an institution that did not arise until Christian missionary endeavors really got off the ground. The anachronism may lie, however, in the connotations we give to the term *church.* To understand this term simply as "congregation" or "assembly," particularly in the sense of the *qahal,* the "assembly" of the faithful who awaited God's end-time salvation (as the term was used at Qumran), would remove the anachronism. Jesus may have spoken of building around the Twelve an eschatological "assembly" of disciples who would await his coming again, and to which he could give specific instructions concerning how to live in the interim and how to be ready for his return.

For this "assembly," this "congregation" of the faithful, Matthew gathers, shapes and organizes a wealth of Jesus traditions to provide guidance for living in the manner that pleases God in the context of a strong and supportive community of disciples.

Reflecting God's character: A core Matthean value. In the Sermon on the Mount (Mt 5—7) Matthew directly and fully addresses the character and ethos that the Christians are to embody. This is a collection of sayings and instructions by Jesus organized according to topic. It does not bear the marks of a single original discourse, for many topics are presented and transitions are wanting. A comparison with Luke 6 is instructive. Luke collects only one-third of the sayings in the Sermon on the Mount in this Sermon on the Plain. Other material collected in the Sermon on the Mount is found scattered in six other places throughout Luke's Gospel. This collection of principle teachings of Jesus became foundational for instruction in Christian discipleship.

There has been much discussion concerning the nature and purpose of the Sermon on the Mount. Some view it as an impossible ethic, meant to drive people to despair of ever attaining righteousness. Indeed, some even take the "greater righteousness" Jesus points to in Matthew 5:20 as something entirely divorced from what follows in Matthew 5:21-48—according to them it is the righteousness that comes by faith, as found in Paul's letters. To view the Sermon on the Mount as an impossible ethic meant to drive people to despair of attaining "their own righteousness" so that they will flee to the cross is to write it off as a cipher for Romans 10:3-4. It also attributes a rather strange mind game to Matthew, who explicitly directs readers to take Jesus' sayings with utmost seriousness as the rule for building a secure life (Mt 7:21-27). It is, after all, not Jesus' *halakha* but the Pharisaic-rabbinic *halakha* that he regards as oppressive and impossible (Mt 23:4). Moreover, this view of the Sermon on the Mount fails to appreciate what the Holy Spirit can accomplish in a disciple's life, molding him or her fully into the character of Jesus so that "the just requirement of the law might be fulfilled"—not bypassed—by those "who walk not according to the flesh, but according to the Spirit" (Rom 8:4 NRSV).

Another view looks at the Sermon on the Mount as an interim ethic meant to be observed only for the short time between Jesus' ascension and return, now rendered impracticable on account of the yawning centuries. Again, the tendency to protect present-day disciples from the rigorous demands of Jesus is prominent, but probably not wholesome. The Sermon on the Mount *is* an interim ethic, since it takes seriously the return of Jesus and the coming judgment (Mt 7:21-23), but it is an ethic for the church as long as the interim exists. It is no less the revelation of the righteousness God seeks in disciples now than it was the revelation of the righteousness God sought in the first followers of Jesus. In affirming this we need not be concerned about conjuring up the specter of works righteousness, the attempt to earn God's favor. Matthew writes to those who have received God's gift of forgiveness, acceptance into God's family and access to God's favor. Matthew calls for the righteousness that "exceeds that of the scribes and Pharisees" as a response to the gift and calling of God, a gift represented by the Beatitudes that precede Matthew 5:17-20. This righteousness is only a reflection of the righteousness of God that first touched the disciples. The love and forgiveness disciples are called to show, for example, responds to and reflects the love and forgiveness that God had first extended to them (Mt 5:38-48; 18:23-35).

The first cardinal teaching of the Sermon on the Mount, which is then echoed throughout Matthew's special material, is that the family of God is called to reflect the character of God.

> You have heard that it was said, "You shall love your neighbor and hate your enemy." But I say to you, Love your enemies and pray for those who persecute you, so that you may be children of your Father in heaven; for he makes his sun rise on the evil and on the good, and sends rain on the righteous and on the unrighteous. For if you love those who love you, what reward do you have? Do not even the tax collectors do the same? And if you greet only your brothers and sisters, what more are you doing than others? Do not even the Gentiles do the same? Be perfect, therefore, as your heavenly Father is perfect. (Mt 5:43-48 NRSV)

The basis for Jesus' teaching against retaliation of any kind—not returning hate for hate or injury for injury—is the character of God, who extends favor to all. Just as God sends the blessings of rain and sun on the whole world, so God's children are to participate in God's work of bringing blessing, extending favor and mercy as God extends them.

The disciples are not called to be doormats but rather to respond actively to the ignorant, the malicious and the hurtful with the favor and love of God, which can transform the enemy into a friend and the arrogant into the penitent. Jesus calls for courageous action, not capitulation. Jesus' followers are called neither to be slaves to evil nor to respond to injuries and to evil on evil's own terms, but to be free in God's love to respond to evil out of God's goodness and healing. In effect, another person's lack of goodness must not have the power to shape disciples' attitudes or actions. God does not respond to us as we deserve but in love and mercy, calling us to repentance and wholeness. Followers of Jesus must reflect this aspect of God's character in order to do the will of the Father in heaven (Mt 7:21).

Matthew takes the command in Leviticus 11:44 to "be holy as I am holy" and rewords it as "be perfect, therefore, as your heavenly Father is perfect" (Mt 5:48). *Holy* might have been laden with the wrong emphases, since this was the heart of the Pharisaic-rabbinic interpretation of Torah. God's "holiness" was taken as a mandate for the separation of the righteous from the sinners, which hindered God's work among the sinners. Matthew chose *perfect* as a new but related term, one that could be filled with mercy and love. *Perfect* is quite closely related to *holy*, given that *holiness* often denotes "completeness" and "wholeness" (and not just something set apart from the ordinary) in the Torah. In this sense God's perfection consists of God's completeness, God's ability to act without being limited by the responses or actions of others. This is what believers are called to reflect in their grants of love and mercy to humans and in their refusal to respond in kind to those who do evil and the like. Because God is "whole," God does not need others to treat God kindly in order for

God to treat them kindly in return. Disciples of Jesus are called to find their wholeness in God so that they too do not need another person to be courteous, understanding or even just in order to seek and to serve God's purposes for that other. For Matthew this "doing of the will of God" is what creates kinship with Jesus the Son and with the Father (see Mt 5:45; 12:49-50).

The Lord's Prayer (Mt 6:9-13) reinforces this community ethos of seeking opportunities to participate in God's work of extending love and mercy to those in need. When a person prayed that God's name might be "sanctified," he or she was not praying that God's name would be holy (which it already is), but that it be kept holy by being honored and revered. Jesus insists that this happens as disciples do

Figure 6.6. An ancient olive tree in the Garden of Gethsemane. (Photo courtesy of Todd Bolen [BiblePlaces.com])

EXEGETICAL SKILL
The Use of Comparative Material in New Testament Exegesis

The texts collected in what we call the New Testament were not written in a vacuum, sealed off from the influence of the world around them and the world behind them. These were not tablets dropped from the sky. They are texts that emerged as real Christian leaders struggled alongside their congregations, trying to encourage and shape these communities in ways that are faithful to the vision of God for God's new people. They were written in the real world to shape disciples in the real world. As such, the close study of the world that was real for them—the Greco-Roman world of the first century C.E., together with the cultural resources available to people in that world—is vitally important for those who want to understand the New Testament texts as their authors intended.

This study can be accomplished in part through reading *about* the first-century world, but it is most illuminating also to read widely *in* the literature *of* that world. The Old Testament, of course, is foundational as a group of texts available to people in the first century, but we must also include the Apocrypha, the pseudepigrapha, the Dead Sea Scrolls, the works of Philo and Josephus, and early rabbinic materials for a complete picture of the wealth of resources enjoyed in Jewish circles, many of which might also have been available or known to the early Christian movement.

Immersing ourselves in the Jewish literature is an essential step on the road to understanding the New Testament in its literary, theological, social and cultural context. But the church also took shape within and included members enculturated in the dominant Greco-Roman culture.[a] Reading select works of Aristotle, Plato, Epictetus, Seneca, Dio Chrysostom, Plutarch and Cicero (to name some of the more important Greek and Latin authors) exposes the New Testament student to the wealth of resources available

---

[a]Indeed, the same should be said about a great many Jews in the first century. Philo, Josephus and the authors of Wisdom of Solomon, 4 Maccabees and *Letter of Aristeas* could never have written as they did were they not deeply immersed in both the Jewish and Greek culture. The investigation of streams of influence on early Christianity has often been fraught with ideological baggage. N. T. Wright points out that in the earlier part of the twentieth century, Judaism was seen as "the dark background against which the bright light had shone" (*Jesus and the Victory of God* [Minneapolis: Fortress, 1996], p. 120), with the result that scholars looked to Greco-Roman religion and philosophy for Christianity's pedigree (seen then as providing a "reputable ancestry" for the faith). After World War II and the horrors of anti-Judaism, Christian scholars reversed the trend completely, with the result that "Jewish ideas were 'good', non-Jewish ones 'bad' " (ibid.). This tendency is still quite evident today whenever scholars or pastors insist on looking primarily to "Jewish backgrounds" for early Christian ideas, language and culture. It appears in even more aggravated form when they look solely to the Old Testament as the body of resources feeding the New Testament, closing their eyes on purely ideological grounds to the extrabiblical Jewish and Greco-Roman literature, whose impact is everywhere apparent.

from the Gentile world for the formation of Christian culture.[b] The near disappearance of classical studies in Western education has seriously impeded our ability to hear Paul or John the Seer or even the rival teachers in Galatia in context. Pastors and other Christian leaders would do well to weave a consistent exposure to more of these primary texts into their long-term plans for continuing education.

Growing in our awareness of these resources enables a number of insights. First, we can begin to assess how early Christian leaders learned from available resources and applied that knowledge to their work in shaping the early church. Second, as the gap narrows between the New Testament's and the ancient world's thought and ethics, we can see more clearly what was truly distinctive about the Christian message and community. Third, we can begin to understand how the early Christians would have made sense of the message they were hearing from their leaders, both by making connections with material they might have previously encountered (not through reading it directly, most likely, but rather through hearing about it as part of their enculturation) and by discerning ways the new message was departing from or playing off familiar topics or teachings.

New Testament scholars have been engaged in this kind of study for centuries, with the result that a critical commentary or scholarly article will often approach the meaning of a New Testament passage, concept or teaching by studying parallels, or comparative texts, in other ancient literature. This is an extremely fruitful enterprise but also one fraught with some dangers—notably the condition whimsically diagnosed as "parallelomania."[c] Students afflicted with this condition heap up alleged parallels to a New Testament passage on the basis of some perceived similarities and then make premature statements about the influence of one text on another, or premature value judgments about the quality of one text over another.

One major problem with parallelomania is that the student does not seek to understand the parallel literature on its own terms, as part of a larger text and system of thought. On the contrary, when confronted with alleged parallels between the New Testament and other literature, the prudent reader should first seek to understand the extracanonical passage fully in its own context and in light of the larger thought world promoted in its family of literature (e.g., Essene, rabbinic, Stoic, etc.). By doing so, false parallels can be eliminated and real parallels will take on greater depth. Second, the careful student will avoid the genetic fallacy. Just because two texts contain a very similar idea or instruction, it does not follow that one used the other, even if one is demonstrably earlier than the other.

---

[b]The mass of literature, both Jewish and Greco-Roman, available from the period can be overwhelming. For suggested starting points, see the reading list of primary sources provided at the end of the chapter two.

[c]Samuel Sandmel, "Parallelomania," *JBL* 81 (1962): 1-13.

Priority does not necessitate causality. Instead, the two works may draw on a common stream of tradition or represent parallel developments of a shared tradition. A parallel text may bear witness that a particular idea or teaching was available in the world of the New Testament author, but it does not necessarily represent the direct source of that thought or teaching. Third, the parallels should inform our reading of the New Testament, not replace it. In the words of Sandmel, "if we make [Paul] mean only what the parallels mean, we are using the parallels in a way that can lead us to misunderstand Paul."[d]

How might this skill look in practice? First, consider Jesus' words about forgiveness in Matthew 6:14-15, commenting on the petition of Matthew 6:12, "forgive us our debts, as we have forgiven our debtors": "For if you forgive others their trespasses, your heavenly Father will also forgive you; but if you do not forgive others, neither will your Father forgive your trespasses" (NRSV). Jesus' teaching on forgiveness is not attested in the Jewish Scriptures, and if we were aware only of biblical literature, we might presume that Jesus is standing apart from the Judaism of his day. However, we find a noteworthy parallel in the Wisdom of Ben Sira:

> The vengeful will face the Lord's vengeance,
> for he keeps a strict account of their sins.
> Forgive your neighbor the wrong he has done,
> and then your sins will be pardoned when you pray.
> Does anyone harbor anger against another,
> and expect healing from the Lord?
> If one has no mercy toward another like himself,
> can he then seek pardon for his own sins? (Sir 28:1-4 NRSV)

Is this a true parallel or merely an apparent one? Both Ben Sira and Jesus are speaking about the relationship between forgiveness on the human plane and the possibility of experiencing forgiveness from God; both warn that those who keep an account of others' sins against them will face God's strict account; both underscore the impropriety of asking for mercy while showing none. Particularly when we take Matthew 18:23-35 into account as we read Matthew 6:14-15, Ben Sira shows itself to be a true parallel.

Ben Sira was a teacher of wisdom who ran a "house of instruction," or a school, in Jerusalem in the first quarter of the second century B.C.E. His writings were very influential in both Palestine and abroad, with the result that some of his instructions were likely to have entered the popular wisdom that later sages like Jesus could draw on. This is not to say that Jesus read Ben Sira, but it is very likely that Jesus learned some of Ben Sira's wisdom from the instructions he received in the synagogue and, per-

---

[d]Ibid., p. 5.

haps, in dialogue with teachers throughout his formative years (see, e.g., Lk 2:46-49). Our awareness of this background is very instructive. It shows us that Jesus neither formulated all of his teachings from "thin air" or in opposition to Jewish sages. It cautions us, as well, that what we might at first presume to be distinctive to Jesus and Christianity *over against* Judaism actually turns out to be very much at home *within* Judaism.[e]

Similarly, when Jesus invites the people to "Come to me, all who are weary and carrying heavy burdens, and I will give you rest. Take my yoke upon you, and learn from me; . . . and you will find rest for your souls. For my yoke is easy, and my burden is light" (Mt 11:28-30 NRSV), he uses language and a literary form very similar to that of the earlier wisdom teacher:

> Draw near to me, you who are untaught,
> and lodge in my school. . . .
> Put your neck under the yoke,
> and let your souls receive instruction;
> it is to be found close by.
> See with your eyes that I have labored little
> and found myself much rest. (Sir 51:23, 26-27 RSV)

The presence of shared motifs—the invitation to "draw near," the metaphor of the "yoke" applied to learning, the invitation to learn, the promise of finding rest after light labor—in a similar situation of inviting people to discipleship suggests that we are again looking at a true parallel that might be informative for how we understand Matthew 11:28-30. Jesus' use of these motifs may have invited the hearers to view him as a teacher of wisdom and of the interpretation and application of Torah, and to view attaching themselves to his group of disciples as a kind of attachment to a wisdom school. Thus by attending to comparative texts, we gain a previously unavailable insight into how Jesus' audience might have viewed him in light of his words and what models were available to them for understanding and relating to this Jesus.

As a final example, and one that will take us into the equally important Greco-Roman side of the equation, consider Matthew 5:43-48. The rationale Jesus gives for loving your enemies (it reflects God's generous character) bears a marked similarity to Seneca's instructions to noble benefactors. In one passage Seneca writes, " 'If you are imitating the gods,' you say, 'then bestow benefits also upon the ungrateful; for the sun rises also upon the wicked' " (*Ben.* 4.26.1). This is at first a striking parallel, but at this point Seneca takes issue with his literary conversation partner: the gods do good to all for the benefit of the good, not the bad. (The bad are

---

[e]An excellent resource in this regard in J. H. Charlesworth, *Jesus Within Judaism* (New York: Doubleday, 1988).

benefited only because they cannot be separated out from the good.) The rain, another sign of divine favor, cannot merely descend on the fields of the just (*Ben.* 4.28.3). Later in his book, however, Seneca himself uses the example of the gods to urge a person to give even to those who have been ungrateful for gifts in the past, even to those "at whose hands we have suffered loss" (*Ben.* 7.31.5). This brings us closer to Jesus' use of the example of God's generosity, as does Seneca's understanding of why the gods are able to give in this manner—"they follow their own nature, and in their universal bounty include even those who are ill interpreters of their gifts" (*Ben.* 1.1.9). Because it is their nature to do good rather than evil, the gods are free to give to whomever they choose. They are not bound or confined in their choice by another's lack of goodness or gratitude. The person who would manifest true generosity in its purest and noblest form, then, take the gods for their models. In a similar manner Jesus teaches that acting in accordance with God's generosity shows a "family resemblance" to God.

It is highly unlikely that Jesus (or Matthew) and Seneca influenced one another either way, but Seneca's text allows us to determine that Jesus' teaching again might resonate at several points with ethical instruction heard elsewhere. By comparing Jesus' teaching with Seneca's, moreover, the distinctive aspect of Jesus' teaching emerges more clearly. What Seneca's pupils might be led to do in the extraordinary case, namely, seek to benefit those who have harmed them, Jesus' disciples are to do as a matter of course. The standard of God is to be the standard of Jesus' disciples in everyday human interactions, not just as an occasional or extreme display of a generous spirit.

Finding comparative materials can be difficult for the beginning student. Fortunately, writers of critical commentaries (such as the Hermeneia series, the Word Biblical Commentary, the Anchor Bible Commentary, the New International Greek Testament Commentary and Eerdmans' Socio-Rhetorical Commentary Series) are profoundly aware of the importance of putting students in touch with comparative texts; so they often include quotations from classical Greco-Roman and Jewish authors (or at least citations the student can look up, read and ponder). The student must remember to use these resources critically, heeding the advice of scholars like Sandmel on the judicious use of comparative texts.

My students often ask me how to continue to deepen their understanding of the New Testament after our introductory classes, and my advice is always to read broadly and thoughtfully in the Jewish, Greek and Latin classics. The more you know about the historical, philosophical, ethical, theological, social and cultural contexts of the first-century world, the richer and more insightful your interpretation of the New Testament has the potential to be.

Readers wishing to develop this skill further on their own might engage one or more of the following exercises, asking the following questions of each set of texts: (1) What points of contact do you find between these texts? (2) Where is the line of thought developed in similar directions, and what divergences occur? (3) Do you think literary dependence is likely, or should we read these merely as mutually illumining witnesses to the topics treated in these texts (i.e., as windows into the thought world and background of the New Testament)? (4) How is your reading of the New Testament passage enhanced or refined by consideration of the comparative text? (5) Does the comparison lend any insights into what the New Testament author was trying to achieve, and how he set about to accomplish this?

1. Wisdom of Solomon 13:5-10; 14:22-27; and Romans 1:18-32.

2. Proverbs 8:22-30; Wisdom of Solomon 7:22—8:4; and Hebrews 1:2-3; Colossians 1:15-20.

3. The Priene Inscription honoring the birthday of Augustus Caesar (available in numerous resources; see, e.g., F. W. Danker, *Benefactor* [St. Louis, Mo.: Clayton, 1982], pp. 215-22) and Luke 2.

FOR FURTHER READING

Bauckham, Richard. "The Relevance of Extracanonical Jewish Texts to New Testament Study," pp. 90-108. In *Hearing the New Testament*. Edited by Joel B. Green. Grand Rapids: Eerdmans, 1995. See especially the extensive bibliography on pp. 105-8.

deSilva, David A. *Introducing the Apocrypha: Message, Context, and Significance*. Grand Rapids: Baker, 2002.

Evans, C. A. *Noncanonical Writings and New Testament Interpretation*. Peabody, Mass.: Hendrickson, 1992.

Sandmel, Samuel. "Parallelomania," *JBL* 81 (1962): 1-13.

works of love and light, which cause others to give glory to God (Mt 5:16). Paul reinforces this interpretation when he writes to Jews who do not observe God's commandments, "the name of God is blasphemed among the Gentiles because of you" (Rom 2:24 NRSV). Just as the disobedience of God's servants leads to the slandering and dishonoring of God's name, so the obedience of God's servants leads to the honoring and hallowing of God's name.

The third petition, "Thy will be done," places the supplicant in submission to that will, just as Jesus submitted himself to God's will in the Garden of Gethsemane (see figure 6.6). The person who prays thus acknowledges the lordship of God over external circumstances and also commits to do the will of God, to seek out how she or he may accomplish God's purposes in the coming day. Finally, the petition regarding forgiveness ("forgive us our debts as we have *forgiven* our debtors"), the only petition to receive direct comment (Mt 6:14-15), speaks to the importance of cultivating God's character within the believer. As God forgives, we must forgive. The parable of the unforgiving steward (Mt 18:23-35) emphasizes that forgiveness is not optional but mandatory. The character of the church, therefore, must be a forgiving character, and unforgiveness is a blight on all its endeavors.

A community of works of mercy. The aspect of the ethos of the new community that Matthew most underscores, placing it as the conclusion to all Jesus' teaching, is doing works of mercy toward those who are in dire circumstances (Mt 25:31-46). There has been much debate concerning the meaning of this passage, and a number of respectable scholars make a case for reading it as a declaration that individuals will be judged based on their treatment of the wandering Christian missionaries, the "least" of Jesus' brothers.[26] Strongest in favor of this reading is that Jesus elsewhere says that Sodom will be better off than those towns that do not receive and give hospitality to the apostles, and that the pitiable conditions described in the vision frequently matched the conditions of itinerant missionaries. Another reading suggests that this vision, the climax of the apocalyptic discourse in Matthew, offers encouragement to the beleaguered Christian community that they will be vindicated at the Last Judgment, when God rewards or punishes all non-Christians on the basis of how they have treated the Christians, Jesus' family, in their midst.[27]

An equally strong case can be made for reading the "least of these my brothers and sisters" as the weakest, neediest members of the Christian community, the least of the "little ones" (Mt 18:6, 10, 14) the community is to care for. Not only outsiders will be judged based on their treatment of these believers but other believers as well will find themselves penned up as sheep or goats depending on whether or not they have responded to the needs of their brothers and sisters.[28] I suspect, however, that Jesus would not have us leave the boundaries drawn so closely around the Christian needy. In Matthew 5:38-48 Jesus moves the hearer past love of neighbors to love of our enemies. Gentiles and hypocrites love those who belong to them: what credit is this to anyone? Is it still possible for Christians to think of doing acts of mercy only toward the "brothers and sisters" within the new community, or must their mercy and kindness reach out to all people in need? If disciples are to reflect the character of God, who sends the gifts of rain and sun on all alike, then they cannot simply see their mission as reaching out to those within the community of faith. Christians are thus called to form a community that cares for the world's needy, those for whom the world's powerful and upwardly mobile have no time or compassion.

There is a certain reciprocity between the flow of kindness established in Jesus' first teaching (Mt 5—7) and his final teaching (Mt 24—25). In Matthew 5—6 God supplies all our needs, reaches out in love to forgive and restore the sinner and sustain the wayward, and calls redeemed sinners to live out of God's character. In Matthew 25 Jesus calls his followers to extend mercy, love and forgiveness to other human beings. When the disciples stand before the judgment seat in chapter 25, they find that in giving to others they have given to Christ, acting as faithful, grateful clients of their own benefactor, rendering to him the ser-

---

[26]See, for example, R. C. Oudersluys, "The Parable of the Sheep and the Goats (Mt 25:31-46): Eschatology and Mission, Then and Now," *Reformed Review* 26 (1973): 151-61; J. M. Court, "Right and Left: The Implications for Matthew 25.31-46," *NTS* 31 (1985): 223-33; U. Luz, "The Final Judgment (Mt 25:31-46): An Exercise in 'History of Influence' Exegesis," in *Treasures New and Old: Contributions to Matthean Studies*, ed. D. R. Bauer and M. A. Powell (Atlanta: Society of Biblical Literature, 1996).

[27]Stanton, *Gospel for a New People*, chap. 9.

[28]See further the positions reviewed in D. A. deSilva, "Renewing the Ethic of the Eschatological Community: The Vision of Judgment in Matthew 25," *Koinonia* 3 (1991): 168-94.

vice to which he called them. Just as Jesus identified with human beings in taking our sins upon himself and restoring us to God's favor, so Jesus continues to identify with those who are in need of love and mercy. The goats failed to recognize that in withholding compassion from the needy around them, they declined their obligation to their benefactor and lord.

Attitudes toward wealth and material pursuits. Like Mark before him, Matthew urges a detachment from ambition to achieve wealth in worldly terms. Within Jesus' sayings Matthew finds two distinct but equally important reasons for this attitude toward money. First, disciples cannot afford to have their commitments and interests divided and their commitment to the community threatened. If we are to remain loyal to God, that loyalty must extend to our very ambitions and desires (Mt 6:19-21, 24). If we join ourselves to the Christian community or if we want to mature in discipleship (Mt 13:7, 22), we cannot be intent on preserving or increasing our material treasure. The rigors of exclusive commitment to the one God and the Messiah, whom the world rejects as subversive and shameful, will not make for capital growth. The rich young man's story shows this most clearly (Mt 19:23-26).

Second, an attitude of detachment from worldly treasure will make it easier to use worldly wealth well; for example, using it to care for the poor (Mt 19:21). The rich young man is called to make an investment in lives, to trust the "bull market" of works of charity to bring "treasures in heaven" (explicitly recalled here from Mt 6:19-21). Only such generosity and compassion leads a person to be "perfect" (a distinctive feature of Matthew's version of this story, recalling Mt 5:48), for such is the generosity of God. This is a theme that will be developed even more fully in Luke and will remain an important aspect of the church's ongoing reflection on the relationship of Christians to worldly wealth (see, for example, *Shepherd of Hermas,* similitude 1; Clement

of Alexandria, "Who is the Rich Man that Shall Enter Heaven?").

Relationships within the community. Matthew 18 has provided one of the earliest sets of instructions on "church discipline" (highlighted by the role of the *ekklēsia* in Mt 18:17), rules for the way Christian communities are to regulate themselves. In this discourse Matthew seeks to direct the community to care for the "little ones." In a world that glorifies strength and those who excel, and that despises the ungifted and weak, the church is to be a place where the weak, the socially powerless and ill-connected, and the ungifted are nurtured. The brothers and sisters are not to hinder the progress of the weak but are to be sure not to make them stumble in their discipleship (Mt 18:6-7). Those who were "little" in their faith are not to be despised but carefully tended and cultivated; those who are straying are sought out, not despised for their lack of firmness and discipline (Mt 18:10-14). Matthew uses the parable of the lost sheep to develop Jesus' concern for the wandering believer— the same parable Luke uses to highlight Jesus' concern for the outsider. Matthew 25:31-46 must also influence the community members' care for their brothers and sisters in need.

The watchword for community relations, and especially conflict, is "forgiveness." Mutual forgiveness is enforced by the community's awareness of having been forgiven much more by God. The forgiving God expects the forgiven to be forgiving in turn (Mt 18:23-35). However, there is also the realistic provision for conflict resolution in Matthew 18:15-17 for those who injure a sister or brother but fail to seek forgiveness. The first direction is to confront the offending sister or brother privately: keeping the matter private between the two believers shows a desire to safeguard the reputation of the offending believer in the church. If this fails to effect reconciliation, the offended disciple should seek the mediation of two or three other believers, recontextualizing the directions of Deuteronomy 19:15 concerning the establishment of a grievance. Finally, the entire local assembly of Christians is called in as an adjudicatory body. Those who refuse to open their hearts to the will of the community, failing to trust the insight of the sisters and brothers, are to be expelled from the assembly. Here Matthew places sayings of Jesus that would more naturally, taken out of the Matthean context, speak about the believers' access to God's favor and authority in prayer: "where two or three are gathered in my name, I am there among them" (Mt 18:20 NRSV). By including this saying in the midst of a discussion about conflict resolution within the church, Matthew underscores the authority of the community of disciples to adjudicate disputes between believers and enforce community discipline: they act with the authority of the Lord who is present in their midst.

Relationships with outsiders. Matthew maintains Mark's strange balance of viewing the community of disciples in a hostile relationship with the world while at the same time being commissioned by Jesus to preach, convert and make disciples of the inhabitants of the world. Indeed, Matthew adds materials that underscore both sides of this tension. Matthew's readers expect the world to respond to them with hatred and violence (Mt 10:24-28, 34-39; 24:9-11), but they also expect that they will reach some and make disciples in every nation (Mt 9:36-38; 28:18-20).

Within this two-sided view of outsiders Matthew includes a strange story that mitigates the mutual antagonism of insiders and outsiders by encouraging the pursuit of peace as far as possible. In Matthew 17:24-27 the collectors of the temple tax come to Peter and ask whether or not his master pays the tax. In the dialogue that follows, Jesus affirms the right of the children of the king-

dom not to pay the tax. That is, the disciples of Jesus are already children of God and have no need of the temple sacrifices to keep that relationship secure. Nevertheless, to avoid giving offense to those outside, they relinquish those rights and pay the temple tax. Disciples are thus taught to make every effort to show solidarity with their unbelieving neighbors, so long as their exclusive commitment to God through Jesus is not compromised.

The eschatological focus of Matthean Christianity. While Matthew shows great interest in the ongoing life of the church and a keen awareness of Jesus' presence in the church (Mt 18:20; 28:20), he also maintains a vibrant eschatological hope. His instructions concerning living together as a church stand side by side with and are often fueled by a sure expectation of Jesus' return. Matthew continues Mark's practice of applying Scriptures not fulfilled in Jesus' first coming to a second coming of the Messiah and to the continuing and future work of Jesus as Christ. Thus early Christian leaders developed an important distinction: not all the messianic and eschatological oracles of the Jewish Scriptures apply to one appearing. The first coming of the anointed One is in humility, the second in power and judgment. Psalm 118:22-23 and Psalm 110:1 (Mt 21:42; 22:44) continue to affirm the exaltation of Jesus after his passion. The signs of the "day of the Lord" envisioned in Joel 2:10-11 will still presage the appearing of the glorified Christ (Mt 24:29). Daniel's vision of the "son of man" coming on the clouds of heaven (Dan 7:13) will yet come to pass (Mt 24:30; 26:64).

These eschatological convictions undergird and motivate the adoption of the community ethos Matthew promotes. The four parables that conclude the last discourse all link doing the will of God with being prepared for meeting the Master at his return. Whether or not the Master is early or late, the disciples must be prepared in any eventuality. How do we prepare? By doing the tasks the Master appointed us in the interim (Mt 24:45), which Matthew expands from the Marcan form by adding a detail about that work: it involves caring for the other servants of the household. How we treat our fellow servants determines how we will be received by the Master at his return. As the foolish bridesmaids found out, there will be insufficient warning to prepare at the last minute. That is, we must be ready—found doing the Master's will—at all times so we will not be caught unprepared and excluded. Life is to be lived with an eye always on the Master's return and the final reckoning. This interim period is a time for fruitful labor on the Master's behalf, putting whatever gifts and resources he has entrusted to us (note—nothing is our own, all was given by the Master) to use for the increase of the Master's kingdom, that is, making faithful disciples, caring for the needy, extending love and mercy to the hungry, naked, sick and imprisoned. Passages like Matthew 7:21-23 and Matthew 25:31-46 leave no room for complacency or new doctrines of election *tout court*. In Matthew's understanding of Jesus' call, membership in the new community is not a "get out of hell free" pass. Rather, becoming part of the community of disciples brings the privilege of knowing God, being nurtured by the presence of Jesus and discovering the way to live so we can be found faithful.

Encouragement for an empowered community. Matthew assures the communities of disciples that their risen Lord has endowed them with authority over their spiritual enemies, that God's presence will always be among them as mediated by the Son, that they would enjoy victory over the hosts of Satan and every power allying itself with the enemy of God: "I will build my church, and the powers of death shall not prevail against it" (Mt 16:18 RSV); "Again I say to you, if two of you agree on earth about anything they ask, it will be done for them by my Father in heaven. For where two or three are gathered in my name, there am I in the midst of them" (Mt 18:19-20 RSV). While, on the one hand, the Christians may suffer marginalization and rejection, they also enjoy close proximity to God and God's power, as well as God's assurance about the future of their community.

Moreover, the Christian community plays a key role in the coming of God's kingdom. The keys to this kingdom are entrusted to the Christian community; people are shut out or allowed into the kingdom as they embrace or spurn the community formed by Jesus. The ways that are pleasing to God are taught only in the church endowed with the Spirit of Jesus: "I will give you the keys of the kingdom of heaven, and whatever you bind on earth will be bound in heaven, and whatever you loose on earth will be loosed in heaven" (Mt 16:19 NRSV); "Truly I tell you, whatever you bind on earth will be bound in heaven, and whatever you loose on earth will be loosed in heaven" (Mt 18:18 NRSV). *Binding* and *loosing* are terms familiar from rabbinic discourse, meaning forbidding and permitting. The church has been entrusted with the knowledge of what is forbidden and what is permitted in light of God's standards and character, and those who have joined themselves to this body have access to that liberating knowledge—and blessed are they who do what they hear!

CULTURAL AWARENESS
Honor Discourse in Matthew

The first-century Christians certainly fell into the category of "minority culture." They were largely without political power, frequently were exposed to the negative and hostile sanctions of those around them, and lacked the same access to goods and services enjoyed by the members of the majority culture as a result. The Jewish subculture, of course, rejected the early Christian claims for Jesus and especially reacted against the emerging tendency among the early Christians to disregard Torah while at the same time claiming to be part of the covenant people of God. The dominant Greco-Roman culture regarded the Christian movement as deviant and shameful because it drew good citizens away from the ideals and values of the Hellenistic world and made them functional atheists. It also drew them away from being fully participating and reliable members of the city and province, creating an enclave of dissent that refused to honor the gods and the emperor, and that shared a dream of civil chaos and revolution (the kingdom of God replacing eternal Rome).[a]

Where we find references to social pressure ("persecution") being aimed at the Christians, this indicates that the larger society was attempting both to pull the Christians back into line with that larger society's cultural values and discourage other members of the society from joining this deviant group. As a leader in the Christian community Matthew tries to address this social pressure to defuse its threat to the believers' commitment and to reaffirm the believers in the Christian understanding of the way things really are and what constitutes the path to honor given the way things really are.

Jesus teaches God's way honorably. Part of the challenge facing the Christian was the fact that their leader, the head of their group whose honor reflected on them all, died a degrading death as an executed criminal and was furthermore labeled a "sorcerer" (one who worked magic through association with demonic powers) and a "deceiver" (one who led Israel away from covenant loyalty) by non-Christian Jews. The crucifixion of Jesus and the labels that were attached to him were aimed at nullifying the appeal of following and identifying with this Jesus, holding him up as a paradigm of disgrace, whose teaching was contrary to the way approved by God.[b] If Christians could be persuaded that Jesus was not the one who taught God's way honorably, their commitment to the Christian group

---

[a]See further David A. deSilva, *Honor, Patronage, Kinship and Purity* (Downers Grove, Ill.: InterVarsity Press, 2000), pp. 44-50.

[b]On labeling and deviancy, see further Bruce J. Malina and Jerome H. Neyrey, "Conflict in Luke-Acts: Labelling and Deviance Theory," *The Social World of Luke-Acts: Models for Interpretation*, ed. Jerome H. Neyrey (Peabody, Mass.: Hendrickson, 1991), pp. 97-122.

would be compromised. As part of his strategy for insulating members of the Christian group from the shaming techniques of the parent body, Matthew affirmed the ultimate leader of the group as a reliable, honorable guide to right knowledge and conduct. Moreover, he underscores Jesus' honor at the expense of the spiritual progenitors of the Jewish Christians with whom the early church was in tension.[c]

First, Matthew underscores Jesus' ascribed honor. The addition of the birth and infancy narratives serves this end admirably. A person's nobility was demonstrated, in the first instance, from the nobility of his or her ancestors, parents, race, city and the circumstances of his or her birth (such as cosmological signs or supernatural occurrences). Jesus enjoys an illustrious ancestry, being connected with David, the founder of the monarchy and head of the leading house of Israel. Jesus is a legitimate "son of David," a claim that bears directly on the claims made concerning his messiahship (cf. Mt 9:27; 12:22-23; 20:30-31; 21:9, 15). Moreover, Jesus enjoys an even more illustrious descent, namely, from God (Mt 1:24-25). His birth is further surrounded by visions and cosmological signs that would be recognized as signs of his uncommon honor and destiny. The adoration of the magi, who revere Jesus by a physical demonstration of *proskynēsis,* confirms his honor. An oracle from Micah is employed to confirm the nobility of Jesus' city of origin, Bethlehem (Mt 2:5-6). Most poignantly, Jesus' honor is affirmed by God's own Self at his baptism: "This is my Son, the Beloved, with whom I am well pleased" (Mt 3:17 NRSV). In all these ways, then, Matthew introduces Jesus as a person of uncommon, indeed unique, honor, against the claims of detractors.

Jesus' honor is even more evident, however, in Matthew's presentation of his deeds of virtue. Jesus' fame spreads in the Gospel through his mighty acts of healing and exorcism (Mt 4:23-25; 8:1-4, 5-12, 14-17; 8:28—9:1, 8, 18-26, 27-31, 32-33; 15:29-31; 17:14-21). Jesus is a mediator of God's gifts of healing; recognizing this, people approach him with deep reverence (see Mt 8:2; 9:18). By responding selflessly to requests for help, Jesus shows himself beneficent and generous, two widely honored traits in the Greco-Roman world. For Matthew these acts of healing also demonstrate Jesus' status as God's anointed One, the Messiah, for Jesus does the works of the Messiah (Mt 11:2-5; cf. Is 29:18-19; 35:5-6; 61:1, which were also brought together as expectations of the Messiah in 4Q521).

Jesus' honor is most clearly established, however, in his death. On the one hand, Matthew shows that Jesus' death is not the deserved and just end of a criminal, but the end result of a process of injustice carried out by deceitful and envious people (see Mt 26:3-5, 14-16, 59-61; 27:18). Even

---

[c]For a much fuller discussion of Matthew's "encomium" on Jesus, see Jerome H. Neyrey, *Honor and Shame in the Gospel of Matthew* (Louisville, Ky.: Westminster John Knox, 1998), chaps. 3-7.

Figure 6.7. A Jewish ossuary from the first century C.E., featuring a common geometric design. After a body had decomposed in a tomb, the bones were collected and placed in an ossuary. (Photo: Sam Renfroe; courtesy of Ashland Theological Seminary)

the wife of Pilate and the centurion in charge of the execution see Jesus' innocence (Mt 27:19, 54). If Jesus' suffering (and the trial and passion narrative is replete with verbal and physical assaults on Jesus' honor) was inflicted unjustly rather than justly, the disgrace does not attach to him but to his enemies (cf. Plato *Gorg.* 508D; Seneca *Constant.* 16.3). On the other hand, Matthew builds on a foundation that has been well laid in the early church—indeed, from the earliest proclamation of Jesus' death as a death "for our sins" (cf. 1 Cor 15:3)—for interpreting Jesus' crucifixion as a noble death rather than a dishonorable execution or unfortunate injustice. Matthew prepares for this interpretation as early as Matthew 1:21, where Jesus' name is chosen for him by God as a summary of his life's achievement: "he will save his people from their sins."

A noble death is a voluntary death embraced because it accords with the virtuous course of action, especially when it brings benefit to others. There is no greater display of generosity and virtue, hence honor, than to lay down one's life for friends or country.[d] Jesus submitted to crucifixion voluntarily both out of obedience to God and out of a commitment to benefit others. Jesus' own noble motives were operating alongside and through his opponents' base motives. The fact that Jesus foresaw his passion and moved steadily toward it demonstrates its voluntary nature (see Mt 16:21-23; 17:9-12, 22-23; 20:17-19; 26:18, 21, 31-32, 45). Jesus was not caught off guard but knew the hour of his betrayal and hand of his betrayer. Jesus' prayer in Gethsemane explicitly depicts Jesus' voluntary acceptance of suffering and death in obedience to God's plan (Mt 26:39, 42), obedience to God being a core virtue.[e] Moreover, Matthew includes a tradition unique to his Gospel concerning Jesus' ability even after his arrest to escape the power of his enemies with the aid of legions of angels (Mt 26:52-53). His silence at his trial—his refusal to offer any defense—confirms his voluntary acceptance of the cross.

The beneficial effects of Jesus' death for others is repeatedly stressed in Matthew. Jesus came to "give his life as a ransom for many" (Mt 20:28 NRSV), and speaks of his blood as "poured out for many for the forgiveness of sins" (Mt 26:27-28 NRSV). Finally, the passion of Jesus was the working out not of the will of Jesus' enemies but of the will and purpose of God to bring benefit to humanity. Matthew's considerable expansion of references to and echoes of Old Testament Scriptures in the passion narrative especially serves this end. Moreover, the final word on Jesus' honor is not the cross but the resurrection. This is God's vindication of God's righteous and approved One (see the theology of resurrection in 2 Macc 7), the final answer to Jesus' detractors' taunt in Matthew 27:43: "Let God deliver him now, if he wants to" (NRSV). Through the lens of Psalm 118:22-23 (see Mt 21:42), Matthew interprets the resurrection and ascension of Jesus as God's appointment of Jesus to the position of highest authority in the cosmos, hence of greatest honor and greater potential for ascribing honor and dishonor. The final word is not human rejection of Jesus but God's election precisely of this rejected One as the cornerstone.

Those Christians nurtured by Matthew's Gospel can be assured of their leader's honor and the folly of Jesus' detractors past and present. This in turn helps to insulate them against the attempts to draw them away from commitment to that leader. Moreover, in reminding the audience of Jesus' death on their behalf, Matthew also reminds them of their debt of gratitude and loyalty to their Patron—their own honor is secure as long as they act honorably toward this exalted Benefactor.

Honor, group values and preserving community in Matthew. In

---

[d]On the pattern of the noble death, see David Seeley, *The Noble Death: Graeco-Roman Martyrology and Paul's Concept of Salvation* (Sheffield, U.K.: Sheffield Academic Press, 1990).
[e]The notion of an obedient death leads to the possibility of it being an expiatory death, as in 4 Macc 6:28-20; 17:20-22.

chapter three we saw that a minority culture would only survive and remain distinctive as long as (1) group members were insulated against the opinion of nongroup members who held to different values and allegiances, and were sensitive only to the affirmation and disapproval of those who shared the group's values, (2) pursuing what was valued by the group was clearly held up as the only sure path to lasting honor, and (3) the experiences of contempt and rejection at the hands of outsiders were constructively reinterpreted in terms of the group's values and worldview. Matthew's Gospel contributes to all three aspects of group maintenance in the early church, and a close survey of these strategies will help us discover how these strategies are at work in other New Testament texts. We will also discover how to put them to work now in the formation of strong and distinctive communities of disciples.

Defining whose approval matters. In keeping with his interest in shoring up the Christians' commitment to the new way taught by Jesus in the face of pressure and rejection from the synagogue, Matthew incorporated many Jesus traditions that would insulate the believers from the approval and disapproval of non-Christian Jews who stood in line with the traditions represented by the Pharisees and scribes before the fall of Jerusalem. Matthew demonstrates Jesus' credibility and honor as a teacher and the Pharisees' dishonor and unreliability as teachers of God's way. Matthew included a striking number of confrontation stories between Jesus and other Jewish teachers (e.g., Mt 9:1-8, 10-13, 14-17; 11:2-6; 12:1-8, 9-14, 24-42; 15:1-20, 21-28; 16:1-4; 19:3-9; 21:15-17, 23-27, 28-32, 33-46; 22:15-22, 23-33, 34-40, 41-46). These confrontations have been rightly analyzed as competitions for honor and, as a result of that honor, the right to speak as authoritative interpreters of God's Law.[f] In each of these confrontations (or challenge-riposte exchanges), a challenge is posed with a view to discrediting the challenged in the eyes of the public and a riposte is launched back in defense or counterattack. Jesus repeatedly emerges as the victor in these exchanges in the eyes of the public. Without exception he is able to demonstrate that his actions and his teachings are truly in accord with God's Law, while his opponents distort and miss God's intentions. A special Matthean emphasis involves Jesus' outright censure (shaming) of the Pharisees (see especially chap. 23, but also the briefer remarks such as are found in Mt 12:39; 16:4), to which the Pharisees can offer no defense (in the world of the Gospel narrative, at least).

The cumulative effect of this stream of material is that the Christian audiences will be insulated against the opinion of the contemporary repre-

---

[f]See Bruce J. Malina and Jerome H. Neyrey, "Honor and Shame in Luke-Acts: Pivotal Values of the Mediterranean World," in *The Social World of Luke-Acts: Models for Interpretation*, ed. Jerome H. Neyrey (Peabody, Mass.: Hendrickson, 1991), pp. 29-32, 49-52.

sentatives of the Pharisees, looking exclusively to Jesus as the teacher of the divinely approved way of fulfilling Torah (see Mt 17:5). Matthew has made these traditions prominent in order to undermine the credibility of the representatives of the non-Christian way of keeping Torah. Following the opinion of the dishonorable is to risk becoming dishonorable. The censure of non-Christian Jews will be nullified as the Christians seek after the praise of the One who taught "the way of God in accordance with the truth" (Mt 22:16 NRSV). Indeed, the installation of Jesus as the eschatological Judge, separating the righteous from the wicked on the basis of the standards he himself taught during his earthly ministry, is the ultimate expression of this conviction.

Many other passages would reinforce this effect. For example, Matthew 11:20-24 and 12:41-42 suggest that those who reject Jesus' message will fare far worse than the worst of paglan cities. Before the judgment seat of God those who opposed Jesus during his ministry and the disciples of those Pharisees who now oppose the Christian way of doing Torah will be condemned. Their lack of honor and virtue will be exposed. In light of God's eternal verdict those who reject Jesus and his followers are shown to be a court of reputation that ultimately does not matter. To give in to its pressures to conform now would only lead to the believer's own condemnation before God's judgment seat. Moreover, the contrast between the few who enter by the narrow gate and the many who enter by the wide gate (Mt 7:13-14) serves to offset the minority (and therefore deviant) status of the Christian group. They are expected to be in the minority since only a small number from the mass of humankind finds the divinely approved way. If the majority, who are entering the broad and easy road to destruction, despise the Christians as dishonorable fools, the Christians will be able to neutralize the force of such pressure to conform by contemplating the ultimate end of the outsiders—destruction. The way of life promoted within the church, even if held as dishonorable by the majority of people, is nevertheless the road to life and eternal honor before the court of God and the Son.

Matthew 6:1-18 proposes a repeated contrast between the praise of people and the approval of God. Jesus warns against engaging in pious behavior for the sake of human approval (specifically here the approval of the "synagogue," a body that does not conceive of piety in the same manner as the Christian community; Mt 6:2, 5). The Christian is instead to seek the approval solely of "your Father who sees in secret" (6:4, 6, 18 NRSV). This is not a command to hide or privatize your faith, but rather a charter for freedom to pursue what God values (as taught by Jesus and his followers) without being pressured by non-Christians to perform pious actions for the sake of their acceptance. These words would also be enormously important for Gentile Christians, who would be pressured by their neighbors to perform the public acts of piety that the Greco-Roman society approved as tokens of loyalty and civic virtue—the prayers of such outsiders is vain babbling, but the one God hears the prayers of Jew and Gentile offered in Jesus' name.

Matthew also preserves traditions that energize the interaction and mutual support of the Christian assembly. As those who do the will of God, they are the family of the Son of God, hence part of God's family (Mt 12:48-50) and partners in the honor of the head of that family. Within that family there is a mandate for applying social pressure "positively" on group members who are straying from commitment to the group and its distinctive values (Mt 18:10-14).[9] Within the group all the faithful must be honored and affirmed as they walk in line with the group's values (Mt 18:10) and on no other basis. The church is also given considerable authority over disputes within the group. After a private confrontation and a meeting with two or three witnesses, the whole Christian community is called to enforce discipline, and the verdict of the community is witnessed by Jesus who is present in their midst; thus the verdict is binding in both realms of earth and heaven (Mt 18:15-18). The church is in a position to enforce the wayward member's conformity with the ethical ideals of Jesus. After all, what member would willingly endure excommunication from the church as long as he or she believed it truly has the authority to bind and loose, and remains the place where the presence of God as mediated by Jesus can be known? If the narrow road is the way to the eternal inheritance of God's kingdom, the church is the gateway to that inheritance. Attachment to the community and vital engagement of its values is therefore a strong assurance also of God's approval of an individual's life and worth, a strong counterbalance to society's claims to the contrary.

Defining the path to true honor. The vast amount of Jesus' teaching that Matthew preserves serves to establish patterns of behavior that ultimately lead to honor before God's court—the only court that counts—and to deter the audience from behaviors that lead to the opposite. We can only look closely at a few passages here, but you are encouraged to be alert to sanctions of honor and dishonor being attached to behaviors throughout Matthew.

Matthew 10:24-39 is a passage especially rich in topics of honor and dishonor. Matthew 10:24-26 contributes to the believers' freedom from the opinion of non-Christians and to their assurance of vindication when all that is now hidden (e.g., the lordship of Christ) becomes manifest (i.e., at the Last Judgment). Matthew 10:32-33, however, uses language of honor and disgrace to sustain loyalty to and confession of Jesus in

---

[9]Note that because of the different contexts into which this parable has been inserted, Matthew makes the "lost sheep" a parable for life within the church while Luke makes it a mandate for evangelism outside the church.

the face of pressure to deny association with his name: "Everyone therefore who acknowledges me before others, I also will acknowledge before my Father in heaven; but whoever denies me before others, I also will deny before my Father" (NRSV). Desire for honor before the eternal court, secured by Jesus' character witness, should lead believers to accept disgrace before the human court on account of their loyalty to Jesus. Here is a new point of reference for honor. The believer must prove him- or herself worthy of Jesus rather than worthy of the affirmation of natural kin or the larger society: "Whoever loves father or mother more than me is not worthy of me; and whoever loves son or daughter more than me is not worthy of me; and whoever does not take up the cross and follow me is not worthy of me" (10:37-38 NRSV). While the way of discipleship may cost a person his or her place in the natural kinship group, and while it may lead to contempt (symbolized in the cross), it is still the way that someone is found worthy of Jesus, and therefore worthy of honor before God.

Using a tradition gleaned from Mark, Matthew promotes the Christian redefinition of true greatness in God's sight as serving rather than seeking precedence over others (Mt 20:24-28). He underscores this new definition of honorable behavior with a number of additional sayings (Mt 18:4; 23:11-12). Taken together, these sayings reinforce for the hearers the essential posture of discipleship—serving rather than self-promotion—as the only path to real and lasting honor. This path is explicitly contrasted with the dominant cultural assessment of honor (what the "rulers of the Gentiles" do, Mt 20:25).

The literary form known as the beatitude, or "makarism," also relates directly to the delineation of who is honorable and what qualities or behaviors are honorable. K. C. Hanson has helpfully defined the makarism as "the public validation of an individual's or group's experience, behavior, or attitude as honorable."[h] He proposes that the opening of a beatitude should be translated not "blessed" or "happy" or "enviable" but "how honorable." We should extend that translation to include "how honored" or even "how favored" since makarisms usually also express the concept of having been specially endowed by God with some gift that bestows honor. These makarisms appear in Matthew 5:3-12; 11:6; 13:16-17; and 16:16-19. The first and most famous set serves to uphold the generally recognized values of mercy, gentleness, peace-making, purity and passionate concern for justice. The final makarism in the series is most striking: it actually makes the experience of contempt and rejection for the sake of Jesus a claim to honor and sign of God's favor (Mt 5:10-12). It becomes the path to honor, therefore, to persevere in the face of the larger society's attempts at

---

[h]K. C. Hanson, "How Honorable! How Shameful! A Cultural Analysis of Matthew's Makarisms and Reproaches," *Semeia* 68 (1996): 81-111.

shaming rather than to acquiesce to their discipline and conform again to the dominant culture.

The counterpart to seeking honor is avoiding disgrace. One behavior that Matthew particularly promotes by invoking topics of dishonor is forgiveness. In the lengthy parable closing the instructions on community life (Mt 18:23-35), a slave who is forgiven a huge debt against the master is freely forgiven. He then goes out and shows no mercy on a fellow slave who owes but a trifling sum in comparison. The master censures the unforgiving slave and throws him into the debtors' prison after all. The parable closes by warning the addressees: "So my heavenly Father will also do to every one of you, if you do not forgive your brother or sister from your heart" (Mt 18:35 NRSV). Matthew thus moves the hearers to practice mutual forgiveness, lest they come to dishonor when they stand before their God who forgave them so great a debt. When confronted with an affront from a fellow believer, they are warned not to think more highly of their honor and desire for satisfaction than God did of God's own when God forgave them their offenses.

As another example, we may look to the eschatological "parables" in Matthew 24:45—25:46. Throughout this passage honor is promised to those who have lived out their lives faithful to Jesus' word; dishonor awaits those who fail to take his word to heart and commit their lives to bearing the fruits of righteousness. In the first parable (24:45-51) the servants who are continually occupied with the business that the master has assigned them will receive honor within the household of the master at his return (24:47). Those who neglect their service will be shamed and cast out from the household (24:51). In the parable of the talents (25:14-30) the language of approval and disapproval comes to the fore as the master praises and exalts those who use what the master has entrusted to them to increase the kingdom, but the one who fails in this regard comes to disgrace, being branded "worthless," "wicked and lazy," and being excluded from the kingdom. Finally, those who have engaged in works of love, deeds of charity and mercy toward the hungry, weak, sick, poor, and imprisoned are pronounced "honored" or "favored" by God (Mt 25:34). Here believers are taught that, ultimately, their honor depends not on networking with the rich and powerful but with responding in mercy and generosity toward the needy and nobodies.

By such means, then, Matthew brings together Jesus traditions that outline the path to honor before the court of God, whose approval and disapproval are to be mirrored and reinforced by the members of the Christian community one for another.

Reinterpreting the non-Christians' display of contempt and rejection. Matthew's repertoire of creative reinterpretation of society's rejection and censure is somewhat limited when set beside his New Testament colleagues (notably Paul, Hebrews and 1 Peter). Nevertheless he does offer some contributions in this regard. First, Matthew preserves sayings that present disgrace and opposition from the dominant culture and the parent religion as experiences to be expected. These should not catch believers unaware, disconfirming their convictions about their place in God's favor and truth. The first disciples were told to expect such attempts at social control (Mt 10:17-18), and the generations of believers that would follow are warned that hostility from outside is inevitable (Mt 24:9-10).

Further, Matthew links the Christians' experience of censure and rejection with Jesus' own experience at the hands of the ungodly (see Mt 10:24-25). He argues that it is fitting for the followers to be treated in the same way as their Master; in fact it would be inappropriate for the world to think more highly of the disciples than of their Master. In this way the believers may also hope to be "like the teacher" in his vindication by God, the ultimate guarantor of Jesus' honor and the honor of his followers.

Finally, we should recall here the sayings included (and extended) by Matthew that pronounce these believers honored, favored and approved when they are subjected to disgrace and persecution for the sake of the name (Mt 5:11-12). The Hebrew prophets provide an argument from historical example: they were maligned and dishonorably treated by their neighbors, but Matthew and his readers knew what honor they enjoyed before God and the community of faith. Likewise, those who conformed to the prophets' example could be assured that they too would stand in honor with them. Given the community's definitions of reality, according to which Jesus himself will come to judge the nations and reward his own, it becomes actually honorable to suffer contempt, reproach, insult and hostility now on his account.

Growing in sensitivity to the use of honor and shame language in the New Testament serves two important ends. First, it opens us up to an important part of what made the texts persuasive for the first hearers. It helps us enter into a flesh-and-blood community struggling with how to keep their self-respect and how to remain faithful to their newfound faith and hope in the midst of real social pressures. Second, as we become more sensitive to the social agendas of the authors, we are equipped to peer more incisively into our social setting. We are better equipped to help fellow Christians as they try to live out their faith in a world that does not agree with the values and ideology of the gospel. We are better equipped to create effective, energizing congregations and support groups that enable individuals to remain faithful to the life and witness God has called them to. And we are better equipped to defuse the messages Christians receive that might dissuade them from wholehearted commitment to this outdated religion and seduce them into having a care first for the things of this life.

FOR FURTHER READING

deSilva, David A. *Honor, Patronage, Kinship and Purity: Unlocking New Testament Culture*. Downers Grove, Ill.: InterVarsity Press, 2000.

———. *The Hope of Glory: Honor Discourse and New Testament Interpretation*. Collegeville, Minn.: Liturgical Press, 1999.

Malina, Bruce J., and Jerome H. Neyrey. "Honor and Shame in Luke-Acts: Pivotal Values of the Mediterranean World," pp. 25-66. In *The Social World of Luke-Acts: Models for Interpretation*. Edited by Jerome H. Neyrey. Peabody, Mass.: Hendrickson, 1991.

———. "Conflict in Luke-Acts: Labelling and Deviance Theory," pp. 97-124. In *The Social World of Luke-Acts: Models for Interpretation*. Edited by Jerome H. Neyrey. Peabody, Mass.: Hendrickson, 1991.

Neyrey, Jerome H. *Honor and Shame in the Gospel of Matthew*. Louisville, Ky.: Westminster John Knox, 1998.

MATTHEW AND MINISTRY FORMATION

Matthew's Gospel most clearly focuses on life in the *ekklēsia*. Therefore it should not be surprising to find that it has much to contribute to the formation of effective ministry, mature disciples and vital communities of faith. How can Matthew accomplish these effects in your own ministry and faith?

To begin with, Matthew's extensive interest in anchoring Jesus and his teaching in the Jewish Scriptures cautions us against devaluing our connection with the Old Testament heritage. Many pastors preach mainly from the New Testament. Seminaries that require only one ancient language as part of their preparation of ministers tend to emphasize Greek for that very reason. Matthew stands as a continual reminder that being a "New Testament Christian" is not enough. The Hebrew Bible remains the Word of God for the churches. Our appreciation of the message and significance of Jesus, of God's standards and desires for God's people and God's world, and of our place in the larger plan of God are all enhanced as we continue in Matthew's tradition of anchoring the New Testament message (and our churches) in the earlier oracles of God. Matthew reminds us that the New Testament has value as the revelation that stands in continuity with the Old Testament, not as its replacement.

Matthew also underscores the importance of Jesus as the Mediator of God's presence in the church and in the world. This emphasis provides an especially valuable resource for the task of pastoral care (whether conducted by the ordained or laypeople). The infancy narratives, which are programmatic for the whole of the Gospel, begin essentially by naming Jesus as Emmanuel, "God with us," and by identifying that presence as saving (rather than damning or condemning) in the name *Y'shua*, "he will save" (Mt 1:21-23). The Gospel closes with the assurance, "I am with you always, even to the end of the age" (Mt 28:20).

Highlighted by the Gospel's beginning and ending, this theme also recurs frequently in the body of the Gospel (e.g., Mt 18:20). Jesus' presence means healing. To those who sit in darkness, Jesus' presence brings light (Mt 4:16); to those who sit in Jesus' presence and learn from him, Jesus brings rest (Mt 11:28-30); to those who allow Jesus to embrace and protect them as a mother hen protects her offspring, Jesus brings the comfort and restoration so desperately needed (Mt 23:37). Matthean ministry is not a work carried on by disciples while Jesus is absent, but the work continued by Jesus in the midst of his disciples.

Additionally, Matthew places a high value on the doing the will of the Father in heaven (Mt 7:21-23), or on fulfilling the Law of God (Torah). This is far from an exercise in legalism, however, since doing God's will means acting in accordance with God's essential character, who loves God's creatures and is generous toward them (Mt 5:38-48). Jesus' followers thus have a distinctive hermeneutical key for fulfilling Torah, namely, embodying God's holiness as love and generosity toward fellow humans rather than seeking to embody holiness through separation from the ordinary or unclean (which tends to result in withholding love and kindness from those in need of God's love). In promoting "religion" of the first kind (a kind that James, who is also deeply informed by the Old Testament prophets, would heartily approve; cf. Jas 1:27), Matthew shows an awareness that we cannot expect to be whole people unless we reach out to others, stand with them in their need and extend God's love and favor. It has been said that God's love and favor are most fully known by us as we give them away to others. This is not just for pastors and counselors but for all people. We must allow (and challenge) all Christians to participate in this doing of God's will, so that they too may know the fullness of living for God. As a corollary to this, Matthew challenges "religious people" of all cultures and ages to consider where their true loyalties lie—with God's requirements or with "the traditions of the elders," those religious customs and ways that so quickly become "law" in church bodies. In this regard Matthew offers further liberation from legalism, freeing congregations to reach out with God's love in new and creative ways as the Spirit leads.

The Sermon on the Mount is a veritable treasure house of insights for leading individual disciples to wholeness. It deals with a host of topics that are central to the care of souls—anger, lust, anxiety, unproductive placement of blame and double-mindedness, among others. Since Jesus' words can be used healthfully and effectively in pastoral care, or misused to reinforce unhealthy behavior patterns and thoughts, some close attention will be given to a few sample topics.

Jesus' first teaching on the true keeping of Torah (Mt 5:21-26) takes the prohibition against murder and claims that this commandment is violated wherever we pronounce another human being a "fool" or "worthless," and wherever we even harbor anger against another person. Jesus' words might be used (unwisely) to counsel the repression of anger, keeping in those ugly feelings and not giving them expression. But Jesus is not teaching his followers to keep it all in, to maintain a calm exterior and keep up civil appearances. Rather, he instructs his followers to be done with it altogether, to give it no place in their hearts. Early on in the textual tradition, but well after the earliest manuscripts, the words "without a cause" begin to appear in this verse (see the KJV, which was based on manuscripts that included this loophole). Some scribes could not accept that Jesus would not allow a person to be angry with a brother or sister for good reason.

Why should Jesus link anger with murder? Anger ceases to regard the other person as a human being. It takes our focus off the extraordinary value of the person with whom we are angry. We cease to see a person; rather, we see an offender, a hindrance, an obstacle. Anger is not the same as murder, to be sure, but both share a common feature in this lack of regard for the other person's humanity. How can disciples approach other people without anger? This is not within the realm of human effort but is the result of coming to the full knowledge of God's love for us and for the other person (the ultimate foundation of the ethic promoted in the Sermon on the Mount). The more we experience the former (God's love for us) the more readily we can participate in the latter (God's love for the other person).

Similar reflections might be generated on the debilitating power of lust, which Jesus equates with adultery. Just as anger dehumanizes its object and prevents us from seeking God's will for that person, so lust looks neither at the value of the whole person nor at the purposes of God that could be accomplished through conversation and relationship. Lust is a very subtle instrument of the adversary. It substitutes a very strong human agenda for God's agenda in human interaction. Where disciples resist yielding to lustful suggestions, inward guilt and shame still might prevent them from engaging in healthy interaction with the erstwhile object of desire that would enable mutual edification as God makes opportunity. It is therefore not without reason that Matthew preserves these sayings of Jesus, and it is incumbent on preachers of the Gospel to examine, embody and proclaim them. Only if a person sees another not with lust but with God's eyes can that person serve God's ends fruitfully and fulfill his or her responsibility to others within the body of Christ.

Jesus' instructions about turning the other cheek merit careful reflection in the context of ministry (Mt 5:38-48). Jesus' sayings could be read as promoting self-abuse, passivity, acceptance of oppression and violation of human dignity, leading the unwise minister to counsel codependency on this basis: "Stay with your spouse and keep praying that the abuse stops. Keep showing love and providing whatever the spouse needs." Such would miss the mark completely. Rather, Jesus counsels disciples to cultivate such rootedness in God's love and generosity that their responses to the ignorant and malicious will not be driven and shaped by the offenders' malice but rather by God's goodness. Ministers and pastoral counselors encounter people daily who are in bondage to patterns of behavior and thought shaped by another's neglect, abuse, hurtfulness and so forth. Matthew directs us to break that bondage, to liberate people from having their lives, attitudes and choices limited and controlled by another person's hurtfulness, whether immediately in the encounter with that hurtful person or years down the road. It is almost a commonplace in counseling that adult children still live out responses to a demanding or abusive parent in their new relationships with spouses, authority figures, peers and others. Jesus equips us to break these patterns, find ourselves in God's love and favor, and live toward others as God directs. This does not mean ignoring injuries or hurts, but it certainly will move us to address them differently—we will seek reconciliation and mutual understanding rather than returning the injury, however subtle the form of our revenge.

Walter Wink offers a perceptive analysis of Jesus' call to "turn the other cheek," "give the undergarment" and "walk the second mile" (Mt 5:38-42).[a] Far from calling his disciples to passivity or to quiet, submissive cooperation with their own oppression, Jesus calls them to meet injustice and oppression creatively and courageously with nonviolent protest. The person struck on the right cheek "robs the oppressor of the power to humiliate" by turning the other, showing that his or her dignity remains unaffected, his or her equality undiminished by shows of force.[b] Peasants driven further and further into destitution, taken to court by their creditors for their last possessions, strip themselves naked in protest against institutionalized economic rapine.[c] A civilian in an occupied land is forced to carry the foreign soldier's burden a mile—and then throws the soldier completely off guard by insisting on carrying it a second mile, taking back "the power of choice" and the dignity of acting on his own initiative.[d]

In all these ways the "powerless are emboldened to seize the initiative,"[e] to find and reaffirm their own personhood and value, while not mirroring the evil—indeed, becoming the evil—that confronts and oppresses them. They are enabled to resist, to expose injustice, to refuse to accept humiliation and to make the oppressor have to think twice, to consider the oppressed person in a new light, and to do all this without betraying their own souls. Jesus' program for nonviolent but active resistance to domination systems challenges us as Christian leaders to continue his prophetic and bold engagement with the "powers" that have institutionalized dehumanizing practices.

A large block of the Sermon on the Mount speaks to the issue of sincerity in religion (Mt 6:1-18), and this passage is of primary significance to those engaged in shaping communities of disciples. Jesus explicitly instructs his own not to engage in religious activities for the sake of human approval. These sayings speak about the practice of using worship and piety to create a public face, a mask, that wins human approval and even esteem, but in so doing we replace the possibility of authentic transformation by the power of God with an inauthentic transformation or formation of appearances. Ministers can help form congregations that do not facilitate this kind of inauthentic Christianity. They can teach the importance of not granting approval or disapproval on the basis of appearances, so that individuals may feel less of a need to put on a good show, hiding who the person really is, not allowing other Christians to have contact with the real person but only the persona, the "mask." Churches especially cannot be places where

---

[a]Walter Wink, *Engaging the Powers* (Minneapolis: Fortress, 1992), pp. 175-93.
[b]Ibid., p. 176.
[c]Ibid., pp. 178-79.
[d]Ibid., pp. 180-82.
[e]Ibid., p. 179.

people must act a certain way and put on a good front to be accepted, but rather places where we can be fully ourselves with one another so that healing and transformation of the person, of the heart, can take place (not just the transformation of the appearance, putting on our "Sunday best"). This might best be done by modeling openness and honesty, and by making honesty rather than pious appearances our expectation of the people under our care.

One particular area in which Jesus' instructions about piety intersect with church life pertains to prayer. Quite a number of Christians just will not pray for others or themselves out loud. These same people frequently admire the pastor's eloquence in prayer and are ashamed of their lack of free-flowing theo-babble. Have people gotten the idea that they may pray (aloud in a group setting, at least) only if they can do it eloquently and beautifully and not simply and from the heart? Are people afraid to pray out loud because they do not think they can use the right language or sound florid enough? Jesus' words to those who model only "beautiful prayer" and those afraid to pray "unbeautifully" are quite direct—"when you pray, do not heap up empty phrases as the Gentile do; for they think they will be heard for their many words" (Mt 6:7 NRSV). Ministers can again model these Jesus traditions by taking care in their prayers to let the heart speak, and not to clothe their petitions in sonorous expressions, if only to encourage people under their care to pray simply, honestly and with the confidence of children of God.

One final observation from the Sermon on the Mount comes from Matthew 7:1-5, where Jesus instructs his hearers to turn away from examining other people's faults and mistakes, and give attention rather to one's own problems. Christian ministers, counselors and caregivers often encounter people who affix blame to others as a standard defense mechanism to deflect looking into their own hearts, acknowledging their debilitating patterns of relating, their insecurities, and so forth. There is a place for examining others' responsibility in relationships (e.g., helping a troubled spouse understand that the relationship cannot be healed by the will and endeavors of only one partner), but there is also the need for focusing on those matters that lie within an individual's control to ameliorate, and to open them up to God for help and healing. Matthew's Sermon on the Mount could be profitably explored from this angle passage by passage. From this and other discourses of Jesus in Matthew, it is clear why the First Gospel should have become the favorite of early Christian leaders entrusted with shaping and nurturing Christian communities.

Matthew preserves traditions that speak of the community of disciples as a kinship group, the family that Jesus has gathered together (Mt 12:46-50; 19:27-29). By using kinship language to characterize the relationships between believers (e.g., "brother or sister" in Mt 18:15, 21), Matthew invites believers to take on the obligations of sisters and brothers toward one another and pursue the quality of relationships held to characterize (well-functioning) families as an ideal for interaction between believers. This will be discussed further in the chapter on John (see also the section on "Kinship and the Household" in chapter three), but we may begin to reflect on this issue now in a preliminary way.

Matthew strongly challenges modern congregations to rethink the common distinctions made between family and church, and to begin treating, valuing and offering themselves to one another as "family" in the best and most whole sense of that word. Matthew also preserves Jesus traditions that speaks of the resistance from natural kinship groups encountered by early Christians (Mt 10:34-38), for which an important countermeasure is provided by the church as kinship group. People bound in the webs spun by dysfunctional (not to mention abusive) family situations can only move toward healing to the extent that they are willing to experience resistance from their natural kinship groups. The church can become a great catalyst for healing to the extent that its members are willing to take up the call to be fully family one to another, to offer that deep level of emotional and material support to one another.

Matthew specifically addresses the shaping of church community, particularly in chapter eighteen. His sculpting of the first-century congregations still offers sage counsel for those who take part in molding congregational life today (a process to which every Christian makes a contribution, whether positive or negative). First, the church is challenged to be a community of forgiveness, a facet underscored in Matthew 6:14-15 as well as Matthew 18:21-35. Jesus' parable of the unforgiving servant leaves no room in the church for grudges, bitterness or other signs of unforgiveness between believers, and taking this to heart would represent an important step toward recovery for many congregations.

Second, Matthew provides instructions for conflict resolution in the church (Mt 18:15-20).[f] Christian communities are frequently crippled by the willingness of believers to share their grievances about another person with everybody except that person, thus spreading dissent and division while not taking the one course that could effect reconciliation. Matthew directs believers away from this destructive behavior and directs churches away from condoning and supporting this approach to interpersonal conflict. When they hear a complaint against another, believers can be trained to direct the plaintiff to speak to that other person directly. If the rift continues, first a small group and then the whole Christian community are called to function as instruments for the reconciliation of individual disciples one to another. Matthew seeks to nurture a community in which all members are committed to one another, especially to reconciling one with another. Matthew prefaces the instructions on community discipline with the parable of the lost sheep. Thus the solicitous concern each believer is to have for the sister or brother who strays from the way of Christ certainly leads toward community efforts at reconciliation and away from an "ecclesiastical court." Nevertheless, community discipline—as well as community "discipling"—is surely in mind.[9]

---

[f] I am grateful to my colleague Dr. Doug Little, professor of pastoral counseling at Ashland Seminary (retired), for highlighting the value of Matthew 18 in this regard.

[9] A text of great importance in the history of the church is Matthew 16:17-19. After Peter's correct confession of Jesus as the Messiah, the Son of God, Jesus announces his intention to build his "assembly" on this "rock," an obvious pun on Peter's name. Whether Jesus intended the "rock" to refer to Peter or to the confession of faith Peter made is a matter of great debate, but Jesus' conferral of the "keys of the kingdom" to Peter (spoken to Peter in the second person singular) gives Peter the unmis-

Matthew's particular application of the parable of the "lost sheep" reminds the congregation that it is to be a community of people watching out for the sister or brother, a community in which members help one another to stay on track, to continue to "walk in line with the truth of the Gospel," to borrow a phrase from Paul. Other New Testament voices also have much to say regarding our responsibility toward one another (Gal 6:1-2; Jas 5:19-20). Out of respect for another's "privacy" or "rights," or out of a philosophy of "minding one's own business," or out of a postmodern sense of "toleration" and "diversity," many believers are reluctant to take up Matthew's challenge to identify the erring, go after the wanderers, and bring them back to the right way. That hesitancy has facilitated many affairs, divorces, acts of dishonesty and acts of abuse. Individuals facing powerful temptations or deep-rooted tendencies need the support, encouragement and commitment of their sisters and brothers if they are to rise victorious over the powers that seek to make shipwreck of their faith.

Finally, Matthew seeks to fashion a community of outreaching love and generosity, where the needs of the "least" will be the focus of believers' attention (e.g., Mt 19:21; 25:31-46). For Matthew following the Lord who gave himself for others means giving ourselves for others, working for the good of all and not just our immediate families. Expecting the Lord's return, moreover, finds positive expression not in futile attempts to calculate the day and the hour, nor in a manufactured eschatological fervor, but in acts of love and mercy that relieve suffering in the present time.

FOR FURTHER READING

Aune, David E., ed. *The Gospel of Matthew in Current Study.* Grand Rapids: Eerdmans, 2001.

Bauer, David R., and Mark A. Powell, eds. *Treasures New and Old: Contributions to Matthean Studies.* Symposium Series. Atlanta: Society of Biblical Literature, 1996.

Betz, Hans Dieter. *The Sermon on the Mount.* Hermeneia. Minneapolis: Fortress, 1995.

Carter, Warren. *Matthew: Storyteller, Interpreter, Evangelist.* Peabody, Mass.: Hendrickson, 1996.

Davies, W. D., and Dale C. Allison Jr. *A Critical and Exegetical Commentary on the Gospel According to Saint Matthew.* 3 vols. ICC. Edinburgh: T & T Clark, 1988, 1991, 1996.

---

takable authority to act as the "gatekeeper," so to speak. This text has become, therefore, a lynchpin in the demonstration of the primacy of Peter and his successors (the popes of the Roman Catholic Church). But what role did Jesus really intend for Peter to have? And for how long? When Matthew preserves the same commission in the plural in Matthew 18:18, giving to the gathered Christian community the same authority to "bind" and "loose" (notably, in regard to membership in the assembly), does he understand authority to be located in Peter and his successors or in the body of the church as a whole? Is Peter's commission one of limited duration, to strengthen his brothers after the resurrection (Lk 22:32) and get the church started (as we see his role in Acts, up to the point he drops off the page in Acts 12), or a perpetual one? This debate, and the proper understanding of Jesus' commission of (and conferral of authority on) Peter, looms large in Catholic-Protestant dialogue.

Gundry, Robert. *Matthew: A Commentary on His Handbook for a Mixed Church Under Persecution.* Grand Rapids: Eerdmans, 1994.

Hagner, Donald. *Matthew 1-13.* WBC. Dallas, Tex.: Word, 1993.

———. Matthew 14-28. WBC. Dallas, Tex.: Word, 1995.

Harrington, Donald. *The Gospel of Matthew.* Sacra Pagina. Collegeville, Minn.: Michael Glazier, 1991.

Keener, Craig. *A Commentary on the Gospel of Matthew.* Grand Rapids: Eerdmans, 1999.

Stanton, Graham, ed. *The Interpretation of Matthew.* Philadelphia: Fortress, 1994.

———. *A Gospel for a New People: Studies in Matthew.* Louisville, Ky.: Westminster John Knox, 1993.

7

THE GOSPEL ACCORDING TO LUKE

Following the Heart of the Father

The Gospel of Luke and the Acts of the Apostles are two volumes of a single written work, Acts being the conscious sequel to Luke. It is therefore unwise, and in the climate of our growing awareness of their connectedness impossible, to read one in isolation from the other. Even though the two volumes are treated in separate chapters of this book, we will have to keep looking forward to Acts as we consider Luke and backwards to Luke as we ponder Acts.

Luke takes the Gospel genre to a new level, applying his literary skill to the narration of Jesus' life and teaching, and weds it to the genre of historiography in the context of his two-volume project. The historian, however, is also the pastor, and Luke has preserved a wealth of Jesus traditions that speak powerfully to the nature of the community of disciples Jesus formed. It is in his Gospel that we find the heart of God for the lost and for the poor most clearly revealed, and the church most forcefully challenged to mirror that heart. It is also in the context of Luke and Acts together that the Gentile Christians find a convincing response to the burning question concerning the legitimacy of the largely Gentile Christian movement as the continuation of Israel, God's historic people. Additionally, it is within these two volumes that the Christians are also assured of their legitimacy with regard

to the Roman order, that they have not joined a shameful, subversive group as so many of their neighbors insinuate but rather a time-honored and legally tolerated religion.

THE HISTORICAL AND PASTORAL CONTEXT OF LUKE'S GOSPEL

Authorship. As in the Gospels according to Mark and Matthew, the author of Luke-Acts never names himself, and so it has fallen to early church tradition to supply this information. Irenaeus (*Haer.* 3.1.1) offers an early witness to Luke, Paul's traveling companion, as the author of these two volumes, and this suggestion is nowhere seriously challenged among early church fathers. The author of Luke-Acts, it must be admitted, actually has "presence" in his text, since in both prologues (Lk 1:1-4; Acts 1:1-2) he speaks of his activity, purposes and methods quite directly. He even names a particular Christian, Theophilus, in these dedicatory prefaces. With such authorial presence and indications of an audience that would be able to ascribe authorship accurately, the church tradition stands a good chance of being correct.

The internal evidence for authorship is less convincing than what we might suspect and what many would claim. First, we often hear or read of the use of richer terminology for medical conditions in Luke-Acts as a proof that these books were written by "the beloved physician" (Col 4:14). The author's vocabulary does not in itself provide proof of his occupation, however, since other nonphysicians in the Hellenistic period use the same variety of terms.[1] What Luke's vocabulary reveals, then, is his higher level of education than his fellow Evangelists. Interestingly, Tertullian refers to the author once as Luke the lawyer, showing that the author's writing also could give the impression of the being part of another profession that is now considered to be highly specialized.

The autobiographical nature of the "we" passages in Acts has often lent support to the traditional view that a fellow traveler of Paul wrote Acts (and thus also the Gospel of Luke).[2] It was common for ancient historians to reveal their own firsthand participation in the history they wrote, since eyewitness involvement in the events was a positive value for ancient historians such as Thucydides and Josephus. ("Armchair historians" were not as credible.)[3] These "we" passages are probably not to be explained as a fictional literary convention used to make the narrative more vivid. If this were so, then the limit of the use of the first-person plural to Acts 16:10-17; 20:5-15; 21:1-18; and 27:1—28:16 would lack a plausible explanation. (Why not write the entire story of Paul this way?) It is more likely that the "we" passages indicate either a firsthand source woven in somewhat awkwardly by the author or, more likely (since the author of Luke-Acts is far from awkward), the author's own involvement in those parts of the story. The problem is, however, that Luke is not the only traveling companion of Paul that could have been present at those points in the story. Again, we rely on the nomination of Luke by early church tradition to disqualify candidates like Epaphras.

One important factor needs to be kept in mind, however, in discussions about authorship: even if Luke, "the beloved physician," did write these two volumes—a position that is quite defensible[4]—it does not mean that he writes without an agenda. Scholars will often argue against authorship by a companion of Paul on the basis of (1) the different picture of the early church and its internal disagreements and resolutions that we get in Acts versus Paul's letters, and (2) divergences from or general avoidance of specific tenets of Pauline theology in Luke-Acts. This is fallacious reasoning. Even if the author of Luke-Acts had personal contact with Paul, he is not therefore a mouthpiece for Paul; just because he tells the story differently and articulates early Christian theology differently does not deny the possibility of close acquaintance with Paul. Not all of Paul's associates thought exactly like Paul on every issue (even Barnabas, in Gal 2:11-14), and a number of them went their separate ways from Paul for reasons that remain somewhat murky (e.g., Mark or Demas). Luke's purpose is not to provide another witness to Paul's perception of events and belief. Rather, he shapes his presentation of the life of Jesus and the growth, mission and faith of the early church in such a way as best responds to the pastoral needs and challenges of his audience. These purposes will be explored more fully below.

---

[1]Henry Cadbury, *The Style and Literary Method of Luke* (Cambridge, Mass.: Harvard University Press, 1920), 1:50-51; Luke Timothy Johnson, *The Writings of the New Testament,* 2nd ed. (Minneapolis: Fortress, 1996), p. 198; Eduard Lohse, *The Formation of the New Testament* (Nashville: Abingdon, 1981), p. 152.

[2]See, for example, the extensive discussion of this feature in Colin Hemer, *The Book of Acts in the Setting of Hellenistic History* (Tübingen: J. C. B. Mohr, 1989), pp. 312-34.

[3]David E. Aune, *The New Testament in Its Literary Environment* (Louisville, Ky.: Westminster Press, 1987), p. 124.

[4]This position has been maintained by such notable historical critics as Martin Dibelius (*Studies in the Acts of the Apostles* [London: SCM, 1956], p. 123) and Robert M. Grant (*A Historical Introduction to the New Testament* [London: Collins, 1963], pp. 134-35).

EXEGETICAL SKILL
Textual Criticism

In the introduction to the Gospels, you were exposed to some discussion of the textual transmission of the New Testament texts. Textual transmission is the process of how the written Word was spread and preserved through endless manual copying from the first through the sixteenth centuries, when the advent of the printing press helped standardize the Greek text (or at least ensure that the same mistakes were preserved in multiple copies). This process, you may recall, produced a veritable sea of variant readings. If you were to set the approximately 5,300 surviving New Testament manuscripts side by side, you would not find any two (of any sizeable length) to have exactly the same text.[a] Textual criticism is the discipline of discerning, from all the available variant readings of a particular phrase or verse, what is most likely to have been the original wording, the wording of the actual author, whose original version is otherwise inaccessible to us. Textual critics attempt to look through all the copies, the copies of copies, and the copies of copies of copies—through all the changes made by countless people keeping the New Testament alive by hand—to discover the most ancient form of the text.

As one scribe copied a manuscript, whether to replace a manuscript that was wearing out or to make a copy for another church or monastery, he would inevitably make mistakes. Many of these mistakes were accidental—mostly tricks of the eye. The scribe would make spelling errors, confuse similar-looking letters or switch letters around in a word or words around in a sentence. As the scribe's eyes moved from original to copy and back again, he might not land at exactly the right place. He might jump either forward or backward in the original to another word that began or ended with the same series of letter he was just copying, thus skipping or doubling words and phrases. In some cases a single scribe would read aloud as multiple scribes wrote down the text. This was considered mass production. A scribe could misconstrue the text as it was being read to them, especially as the Greek vowels and diphthongs came to be pronounced more and more alike.

Not all changes are accidental, however. Many scribes sought to be helpful by making intentional "corrections" of the text as they copied. One very common "correction" involved harmonizing the phrasing in one passage with what was known or remembered from another. For example, scribes would correct Old Testament quotations in the New, bring Mark or Luke into closer harmony with Matthew, or conform an expression in one Pauline letter to an expression from another. Sometimes a scribe who was comparing

---

[a]Bart Ehrman, "Textual Criticism of the New Testament," in *Hearing the New Testament: Strategies for Interpretation,* ed. Joel B. Green (Grand Rapids: Eerdmans, 1995), pp. 129, 131.

two or manuscripts as he copied would harmonize the variants, conflating the readings into a new reading. Scribes would also frequently seek to improve the grammar and style of the text or correct any perceived errors or discrepancies. Sometimes, they would even make theologically motivated omissions, changes or insertions (some of which may have started out as marginal glosses, later getting copied as part of the text itself). The textual critic sifts through all the variants at a given place in the text and attempts to discern which reading is most likely the original reading of the text, the one given by the author and later changed in the process of transmission (copying).

Textual critics use a variety of witnesses to the various readings. First, there are the Greek manuscripts. The oldest of these are generally the *papyri* (second through fifth centuries), manuscripts written in Egypt and preserved on account of the dry conditions of the land there. These are the earliest manuscripts, but all are located in one small part of the Mediterranean. Next come the *uncials* or *majuscules,* which are so named because they are written in all capital letters, mostly without word breaks or punctuation. These date from the fourth to the ninth century. Some of the most important witnesses, the major codices of the fourth and fifth centuries (Sinaiticus, Alexandrinus and Vaticanus), belong to this class. Finally, there are the *minuscules,* which employ lower case letters, word breaks and some punctuation. These tend to be from the ninth century and later. The uncials and minuscules come from a variety of locations, which tend to be grouped as Alexandrian, Caesarean, Byzantine, Antiochene and Western.

Text critics also examine the early translations of the New Testament, called "versions." Some of these are as early as the second and third centuries. Through reconstruction of the Greek that would have led to the translation, they arrive at a secondary witness to early Greek manuscripts. The most important of these versions are the Old Latin, Vulgate, Syriac and Coptic, each of which can be located in a specific part of the Mediterranean. Another kind of resource is found in the quotations of the New Testament by early church fathers. Some of these wrote running commentaries on whole books of Scripture (like Origen, Chrysostom and Augustine); others give quotations in the course of their doctrinal or ethical expositions. Either way, they provide a valuable tertiary witness to the state of the New Testament text at the time of their writing (which can usually be dated very precisely). Critics use this kind of resource very carefully, however, since oftentimes a church father will quote from memory, the result being something of paraphrase rather than a witness to the actual wording of the passage. The church fathers also have clear geographical locations, which is of great value in weighing variants.

In their quest for the "original" text of the New Testament, text critics evaluate both the "external" and "internal" evidence provided by these variants. External evidence pertains to the evaluative weight of the manuscripts where a variant appears. Most text critics reject deciding for or against a variant on the basis of the number of manuscripts that contain that particular reading, since the vicissitudes of textual history render this criterion unreliable. There might have been three ancient manuscripts ultimately behind two different readings. Manuscripts X and Y read "he will conquer kings" while manuscript Z reads "he will conquer princes." Let's say no scribes ever copied X and Y, however, but 500 copies were produced on the basis of Z. Does this mean that there are 501 (Z and family) witnesses against 2 (X and Y)? According to textual critics, it is rather a case of 2 witnesses (X and Y) against 1 (Z). This is the major argument against the Majority Text, which the most conservative students (and champions of the King James Version) still seek to elevate as the best text of the New Testament, since the majority of surviving manuscripts bear witness to its readings.[b]

Instead, scholars weigh the evidence according to the following criteria:[c]

1. The antiquity of the reading: The older a variant is, the better its chances of being closer to the original than its younger counterparts, unless it can be demonstrated that the reading should be discarded on internal grounds.

2. The geographic distribution of the witnesses to the various readings: If a reading is attested in manuscripts coming from different regions, it is less likely to be a local variation. This must be tempered, of course, with consideration of the antiquity and general reliability of each text.

3. The relationships between witnesses: Those manuscripts that are copies of "manuscript X" do not count as separate witnesses, nor does widespread distribution count if it can be demonstrated that the manuscripts are "genetically related" by virtue of being copied from the same source or family of sources.

4. The reliability of each textual witness: For example, does manuscript X tend to have a lot of scribal errors or show a harmonizing tendency? If so, this will count against its "credibility" when set alongside a manuscript that tends not to show such patterns of intentional or accidental change.

Bart Ehrman succinctly summarizes the above: "readings found in the oldest, most widespread, and best manuscripts are more likely to be original than their variants."[d]

Alongside the external evidence, the text critic sets the internal evi-

---

[b]Ibid., p. 133.
[c]See Arthur G. Patzia, *The Making of the New Testament* (Downers Grove, Ill.: InterVarsity Press, 1995), pp. 146-47; Ehrman, "Textual Criticism," pp. 134-35.
[d]Ehrman, "Textual Criticism," p. 135.

dence, which to a large extent involves trying to explain how one of the variants would have given rise to the other variants by positing any of the accidental errors or intentional changes discussed above. Can an omission be explained by a scribe's eye skipping to the next word starting or ending with a similar string of letters? If so, the omitted words were probably the original. Are variants to be explained by the scribe harmonizing Luke to Matthew? Such variants probably ought to be discarded as "editorial." Is one variant more in keeping with the style, vocabulary and thought represented elsewhere by the author of the text? Such a variant usually is preferred to its alternatives, if the latter violate the author's stylistic, linguistic and theological tendencies. In general, text critics follow two rules as they sort out internal evidence:

1. The shorter reading is to be preferred (since it is more likely that words, explanatory glosses and the like would be added rather than deleted, except where the accidental omission can be detected).

2. The more difficult (less harmonized or potentially awkward) reading is to be preferred (obviously not if it is nonsense, but in general scribes sought to make the text easier to understand rather than more difficult, hence the easier reading of two intelligible ones is more likely to be the scribal change).

A famous example of a theologically motivated corruption ("improvement") of the New Testament is found in older English translations of 1 John 5:7-8 (like the KJV): "For there are three that bear record *in heaven, the Father, the Word, and the Holy Ghost: and these three are one. And there are three that bear witness in earth,* the spirit, and the water, and the blood: and these three agree in one." The italicized words are now relegated to a footnote in modern translations, since that passage was invented and inserted into the original text. The external evidence is overwhelmingly against these verses being original to John. They are absent from all Greek manuscripts, except for four late minuscules (eleventh to sixteenth centuries—and in the earlier two of these, the words are inserted by a later hand into the text in the form of a gloss) and all versions, except for some post-Vulgate Latin manuscripts. In the fourth and fifth centuries some Latin fathers begin to quote these words as Scripture, and they became fixed in the Latin text tradition. The internal evidence is also against it: the omission of such a useful trinitarian verse by scribes and translators in every corner of the Mediterranean defies explanation. Its inclusion is readily explicable, however, as a pious expansion inspired by the phraseology of the three witnesses of the water, blood and Spirit, perhaps first written as a gloss and finally copied as if it were part of the text itself.[e]

---

[e]For a comprehensive discussion, see Raymond E. Brown, *The Epistles of John,* AB 30 (Garden City, N.Y.: Doubleday, 1982), pp. 775-87.

For a more detailed example, we turn to the Lucan form of the Lord's Prayer (Lk 11:2-4).

[2]When you pray, say
Father,
let your name be sanctified;
let your kingdom come;
[3]keep giving to us each day our daily bread;
[4]and forgive to us our sins,
for indeed we ourselves forgive every one indebted to us;
and do not lead us into temptation.

The first variant is a mere spelling error in the Greek word for "pray," but it is fairly widely attested. The spelling variant actually produces a change of the verb's mood, but in context it would be translated the same either way (just being treated as an error). Since Luke tends to get his verb moods right, text critics tend to give him the benefit of the doubt here. The second variant is a lengthy addition between the words "pray" and "say." A single manuscript (Codex Bezae, symbolized by "D") reads: "When you pray, do not babble as the rest: for some people think that they will be heard by their abundant speech; but praying, say," then the Lord's Prayer begins. Since this reading is attested in a single fifth-century manuscript (one that is known anyway for abundant omissions and additions, thus not a very reliable witness), and since it represents a clear attempt to incorporate advice from Matthew into Luke's teaching on prayer, there is no doubt that it is a scribal addition.

As the prayer begins we find many variants that appear as the result of scribes conforming the Lucan form of the Lord's Prayer to the Matthean form, which was the form that entered common liturgical and personal usage. "Father" is attested in a third-century papyrus numbered P[75], the fourth-century codices Sinaiticus and Vaticanus, the Vulgate, a Syriac translation, a seventh-century Latin translation and Marcion (second century) and Origen (third century). The eighth-century codex L expands this to "our father," while the vast majority of Greek manuscripts, as well as the Syriac and Coptic translations, read "our father in heaven." In view of the antiquity and wide geographical distribution of the shorter reading, and the tendency among scribes to harmonize, the reading "Father" stands the better chance of being original. Conversely, were "Our father in heaven" original, we would have no reasonable explanation for a scribe's omitting from the Lucan form of the Lord's Prayer what he allowed to remain in the Matthean form (hence, theological tinkering with the prayer is not the issue).

This reasoning would also pertain to the variants that introduce "your will be done" or "your will be done on earth as in heaven" into verse two and add "but deliver us from evil" at the end of the prayer. It also holds for the variants that represent the replacement of Lucan diction with the Matthean equivalents: "give" for "keep giving" and "today" for "each day" in verse 3, "debts" for "sins," "we forgave" for "we also forgive," and "our debtors" for "every one indebted to us" in verse 4. The manuscript tradition bears strong witness to the attempts of some scribes to resist harmonizing and the ease with which many others gave way to harmonizing.

A number of variants, which clearly have no claim to being "original" to Luke, nevertheless provide interesting windows into early Christian theology and usage. In place of "let your kingdom come," we find in two late Greek minuscules (twelfth- and thirteenth-century) "let your holy Spirit come upon us and let it cleanse us," a reading given much earlier attestation, however, in the writings of the fourth-century church father Gregory of Nyssa. This shows a tendency in some pockets of the early church to understand the coming of God's kingdom as present in a very real sense when the Holy Spirit comes upon the gathered assembly of believers, cleansing them for the encounter with the Almighty.

Textual criticism thus takes the student into the "real world" of how the New Testament was kept alive, used, read, interpreted, corrected *and* corrupted over the centuries. Unfortunately, the tools textual critics use are not very accessible or user-friendly to the nonspecialist. If any exegetical skill merits the label *discipline*, it is this one. First, it presupposes a firm grasp of the Greek language. While some modern Bible translations include the occasional footnote, "some ancient manuscripts read . . . ," the real storehouse of textual variants is in the large blocks of material at the bottom of the page of the Greek New Testament.[f] Second, in the interests of economy, every Greek manuscript and other witness has its own symbol *(siglum),* and so the user must frequently turn to the list of *sigla* in order to find out what actual manuscripts support each variant and to learn a rather complex system of typographical symbols for different kinds of variants (omissions, insertions, transpositions of words and so forth) and abbreviations of families of manuscripts, early translation and church fathers.[g] Nevertheless, the student who is able to learn Greek is certainly also able to master these symbols and abbreviations, and so begin to explore the "critical apparatus" of textual variants with profit.

Since textual criticism is, admittedly, a rather specialized field of study, most serious Christians will not probably not have the leisure to engage

---

[f]Specifically, the *Novum Testamentum Graece,* 27th ed. (Stuttgart: Deutsche Bibelgesellschaft, 1993). This is readily available in the United States through the American Bible Society (1-800-32-BIBLE; <www.americanbible.org>), as is Bruce M. Metzger's *A Textual Commentary on the Greek New Testament* (Stuttgart: United Bible Societies, 1971).
[g]*Novum Testamentum Graece,* pp. 684-718; 44-79 respectively.

the discipline directly. It is at least essential for those who teach and preach the Word to understand the evaluative processes and decisions that stand behind the reconstructed Word on which almost all modern translations are based. An indispensable resource for this is Bruce M. Metzger, *A Textual Commentary on the Greek New Testament* (Stuttgart: United Bible Societies, 1971), a discussion of all important variants in canonical order, explaining the decisions made by the small group of textual critics largely responsible for the major critical Greek editions of the New Testament (the basis of the RSV, NRSV, JB, TEV, NIV and so many other English translations). Nearly every verse of the New Testament has textual variants, most of which are minute matters of spelling or omission of little words (definite articles and the like), though some are highly significant.

Textual variants are everywhere in the Greek New Testament, so any passage would provide considerable material for practice in this skill. The following might be interesting places to begin:

1. Look closely at the variants to the eucharistic words in Luke 22:17-20, which hold considerable significance for the soteriology and sacramentology of Luke (perhaps with the aid of Metzger's *Textual Commentary,* pp. 73-77).

2. Review the textual history of John 7:53—8:11.

3. Review the textual variants surrounding the ending of Mark (Mark 16:8 and the additions that follow).

4. Look at the variants in the story of the conversion and baptism of the Ethiopian eunuch (Acts 8:34-40), paying special attention to the additions in Codex Bezae (D). Codex Bezae habitually adds substantially to Acts (see also, for example, Acts 11:1-2; 13:33; 14:1-2; 16:38-40; 19:14). What interests do you detect in this particular expansion of Acts?

Ask of the variants in each passage: (1) What theological or other interests might the variants reveal? (2) How would I account for the different variants? (3) Why did textual critics reach the decisions they did about the "original" form of the text?

FOR FURTHER READING

Aland, Kurt, and Barbara Aland. *The Text of the New Testament: An Introduction to the Critical Editions and to the Theory and Practice of Modern Textual Criticism.* 2nd ed. Grand Rapids: Eerdmans, 1989.

Comfort, Philip W. *The Quest for the Original Text of the New Testament.* Grand Rapids: Baker, 1992.

Comfort, Philip W., and David P. Barrett. *The Complete Text of the Earliest New Testament Manuscripts.* Grand Rapids: Baker, 1999.

Ehrman, Bart. *The Orthodox Corruption of Scripture: The Effect of Early Christological Controversies on the Text of the New Testament.* New

York: Oxford University Press, 1993.

———. "Textual Criticism of the New Testament," pp. 127-45. In *Hearing the New Testament: Strategies for Interpretation*. Edited by Joel B. Green. Grand Rapids: Eerdmans, 1995.

Metzger, Bruce M. *The Text of the New Testament: Its Transmission, Corruption, and Restoration*. 3rd ed. New York: Oxford University Press, 1993.

———. *A Textual Commentary on the Greek New Testament*. Stuttgart: United Bible Societies, 1971.

Patzia, Arthur G. *The Making of the New Testament*, pp 137-50. Downers Grove, Ill.: InterVarsity Press, 1995.

Circumstances and purposes of composition. Luke-Acts is the only New Testament narrative that supplies a specific reader. It addresses itself specifically to Theophilus, whose name means "friend of God" (*not* "God-lover" or "God-fearer"). The simplest explanation of the mention of Theophilus in the prologue of each volume is that Theophilus provided support for Luke to do his investigations and writing. Luke would then be following the convention of the dedicatory preface by naming his literary patron, just as Josephus does in his historical writings. The name Theophilus need not be taken as a symbol for the body of Gentile God-fearers who attached themselves to the synagogue and then the church: the name would be reasonable enough as a real name in antiquity. He is already a convert, for he has already heard the Christian message and "been instructed" in the Christian gospel. Luke writes to reinforce his confidence in the church's teaching and God's promises. The form of address, "most excellent," may indicate an official in the Roman administration (converts were to be found even among "Caesar's household," according to Phil 4:22),[5] or it may simply be a token of the respect and honor due one's patron.

As in the case of Josephus the literary patron to whom the work is "addressed" does not represent the sum total of the audience. While Theophilus is explicitly named and undoubtedly read the volumes carefully, he will have friends within the larger Christian community with whom he will share the work. When Luke addresses Theophilus, he may also have in mind other such well-placed Christians of means in the early church—those few but important figures who came to Christianity from the upper rungs of the social ladder on whom the churches largely depend for their meeting places and the like. Luke's words about possessions, wealth and the necessity of caring for the less fortunate are potent reminders to these patrons about the special challenge and charge God has placed on them.

Luke wrote, however, for an even wider audience, and Theophilus may well have also underwritten the costs of copying the volumes and circulating them among Christian communities like his own—those that included a large Gentile Christian segment and were con-

---

[5]It has been suggested that Theophilus was a magistrate involved in the trial of Paul, but this has not won wide acceptance and depends too much on the view that Acts was a "legal brief" in defense of Paul—to the neglect of so many other clear goals for Acts.

nected closely with the Pauline mission, and for whom the message would be most relevant and the medium most pleasing. Both volumes were eventually spread throughout the early church (though not as quickly, universally or uniformly as Matthew). So we will need to inquire into how Luke-Acts addresses those concerns and issues that the early church as a whole wrestled with in the last decades of the first century.

We cannot be reasonably certain about the location of composition. Some have weighted Ephesus as likely, given the fact that Paul gives his farewell to the elders of that church in the narrative of Acts. There is little reason, however, to favor one city over another. But it is reasonable to favor an urban setting over a rural one, since Christianity spread as an urban phenomenon and only reached out into the rural areas much later, and to favor an original setting in a community closely connected with the Pauline mission, given the importance that Luke attaches to this apostle, his mission and the questions raised in the early church in connection with his mission.

With regard to date, some argue for a pre-70 date for Luke and Acts based on the absence of references to (1) the fall of Jerusalem (which is actually a specious argument, as will be seen below), (2) the persecution in Rome under Nero, and (3) the death of Paul.[6] Two out of three of these, however, have been seen reflected in the text by other scholars. For example, the ominous words of Acts 20:25 can be taken as a sign of the author's and audience's awareness of Paul's fate in Rome. The last quarter of Acts foreshadows a final verdict

of guilty and of a final (if undeserved) sentence of death, and indeed the limitation placed on the amount of time spent by Paul in Rome "unhindered" combines with these narrative signals to confirm that the author and readership knew of Paul's untimely death at the end of those two years in Rome.

Luke's Gospel, moreover, is the most explicit of all three Synoptic Gospels concerning the destruction of Jerusalem. The changes made by Luke from Mark's presentation of Jesus' eschatological discourse all move in the direction of bringing Jesus' words closer in line with the events of 70 C.E. By examining the Gospel parallels closely (i.e., performing redaction criticism), we can see that Luke clarifies what Mark and Matthew cryptically called the "abomination of desolation" (Mt 24:15// Mk 13:14). Luke interprets this saying of Jesus as a reference to the siege of Jerusalem (rather than, say, a desecration of the temple): "But when you see Jerusalem surrounded by armies, then know that its desolation has come near" (Lk 21:20 NRSV). Where Matthew and Mark refer to "great tribulation such as has not been since the beginning of the world until now" (Mt 24:21//Mk 13:19), Luke writes: "they will fall by the edge of the sword and be taken away as captive among all nations; and Jerusalem will be trampled on by the Gentiles, until the times of the Gentiles are fulfilled" (Lk 21:24 NRSV). What Matthew and Mark leave as a general prediction of suffering, Luke now specifies as the suffering of those who endure the siege of Jerusalem and its aftermath. Luke's omission of the instruction "pray that your flight may not be in winter"

---

[6]See, e.g., Donald Guthrie, *New Testament Introduction* (Downers Grove, Ill.: InterVarsity Press, 1970), pp. 340-45, who clearly favors this position. He also argues that the interest in the controversy over the necessity of circumcision is a sign of Acts having been written closer to the time when that debate was still fresh. The importance of that debate in Acts, however, lies not so much in the practical issue itself. Rather, the story of the movement of the Spirit among the Gentiles and the process by which the Jerusalem leadership came to recognize the validity of Gentile Christianity as part of the new people of God contributes chiefly to the legitimation of Gentile Christianity, which is one of Luke's main concerns and achievements. An eloquent defense of an early date is offered by Hemer, *Book of Acts,* pp. 365-410. Especially important are the indications of an early date discussed on pp. 376-82. Hemer is well aware that most if not all of these indications are also consonant with a later date, and it is their accumulation that carries force for him.

(Mk 13:18) may represent his knowledge that the siege actually occurred over the summer of 70 C.E.

Additionally, for the first time in a Gospel we have explicit explanations offered for the event, suggesting that one of Luke's minor purposes is to explain how God could have allowed God's holy city to be destroyed and God's holy place to be trampled as it had been. The major explanation given for the fall of Jerusalem is that the people did not respond to God's agent of salvation or to his apostles who called for repentance and response in the wake of his resurrection in a suitable way:

> The days will come upon you, when your enemies will set up ramparts around you and surround you, and hem you in on every side. They will crush you to the ground, you and your children within you, and they will not leave within you one stone upon another; because you did not recognize the time of your visitation from God. (Lk 19:43-44 NRSV)

Not all who favor a date after 70 C.E. do so because of a commitment to the belief that Jesus could not predict the fall of Jerusalem,[7] but because of a commitment to the belief that Mark and Matthew preserve the more original form of Jesus' prediction, which Luke alters in recognition of the fact that the predictions came true in 70 C.E. and out of a desire to lead his readers to understand the siege of Jerusalem in this way. Such an interpretive move on Luke's part strongly suggests that we should place the writing of the Gospel and Acts in the period after the destruction of Jerusalem. The absence of explicit treatment of any of the three subjects listed above is best explained as a decision reached by Luke on the basis of his purposes for writing and the scope of his work, which was the progress of the Gospel from Jerusalem to Rome achieved by 60 C.E. This would render any explicit mention of the events of the mid- to late-60s out of place and superfluous.[8]

Purposes and special emphases. Luke and John are the only Evangelists that make explicit statements about the purpose of their work. Luke claims that he writes "an orderly account" that he hopes will enable Theophilus, and presumably his wider readership as well, to "know the truth [*asphaleia*] concerning the things about which you have been instructed [*katēchēthēs*]." Luke's goal is not merely historical, although he does make certain recognizable claims to be writing "history," as it would have been understood in the first century. Luke writes to confirm the commitment made and instruction received by Theophilus and other readers like him as they joined the Christian movement.

What kind of confirmation would Theophilus and other members of the Gentile-dominated churches of Asia Minor and Greece have needed, given the content and emphases of the narratives Luke has provided? Fundamentally, the questions appear to have been, How do we know that, having joined this small religious group, we are actually standing in the center of God's will? How can we be sure that we are part of God's people, and that we are doing the right things to please God? Because of the alternative expressions of faithfulness and obedience to the one God available in the synagogue and among the more conservative Jewish Christian circles, and because of the divisions within early Christianity concerning the relationship of Christians to Torah and the like, Gentile Christians would have had ample opportunity to question what they had been

---

[7]Against Guthrie's sweeping claim that "if a predictive element in the ministry of Jesus is allowed, the whole basis of this generally held dating collapses" (*Introduction to the New Testament,* p. 346).

[8]Thus Aune, *New Testament,* p. 118, among others.

taught. Perhaps this best accounts for Luke's expansion of the scope of his work from "Gospel" to "church history," responding to these questions by telling a story about God's mighty acts not only accomplished in Jesus' story but also "among us" (Luke 1:1), showing his readers how they stand at the crest of God's plan for redemption.

As we study the whole of Luke-Acts, we find that Luke is especially intent on confirming Gentile Christian readers in the certainty (in the sense of reliability) of the promises of God. The special problem here is that of theodicy, explaining how God did in fact fulfill God's promises to the house of David (see Acts 15:16-18) despite the fact that the majority of Jews did not accept the means of fulfillment and despite the fact that Jerusalem now sits in ruins. This is important insofar as it has direct bearing on God's reliability now for those who have trusted in God's promises in Christ, whether Jew or Gentile. Luke's special emphasis on the role of the Spirit of God in the ministry of Jesus, the life and movement of the early church, and the ongoing life of Luke's readers serves also to help legitimate the path the church is on and the place of Gentiles in that body. The Spirit is the driving force and the continuity between each stage in God's unfolding drama of salvation. This continuity is also confirmed as Luke contributes to the church's Christocentric reading of the Jewish Scriptures, extending this reading into the life of the early church and its ongoing mission. Not just Jesus but also the mission of the church fulfills the promises and prophecies of the Jewish Scriptures.

Like Mark and Matthew, Luke also seeks to demonstrate how God's law is indeed fulfilled in those who walk in acts of mercy, love and compassion, but who do not occupy themselves with dietary restrictions, sabbath observances and the like. Also like his fellow Evangelists, Luke seeks to contribute to the shaping of the ethos of the Christian community. Some of his strongest emphases fall on making the church a place for the penitent to experience restoration and the place where relief and help is found for those in need.

Another major interest of Luke-Acts is the clarification of the position of the church with regard to the Roman Empire. On the one hand, Luke does not allow Christians to embrace the Roman imperial ideology. There is no move toward coexistence through compromise on that level. On the other hand, he also seeks to demonstrate that Christians are not fundamentally at odds with the Roman order. He emphasizes Jesus' *innocence* in the eyes of Pilate, Herod and the centurion, just as he will emphasize Paul's innocence in the eyes of every Roman official before whom Paul is brought. Christianity is consistently presented as an entity within the historical (and divinely guided) development of Judaism—whatever Jews think of this arrangement—which means that its fundamentally different ideology should be tolerated as a form of that longstanding opponent of polytheism. Contrary to popular slander concerning the Christ-followers, Luke presents Christians as a group of noble people committed to virtue and orderly living, not to political subversion and disturbance of the public order.

How Luke accomplishes each of these goals will be treated at length in "Luke's Message" (pp. 316-33)

Structure. It is vitally important to read Luke within the context of the author's larger project. Acts is not an independent writing, a fact that our canonical order conceals. Without reading Luke as part of Luke-Acts, we can easily make mistaken claims about Luke and his audience. For example, on the basis of Luke alone we could observe that the author is less interested in the fulfillment of Old Testament prophecy in the life of Jesus than Matthew, but if we include Acts it will be clear that Luke is as vitally concerned with anchoring the life and ministry of Jesus in the oracles of God as Matthew.

An Outline of Luke's Gospel

Introductory Material: 1:1—2:52

    Prologue: 1:1-4

    Announcement of the birth of John the Baptist: 1:5-25

    Announcement of the birth of Jesus: 1:26-56

    Birth of John: 1:57-80

    Birth of Jesus: 2:1-52

Jesus in Galilee: 3:1—9:50

    Preparation for ministry: 3:1—4:13

        John the Baptist and Jesus: 3:1-22

        Genealogy: 3:23-38

        Temptation: 4:1-13

    Inauguratory Sermon: 4:14-30

    Galilean ministry: 4:31—9:50

Journey to Jerusalem: 9:51—19:27

Jesus in Jerusalem (and environs): 19:28—24:53

    Jerusalem ministry: 19:28—21:38

    Passion narrative: 22:1—23:56

    Resurrection appearances in Judea: 24:1-53

This connection is also borne out by the overall structure of both books, in which Jerusalem, the historic, holy city of God and the center of God's interaction with humanity, stands at the center of the movement of the whole.[9]

Luke—*to Jerusalem*
Introduction: Luke 1—2
Judean ministry outside Jerusalem: Luke 3:1—9:50
Journey to Jerusalem (which contains most of the special materials): Luke 9:51—19:27
Jerusalem: Luke 19:28—24:52

Acts—*from Jerusalem to the ends of the earth*
Jerusalem: Acts 1:1—8:1
Judea and Samaria and Galilee: 8:1—9:31 (9:32-43 is transitional)
"To the ends of the earth": 10:1—28:31

The literary character of Luke-Acts. Luke-Acts contains the most literary Greek of the New Testament narratives, more on par with the rhetorically adept letter to the Hebrews. The author's vocabulary and his competency in the rhetorical and narrative arts betrays an intentional education. He is able to use a variety of Greek styles, whether he is imitating the style of the Septuagint in his infancy narratives or the style of courtroom rhetoric in the prosecution and defense speeches in Acts. Luke consistently corrects and improves Mark's grammar and style, placing a greater emphasis on syntax (the subordination of clauses) over against the use of simple and compound sentences. He shows a high level of awareness of the literary conventions of the genre of historiography, a fact that will merit extended scrutiny within the discussion of Acts.

---

[9]Johnson, *Writings of the New Testament,* pp. 204-5.

LUKE'S USE OF OTHER EARLY CHRISTIAN RESOURCES

In his prologue Luke presents his history of Jesus and the early church as the result of his careful investigation of the subject matter. This may have involved the questioning of eyewitnesses, many of whom would have been alive in the decade after the fall of Jerusalem and available for questioning. It is not necessary to assume that these persons' names have come down to us, or, if they have, that they were major players in the drama Luke tells. He also makes reference to earlier written works, regarding his work as the successor and perhaps more perfect account of Christian origins. At the very least, he shows signs of being aware of previous Gospels and gives evidence of having used these resources critically.

Luke and Mark. One widely recognized resource for Luke, as for Matthew, is Mark's Gospel. Luke's essential agreement with the witness of Mark is reflected in the large blocks of material from Mark that Luke has incorporated into his own Gospel:

Luke 3:1—4:15 = Mark 1:1-15
Luke 4:31—6:19 = Mark 1:21—3:19
Luke 8:4—9:50 = Mark 4:1—9:40 (minus Mk 6:45—8:20)
Luke 18:15-43 = Mark 10:13-52 (note absence also of Mk 9:41—10:12)
Luke 19:29—22:12 = Mark 11:1—14:16
Luke 22:13—24:12 = Mark 14:17—16:8[10]

These blocks do not indicate anything like verbatim agreement, however, since Luke is intent on improving Mark's diction, grammar and style as well as editing Mark's content in some more substantial ways.

We will also immediately notice that two major blocks of Mark's material were not incorporated into Luke (Mk 6:45—8:20; 9:41—10:12), with the result that Luke incorporates markedly less of the Second Gospel than Matthew. Why? Were these passages absent from Luke's copy of Mark, as some have suggested? The German scholars Hans Conzelmann and Andreas Lindemann propose more plausibly that Luke omitted this material for theological reasons. Luke wanted to eliminate Jesus' ministry to regions outside of Jewish territory, limiting the focus of his work to Galilee and Judea. In this way Luke streamlines the picture of a ministry to Israel (Jesus' focus on enacting God's faithfulness to Israel and rebuilding the house of David) prior to a Gentile mission.[11] While this fails to account for Luke's inclusion of the exorcism of the Gadarene demoniac, it is otherwise a rather solid explanation. It is more difficult to account for the omission of Mark 9:42—10:12. These verses contain some of the more difficult and harsh sayings of Jesus, but Luke does not elsewhere shy away from the challenge of Jesus' message, so it is difficult to think that he would do so here.

Luke's method is to follow Mark for a long section, then switch to his other sources for a large block of text and keep moving back and forth between his sources rather than try to integrate them more closely. Thus we observe that for extended sections Luke has nothing comparable to Mark, as in Luke 1:1—2:52 (the infancy narratives), 3:1—4:30 (different traditions of the work of John; the temptation and Nazareth sermon), 6:20—8:3, 9:51—18:14, 19:1-28 (Zacchaeus; parable of the pounds), and 24:8-53 (the resurrection narratives).

Luke retains the so-called messianic secret motif found in Mark. In addition to including in his Gospel those episodes in Mark where Jesus commands to others to be silent con-

---

[10]This material is conflated from Lohse, *Formation of the New Testament,* p. 147; and Raymond Brown, *Introduction to the New Testament* (Garden City, N.Y.: Doubleday, 1997), p. 263.

[11]H. Conzelmann, and A. Lindemann, *Interpreting the New Testament* (Peabody, Mass.: Hendrickson, 1988), pp. 231, 234.

cerning his identity or his miracles, Luke adds a number of nuances to Mark's overall presentation. Especially noteworthy is Luke's claim that Jesus' meaning was hidden from the disciples by divine agency (Lk 9:45; 18:34). Luke, like Mark, expresses in this way the conviction that Jesus' messiahship cannot be understood apart from his crucifixion and resurrection. Indeed, it is only after the crucifixion and resurrection that a true reading of the Scriptures becomes possible:

> Then he opened their minds to understand the scriptures, and said to them, "Thus it is written, that the Messiah is to suffer and to rise from the dead on the third day, and that repentance and forgiveness of sins should be proclaimed in his name to all nations, beginning from Jerusalem. (Lk 24:45-47 NRSV; cf. 24:27, 32)

Like Matthew, Luke agrees with Mark's teaching about Jesus' messiahship and the meaning of following such a Messiah. He even retains two of Mark's three parallel teachings concerning Jesus' messiahship and Christian discipleship. The first two passion predictions in Luke are followed by teachings on discipleship, as in Mark (cf. Lk 9:20-22/9:23-26; 9:43b-45/9:46-48 with Mk 8:31-33/8:34-38; 9:30-32/9:33-37). Luke only breaks the pattern with the third passion prediction (Lk 18:31-34; cf. Mk 10:32-35), eliminating the episode of James's and John's unseemly request and postponing this second argument concerning who is the greatest to the Last Supper (Lk 22:24-27; cf. Mk 10:41-45). This minor difference aside, it is clear that Luke would support essentially the same definition of Jesus' messiahship and the contours of Christian discipleship that were so prominent a feature of Mark's message.

Both Matthew and Luke have significantly altered Mark's presentation of the disciples, mitigating Mark's rather sharp portrayal of their slowness of mind and lack of loyalty. Luke does this first by attributing to divine agency the veil that lay over their minds concerning Jesus' passion predictions, adding to each declaration of the disciples' ignorance the explanation that "the meaning was concealed from them, so that they should not understand" (Lk 9:45; 18:34). Luke emphasizes the disciples' steadfastness rather than their desertion. Jesus identifies them at the Last Supper as "those who have stood by me in my trials" (Lk 22:28 NRSV) rather than as those who would soon desert him, as in Mark and Matthew. Luke does not say at the arrest that "then all the disciples forsook him and fled," as do Mark and Matthew. At the crucifixion, not only the women but "all those known to him" stood off in the distance, watching the passion (Lk 23:49). The failure to watch and pray in the garden is minimized by Luke, who changes Mark's three naps to one, adding the explanation that they were "sleeping because of grief," not mere weakness (Lk 22:45). It is difficult to get into the mind of the Evangelist to explain these changes, but one possible explanation involves Luke's desire to show the disciples as reliable witnesses to *all* of Jesus' ministry, including his arrest and crucifixion.

Luke also differs from Mark in his portrayal of Jesus. In Luke, Jesus is less given to emotion and is more clearly master of the emotions. References to Jesus acting out of pity or experiencing anger or love are frequently dropped. The substitution of Psalm 31:5 ("Into your hand I commit my spirit") for Psalm 22:1 ("My God, My God, why have you abandoned me!") as Jesus' last words before his death completes the picture of the self-controlled philosopher-sage who is not swayed by the power of the emotions. This would be more suitable for a Gentile Christian audience, who would be familiar with the popular philosophical evaluation of the emotions as a hindrance to virtuous action. For the sake of the same audience Luke removes references to Aramaic words that were part of the tradition (*Ephphatha*, *Talitha cumi*, etc.).

Luke's preface (Lk 1:1-4) also changes the way the Jesus traditions are read since it contains several signals that lead readers to encounter the two-volume narrative that follows within the context and conventions of ancient historical writing rather than as a free-standing biography. It remains true that the first book (Luke) follows the format and interests of a *vita*, but the presence of the second volume and the nature of the preface now brings Jesus' story and the church's story together in a mutually informative and interpretive manner.

Luke and Q. Luke shares a large body of Jesus' sayings with Matthew, together with a few narratives like the temptation story and the preaching of John. This represents the block of tradition or the sayings source known as Q. Luke frequently sets these sayings in a new setting and interpretative context that shows Luke's distinctive interests and interpretation or application of the words of Jesus. We often observe a marked difference between Luke's use and Matthew's interpretation of the same saying. For example, Luke applies the parable of the lost sheep (Lk 15:3-7) as a testimony to God's heart for reaching out to the lost, while Matthew uses this same parable to commend careful shepherding of the weak members of the church (Mt 18:12-14). Similarly, Luke's version of the wedding banquet (Lk 14:15-24) speaks to the obstacles of responding to God's invitation, and supports the exhortation to become detached from worldly pursuits and wealth to be free to be a disciple.

Figure 7.1. A mosaic from the floor of a villa in Sepphoris, featuring scenes from Greek mythology (a scene of Hercules is in the center; the god of wine, Bacchus, is featured prominently as well). If this is indeed from the dining room, three couches would have been placed around this mosaic, as servers brought food to the guests "reclining" (heads pointed toward the center) around these couches. (Photo courtesy of Todd Bolen [BiblePlaces.com])

Luke's Special Material (L)

Luke contains more material unique to his Gospel than does Matthew. Some of these passages may have been part of the Q tradition that Matthew decided not to include. Much of it probably flowed to Luke and the communities he had been a part of through separate streams of tradition. These passages contribute considerably to Luke's distinctive contours and emphases.

1. The infancy narratives (Lk 1—2)
2. Luke's distinctive genealogy (Lk 3:23-38)
3. Five miracle stories
   Miraculous catch of fish (Lk 5:1-11; cf. Jn 21)
   Raising the son of the widow of Nain (Lk 7:11-17)
   Healing of the crippled woman (Lk 13:10-17)
   Healing of the man with dropsy (Lk 14:1-6)
   Healing of the ten lepers (Lk 17:11-19)
4. Other vignettes
   Mary and Martha (Lk 10:38-42)
   Zaccheus (Lk 19:1-10)
5. Fourteen distinctive parables
   The two debtors (Lk 7:40-43)
   The good Samaritan (Lk 10:29-37)
   The insistent friend at midnight (Lk 11:5-8)
   The rich fool (Lk 12:13-21)
   The barren fig tree (Lk 13:6-9)
   Building a tower (Lk 14:28-30)
   Preparing for war (Lk 14:31-32)
   The lost coin (Lk 15:8-10)
   The father and the two sons (Lk 15:11-32)
   The prudent steward (Lk 16:1-9)
   The rich man and Lazarus (Lk 16:19-31)
   The servant's duties (Lk 17:7-10)
   The unjust judge (Lk 18:1-8)
   The Pharisee and the tax collector (Lk 18:9-14)
6. Certain episodes in the passion narrative, like the trial before Herod and the words from the cross (Lk 23:6-12, 34, 40-43, 46)
7. The resurrection appearances, especially the Emmaus experience (Lk 24:13-53)

Matthew, however, uses this parable to reinforce both the message of the parable of the wicked tenants and the need to bear proper fruits once one has been admitted to the new people of God (Mt 22:1-14).

Because of Luke's tendency to use blocks of Mark's material, retaining their original order quite closely, it is thought that he would have done the same with Q. Thus reconstructions of Q generally follow the Lucan order of these sayings since Matthew appears to have been more of a topical arranger of the traditions he included.

LUKE'S MESSAGE

The faithfulness of God to Israel. One of the primary features of Luke's work is an emphasis on God's faithfulness to Israel and, thereby, the confirmation of God's reliability toward the new people of God made of some Jews and many Gentiles. The eternal promises made to Israel cannot simply be rescinded, such that God has cast off God's people, proving unreliable toward them. It must be shown that God was faithful but that the people were not all open to God's fulfillment of those promises, rejecting God's anointed One and cutting themselves off from the people of God. In effect, the people of God remain unchanged in Luke's understanding of salvation history: many cut themselves off through their rejection of Jesus and his messengers while many join themselves to the people of God through their acceptance of Jesus. The criterion for belonging to that people is a positive response to the "prophet like Moses" that God raised up (Acts 3:22-26).

Acts 15:16-18 offers a programmatic statement of this theme:

> After this I will return,
> and I will rebuild the dwelling of David,
>   which has fallen;
> from its ruins I will rebuild it,
> and I will set it up,
> so that all other peoples may seek the
>   Lord—
> even all the Gentiles over whom my
>   name has been called. (see Amos
>   9:11-12 LXX)

This provides the outline for Luke's presentation throughout Luke-Acts: Jesus comes to Israel as the fulfillment of God's promise and sure sign of God's faithfulness to those promises; the house of David is restored as the church grows through Jerusalem, Judea, Galilee and Samaria (all formerly belonged under the rule of David); then the gospel spreads to the Jews scattered among the nations; finally, the Gentiles themselves are brought into the people of God through the preaching of the gospel.

The demonstration of God's faithfulness to the house of David and to Israel begins in the early chapters of Luke. Indeed, this more than anything else is the driving rhythm of the birth narratives in Luke 1—2. Luke even imitates the Greek style of the Septuagint as a means to connect these narratives to those Scriptures, in effect showing that in the births of John and Jesus the story of God's acts on behalf of God's people continue.

Luke links both families to two principal families of Israel, two families that received specific promises from God. John is of strict Aaronic descent, since both his mother and father are of priestly and Aaronic descent (Lk 1:5). Jesus is of Davidic descent through Joseph (Lk 1:27; 2:3-4). Both families, moreover, are true Israelites, being completely Torah-observant (Lk 1:6; 2:21, 22-24, 27, 39, 41-42). Throughout these first two chapters the characters celebrate God's faithfulness to the promises God made, a faithfulness that comes to expression in the gift of these two children. With regard to the birth of John, the angel Gabriel weaves Malachi 4:5-6 into the announcement of his conception:

> He will turn many of the people of Israel
> to the Lord their God. With the spirit
> and power of Elijah he will go before
> him, to turn the hearts of parents to
> their children, and the disobedient to
> the wisdom of the righteous, to make
> ready a people prepared for the Lord.
> (Lk 1:16-17 NRSV)

This scriptural promise is incorporated also into Zechariah's song at John's circumcision and naming: "You, child, will be called

Differences Between the Greek and Hebrew Texts of the Old Testament

The quotation in Acts 15:16-18 comes from the Septuagint version of Amos 9:11-12. The Septuagint is a name commonly given to the translation of the Hebrew Scriptures into Greek that took place through a variety of translators with a variety of translational philosophies and aptitudes. The Torah was translated rather literally and completed by the mid-third century B.C.E. The historical and prophetic books were translated with greater variety and degrees of accuracy by the early second century B.C.E. The writings seem to have been available in Greek by 100 B.C.E. These Greek translations became the primary means by which Greek-speaking Jews and the early Christians had access to the Hebrew Bible.[a]

At many points the Septuagint translation differs markedly from the Masoretic text (the Hebrew text as it has come down to us). For example, the Masoretic text of Amos 9:11-12 states that the fallen dwelling of David is rebuilt in order that it "may possess the remnant of Edom and all the nations that are called by my name." The Hebrew text suggests a new empire with Jerusalem at its center; the Greek version speaks rather of a great conversion of the Gentiles to the worship of the one God. The latter, of course, is more congenial to the Christian hope, freed of political nationalistic ties.

Another famous example of a significant difference between translation and original being used with profit by early Christians is Psalm 40:6-8. Compare the quotation of this psalm in Hebrews 10:5-7, where the author followed the Septuagint text, with Psalm 40:6-8 as it appears in your Old Testament, which is based on the Hebrew text. What differences do you observe? How do these differences become significant for the way the author of Hebrews interprets the Psalm in Hebrews 10:1-10? Could he have made the argument work based on the Hebrew text?

---

[a]For a recent, thorough and reliable introduction to the Greek versions of the Old Testament, see Moisés Silva and Karen Jobes, *Invitation to the Septuagint* (Grand Rapids: Baker, 2000).

---

the prophet of the Most High; for you will go before the Lord to prepare his ways" (Lk 1:76 NRSV). The gift of John to the barren couple, then, represents God's way of fulfilling his announcement of a forerunner to God's anointed One.

Gabriel also connects the advent of Jesus with the fulfillment of the promises God made to David, weaving into his announcement the promise of a perpetual kingdom under a descendent of David (2 Sam 7:14-16), to whom

God will relate as parent to child (2 Sam 7:14; Ps 2:7): "He will be great, and will be called the Son of the Most High, and the Lord God will give to him the throne of his ancestor David. He will reign over the house of Jacob forever, and of his kingdom there will be no end" (Lk 1:32-33 NRSV). God's promises to Abraham (Lk 1:54-55, 72-73) and promises to David (Lk 1:32-33, 69) are both singled out— even more explicitly than in Matthew—as being fulfilled in Jesus' birth:

He has helped his servant Israel,
in remembrance of his mercy,
according to the promise he made to our
ancestors,
to Abraham and to his descendants
forever. (Lk 1:54-55 NRSV)

Blessed be the Lord God of Israel,
for he has looked favorably on his
people and redeemed them.
He has raised up a mighty savior for us
in the house of his servant David,
as he spoke through the mouth of his
holy prophets from of old,
that we would be saved from our
enemies and from the hand of all
who hate us.
Thus he has shown the mercy promised
to our ancestors,
and has remembered his holy covenant,
the oath that he swore to our ancestor
Abraham. (Lk 1:68-73 NRSV)

The point of these songs is that God has indeed been faithful to all the promises God made and reliable in every respect. The fruit of God's faithfulness is the good news of salvation provided in Jesus.

As the birth narrative continues, Luke reinforces this theme as the angel declares to the shepherds that Jesus' birth is good news to "all the people," that is to the whole people of Israel (Lk 2:10-11: note, this should *not* be translated "to *all* people," as in the KJV). Jesus is the "consolation of Israel" (Lk 2:25), the one whose coming is God's salvation

which you have prepared in the
presence of all peoples,
a light for revelation to the Gentiles
and for glory to your people Israel.
(Lk 2:31-32 NRSV)

Finally, the prophetess Anna connects Jesus' birth with "the redemption of Jerusalem" (Lk 2:38). Jesus' miracles during his ministry cause onlookers to declare that "God has

looked favorably on God's people" (Lk 7:16), that is, God has turned again to restore the fortunes of Zion.

As the drama unfolds, what Luke depicts is not a turning of God away from Israel to the Gentiles but the decision of many Jews to cut themselves off from the people of God by rejecting God's prophet. This will be developed explicitly in Peter's sermon in Acts 3:22-26 and Stephen's speech in Acts 7, but it is already introduced within the Gospel narrative at Luke 7:30. There, "by refusing to be baptized by [John], the Pharisees and the lawyers rejected God's purpose for themselves" (NRSV) whereas those who responded favorably to John's message "acknowledged God's justice," that is, God's faithfulness to God's promise to bring salvation (Mal 3:1). On the other hand, wherever Jews accept Jesus and Jesus' messengers, the "fallen house of David" is being restored. Luke shows this part of the promise being worked out in the first half of Acts as the church grows throughout Judea, Galilee and Samaria (Acts 9:31): in each region that formerly belonged to the kingdom of David, the reign of Jesus, the son of David, is established and the people restored.

The Gentiles in God's redemptive plan. As the programmatic statement in Acts 15:16-18 makes clear, Luke is also interested in developing the universal scope of the gospel. He stresses that from the very beginning God's purpose involves all nations, and God's provision in Jesus is for all people, not Jews only. This has roots in the infancy narrative, as Simeon calls attention to Jesus' role as "a light for revelation to the Gentiles" (Lk 2:32), recalling two relevant passages from the servant songs of Isaiah that speak of the servant of God as God's "covenant to the people and light to the nations" (Is 42:6) and of the servant of God who will "raise up the tribes of Jacob and restore the survivors of Israel," and be given as "a light to the nations, that my salvation may reach to the end of the earth" (Is 49:6 NRSV).

Luke's genealogy also serves this purpose (Lk 3:23-38), going back beyond Abraham, the particular ancestor of the Jewish nation, to Adam and even to God, stressing the oneness of all people in the common ancestry of all races and nations.

This interest in the universal scope of God's purpose also has roots in John the Baptist's ministry, or, perhaps more accurately, in Isaiah 40. Luke does not merely quote the one verse found in the other Gospels to describe John's ministry (Is 40:3), but quotes three full verses in order to arrive at the verse that really interests him—"and all flesh shall see the salvation of God" (Lk 3:6 NRSV; Is 40:5).

Luke has also repositioned Jesus' sermon in the Nazareth synagogue, making this the inauguration of Jesus' public ministry. The episode now takes on the qualities of a programmatic statement about Jesus' ministry and its significance. And one prominent feature of the exchange between Jesus and the residents of Nazareth concerns God's saving purposes directed toward Gentiles—notably without any corresponding saving activity among Israel—during the period of its rebellion against God under Ahab and the worship of Baal (Lk 4:25-29). In this way Luke calls to mind God's interest in pouring out God's favor on Gentiles from of old, such that what the church experienced in the second half of the first century was not to be seen as a deviation from God's character and activity, but as its ultimate fruition. Interestingly, Luke alone among the Evangelists portrays Jesus' rejection at Nazareth as a direct result of his declaration of God's salvific purposes toward Gentiles.

It has been suggested that the mission of the Seventy-two (or the Seventy, in some manuscripts), which is unique to Luke among the Evangelists, also hints at a Gentile mission even though these missionaries are still sent to Israel (Lk 10:1-20). The twelve apostles could represent emissaries to the twelve tribes of Israel, while the seventy or seventy-two disciples sent out later could represent witnesses to the seventy or seventy-two Gentile nations/tribes as they were then enumerated. A second possibility, which need not exclude the first, is that the number of missionaries is meant to recall the translators of the LXX (numbered also seventy or seventy-two in different stories). Just as the LXX translators were acting in a way as missionaries, paving the way for the Jewish Scriptures to reach Gentiles, so the seventy or seventy-two Jesus sent out would eventually have the same goal.

God's compassion for the outsider and the non-Jew's capacity to respond with faith and love are also present in Jesus' dealings with or use of outsiders as models for insiders. For example, the centurion in Luke 7:1-10 remains a model for trust in Jesus. The Samaritan, regarded as a non-Jew by Judeans and Galileans, is the hero of a miracle story, being the only healed leper to return to give thanks to Jesus (Lk 17:16-18), and another Samaritan is the hero of a parable on how to fulfill the Torah itself, being the model of compassion and love for the neighbor (indeed, even for one's ethnic enemy; Lk 10:30-37). All of these hints become part of the explicit agenda of Jesus' followers after the resurrection, when Jesus commissions them to proclaim "forgiveness of sins . . . in his name to all nations, beginning from Jerusalem" (Lk 24:47 NRSV).

When we arrive at Acts, God's longstanding purposes to include the Gentiles in the people of God are heavily underscored. While the Gospel foreshadows this theme, a major goal of Acts is to show how this purpose is worked out so that God's hand is unmistakably seen at work behind this movement. There, the missionaries of Jesus will themselves fulfill the destiny of Jesus to be a "light to the Gentiles," embodying his mission in their own (Lk 2:32; Acts 13:47; 26:17-18).

God's faithfulness is thus established at every point in Luke-Acts: God has been faithful to the historic people of God, fulfilling through John and Jesus the promises made to their ancestors. The people of God itself, however, is being redefined based on the individual's acceptance or rejection of God's Messiah, God's Servant. The Gentiles who have been called by God's name may rest assured that God will be faithful to them, just as God was to Israel: the challenge will be, rather, to remain faithful to God.

The fulfilling of "Moses and the Prophets" in the church. Luke-Acts shares with other New Testament authors the conviction that the Old Testament finds fulfillment in the Christian movement in two ways: first, the story of Jesus fulfills the prophetic oracles of God; second, the followers of Jesus fulfill the essence of God's law. With regard to the former, Luke makes an important contribution by showing how the Old Testament Scriptures continued to be fulfilled as the church took up and expanded its mission. With regard to the latter, Luke shares with other early Christian authors the conviction that the prophets elevated what was most essential in Torah, such that attention to the "weightier matters" of mercy, compassion and social justice is really what God values and what God requires of all God's people.

Unlike his Synoptic counterparts, Luke postpones any heavy emphasis on how the Old Testament paradigms and promises are taken up in the life of Jesus until after the resurrection, again pointing to his conviction that those texts can only be understood in light of that crowning event. Especially programmatic in this regard is Luke 24:44-47, in which Jesus explains his earlier passion predictions:

> "These are my words that I spoke to you while I was still with you—that everything written about me in the law of Moses, the prophets, and the psalms must be fulfilled." Then he opened their minds to understand the scriptures, and he said to them, "Thus it is written, that the Messiah is to suffer and rise from the dead on the third day, and that repentance and forgiveness of sins is to be proclaimed in his name to all nations, beginning from Jerusalem." (NRSV)

Scripture is woven into the infancy narratives, expressing Luke's conviction that the births of John and Jesus fulfilled a host of Old Testament paradigms and predictions. Almost every clause in the songs of Mary, Zechariah and Simeon resonates with specific Old Testament texts, and the words of Gabriel consistently incorporate Old Testament promises. Luke also records how many new texts from the Old Testament, now being read messianically, were brought into the discussion of Jesus' significance by the early church. A prime example is Luke 4:16-21, where another Isaianic Servant Song (Is 61:1-2) is placed on Jesus' lips at the outset of his ministry as a sort of summary statement of what his work was all about. In Acts 4:26-30, Psalm 2, which functions prominently as a messianic psalm in early Christian discourse, is related specifically to Jesus' trial (in which the "kings of the earth" participated through the actors Pilate and Herod), execution and vindication. Psalm 16 (Acts 2:25-32) is brought forward as a witness to Jesus' resurrection, since it could not be applied to David who died, was buried and whose bones are still to be found in their place. What was originally an assurance that God would protect David from dying at the hands of his enemies in the first place is now read as a promise that God would not allow his anointed One to remain in the grave once dead.

The Torah, prophets and psalms speak not only to the life, death and resurrection of Jesus, but also to the preaching of the early church and its mission from Jerusalem to all nations, the fulfillment of which is the premise of Acts. This conviction that the Scriptures speak not only of Jesus but to the experience of those who receive the proclamation, persists throughout Acts:

All the prophets testify about him that *everyone who believes in him receives forgiveness of sins through his name.*" (Acts 10:43 NRSV)

To this day I have had the help from God, and so I stand here, testifying to both small and great, saying nothing but what the prophets and Moses said would take place: that the Messiah must suffer, and that, by being the first to rise from the dead, *he would proclaim light both to our people and to the Gentiles* [i.e., through his missionaries]. (Acts 26:22-23 NRSV)

Specific events in the life of Jesus and the church continue to be related to the Old Testament. Not only is Judas's treachery explained as the fulfillment of the prophets, but now finding a replacement for him is mandated by Old Testament texts (Acts 1:16). The experience of Pentecost, the outpouring of the Holy Spirit on the followers of Jesus, is interpreted specifically as a fulfillment of Joel 2:28-32 (Acts 2:16: "This is what was spoken through the prophet Joel"). The ancient oracles of God continue to speak to and be cited as fulfilled in the growth and movement of the early church as the Acts narrative unfolds, down to the climactic announcement of the missionaries' complete focus on a Gentile mission as the Jews in Rome reject the message, reenacting the pattern established during Isaiah's ministry (Acts 28:26-28; Is 6:9-10). In this way Luke continues and greatly extends the work of other early Christian leaders who saw in these correspondences between ancient oracle and current event the sure sign that God was at work in Jesus and the church.

"Moses and the Prophets" reveal not only God's will for history, worked out by God's hand, but also God's will for the people called by God's name, worked out by the obedience of each individual to God's law. Luke shares with Mark and Matthew the understanding

Figure 7.2. Remains of the Roman road connecting Jerusalem and Emmaus (Lk 24:13). (Photo courtesy of Daniel Frese [Bible-Places.com])

that God's Torah is kept only where mercy and love are the central interpretative values rather than holiness as separateness from the outcast, the unclean or the person in need. Luke underscores this point more boldly than Mark and Matthew by including two additional healing stories set on a sabbath. To the episode of the man with the withered hand (Lk 6:6-11), common to all three Synoptics, Luke also adds the stories of the healing of the crippled woman (Lk 13:10-17) and the man with dropsy (Lk 14:1-6). Luke is thus highlighting what the other Evangelists, and no doubt Jesus, taught with regard to keeping Torah. The real model of being in line with God's rhythm of life is not the rigid separation of work and rest (which distinguishes the Jew from the remainder of the world as well), but always to be engaged in mercy and acts of compassion—certainly never to withhold mercy and compassion for the sake of any rigid observance of a commandment. That automatically puts one out of order with regard to God. This emerges forcefully in Luke 13:10-17, where Jesus' critic addresses the crowd: "There are six days on which work is to be done—come and be healed on those days!" Jesus replies by reasoning from the "lesser" case to the "greater" case, a common form of argumentation in both Jewish and Greco-Roman discourse. If a person considers it permissible to untie an animal and lead it to water on the sabbath, it stands to reason that it is permissible to "untie" a person from an affliction. It is therefore false to think that withholding compassion for the sake of not doing work on the sabbath and thus resting with God is actually a true reflection of what God is doing. God is the merciful and compassionate One, and so mercy and compassion are never out of season, never a violation but always the fulfillment of God's commandment. Those who oppose Jesus' teaching on what truly puts a person in line with God's heart are here explicitly "put to shame" (Lk 13:17).

This view of the true keeping of Torah comes to expression again in Jesus' "Sermon on the Plain" first in his statement of the Golden Rule: "do to others as you wish as you would have them do to you" (Lk 6:31 NRSV). The negative version of this maxim functioned for Hillel as a concise summary of the whole Torah. Even more to the point, however, is Luke 6:36: "Be merciful, just as your Father is merciful." Behind this expression we can readily hear the core command of the Levitical Holiness Code: "be holy, for I am holy" (Lev 11:44-45). Whereas Matthew has restated this command using the terminology of wholeness ("Be perfect as your father in heaven is perfect," Mt 5:48), Luke has rewritten it to highlight God's mercy as the central characteristic of God that is to be reflected in the people of God.

This emphasis on mercy is highlighted in the special materials found only in Luke especially in the parable of the good Samaritan (Lk 10:29-37). Some have excused the priest and the Levite on the grounds that they were keeping themselves ritually clean for the performance of their duties in the temple. The priest, however, is specifically said to be "going down," that is, away from Jerusalem (in the Old Testament and New Testament, one "goes up" to Jerusalem), and so has no pressing reason to avoid ritual defilement. The only one who does keep the law, namely, to "love one's neighbor as oneself," is the Samaritan, the person with no connection to the Jerusalem temple or even its definition of the people of God. The Samaritan is presented as the model of doing Torah, and this example is one of wholehearted commitment to provide for a fellow human being in need.

Finally, we should consider the special Lucan parable of the rich man and Lazarus (Lk 16:19-31). For an extended period of time Lazarus sits at the gate of the rich man's house, but the rich man does nothing to relieve the heavy need of his neighbor. When the rich man finds himself in hell and quite without hope, he begs Abraham at least to send Lazarus to his brothers so that they may be warned of the fate that awaits them if they do not open their hearts to their neighbors and devote themselves to acts of mercy and compassion. Abraham replies: " 'They have Moses and the prophets; they should listen to them.' He said, 'No, father Abraham; but if someone goes to them from the dead, they will repent.' He said to him, 'If they do not listen to Moses and the prophets, neither will they be convinced even if someone rises from the dead'" (Lk 16:29-31 NRSV). This expresses Luke's conviction that "Moses and the prophets" clearly command mercy and care for the poor and warn of the consequences of the failure to do so. Again the essential mandate of the Torah and the prophets is named as love, mercy, compassion and relief for those in any kind of need.

The hallmark of the new community: Restoration of the sinner. Luke especially commends two qualities for the Christian community to embody. The first is the willingness and desire to reach out to the sinner who repents. The availability of repentance from sin and the possibility of a restored relationship with God is central to the proclamation of John the Baptist, who will "give knowledge of salvation to God's people in the forgiveness of their sins" (Lk 1:77; cf. Lk 3:3), which is the fruit of God's own mercy and desire to restore the fallen. This becomes even more prominent in the ministry and teaching of Jesus, who comes to "proclaim the acceptable time of the Lord" (Lk 4:19), the time when God turns in favor again toward God's people. Jesus regards his own ministry as especially one of reaching out to the lost and bringing them back to the knowledge of and obedience to God. To the

Figure 7.3. A traveler's earthen flask from the Roman period, featuring the concentric design of Roman pottery and two loops for a leather or rope strap. Such flasks, as might have been assumed by Jesus' audience to have been carried by the Good Samaritan, were used to carry water or wine, and smaller ones for carrying oil, on journeys. (Photo: Sam Renfroe; courtesy of Ashland Theological Seminary)

Pharisees who criticize him for eating with sinners, Jesus replies "Those who are well have no need of a physician, but those who are sick; I have come to call not the righteous but sinners to repentance" (Lk 5:31-32 NRSV). These last two words appear only in the version of the saying preserved by Luke, who thereby emphasizes Jesus' work in turning the sinner from sin to the ways to God.

Luke alone preserves the story of the penitent woman who anoints Jesus with precious ointment (Lk 7:36-50). Some have suggested that this is a Lucan reworking of the story of the anointing at Bethany (cf. Mk 14:3-9), such that what Mark and Matthew read as a messianic anointing before the passion, Luke reads as the grateful and lavish act of love of a forgiven sinner. Jesus' words about those who are forgiven much loving much seem to indicate that the woman has come not seeking forgiveness, but rather to express gratitude and love in the wake of experiencing forgiveness. What is perhaps most striking in this story is the Pharisees' failure to recognize the core value of restoring and welcoming the penitent, insisting instead on the separation of the righteous. Their understanding of what it means to be a prophet leads them to expect Jesus to repulse such a woman, and his openness to her calls into question his divine anointing in their eyes. Nevertheless, the reader knows that Jesus is the one doing the work of God in the story. The reader will be challenged to distance himself or herself from the attitude of the Pharisees who understand "righteousness" as the refusal to associate with undesirables and so become rather sparing in their ability to love God or people.

The three parables of chapter 15 pursue this theme as well. Again in response to the Pharisees' criticism of his welcoming sinners to table fellowship, Jesus points to God's heart for the lost, reflected in the earnest search of a shepherd for a lost sheep, a woman for a lost coin and a father's welcome for a lost and wayward son. Those opposed to Jesus' calling of the sinner (indeed, to God's attempts to restore the sinner) are put to shame at the end of the chapter. They are seen to be reflected in the elder son who refused to share in the father's joy, standing off at a distance and grumbling against the father's mercy (Lk 15:25-32). The story of the conversion of Zaccheus (Lk 19:7-10), who turns from legal robbery to become a benefactor of the community, and the repentance of the criminal on the cross (Lk 23:40-43) round out this very prominent theme in Luke, keeping the restoration of the penitent at the center of Jesus' ministry to the very end. This becomes the work of the church in what is in effect Jesus' commission to the church in Luke 24:47, namely, that "repentance and forgiveness of sins should be preached in his name to all nations." Acceptance of the outsider who turns from sin to the Lord is, of course, also to be mirrored by acceptance and restoration of the penitent brother or sister who offends within the community (Lk 17:3).

In sum, the church is to reflect the character and heart of Jesus, not by separating itself from sinners but by reaching out to them, calling them to repentance and newness of life, being the agent of God's continued restoration of the lost and wayward, and thus becoming the source of ongoing joy in heaven.

Christians and the proper use of wealth. If one hallmark of the Christian is a heart that reaches out to the lost, according to Luke, the other is the proper use of money in the care for the poor. God's own heart for the poor, the weak and the oppressed is evident as early as the song of Mary:

> He has brought down the powerful from
> their thrones,
> and lifted up the lowly;
> he has filled the hungry with good
> things,
> and sent the rich away empty. (Lk
> 1:52-53 NRSV)

The Lucan version of the Beatitudes, now with their corresponding woes, also attests to God's special concern for the poor, those who mourn and those who hunger, to whom God has given the promise of relief. To those who now are rich, who eat their fill and laugh, there are only the stark words: "you have received your consolation . . . you will hunger . . . you will weep" (Lk 6:24-26). God's heart is also at the heart of Jesus' ministry as Luke depicts it. Jesus came as the Isaianic Servant who has been anointed

> to bring good news to the poor . . .
> to proclaim release to the captives
>   and recovery of sight to the blind,
>   to let the oppressed go free,
> to proclaim the year of the Lord's favor.
>   (Lk 4:18-19 NRSV)

How does Luke instruct disciples to respond to Jesus? How are they guided to live out their repentance from sin and rededication to God? As early as John's preaching we find Luke already giving clear direction in this regard: "And the crowds asked him, 'What then should we do?' In reply he said to them, 'Whoever has two coats must share with anyone who has none; and whoever has food must do likewise' " (Lk 3:10-11). This theme resonates throughout Luke. In fact, Luke frequently brings sayings and parables that, in Mark or Matthew, speak to some other issue into the orbit of commending care for the poor and investing resources in the relief of the needy. For example, when a Pharisee takes exception to Jesus' disregard for ritual purification before meals, Jesus replies: "You Pharisees clean the outside of the cup and of the dish, but inside you are full of greed and wickedness. You fools! Did not the one who made the outside make the inside also? So give for alms those things that are within; and see, everything will be clean for you" (Lk 11:39-41 NRSV). In the Marcan and Matthean parallels, the climax is a broad redefinition of purity and pollution as a

general ethical matter (and in Mark the setting aside of dietary laws; Mk 7:1-23; Mt 15:1-20). In Luke, however, uncleanness is very specifically redefined as "greed and wickedness," and purity is the result specifically of giving aid to the poor. Luke uses the debate over ritual washing of utensils to reinforce his distinctive emphasis on how the believer is to relate to material possessions and the acquisition and distribution of this world's wealth.

Among the special Lucan materials we find the parable of the foolish rich man (Lk 12:13-21). In response to being summoned by someone to become arbiter in an inheritance dispute, Jesus points to the folly of storing up wealth as the world counts it but being found poor toward God on the day when the naked soul stands before God. How does an individual become rich toward God? While Matthew also counsels laying up treasures in heaven (Mt 6:19-21), only Luke adds a clear and specific direction how to lay up treasure in heaven: "*Sell your possessions, and give alms.* Make purses for yourselves that do not wear out, an unfailing treasure in heaven, where no thief comes near and no moth destroys. For where your treasure is, there your heart will be also" (Lk 12:33-34 NRSV).

This startling injunction to "sell your possessions, and give alms" in Luke 12:33 is reinforced and echoed in at least three other places. First, Luke concludes his discussion of counting the cost of discipleship with the saying: "So therefore, none of you can become my disciple if you do not give up all your possessions" (Lk 14:33 NRSV). Discipleship means laying no further claim to your possessions as your own, but putting them entirely into God's discretionary fund. Luke preserves the challenge to the rich young man, "Sell all that you own and distribute the money to the poor, and you will have treasure in heaven; then come, follow me" (Lk 18:22 NRSV). Since this same challenge has been issued to all disciples twice before, the hearer will not suppose that Jesus had directed it only at this particular rich person but rather to all who become part of the community of faith. Finally, we encounter the positive counterpart to this rich man in Luke 19:7-10. Zaccheus, a model convert, does not sell *all* his possessions, but he does sell half of them and give the proceeds as alms for the poor. The pattern of Zaccheus is perhaps given as a model of how Jesus' sayings about possessions and laying up treasures in heaven may be applied in everyday life. Jesus calls us to cut away excesses in order to provide for others' necessities, to "live simply so that others may simply live." In a way Zaccheus poses a much more potent challenge to the reader than the rich young man. While few if any could sell *all* their possessions and give to the poor, it would be possible, though difficult, for many to give away a large portion of their possessions and still provide for their necessities, making it all the more real a challenge.

Further reinforcing this line of exhortation, Luke includes sayings about how to give a dinner that will have eternal significance:

> When you give a luncheon or a dinner, do not invite your friends or your brothers or your relatives or rich neighbors, in case they may invite you in return, and you would be repaid. But when you give a banquet, invite the poor, the crippled, the lame, and the blind. And you will be blessed, because they cannot repay you, for you will be repaid at the resurrection of the righteous. (Lk 14:12-14 NRSV)

Jesus trades here on the idea of reciprocity: giving has no merit in God's sight as long as we spend our resources on those who will return the same to us another day. Treating the needy to hospitality and a meal, however, yields significantly greater rewards, though beyond the earthly circle of reciprocity.

This countercultural advice is immediately followed by Luke's version of the parable of the banquet (Lk 14:16-24). One of the guests at the dinner Jesus had been invited to exclaims "Blessed is anyone who will eat bread in the kingdom of God!" (Lk 14:15 NRSV). Jesus answers with the parable. While in Matthew the same parable (in a heavily redacted form) was used to address issues of salvation history, here the parable is used to explain that despite exclamations of blessedness about being in God's kingdom and other such religious platitudes, when the time comes to be called to the table those invited will be too occupied with worldly concerns to respond. In the context of a discussion of care for the poor, it is noteworthy that two out of three excuses have to do with buying and too much concern for worldly business to answer the host's invitation. The host therefore turns to new invitees: the poor and the lame and those without such pressing business. Jesus' use of the parable in Luke's version appears to show how the worldly minded simply cannot respond to the invitation of Jesus, so they will not "eat bread in the kingdom of God." This parable will be played out a little later in the rich man's sorrow at learning the cost of responding to Jesus' invitation (Lk 18:23).

Luke devotes much of chapter 16 to two parables (the prudent steward, and the rich man and Lazarus) that explore further the issue of the proper use of wealth and the danger of not using wealth well. The parable of the steward (Lk 16:1-8) is one of "accounting," hence it looks ahead to the final judgment.[12] The steward is faced with a crisis, namely, the fact of impending judgment. How will he plan for and survive that day of reckoning? He uses what he can, the master's accounts, to make friends for himself among his master's debtors so they will be indebted to the steward and obliged to return the favor by helping him out

---

[12]See, further, David A. deSilva, "The Parable of the Prudent Steward," *Criswell Theological Review* 6 (1993): 255-68.

later when he is in need (see "Patronage" section on pp. 334-37).

This is a strange parable, to be sure, perhaps one of the strangest attributed to Jesus in the canonical Gospels, but the moral lesson Luke preserves is clear enough: "the children of this age are more shrewd in dealing with their own generation than are the children of light. And I tell you, make friends for yourselves by means of dishonest wealth so that when it is gone, they may welcome you into the eternal homes" (Lk 16:8-9 NRSV). Those who hear Jesus' words are challenged to act with similar shrewdness in the face of the judgment that awaits them, namely, judgment before the throne of God.

How are they to do that? Luke's answer may not seem very clever to people of the worldly mind. They are to make friends through their use of their money. But what kind of friend will be able to welcome the hearers into "eternal homes." Who does Jesus have in mind? The second parable clarifies this question (Lk 16:19-31). Had the rich man opened his heart to Lazarus and relieved his want, then at their deaths Lazarus could have welcomed the rich man into heaven. As it stands the rich man did not act wisely in the face of the judgment, and so he was excluded. In Luke's eyes at least, the way to be "faithful with the dishonest wealth" so you will be entrusted with "true wealth" is to use money to relieve those in need, to make friends by sharing with the poor, sharing possessions being the essence of friendship in ancient ethical treatises.

This dominant Lucan theme of the necessity of relieving yourself of extra baggage by giving aid to those who lack daily necessities may shed light on Luke's version of the saying about the narrow gate: "Someone asked him, 'Lord, will only a few be saved?' He said to them, 'Strive to enter through the narrow door; for many, I tell you, will try to enter and will not be able' " (Lk

13:23-24). In Matthew we find two gates—a narrow one and a wide one, each opening onto a different vista, as it were. In Luke, however, we find only *one* gate through which *not* all can enter. What prevents some from being able to enter, even though they seek to do so? Is it because they cannot "fit" through the gate, quite possibly because of their baggage? This would certainly account for the rich young man, who becomes discouraged about entering into the kingdom on account of his wealth. This is further reinforced by the image of the camel trying to squeeze through the "eye of the needle," which remains easier than for the rich person to squeeze into the kingdom of heaven (Lk 18:25). Zaccheus again emerges as a model that solves the problem and shows how God can make possible the impossible. If this reading is correct, it bears a striking resemblance to the teaching of the *Shepherd of Hermas*. This early Christian writing was so well regarded in some areas of the church that it was included in a number of canonical lists and was included with the Epistle of Barnabas at the end of the New Testament in Codex Sinaiticus. Hermas has a vision of the building of a great tower, representing the church. Some stones are round and smooth, and cannot be fitted into the tower as they stand. An angel explains to Hermas that these are rich people, who must first have the excess trimmed through almsgiving before they can be fitted into the tower.

The teaching in Luke concerning the proper use of wealth will be reinforced by the portrait of the early church painted in Acts 1—5, where the perfect ideal of friendship (according to which "friends hold all things in common") is actualized.[13] Especially noteworthy is Acts 4:32-35:

Now the whole group of those who believed were of one heart and soul, and no one claimed private ownership of any

---

[13]See Aristotle *Eth. Nic.* 8.9.1

possessions, but everything they owned was held in common. With great power the apostles gave their testimony to the resurrection of the Lord Jesus, and great grace was upon them all. There was not a needy person among them, for as many as owned lands or houses sold them and brought the proceeds of what was sold. They laid it at the apostles' feet, and it was distributed to each as any had need. (NRSV)

Luke's teaching about wealth is not a matter of a salvation by merit, or buying one's way into the kingdom. Luke alone records the words of Jesus: "when you have done all that you were ordered to do, say, 'We are worthless slaves; we have done only what we ought to have done!' " (Lk 17:10 NRSV). It is, however, serious and sober counsel about being obedient to God and reflecting the heart of God, who is merciful and compassionate.

The church and the Roman order. Luke has a two-sided agenda as he depicts the relationship of the church to the Roman imperial administration. On the one hand, he is most intentional about depicting Christians as acting well within their legal bounds. They are presented as the legitimate heirs of Judaism, and so should also succeed to the privileges and toleration granted the parent religion, at least officially (mob hostility and the like would always work against the Jew and the Christian). The Roman authorities throughout Acts recognize this, serving perhaps as a set of precedents for Christians to use when they come under official scrutiny. They are also "just" and "innocent" of any crimes against the state or society. Throughout the narrative of Jesus' trial and execution, Luke stresses his innocence in the eyes of Roman authorities. Pilate and Herod agree that Jesus has "done nothing deserving of death," and that no base for an accusation is to be found in him (Lk 23:4, 14-15, 20, 22); the centurion concurs that "surely this man was

just" or "innocent" (Lk 23:47). Similarly in Acts, Paul's innocence in terms of Roman law will be repeatedly stressed (Acts 18:13-15; 23:28-29; 25:8, 18-19, 25; 26:31-32). Luke thus makes a claim on behalf of all Christians (largely to assure Christians themselves) that they are still responsible citizens and have not become "enemies of the Roman order."

While Luke is intent on showing that Christianity is not a revolutionary movement in the sense of being *actively* subversive or engaged in illegal practices, he does not allow Christianity to become another cipher for the civil religion. It is never purely and uncritically pro-Roman. As early as the infancy narratives Luke is establishing a contrast between the declaration of the good news of a golden age as promulgated by imperial propaganda and the true good news of God's salvation made available not in the emperor but in Jesus. Even in the New Testament document that is most intentional about depicting Christians as well within their legal bounds, the Christian movement remains subversive where the Roman ideology is concerned. In this regard the charge leveled against Paul in Acts 17:7 is a valid indictment of every Christian: "they are all acting contrary to the decrees of the emperor, saying that there is another king named Jesus" (NRSV).

The fourth Eclogue by Virgil, a poet in Augustus's court, is a frequently cited example of how the dominant cultural ideology presented the rise of the emperors as the dawning of the Roman golden age. The birth of an heir to Augustus's throne, which promised a smooth succession and continued peace, is greeted as the birth of the one who will restore the golden age. The Romans shared the view that history was divided into four periods or ages: golden, silver, bronze and iron. Each age was a step toward decline from the previous age. At the nadir, the iron age, the restoration would happen and the golden age would return. It is easy to see how this same model could fuel political propaganda (e.g., for Virgil and his patron, Augustus), and revolutionary and apocalyptic aspirations (e.g., for Daniel, whose iron age is followed not by a return to a golden age under a glorified Gentile king, but a new kingdom of God, ruled by God's holy ones). Luke presents Jesus as the One born to usher in the true golden age, the time of God's favor, in intentional opposition to the hopes and dreams that were being (at about the same time!) heaped on the heirs and heirs apparent of Augustus.

Another important source for the way Augustus and his reign were viewed in the provinces, one that preserves striking parallels to Luke 1 and 2, is the Priene Inscription.[14] The inscription is not completely preserved, so some scholarly reconstruction (based on other available decrees honoring the emperor and considerations of how many letters could fit in the missing spaces) has been necessary. The inscription praises Augustus's birth and rise to power as the provision of providence, indeed as its most generous and thoughtful gift that surpasses all previous favors and leaves no hope of ever being surpassed. Augustus is said to have been filled by this providence "with virtue for the benefit of humanity," a savior "for us and for those who come aft[er us]," one who "makes an end to war and [adorns peace]." His birthday ("the birthday of the god") is lauded as "the beginning of his good news (*euangelion*)," and therefore it is proposed that a new calendar be introduced into the province with that day as the beginning of the year.

In contrast to such propaganda, Luke declares that the birth of Jesus truly means "good news" (*euangelion*) to the people of Israel and peace for all people who respond to God's favor (Lk 2:11-14). Jesus alone is the Savior and Benefactor of the human race. In Jesus all former hopes for a time of blessedness find fulfillment, and his provision for deliverance and wholeness makes it impossible ever to hope for better. Jesus is the One who has the message of "the good news of the kingdom of God" (Lk 4:43), the reign of peace which shows the pax Romana up for what it is—in words placed on the lips of the chieftain of the British tribes, "to violence, robbery, and rapine they give the lying name of 'government'; they create a desert and call it 'peace' " (Tacitus *Agricola* 30).

SPECIAL EMPHASES IN LUKE

The death of Jesus in Luke-Acts. Does Luke share the view of most other New Testament authors that Jesus' death has significance as a sacrifice of atonement or as a ransom? When we look at Luke's version of Jesus' response to the status-seeking of the disciples, we find that the passage (now displaced to the Last Supper, Lk 22:24-27) lacks the clear redemptive emphasis that was found in Mark 10:35-45. When Jesus appeals to his own example as the model for his disciples, he does not conclude by saying that "the Son of Man came not to be served, but to serve *and to give his life a ransom for many*," but rather "but I am among you as one who serves" (NRSV). Does this suggest that Luke is trying to downplay the redemptive effect of Jesus' death, making his death more the death of the righteous One who dies innocently and so is raised up by God? Some say that this is the case, but Luke's shift of emphasis in Luke 22:24-27 could be due either to (1) a different tradition about Jesus' response to the disciples' jockeying for precedence (the whole saying in Lk 24:27 is markedly different from its parallels), or (2) a desire to keep the focus of the passage wholly on Christian discipleship rather than concluding with a christological statement that might blunt the impact. That is to say, the emphasis is left on Christ's mission as serving, which the disciples can imitate, not on ransoming, which the disciples cannot imitate.

---

[14]The text of this inscription can be found in F. W. Danker, *Benefactor: Epigraphic Study of a Graeco-Roman and New Testament Semantic Field* (St. Louis, Mo.: Clayton, 1982), pp. 215-18.

One important passage where a redemptive death for others is still very much present is Luke 22:17-20, the institution of the Lord's Supper. Unfortunately, this passage is full of textual problems, but most of these involve attempts to conform the strange order of the meal (cup, bread, cup again) to the more typical order of bread and cup known from the other Gospels, from Paul, and from early Christian liturgy. Only D (Codex Bezae, well known for the license it takes with Luke and Acts), several early Latin versions and one Syriac version actually omit the relevant words concerning the body "given for you" and the blood "poured out for you," and so the text is probably best retained in its longest form as a witness to Luke's comfort with the redemptive overtones of the death of Jesus.

Worthy of strong consideration, however, is the near-complete lack of an interpretation of the death of Jesus as an atoning sacrifice in the evangelistic sermons of Acts. There, the death of Jesus is consistently the rejection of the righteous One, and the way to salvation is repentance from complicity in that rejection and a new acceptance of Jesus as the prophet like Moses whom God raised up as Lord and Messiah to bless the people by turning them from their "wicked ways" (Acts 2:22-39; 3:12-26). Forgiveness of sins is proclaimed through this man (Acts 13:38), but it is not said to come through his blood or explained with reference to a sacrifice. The only hint of a "ransom" soteriology occurs in Acts 20:28, where God is said to have "obtained" the church "with the blood of his own Son."

This again need not signal Luke's *rejection* of such an interpretation of Jesus' death, but rather it signals his interest in exploring other aspects of the significance of that death, for example, the significance of the rejection of God's righteous One for the redefinition of the people of God, of which the Gentiles now find themselves the larger constituency.

The Holy Spirit in Luke-Acts. Among the Evangelists, Luke is known as the theologian of the Holy Spirit. The role of the Holy Spirit is indeed prominent in Luke-Acts, appearing on the stage or referred to by another character no fewer than seventy times in the drama. Significantly, the Holy Spirit is more than twice as prominent in Acts (after Jesus has ascended) as in Luke (while Jesus is present in bodily form with the disciples).

Jesus is the mediator by whom others will experience the fullness of the Holy Spirit (Lk 3:16), being himself anointed with the Spirit for this purpose (Lk 3:22; 4:1, 16-19; Acts 10:38), and, indeed, having been fathered by the Spirit (Lk 1:35). The Holy Spirit is the best of all good things a person could—and should—ask from God (Lk 11:13). This gift will be poured out on all Jesus' disciples (Acts 1:5; 2:1-11). The Holy Spirit is the content of the divine promise intended, as Peter says in his first sermon, for all whom the Lord calls to himself (Acts 2:17, 33, 38-39). Wherever the word is proclaimed and people turn to God, there the Holy Spirit falls on the new disciples through the agency of the apostles (Acts 8:15-17; 9:17; 19:1-6). The Holy Spirit even falls on Gentiles who call on Jesus (Acts 10:44-45, 47; 11:15-16). It is this outpouring of the Holy Spirit on the Gentile Christians that provides the decisive evidence for God's full acceptance of them on the basis of their joyful reception of the word, and thus the position that the church must take on the question of whether or not Gentiles Christians must become Jews in order to be acceptable to God (Acts 11:12; 15:8, 28).

The Spirit is credited with having announced ahead of time how God would work out God's purpose for humanity, and forewarned of the resistance the agents of that purpose would meet. The Spirit testified to Judas's betrayal and the need to replace him (Acts 1:16), to the conspiracy of the "kings of the earth" (in the persons of Pilate and Herod) against God and God's anointed (Acts 4:25). The Spirit bore witness through Isaiah that ethnic Jews would not respond to God's invitation in Jesus, thus legitimating the Gentile turn that the early Christian mission took (Acts 28:25-26).

The Spirit continues to provide this ministry of foretelling in the early church, as when Agabus predicts the famine that would encompass the Mediterranean (Acts 11:28) and that Paul would be arrested by the Jews in Jerusalem and handed over to the Roman authorities (Acts 21:11), about which indeed the Spirit forewarned Paul elsewhere (Acts 20:23).

Prominent in Luke is the theme of the Holy Spirit's direction of the actors in the early Christian drama, the constant reminder of God's hand at work bringing to reality the divine plan. Thus the Spirit leads Simeon into the temple at the right time to meet and acclaim Jesus, whom Simeon identifies as the One whom God promised to show Simeon before the old prophet's death (Lk 2:27). The Spirit will lead John and empower his preaching (Lk 1:15). The Spirit leads Jesus into the desert to be tested (Lk 4:1). In Acts the Spirit's guidance becomes far more "intrusive" into the human sphere. The Spirit guides Philip to the Ethiopian official to convert him, then snatches Philip away to bring him to Azotus (Acts 8:29, 39). The Spirit instructs Peter to accompany the three men sent for him from Cornelius (Acts 10:19-20), thus orchestrating this important conversion of a Gentile to the faith. The Spirit takes an especially active role in guiding Paul and his team away from the provinces of Asia and Bithynia, leading them to preach in Macedonia and Greece (Acts 16:6-10). The story of the early church thus becomes the story of how God was re-creating the "people of God," and since God stood behind every move and development, the shape that the movement takes is thereby legitimated (at least for those "inside" the group).

Another major task of the Spirit is to empower and direct public testimony to God's activity among humankind. Thus it is the Spirit that prompts Elizabeth to confirm for Mary what God is doing in her (Lk 1:41) and Zechariah to declare the prophetic significance of the birth of his son (Lk 1:67). The Spirit will teach the disciples what to speak when they are brought before authorities to account for their words and deeds (Lk 12:12). The Spirit empowers the witness of the disciples to reach the ends of the earth (Acts 1:8), a work that begins powerfully at Pentecost (Acts 2:2, 17-18) and continues in the courageous testimony of Peter and the other disciples in the face of the hostility and punitive measures of the Jewish authorities (Acts 4:8, 31). The Spirit's empowerment is also seen in the selection and commissioning of Paul and Barnabas (Acts 13:2-4) and of the elders in Ephesus (Acts 20:28).

The Holy Spirit's fellowship is a source of joy (Lk 10:21) and comfort (Acts 9:31), but the presence of the holy also continues to be fraught with danger for those who approach unworthily. It is no longer a matter of physical defilement inviting the unleashing of the destructive power of the holy, but the defilement of the relationship the Spirit has deigned to have with human beings through lying in the presence of the Spirit of truth (Acts 5:3, 9), through slandering the activity of the Holy Spirit as the work of the unholy forces of the cosmos (Lk 12:10) or through mistaking the Spirit as a commodity to be traded and the means by which a person could increase his or her status in a community (Acts 8:18-24).

Luke never allows believers to drift into a focus on the charismatic in and of itself. He never allows them to become mere connoisseurs of the miraculous; he always calls them back to the doing of the will of God. For example, when the seventy sent out by Jesus return titillated by the fact that "Lord, in your name even the demons submit to us," Jesus responds soberly: "do not rejoice at this, that the spirits submit to you, but rejoice that your names are written in heaven" (Lk 10:17-20 NRSV). The Holy Spirit is indeed the gift that God seeks to give to all who ask, to all who

The Role of Women in Luke-Acts

Luke features the role of women in Jesus' ministry and the life of the early church more fully than the other Synoptic Evangelists. The witness of Simeon to the significance of the infant Jesus is paralleled by the testimony of the prophetess Anna (Lk 2:25-35, 36-38). Jairus' daughter is counterpoised by the widow's son (Lk 7:11-14), and Jesus responds to the grief of a mother as well as that of a father. This complementarity extends even to the examination and demise of Sapphira along with her husband: she was independently accountable for bearing accurate witness (Acts 5:1-11). It also extends to featuring women as models for discipleship in Jesus' parables of the lost coin (Lk 15:8-10), who exemplifies the joy that should be felt when a sinner returns to the paths of righteousness (and notably also exemplifies the joy of God and the angels at such repentance), and the persistent widow (Lk 18:1-8), a model for persistence in prayer.

A woman shows Jesus the love and hospitality that Simon the Pharisee ought to have shown (Lk 7:36-50). Women are the financial supporters of Jesus' ministry (Lk 8:1-3) and faithful witnesses to his suffering, burial and resurrection—indeed, they are the first to proclaim the resurrection (Lk 23:49—24:12). Priscilla is a teacher and coworker of Paul, who together with her husband Aquila was responsible for teaching the gifted orator Apollos "more accurately" about the faith he preached (Acts 18:1-2, 24-28). The fact that Luke names Priscilla first (Acts 18:26), which is certainly unusual, suggests that she was the more visible and prominent of the pair in public ministry.

The story of Mary and Martha in Luke 10:38—11:1 may address Jesus' view concerning the proper work for women to be doing. Women typically prepared food and served guests, and Martha expressed dismay that Mary would not conform to these expectations and help her in the kitchen (see figure 7.4). Jesus, however, confirms Mary's right to sit at Jesus' feet, that is, to take on the role of a disciple along with Jesus' male disciples. In so doing he also tries to free Martha from being preoccupied with those duties that cultural expectations have fixed in her mind as her proper concern and to join her sister in the circle of disciples. The presence of women alongside Jesus during his ministry and alongside the Twelve after his ascension (see Acts 1:14) testifies to the "success" of this parable: both women and men in Jesus' circle got the point.

"call upon the name of the Lord," but that gift is one that equips disciples for service and witness, not one that should feed spiritual power trips or self-aggrandizement of any kind.

The "Delay of the Second Coming" in Luke. In Luke's account of Jesus' teaching, there is a pronounced emphasis on combating expectations of God's final intervention happening immediately. This would have been quite appropriate in the context of Jesus' own ministry, since ancient people typically looked for a person identified as the Messiah to act at once to bring about God's purposes for the nation of Israel, leading the nation in a successful revolt against the Gentile overlords and restoring political independence. It was also quite appropriate for Luke's context of ministry, as the church had to adjust its expectations concerning the length of the interim between Jesus' ascension and return. Synoptic comparison (or redaction criticism) is the tool that has unearthed this insight. First, the Lucan form of the parable of the talents (Lk 19:11-27; cf. Mt 25:14-30) reveals a specific interest in this

Figure 7.4. The reconstructed kitchen of a house at Qatzrin, with cookware and clay oven. In such a kitchen, Martha prepared a dinner worthy of her guests. (Photo courtesy of Qatzrin Park and Todd Bolen [Bible-Places.com])

question. In Matthew the parable occurs in the context of a discourse on the last judgment (Mt 24—25), and addresses the question of what will make for approval or censure on that day. Luke, however, presents the parable as addressed to those who "supposed that the kingdom of God was to appear immediately" (Lk 19:11). Now the parable speaks of the need for disciples to set their minds on persevering in fruitful labor during the interim period.

As we compare the opening of the parable of the wicked tenants in Matthew 21:33 with its counterpart in Luke 20:9, one observes that the Lucan form adds a small detail: "A man planted a vineyard, and leased it to tenants, and went to another country *for a long time*" (Lk 20:9 NRSV, emphasis added). This is a minor adjustment, but one that reinforces the "attitude adjustment" Luke is attempting to achieve among the churches.

Finally, when we compare Luke 21:8, Mark 13:6 and Matthew 24:5 (parallels from the "Apocalyptic Discourse" of Jesus), we find that, while Matthew and Mark preserve sayings in which Jesus warns believers to beware those who falsely claim to be the Messiah, Luke adds a second form of deception that might lead the believers astray. Not only are the believers to look out for the many who "will come in my name and say, 'I am he!' " but also for those who say *"the time is near"* (Lk 21:8 NRSV).

This survey of three passages in Luke's Gospel, comparing the precise wording in Luke with the wording in Matthew or Mark, shows that Luke was concerned not only to discuss end-time events but also to prepare the audiences for fruitful living in the time between the present and that second coming. In Luke, particularly in the way he has framed the parable of the talents, the interim period becomes not merely a time for waiting but a time for fruitful service, for declaring the provision God has made for every nation, and for laying up treasures in heaven. In this way redaction analysis can make us aware of a distinctive concern of a particular Gospel. The small variations are not insignificant, nor are they to be harmonized with the forms of the sayings in other Gospels, for they are clues to the pastoral purpose and message of the particular Evangelist.

CULTURAL AWARENESS
Luke and Patronage

Luke is clearly aware of patronage and reciprocity relationships and expectations, and not merely from the statement in Luke 22:25 that in the Gentile world, "those in authority over them are called benefactors." How does knowledge of the workings of patronage in the ancient world help us to become more sensitive and insightful readers of Luke's Gospel? More than any other Gospel, God's favor is underscored in Luke. The infancy narratives abound with the phrases "you have found favor with God" and "God has looked favorably" (Lk 1:25, 28, 30). Throughout, God is portrayed as the Patron whose favor and benefits are sought in prayer, and whose favorable response to prayer is assured (Lk 1:13). God answers the fervent prayer of Elizabeth and acts to take away the shame attached to the barren woman; God shows favor unasked toward Mary, electing her to be the mother of the Son of God. Jesus will later teach his followers concerning prayer:

> Ask, and it will be given you; search, and you will find; knock, and the door will be opened for you. For everyone who asks receives, and everyone who searches finds, and for everyone who knocks, the door will be opened. Is there anyone among you who, if your child asks for a fish, will give a snake instead of a fish? Or if the child asks for an egg, will give a scorpion? If you then, who are evil, know how to give good gifts to your children, how much more will the heavenly Father give the Holy Spirit to those who ask him! (Lk 11:9-13 NRSV)

God's favorable reception of their petitions is assured, and God has prepared the greatest benefaction of all for those who ask. Whereas Matthew leaves this open ("God will give good things to those who ask"), Luke names this gift as the Holy Spirit.

The songs in the infancy narratives are primarily songs about God's patronage. On the one hand, they represent the response of gratitude to God for God's favor. Mary's Song begins with praise to God for God's gift:

> My soul magnifies the Lord,
> and my spirit rejoices in God my Savior,
> for he has looked with favor on the lowliness of his servant.
> Surely, from now on all generations will call me blessed;
> for the Mighty One has done great things for me,
> and holy is his name. (Lk 1:46-49 NRSV)

Zechariah likewise pronounces a blessing on God for benefits received:

> Blessed be the Lord God of Israel,
> for he has looked favorably on his people and redeemed them.
> He has raised up a mighty savior for us. (Lk 1:68-69 NRSV)

These songs, however, also tell us how God's patronage works and to whom it is directed. Mary's Song continues:

> His mercy is for those who fear him
>   from generation to generation.
> He has shown strength with his arm;
>   he has scattered the proud in the thoughts of their hearts.
> He has brought down the powerful from their thrones,
>   and lifted up the lowly;
> he has filled the hungry with good things,
>   and sent the rich away empty.
> He has helped his servant Israel. (Lk 1:50-54 NRSV)

God's patronage is directed not toward human elites but the human poor, the non-elites who suffer want and hunger, over whom the mighty exercise their power. God is celebrated in this song specifically as the patron of the weak and the poor, a portrait that ties in very closely with Luke's overall emphasis on caring for the poor. God is also celebrated as the trustworthy Patron of Israel in both Mary's and Zechariah's Songs, for God has brought the help God's client people needed so desperately.

Into this celebration of God's favor and beneficence, Luke 2:1 comes as a striking intrusion. Luke introduces here Emperor Augustus, the other contender for the title Patron of the World, who is hailed everywhere as savior and benefactor, whose divine worship is intended as a response of gratitude to match the magnitude of the emperor's gifts. Luke's nativity story is in many ways a counterclaim against the imperial ideology of the emperor as the vehicle of divine salvation. Jesus is the one who will bring salvation, whose birth heralds the coming of an age of peace and well-being:

> I am bringing you good news of great joy for all the people: to you is born this day in the city of David a Savior, who is the Messiah, the Lord. . . .
>   "Glory to God in the highest heaven,
>   and on earth peace among those he favors!" (Lk 2:10-11, 14 NRSV)

Jesus is God's answer to the pax Romana, the one whose advent brings "peace on earth." He is the one who is to be courted as the benefactor of the human race.

Luke 7:2-10 is singularly illustrative of patronage-brokerage-clientage relationships and roles, and the ways that networks of favor could be used to allow one person to get what (it is believed) another person has. This version differs significantly from the Matthean parallel in that the centurion never actually encounters Jesus except through mediators. Before reading on here, read Luke 7:2-10 and try to untangle the web of patron-client relationships that have been formed and are being formed in this passage. Ask yourself, Who has benefited whom? Who is seeking a benefit from whom? How are brokers being used in this passage?

The centurion needs a favor that only a deity can supply—a timely and miraculous healing. Having heard about Jesus' acts of healing, he considers Jesus to be able to provide this favor (whether on his own power or as effective broker of divine gifts). But how should the centurion, an officer of the unwelcome Gentile occupying force, approach a Galilean wonderworker to maximize his chances of securing this favor? Among his resources are Jesus' fellow Jews, whom the centurion has previously indebted to him by building a synagogue for the community. The time is right for them now to repay the favor with a favor—acting as brokers to secure Jesus' favor on the centurion's behalf. He asks the elders, those Jesus would most naturally respect and would be most naturally inclined to consent to do a favor, to present his petition. They do this for the centurion, adding the character witness that the centurion will be a worthy recipient of favor. The centurion further displays the respect he has for and the trust that he places in Jesus by sending his "friends" (members of the closer circle of his clients) to him with another message. Jesus is most impressed with the centurion's "faith"—the trust that the centurion places in Jesus' ability to connect him with divine favors—and grants the desired benefit.

Luke also has some challenging things to say about brokerage. First, he shares with other New Testament authors the conviction that Jesus is the one who mediates the favor of God. We gain access to God only through the Son, and apart from Jesus there is none who can secure for us God's favor: "All things have been handed over to me by my Father; and no one knows who the Son is except the Father, or who the Father is except the Son and anyone to whom the Son chooses to reveal him" (Lk 10:22 NRSV). Even more succinctly, Jesus claims that "whoever receives me receives him who sent me" (Lk 9:48). Entering into a relationship with Jesus as one's personal patron means that he or she now enjoys as a patron the One who is able to grant access to the highest Patron of all, namely, God.

In the context of this saying, however, the audience will have their expectations about brokerage turned upside down: "An argument arose among them as to which one of them was the greatest. But Jesus, aware of their inner thoughts, took a little child and put it by his side, and said to them, 'Whoever welcomes this child in my name welcomes me, and whoever welcomes me welcomes the one who sent me'" (Lk 9:46-48 NRSV). People were used to seeking the favor of greater or more powerful people in their area as a means of gaining access to even greater and more powerful patrons. The weak or little people, however, were never courted as mediators of God's favor, as brokers of greater patrons. This is precisely what Jesus is declaring. Those who welcome the child, the little one, the weak one, will in fact welcome Jesus. The brokers of access to Jesus are in fact the nobodies, the insignificant people, the ones the world holds cheap! What a reversal of the worldly mindset! Followers of Jesus are thus urged to care for these non-elites, these weak ones, because Jesus has conferred on them the honor of being Jesus' brokers.

We may observe in closing how the healing of the ten lepers (Lk 17:11-19) highlights the importance of gratitude as a necessary response, the sign of the honorable client who knows how to return honor and thanks for benefits received (cf. Lk 1:46-49; 2:20; 7:16; 18:43; 19:37): "one of them, when he saw that he was healed, turned back, praising God with a loud voice. He prostrated himself at Jesus' feet and thanked him. . . . Then Jesus asked, 'Were not ten made clean? But the other nine, where are they? Was none of them found to return and give praise to God except this foreigner?' " (NRSV). It is an odd story, for all ten—the honorable and dishonorable clients—are healed. Only one, however, is commended by Jesus, and that is the one who showed gratitude.

FOR FURTHER READING

Danker, F. W. *Benefactor: Epigraphic Study of a Graeco-Roman and New Testament Semantic Field.* St. Louis, Mo.: Clayton, 1982.

deSilva, David A. *Honor, Patronage, Kinship and Purity: Unlocking New Testament Culture,* chaps. 3 and 4. Downers Grove, Ill.: InterVarsity Press, 2000.

Lull, D. J. "The Servant-Benefactor as a Model of Greatness (Luke 22:24-30)," *NovT* 28 (1986).

Moxnes, H. "Patron-Client Relations and the New Community in Luke-Acts." In *The Social World of Luke-Acts,* ed. Jerome H. Neyrey. Peabody, Mass.: Hendrickson, 1991.

EXEGETICAL SKILL
Interpreting Parables

The parables of Jesus are perhaps the best known and most popular facet of the Jesus tradition, capturing the imagination of people from earliest youth and inviting the production of countless devotional books. But how should we interpret a parable? How might an interpreter approach them to unlock their meaning in the most reliable and authentic manner?

Since the early patristic era the allegorical interpretation of parables has been a favorite method, and can still be heard in sermons today. Augustine set the high water mark for this kind of interpretation when he interpreted the parable of the good Samaritan thus (found in his *Quaest. Evan.* 2.19): Adam went down from the state of blessedness (Jerusalem) to a mortal state (Jericho, representing the moon, which grows, wanes and dies, thus representing Adam's mortality). The devil and his demons stripped Adam of his immortality, beat him by leading him to sin and left him half dead (able to know God, and thus alive, but wasted by sin, and thus dead). The Old Testament Law and sacrifices could do nothing for him, but Jesus (the Samaritan) restrained sin in humankind (the binding of the wounds) and brought hope (oil) and exhortation to zealous improvement (wine). Through the incarnation (the beast of burden) Jesus bore up humanity and brought it into the church (the inn), entrusting it to the teachings of Paul (the innkeeper) and providing for its care the two commands of love, or alternatively, the promise of this life and the life to come (the two coins). Read this way the parable becomes a teaching about salvation history from the Fall of humankind down to the ministry of Paul and the founding of the church, and about the means to salvation.

Many readers and practitioners of this form of interpretation were, no doubt, impressed with the intricacies of theology that a parable could be made to reveal. Others, however, sensed that the parable's meaning was itself lost and buried beneath the veil of the interpretation. Toward the end of the nineteenth century, Adolf Jülicher published his arguments for rejecting the allegorical interpretation.[a] He was followed closely by C. H. Dodd and Joiachim Jeremias, who blamed the Evangelists for introducing allegorical interpretation into the reading of parable.[b] Dodd takes Mark to task, for example, for wrongly introducing an allegorical interpretation of the kinds of soil in the parable of the sower, which as a whole is merely meant to "conjure up a picture of the vast amount of wasted labour which the farmer must face, and so to bring into relief the satisfaction that the harvest gives, in spite of all."[c]

The interpretation of a parable became a search for the one point of comparison between the parable and the issue, situation or concept addressed by Jesus. Jülicher would have the interpreter seek a moral generalization. Jeremias and Dodd rightly urged interpreters rather to look first for the way the parable would have been heard in the life setting of Jesus' ministry, and how the parable posed a challenge in that setting. Jeremias and Dodd sought to recover the original form of the parable by stripping away any introductions, conclusions and interpretative remarks, which they held to derive from the Evangelists (although Dodd would occasionally find elements of original application still preserved by the tradition, e.g., the comparison of the response to John the Baptist and Jesus in Luke 7:31-35). Their focus, then, was on the interpretation of the recon-

---

[a]Adolf Jülicher, *Die Gleichnisrede Jesu*, 2 vols. (Tübingen: J. C. B. Mohr, 1988-1989).

[b]C. H. Dodd, *The Parables of the Kingdom* (New York: Charles Scribner's, 1961); Joachim Jeremias, *The Parables of Jesus* (London: SCM Press, 1954).

[c]C. H. Dodd, *Parables of the Kingdom*, p. 8.

structed parable, and they have been followed closely in this regard by John Dominic Crossan.[d]

A consensus began to emerge that (1) parables are not allegories, and all allegorical interpretation is to be avoided, (2) most if not all indications of a parable's original context are products of the Evangelist or tradition, and not historically reliable, (3) the interpreter nevertheless needs to investigate how the parable would have been understood by Jesus' hearers to arrive at an authentic hearing, and (4) a parable seeks to make only one point.

Scholarship is always performing self-checks on any consensus, which is one of its healthier operations, and points (1), (2), and (4) above have come under considerable fire. David Flusser conducted an extensive comparison of Jesus' parables with the parables told by rabbis (and preserved across the centuries).[e] He suggests that many of the interpretive contexts provided by the Gospel tradition are probably original, since, in the rabbinic tradition as well, parables are rarely free-floating, but more often connected with some question, incident or situation. This context has often become part of the fixed tradition of rabbinic parables. More recently Craig Blomberg has observed the regular use of allegory by rabbis interpreting or formulating their parables, suggesting that the reaction of Jülicher and his followers against allegory was too strong and sweeping. A strong case can be made by the use of these comparative texts that the Evangelists preserve Jesus' own "allegorical" interpretation in their interpretations of the parable of the soils and the parable of the wheat and the tares, and are not introducing a foreign method of interpretation to Jesus' more simple parables. Blomberg further argues that parables made one main point in connection with each of its main characters, a tenet that bears out quite well in his analysis of individual parables. Where scholars criticize Luke's interpretation of the parable of the unjust judge (Lk 18:1-8) as unoriginal, for example, they have focused on one point (the generosity of God, derived from a "lesser to greater" argument) to the exclusion of another authentic point highlighted by Luke in 18:1 (persistence pays off, the point learned from the examination of the widow's actions in the parable).[f]

Fundamentally at issue is the degree and nature of allegorical interpretation, and a concern not to import content foreign to Jesus' intentions for his historical setting. Augustine obviously violated this principle, bringing Paul into pre-32 C.E. Jesus speech. Nevertheless, a reading of the wicked

---

[d]John D. Crossan, *In Parables: The Challenge of the Historical Jesus* (New York: Harper & Row, 1973).
[e]David Flusser, *Die rabbinischen Gleichnisse und der Gleichniserzähler Jesu; 1 Teil: Das Wesen der Gleichnisse* (Bern: Peter Lang, 1981).
[f]Craig L. Blomberg, *Interpreting the Parables* (Downers Grove, Ill.: InterVarsity Press, 1990), p. 93.

tenants parable in which the tenants "stand for" the religious leaders of Jerusalem, the slaves "stand for" the prophets and the son "stands for" Jesus is almost inevitable but still quite in keeping with the life setting of that parable in the context of Jesus' conflict with other religious authorities. Since allegory already was a feature of Old Testament parables (e.g., Nathan's parable in 2 Sam 12:1-10 and the vineyard song in Is 5:1-7), it should not be surprising to find Jesus and the Evangelists using this less complex kind of allegory in the formulation and interpretation of parables as well. However, an interpretation of a parable should not impose arbitrary meanings that would have been foreign to Jesus' audience. The appropriateness of allegorical reading becomes a matter of degree: major symbols can represent some feature of reality, but minor details are not to be pressed into the service of allegory.

The history of parable research then suggests the following guidelines for interpreting parables:[9]

1. Seek to hear the parable from within the context of Jesus' ministry in first-century Palestine. What connections or associations would the hearers have made? What would have shocked them, given their social and cultural assumptions and relations? This requires attentiveness to the art of the parable itself, such as structure and parallelism, as well as investigation of the cultural and social realities that appear in the parable (e.g., inheritance rights, the vulnerability of widows, the role of a steward in a household, the relationships between absentee landlords and tenant farmers, and the like). These matters would have been self-evident to the first hearers, but we need to recover this assumed context with care and effort.

2. How does the particular Evangelist lead us to understand the parable? What clues for interpretation are given by the context provided by the Evangelist, which in some cases may indeed be the original context that was related as part of the Jesus tradition? What other clues for interpretation are offered, for example in the reactions of various parties to the parable? How might the Evangelist have adapted and applied the parable in light of his distinctive interests and pastoral concerns (redaction criticism is at work here)?

3. How are the hearers led to respond to the parable (try to think both of Jesus' original audience and the Evangelist's audience)? With a value judgment? With a summons to decisive action? With deeper understanding of the ways of God with humanity? With a call to emulation or nonemulation? Several of these may be at work in a single parable and might

---

[9]These are adapted from K. R. Snodgrass, "Parable," in *Dictionary of Jesus and the Gospels*, ed. Joel B. Green, Scot McKnight and I. Howard Marshall (Downers Grove, Ill.: InterVarsity Press, 1992), p. 598; and Dodd, *Parables of the Kingdom*, pp. 11-20.

be different for various sectors of the audience. Dodd rightly notes that "the parable has the character of an argument, in that it entices the hearer to a judgment upon the situation depicted, and then challenges him [or her], directly or by implication, to apply that judgment to the matter in hand."[h]

4. Check your interpretation against the rest of the preserved Jesus traditions, particularly within the Gospel where the parable appears. Is there explicit testimony elsewhere to the meaning or meanings you find in the parable?

5. Don't press the details as Augustine did. Parables are stories, and stories need detail to work. The details tend to be part of the medium rather than the message. For example, the robe, sandals and ring in the parable of the father and his two sons are the narrative accouterments of the son's acceptance back into the father's household, not symbols for righteousness, the preaching of the gospel and the wedding of the Lamb.

6. Dodd affirmed that "a just understanding of their original import in relation to a particular situation of the past will put us on right lines in applying them to our own new situations."[i] How does the challenge or insight that the parable introduced into its ancient context address the questions and issues faced by a modern disciple or community of disciples?

Because many parables are discussed in the course of these three chapters on the Synoptic Gospels, no additional examples are given here. Rather, you are invited to examine the interpretations of parables given throughout these chapters and to evaluate their appropriateness in light of the guidelines given above and in light of the issues raised in the history of scholarship. In addition you may wish to try this procedure on a familiar parable in the following exercise, using two or three critical commentaries to help you in your investigation.

EXERCISE

The Father and His Two Sons (The Prodigal Son)

1. Move toward a first-century hearing of the parable: what did it mean for the son to ask for his share of the inheritance from his living father? How would Jesus' audience regard a Jew's decision to travel to a distant country (i.e., leave Israel)? Who domesticates pigs, and how would the audience regard a Jew who associated so closely with such people, and with such work? What dynamics of honor and shaming are at work in the story, and how do these help to explain the audience's surprise at the father's

---

[h]Dodd, *Parables of the Kingdom*, p. 11.
[i]Ibid., p. 157.

extravagant response to the wayward son (and the unsurprising response of the older brother)?

2. What clues does Luke preserve of the original context of this parable in the life setting of Jesus' ministry? Is this a credible context, or does it sit in some tension that suggests that Luke has created an artificial setting? If it is credible, what point is Jesus making with this parable, and how would it speak differently to the different constituents of Jesus' audience? What correspondences exist between the parable and the people and positions reflected in Jesus' situation? For example, where will different sectors of the audience see themselves in the parable, and what message do they get? How well does the parable answer the challenges of that context (i.e., Lk 15:1-2), and what is its argumentative force in that context?

3. What is the impact the parable seeks to have on its audience, both in the life setting of Jesus and in the context of Luke's audience?

4. How well does the rest of the body of Jesus traditions preserved in Luke resonate with and thus confirm your conclusions about this parable?

5. Given your understanding of the parable in its ancient context, what challenge or insight do you perceive that the parable brings to specific questions and issues in your own context of ministry?

For additional practice, you can apply the same procedure outlined in this section to any of the parables in the Synoptic Gospels.

FOR FURTHER READING

Bailey, Kenneth E. *Poet and Peasant: A Literary Cultural Approach to the Parables in Luke.* Grand Rapids: Eerdmans, 1976.

———. *Poet and Peasant and Through Peasant Eyes: A Literary-Cultural Approach to the Parables in Luke.* Combined ed. Grand Rapids: Eerdmans, 1983.

Blomberg, Craig L. *Interpreting the Parables.* Downers Grove, Ill.: InterVarsity Press, 1990.

Dodd, C. H. *The Parables of the Kingdom.* New York: Charles Scribner's, 1961.

Jeremias, Joachim. *The Parables of Jesus.* London: SCM Press, 1954.

Snodgrass, Klyne R. "Parable," pp. 591-601. In *Dictionary of Jesus and the Gospels.* Edited by Joel B. Green, Scot McKnight and I. H. Marshall. Downers Grove, Ill.: InterVarsity Press, 1992.

Via, Dan O., Jr. *The Parables.* Philadelphia: Fortress, 1967.

LUKE AND MINISTRY FORMATION

Shaping a community of restoration. Luke's compilation of sayings and parables focused on the heart of God for the lost clearly indicates his desire to nurture the same heart among communities of disciples. The church that takes Luke's word to heart will be a community of mercy and love, actively seeking the restoration of fallen people, reflecting the character of the God who called the community together. Luke gives his successors, namely, contemporary Christian leaders, the ongoing task of building up the sort of community that can become a place for the healing of the broken. Only as individual church members are won over to the vision of a God who seeks and saves the lost, who heals the broken hearted, and who yearns to impart his holiness and wholeness to our fragmented and broken selves will a church fulfill its service to God and to the world.

One of the obstacles to achieving this end is our tendency within the church to mask our own fallenness and brokenness, to put on our best face at church, and not trust one another to help us seek God's full restoration of our own lives. We act like Simon the Pharisee, who may indeed believe he has little to be forgiven, and so we are not free to lavish love on others like the woman who knew she had been forgiven much and forgiven deeply (Lk 7:36-50). That story encourages us to face the sins that weigh us down, to own them so that we can be released from them and experience the freedom to express the love and gratitude that follows. It also directs the community of faith to respond to such vulnerability as Jesus did rather than as Simon did. That is to say, the community cannot respond to someone who would work through serious hurt or vulnerability to temptation by suggesting that such activity is out of place among respectable people. Only as the church takes on the character of a "Sinners Anonymous" group will we see deep, inner transformation happen.[a] When such a community ethos is in place, the church will become once again a haven for all who seek to flee from sin and the wrath to come, where those who have not yet encountered God's heart may find not condemnation but love, restoration and freedom from a harmful way of life lived apart from God.

Luke seeks to nurture a community that values and invests itself not only in facilitating the restoration of the sinner and the lost, but also in the liberation of those bound by cycles of poverty or oppression in any form (Lk 4:16-19). The parable of the rich man and Lazarus (Lk 16:19-31) and the example of Zaccheus (Lk 19:1-10) declare that we cannot be whole until we become sensitive and responsive to the needs of our destitute brothers and sisters. The plight of the poor is a social sickness, and as long as our hearts remain hardened to others in need, with our blinders on and our focus elsewhere, we ourselves participate in that sickness.

---

[a]Part of the success of Alcoholics Anonymous, of course, is due to the fact that all its members identify themselves as people in need of deliverance from addiction to alcohol, and to the fact that its members encourage and support one another in a most intentional way to keep each other from giving in to the craving for a drink. The organization, founded to a large extent on New Testament principles, can now teach much to churches that have lost that focus and energy.

Luke's Gospel, like the Fourth Gospel, gives more attention to the role of Samaritans in Jesus' ministry. The animosity between Jews and Samaritans is well documented in the New Testament (Mt 10:5; Lk 9:51-56; Jn 4:9; 8:48) and has deep roots in the history of Israel (the tensions and strife between the divided kingdoms of Israel and Judah, with their rival cult centers of Gerizim and Jerusalem; the diverging of the stories of Israel and Judah as each was subjected to a different experience of exile and return). Nevertheless, Samaritans are prominently featured in Luke's Gospel as exemplary models of discipleship (Lk 10:33; 17:16) and in Acts as the target of the Christian mission (Acts 8). In this way Luke provides a model for how Jesus' disciples are to look on those who are designated "enemies," who are "not our kind," who live on the "wrong side" of some set of tracks by the standards of ethnicity, religion, nationality, sexual orientation and so forth. Jesus and the early church looked at the Samaritans from the point of view of the plan of God, which sought the restoration of the house of David, of which the Samaritans—despite the strenuous objections of Jews—were nevertheless a part, and strove for their redemption and their inclusion. So as we continue to heed God's call to bring his salvation to all, we are boldly challenged to cross those humanly drawn boundaries in outreach and to look on each person not through the lens of any human prejudice, nor to respond to them in kind when they speak to us out of their prejudice (see Lk 9:51-56), but to seek their redemption in God's love.

Freeing believers from national ideologies. It was easy for people living in the first-century Mediterranean world to buy into the myth of their society, namely, the myth of the Roman peace. All the visible symbols of the deified emperors and the deified goddess Roma, the civic festivals and holidays built around the family of the emperor, and the public discourse about the great debt the world owed Augustus and his family conspired to lull people into believing in that ideology. Things have not changed much. Whether we live in China, Germany, Latin America or the United States, we are born and bred into an ideology that promotes and supports the values, powers and systems of that society.

Luke provides a paradigm for an essential task of the Christian leader: the clear articulation of a distinctively Christian ideology. This invites disciples to discover where the values and assumptions they have imbibed since childhood differ from God's values and purposes for humanity and for Christian community. In effect, this means liberating disciples from reducing their response to the Gospel to what fits neatly into the value structures, expectations and institutions of the secular society. Like Luke's readership, modern churches will be enabled to take up a revolutionary witness (though, also like Luke's communities, without bloody revolution). This is perhaps one of the most pressing tasks for American Christianity, whose distinctive history (with its ideology of the "Christian nation") has tended to reduce Christianity to a civil religion. Christians from around the world, however, can identify with this task just as readily—from disciples who confront the conjunction of Shinto and political ideology in Japan to disciples in Taiwan learning how to disentangle themselves from ancestor worship while still honoring their families, often at the cost of rousing significant disapproval and suspicion.

Money. A pastor need never be embarrassed to preach about money. He or she is only following Jesus' example, especially the example set in Luke's Gospel. Wealth is an even greater idol in the modern world than mammon was in the ancient world. This is, of course, a special danger in America, Europe and everywhere that new capitalist markets have arisen and global corporations established their presence, making the promise of wealth now so much more accessible to so many more people. Because of the idolization of the abundance of wealth, however, even people in the Western world who live at a level far above the well-to-do in third-world countries consider themselves and are looked upon by others as "poor." Within a culture that claims "more for me" it is difficult even to hear Luke's word "share with all."

Before an individual can respond to the Gospel like Zaccheus, he or she must unlearn the definitions of *enough* and *sufficient* that our society offers (if it understands these words at all) and learn a definition that is truly in keeping with human need rather than human wants and expectations. This is a difficult task when the entire advertising industry lives by training us to "need" more. We must learn that to love our neighbor as ourselves, we must use our possessions as much for our neighbor's good as for our own.

Luke is keenly aware of the divisive power of money. The hoarding of wealth cut off the rich man from Lazarus because the rich man valued money more than the life of his neighbor. Covetousness over an inheritance pitted one sibling against another (Lk 12:13-15)—they valued money more than kinship. For years Zaccheus was cut off from his fellow Jews on account of his valuing of money over solidarity with his people. How many close relationships are destroyed over money? How much bitterness and tension creep into a relationship or even into the church through competition for control over how money is spent? Luke's solution is simple, from a theoretical standpoint. A Christian's wealth belongs to the Lord, to be used as the Lord directs for the good of all rather than the good of the "owner." This attitude enabled the quality of fellowship found in the early church, the realization of God's desires for human community (Acts 2:42-47; 4:32-37). Ultimately the true good of the one can only be achieved in concert with the good of all.

Prayer. Luke underscores the importance of prayer and waiting on the Lord throughout both volumes, sounding a reminder to pastors and laity that is always timely. Jesus prays throughout the Gospel at key points in his life and ministry: he prays at his baptism (Lk 3:21), at his transfiguration (Lk 9:29), in the garden for strength before his passion (Lk 22:39-46) and on the cross, both for others and himself (Lk 23:34, 46). He renews himself through prayer in the midst of his hectic ministry, withdrawing even from expectant and needy crowds who clamor for his attention (Lk 5:16). Jesus models the need to keep ourselves close to the heart of God and refreshed by God's presence so our ministry will flow from God's power rather than consume us. Jesus seeks God's guidance in an all-night prayer vigil before selecting the twelve (Lk 6:12), and prays for his own disciples to remain firm through times of testing (Lk 22:31-32). Throughout the Gospel, Jesus reveals himself as a person of prayer whose prayer life is so powerful that the disciples want to learn to pray from him (Lk 11:1).

Luke 11:5-13 assures us that God hears and is already favorably disposed toward us, even more than a good human parent toward his or her child. The parable of the unjust judge in Luke 18:1-8 encourages us to persist in prayer, for if a corrupt, human judge will eventually be moved to use his position to vindicate a persistent lobbyist, how much more will the good Judge of all vindicate his people. Luke does not turn these into blanket statements about how God will fulfill any prayer that we offer, however. Rather, he intends these sayings to spur us on to pray specifically for the Holy Spirit (Lk 11:13) and for justice (Lk 18:7)—two petitions which Luke says God will not disappoint. This leads us to devote considerable energy in our corporate and individual prayers to seeking the guidance and empowerment of the Spirit for the advancement of God's purposes, and to crying out before God on behalf of all who suffer injustice and oppression (e.g., our sisters and brothers throughout the world who suffer for the sake of their confession). As in Mark, prayer remains the way to find strength to overcome trial and weakness, and to remain firm in our loyalty and walk during the interim between Jesus' ascension and return (Lk 21:36; 22:40).

In Acts, prayer becomes even more prominent. Believers are always "devoted to prayer" (Acts 1:14; 2:42), and Christians frequently enjoy significant times of prayer together (Acts 12:5, 12; 16:25; 20:36; 21:5). In the face of the challenges of witness in an unsupportive society, the disciples find renewed courage and vision by means of praying together (Acts 4:23-31). Prayer always precedes receiving direct and timely guidance from God, often in the form of dreams or visions (Acts 9:11-12; 10:9). If we take the apostles as our models, then ministers will be first and foremost women and men of prayer. Just as the apostles, faced with a myriad of tasks and responsibilities, decided that prayer and proclamation of God's Word was their first priority, so Luke challenges the leaders of God's church today to make prayer the center of their ministry. If the busyness of ministry threatens to shorten or eliminate our seasons of prayer, we can be sure that the effectiveness of our ministry will be proportionately diminished. Ministers and other Christian leaders will also not only pray alone (a side effect of our privatization of religion) but will spend significant time in prayer together with other ministers, lay leaders and prayer partners.

Stability and the single mind. The story of Mary and Martha speaks in a timely way to an increasingly phrenetic and frantic society (Lk 10:38-42). Jesus points Martha—and all of us who are so very much like Martha—to the core necessity of life. If we possess this one thing, it gives life to all that we do; if we lack it, we cannot compensate for that lack no matter how much we do. The *one* needful thing is to sit at Jesus' feet, spend time in his presence undistracted and listen for his word. This is a hard word for many people, myself included, to accept. It is a hard word to believe in an active society where *doing* and visibly *achieving* are emphasized so strongly. But if anything must suffer this day, Luke says that it cannot be our spending time with God. We have books to read, committee meetings to attend and leaves to rake, but first and above all, we have to sit at Jesus' feet, wait on the Lord and seek God's face.

This word is echoed in the psalms of ancient Israel: "Wait for the Lord," "Seek God's face," "*One thing* have I desired, to gaze upon the beauty of the Lord and learn from God in God's temple" (Ps 27: 14, 8, 4). From a worldly point of view to "wait" on the Lord when there is work to be done seems like procrastination or worse. Jesus' challenge to Martha and to all who resemble her more than her sister is to reverse that mindset and to let the way we spend our time help us to be guided in all things by God's Spirit, not driven in all things by the demands of our studies, our congregations or our own ambitions.

Luke speaks not only to religious professionals but to everyone who would make progress in discipleship, to everyone who seeks to leave behind old pains and the patterns they have engraved on their mind and heart. Inner healing, formation in the image of Jesus, growth in discipleship: all depend on spending time in God's presence, sitting at the feet of Jesus. Ultimately, that is the place where lives are reordered, hearts healed, balance attained and stability found. Our hearts will never find rest until they rest in God, and rest means spending time resting in God's presence.

FOR FURTHER READING

Bock, Darell L. *Luke*. 2 vols. BECNT. Grand Rapids: Baker, 1994, 1996.

Cadbury, H. J. *The Making of Luke-Acts*. Peabody, Mass.: Hendrickson, 1999.

Fitzmyer, Joseph A. *The Gospel According to Luke*. 2 vols. AB. Garden City, N.J.: Doubleday, 1981, 1985.

Green, Joel B. *The Gospel of Luke*. NICNT. Grand Rapids: Eerdmans, 1997.

Johnson, Luke Timothy. *Luke*. Sacra Pagina. Collegeville, Minn.: Michael Glazier, 1991.

Marshall, I. Howard. *The Gospel of Luke*. NIGTC. Grand Rapids: Eerdmans, 1978.

Neyrey, Jerome H., ed. *The Social World of Luke-Acts: Models for Interpretation*. Peabody, Mass.: Hendrickson, 1991.

Nolland, John. *Luke*. 3 vols. WBC. Dallas: Word, 1989, 1993, 1999.

8

THE ACTS OF THE APOSTLES

Following the Leading of the Spirit

Luke wrote the Acts of the Apostles explicitly as a sequel to his Gospel, and we can only grasp his pastoral and theological program as we read both documents together. For this reason the chapter on the Gospel of Luke above dedicated a fair amount of space to themes developed in Acts, and this chapter on Acts will necessarily keep looking back to Luke.[1] In his preface to the "first book" (Lk 1:1-4) Luke expressed his desire to give the reader "certainty" about the instruction received in the Christian message. We often read this certainty as denoting historical accuracy, as if carefully researched detail and absolute factuality were the author's main objective. While Luke has acted as a reliable historian (by ancient standards, at least), the certainty that the author needs to give the reader is less about impersonal facts and more about the reliability of the Gospel itself.

Acts is an authenticating document. It locates the Christian movement squarely within the unfolding drama of God's chosen people, effecting a smooth transition from the usual authorities of Judaism to the new authorities of the new community. It locates the Gentile believers, formerly strangers to God's people

and the story of that people, within that unfolding drama of salvation. Rather than answering questions of mere antiquarian interest, Luke wants to explain for Theophilus and his fellow believers how they can be sure that they are part of God's plan, and that the Christian movement is the legitimate avenue by which God is bringing the Gentiles into God's plan and people. We look then for Acts to do much more than simply provide the data for a reconstruction of early Christian history. We look to Acts to provide a *sacred* history that gives the church identity after the work of the first generation apostles is essentially complete. We look to Acts for reflection and theology in the form of historiography, telling a Gentile church how it fits in with the people of God's own choosing.

THE GENRE OF ACTS: ACTS AND ANCIENT HISTORIOGRAPHY

The ancient reader of Acts would probably have understood this work as a piece of historiography. Indeed, the church assigned it a title that reflects the specific and well-established subgenre of the "acts" (*praxeis*) of an important person or group of people.[2] They would

---

[1]In an effort to be economical, topics treated fully in chapter seven will not be repeated here. Acquaintance with that chapter is assumed.

[2]David E. Aune, *The New Testament in Its Literary Environment,* LEC 8 (Louisville, Ky.: Westminster Press, 1987), p. 78. See the extensive study of Acts as an example of Hellenistic historiography, with an impressive defense of the historical reliability of Acts (in regard to the standards of ancient historiography), provided by Colin Hemer, *The Book of Acts in the Setting of Hellenistic History* (Tübingen: J. C. B. Mohr, 1989).

have taken it seriously as an attempt to reconstruct and narrate past events, and not merely as a piece of edifying fiction or a "romance."[3]

Acts shares a number of features with works of ancient historiography. It is these literary clues that would have led readers to identify Acts as part of this genre. First, Luke's prefaces would have raised this signal. Prefaces to historiographical works included the conventional topoi of "the praise of history, the claim of impartiality and the permanent value of the subject." Prefaces would often include "(1) requests and dedications; . . . (2) apology for defective style; (3) comments on the value and utility of history; (4) mention of predecessors (often critical); (5) assurance of impartiality; (6) use of appropriate methodology; and (7) reason(s) for choice of subject."[4] Luke 1:1-4, the preface to the two-volume work, fulfills many of these expectations and employs several of these topics (at least those numbered 1, 4, 6 and 7). Multivolume works employed prefaces at the beginning of each book "to recapitulate the previous book and summarize the next,"[5] something we see in Acts 1:1-2.

Comparing the prefaces in Luke-Acts with the two books of Josephus's *Against Apion* (technically an apologetic text that works mainly from historical topics) yields some amazing similarities. In the preface to *Against Apion* bk. 1, Josephus addresses his patron as the "most excellent Epaphroditus," provides a brief discussion of the reasons for writing (that is, what prompts the book), and announces his intention to set forward a true perspective on the Jewish people, specifically its antiquity and nobility. In the preface to book two, he again addresses the "most honored Epaphroditus," summarizes the contents of "the former book," and announces what book two will go on to do. These are parallel to Luke 1:1-4 and Acts 1:1-2 in every way.

Other features shared by Luke-Acts with ancient historiography include "synchronisms" (attempts to locate an event by different methods of dating, e.g., the reigns of kings from various different kingdoms, lists of people who have held a particular priesthood down through the centuries and the like) such as found in Luke 3:1-2, the use of a genealogy of Jesus in ascending order back to an illustrious ancestor (indeed, back to deity), which is typical of Greco-Roman histories, the use of summary statements as opportunities to effect smooth transitions between narratives, and an interest in how murky divine oracles worked themselves out in actual history.[6] We might also remember here how Luke includes himself as a participant in certain stretches of the history, since firsthand involvement was particularly valued in a historian.[7]

All this is to say that Luke signals his intention to write a work that would have been shelved under "nonfiction" in an ancient library, and specifically categorized under "historiography." We must, however, carefully consider what people expected of their nonfiction historiography in order to evaluate properly the historicity of Acts. There were several kinds of historiography:

1. historical monographs, which provide an orderly account of a single, connected stream of events, like the Peloponnesian War or the Jew-

---

[3]This alternative was suggested by Richard Pervo in his *Profit with Delight: The Literary Genre of the Acts of the Apostles* (Philadelphia: Fortress, 1987). While it is true that Acts contains many motifs familiar from poetic and fictional works, Lucian wrote that history needs to be written artfully and poetically (*How to Write History* 45, 53). Employing the elements of good fiction does not make the book fictional but rather a well-told history.

[4]Aune, *New Testament in Its Literary Environment*, pp. 89-90.

[5]Ibid., p. 89.

[6]Ibid., pp. 86, 121.

[7] See also the "I" passages in Ezra and Nehemiah, woven into the Chronicler's history (ibid., p. 101).

ish War, from their causes to their conclusion

2. the general history of a given people from their origins to the recent past

3. antiquarian history, which might focus on ethnography, local history, genealogy or geography, often embedded in a general history[8]

Acts would probably best be considered a monograph on the spread of the Gospel from Jerusalem to Rome, since this stream of events holds together the whole and is programmatically announced (Acts 1:8), summarized (e.g., Acts 9:31) and presented as the outworking of divine oracles at various points in the narrative (e.g., Acts 15:14-18).

On the one hand, the ancients valued truthfulness in a historical narrative. Cicero wrote, "the first law of history is neither to dare to say anything false nor to falsify anything true."[9] Nevertheless, the various subgenres of historiography could also serve ideological ends rather than strict historical interest. Josephus's *Jewish War*, for example, tries to demonstrate the essentially law-abiding and peaceful nature of the Jewish people, save for a few bands of revolutionaries. Josephus's *Antiquities of the Jews* and Hecataeus of Abdera's *History of Egypt* try to establish the antiquity and therefore superiority of a particular culture (in both cases in an environment of vocal detractors of their race). The Deuteronomistic history (Joshua through 2 Kings) presents history in the service of teaching an important lesson about fidelity to Torah and the Jewish way of life, aiming to shape the readers' behavior in the present. In short, ancient historians are frequently more interested in history for what makes history meaningful than concerned with "just the facts."

While some scholars dismiss the historicity of Acts entirely, close scrutiny of the itineraries in Acts against the itinerary reflected in several of Paul's letters (mainly Philippians, 1 Thessalonians and the Corinthian letters) suggests that these primary sources can confirm many of the details of Acts.[10] If Acts is shown to be largely (though not perfectly) reliable where it can be checked, we should not be too quick to dismiss its potential for yielding historical outlines for other pieces in the puzzle of early church history. We also cannot dismiss the ancient author and reader as naive with regard to the line between historical truth and creative fantasy. Truthfulness, as well as usefulness and entertainment value, was clearly a high priority among ancient historiographers.

Given the concerns and questions that generally motivate historical investigation, or at least are ancillary to it, it would be both anachronistic and reductionistic to insist on an absolute, one-to-one correlation between the narrative of Acts and the actual events. A reflection of "just the facts" is both far more and far less than Acts, as an example of ancient historiography, seeks to provide. It is a witness to the *character* of the early church and rooted in reflection about the early church, but it does not seek to be an impartial and disinterested history of that church. We may compare it with the Gospels. No one of them is *the* definitive history of Jesus, and their multiplicity attests to their deeper interests in Jesus' ministry than merely reconstructing facts. Acts is one witness, but it should not be privileged as the perfect witness. For example, if only one of our four Gospels came to us, we might be tempted to make of that one Gospel the absolute and infallible history of Jesus. But what a different and one-sided picture that would be when set aside the richness reflected in the four Gospels!

We will approach Acts, therefore, as a story

---

[8]Aune, *New Testament in Its Literary Environment*, pp. 87-89.
[9]Quoted in William H. Lucey, *History: Methods and Interpretation* (Chicago: Loyola University Press, 1958), p. 15.
[10]See Hemer, *Book of Acts*, pp. 244-76.

about the past that seeks to have a direct impact on thought and behavior in the author's and audience's present. Luke, first and foremost, selects what to include and what not to include based on his interests in that story and the usefulness of that story for his pastoral goals. Luke shapes the story to highlight what he perceives to be the patterns in that story, and these too are central to his overriding pastoral concerns. Luke interprets the flow and significance of the early church's story for those readers who have joined themselves to that story, and this guides his "historical" presentation. Several specific historical problems will be discussed in the course of this chapter, and these will further refine our understanding of the nature of the "history" Luke tells. It is important for us to realize up front, however, that he tells this story well within the generic expectations of the ancient historiographer.

THE SPEECHES IN ACTS

A specific question regarding the historicity of Acts centers on the speeches. As much as 30 percent of the book consists of speeches: evangelistic sermons in Acts 2, 3, 13 and 17; speeches in a council's deliberations in Acts 15; a farewell speech in Acts 20; defense speeches in Acts 22, 24 and 26. We might at first expect these to be verbatim reports of what each character said. There is no evidence, however, that the apostles' speeches were treated in the same way as Jesus' sayings, which were carefully preserved and handed down either within pronouncement or controversy stories (as in the oral traditions behind Mark) or independently of a narrative (as in most of the sayings in the Q stratum). Moreover, how could we expect Christians to learn, let alone preserve verbatim, the advice of Gamaliel (given behind closed Sanhedrin doors), the proceedings in Ephesus (the words of Demetrius the silversmith and the town clerk)

or the remarks of the flattering Tertullus, the lawyer who accused Paul before Felix?

There is a tradition concerning speeches and dialogue in ancient historical writing going back to Thucydides, an historian of the fifth-century B.C.E. In the prologue to his *History of the Peloponnesian War,* Thucydides writes: "I have made use of set speeches some of which were delivered just before and others during the war. I have found it difficult to remember the precise words used in the speeches which I listened to myself and my various informants have experienced the same difficulty; so my method has been, while keeping as closely as possible to the general sense of the words that were actually used, to make the speakers say what, in my opinion, was called for by each situation" (*War* 1.22.1). This philosophy persists into the second century C.E., as seen in Lucian's advice on the subject: "If some one has to be brought in to give a speech, above all let his language suit his person and his subject. . . . It is then, however, that you can exercise your rhetoric and show your eloquence" (*How to Write History* 58, LCL).

The speeches in the *History* reflect Thucydides' own style rather than the different styles of different speakers, and, on the whole, they were created by him—an act that he saw as completely consonant with his goals as an historian.[11] The speeches in Josephus's *Jewish War* likewise reflect Josephus's own style, showing them to be largely his compositions rather than verbatim reports of others' speeches. This practice of creative quoting extends even to reports of treaties, letters and inscriptions where historians' versions of these can be compared with the actual texts they purport to reproduce. The standard for ancient historiography, then, was that speeches must be appropriate to the setting, speaker and occasion. If at all possible, the content (the gist) of the speech must

---

[11]Aune, *New Testament in Its Literary Environment,* pp. 92.

The Kerygma—The Proclamation of the Gospel

The evangelistic sermons in Acts provide important witnesses to the basic form of the apostolic message, called the *kerygma,* the Greek word for "proclamation." This basic pattern is consistent between Paul, the sermons in Acts, and as Paul claims, across the witness of the apostles ("Whether then it was I or they, so we proclaim and so you have come to believe," 1 Cor 15:11 NRSV).

A survey of witnesses to the kerygma in the New Testament produces a macropattern that can be construed as the following:

A. These events are foretold in Scripture

B. Jesus is connected to an Old Testament type

B1. descendant of David

B2. "Prophet like Moses"

C. John the Baptist as forerunner

D. Jesus' ministry

E. Jesus dies

E1. for us

E2. according to the Scriptures

F. Jesus is buried

G. Jesus is raised on the third day

G1. according to the Scriptures

H. Jesus appears to the disciples, who becomes "witnesses"

I. Jesus is exalted by God

J. Jesus provides assistance to believers from this new position

K. Jesus will return as Judge

The earliest datable witness to the kerygma is 1 Corinthians 15:3-8, where Paul recalls "the good news that I proclaimed to you" (1 Cor 15:1), which was in turn something he received (1 Cor 15:3). He uses the technical terminology of "receiving" and "handing on" a fixed tradition, showing both the common ground here between Paul's proclamation and the preaching of the other apostles and the fact that this distilled essence of the good news predates Paul's preaching in Corinth. This pattern is fairly simple, focusing on the central events in the macropattern (E/E1/E2, F, G/G1, H). That Paul is aware of the other elements is amply attested throughout his letters. For example, Roman 8:31-34 combines elements E/E1, G, I and J (in the form of making intercession for us, Rom 8:34), and does so in such a way that suggests this is foundational material that Paul assumes his readers (who have not yet heard Paul preach) will already know. The importance of topic K in Paul cannot be overestimated: the return of Christ, together with the cross and resurrection, provide the fixed compass points for all of Paul's theological and ethical excursions.

Turning to the presentations of the kerygma in the missionary sermons (and shorter proclamations) in the first half of Acts, we can observe how each sermon invokes a selection from these topics:

Acts 2:22-36: A, B1, E, G, H, I

Acts 3:13-26: A, B2, E/E1, G, H, I

Acts 10:37-41: C, D, E, G, H, K

Acts 13:26-41: A, B1, C, E, F, G, H

Acts 4:10-11: E, G, (I)

Acts 5:30-32: E, G, H, I

The death, resurrection and witnesses remain central topics; connections with the Jewish Scriptures and tradition (combining A and B) and the topic of exaltation also emerge as vitally important. The weighting and development of the topics differs, of course, from sermon to sermon, but the repertoire of topics remains fairly consistent. C. H. Dodd described the *kerygma* as "a proclamation of the death and resurrection of Jesus Christ, in an eschatological setting from which those facts derive their saving significance," and the evidence continues to bear this out.[a]

The importance of these topics and the fact that they are representative not merely of Paul's preaching but of apostolic preaching more broadly can be seen from their pervasive influence on the discourse of the New Testament. The author of 1 Peter, for example, gives attention to topics A, E/E1/E2, G, I and K in the course of his letter, again in such a way that suggests the audience's familiarity with and acceptance of these topics as foundational elements of their faith. Mark's framing of the story of Jesus would be expected to give attention to the narrative elements, which it does as far as it goes (C, D, E, F, G), but Mark is also at pains to include A, B and, through the inclusion of particular sayings of Jesus, E1/E2, I and K (lending to the view that Mark's Gospel is a narrative expansion of the kerygma). This is not to minimize the differences in nuance between authors.[b] Paul, for example, uses the title "Son of God" to speak of Jesus' messiahship, whereas the speeches in Acts do not. Paul specifically connects Jesus' death with our deliverance from sin, while Acts does not make this connection explicit (though 1 Peter and Mark do).

Awareness of the elements of the kerygma help us read the New Testament in a number of ways. First, the reconstruction of the kerygma provides a window into the historical reality of early Christian evangelistic preaching in the decades prior to the appearance of our first written texts. Second, it helps address the historical-ideological question of the relationship of Paul's gospel to the Jesus of history. Some have taught that Paul replaced the message of Jesus with a mystery cult myth centered on Jesus' death and resurrection, and thus he became the "real" founder of Christianity. But it appears from the presence of the kerygma in many different streams of tradition that Jesus' death and resurrection were central to the proclamation of many different apostolic voices, including those who knew the Jesus of history, and this argues for a greater continuity between Jesus and the apostolic preaching. Third, it helps us rhetorically. Where we find elements of the kerygma invoked by a particular author, we see that he is really appealing to the fundamental logic of the Christian community, the foundational topics of Christian discourse that provide important common ground (and thus starting points for argumentation) between author and audience.

---

[a]Dodd, *Apostolic Preaching*, p. 24.
[b]See ibid., pp. 25-26.

be accurately conveyed, but the expression was left to the ingenuity of the writer.

This model accounts well for the speeches we find in Acts. Luke may have heard some of the speeches or had models of early Christian evangelistic sermons available to him.[12] He would have had to rely on reports of other informants for the proceedings of many of the speeches and trials, and would have been perfectly free to invent something appropriate where actual memory was inaccessible. Luke would have honored reminiscences of the general tenor of what was said, for example, central Old Testament texts or other topics used in evangelistic sermons, making his work a witness to the character and content (though not the exact words) of early apostolic preaching. He would have preserved critical decisions rendered by important magistrates, the sorts of charges brought against the Christian missionaries in Jerusalem and abroad, and the basic strategies of defense speeches. He also would have been free to apply his own rhetorical skill in the reconstruction of an appropriate speech conveying whatever information was known to have been spoken. Moreover, he would have been in keeping with the best of the historiographic tradition to use these speeches as a means to communicate his own understanding of the significance of the events being discussed, such as the death and resurrection of Jesus, the outpouring of the Holy Spirit, the significance of joining or not joining the community of disciples gathered around Peter (in the early speeches of Acts, including Stephen's speech), the significance of the calling and ministry of Paul (in the defense speeches), and the like.[13]

THE PURPOSES OF ACTS

Like the Gospels, Acts is not a timeless history of the early church, far removed from all the concerns of its own time and place in the ancient Mediterranean. Rather, the pastoral concerns of Christians around the Mediterranean guide Luke as he selects material and shapes the story that will help them understand where they stand in God's plan. Determining a narrative's purpose is a tricky enterprise. Letters give direct information about the situation being addressed and how the author hopes to affect that situation. A narrative does not so readily give clues as to its readers' questions and author's purposes. An important place to start, however, is with themes and concerns that recur throughout the narrative like refrains in a song. These point to the larger concerns of the author and thereby the purposes that guided his crafting of the narrative.

A major concern of Acts is the legitimation of the Christian movement and the precise form it takes as a predominantly Gentile movement. Luke consistently shows how God authorizes each step taken by the church, either through prophetic fulfillment or the specific guidance of the Spirit. In the evangelistic speeches, Old Testament prophecies serve especially to validate story of Jesus, a strange Messiah who suffers and is then vindicated through resurrection from the dead. Even more attention is given, however, to the fulfillment of divine oracles and commands in the church's mission to Jews and Gentiles.

As part of this task of legitimation, Luke seeks to explain the embarrassing fact that the bulk of Jews are not found among the alleged heirs of the promises, the church. Luke addresses this in the first seven chapters when he

---

[12]C. H. Dodd argues that Luke shows signs of having used source material that was originally written in Aramaic for the speeches in Acts 2, 3, 10 and 13 (*The Apostolic Preaching* [New York: Harper & Row, 1964], pp. 19-20). At the very least, these minisermons as Luke reconstructs them might indeed bear witness to the pattern of early Christian missionary preaching.

[13]On the speeches in Acts as an important means by which Luke conveys his theology and interpretation of history, see Aune, *New Testament in Its Literary Environment,* pp. 126-27.

shows how the official spokespersons of Judaism (the temple priests and the Sanhedrin) cease to speak for the one God, being succeeded in that role by Jesus' apostles. He also addresses it as he redefines the membership requirements of the people of God. He thus seeks to establish continuity—a clear succession—between the new community and the old, so that his readers will be secure in their hope of being grafted into the people of God. Luke's attempt to depict the Jerusalem apostles

narrative that the Christian movement is a legitimate development within Judaism, and, indeed, is *the* legitimate continuation of Judaism. Christianity is not a novel superstition but the heir of a religion which enjoys a claim to great antiquity, one of the factors that rendered a religion respectable. Moreover, Christians are not a subversive group, nor a danger to the Roman peace. Wherever Roman authorities had occasion to hear cases against the early leaders of the church, they recognized that the

Figure 8.1. The interior of the Julia Curia, the hall where the Roman Senate met, the center of empire. (Photo courtesy of Todd Bolen [BiblePlaces.com])

as standing wholly behind the Gentile mission (thus not reporting any disputes between Paul and Jerusalem authorities on this point) also supports this goal.

Acts also has a clearly apologetic purpose, not, as a few have alleged, as a legal brief for Paul's final trial but rather for the Christian movement as a whole. Luke provides much information about how outsiders—and Roman authorities in particular—view the Christian movement. Luke contends throughout his

case lay outside their purview. These figures should be a model for the authorities of all ages, and with the strong regard for precedent in Roman law, they might have been an arsenal of defense should a new generation of Roman authorities be made to inquire about the "followers of the Way."

I have not yet mentioned in this discussion Luke's desire to provide early Christians with a detailed account of their origins. This is intentional, *not* because Acts does *not* offer many re-

Luke's Geography

We noticed in the chapter on Luke that Luke organizes his two-volume work by constructing a very definite sense of movement. The Gospel moves to Jerusalem, emphasized by Luke's framing of so many of his "special material" within a lengthy journey toward Jerusalem (Lk 9:51—19:27). Acts begins in Jerusalem and moves out "to the ends of the earth," according to the programmatic statement of Acts 1:8. The centrality of Jerusalem in Luke's mental map is highlighted both in the amount of attention given to events in that city both in Luke 19:28—24:52 and in Acts 1:1—8:1 and in the conviction that God himself was behind the actions there (the death and resurrection of Jesus, the empowering of the disciples as witnesses).

Luke's sense of geography may also function as a sort of subtle, covert operation within his larger war on Roman imperial ideology. For Luke, Jerusalem is still the center of the world, since it is the center of God's activity in the world. From the point of view of Greece and Rome, the central events of redemption indeed happened "in a corner" (Acts 26:26), but Luke disagrees with such an imperial perception of geography. On the contrary, the gospel reaches Rome as it spreads out from the center (Jerusalem) to the "ends of the earth" (using a phrase borrowed from Is 45:22; 52:10). Rome, of course, views itself as the center of the world, and Luke reflects this to some extent since Acts climaxes with Paul's mission there. Nevertheless, there is still an unmistakable tension between Luke's emphasis on Jerusalem and the spread of the gospel as a movement out from this holy center to the periphery (of which Rome represents an extreme), and the dominant culture's view of Rome as the center of the world.

liable insights into that story but because Luke-Acts, as a whole, seeks to do much more than talk about the past. Its interest and purposes are not those of the archivist or antiquarian but of the pastor who knows how to use stories about the past to shape a community's awareness of its identity, its place in God's unfolding plan and its values.

THE STRUCTURE OF ACTS

We can easily divide Acts into episodes, thanks to the shifts of scene and action, and even larger sections thanks to Luke's use of summary statements and the like. The overall structure that gives shape to the whole of Acts could be conceived in a number of ways, but the most profitable seems to be to understand it as a working out of the programmatic statement in Acts 1:8: "you will receive power when the Holy Spirit has come upon you; and

you will be my witnesses in Jerusalem, in all Judea and Samaria, and to the ends of the earth" (NRSV). This yields the basic plot that then unfolds in greater detail. In the first seven chapters, the Holy Spirit moves mightily to empower the apostles' witness in Jerusalem. Chapters 8 and 9 expand that horizon to include Samaria and Judea. Chapters 10 through 28 speak of the movement of this testimony across the ethnic barrier of Jew versus Gentile and across the geographic barrier of the land of Israel to Rome, the center of the empire.

Luke's programmatic rehearsal of Old Testament prophecy in Acts 15:15-18 serves as a midcourse reminder of this overall movement:

This agrees with the words of the prophets, as it is written,

"After this I will return,
and I will rebuild the dwelling of David,

which has fallen;
from its ruins I will rebuild it,
and I will set it up,
so that all other peoples may seek
the Lord—
even all the Gentiles over whom my
name has been called.
Thus says the Lord, who has been
making these things known from
long ago." (NRSV)

Looking back to the Septuagint version of Amos 9:11-12, Luke sees the history of the early church announced beforehand in the purpose of God. Through the proclamation of Jesus as Messiah, God would restore Israel, hence the mission in Jerusalem, Judea, Samaria and even to the eunuch, "cut off" from God's people but now restored through the gospel. This also accounts for the mission to Diaspora Jews, with Paul always going first to the Jews, then to the Gentiles. After the work is done rebuilding the fallen house of David, the building of the people of God continues through the mission to the Gentiles.

THE MESSAGE OF ACTS

Acts is an authenticating story: Luke wants to show the legitimacy of the Christian movement as it had taken shape by the end of its first generation. Many non-Christians could point to the phenomenon of early Christianity and call its legitimacy into question. "It is a new Gentile cult, with none of the respectability of the ancient religions handed down from antiquity." "It is an illegitimate offshoot of Judaism, having lost all rootedness in the law of Moses, the core of the religion of the Jewish people—'Judaism Lite.' " "It is a band of disorderly rabble, followers of a failed revolutionary." "Whatever it is, God is not in it." Luke's narrative of Jesus' ministry and the church that grew up in his name paints a picture that shows how all these criticisms prove unfounded. God *is* behind this particular movement. It *is* the legitimate continuation of the ancient, historic people of God. It is *not* a scurrilous movement of subversive elements. In this section we will explore how Luke reassures his readers about the legitimacy of the movement they have joined on all these counts.

Who is the legitimate bearer of divine authority? The first seven chapters of Acts portray something of a power struggle between the temple authorities and the leaders of the Christ followers in Jerusalem. People entering the temple precinct encounter not one channel to God, but two—and these are clearly in competition with each other during these early chapters. The nature of access to the divine is different, as is the nature of the authority enjoyed by each group's leaders. Luke addresses here a classic question of legitimation—which group has God authorized to direct God's people?

Sociology of religion distinguishes three types of authority or legitimation. The first is *traditional* legitimation. An institution or figure has authority over the people because of its connection with a longstanding tradition. Such, for example, is the monarchy: a certain family has always ruled, therefore it is expected in each generation that a member of this family will direct the affairs of state. The temple enjoyed traditional authority. This was the house built long ago to be the place of meeting between humanity and the one God. Its priests have always directed the way worshipers come before God. Because they were the successors to the traditional offices, the priests and Sanhedrin held sway over the people. Another sort of authority is called *functional* legitimation. A person (or institution) has power or authority over the people because he or she got the job done (or the results of its efficacy are clearly seen). Paul uses this sort of legitimation for his authority over the Corinthians (see especially 2 Cor 3:1-3). Rather than claim the traditional authority of being appointed as an apostle, Paul points to the results of his ministry—the very existence

An Outline of Acts

Prologue, commissioning of the apostles and restoration of the Twelve: 1:1-26

The rebuilding of the "house of David": 2:1—9:31

> The Holy Spirit descends; the first major evangelistic crusade of Peter: 2:1-47
>
> Healing a lame man; the second evangelistic sermon of Peter: 3:1-26
>
> Opposition from Sanhedrin; apostles' prayer for boldness and renewed empowerment by the Holy Spirit: 4:1-31
>
> Transitional summary; Barnabas, Ananias and Sapphira: 4:32—5:11
>
> Transitional summary; confrontation with the Sanhedrin; concluding summary: 5:12-42
>
> Selection of the Seven; Stephen's ministry; Saul's persecution of the Christians: 6:1—8:3
>
> Philip's ministry; evangelization of Samaria and the eunuch: 8:4-40
>
> Saul's conversion and commission; concluding summary: 9:1-31

The firstfruits of the Gentile mission: 9:32—12:25

> Prelude: Peter's miracles: 9:32-43
>
> The Cornelius episode: 10:1-48
>
> Peter's defense of the outreach to Cornelius: 11:1-18
>
> Herod Agrippa's persecution of Peter; Peter's deliverance and Herod's death: 12:1-25

Paul's missionary journeys: 13:1—21:14

> Paul's first missionary journey: 13:1—14:28
>
> The Jerusalem apostles' decision about Gentile Christians: 15:1-35
>
> Paul's second missionary journey: 15:36—18:22
>
> Paul's third missionary journey; farewell discourse; return to Jerusalem: 18:23—21:14

Paul's journey to Rome: 21:15—28:31

> Paul's arrest and hearings in Palestine: 21:15—26:32
>
> Paul's journey to and ongoing work in Rome: 27:1—28:31

We could certainly construe the major sections differently. This outline highlights Paul's three missionary journeys, an understanding driven more by tradition than by inherent structural markers. We could, however, restructure the outline in such a way as to highlight Acts 15 as the climax to the movement of the plot begun in Acts 10, setting those chapters apart as a major section.

One striking observation that emerges from the outline of Acts is its parallelism with the Gospel of Luke. In both there is an emphasis on the "journey" made by God's agents, following God's plan (for Jesus, to Jerusalem; for Paul, to "the ends of the earth"). There are passion predictions along the way (see Acts 20:22-23; 21:10-14), fulfilled in the climactic arrest and multiple hearings of Paul (reminiscent of Jesus' hearings before both Herod and Pilate). Luke subverts the outcome by telling not of Paul's execution but of his triumphant proclamation of the kingdom of God in the heart of the empire.

---

of the Corinthian congregation—as all the support for his claim to authority that he needs. The third type of authority is supported by *charismatic* legitimation. A person or small group has special abilities far beyond what is considered natural and is thought of as having been especially anointed by God because of these supernatural qualities. Because of the evidence of direct divine anointing and the charismatic figure's promise that all who follow him or her will be that much closer to God's will and power, people willingly follow. This is the sort of authority exercised by the apostles in the early Christian group.

Luke presents the conflicts between the apostles and temple authorities as a struggle over which group has been anointed by God to direct God's people, to give definition to that people and therefore take God's people on in the next stage of God's "plan" (the "purpose of God" or "plan of God" being a major theme of Acts). In these early chapters Luke takes pains to show that God's anointing rested on the twelve and the community formed around them in Jesus' name. Because God's power and Spirit rest there, they constitute authentic Judaism. If the majority of ethnic Jews have gone a separate way, that is because, Luke would explain, they did not understand the succession that took place in Jerusalem around 30 C.E.

Acts begins with a succession scene strongly reminiscent of the passing of the torch from Elijah to Elisha. Jesus, the prophet par excellence empowered by God (a model established in Lk 4:16-30), is taken up into heaven while his disciples and companions look on.[14] Like Elisha, they will receive a "double portion" of the Spirit to carry on the work of God.[15] In chapter 1 the core of the new "people of God" waits for the promised power from on high (Acts 1:8); in chapter 2 the transfer of charisma occurs as God pours out the Holy Spirit on the disciples (Acts 2:1-4). This story establishes the charismatic legitimacy of the disciples' authority to act on God's behalf in the world. The reality of this anointing is demonstrated as they testify to Jesus in the native languages of the Jewish pilgrims that have come to Jerusalem

for Pentecost. In response to the powerful oration and the evident presence of divine power, thousands join the fledgling group (Acts 2:37-42). The "success stories" of the opening chapter of Acts, with thousands being won over and more joining daily (Acts 2:41, 47), are presented as a testimony to God's purpose and power at work in the early Christian church and mission. It was "the Lord" who added to the community's number daily.

The charismatic authority of Peter and John is enhanced as they publicly heal the man lame from birth (Acts 3:1-11), which gives them an opportunity to testify again to the salvation of God made available in Jesus. Here the conflict erupts in earnest. The temple authorities act against the apostles, shutting them up in prison and examining them the next day (Acts 4:1-3). They inquire specifically concerning the source of the disciples' authority (the "power" and "name" behind their actions) to do what they have been doing (Acts 4:7). Peter, whose anointing Luke explicitly calls to mind by saying he was "filled with the Holy Spirit" (Acts 4:8), uses the occasion to testify further to Jesus. The authorities see that something greater is at work in these men. Their confidence to speak before the Sanhedrin does not come from any special training in Scripture and argument (for they are "uneducated and ordinary men," Acts 4:13) other than what they have learned from their connection with Jesus and from the obvious fact that some spiritual power is moving through them (of which the healed man is evidence enough even for them, Acts 4:14).

The temple authorities, therefore, do the only thing they can—they seek to contain their influence as much as possible. They attempt to implement "damage control" by ordering the disciples not to proclaim the name of Jesus any more (Acts 4:16-18), but the

---

[14]Luke Timothy Johnson, *The Writings of the New Testament,* 2nd ed. (Minneapolis: Fortress, 1996), p. 222.
[15]In the sense that the firstborn son inherited a double share in an inheritance, not twice what the master had.

charismatic authorities cannot yield to the traditional authority. The disciples' commission comes directly from God, and they cannot disobey God in favor of obeying mere human authority (quite the stab at the high priest and his council; Acts 4:19-20). After this encounter God's authorization of the disciples is confirmed by a second impressive outpouring of the Holy Spirit on them (Acts 4:31). With these multiple scenes of God's pouring out of the divine charism, Luke thus reinforces for the reader that the true spokespersons for God in this struggle are Jesus' followers. Their lack of connection with the official religious structures of Judaism is more than compensated for by their direct empowerment by God.

Luke then shows the disciples exercising judicial authority within the new community. The strange story of Ananias and Sapphira serves to augment the reader's awareness of the apostles' charismatic legitimation. This unhappy couple drops dead in the apostles' presence because the apostles are saturated with the power of the Holy God, before whom no unrighteous person may stand. In the temple precincts the expectation of dropping dead only accompanies unauthorized or improper entry into the holy of holies. The location of that powerful yet dangerous divine presence is thus shown to have shifted. An aura of holiness is now clearly discernible around the apostles, arousing fear and awe in the people (Acts 5:11). So great is the public awareness of Peter's anointing with divine power that people expect even his shadow to heal the sick who are placed in his path (Acts 5:14-15).

The group continues to grow, and the influence of the disciples increases. So the temple authorities must take more decisive action. Luke attributes this to jealousy (Acts 5:17), showing again that the heart of the conflict is a struggle for authority in the eyes of the people as the duly appointed representatives of God. The temple authorities cannot resist the apostles, for God is clearly on their side. Not even

the prison doors will cooperate (Acts 5:19-20). The power of the officials (they are hardly "authorities" by this point in the narrative) has now eroded to the point that they cannot act violently against the disciples, so strong is their support base among "the people" (Acts 5:26). Once more, in a private hearing before the Sanhedrin, the disciples claim that they must obey God and not yield to the temple officials' demands (Acts 5:29). Their persistence in the face of threats and punishment lend great credibility to their claim that divine necessity drives their actions. Their final word to the council recalls the disciples' anointing with God's Spirit and introduces the criterion for having this anointing—obedience to the purposes of God in raising Jesus (Acts 5:30-32).

Luke then provides a very strategic and important scene, bringing one of the rivals and opponents of the disciples to center stage. Gamaliel settles the dispute with an ironic pronouncement that proves—from the lips of an enemy—the very point Luke is trying to make. If God is behind the movement, it will grow and no human power can stop it (Acts 5:38-39). Acts' ongoing success story of the gospel in every land will demonstrate that the Christian movement is authorized by God and is the legitimate development of God's people because it enjoys God's legitimation.

Although Luke signals the beginning of a new section at Acts 6:1, the Stephen episode remains closely connected to this struggle. Stephen makes explicit what the first five chapters have demonstrated implicitly: the temple with its priesthood is no longer the means to approach God. Indeed, Stephen goes even further, calling into question God's legitimation of the temple in the first place:

> Yet the Most High does not dwell in houses made with human hands; as the prophet says,
> "Heaven is my throne,
> and the earth is my footstool.

What kind of house will you build for
me, says the Lord,
or what is the place of my rest?
Did not my hand make all these things?"
(Acts 7:48-50 NRSV)

Earlier, the Jewish leaders had protected the temple and eliminated Jesus; now the people choose to reaffirm the sacredness of the temple by rejecting Jesus' witness, stoning Stephen outside the gate (Acts 7:55-60). Nevertheless, their efforts cannot negate God's authorization of the leaders of the new community, nor can their zealous persecution of those who dare question the divine sanctioning of the temple restore to its leaders the authority they have lost to the apostles. As Acts continues, the movements of God are all found within and behind the movements of these apostles, and the issue is thus settled in the plot of the narrative.

Jesus and the church in the will of God. As mentioned before, Luke portrays the development of the Christian movement as unfolding just as it should have, moving right on track with regard to the "plan of God." Every major step in the mission of the church is rooted in this divine plan (see especially Acts 2:23; 4:28; 26:22-23), mostly as that plan was revealed in Scripture, sometimes as revealed in God's hand at work through coordinating crucial events (for example, through giving simultaneous dream-visions in Acts 9:1-16; 10:9-16, 30-33). Through both means of "proof," Luke especially shows that the growth of the church from a Jewish movement to a universal movement took place by the express direction of God.

1. Jesus in the will of God. As an essential first step in anchoring the movement in the "plan of God," Luke sets out to show that the peculiar shape of Jesus' messiahship is in fact the precise form God meant for it to take from long ago. This interest began in the Gospel (e.g., Lk 24:25-27), but moves forward appreciably in the speeches and sermons of Acts.

First, the notion of a suffering Messiah was an especially difficult concept. Psalm 2, a "royal psalm," becomes a witness to the hostility that Jesus faced (Acts 4:24-28), while Psalm 118:22 ("the stone that the builders rejected") affirms the rejection of Jesus by the leaders of Jerusalem as part of God's plan, not a sign of Jesus' failure (Acts 4:11). The Servant Song in Isaiah 52:13—53:12 provides another aid for integrating Jesus' crucifixion into a conception of messiahship (Acts 8:32-35). In addition to providing specific quotations Luke also makes a general affirmation that the suffering of the Messiah is part and parcel of the Old Testament witness (see Acts 13:27, 29; 17:3, 11).

Second, Luke provides ample testimony from the Scriptures to the resurrection of the Messiah. In Peter's first sermon as well as Paul's sermon in Pisidian Antioch, Psalm 16 provides an especially important witness:

I saw the Lord always before me,
for he is at my right hand so that I will
not be shaken;
therefore my heart was glad, and my
tongue rejoiced;
moreover my flesh will live in hope.
For you will not abandon my soul to
Hades,
or let your Holy One experience
corruption. (Acts 2:25-27 NRSV)

Peter reasons that this cannot apply to David, as commonly thought, since David's corpse rotted in the grave; rather, it must point ahead to David's successor, the Messiah. Luke also introduces Psalm 110:1 (also prominent in Hebrews) as a witness to Jesus' exaltation to glory after his sufferings (Acts 2:34-36). Another key Old Testament text both for Luke's understanding of Jesus and for his redefinition of who constitutes the "people of God" is the prediction of Moses that "The Lord your God will raise up for you from your own people a prophet like me" (Acts 3:22; see Deut 18:18). The intentional pun on resurrection ("God will

The Picture of the Early Christian Community

Luke portrays the group that forms around the Twelve as a community that embodies the Greco-Roman and Jewish ideals of friendship and civic virtue (Acts 2:42-47; 4:32-36). We find in the early church no unsavory characters disturbing the peace of Jerusalem or promoting the social agitation and division that accompanied other messianic movements. Instead we find a model community resembling those most praised by ancient philosophers. The Christians are unified in mind and purpose, gathered around a common set of values and hopes. This unity extended to treating their goods as common property, making them a community of friends of the highest order. Aristotle said that "all things are common property for friends," and Luke emphasizes the achievement of this ideal. Indeed, this achievement also witnesses to the divine presence and power in the community! The early church also fulfilled the Deuteronomistic ideal of the elimination of poverty within the people of God (see Deut 15:4-11; cf. Acts 4:34). Moreover, the group was not a sect that cut itself off from the welfare of others but rather extended their generosity to the larger society. Luke closes his first description of the group by noting that "they had favor toward all the people" (Acts 2:47). This would be a more likely reading given the meanings of the preposition *pros* than we find reflected, for example, in "having the goodwill *of* all the people" (NRSV), which would be more naturally expressed by *para*.

raise up"/"God raised up his servant") especially allows the prophecy to be connected with Jesus, whom God has in fact raised up for the salvation of the people.

2. *Rebuilding the house of David.* While many early Christian writers anchor Jesus' ministry in the Old Testament, Luke takes the important next step of showing also how the mission of the church works out the preannounced purpose of God. This process begins with the interpretation of Judas's defection and the election of a replacement to complete the Twelve (Acts 1:16-18, 20-21), and presses on in the interpretation of the pouring out of the Holy Spirit at Pentecost as the end-time anointing of the Holy Spirit foretold in Joel 2. Already in the prophecy of Joel, Luke finds a warrant for the church's universal mission: "everyone who calls on the name of the Lord will be saved" (Acts 2:21).

As we have already seen in the chapter on Luke, Acts 15:15-18 is the central, programmatic statement that clarifies the plot of the book of Acts. In that passage James cites a somewhat altered version of Amos 9:11-12 as a summary of God's purposes for humanity. First, God would rebuild the fallen house of David, after which all the nations over whom God's name was invoked would be gathered into the reconstituted people of Acts. This is the basic outline of the plan of God that will be worked out in the church's story.

The first step in the church's mission, then, must be the fulfillment of God's promise to Israel and the restoration of the house of David. We return here to the crucial importance of the prophet like Moses, introduced by Luke in Acts 3:21-26. In this sermon Luke first affirms the manner in which God has been faithful to God's promises to Israel: "You are the descendants of the prophets and of the covenant that God gave to your ancestors, saying to Abraham, 'And in your descendants all the families of the earth shall be blessed.' When God raised up his servant, he sent him first to you, to bless you by turning each of you from your wicked ways"

(Acts 3:25-26 NRSV). The "sending" of Jesus here actually comes *after* his resurrection. The blessing becomes available as the Jewish hearers repent, turn from their sin (their rejection of Jesus) and commit themselves to follow the anointed One of God. This pattern also undergirded Peter's first sermon, when he gave the house of Israel its first opportunity to repent and reclaim their place in the people of God, acknowledging God's act in making Jesus "both Lord and Messiah" (Acts 2:36).

By finding themselves on the outside of God's plan, however, since they have been party to the rejection of the Messiah, the Jewish hearers must act positively to regain their place in the people of God. Here the second point of the prophet like Moses prophecy comes to the fore: "You must listen to whatever he tells you. And it will be that everyone who does not listen to that prophet will be utterly rooted out of the people" (Acts 3:22-23 NRSV). Thus Luke has discovered in Scripture an important criterion for belonging to the people of God—obedience to the prophet like Moses whom God would raise up, no longer understood as Joshua but now, in the context of God's eschatological fulfillment of God's promises, as Jesus. After the coming of this end-time prophet, Israel's boundaries are defined solely by positive or negative response to him.

Stephen's speech develops this paradigm further, reading Moses as a type for Jesus (Acts 7:25-37, 51-53).[16] Repeating the prophecy from Deuteronomy (Acts 7:37; Deut 18:18), Stephen correlates Moses' career with that of Jesus. Just as Moses was not recognized as God's agent of deliverance by the Hebrews (Acts 7:25), so Jesus was not recognized by his generation as God's agent (cf. Acts 13:27). After the people rejected Moses' authority as "a ruler and a judge" over them (Acts 7:27, 35), God sent Moses a second time to the people to bring them deliverance through his hand (Acts 7:35-

36). The description of Moses as one "whom they rejected" but whom God "sent as both ruler and deliverer" is clearly the type of Jesus. The verbal similarity with Peter's declaration is unmistakable—"this Jesus whom you crucified God has made both Lord and Messiah" (Acts 2:36). Just as Moses was rejected the first time by the people, so Jesus was rejected and killed by the people; just as Moses was brought back to the people to bring them God's deliverance, so Jesus was also raised up to bring blessing to the house of Israel (Acts 3:26). Just as the people rebelled against Moses in their desire to return to Egypt and idolatry, so the people reject and kill those who proclaim Jesus' resurrection and offering of deliverance. Finally, the end result of those who rebelled against Moses' authority was to "worship the host of heaven" (Acts 7:42), to become themselves pagans; so those within the house of Israel, therefore, who reject Jesus, are "cut off from the people."

Luke's answer to the question of the overwhelming minority of Jews who attached themselves to Jesus is that it is not God who has rejected God's people and so proven unreliable, but they who have "rejected God's purpose for themselves" (Lk 7:30). Luke has underscored this in the conclusion of Acts, having reduced the amount of the quotation of Isaiah 6:9-10 in Luke 8:10 (compare his source, Mk 4:10-12) and giving it full attention in Acts 28:25-28. There, the prophecy of Israel failing to perceive and heed the message of God is applied to the synagogue's response as a whole to the gospel, and therefore their rebellion against God and their falling away from the people of God. At this climactic point Paul declares again that "this salvation of God has been sent to the Gentiles; they will listen" (Acts 28:28 NRSV). The rejection of the gospel by most Jews is, for Luke, not a cause for questioning the legitimacy of the Christian proclamation as the true successor of the promises of God: it is rather a matter of pro-

---

[16]Johnson, *Writings of the New Testament,* p. 209.

phetic record. God's promises to Israel have not failed; rather, those who reject God's activity in his anointed One "judge [them]selves to be unworthy of eternal life" (Acts 13:46).

Negatively, Old Testament Scriptures emerge that support a definition of the people of God as constituted only by those who respond favorably to the message about Jesus, but positively the house of David indeed achieves restoration in the Acts narrative. As the apostles preach to the crowds of pilgrims gathered for Pentecost, they begin their mission to restore Israel. Luke leaves the story of the thriving church in Jerusalem to speak next of the mission in Samaria. In David's time Samaria, the territory of the ancient northern kingdom that split off from David's heirs after Solomon, was part of David's "house." As the Samaritans also respond favorably to the preaching of the apostles, the ancient kingdom of Israel (the ten northern tribes) is restored to the house of David. Even the conversion of the eunuch in Acts 8:26-40 has a special role in this story, since it is promised in Isaiah 56:3-5 that in the restoration even the eunuch, excluded from the people of God by Deuteronomy 23:1, would find a place in the people of God. Thus we see in this solitary figure the beginnings of the church's moving beyond the boundaries of the historic Israel to include all those for whom the Scriptures promised inclusion in the messianic age. With Acts 9:31 the rebuilding of the house of David is essentially complete (although Paul will continue to reach out to Diaspora Jews, scattered after David's kingdom's demise, and hence part of the promise): "The church throughout Judea, Galilee, and Samaria had peace and was built up. Living in the fear of the Lord and in the comfort of the Holy Spirit, it increased in numbers" (NRSV). In every region formerly belonging to David's kingdom, the reign of Jesus, the son of David, has been established and the people restored.

3. *"A light to the Gentiles."* Early Christian leaders and teachers subjected the place of Gen-

tiles in God's plan of salvation to intense debate, particularly regarding the acceptability of Gentile Christians within the "people of God" *as* Gentiles. The debate between Paul and Peter at Antioch (Gal 2:11-14) records but one window into this debate. The situation behind Galatians as a whole reflects the ongoing uncertainty in the church about what God would require of Gentiles to be incorporated in God's people. Did they have to become Torah-observant Jews to be saved in Christ? Was it necessary for them to observe the dietary regulations of Torah for Jewish Christians safely to have fellowship with them? Luke offers Gentile Christians the strong assurance that God has fully accepted them into God's people on the basis of repentance and belief in Jesus, and thereby Luke also offers a corrective to Jewish Christians who would continue to dispute this point.

Old Testament prophecy attests to the hope that the Gentiles would be called to worship the one God. This motif, announced in the opening chapters of the Gospel of Luke, becomes a dominant motif in Acts, where Luke underscores God's longstanding purposes to include the Gentiles in the people of God. In his first sermon, addressed to the Jewish pilgrims gathered for Pentecost, Peter invokes the promise in Joel that "everyone who calls on the name of the Lord will be saved" (Acts 2:21). In the context of Joel the promise was limited to those in Israel, for the prophet goes on to speak of those in Jerusalem who will be delivered. In the setting of the early church, however, *all* takes on its full universalist coloring, including Jew and Gentile. The universal scope of this prophecy emerges again in Peter's conclusion: "the promise is for you, for your children, and for all who are far away, everyone whom the Lord our God calls to him" (Acts 2:39 NRSV).

This universal scope becomes all the more explicit in the mission of Paul and Barnabas, who regard their activity as the fulfillment of Isaiah 49:6, a text also spoken over the infant Jesus' head by Simeon: "I have set you to be a

Figure 8.2. A statue of Artemis of the Ephesians (Acts 19:21-41), worshiped in Asia Minor not as the Greek goddess of chastity and hunting but as a fertility goddess. (Photo courtesy of the Ephesus Museum, the Turkish Ministry of Art and Culture, and Todd Bolen [BiblePlaces.com]).

light for the Gentiles, so that you may bring salvation to the ends of the earth" (Acts 13:47; see also 26:23). Jesus is the light that will enlighten the nations precisely through the Gentile mission of the church. Climactically, James interprets Amos 9:11-12 at the apostolic council as a promise that the restoration of the house of David (effected by the building up of the church in Judea and Samaria) must lead directly to the expansion of the people of God to include all the nations (Acts 15:16-17).

The question of the legitimacy of the Gentile mission, and the setting aside of the Mosaic covenant, will not be settled quite so easily as this, however. In addition to the appeal to prophecy Luke constructs an elaborate episode near the heart of his narrative that shows the hand of God unmistakably at work in moving the Christian movement toward Gentile inclusion. This is the famous story of the conversion of Cornelius and his household (Acts 10). In preparation for this step God sends Peter a dream-vision in triplicate (Acts 10:9-16), with the message that whatever God has declared clean must not be considered unclean by human beings. The previous day, while the centurion was in prayer, an angel had instructed Cornelius to send for Peter, telling him precisely where to find the apostle (Acts 10:3-6, 30-33). Moreover, the Holy Spirit alerts Peter to the approach of Cornelius's servants and instructs Peter to go with them, claiming also to have sent Cornelius's servants to Peter (Acts 10:19-20). As in the double vision that surrounded the conversion of Saul (Acts 9:3-6, 10-16), so here Luke presents God as orchestrating the human drama directly in order to accomplish God's purposes within that drama.

Hearing about God's message to Cornelius, Peter comes to understand the meaning of the vision he himself received: "I truly understand that God shows no partiality, but in every nation anyone who fears him and does what is right is acceptable to him" (Acts 10:34-35 NRSV). God confirms this and shows God's own acceptance of the Gentile believer as "clean" by pouring out the Holy Spirit on the whole household (Acts 10:45-48). The "circumcised believers" may be "astounded that the gift of the Holy Spirit had been poured out even on the Gentiles," (10:45), but Peter rightly draws the conclusion: "Can anyone withhold the water for baptizing these people who have received the Holy Spirit just as we have?" (Acts 10:47 NRSV). God had made the first move toward Gentile inclusion, and this becomes the warrant for Peter to identify this movement of the church in a Gentile direction as part of the plan of God (and an outworking of God's true and impartial character, as Peter confessed in Acts 10:34-35). Luke makes two crucial points through this episode. First, God does not honor the distinction between Jew and Gentile, and the value judgments attached to that distinction. Second, joyful hearing of the word itself cleanses the heart so that the Holy Spirit, which makes its home in no unclean thing, may enter in. This work of God makes it possible then for Gentile Christians to claim continuity with the historic people of God, and they indeed find themselves the heirs of that people.

The importance of this episode comes through in Acts 11, when Peter is called to account for his revolutionary move. After Peter testified to God's initiative in the episode (see Acts 11:17), the whole Jerusalem church acknowledged the decisive step in salvation history that God, not Peter, had taken. Luke emphasizes the ongoing guidance and power of the Holy Spirit, orchestrating the spread of the gospel to Gentile territories and Gentile audiences (Acts 13:2; 15:28; 16:6; 20:22), reminding the readers throughout that the Gentile mission is God's mission, not the mission of potentially misguided human preachers. The climax of this segment comes with Acts 15, the episode that brings the question of the Gentile mission to a head—and to resolution. After the more conservative Jewish Christians begin teaching Gentile Christians that they must be "circumcised according to the custom of Moses" and "keep the law of Moses" (Acts 15:1, 5), all the main characters assemble for this meeting of the minds. Peter opens the deliberations with a recollection of the lessons God taught the church in the Cornelius episode (Acts 15:7-11). Paul and Barnabas provide corroborating testimony concerning the work of God among the Gentiles on their first missionary journey (Acts 15:12). James draws the appropriate conclusion (Acts 15:13-21). In this episode Luke has effectively tied the Gentile mission to the Jerusalem apostles, the core around which God was forming and renewing his people.

The narrative of Acts, with its appeal to several key Old Testament texts and its emphasis on the explicit direction and guidance of the church's mission by God through the Holy Spirit, serves to legitimate the shape of the church at the time of Luke's writing. A funda-

Early Christian Missionary Preaching

Acts preserves two distinct kinds of missionary strategy. I say "strategy" because the texts of the sermons as Luke provides them are far too short to be considered complete speeches (the longest might take three minutes to read out loud!). Acts 2, 3 and 13 contain examples of an evangelistic strategy suited to a Jewish context. These speeches reflect a strategy of seeking to connect the content of particular Jewish scriptural texts with the figure of Jesus as prophecies that anticipate the shape of his messiahship, such that the ancient promises are now made available to God's people.

Acts 14 and 17 contain examples of the evangelistic sermon suited to a Greco-Roman context presupposing no familiarity with the Jewish Scriptures. Here, the strategy involves the presentation of the one God who stands above all those lesser shadows of divinity worshiped in the traditional Greco-Roman cults. In this regard early Christian discourse resembles the theology of many high-minded Greek or Latin philosophers, who were basically monotheists, seeing in the multiplication of deities merely facets of the one true God. The approach taken in these speeches is corroborated to some degree by such statements in Paul's letters as 1 Thessalonians 1:9-10: "you turned to God from idols, to serve a living and true God." In line with this strategy Jesus is the one who has made this God known and the agent of the one God's judgment of the world. Of course, the New Testament epistles make it clear that those who responded favorably to such an initial contact would then receive a thorough grounding in the Jewish Scriptures and in a Christ-centered interpretation of those texts (see also the textbox on the kerygma).

Both kinds of missionary sermon succeed in finding points of contact between the worldview of the audience and the message about Jesus, God's anointed—a certain cultural and philosophical sensitivity that ensures a meaningful hearing of the word.

---

mentally Gentile movement finds itself squarely in the plan of God and in the historic people of God, ethnic paradox notwithstanding.

Creating a proper Christian "image" for insiders and outsiders. Luke desires to reflect a certain picture of the Christian movement to the outside world. He may have hoped to accomplish this directly through outsiders reading his work, but he would more likely accomplish his goal indirectly by the way Christians would present themselves after digesting his material.

One main aspect of this is his presentation of Christianity as a development within Judaism—indeed as *the* form of Judaism standing most in continuity with the ancient expression of that faith, seen in Luke's claim that the Law and the Prophets attested to the Christian's

hope. Paul, for example, does not present himself as an innovator, an inventor of a new mystery cult or religious group. He consistently anchors his missionary work and his own faith in the historic expression of Israel's faith. Thus we read in his defense speeches: "Brothers, I am a Pharisee, a son of Pharisees. I am on trial concerning the hope of the resurrection of the dead" (Acts 23:6 NRSV). The debate between Christians and non-Christian Jews is relegated in the verses that follow to the level of the debate between the Pharisees and the Sadducees (Acts 23:6-9). In his further defense speeches Paul underscores the continuity between the ancient hope of Israel "laid down in the law and the prophets" and the way of life and belief espoused by "the

Way" (see Acts 24:14-15; 26:4-8, 22-23). Paul, the Pharisee of Pharisees who should of all people know genuine Judaism when he sees it, sees it in the Christian movement.

Such a presentation continues to foster the assurance of Gentile Christian readers that the community to which they have attached themselves enjoys great antiquity (which was highly revered by the more intellectually minded people of antiquity) and the legal status of Judaism originally sanctioned by Julius Caesar and further ratified by Augustus. While this did not guarantee the Gentile convert protection (for it was odious to the population to have their neighbors withdraw from the civic displays of loyalty and solidarity), it nevertheless served an important *internal* function. Often it is more important to regard oneself as legitimate than be regarded as legitimate.

A second feature of this image emerges in the response of authorities—especially Roman authorities—to Christians throughout Luke-Acts. Because no Roman authority actually declares a Christian guilty, these figures tacitly acknowledge the group's right to exist in peace, "without hindrance," like Paul at the end of Acts. In Jesus' trial Pilate repeatedly announces the absence of solid grounds for an accusation against Jesus, and therefore there was no basis for the treatment he was about to receive (Lk 23:4, 14-16, 22). Herod Antipas, despite his contemptuous treatment of Jesus, offers Pilate no insight as to Jesus' guilt (v. 15). The centurion in charge of the crucifixion detail, observing the way Jesus faced death, believes him to be "just" or "righteous" (*dikaios,* Lk 23:47), certainly not deserving a criminal's execution. In the early chapters of Acts the figure of Gamaliel offers the wise counsel concerning the Christian movement: if it is from God, no human authority can resist it, and if it is of merely human origin it will come to nothing like so many other messianic movements (Acts 5:34-

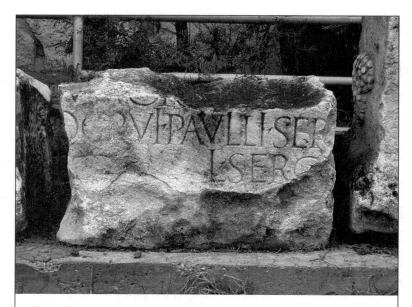

Figure 8.3. An inscription bearing the name of the proconsul Sergius Paulus, whom Paul and Barnabas encountered in Cyprus (Acts 13:4-12). (Photo courtesy of the Pisidian Antioch Museum, the Turkish Ministry of Art and Culture, and Todd Bolen [BiblePlaces.com])

39). He appears to be a model for how a sensible Jewish authority should respond to this messianic Jewish sect, in striking contrast to the rancor of the Sadducees in the Sanhedrin.

The career of Paul highlights the innocence of Christianity before Roman law. Sergius Paulus (see figure 8.3), proconsul of Cyprus, does not see Paul as an enemy of the Roman order (Acts 13:6-12), but rather receives Paul's message with faith. The authorities in Philippi are embarrassed by their treatment of Paul and Silas, and end up apologizing to them (Acts 16:35-39). Lucius Gallio, proconsul of Achaia, observes that the whole affair of Christianity is an inner-Jewish matter and not under the jurisdiction of a Roman magistrate since it was wholly concerned with Jewish faith and practice, and not disruptive of the Roman peace (Acts 18:12-17). The Jews from Asia, the enemies of Paul's mission who stirred up trouble for him from Pisidian Antioch on, accuse him of trampling Torah and defiling the temple, while Jewish authorities and lay persons alike conspire to assassinate him. However, when he stands before Roman authorities or the Roman-approved Agrippa II, he consistently receives the verdict of "innocent" (Acts 23:28-29; 25:18-19, 25; 26:31-32). The climax of these declarations comes from Herod Agrippa II, conversing with the Roman governor Festus and Agrippa's sister Bernice: "This man is doing nothing to deserve death or imprisonment. . . . This man could have been set free if he had not appealed to the emperor" (Acts 26:31-32 NRSV).

In the Roman legal system, precedents were eagerly sought out and were used to decide cases not strictly covered by Roman law. Pliny the Younger, who was governor of Bithynia and Pontus in 110-111 C.E., left us an immensely valuable correspondence between himself and Emperor Trajan, showing just how important and weighty precedents were. The outcome of each of these trials gave Christians, especially Gentile Christians, confidence of their legal status within the empire, although their usefulness as actual legal precedents to support their legitimacy in Roman eyes is dubious. By means of these stories Luke fostered a self-understanding whereby Christians would not think of themselves as automatically stepping out of bounds with regard to Roman law because they became Christian. Such a view is highly consonant with what we find in Romans and, somewhat wistfully, in 1 Peter, but rather distant from the picture of the Christian in the world that we find in texts like Philippians, Hebrews and Revelation.

ACTS AND HISTORY: PAUL AS A TEST CASE

Although there is only one first-century narrative of the story of the early church (as opposed to four narratives of the ministry of Jesus, which can serve as checks for one another), the letters of Paul provide a considerable amount of material that has served as a check for Acts. A person's own tendencies toward harmonizing the sources or the conflicts within the canon especially emerge in discussions of how the Paul of Acts relates to the Paul of the letters.

Luke's acquaintance with the correct terms for Roman administrators in the various provinces and the boundaries of those provinces during Paul's active period has gone a long way toward establishing his general credibility as a historiographer, at least in terms of the then-current standards.[17] Luke's acquaintance with Palestinian history shows occasional lapses (e.g., the date of the census of Quirinius and the date of the revolt of Judas the Galilean

---

[17]These have been confirmed in William Ramsey, *The Bearing of Recent Discoveries on the Trustworthiness of the New Testament* (London: Hodder & Stoughton, 1915); *St. Paul the Traveler and Roman Citizen* (London: Hodder & Stoughton, 1896); A. N. Sherwin-White, *Roman Society and Roman Law in the New Testament* (Oxford: Clarendon, 1963), pp. 86-93; and Colin Hemer, *Book of Acts,* pp. 101-220.

EXEGETICAL SKILL
Historical Criticism

It might be somewhat misleading to deal with historical criticism in a small section like this since, in effect, this entire book is written from a historical-critical paradigm. My goals throughout concur with the best intent of historical criticism for the interpretation of Scripture, namely, to bring to life as fully as possible (1) how the text was shaped by the situations and resources contemporary with the first-century Christians, and (2) how those first Christians heard its message and challenge within those situations. The historical-critical paradigm embraces many exegetical tools, including textual criticism, genre and literary analysis, analysis of the historical situation presupposed by the text, analysis of the words and grammar of the text, and reading a passage in light of its literary context and philosophical, cultural and theological background.[a]

Historical critics attempt to discern what actually happened in the history to which the text bears witness as well as in the circumstances of the production of the text. First and most basically, the historical critic faces a "task of elucidation."[b] Are there historical persons, events, institutions or artifacts that the text mentions and that we need to know in order to understand the text? How much can we learn about the realities of which the text speaks? Second, the student has the task of testing the historical accuracy of the passage under investigation.[c] How reliable is the data provided by the text about the historical realities it reports? Are there discrepancies between biblical texts speaking of the same event or phenomenon? Do we discover discrepancies when comparing the history reflected in the biblical texts with the history reflected outside those texts, for example, in other historians (Josephus, Tacitus, etc.) or inscriptions and the like? A third facet of historical criticism, and one that deeply engages authors of Old and New Testament introductions, involves discerning the historical circumstances of the composition and reception of the text. What can be known about the author, his or her situation, and the factors that motivated and shaped the composition of the text?

Historical criticism is not new. The second-century scholar Tatian faced it head on when he attempted to create one Gospel out of the four (his *Diatessaron*, the first harmony of the Gospels). The early critics Celsus and Porphyry used historical criticism to discredit the Christian Scriptures, pointing out contradictions between the texts or between a text and known history. In response early apologists often took up the strategy of harmonization. Augustine provides but one example of this as he reconciles the "six

---

[a]Edgar Krentz, *The Historical-Critical Method* (Philadelphia: Fortress, 1975), p. 2.
[b]I. Howard Marshall, "Historical Criticism," in *New Testament Interpretation: Essays on Principles and Methods*, ed. I. H. Marshall (Grand Rapids: Eerdmans, 1977), p. 126.
[c]Marsall, "Historical Criticism," p. 126.

days later" with the "eight days later" in the Synoptic accounts of the Transfiguration (*On Christian Doctrine* 3.35.50). Sometimes we can harmonize different accounts without doing injustice to either. The visits of Paul to Jerusalem in Acts 9—15 and Galatians 1—2 offer a good example of this.

At other times, however, a serious historical improbability results. For example, it is highly improbable that Jesus cleansed the temple twice, once at the beginning of his public ministry (as in John 2) and once near its climax (as in the Synoptics). Even within the three Synoptic Gospel accounts of this event we find irreconcilable differences. (Did Jesus follow Matthew's order of triumphal entry, indicting the temple, leaving Jerusalem, cursing the fig tree, or Mark's order of triumphal entry, leaving Jerusalem, cursing the fig tree, indicting the temple?) Since harmonization fails to treat each text with the same respect, we are given an invitation to probe more deeply into the precise nature of the New Testament authors' interest in the history about which they write, namely, how it was guided by their sense of the significance of that history. We shift our focus to seek in these details the clues to the authors' interpretation of why that history was important, eventful or paradigmatic. When we consider that the first aim of New Testament narratives was to elucidate the significance of Jesus and his teachings for his followers and their lives together, we will allow them greater flexibility in their shaping and arrangement of traditions rather than force on these texts our expectation that "truth" must also mean "strict historicity."

Historical criticism is not a wholly objective or value-free enterprise, however. We need to understand and scrutinize the presuppositions that guided many of its nineteenth- and twentieth-century practitioners. Ernst Troeltsch set the agenda for modern historical investigation of the Bible in the late nineteenth century. History, he argued, was the quest for the probable and was always open to criticism and correction. Historians would therefore approach the history narrated in Scripture with a degree of skepticism and doubt, treating Scripture as any other historical source that reflected the historical realities through lenses of different qualities. When examining that source alongside other sources from the period, the historian observes two main principles. The first is the principle of analogy: the historian's present experience determines what is probable and plausible for past experience. The second is the principle of correlation: historical facts have causes and effects within the natural fabric of society and the environment.[d] The effect of these principles, of course, is to exclude the unique historical event and the supernatural intervention.

Here historical criticism reveals its lineage. It is a child of the Enlightenment, that period of energetic intellectual ferment that gave rise to the modern scientific study of social and natural phenomena, forged with a

---

[d]Summarized from Krentz, *Historical-Critical Method*, p. 55.

dogmatic antisupernaturalistic bias. Admitting the supernatural into a student's explanations or reconstructions meant that he or she was not "playing by the rules" of scientific inquiry. Indeed, the scientific worldview and ethos legitimated the a priori bracketing of the supernatural as proper and intellectually responsible "scientific rigor." This process, however, merely served to authenticate and legitimate a naturalistic worldview over against a supernaturalistic worldview, and thus to continue to provide a grid by which our experience is limited and defined.[e] The fact that many people in the Western world go through their whole lives without witnessing a miraculous healing or other intervention of the supernatural is perhaps more a testimony to what the Western worldview will allow a person to see or experience than a testimony to the illusionary nature of the supernatural.

Krentz writes that "the critical biblical scholar will not only question the texts, but himself—his methods, his conclusion, and his presuppositions,"[f] and nowhere is this more necessary than in the presupposition that the historian must eliminate the possibility of divine action.[g] Rather than open the door to methodological anarchy, however, those who insist that the miraculous be taken seriously as a historical possibility also insist that special care be taken when seeking to establish the historical probability of the miraculous or supernatural. The investigator must especially weigh the reliability and number of witnesses as well as the contextual appropriateness of the miracle (something that readily sets the miracles in the canonical Gospels apart from those in the Infancy Gospel of Thomas, for example).[h]

The following may serve as a basic outline for the method of investigating the history told *by* the text (similar steps would be taken when weighing the questions surrounding the history *of* the text's composition):

1. Gather all the ancient sources that have bearing on the event or phenomena under investigation. It is vitally important to make use of extrabiblical evidence (other literary works, especially those by historiographers, as well as inscriptions, coins and archaeological evidence) to illumine the history with which the New Testament claims to intersect.

2. Evaluate how fully and reliably each source contributes to the picture of the past. At this point, Krentz very helpfully distinguishes between two avenues of interrogation[i] the student must pursue:

---

[e]I have explored the ideological functions of modern biblical criticism and the inappropriateness of the a priori denial of the miraculous in my article, "The Meaning of the New Testament and the *Skandalon* of World Constructions," *Evangelical Quarterly* 64 (1992): 3-21.

[f]Krentz, *Historical-Critical Method,* p. 54.

[g]Among those who call for such a modification are Krentz (*Historical-Critical Method,* p. 69); D. A. Hagner ("The New Testament, History, and the Historical-Critical Method," in *New Testament Criticism and Interpretation,* ed. D. A. Black and D. S. Dockery [Grand Rapids: Zondervan, 1991], pp. 83-91), Marshall ("Historical Criticism," pp. 134-35), and deSilva ("Meaning of the New Testament," pp. 12-21).

[h]Hagner, "New Testament," pp. 87-88; Marshall, "Historical Criticism," pp. 134-35.

[i] Krentz, *Historical-Critical Method,* pp. 42-43.

The Acts of the Apostles

a. External criticism: what are the "credentials" of the witness? Who actually produced the source text? How credible is this witness with regard to the material he or she claims to speak about? Has this person's witness been preserved intact, or tampered with by copyists and later editors?[j]

b. Internal criticism: what was the original sense of the text as it was heard or read by its first audience? What level of internal consistency do you observe in the author's treatment of the historical questions, both in its own right and in comparison with other sources?

3. Weigh the differences between and convergences of the available sources, taking into account the credibility and purposes of each source.

4. Present the most plausible reconstruction of the recovered "facts," or the history, reflected by the differing sources and the evidence for your decisions and evaluations. Part of this should include some accounting for the purposes or causes of divergences between sources.

Luke Timothy Johnson offers a paradigm of the sensible application of this model to the historical investigation of Jesus' life and ministry.[k] Here I will suggest a few exercises you might try as a means of orienting yourself to historical inquiry. The section "Acts and History: Paul as a Test Case" will probe some larger historical issues using these procedures. For readers wishing to practice historical-critical inquiry, try the following exercises:

1. Acts 17—18 and 1 Thessalonians 2:17—3:6 appear to narrate the same travel itinerary of Paul and his companions. What really happened in the team members' various movements between Thessalonica and Corinth?

a. Trace the movements of Paul and all the members of his team mentioned in Acts 17:1—18:5. Do the same for 1 Thessalonians 2:17—3:6.

b. Compare your outlines. Where do the itineraries agree? Are there any points where the outlines do not agree? Pay close attention to the movements of Timothy and Silas. At what point do they part company with Paul (in Thessalonica or in Athens)? At what point do they rejoin Paul? What movements would each member have to make in order to accommodate all the data in both accounts? (This is harmonization.) Is this a more plausible solution to preferring one account over the other?

c. Consider the credibility of both authors. What access would Luke have to this information, and how fresh would this information be (even if Luke writes in 62 C.E., the earliest possible date, but all the more if he

---

[j] From our study of textual criticism, we are already familiar with how a biblical text might come to be altered by later scribes. A famous case of the later corruption of an extrabiblical source is Josephus's "testimony" to Jesus (*Ant.* 18.3.3). While Josephus may well have mentioned Jesus and the movement that sprung up in his name, the declarations about Jesus being in fact the Christ, appearing to his disciples after his death and being the subject of many Old Testament prophecies are surely the pious addition of a Christian scribe. This baptizing of Josephus is akin to the baptizing of Seneca effected by the pseudonymous "Correspondence of Paul and Seneca"—scribes just could not leave their favorite Greco-Roman authors pagan!

[k] Luke Timothy Johnson, *The Real Jesus* (San Francisco: HarperSanFrancisco, 1996), pp. 105-40.

373

writes after 70 C.E.)? What access would Paul have to this information, and what credentials does he have as a "witness" to these data?

d. Formulate a hypothesis for the detailed travels of Paul, Silas, Timothy and possibly some other unnamed sisters and brothers between Thessalonica and Corinth, and support your evaluation of the evidence. If you can work with others, present your case and critique one another's cases.

2. In Acts 12:20-23, we read about the death of King Herod. This raises a question: how did Herod die?

a. First, we need to know which King Herod the text writes about. Was it Herod the Great? Herod Antipas, his son; Herod Agrippa I, his grandson; or Herod Agrippa II, his great-grandson?

b. Second, we need to gather all the relevant sources, which turns out to be two: Acts 12:20-23 and Josephus *Antiquities* 19.8.2.[1]

c. Third, carefully study each account separately. How internally consistent is each account? Compare the two accounts. Where do they converge? On what points do they differ? How do the points of convergence between both accounts help to establish a bare minimum of recoverable history? Which offers the more plausible explanation for the king's stomach problems? What are the different viewpoints of the death of Herod reflected in these accounts (in light of the larger depiction of Herod Agrippa in both works)?

d. Fourth, consider the aims of each author and the claims each has to providing an accurate depiction of these events. Consider, at this point, Josephus's claim to personal acquaintance with Agrippa II through sixty-plus letters, some of which attest to Agrippa II's review of Josephus's work (see Josephus *Life* 65). Who seems to be in the better position to know and more intent on passing on the "facts" of secular history? How much historicity can we accord Agrippa's death-bed speech in Josephus given his general approach to speeches?

e. Finally, dare to make a hypothesis concerning the circumstances and manner of Agrippa I's death. Again, if you are able to work with others, present your case and critique one another's cases. To what extent is the Acts account confirmed by extrabiblical sources? What remains unclear?

3. Acts gives three accounts of Paul's conversion/commission (Acts 9:1-9; 22:4-16; 26:9-18), and Paul provides a brief account of his own (Gal 1:15-16). Evaluate these sources and attempt to reconstruct what "really happened" on the road to Damascus to turn Paul from persecutor to preacher. Pay special attention to the experience of the men who accompanied Paul, the actual words attributed to Jesus and who gives Paul his commission.

---

[1]The latter text should be readily accessible in any seminary library or through an online resource, such as <http://wesley.nnu.edu/josephus> or <http://www.ccel.org/j/josephus>.

in Acts 5:37),[17] but Josephus, on whom we rely greatly for intertestamental and New Testament period history, will do as much. Moreover, in an previous exercise we have observed the discrepancies between Acts 17:10-15; 18:5 and 1 Thessalonians 3:1-3. While the discrepancies are rather slight, and while the similarities serve to affirm the basic reliability of the travel itineraries of Acts, we cannot ignore them either. We must be prepared both to affirm and to critique Luke's history in terms of the standards of the genre of ancient historiography within which he works.

Acts and the "Historical Paul." How accurate is Luke's presentation of Paul? How well does it accord with the testimony of Paul's undisputed letters? When Paul circumcises Timothy out of regard for the Jews they would encounter in their missionary travels (Acts 16:3) and undergoes a rite of purification and pays for the shaving of the heads of some men who had taken a Nazirite vow (Acts 21:23-26), is this inconsistent with his self-portrait in his epistles? Guthrie rightly argues on this point that being a Jew to Jews and making concessions in indifferent matters to the "weak" (solid Pauline principles; see 1 Cor 9:20; 10:32-33) explain his actions in Jerusalem in Acts 21, and that Paul never argued against circumcising Jews or Jewish Christians.[18] Others regard the depiction of Paul as the persuasive orator and miracle worker in Acts to be inconsistent with Paul's own testimony that he refuses to rely on eloquence or showmanship for apostolic credibility. On the one hand, the different situations and audience issues can account for this quite easily. Paul may have deliberately adopted a different style when preaching in Corinth, the Mecca of showmanship. Moreover, Paul's emphasis on his weak appearance does not mean he is ignorant of

oratory and its conventions—just that he downplays flashy delivery and style in favor of content and inner conviction. Finally, on this point we must allow that Luke's style and rhetorical finesse is really what comes through in the speeches of Acts. While this may indeed be inconsistent with Paul's own style of oratory, it is not inconsistent with the practice of ancient historiography.

Perhaps the most important issue is the difficulty scholars have reconciling the accounts of Paul's visits to Jerusalem in Acts with his firsthand and rather solemn deposition written in Galatians 1—2.[19] Closely related to this is the striking difference between the record of the debates over the circumcision of the Gentile Christians and the necessity of circumcision for table fellowship reflected in Galatians and the way this issue is worked out in Acts 10—15.

In Galatians 1—2 Paul stresses the independence of his message and apostolic authority from any human source or agency. Because he is at odds with teachers who appear to be associated with Jerusalem, he distances himself from the Jerusalem apostles as a possible source for his commission while also affirming their confirmation of his commission by God. This rhetorical strategy must be kept in mind because it may color Paul's own presentation of the "facts." Nevertheless, Paul claims that after his conversion he first visited Jerusalem three years later to meet with Peter and James only (Gal 1:18-24). His next visit was "after fourteen years" (whether to take this as fourteen years after his conversion or fourteen years after the first visit is another problem). At this meeting Paul explained his gospel privately to the Jerusalem leaders (James, Peter and John are specifically mentioned), received from them the acknowledgment of his com-

---

[17]Raymond Brown, *Introduction to the New Testament* (Garden City, N.Y.: Doubleday, 1997), pp. 321.
[18]Donald Guthrie, *New Testament Introduction* (Downers Grove, Ill.: InterVarsity Press, 1970), p. 356.
[19]See the discussion of this problem in Hemer, *Book of Acts*, pp. 247-51.

Figure 8.4. The acropolis of Athens, featuring the Temple of Athena (the Parthenon), overlooking the city. (Photo courtesy of Todd Bolen [BiblePlaces.com])

mission to preach to the Gentiles and agreed to remember the poor in Judea as part of his mission work (the only stipulation laid on his mission work by the "pillars"). It was of decisive importance to him that on that occasion the leaders said nothing about the necessity of circumcising Titus, whom Paul had taken along with himself and Barnabas (Gal 2:1-10).

After this meeting, however, Paul, Peter and Barnabas have a falling out at Antioch (Gal 2:11-14). Influenced by some men "from James," Peter, Barnabas and the other Jewish Christians at Antioch begin to have table fellowship only with one another, and not with the Gentile Christians as well. Paul reproaches Peter to his face for his behavior, since they both knew that Jews and Gentiles were justified by God on the same basis of trust in Jesus

(Gal 2:15-16).

In Acts Paul visits Jerusalem, meets the "apostles" and is authenticated by Barnabas, and exercises a visible ministry in Jerusalem until he must flee (Acts 9:26-30). He visits Jerusalem a second time to deliver alms collected in Antioch for famine relief in Judea, giving these to "the elders" (Acts 11:27-30). He visits Jerusalem a third time after the issue of whether or not Gentiles need to be circumcised to be saved comes to a head (Acts 15:1-5), and he has a rather passive role in the "apostolic council" of Acts 15:6-35, bearing witness to the work of God in Syria and Asia Minor, and taking the apostles' decision (that Gentiles need not be circumcised and keep the Torah, but had at least to avoid meat sacrificed to idols, blood, fornication, and meat from a strangled animal) back to the churches there.

Every attempt to reconcile these accounts faces a number of conundrums and must answer some difficult questions. Among the more significant are the following:

- On Paul's first visit to Jerusalem, did he meet with two people only, as Paul claims in Galatians, or the larger circle of apostles, as Luke recounts (if we identify these two visits as the same: if not, larger problems emerge)?

- Does Galatians 2:1-10 recount the same visit to Jerusalem as Acts 11:27-30 or Acts 15:6-35? If it is to be identified with the Acts 11 visit, why is Luke's report so different, focusing only on the delivery of relief to the Jerusalem church elders and saying nothing about the meeting between Paul,

Barnabas, Peter, John and James? If it is not to be identified with that visit, why does Paul not speak of this interim visit to Jerusalem in Galatians, where he seeks very intentionally to lay out the exact extent of his dealings with the Jerusalem church powers?

- If Galatians 2:1-10 is to be identified with the visit in Acts 15, what are we to do with the notable discrepancies? Paul speaks of a private meeting with the apostles; Luke tells of the convening of a more general assembly. In the Galatians account the issue is the legitimation of Paul's ministry; in Acts the issue is the necessity of Gentile Christian observance of Torah, starting with circumcision. In the Galatians account Paul goes away with only one stipulation placed on his work; in Acts, four Torah-based stip-

Figure 8.5. The Areopagus, as seen from the acropolis of Athens (Acts 17:16-34). (Photo courtesy of Todd Bolen [BiblePlaces.com])

The Gallio Inscription
CORNERSTONE OF NEW TESTAMENT CHRONOLOGY

The New Testament authors, unlike typical historians, give their readers very few dates. Luke sets the beginning of Jesus' ministry very precisely in the fifteenth year of the reign of Tiberius (Lk 3:1), which we would count as 29 C.E. (see figure 8.6). It is not until Acts 12 that we get another precisely datable event, the death of Herod Agrippa I in 44 C.E. After that, we are again afloat in a dateless sea of events until we arrive at Acts 18:12—and that rather as an accident than as the design of the author. Luke reports that Gallio, whom we know to be Lucius Junius Gallio, the brother of Lucius Annaeus Seneca, the famous philosopher and tutor to Nero, was proconsul of Achaea (Greece) at some point during Paul's stay in Corinth. Because of the chance survival of an inscription at Delphi, we also know that Gallio was proconsul there near the beginning of 52 C.E.[a] Senators served as proconsuls for one year (or two years at the maximum), so that Gallio's term of office was most likely June 51 to June 52, with the possibility that his stay was extended one year in either direction. On this slender thread hangs the whole basis for reconstructing a chronology of the life, missionary activity and letter writing of Paul the apostle!

[a]The text of this inscription can be found in C. K. Barrett, *The New Testament Background: Selected Documents* (Hew York: Harper & Row, 1961), pp. 48-49. This book is an excellent, all around beginning resource to important ancient witnesses to the world of the New Testament.

---

ulations are laid on all Gentile believers.

- While Paul also regarded fornication as incompatible with the new life in Christ (1 Cor 6:12-20), would the Paul who insisted that all foods are clean when received with thanksgiving and who defended, in principle, the innocuousness of eating the meat that had been sacrificed to idols have accepted the four stipulations on Acts 15:29 (contrast with Rom 14:3-4, 14; 1 Cor 8:1-9; 10:25-31)?

Other questions arise specifically concerning the role of Peter in these proceedings:

- Why doesn't Luke tell of the disagreement between Peter and Paul in Antioch?
- Why does Peter speak almost the same words at the apostolic council as Paul spoke to his face at Antioch (against Peter's position there, cf. Acts 15:7-11 with Gal 2:15-16)?

- How could the apostle who had the visions of Acts 10:9-16 and who championed the Gentile mission in Acts 11 turn around and withdraw from the Gentiles as "common" or "unclean" in Antioch (Gal 2:1-10)?

These by no means exhaust the kinds of historical questions that arise when we set Acts side by side with Paul's own testimony. Many of these difficulties and questions are answerable, however, if we are prepared to allow that Luke's selectivity in reporting may be a much more important issue than his accuracy. Even an accurate report can present a very idiosyncratic picture by virtue of its selection of what to include and what to exclude. Luke has chosen not to include anything that suggests division and uncertainty within the inner circle of apostles where the inclusion of the Gentile Christians is concerned. Deeply concerned with giving his Gentile Christian

Figure 8.6. A denarius of Tiberius (14-37 C.E.), reigning emperor during the time of Jesus' public ministry. It was such a denarius that the Synoptic tradition envisages Jesus requesting and examining when he responds to the question about paying taxes to Caesar (Mt 22:15-22; Mk 12:13-17; Lk 20:20-26). The inscription reads "Augustus Tiberius Caesar, Son of the Divine Augustus." A seated female figure, representing either the figure of Peace or Livia (Tiberius's mother), is featured on the reverse along with the emperor's title of *Pontifex Maximus*, "highest priest." (Photo courtesy of Superior Galleries, Beverly Hills)

readers certainty and security about their place in the people of God, it would not suit him to tell of the sharp division between Peter and James on the one hand, and Paul on the other on this issue. Nor would it help to recall the ways that key figures like Peter may have vacillated on this issue. Luke may not have been privy to information about the private meeting between Paul, Barnabas, Peter, James and John. Paul only speaks of this once and only when absolutely pressed. Luke would have found nothing edifying, as far as his purposes were concerned, to speak about the Antioch incident (Gal 2:11-14) or any other sign that the Jerusalem leaders who received the initial anointing of God had doubts about the status of Gentiles in the church. Instead, he tells enough of the story (granted, also with some inconsistencies and alterations, especially where speech is concerned) to present a pic-

ture of the apostles moving in harmony and unity, agreed with the basic Pauline position concerning the place of Gentile Christians in the people of God, but even going so far as to have Peter and James articulate themselves what Paul taught on this subject.

Acts and the theology of Paul. Scholars examine the theology of Acts vis-à-vis the theology of Paul for telling points of similarity, contradiction or lack of overlap entirely. For example, it is true that Acts does not present Paul as the champion of "justification by faith in Christ" as opposed to justification "by means of works of the law," Acts 13:38-39 being but a faint echo of this major theme of Galatians and Romans. Moreover, there is nothing in Acts of Paul's theology of suffering, of power made perfect in weakness, which dominates 2 Corinthians. At places there are notable tensions, as for example in the treatments

379

of natural theology in Acts and Romans. God has left visible traces of God's self in creation so people might perhaps find God through natural revelation. How does God respond to the failure of the Gentiles to achieve this knowledge? In "Paul's" sermon on the Areopagus, he claims that God has overlooked former ignorance but now calls for repentance and will hold the disobedient accountable. In Romans 1:18-32, however, Paul himself claims that the debauchery rampant among the Gentiles results from God's punishment of their willful disobedience. Even if we claim that the different settings (an evangelistic sermon versus a letter to established converts) render the differences intelligible, the differences nevertheless remain.

Despite divergences, however, there are also striking consonances between the theological outlook of Acts and that of Paul. For example, both find it necessary to demonstrate God's faithfulness to Israel, and both point to the Jewish Christian mission and remnant as evidence (see Rom 9—11). Both understand the "plan of God" to involve the collection of a remnant from Israel into which the Gentiles are grafted by faith in Jesus. Both Luke and Paul understand the pouring out of the Holy Spirit as the "promise" of God (Acts 2:38-39;

Gal 3:14), a rather distinctive interpretation. Both depict the conversion of Gentiles as a turning away from empty idols "to a living God" (Acts 14:15; 1 Thess 1:9-10). Both underscore that God provides deliverance for Jews and Gentiles by the same means, namely, "the favor of the Lord Jesus" (Acts 15:11; Gal 2:15-16), although in Acts Peter gives voice to this conviction.

Taken together the theology of Acts suggests an author who has been informed about Paul's theology, quite possibly firsthand during extended travels together, who nevertheless does not see himself merely as the mouthpiece of the apostle. The sermons and speeches of Acts provide Luke with an opportunity to preach *his* interpretation of salvation history, and not merely record the proclamation of others. The Areopagus speech especially, which Luke did not witness, would have provided a fine opportunity for Luke to create a speech appropriate to the occasion. Moreover, the differences in the reports of events are of such a kind as we might expect between one who was a major player in those events and who knew far more of what went on behind closed doors and another who told the story of those events at some remove in terms both of the action and the time.

EXEGETICAL SKILL
Rhetorical Criticism (1)—Judicial Topics

The mode of analysis called rhetorical criticism invites us to look closely at the kinds of arguments a New Testament author put forward, the different ways he works on the audience to bring them in line with his pastoral goals for them, the ends the author may have in view as he writes a particular section, and the way he has arranged all the pieces of his text strategically to move the hearers from wherever they are to wherever he needs them to be in order to respond to the challenges of their situation the way the author deems faithful. It equips us, in effect, to understand how a New Testament book works to effect the desired end in a specific set of circumstances. The obvious pastoral gain of this kind of analysis is that rhetorical analysis also informs us about how to bring those desired ends to life in a new set of circumstances, namely, in the congregations we serve.

The Greeks and Romans made persuasion an art and a science. The efficient running of a city, the administration of justice and the promotion of civic values all depended on the ability of private citizens to argue their case effectively. Already by the time of Aristotle, public speaking had so developed its own set of rules that he could write a lengthy book based on his observation of successful oratory (*The Art of Rhetoric*, still the starting point for detailed study of the ancient art). After him arose many who sought to provide the young citizen and student with a manual on this discipline that was regarded as the key to success, leaving us with a wealth of insight into the state of argumentation and persuasive artistry during the intertestamental and New Testament period.[a] In addition to such resources we also have a large body of actual speeches by such masters as Demosthenes, Cicero and Dio Chrysostom, showing us the theory in practice, providing both confirmation and refinement of the picture we get from the textbooks.[b] By studying classical rhetoric we can become adept at discerning how a New Testament author hopes to influence his audience, through what means and to what end.

The art of oratory took shape within the institutions of the Greek city and were developed to meet the specific needs of specific occasions and contexts. In the council chamber citizens gathered to make decisions about what actions should be taken in the future, and how the city (or some of its constituents) should respond to some need or situation. This became the home for *deliberative* oratory—speeches aimed at weighing the pros and cons of one course of action over another and urging a particular response. The public forum provided a place for ceremony, for remembrance of the dead, and hence for *epideictic* oratory. The funeral eulogy is the prototype of this kind of rhetoric, where the deceased would be praised for their virtues or perhaps condemned for their vices, with the result that the gathered audience would be reminded of what values and kind of life led to honor and what kind of life led to dishonor. Finally, the courtroom provided an arena for crimes to be uncovered and punished, and

---

[a]See, for example, the *Rhetoric ad Alexandrum* (wrongly attributed to Aristotle), the *Rhetorica ad Herennium* (wrongly attributed to Cicero), Cicero's numerous works on oratory (*De Oratoria, Brutus, De Inventione*) and Quintilian's *Institutio Oratoria*. All of these are available in the Loeb Classical Library editions (Cambridge, Mass.: Harvard University Press).

[b]Argumentation was not neglected among the Hebrew-speaking population either. We find especially in the wisdom tradition (reflected in Proverbs, Ecclesiastes and Ben Sira) and the rabbinical tradition (reflected in the debates recorded in Mishnah and Talmud) another kind of theory of argumentation being developed, overlapping at many points with the argumentative strategies found in Greek and Latin literature. Both kinds of rhetoric and argumentation need to be studied in order to appreciate fully the ways in which a New Testament author, often writing in Greek to Gentile Christian and Hellenistic Jewish Christian audiences, develops a position, motivates action or establishes guilt and innocence.

thus for *forensic* or *judicial* rhetoric—the attempt to prove that some person did or did not commit some blameworthy action in the past.

While the three basic genres of oratory developed in these everyday settings, they did not remain limited to those historic settings. People would use deliberative topics wherever some group needed to make a decision about a future course of action. Forensic rhetoric could be employed outside the setting of a legal court wherever issues of blame or innocence were involved. Epideictic rhetoric moved beyond the public forum very early because praise or censure of a living individual was already an essential element of legal speeches and deliberative speeches by Aristotle's time. Prosecutors frequently engaged in censure of the defendant and his defender in order to undermine their credibility; an orator in the council chamber frequently praised those figures who pursued a course of action similar to the one he was promoting. This observation raises the important point that a speaker could mix different kinds of oratory in order to achieve his or her ends.[c] A deliberative speech, for example, could employ both epideictic and forensic topics along the way. The task of a nuanced rhetorical analysis is not merely to decide that a speech is deliberative (for example), but to discern the ways in which deliberative, epideictic and forensic topics, if present, advance the author's goals for the readers he (or she) addresses.

Acts provides examples of several different species of rhetoric. The evangelistic sermons, while largely epideictic (highlighting the significance of Jesus), ultimately serve a deliberative goal—to motivate the hearers to join the new community of believers. Acts 15 presents a series of speeches even more overtly deliberative in nature, as the Christian "council chamber" members debate whether or not they will require Gentiles to be circumcised. Acts 22, 24 and 26, moreover, provide us will full-fledged judicial (defense) speeches and one speech for the prosecution. The latter two will provide us with a springboard from which to dive into ancient rhetoric, and to see how an awareness of classical rhetoric can help the student of the New Testament analyze the strategies employed in the text.

In Acts 24:2-8 Tertullus, the hired mouthpiece for the prosecution, presents a brief speech accusing Paul. The opening of this accusation reflects the important advice of teachers of oratory that a speaker render his audience "attentive, receptive, and well-disposed" (Pseudo-Cicero *Rhet. ad Her.* 1.3.6). There were several ways a speaker could secure goodwill. He might speak (modestly, of course) of his own services to the

---

[c]"The end [goal] of the deliberative speaker is the expedient or harmful; for he who exhorts recommends a course of action as better, and he who dissuades advises against it as worse; *all other considerations, such as justice and injustice, honour and disgrace, are included as accessory in reference to this*" (Aristotle *Rhet.* 1.3.5, emphasis added; see also Pseudo Aristotle *Rhet. ad Alex.* 1427b31–35; Pseudo Cicero *Rhet. ad Her.* 3.8.15).

people and his own nobility of conduct in general, or he might seek to elicit pity. The speaker might secure goodwill for himself by revealing the base motives of the opponent. Tertullus seeks to gain Felix's attention and good will by opening with words about the judge. The author of the *Rhetorica ad Herennium* advised setting forth "the courage, wisdom, humanity, and nobility of past judgments they have rendered" and revealing "what esteem they enjoy and with what interest their decision is awaited" (1.4.9). This is precisely what both Tertullus, and to a lesser extent Paul, will do (Acts 24:2-4, 10).

The specific charge is an attempted profanation of the temple (Acts 24:6; see 21:27-30), but to make this charge stick Tertullus uses a common technique. In a few brief strokes he attempts to paint a picture of Paul's "manner of life," to show that it is wholly consonant with and strongly suggestive of criminal activity (see *Rhet. Her.* 2.3.5). He therefore alleges that Paul's character is "pestilent," that his principal activity is disturbance of the peace and that he is a leader of a subversive faction called the "Nazarenes" (Acts 24:5). Only his conclusion is unlikely—the attorney for the prosecution would not offer the defendant as his only witness but would rather call on third parties. It must be said that Luke has only given Tertullus a bare bones opening statement, serving mainly to set the stage for Paul's apology (defense speech).

Paul addresses these various charges and character slurs by means of a variety of appropriate defense strategies. After a brief, reserved but nonetheless respectful expression of confidence in Felix's judicial savvy, Paul denies the factuality both of the charge of sacrilege (Acts 24:13) and of his conducting himself in a disruptive fashion or agitating the people (Acts 24:12). The point at issue (technically, the *stasis*) between Paul and his opponents, then, is what the theorists would call "conjectural"— whether or not a criminal act has actually been committed (see *Rhet. Her.* 1.11.18; see Aristotle *Rhet.* 3.17.1). Paul will admit, however, to being a member of "the Way," although he denies the applicability of the label "sect" (i.e., divisive splinter group or faction—a derogatory label in the ancient world; Acts 20:14).

This provides him with an opportunity to discuss the topic of "manner of life." Just as prosecutors will try to establish that a defendant's manner of life is consonant with criminal activity, so the defense seeks to show that it is neither consonant with nor suggestive of criminal activity. Thus in Acts 24:14-16 Paul depicts his way of life as completely consonant with the values and piety of Judaism. With regard to the specific charge made against him of profaning the temple and coming to Jerusalem as an agitator, Paul supplies an alternative view: he came bearing alms (an act that would be universally regarded as pious and virtuous) and quietly participating in the rites appropriate to the sacred place (Acts 24:17-18). Paul closes by challenging the prosecution to come up with witnesses that can prove the fact of the charge laid against him, and he does so in a style that conveys indignation at the charge and the whole proceeding—another well-worn legal tactic.

When we turn to Acts 26, we find that the specific charge of profanation of the temple is largely buried under other "points of disagreement" between Paul and the Jewish authorities (see Acts 25:7-8, 14-19, 25-27). Paul's ministry as a whole is now, therefore, on trial, so that Agrippa and Festus may decide if there is a criminal charge to lay against him. Paul opens, as we now would expect, by attempting to capture a favorable hearing (again secured by speaking well of the judge, expressing confidence in Agrippa's competence and asking for a patient hearing; Acts 26:2-3). In Acts 26:4-8, Paul introduces the topic of "manner of life," claiming that many Jerusalemites can bear witness to his former pious and strictly Torah-observant conduct.

The focus of Paul's defense, however, is on his obedience to a commission from God to engage in the work for which he has been brought to trial. Paul's defensive strategy reflects a case that would be labeled "juridical," that is, the defense admits that an action happened, but the jury is called on to decide whether it was right or wrong. The author of *Rhetorica ad Herennium* writes about two kinds of juridical cases. In the "absolute type," the defense maintains that the act in and of itself was right. In the "assumptive type," the defense acknowledges the charge and pursues one of the following lines of defense:

- pleading for pardon, often showing that the act was performed as a result of ignorance, constraint or accidental

- shifting the question of guilt, showing that a person was driven to the act by the crimes of others

- rejecting the responsibility for the action, showing how it lies with another person or in the circumstances

- comparing the course taken with the alternative course (the act chosen may have been illegal but was the only available alternative was much more harmful, dishonorable or something similar; *Rhet. Her.* 1.14.24; 1.15.25)

We could construe Paul's defense in one of two ways. It might suit the last kind of assumptive case. Paul asserts that, whatever the charges that may be brought against him, he was acting out of obedience to a command from God. Any other course he might have taken therefore would have been a worse one, for it would involve being "disobedient to the heavenly vision" (Acts 26:19). On the other hand, we could consider this an "absolute" case: since Paul acted on the direct command of God, his actions must be considered right and therefore not actionable. Either way, Paul understands the importance of establishing God's intervention as a true fact of the case. He therefore astutely devotes significant space contrasting his energetic opposition to the Christians before the Damascus road experience (Acts 26:9-12) to his activity on behalf of the Christian message after that experience (Acts 26:19-23). Such a striking difference between the "before" and the "after" renders the story of his divine commissioning more plausible, which is key to his defense.

Even a basic grasp of one rhetorical theorist's treatment of defense topics (we have focused on the *Rhet. ad Her.*) has enabled us to understand more fully the persuasive strategy behind each component of these speeches. The more you read in classical rhetorical theorists, the more equipped you will become to discern how the biblical text works as a well-arranged series of arguments and appeals, and how it is designed to move the hearers closer to the decision the author wants them to make. In the chapters ahead we will continue to delve into the different kinds of appeal an author might make and study these at work in the other two major kinds of oratory: deliberative speech and epideictic speech.

Readers wishing to practice the analysis of judicial topics should turn to 2 Corinthians 1:15—2:11; 7:5-16, two passages that contain a great deal of judicial rhetoric. What charge has been leveled against Paul that he must now defend himself? What kinds of judicial proofs does he offer (e.g., oaths and witnesses)? What topics of defense does he use as he explains why, even though he did indeed change his travel plans and wrote a rough letter to the church, he did not act in a blameworthy fashion, but only in their best interests (look particularly to 1:23; 2:1, 3, 5, 9; 7:8-12)?

FOR FURTHER READING

Aristotle *The Art of Rhetoric*

Cicero *On Invention (De inventione)*

Pseudo-Cicero *Rhetoric to Herennius (Rhet. ad Her.)*

Quintilian, *Institutes of Oratory (Institutio Oratoria)*

Kennedy, George A. *New Testament Interpretation Through Rhetorical Criticism.* Chapel Hill: University of North Carolina Press, 1984.

Mack, Burton L. *What Is Rhetorical Criticism?* Minneapolis: Augsburg Fortress, 1990.

Porter, Stanley E. *Handbook of Classical Rhetoric in the Hellenistic Period.* Leiden: Brill, 1997.

ACTS AND MINISTRY FORMATION

Since Luke-Acts forms a continuous whole, we had the opportunity to reflect on the contribution of Acts to a number of ministry issues (like the centrality of prayer for a vital, God-directed and God-empowered ministry) in the course of the chapter on the Gospel of Luke. Luke's second volume, however, raises several additional topics of particular importance for Christian ministry and discipleship.

First, Acts reminds us of the communal context of Christian discipleship. Conversion to faith in Jesus meant joining a community of Christ followers and growing into Christian maturity by means of constant association with and mutual sharpening of other believers (Acts 2:44, 46-47). In Acts a person cannot join with Christ without also joining the people of God as it was being renewed in Christ. Luke presents the church as the place where two Old Testament ideals find fulfillment. First, the church is where "brothers and sisters dwell together in unity" (Ps 133:1), enjoying the goodness, the peace, the pleasantness that God intends for humankind. Seeking God together with their whole hearts and spending significant amounts of time together in that pursuit, they find themselves in harmony with one another. Churches where Christ followers still get together "day by day" for prayer, study, sharing of meals and worship will find that God would still add "day by day" to their numbers, for such is the quality of community that thirsty human souls seek. Obviously, Luke knew that harmony cannot be sustained at all times. By Acts 6:1 we find the more familiar church scene of two factions complaining against one another. Whenever such conflicts arise, however, leaders and congregation need to act decisively and openly together to work for the restoration of harmony through the resolution of any legitimate grievance.

Second, the church is the place where "there was not a needy person" (Acts 4:34; cf. Deut 15:7-11; Acts 2:44-45; 4:32-37; 20:34-35), since the sharing of ideals took on flesh in the sharing of possessions whenever a need arose. Especially in Western culture, where *mine* and *more* are among the first words our children learn, we need to work hard to inculcate the alternative Christian watchwords of *ours* or *God's* and *enough* where possessions are concerned.

Acts, perhaps even more obviously, holds up a model of the church in mission. Witness and evangelism are driving forces in the Christian community and primary concerns of Christian leadership. Although community maintenance is also properly valued throughout the New Testament, Acts particularly challenges us to the increase of the kingdom and the realization of the commission to be witnesses to every corner of the earth. Decisions about witness and evangelism are not human decisions, according to Luke. Every step of the way, the church's outreach is God's to direct, and we discover God's direction in the context of rich, committed personal, group and congregational prayer as well as openness to other ways God might communicate God's will. Many churches try different forms of outreach only to be discouraged by their failure to bear fruit. In part, failure may be due to our impatience or discomfort with seasons of prayer and listening to God in the company of other believers, seeking together God's will. Our privatization of prayer and things religious works hard here against Luke's depiction of the fruits of corporate prayer, although many churches are rediscovering the power and pleasure of the latter. Nevertheless, Acts suggests that we find the ministries that God wants our churches to exercise and then devote ourselves to God's will rather than set up an array of ministries and then ask God to bless them.

A related and broader issue that Acts raises is the discernment of God's will where no Scripture or dominical command exists, or where Scripture seems to give contradictory testimony. In Acts this emerges around the question of the necessity of circumcision for belonging to the people of God, for which both sides could assemble impressive proof texts (and did, as we will see in Paul's letters). We could all wish to receive direction from God as Paul did in his Damascus Road experience. Nevertheless, the process for most churches may more often resemble the process of Acts 10—15. God's Spirit begins to plant suggestions in various leaders and other Christians. These suggestions bear fruit and the unmistakable sign of God's hand at work. Others raise objections, and eventually the whole church must weigh all the evidence and come to agreement together. Unfortunately, so many have used religious language to legitimate their own agendas, this whole process of discernment has fallen into disrepute. One possible safeguard emerges, however, from Acts 15: the signs of God's hand at work were unmistakable even to those who raised vociferous objections. There was no quibbling over whether or not God was behind the movement toward Gentile inclusion, no empty appeals to "God's will" or "God's blessing of the ministry" to push for the pro-Gentile agenda. God's hand was most evident in the unanimity and harmony of the final resolution, perhaps the best evidence of all.

Many churches struggle with finding appropriate leaders for the ministries of the church. In most of the churches to which I have belonged, the basic model is that ministry roles become vacant and volunteers come forward to fill them (and even that can require much cajoling during the announcement time). Acts presents a very different model. On one occasion the Christian community selects those who, in their collective opinion, possess the necessary character to fulfill the ministry well (Acts 6:1-6). On two other occasions God announces God's choice for a particular ministry. Both of these occasions are surrounded by prayer, although the medium of discernment differs (Acts 1:24-26; 13:1-3). The church leaders authorize the choices and empower them for the work to which they are called through prayer and the laying on of hands (Acts 6:6; 13:3). For such a model to work, Christ followers need to understand themselves as servants of God and the church, to serve and do as the community and the Master direct. Talk of "comfort zones" or "other commitments" does not come up in these narratives. The congregational aspect of selection would have a number of benefits. First, the person in the ministry role would know he or she has the support of the congregation, and this can be an effective empowerment for ministry. Second, the whole church would know it is behind that person's ministry, and this can be an effective preventative for backbiting, envy or power plays. The congregation as a whole, however, also plays a role in the discernment of God's choice, and so the same benefits ensue.

Those who carry out the work of God in a world where people do not consistently seek what God values will inevitably encounter opposition.[a] The New Testament offers many examples and encouragements to persevere in the face of opposition to our witness to God's purposes and values, and in the face of the hardships we may encounter as we serve God's design. Acts adds to this armory of the Christian the last word on human authority: wherever it conflicts with God's command, "we must obey God rather than any human authority" (Acts 5:29 NRSV; cf. 4:19-20). Acts is far from a revolutionary text. It does not encourage stepping out on the wrong side of the law to witness but positively values keeping yourself, your ministry and your congregation on the right side of the law, innocent in the eyes of the proper authorities. Nevertheless, even the text that is the most irenic toward secular authority will not allow us to justify sacrificing obedience to God's purposes and vision for humanity for the sake of approval, acquittal or peace with the government.

Acts presents corporate prayer as the greatest resource for facing opposition and the cost of true discipleship. Gathered together in the honest, heartfelt expression of their need in their situation, the disciples find strength in one another, in their corporate affirmation of God's character, power and purposes, and in God's own empowerment of God's witnesses and servants (Acts 4:23-31). Such a picture takes us back to the importance of Christian community—singly, we can be defeated; together, our strength in God multiplies exponentially. The disciples' response to being punished by the authorities uncovers a secondary resource. To them a degrading flogging became a sign that they were "worthy to suffer dishonor for the sake of the name" (Acts 5:41). If we seek God's approval above and beyond any worldly tokens of status, and if we fear God's disapproval more than any worldly disgrace, we will be free to obey God as boldly and effectively as the heroes of Acts (Acts 5:42). Where society's attempts to mute our witness become further encouragements to witness, how can the purposes of God fail in our world?

As in the Gospel of Luke, so Acts again underscores the importance of articulating and understanding our continuity with the people of God throughout history, particularly Israel. Many Christians (and many pastors) show but a shallow awareness of how the "new people of God" connect with the Old Testament revelation. For Luke and his readers this was a pressing issue of the legitimacy of the church. Certainly after the legalization of Christianity and its adoption as the state religion of a Gentile empire, that impetus disappeared. Nevertheless, failure to connect the Christian faith with the revelation of the Old Testament

---

[a]We should not, however, infer the opposite, though I have met pastors who took encountering opposition as a sufficient sign that they were doing God's work.

would still make of the church a Gentile cult rather than a new stage in the development of God's ongoing purposes for humanity. While we will do so for different reasons than Luke, perhaps, we must still follow his example of searching out the Old Testament for clues to our identity and mission as part of God's people.

Luke-Acts says much about God's faithfulness to the Jewish people, sending Jesus first to them as the fulfillment of the promises to Abraham and David, sending Jesus' missionaries first to Jews as part of the renewal of the people of God. What about our faithfulness to the Jewish people? In the modern theological environment many Christians question whether or not the Jews need the Gospel, indeed whether it is even proper or appropriate to evangelize Jews. Many notable theologians and biblical scholars have argued that since God's covenant is eternal, those to whom the covenant was made may and should continue to rest in that covenant, while the Gentiles flock to God through Jesus. No doubt the lingering sorrow over the atrocities of the Holocaust—and the gross devaluation of the Jewish people and their faith that led to such genocide— drives this position to some extent. However, Acts would have us question whether such overcompensation is really the most faithful solution to modern anti-Judaism. In an (impossible) attempt to redeem ourselves after the Holocaust, are we in fact adding to the atrocities by now trying to deny Jews the Gospel? These are complicated theological issues demanding much fuller exploration on the part of all Christians; I merely note here that Acts would have some bearing on this question.

For those who do believe that it remains the duty of Christians to take the good news about Jesus to the Jewish people, it must be said that Acts may no longer offer the best models. First, any speech that attempts to replicate Peter's charge "this Jesus whom you crucified" and to call Jews to repent of this clearly misses the mark. Moreover, the sermons in Acts addressed to Jewish audiences tend to rely very heavily on proofs from Old Testament prophecy being fulfilled in the life, death and resurrection of Jesus. We should remember, however, that the first disciples were not won to Jesus by discussions of Old Testament interpretation but by their living encounter with him, after which they could not help but read the Old Testament as a witness to Jesus as the one in whom all God's promises find their "Yes" (2 Cor 1:20). Christian evangelists should also be aware that the fruits of Old Testament scholarship (scholarship in the Hebrew Bible), calling people to look now first to the context of ancient Israel for the fulfillment of all messianic prophecies, have thoroughly penetrated the consciousness of the Jewish people as well. Trying to convert Jews to Christianity by pointing to Jesus' fulfillment of prophecy is probably a dead end at this point, given the antimissionary literature that exists on this topic. It is well to remember, then, that the heart of evangelism entails bringing people to an encounter with the living Jesus, which is of more value than all the arguments from prophecy in the world; and this ultimately is also what convinced the first Jewish disciples.

FOR FURTHER READING

Barrett, C. K. *A Critical and Exegetical Commentary on the Acts of the Apostles.* 2 vols. ICC. Edinburgh: T & T Clark, 1994, 1997.

Bruce, F. F. *Commentary on the Book of Acts: The English Text, with Introduction, Exposition, and Notes.* 2nd ed. NICNT. Grand Rapids: Eerdmans, 1988.

Dibelius, Martin. *Studies in the Acts of the Apostles.* London: SCM Press, 1956.

Fitzmyer, Joseph A. *The Acts of the Apostles.* AB 31. Garden City, N.Y.: Doubleday, 1998.

Haenchen, Ernst. *The Acts of the Apostles.* Philadelphia: Westminster Press, 1971.

Hemer, Colin. *The Book of Acts in the Setting of Hellenistic History.* Winona Lake, Ind.: Eisenbrauns, 1990.

Hengel, Martin. *Acts and the History of Earliest Christianity.* Philadelphia: Fortress, 1979.

Johnson, Luke Timothy, *The Acts of the Apostles.* Sacra Pagina. Collegeville, Minn.: Michael Glazier, 1992.

Winter, Bruce, ed. *The Book of Acts in its First Century Setting.* 6 vols. Grand Rapids: Eerdmans, 1993-1997.

Witherington, Ben, III. *The Acts of the Apostles: A Socio-Rhetorical Commentary.* Grand Rapids: Eerdmans, 1998.

9

THE GOSPEL
ACCORDING TO JOHN

Following the One from Above

Like the other Gospels, the Fourth Gospel took shape in response to the questions, concerns and challenges facing first-century Christians. Nevertheless, the way the author brings the readers into contact with eternity—both in the One "from above" who came in the flesh and returns to the Father, and in the proximity of eternal life for those who receive him—gives this Gospel more of a timeless quality. Perhaps this accounts for its tendency to emerge as the favorite Gospel of modern readers, the one most often shared as a separate tract.

John has always stood apart from the other Evangelists as the "spiritual" Gospel. While Matthew, Mark and Luke certainly make significant contributions to the church's reflection on the significance of Jesus and his ministry, John does seem to offer even more extended and sophisticated reflection on the relationship of the One from above to the Father, the relationship of the many children to the Son, and the values that are to characterize disciples in this world. Earlier assessments of the lack of historical value to John's Gospel have given way to a more balanced assessment of the tradition behind this Gospel, but we are still struck more by the Gospel's focus on the meaning and moment of the incarnate Word than by its contributions to a "life of Jesus."

THE HISTORICAL AND PASTORAL SETTING OF JOHN'S GOSPEL

Authorship. Like the Synoptic Gospels, the Gospel of "John" actually does not name its author. Unlike Matthew and Mark, however, a kind of authorial presence is felt throughout the Fourth Gospel in the references to the Beloved Disciple, whom early church tradition identified by the late second century with John the son of Zebedee. Writing in the late second century, Irenaeus provides our earliest explicit witness: "Afterwards [i.e., after the other three Evangelists had written their work], John, the disciple of the Lord, who also had leaned upon His breast, did himself publish a Gospel during his residence in Ephesus in Asia" (*Haer.* 3.1.1). Shortly after Irenaeus, the author of the Muratorian Canon also attributes the Fourth Gospel to John the son of Zebedee.[1]

Many students of the Fourth Gospel cannot

---

[1] Paul N. Anderson makes a suggestive observation concerning Johannine authorship based on Acts 4:19-20 (see Anderson, *The Christology of the Fourth Gospel* [Valley Forge, Penn.: Trinity Press International, 1997], pp. 274-77; "Interfluential, Formative, and Dialectical—A Theory of John's Relation to the Synoptics," in *Für und wider die Priorität des Johannesevangeliums*, ed. P. L. Hofrichter [Hildesheim: Georg Olms, 2002], pp. 47-48; "John and Mark: The Bi-Optic Gospels," in *Jesus in Johannine Tradition*, ed. R. T. Fortna and T. Thatcher [Louisville, Ky.: Westminster John Knox, 2001], pp. 187-88). Having been brought before the Sanhedrin, Peter and John make the following response: "Whether

simply accept the claims made by the tradition. First, Irenaeus himself shows some confusion concerning his knowledge of "John." On the one hand, he claims to have been a student of Polycarp in his youth (early second century), and identifies Polycarp as a student of John the apostle. But he also claims that Papias was a student of John the apostle (*Haer.* 5.33.4), while in Papias's case this John is John the "Elder," not the apostle (Eusebius *Hist. Eccl.* 3.39.4). If Irenaeus was wrong with regard to Papias, he might well have been mistaken also with regard to Polycarp's teacher. We should also recall that the acceptance of or desire to promote a text as orthodox led to attributions of apostolic authorship (and not always the reverse!). With regard to John in particular, Irenaeus and others were busily trying to reclaim the text for the apostolic witness in the face of energetic uses of the text by Christian Gnostics to promote their own beliefs.

Second, the internal evidence itself does not lead us unambiguously to identify the Beloved Disciple with John the son of Zebedee. The sons of Zebedee are themselves mentioned only once (Jn 21:2). The Beloved Disciple comes to be identified with John by a process of reasoning riddled with problems. Noticing the association of Peter and John in Acts 3—5 and association of Peter and the Beloved Disciple in John 20—21, we could equate John with the Beloved Disciple. But this is by no means necessary or even sound. (Acts is a literary product of a different author.) Indeed, the Beloved Disciple's close association with Peter may be an attempt to underscore the reliability of his witness for the

sake of the Christians that stood in line with the Johannine tradition. The source of their traditions about Jesus was thus seen to stand as close to Jesus as Peter, regarded as the first of the apostles in many Christian circles.[2] Noticing that the Beloved Disciple is present for the Last Supper in John, it seems reasonable to conclude that he is part of Jesus' inner circle *within* the Twelve, but this assumes that only the Twelve were with Jesus for the scenes of the farewell discourse (the lingering influence of Da Vinci's portrayal of the last supper?), the arrest and the trial. The Synoptics give this impression by referring to the Twelve throughout that scene, but not John.

What then can we determine from internal evidence? First, the witness of Jesus who brought these traditions to the communities is not the same person as the actual writer/editor who has produced the Fourth Gospel in the form that we have it. In John 19:34-35 the Evangelist testifies to the reliability of the Beloved Disciple's witness to the crucifixion, identifying him as the source of the tradition. John 21:24 could also be read as a testimonial by the author (or, in this case, redactor) concerning the Beloved Disciple, and the "things" written by him refer to written sources left behind by the Beloved Disciple, not the Gospel itself. The Beloved Disciple emerges, then, as the source of the tradition and probably its chief interpreter, and in that sense deserves the title "Evangelist," but he is not the final author.

Who is the Beloved Disciple? Early tradition is unanimous in identifying him as John the apostle, but what would internal evidence suggest? The Evangelist himself supplies six

---

it is right in God's sight to listen to you rather than to God, you must judge; for we cannot keep from speaking about what we have seen and heard" (Acts 4:19-20 NRSV). The second half of this response has a distinctively Johannine ring. The same idiom of "what was seen and heard"—both elements, in that order—appears also in 1 John 1:3 and John 3:32. Apart from the question of the historicity of the scene in Acts 4, this passage may reflect Luke's awareness of the distinctive topics of Johannine tradition, since he placed on John's lips words that would have been quite appropriate for him. Again, the observation is only suggestive, but it does support the idea that Johannine tradition is based on the eyewitness tradition of a close disciple of Jesus. See Craig Keener, *The Gospel of John* (Peabody, Mass.: Hendrickson, 2003), 1:82-114, for a thorough defense of Johannine authorship.

[2]Robert Kysar, "John, Gospel of," *Anchor Bible Dictionary,* ed. David N. Freedman (Garden City, N.Y.: Doubleday, 1992), 3:919.

candidates in John 21:2, since the Beloved Disciple later appears to be present in this scene: "Simon Peter, Thomas called Didymos, Nathanael from Cana in Galilee, the sons of Zebedee, and two others of his disciples were together." Peter is ruled out since he refers to the Beloved Disciple, leaving James, John, Thomas, Nathanael and two unnamed candidates. Interestingly, the description of a "disciple whom Jesus loved" only appears in the second half of the Gospel (Jn 13:23; 19:26-27; 20:1-10; 21:7, 20-24), after the raising of Lazarus. The fact that Lazarus is the only person who is explicitly identified as the "one whom Jesus loves" (Jn 11:3, 36) has suggested to some that he was the Beloved Disciple. Was he next to Jesus at the meal mentioned in chapter 13 because he was hosting it at his house in Bethany? The expectation that the Beloved Disciple would not die would be especially credible if he was the one that Jesus had raised from the dead, and so was thought to participate already in eternal, unending life. It is still a misunderstanding but now a more intelligible one.[3] Lazarus may or may not have been the Beloved Disciple, but internal evidence points to him more plausibly than to the son of Zebedee, who may indeed play a very minor role in this Gospel.

The Beloved Disciple is very much at home in Judea and especially Jerusalem. He is sufficiently well known to the high priest to gain access to the night trial of Jesus. He probably stood outside the circle of the Twelve but was nevertheless a faithful witness—in many ways, more faithful than the Twelve—to the passion and resurrection of Jesus (Jn 19:35). His familiarity with Palestine, especially Judea, and with Jewish festivals and Scriptures derives from his own long experience of the same. He shows a thorough awareness of local features of Judean life, including the surprising mention of a pool with five porticoes. Scholars had long thought this a fabrication, until one was actually unearthed in the northeast portion of Jerusalem (see figure 9.3). He might indeed have also been given the fairly common Jewish name John (Yohanan), which would more than explain the ease with which he was assimilated to the son of Zebedee by Irenaeus, Clement of Alexandria and all who read and accepted their statements about the Fourth Gospel.

Location and date. The Fourth Gospel gives no clear indication of the place of composition, and the Johannine Epistles do not help in this regard. Its connection with Revelation (written about 93-95 C.E.), addressed to the seven churches in the province of Asia, suggests that a city in western Asia Minor is a likely provenance. The traditional association of this Gospel with Ephesus therefore would seem as likely as any suggestion. The strong Palestinian influences on the Gospel (the knowledge of Judean and Samaritan geography, the Semitic idiom, the familiarity with the temple and its rites) have led some to suggest Israel as the place of composition, but the evidence merely points to the origin of the Beloved Disciple and his tradition (and perhaps the actual author as well) in Palestine. The stamp of the Beloved Disciple's native land would not fail to make an impression on his work and remain a part of his witness.

Some students had formerly dated John to the mid- or even late-second century, but the discovery in Egypt of a papyrus fragment of part of John (P[52], or Rylands Papyrus 457, con-

---

[3]Ben Witherington III, *John's Wisdom* (Louisville, Ky.: Westminster John Knox, 1995), p. 13. Anderson suggests another plausible explanation for the need to explain the death of the Beloved Disciple. In his view John 21:23 deals with the problem that none of the original disciples had indeed lived to see the parousia, as the Jesus saying found in Mark 9:1 would have led early Christians to expect. Mark deals with this problem in his own way by placing the saying right before the Transfiguration, so that Peter, James and John do at least see Jesus in his glory ("John and Mark," p. 184).

taining John 18:31-33, 37-38),[4] coming from the first half of the second century, sets the latest possible time of composition very early in the second century or late in the first century. Most students tend to place John late in the first century.[5] One reason for this is that John appears to reflect a lengthy process of reflection on and development of Christology. In effect, Clement of Alexandria's view has long tenure: "But, last of all, John, perceiving that the external facts had been made plain in the Gospel, being urged by his friends, and inspired by the Spirit, composed a spiritual Gospel" (Eusebius *Hist. Eccl.* 6.14.7). An exalted Christology, though, is no guarantee of late date, as the hymn in Philippians 2:5-11 (which could predate Paul's letter and thus come from the early 50s or even before) and Hebrews 1:1-4 (if written before the fall of the temple) attest.[6]

A stronger reason for dating the Fourth Gospel toward the end of the first century is the reflection within the narratives of organized expulsion from the synagogue (Jn 9:22, 34; 12:42-43). While hostility between Jewish Christian and non-Christian Jew was a reality from the start, actual expulsion from the synagogue is probably a later step, the formalization of the parting of the ways that was taking place in the decades following the fall of temple.[7] In addition, the Gospel and epistles of John both show evidence of countering early expressions of docetic Christology

similar to those attacked by Ignatius of Antioch in 110-111 C.E.

The setting and purpose of John's Gospel. As with our discussions of the other Gospels, probing the setting and purpose of the Fourth Gospel is a shadowy venture. We are almost entirely dependent on the text of the Gospel itself for indications of the life circumstances and burning questions of those it was addressed to (reinforced, however, by clearer indications of the challenges facing churches from the epistolary literature of the New Testament). This has become even more shadowy in the light of recent suggestions that limiting a Gospel's audience to a small circle of readers whose exact circumstances can be identified is based on a flawed model of how the Gospels were written and disseminated.[8]

In spite of those well-argued suggestions we need not abandon the search for a Gospel's context completely. Since each Gospel is distinctive, each gives indications of addressing certain needs that would be appropriate for certain kinds of audiences facing certain kinds of concerns or questions. This is all the more true for the readership addressed by John, for which we have the testimony of several epistles, suggesting a circle of communities particularly influenced by (and now in debate over) the traditions of the Beloved Disciple. While there is no need, of course, to limit the author's intended readership to these communi-

---

[4]See Phillip W. Comfort and D. P. Barrett, *The Complete Texts of the Earliest New Testament Manuscripts* (Grand Rapids: Baker, 1999), pp. 355-58 for a brief introduction and an edition of the Greek text. Images of P[52] are readily available on the page at the John Rylands University Library where it is stored <http://rylibweb.man.ac.uk/data1/dg/text/fragment.htm> also <http://rylibweb.man.ac.uk/data2/spcoll/greek>.

[5]J. A. T. Robinson has proposed, on the other hand, that John predates the other Gospels (*The Priority of John* [London: SCM Press, 1985], pp. 1-122).

[6]See Kysar, "John" p. 919; D. A. deSilva, *Perseverance in Gratitude: A Socio-Rhetorical Commentary on the Epistle "to the Hebrews"* (Grand Rapids: Eerdmans, 2000), pp. 20-21; Luke Timothy Johnson, *The Writings of the New Testament,* 2nd ed. (Minneapolis: Fortress, 1996), p. 470.

[7]J. Louis Martyn, *History and Theology in the Fourth Gospel* (Nashville: Abingdon, 1979); Raymond Brown, *The Community of the Beloved Disciple* (New York: Paulist, 1979); and Paul N. Anderson, "The *Sitz im Leben* of the Johannine Bread of Life Discourse and Its Evolving Context," in *Critical Readings of John 6,* ed. R. A. Culpepper (Leiden: Brill, 1997) all bear witness to the importance and timing of these developments for the formation of the first edition of the Fourth Gospel.

[8]R. J. Bauckham, ed., *The Gospels for All Christians* (Grand Rapids: Eerdmans, 1998).

EXEGETICAL SKILL
Narrative Criticism

A great deal of New Testament study is based on what we might call the "historical-critical" paradigm. This model drives us to discover the historical and social situation behind a particular text or the process by which a text came to be written and put together in the form with which we are now familiar, or the way that the text contributed to the situation of its actual readers or hearers. In short, it encourages us to attend to the world behind the text. But a one-sided emphasis on this pursuit often causes us to neglect or forget the world that the text itself creates and the impact that text has on its readers as they are invited into and guided in their interaction with that world. Here, narrative criticism has breathed new life into the study of the Scriptures, for it invites precisely this attention to the story—the characters, plot and other literary features an author uses to create a story world—and to the effects the text invites and encourages in its readers.

Narrative criticism of the New Testament is fueled by the concepts that literary critics in the field of secular literature have used for decades. These include the following:[a]

- The "implied author." While historical-critical inquiry leads us to seek the real author of a text, narrative criticism studies the author implied by the text. What does the reader learn about the person telling the story from the story itself? What beliefs and convictions does he or she hold? What is the implied author's social location (that is, what does the story tell us about the author's acquaintance with or relationship to technology, politics, history, wealth, education and the like)? In other words, what is the reader's *impression* of the author from reading the story, independent of any known, recoverable facts about the actual author?

- The "implied reader." Again in contrast with historical-critical inquiry, we are concerned here with the way the reader is constructed by the text itself. This is the search for the ideal reader, the reader who will respond positively to all the cues given in the story, and who will make all the responses a text invites.

- The process of reading. A reader moves through a text in sequential order from beginning to end. The sequence of a text therefore is itself very

---

[a]This list is adopted from Mark Alan Powell, "Narrative Criticism," in *Hearing the New Testament: Strategies for Interpretation,* ed. Joel B. Green (Grand Rapids: Eerdmans, 1995), pp. 239-55. More extensive discussions of each concept can be found in Mark Alan Powell, *What Is Narrative Criticism?* (Minneapolis: Fortress, 1990); Elizabeth S. Malbon, "Narrative Criticism: How Does the Story Mean?" in *Mark and Method: New Approaches in Biblical Criticism,* ed. J. C. Anderson and S. D. Moore (Minneapolis: Fortress, 1992), pp. 26-36; S. Chatman, *Story and Discourse: Narrative Structure in Fiction and Film* (Ithaca, N.Y.: Cornell University Press, 1978). For a groundbreaking study that applies narrative criticism to John's Gospel, see Alan Culpepper, *Anatomy of the Fourth Gospel* (Philadelphia: Fortress, 1983).

important for the ways a story unfolds for and impacts its readers. This involves taking care to relate the passage studied to the material that has come before (from the beginning) and will follow to the end, a set of questions we have already studied more closely under the "Reading in Literary Context" section in Mark. What is assumed that the reader knows from the story read up to this point? What is assumed that the reader knows from outside the text to make sense of the references and material the author includes? What is not necessarily assumed that the reader knows (e.g., material from the other Gospels)? How does the passage foreshadow what will come later in the narrative (thus potentially causing the reader to make a connection back to the passage you are studying)? What connections does the author make or will the reader supply to make sense of the story as it unfolds?

- Structure. Are there clues to how the reader will understand the structure of the narrative, or smaller parts of the narrative, perhaps signaled through repetitions of phrases, divisions into episodes, established patterns of question and answer, challenge and response, and the like?

- Focus. How does the author heighten the reader's focus on particular elements of the narrative through repeated references to that event or character, or through expanded and lengthy treatment of that event or character? By mapping out those points that receive detailed attention or that are brought to mind at several points throughout the narrative (e.g., consider the crucifixion: referred to in the passion predictions, narrated at length and referred to in retrospect), we can learn the implied author's points of greater concern, which are also expected to have the greater impact on the implied readers. The astute narrative critic will also pay heed to those elements that are underplayed or neglected in the story. What does the author's limiting of the reader's focus in those directions say about the author, the author's interests and the experience he or she is shaping for the reader?

- Plot. As a story moves forward, a plot unfolds, and this plot provides the essential energy that moves a reader from beginning to end. What is the plot of the passage? What is driving the plot? Is it conflict between characters? Is it some kind of quest or mission on the part of some characters? How does the plot build up to a climax and resolve itself? If there is some unresolved part of the story, how will the readers create resolution (a wonderful example of Jesus leaving an open-ended plot for his own audience to fill in is found in Mt 21:33-41)?

- Characterization. Characters are as essential to a narrative as its plot. Who are the characters in the story? How are they portrayed? That is, what does the reader know about them from their own words, thoughts and deeds, and from the opinions other characters have of them? Is there discernible change or development in particular characters as the narrative moves forward?

- Point of view. From whose perspective is the narrative told? Are there shifts in perspective within the narrative from, for example, the narrator to the crowds to Jesus' opponents to disciples? Whose point of view does the author wish the readers to accept as reliable? For example, if some characters think ill of one character, but God or the narrator speak well of the character, whose opinion will the reader credit, and how will that affect the characterization of the others? In effect, study of point of view invites us to look closely at how the evaluations and sympathies of the reader are being guided (and thus also limited) by the author throughout the narrative.

- Setting. What is the backdrop against which the drama plays itself out (e.g., the time and location), and what evocations will this setting have for the implied readers? How will the setting and its evocations affect the way readers experience the drama that takes place there? (Jesus' overturning of the tables in the outer court of the temple would have a different effect and meaning if it happened in the streets; Jesus' death has certain effect because it occurs during Passover).

- Irony. Irony occurs when the reader knows more than the characters in a drama and is able to see their misperceptions of events in the drama. In effect, the reader can see how the characters are "reading" events, and how that reading differs from a true reading, given the knowledge shared by author and reader.

- Symbolism. Literature is replete with figures of speech like simile (as in "the kingdom of God is like . . .") and metaphor (as in "I am the vine . . ."), in which one thing is illuminated by comparison with another thing. Moreover, characters, actions and settings in a drama can themselves become symbols inviting the reader to attach certain "meanings" to them.

- Intertextuality. How does the narrative build its meaning and effects on other texts available for the reader? This is part of the "assumed knowledge" of the "implied reader," but it takes on a greater level of specificity as the text points to other specific texts "out there," beyond the world of the narrative. The most commonly noticed are references to the Old Testament in the New Testament narratives, whether explicit attention is drawn to the older text ("as it is written . . .") or characters, motifs and phrases are just dropped into the new text without the author referring explicitly to the source. This is such an important area of study, it will be the subject of special attention in two later chapters.

Of all the New Testament narratives, John especially invites this mode of analysis because the author has provided us with some of the most extensive and finely crafted stories of the New Testament. As a preliminary model we will look in detail at John 4:1-42 (though space limitations prevent a thorough analysis of all the features listed above). This is just one episode within the larger narrative of John, but it is unified by setting (Jesus moves into Samaria at the beginning, all the action happens in Sychar, and Jesus leaves Samaria at the end), by consistency of characters (Jesus, the disciples and the Samaritan woman), and by plot, namely, the revelation of God's Christ to the Samaritans, beginning with the single woman and concluding with "many."

The narrator gives considerable attention to setting, locating Jesus at Jacob's well in Sychar at noontime. The reader is thus reminded of the spiritual heritage of Samaria, a region that was the scene of many patriarchal narratives, as well as the inheritance of Jacob and his sons (a point of intertexture, since those stories about Jacob's sojourn here are implicitly recalled). We are on historic if not holy ground here. The timing is also significant: women tended to draw water early in the day rather than in the heat of the day. The author will narrate a story in which many things are "out of place"—a Jew speaking with a Samaritan as if on terms of friendship, a man talking freely in public to a woman who is not his wife—and this may be a way the author foreshadows the improprieties yet to come. It is consonant with the "out of placeness" of Jesus himself, who belongs to the realm above, as well as the "out of placeness" that characterizes the reader/disciple, who does not belong to the world.

The plot opens by means of a request—"Give me a drink" (Jn 4:7)—and is advanced through the dialogue that follows. The movement here is from misunderstanding to understanding, from failure to recognize Jesus to recognition of Jesus on the part of the woman, but it is also a movement toward the woman on Jesus' part as he moves past the typical expectations, misunderstandings and distractions on the way to revealing himself to her. Indeed, misunderstanding and irony are favorite literary techniques of the author of John. The woman will have to work past misunderstandings at verses 11 and 15, while the disciples themselves will be ushered past a misunderstanding at verse 33. These misunderstandings invariably involve apprehending Jesus' words at the literal, physical, mundane level, and failing to grasp their true, symbolic or spiritual meaning until the misapprehension is pointed out by Jesus. The reader of John 4, moreover, has already encountered this pattern in John 2:18-22 and 3:1-12, and will encounter it again throughout the episodes that follow (see, for example, Jn 6:41-42, 52-60; 7:32-36; 8:21-22). This very pattern of stumbling over the words of Jesus at the literal level and having to move past them to a symbolic understanding mirrors the stumbling over the very revelation of God in the "Word made flesh" at the human level (Jesus, the carpenter's son, born in Nazareth) and the need to move to a deeper understanding of who Jesus is as the one from above. The narrative thus comes to mirror the process of coming to faith or failing to come to faith.

Irony is not as prominent in this episode as elsewhere (for other examples, see Jn 7:27; 11:49-52; 19:2-3, 14), although a hint of it is present in John 4:12, where the author and the reader know what the Samaritan woman at this point does not, that Jesus is indeed "greater than our ancestor Jacob." This is such a satisfying narrative, however, because the woman does indeed come to share in the author's and reader's knowledge about Jesus, and she participates in transmitting that knowledge to her neighbors.

In the middle of the episode the woman leaves and the disciples enter. The one-on-one encounter between Jesus and the woman is given greater scope than the following two scenes (Jesus and the disciples; Jesus and the Samaritans) combined. In the scene with the disciples, Jesus says that the doing and completing of the work of God is what nourishes him. This is a commentary on what Jesus has been about in verses 7-26. And it sounds a theme that the larger narrative will continue to develop as the followers of Jesus (with whom the reader is asked to identify) are urged by Jesus to labor for the bread that lasts rather than physical bread (in a dialogue in which food, the doing of God's work, believing in Jesus, and receiving Jesus as the "bread of life" are all combined; Jn 6:26-40). In effect, the narrative invites the readers who recognize Jesus as the revelation of the Father to embody Jesus just as they embody the food they eat. The result is that they will continue to do the work of God that Jesus began. Later, the metaphor of the vine and branches will articulate the same set of meanings in a different way (Jn 15:1-11).

Using the imagery of sowing and reaping a harvest, Jesus invites the disciples to participate in the work that Jesus has been doing among the Samaritans and to continue to expand that work. They go only where others have gone before, and the expectation is created that many fields are ripe for harvesting. Here the story in the text is only fulfilled in the story of the disciples and the readers who identify themselves with the disciples. A narrative expectation is created that is fulfilled in a preliminary and partial way in John 4:39-42, and that is supported again in John 10:16 in the metaphor of the shepherd and his flocks, and that emerges in a new context in John 12:20-24, when Gentiles come seeking Jesus. This movement gives moment to the crucifixion, which from the start has been presented as the means by which the harvest would be gathered (see Jn 3:14-15; 11:51-52; 12:32), and opens out into the work of the disciples not narrated but foreseen within the world of the narrative.

This analysis has not taken into account the meaning of important symbols like "running water" and "food," nor has it paid direct attention to characterization and character development (to which the author gives considerable attention) or attempted to reconstruct the implied author and reader, although some scattered observations are relevant to those tasks.

Nevertheless, I have tried to show in a brief way how attention to the elements of narrative criticism can contribute to our understanding of a story and our ability to enter into the world the story creates and the effects it seeks to have on readers. Such analysis is an invaluable complement to the study of the world outside and behind the text, for ultimately the story itself often carries home the deeper meaning of the sacred text and achieves the author's goals for our formation as disciples.

John's Gospel provides an excellent field to practice narrative criticism because the fourth Evangelist crafts such full and rich episodes in comparison with the briefer narratives in the Synoptic Gospels. The reader is invited to explore the following episodes, working through each of the twelve literary-artistic concepts described in this section, especially the last ten concepts (the investigation of the implied author and implied reader really requires an investigation of the entire text): John 3:1-21; 6:1-71; 9:1-41; 11:1-57. With each passage remember that the episode is part of the narrative movement of a larger whole. The skill of narrative criticism necessitates the investigation of literary context as well (see "Exegetical Skill: Literary Context" in the chapter on Mark).

FOR FURTHER READING

Beardslee, William. A. *Literary Criticism of the New Testament.* Philadelphia: Fortress, 1969.

Booth, William C. *The Rhetoric of Fiction.* 2nd ed. Chicago: University of Chicago, 1983.

Culpepper, R. Alan. *Anatomy of the Fourth Gospel: A Study in Literary Design.* Philadelphia: Fortress, 1983.

Kingsbury, Jack D. *Matthew as Story.* 2nd ed. Philadelphia: Fortress, 1988.

Kurz, William S. *Reading Luke-Acts: Dynamics of Biblical Narrative.* Louisville, Ky.: Westminster John Knox, 1993.

Moore, Stephen D. *Literary Criticism and the Gospels: The Theoretical Challenge.* New Haven, Conn.: Yale University Press, 1989.

O'Day, Gail R. *Revelation in the Fourth Gospel: Narrative Mode and Theological Claim.* Philadelphia: Fortress, 1986.

Powell, Mark Allan. *What Is Narrative Criticism?* Minneapolis: Fortress, 1990.

Rhoads, David, and Donald Michie. *Mark as Story: An Introduction to the Narrative of a Gospel.* Philadelphia: Fortress, 1982.

Staley, John L. *The Print's First Kiss: A Rhetorical Investigation of the Implied Reader in the Fourth Gospel.* SBLDS 82. Atlanta: Scholars Press, 1988.

Stibbe, M. W. G. *John as Storyteller: Narrative Criticism and the Fourth Gospel.* Cambridge: Cambridge University Press, 1992.

ties, the way the preserved traditions have taken shape and the final form they are given provide windows into the story and struggles of at least the bearers of that tradition if not their audience as a whole.

The quest for the historical Johannine communities, as it were, peaked with the work of Raymond Brown.[9] In his two-volume commentary on John, Brown discerned several distinct stages in the composition of the Gospel of John corresponding to stages in the history of the Johannine community. According to his reconstruction we find at the core of the community (or perhaps better, the circle that carries the Johannine tradition) the Beloved Disciple, whose ongoing reflection on and preaching about Jesus' significance stood at the center of a community of believers that was nurtured by him. This circle had its roots in Palestine, where it endured a long quarrel with non-Christian Jews. This stage is reflected in the selection, preservation and expansion of Jesus traditions focusing on points of dispute concerning claims about Jesus' significance as well as in the persistence of a dualistic mode of thinking about people and life in this world similar to that encountered in another sect, namely, the Qumran community.

At some point, perhaps in connection with the first revolt, the circle resettled in Syria or, more likely, Ephesus in Asia Minor. There it continued to encounter opposition from non-Christian Jews, even being shut out of the synagogues for their radical confession of Jesus as God's Son.[10] The conflicts between church and synagogue reflected in the oracles to the churches in Smyrna and Philadelphia in Revelation 2:9-11 and 3:8-10, a text emanating from the Johannine circle, attest to this ongo-

ing tension over "who Jesus is." The tradition also suggests tensions between Johannine Christians and those who were disciples in secret for fear of the Jews (Jn 9:21-23; 12:42-43; 19:38), Christian Jews who refused to make a bold and open confession (in the eyes of the Beloved Disciple and the Evangelist, at least). The openness to Gentile mission reflected in John 10:16 and 12:20-32 also suggests that the tradition had some time to ferment in regions where such a mission would be a reality, such as Asia Minor.

The ongoing history of the communities guided by the bearers of this Johannine tradition after the composition of the Gospel can be seen in the Johannine letters. As with so many local congregations the story is not always a happy one. First, these communities faced a heart-wrenching schism surrounding the rise of docetist interpretations of the incarnation and passion, which denied the reality of the divine Logos (or Christ, or Son) actually becoming flesh and suffering in the flesh. Such a view has strong ideological ground in the Greco-Roman view that the gods are impassible, that is, that they cannot suffer at the hands of human beings, nor be acted on by the material creation. It may, however, also arise from some very practical and pastoral interests connected with the increased pressure on Christians from local Gentile populations and local officials leading to the threat of persecution for failure to worship the emperor. If the Christ did not suffer in the flesh, neither should his followers have to suffer![11] Anderson makes a good connection between docetism and martyrdom from the writings of Ignatius of Antioch: "If our Lord suffered these things only in appearance, then I am in chains only in ap-

---

[9]Brown's reconstruction will be supplemented here with insights drawn from Anderson's "Interfluential, Formative, and Dialectical," pp. 30-32; *Christology of the Fourth Gospel*, pp. 257-61; and *"Sitz im Leben,"* pp. 28-57.

[10]From the non-Christian Jewish point of view, such a confession might well have appeared to be a wandering away from the central tenet of the faith—"Hear, O Israel: the LORD our God, the LORD is One" (Deut 6:4). See further, Anderson, *"Sitz im Leben,"* pp. 33-34.

[11]Anderson, *"Sitz im Leben,"* pp. 40-43.

pearance! And why am I giving myself over to death, fire, sword, and wild animals?" (*Ign. Smyrn.* 4:2).[12] Finally, we find clear indications of inner-Christian debates concerning the nature of authority in the church, exemplified by 3 John and the problems between the Elder and Diotrephes, the latter representing a hierarchical model of authority in the church.

What kinds of pastoral concerns, then, did the Fourth Gospel address? For what kinds of pastoral concerns would the Fourth Gospel have been an effective response? The Gospel of John is frequently used in our century as an evangelistic tract. Was it written to be so used in the first century? Students are divided on this question. Some regard both the making of new converts and the strengthening of Christian believers as of equal importance to the Evangelist.[13] Others deny the work any missionary thrust, while still others promote evangelism of outsiders as the Gospel's primary objective.[14] This Gospel has its own purpose statement in John 20:31: "These are written so that you may come to believe that Jesus is the Messiah, the Son of God" (NRSV). To the English reader this might appear to solve the question, but there is a hidden problem in the Greek. The manuscript evidence is about equally divided between reading the verb *believe* as an aorist—"in order that you might believe," or possible even "come to believe"—and a present continuous action—"in order that you may keep on believing." The former reading favors an evangelistic thrust,

the latter a faith-sustaining thrust. This problem is complicated by the likelihood that John 20:30-31 originally constituted the ending to the Gospel only in its "first edition" (see pp. 404-9). At that stage, in dialogue (and debate) with the synagogue, the Fourth Gospel might well have functioned as a repository of evangelistic materials.[15]

Although the Fourth Gospel preserves, then, traces of evangelistic interests, its present form shows some distance from those ends. For example, consider the responses of many unbelievers in the Gospel. Although the disciples have a responsibility to bear witness to the world (Jn 15:27; 17:18), and several individuals (like the Samaritan woman and the man born blind) come to faith in the Gospel, many other outsiders get progressively more mired and confused as they inquire into Jesus, which is not a hopeful sign for an unbelieving reader. In many ways, episodes such as those that fill chapters 6-8 seem better suited to explaining the failure of mission rather than motivating conversion.

In its present form, then, it is most likely that the Fourth Gospel primarily addresses a Christian readership. John's Gospel reflects the need to assure Christians (especially Jewish Christians) in the face of opposition and criticism from non-Christian Jews who rejected their claims about Jesus' significance and were in the process of excluding more and more of those who were too far from the center of pharisaic Judaism.[16] The "Jews" in John's Gos-

---

[12]This might also lend some poignancy to the insistence in 1 John that Christ came not only in water but also in blood (1 Jn 5:6), and to what it would mean for the disciple to have this witness of the Spirit, the water and the blood in him- or herself as well (1 Jn 5:10).

[13]C. K. Barrett, *The Gospel According to St. John,* 2nd ed. (Philadelphia: Westminster Press, 1978), p. 26; George R. Beasley-Murray, *John,* WBC (Dallas: Word, 1987), p. lxxxix.

[14]Raymond Brown, (*The Gospel According to John,* AB [Garden City, N.J.: Doubleday, 1966], 1:73-78) is typical of the first kind, Witherington (*John's Wisdom,* p. 32) of the second.

[15]I agree with Witherington (*John's Wisdom,* p. 4) that even in its earliest edition it would be better to regard the Fourth Gospel as a resource to assist believers in evangelism (and to assist them to endure opposition and rejection when they bear witness to Jesus) rather than as something to be handed out as a missionary tract.

[16]Barrett, *Gospel According to St. John,* pp. 63-64; Brown, *Gospel According to John,* 1:71-75; Beasley-Murray, *John,* p. lxxxix; Kysar, "John," p. 918.

pel refer in the main to the religious authorities and others who were hostile to Jesus, the representation in the text of the author's contemporaries who were pressuring Christian Jews either to hide or renounce their convictions about Jesus as the Messiah or risk excommunication from the synagogue and suffer dislocation from their social networks.[17]

Some suggest that the fourth Evangelist writes specifically to encourage Jewish Christians in the wake of the introduction of the "Benediction Against Heretics" into the synagogue liturgy, presumably around 85 C.E., as a means of driving "heretics" from the synagogue.[18] We cannot be so precise, however, about the actual date and extent of the implementation of this change to synagogue liturgy. Moreover, hostility between non-Christian Jews and Christian Jews began much earlier and was not necessarily settled quickly throughout the Mediterranean by a universal policy issued in or around 85 C.E.[19] Nevertheless, the Evangelist was in fact quite concerned about the effect of the synagogue's negative evaluation of Jesus and those who followed him. Expulsion from the synagogue is a recurrent concern in John 9:22, 12:42 and 16:2, and twice this eventuality is linked with the open confession of Jesus. The Fourth Gospel preserves much material that would have been highly effective in providing special insulation with regard to the evaluation of non-Christian Jews, and even more specifically with regard to this issue of having to choose between honoring Jesus and being honored or affirmed by the synagogue.

Although a major force behind the Johannine Epistles, the refutation of heretic Christians is probably not a driving force behind the composition of the Fourth Gospel. Rather, John appears to have the more constructive purpose of deepening Christians' reflection on the significance and richness of the treasure they have received in Jesus, and to encourage them to keep their hold on this treasure. The words and stories about Jesus are concerned with keeping the disciples "from stumbling" (Jn 16:1) in the face of opposition. We catch a glimpse of the need to strengthen or educate believers in their confession from the aftermath, as it were, of the community's story as seen in 1-2 John, and in the mention of other interpretations of the Gospel available to Christians in Asia Minor (such as the preaching of the Nicolaitans in Revelation 2). Moreover, from the amount of space given to relevant traditions and even the doubling of this material in chapters 13-17, the Fourth Gospel clearly seeks to affirm or construct a particular ethos for the Christian communities, an ethos marked by love, mutual help and service, and unity.

A different purpose or set of purposes may need to be considered for John 21, which has the appearance of an epilogue or appendix added after the main body of the Gospel was completed (see the perfectly adequate conclusion in Jn 20:30-31, now with a secondary conclusion in Jn 21:24-25). In this appendix the author deals with the death of the Beloved Disciple, which may have surprised and dismayed the community. The author may have known the rumor that the Beloved Disciple would not die until Jesus returned to have been current among the communities that followed the Johannine tradition. A second pur-

---

[17]Brown, *John*, 1:71, 74-75.

[18]"For apostates let there be no hope . . . and let the Nazarenes and the heretics perish as in a moment, let them be blotted out of the book of the living and let them not be written with the righteous. Blessed art Thou, O Lord, who humblest the arrogant" (translation from Everett Ferguson, *Backgrounds of Early Christianity*, 2nd ed. [Grand Rapids: Eerdmans, 1993], pp. 543-44).

[19]D. A. Hagner, "The *Sitz im Leben* of the Gospel of Matthew," in *Treasures New and Old: Recent Contributions to Matthean Studies*, ed. D. R. Bauer and M. A. Powell (Atlanta: Scholars Press, 1996), pp. 27-62.

John's Gospel and the Role of John the Baptist in God's Plan

No Gospel gives more attention to the identity and role of John the Baptist than the Fourth Gospel—more than is needed simply to record his witness to Jesus' significance. This has led some to suppose that one of the minor purposes of John's Gospel is to clarify the relationship between John the Baptist and Jesus, showing the latter to be the successor and superior to John.

What happened to the followers of John the Baptist that did not become followers of Jesus? We know from Acts 19:1-7 that John the Baptist continued to have followers long after Jesus' resurrection. A sect emerges in late antiquity called Mandaism, whose extant writing, though from a much later period, claims that John the Baptist was God's light for the world and the divine redeemer. Followers of this sect exist even to the present day. In the Fourth Gospel, however, John the Baptist himself is made repeatedly to bear witness to Jesus' precedence in God's economy and to accept the diminution of his own honor and following in favor of the increase of Jesus' honor and following (Jn 1:8-9, 20, 30; 3:28, 30; 10:41). The Fourth Gospel, then, may give so much attention to John the Baptist's witness to Jesus' superiority because its author is aware of a tendency to elevate John to the detriment of Jesus.[a] While positively valuing the Baptist, the author nevertheless seeks to secure John as a clear witness to the surpassing authority of Jesus.

---

[a]Brown, *Gospel According to St. John*, pp. 67-70; Beasley-Murray, *John*, p. lxxxix.

---

pose of this chapter would be to establish the relationship between Peter, representing the established leadership of the wider church, and the Beloved Disciple, who may not have had a part in the apostolic circle or, apparently, the emerging church hierarchical structure. On the one hand, the episode highlights the importance of the community's founder. On the other hand, it may serve to reconcile the community to the authority of the larger church as Johannine Christianity came fully into the mainstream.[20]

THE RESOURCES BEHIND THE FOURTH GOSPEL

Literary sources and the composition of John. Source Criticism—the attempt to discover literary sources used by and incorporated within the New Testament texts as we now have them—flourished in the late nineteenth and early twentieth centuries, and was rigorously applied to the Fourth Gospel by Rudolf Bultmann, whose work and observations remain foundational for the study of John even for those who reject his source theory. Several indicators can point to an author's use of sources. For example, the style and customary vocabulary of the text might suddenly change, or uncharacteristic themes and topics might be introduced in a particular section but then go undeveloped and unmentioned throughout the remainder of the work. Additionally, we might detect a "bump" in the flow of the narrative (the technical term is *aporia*), suggesting a literary seam. Passages articulating a theology or ideology different from (even contrary to)

---

[20]Raymond E. Brown, *The Epistles of John*, AB 30 (Garden City, N.Y.: Doubleday, 1982), pp. 70-71.

An Outline of John's Gospel

Prologue: John 1:1-18

The "Book of Signs": John 1:19—12:50: Jesus' ministry to the world

The "Book of Glory": John 13—20

    Jesus' instructions to his followers: 13:1—17:26

    Passion and resurrection appearances and conclusion: 18:1—20:31

Epilogue: John 21:1-25: Additional(?) resurrection appearance and conclusion

---

other passages in the book might suggest that sources with different viewpoints have been brought together. Sometimes, we actually have access to a text that might have served as a literary source for another (as in the case of Mark in regard to Matthew and Luke, or Jude in relation to 2 Peter).

Identifying and making a convincing argument for the use of non-Johannine sources by the fourth Evangelist is made difficult by several factors. First, we have no independent witnesses to the traditions found in John and therefore no basis for comparison. Second, the Evangelist has given his material a fairly uniform style and vocabulary throughout, thus removing two important criteria for discerning and defending proposed sources.[21] Nevertheless, there are still a number of bumps and seams in the Gospel that suggest places where older resources have been brought together into the form of the narrative as we now have it.

- The transitions within the prologue between material celebrating the "Logos" and derivative material speaking about John the Baptist and his relationship to the "Word" (Jn 1:6-8 and 1:15) suggest at least the revision of an earlier Logos hymn.
- The geographical *aporiai* in John 4—7 sug-

gest seams in composition. Jesus goes from Galilee in chapter 4 to Jerusalem in chapter 5, and then he is suddenly introduced as going to the other side of the Sea of Galilee in chapter 6 (a far cry from Jerusalem), appearing again in Jerusalem at the opening of chapter 7 with no intervening explanations of these shifts in setting. Bultmann solved the problem by reordering the chapters so that the episodes in Galilee and the episodes in Jerusalem are gathered together (followed by a return to Galilee later in chap. 7, explicitly as a reaction to the increased hostility he met in Jerusalem in chap. 5).

- A lengthy upper room address by Jesus appears to be brought to a close in John 14:31, only to be followed now by another three chapters of upper room discourse.
- John 20:30-31 provides a perfectly adequate conclusion to a Gospel, making chapter 21 appear to be a later addition.

We could add to this list several theological statements found in self-contained passages that stand in some tension with the rest of the Gospel (e.g., Jn 6:53-58, if this is read as a reference to participating in the rite of holy Communion).

Such *aporiai*, along with other literary ob-

---

[21]Kysar, "John," p. 921; Eduard Schweizer, *Ego Eimi* (Gottingen: Vandenhoeck, 1939), pp. 82-112. See the thorough critique of Bultmann's arguments for sources based on style in Anderson, *Christology of the Fourth Gospel*, pp. 70-166. The exception, not surprisingly, is John 7:53—8:11, which we have already seen should not be considered an original part of the Fourth Gospel but rather a later interpolation intended to preserve an important part of the oral Jesus tradition from oblivion.

servations, led Bultmann to propose a number of sources woven into a single Gospel by the fourth Evangelist:

- A "signs source." The enumeration of the first and second signs in John 2:11 and 4:54 might be indications of an earlier text that related a series of numbered signs as a testimony to Jesus' miracles. This would have been an evangelistic document meant to inspire belief among the unconverted by the stories of Jesus' miracles and won-

an original farewell discourse. Moreover, the material in John 15:26—16:33 largely duplicates topics previously encountered in chapter 14 (e.g., the coming of the Spirit, the function of the Spirit, the departure of Jesus and Jesus' purpose behind telling the disciples what will happen in advance).[22] Together, these observations suggest that two different bodies of Jesus traditions, largely overlapping in subject matter, have been joined into the "farewell

Figure 9.1. A street in Beth Shean (Scythopolis) lined with colonnades. Scythopolis was an impressive, Hellenized city between Samaria and Galilee. (Photo courtesy of Todd Bolen [BiblePlaces.com])

ders. John 20:30-31, which makes reference to a collection of signs, would have been the original conclusion to this evangelistic tract.

- A "discourse source." The main indication for such a source is the strange literary seam at John 14:31, which seems to end

discourse." The fact that they were not better blended together actually suggests the high regard the redactor had for the traditions passed down from the Beloved Disciple.

The full extent of the discourse source or sources, however, is more difficult for scholars

---

[22]Additionally, observe that Jesus says "none of you asks me, 'Where are you going?' " (Jn 16:5 NRSV) after both Peter and Thomas have raised this very question (Jn 13:36; 14:5). This literary problem would also be resolved, then, if we posit a second discourse source being introduced after chapter fourteen is over (Bart D. Ehrman, *The New Testament: A Historical Introduction to the Early Christian Writings* [Oxford: Oxford University Press, 1997], p. 144).

Figure 9.2. Bethany and Bethphage. Lazarus, Martha and Mary made their home in Bethany. These villages also figure prominently in the story of the triumphal entry and passion week. (Photo courtesy of Todd Bolen [BiblePlaces.com])

to determine.[23] Would it contain some of the other self-disclosure speeches of Jesus in John 6—10, with this material placed in the context of debate with the world and no longer in the original context of the private teaching of Jesus to his disciples? At the very least the likelihood that John 15—16 belongs to an earlier written collection of Johannine Jesus traditions opens up the possibility.

- A passion source. Bultmann explained the distinctive flavor of John's passion narrative by suggesting a passion source independent from but following the same basic outline (as we would expect) as the Synoptic Gospels' passion source. Whatever its prehistory of this tradition, John 19—20 is now so infused with all the distinctive characteristics of the rest of the Gospel that defense of a non-Johannine passion source is especially difficult. Each scene reflects the Beloved Disciple's perception of Jesus and the significance of his death as well as the Beloved Disciple's understanding of the world that rejected Jesus.

---

[23]Bultmann proposed an extensive discourse source or sayings source, but this has not been successfully demonstrated (Kysar, "John," p. 922; Bultmann's theory is succinctly discussed in Eduard Lohse, *The Formation of the New Testament* [Nashville: Abingdon, 1981], pp. 172-74; Beasley-Murray, *John*, p. xxxviii). Beasley-Murray suggests that the discourses have their origin in the preaching of the Beloved Disciple, but then admits the impossibility of trying to reconstruct an oral source from its only surviving literary witness.

John's Style

From the standpoint of style it might be difficult to tell whether a two- or three-verse excerpt from a Synoptic Gospel came from Mark, Matthew or Luke. It is the rare passage in John, however, that might be mistaken as the work of one of his canonical peers. John uses a distinctive vocabulary, displaying great interest in symbolic words like *light, darkness, truth, lie, above, below, vine, door,* the imagery of shepherding and the like. Equally distinctive is John's style, especially with regard to Jesus' speech. Jesus speaks often in mysterious riddles, often in lengthy, repetitious self-revelations. The style of these discourses is often poetic and rhythmic, and marked by antithetical development of themes. John's dualism and dualistic mode of thought is very much evident in the style of the discourses.[a]

John tends to construct lengthy dramatic stories, often divisible into episodes, and he makes frequent use of irony, puns (like born from above/born again), and misunderstanding as he advances his dialogues (see Jn 3:1-10; 4:1-42; 6:22-59; 7:33-35; 8:21-22). A strongly Semitic syntax underlies the Greek, a reflection of the author's own Palestinian roots, however, rather than evidence of a Semitic "original."[b]

[a]Kysar, "John," pp. 915-16; Raymond Brown, *Introduction to the New Testament* (Garden City, N.Y.: Doubleday, 1997), pp. 333, 335-37.
[b]For details, see Lohse, *Formation of the New Testament,* pp. 182-83.

- An epilogue. John 21 presents something of an appendix, with verses 24-25 providing a new (and redundant) conclusion to the whole, even showing awareness of John 20:30 (Jn 21:25 resumes the "many other works" theme). It is possible that the last chapter was added at a later stage in the Gospel's history, addressing some new concerns that arose in the interim, such as the death of the Beloved Disciple or the assimilation of the Johannine communities into the mainstream of the Christian movement, represented by Peter's pastoral leadership.[24]

Source theories have dominated conversations about the composition of the Fourth Gospel for some time, but in recent decades the luster of this particular solution to the *aporiai* and other tensions within the Gospel has seemed to fade. Again, the striking unity of the Johannine style, themes and topics makes for a difficult upstream swim for any source theory. The theological tensions present within the Gospel may reflect the ongoing reflection on the tradition by the leaders in the Johannine tradition over decades. In addition, the ongoing interpretation and application of the tradition to face new challenges decade after decade points not to a multiplicity of authors or sources but a multiplicity of situations being freshly addressed.[25] In other words, the tensions within the Fourth Gospel might have emerged more through its bearers commenting on their own tradition than through the incorporation or correction of non-Johannine sources.[26]

[24]Brown, *Epistles of John,* pp. 70-71, 106-12.
[25]Anderson, "Interfluential, Formative, and Dialectical," p. 24.
[26]Anderson, *Christology of the Fourth Gospel,* pp. 257, 263-64.

The very real *aporiai* and other tensions in the narrative can be dealt with much more simply in a theory of multiple, successive editions of the Fourth Gospel (rather than the use of non-Johannine sources).[27] The first edition was composed in a setting where the primary purposes were to convince non-Christian Jews of the validity of Jesus' messiahship (which would explain the emphasis on signs and the original conclusion, Jn 20:30-31) and to deal with the hostility of the synagogue against Christian Jews. Later editions incorporated other Johannine traditions developed in light of the ongoing challenges facing the community, such as the interpretation of Jesus' feeding miracle and the implications of discipleship (chap. 6) and the death of the Beloved Disciple (chap. 21), and as an attempt to preserve traditions not included in the original Gospel, such as the larger body of teachings now found in chapters 15-17. The Beloved Disciple, whatever his identity, provided many of the traditions and perhaps even committed some of these to writing (which would explain the reference to his scribal activity in Jn 21:24). A disciple of his, or perhaps the Beloved Disciple himself, composed the first edition of the Gospel. Another disciple of his would then have made further expansions on the Gospel after the death of the Beloved Disciple to provide for the ongoing nurture and guidance of the communities that have depended on this witness, and to share that witness with the wider church.

The Synoptic Gospels? Robert Kysar called John the "Maverick Gospel." Set next to the Synoptics with their vast store of shared material and their rather similar style and focus, John certainly seems to speak about Jesus in his own way, in his own idiom and with his own material. On the one hand, it is the same basic story. The Messiah, announced by John the Baptist, goes about the land gathering disciples, teaching, performing wonders. As opposition grows the Messiah is arrested after a final evening with his disciples, tried before Jewish and Roman authorities, crucified and buried. The end of the story is also the same: the Messiah overcomes death through resurrection and is reunited with his disciples before ascending to heaven.

Yet in its particulars, it is also a different story.

- The "cleansing of the temple" story appears near the outset of Jesus' public ministry rather than as a precipitating factor near the end.

- John narrates what was largely a Judean ministry. From chapters 8 through 20, John suggests no movement outside of Judea. This stands in stark contrast with the Synoptic picture of a lengthy Galilean ministry leading up to a one-week Jerusalem ministry.

- Jesus' ministry incorporates at least three Passovers in John, not just one as in the Synoptics. This also contributes to the Jerusalem-centered focus of the Gospel, since Jesus already visits Jerusalem twice by the end of chapter 7.

- Jesus' ministry overlaps considerably with John the Baptist's in John's Gospel, as opposed to Mark, for example, where Jesus begins preaching only after John is put in prison.

- There are no exorcisms in John (save for the "big one" in Jn 12:31), and relatively few healings compared to the other Gospels. Those that are narrated are expanded at length by additional episodes and conversations about the significance of the healing.

- John tells of the trial before Annas but gives no detail about the trial before Caiaphas.

- Jesus has a significant dialogue with Pilate (very different from Mk 15:2-5).

- Simon of Cyrene has no role in this passion.

---

[27]A two-edition composition history is championed by Barnabas Lindars (*The Gospel of John*, NCB [Grand Rapids: Eerdmans, 1972], pp. 46-54) and by Paul N. Anderson in the works previously cited.

Stories and Sayings Common to John and the Synoptics

STORIES SHARED BY THE TWO TRADITIONS
- cleansing of the temple (Jn 2:13-22//Mk 11:15-19)
- Jesus heals the official's son/servant (Jn 4:46-54//Mt 8:5-13)
- Jesus feeds the 5,000 (Jn 6:1-14//Mk 6:32-44)
- Jesus walks on water (Jn 6:16-21//Mk 6:45-51)
- anointing at Bethany (Jn 12:1-8//Mk 14:3-9)
- entry into Jerusalem (Jn 12:12-19//Mk 11:1-10//Mt 21:1-11)
- miraculous catch of fish (Jn 21:4-8//Lk 5:1-11)
- significant features of the arrest, trial and crucifixion story

SAYINGS SHARED BY THE TWO TRADITIONS
(not necessarily in application or placement)
- rebuilding of the temple in three days (Jn 2:19//Mk 14:58; Mark attributes this to a "false witness," however)
- requirements for seeing the kingdom of God (Jn 3:3, 5//Mt 18:3)
- prophets are not without honor except in their native land (Jn 4:44//Mk 6:4)
- "Those who love their life will lose it, and those who hate their life in this world will keep it for eternal life"; necessity of following Jesus (Jn 12:25-26//Mk 8:34-35)
- "servants are not greater than their master" (Jn 13:16; 15:20//Mt 10:24; in Jn 15:20, the context and meaning is the same as in Mt 10:24; at Jn 13:16, the Evangelist has used the same saying to reinforce an instruction about servanthood as the ethos for discipleship)
- "Whoever receives one whom I send receives me; and whoever receives me receives him who sent me" (Jn 13:20//Mt 10:40)
- "All things have been handed over to me by my Father; and no one knows the Son except the Father, neither does anyone know the Father except the Son and anyone to whom the Son chooses to reveal him" (Mt 11:27//Lk 10:22; see Jn 1:18; 3:35; 7:29; 10:15; 13:3; 17:25)
- predictions of Judas' betrayal, Peter's denial, disciples' desertion (Jn 13:21-30, 38; 16:32// Mk 14:18-21, 27-31)
- "Ask and you will receive" (Jn 16:24//Mt 7:7-8)
- forgiving and retaining sins (Jn 20:23//Mt 16:19; 18:18)

OTHER NOTEWORTHY RESONANCES
- "Father, save me from this hour" and drinking the cup the Father holds out (Jn 12:27; 18:11// Mk 14:36; in John, however, Jesus never actually asks for the hour or cup to pass)
- passion predictions (Jn 13:33; 14:3, 28-29 [see also 12:32-33]//Mk 8:31; 9:31; 10:33-34)
- objection to Jesus based on his lineage (Jn 6:42//Mk 6:3)
- objection that Jesus is possessed (Jn 8:48-49//Mk 3:22-30)

(Jesus is "carrying the cross by himself" according to Jn 19:17.)

- The time of the crucifixion is different: noon in John 19:14, but 9 a.m. in Mark 15:25.

- In John, Jesus dies on the day of preparation, so that the Last Supper does not take place on Passover as in the Synoptic Gospels; there is also no institution of the Lord's Supper.

- Jesus' body is prepared for burial immediately in John, whereas in the Synoptics the women do not try to apply the spices until after the sabbath.

In addition to the differences in plot there are also significant differences in the speech attributed to Jesus.

- Very little of the speech attributed to Jesus in the Synoptic Gospels appears in John, and vice versa.

- John presents well-developed discourses on clearly identified topics (bread of the world, light of the world, resurrection and life, and so forth), not discrete sayings loosely combined as in the other Gospels.

- None of the Synoptic parables appear in John, being replaced by similitudes of a rather different sort, proceeding by the unfolding of images (like a vine) rather than the telling of a story (like the story of an absentee landlord and his bad tenants in a vineyard).

- The Synoptic Jesus proclaims the coming and nature of the kingdom; John's Jesus proclaims his own coming and significance. Unlike the presentation of Jesus in Mark, Matthew or Luke, in John Jesus is not shy about making messianic claims (Jn 4:26; 9:35-37).

Given both the points of convergence and divergence between John and the Synoptic Gospels, what can we say about their interrelationship? On the one hand, the Beloved Disciple and the fourth Evangelist would probably have had acquaintance with a much broader body of Jesus traditions than those found in the Fourth Gospel (witness John 20:30), and it also stands to reason that there would be a high degree of overlap between the traditions known to them and the traditions known to Mark, Matthew and Luke. That is to say, the Johannine community and its leaders probably encountered many of the traditions during their oral transmission phase that have come down to us in written form in the Synoptic Gospels. The reverse is also probably the case, namely, that the traditions currently preserved in Mark, Luke and to a lesser extent Matthew were influenced by Johannine traditions during their oral transmission phase as well.[28] There has been a consistent tendency to assume that because John's Gospel might indeed be the last Gospel written (at least, finalized), any similarities between it and the other Gospels indicate literary dependence on John's part. Those who follow such a line of argument fail to appreciate the complexities of how traditions could be *mutually* formative during the long decades of oral transmission.

An interesting case in regard to possible Johannine influence *on* the Synoptic Gospels is Luke's Gospel. Luke departs from Mark and sides with John at least three dozen times, pointing to Lucan awareness of—and at many points, preference for—the Johannine Jesus traditions (in their oral stages). This would be quite in keeping with Luke's claim to have investigated the Jesus tradition from a number of different written and oral sources. John, on the other hand, does not seem to have borrowed any themes characteristic of Luke. (Unless Luke's emphasis on Samaritans and women in Jesus' ministry was an influence that flowed in the direction of Luke to John, rather than vice versa.)[29] Another concerns the appearance in the Q source of a saying

---

[28]Anderson, "Interfluential, Formative, and Dialectical," p. 19; *"Sitz im Leben,"* pp. 8-11.
[29]Anderson, "Interfluential, Formative, and Dialectical," pp. 19, 43-47.

that is much more at home in Johannine than Synoptic discourse. In Matthew 11:27 (Lk 10:22), Jesus declares: "All things have been handed over to me by my Father; and no one knows the Son except the Father, and no one knows the Father except the Son and anyone to whom the Son chooses to reveal him" (NRSV). This saying combines otherwise distinctively Johannine motifs and language (see Jn 1:18; 3:35; 7:29; 10:15; 13:3; 17:25). Did the preachers who passed down the Q tradition learn this saying from contact with Johannine Christianity?[30]

The Evangelist may even have been acquainted with Mark and/or the other Gospels in written form.[31] This would not mean, however, that he used it as a source, per se.[32] The verbal agreements between Mark and John are also not so great as to necessitate (or even render probable) literary dependence (the longest is Mk 14:7-8//Jn 12:7-8). Indeed, out of forty-five points of contact between John 6 and Mark 6 and 8 in the narratives of the miraculous feedings, none are such as to suggest literary dependence.[33] The significant differences in the use of (or form of) some sayings is again easier to explain on the basis of independent development of the same (oral) traditions.

The possibility that John knew one or more of the Synoptics has led to several different theories about John's purposes in offering the

Fourth Gospel. Clement of Alexandria had already offered the view that John wrote to supplement the other Gospels, in particular by providing a more "spiritual" perspective on the deeds recounted so thoroughly elsewhere. This view encounters two problems. First, we have come to understand that the Synoptic Gospels are equally spiritual (in the sense of providing theological reflection on the significance of Jesus' story) and that John's Gospel is equally historical (in the sense of offering information not found in the other Gospels). Moreover, John does not preserve the "history" of the Synoptics without significant modifications. Finally, the inclusion of a fair amount of material also found in the Synoptics shows that John regarded his Gospel not merely as a supplement to be read alongside the others.

Others have suggested that John wrote his Gospel as a supplement or as an intentional correction of what was found in Mark or the Synoptic tradition. Some evidence that points in the former direction would be the fourth Evangelist's selection of materials. That, in the first edition of John at least, he chooses to narrate the signs that are not already included in Mark (the feeding in Jn 6 belongs to the second edition, and clearly duplicates a sign also narrated in Mark), suggests some knowledge of what Mark had included and a desire to write "around" that material.[34] Nevertheless, to

---

[30]Anderson would answer this in the affirmative ("Interfluential, Formative, and Dialectical," pp. 48-50). Another explanation for this particular saying, based on the criterion of multiple attestation, would be that Jesus himself said something like this, so that mutual influence would not be necessary.

[31]This view has been defended most recently in Richard Bauckham's "John for Readers of Mark" (in *The Gospels for All Christians*, ed. Richard Bauckham, [Grand Rapids: Eerdmans, 1998], pp. 147-71). According to Bauckham, John knew Mark's work and wrote for people whom he assumed would know Mark's work.

[32]Marianne Meye Thompson, "John, Gospel of," *Dictionary of Jesus and the Gospels*, ed. Joel B. Green and Scot McKnight (Downers Grove, Ill.: InterVarsity Press, 1992), pp. 368-383. 375; Lohse, *Formation of the New Testament*, p. 168; Brown, *Introduction to the New Testament*, p. 365; Beasley-Murray, *John*, p. xxxvii. Had John used Mark as a source, he would have done so in a completely different manner from both Matthew and Luke. The latter eliminate narrative details and theologizing comments found in Mark. John has as many details if not more, and often the details are different. John, then, seems to stand in relation to his own tradition as Mark does in relation to the Petrine tradition—as the first attempt to put an orally developed tradition in writing, with an abundance of detail (thus Anderson, "Interfluential, Formative, and Dialectical," pp. 26-28, 36).

[33]Anderson, *Christology of the Fourth Gospel*, pp. 98-102; "Interfluential, Formative, and Dialectical," pp. 25-26, 35.

[34]Anderson, "Interfluential, Formative, and Dialectical," p. 40.

regard John as a supplement to the Synoptics represents a shallow estimation of its contribution (and its independent voice and vision). A strong case can be made that the Fourth Gospel seeks to correct Synoptic traditions about the place and significance of the miraculous in the Christian life. All five Synoptic feeding stories conclude the episodes of miraculous feeding with the observation that "they ate and were satisfied" (see Mk 6:42; 8:8). In John

Figure 9.3. Excavations of the Pools of Bethesda in Jerusalem, spoken of in John 5:1-9. The fifth portico, so long regarded as symbolic, actually cuts across the middle, separating the two pools. (Photo above courtesy of Todd Bolen [BiblePlaces.com]; photo below courtesy of the Holyland Hotel and Todd Bolen [BiblePlaces.com])

6:26, Jesus criticizes the crowd for following him specifically because "they ate and were satisfied" rather than because they understood the meaning of the event. The focus on the power of God to fix problems or provide material assistance is presented as off-focus from the true significance of the miracle as sign of who Jesus was.[35] Again, however, it would be too shallow an estimate of the Evangelist's aims to say that he wrote only in order to correct Synoptic traditions, as if his interests were driven by and limited by what he found in the Synoptics. But the Fourth Gospel does provide important evidence of dialogue and counterpoint within the early church where the meaning of Jesus is concerned.

It seems best to conclude that while John had many traditions at his disposal that were also incorporated in other Gospels by other Evangelists, his purpose was to commit to writing the tradition about Jesus that was most central to his own understanding of Jesus and the understanding shared among those churches shaped by the witness of the Beloved Disciple. That is to say, the fourth Evangelist wrote in order to provide the churches with the same thing the Synoptic Evangelists independently sought to provide—a coherent presentation of those traditions deemed most important and relevant to the life of faith and the nurture of the Christian churches, and a word painting of Jesus that reflected the Jesus known through the witness of the Beloved Disciple and the ongoing work of the Paraclete in the community's midst.

Broader formative influences. During the nineteenth century and the first half of the twentieth, students of John sought for John's resources mainly in non-Jewish literature. Connections between John and the Greco-Roman milieu begin with the introduction of the Logos in John 1:1, the term also applied by

Stoic philosophers to the divine principle ordering the universe, the mediator, in effect, between God and the visible, physical realm.

Special attention was given, however, to the connections between John and Gnosticism. It was common to observe the parallels between the movement of the "Son" in John with the Gnostic "redeemer myth" of a savior who descends into this world from above, enlightens those who share in the divine mind, and leads them into the realm above. The relationship of this pattern to John's Gospel is somewhat complicated, however, by the fact that the bulk of witnesses to Gnosticism in the West actually show dependence on John's Gospel, and those that derive from the East tend to date from much later than the Gospels. A safer hypothesis would be that John would resonate with a kind of proto-Gnosticism, speaking strongly to those seeking the savior who would lead them to the realm that is beyond, rather than that John drew heavily on full-fledged Gnostic thought.

The discovery of the Nag Hammadi Library in 1945, an important collection of Gnostic scriptures, has enabled students to look more closely at the connections between John and Gnosticism. Perhaps the most striking parallel to emerge is the form of the "revealer discourse," in which a divine being speaking in the first person reveals him- or herself to the hearers with a series of "I am" statements. The Gnostic text titled "Thunder, Perfect Mind" exhibits this form most fully, promising everlasting life and freedom from ever dying again to those who find the deity.[36]

The second half of the twentieth century, however, witnessed a resurgence of interest in the Jewish milieu of John's Gospel. This was fostered by the discovery of the Dead Sea Scrolls in 1947 and by increased attention being given to the Jewish pseudepigrapha. "The

---

[35]Anderson, *Christology of the Fourth Gospel*, p. 257; *"Sitz im Leben,"* pp. 28-29.
[36]See *The Nag Hammadi Library in English*, ed. J. M. Robinson (San Francisco: Harper & Row, 1978), pp. 295-303.

thoroughgoing Gnostic interpretation of the Fourth Gospel is in no small degree due to a scholarly minimizing of the Jewish relations that it exhibits."[37]

The career of Wisdom in *1 Enoch* 42, for example, provides ample background for the rejected revealer from above who came to walk on earth and returned to the heavenly realm. Moreover, the self-revelation of Lady Wisdom in Proverbs 8, not to mention the "I am" statements made by God throughout Isaiah 40—55, by which God reveals God's character, acts and eternity, also provide sufficient background for John's development of the same on Jesus' lips. The importance of wisdom discourse in Gnostic literature, moreover, suggests that Gnostic revealer discourses may be dependent on these same sources, such that in John and the earliest Gnostic texts we have a case of mutual dependency on common resources, developed in different directions.

Another factor not to be neglected is the mediation of Greco-Roman ideas via Hellenistic Judaism. Philo of Alexandria blends the Stoic idea of the Logos with the Jewish conceptions of God as Creator and Sustainer of creation, using a mediator to effect both.[38] Philo thus interprets the Stoic Logos in light of the intertestamental Wisdom tradition, which again provides a major background for John's presentation of the Logos (and early Christian Christology more generally, as in Col 1:15-20 and Heb 1:1-4).

The Jewish Scriptures themselves provide an obvious resource for John's expression of the meaning of Jesus as light, shepherd, and fountain of living water, all of which are images for God or God's Word. These images are also shared by Jewish apocalyptic writers contemporary with the fourth Evangelist, as in, for example, *2 Baruch* 77.11-16, where the Torah is praised as the lamp, shepherd and fountain that will guide and sustain Israel after the temple's destruction. Both church and synagogue are thus seen to draw on the same resources for the nurture and sustenance of their respective groups. Moreover, John, like Matthew, presents a christological reading of the Old Testament, according to which Jesus embodies the fullness of the Old Testament revelation and especially the significance of the Jewish festivals.

The Dead Sea Scrolls cast a new light on the dualism encountered in the Fourth Gospel (as well as in the epistles of John). Both the *Rule of the Community* (1QS) and the Gospel of John use pairs of opposites like light and darkness, truth and iniquity (or lies), to differentiate between group members and outsiders at the very level of their being as belonging almost by nature to light or darkness. Both also prescribe love for fellow members of the community and, as a correlate, emphasize separation from the "children of darkness" or the "world."

The literature of Qumran also sheds important light on the role and work of the Holy Spirit, at least as it was conceived by one other Jewish sect. According to J. L. Price, "Jewish apocalyptic and wisdom books provide an intelligible background for John's conception of the divine Spirit as a quasi-personal teacher, guide and revealer of God's mysteries to his chosen ones. But the Qumran complex of ideas which defines the Spirit both as a God-appointed, cosmic-defender and advocate, and as a witness within certain men to 'the truth' . . . affords a particularly close analogy to the forensic activities of John's *paraklētos.*"[39]

Since the recovery of the Dead Sea Scrolls, students of John have been surprised by John's

---

[37]Beasley-Murray, *John,* p. lv.

[38]See Philo *Quaest. in Ex.* 2.68; *Fug.* 95-98, 100-101; references in Thompson, "John," p. 376.

[39]J. L. Price, "Light from Qumran upon Some Aspects of Johannine Theology," in *John and the Dead Sea Scrolls,* ed. J. H. Charlesworth (New York: Crossroad, 1990), pp. 23-24. See also A. R. C. Leaney, "The Johannine Paraclete and the Dead Sea Scrolls," in *John and the Dead Sea Scrolls,* ed. J. H. Charlesworth (New York: Crossroad, 1990), pp. 38-61.

The Fourth Gospel and the Historical Jesus

Critical research of the life of Jesus from the First Quest through the Jesus Seminar has tended to discount the historical value of John's Gospel, almost uncritically accepting Clement of Alexandria's view of the text's purpose. Nevertheless, there have been significant voices (like J. A. T. Robinson and Craig Blomberg) who have argued in favor of the historical value of John alongside the other Gospels. John has been found to exhibit surprising accuracy on the level of the smallest details, like the pool with five porticoes, formerly thought to be a fiction (perhaps a symbol for the Torah) until the pool of Bethesda (see figure 9.3), sporting four porticoes around its perimeter and a fifth across the middle, was excavated in Jerusalem. Such details have strengthened the Gospel's explicit claims to preserving eyewitness testimony (Jn 1:14; 19:35; 21:24).[a]

While the Fourth Gospel may spend more time than the Synoptic Gospels reflecting on the significance of Jesus as displayed in his works, it nonetheless contains traditions with value for the student of the life of Jesus. More scholars are beginning to view a two or three year ministry more probable, with Jesus moving in and out of Jerusalem on several occasions, rather than making a single, climactic journey. The portrayal of John the Baptist's and Jesus' ministries overlapping, perhaps even being in competition, and the presentation of some of Jesus' first disciples as former disciples of John the Baptist, are increasingly regarded as more plausible.[b]

At certain points John may contain a more correct remembrance of the story of Jesus and may be of greater use for historical Jesus studies. Anderson argues forcefully for the historical placement of the cleansing of the temple early in Jesus' public ministry, as in John, with a public ministry that includes several visits to Jerusalem.[c] From this perspective the cleansing of the temple in Mark (and in Luke and Matthew) might result rather from the geographical grouping of materials than from chronological accuracy. (We might recall Papias' critique of Mark on precisely this point, that he did not write things down "in order.") Anderson points out that John 2:20, which states that at the time of the cleansing the temple had been under renovations for forty-six years, would place the event in 27 C.E., hence early in Jesus' public ministry (the crucifixion tends to be dated between 29 and 33 C.E.).

Whatever our decisions about particular historical questions are, it is the case that the Fourth Gospel has been too easily and quickly set aside by many Jesus historians. It has much to contribute to the conversation about the historical Jesus as an independent and valuable source.[d] The deeply entrenched idea that the Synoptics preserve a "three-against-one" witness against John also needs to be debunked since Matthew and Luke are dependent on Mark. Mark and John present "two parallel perspectives on Jesus' ministry."[e]

---

[a]Anderson, "John and Mark," p. 176.
[b]Thompson, "John," p. 375; Anderson, "Interfluential, Formative, and Dialectical," p. 38.
[c]Anderson, "Interfluential, Formative, and Dialectical," pp. 28 n.15, 42-43; "John and Mark," p. 183.
[d]C. H. Dodd, *Historical Tradition in the Fourth Gospel* (Cambridge: Cambridge University Press, 1963), p. 423.

This renewed interest in the historical value of John extends to the discourse material as well. Ben Witherington suggests that the discourses themselves preserve not later Christian reflection on Jesus' words and significance but rather Jesus' private teachings to his disciples.[f] The Evangelist has set this material in the context of public disputes. Hence the words are authentic, but the setting is fictive, representing the later church's situation as it bears witness to Jesus but meets with rejection and exclusion.[g] The farewell discourses, on the other hand, represent precisely the kind of private teaching Jesus might have given his inner circle of followers, depicted by the Evangelist in an appropriately private setting.

Other scholars are more apt to attribute these reflections on the significance of Jesus' works or signs to the preaching activity of the Beloved Disciple.[h] The possibility that some of the discourse material derives not from the historical Jesus might disturb some modern Christians, but it might not have raised a problem for the first-century Christians in the circle of the Johannine communities, for they believed that the "historical Jesus" continued to teach and to reveal himself and the Father long after his ascension through the teaching ministry of the Paraclete, the Holy Spirit, communicating words he could not share during his earthly ministry (Jn 14:26; 16:12-14).

---

[f]Witherington, *John's Wisdom*, p. 37
[g]Ibid.
[h]Beasley-Murray, *John*, p. xlii; Brown, *Gospel According to John*, pp. xxxiv-xxxv; Barrett, *Gospel According to St. John*, p. 26.

---

affinities with the Palestinian Jewish milieu, connections previously unknown. Raymond Brown looks to the scrolls as offering consistently "better parallels to John than do any of the non-Christian elements in the Mandaean documents . . . or the examples in Philo and the *Hermetica*."[40]

JOHN'S MESSAGE

The identity and significance of Jesus. Perhaps the most important contribution of the Fourth Gospel is its extended reflections on the identity and significance of Jesus. This focus occupies most of the Gospel, which from its outset declares Jesus to be the very Word of God in the flesh, the perfect Mediator of the knowledge of God: "whoever has seen me has seen the Father" (Jn 14:9). We will consider John's contribution to early Christology by considering Jesus first as the "One from above," then as the fulfillment and embodiment of the Old Testament revelation and finally as the revealer of the great "I am."

1. Jesus, the One from above. Far from imposing foreign schemes like the Gnostic redeemer myth on the early church's reflection on Jesus, the Fourth Gospel represents a natural out-

---

[40]Raymond E. Brown, "The Dead Sea Scrolls and the New Testament," in *John and the Dead Sea Scrolls*, ed. J. H. Charlesworth (New York: Crossroad, 1990), p. 7. Pierre Benoit concurs, claiming that "it is no longer necessary to invoke Greek Gnosticism as the original milieu of the Fourth Gospel, since now we have one, which is more ancient and closer, in Palestine itself" ("Qumran and the New Testament," in *Paul and the Dead Sea Scrolls*, ed. J. M. O'Connor and J. H. Charlesworth [New York: Crossroad, 1990], p. 17).

working of other early Christian witnesses to Christology. Many passages in the New Testament make similar claims about Jesus (Phil 2:5-11; Col 1:15-20; 1 Tim 3:16; Heb 1:1-4). Even Mark, who seems to present a Jesus who is reluctant to make claims about his messiahship, presents Jesus as the "Son of God" (Mk 1:1) and as the one who, like the one God, makes the winds his messengers and controls the waves of the sea. John, however, brings a greater focus and depth to these preliminary attempts to speak of Jesus' relationship with God the Father.

The Fourth Gospel opens with a hymn about the Logos, the "Word" of God. John makes lofty claims indeed concerning the nature and work of this Logos:

> In the beginning was the Word, and the Word was with God, and the Word was God. He was in the beginning with God. All things came into being through him, and without him not one thing came into being. . . .
>
> He was in the world, and the world came into being through him; yet the world did not know him. He came to what was his own, and his own people did not accept him. (Jn 1:1-3, 10-11 NRSV)

Convinced that Jesus *returned* to the Father at his ascension, early Christian authors began to seek out witnesses to the activity and character of the Son before he left the Father in the first place. John, like the author of Hebrews (see Heb 1:1-4), looks to the Jewish understanding of the person and work of Wisdom for this witness.

In the early Jewish wisdom tradition (represented by the collection known as Proverbs), Wisdom already takes on a personal appearance. The abstract quality becomes a "she," a personal coworker of God. Proverbs 8 provides a self-disclosure statement by Wisdom, who presents her virtues, attributes and bene-

fits. Toward the end of this poem, we read:

> When [God] established the heavens, I
>   was there . . .
> when he marked out the foundations of
>   the earth,
>   then I was beside him, like a master
>   worker;
> and I was daily his delight,
>   rejoicing before him always. . . .
> For whoever finds me finds life
>   and obtains favor from the LORD;
> but those who miss me injure themselves;
>   all who hate me love death.
>   (Prov 8:27, 29-30, 35-36 NRSV)

Wisdom was God's partner in creation itself, a tradition kept alive in the Wisdom of Solomon, a text from the turn of the era. Wisdom was "present when [God] made the world" (Wis 9:9 NRSV). But Wisdom does not remain in heaven. "Solomon" prays that Wisdom would descend to him for his aid:

> Send her forth from the holy heavens,
> and from the throne of your glory
>   send her,
> that she may labor at my side,
> and that I may learn what is pleasing
>   to you. (Wis 9:10 NRSV)

According to a first-century stratum from *1 Enoch*, "Wisdom went out [from heaven] to dwell with the children of human beings, but she found no dwelling place. So Wisdom returned to her place and settled permanently among the angels" (42.2).

Jewish speculation about Wisdom, then, provides an enormously important resource for early Christian reflection about Jesus' larger career. The fourth Evangelist identifies Jesus as the incarnation of God's agent in creation, the Word (Jn 1:1-3). Like Wisdom, John's Logos makes a pilgrimage from heaven to labor alongside human beings and teach what is pleasing to God (Jn 1:9-10; 14:21). While Jesus himself returns to the Father, the Holy

Spirit is poured out on the believers to continue to labor beside them, guide them wisely and guard them. Moreover, having met with widespread rejection and hostility, the Logos, like Wisdom, returns to the realm on high.

The author of Wisdom of Solomon writes concerning this figure of Wisdom:

> [She is] a pure emanation of the glory
>   of the Almighty. . . .
> For she is a reflection of eternal light,
> a spotless mirror of the working of God,
> and an image of his goodness. (Wis 7:25-26 NRSV)

Again, we find a clear echo of this in John's presentation of Jesus. Just as people could look to Wisdom to see the perfect reflection of God—that is, just as they could know God through pursuing Wisdom—John now claims that they know God by looking at Jesus. It is Jesus who shows the Father, who reveals God: "whoever has seen me has seen the Father" (Jn 14:9; cf. 14:7; 15:24).

Some have found the Jewish concept of agency to be a helpful model to explain this relationship, and especially to preserve the monotheism of the Fourth Gospel. "The one who is sent is like the one who sent him" (*m. Berakot* 5:5), so that to encounter the one sent is, in effect, to encounter the sender (Jn 12:45; 14:7-9).[41] This model also explains the dependence of the Son on the Father, as the former must act out the Sender's commission exactly and unerringly (see Jn 3:35; 5:19). Disrespect shown the Son becomes dishonor shown the Father: "Anyone who does not honor the Son does not honor the Father who sent him" (Jn 5:23 NRSV; cf. 3:36). God, however, upholds his own honor, and the honor of his agent (Jn 8:49-50). But Jesus is more than just an agent: he is the unique revelation of the Father and the place where human beings encounter God for salvation or judg-ment. It is only the word *like* in the definition of the agent given above that makes it slightly too weak a concept to fully explain the mystery of Jesus in the Fourth Gospel.

According to the author of Proverbs 8, those who gain Wisdom enjoy God's patronage and find life. Failure to gain Wisdom, however, means death. This reverberates in John, who presents an encounter with Jesus as determinative for whether or not a person enters into life or remains under the power of death (Jn 3:36; 5:21-24, 40; 6:51-54). Jesus is now the face of the one Mediator of God's favor (Jn 1:18; 3:17, 35-36; 5:37-38; 13:20; 14:6). In John, an encounter with this Jesus determines one's identity in this life and future in the next (Jn 3:17-21, 36; 5:24; 6:40; 8:24, 47; 12:44-50; 16:11, 33). Is this person to be a child of light or continue in darkness? Is he or she to remain under sin and judgment or move into life and freedom from judgment? It is perhaps this emphasis on encounter and decision that has made John such a popular evangelizing tool.

John's presentation of Jesus, then, draws heavily on Jewish wisdom traditions. John perceives in Jesus what had previously been attributed to the faceless Wisdom. The Word of God remains the Mediator of God in creation, revelation and in extending God's favor to humanity. It is the Word made flesh, Jesus, who alone is able to "exegete" the Father. Not Torah nor any other source can make God known or interpret God as can the Son (Jn 1:18), though Torah remains an important witness to the Word made flesh (Jn 5:39, 46-47).

The *sign*, the term used to denote the miraculous deeds of Jesus, is the tool Jesus used to reveal his true status, honor and authority to his disciples. The miracle is not merely a beneficial act: it has not achieved its goal unless it stimulates belief among the witnesses and leads them to recognize God at work in and revealing God's self through Jesus. Thus

---

[41]See Thompson, "John," pp. 377-79 for numerous other references and further discussion.

the transformation of water into wine becomes "the first of his signs . . . reveal[ing] his glory; and his disciples believed in him" (Jn 2:11 NRSV). The greatest sign, of course, would be Jesus' resurrection, the sign he gave to his critics in the temple (Jn 2:18-19). Many are credited with believing in Jesus on account of the signs he performed (Jn 2:23; 4:53; 11:47-48; 12:10-11, 17-18). Others at least suggest that the signs may be taken as indicators of Jesus' messiahship (Jn 7:31; 9:16). Jesus himself points to his "works" as proof that he has been sent by the Father, the evidence that substantiates his claims to be the Son of God and to speak the truth on behalf of God (Jn 5:36; 10:38; 11:42).

Nevertheless, the value of signs is ambiguous. A miracle can reveal the divine or merely gratify human desires (Jn 6:26). Not all recognize the miracles as signs, nor do the signs guarantee that "revelation" happens. John 2:24-25 criticizes the shallowness of belief based on signs, for Jesus does not trust these "believers." When the official of Capernaum comes to Jesus, he responds not with praise of the official's faith (as in Luke and Matthew), but with an expression of frustration: "Unless you see signs and wonders you will not believe" (Jn 4:48 NRSV). A sign can be misunderstood or overlooked. The crowd fed by Jesus on the hillside experienced the miraculous provision of food but did not perceive that this was a sign, a failure that is played out as these same people immediately demand a sign from Jesus after he had just fed 5,000 (Jn 6:26, 30-31). Perhaps the most negative comment on the value of signs is found in John 12:37-40:

> Although he had performed so many signs in their presence, they did not believe in him. This was to fulfill the word spoken by the prophet Isaiah:
> "Lord, who has believed our message,
>   and to whom has the arm of the
>   Lord been revealed?"

> And so they could not believe, because Isaiah also said,
> "He has blinded their eyes
>   and hardened their heart,
> so that they might not look with their
>   eyes,
> and understand with their heart and
>   turn—
> and I would heal them." (NRSV)

The signs did not bring about faith, and the Son is still rejected by the world and executed. While on the one hand John preserves these accounts of Jesus' proofs of his identity—his credentials, as it were—he is reluctant to portray them as an adequate foundation for faith. Perhaps Jesus' words to Thomas pronounce the final word on the value of signs in John: "Have you believed because you have seen me? Blessed are those who have not seen and yet have come to believe" (Jn 20:29 NRSV). The most important sign of all—the resurrection—is not one that can be confirmed by sight, but it is only this sign that allows us to truly know who Jesus is, where he has come from and where he is going.

For all the claims made by John on Jesus' behalf, the humanity of Jesus is never sacrificed, as some might claim: the prologue makes emphatic the Word's *becoming* flesh, not merely inhabiting flesh. Jesus experiences a full range of emotions, just as in Mark, including grief (Jn 11:33-35), fatigue (Jn 4:6), anguish (Jn 12:27; 13:21), irritation (Jn 2:4; 6:26; 7:6-8; 8:25) and suspicion (Jn 2:24-25). He remains thoroughly human as well as divine, perhaps more so in both directions in this Gospel than any other. As such, Jesus himself is a sign of God. To look past the human teacher and see the Father is essential to the reception of the revelation of God, to coming to a saving faith and to come into possession of eternal life.

2. Jesus, Torah and the Jewish festivals. John is closely attuned to the major symbols of Juda-

Figure 9.4. Mt. Gerizim, the sacred mountain of the Samaritans to this day (see Jn 4:19-24). (Photo courtesy of Todd Bolen [BiblePlaces.com])

ism (temple and Torah) and the liturgical rhythm of the Jewish calendar. This symbolic and liturgical environment provides an essential background for understanding John's presentation of Jesus' significance.

First, Jesus is presented as the new temple. Jesus' words to Nathanael point in this direction: "Very truly, I tell you, you will see heaven opened and the angels of God ascending and descending upon the Son of man" (Jn 1:51 NRSV). This statement refers to Jacob's vision in Genesis 28:12-17, where Jacob lies down and dreams of angels ascending and descending a celestial ramp, and thereafter he receives a word from God. On waking he declares, "Surely the LORD is in this place—and I did not know it! . . . How awesome is this place! This is none other than the house of God, and this is the gate of heaven" (Gen 28:16-17 NRSV). For John, it is the Son of Man, Jesus, who becomes the house of God (the temple), and who is the gate of heaven (cf. Jn 10:7-9; 14:6). The Lord was present in the world in Jesus, and many "did not know it." John stages

the "cleansing of the temple" at the very outset of Jesus' ministry to underscore this theme of replacement. Jesus' body will now be the temple, the place of mediation and encounter between God and humanity (Jn 2:19-21). Both Jerusalem and Mount Gerizim (see figure 9.4) are rejected as places where God is encountered. The longstanding feud between Bethel and Zion is pointless, for only in Jesus do we encounter God, and only Jesus supplies the Spirit, without which we cannot offer true worship (Jn 4:21, 23).

For John the Jewish Scriptures had value as a witness to the Word made flesh (Jn 5:39). Those who call themselves Moses' disciples without being also Jesus' disciples (Jn 9:28-29) are, in John's view, merely deluding themselves: Moses (the voice of Torah) will accuse those who reject Jesus (Jn 5:45-47). Those who reject Jesus do not read the Scriptures correctly, even drawing a dramatically wrong conclusion from the Torah: "We have a law, and according to that law he ought to die because he has claimed to be the Son of God" (Jn

19:7 NRSV). On the contrary, John avers, "by that law" all ought to come to faith in Jesus (Jn 5:39). Nevertheless, John, like the other Evangelists, notes that Jesus' very rejection is itself attested in Scripture. In John 12:37-40, for example, not only Isaiah 6:9-10 but also the famous Suffering Servant song (Is 53:1) is cited to this end. As Johnson eloquently sums up the matter, "The functions of Torah are totally subsumed by Jesus: he reveals God's will, he judges, he offers the spirit, he gives light, he sets free, he gives life. What; Torah was as a text, Jesus is as living Son: God's Word."[42]

Finally, the fourth Evangelist forges more explicit links between the events in Jesus' ministry (and Jesus' words) and Jewish festivals than any other New Testament author. The proximity of each particular festival casts a special, interpretative light on Jesus' actions and words, even as Jesus' actions and words show that the essence of the festival is captured in his person.

Jews associated Pentecost (Shavuot) with the giving of the law on Mount Sinai "on the third new moon after the Israelites had gone out of the land of Egypt" (Ex 19:1 NRSV). While the timing is not exact, the agricultural festival of Shavuot was close and available for this religious overlay. The unnamed "festival of the Jews" (Jn 5:1) is probably this festival of Pentecost, or Weeks, which focused on the giving and keeping of the Torah. John makes this feast the setting for a discussion of Jesus' authority and relationship to Torah. Jesus heals the lame man laying beside the pool of Bethzatha and tells him to "Stand up, take your mat and walk" (Jn 5:8-9 NRSV), which the man immediately does in violation of the prohibition to do any work on the sabbath (Jn 5:9-10). When accused of violating Torah, the man replies in self-defense, "The man who made me well said to me, 'Take up your mat and walk' " (Jn 5:11 NRSV). By healing the man, Jesus demonstrated his authority, and the man understood Jesus' authority to override the authority of Torah. If Torah said "do not work," but Jesus said "work," it was clear whom to follow. The ensuing debate between Jesus and his critics ends with the declaration that Moses and the Scriptures are Jesus' witness—indeed, the "Father's testimony" on behalf of the Son is none other than the Scriptures themselves. The true celebration of *Simchat-hattorah* (The Joy of Torah) therefore, can only happen when that Torah is read as a witness to Jesus.

Passover celebrates the foundational event in the story of Israel—the deliverance of the Hebrews from bondage in Egypt. This was the beginning of their story as a nation and the central redemptive act of God on their behalf. Here God committed God's self to them: "out of Egypt have I brought my son" (Hos 11:1). It was rich in sacrificial symbolism, particularly in the sacrifice of the paschal lamb, the lamb whose blood redeemed the firstborn of each family. When narrating the miracle of the feeding of the 5,000, John includes the detail that "the Passover, the feast of the Jews, was at hand" (Jn 6:4). The story that follows must be read in light of this feast, an association that remains close to the surface as Jesus contrasts the manna eaten by the Israelites in the wilderness with the true bread from heaven, which he provides. This discourse about the bread of life takes a paschal turn as Jesus speaks now of his own flesh as this life-giving bread and points ahead to his death as the new Passover sacrifice that brings the children of God out of slavery in the world to the eternal inheritance of the children of light (Jn 6:49-58). This is foreshadowed in the first Passover in John (Jn 2:13), which includes the first "passion prediction" in John (Jn 2:19), and is most fully developed in John 18—19, the third and final Passover. Jesus' passion is bathed in paschal

---

[42]Johnson, *Writings of the New Testament,* p. 491.

imagery. He is sentenced to die, and in fact does die, on the day of preparation for the Passover. The different time of Jesus' death in the Fourth Gospel serves to highlight Jesus' significance as the Lamb of God that takes away the sins of the world (Jn 1:29), the new Passover Lamb (Jn 19:14-16). The hyssop used to give Jesus vinegar is an image from the first Passover, when branches of hyssop were used to sprinkle the blood of the lambs on the doorposts and lintel (Jn 19:29). Just as the Passover lambs were not to have any bones broken (Ex 12:46), so none of Jesus' bones are broken (Jn 19:36).

The autumn festival of Succoth, or Booths, retained much of its agricultural significance. At this festival the people sought God's gift of rain for the coming season. For seven consecutive days the priests went to the pool of Siloam (see figure 9.5) to draw water, singing Isaiah

Figure 9.5. The Pool of Siloam, where Jesus sent the blind man to wash his eyes and be healed (Jn 9:1-7). (Photo courtesy of Todd Bolen [Bible-Places.com])

12:2-6 ("with joy you shall draw water from salvation's living springs"), and processed to the temple where they poured out the water as a libation, symbolizing the people's dependence on God for the rains, and thus for life itself. This festival was also laden with hopes for the coming age, and the living waters that would flow out from Jerusalem (Zech 14:8). On the eighth day, the climax of the festival on which no libation was performed, Jesus is portrayed as standing up and shouting to the masses assembled in the temple: "Let the one who believes in me drink. As the scripture has said, 'Out of the believer's heart shall flow rivers of living water'" (Jn 7:38 NRSV). John thus presents Jesus as the answer to the petitions of the previous seven days' libations, indeed as an eschatological fulfillment since the water is not merely the annual rain but the life-giving Spirit (cf. also Jn 4:13-14).

Another aspect of this festival involved the lighting of huge golden lamps, symbols of God's leading the people by the cloud and the pillar of fire. In the very next scene (remembering that John 7:53—8:11 is a later insert, interrupting the flow of the original narrative), Jesus says, "I am the light of the world. Whoever follows me will never walk in darkness but will have the light of life" (Jn 8:12 NRSV; cf. Is 60:14-22; Zech 14:7). God's shepherding of the people Israel thus continues in the good Shepherd, whose followers walk in the light of the Lamb.

The feast of dedication, or Hanukkah, celebrates the purification of the temple after its desecration by the pagan cults of the Hellenizers and their Gentile partners (brought to an end in 164 B.C.E.). In the context of this feast Jesus declares:

Can you say that the one whom the Father has sanctified and sent into the world is blaspheming because I said, "I am God's Son"? If I am not doing the works of my Father, then do not believe me. But if I do them, even though you do not believe me, believe the works, so that you may know and understand that the Father is in me and I am in the Father. (Jn 10:36-38 NRSV)

The sanctification of the temple is no longer essential, because Jesus has come into the world as the one consecrated by God. If the temple was honored as the place where God dwelled, how much more should Jesus be honored, in whom the Father dwells and who dwells in the Father? At this festival we return to the theme of the new temple. The former role of the temple—the place where God would dwell and meet God's people—is now assumed by Jesus, in whom God does indeed dwell fully, perfectly and bodily. Jesus is the consecrated place for encounter with God.

3. The "I am" sayings. Much scholarly discussion has focused on the "I am" sayings that appear throughout the narrative. The prevalence of these sayings gives John's work the appearance of a discourse of a divine revealer. In most instances Jesus is presented as "exegeting" his own significance in light of Old Testament images. While these sayings resemble the self-revelation discourses in the Hermetic literature (as in the tractate "The Thunder, Perfect Mind," Codex 6.2), the primary background is almost certainly provided by divine speech in the Jewish Scriptures, beginning with Exodus 3:14: "I am what I am" ("I am the one who is" LXX). The form is also common throughout Deutero-Isaiah: "I, the LORD, am first, and will be with the last" (Is 41:4 NRSV); "that you may know and believe me, and understand that I am" (Is 43:10; see also vv. 11-13); "even to your old age, I am" (Is 46:4; see also 43:25).[43] Also worthy of comparison is the self-disclosure speech of Wisdom in Prov-

---

[43]Brown, *Gospel According to John*, 1:533-38; Beasley-Murray, *John*, p. lix.

erbs 8, all the more as Jewish speculation concerning the cosmic role of Wisdom provides an important background for early Christian discussions concerning the pre-incarnational role of the Son.

John clearly intends for the readers to hear a resonance between Jesus' words and God's revelation of God's name in Exodus 3:14. In the episode where the "Jews" say to Jesus, "You are not yet fifty years old, and have you seen Abraham?" Jesus replies, "Very truly, I tell you, before Abraham was, I am" (Jn 8:57-58 NRSV). Jesus' audience then attempts to stone Jesus for blasphemy: there is no misunderstanding of Jesus' meaning on their part. This absolute use of "I am" as Jesus' self-identification with the divine Name appears again in the arrest scene: "Jesus, knowing all that was to happen to him, came forward and asked them, 'Whom are you looking for?' They answered, 'Jesus of Nazareth.' Jesus replied, 'I am he'" (18:4-5 NRSV). Notably, the "he" at the end of "I am he" is not explicit in the Greek text, so that the echo of the divine Name is all the more obvious. Understanding Jesus' essential oneness with the Father is, for John, a prerequisite for experiencing the benefits of his ministry:

> You are from below, I am from above; you are of this world, I am not of this world. I told you that you would die in your sins, for you will die in your sins unless you believe that I am [he]. . . . So Jesus said, "When you have lifted up the Son of Man, then you will realize that I am." (Jn 8:23-24, 28 NRSV; cf. Jn 10:30)

Jesus identifies himself as "the bread of life," a bread that frees those who partake of it from future hunger (Jn 6:35). This is developed in explicit contrast to the earlier bread of God's provision, the manna in the wilderness (a miracle repeated by Jesus who provided such bread in the wilderness as well). That bread sustained life only for a short while; Jesus sustains life be-

yond death through the resurrection of believers at the last day. Jesus also identifies himself as "the light of the world" (Jn 8:12) This image comes from the Servant Songs of Isaiah, which celebrate the Servant of God as the light for the world (Is 42:6; 49:6), now applied to Jesus, the fulfillment of that scriptural hope as well (cf. Jn 1:4-5, 9; 9:5). Jesus also embodies the hope of pious Jews for the life of the world to come: "I am the resurrection and the life. Those who believe in me, even though they die, will live, and everyone who lives and believes in me will never die" (Jn 11:25-26 NRSV; cf. also Jn 5:21, 24, 29; 6:27). Jesus grants resurrection and vindication at the last day. Jesus also reveals himself as "the way, and the truth, and the life," the only means of access to the Father (Jn 14:6).

In another self-disclosure passage, Jesus declares, "I am the good shepherd. The good shepherd lays down his life for the sheep. . . . I am the good shepherd. I know my own and my own know me, just as the Father knows me and I know the Father. And I lay down my life for the sheep" (10:11, 14-15 NRSV). This introduces an image derived from the prophetic writings used to describe God's dealings with Israel. In contrast to false shepherds, God is a Shepherd who cares for God's flock (Is 40:11; Jer 23:3; Ezek 34:11-16). God also promises to raise up shepherds, particularly one "righteous branch" (Jer 23:4-6). Ezekiel preserves an especially apt image: "I will set up over them one shepherd, my servant David, and he shall feed them: he shall feed them and be their shepherd" (Ezek 34:23 NRSV). John identifies Jesus as this Shepherd-Messiah, whose shepherding is also the shepherding of God. Jesus goes on to identify his shepherding to include the calling together of sheep from many folds, so that there will be "one flock, one shepherd" (Jn 10:16). Under Jesus' shepherding, the ideal of one people (made from all the nations of the world) serving the one God will be fulfilled (Jn 11:51-52; cf. Rom 3:29-31).

Eschatology in the Fourth Gospel

John's statements about the believers' enjoyment of their eternal rewards have been a matter of considerable debate in scholarship. On the one hand, believers "have" eternal life in the present (Jn 3:36). Believers have already passed from death to life, possessing eternal life now (Jn 5:24). Deliverance and judgment, salvation and condemnation are already being determined in an individual's encounter with Jesus (Jn 3:18). On the other hand, they still look forward to resurrection to the life of the world to come (Jn 11:23-26), to being "raised up on the last day" (Jn 6:39-40, 54), to a future judgment (Jn 12:48), and to eternal life beyond death in this world (Jn 12:25).

One solution to this tension has been to regard one side as a secondary intrusion into the Fourth Gospel. According to this view a later editor has tamed an unorthodox eschatology that overly stressed the present enjoyment of eternity. The difficulty with this, of course, is the stylistic and linguistic consistency of the Gospel, which removes two important criteria for detecting an editor's hand. Another solution, more plausible to this author, is that John reflects the "already and not yet" tension of Christian life in the same vivid way it appears in Pauline and post-Pauline literature. John's statements are not at odds with but rather reflective of a worldview in which the believer lives at the very threshold of the two ages and is vitally connected with the Lord who has already triumphed and passed into the eternity of God's realm "above."

Another significant use of Old Testament imagery in a self-disclosure speech appears in John 15, where Jesus declares:

> I am the true vine, and my Father is the vinegrower. He removes every branch in me that bears no fruit. Every branch that bears fruit he prunes to make it bear more fruit. . . . Abide in me as I abide in you. Just as the branch cannot bear fruit by itself unless it abides in the vine, neither can you unless you abide in me. I am the vine, you are the branches. Those who abide in me and I in them bear much fruit, because apart from me you can do nothing. (Jn 15:1-2, 4-5 NRSV)

The image of Israel as a vine of God's planting is very familiar to readers of the Jewish Scriptures. The psalmist says of God:

> You brought a vine out of Egypt;
> you drove out the nations and planted
>   it.

> You cleared the ground for it;
>   it took deep root and filled the land. . . .

> Turn again, O God of hosts; . . .
> have regard for this vine,
>   the stock that your right hand
>   planted. (Ps 80:8-9, 14-15 NRSV)

Jeremiah addresses Israel with the voice of the Lord:

> I planted you as a choice vine,
>   from the purest stock.
> How then did you turn degenerate
>   and become a wild vine?" (Jer 2:21
>   NRSV)

And of course Isaiah 5:1-7 compares Israel with a vineyard of God's planting and its inhabitants as God's vines. In the Fourth Gospel, however, Jesus himself emerges as the "vine," and only those who cling to Jesus as branches to the vine belong to the vineyard of God's planting, which God continues to tend as the "vinegrower."

John has brought together a vast amount of material, then, aimed at helping readers see Jesus as the embodiment, fulfillment and point of connection with the sum total of the Jewish religious heritage. This pervasive demonstration will assist readers to regard Jesus himself as the focal point of their spiritual hope, their identity as the people of God and their eternal destiny, and so cling to him above all else. Such a demonstration would be particularly timely and on target for an audience that is aware of its displacement from its religious heritage, encouraging them that, rather than losing anything, they have entered into the fullness of their inheritance among the people of God.

The death of Jesus as the hour of glorification. All four Evangelists present Jesus' execution in a way that brought out its nobility and negated its disgrace. John, however, intensifies the nobility of the cross by making it nothing less than the hour of Jesus' glorification. The crucifixion begins the process of Jesus' exaltation; John would have its nobility completely overshadow the stark realities of an executed criminal's body nailed up for shameful display. Like the other Evangelists, John uses clearly recognizable topics that present the crucifixion as a noble death. Like the brave soldier's death on the battlefield, Jesus' death is voluntarily embraced, enacts virtue and brings benefit to others.

Throughout the passion narrative John presents Jesus' enemies as trying to degrade him: he is bound (Jn 18:12, 24); his face is struck (Jn 18:22); he is flogged and then taunted by the soldiers by means of the crown of thorns and the mocking tokens of honor (Jn 19:1-3); he is made to carry the crossbeam (Jn 19:17) and finally affixed to the cross, naked, powerless to stop the soldiers from casting lots for clothing (Jn 19:23-24). Despite appearances, however, John claims that Jesus' death is not an act inflicted on him but voluntarily chosen by himself for the sake of accomplishing a noble and beneficent goal. Aristotle had considered it one mark of courage to voluntarily "submit to some disgrace or pain as the price of some great and noble object" (*Eth. Nic.* 3.1.7). John's use of this topic transforms Jesus' endurance of degradation and suffering into a mark of courage, an honorable virtue.

John shows Jesus' death to be voluntary first as Jesus claims to have authority over his own life, both with regard to laying it down and even taking up his life again. (Jn 10:17-18). When Jesus "gives up" his spirit, the reader may recall this earlier claim concerning the voluntary character of the death. As in the Synoptic Gospels, the voluntary nature of the death is also demonstrated by Jesus' foreknowledge of the passion, seen both in the Johannine passion predictions (Jn 7:33-36; 8:21-29; see also Jn 3:14; 12:32) and in the concept of the "hour" that Jesus knows and freely accepts (Jn 2:4; 12:23; 13:1; cf. "my time" in Jn 7:6, 8). Jesus does not come to his death because his enemies prevail. Indeed, they are continually foiled in their attempts to arrest Jesus until his hour arrives. John also underscores Jesus' knowledge of the identity of the betrayer and the time of betrayal (Jn 6:71; 13:11), going so far as to portray Jesus as ordering Judas to perform the deed at a specific time, orchestrating his own sacrifice (Jn 13:18-19, 21-30). This heightens the perception of Jesus not as victim but as a willing benefactor who is even proactive in his death. As the passion unfolds, Jesus remains a powerful figure both in his encounter with the soldiers and with Pilate. John is thus careful to show that Jesus never loses his power or authority. Everything he suffers, he endures voluntarily because he has undertaken to achieve a noble goal.

The nobility of that goal comes from the fact that Jesus dies on account of obedience to God, his Father. The cross is the accomplishment of the Father's work as well as an opportunity for the Son to bring honor to the Father. Rather than pray that the cross might

The Sacraments in the Fourth Gospel

Paul's churches practiced baptism as an initiation rite and celebrated the Lord's Supper as an ongoing rite within the community of believers. It is highly likely that the authors of the Synoptic Gospels also assumed the same practices to be common and familiar among their readership. What about John? Did he assume and support these two rites as part of the life of the church?

With regard to baptism, there is no account of Jesus' baptism by John. As the event that launches Jesus' public ministry in Mark, Matthew and Luke, it is most conspicuous by its absence in John. Moreover, the Evangelist distances Jesus from the act of baptizing, saying that only his disciples were baptizing people (Jn 4:1-3). On the other hand, John 3:3-8 seems to assume the practice of baptism in speaking of being born "by water." Here John does not denigrate the importance of water so much as affirm the indispensability of the Spirit. The latter is the "immersion" that brings eternal life. The Spirit must remain the focal point as far as entry into the community is concerned (Jn 1:26-34; 3:5).[a]

Another glaring omission occurs on the eve of the Jesus' passion. The disciples gather for a last meal with Jesus, but Jesus does not take bread and wine and institute a perpetual memorial as in the Synoptic and Pauline traditions. Does this imply that John was antisacramentarian? It has been difficult for scholars to reconcile the absence of a Lord's Supper scene in John with the conclusion of the "bread of life" discourse in John 6, where Jesus speaks of the necessity of "eating the flesh" and "drinking the blood" of the Son of Man in order to have life and experience eternal life "on the last day" (Jn 6:53-54). This passage is most often read as a strong affirmation of the Eucharist—so strong that Bultmann insisted that it was an interpolation by a later editor, rightly noting that the idea that a person must partake of the sacrament of communion in order to have eternal life is incompatible with the soteriology of the Gospel as a whole, which requires only "believing."[b] Bultmann read Ignatius of Antioch's statement about "breaking one bread" as "the medicine of immortality" as a near-contemporary, comparative text, suggesting that both Ignatius and the editor who added John 6:51-58 ascribed a quasi-magical quality to the Eucharist, like found in the mystery religions.

Peter Borgen has shown, however, that John 6:31-58 has both stylistic and thematic unity as a midrash on the theme of manna, so that there is little ground for setting John 6:51-58 aside as a pro-Eucharistic interpolation.[c] This passage also does not adequately compensate for the absence of institution of the Lord's Supper in John 13 (a primary rationale given for its interpolation). It is quite plausible, however, that John 6:53-58 is not meant to be understood as a text about participating in the Eucharist, although the whole "bread of life" discourse has obvious relevance and meaning for readers who themselves practice communion.

---

[a]Paul N. Anderson, "Was the Author of the Fourth Gospel a Quaker?" *Quaker Religious Thought* 76 (1991): 35.

[b]Rudolf Bultmann, *The Gospel of John,* trans. George R. Beasley-Murray (Philadelphia: Westminster Press, 1971), pp. 218-19.

[c]Peder Borgen, *Bread from Heaven* (Leiden: Brill, 1965), pp. 20-42.

Anderson forcefully argues that this passage should be read as a call to follow Christ even into places of suffering and death.[d] Drinking the "cup" symbolized costly discipleship in the Synoptic tradition (Mk 10:35-45) in a context overshadowed by a passion prediction (Mk 10:32-34). The context of John 6:51, where Jesus has just spoken of giving his flesh for the life of the world through his own impending passion and death, creates a similar setting for reading these verses as a discussion about discipleship. Eating Jesus' flesh and drinking his blood then would be related to the appropriation of his sufferings in some way, but not necessarily by means of the Eucharist.

Turning to Ignatius of Antioch, Anderson finds first that the "medicine of immortality" has more to do with maintaining fellowship with the one bishop in the one church celebrating the one meal together (hence, unity and solidarity with the orthodox church) than with the partaking of the food itself, and that the Eucharist and suffering for the sake of the name are closely linked.[e] Ignatius writes of heretics who abstain from the Eucharist because they do not accept that Christ suffered in the flesh, the central meaning of the sacrament (*Ign. Smyrn*. 7:1). Ignatius uses the language of desiring "God's bread, which is the flesh of Christ" and craving to drink "his blood, an immortal love feast indeed" as a means of describing his "passion for death," his desire to be martyred for Jesus in Rome and so attain to eternal life (*Romans* 7:2-3). Therefore, John 6:53-58 could be heard to urge the appropriation of Jesus' death, quite probably in the form of being willing to suffer with Jesus in the face of hostility from non-Christians, as the path to eternal life. The crowd that was scandalized by the talk of the Messiah dying (giving his flesh for the life of the world) will be further scandalized by the implications of this messianic model for the disciples of such a Messiah (strikingly similar then to Mark's presentation of the relationship of Jesus' messianic mission and the cruciform shape of discipleship).

Since the Johannine circles geographically overlapped to such a high degree with other Christian circles (especially if the center was located in Syria or Ephesus), it is likely that the author and his circles were at least familiar with the rites, and probably practiced them as well. The absence of any actual polemic against baptism or celebration of communion should caution us against reading John as antisacramentarian. On balance, the silences about the rites themselves should probably be understood as a signal of John's fundamental preoccupation with the greater "sacrament," the Word made flesh, the revelation of God and the access to the Father made present and visible in the incarnation of Jesus, and with the meaning of being joined with him. John explores the significance of being born anew (ritually connected with baptism but made effective by infusion with the Holy Spirit) and being joined with Christ (ritually enacted in communion but practically in enduring the cost of discipleship), just as he commits far more space to exploring the significance of Jesus rather than cataloguing his various deeds and sundry teachings on topics other than his own person and work.

---

[d]Anderson, *Christology of the Fourth Gospel,* pp. 119-36.
[e]Ibid., pp. 119-24.

be avoided, as in the Synoptics, Jesus prays in John: "Father, glorify your name" (Jn 12:28). By allowing himself to be "lifted up" on the cross, Jesus will draw all people to himself, realizing God's desire to "gather together the scattered children of God" (Jn 11:52; 12:32). The nobility of the cross is established, secondly, from the benefit that Jesus brings to others by means of his death. John expresses this through hints of atonement language, as in John the Baptist's declaration that Jesus is the "Lamb of God who takes away the sin of the world" (Jn 1:29 NRSV), placing his death within the framework of the sin offering that restores the relationship between God and the sinner. His death is a saving death that brings the gift of eternal life to those who believe, a costly manifestation of God's love for humanity (Jn 3:14-17). As the good or noble Shepherd, Jesus lays down his life on behalf of his sheep (Jn 10:11, 15) in order to bring them the gift of this more abundant life (Jn 10:10).

Because Jesus honors the Father in this death, Jesus also anticipates that God will honor him through it (Jn 13:31-32; 17:4-5). John's depiction of Jesus' death as an act that honors God and brings honor to Jesus has special meaning as we consider that Peter's martyrdom is referred to also as an act that will bring honor to God (Jn 21:19). Jesus provides an example for the believers to follow, namely, seeking honor from God and seeking to honor God in obedient service, even if this means being shamed and afflicted by nonbelievers. Just as Jesus' honor remained intact through his passion, so the honor of believers will remain untarnished by the assaults of non-Christians as long as they remain loyal and obedient to the God who

drew them to himself in Jesus. As in the Synoptic Gospels, so the fourth Evangelist also maintains that following a suffering Messiah will mean embracing hostility and marginalization for the sake of his name (Jn 15:18-21; 16:33; quite possibly 6:51-58 as well).[44]

The second Paraclete—the Holy Spirit in John. Like Luke, John places a strong emphasis on the person and role of the Holy Spirit. John testifies to Jesus as the one on whom the Holy Spirit remains and the one who baptizes with the Holy Spirit (Jn 1:32-34). Jesus speaks of the Spirit early in the Gospel as the source of the new birth that makes people the children of God and allows them to see the kingdom of God (Jn 3:3-8). The Spirit is essential for the true worship of God, surpassing any claims to holiness and propriety for worship made by geographical locations. Thus the proper worship of God cannot be limited to Mount Zion and Mount Gerizim, and indeed both are surpassed and replaced by worship in the Spirit (Jn 4:21-24). The Evangelist intrudes on his narrative to explain for the readers that the "living waters" that Jesus would cause to well up within the believer are in fact the indwelling of the Spirit (Jn 7:39), which Jesus would send on believers after his return to the Father.

Jesus' farewell discourse expands further on the role of the Spirit. The Spirit is the gift of God sent to the believer at Jesus' request:

> If you love me, you will keep my commandments. And I will ask the Father, and he will give you another Advocate, to be with you forever. This is the Spirit of truth, whom the world cannot receive, because it neither sees him nor knows him. You know him, because he

---

[44]Docetism, with its assertion that the Christ never truly suffered and that the passion was somehow a matter of appearances rather than reality, was ideologically based in the conviction that the divine could not suffer at the hands of or be acted on by created things. Paul Anderson has also shown, however, that docetic Christology was also practically motivated by the desire to justify cooperation with the demands of an unbelieving society and to avoid persecution for the sake of Jesus ("*Sitz im Leben*," p. 45). Ignatius of Antioch, a bishop being transported to martyrdom in 110-111 C.E., makes this connection explicit (*Smyrn.* 4.2).

abides with you, and he will be in you. I will not leave you orphaned; I am coming to you. (Jn 14:15-18 NRSV)

Life in the Spirit is thus compatible only with obedience to Jesus' commandments, which John encapsulates primarily in the simple yet comprehensive "love one another as I have loved you" (Jn 15:12). Jesus calls the Spirit "another Paraclete" (an advocate, guide and encourager), implying that Jesus' own role was also that of Paraclete. The coming of the Spirit fulfills Jesus' promise "I will come to you," for the Spirit makes Jesus' presence known among the believers. This sending of the Spirit is also the fulfillment of the announcement made at the outset by John the Baptist about the role of Jesus (Jn 1:32-34); it is also the realization of the "new birth" by which fleshly human beings can enter into their new inheritance as children of God (Jn 1:12-13; 3:3-8). The reminder in chapter 14 that the world cannot receive the Spirit reinforces the essential dualism laid out in those earlier chapters between those born of the Spirit and those born merely of the flesh.

Jesus' return to the Father means great advantage, not disadvantage, for the believers:

> It is to your advantage that I go away, for if I do not go away, the Advocate will not come to you; but if I go, I will send him to you. And when he comes, he will prove the world wrong about sin and righteousness and judgment: about sin, because they do not believe in me; about righteousness, because I am going to the Father and you will see me no longer; about judgment, because the ruler of this world has been condemned. (Jn 16:7-11 NRSV)

The word rendered "prove" is perhaps better translated as "convict," given the forensic (courtroom) imagery of crime and judgment in this passage. The Spirit's role is conceived here as that of a witness. The Spirit bears witness to the sin of the unbelieving world because that world is unable to receive God's Holy Spirit. The Spirit bears witness to righteousness, that is, the righteousness of Jesus who truly taught God's way and now has been welcomed back to the right hand of God (or better, the bosom of the Father). The Spirit bears witness that the ruler of this world, Satan, stands condemned in the wake of Jesus' death and resurrection, and all who continue in his work also stand under judgment on account of their rejection of Jesus.

Within the community the Spirit bears witness to Jesus and makes Jesus' continued presence among and guidance of the community possible:

> I have said these things to you while I am still with you. But the Advocate, the Holy Spirit, whom the Father will send in my name, will teach you everything, and remind you of all that I have said to you. (Jn 14:25-26 NRSV; cf. also Jn 15:26)

> I still have many things to say to you, but you cannot bear them now. When the Spirit of truth comes, he will guide you into all the truth; for he will not speak on his own, but will speak whatever he hears, and he will declare to you the things that are to come. He will glorify me, because he will take what is mine and declare it to you. All that the Father has is mine. For this reason I said that he will take what is mine and declare it to you. (Jn 16:12-15 NRSV)

The Spirit is the teacher of the believers who will guide them into the full truth about Jesus (an assurance on which 1 John relies heavily, as in 1 Jn 2:20, 26-27; 3:24). The Spirit will not only *remind* the believers about what Jesus had already said to the disciples during his time in the world. According to John 16:12-14, the presence of the Spirit among the believers allows Jesus also to *continue* instructing the dis-

The Portrayal of Peter in John

The characterization of the disciples in the Gospels has always been a matter of great interest, given their importance as leaders in the early church, transmitters of Jesus' teachings and interpreters of his mission and his vision for the community called together in his name. It is thus especially interesting when a disciple—especially one as prominent and important in the story of the early church as Peter—is presented in a somewhat dim light. Does the Fourth Gospel portray Peter, the "rock" on whom Christ built his church according to the Matthean tradition (Mt 16:17-19), in a somewhat deconstructionist manner? Does he seek to criticize in the person of Peter the growing tendency in the early church to locate the repository of authority for the community of faith in a church office and its incumbent?

Paul Anderson would answer these questions in the affirmative,[a] pointing to the following evidence in the Fourth Gospel:

- Peter is conspicuous in his misunderstanding of Jesus' demonstration of servant leadership in John 13:6-10. This observation is strong indeed, but Peter is presented in no worse light that James and John(!) in Mark's Gospel (Mk 10:35-45). All of the Twelve and all who would lead in the church since their passing have had to wrestle with Jesus' countercultural leadership model.
- Peter misunderstands his commission in John 21:15-17. But this observation, it seems to me, misses the mark. The point of the threefold commission is clearly patterned after the threefold denial and, if anything, speaks to the importance of Peter for Jesus and the growth of the church. Indeed, *Peter* is the one commissioned to tend the sheep and feed them; the Beloved Disciple is not given any specific commission or responsibility for the church in that scene or any other.
- Peter is seen "returning the keys of the Kingdom to Jesus" when he says "You [alone] have the words of eternal life" (Jn 6:68 NRSV). Authority, access to truth, access to the words of life always remains with Jesus, never with his representative(s) on earth. If it could be shown that the Fourth Evangelist knew of Peter's commission in Matthew 16:17-19, this point would be more significant in terms of deconstructing a Petrine model of leadership. However, at the very least this statement does resonate well with John's conviction that Christ, and then the Spirit, remain perpetually the source of teaching and guidance in the church.
- Jesus entrusts all of his disciples with the commission to forgive sins in John 20:23 rather than just Peter (Mt 16:19), broadening authority to the whole community rather than restricting it to a single figure or official. While this is correct, we should note that the same movement appears within the Matthean tradition. Matthew 18:18-20 also shows Jesus giving the authority to bind and loose to all the disciples, locating that authority in the gathered community where Jesus is present. John cannot be said to oppose Matthew, then, on this point, but the absence of any tradition parallel to Matthew 16:17-19 is consonant with John's opposition to the development of monarchical church leadership in favor of Christocracy in the church.

---

[a]Anderson, *Christology of the Fourth Gospel,* pp. 221-51; "Interfluential, Formative, and Dialectical," pp. 52-57; and *"Sitz im Leben,"* pp. 50-57.

ciples because they are unable to receive it all during the span of his time with them in the flesh. This understanding of the teaching role of the Spirit, the mediator of the words Jesus would continue to speak, may be highly significant for understanding the source of Johannine discourse material. These discourses may contain "authentic" Jesus sayings (as the fourth Evangelist would view them), spoken by the glorified Jesus and communicated to the churches by the Holy Spirit after the ascension.

Jesus' absence from sight does not mean therefore that he is unavailable to the church. On the contrary, he is even more available to them now that he has returned to the Father. The Father and Jesus make their home with the believers (Jn 14:23), and the Spirit continues to make Jesus' presence known and instruction real. The real leader of the church remains, for the authors of John and the Johannine Epistles, Christ through the Spirit.[45] This conviction may shed light on the situation behind 3 John, where a certain Diotrephes exercises a strong hand in the oversight of a particular Christian community or house church. Diotrephes, who "loves to be first," seems to represent a leadership model in which the doctrinal and ethical health of the church is assured by the oversight of a presiding officer. The Elder, on the other hand, represents a model of leadership in which the Spirit continues to provide effective and sufficient protection of the truth and of conduct, as the Spirit's guidance is discerned by the community of faith. Authority resides not in an office or its incumbent but in the Paraclete who continues to teach and guide the community through all its members.[46] "All" have this anointing, and need no one to "teach" them (1 Jn 2:20-21, 24, 27; a clear application of the

traditions found in Jn 14:26; 16:12-14).[47]

This raises an important issue for ministry in the church. Is the Spirit enough to ensure that the church will go in the right direction? Or do we ultimately rely on an institutionalized authority structure to maintain the boundaries and keep the church on track? An easy answer to such questions is excluded by the mere fact of the variety of answers to these questions found within the pages of the New Testament. Rather, we are invited to wrestle with both sides of this tension and strive to preserve balance between them in the life of the church.

John's cultivation of the ethos of the Johannine community. Jesus' farewell discourse in John directly address the insiders, those who identify themselves as Jesus' disciples. As such, they have much to tell us about who we are to be as Jesus' followers. It is quite striking how closely John ties each aspect of the community's ethos specifically with imitating Jesus' example. For almost every facet of the Christian walk that John holds up for us, Jesus is presented as our example, particularly with regard to the values of servanthood, Christian love and Christian unity, but also notably in the encouragement of ongoing witness and obedience in the face of the world's hostility and rejection. John thereby helps us grapple with the issue of what it means to have Christ formed in us, to borrow a phrase from Paul.

The readers of the Fourth Gospel are called most dramatically to be servants one to another, specifically following Jesus' example in John 13:2-17. In this scene Jesus takes on the role of a domestic slave, bending down to wash and dry the disciples' feet. After resuming his place at the meal, Jesus says:

> Do you know what I have done to you?
> You call me Teacher and Lord—and you

---

[45]See Gary Burge, *The Anointed Community* (Grand Rapids: Eerdmans, 1987).

[46]Anderson, "Was the Author," pp. 32, 41-42; "Interfluential, Formative, and Dialectical," pp. 52-57.

[47]See also 1 Jn 3:24—4:6, where the Spirit-led community, not a single official, is entrusted with testing and discernment.

are right, for that is what I am. So if I, your Lord and Teacher, have washed your feet, you also ought to wash one another's feet. For I have set you an example, that you also should do as I have done to you. Very truly, I tell you, servants are not greater than their master, nor are messengers greater than the one who sent them. (Jn 13:12-16 NRSV)

Jesus employs a "greater to lesser" argument: If Jesus, the master, acts as a servant to those whom he loves, how much more should the disciples, the servants, accept the role of servant one to another. In this, John reflects very closely the Synoptic teachings on discipleship as servanthood, which are also based on the model of Jesus (see Mk 10:42-45; Lk 22:24-27, the latter notably also in the setting of the last meal).

The readers of the Fourth Gospel are also called to love one another as Jesus loved them and left them an example of love's expression:

I give you a new commandment, that you love one another. Just as I have loved you, you also should love one another. By this everyone will know that

Figure 9.6. An earthenware footwashing basin from the sixth century C.E., of a type known also from the first century. The foot rested on the raised ledge while water was poured over it, the basin acting as a receptacle. (Photo: Sam Renfroe; courtesy of Ashland Theological Seminary)

you are my disciples, if you have love for one another. (Jn 13:34-35 NRSV)

This is my commandment, that you love one another as I have loved you. No one has greater love than this, to lay down one's life for one's friends. You are my friends if you do what I command you. (Jn 15:12-14 NRSV; see also Jn 10:11, 15)

While Jesus alone lays down his life in order to bring salvation to his friends, his followers are called to show the same degree of love one to another. Such challenges seek to intensify the affection and mutual support within the community so that the encouragement and affirmation from within outweighs the censure and discouragement from without. This is precisely what the author of 1 John calls for in the aftermath of a bitter schism. The community requires solidarity and mutual support at all times in order for Christian commitment to be maintained. Only when the followers of Jesus experience true and abiding love among the fellowship of the believers will they be able to persist in their commitment.

Just as Jesus was rejected by the world and endured its hostility, so the readers of the Fourth Gospel are called to endure the world's rejection and hostility:

If the world hates you, be aware that it hated me before it hated you. . . . . Because you do not belong to the world, but I have chosen you out of the world—therefore the world hates you. Remember the word that I said to you, 'Servants are not greater than their master.' If they persecuted me, they will persecute you; if they kept my word, they will keep yours also. But they will do all these things to you on account of my name, because they do not know him who sent me. (Jn 15:18-21 NRSV)

John, like other New Testament authors, wants to motivate the believers to lay aside concern for the opinion of unbelievers so they will be free to persevere in their commitment to God through Jesus. The disciples receive no more than the master endured, and the believers should not expect to be treated with greater justice than their Lord. Matthew makes similar use of the same saying—one of very few sayings shared by John with the Synoptic tradition (Mt10:24). Moreover, John's claims about the outsiders' ignorance of God and their folly in opposing and rejecting Jesus serve to disarm the sting of the outsiders' shaming of and opposition to believers. The unbelievers are the disprivileged ones, for they have not been chosen by God for a special knowledge of God and a privileged destiny among the children of God. Moreover, Jesus declares that he has overcome the world, the source of opposition to the disciples. The unbelievers' hostility is merely annoyance from an already-defeated enemy, and the believers are invited to share in Jesus' victory by sharing in his unyielding witness to God's truth in this world (Jn 16:33). Such considerations will certainly help insulate the believers from the society's social sanction of shaming and make it less likely that believers will seek to relieve that shame by conforming again to the values and convictions of the outside world.

In the face of the world's hostility it is all the more essential that the believers pursue unity within the community of faith, just as Jesus and the Father enjoy unity with one another (Jn 17:11, 20-23). Jesus' own prayer for his followers is that they be united with one another, that there be no place given to division and disunity. This is to be the church's witness to the world that Jesus was indeed sent by God! The same unity enjoyed by the Son and the Father—one that is not maintained without humility and submission—is also to characterize the community of believers, who will find unity when each member is submitted to God.

Despite the world's hostility and anticipated rejection, the readers of the Fourth Gospel are sent out into the world to witness. This again occurs in imitation of Jesus, who was sent by God into the world as the revealer of the truth and light: "As you have sent me into the world, so I have sent them into the world" (Jn 17:18; cf. Jn 20:21). The community of the Beloved Disciple, and all believers, are called to continue to pronounce Jesus' testimony to the truth, to "make the good confession" as Jesus did before Pilate and the world, to point the world to its God and the one mediator between God and creation, Jesus the Word made flesh.

Finally, John grounds the believers' sense of honor and self-worth specifically in their connection with Jesus, the Son. He leads readers to distance themselves from those who hide or mute their Christian confession on account of "fear of the Jews," which is properly understood as concern for their standing in the eyes of the non-Christian population (see Jn 9:22; 12:42-43; 19:38). John presents caring about the praise of humans, specifically non-Christians, as the greatest hindrance to attaining the praise that comes from God, which is, of course, a much higher and lasting good. The believers attain this greater honor by serving Jesus: "Whoever serves me must follow me. . . . whoever serves me, the Father will honor" (Jn 12:26 NRSV). This service consists in embodying the core values John develops throughout the Gospel—mutual love and service, unity within the church and bold testimony in the world to the truth of God revealed in Jesus. Rather than use honor discourse to promote a wide variety of behaviors and curtail a wide variety of other behaviors, John simply focuses the believers on the honor they enjoy as members of the family of God and urges them to preserve that honor through continued loyalty to Jesus, acceptance of his message, and faithful service to him in the person of the sister or brother. Service within the community replaces human status seeking, as the believers are assured the honor which God ascribes to them.

CULTURAL AWARENESS
Kinship Language and the
Interpretation of John's Gospel

The Fourth Gospel shares the vision of other New Testament authors that the believing community forms a new kinship group. Believers share in a common birth, a new beginning in a new family with a new Father: "To all who received him, who believed in his name, he gave power to become children of God, who were born, not of blood or of the will of the flesh or of the will of man, but of God" (Jn 1:12-13 NRSV). Later, in the conversation with Nicodemus, Jesus says: "no one can see the kingdom of God without being born from above. . . . [N]o one can enter the kingdom of God without being born of water and Spirit. What is born of the flesh is flesh, and what is born of the Spirit is spirit" (Jn 3:3, 5-6 NRSV). Descent in terms of the flesh (in terms of family and ethnic group) is without value in God's sight. What matters alone is being born of the Spirit. The way to this new birth is through believing in the light that is Jesus and walking in that light, that is, following Jesus' commandments and example: "While you have the light, believe in the light, so that you may become children of light" (Jn 12:36 NRSV).

As a new family the believers are called to enact the values of kin toward one another. The Christians are repeatedly urged to "love one another" (Jn 13:34; 15:17), specifically after the example of Jesus, who valued the well being of his sisters and brothers above his own life (Jn 15:12-13). Just as it would be disgraceful for us to "love" our natural kin only as long as that love cost nothing, so the people joined by the blood of Jesus are to "go the distance" in loving each other. Putting one another ahead of our comfort level, our attachment to our money, even our personal safety—this is the kind of love for one another that, for John at least, sums up all of Jesus' teaching. This is to be the church's essential mark, so that the world would recognize our connection with Jesus by the love we show one another (Jn 13:35).

Turning to the closely related Johannine Epistles we again find that love of the brothers and sisters is an essential characteristic of those who are "in the light." Without such love, we are still "in darkness" (1 Jn 2:9-11). Loving the family of God is the indication of being "born of God" (1 Jn 4:7) and also of loving God. For John as for other ancient moralists, love for siblings is the best proof of love for one's parents. Those without such love for fellow believers show themselves to be "children of the devil" (1 Jn 3:10). This love must be practically demonstrated. First John provides a simple way in which "laying down one's life" for the sisters and brothers (Jn 15:12-13) can be enacted: "How does God's love abide in anyone who has the world's goods and sees a brother or sister in need and yet refuses help? Little children, let us love, not in word or speech, but in truth and action" (1 Jn 3:17-18 NRSV).

Just as harmony or unity is a core value for natural families, so John stresses its importance for the Christian family. Just as the Father and the Son exhibit perfect agreement and harmony (Jn 17:11, 21), and exhibit a complete sharing of goods (Jn 17:10), so the disciples are to exhibit unity among themselves in the bond of love. Again, this redounds to the honor of the whole household, including the world's recognition of the Son as the Father's emissary (Jn 17:21).

Kinship language contributes greatly to John's presentation of Jesus' honor in this Gospel. The author accomplishes this not by arguing for Jesus' honor in terms of noble descent from the house of David or birth in a city with a noble heritage, as does Matthew. Rather, he relativizes all worldly claims to honor in an appeal to Jesus' divine lineage and heavenly origin. This is very much in keeping with his claim that birth into God's family replaces birth into one's family of origin (Jn 1:11-13) and with his negation of the spiritual or salvific value of claims to physical descent from Abraham. As in the other Gospels Jesus' location in a particular natural kinship group (the son of an artisan in Nazareth) hinders his neighbors from understanding his place and role in the family of God: "Is not this Jesus, the son of Joseph, whose father and mother we know? How can he now say, 'I have come down from heaven'?" (Jn 6:42 NRSV).

In John, Jesus gives considerable space to deconstructing the reliance of the "Jews" on their kinship with Abraham for their place in the family of God (compare the briefer treatment of this theme in Mt 3:9; 8:11-12). Belonging to the offspring of Abraham "by means of blood, flesh, or human desire" (Jn 1:12-13) does not make an individual part of God's family. Rather, that person must receive Jesus' testimony and be born from above in order to become a free child within the household of God.

John 8:31-45 contains a conversation between Jesus and "the Jews who had believed in him" that utilizes the topic of "likeness" extensively and combatively. Jesus claims that following his word will make these Jews free, but that implies that they are currently slaves. They invoke their noble ancestry from Abraham to deflect this implication. Jesus explains that their innate drive to sin—in particular, to kill Jesus because his word "has no place in them"—reveals their slavery to sin and alienation from the Father. Here again the Jews rest on the claim "Abraham is our Father," to which Jesus responds, "If you were Abraham's children, you would be doing what Abraham did, but now you are trying to kill me, a man who has told you the truth that I heard from God. This is not what Abraham did. You are indeed doing what your father does" (Jn 8:39-41 NRSV). The Jews may suggest an insult to Jesus, whose lineage we know to be irregular, to say the least ("They said to him, 'We are not illegitimate children'"). They go on to claim that God is their father, but Jesus refutes it: their rejection of

God's emissary shows that they are not of God's household. Rather, "You are from your father the devil, and you choose to do your father's desires. He was a murderer from the beginning and does not stand in the truth, because there is no truth in him. When he lies, he speaks according to his own nature, for he is a liar and the father of lies" (Jn 8:44 NRSV). The Jews' rejection of Jesus and his word of truth thus shows them to be offspring of the liar. Throughout this exchange, then, claims to a certain parentage and attributions of alternative parentage provide the basis for challenges to and defenses of behavior and honor.

EXEGETICAL SKILL
Social-Scientific Criticism (1)—
Orientation to the Larger World

Social-scientific analysis of the New Testament, sometimes also referred to as "sociological exegesis," provides us with tools to get at the "real life" situations and issues within and behind the biblical text. This discipline arose in part as a reaction against avenues of interpretation that treated the Bible mainly as a source for ideas and theology, neglecting the flesh-and-blood dimensions of the text and the story it told. The kinds of questions asked by social-scientific interpreters and the models they bring to the Scriptures all seek to uncover information about the economic systems, the power structures and the social dynamics behind the text to illumine more fully the situation addressed by the text. Social-scientific analysis also seeks to uncover more fully how the text acts back on that situation, shaping the social dynamics, the distribution of power, the flow of resources and the like.

Social-scientific interpretation tends to proceed in one of two principle modes. The first is social description, the goal of which is to help the readers arrive at a more thorough insider's knowledge of the social, cultural, political, economic and ecological situation behind a New Testament text. The second involves the use of social-scientific models to explain the behaviors, structures, authority claims and cultural patterns encountered in a particular text. The best scholars combine these modes in their work, using one to enhance and correct the other.

Social-scientific interpretation is one of the main tools undergirding this New Testament introduction. As such, you have already encountered its fruits in the chapters on the Synoptic Gospels and Acts, for example in the analysis of the group-forming and group-maintaining functions of Matthew, or the questions of the legitimation of authority in Acts. You have encountered it in the study of the cultural background of the New Testament and the ways that a growing awareness of key cultural assumptions and values can open up the New Testament to us "foreigners" in illuminating ways. You will continue to encounter it prominently in the chapters that follow. Along the way, however, I will use several "Exegetical Skill" sections to introduce you to some specific sets of questions or specific models that you may find useful for your own investigations of the New Testament. Hopefully, these will spur you on to learn more about this discipline and to acquaint yourself with its broader spectrum of investigative techniques.[a]

How does the text encourage readers to respond to the "Word" in the "world"? One way for us to begin to think sociologically about a text is to consider the ways the author is trying to model or shape the relationship between the reader and other people in the "real world." Although social-scientific analysis is deeply rooted in the historical-critical paradigm, at this point it can also feed off the results of narrative criticism, for we are thinking here about the way people are likely to respond in the "real" world based on how fully they embody the responses of the "implied" or "ideal reader."

We come to the text now with a new set of questions: Does the author encourage the formation or maintenance of a group that can be marked off from other social bodies? If so, how? How does the author suggest that the group is related to other social groups "out there" in society? How does the author nudge the group members to respond to one another within the group and to other groups? That is, what kinds and qualities of social relations and responses does the text nurture?

To answer such questions, interpreters often find it helpful to turn to the work of sociologists of religion, who study the behavior of sects and other group cultures in the modern world, and who construct models of how sectarian groups preserve their own identity and respond to the world around them. At this point it is imperative to observe an admonition that critics of the social-scientific method often direct toward its proponents. A model is misused if the data in the text are stretched or manipulated to make the text fit the model, or if assumptions derived from the model are imposed on the text without internal support from the text. That is to say, models should only be used to help us make observations about the text and its social dynamics. They never should be imposed on the text.

---

[a]An excellent introduction to this discipline in all its complexity and richness is J. H. Elliott, *What Is Social-Scientific Criticism?* (Minneapolis: Fortress, 1993). Two fine surveys of landmark works in the discipline and the models and techniques these employ are B. Holmberg, *Sociology and the New Testament* (Minneapolis: Fortress, 1990), and chapter five of V. K. Robbins, *The Tapestry of Early Christian Discourse: Rhetoric, Society, and Ideology* (London: Routledge, 1996). For a briefer introduction, see David A. deSilva, "Embodying the Word: Social-Scientific Interpretation of the New Testament," in *The Face of New Testament Studies,* ed. Scot McKnight and Grant Osborne (Grand Rapids: Baker, 2004).

Since the 1970s, students of the Bible have been mining the work of sociologists to find tools that will help them discover more about the world behind the texts and to articulate and even predict more clearly the kind of group a particular scriptural text is trying to shape. Brian Wilson's typology of sects provides one such helpful heuristic tool.[b] Wilson finds that sectarian groups orient themselves to the society around them in seven basic ways, according to the objectives set by the group and the means by which the group seeks to achieve those ends.

- Conversionist. The group wants to bring the world in line with the standards it regards as right and true, and seeks to do so through the conversion of individual people. As more and more people are won to the group, the group gets closer and closer to the transformation it seeks.

- Revolutionist. The present order is itself the source of dissonance between "the way things are" and "the way things ought to be." The group therefore looks forward to the complete overthrow of the present system, which might come through divine means, armed revolution or a combination of the two, and to its replacement by the leadership of the group.

- Reformist. The problem with the world is bigger than individuals, but not so bad as to require a completely new start. Reformist groups believe they can make the world right by working to change the system from within.

- Introversionist. Rather than actively seeking to change outsiders into insiders or making the society a better place, introversionist groups tend to withdraw and focus on perfecting themselves in the values the group espouses. The group achieves its goals by remaining "pure" from the outside world.

- Thaumaturgical. The focus here is not so much on changing the world but on finding supernatural help for coping with specific problems that life throws in the way of the group members. This kind of response is fostered wherever members are led to expect miraculous healing, deliverance from danger, recovery from loss and the like.

- Gnostic-Manipulationist. This term is slightly misleading, because it really has nothing to do with the early movement known as Gnosticism. The term really has to do with finding the right "knowledge" or

---

[b]The following is taken from B. R. Wilson, *Magic and the Millennium: A Sociological Study of Religious Movements of Protest among Tribal and Third-World Peoples* (New York: Harper & Row, 1973), pp. 22-26, as summarized in Robbins, *Tapestry of Early Christian Discourse*, pp. 147-50. See also Robbins, *Tapestry*, pp. 250-59, 176-79 for more examples of how this model has been used to open up New Testament texts in new ways.

"know-how" (Greek, *gnōsis*) to manipulate circumstances to one's advantage. These sects tend to accept the goals shared by the larger society (like health, wealth and happiness) but promote a "better" way to achieve those goals. The preachers of the "health and wealth gospel" nurture this kind of response.

- Utopian. Rather than overturning or reforming the present order, a utopian group pours itself into constructing an alternative order in which God's ultimate principles and values undergird that order.

These categories are by no means mutually exclusive. Introversionist and utopian responses are highly compatible, as are introversionist and revolutionist responses. Thaumaturgical responses are compatible with every other form of response. It is very rare for a group to be fit neatly into any one category. More often a group will exhibit elements of several kinds of response to the world, with different degrees of prominence given to each kind of response. This is exactly what we would expect from a three-dimensional, real-world phenomenon like a social group.

Responses to the world in John. How do these categories help us answer the questions we introduced in the previous section? First, John quite clearly identifies a particular group that is set off from the rest of the world. As early as the prologue we find the encounter with the Word setting off those who become "children of God" from those who reject the light (Jn 1:10-13), a distinction reinforced by the imagery of family binding together the group that received the Word in Jesus. John will return again and again to this separation of people of light from people of darkness, children of God from children of the devil, throughout the Gospel. The highly dualistic mode of John's language and the way he leads his audience to see the world in terms of stark dichotomies feeds an ideology of separation from the surrounding society as a distinct social group. The Christian group is seen as set apart from the synagogue, largely thanks to the synagogue's own actions against what it perceived to be deviants. (Here is a whole field for fruitful sociological inquiry; see especially John 9.) It is also set apart from the "world," which is presented as irretrievably hostile to the Son and to those who are gathered to the Son (chaps. 15-16).

What kinds of goals and means of attaining those goals does the Gospel nurture for this group of disciples (to the extent that the disciples in the "real world" will accept and reflect the author's vision for the disciples in the text world)? From our study of John 4 we can already see that John nurtures a conversionist response to some degree. Individuals can indeed break through the darkness and encounter the light, and the disciples are invited to participate in the harvest that the Son began to recap. Nevertheless, there is no expectation that converting people will correct all that the group perceives to be amiss with the world.

While most New Testament texts nurture a strong revolutionist response, looking forward to the time when God will overturn the kingdoms of the world and establish the kingdom of the Son, John has largely muted this kind of response. Part of this is due to his realized eschatology, which could be viewed as "realized revolution." The "ruler of this world" is driven out at the crucifixion in some sense (Jn 12:31), but the world remains largely unchanged and unredeemed. Jesus' kingdom is "not of this world" (Jn 18:36) but seems to exist beyond this world, with little expectation for this world coming under his sway being nurtured.

Neither does the Gospel point its followers in reformist directions. Unlike the Synoptic Gospels, wherein Jesus gives ample prescriptions for the redistribution of wealth and the reformation of oppressive economic institutions, John has none of this. Rather, the constructive attentions of the group are directed inward in a utopian thrust, supported (but not overshadowed) by introversionist leanings. The disciples are very much aware of their separation from the world, not only on the basis of their identity as people of light in the midst of darkness but also on the basis of the hostility of the world toward the group, interpreted as the world's rejection of those who are not its own. Separation from the world, however, does not become an end in itself but the framework for the construction of an alternative order in which God's commandments fully shape relationships between people and God's values are fully reflected in the group. The values of love and unity are prominent pillars for this alternative community, and the Holy Spirit is its guiding force.

To what extent does John encourage thaumaturgical responses? On the one hand, Jesus performs several healings and even a resuscitation, with the result that both author and audience are seen to assume the possibility of the supernatural reaching in to fix life's problems. John even fosters the expectation that the disciples will do "greater works than these" (Jn 14:12) and that whatever the disciples ask for (the lack of limits here is astounding) will be done for them by the Father (Jn 14:13-14). On the other hand, John presents these miraculous events as signs pointing the discerning toward a true knowledge of Jesus, impelling them toward a commitment to Jesus and his way. While God's power and intervention is available as a resource for a group experiencing the hostility of outsiders, the goal is never just fixing life's ills, but the manifestation of the Son's glory in the world as signs calling for faith. This presentation is significantly different from the more practical and problem-focused advice of James 5:13-18.[c]

---

[c]Indeed, the fourth Evangelist's attitude toward the miraculous may be even more ambivalent than this. The miraculous feeding of the 5,000 produces only negative results, such that the fact that they "ate and were filled" (Mk 6:42; 8:8) becomes a problem in John, where the crowd only seeks Jesus be-

Thaumaturgy thus serves something like a gnostic-manipulationist response, but here our use of the model has to be highly qualified because John's group is nothing like the gnostic-manipulationist sects Bryan Wilson observed. Knowledge is crucial in John. Those who "know . . . the only true God, and Jesus Christ whom [God has] sent" are those who achieve the principal goal of "life" and "eternal life" (Jn 17:3 NRSV). In a sense John does accept the goals and values of the synagogue, and from that point of view he can be said to promote a better knowledge with regard to attaining those goals. It is not, however, manipulationist in Wilson's sense of that word.

This all-too-brief analysis (a proper one would work through the text passage by passage) does give us an overview of the kind of group the Fourth Gospel seeks to shape. I would identify "utopian" as the description that best matches John's principle goals—the nurturing of a social group in which God's values and ideals are fully embodied in inner-group relationships, a bold witness to a better alternative to the other systems of relationships offered by the world. The concerns and methods of introversionist groups are also attested, and perhaps this should be seen as the secondary description of the author's goals. Elements of conversionist and gnostic-manipulationist responses to the world are also present, but clearly subservient to the utopian goals, with thaumaturgical responses being subordinated, in turn, to those. This is a very different configuration of responses than we would find in any other Gospel and most any other New Testament text, which suggests that Wilson's typology can help us recover a sense of the variety within the early Christian movement. It will also help us identify more precisely the ways specific New Testament texts can be used faithfully and effectively to shape timely and appropriate responses to the world among our contemporary churches in their diverse circumstances.

This discussion of a complex social-scientific model (the seven types of sectarian response to the world) has been admittedly too brief, and the reader is encouraged to dig deeper by means of reading Vernon Robbins's treatment of this topic (see footnote 67) o Bryan Wilson's original materials. As a beginning exercise, explore the following shorter books: Titus, 1 Peter, James, 1 John. What kinds of responses do each of these texts nurture among the audience, and what specific clues in the text have led you to your conclusions? How do you have to modify Wilson's types to account adequately for the data you uncover (remember: social-scientific models are not absolutes; they always need to be adapted to the peculiar features of real-life groups under investigation)?

---

cause they ate and were filled (Jn 6:26)—but not because they understand anything about his significance or the importance of receiving him in a deeper sense. John might, indeed, no longer have a place for the miraculous. See further, Anderson, *Christology of the Fourth Gospel*, pp. 257, 261; *"Sitz im Leben,"* pp. 28-29.

FOR FURTHER READING

The following books and articles will expose you to a broad range of social-scientific models and avenues of inquiry into the world in front of and behind a text. They will also expose the specific impact a text has on social relationships within a group and between its audience and other groups. Some are geared more toward providing essential information about the social environment of early Christianity; others offer examples of social-scientific models and insights at work in the exploration of specific New Testament texts. As a starting point, I recommend Elliott's *What Is Social Criticism?* Holmberg's *Sociology and the New Testament* and Kee's *Knowing the Truth.*

Berger, Peter L. *The Sacred Canopy: Elements of a Sociological Theory of Religion* (New York: Doubleday, 1967).

deSilva, David A. "Embodying the Word: Social-Scientific Interpretation of the New Testament." In *The Face of New Testament Studies.* Edited by Scot McKnight and Grant Osborne. Grand Rapids: Baker, 2004.

———. "The Epistle to the Hebrews in Social-Scientific Perspective." *Restoration Quarterly* 36 (1994): 1-21.

———. "The Social Setting of the Apocalypse of John: Conflicts Within, Fears Without." *Westminster Theological Journal* 54 (1992): 273-302.

Elliott, John H. *A Home for the Homeless: A Sociological Exegesis of 1 Peter, Its Situation and Strategy.* 2nd ed. Philadelphia: Fortress, 1990.

———. *What Is Social-Scientific Criticism.* Minneapolis: Fortress, 1993.

Holmberg, Bengt. *Paul and Power: The Structure of Authority in the Primitive Church as Reflected in the Pauline Epistles.* Philadelphia: Fortress, 1980.

———. *Sociology and the New Testament.* Minneapolis: Fortress, 1990.

Kee, Howard C. *Knowing the Truth: A Sociological Approach to New Testament Interpretation.* Minneapolis: Fortress, 1989.

Meeks, Wayne A. *The First Urban Christians: The Social World of the Apostle Paul.* New Haven, Conn.: Yale University Press, 1983.

Neyrey, Jerome H., ed. *The Social World of Luke-Acts: Models for Interpretation.* Peabody, Mass.: Hendrickson, 1991.

Stambaugh, J. E., and David L. Balch, *The New Testament in Its Social Environment.* Philadelphia: Westminster Press, 1986.

Theissen, Gerd. *The Social Setting of Early Palestinian Christianity.* Philadelphia: Fortress, 1978.

———. *The Social Setting of Pauline Christianity: Essays on Corinth.* Philadelphia: Fortress, 1982.

JOHN AND MINISTRY FORMATION

The Fourth Gospel begins to contribute to the formation of ministers and counselors and others who reach out to bring the light of Christ to people in need by presenting the model of the good Shepherd, Christ, the minister par excellence. Each of Jesus' encounters with individuals in the Fourth Gospel says much about the task and art of ministering healing. The encounter with the Samaritan woman provides an especially fruitful case study. Jesus must himself first set aside long-standing social, ethnic and religious barriers to reach this woman. Ministers too are called to leave their own prejudices at the cross and to dispel any prejudices that will block the hearts of those they help against the counselor or minister. Our social location and ethnic identity should not dam or determine the flow of the living water that Jesus provides by means of our ministry.

Jesus also moves the conversation forward to expose the relational brokenness (indeed, the sin) in the woman's life. Something is clearly not whole with a woman who has already endured five marriages—such a string of failed relationships cannot help but leave deep emotional scars and reveals some deeper problems that the woman has tried (and is trying) to deal with through a sexual relationship, but that cannot be healed in this way. The endless repetition shows a woman at work trying to deal with some personal issue, but she is obviously failing to get at the heart of it since she is trying to solve it through an improper means. At this point things are getting too close to home for the woman, and she throws up a religious question that might throw the prophet off track. The question is poised to protect the woman by trying to raise barriers between herself and Jesus ("We Samaritans say . . . You Jews say . . ."). Jesus again cuts through the re-erected barriers and allows her to see that what for her is a distant hope becomes fulfilled reality in the encounter with Jesus. In many ways this is a pattern ministers and counselors may find themselves repeating in many encounters.

Jesus' encounter with the lame man at the pool of Beth-zatha shows us another figure in need of healing but trapped in a cycle of failed attempts. His own resources are insufficient for gaining the healing he wants, and the endless attempts to find wholeness through the same impossible means has led to a condition of hopelessness and self-pity (and who can blame him after thirty-eight years). Again Jesus breaks in with a new healing power, and he achieves what the futile patterns of coping never could. Pastoral counselors are familiar with the cycle of seeking solutions to a problem in the wrong places. John 4 and 5 provide two mutually reinforcing stories that speak of breaking the pattern and finding wholeness when Jesus enters into and works on a person's brokenness in new, life-giving ways.

John 21 preserves something of a counseling session arranged by Jesus for Peter. Jesus lights a charcoal fire, taking Peter back to the scents in his nostrils that night when he denied Jesus (Jn 18:18). This time, however, Jesus gives Peter the opportunity to confess his love for Jesus three times and empowers him with a commission three times to look after Jesus' followers. Jesus allows Peter to go back, as it were, and relive the scene and do it right this time, releasing him from the guilt and shame of his failure. We find similar techniques at work in a number of counseling methods: the minister takes the parishioner back into those situations that have been painful and have adversely affected his or her psyche, only this time the parishioner is made aware of Jesus' presence in that situation and is allowed to act on that situation from the new position of security and strength.

Another important resource found in the Fourth Gospel is the Evangelist's use of powerful images in his pastoral response to the church. These images—light and darkness or "new life" to describe the work of Christ in the person and in the world—can still be used to great effect in ministry situations. John opens with the images of light piercing and searching the darkness, calling to mind the psalmist's cry:

> Search me, O God, and know my heart;
> test me and know my thoughts.
> See if there is any wicked way in me,
> and lead me in the way everlasting. (Ps 139:23-24 NRSV)

This may be a fruitful image for those who seek healing, those who may invite the light of God to shine within them in order to illumine what needs to be exposed and healed, what requires the life-giving light of Jesus. John also opens with the assurance that the darkness is not too powerful for God's light—the light is stronger, able to deliver any person from the darkness that clouds the heart and mind as a result of living with the long-term effects of sin, broken relationships, abuse, inferiority and the like. Such imagery and assurances can also strengthen disciples for witness and social action in the service of bringing God's justice, peace and healing to this broken world, dispelling the darkness with the light of Christ.

Another pervasive image is that of the new birth. John introduces this image in the prologue (Jn 1:12-13) and develops it further in Jesus' dialogue with Nicodemus (Jn 3:3-8). So much of what restrains people in relationships and keeps them bound to harmful patterns of living comes from their inheritance from our first birth, their birth "according to blood and the will of the flesh" (Jn 1:13). Jesus offers a new birth—a second chance to have our identities and selves shaped, but this time by our interactions with a new family, particularly God the Father. Jesus offers to us and those to whom we would minister a new identity and security, a safe place from which to look at the residue of our first birth and the life we have lived since. We are invited, with Jesus, to observe the Father's working and being, and thereby learn new patterns of being and living. We pattern our lives after our heavenly Parent's character and cues, replacing imperfect cues from earthly families. We are invited into the freedom of a new destiny and a new inheritance, a new life as we live out of this second birth and the character formation we receive from being with God.

So far we have focused on individual-oriented ministry, but John also provides us with a grand vision for the shaping of a Christian community, a vision that all believers are called to nurture together. John 13—17, with its instructions to believers for the sort of community they are to form, points us to the church as the environment where healing can happen and that can support healing if we only take Jesus' instructions seriously. If we as a church begin to open ourselves to loving one another, serving one another and pursuing unity rather than division (even if that means an emphasis on serving and loving rather than doctrinal litmus tests), then we will be creating the place where deep, personal sharing can occur (which requires trust), and where those engaged in seeking the new life to which Jesus calls them will find support and encouragement for the journey.

The new birth and new life require new family, and only the church can provide that. Taking Jesus' words to heart and modeling what we do as a church after what we see the Father and the Son doing will lead us away from being just another, larger, dysfunctional family and closer to being that family where the Spirit is the Teacher and Counselor, leading us into truth and life. Jesus' prayer on behalf of the church cannot fail to impress us with the importance of unity in the church, not only within the local congregation but across denominational and national boundaries. The global Christian community must reflect the relationship of the Father and the Son. Therefore unity and love, the values John presents as defining the relationship of the Father and the Son, are the core values promoted by John.

The Fourth Gospel also calls us, especially in our role as ministers one to another and the world, to abide in Jesus and bear fruit (Jn 15:1-11). Our methods-oriented and results-oriented mentality, where we have a program for every need and we measure effectiveness by numbers, can quickly move ministers away from being centered in Jesus and to relying on their own energy and the effectiveness of various programs to produce results. John reminds each of us, however, that our effectiveness comes from one source alone—our connectedness, our rootedness in Jesus. Jesus' love and friendship are the wellspring from which all effective ministry flows, and they sustain ministers through a lifetime of effective service. The fourth Evangelist helpfully—indeed, salvifically—reminds ministers in all areas of service that their most precious resource, the one most to be protected and cultivated, is their connectedness with the heart of Christ.

For Further Reading

Anderson, Paul N. *The Christology of the Fourth Gospel: Its Unity and Disunity in the Light of John 6.* Tübingen: Mohr Siebeck, 1996; Valley Forge, Penn: Trinity Press International, 1997.

———. "Was the Author of the Fourth Gospel a Quaker?" *Quaker Religious Thought* 76 (1991): 27-43.

———. "Interfluential, Formative, and Dialectical: A Theory of John's Relation to the Synoptics," pp.19-58. In *Für und wider die Priorität des Johannesevangeliums.* Edited by P. L. Hofrichter. Hildesheim: Georg Olms, 2002.

———. "John and Mark: The Bi-Optic Gospels," pp. 175-88. In *Jesus in Johannine Tradition.* Edited by R. T. Fortna and T. Thatcher. Louisville, Ky.: Westminster John Knox, 2001.

————. "The *Sitz im Leben* of the Johannine Bread of Life Discourse and Its Evolving Context," pp. 1-59. In *Critical Readings of John 6*. Edited by R. A. Culpepper. Leiden: Brill, 1997.

Barrett, C. K. *Essays on John*. Philadelphia: Westminster Press, 1982.

————. *The Gospel According to St. John*. 2nd ed. Philadelphia: Westminster Press, 1978.

Beasley-Murray, George R. *John*. WBC. Dallas: Word, 1987.

Blomberg, Craig. *The Historical Reliability of John's Gospel*. Downers Grove, Ill.: InterVarsity Press, 2001.

Borgen, Peder. *Bread from Heaven: An Exegetical Study of the Concept of Manna in the Gospel of John and Writings of Philo*. Leiden: Brill, 1965.

Brown, Raymond. *The Community of the Beloved Disciple*. New York: Paulist, 1979.

————. *The Gospel According to John*. AB. 2 vols. Garden City, N.J.: Doubleday, 1966, 1970.

Bruce, F. F. *The Gospel of John*. Grand Rapids: Eerdmans, 1983.

Bultmann, Rudolf. *The Gospel of John*. Translated by George R. Beasley-Murray. Philadelphia: Westminster Press, 1971.

Charlesworth, James, ed., *John and the Dead Sea Scrolls*. New York: Crossroad, 1990.

Dodd, C. H. *Historical Tradition in the Fourth Gospel*. Cambridge: Cambridge University Press, 1963.

————. *The Interpretation of the Fourth Gospel*. Cambridge: Cambridge University Press, 1953.

Keener, Craig S. *The Gospel of John: A Commentary*. 2 vols. Peabody, Mass.: Hendrickson, 2003.

Kysar, Robert. *The Fourth Evangelist and His Gospel*. Minneapolis: Fortress, 1975.

————. "John, Gospel of." *Anchor Bible Dictionary*. 3:912-31. Edited by David N. Freedman. Garden City, N.Y.: Doubleday, 1992.

————. *John, the Maverick Gospel*. Rev. ed. Louisville, Ky.: Westminster John Knox, 1993.

Martyn, J. Louis. *History and Theology in the Fourth Gospel*. Nashville: Abingdon, 1979.

Morris, Leon. *The Gospel According to John*. NICNT. Grand Rapids: Eerdmans, 1971.

Painter, John. *The Quest for the Messiah: The History, Literature, and Theology of the Johannine Community*. 2nd ed. Nashville: Abingdon, 1993.

Robinson, John A. T. *The Priority of John*. London: SCM Press, 1985.

Schnackenburg, R. *The Gospel according to St. John*. 3 vols. New York: Crossroad, 1968-1982.

Talbert, Charles H. *Reading John*. New York: Crossroad, 1994.

Thompson, Marianne Meye. "John, Gospel of," pp. 368-83. In *Dictionary of Jesus and the Gospels*. Edited by Joel B. Green and Scot McKnight. Downers Grove, Ill.: InterVarsity Press, 1992.

————. *The Humanity of Jesus in the Fourth Gospel*. Philadelphia: Fortress, 1988.

Witherington, Ben, III. *John's Wisdom: A Commentary on the Fourth Gospel*. Louisville, Ky.: Westminster John Knox, 1995.

10

THE EPISTLES OF JOHN

Painful Breaches of the Bond of Unity and Love

The three letters of "John" provide a kind of sequel to the Gospel of John in a manner similar to the way Acts continues the story of Luke. Here, however, the sequel does not concern the immediate post-Easter efforts of the Jerusalem church, but the story of the communities most directly and deeply influenced by the Gospel of John. Each of these letters addresses very specific challenges in very specific situations within the life of specific communities, so that the category "general epistles" applies even less to these texts than to Jude and 2 Peter.

The sequel is a tragic one. As the history of Christian thought in the second and third centuries would show, the Fourth Gospel admits of several different lines of interpretation. The letters of John witness to an early split within the church over the interpretation of that tradition. The author of these epistles contends for the importance of the humanity of Christ, the salvific significance of his death and the basis for Christian love that Jesus' death provides. The separatists place far more emphasis on the significance of the revelation of God breaking into the world by means of Jesus as a vehicle for the Christ, but neither fully enfleshing their Christology nor their responsibility to other Christians. The church's selec-

tion of these letters for the canon, but not any missives of the separatists, stands as another witness to the importance of the cruciform Christ and thus to the cruciform life of the disciple who would confess this Christ.

INTRODUCTION TO THE JOHANNINE EPISTLES

The Johannine Epistles in the life of the "Johannine community." In a way that no text does for the Synoptic Gospels, the Johannine Epistles provide vivid windows into the lives of the communities addressed by the Fourth Gospel. That the three letters of John derive from the environment of Johannine Christianity hardly requires demonstration. Anyone reading casually or devotionally through the New Testament immediately notices the similarity between the Fourth Gospel and 1 and 2 John.[1] The shared, distinctive vocabulary (*word, beginning, light, life, truth, abiding, world, water* and *blood, joy, victory* and so forth) and the shared emphasis on the commandment to "love one another" as the heart of Christian ethics and obedience make such a connection unmistakable.

The author of 1 John shows deep affinities with the Christology and ethics of the Fourth Gospel. Both emphasize the need to believe in

---

[1]Extensive listings of parallels can be found in Raymond E. Brown, *Epistles of John*, AB 30 (Garden City, N.Y.: Doubleday, 1982), pp. 755-59.

Jesus (and, notably, both understand this as a certain kind or quality of confession that reflects the Johannine understanding of Jesus' significance). Both speak of the importance of "walking in the light" and turning away from all such deeds as belong to the darkness and show enmity with the light. Both emphasize the single command to "love one another" even to the point of laying down one's life for a brother or sister (1 Jn 3:16-18; Jn 10:11; 15:12-13). Both stress the incompatibility of love of God and friendship with the world (1 Jn 2:15-17; 3:13-14; 5:4-5). Both speak of the Holy Spirit as an essential resource available to the believers to teach them the truth about Jesus, a factor that 1 John especially relies on to reassure the remnant that they have made the right decision (1 Jn 2:20, 26-27).

Nevertheless, it is equally clear that the epistles address specific developments in the life of the circles of Christian communities that adhere to the Johannine tradition. The traditions collected together in the Fourth Gospel speak to the debate between Christians and non-Christian Jews concerning the identity and significance of Jesus as well as delineate the foundational ethic for the Christian community (a primary function of Jn 13—17). First and Second John, however, address an internal division within the Christian community—one that is wholly explicable on the basis of rival interpretations of the traditions found in the Fourth Gospel.[2]

The Gospel of John stresses both the humanity and the divinity of Jesus. Neither could be lost to view. The Gospel had placed greater emphasis on affirming a high Christology in the face of outsiders (at least, in the traditions) who fail to ascribe divinity to Jesus. The epistles, however, address an inner-church debate in which some Christians, nurtured on the traditions of the Fourth Gospel, push affirmations of the divinity of the Christ too far, forgetting the importance of the deeds and death of the human Jesus.[3] The opening of 1 John parallels the prologue to the Gospel with its emphasis on "the beginning," but now the tangible life of the Son in the flesh is emphasized as a response and corrective to a development of the Gospel tradition that attaches too little weight to what was accomplished in the "flesh" of Jesus.

The more progressive Christians could not remain united with their more traditional sisters and brothers, and so they split off to form their own congregation (1 Jn 2:18-19). In the opinion of the author of 1 John, they broke the bond of love and unity by leaving the community, initiating the schism and the divisive competition now for adherents.[4] Convinced that they now bear the true heritage of the Beloved Disciple, these secessionists now undertake a mission of their own in an effort to draw other Christians from the sphere of Johannine influence into their way of thinking and into their fellowship (2 Jn 7-11). Each of the three epistles of John contribute in some way to the community leaders' attempts to curtail the success of these proselytizing secessionists.

---

[2]This was established definitively in Brown, *Epistles*, pp. 47-103, and is followed by Kysar ("John, Epistles of," *Anchor Bible Dictionary*, ed. David N. Freedman [Garden City, N.Y.: Doubleday, 1992], 3:905); Stephen Smalley (*1, 2, 3 John*, WBC [Waco: Word, 1984], p. xxvi), who, however, thinks the author fights against two different deviations, one in the direction of a low Christology, the other in the direction of an excessively high Christology; and John Painter ("The 'Opponents' in 1 John," *NTS* 32 [1986]: 48-71) among others.

[3]The author of 1 John, in fact, now uses the labels that were used within the Johannine tradition to vilify non-Christian Jews to label Christian secessionists as enemies of the Gospel (e.g., "darkness," "liars," "belonging to the world"; see Raymond E. Brown, *The Community of the Beloved Disciple* (New York: Paulist Press, 1979), pp. 133-34; *Epistles of John*, p. 92; Smalley, "Opponents," p. xxvii).

[4]Brown, *Epistles of John*, p. 55; Painter, "Opponents," p. 50. These "antichrists" appear now to be acting as "false prophets" as well, trying to lure their former sisters and brothers away from the traditional Johannine faith (1 Jn 4:1-3).

Chronology of the Johannine Epistles and the Fourth Gospel. The biblical-studies equivalent of the familiar chicken-and-egg question is, which came first, the Fourth Gospel or the Johannine Epistles? The question is greatly complicated by the likelihood that the traditions that contributed to the Fourth Gospel nurtured Christians for decades before the Gospel was written, and that the Gospel itself went through a number of revisions after it was originally composed.[5] Even if 1 John came after the Gospel, it is still therefore possible that 1 John could impact the Gospel at the stage of its redaction (a likely enough situation, since the community leaders would want to ensure that future readers of the Gospel would not make some of the same errors that the secessionists did).

Some suggest that the epistles, especially 1-2 John, were written first. They point to the absence of any direct quotations of the Fourth Gospel, the author preferring simply to make use of the terminology and thought of the traditions that stand behind it. Moreover, 1 John reflects an older Jewish apocalyptic framework than the Fourth Gospel.[6] But the latter, at least, only proves that the author knew older Jewish apocalyptic traditions in addition to the traditions of the Fourth Gospel. Kenneth Grayston regards 1 John as reflecting a stage in the tradition history behind the Gospel that reflects the same situation that stands behind John 13—17 with its emphasis on love and unity.[7] He places the opponents in the context of the debate among Jewish Christians earlier in the community's history. This mistakenly assumes, however, that John 13—17 must reflect a situation of internal division and schism, but Christian preachers do not only preach love and unity when some church members are seceding from the congregation.[8]

The more promising solution is to regard these epistles as later than the Gospel, with the proviso that 1 John has probably exercised some influence on the final form of the Gospel at an editing stage.[9] This position allows for the most logical progression in the collective history reflected behind the individual documents, moving from formation of the tradition in dispute with outsiders to the defense of the tradition in dispute with insiders who want to press it too far. The fully developed Gospel tradition, moreover, stands at the center of the dispute between the author of 1-2 John and the separatists, and it can be taken for granted by both sides. Were the Gospel written after the schism, moreover, we should have expected the leaders (such as the author of 1 John) to present a Gospel more thoroughly insulated from the kinds of misinterpretations pursued by the secessionists. The history of the second century, however, tells

---

[5]Brown, *Epistles of John*, p. 73.

[6]For fuller arguments for the priority of the Johannine Epistles, see the introduction to Georg Strecker, *The Johannine Epistles*, Hermeneia (Minneapolis: Fortress, 1996).

[7]Kenneth Grayston, *The Johannine Epistles*, NCB (Grand Rapids: Eerdmans, 1984), pp. 10-14.

[8]The Fourth Gospel is mainly concerned with the external hostility of the synagogue and the world at large, and thus the task of building up a strong community over against external "enemies." There are points, of course, where the Gospel shows an awareness of the devil among the Twelve, and the many disciples who fall away due to their inability to comprehend Jesus' teaching, notably teaching about himself (Jn 6:60-71). Nevertheless, these are merely suggestive and underdeveloped hints of the reach of the tentacles of the devil and world within the community rather than reliable signs of real, observable inner-community division.

[9]See, most fully, Brown, *Epistles of John*, pp. 30-35. Paul Anderson also locates the epistles between the first and second editions of the Gospel, the first having been written to respond to the tensions with the synagogue and the pressure on Jewish Christians to hide their faith in Jesus or renounce it altogether; the second was written after the threat of persecution of Gentile Christians increases and docetism, with its denial of Christ's actual suffering (and hence the need for disciples to suffer), has run its course ("The *Sitz im Leben* of the Johannine Bread of Life Discourse and Its Evolving Context," in *Critical Readings of John 6*, ed. R. A. Culpepper [Leiden: Brill, 1997], pp. 42-43).

us the Gospel was still quite susceptible to this kind of reading, and so we can surmise that the most the author of 1 John could do was interject a few restrictive claims into the fairly well fixed Gospel.

It is, moreover, likely that the three letters were written at about the same time as one another, though to different audiences. First John addresses the most proximate audiences of the author's circle, seeking to insulate them against the secessionists' position and consolidate their allegiance in the wake of the schism.[10] Second John addresses a more distant house church (or perhaps a set of churches) to warn them about secessionist missionaries, shaping the Christians' perceptions of those missionaries in advance of their coming to assure their rejection. Third John may well postdate the other letters, seeking to secure hospitality for the author's missionaries in a locale where one church leader has blocked the author's envoys from receiving hospitality (perhaps as part of an attempt to keep his church free from *any* contamination from the disruptive schism).

Authorship, date and setting. The similarity in form, especially in the opening and closing, tends to favor the position that the same person wrote 2 and 3 John, a person who refers to himself only as the "Elder."[11] The difference in literary form has led some scholars to propose that a different person closely related to the Elder wrote 1 John, but authors did not limit themselves to a single genre of written expression in antiquity, any more than we do today. The person who composes sermons also routinely composes letters. The impressive amount of shared vocabulary between 1-2 John, coupled with the fact that there is little or no verbatim correspondence (such as a copier or forger might produce), supports common authorship for 1-2 John, hence for all three letters.[12]

A much more challenging question concerns whether or not the author of the epistles was also the author of the Fourth Gospel.[13] The late-second-century canonical list known as the Muratorian fragment attributes both the Gospel and several letters, one of which is clearly 1 John, to the same author, and this would tend to represent the majority opinion of the early church. Martin Hengel defends the traditional view of the early church that one author, actually named John, stands behind all four texts.[14] It is noteworthy, however, that as late as Eusebius we find 2-3 John among the disputed books of the canon on account of their attribution to the Elder John, who would seem to be different from the apostle John that was by then universally assumed to stand behind the Gospel and 1 John, a possibility that Eusebius admits (see *Hist. Eccl.* 3.24.17; 3.25.2-3).

The similarities in vocabulary and style (in the sense of grammatical features of the text) between the Gospel and epistles still tend to suggest common authorship to readers, and

---

[10]The addressees, however, are probably not the members of the author's own congregation. First, the communication is written rather than oral: even without the epistolary trappings, writing implies dissemination over a distance. Moreover, while the author can refer to himself and the audience as a "we" (Brown, *Epistles of John*, p. 31), he can also address them as a "you" distinct from and needing to side with the "we" around the author (as in 1 Jn 1:3; probably Jn 4:4-6) as opposed to the "they" composed of the secessionists.

[11]Smalley, *1, 2, 3 John*, p. xxii; Grayston, *Johannine Epistles*, p. 6.

[12]Smalley, *1, 2, 3 John*, p. xxii; Brown, *Epistles of John*, pp. 14-19. Grayston proposes a theory of multiple authorship, with a group of writers apparent behind the "we" of the first section and a single author, whose hand begins to become apparent with the first person singular pronouns and verbs forms in Jn 2:1-2, 7-8, etc. (*Johannine Epistles*, p. 3). A single author writing on behalf of a "we" group, however, would produce the same result, making this more complex theory unnecessary.

[13]See the extensive treatment of this question in Brown, *Epistles of John*, p. 19-30.

[14]Martin Hengel, *The Johannine Question* (Philadelphia: Trinity Press International, 1989).

this impression is especially borne out when the epistles are compared strictly with the discourses rather than the narratives in the Fourth Gospel.[15] Some differences in vocabulary can largely be explained by a shift in genre from narrative to discourse and in focus from Jesus traditions encapsulating disputes with non-Christian Jews to material addressing a controversy over Christology and ethics among Christians. Other differences, however, are less easy to explain. Key terms in the Gospel (like *glory* and *glorify*), for example, are also absent from 1 John, just as 1 John shows the development of new, important terms within the tradition not found in the Gospel (like *seed* and *anointing*).[16] Shared words can also be used quite differently. The unusual term *parakletos* denotes the Holy Spirit in John's farewell discourse, for example, but it denotes Jesus in 1 John 2:1. *Word* (*logos*) appears to denote the message of the Gospel in 1 John rather than the pre-incarnate Son, as in the prologue of John's Gospel.

Differences in thought and emphasis, which suggest at least a very different situation, also tend to point to different authors. For example, features attributed to Jesus in the Fourth Gospel, like being "light" or giving the command to "love one another," the epistles attribute to God. First John places much more emphasis on the atoning value of the death of Jesus than found in the Gospel. Similarly, the emphasis in 1 John falls on the physical, tangible nature of the Christ, whereas the Gospel emphasizes the manifestation of God's glory through the Word made flesh. First John shows a greater awareness of apocalyptic topics and expectations (Christ's "appearing," the coming "antichrist," implicit expectation of judgment at Christ's *parousia*), although the realized eschatology that is more characteristic of the Gospel is not absent (see especially 1 Jn 3:14).

Although I would hardly agree with Grayston's bold claim that "any thoughtful reading" shows that "the Epistle is written well below the level of the Gospel,"[17] it seems much more probable that the author of the epistles did not also write the Fourth Gospel, although he may well have had a hand in editing it, heightening the Gospel's attention to future eschatology, the reality of the death of Jesus (the water and the blood), and so forth.[18]

Who then is this Elder? Irenaeus (*Haer.* 1.16.3) names him as John the disciple, but ascription of apostolic authorship was central to promoting a book's acceptance as authoritative, just as the acceptance of a book as authoritative all but carried with it the assumption that it was written by an apostle (or as in the case of Mark and Luke, under the auspices of an apostle). The fact that 2-3 John, at least, remained disputed shows that there was no sure tradition for associating these texts with an apostle. (The association of 1 John with an apostle on the strength that the author did *not* identify himself as the Elder is an obviously weak argument from silence.)

Identification of this author is further complicated by the ultimate anonymity of the author of the Fourth Gospel. While early church traditions identify the Beloved Disciple as John, we have seen that a wealth of internal evidence points away from the Galilean fisherman toward a member of the Jerusalem elite (who still may have been named Johanan!).

---

[15]Smalley rightly emphasizes the commonalities between the farewell discourse (Jn 13—17) and 1 John as the greatest concentration of shared vocabulary and themes (*1, 2, 3 John*, pp. xxix-xxx).

[16]Grayston, *Johannine Epistles*, p. 8.

[17]Ibid., p. 9.

[18]We cannot be dogmatic on this point, however. After his exhaustive study, even Raymond Brown must admit that the evidence cannot *prove* that one author could not have written both the Fourth Gospel and the epistles (*Epistles of John*, p. 30).

Later church tradition may have identified two originally different disciples named John, one being numbered among the Twelve. Eusebius's account of a statement by Papias distinguishes between two Christian leaders named John in Ephesus (*Hist. Eccl.* 3.39.4), each standing at a different level in regard to the Jesus tradition—the presbyters or "elders" (among whom Aristion and John are named) passed on the words of the Lord's disciples (among whom another John is named alongside Peter, James and etc.). *Elder (presbys)* may have a specialized meaning, but the term could also simply denote an older member of the community or a leader (leading roles normally falling to senior members anyway). Ultimately, then, all we can say is that the author was a respected teacher and leader within the circle of communities that ultimately drew their inspiration from the Beloved Disciple.[19]

Recognizable quotations in other authors provide the customary evidence for the latest possible date of composition. In this case Polycarp's *Letter to the Philippians* provides this. In this letter Polycarp writes that "everyone who does not confess Jesus Christ to have come in flesh is antichrist" (7.1), a striking recontextualization of 1 John 4:2 (with minor modifications). Since Polycarp immediately goes on to speak of those who are "of the devil" (familiar from 1 Jn 3:8, 10), this is taken as evidence

that he knew 1 John.[20] Polycarp wrote his *Letter to the Philippians* immediately after Ignatius passed through on his way to martyrdom at Rome sometime between 110 and 117 C.E.[21] This would establish c. 110 C.E. as the latest date of composition. Given a date of 85-90 C.E. for the Gospel, the epistles would fall between these two dates.

Most scholars locate the author and the congregations he seeks to influence in Asia Minor, specifically in and near Ephesus. This is mainly based on the early church traditions that locate John in Ephesus and on the very clear connection between the book of Revelation and the churches in Asia Minor. Some scholars suggest Syria, given the more thoroughly Jewish milieu of the Gospel's thought and the firsthand knowledge of Palestine evidenced in the Gospel tradition. Since these are characteristics of the *traditions*, however, they are not sufficient to determine the location of the authors at the end of the first century: the center may well have shifted from Syria or Palestine to Ephesus well before the Gospel took shape.[22]

Genre and purpose. Although always called a "letter," 1 John actually lacks the usual signals of a letter. It has no epistolary prescript (e.g., "the Elder to the churches, greetings") and none of the usual formalities that end a letter (personal greetings, prayers and prayer

---

[19]This may seem to give away too much, especially for those who accept the early church's insistence that apostolicity is determinative for canonicity. Even without a name, however, the status of the Beloved Disciple as a witness to Jesus' earthly ministry and resurrection, and his obvious commitment to Jesus for the remainder of his lifetime, grants him the status of an apostle by the criteria of Acts 1:21-22. The close association of the thought of the epistles with the traditions he preserved shows them also to have been written "under his auspices" as much as Mark and Luke could be said to have been authorized by Peter and Paul respectively.

[20]Other early patristic references include *Epistle to Diognetus* 10:3 ("How will you love the one who thus loved you beforehand?"; cf. 1 Jn 4:19) and Justin *Dialogue with Trypho* 123.9 (cf. 1 Jn 3:2). Both of these are dated in the middle of the second century.

[21]The present form of the letter may represent the conflation of two different letters, one written before Polycarp had any news of Ignatius's actual death (*Phil.* 13.1) and one written after Ignatius's death became known and he joined the ranks of the martyrs (*Phil.* 9.1; see W. R. Schoedel, "Polycarp, Epistle of," in *Anchor Bible Dictionary*, ed. David N. Freedman [Garden City, N.Y.: Doubleday, 1992], 5:390-92, especially p. 390). In this case the reference to 1 Jn would fall in the second, later letter, which still holds the example of Ignatius and his companions as a vivid, recent memory.

[22]See, further, Grayston, *Johannine Epistles,* pp. 27-28; Smalley, *1, 2, 3, John,* p. xxxii; Kysar, "John, Epistles of," p. 909; Brown, *Epistles of John,* pp. 101-2.

The Structure of 1 John

The structure of 1 John is not easy to discern, all the more as the author moves almost in a spiraling fashion through his themes rather than in a linear development. Overall, scholars have tended to observe the following major breaks in the epistle:

1:5 (beginning of body after prologue; topics of light and darkness)

2:18 (introduction of the apocalyptic topics and themes, applied to the secessionists)

2:29 or 3:1 (introduction of ethical topics of sin versus righteousness)

4:1 (introduction of tests for discernment of the spirits) or 4:7 (reintroduction of obligation to love one another and major development of this theme)

5:1 (resumption of topics of right belief, centered on the themes of blood and witness)

5:13 (summary of epistle and concluding admonitions)

It is possible that Jn 5:14-21 is a later addition,[a] but again the lexical, thematic and stylistic consistency with what precedes it makes this impossible to demonstrate. A fuller sampling of various outlines can be found in I. Howard Marshall's *Epistles of John* and Raymond Brown's, *Epistles of John*.[b]

---

[a]Eduard Lohse, *The Formation of the New Testament* (Nashville: Abingdon, 1981), p. 188.

[b]I. Howard Marshall, *The Epistles of John*, NICNT (Grand Rapids: Eerdmans, 1978), pp. 22-26; Brown, *Epistles of John*, p. 764.

---

requests, and the like). It is nevertheless a written communication addressing specific addressees (even if this should include a wide circle of addressees in the sphere of influence of the Johannine traditions) in the light of specific developments and challenges in their local situation. Whether we decide to name it a homily, tract or handbook makes little difference, as long as its basic situational character remains in the forefront.

First John seeks to purge any possible leftover influences of the secessionists' way of thinking. The author tries to consolidate and secure the neighboring congregations for his own group's understanding of the faith, providing a sort of prophylaxis against secessionist influence beyond the author's local congregation. Finally, there was great need for healing: the schism meant internal turmoil and hatred, and now what was needed was love and mutual support within the remnant, attitudes that the address seeks to nurture.

By contrast, 2-3 John are almost textbook examples of the Greco-Roman letter form (both of the mixed type, since they seek to achieve several aims). Indeed, an inventory of the epistolary styles and topics invoked in each letter points to the various aims of 2 and 3 John.[23]

Both 2 John 1-4 and 3 John 1-4 open as letters of the *friendly* type, using its topics of mutuality and appreciation for the virtue of the recipients to establish connectedness and goodwill between author and recipient(s). This is especially appropriate given the situation of competing groups within the Johan-

---

[23]It thus becomes clear than 2 John, for example, is not merely the attempt of an inferior author to convey the essential meaning of 1 John (as in Grayston, *Johannine Epistles*, p. 7).

455

nine circles and the author's desire to reinforce relations between his own group and the satellite congregations.

Second John 5-11 modulates into an *advisory* type, touching on two major topics: (1) the conduct that should characterize inner-community relations, and (2) the response to be given to representatives of the secessionist movement. The latter topic requires that some background information be given to the readers, information that is, however, highly colored and so could be said to blend in topics of vituperation to prejudice the audience against the rival group.

Third John 5-8 resembles the *praising* type, as the Elder lauds a certain Gaius for his hospitality toward and material support of the Elder's emissaries. Encouraging Gaius's continuing investment in this role is all the more urgent, since Diotrephes, the leader of a neighboring house church, refuses the Elder's emissaries. One of the primary purposes of 2 John,

Figure 10.1. Interior of a house in Pompeii showing the standard arrangement of rooms around an open courtyard, or *atrium*, often containing a decorative pool. We may imagine some early Christian house churches meeting in a wealthy home such as this. (Photo courtesy of William Krewson [BiblePlaces.com])

then, is to maintain Gaius's commitment to hospitality for the messengers of the genuine interpretation of the Johannine tradition.

Third John 9-11 modulates into the *vituperative* type, as the Elder criticizes Diotrephes for his refusal to extend hospitality to—and his refusal to allow anyone connected with his house church to shelter and support—the Elder's emissaries. It is likely that this reflects Diotrephes' solution to the problem of the schism and the dangers of deception, namely, refusing to give quarter or platform to anyone coming from that infected congregation.[24]

Third John 12 resembles the *commendatory* type, as indeed the Elder recommends Demetrius to Gaius as a reliable messenger and representative of the Elder himself.[25]

THE MESSAGE OF THE JOHANNINE EPISTLES

Believing and loving: The practical consequences of Christology.

First John has a strange appeal for those who want to make assent to certain beliefs central to defining who is or is not a genuine Christian. This same dimension of the text leads those who place greater stock in "living in love" or "preserving the unity" of the church, two other cardinal values even within the Johannine tradition (see Jn 14—17), to find 1 John less congenial. But the author of 1 John is not actually dealing with two separate realms of Christian reality as he focuses here on *believing* and there on *loving*. Rather, the core christological affirmations he regards as determinative for being "in the light" or "in the truth" are of such importance precisely because they become the ground and basis of Christian love and unity.

What precisely was the Christology opposed by the author and espoused by the secessionists? One difficulty in arriving at an answer is the author's obvious bias against presenting the rivals' position dispassionately and completely. Instead, he presents slogans or claims or negations that may reflect the rivals' Christology but in no way explain it. His strategy is not to lay out the opposing arguments and deconstruct them but to pillory them through counterassertion and labeling. Nevertheless, through the polemic we discover an emphasis on the importance of affirming that the "Son of God," or the "Christ," is none other than Jesus,[26] that Jesus is Christ having "come in the flesh" (1 Jn 4:2), and that Christ Jesus came "not in water only, but also in blood" (1 Jn 5:6). The rivals would debate these points, or at least give them a different interpretation. Although some have argued that the rivals are non-Christian Jews or lapsed Christian Jews, the main proposals regard them as Christians who have arrived at a different view of Jesus' role in God's dealings with humanity than the

---

[24]Brown, *Epistles of John,* p. 738. Paul Anderson sees Diotrephes, "who loves to be first," as an example of the emerging hierarchical organization of and location of authority within the church. Such authority is radically different from the Elder's (and Johannine tradition's) model of a Spirit-led and Spirit-taught church in which authority remains with Christ and truth is discerned by the community in submission to the Paraclete. The debate between the Elder and Diotrephes, then, would be ecclesiological, not doctrinal. (The suggestion that Diotrephes is a docetist, for example, has no basis in 3 John.) See Paul N. Anderson, "Interfluential, Formative, and Dialectical," in *Für und wider die Priorität des Johannesevangeliums,* ed. P. L. Hofrichter (Hildesheim: Georg Olms, 2002), pp. 31-32.

[25]Definitions and examples of these various types are given by the ancient author known as Pseudo-Demetrius, quoted in A. J. Malherbe, "Ancient Epistolary Theorists," *Ohio Journal of Religious Studies* 5 (1977): 1-77. See the brief introduction to this mode of analysis in "Exegetical Skill: Epistolary Analysis" in the chapter on the Thessalonian correspondence. A more detailed analysis of these two letters through a judicious blend of epistolary and rhetorical analysis can be found in D. F. Watson, "A Rhetorical Analysis of 2 John According to Greco-Roman Convention," *NTS* 35 (1989); and "A Rhetorical Analysis of 3 John: A Study in Epistolary Rhetoric," *CBQ* 51 (1989).

[26]The use of the article with "Son of God" and "Christ" but not with the proper name "Jesus," as is common, suggests that "Son of God" and "Christ" are the subjects of the creedal affirmations and "Jesus" the predicate nominative of 1 Jn 2:22; 4:15; 5:1.

Christological "Slogans" and Source Criticism of 1 John

Scholars have long noted the terse statements that run throughout 1 John, which stand out from their context like maxims or slogans that are receiving commentary or discussion. In the heyday of source criticism (the early part of the twentieth century), the tendency was to view these sloganlike statements as part of an older source that the author used as he wrote his address.[a]

Source criticism of 1 John lost credibility for two principal reasons. First, source critics tended to leave out obvious sloganlike sentences in 1 John from their reconstructed sources because those particular slogans did not suit the rhythm, structure or viewpoint of their hypothetical reconstructed source. Such selectivity on the basis of content rather than form seriously undermined the scholarly integrity of their work. Second, the criteria source critics used to include or exclude particular material as part of their sources did not withstand close scrutiny: the criteria determined the results ahead of time; indeed the criteria were even influenced by the picture of the sources or situation that the source critic expected to uncover.

The work of source critics in uncovering these sloganlike sayings, however, has been of great value, since it is very likely that among them we can find statements made by the secessionists that the author of 1 John is reinterpreting, countering and otherwise engaging in an effort to undermine his rivals' influence both locally and throughout the network of communities linked by common allegiance to the Johannine traditions.

---

[a]See the discussion of E. von Dobschütz and Rudolf Bultmann's source theories in Brown, *Epistles of John*, pp. 36-43.

---

author and his group would endorse.

Kenneth Grayston has suggested that this is a low Christology, with the rivals denying any significant dependence on Jesus for their connection with the Father (which they enjoy by virtue of their own possession of the Spirit, the real mediator of salvation).[27] The man "Jesus" is not an indispensable part of God's plan for salvation, they reason. This is not necessarily opposed to but rather complements the view of Raymond E. Brown, who suggests that the rivals failed to identify the man, Jesus, sufficiently closely with the pre-incarnate Son, the Christ. Reference is frequently made to Irenaeus's description of the opinion of the late-first-century Jewish Christian heretic Cerin-

thus, who is said to have claimed that Jesus was merely the son of human parents, and that the Christ, who came from the Almighty Power, descended on him in the form of a dove, and after this [Jesus] proclaimed the unknown Father and worked miracles, but finally the Christ separated from Jesus, so that it was Jesus who suffered death and experienced the resurrection, but the Christ, as a spiritual being, remained without suffering.[28]

The denial of Jesus as the Christ having come in the flesh (1 Jn 4:2) would seem to be illuminated by such a belief, though we cannot be sure how closely the opponents of the author of 1 John reflect views attributed to Cerinthus a century later.

---

[27]Grayston, *Johannine Epistles*, pp. 12, 16, 19.
[28]Irenaeus *Against Heresies* 1.26.1 (as quoted in Lohse, *Formation of the New Testament,* p. 189).

In particular, the rivals could locate the salvific act in the revelation of the Son at Jesus' baptism (a ritual act by which the Christians too can come to share in God's nature as Spirit) and fail to ascribe salvific importance to the bloody death of Jesus on the cross.[29] Even the most famous verses of the Fourth Gospel—John 3:16-17—could be seen to ascribe saving significance to the *sending* (Jn 3:17, perhaps seen as a synonym explaining the *giving* in Jn 3:16) of the Son rather than the dying of Jesus. Indeed, the close linkage between the witness of John the Baptist and the Word becoming flesh in the prologue of John's Gospel could have been read as a further indication that the incarnation happened at the baptism of Jesus (thus connecting with Cerinthus's position at this point) rather than at the conception of Jesus by Mary thirty years prior.[30] The rivals' position would not be Gnostic but would certainly represent a step forward in the trajectory that would lead to second-century Gnosticism (tellingly dependent on the interpretation of John's Gospel), even beginning to develop the implications of the Fourth Gospel in ways that would be more conducive to Gnostic thought later on.[31]

It is precisely in statements concerning the death of Jesus as the supreme moment of the revelation of God's character that the twin concerns of "believing" and "loving"/"walking in the light" converge. The unifying theme of the author's ethics is the believer's reflecting God's character and essence in the world. The believers are to "walk in the light as he himself [namely, God, 1:5] is in the light" (1 Jn 1:7 NRSV). They "purify themselves, just as he is pure" (1 Jn 3:3 NRSV). They do "what is right-

eous," even as "he is righteous" (3:7 NRSV). Just as the believers will one day "be like him" since they "will see him as he is" (3:2 NRSV), so they are called to live now after the pattern of the One they will one day fully and perfectly reflect.

"No one has ever seen God," however (1 Jn 4:12 NRSV; significantly, compare Jn 1:18). This reflection of God is refined and given more precise content as the "imitation of Jesus." The believer "ought to walk just as he walked" (1 Jn 2:6 NRSV), the shift to the past tense, as well as the notion of walking, suggesting a shift of subject from the unseen God-as-Father to the observable God-made-flesh. And most prominently, the "love" of the God who "is love" (1 Jn 4:8) is demonstrated precisely in the self-giving act of Jesus on the cross:

> We know love by this, that he laid down his life for us—and we ought to lay down our lives for one another. (1 Jn 3:16 NRSV)

> God's love was revealed among us in this way: God sent his only Son into the world so that we might live through him. In this is love, not that we loved God but that he loved us and sent his Son to be the atoning sacrifice for our sins. Beloved, since God loved us so much, we also ought to love one another. (1 Jn 4:9-11 NRSV)

In the context of the latter passage it becomes clear, then, why the author would be so adamant concerning the belief "that the Father has sent his Son as the Savior of the world" and why this confession would be prerequisite

---

[29]Brown, *Johannine Epistles*, pp. 50-55, 73-79, especially p. 75.

[30]Brown, *Epistles of John*, p. 77.

[31]Ironically, the importance of the Johannine writings increased as the threat of their distortion at the hands of Gnostic Christians increased throughout the second century. First John provided a handle on reclaiming the Gospel of John for the "Great Church" (those Christians who held to what would later come to be identified as the orthodox position; see also Brown, *Epistles of John*, p. 103, n. 242), and it became increasingly important to make John part of and witness for the Great Church over against Gnostic appropriations of it.

1 John and the Letters of Ignatius on Love

One of the best known Christian leaders from the postapostolic era is Ignatius, who was the bishop of Antioch during the first decade of the second century. Ignatius has left seven letters behind, all of them written as he was being transported from Antioch to his execution in a Roman arena. In a letter to the Christians in Smyrna, written at about the same time as 1 John (perhaps up to a decade later), Ignatius warns against listening to the teaching of certain Christians who deny the reality of Jesus' coming and truly suffering in the flesh. Ignatius draws on Luke's resurrection appearances, pointing out that Jesus was indeed still "flesh" after the resurrection: unlike a phantom, he could be touched by the disciples, and he even ate and drank in their presence as if to prove his corporeality, however transformed it had become (*Ign. Smyrn.* 1-6).

Of special interest is the connection between Christology and ethics that Ignatius makes:

> Let no one deceive you. . . . If they do not believe in the blood of Christ, theirs will be the judgment. . . . Learn how contrary to the opinion of God are those who think differently concerning the favor of Jesus Christ that came to us: Love is not a concern to them, neither toward the widow nor the orphan, nor the afflicted, neither the prisoner nor freed person, neither the hungering nor thirsting. (*Ign. Smyrn*. 6.1-2, translation mine)

The position of Ignatius's opponents is not identical with that of the Johannine secessionists, but the comparison is illuminating, particularly in the implicit connection made by Ignatius between a failure to ascribe significance to the flesh and blood of Jesus and a failure to relieve (the bodies of) those in need.

---

to the mutual abiding of God in the believer and the believer in God (1 Jn 4:15). Only in the voluntary death of Jesus does the author find definitive proof of "the love that God has for us" (1 Jn 4:16 NRSV), and thus the basis and standard for the love that is to infuse the Christian community. It is the "basis" in that we are bound to love one another in gratitude and obedience to the God who so loved us. It is the "standard" in that it reveals the nature and measure of the depth and character of the love that reflects God, that shows one to be engendered by God. This love manifests itself in the same kind of real, costly, other-centered acts of devotion, caring and support that is observed in Jesus' laying down of his own life for his friends (1 Jn 3:16-18; cf. Jn 15:12-13).

As we continue to wrestle within and across denominations with "who Jesus is," 1 John cautions us not to move away from central, indispensable affirmations that capture the essence of the character of this God we worship. It also, perhaps too subtly, cautions us against a loveless commitment to beliefs or orthodoxy. For the author orthodoxy ultimately serves the promotion of selfless love for the sisters and brothers. Merely "believing" certain facts about Jesus does not make us children of God. Rather God is looking for belief that reflects the loving, just and holy character of the divine Parent in real-life interactions within the community of faith.

Sin and righteousness. First John's statements about sin in the believer's life resist easy systematization. In large measure this is due to the polemical situation in which the author writes; he must affirm his own understanding of the Johannine tradition while correcting or undermining the view of the secessionists. To some extent, however, it must also be due to the paradoxical nature of the disciple's existence as, in Luther's words, "simultaneously righteous and sinful."

On the one hand, the Elder is quite adamant that sin has no place in the life of the genuine disciple of Christ:

- Everyone who remains in him [i.e., Christ, 3:5] does not sin/continue to sin. (1 Jn 3:6)
- Everyone who keeps on sinning has neither seen nor known him. (1 Jn 3:6)
- The person committing sin is from the devil. (1 Jn 3:8)
- All who have been born of God do not practice sin, because God's seed remains in them, and they are not able to continue to sin because they have been born of God. (1 Jn 3:9)

Whether or not someone keeps on sinning or practices what is right shows his or her true lineage, whether he or she is from God or the devil.

On the other hand, the author also takes for granted not only that believers "have sinned," for to say otherwise is to speak against the truth of God (1 Jn 1:8, 10), but also that they will commit sins, though he would hope otherwise (1 Jn 2:1). Moreover, God clearly expects that this will happen, having provided Jesus Christ as our ongoing Advocate (*paraklētos*), whose death is effective not only for past but also future sins (1 Jn 2:2). To complicate matters further there are apparently some sins that do not lead to death, and concerning which the prayers of Christians can be effective, and sin that leads to death, for which Christians are not enjoined even to pray (1 Jn 5:16-17).

Certain statements about sin reflect the secessionists' mistaken understanding. First

John 1:8, 10 often seem to fall into this category. The opponents may well have claimed sinlessness, perhaps by virtue of their being in fellowship with God and being born of God. Their understanding of sin may be conditioned by the Fourth Gospel's apparent equation of sin with unbelief, or rejection of the revelation of God in Jesus (Jn 9:41; 16:8). Alternatively they may regard belief as the complete cure for the problem of sin, to the exclusion of the mastery of the passions of the flesh, conformity to the mind of Christ exhibited in his selfless death, or amendment of life in general. Something of this nature appears to stand behind the Elder's transformation of their claim to "be born of God" and therefore sinless into a test: only those who do what is right and do not sin (i.e., who love the sisters and brothers) can be shown to be born of God (1 Jn 3:7-10). Sin can no longer be "natural" for the believer—it is a violation of his or her new nature, and if sinning comes naturally it is perhaps a sign that the person does not truly have this new nature, does not have "God's seed."

The Elder understands that belief without a transformed life profits a person nothing. The "world," which takes on a near-demonic power in 1 John, is destined to fade away with the pursuits, values and ambitions that belong to it. Believers need to allow their experience of fellowship with God and of God's love to disentangle them from that complex web so that they do not share the fate of the world (1 Jn 2:15-17). Within this larger paradigm of a high commitment to moving from belief in Christ to a close and complete reflection of the character and values of God in relationships and life ("conquering the world," in other words), the Elder acknowledges the potential of failure, and affirms that failures along this path do not disqualify the Christian from fellowship with God or from continued pursuit of righteousness. He insists, however, that confession and forgiveness (rather than denying the reality of sin) are the proper responses to disobedience on the part of the Christian.[32]

Despite the apparent emphasis in the Johannine literature on belief, which have given rise to several strains of Christianity in which "belief" and "rebirth" are the central and perhaps only significant prerequisites for salvation, the Elder joins the many other apostolic voices that underscore the importance of what later theologians would label "sanctification." Succinctly put, "all who have this hope in him," namely, the hope of attaining the future state of the children of God (1 Jn 3:1-2), "purify themselves, just as he is pure" (1 Jn 3:3 NRSV). The Elder's legacy is that every claim to know God or to be born of God (e.g., "born again") must be borne out in a transformed life, a life that now falls in line with the character of God and God's desires for human community.

The tests in 1 John continue to point new generations of readers to look at how people interact with and invest in other believers for the evidence to back their claim to "knowing God." The Johannine Epistles, therefore, stand as a perpetual reminder that what we confess with our lips must show forth in our lives and relationships. If a person makes lofty claims to divine knowledge without being committed to mundane relief of human need (1 Jn 3:16-18) or to the support of fellow believers (1 Jn 2:9-11; 2 Jn 5-6), what does that person truly know of God's love?

Hospitality: The dangers of openness, the dangers of isolationism. The theme of hospitality connects and pervades the second and third letters of the Elder. Second John warns a sister church about the secessionist missionaries that have left the author's congregation and now seek to take their alternative understanding of Christ, salvation and the Christian life to other congregations. The mandate is clear: do not allow such people to use the house church as a venue for purveying aberrant teachings (2 Jn 10-11). Refusing the secessionist missionaries hospitality constitutes the author's strategy for preserving the sister congregation from the kind of heart-wrenching disruption that befell his own congregation.

The Elder experiences this policy from the other side in 3 John, where his own emissaries are refused hospitality and a venue at the house church governed in some sense by Diotrephes. The Elder presents Diotrephes as acting out of a self-promoting arrogance, maintaining his preeminence in his local congregation by keeping out the Elder and his emissaries. However, it may well be that Diotrephes does this to protect his house church—his clients—from potentially heterodox teachers.[33]

These two letters thus place the readers between the duty to refuse hospitality to those who misrepresent God and God's message and the duty to offer hospitality to those who faithfully represent God and God's message, and thus should be received and sent away "in a manner worthy of God" (3 Jn 6). Fulfilling both obligations could not have been easy and called for great discernment. Second John is written to prevent the danger of being so open that the congregation is exposed to persuasive words that would ultimately harm their faith and their progress in discipleship. At the other extreme the case of Diotrephes shows the danger of isolationism. In trying to shut out error he also shut out the nurturing voices of the El-

---

[32]Painter, "Opponents," p. 56.

[33]It is most probable that Gaius, the explicit addressee of 3 John, and Diotrephes belong to different house churches rather than represent two householders in the same church. The amount of information that the Elder includes about events in Diotrephes' church would be unnatural and redundant if Gaius were also a member of the same house church. If Gaius were part of that community, the use of "among them" in verse 9 would also be unnatural (Brown, *Epistles of John*, pp. 729-30). Moreover, we would expect a different treatment of the "putting out of the church" theme if the Elder were asking Gaius to risk this himself out of fidelity to the Elder.

der and other genuine sisters and brothers in the faith. In the face of diversity, innovation and dissension within a larger community of churches, cocooning one's church may be an attractive means of avoiding being led astray. It is, however, an option ultimately rejected by the Elder, who calls for discernment, and not complete isolationism.

In the pluralistic culture from which I write, these two letters seem at once highly relevant and highly parochial. It would be easy to use them to exclude all viewpoints with which we disagree, shutting our ears and, as much as possible, our congregations' doors to understandings of our Christian calling that we do not affirm. New Testament history, however, is full of fruitful dialogue and debate between sisters and brothers of good faith who wrestled with each other's views and profited from the open dialogue in the end. Second John surely cannot be used in a spirit that would be contrary to that exhibited in the apostolic conference in Jerusalem, for example. Nevertheless, 2 John (as much as Paul in Gal 1:6-10) reminds us that there are boundaries beyond which the faith expressed and the ethic taught are no longer Christian. The Elder summons us to consider in prayer and in questing dialogue with other Christians where those lines are—not for the purpose of refusing to dialogue with people across those lines but of recognizing that when we dialogue across those lines we are engaged in evangelism. Third John stands next in the canon to warn us against the dangers of drawing those lines so narrowly or in such a way that we find the representatives of the apostolic witness on the other side from us.

EXEGETICAL SKILL
Exploring Ideological Texture in a Text

All exegetical methods explored in this book are driven by questions that an interpreter wants to answer. For example, behind redaction analysis lie questions such as "what are the distinctive emphases and interests of this text?" The question leads to a rather well-defined methodological procedure for arriving at data that can contribute to an answer. Exploring the "ideological texture" in a text is also driven by questions, but it has not yet produced a set of procedures comparable to the use of Synoptic comparison in redaction analysis. Rather, the questions themselves provide lenses to sift through the text and recover data that can be put to answering those questions.

Ideological criticism actually encompasses a much larger project or set of projects.[a] At one level the investigator wants to understand how the ideology of interpreters affects the way the text is interpreted and the manner and ends to which it is applied. The investigator seeks to understand how cultural location, ethnicity, social location, gender and other factors constrain an interpreter and contribute to the results of any investigation of the text (viewed negatively, as limiting or constraining interpretation;

[a]For more detailed orientation to this area of investigation, see Vernon Robbins, *Exploring the Texture of Texts* (Valley Forge, Penn.: Trinity Press International, 1996), pp. 95-119; and *The Tapestry of Early Christian Discourse* (London: Routledge, 1996), pp. 192-99, 222-29.

viewed positively, as opening up alternative readings of the text). This mode of analysis can be applied to other interpreters in the history of interpretation or the contemporary scene, and it can be applied (and at some point *must* be applied) to oneself as interpreter.

At another level ideological criticism seeks to uncover the ways ideology shapes the text itself and works through the text on the readers in their situation.[b] This is our focus here. Ideological analysis of a text is an outgrowth of the awareness that the New Testament texts are *rhetorical* texts, that is, they seek to persuade, affirm, and limit and constrain readers to respond to situations and other ideas in certain ways, and not in other ways. This already reveals something of the ideology of the interpreter, since many also approach the New Testament texts as timeless revelations from God without any concern for meaning in its original context. Others might also resist any hint that the New Testament authors are manipulating their audiences or presenting their rivals in anything but an absolutely accurate manner, uncolored by the situation of hostility or rivalry. Even to raise questions about ideology in the text, therefore, presupposes a certain set of decisions about how the New Testament texts function as the word of God and what is possible or ethical for New Testament authors to do.

Exploring the ideology within a text involves asking, among others, questions such as the following:

- What are the interests and aims of the author and the group represented?

- How does the author address questions of authority? Often this emerges where the author points out the "weight" or legitimacy of his own authority, or where he undermines the authority of anyone who works against his interests.

- What other groups or parties are detectable through the text? What are their interests and aims? How does the author make room for or marginalize these other groups, their voices and their agendas?

- How does the discourse attempt to shape or control the readers' perceptions of reality, interpretations of a particular phenomenon or situation, and the like? How do such attempts facilitate the co-optation of the readers' support for the author and his interests and aims?

- What concerns and aims might be present among the readers, and how does the author address, marginalize or replace these concerns or aims? What is the effect of the author's treatment of these concerns or aims?

---

[b]See Robbins, *Exploring the Texture,* pp. 110-19; J. H. Elliott, *What Is Social-Scientific Criticism?* (Minneapolis: Fortress, 1993), p. 74.

- How does the author delineate the options or alternatives available to the readers in their situation? Relevant here are also questions of how the author limits options and places positive and negative valuations on these options. How does this delineation and valuation, once again, facilitate the co-optation of the readers' support?

There is no formal methodological procedure in place for answering these questions.[c] Rather, ideological criticism invites the interpreter to repeated close readings of the text from the standpoint of these questions. The mere act of posing new questions of the very familiar texts is one of the most important aspects of exegesis, for the new questions mean that new angles of the text are being brought to light, new data gathered and new conclusions attained (which, in many instances, reinforce historical conclusions).

Although the questions might be uncomfortable to ask of texts regarded as inspired Scripture, the questions in themselves do not challenge the inspiration or authority of Scripture. Whether we approach these questions from a hermeneutic of trust or hermeneutic of suspicion, whether we investigate them with a view to negating or limiting Scripture's voice in the contemporary scene or with a view to learning from it to carry on its ideological agendas—these matters belong to the realm of the ideology of the interpreter.[d]

Ideological texture in 1 John: A window into the pastoral strategy of the Elder. Signs of an agenda are apparent as early as the purpose clause of 1 John 1:3. The author writes "in order that you [the readers] may have fellowship with us." Although we ought not press the matter too far, the author's choice of an aorist subjunctive rather than a present subjunctive is somewhat surprising, suggesting that the author is not merely writing in order that fellowship may be "continued" but rather that it is in

---

[c]Certain advanced disciplines, like the structural analysis of a text with a view to determining the author's convictions, can certainly assist this line of investigation and bring considerable methodological rigor to the enterprise. See the work of Daniel Patte, especially *Structural Exegesis for New Testament Critics* (Minneapolis: Fortress, 1990).

[d]Here my own ideological convictions, and those of my community of interpretation, come to my own attention. As a Christian working with and teaching those who for the most part identify themselves with evangelical Christianity, talking about the ideology of a New Testament author can be rather awkward—even threatening. This does not mean, however, that evangelical Christians should ignore the fact that authors have ideologies and strategies for persuasion. Rather, this mode of investigation calls us to redefine what it means to call these writings the word of God. This question is frequently resolved with reference to the divine authorship of the texts, but it might be more useful to think of the phrase "word of God" expressing the conviction that one recognizes these texts to have legitimate authority over the reader. The evangelical reader would, then, tend to align himself or herself with the ideology of the human author, expressing a certain loyalty to that author as God's spokesperson in a particular situation. We would not do this, however, as if the author were not ideologically motivated. Rather we are aware of the ideologies that tug and pull in the situation surrounding the text and aware that the evangelical interpreter will tend to give authority to the voice of the author rather than the voice of the author's rivals when the time comes for application. This is, however, strictly a matter of ideological commitment—another interpreter might with equal conviction seek to restore the voices of those rivals and let them speak anew.

some question and needs to be secured. The fact that the author must write to this audience tells us that he (or she) is not present with the readers and therefore may not be merely exercising pastoral care in the wake of schism. Rather, the author may be seeking to secure this readership for his own party in the wake of a schism in which two rival parties are now moving beyond the author's local congregation where the split occurred. It is noteworthy in this regard that the author says the separatists went out "from us" rather than "from you" (1 Jn 2:18-19), all the more as the author routinely distinguishes an "us" (meaning the author and his circle or group) and a "you" (meaning the readers). It is the "you" group that now must be on guard against the other voices (1 Jn 2:20-24). Thus we already see that there are indications of multiple, contrary voices in the setting addressed by the author, and so we are invited to investigate how the author will guide the hearers/readers to encounter these divergent voices.

Alongside this human agenda, however, the author invokes the unseen agenda of God's love, which the author and his group facilitate. At several points the author refers to God's love "being perfected" (i.e., achieving its goal) in the believer. When we "keep his word," which is synonymous with "keeping his commands" (1 Jn 2:5), when we love one another as Christ loved us (1 Jn 4:12), when fellowship with God through love of the brothers and sisters has reached such a state that no fear of judgment remains (1 Jn 4:17-18), God's love has achieved its agenda in the lives of that human community. The author gains considerable legitimation of his authority and voice from his presentation of his own agenda as working alongside and in support of God's agenda in the addressees' lives.

From the outset (as one would expect in light of ancient rhetorical conventions) the author prepares the hearers to receive his speech as the authoritative voice in the situation of multiple voices. The author's party's message concerns "what was from the beginning" (1 Jn 1:1), reminding them of commands and messages the readers have had "from the beginning" (1 Jn 2:7; 3:11). By implication, whatever the author says will be rooted in the original, and thus authentic, message concerning the Gospel, whereas anyone who speaks otherwise will be seen as an innovator (something that would not be regarded as positive in traditional societies).

Moreover, the author repeatedly stresses the firsthand experience he and his party had with the key events and experiences that stand at the root of this message. They have seen, heard and even touched the relevant content (we naturally think of an experience with the incarnate Son at this point), and this "material witness" card in favor of the author's party's testimony is repeatedly played (1 Jn 1:1-3, 5; 4:14). The author presents himself and his group as the reliable eye- and ear-witnesses through whom the readers can be connected with the ancient, authentic message: "this is the message we have heard from the beginning and we announce to you" (1 Jn 1:5). It is noteworthy, however, that the Spirit and God also emerge as witnesses to the author's affirmations about Jesus (1 Jn 5:6-10), over against the affirmations or negations being made by other voices. Part of the author's strategy is clearly to claim the right to speak on God's behalf in this situation.

Relevant here are the subtle ways the author aligns the audience with his own party. First John 2:12-14 may be taken as an example. The author addresses the hearers in triumphant terms, speaking of their prior knowledge of the Father, or "the One who is from the beginning," of their enjoyment of the gift of having been forgiven their sins, and of their victory over the cosmic enemy, the "evil one." The significance of the "blood of Jesus" appears to be a subject of contention between the author's party and the rival party (see 1 Jn 5:6), but the author prepares the hearers to stand by their current understanding of that blood by celebrating "with them" the benefits it has brought them (1 Jn 1:7). By speaking of their knowledge of "the One from the beginning" and perhaps specifically attributing this to the elders (the respected ones) among the readers, the author makes them natural allies of his message, which also testifies concerning that which "was from the beginning" (1 Jn 1:1; 2:13-14; see also 2:21, which similarly claims that the addressees' prior knowledge should align them with the author against the other voices). He appeals to their own previous experience and knowledge for the legitimation of his own message. Finally, he presents their situation as one of conflict with the "evil one," whose symbolic power will be harnessed throughout to characterize those positions not held by the author. Since they already have conquered (1 Jn 2:13-14), they will be attuned to preserving their victory, a stance that will be amenable to the dominant figure the author uses—"remaining," or "abiding" in what the community of hearers already have learned. Indeed, as we will see, the use of *abides* *(menei)* throughout this epistle promotes a conservative response to the innovations that have rent the author's congregation asunder.

How then are other voices brought into the text, and where are their aims discernible? The first clear reference to the "other side" of the split in the author's community is 1 John 2:18-19. The author uses the community's apocalyptic framework of expectations to label and neutralize the other voices. The hearers know of the expectation of "antichrist," and the author now introduces the secessionists as the fulfillment of that expectation and as the proof of living in "the last hour." The author uses shared knowledge about "the last hour," in effect, to close the distance between himself and the readers, and to create an unbridgeable distance between the separatists and the readers. The fact of the split becomes proof that these other parties are not of "us" (namely, the author's community of authentic Christianity, 1 Jn 2:19), but in the web of associations the author is spinning, to be *not of us* is also to be *not of God* and *of the world.* Furthermore, these other voices are identified as "the liar," presented as the synonym of "the antichrist" in 1 Jn 2:22, on account of their convictions concerning Jesus. They are, simply, "the ones [potentially] deceiving" the hearers (1 Jn 2:26), which presents them as the clear and present danger to remaining in the truth, since they seek to lead people currently "in the truth" toward "the lie." All this shows the author's strong commitment to marginalizing those other voices rather than making any room for them in the situation.

At this point, however, it is important to consider those other voices apart from the author's coloration of their portrait.[e] They were likely Christians from within the author's congregation, nurtured in the same body of Johannine traditions. Perhaps because they were Gentile Christians lacking the Jewish roots in the traditions of the Fourth Gospel, they developed this tradition in a direction that was ultimately deemed unacceptable by and incompatible with the author's understanding of that tradition.[f] Rather than trying to deceive, the rivals no doubt thought they could enlighten, taking Christianity to its next logical step as it moved from the backwater of Galilee into the major centers of the Greco-Roman world. In other words, they might look very different from the author's presentation of them. This presentation is not driven by journalistic conventions (in their

---

[e]Paul Anderson argues that we actually have references to two different groups of secessionists in 1 John ("*Sitz im Leben*," pp. 36-37, 46-47). Anderson connects the "denial of the Father and the Son" with lapsed Jewish Christians, since pressure from the non-Christian Jews (who had no place for the Son) would have led these former disciples to "deny the Son" (and thus lose the Father as well, according to the author). He then connects the denial that "Jesus Christ has come in the flesh" with a later docetist movement within Johannine Christianity reflecting the interests of Gentile Christians wishing to avoid persecution "in the flesh" by denying that the Christ they follow suffered truly "in the flesh." While retroversion to the synagogue would certainly provide one very plausible context for language about "denying the Son" and thus losing "the Father," Anderson's arguments that this *must* be the case are less convincing. He argues, in part, from the timing of the appearing of these antichrists in the author's presentation, with the author stating that the secessionists of 1 John 2:18-25 already "went out from us," while the second group is newly arisen.

It is true that the secessionists in 1 Jn 2:18-25 already "went out from us" (1 Jn 2:19), but this does not mean they were unavailable to the community that remained behind. Indeed, their continued efforts to win over their friends would be a logical cause for the author's admonition to "test the spirits to see if they are God's." The secessionists of 1 Jn 2:18-25 who "went out from us" would then be identical with the "many false prophets" who "have gone out into the world," denying that "Jesus Christ has come in the flesh" (1 Jn 4:2). Additionally, the author describes the negative influence in both passages as the antichrist that was expected to come, and that is currently present (the perfect tense in 1 Jn 2:18, which speaks of a complete action with ongoing results, corresponds completely with the present tense on 1 Jn 4:3): "As you have heard that antichrist is coming, so now many antichrists have come" (1 Jn 2:18 NRSV). "This is the spirit of the antichrist, of which you have heard that it is coming; and now it is already in the world" (1 Jn 4:3 NRSV).

If the simpler solution is to be preferred, we should understand 1 Jn 2:18-25 and 1 Jn 4:1-3 to describe the same group of people threatening from outside the doctrinal and ethical purity of the congregation. The denial that "Jesus is the Christ" in 1 Jn 2:22 is further developed in 1 Jn 4:1-3; the language about denying the Son restates in familiar terms the implications of denying that Jesus is the Christ (indeed, the Christ come in the flesh).

[f]This is the view of Brown, *Epistles of John*, pp. 50-55, 69-86, 103; see also Painter, "Opponents," p. 49.

ideal form) of presenting the facts in and of themselves, but by ideological strategy, presenting the facts in a way that will direct the readers' response the way that the author desires.

When we turn to consider how the author shapes the readers'/hearers' perceptions of reality and delineates the options available to them in their situation, we are struck at once by the stark dualism of the text.[9] The author posits assertion after assertion, entering the situation with an assumption of absolute authority to divide light from darkness, to distinguish truth from falsehood, to define what is "of God" and what is "of the world." The dichotomies of "light" and "darkness" (beginning at 1 Jn 1:5), "doing the truth" and "lying" (beginning at 1 Jn 1:6), and "God" (or "the Father") and "the world" (beginning in earnest at 1 Jn 2:15) set up a framework where a thing will either be good or bad, beneficial or harmful. This intensely oppositional construal of reality facilitates the co-optation of the addressees, if they accept this view as indeed authoritative and reliable, by preventing them from regarding the alternatives (the author's gospel versus the secessionists' gospel) as real alternatives. In the choice between light and darkness, truth and falsehood, righteousness and sin, being born of God or belonging to the world and the devil, there is really only one choice for those who share the author's positive evaluation of light, truth, righteousness and God, and negative evaluation of darkness, falsehood, sin, and the world and the devil.

These oppositional pairs become a principal tool for the author's "imposition" of his own view of the situation on the addressees, replacing any alternative view. They also provide the coordinates by which positive and negative valuations may be assigned within that view. For example, "light" is equated early on with "God" (1 Jn 1:5), obviously underscoring the positive value of "light" as in some way sharing the divine essence, and the negative value of darkness as opposed to the divine essence. "Darkness" is qualified as "passing away" (1 Jn 2:8) as is the world, incidentally, aligning "world" with "darkness" against "light" and "God" (1 Jn 2:17). Thus anything pertaining to "darkness" or "world" results in "death" (1 Jn 2:17; 3:14-15), a clearly negative consequence. In opposition to this the author posits numerous characteristics and behaviors that lead to "abiding forever" (1 Jn 2:17) or "eternal life" (1 Jn 2:25; 3:14; 5:11-13), the positive counterpart. The author can now use the oppositional pairs (light-darkness, truth-lie, God-world and so forth) to promote the audience's self-identification with the author's group's understanding of the gospel and

---

[9]Scholars correctly note that certain distinctive and pervasive features of the style of 1 John, namely, its use of "repetition and spiral-like progression," synonymous parallelism and antithetical parallelism (Kysar, "John," pp. 902-3), very directly serve the ideological agenda of the author. Kysar aptly observes here that the author's style "has the effect of reinforcing certain themes and fixing certain images in the readers' minds."

Christian life—and indeed to ally itself with the author's group—over against any rival.

Thus anything that shows a person to be aligned with "God" or "of God" (*ek tou theou*) emerges as a positive and beneficial trait or behavior, and anything that shows a person to be "of the world" (*ek tou kosmou*) or its underlying power, the "evil one" (1 Jn 5:19), emerges as a highly negative and harmful element in the situation. Of course, every one among the addressees would want to show themselves to be engendered of God rather than of the world. They are thus disposed to identify themselves with all that the author predicates of the category "being born of God": doing righteousness (1 Jn 2:29) rather than doing sin (1 Jn 3:9; 5:18); confessing Jesus as the Christ having come in the flesh (1 Jn 4:2; 5:1); walking in love toward the sisters and brothers (1 Jn 4:7-11). Perhaps most striking in the study of the "politics" of the text in this regard is 1 Jn 4:4-6:

> Little children, *you are from God,* and have conquered them; for the one who is in you is greater than the one who is in the world. *They are from the world;* therefore what they say is from the world, and <u>the world listens to them</u>. *We are from God*. <u>Whoever knows God listens to us,</u> and <u>whoever is not from God does not listen to us</u>. From this we know the spirit of truth and the spirit of error. (NRSV)

This amazing passage accomplishes a number of things in terms of ideological texture. First, it posits a strong association of the hearers/readers with the author's group over against the rival party using the "of God-of the world" opposition (see italicized words). Second, it predisposes the addressees against "listening" to the rivals or accepting their message, since that would signify that they too were "of the world," with all its negative valuations and consequences, and disposes them to listen to the author and his group because that would affirm them in their connection with God (see underlined words).

Another powerful oppositional pair is *truth* versus *falsehood*. The author firmly locates the audience, along with himself, in "truth." The right agenda with regard to knowing the truth is to "abide" or "remain" in that truth, and so the verb "to abide" or "to stay" (*menein*) becomes one of the more prominent verbs in 1 John. The opposite of abiding is "being deceived," the action that can move a person away from truth into falsehood (1 Jn 1:8; 2:26; 3:7; 4:6). In the author's situation nothing could be better crafted than this to keep an audience in his camp. The path to life is to "remain" or hold on to "that which you heard from the beginning" and to see that "what you heard from the beginning remains in you" (1 Jn 2:24). Whatever would lead the audience away from their present understanding of the Johannine tradition is named "deception," that which threatens their abiding in the truth and which derails them into the lie. The secessionists will not stand a chance.

The letter further stacks the odds against the secessionists getting a hearing by providing a large number of "tests" by which the addressees can tell truth from falsehood. For example, the author writes, "Whoever says 'I have come to know [God],' but does not obey his commandments, is a liar, and in such a person the truth does not exist" (1 Jn 2:4 NRSV). These "commandments" are identified as having a certain belief in Jesus as Son and Christ (1 Jn 2:23; 5:1), and loving the sisters and brothers (1 Jn 3:23), two stances and behaviors that are also aligned with "walking in light" and being "born of God," and, in short, all the other positive markers in 1 John. Thus when the secessionists arrive in the community of addressees and begin to speak of nuancing the community's belief in Jesus or of the need to remain separate from the author's influence through breaking fellowship (violating the "love of the brothers and sisters"), the addressees will be prepared to reject their claim to speak on God's behalf. Rather than seriously entertain their innovations as a viable alternative, they are being poised, at least, to consign them to the column of "liar" (1 Jn 2:4), "false prophet" (1 Jn 4:1) and even "antichrist" (1 Jn 2:22). If the addressees accept the validity of these tests, in other words, they will effectively play out the author's agenda for them, since these are tests the secessionists will fail by definition (see also 1 Jn 1:6; 1:8, 10; 2:9, 23; 4:2-3).

Affirmed that they have the truth, the audience will be intent to preserve their advantage, both guarding against being deceived and striving to remain in the sure sphere of light and truth in which they find themselves by virtue of their religious experience up to this point in their history. Indeed, the author's appeal to the "anointing" *(chrisma)* that they received is an overt appeal to their own religious experience as a natural ally with the author's group. To depart from the teaching they have received would be to betray their own interior conversation with God (1 Jn 2:27). The positive path of "abiding" is further delineated by the author as walking as Christ walked (1 Jn 2:6), the theme of "imitation of Christ" running throughout 1 John; "doing God's commandments" (1 Jn 3:24), further clarified as "loving one another" (1 Jn 4:12); and confessing that the Son of God is Jesus (1 Jn 4:15). As the addressees continue to focus on these things, the author assures them that they will remain in God and the Son, *and* God will remain in them (1 Jn 4:12, 13, 15, 16).

The addressees are thus invited into a textual world where everything is black and white, strangely simple and uncomplicated: a succinct core of convictions and behaviors (an acknowledgment of Jesus as Son of God and Christ, and a commitment to other-centered love within the community of those who are of God) is linked to everything positive and beneficial, and the negation of these core values linked to everything negative and disadvantageous. They are then invited to place this grid on the realities they encounter in all of its complexities, and resolve those complexities in favor of the solutions proposed in the text.

To continue to develop your own skills in discerning and analyzing "ideology within the text," probe one or more of the following shorter books (each is especially suited to this kind of analysis—two opposing voices are so evident in the situations behind these texts) using the questions raised earlier in this section: Galatians, 2 Peter, Jude. Revelation, of course, represents an ideological tour de force. Keep in mind the questions outlined above as you read and study that text as well.

THE JOHANNINE EPISTLES AND MINISTRY FORMATION

The discussion of the message of these letters already has taken us into the contributions that the Johannine Epistles can make to discipleship and effective ministry, from the insistence that authentic beliefs bear their fruit in transformed lives to the challenges of accurately and humbly drawing boundaries that are necessary to preserving the faith from distortion, while allowing for the kind of fruitful and dynamic dialogue that is necessary to clarify the faith and its implications in every new setting and time.

One other contribution 1 John makes is in the integration of eschatology with discipleship. While we have noted that the Elder has a more overtly apocalyptic outlook than the fourth Evangelist, he consistently uses that outlook to shape and motivate the way believers live out their lives in the present. Antichrist is coming (1 Jn 2:18); the world will pass away (1 Jn 2:17); believers conquer the world and the devil who stands behind it (1 Jn 5:4-5); believers will be changed when they see Christ "as he is" (1 Jn 3:2).

All of these statements are at home within the thought world of Jewish Christian apocalypticism. But for the Elder they call for careful engagement in the present. In the Elder's version of realized eschatology, antichrist is already to be resisted in the encounter with the "many antichrists" (1 Jn 2:18-19), none of whom have the grandiose stature of the apocalyptic archenemy, but each is a dangerous reef that can shipwreck faith. Victory over the world is something to be safeguarded by remaining in the faith as passed down by the conservators of the apostolic tradition (1 Jn 5:4-5) rather than being derailed by innovations and deviations, and by continuing to disentangle oneself from covetousness, lust and the pride that comes from possessions (1 Jn 2:15-17).[a] The final eschatology of the believer, namely, to be "as Christ is," sets the full agenda for the mundane history of the believer, who will daily seek to purify himself or herself to become pure as "he is pure," moving steadily toward the full reflection of Christ.

---

[a]The third of these is traditionally translated "pride of life," but *bios* ("life") is used in 1 Jn 3:17 as well, where we find the translation "this world's goods" *(ton bion tou kosmou)*.

The Elder thus provides a paradigm for how apocalyptic expectations ought to affect individual disciples and communities of faith. Just as statements about the nature and work of Christ must take on flesh in the lives of the believers who make those statements, so also statements about the Christian hope must lead to vital engagement in the present. In this way apocalyptic expectations do not become a substitute for spiritual formation, investment in ministry and social action, but rather a catalyst for the same.

There is a reason, however, why I chose to highlight "ideological analysis" as the exegetical skill in this chapter, and that is because the Johannine Epistles could easily contribute as negatively to healthful ministry formation as they could positively, wherever the ideological arsenal of the Elder is adopted inappropriately in the life of an individual disciple, a congregation or an entire denomination.

First, there is the danger of equating conservatism with faithfulness to the gospel. While he clearly understands there to be an inviolable and essential core to the apostolic gospel, the Elder does not promote conservatism for its own sake. His rhetoric, however, can easily be used to maintain an "old" way of thinking or a "traditional" way of doing things in any new situation, almost for its own sake. The Judaizers, Paul's rivals, also could have claimed to be remaining or abiding in "that which was from the beginning" as they maintained the validity of the Torah of God for the people of God. There *are* matters to "abide" in that are traditional, and there *are* developments that call for bold breaks with "the way it has always been done." It takes wisdom to discern the difference between resisting basic perversions of the message (to remain within the apostolic faith) and being so conservative that we miss what God is doing or teaching anew.

Second, to name the elephant in the Johannine living room, there is the danger of how the Elder's rhetoric will be applied to new schisms and to denominationalism in general. First and Second John provide an arsenal of ideologically charged material that Christians, in any contemporary situation of dissension and split, can use to legitimate their own position and condemn outright those who leave (or who feel it no longer possible to remain). Used this way, 1-2 John are uncomfortably self-serving, and what branch of the Christian church has failed to use the rhetoric of 1 John to insulate its members against those who have challenged its beliefs and ethics and left it behind? Roman Catholics have applied it to Protestants. As Protestant groups continued to splinter and multiply, the occasions for preaching out of 1 John to assure the "faithful" and condemn the "splitters" have multiplied, insulating those who remain from any doubts raised by those who left, erecting higher and higher walls between parts of the body of Christ.

Therefore 1 John is also an occasion for mourning. It is a prototype of the breach of Christian love and unity so deeply valued by the carriers of the Johannine tradition. In effect, it marks the failure of even the early church to "be the church." When reading a text like 1 John it is important to hear it not merely as a word spoken to us as if we were the "you" in the text, but also about us as if we were the "they." Are we guilty of breaking the new commandment, of failing to love the brothers and sisters, of breaking the bond of Christian love and unity?[b] Even if a body of Christians has separated from our own, can we simply apply the rhetoric of 1 John to denounce them, or does it also denounce our failure to love and to work together for the harmony of the body? Are there paths toward recovery of this unity and love—in practice if not in polity—such that we can take steps to move toward answering Jesus' own prayer in John 17?

On the one hand, there may be times when a church split really does entail matters that even the Elder would agree are essential to defining Christian faith, and that such splits may warrant the kind of rhetoric we find in 1 John. That being said, most church splits of which I am aware do not concern matters of such import. Many splinterings may occur surrounding highly valued matters of practice, belief or polity, but not over issues that threaten the core identity of Christian discipleship. As we continue to disagree on these highly valued matters, therefore, it would appear prudent to keep these disagreements in perspective and be more eager to maintain love toward our sisters and brothers—even when church polities must divide and separate—than use the rhetoric of 1 John to disavow our connectedness in Christ.

[b]It is important to consider that even though the author condemns the secessionists for not "loving the brothers and sisters," it is highly probable that they, like the author, simply defined the circle of sisters and brothers to exclude the other (Brown, *Epistles of John,* p. 85). The secessionists' "hatred" of the brothers and sisters may amount to no more than their rejection of the author's community (while still maintaining love and support for their fellow secessionists).

FOR FURTHER READING

Brown, Raymond E. *The Community of the Beloved Disciple.* New York: Paulist Press, 1979.

————. *The Epistles of John.* AB 30. Garden City, N.Y.: Doubleday, 1982.

Bultmann, Rudolf. *The Johannine Epistles.* Hermeneia. Philadelphia: Fortress, 1973.

Grayston, Kenneth. *The Johannine Epistles.* NCB. Grand Rapids: Eerdmans, 1984.

Kysar, Robert. "John, Epistles of." *Anchor Bible Dictionary.* 3:901-12. Edited by David N. Freedman. Garden City, N.Y.: Doubleday, 1992.

Lieu, Judith. *The Second and Third Epistles of John..* ICC. Edinburgh: T & T Clark, 1986.

Marshall, I. Howard *The Epistles of John.* NICNT. Grand Rapids: Eerdmans, 1978.

Mitchell, Margaret M. "Diotrephes Does Not Receive Us." *JBL* 117 (1978): 299-320.

Schnackenburg, Rudolf. *The Johannine Epistles: Introduction and Commentary.* New York: Crossroad, 1992.

Sloyan, Gerard S. *Walking in the Truth: Perseverers and Deserters. The First, Second, and Third Letters of John.* Valley Forge, Penn.: Trinity Press International, 1995.

Smalley, Stephen. *1, 2, 3, John.* WBC. Waco: Word, 1984.

Smith, D. Moody. *First, Second, and Third John.* Interpretation. Louisville, Ky.: John Knox Press, 1991.

Thompson, Marianne Meye *1, 2, 3 John.* Downers Grove, Ill.: InterVarsity Press, 1992.

Watson, Duane F. "A Rhetorical Analysis of 2 John According to Greco-Roman Convention." *NTS* 35 (1989): 104-30.

————. "A Rhetorical Analysis of 3 John: A Study in Epistolary Rhetoric." *CBQ* 51 (1989): 479-501.

11

A PROLOGUE TO THE STUDY OF PAUL'S LETTERS

The second half of the New Testament is dominated by the figure of Paul, the hero of Acts and the reputed author of the majority of the letters found in the New Testament.[1] His representation in the canon threatens to eclipse the importance of other key apostles and ministers of the Word, such as Peter, James and John, but this representation may not be entirely unwarranted given Paul's importance in championing the mission to the Gentiles and his tireless and unsurpassed efforts in founding and nurturing churches from Antioch to at least as far as Rome.

Although our focus remains primarily on the texts of the New Testament, we will briefly consider Paul's road to faith in Christ and his career as "Apostle to the Gentiles" insofar as this will serve the study of the letters themselves. Such a prologue will assist the student to grasp Paul's distinctive and radical understanding of the significance of Christ with respect to the binding power of the law and the value of distinctions between Jew and Gentile, a theme that dominates several cardinal letters. It will also provide a sufficient chronological framework on which to hang the subsequent discussions of the individual Pauline letters and the events to which they refer.

CHALLENGES IN THE STUDY OF PAUL'S LIFE

Reconstructing Paul's career is complicated by a number of factors. First, his letters, focused as they are on the challenges confronting his congregations rather than biographical reminiscences, do not give a complete picture of his movements or activities. What biographical data can be gathered are the result of incidental comments about Paul's whereabouts and travels or of intentional use of particular episodes to make some point relevant to his congregations' situation. Second, although Acts does provide a possible framework for most of Paul's missionary endeavors and movements, it is still a selective source telling only of certain episodes and leaving yawning gaps in Paul's story (for example, the entirety of Paul's youth and education, the space between his conversion and first missionary journey, details of his eighteen months in Corinth or his three years in Ephesus, and the like). That Acts leaves Paul in Rome under house arrest is also a cause for sorrow for the historian, who would prefer to have firm, first-century sources for what happened after those two years in Rome (whether they ended in Paul's execution or whether Paul continued his

---

[1] Pauline authorship of Romans, 1-2 Corinthians, Galatians, Philippians, 1 Thessalonians and Philemon, at least, is not seriously disputed. The authorship of the remaining six letters (Ephesians, Colossians, 2 Thessalonians, 1-2 Timothy and Titus) is contested and will be discussed in the appropriate chapters.

missionary endeavors for some years after that detention). Third, there are relatively few dates on which to hang a "life of Paul," and the primary dates are entirely dependent on synchronisms in Acts linking Paul's story with known characters from Roman history. These dates are (1) 51 C.E.: Paul is brought up on charges before the consul Lucius Junius Gallio in Corinth, (2) 58-60 C.E.: Paul is imprisoned in Caesarea during the last part of the governorship of Felix and the beginning of the administration of Porcius Festus.

we are bound to be disappointed. However, when we set the information we do possess about and from Paul alongside the information we have about other prominent personalities from antiquity, we must count ourselves fortunate. Paul's letters and Acts provide us with qualitatively and quantitatively superior data for understanding Paul's life and thought than we have for most kings and emperors. We can glimpse far more of Paul's mind and religious experience than we can of any other first-century Christian. In light of this it is not surpris-

Figure 11.1. A street from Pompeii, showing the close layout of rows of shops and services. Paul the tentmaker may have worked out of a shop such as one of these. (Photo courtesy of William Krewson [Bible-Places.com])

Other phases of Paul's career can then be arranged in relative chronologies and then fitted around these two known pillars, together of course with the date one chooses for the execution of Jesus (which tends to be placed between 29 and 33 C.E., usually in the earlier part of that span).

When we compare the information we have with the information we would like to have,

ing that inquiry into the life and thought of Paul occupies New Testament scholarship more than inquiry into any other figure save Jesus himself.

PAUL'S PRE-CHRISTIAN EXPERIENCE

What does Paul choose to reveal about his own early life and conversion? Brief autobiographical statements appear in Galatians 1:13-

The Relative Value of Acts and Paul's Letters as Historical Sources

Whether we read Luke and Acts together (as is fitting, given the author's consciousness of writing Acts as a sequel to Luke) or move through the New Testament in strict canonical order, Acts tends always to be treated before Pauline literature. The letters of Paul and the data they contain, therefore, tend to be read within the framework of Acts and thus effectively subordinated to Acts. It is important to bear in mind as a corrective, however, that Paul's letters rather than Acts provide us with our primary source material for understanding Paul and his ministry. All of Paul's undisputed letters are earlier than Acts and reflect the perspective of a participant, not a historiographer. Paul provides firsthand reflections on his life before conversion and on the meaning of his conversion in his letters, especially Galatians, and such firsthand accounts should be privileged over secondhand reports such as found in Acts. Paul's letters give us glimpses into the conflict over the basis for Gentile inclusion in the church before the issue was resolved; Acts writes from the perspective enjoyed after its resolution, at least twelve but more likely twenty to thirty years after that resolution was achieved. The author of Acts is not interested in remembering the difficult confrontations between Paul, Peter and Barnabas on this issue, presenting a much more unified picture of the major players that was only possible in hindsight.

While Acts is of great value for considering the history of Christian origins, it is a theologically and ideologically motivated reconstruction of that history. Paul's letters, of course, are also so motivated, but at least they come directly from one of the major players in those first decades of the growth and formation of the Christian movement. In any study of Paul, then, Paul should be allowed to speak for himself first, and data from his letters should be analyzed as of primary importance; then Acts can be safely introduced as a secondary and corroborating witness.

16; 2 Corinthians 11:22 and Philippians 3:5-6. From these we learn that Paul was brought up to be a Jew of Jews from his birth. He was of solid Israelite stock, tracing his lineage through the tribe of Benjamin (Phil 3:5), which produced the first Israelite king, after whom Paul (Saul) was named. His parents piously inscribed him within the covenant through circumcision when he was eight days old (Phil 3:5), the appointed time for this rite. The self-description "a Hebrew sprung from Hebrews" (Phil 3:5) may refer either to the purity of his genealogy (no intermarriage with Gentiles, something not unknown in the Diaspora, see Acts 16:1-3) or more likely to the language spoken by his parents and himself at home, a mark of their commitment to preserving their ancestral way of life. Although Paul does not himself refer to his Roman citizenship, the author of Acts appears to have no motive for inventing this fact. Indeed, several key events in Paul's life (e.g., his being sent to Rome for trial) are inexplicable without it. Part of his parents' legacy to him, then, was the gift of being a citizen not only of Tarsus but also of Rome, which would give him specific legal rights and, theoretically at least, the assurance of due process.

The author of Acts speaks of Paul receiving formal education in Jerusalem "at the feet of Gamaliel" (Acts 22:3; see 5:34), a respected teacher whose name is also well at-

477

tested in rabbinic literature. Such an education would be in keeping with Paul's parents' dedication to piety as well as to Paul's own witness to his training as a Pharisee and his intense zeal for the traditions of the elders (Phil 3:6; Gal 1:14). Our views of Paul's education have to reckon with the data of Paul's literary legacy—his facility in Old Testament and intertestamental Jewish traditions, his skill in argument (not only in terms of what would come to be known as rabbinic exegetical procedures but also the kinds of argumentation promoted by Greek and Latin rhetoricians), his proficiency in the art of letter writing, his familiarity with popular philosophical and ethical topics, and his mastery of the Greek language.[2]

Training in all of these areas would have been available to Paul in Jerusalem, which was a cosmopolitan city connected with the Greco-Roman world, not isolated from it.[3] The Hellenization of Palestine made substantial progress during the Greek and Hellenistic periods, and was given renewed attention during the period of Roman domination.[4] In the setting of Gamaliel's school, perhaps similar to what we would have found in the school of Yeshua Ben Sira two centuries before, Paul would have learned not only of Torah and its rules of application but the art of

argumentation[5] and the wisdom tradition (which combined Greek, Egyptian and Jewish wisdom), and he quite probably continued his study of Greek as well. Fluency in Greek would have been of great importance as the means to communicate with and instruct Greek-speaking Jews from the Diaspora residing in Palestine, visiting during pilgrimages or encountered in a teacher's travels away from Palestine. Conversations with Jews from the Diaspora would have afforded ample opportunity for Paul to learn more of Greco-Roman philosophy and ethical traditions, as would debates with Gentile philosophers resident in Palestine. The essential skill of letter writing would not have been neglected, and the Hellenistic letter form had been practiced in Jerusalem at least since the rise of the Hasmoneans.[6]

Paul characterizes himself as passionately zealous for the Torah prior to his encounter with Christ. He devoted himself to the Pharisaic way of life, being fully dedicated to Torah as interpreted and extended through the oral traditions that eventually multiplied and became associated with rabbinic Judaism. He calls to mind his devotion to the covenant at Galatians 1:14, where he remembers that his own passion for the law outstripped many of his comrades of the same age, perhaps referring to his fellow

---

[2]Martin Hengel speaks of Paul receiving a Jewish education in Greek, both aspects being important to consider (*The Pre-Christian Paul* [London: SCM Press, 1991], p. 38). While he was thoroughly acquainted with Greek language, argumentation and the like, his education would have been based on the Septuagint and other Jewish writings in Greek, rather than on Hesiod and Homer, the standard fare of Greek education among Gentiles.

[3]See ibid., pp. 57-61. Jewish education in Greek, including the art of argumentation, was pursued in Jerusalem at least from the time of Herod.

[4]See the landmark studies by Martin Hengel: *Judaism and Hellenism*, 2 vols. (Philadelphia: Fortress, 1974); *Jews, Greeks, Barbarians* (Philadelphia: Fortress, 1980); *The Hellenization of Judaea in the First Century After Christ* (London: SCM, 1989).

[5]Even if this did not include training specifically in the Greek art of rhetoric, Jewish traditions of argumentation—especially as seen in the more fully developed forms of wisdom literature (see David A. deSilva, *Introducing the Apocrypha* [Grand Rapids: Baker, 2002], pp. 169-75)—would have given Paul an ample foundation on which to keep building as he encountered and absorbed Greco-Roman rhetorical strategies in his missionary work. The ways that insights from rhetorical criticism come to bear on the interpretation of Paul's letters (and other New Testament discourses) will be explored in several "Exegetical Skill" sections in the chapters that follow.

[6]On ancient letter writing and its application to the analysis of New Testament epistles, see the section "Exegetical Skill: Epistolary Analysis" in chapter thirteen on the Thessalonian Correspondence.

students in Jerusalem.[7] Moreover, despite persistent readings of Romans 7:14-25 as Paul's confession of inadequacy to keep the Torah, Paul claims that he lived in perfect conformity with the demands of Torah—"as to righteousness under the law, blameless" (Phil 3:6 NRSV). Torah would certainly not have represented a lifeless religion for Paul. Rather, Torah was the gift of God to Israel, sanctifying Israel and inviting Israel into a covenant relationship with God. The doing of Torah was a response to God's choice of Israel to be God's own, the path to security and peace for the nation and the path to life for the individual. As a Pharisee, Paul would have shared in the hope for the resurrection and the life of the world to come as the reward for fidelity to the covenant. This apocalyptic framework would provide an important resource for making sense of his encounter with Jesus, the resurrected one.

Paul's zeal for God and for the covenant manifested itself—indeed, as Paul himself seems to think, climaxed—in persecuting the early Christian movement. The connection between zeal and persecution is evident in both Galatians 1:13-14 and Philippians 3:6, and is also well attested in the history of Judaism. As models for this kind of zeal Paul had Phinehas, who manifested "zeal" by killing an Israelite male and his Midianite concubine, defending the boundaries of the people of God (Num 25:1-13). Phinehas's zeal atoned for Israel's transgression and turned away God's wrath. As further examples of zeal Paul had the heroes of the Maccabean revolt, Mattathias and his son Judas Maccabaeus. After killing a Jew as he stepped forward to break faith with the covenant by offering a pagan sacrifice, Mattathias and his family gathered together in their guerilla force "everyone who is zealous for the law and supports the covenant" (1 Macc 2:27 NRSV). Their zeal burned against deserters of the covenant, enforcing obedience to Torah or depriving the renegades of life (1 Macc 2:44-47). Thus they too "turned away wrath from Israel" (1 Macc 3:8).[8]

Paul thus acted as a watchdog for the ancestral ways and joined those who saw the Jesus movement (particularly as it came to expression among repatriated Diaspora Jews like Stephen) as a threat to Jewish identity, perhaps as the same sort of apostasy from Torah that had traditionally precipitated God's wrath and visitation of vengeance through some foreign power. Rome's presence in Judea made it an ever-present candidate for use by divine vengeance.[9] Paul was thus seeking to protect Israel's covenant loyalty and place in God's favor through punishing those who threatened to violate that covenant bond and incur God's wrath against the whole people.[10] Nor was

---

[7]James D. G. Dunn insightfully points out that *Judaism* was a term apparently coined by Jews in opposition to Hellenism (*The Theology of Paul the Apostle* [Grand Rapids: Eerdmans, 1998], p. 347). The first literary occurrence of the term is 2 Macc 4:13, where the word represents the Jewish way of life specifically as something set apart from and distinct from the way of life of the Greeks (which was being foisted and even forced on Jerusalem and Judea by its Hellenizing Jewish elites). On this point, see also deSilva, *Introducing the Apocrypha*, pp. 276-78. Paul's use of the term may signal his awareness of the importance of maintaining the distinctiveness of this way of life, thus maintaining the boundaries that marked Israel off as "holy," and the importance that such "boundary issues" would have throughout his career (as in Antioch, Galatians, the Jerusalem conference and Romans).

[8]See, further, deSilva, *Introducing the Apocrypha*, pp. 257-58, 265; Dunn, *Theology of Paul*, pp. 351-52.

[9]The author of the *Psalms of Solomon*, in fact, understood the Roman invasion of Jerusalem in 63 B.C.E. and the havoc Pompey wrought there as divine chastening for the transgressions and injustice of the later Hasmonean kings and the aristocracy.

[10]From this N. T. Wright concludes that Paul was a Shammaite Pharisee, which indeed would have made him a member of the "strictest sect" of his religion (*What Saint Paul Really Said* [Grand Rapids: Eerdmans, 1997], pp. 26-29; see Acts 26:5). The school of Shammai was indeed stricter in its application of Torah than the school of Hillel, and the fact that Paul studied under Gamaliel (a Hillelite) would not preclude his moving away from his teacher's opinions to follow the stricter application of the Shammaite Pharisees. Such a shift would also help explain the distance between Gamaliel's "live, let live and leave it to God" policy (Acts 5:38-39) and his former student's policy of "ravaging the church" (Gal 1:13).

Paul alone in this. Long after his conversion we find other Jewish Christian preachers still very much sensitive to this sort of pressure from their fellow Jews (Gal 5:11; 6:12-13). The same theological motivations that drove Paul continued to drive more zealous followers of Torah in Judea and throughout the Diaspora. Their motivation was quite sincere; they saw themselves as the protectors of the covenant. It was indeed when his zeal for Torah was at its most fevered pitch and his opposition to the Jewish Christian movement in its full strength that the inexplicable happened.

PAUL'S ENCOUNTER WITH THE LIVING CHRIST

The turning point in Paul's life, by his own recollection, was God's revelation of God's Son to him, even "within" him (Gal 1:15-16; see also 1 Cor 15:8). Scholars have debated whether this should be considered a conversion or a prophetic call,[11] but the debate misses the point. It was both at the same time.[12] Paul immediately left those pursuits that were incompatible with the revelation of Jesus as the Messiah (e.g., the persecution of his followers), came to a new understanding of who Jesus was in God's plan for God's people and radically shifted his allegiance from Torah to Jesus as Messiah. From that standpoint it was a conversion. Paul also understood the revelation as a commission to proclaim the good news about Jesus to the Gentiles, and from that standpoint it was a call.

It would be a mistake, however, to think of Paul's conversion in terms of "personal decision for Christ." It is more an encounter with divine destiny and an acceptance of that destiny. In other words, God had decided for Paul, revealed to him the errors in his understanding and direction (hence, converted him), and personally revealed what Paul's task was now to be (hence, commissioned him). Paul gives nothing of the details of this experience, which are supplied entirely by the author of Acts. Nevertheless, the double emphasis in Acts on Paul's changed understanding of Jesus and the "followers of the Way" in the plan of God, and his awareness of a divine commission communicated through that encounter (especially clear in Acts 26:12-18), is entirely in keeping with Paul's own understanding (as in Gal 1:13-16).

How then did Paul's encounter with Jesus, risen and glorified, change Paul's mind about his most fundamental convictions? As a starting point we can inquire into the preparation Paul had for this conversion and calling. It is frequently affirmed that Paul had long been dissatisfied with his religion and even felt empty with the Torah-observant way of life. Indeed, his persecution of the Christian movement is often portrayed as a desperate attempt to rekindle his faith in the old time religion.

---

[11] See, for example, Krister Stendahl, *Paul Among Jews and Gentiles* (Philadelphia: Fortress, 1976), p. 7. Stendahl shies away from calling Paul's experience a conversion because he does not want to say that Paul changed *religions* as a result of encountering Jesus: Paul was still responding to "the same God." The latter observation is essentially correct. Paul did not leave behind the faith of Abraham in order to embrace the faith of Christ, and he saw himself rather as embracing the fulfillment of what God had promised and been driving toward all along (so, correctly, D. A. Hagner, "Paul and Judaism: Testing the New Perspective," in *Revisiting Paul's Doctrine of Justification,* ed. Peter Stuhlmacher [Downers Grove, Ill.: InterVarsity Press, 2001], p. 93). Nevertheless, if we allow that conversion can happen as one moves between groups that have different expressions and understandings of a single religion, then Paul was certainly converted. If joining the Essene community would have constituted conversion for a Pharisee, joining the Christian community would have done so all the more since Saul the Pharisee came to embrace the beliefs and practices of a distinct group that he had formerly opposed, and even persecuted.

[12] Seyoon Kim engaged James D. G. Dunn in a debate concerning the question of which came first, conversion or commission (see Kim, *Paul and the New Perspective* [Grand Rapids: Eerdmans, 2001], pp. 4-13, 36), but the essential point is that the encounter with the risen Jesus, the glorified Christ, changed both Paul's understanding of what God was doing in his generation and of what Paul's role as a servant of God would be.

Such affirmations, however, have no basis in Paul's own statements about his pre-Christian life.[13] On the contrary, his strict adherence to Pharisaism gave him a healthy self-image free from the debilitating effects of guilt. He was "blameless" before Torah, after all (Phil 3:6); it was only after his conversion that he regarded himself as the least of the apostles. Therefore, we will not find reliable insights into Paul's conversion if we pursue this psychologizing line of thought.

A better starting point would be Paul's prior acquaintance with the Christian proclamation. He was certainly informed about the Way, at least enough to devote himself to silencing its preachers and pressuring its adherents to leave off their deviant way of life. He knew that it presented a threat to what he held most dear, namely, Torah and the integrity of the Jewish covenant with God through Torah. Jesus, who had been recently crucified as a blasphemer, had himself profaned the sabbath, violated purity regulations, and claimed far too much authority for himself (e.g., the authority to forgive sins). He even may have claimed to be the Messiah, as the Sanhedrin had said. He had violated Torah (at least as Paul and the Pharisaic party interpreted it), stood condemned under Torah and had been justly executed under its curse.[14] To proclaim such a person now as the "Righteous One" was clearly an affront to the definition of righteousness by Torah's standards. Indeed, what could be the end result of this movement except widespread relaxation of Torah's commands in the name of this crucified one, with the sequel that Israel would

Figure 11.2. A statue of Paul outside the Vatican Museum, with the two constant symbols of his iconography: the book, representing his literary legacy, and the sword, representing his martyrdom. (Photo courtesy of William Krewson [BiblePlaces.com])

again be punished for tolerating such flagrant violations of the covenant?

So now to be confronted with the risen Jesus must have sent Paul into the deepest throes of cognitive dissonance. His former interpretation of the world and God's action in that world, which had seemed so secure and certain, were violently and irreparable shaken. For Jesus to be alive—and glorified, no less—

---

[13]Hengel rightly opposes looking for psychological explanations for Paul's conversion, for example in a supposed discontentment with Torah, in alleged inner struggles and the like (*Pre-Christian Paul*, p. 79). Philippians 3:6 betrays no such struggles. Not the deficiencies of his religion but an unexpected encounter with the divine best explains the radical change.

[14]This curse pertains not only to the curse pronounced on "anyone hung on a tree" (Deut 21:22-23), a text applied to victims of crucifixion during the Roman period (see 1QT 64:7-12; Hengel, *Pre-Christian Paul*, p. 83), but more broadly to the curse pronounced on "anyone who does not uphold the words of this law by observing them" (Deut 27:26 NRSV; Hengel, *Pre-Christian Paul*, p. 84). Jesus' frequent conflicts with the Pharisees over matters of *halakha*—over how to walk in the way of the law—showed him to be at odds with walking according to Torah as Paul the Pharisee understood it and thus at odds with Torah itself from his point of view.

meant that God had vindicated Jesus against the claims of his enemies (the authorities Paul revered and followed). God had approved Jesus and shown that Jesus was righteous in God's eyes. It is, as it were, that in the Damascus Road christophany, God said once again: "This is my beloved Son. Listen to him!" What was proclaimed at Jesus' baptism and transfiguration was announced to Paul by means of encountering Jesus resurrected and glorified by God, vindicated by God along with all his claims and teachings.

The connection between resurrection and divine vindication of the righteous Person unjustly killed was well established in Jewish thought before Paul's time. We may look to the expressions of hope for the martyrs in 2 Maccabees 6—7 (a text known, if not written, in Palestine in the late second-century to early first-century B.C.E.) and Wisdom of Solomon 3:1-9.[15] If Jesus is truly righteous in God's sight, and if Jesus was condemned under Torah as a transgressor and blasphemer, then Torah itself could no longer be seen to reveal God's righteousness fully or reliably, nor make its devotees righteous before God. The problem for Paul was not that Torah *could* not be obeyed but that Torah was not the final and ultimate revelation of God's righteousness. Jesus was that revelation. A critical change in Paul's mind, then, is that the center of authority and revelation shifts from the Torah to Jesus.[16]

If Jesus was righteous before God, then his followers must be correct in their acclamation of him as Messiah and in taking their bearings from his teachings above (or, rather, as the interpretive key to) Torah. Encountering Jesus as the *resurrected* One, furthermore, signaled to Paul that he had entered into the last days. Judaism had quite a number of diverse eschatological frameworks, but at the end of most of them was the resurrection of the righteous to eternal life after the final triumph of God over all the enemies of God's people. Jesus' resurrection becomes the first fruits of this end-time harvest, a conviction shared by Paul, the author of Hebrews and the author of Revelation. It places the world near its final consummation. This nearness of the end dominates Paul's thought, ethics and writing (see, e.g., Rom 13:11-14; 1 Cor 7:29-31; 1 Thess 4:13—5:11; 2 Thess 2:1-15). There was also a tradition in Judaism that in the age of the Messiah a new Torah would be given, a perfected "Torah of the Messiah" (= "law of Christ" in Gal 6:2). Paul was prepared, once the Messiah had been identified and the breaking in of the age to come had been established, to encounter a new and more perfect guide to God's will—one that actually *enabled* obedience, not merely outlined what was required. This he found in the Holy Spirit.

Much of Paul's theological orientation can be traced back, therefore, to his encounter with the risen Jesus.[17] Of course, it would remain for him to wrestle with the implications of this revelation for the remainder of his life in the variety of the situations he encounters, but the fundamental lines are drawn in this encounter—hence he can truly claim that his gospel came through a "revelation of Jesus Christ" rather than through human agency (Gal 1:11-12).

This revelation of Jesus as the Messiah and the experience of being chosen and called by God to preach the good news to Gentiles are not so disjointed as might perhaps appear at first. Part of the Jewish hope for the messianic age was that the Gentiles would come to wor-

---

[15]See deSilva, *Introducing the Apocrypha*, pp. 142-44, 277.

[16]See J. C. Beker, *Paul the Apostle* (Philadelphia: Fortress, 1980), pp. 182-89. God's resurrection of this crucified Christ signaled the end of the Torah's jurisdiction and that God's saving acts were now moving into a new stage.

[17]See the thoroughgoing attempt to demonstrate this in Seyoon Kim, *The Origins of Paul's Gospel* (Grand Rapids: Eerdmans, 1982); and *Paul and the New Perspective*.

ship the one God of Israel, bringing their glory to Jerusalem. Paul himself cites some of the oracles of God that fed this hope in Romans 15:9-12:

> As it is written,
> "Therefore I will confess you
>   among the Gentiles,
> and sing praises to your name";
> and again he says,
> "Rejoice, O Gentiles, with his people";
> and again,
> "Praise the Lord, all you Gentiles,
> and let all the peoples praise him";
> and again Isaiah says,
> "The root of Jesse shall come,
> the one who rises to rule the Gentiles;
> in him the Gentiles shall hope."
> (NRSV)

Paul's own nurture in the Old Testament Scriptures would naturally lead him to connect the coming of the Messiah with the arrival of the time for the ingathering of the Gentiles.[18] What was special to his own calling was that he should take part in this mission to the Gentiles as an ambassador of the Messiah. The author of Luke-Acts effectively captures the connection of Old Testament hope and Pauline mission by using Isaiah 49:6 to illumine both the significance of Jesus and the mission of Paul: "I have set you to be a light for the Gentiles, so that you may bring salvation to the ends of the earth" (Acts 13:47 NRSV; Lk 2:32; see also Acts 26:18).

Paul's commission to proclaim good news to the Gentiles connects also with Paul's realization that the Torah has been superceded by Christ as authority. The Torah essentially kept Jew and Gentile separate, maintaining the "dividing wall of hostility" between Jew and Gentile (Eph 2:14-15). That the Torah appeared to have come to the end of its course in the resurrection of Jesus certainly gave impetus now to calling the Gentiles, kept for so long at bay from the promises of God, home to their Creator and Savior. This ingathering of the Gentiles would ultimately hale, for Paul, back to the *Shema* itself, the creed of Israel: "Hear, O Israel: the LORD your God, the LORD is One" (Deut 6:4). The dividing wall of Torah, erected between Jew and Gentile, seemed to belie this essential truth. As Paul remarks in Romans, "Is God the God of Jews only? Is he not the God of Gentiles also? Yes, of Gentiles also, since God is one" (Rom 3:29-30 NRSV). The oneness of God was to be replicated in the oneness of God's people (Gal 3:19-28).[19] Paul became convinced through his encounter with the risen Lord that he was the one to bring the promises of God to the Gentiles—the promises given long ago to the Gentile Abraham—by announcing this new act of God's favor, the arrival of the Messiah and the possibility of salvation through trust in this Mediator of God's favor.

It would be a mistake, however, to consider Paul's experience of the risen Christ entirely in terms of intellectual developments and changes in vocation. It is clear that the encounter also opened up Paul to the experience

---

[18]See Wright, *What Saint Paul Really Said*, pp. 36-37. Wright couches this in terms of the expectation of the resurrection of the righteous, the eschatological restoration of Israel, after which the Gentiles would be brought to the worship of the one God. Encountering *Jesus* resurrected, Paul saw that God had done for Jesus what Paul expected God to do for all Israel—reversing their predicament under the Gentiles (reflected in Jesus' crucifixion) and bestowing the resurrection from the dead. As Messiah, Jesus embodies Israel's destiny (thus the importance in Paul's thought of participation in or being joined with Christ to share in that destiny). Identifying the resurrection of Jesus, then, with the restoration of Israel, Paul came to understand that God had begun to fulfill God's end-time promises, which meant that the time for the ingathering of the Gentiles had arrived. Here again the conversion quite naturally becomes a commission.

[19]Another important stream of tradition that would feed this expectation concerns the universal dominion of the Messiah, reflected in Psalm 2:7-8; 72:8; 89:27 (Wright, *What Saint Paul Really Said*, p. 55). From this angle, again, Paul would be led to expect one Lord for Jews and Gentiles.

Paul's Gospel and the Historical Jesus

If you browse the books on Christianity in the religion section of a major bookstore, you can almost always find a book that promises to demonstrate that Paul, having transformed Jesus from a Jewish teacher into a semipagan cult figure, was the real founder of Christianity. Such books are merely the extreme (and rather sensationalistic) manifestation of the often-made observations that, on the one hand, Paul does not seem to be as concerned with the teachings of Jesus as we would expect, and that, on the other hand, Paul seems to be far more concerned with the person of Jesus, and with the meaning of his death and resurrection, than Jesus ever was.

These observations, however, need to be tempered by two essential considerations. The first is that Paul's teachings are thoroughly leavened by the words of Jesus.[a] Paul rarely quotes Jesus' words directly. He does quote the words of Jesus at the Last Supper as part of his own teaching on how the celebration of the Lord's Supper is to be observed (1 Cor 11:23-26; see Mk 14:22-25; Lk 22:17-20; Mt 26:26-29). The way Jesus addressed God as "Abba! Father!" (see Mk 14:36) becomes the way Paul anticipates that believers, adopted by God's Spirit, will also address God (Rom 8:15; Gal 4:6).

More often, Paul appeals to the words of the Lord without the use of a direct quote. For example, Paul's focus on the debt of Christians to "love one another" and his conviction that the summary and fulfillment of the whole Torah is found in the command to love your neighbor as yourself, reflects a knowledge both the "new commandment" of Jesus (Jn 13:34-35; 15:12) and Jesus' summary of the law (Mt 22:37-40). Romans 12:14-21 instructs readers to "bless those who persecute you" (cf. 1 Cor 4:12), to refuse to "repay evil for evil," and instead to "overcome evil with good." Paul has thus thoroughly digested and incorporated Jesus' distinctive teaching about how to respond to people who offer insult and hostility (see Lk 6:28-35; Mt 5:38-41).

Paul frequently refers to authoritative pronouncements by Jesus when making his own case. Jesus' teaching about divorce (Mk 10:9-12//Mt 19:6, 9) is authoritative for Paul's converts (1 Cor 7:11). Paul claims the same right that Jesus extended to all preachers of the Gospel (1 Cor 9:14; Lk 10:7), even if he does not make use of it. Paul's declaration that "nothing is unclean in itself," about which he is "persuaded in the Lord Jesus" (Rom 14:14 NRSV), is a lesson from the Jesus tradition (Mk 7:14-23), and Paul's conclusion that "everything is indeed clean" (Rom 14:20 NRSV) agrees with Mark's interpretative note on that story that "thus he declared all foods clean" (Mk 7:19 NRSV).

Paul's eschatological orientation, moreover, is entirely in keeping with Jesus' own. Both make central to their ministries the proclamation that God's reign is dawning (Mk 1:14-15; 14:25; Lk 10:9, 11; Rom 14:17; 1 Cor 4:20; 6:9-10; 15:24, 50). Certain particulars of Paul's eschatology seem to derive directly from the Jesus tradition. Thus 1 Thessalonians 4:15-17 can be viewed as an expansion of Matthew 24:30-31, explicating how *all* the elect, both dead and living, will be

---

[a]See Kim, *Paul and the New Perspective*, pp. 260-69; D. L. Dungan, *The Sayings of Jesus in the Churches of Paul* (Philadelphia: Fortress, 1971); D. C. Allison, "The Pauline Epistles and the Synoptic Gospels: The Pattern of the Parallels," *NTS* 28 (1982); David Wenham, *Paul: Follower of Jesus or Founder of Christianity* (Grand Rapids: Eerdmans, 1995).

gathered. In 1 Thessalonians 5, Paul uses the image of the thief for the unexpected coming of the Lord (1 Thess 5:2, 4; Mt 24:42-44), urges disciples to "be watchful," and presents "drunkenness" as a negative image of being unprepared (1 Thess 5:7; Mt 24:49-50).

Paul exhibits, therefore, a thorough knowledge of, respect for and use of Jesus traditions now known especially through Mark and through the Q tradition (the material shared by Matthew and Luke), and he regards these traditions to be authoritative and formative for the communities of Christ followers in his orbit.

The second consideration is one of timing. Paul looks back on the cross and resurrection, the initiating act of the new creation. He encounters Jesus as the exalted Lord on the road to Damascus, and not merely as a Jewish teacher walking through the hills of Galilee. Looking out after the death and resurrection of Jesus, Paul stands at a different and significantly advanced place in salvation history compared to where the disciples stood as they walked with Jesus prior to the cross. The fact that God resurrected—and this was the first time anyone had been resurrected—a man who died accursed by the Torah (by being convicted of blasphemy, if not also by the fact of crucifixion) meant that both Jesus' death and resurrection had profound implications for who Jesus was in the scheme of things, for the role of the Torah in regulating the people of God, and for understanding the present time as the time God would fulfill his promises to Abraham at last by bringing the knowledge of God to the Gentiles.

Paul could not simply repeat the teachings of Jesus; he also had to "actualize" the achievement of Jesus in his death and resurrection.[b] Notably, however, he does so in a way that still shows close connection with the Jesus traditions. Jesus' interpretation of his own death as a giving of his life as a "ransom for many" (Mk 10:45 and, especially, the words of institution at the Last Supper) led quite naturally to Paul's theology of the cross as an atoning sacrifice, a redemption, a death "for us" that rescues us "from the present evil age" (Gal 1:4). Paul's lofty understanding of Jesus not only as a teacher but as a revealer of the Father (2 Cor 4:4-6; Col 1:15-20) grows out of Jesus' own words about his role in making the Father known (Mt 11:27; Jn 14:9-11). Even Paul's understanding of his mission to the Gentiles corresponds closely to Jesus' vision for many Gentiles coming to sit at Abraham's table, even while the natural descendants of Abraham are shut out (Mt 8:5-13), not to mention the "great commission" of Matthew 28:18-20.

FOR FURTHER READING

Allison, Dale C. "The Pauline Epistles and the Synoptic Gospels: The Pattern of the Parallels." *NTS* 28 (1982): 1-32.

Dungan, David L. *The Sayings of Jesus in the Churches of Paul.* Philadelphia: Fortress, 1971.

Kim, Seyoon. *Paul and the New Perspective,* pp. 259-91. Grand Rapids: Eerdmans, 2001.

Wenham, David. *Paul: Follower of Jesus or Founder of Christianity.* Grand Rapids: Eerdmans, 1995.

Wright, N. T. *What Saint Paul Really Said,* pp. 167-84. Grand Rapids: Eerdmans, 1997.

---

[b]Wright, *What Saint Paul Really Said,* p. 181.

of the love of God in a new and overpowering way, shown in Jesus and his self-giving death (Gal 2:20).[20] This element, too, holds together his conversion and commission: "the love of Christ urges us on, because we are convinced that one has died for all; therefore all have died. And he died for all, so that those who live might live no longer for themselves, but for him who died and was raised for them" (2 Cor 5:14-15 NRSV). Encountering Christ was for Paul both a profound religious experience of reconciliation with God *and* a vocation to act as God's ambassador of reconciliation (2 Cor 5:18-20).

It is common to end any discussion of Paul's spiritual odyssey here, but Paul's conversion and call set him on a lifelong journey.[21] Twenty years later his converts would read of his ongoing quest to know more and more of the fellowship of Christ's sufferings, which he had in abundance as a result of his missionary work, and striving always to conform more and more to Christ's example. Even as he was engaged in the task of evangelism and church formation, he was equally aware of his own progress in discipleship, pressing on to take hold of the prize (Phil 3:14; see also 1 Cor 9:24-27). He came to his understanding of the role of the Spirit and spiritual gifts in the life of the believer by becoming more and more sensitive to the leading of the Spirit and experiencing its power to defeat the cravings of the fleshly nature, a power that the Torah had not given him. His encounter with Christ had opened him up to a level of authenticity in his experience of God that surpassed by far what had been bequeathed to him by his heritage, and into which he now tirelessly invited other people across the Mediterranean with the same zeal he once showed in his pursuit—and attainment—of righteousness under the law.

THE MINISTRY OF THE APOSTLE TO THE GENTILES

In Galatians, Paul tells us a little more about his early life as an apostle to the Gentiles. Immediately after his encounter with Christ he went into Arabia, most likely to begin his mission, to respond in obedience to the divine commission. The designation "Arabia" points toward the neighboring Gentile kingdom of the Nabateans, not toward desert wastelands where Paul sought a clearer sense of his calling in meditation and solitude.[22] After this he returned to Damascus, again presumably to preach, where he was forced to flee for his life (2 Cor 11:32-33; Acts 9:19-25).[23] Only then did he make a visit to Jerusalem, to see Peter especially (Gal 1:18-20). For eleven years more he preached in Syria (Syrian Antioch was an important and persistent center for Paul's work) and Cilicia (Paul's native city of Tarsus was to be found here as well), carrying on his ministry in those Gentile regions (Gal 1:21-24).

Prompted by revelation he visited Jerusalem a second time in order to assure himself that he was working in concert with the original apostles of Jesus, and, as Paul will argue in Galatians, he found himself to be working more in concert with the Spirit of God than even these Jerusalem pillars (Gal 2:1-10), one of whom would falter in his commitment to the Gentile mission (Gal 2:11-14). After the private meeting with Peter, James and John in Jerusalem, which most historians would date

---

[20]Raymond Brown, *Introduction to the New Testament* (Garden City, N.Y.: Doubleday, 1997), p. 449.

[21]See Ben Witherington III, *The Paul Quest* (Downers Grove, Ill: InterVarsity Press, 1998), pp. 79-87, who does not fall into this trap.

[22]Witherington, *Paul Quest,* pp. 308-9.

[23]This event is dated to 37-39 C.E. Damascus was not under the jurisdiction of King Aretas before the succession of Caligula in 37 C.E., and Aretas himself died prior to 40 C.E. See Robert Jewett, *A Chronology of Paul's Life* (Philadelphia: Fortress, 1979), pp. 30-33.

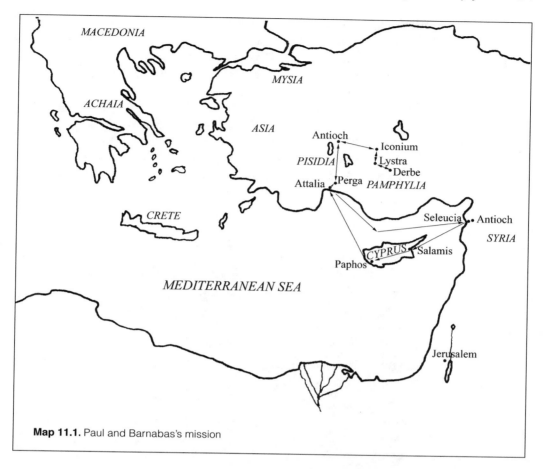

Map 11.1. Paul and Barnabas's mission

in 47-48 C.E.,[24] Paul and Barnabas evangelized in the regions of Lyconia and Pisidia, specifically targeting Pisidian Antioch, Iconium, Lystra and Derbe, returning to each city in reverse order on the way back to Syrian Antioch.[25] Here we are entirely dependent on Acts for our information (Acts 13—14), with a corroboration in 2 Timothy 3:11.[26] At the same time the question of Gentile inclusion in the church and whether or not they should be circumcised and taught to observe the Mosaic law reached a fevered pitch. It is probably shortly after Paul and Barnabas returned to Antioch that Paul learned of a Jewish Christian mission interfering with the churches he planted, prompting the writing of Galatians and, shortly after, a meeting of the leaders of the Christian movement and mission in Jerusalem to decide this question (Acts 15).

---

[24]See, for example, Becker, *Paul the Apostle,* p. 31; Witherington, *Paul Quest,* pp. 314-18; Loveday Alexander, "Chronology of Paul," in *Dictionary of Paul and His Letters,* ed. Gerald F. Hawthorne and Ralph P. Martin (Downers Grove, Ill.: InterVarsity Press, 1993), pp. 122-23.

[25]For glimpses into Paul's missionary preaching, see "Paul's Preaching to the Galatians" in chapter twelve on Galatians. Galatians 3:1-5; 4:13-15; 1 Corinthians 2:1-5; and 1 Thessalonians 1:9—2:12 provide firsthand reminiscences of Paul's preaching and practice in these missionary encounters.

[26]This reference loses its force, obviously, if 2 Timothy is read as pseudonymous *and* as dependent on Acts.

After resolution was achieved, Paul and Barnabas returned to Syrian Antioch, where they parted company. Paul now traveled with Silas (the Silvanus that wrote as coauthor of 1 and 2 Thessalonians) back through Syria and Cilicia, strengthening the churches there and spreading the report of the decision of the Jerusalem leaders regarding Gentiles and Torah. Again, we are wholly dependent on Acts 15:30-41 here. In Lystra, Paul and Silas encountered Timothy, whom they took with them to help in their missionary endeavors. The three of them pushed westward into Macedonia, evangelizing Philippi, Thessalonica and Berea. Paul went on to Athens alone and then to Corinth, where Silvanus and Timothy rendezvoused with him. For this series of events the Acts narrative is amply supported by data from 1 Thessalonians (compare the movements of the team members in

Figure 11.3. A page from P[46], a collection of the letters of Paul dating from about 200 C.E., and therefore a vitally important witness to the text of the New Testament. This page shows the last line of Romans, which ends at Romans 16:24 (with greetings from "Quartus, the brother") in this manuscript. Romans 16:25-27 actually appear earlier (right after Rom 15:33). Romans is surprisingly followed in this collection by the Epistle to the Hebrews, with Hebrews 1:1-7 occupying most of this page. (Photo courtesy of the Papyrology Collection, Graduate Library, The University of Michigan)

Map 11.2. Paul's Aegean mission

Acts 16—18 with 1 Thess 2:1-2; 3:1-6), written by Paul from Corinth.

According to Acts, Paul and his team stayed in Corinth for at least eighteen months. During that time Paul was brought up on charges before the Roman proconsul of Achaia, Lucius Junius Gallio, connecting at last with a firm date known from Roman sources (51 C.E.). This dating would incidentally correspond with the expulsion of (some) Jews from Rome under Claudius, most probably to be dated to 49 C.E. (see Acts 18:2), the motive for Aquila and Pricilla's sojourn in Corinth, giving Paul the opportunity to meet and befriend them there. At the end of his stay in Corinth, Paul traveled back to Jerusalem via Ephesus and a sea voyage thence to Caesarea. After "greeting the church" in Jerusalem, he returned to Syrian Antioch and the churches he founded in Galatia and Phrygia (Acts 18:18-23).

The next phase of Paul's career is centered in Ephesus, where, the author of Acts informs us, Paul spent more than two years (Acts 19:8-10). It is a noteworthy correspondence that Apollos is said to have visited the Christians in Corinth while Paul was in Ephesus (Acts 19:1), a visit also well attested by Paul himself (1 Cor 1:12; 3:4-7). It is at this point, however, that it becomes more difficult to fit the movements reflected in Paul's letters neatly into the itinerary of Acts. The author of Acts will speak of only one more visit by Paul to Corinth: at the end of his stay in Ephesus, Paul travels to Macedonia, then Greece, then back through Macedonia (Acts 20:1-4) and on to Jerusalem. From Paul's writings (see especially 1 Cor 16:5-9; 2 Cor 1:15-17; 13:1) it is clear that he made at least one other visit to Achaia during his stay at Ephesus. The more complicated movements of Paul and his emissaries reflected in 1-2 Corinthians, as well as the composition of those texts themselves,[27] are all to be dated to this period; they fill out the story of Paul's challenges and activities during these years exponentially.

Once Paul achieves reconciliation with the Corinthian Christians, he makes a journey through Macedonia and Achaia to gather a collection (2 Cor 8:1-6, 16-24; 9:1-5). This is perhaps the journey envisioned in Acts 20:1-4, though the list of names there does not include Titus, who clearly was also involved. This project, about which Acts is silent, is a prominent topic in Paul's own letters and a matter of great concern for him (see Rom 15:25-29; 1 Cor 16:1-4; 2 Cor 8—9). No doubt it symbolized, in part, the unity and reciprocal relationship that existed between his largely Gentile churches and the Judean Christian community. Paul writes Romans at the conclusion of the collection project, probably from Corinth itself, and bears witness to his plans to return forthwith to Jerusalem with the funds and, after that, to journey to Rome and begin a mission in the West. Here, however, the framework of Acts supplies essential information about what transpired on Paul's return to Jerusalem.

Bear in mind that many events in Paul's career are beyond recovery or precise placement in any reconstruction of his ministry. The catalog of hardships in 2 Corinthians 11:23-27 is quite informative in this regard. Here Paul speaks of having endured at least several imprisonments, five disciplinary floggings under the jurisdiction of the synagogue,[28] a stoning and three shipwrecks (one of which involved a whole night and day adrift on the sea). This catalog was written well before any of the hardships endured in connection with the arrest in

Jerusalem and four years of detention that followed, but Acts certainly does not record all of them. For instance, Acts records only one shipwreck, and that on the journey to Rome—after the three Paul mentions in 2 Corinthians 11:25. Similarly, Acts only shows Paul in prison once during these earlier years (in Philippi), whereas Paul already speaks of imprisonments in the plural before his fateful arrest in Jerusalem (2 Cor 11:23). This has made it difficult to reach certainty about the location from which Paul wrote the Prison Epistles (Ephesians, Philippians, Colossians, Philemon).[29] Did these come from the detentions in Rome or Caesarea, or might they be set within the context of some other imprisonment not specified by Acts?

Paul's new stance toward the Torah made him persona non grata with non-Christian Jews and, indeed, many Jewish Christians in Judea. The words attributed to James in Acts 21:20-21 reflect the anti-Pauline sentiments in Jerusalem: "They have been told about you that you teach all the Jews living among the Gentiles to forsake Moses, and that you tell them not to circumcise their children or observe their customs" (v. 21 NRSV). In other words, Paul is regarded as an apostate Hellenizer out to destroy the distinctive way of life and identity of the Jewish people. He is painted in the same hues as the radical Hellenizers who brought so much grief to Israel prior to the Maccabean Revolt, a portrait completed by the suggestion that he profaned the temple by bringing a Gentile friend into the court of the Israelites. Paul himself does not appear to have counseled Jews in the Diaspora to relinquish any of their ancestral customs—as long as their practice did not betray the nature

---

[27]See the discussion of these events in chapter fourteen, "The Corinthian Correspondence." In all, Paul wrote at least four letters to Corinth, two of which have not been preserved. Canonical 1 Corinthians was written from Ephesus; 2 Corinthians after Paul had left Ephesus and begun his visit through Macedonia on the way to Corinth. See Witherington, *Paul Quest,* p. 330.

[28]Under Roman law, ethnic groups were allowed to regulate their own communal life and administer discipline according to their native laws as long as this did not interfere with Roman law. As a Jew, Paul would have been subject to the discipline of the Jewish community.

[29]The authenticity of Ephesians and Colossians is often questioned; see the discussion of the arguments for and against authenticity in chapter eighteen.

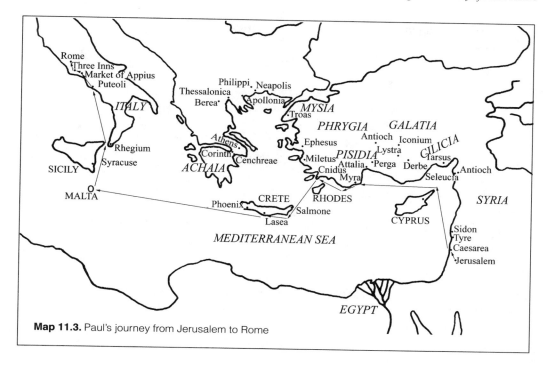

Map 11.3. Paul's journey from Jerusalem to Rome

of the one, new body of Jews and Gentiles united by Christ (e.g., by refusing to have table fellowship with Gentile Christians). His strong statements about circumcision's lack of real value in God's sight, and his insistence that Jewish and Gentile Christians could eat together, meet in one another's homes, and the like, would have been basis enough for opposition back in Jerusalem.

A riot in Jerusalem leads to Roman intervention, several hearings in Jerusalem and Caesarea Maritima (the Roman provincial capital), and a two-year detention in the garrison at Caesarea. This culminated in Paul's appeal to be heard by the curia in Rome, an arduous journey and a further two years' detention awaiting trial.[30] This phase occupied Paul from late 57 to 62 C.E. Paul's post-62 C.E. career is more problematic because the narrative framework of Acts ends with Paul under house arrest in Rome. Several scenarios suggest themselves. First, Paul's detention in Rome might simply have ended in his execution. Early church tradition, however, speaks of Paul's acquittal in that first trial, a period of further ministry (perhaps involving his intended mission to Spain;[31] perhaps involving a change of plans and further work in the eastern Mediterranean), and a second imprisonment in Rome in connection with the persecution of Christians there in 64 C.E., ending with decapitation. This last phase of Paul's life becomes most important for the discussion of the Pastoral Epistles (most notably 2 Timothy) and for the question of whether or not a plausible setting can be found for them in Paul's ministry.

---

[30]Imprisonment or detention was rarely used as a punishment under Roman law, quite unlike the American penal system where it is a primary form of punishment. Rather, detention in some form was imposed on those accused and awaiting trial to determine guilt or innocence of crime. See Albert A. Bell Jr., *Exploring the New Testament World* (Nashville: Thomas Nelson, 1998), pp. 8-11.

[31]This tradition appears to be supported by *1 Clement* 5:5-7 and is followed by Adolf Deissmann, *Paul* (New York: Harper & Brothers, 1957), p. 248.

FOR FURTHER READING

Becker, Jürgen. *Paul: Apostle to the Gentiles.* Louisville, Ky.: Westminster John Knox, 1993.

Beker, J. Christiaan. *Paul the Apostle: The Triumph of God in Life and Thought.* Philadelphia: Fortress, 1980.

Bornkamm, Günther. *Paul.* New York: Harper & Row, 1971.

Bruce, F. F. *Paul: Apostle of the Heart Set Free.* Grand Rapids: Eerdmans, 1977.

Deissmann, Adolf. *Paul: A Study of Social and Religious History.* New York: Harper & Brothers, 1957.

Dictionary of Paul and His Letters. Edited by G. F. Hawthorne and R. P. Martin. Downers Grove, Ill.: InterVarsity Press, 1993.

Fee, Gordon D. *God's Empowering Presence: The Holy Spirit in the Letters of Paul.* Peabody, Mass.: Hendrickson, 1994.

Hengel, Martin. *The Pre-Christian Paul.* Valley Forge, Penn.: Trinity Press International, 1991.

Hengel, Martin, and Anna Maria Schwemer. *Paul Between Damascus and Antioch: The Unknown Years.* Louisville, Ky.: Westminster John Knox, 1997.

Jewett, Robert. *A Chronology of Paul's Life.* Philadelphia: Fortress, 1979.

Lüdemann, Gerd. *Paul: Apostle to the Gentiles. Studies in Chronology.* Philadelphia: Fortress, 1984.

Meeks, Wayne. *The First Urban Christians: The Social World of the Apostle Paul.* New Haven, Conn.: Yale University Press, 1983.

O'Connor, Jerome M. *Paul: A Critical Life.* Oxford: Clarendon, 1996.

Ridderbos, H. N. *Paul: An Outline of His Theology.* Grand Rapids: Eerdmans, 1975.

Roetzel, Calvin. *The Letters of Paul: Conversations in Context.* 2nd ed. Atlanta: John Knox Press, 1985.

Sanders, E. P. *Paul.* New York: Oxford, 1991.

Westerholm, Stephen. *Preface to the Study of Paul.* Grand Rapids: Eerdmans, 1997.

Witherington, Ben, III. *New Testament History: A Narrative Account.* Grand Rapids: Baker, 2001.

——— *Paul's Narrative Thought World.* Louisville, Ky.: Westminster John Knox, 1994.

——— *The Paul Quest: The Renewed Search for the Jew of Tarsus.* Downers Grove, Ill.: InterVarsity Press, 1998.

12

THE LETTER TO THE GALATIANS

Walking in Line with the Spirit

One of the more pressing sets of questions with which the early church had to wrestle had to do with the requirements for joining the people of God and the ongoing validity of the Torah (the Jewish law) as the code that should regulate the life of the church. The voices of those who argued that circumcision, the rite of entrance into the covenant people since Abraham, remained an essential mark of those who belonged to God's new covenant are not well represented in the New Testament. However powerful these voices might have been, they were pushed to the margins by Paul and his growing influence in the church, Galatians providing perhaps the strongest statement against such voices.

For Paul, circumcision belongs to that limited period of time between the giving of the promise to Abraham and the coming of Jesus, in whom the promised inheritance came to all who believed, whether Jew (the circumcised) or Gentile (the uncircumcised). The Torah as a whole similarly belongs to that interim period, when humanity was still in its adolescence with regard to its knowledge of the one God. With the coming of Christ and the pouring out of the Holy Spirit into the hearts of the believers, however, humanity came of age in its relationship with God. Galatians bears testimony to the importance of the Holy Spirit in the life and experience of the early church. It is the Spirit, poured out on those who trust Jesus Christ, that makes someone a child of God

and therefore part of the one people of God. The Spirit, guiding the believer like a constant friend, leads the believer into conformity with God's righteousness, making Christ take shape in him or her. To seek to bring back the "old ways" of trying to walk in line with God shows an essential failure to grasp the promise and privilege of the new way God has opened up, a failure that brings out Paul's emotions in this letter like no other.

THE HISTORICAL SETTING OF THE GALATIAN CHURCHES

Galatians in the career of Paul. Galatians gives us more firsthand information about Paul's early career as a Christian missionary than any other text. The challenge is to understand how the events described in this account coincide with the events described in the secondhand account by Luke known as the Acts of the Apostles. We have already considered Acts on its own terms and the nature of ancient historiography. While seeking to provide a reliable account of Christian origins, Luke nevertheless is highly selective: he organizes his material according to the patterns and development he wishes to highlight, and he has his own perspective on and interpretation of the events he narrates. Scholars tend to approach this question from one of three basic positions:

- Acts and Galatians are both completely historically reliable; they can and must be harmonized (i.e., Galatians must be read within the framework of Acts).

- Acts and Galatians are both generally reliable but must be read and evaluated in terms of the authors' different aims, perspectives, knowledge of events and principles of selection. Together, each can *contribute* to a reliable picture of the history of the early church. Privilege of place tends to be given to Galatians as a firsthand testimony to events.

- Acts and Galatians are documents written to tell "history" in a way that supports the authors' agendas. (Usually this is applied far more forcefully to Acts than to Galatians.) The framework of Acts is open to revision because it reflects more of Luke's idealized portrait than the "facts." Privilege is always given to Galatians.

This introduction proceeds mainly from the second theoretical position, although the results suggest that the two texts are highly complementary.

Both Galatians and Acts speak clearly about Paul's former opposition to the Jesus movement in Palestine (Gal 1:13, 23; Acts 8:3; 9:1-2) and about Paul's encounter with the glorified Christ (Gal 1:15-16; Acts 9:3-6). Both understand this encounter to involve Paul's commission to preach the gospel (Gal 1:15-16; Acts 9:15). At this point, Paul's selectivity is more apparent: he denies conferring with "flesh and blood" (Gal 1:16), by which he means to emphasize the independence of his gospel from the Jerusalem apostles and his utter dependence on God for his message and commission. His omission of any mention of Ananias (see Acts 9:10-19) is therefore understandable as being beside the point and potentially damaging to his claims. Both accounts agree that Paul continued on in Damascus for a time, though Luke gives the impression of a much shorter stay there (Gal 1:17; Acts 9:20-25).

We come, then, to the question of Paul's visits to Jerusalem.[1] Luke speaks of three visits in Acts 9—15: the first occurs shortly after Paul's conversion (Acts 9:26-30); the second occurs in connection with famine relief funds taken up in Antioch (Acts 11:27-30); the third occurs in connection with the "apostolic conference" deciding the question of whether or not Gentile converts need to be circumcised and keep Torah (Acts 15). Paul speaks of two visits in Galatians: the first occurs three years after his conversion (Gal 1:18-20); the second occurs fourteen years after either his conversion or the first visit (Gal 2:1-2). In chapter eight (on Acts) I posed a series of questions with regard to sorting out these data. Here I will lay out my own responses to those questions.

In Galatians 1—2, Paul very carefully lays out a case that demonstrates his independence from the Jerusalem apostles. He is intent on detailing his interactions with them precisely and putting the proper spin on those visits so that no one can accuse him of being a "derivative" apostle, answerable to Jerusalem rather than to God. To omit mention of a visit (e.g., the famine relief visit, if Luke is correct about that visit), especially when he invokes oaths about the truthfulness and completeness of his information (Gal 1:20), would leave Paul open to immediate disconfirmation and loss of the debate in Galatia. Even if Luke had invented the famine-relief visit, it would still be wrong to identify the visit in Galatians 2:1-10 with the apostolic conference in Acts 15:

- The visit Paul narrates was a private meeting that focused mainly on confirming Paul's calling as apostle to the Gentiles; Acts 15 describes a more open meeting, focused mainly on the question of what Gentile converts were required to do to be part of the new people of God.

---

[1]An excellent review of this problem in Pauline biography can be found in R. P. Longenecker, *Galatians,* WBC 41 (Dallas: Word, 1990), pp. lxxiii-lxxxiii.

- The outcome of the visit Paul narrates is the confirmation of Paul and Barnabas as agents of God's gospel (the former being more in doubt than the latter, given Paul's past) and the admonition to "continue to remember the poor" (Gal 2:10); the outcome of the meeting in Acts 15 was the delineation of a minimum number of purity requirements for Gentile converts (abstaining from food sacrificed to idols, fornication, eating blood and eating meat that had been slaughtered by strangulation).

- The events in Galatians (let alone Paul's activities prior to Galatians) must logically predate any such decision that was reached in the meeting narrated in Acts 15, since that ruling would have direct bearing both on the question of circumcision raised in Galatia and the question of table fellowship with the Gentile Christians raised in Antioch (Gal 2:11-14).

Paul, then, visited Jerusalem for the first time after his conversion/commission by the glorified Christ three years (or in the third year) after that event. Paul speaks of this as a private meeting to get acquainted with Peter and, to a lesser extent, James, staying only two weeks. Since Paul regards himself as "still unknown by face" to the churches in Judea (Gal 1:22), Luke may have colored his depiction of this visit (Acts 9:26-30) with stories of Paul openly preaching and debating in Jerusalem as a means of making his transformation more dramatic and vivid. Luke also suggests that with Barnabas's help Paul was introduced to the whole circle of apostles and was, in effect, incorporated into their group for the duration of his stay in Jerusalem (Acts 9:27-28).

After leaving Jerusalem, Paul returned to work in the regions of Syria (the home of Antioch) and Cilicia (the home of Tarsus), Paul providing a more generalized account of this than Luke (Gal 1:21; Acts 9:30; 11:25-26). The work in Antioch, in particular, sets the stage for a second visit to Jerusalem. Luke looks on this from the outside, underscoring the visit as part of a famine relief program (Acts 11:27-30). The phrasing of Galatians 2:10, in which the Jerusalem apostles urge Paul and Barnabas to "continue to remember the poor" while Paul asserts that he had already been eager to do this very thing, would complement the "relief fund" aspect of this visit. Paul, however, looks at the visit as an insider, being privy to the meeting with James, Peter and John. While Paul is intent on demonstrating his essential independence from these Jerusalem "pillars," this also affords him an opportunity to affirm the validation of his calling by them at the same time.

Subsequent to this, Paul evangelizes the Galatians. Scholars have endlessly debated whether the Galatian churches were located in south Galatia or north Galatia.[2] Generally, those who favor locating these churches in northern Galatia identify the meeting in Galatians 2:1-10 with the meeting in Acts 15 (if they do not abandon the framework of Acts altogether). Acts gives no details about Paul's activities in the cities of north Galatia (Ancyra, Pessinus and Tavium), merely mentioning that Paul and his team "went throughout the region of Phrygia and Galatia" in Acts 16:6 (the initial, evangelizing visit) and returning to "the

---

[2]On locating these churches in the northern territory of Galatia, see J. B. Lightfoot, *St. Paul's Epistle to the Galatians,* 10th ed. (1890; reprint, London: Macmillan, 1986); J. Moffatt, *An Introduction to the Literature of the New Testament,* 3rd ed. (Edinburgh: T & T Clark, 1918), pp. 83-107. W. M. Ramsey made the classic case for locating these churches in the southern cities of Galatia in his *Historical Commentary on St. Paul's Epistle to the Galatians,* 2nd ed. (London: Hodder & Stoughton, 1900); see also E. deWitt Burton, *A Critical and Exegetical Commentary on the Epistle to the Galatians,* ICC (Edinburgh: T & T Clark, 1921); Colin Hemer, *The Book of Acts in the Setting of Hellenistic History* (Tübingen: J. C. B. Mohr, 1989), pp. 277-307. An exceptional summary of the issues involved and of the positions taken can be found in Longenecker, *Galatians,* lxiii-lxxii.

region of Galatia and Phrygia" in Acts 18:23) to strengthen the disciples there. According to the "south Galatian hypothesis," the churches addressed by Paul's letter to the Galatians were Derbe, Lystra, Iconium and Pisidian Antioch, an evangelization effort described in detail in Acts 13—14.

Both sides have their merits and difficulties, and they have been championed by careful and astute scholars. The term *Galatians* would be a more appropriate designation for residents in north Galatia, if an ethnic designation (e.g., "Celts") had been intended, but it is also perfectly appropriate for residents in south Galatia given their Roman provincial designation. Indeed, what other single title could unite those south Galatian churches, which ethnically would be quite disparate?[3] Paul himself claims to have preached to these people on account of an illness (i.e., his plans to preach elsewhere were deferred on account of sickness, with the result that he evangelized where he was laid up). This does not fit the picture we find in Acts 13—14 of Paul's ministry in south Galatia, but because Acts is completely silent about (alleged) activities in north Galatia, it would not pose a stumbling block to a north Galatian mission. On the other hand, when we consider Luke's more stylized and secondhand depiction of Paul's missionary work in each city, particularly in south Galatia (that is, prior to Luke's acquaintance with Paul), this discrepancy can be explained as a result of Paul's intimate recollection of the facts and Luke's inferior access to those facts and other authorial interests.

On balance, I favor locating the Galatians crisis in the south Galatian cities, early in Paul's career and prior to any conference on the topic of Gentile responsibility to keep Torah. Such an agreement would have been the perfect trump card for Paul if the Galatian crisis developed *after* the apostolic conference.[4] Our decision, however, will hardly affect our appreciation of the issues raised in the situation behind Galatians or in Paul's response.

Paul's preaching to the Galatians. In contrast to the narrative of Acts, Paul appears not to have intended to preach to these specific congregations but was impeded from fulfilling his purpose (presumably to go further) and made the best of the limitations imposed on him by his health (Gal 4:13). Here Paul displays a truly positive and Spirit-led response to the frustrations of being hindered in his plans by sickness, seeking out God's provision of otherwise unexpected opportunities. The Galatians responded favorably to Paul's preaching, despite his bodily ailment. Paul himself regards this to be extraordinary since those brought up in Greek culture came to expect a good show from public speakers. Manner of presentation, physical grace and poise, and vocal beauty were all as important as what was said. Indeed, those who lacked the physical presence, voice and declamatory power could expect to receive ridicule and public scorn rather than an attentive hearing. Rather than despise the speaker, however, the Galatians and Paul formed a deep bond of loyalty and devotion during that visit (Gal 4:15), making their subsequent departure from Paul's

---

[3]Burton, *Epistle to the Galatians,* p. xxix.

[4]Longenecker adds several important observations based on Paul's traveling companions, tipping the balance in this direction (*Galatians,* pp. lxx-lxxi). First, he notices the absence of any mention of Timothy, who is linked with Paul throughout the so-called second missionary journey and is mentioned in every undisputed Pauline letter, except Galatians. This suggests that Paul evangelized Galatia *and* wrote Galatians before he teamed up with Timothy. Second, Longenecker observes the prominent role played by Barnabas in Galatians. True, Barnabas was a well-known evangelist in his own right, like James, John and Peter (none of whom the Galatians need have met for those references to be meaningful). However, the inclusion of Barnabas in Galatians 2:9 and, more especially, the climactic nature of Barnabas (of all people!) being carried away in Peter's hypocrisy in Antioch (Gal 2:13) would have more force if he was personally known to the Galatians.

message all the more surprising and hurtful for the apostle.

What exactly did Paul preach when he was in Galatia? The central feature of his gospel here, as in Corinth, was Christ crucified (Gal 3:1; see 1 Cor 2:2). What significance could this possibly have had for the Gentile Galatians? Jesus as the Christ, or Messiah, was a foreign concept, and crucifixion a sign of utter degradation. Greek culture, however, could envision a divine being suffering excruciating torments, and this specifically on behalf of humanity. The myth of Prometheus, for example, typifies this pattern. Throughout Galatians, Paul refers to Jesus as one who, in death, "gave himself on behalf of our sins" (Gal 1:4), who "loved me and gave himself up for me" (Gal 2:20), who rescues believers "from the present evil age" (Gal 1:4). The condensed, formulaic nature of these verses suggests that Paul had used them before and could assume the Galatians' familiarity with these concepts from his earlier visit. Paul presented Christ's crucifixion in terms of a benefactor who poured himself out completely in order to bring benefit to his clients. This terminology of "giving oneself," or "pouring oneself out," is frequent in inscriptions honoring benefactors. The shameful death of the cross was thus transformed into a noble act of supreme generosity and benefit.

Dying "for our sins" (Gal 1:4), Christ removed the obstacles to standing before a favorable God rather than an angry Judge. The thought of dying to "rescue us from this present evil age" introduces Paul's apocalyptic framework into his message early and forcefully. An apocalyptic worldview tends to see this world and its history as a temporary phenomenon, one in which the justice of God and the rewards of God for the righteous cannot fully be manifested. The death and resurrection of the Messiah signaled, for Paul, the beginning of the end of this current age and the imminence of the inception of the "age to come," a better, eternal age in which God's purposes are completely fulfilled and God's people enjoy their full reward. Christ's death was therefore an act that brought rescue *from* this world and its fate (judgment) *for* the benefits of living with God in the age to come.

The way to join oneself to this Christ was by "faith," trusting in the efficacy of his death on behalf of others to connect people with God. Those who are "of faith" trust that Jesus is a competent patron, able to procure the favor of the ultimate Patron, God. They trust that the provisions they receive by virtue of their association with Christ (for example, the Holy Spirit) are sufficient to bring them where God wants them to be. Comprehended within this faith is uncompromising loyalty and obedience to Jesus. The response of gratitude toward Christ and the God he makes known would require a complementary turning away from idols and all their trappings (as in 1 Thess 1:9-10), and Paul would have had a wealth of anti-idolatry polemic at his fingertips from the writings of Hellenistic era Jews (for example, the Letter of Jeremiah, the Wisdom of Solomon and the like). Moreover, Greek and Roman philosophers had long emphasized the essential oneness of God, who was worshiped imperfectly under a vast array of partial guises and inadequate representations. Paul could connect this with his own understanding that the one God of the Jews was also the one God of the Gentiles. His cosmopolitan approach would certainly have been more appealing than the traditional Jewish appeal that stressed the ethnic particularity of the one God and the way of life by which one could please him.

The indisputable sign for Paul of the efficacy of Jesus' work is the Galatians' reception of the Holy Spirit. Their response of trust on hearing Paul's preaching of the gospel resulted in the pouring out of God's Holy Spirit on them (Gal 3:1-5). By all accounts of the human exuberance and divine manifestations that this entailed, the Galatians would have been quite aware that a decisive change had occurred, that they had in fact received the Spirit of God. This should have been enough to show that God had approved them as part of God's family. These Gentile converts were no longer unclean, no longer outside the people of promise, since God had made known God's own acceptance of them into that household.

The rival teachers and their mission. Paul left Galatia with the conviction that his work among the Galatian converts rested on a firm foundation. What happened to shake that foundation in the months that followed his visit? On the one hand, we cannot assume that Paul had left every question answered. As the Galatian converts continued in their new life, reflecting more on their experience and, as is quite likely, on the Scriptures, new questions would have emerged. On the other hand, it is apparent that other teachers encountered the Galatian Christians, raising new questions and addressing other questions in a way that called Paul's work among them into question. Paul never names these rival teachers, but he speaks frequently of "those who are upsetting you" (Gal 1:7; 5:10), who "pervert the gospel of Christ" (Gal 1:7), who "court" them (Gal 4:17), who "trip you up from obeying the truth" (Gal 5:7), whom Paul wishes would go ahead and castrate themselves (Gal 5:12). Paul ascribes to these rival teachers the base motives of wanting to make the Galatians dependent on them for their inclusion into God's people (Gal 4:17), of seeking to make a good showing to enhance their own honor in certain circles by getting the Galatians to accept circumcision (Gal 6:12-13), and of being too cowardly to endure the opposition that preaching the true gospel brings (Gal 5:11; 6:12).

Who then are these rival teachers? Scholars are almost unanimous in affirming that they represent another mission by Christian Jews to Gentiles, one that taught Torah observance as a corollary to coming to Christ.[5] This mission may have begun independently of any concern for what Paul was doing, but it appears in Acts and Galatians largely as a cleanup mission, whose teachers followed along Paul's tracks trying to bring Gentile Christians into conformity with Torah and circumcision. In effect, they wanted to preserve fully the Jewishness of the new Christian movement and keep it firmly anchored within Judaism. Judaism, after all, could tolerate messianic sects—just not the negation of its most central identity markers (like circumcision and Torah obedience).

The activity of this mission is reflected in Acts 15:1-4, which tells of Jewish Christians from Judea coming to the churches served or founded by Paul and Barnabas, and seeking to impose circumcision and Torah observance on the converts there. Paul refers to this rival mission in Philippians 3:2-21 as a foil for his own, positive model of discipleship. Galatians, however, provides the fullest picture of the rival mission, together with the fullest refutation of their gospel. They were no doubt motivated theologically. The rival mission wanted to preserve the integrity of the covenant, setting the work of Christ within the context of this covenant (Torah). Christ would still be the one who brought light to the Gentiles, who effected the ingathering of the nations in the end time, but Christ would accomplish this by bringing the Gentiles into

---

[5]The other options in the history of scholarship are that the rival teachers are Gentile Christians who have adopted the Jewish way of life, or that they are non-Christian Jews. The latter position has recently been revived by M. D. Nanos (*The Irony of Galatians: Paul's Letter in First-Century Context* [Minneapolis: Fortress, 2002], p. 193), though it renders Gal 6:12 difficult to explain. The Gentile and Jewish Christians are still attached to the synagogue, he postulates, with the non-Christian Jews calling the Gentile Christians, who laudably seek to be "righteous," to take the necessary step of circumcision so as to separate themselves from the pagan world to which they still belong (pp. 317-18). Nanos still understands, like those who regard the "influencers" to be Jewish Christian teachers, the Gentile Christians to regard circumcision and full inclusion into the Jewish people as complementary to their faith in Jesus (p. 227).

Figure 12.1. A beautiful mosaic from the floor of the synagogue in Tiberius, dating from the fourth or fifth century C.E. The iconography depicts central cultic symbols: the ark where the Torah scrolls were deposited, the seven-branched *menorah*, a knife for sacrifices, a shovel for incense and a *shofar*. (Photo courtesy of Todd Bolen [BiblePlaces.com])

the Jewish people wholesale through circumcising them and getting them to take on themselves the "yoke of Torah." They were also concerned about the unity of the church. Like Paul, they sought to enable Jew and Gentile to come together in Christ in one worshiping body, the one body of the redeemed. Unlike Paul, they believed it was essential that the Gentiles, not the Jews, alter their behavior to make that fellowship possible.

The rival teachers were socially motivated by their zeal for the Torah and their commitment to keep God's people distinct from all the other peoples of the earth—to enact the Levitical standards and definitions of holiness, in other words. The rumor about Paul in Jerusalem (see Acts 21:20-21) is that he leads Jews to abandon the Torah and forsake the covenant. This is not entirely inaccurate. Paul himself became a Jew to Jews and a Gentile to Gentiles, violating Torah's standards of purity

(especially the pharisaic interpretation of these standards) by eating with his Gentile converts, perhaps even eating food improper for Jews. He encouraged his Jewish coworkers to do the same, setting aside for the sake of the mission and the gospel those restrictions within Torah designed to keep Jews from freely associating with Gentiles, and hence being polluted by those contacts. Moreover, he encouraged his Jewish converts to do the same with regard to his Gentile converts, to "welcome one another as Christ welcomed you" (Rom 15:7). Paul might well have been seen to promote apostasy from the covenant. While he lacked the political power of a Jason or Menelaus to enforce Hellenization, he appeared to be succeeding in loosening Torah so that Jews and Gentiles were freely mingling together. The boundaries were threatened, and those wishing to preserve the integrity (the wholeness) of the organism of Judaism had to act decisively.

The "New Perspective" on Paul and Early Judaism

Pauline studies have undergone something of a paradigm shift during the last quarter of the twentieth century, principally thanks to the insights and energies of those who promote a "new perspective" on Paul and early Judaism. This new perspective grows out of a recognition that much interpretation of Paul and Judaism in the modern era has been distorted through the ongoing influence of Luther's interpretation of Paul against the backdrop of a Catholicism that called for meritorious works as the means of achieving salvation. In Luther's writings Judaism became the graceless, externalistic, legalistic foil to Paul's religion of grace, the Spirit and love. The caricature of early Judaism fed the caricature of the Jewish people, and the extreme end of such denigration manifested itself in the Holocaust.

The horrors of the Holocaust precipitated a reevaluation of the perception of Judaism in the New Testament texts and their interpretation. Although several scholars had urged already that Judaism was also a religion of grace, it was E. P. Sanders who forcefully brought widespread attention to this understanding. He showed consistently that in all its diversity early Judaism was a religion of grace. The election of Israel was an act of divine grace; the giving of the Torah, the covenant that bound God and Israel to one another, was an act of divine grace. Doing the law was not understood as the means by which God's favor could be earned but as the proper response to God's favor already given in election and in the covenant. It had to do with the maintenance of an elect status bestowed by God, not with the acquisition of such status. Moreover, God had generously made provisions for failure to observe the covenant in the form of sacrifices, so that forgiveness and reconciliation remained available. Such provisions show that flawless performance was not expected. Sanders described Judaism as a religion of "covenantal nomism," the regulation of life by a law *(nomos)* within the framework of a graciously bestowed and maintained covenant relationship.

How, then, can we understand Paul's polemics against Judaism if the "new perspective" is correct thus far? An important insight that has emerged is that Paul does not oppose "grace" to "good works" in any way.[a] Rather, the works that are the target of Paul's polemic, often more fully expressed as "works of the law," involve those covenant obligations that pertained strictly to Israel under the Torah—the pedagogue and guardian whose time is past (Gal 3:23—4:7). Persevering in "works of the law" is a problem because the purpose of these laws was largely to mark off the Jewish people from the nations (see the powerful expressions of this in *Jub* 22.16 and *Letter of Aristeas* 139, 142). Remaining holy to the Lord entailed remaining distinct and separate from people who did not live by Torah, which meant the Gentiles and, quite often, unobservant Jews. A corollary of distinctiveness was ethnic pride in Torah as a sign of God's special favor toward the Jews (thus Paul's castigation of "confidence in the flesh" and of "boasting" in the law). This was a problem for Paul since, with the death and resurrection of Jesus, God had manifested God's desire to extend the promise and the blessing to all the nations, something that

---

[a]See James D. G. Dunn, *Romans 1-8*, WBC 38 (Dallas: Word, 1988), pp. lxvii-lxx; *The Theology of Paul the Apostle* (Grand Rapids: Eerdmans, 1998), pp. 354-59, 365.

"zeal for the Torah" quite thoroughly inhibited. At such a stage in salvation history, insisting on the "works of the law" ran against God's purposes for the present era. In trying to remain "true" to the law, non-Christian Jews (and Judaizing Christians) had in fact betrayed the Law, not observing that its goal had been reached in the coming of Christ. Insisting on "works of the Torah" meant trying to reerect the "dividing wall of hostility" at a time when God tore it down in Christ and in the outpouring of the Spirit (cf. Gal 2:18; Eph 2:11-16), thus acting in open defiance of God.

The new perspective has certainly brought many benefits to the study of the New Testament and early Judaism. It has taught us to try to understand early Judaism on its own terms as a prerequisite to interpreting Paul. It has given us good cause to reexamine some long-held views of Pauline theology that may have more to do with Reformation-era debates than with Paul's challenge to some streams of Jewish Christianity. Even though some of the statements that have come out of the new perspective are more extreme than the evidence necessitates, this is exactly what we would expect—and should be prepared to allow—after the pendulum has been swinging so long and so hard in the opposite direction. Nevertheless, its leaven, with some modifications, will be evident throughout our discussions of Galatians and Romans.

FOR FURTHER READING

Dunn, James D. G. *Romans 1-8.* WBC 38A. Dallas: Word, 1988.

———. *Romans 9-16.* WBC 38B. Dallas: Word, 1988.

———. *The Theology of Paul the Apostle.* Grand Rapids: Eerdmans, 1998.

Kim, Seyoon. *Paul and the New Perspective.* Grand Rapids: Eerdmans, 2001.

Sanders, E. P. *Paul and Palestinian Judaism.* Philadelphia: Fortress, 1977.

———. *Paul, the Law, and the Jewish People.* Philadelphia: Fortress, 1983.

Stuhlmacher, Peter. *Revisiting Paul's Doctrine of Justification: A Challenge to the New Perspective.* Downers Grove, Ill.: InterVarsity Press, 2001.

Wright, N. T. *What Saint Paul Really Said.* Grand Rapids: Eerdmans, 1997.

The rival mission considered Paul's activity as a threat to the larger group (the Jewish people), which had to be preserved. These teachers were also acutely aware that apostates could be persecuted by the zealous (as Paul himself had done prior to his conversion; Gal 1:13-14, 23). Such zeal was firmly rooted in the tradition of Phinehas, who struck down an Israelite and his Moabite concubine and so won for himself a covenant of priesthood and saved Israel from being destroyed by a plague for its apostasy (Num 25:1-13). It was rooted in the tradition of Mattathias and his sons at the outset of the Maccabean Revolt, as they purged apostates from the midst of Israel and thus "turned away wrath from Israel" (1 Macc 2:15-28, 42-48; 3:6, 8). A significant movement within Jewish Christianity, therefore, wanted to make it clear to both non-Christian and Christian Jews that the Jesus movement was in no way a movement that promoted apostasy. By reinforcing Jewish (Christian) adherence to the Torah, and all the more by bringing Gentiles to the light of the Law, the rival teachers could save themselves, the church in Judea, and the churches in the Diaspora where Jewish communities were strong, from the intramural persecution that perceived apostasy could invite. We see evidence for this clearly in the references to persecution throughout Galatians (1:13-14; 4:29; 5:11; 6:12). Where the word of the cross causes persecution while the preaching of circumcision relieves persecution, only Jews could be doing the persecuting, and the rival teachers would certainly alleviate pressures from that quarter.

The "gospel" of the rival teachers. What was the content of the rival teachers' corrective message? They have left no testimony of their own, but we can reconstruct likely elements of their message from two sources. First, Paul's response to their message surely highlights the topics (like circumcision or the value of Torah observance) and the specific positions (like circumcision as the manner by which one joins the family of Abraham, or Torah as the divinely given means for mastering the passions of the flesh) that his rivals used in their presentation of their case. Second, this information can be supplemented by investigating primary texts that display Jewish reflection about these topics or that advance positions similar to those Paul feels compelled to address in Galatians. There are many texts that bear witness to Hellenistic Jewish attempts to build bridges with Greek culture, explaining the benefits and wisdom of keeping Torah, of circumcision and the like. It is likely that the rival teachers would have drawn on such well-articulated and widely attested arguments as resources for their own attempts to bring Gentiles over to the Jewish way of life.

1. The fuss about foreskins. For Gentiles the Jewish rite of circumcision was not one of the more admirable features of that way of life, though it was certainly the best known (alongside avoidance of pork and avoidance of all work on the sabbath). It amounted to a mutilation of the human form and was often disparaged as barbaric.[6] Why would circumcision

suddenly be so appealing, so pressing an option, for the Gentile Christians in Galatia?

According to the Jewish Scriptures circumcision was an immensely positive and powerful ritual. The Galatian Christians no doubt encountered these Scriptures first in Paul's own instruction of his converts, teaching them that these texts were an essential resource for knowing the one God and for understanding the believer's place in God's family. The rival teachers would have been able to ground their message in the sacred Scriptures themselves. After all, did it not say that the promises were given to Abraham and his children? And how did one become a part of the family of Abraham? How does one become an heir of the promises given to Abraham? The Scriptures are unambiguous on this point—through circumcision.

When God made the covenant with Abraham, promising him that he would be the "ancestor of a multitude of nations," God commanded circumcision as the absolute, unavoidable and essential sign of that covenant.

> This is my covenant, which you shall keep, between me and you and your offspring after you: Every male among you shall be circumcised. . . . Any uncircumcised male who is not circumcised in the flesh of his foreskin shall be cut off from his people; he has broken my covenant. (Gen 17:10, 14 NRSV)

Those Gentiles who wish to join God's people must likewise circumcise themselves: this was the means by which the Gentile sojourner was made fit to participate in the life and worship of the community of Israel (Ex 12:48-49). Moreover, one must be circumcised to have any part in the heavenly Zion, the life of the age to come, for it is written:

> Awake, awake,
> put on your strength, O Zion!

---

[6]See Philo *Spec. Leg.* 1.1.1-2.

Put on your beautiful garments,
O Jerusalem, the holy city;
for the uncircumcised and the unclean
shall enter you no more.
(Is 52:1 NRSV)

Likewise Ezekiel, speaking of the heavenly temple, says:

Thus says the Lord GOD: No foreigner, uncircumcised in heart and flesh, of all the foreigners who are among the people of Israel, shall enter my sanctuary. (Ezek 44:9 NRSV)

God's own word demonstrates that circumcision is the means of joining the family of Abraham and the people of God. Indeed, it is key to participation in the age to come. Circumcision, however, has great moral significance as well, as do all of the Jewish laws and customs when viewed symbolically and observed in both mind and both (see Philo *Migr. Abr.* 89). Circumcision "is a symbol for the cutting away of pleasures and the passions" of the flesh that lead the reason astray from its proper course, as well as an acknowledgment that the human male is not capable of producing offspring without the help of God, and therefore also a remedy for pride (Philo *Migr. Abr.* 92; *Spec. Leg.* 1.2.9-11; *Quaest. in Gen.* 3.48). The rite may also be seen as a symbolic initiation into a way of life that will make for mastery of the passions—those desires, sensations and emotions that belong to our human nature and so often hinder us from following the dictates of virtue and righteousness.

2. *Torah as the way to perfection.* Circumcision is a good beginning, but it is only an initiation. God's covenant was made with Israel in the Torah, and all who hope to share in the blessings of Israel and avoid the curses on the disobedient must submit to the yoke of Torah, as it stands written, "Cursed be everyone who does not walk in all the things written in the book of the law, to do them" (Deut 27:26). The person who keeps the commands of Torah will live to God by means of Torah (Lev 18:5).

The way of life prescribed by Torah, however, is far from a collection of barbaric, ethnocentric rules. For the person who is confused about how to make progress in living a God-pleasing life of virtue, as the newly converted might certainly be, Torah provides the God-given guide for the perplexed. Jewish apologetic for the Torah focused on the virtues that a Torah-observant way of life nurtured. Although there are many texts that speak to this topic (*Letter of Aristeas* and the works of Philo being among the more famous), 4 Maccabees provides perhaps the most informative background.

Four Maccabees presents itself as a philosophical "demonstration" of the thesis that the mind that has been trained by following Torah masters the passions of the flesh (4 Macc 1:1, 13-17). Rising above these passions was a central topic of Greco-Roman philosophical ethics, since the passions—whether emotions like fear or anger, sensations like pleasure or pain, or desires like greed or lust—were deemed the most potent enemy of living a virtuous life. Unchecked, the passions of the flesh would clamor louder than the reasoning faculty, derailing a person's commitment to virtue and ability to walk in line with virtue.[7] The battle against these forces became the true battle for honor, the truly noble athletic competition. The Jewish law, however, provides a complete exercise regimen for the strengthening of the rational faculty and the subduing of the passions. The dietary laws and prohibitions against coveting teach self-control (4 Macc 1:31—2:6); the regulations concerning debt release and leaving the gleanings of the har-

---

[7]See David A. deSilva, *4 Maccabees*, Sheffield Guides to Apocrypha and Pseudepigrapha (Sheffield: Sheffield Academic Press, 1998), pp. 52-58.

vest subdue greed (4 Macc 2:7-9); limits on vengeance and actions against enemies subdue the passion of enmity or hate (4 Macc 2:14). Torah is lauded as that which "teaches us self-control, so that we master all pleasures and desires, . . . courage, so that we endure any suffering willingly; . . . justice, so that in all our dealings we act impartially, and . . . piety, so that with proper reverence we worship the only living God" (4 Macc 5:23-24 NRSV).

This is precisely the kind of argumentation that the rival teachers would have had ready at hand to use when they encountered the Galatian converts, still painfully at the mercy of their fleshly impulses and desires. The final chapters of Paul's letter, far from being an appendix providing some moral guidance, is a necessary part of his counterargument.[8] Indeed, the whole driving force of the situation behind Galatians may have been the believers' quest for a reliable guide to virtue and for the discipline that would develop virtue in their lives and inhibit vice. The rival teachers presented the Torah as the best trainer in virtue, the way to perfection in terms of ethical progress, a proven discipline for mastering the "passions of the flesh." Paul then would have to demonstrate that the Galatians had already received all that they needed to rise above the passions and embody the virtues that God sought for in God's people.

3. *Whom should the Galatians trust?* Both Paul's defensive mode in Galatians and the time-honored practice of attacking the credibility of rivals in order to make room for one's own position make it highly likely that the rival teachers had also called Paul's authority and reliability into question. Judging from Paul's response, their attack on his credibility probably contained the following elements:

• The rival teachers came representing the Jerusalem apostles, who supported a much stricter observance of Torah than Paul. James was well known for his piety, even among non-Christian Jews. Peter had wavered on this issue, but the rival teachers might even have cited the Antioch incident to prove that Peter had come to his senses and remained true to the original, Torah-observant gospel (Gal 2:11-14).

• Paul's apostleship and knowledge of the gospel are dependent on the Jerusalem pillars, and his travels to Jerusalem demonstrate his dependence. If Paul's message differs from what the rival teachers claim to be the message of the Jerusalem church, then it is Paul who has been an unreliable and unfaithful messenger (Gal 1—2).

• Paul preaches to suit the audience—he is a people pleaser (Gal 1:10). He preaches circumcision in other instances, but he probably thought that would make his message less welcome or successful here, so he left it out (Gal 5:11; 6:17).

Unlike Paul, the rival teachers would give the Galatians the whole truth about the gospel. Even though it involved difficulties, like the rite of circumcision, they would not keep anything back from the Galatian Christians just to win their assent or avoid more difficult arguments. The Galatians could trust them to bring them the next step in their journey toward righteousness.

PAUL'S RESPONSE IN GALATIANS

What is at stake in Galatia? The rival teachers present circumcision and some degree of Torah observance as completely complementary with the Galatian converts' trust in Jesus. Indeed, it is the next step forward in their spiritual journey to becoming full-fledged children of Abraham and in their ethical journey to a transformed life of virtue. What the rival

---

[8]This is the central thesis of J. M. G. Barclay, *Obeying the Truth: Paul's Ethics in Galatia* (Minneapolis: Fortress, 1981), an exceptionally well-written and helpful investigation of this question.

teachers would join together, Paul radically rends asunder as he opens his letter.

After his customary expansion of the epistolary greeting formula ("Sender to Recipient, greetings"), Paul usually opens a letter with a thanksgiving or benediction (cf. Rom 1:8; 1 Cor 1:4; 2 Cor 1:3; Phil 1:3; 1 Thess 1:2; Philem 4). Here, however, he opens with an expression of shock and amazement (Gal 1:6). For him, the course of action they are contemplating is not a complement to their faith in Jesus but an act of desertion and repudiation of their divine Benefactor. The message of the rival teachers is not a second installment of the gospel but a different gospel, which is not truly another gospel at all but a perversion of the true gospel (Gal 1:7). With two solemn curse formulas (Gal 1:8-9) Paul underscores the complete incompatibility of the message they are hearing with the gospel they had received. This opening is rhetorically effective indeed. It captures the hearers' attention (the main goal of the exordium, or opening of a speech) by presenting their situation as one of the gravest peril, forcing them to be open to reconsidering the relationship between faith in Jesus and circumcision.

But why should Paul consider these so fundamentally at odds? The answer seems to lie in Paul's understanding of the universal scope of God's new outpouring of favor. God was at last bringing together Jew and Gentile into one, united people (Gal 3:28)—the oneness of the God who is God both of Jew and Gentile (Rom 3:29) being reflected in not only the new people being formed in the name of Jesus but also the single basis on which both Jew and Gentile were brought into that united people (Gal 2:15-16). That basis is not Torah, the observance of which had functioned to keep Jew separate from Gentile for a limited amount of time, for "all flesh shall not be justified by works of law" (Gal 2:16), which pertains only to Israel. Rather, that basis is God's generosity toward all as expressed in Jesus' death on behalf of humanity, and that death fulfills the promise made to Abraham at last by making him the spiritual ancestor of many nations.

Paul consistently sets "grace" in opposition to "works of Torah"[9] at key junctures throughout Galatians (Gal 2:21; 5:4), in part because Torah was a necessary trapping of human "immaturity," and in part because what God has graciously done in Jesus *for all* now makes possible what Torah had not made possible, namely, a life lived truly to God, for God and in the power of God. Paul's own story is a living example of this premise, for it is precisely when he was most fully engaged in the works of Torah that he was God's enemy, and it was precisely then that God graciously transformed Paul into an apostle of God's righteousness in Christ. After Jesus' death a *return* to works of Torah as if they could *add* to what Jesus had done would amount to a repudiation of Jesus' ability to connect us to God and an insultingly low evaluation of the potential of the Spirit, the promised gift won for us at such cost, to transform our lives.

What is at stake for Paul, then, is ultimately the meaningfulness of Jesus' death on the cross, "for if righteousness is through the law, then Christ died gratuitously" (Gal 2:21). The

---

[9]Paul's polemic against "works of the law" is not a polemic against "good works," as this is commonly but erroneously understood. Rather, Paul opposes the continued observance of a boundary-maintaining code, not only in the observance of the more obvious differentiators like circumcision, kosher laws and sabbath, but also as an entire body of laws given to *Israel* as a mark of her distinctiveness and separation from the Gentiles (see Dunn, *Theology of Paul's Letter,* pp. 354-59). It is not in maintaining the ethnic identity of Israel (through such "works of Torah") that we are conformed to God's character or brought in line with God's purpose, but only through faith in Jesus, which results in the life of the Spirit being born in us so that we are born to life before God. Paul certainly expects the Spirit to produce all manner of "good works" in the life of the disciple (Rom 2:6-11; 6:12-13; Gal 5:13-25; Eph 2:10).

The "Faith of Jesus Christ" in Galatians

The phrase "the faith of Jesus" or "the faith of Christ" or some equivalent appears at several crucial points in connection with how Paul understands justification to come to human beings (see Rom 3:22, 26; Gal 2:16, 20; 3:22; Phil 3:9). In Galatians we find it in the following contexts:

> Knowing that a person is not justified by works of law except through *the faith of Jesus Christ,* even we [Jewish Christians] have believed in Christ Jesus in order that we might be justified on the basis of *the faith of Christ* and not on the basis of works of law. (Gal 2:16)

> But Scripture has shut all things up together under sin, in order that the promise might be given on the basis of *the faith of Jesus Christ* to those who trust. (Gal 3:22)

The traditional Protestant interpretation of this phrase has been to read it as "faith in Jesus," so that the Christian's faith is what is operative at every turn.

A careful study by Morna Hooker, however, brought the grammatical ambiguity of the phrase forcefully to the attention of scholarship, and an endless string of articles and books now sport the words "the faith of Christ" in the title in response to this question. According to her, and to many who have accepted her conclusions, Paul uses this phrase to draw attention to Jesus' own faithfulness toward God as the effective cause by which the possibility of justification has come into the world. This is certainly brought to the fore in Romans (see Rom 3:22-26; 5:18-19) and so deserves careful consideration as an option here as well. This has the advantage of avoiding the redundancy inherent in the traditional interpretation: for example, "in order that the promise might be given on the basis of believing in Jesus Christ to those who believe [in Jesus Christ]" (Gal 3:22). It also has the advantage of observing the parallelism between "faith of Jesus" and "faith of Abraham" in Galatians. No one would suggest that we translate the latter as "believing in Abraham." And to the incredulous question of James Dunn—"Did Christ also 'believe' as Abraham did?"[a]—we would have to answer, Yes, in fact Christ *did* believe in the God who gives life from the dead and walked forward in obedience accordingly.

Taking issue with Hooker, Dunn noticed that *pistin theou* unambiguously means "faith in God" in Mark 11:22—the context clarifies the grammatical ambiguity.[b] He finds similar contextual clues in Galatians that would lead him strongly to affirm "faith in Christ" as the proper understanding. Thus in Galatians 2:16, Paul speaks of himself and other Jewish Christians "believing in Christ Jesus" as a contextual indicator that "faith of Jesus Christ" must also denote the believers' faith. Stuhlmacher also claims this to be "unambiguously" the meaning of "faith of Christ" in this passage.[c] For this to be true, however, we have to accept the redundancies of both Galatians 2:16 and 3:22 as Paul's desire to repeat himself and make his emphasis clear,[d] rather than

---

[a]Dunn, *Theology of Paul's Letter,* p. 382
[b]Ibid., pp. 379-85.
[c]Stuhlmacher, *Revisiting Paul's Doctrine of Justification,* p. 65.
[d]Dunn, *Theology of Paul's Letter,* p. 381.

connect the references to "believing" to the Christians and the references to "faith/faithfulness" to Christ—an equally plausible and certainly a more rhetorically elegant solution.

The problem is largely solved if we are willing to see an emphasis both on Jesus' faith/faithfulness and our trust in and faithfulness toward Jesus. Dunn, in fact, admits that there is more cause for reading both Jesus' faith/faithfulness and our trust in Romans 3:22-26.[e] All of this is also perfectly in keeping with the kinds of patron-broker-client relationships being articulated in these passages. Jesus acted in faithful obedience toward God and secured benefits for those who, in turn, trust Jesus' efficacy as a mediator of God's benefits and walk forward faithfully in that trust. We will return to this important theological question in chapter sixteen (on Romans), the other text in which the phrase plays a prominent role in Paul's explanation of how God's righteousness is revealed.

---

[e]Ibid., p. 383.

---

very "grace/favor/gift of God" extended through Jesus is at stake (Gal 2:21). Will the Galatians appreciate and accept what God has done for humanity in the cross of Christ? Will they trust the efficacy of that single act of costly obedience to join them to the family of Abraham and the family of God without trying to turn the clock back to a time before Jesus' death? Will they place sufficient value on the resource God has provided in the Spirit—ever so much more effective and empowering a guide to the heart of God than Torah—to lead them into righteousness? All of these questions are wrapped up in the catchwords *grace* and *trust* that so dominate this letter.

Whom should the Galatians trust? Paul is mainly occupied in the first two chapters of Galatians with explaining why he should be trusted, most likely because he has learned that his rivals have suggested that he is not entirely trustworthy. He spends a great deal of space recounting his own direct commissioning by God and affirms his refusal to adapt his message out of a desire to "please" people, which he considers incompatible with being Christ's slave (Gal 1:10). The narrative that he crafts in Galatians 1:11—2:14 is not an attempt at autobiography. Rather, it is Paul's attempt to restore his credibility in the eyes of his converts. To do this he turns to a narrative demonstration, setting the facts of his past conduct and interaction with the Jerusalem apostles straight and giving these facts their proper interpretation. In this defense Paul is intent on demonstrating the following:

- His commissioning and message come directly from God, and so they must be deemed more authentic and authoritative than all rivals.
- His authority is not dependent on or derivative from the Jerusalem apostles.
- Nevertheless, he has worked collegially with them and his apostleship has been recognized as valid by them.
- He is the one who, in the face of any and all pressures, has walked "straightforwardly in line with the truth of the gospel" (Gal 2:14), the truth God revealed to him and reveals through him, and so he is most plausibly the one doing that now in the Galatian situation.

EXEGETICAL SKILL
Rhetorical Criticism (2) — Appeals to "Ethos"

As he analyzed effective oratory, Aristotle discovered that effective speakers would use three different kinds of proof. One, of course, is proof of a more formal and logical kind—the examples, analogies and supporting arguments marshaled in support of a position defended or course of action urged. The other two kinds of proof might seem less obvious. A speaker could enhance the persuasive effects of an address by "putting the hearer into a certain frame of mind" (*Rhet.* 1.2.3), that is, arousing emotions in the hearers that will move them in the direction the speaker wishes them to go. These are called appeals to pathos, or emotion. Of paramount importance, however, is the speaker's demonstration of his or her "moral character":

> The orator persuades by moral character when his speech is delivered in such a manner as to render him worthy of confidence. . . . But this confidence must be due to the speech itself, not to any preconceived idea of the speaker's character. . . . Moral character, so to say, constitutes the most effective means of proof. (*Rhet.* 1.2.4)

This observation would still hold true four hundred years later, as Quintilian compiled his compendium of wisdom and technique learned from a lifetime of successful public speaking:

> But what really carries greatest weight in deliberative speeches is the authority of the speaker. For he, who would have all men trust his judgment as to what is expedient and honourable, should both possess and be regarded as possessing genuine wisdom and excellence of character. (*Inst. Orat.* 3.8.13)

These rhetorical theorists are only recording what, on reflection, all would recognize as common sense. A speaker must have our trust and confidence if she or he is to persuade us to do anything; conversely, questions about a speaker's credibility prove the quickest and most effective means to undermining his or her message.

A speaker should show throughout a speech that he or she possesses "good sense, virtue, and goodwill" (Aristotle *Rhet.* 2.1.5). We trust those whom we deem well-disposed toward us, rather than those who seem antagonistic or derogatory; we trust those who embody the values we hold dear; we trust those who speak and reason sensibly, and who seem knowledgeable about those matters they speak of. In an environment of competing speakers (like Galatians), calling the credibility of the rival speakers into question also contributes to effective persuasion, since a speaker is as much concerned to defuse the persuasive power of opponents as to enhance his or her own. As we probe the rhetorical strategy of texts more deeply, therefore, we will attend not only to the logical arguments advanced but also to the ways a speaker establishes his or her own credibility within the speech and, where applicable, seeks to erode the credibility of rival speakers in that situation.

While these appeals to ethos can and do appear throughout an address, rhetorical theorists suggest that we should be especially alert to them at the beginning (the *exordium*) and at the end (the *peroratio*) of an address. While the main purpose of the opening of an address is to announce the theme and to capture the hearers' attention, showing that the question at hand is one of importance, the speaker will also address "all that helps to destroy or create prejudice" (Aristotle *Rhet.* 3.14.6-7; see also *Rhet. ad Alex.* 1436a33-37). Similarly, a conclusion to an address should "dispose the hearer favourably towards oneself and unfavourably towards the adversary," while also providing a summary statement of the speech and arousing the appropriate emotions in the audience (Aristotle *Rhet.* 3.19.1).

As we turn to Galatians 1:1-10 and 6:11-18, undisputedly the opening and closing of this address, we find Paul attending rather closely and extensively to appeals to ethos.

- Galatians 1:1: As Paul expands his self-designation as the sender of the letter, he emphasizes his direct authorization by God to act as an apostle of the gospel, denying that he relies on any human authorization. It is highly likely, given the extensive treatment of this subject in Galatian 1:11—2:10, that Paul is already working to "destroy prejudice" against himself.

- Galatians 1:7: Paul begins to create prejudice against the rival teachers by referring to them as "agitators" among the Galatians and perverters of the Gospel (see also Gal 5:7, 10), going so far as to call down a curse on them (v. 8). Creating distance between the hearers and these rival speakers will continue to be a major goal throughout Galatians.

- Galatians 1:10: Paul concludes the *exordium* by affirming his freedom from courting human opinion, and therefore he affirms his complete reliability as a proclaimer of truth. Unlike his opponents (see below), he will not be swayed from holding to the true gospel because that gospel might make him unpopular or even bring him hardship. He understands that being a people-pleaser is incompatible with being a reliable servant of Christ.

- Galatians 6:12: Paul suggests that the rival teachers are operating out of selfish and cowardly motives, not because they are well disposed toward the Galatians. A desire to avoid persecution (from non-Christian Jews) motivates them to circumcise the Galatians in order to make both the Galatians and the gospel palatable to other human beings. They are conforming the gospel to what will look good to the people they fear. Acting from selfish motives rather than for the good of the Galatians, the character of the rival teachers will be diminished in the church's eyes.

- Galatians 6:13: Moreover, the rival teachers are themselves insincere, failing to keep the Torah themselves even as they attempt to fasten this yoke upon the Galatian converts.[a] They are promoting circumcision not because they are wholeheartedly devoted to Torah, but because this will enhance their prestige in the eyes of their significant others, the larger Jewish population. (They want to "boast in your flesh.")

- Galatians 6:14: Paul, however, is free from such selfish motives as trying to make the Galatians into a trophy for himself.

- Galatians 6:17: Finally, Paul points to his own scars as proof of his sincerity and reliability. Unlike the rival teachers, he is willing to suffer beatings and whippings for telling the truth about what God has done in Jesus, however unpopular this has made him with those same people whom the rivals fear.

Before reading the remainder of "Whom should the Galatians trust?" experiment with identifying appeals to ethos in the body of the letter (Gal 1:11—6:10), especially in Galatians 1:11—2:14; 4:12-20; 5:2-12. Where does Paul speak about the rival teachers? What motives does he ascribe to them? Are these motives noble or base? Where does Paul speak about his own motives? How does he convey a sense that he can be trusted to tell the truth, even when others are lying? How does he impress on the hearers that his gospel is authoritative? Why, in a situation of conflicting messages about the gospel, should the Galatians trust Paul's version? How does Paul convey a sense of goodwill toward the hearers so that they will know he is well-disposed toward them? How does Paul render the hearers well-disposed toward him as well? As you engage any text from the vantage point of such questions, you are exploring a fundamental aspect of that text's persuasive strategy and power.

---

[a]Exactly what Paul has in mind here is unclear. Nanos suggests that Paul refers to the commandment to love one's neighbor as oneself (*Irony of Galatians,* pp. 227-28). It is not that the rival teachers are lax in their Torah observance but that they are seeking their self-interests as they pressure the Galatian Gentile Christians to do what is against their own best interests in Christ.

Paul begins the body of his letter with the customary verb "I want you to know" (*gnōrizo*, Gal 1:11). The first major point he must stress is the divine origin of the gospel he originally brought to the Galatians (Gal 1:11-12). The first and best reason they should resist the leading of the rival teachers is that Paul brought them exactly and fully the message God had for them. As proof of this bold claim, he reminds them of the encounter that turned his own life around. Paul had been more on fire for the Torah than his rivals could ever be. He was so zealous for the covenant that he persecuted Jewish Christians as threats to that covenant (in the tradition of Phinehas and Mattathias). Paul emphasizes his former self to make two points: first, no one can pretend to know more about the Torah-observant way of life than Paul; second, only God indeed could have turned such a person into what he is now, a preacher of a Torah-free gospel (Gal 1:15-16, 23-24).

The revelation of Jesus Christ that God granted Paul was all at once a conversion, a commission and a communication of the gospel. While Paul doubtless would continue to work out the implications of that communication for decades, he insists that the whole gospel was given to him there *in nuce*. He did not rely, in other words, on any human being teaching him about God's plan in Christ. As support he asserts that he neither "conferred with flesh and blood" nor "went up to Jerusalem" to consult the human leaders of the Jesus movement; instead he spent three years on his own (Gal 1:16-17), preaching the gospel in the Nabatean kingdom. Only then did he go to Jerusalem to make Peter's acquaintance, meeting James the Lord's brother as well (but no other!), staying a mere two weeks. Paul went not as a schoolboy but as a fellow apostle and preacher of the gospel. At this point Paul in-vokes a solemn oath (Gal 1:20), alerting us again to the fact that he is making a quasi-formal case and not merely sharing his faith journey. The next eleven to fourteen years (depending on how we count the "fourteen years" in Gal 2:1) are spent preaching in Syria and Cilicia, so that he remained "unknown" by face to the Christians in Judea.

The narrative thus far shows Paul's independence of the Jerusalem leadership and dependence on God for his commission and for the message he proclaimed (the first two points listed above). As Paul recounts at length this private meeting between James, John and Peter on the one hand, and himself and Barnabas on the other hand, Paul moves to the third point, namely, the Jerusalem apostles' validation of his apostleship and message.[10] Paul insists that he goes to Jerusalem at the behest of God ("according to a revelation," Gal 2:2), rather than as a lackey of the Jerusalem apostles. There he lays out the gospel he had been preaching (Gal 1:21-24), bringing along an uncircumcised Gentile convert named Titus (Gal 2:1, 3). If the Jerusalem apostles felt the need to correct or supplement any aspect of Paul's gospel, that would have been the occasion. Instead, seeing the hand of God to be at work in Paul and Baranabas's missionary endeavors just as in their own (Gal 2:8), and understanding this to be an outworking of God's favor (Gal 2:9), the Jerusalem apostles affirmed Paul and Barnabas as partners in mission and "added nothing" to Paul's message (Gal 2:6). Why, then, should anyone be calling for circumcision of Gentiles now? The Galatians should take this as evidence that Paul's gospel has the recognition of the Jerusalem apostles, whatever the rivals may have said to the contrary.

Where then comes the impetus toward Torah-observance or bringing the Gentile con-

---

[10]For a fuller investigation of this tightrope Paul is walking, see James D. G. Dunn, "The Relationship Between Paul and Jerusalem according to Galatians 1 and 2," *NTS* 28 (1982): 461-78.

verts under the strict tutelage of that out-moded guardian? According to Paul, "certain false brothers" already made their presence and wishes known at that private meeting with the apostles (Gal 2:4), presumably raising the suggestion that Titus needed to be circumcised. Paul paints these people as enemies of the "freedom" that Christ has brought to Paul's converts, wishing to "enslave" them afresh. Paul, however, firmly resisted them at that time, emerging as the champion of the "truth of the gospel," preserving that truth for the Galatians to enjoy subsequently. Because Titus went away uncircumcised, the Jerusalem apostles would be understood to concur with Paul, not the false brothers.

The narrative demonstration concludes with the painful "Antioch incident." Paul must display his own constancy by describing the inconstant behavior of his apostolic colleagues. Both Jewish and Gentile Christians were part of the church in Syrian Antioch, and they displayed their unity, among other ways, by eating at a common table. Peter himself appears to have understood that such an arrangement, though in violation of Jewish purity regulations, was perfectly in keeping with the purity of the new people God had formed from Jews and Gentiles. The "truth of the gospel"—the "one body" fashioned by God out of Jew and Gentile, slave and free, male and female, all of whom are equally acceptable to God on the basis of Jesus' death—was being lived out as Peter, Paul, Barnabas, Jewish Christians and Gentile Christians all shared the common life of the Spirit and had fellowship at table as one people, one body.

At some point people from James (or claiming to be from James) arrived at Antioch and pressured Peter to return to a more respectable way of life for an "apostle to the circumcision."

It is clear from this that the "agreement" described in Galatians 2:6-10 did not settle the issue of how Jews and Gentiles were to regulate their behavior in a mixed congregation. From the perspective of the "people from James," the gospel did not free Jewish Christians from keeping kosher, whatever else it might mean for their lives. Peter yielded to their pressure and began eating at a separate, kosher table.[11] This withdrawal apparently stung the conscience of the Antiochene Jewish Christians, who all gave in to the pressure to observe kosher laws and eat separately from the Gentile converts.

The people from James were concerned only about the Christian *Jews'* adherence to Torah, and quite possibly only Peter's behavior. It was not their intent to make the Gentiles into Jews. The message this sent to the Gentiles, however, was quite clear: You are not really acceptable to God on the basis of your trust in Jesus and your reception of the Spirit; if you want to find acceptance before God, and enjoy fellowship with God's people, you must make yourselves clean by circumcision and Torah-observance. Paul confronts Peter (and the other Jewish Christians as well), accusing them of not living in line with "the truth of the gospel" (Gal 2:14). Paul understood that the Christian Jews' action placed an unspoken requirement on the Gentiles, undermining the sufficiency of the saving act of Jesus. Once again Paul courageously and uncompromisingly stands up for the truth of the gospel—at a time when even Peter and Barnabas had been pressured by concern for human opinion to depart from walking in line with that gospel. Other than Paul, then, whom can the Galatians trust to tell them the truth of God, unaffected by concern for human approval?

The Antioch incident provides a close anal-

---

[11]J. L. Martyn suggests that Peter did so out of regard for his own mission to the Jews in Antioch, the people from James having pointed out how detrimental to his witness his nonobservant lifestyle would be (*Galatians*, AB 33A [Garden City, N.Y.: Doubleday, 1997], p. 242).

ogy to the Galatian situation (though it does not make any statement about the identity of the rival teachers).[12] Paul avers that the rival teachers, like Peter, seek to uphold the old boundaries drawn around the Jewish people by the Torah because they are afraid to tell their fellow Jews the truth about God's abolition of those boundaries in his new outpouring of favor in Christ. They do not, in other words, "walk in line with the truth of the gospel." Just as Paul spoke the truth in Antioch—quite possibly to his own hurt in terms of losing that argument—he will speak the truth in Galatia, without consideration for his own advantage or what is politic.

Who is the heir of the divine promises? Abraham was regarded as the common ancestor of the Jewish people, the people of God. To be a child of Abraham, then, was to be part of God's people. The rival teachers had a strong argument in favor of circumcision, insofar as this was prescribed in Scripture as the prerequisite for being part of Abraham's family. For Paul, however, it was Abraham's trust in God and not his circumcised flesh that made him the recipient of God's promise and resulted in his being accounted "righteous" in God's sight. In this way Abraham could indeed become the ancestor of many nations, the vehicle for God's blessing "all the nations" (Gal 3:8). Circumcision marked a person as a Jew; trust marked a person as an heir of Abraham, whether Jew or Gentile.

Paul invokes the strongest proof for this claim at the outset of his body of proofs (Gal 3:1—4:21), pointing to the Galatians' own reception of the Holy Spirit. Theorists advised that a strong argument, if not the most compelling, should be placed up front. This way the speaker would convince the audience early on, with all following proofs serving to confirm the hearers in their decision. The Gala-tians had received the Holy Spirit on the basis of their response of trust to the hearing of the gospel (Gal 3:2-5). This proves God's complete acceptance of them as Gentiles purely on the basis of their commitment to Jesus.[13] Their trust in Jesus was enough to render them holy to the Lord; there was no need to perform the traditional rites by which Jews had kept themselves holy to the Lord and distinct from the Gentile nations.

Paul, moreover, identifies this Holy Spirit as the very content of the blessing of Abraham that was promised to the nations, the promised gift (Gal 3:14). On what basis could Paul make this identification? First, in the experience of the early church, the Spirit came to all who trusted in Jesus, whether Jews or Gentiles. It was as universal in scope as had been the promise to Abraham: "in you all the nations will be blessed" (Gen 12:3; Gal 3:8). Second, the Spirit signified the believers' adoption by God as sons and daughters (Gal 4:6-7). The phenomenology of being filled with the Spirit led the early Christians, who thereafter called on God as "Abba, Father" (Gal 4:6), to understand this as a spiritual begetting by God's own self, making them spiritual children of Abraham (Gal 3:26-29; 4:21-28) just like Isaac was the spiritual child of Abraham, having been born on the basis of God's promise rather than the deeds of flesh. Paul draws on the powerful image of the ritual of baptism, asserting that in that ritual Christ covered them like a garment and former distinctions were no longer of any value, any meaning (Gal 3:26-28). Humanity was no longer to be divided into opposing dyads—Jews on the one hand, Greeks on the other; slaves on the one hand, free on the other; male on the one hand, female on the other. People were no longer to relate to one another based on the divisions and prejudices inherent in these divisions. Rather, these op-

---

[12]Ben Witherington III, *Grace in Galatia* (Grand Rapids: Eerdmans, 1998), p. 24.
[13]A similar point is made by the extensive episode of Cornelius and its interpretation in Acts 10—11; 15.

positions and dyads have been resolved in Christ, with whom each Christian has been clothed, so that "Christ's" becomes the only term of significance to define the identity and belonging of each. The Galatians may be sure, therefore, that they are Abraham's children and heirs of the promise since they have been fully immersed in Christ.

Paul reminds the Galatian converts of these formative experiences (which probably also entailed their ongoing awareness of the operation of the Spirit in their lives and in their congregational life), asking them what more they could possibly hope to gain by attending to such material concerns as circumcision or food regulations (Gal 3:2-5). Paul relegates the realm of Torah's efficacy to the sphere of the "flesh," which is a catchword throughout Galatians for all that is impotent to effect God's righteousness (as in Gal 4:21-31) and even all that actively opposes the realization of God's righteousness (as in Gal 5:13-25). He presents them with the absurdity of their situation: they have already received the Spirit and can only make progress by heeding the Spirit, not by submitting to something of merely fleshly power.

Paul's argument proceeds by creating a matrix of antinomies, of contrasting irreconcilable pairs. The first of these focuses on the "blessing" versus the "curse" (Gal 3:6-14). Abraham is identified as the vehicle for God's blessing for all people (Gal 3:8), and Abraham's "trust" in God and "faithfulness" toward God qualify him for "blessing." All who show the same trust in God's ability and desire to bestow favor rather than by performing some ritual act on the flesh of the foreskin share in the "blessing" together with "faithful Abraham" (Gal 3:9). The Torah, on the other hand, becomes the vehicle for "curse." Here, Paul may well turn a verse used by the rival teachers— "Cursed be everyone who does not remain in all the things written in the book of the law, to do them" (Deut 27:26)—on its head. This text would more naturally be read to promote Torah-obedience, threatening the curse on those who neglect its decrees.[14] Paul uses it, however, to assert Torah's essential character as "curse" rather than "blessing," which in any case belongs to the promise and to trust. As support for this assertion, Paul brings together two Scriptures that (somewhat artificially)

---

[14]A major crux of interpretation emerges here as one must decide if those who rely on works of the law are "under a curse" because it is categorically impossible for anyone to do all the commandments without misstep (the traditional interpretation, recently upheld by Seyoon Kim (*Paul and the New Perspective* [Grand Rapids: Eerdmans, 2001]. pp. 141-43) or for some other reason. According to the proponents of the new perspective, Jews did not understand Torah as a collection of laws that they had to fulfill perfectly or else fail to attain God's favor. Rather, the commandments of Torah constituted the way of life they were to embody in response to God's favor, and the sacrificial system was God's provision for imperfect people trying to live out this pattern of life. The "curse" of the law did not fall on those who failed to do everything perfectly but on those who sinned willfully, or committed idolatry—in short, those who turned away from the covenant God.

Against this new perspective Kim argues that Jewish rabbis did indeed think that failing to keep one commandment would result in the curse, or in death. Kim refers the reader to Rabbi Gamaliel's weeping at the implications of "he that does them shall live," that one must do *all* the commandments in order to live, and not just one (*b. Sanhedrin* 81a.). Of course, Rabbi Akiba later retorts that in doing each one individually is life. Even if Gamaliel's response is to be interpreted as Kim suggests, then, it is countermanded within the tradition itself.

In invoking Deuteronomy 27:26; 28:58, Paul may be thinking beyond the performance of individual commandments and considering the observance of the entirety of the Law. This would include heeding the prophet whom God would "raise up" after Moses (Deut 18:18, understood in early Christian discourse to refer to Christ, as in Acts 3:22-23), and the model of Abraham, whose trust in God the readers of Torah are taught to imitate. Through their zeal for the Torah and their resistance to what God was doing in Christ in the new phase of salvation history, Israel had made itself an enemy of God (Rom 10:2-4; 11:28), refusing to submit in obedience to God. As such, their "doing" of Torah was only partial and misguided, so they did not in fact "observe and obey all the things written in the book of the law" (Deut 27:26; 28:58, as given in Gal 3:10 NRSV). In trying to keep the Sinai covenant alive after Christ in the way that was appropriate before Christ, they actually turned away from the covenant and fell under the curse.

drive a wedge between "trust" and the Torah. Habakkuk 2:4 bears witness that "the righteous person will live on the basis of trust," which is a different mode of living than found under Torah, where "the one who does them [the works of Torah] will live by means of them" (Lev 18:5). If someone hopes to be a "righteous person," then, he or she is compelled to look to the path opened up by trust in Jesus and by the gift of the Spirit.

The death of Jesus removes humanity from the sphere of the curse. The Messiah himself died under Torah's curse as a sinner, since "cursed is everyone who hangs on a tree" (Deut 21:23),[15] but he did so in obedience to the God who raised Jesus and thereby showed Torah itself to be out of alignment with God's righteousness. This decisive act brought to an end the period of the Torah's authority, and it is this topic that dominates the remainder of the proof section of the letter.

The promise given to Abraham and the fulfillment of that promise in the pouring out of the Spirit on all who are "in Christ" (Gal 3:14) make the promise, and not the law, the central focus of Paul's model of salvation history. For Paul, the period between the giving of the Torah and the "fullness of time" (Gal 4:4), when Christ came and died, constituted a great parenthesis in the plan of God. With regard to its ultimate value, Paul poses an argument from analogy. Once a person's will is made and ratified, no one can add to it. Therefore, when God bequeathed his inheritance to Abraham and his "seed," the Torah that was added 430 years later cannot be taken as an amendment to that promise. It must have some other, more limited role. The promise, however, comes independently of Torah to Abraham and to his "seed," which Paul takes not in the collective sense (the many "offspring") but in a singular sense (the one "offspring," Christ). All who are in Christ therefore are incorporated into the promise quite apart from Torah's stipulations.

The period of the Law, then, is likened to the time during which an heir is a minor child. The Torah pressed on Israel like a pedagogue—a household slave in charge of disciplining his master's young children, escorting them back and forth from their lessons, and the like—corraling and hemming in the children under his care. For such children life is no different from the life of a slave. At this point two more antinomies are introduced that will be used to much effect throughout the remainder of the letter: "slavery" versus "adoption," and "slavery" versus "freedom." At the same time the non-Jews were "slaves" as well to the "elemental principles (or spirits) of the cosmos" (Gal 4:3, 9), powers that pose as gods, or at least exercise that level of power over human beings, but are none at all (Gal 4:8). What Paul has in mind by these "elemental principles" (*stoicheia*) is a matter of some debate: at least the term denotes that which guides, limits and constrains human beings in their thoughts, behaviors and interactions, keeping them in a form of ideological and systemic bondage.

A decisive turning point in history has already passed, however—the "fullness of time" (Gal 4:4) when "faith came" (Gal 3:23, 25). Genesis 49:10 speaks of a critical juncture in the shepherding of the people of God: "The scepter shall not depart from Judah *until he comes* whose right it is." This coming one, for Paul, was Christ, whose coming spelled the end of the period of Torah ("until the offspring would come to whom the promise had been made," Gal 3:19 NRSV).[16] Drawing on these traditions of the advent of a particular figure whose coming would signal a decisive shift in salvation history, Paul declares that Jesus' death and resurrection mark a kind of rite of passage from which there is no turning back. Wherever

---

[15]Martin Hengel, *The Pre-Christian Paul* (Valley Forge, Penn.: Trinity Press International, 1991), p. 83.
[16]N. T. Wright, *What Saint Paul Really Said* (Grand Rapids: Eerdmans, 1997), p. 54.

the gospel is preached and received in faith, and wherever the Holy Spirit is poured out by God on the converted, people come of age, as it were. Their time of minority, when they are subject to these slavish pedagogues and stewards, comes to an end, and they receive the freedom of children who have reached their maturity and enter into their inheritance. A new relationship opens up between humans and God through Jesus, the relationship based on the Spirit of God dwelling in the human heart.

In light of this model of history, Paul's indignation at the thought of imposing Torah observance on Gentile converts becomes more comprehensible. Such a move would amount to a retroversion to a bygone era. Just as the adult cannot again be a child, the person who drinks deeply of God's Spirit cannot again look backward to the Torah for the way forward. More insidiously, turning back to the "works of Torah" would repudiate the freedom, the new and glorious status of "heir" and "son or daughter," that Christ won for the believer through his death "under the Torah" (Gal 4:4-5). In light of these considerations, it is incomprehensible to Paul that his Galatian converts would seriously contemplate taking on the yoke of Torah, that passé pedagogue.

Paul may have encountered the charge that to neglect Torah on account of Christ is to make Jesus into an agent of transgression (Gal 2:17). Paul asserts that this would only be true if someone were to reestablish Torah as the guiding principle of his or her life after coming to faith (Gal 2:18). Only the return to Torah makes a person a sinner. In Christ, however, a person is dead to Torah. For Paul, all that matters now is cultivating the life of the Spirit within us, or as he puts it, all that matters is Christ living in and through the believer—this is the new creation (Gal 2:20; 4:19; 6:15; cf. 2 Cor 5:16-18).

Paul concludes his proof from scriptural arguments with an allegorical reading of the Sarah and Hagar episodes of Abraham's story (Gal 4:21-31), thus returning to the theme of Galatians 3:6 (Abraham "believed God" with regard to God's promise of offspring) and to the question of who is the heir of the divine promises. Abraham sired Ishmael with his wife's female slave, Hagar. Later, he sired Isaac with his wife Sarah. Paul aligns Ishmael, the enslaved child born by fleshly power, with the earthly Jerusalem and all that belong to her, and Isaac, the freeborn child conceived by the power of the Spirit and promise, with the heavenly Jerusalem and all that belong to her. In so doing he has radically rewritten the genealogy of the Jewish people, who trace their lineage naturally from Isaac, not Ishmael. He contends, however, that the lesson to be learned from the story is that those who are born on the basis of God's promise and the Spirit are the ones who inherit the blessing of Abraham (Gal 4:30-31), which corresponds to the Gentile Galatian Christians, and *not* to the rival teachers, who still labor in slavery and seek to enslave the converts as well.

This may seem like a bit of fast and loose exegesis—one that would have earned low scores in an introductory course on the Old Testament. Yet there is actually a high level of sophistication in Paul's use of the Scriptures, especially in his choice of Isaiah 54:1-2 as the "confirmation" of his reading. Sarah, the freeborn woman, was barren and could be understood at one level as the one addressed by the quotation from Isaiah. This text from Isaiah, however, follows immediately after the famous Servant Song (Is 52:13—53:12), in which the righteous one bears the sins of many, ransoms many, makes many righteous and sees his offspring despite being cut off from the land of the living—indeed, engenders offspring precisely in being offered up for sin. Thus it is Jesus, the servant who brings blessings to many, who are then accounted his offspring, who permits this flourishing of offspring for the barren one, multiplying endlessly the children and heirs of Abraham. Paul brings this argumentation back to bear on the immediate situation: the Galatians must expel the rival teachers along with their "other gospel," and so continue to walk in "the freedom for which Christ has set them free" (Gal 4:30; 5:1).

How do we now live to please God? However much some scholars are skeptical about the application of rhetorical criticism to Pauline letters, it is clear that Galatians is meant to affect what the Galatians are about to do in their situation, and thus it serves a "deliberative" purpose. That purpose is stated negatively in Galatians 5:1, dissuading the Galatian converts from the course of action the rival teachers promote: "For freedom Christ has set us free. Stand firm, therefore, and do not submit again to a yoke of slavery" (NRSV). The philosopher and statesman Dio Chrysostom defined freedom as "the knowledge of what is allowable and what is forbidden, and slavery as ignorance of what is allowed and what is not" (*Or.* 14.18). Freedom is not autonomy or absolute license to do what one wishes in every situation (*Or.* 14.3-6), rather it is an opportunity to conform to the absolute law of God. Slavery, on the other hand, consists in being unclear about the laws God has laid down for humankind, being bound instead by ever-multiplying human-made laws (*Or.* 80.5-7). For Dio, following local, ethnic or national laws while remaining ignorant of "the ordinance of Zeus" is "the grievous and unlawful slavery under whose yoke you have placed your souls" (*Or.* 80.7). Paul now classes the Torah with such second-rate law codes, calling it also a "yoke of slavery," relegating it to the period of humanity's ignorance of the law of God written on the heart by the Spirit.

What is the divinely ordained norm for living and the divinely given means to attain a righteous life (to be "justified" against the margin of God's righteousness)? Those who seek "to be justified (*dikaiousthe*) by law" (Gal 5:4), to be "brought in line with God's standards" by performing circumcision and observing other "works of Torah," have grossly undervalued God's gift of the Spirit. This affront to the Giver stands behind Paul's dramatic language of the grace relationship between the believer and Christ being broken. Righteousness remains God's goal for the believer (Gal 5:5), but righteousness (*dikaiosynē,* a word closely related to *justification*) does not come through Torah. God is One, but Torah had not brought humanity together to reflect the oneness of God. It had not effected God's purpose for humanity as expressed in the promises given to Abraham, that God's blessing should extend to all nations. Now God effects justification—God makes people righteous—through the Spirit. God sends the Spirit into Jew and Gentile alike to bring all who believe into conformity with God's character and will, transforming them into the image of the righteous One, Jesus himself (Gal 2:20; 4:19) and causing the people of God to reflect the unity of the one God (3:28).

In a second thesis statement, written in conscious imitation of the first (Gal 5:1), Paul speaks of the proper, positive use of this freedom: "You were called to freedom, brothers and sisters: only not freedom to give the flesh an opportunity; rather, through love serve one another" (Gal 5:13). The freedom Christ gives is not an occasion for the flesh to take control, leading a person deeper and deeper into vice, but an occasion for the Spirit to guide the believer into all virtue.

As Paul weaves together topics of freedom and slavery, flesh and Spirit, he creates a discourse that is very much at home in Hellenistic Jewish ethics. Philo, for example, also regarded "flesh" and "Spirit" as two guiding principles that competed for the allegiance of human beings: "the race of humankind is twofold, the one being the race of those who live by the divine Spirit and reason; the other of those who exist according to blood and the pleasure of the flesh. The latter species is formed of earth, but the former is an accurate copy of the divine image" (*Who Is the Heir of*

Criticisms of the "New Perspective"

The "new perspective" has not been greeted with unanimous support and approval. Indeed, some have regarded it as a dead end in the study of Paul, leading many astray from the time-honored truth about Paul. Some basic cautions raised by a number of scholars are well worth considering.

First, Sanders's characterization of the various Judaisms of the first century as "covenantal nomism," with its emphasis on grace rather than performance of works with a view to earning justification, has come under fire. There are some stunning examples of a doctrine of earning justification (acquittal at the judgment) by the doing of works, where the individual earns eternal reward or punishment by doing or transgressing God's law. *Fourth Ezra,* as Sanders already knew, explicitly affirms that having "a storehouse of works" with God brings a reward (*4 Ezra* 7:77; 8:33). When Ezra claims that God will show his righteousness and goodness by showing mercy to those who "have no store of good works" (*4 Ezra* 8:32, 36), he is soundly corrected by God (*4 Ezra* 8:37-40). A text from Qumran, 4QMMT, explicitly claims that doing the "works of the law" as outlined by the author of this text leads to justification before God "at the end time" (4QMMT 30): "It will be reckoned for you as righteousness when you perform what is right and good before Him" (4QMMT 31).[a] Moreover, *m. Aboth* 3:16 declares that "the world is judged by grace, yet all is according to the excess of works." Critics therefore claim that it simply will not suffice to characterize Judaism in all its diversity as "covenantal nomism."[b]

This is an apt critique, but it begs the question of what we are to do with New Testament texts that affirm that works matter at the judgment and are determinative for eternal destiny. The visions of the last judgment in Matthew 25:31-46, Romans 2:5-11, 2 Corinthians 5:9-10 and Revelation 20:12 all say that people will be judged according to their deeds. Paul also speaks of (bad) works resulting in exclusion from the kingdom (e.g., Gal 5:19-21; 1 Cor 6:9-11). Of course, there are ingenious ways of explaining each of these as not affirming judgment on the basis of works (at least, not for Christians), but this comes across as special pleading. While Sanders's claims require some nuancing, the attempts to redraw a picture of Judaism as at least semi-Pelagian *in contrast to Christianity* (that is, to serve once more as a foil to Christianity) seem to be fueled by ideology rather than critical assessment.

Second, many scholars take issue with the tendency of some proponents of the new perspective to regard the doctrine of "justification by faith" not as a core element of Paul's theology but as an argument that Paul developed to explain the specific question of how "Gentiles can be equally acceptable to God as Jews."[c] While it is true that the topic and language of "justification by faith" comes to the fore only in Galatians and Romans, where the question arises concerning how the new people of God should be defined, Stuhlmacher points out that Paul's doctrine of justification grows out of the early Christian confession of Jesus' death as a death "for our sins" (1 Cor 15:3), an interpretation based on Isaiah 52:13—53:12, where the Messiah bears the sins

---

[a]Geza Vermes, *The Complete Dead Sea Scrolls* (New York: Penguin, 1997), p. 228.
[b]See D. A. Carson, P. T. O'Brien and M. A. Seifrid, eds., *Justification and Variegated Nomism,* vol. 1, *The Complexities of Second Temple Judaism,* WUNT 2/140 (Grand Rapids: Baker, 2001).
[c]See Dunn, *Theology of Paul's Letter,* p. 340.

The Letter to the Galatians

of many and "shall make many righteous" (Is 53:11 NRSV).[d] The confrontation with Jewish Christians in Antioch and Galatia certainly contributed to Paul's teaching on justification by faith, but this was not its origin and exhaustive purpose.

This criticism reflects a longstanding debate in Pauline studies about the "core" of Paul's gospel. Already in the early twentieth century Albert Schweitzer had relegated justification by faith to the status of a "secondary crater" at the edge of the main impact of Paul's message, which was "participation in Christ." Attempts to absolutize the doctrine of justification by faith as the core of Paul's thought, however, suggesting that it emerges complete from the Damascus Road encounter without further development,[e] seem to be another case of special pleading—again in favor of recovering a central tenet of Reformation theology.

A more significant problem emerges from the new perspective on justification, however, where "justification by faith" is understood to be a matter of relevance for Gentiles only, and not for Jews as well. This extreme line of argument tends to be pursued in support of a "two covenant" theology, according to which Jews do not need the gospel but only to be faithful to Torah. Such a view is an understandable development as scholarship seeks to undermine anti-Semitism at every turn, but it is certainly not true to Paul's theology (see Gal 2:15-16).

Third, but closely related to the first and second criticism, many scholars react against Dunn's suggestion that "works of the law" refers specifically to "boundary markers" that separate Jews from Gentiles (e.g., circumcision, sabbath, dietary laws). Rather, these scholars insist that Paul's attack on "works of the law" should continue to be seen as an attack on human achievement in general, against all attempts to establish our own righteousness by measuring up to some set of expectations in which individuals could "boast." To be fair, Dunn does in fact consider "works of the law" to include the ethically relevant precepts of Torah, but he sees Paul reacting against Torah as the *Jewish* law as opposed to the norm God now provides in the Spirit for both Jews and Gentiles. Dunn also believes that the broader understanding of the failure of all human attempts to achieve righteousness before God on human strength represents a viable outgrowth and application of Paul's critique of pursuing works of Torah and boasting in ethnic privilege. This is just not Paul's original sense.

From such debates it becomes clear that the new perspective has reopened several historical and theological questions of the highest importance, and in which many scholars have a considerable personal and theological investment.

FOR FURTHER READING

Carson, D. A., Peter T. O'Brien and Mark A. Seifrid, eds. *Justification and Variegated Nomism.* Vol.
1: *The Complexities of Second Temple Judaism.* WUNT 2/140. Grand Rapids: Baker, 2001.
Kim, Seyoon. *Paul and the New Perspective.* Grand Rapids: Eerdmans, 2001.
Stuhlmacher, Peter. *Revisiting Paul's Doctrine of Justification: A Challenge to the New Perspective.*
Downers Grove, Ill.: InterVarsity Press, 2001.
Westerholm, Stephen. *Israel's Law and the Church's Faith: Paul and His Recent Interpreters.* Grand
Rapids: Eerdmans, 1988.

---

[d]Stuhlmacher, *Revisiting Paul's Doctrine of Justification*, pp. 21-22.
[e]Kim, *Paul and the New Perspective,* pp. 56-57.

Divine Things 12.57). Like Paul, Philo understood "freedom" to be realized as an individual lived according to the divine Spirit and leading of God, which puts "a check upon the authority of the passions," while "slavery" exists wherever "vice and the passions have the dominion" over the person (*Every Good Person is Free* 17). A major difference between the two authors is the role of Torah: for Philo, the study and doing of Torah was the path to freedom; for Paul, the death of Jesus and the gift of the Spirit made this freedom possible apart from Torah.

By means of the Spirit the death of Jesus becomes something in which the believer can participate. Paul declares that he was "crucified together with Christ," with the result that Christ now lived in him (Gal 2:19-20). Similarly, the disciple who belongs to Christ crucifies the power of "the flesh with its passions and desires" and thus is mastered by them no longer (Gal 5:24). The infusion of the Spirit into the life of the believers brings Christ's life into theirs, which mystically effects their dying to the power of the flesh and their living to God. With Paul they are crucified to this present evil age, and the power of the present evil age is crucified to them (Gal 6:14), and they come to life as part of the new creation of God. As they fall in line with the Spirit, like soldiers marching according to the orders prescribed by their general, they find the power of the flesh nullified and the fruits of righteousness multiplied in their lives (Gal 5:16, 18-23, 25).[17]

The stakes and risks of such an approach remain very high. The absence of written laws does not mean that a person can fool God, using the freedom from law as an opportunity to "sow to the flesh," finding room for self-indulgence and the temporary pleasures of sin (Gal 6:7-10). Those who abuse their freedom to indulge the flesh (whether in terms of indulging our bent toward strife and divisiveness in community, toward sexual indiscretions or any such thing) "will not inherit the kingdom of God" (Gal 5:19-21).[18] In the absence of the "guard rails" of Torah, the life of the Spirit calls for complete honesty with ourselves, our Christian family and God if we are truly to follow the Spirit and move forward into the righteousness that God would form in us. It requires a heart that wishes to go where and as the Spirit directs, that does not resist the Spirit in order to protect some areas of fleshly indulgence.

The risks of such a walk, however, are the risks that attend maturity. In our childhood, our guardians keep us from danger and make many moral decisions for us; as adults, we must find that moral faculty fully formed within us and be responsible before our own conscience for our actions. So now, Paul's analogy would affirm, Christians are entrusted by God to be responsive to the Spirit and responsible to the Spirit. They no longer need to be hemmed in by rules like children but are free to seek righteousness in the context of their mature relationship with God through the Spirit. This corresponds to the "writing of the law on the hearts" of God's people that was the burning hope of prophets like Jeremiah (Jer 31:31-34), and to the "circumcision of the heart" (Deut 10:16; 30:6; Jer 4:4) that symbolized obedience from the inner person in response to God's favor and fellowship.

The focal point of the Spirit-led ethic is clearly "love." Rather than being circumcised or not, what ultimately counts is "faith working through love" (Gal 5:6), the use of freedom to "serve one another through love" (Gal 5:13). Paul elevates the command to "love your

---

[17]Martyn makes the important observation that it is the Spirit's war against the "impulsive desire of the flesh," not the believer's war (*Galatians*, pp. 530-31, 534-35). The Spirit is not a resource that can help us in our battle, rather we have been drafted to fight in the Spirit's battle, to "fall in line" with the Spirit as with a commander (Gal 5:25).

[18]See also Jas 1:14-15 on the importance of not allowing desire to come to full term and give birth to death for the person.

neighbor as yourself" (Lev 19:18; Gal 5:14) as the sum total of the law. To walk in love toward others is to fulfill all that is enduring about Torah, indeed, to fulfill the "law of the Messiah" (Gal 6:2). Paul may have known of Jesus' famous summary of the law as love for God and love for neighbor (see Mt 22:36-40). Following the Spirit, Christians will be transformed into a community of mutual investment, care and support rather than mutual hostility and detraction (Gal 5:15), where members are poised against one another in pride, envy and provocation (Gal 5:26). As we examine the specific "works of the flesh" that Paul has selected to exemplify that way of life, we find that most if not all of these display an absence of love for the other. Unsanctified sexual indulgence objectifies the other, using him or her for self-gratification rather than serving God's desires in dealing with the other; strife and competition tear down the other rather than seek his or her good; drunken parties and revels stupefy the individual to the needs of the other and anesthetize them to the prompting of the Spirit to build up the other (Gal 5:19-21).

Similarly, the "fruit of the Spirit" manifests itself relationally as well. Several of the virtues listed in Galatians 5:22-23 have direct bearing on relationships between believers and those outside the community of faith, especially *love, kindness, goodness, faithfulness* (the more likely sense of *pistis* in this context, rather than "faith" or "belief" toward God), and *gentleness/meekness*. The first three orient the disciple beneficently toward others, teaching them to seek the good and serve the interests of their neighbors, and to restrain their aggressive and self-assertive tendencies ("gentleness"). *Peace* is something of a transitional virtue, combining the ideas of harmony and concord between people and the idea of well-being and wholeness within a person. The other manifestations of the Spirit's fruit are, perhaps, more personal than relational virtues. *Joy* springs from an awareness of God's love and beneficence toward the believer whose grateful heart remains mindful of God's gifts in the midst of all circumstances. *Patient endurance* bespeaks the courage of the disciple, both in the face of the rigors of discipleship (e.g., resisting temptation, seeking steady and sure growth toward the likeness of Jesus) and in the face of the hostility of unbelievers. *Self-control* involves the mastery of the passions and is often seen as the foundation for all the virtues since the passions of the flesh are the primary hindrance to every virtue (as in 4 Macc 1:30-31).

Paul certainly does not intend to offer a new Torah in these chapters, but he focuses on how the Spirit transforms human community, what the signs are of the Spirit's work in producing a community where the ideal of love is realized, and what the symptoms are when the "flesh" exerts its power again. Love shows itself where the sinner is gently reclaimed, where believers invest in one another enough to "bear one another's burdens" (Gal 6:1-2); love shows itself where believers refuse to regard a sister or brother as a spiritual trophy of any kind, as if the conversion or transformation of another person could become a claim to honor for oneself (as the rival teachers are doing, in Paul's mind; Gal 6:4-5, 13). Love manifests itself in the sharing of resources between believers who bring more of the truth of God to light for one another (Gal 6:6). Where love is made real, God's transforming Spirit is truly at work, bringing believers into conformity with God's righteousness.

Paul gives a summation of his position in Galatians 6:14-16. The boundaries of Israel, the people of God, have been redrawn by the decisive act of God in Christ at the close of this present evil age. Among the children of Abraham inclusion in the household of God does not happen through circumcision. What matters is the emergence of the new creation in each person and in the community of faith: a dying to the world with Christ and rising to new life, the life of the Spirit reforming the person, forming Christ within the believer.

GALATIANS AND MINISTRY FORMATION

Integrity: Walking in line with the truth. Paul's authority is rooted in the message itself and his faithfulness to that message. Human credentials or legitimation by some governing body add nothing to this root authority. Moreover, Paul presents a living example of the courage of the genuine minister of the gospel, who refuses to conform the gospel to the expectations or demands of church or society, who refuses to avoid confrontation where the truth of the gospel is not being lived out in the church.

Following Paul's pattern, we are instructed that our own persuasive power and authority likewise come from our fidelity to that message, and we must refuse to accommodate that message to suit the tastes of our congregations or the society around us. If we did accommodate the message, we would preach a mere human gospel, one that has been circumcised and emasculated of its transformative power. Rather, we are called to preserve the challenge that the gospel poses to the world and call our constituencies to conform to the gospel, not vice versa. This is the gospel that has power from God to transform, to justify, to bring us in line with God's own righteousness.

We must seek to please God, not people. Here is a great challenge to ministry, for in the day-to-day practice of ministry, in the week-to-week business of running a church or performing a teaching ministry or even engaging in pastoral counseling, the temptation will always be present to please people—those people who employ us, who pay us, who recommend us, who use their influence for us. Paul challenges us to remember that in every encounter, in every decision, in every intervention there is One whom we must please, there is One to whom we, as slaves of Christ, are answerable.

Finally, if we are to have powerful ministries, we must walk straight in line with the gospel, conforming our own conduct to the message. Paul consistently measured himself *and* his fellow apostles by whether or not they were walking toward the truth of the gospel, or behaving in ways that were out of line with that gospel. Our congregations and constituents will do the same. Nothing can undermine a minister's credibility faster and more completely than merely "talking the talk" while not "walking the walk." There are two main stumbling blocks to integrity at this point: the double heart that still makes room for the flesh (Gal 5:13-26) and the cowardly heart that shrinks back from living by the gospel, yielding instead to the expectations and pressures of other people (Gal 2:11-14; 5:11; 6:12-13). Paul's example encourages us that it will never be truly inexpedient to walk in line with the truth of the gospel, even if it should entail persecution in some form.

The importance of the experience of God. Paul's argument stands or falls depending on his converts' awareness of the Holy Spirit in their hearts and their awareness of the Spirit's work within them and between them (Gal 3:1-5). In our endeavors to know the truth and make it known, Paul reminds us not to neglect the surpassing importance of the experience of the holy One. This is the bedrock of Paul's proof, and it is often the bedrock of our personal perseverance in faith. In my own experience of the academic study of religion—first in seminary, then in graduate studies, then as part of the guild of biblical scholarship—it is ultimately not the "facts" I knew or even the "faith convictions" that I had, but the experience of a relationship with God and the awareness of God's Spirit at work within me that provided a center for my faith, that, at times, even kept me "in the faith." In the face of the challenges posed to faith throughout the course of a life, faith must be more than doing the right rituals and knowing the right doctrines: it must be grounded in a living, ongoing relationship with God through the Spirit.

Paul's reliance in Galatia on the converts' awareness of this Spirit urges us to value the experience of God in our times of worship and to cultivate in individuals an awareness of God's presence and of God's hand at work in our lives. Minister and parishioner, counselor and counselee, teacher and student alike must be able to find the irrefutable signs of God's love, acceptance and favor in their lives, and our life together as a Christian community should be directed toward cultivating transforming encounters with the living God. Without the active presence of God's Spirit in our lives, we lack, in Paul's view, the very inheritance promised in Christ and the key to our transformation into the likeness of Christ.

The hope of righteousness: God's norms versus human regulations. God yearns to impart God's righteousness to God's children, having given the Spirit to bring us fully in line with God's character and goodness. Paul draws our attention in Galatians to three principal hindrances to attaining the hope of righteousness. There are the "elementary principles of this world" (*ta stoicheia tou kosmou,* Gal 4:1-11), the imposition of a religious law code, religious rites and other regulations (Gal 3:3, 21; 4:21-31; 5:1-6), and the "flesh with its passions and desires" (Gal 5:19-21, 24).

The last of these is perhaps the most obvious, since it is the most close at hand for each of us. Every disciple is familiar with the impulses of the flesh. When another person affronts us somehow or hinders our plans, the impulse of the flesh orients us toward that person as an enemy or obstacle and sparks anger and conflict rather than cooperation and resolution. Trained to value self-gratification, especially the gratification of sexual impulses, the flesh looks for opportunities at every turn. The flesh leads us to overindulge in food and material comforts, to seek our own comfort before the very survival of others. In short, the flesh insists on its own way, placing its desires above the needs and welfare of the other and the group, and above the just requirements of God.

By *flesh,* Paul does not simply mean the "meat" of our physical person. He recognizes it as a powerful force in the life of a human being that can manifest itself in thought, word and deed, with the mind and soul as well as the body. He also recognizes that it is not identical with the person; it is not the whole person, and it is not even the part that is the person in the truest sense (that part that can assent to the flesh or yield to the Spirit). The power of the flesh is probably what makes the removal of the bridle of law (in some form) all the more frightening and risky. What is to save us from being swallowed up by our own desires, passions and impulses if not rules carefully laid out? Paul confidently speaks, at this point, of the Spirit, the divine Spirit poured into our hearts. Regulations could never tame the passions of the flesh, but the Spirit of God can. Yielding to this Spirit in each new moment is now the divinely prescribed path to righteousness.

Larger, more systemic hindrances to walking in line with God also confront the believer. Paul names the *stoicheia* as spiritual forces exercising authority over the human race. These *stoicheia* masquerade as absolutes, thus enslaving people. They represent the power of the basic principles of the world's way of doing things, the domination systems that we take for granted and deem irreplaceable realities. They represent the ideologies of nationalism, of militarism, of economics (whether capitalism, socialism or communism), even of religion and its limits, and the ways these ideologies shape our society and control and constrain us.

Sociologist Peter Berger describes with remarkable perspicuity how people are programmed from birth (socialized) in their society's self-preserving values, ideals and behavioral norms, so that each individual member of society will do his or her part to keep that society functioning more or less without question.[a] Indeed, there are social and internalized constraints against even raising those questions. This socialization limits the options we perceive for our responses, our relationships, even our ambitions. Paul was indeed perceptive to describe our condition as human beings in society as a kind of slavery or as that of children under various disciplinarians and guardians (Gal 4:1-11). We are presented with the challenge of discerning how these *stoicheia* (we could think of these glibly as whatever "isms" are relevant to our particular social context) have been operative in our lives *and* in the life of the church, so we can become ever more free to respond to one another and to the world from the ideals and values taught by God. The importance of the Spirit here cannot be overestimated: only by hearing and following the Spirit, often in conjunction with studying the Scriptures, can we break out of the boxes our society constructs around our minds from birth.

The final hindrance, and the one treated most prominently in Galatians, is the tendency of religious-minded people to replace (or at least "supplement") the living, vibrant relationship with God and the direction of the Holy Spirit with a code of laws, regulations and traditions, exchanging the power of godliness for the outward forms of "righteousness." This is righteousness with regard to human norms, however, which is not the same as being righteous with regard to God's norms. It is all too easy to add our own agenda and our own requirements to the gospel and thus pervert the gospel. Good motives may stand behind this endeavor, usually the desire to "certify" that people are indeed part of God's family by some means that can be observed or spoken, or to "ensure" that Christians live in line with God's requirements. Many believers, congregations and whole denominations have willingly exchanged the state of having come of age for a return to old (or newly invented) pedagogues.

---

[a]Peter L. Berger, *The Sacred Canopy: Elements of a Sociological Theory of Religion* (Garden City, N.Y.: Doubleday, 1967), chaps. 1 and 2; *Invitation to Sociology* (Garden City, N.Y.: Doubleday, 1963), chaps. 4 and 5.

The rival teachers have not been alone in deeming trust in Jesus to be inadequate proof that someone belongs to God's people, or deeming the Spirit to be an insufficient guide to righteousness. Church history is full of examples of attempts to circumscribe the people of God in ever narrower circles, developing new lists of requirements for belonging to the "true" church or being "true" Christians, erecting more and more boundaries between people in the name of preserving the truth and the sanctity of the people of God. If a divinely sanctioned boundary marker like circumcision, however, was rendered invalid by the death and resurrection of Jesus, and by the pouring out of the Holy Spirit on those who trusted Jesus, how much less valid will be the boundary markers that divide Christian from Christian today. "Hold to these beliefs, not those; be baptized this way, not that; associate with these people, not those; behave this way, not that." The Spirit will direct our beliefs, our practices, our relationships, our behaviors, to be sure, for the Spirit wars against the flesh and its designs for our lives. We cannot, however, codify the Spirit—that is, generate a list of requirements that can functionally replace the Spirit—any more now than Paul's rivals could then.

Paul challenges us to embrace the freedom of living by the Spirit, trusting this gift of God to bring us fully in line with the character and standards of God, to transform us into the likeness of Jesus, the image of the Father. He challenges us to use this freedom responsibly as spiritual adults. Christian freedom is never an occasion for self-service but always an occasion to serve and to love beyond the limits set on us by our upbringing, socialization and customs. The righteousness that God imparts will be manifested in the character of our Christian community. Are we other-centered or self-centered? Are we marked by cooperation or competition? Do we accept one another on the same basis that God accepts us— trusting Jesus—adding nothing as a requirement for fellowship in the one body? Do we live out the vision where ethnic, social and gender distinctions—and the hierarchical evaluations, limitations, abuses or avoidances that are fostered by such distinctions—are transcended in the one family of God's children and heirs? Only by following the Spirit will we, as a Christian community, arrive at the full freedom and glorious inheritance of the sons and daughters of God.

FOR FURTHER READING

Barclay, John M. G. *Obeying the Truth*. Minneapolis: Fortress, 1991.

———. "Mirror-Reading a Polemical Letter: Galatians as a Test Case." *JSNT* 31 (1987): 73-93.

Barrett, C. K. *Freedom and Obligation*. London: SPCK, 1985.

Betz, Hans Dieter. *Galatians*. Hermeneia. Philadelphia: Fortress, 1979.

Bruce, F. F. *Galatians*. NICNT. Grand Rapids: Eerdmans, 1982.

Dunn, James D. G. *The Epistle to the Galatians*. Peabody, Mass.: Hendrickson, 1993.

———. *The Theology of Paul's Letter to the Galatians*. Cambridge: Cambridge University Press, 1993.

Hays, R. B. "Christology and Ethics in Galatians: The Law of Christ." *CBQ* 49 (1987): 268-90.

Hooker, M. D. "PISTIS CHRISTOU." *NTS* 35 (1989): 321-42.

Longenecker, Richard N. *Galatians*. WBC. Dallas: Word, 1990.

Matera, Frank J. *Galatians*. Sacra Pagina. Collegeville, Minn.: Liturgical Press, 1992.

Martyn, J. Louis. *Galatians*. Anchor Bible 33A. Garden City, N.Y.: Doubleday, 1997.

Schüssler Fiorenza, Elisabeth. "Neither Male nor Female: Gal 3:28—Alternative Vision and Pauline Modification." In *In Memory of Her* (New York: Crossroad, 1984).

Witherington, Ben, III. *Grace in Galatia: A Commentary on Paul's Letter to the Galatians*. Grand Rapids: Eerdmans, 1998.

13

THE THESSALONIAN
CORRESPONDENCE

Living in the Light of the "Day"

In 1-2 Thessalonians, Paul, Silvanus and Timothy encourage a community of relatively new believers to persevere in their commitment to love and support one another and to remain faithful to Jesus. The believers' non-Christian neighbors are trying to undermine this commitment by shaming and harassing the converts, seeking to draw them back to the "respectable" lives they used to lead. So they can resist these pressures, Paul and his team focus these Christians on the honor they enjoy now in the eyes of other Christian congregations and on the deliverance they will enjoy on the Day of Judgment. The apostle also addresses several other pastoral concerns in these letters, consoling the believers concerning Christians who have passed away and admonishing the idle to continue to contribute to the congregation and society through an orderly life and productive labor.

These letters, among the earliest of the Pauline letters that have survived, provide us with a first-person testimony concerning Paul's early missionary practice and persona. They also allow us to hear something of Paul's message apart from the debates over the circumcision of converts that led to the prominence of "justification by faith as a gift" in Paul's writings. Here, apart from those polemical situations, conversion from idol worship to the apocalyptic gospel of the returning Christ held center place.

THE CITY OF THESSALONICA

Thessalonica lies about one hundred miles west of Philippi along the Via Egnatia. The city enjoyed a long history before the advent of the Romans in 168 B.C.E. Perhaps because it was an important port city on the Aegean Sea, it was named the Roman capital of Macedonia in 146 B.C.E. Even after Roman domination was established, the city was not restructured as a Roman colony, and it so retained more of its Greek identity into the Roman period.[1] The city continued to be governed according to a Greek constitution, with a council composed of local aristocrats and a gymnasium complex for the education of the young as well as the promotion of Greek culture, religion and athletics. Like Philippi, Thessalonica had also supported Antony and Octavian against Brutus and Cassius in 42 B.C.E. The citizens especially revered Antony, although they quickly expressed their loyalty to Octavian after the defeat of Antony at Actium in 31 B.C.E.[2]

In addition to being a thriving commercial

---

[1]Raymond Brown, *Introduction to the New Testament* (Garden City, N.Y.: Doubleday, 1997), p. 457; Holland Hendrix, "Thessalonica," *Anchor Bible Dictionary,* ed. David N. Freedman (Garden City, N.Y.: Doubleday, 1992), 6:524.
[2]Hendrix, "Thessalonica," p. 524.

port city, Thessalonica was a city full of idols, from which a convert to Christianity would have to turn (see 1 Thess 1:9-10). Inscriptions, carvings and other archaeological finds bear witness to benefactor cults, including the cult of Rome and her emperors. Coins minted at the turn of the era show the deified Julius on one side and Augustus on the reverse. An older temple was rededicated to the deified Augustus and his successors. Even Roman benefactors received cultic honors.[3] The existence of an official called an *agonothete* suggests that athletic games or contests were held in the city in honor of the emperor on a regular basis. All of this adds up to a strong commitment to Roman imperial ideology in this city.

We also find evidence of the worship of the traditional Greco-Roman divinities (including the cult of Dionysus, which was prominent in this region), mystery cults like those of Isis, Osiris and Sarapis, and the local cult of Kabiros.[4] The latter is a religious phenomenon peculiar to Macedonia and Thrace. Kabiros was a kingly figure murdered by his brothers, but he lived on in the divine realm and his return was expected by devotees. He served as an official patron deity for the city, and his favor was courted especially by craftspeople and merchants.[5] The details of the cult are, as with most mystery religions, exceedingly difficult to discern with certainly, since we only have inscriptions, statues and carvings as evidence rather than literary texts devoted to telling the myth or describing the worship. Nevertheless, the basic contours of a deity who died, lives on and will return again could not help but resonate with Paul's gospel of a murdered, rising and returning Lord.

THE FORMATION OF THE CHRISTIAN COMMUNITY IN THESSALONICA

In the late 40s, after evangelizing Philippi (1 Thess 2:2; cf. Acts 16:11-40), Paul and Silas traveled westward along the Via Egnatia toward Thessalonica. Paul preached for three sabbaths in the synagogue, after which the fledgling group of believers moved its focal point to the house of Jason, a propertied convert (his ethnic background, whether Jewish or Gentile, is uncertain), from which point the group could be nurtured and grow.[6] Acts 17:2 has been mistakenly read to signify that Paul only spent three weeks in Thessalonica, but in fact it indicates that he persisted in his synagogue-based mission only for the first three weeks of his stay. Given the fact that he plied his trade while in the city to support himself (1 Thess 2:9; 2 Thess 3:7-9) and also received supplemental support from his friends in Philippi several times, he was no doubt active in the city for at least a few months (Phil 4:16).[7] First Thessalonians gives the impression of a primarily Gentile congregation (see especially 1 Thess 1:9-10) but not necessarily exclusively so. Paul may have gathered some converts from the synagogue.[8]

---

[3]Ibid., pp. 524-25.

[4]Charles Edson, "Cults of Thessalonica," *HTR* 41 (1948): 153-204; Holland Hendrix, "Thessalonicans Honor Romans" (Ph.D. diss., Harvard University, 1984); K. P. Donfried, "The Cults of Thessalonica and the Thessalonian Correspondence," *NTS* 31 (1985): 336-56; Robert Jewett, *The Thessalonian Correspondence* (Philadelphia: Fortress, 1986), pp. 126-32.

[5]Jewett, *Thessalonian Correspondence,* pp. 128-29; C. A. Wanamaker, *The Epistles to the Thessalonians,* NIGTC (Grand Rapids: Eerdmans, 1990), p. 5.

[6]Abraham J. Malherbe, *Paul and the Thessalonians* (Philadelphia: Fortress, 1987), pp. 12-15.

[7]E. J. Richard, *First and Second Thessalonians,* Sacra Pagina 11 (Collegeville, Minn.: Liturgical Press, 1995), p. 10.

[8]I disagree with B. R. Gaventa's suggestion that 1 Thess 2:14-16 is evidence that Jewish Christians were not present in 1 Thessalonians (*First and Second Thessalonians,* Interpretation [Louisville, Ky.: John Knox Press, 1998], p. 3). Paul's polemics in 2:14-16 does not mean that Jewish Christians would be absent from the congregation, merely that all the Christians in Thessalonica were experiencing the same kind of harassment that the Judean Christians had experienced from their fellow citizens.

It is possible that Paul's shop was located in an *insula,* an apartment building with living quarters on the upper floors and artisans' shops on the main floor opening onto the street.[9] Such a location would also afford him access to other artisans and those who frequented the busy center of the pre-industrial city, and it would be a suitable venue in which to share the good news. Artisans and manual laborers were certainly part of the church (see 1 Thess 4:11), along with those who were relatively well off (like Jason, the owner of a sizeable home in the city, no less expensive then than now) and those who were poor (yet still charitable).

The Christian group grew thanks to the hospitality of Jason and the leadership of Paul, until the latter was forced to leave before he would have wished (1 Thess 2:17).[10] Paul uses the image of being "bereft" (1 Thess 2:17), a metaphor of mourning over a separation that is not willed by the parties involved. This image confirms the impression of hasty and untimely departure we get from Acts 17:5-10. Paul and his team depart from Thessalonica for points west—Berea, Athens and eventually Corinth (Acts 17:10—18:17), where Paul would stay for almost two full years and where he would write 1 Thessalonians.[11] This itinerary is fairly well reflected in 1 Thessalonians 2:17—3:6, save for one detail.[12] In Acts 17:14-15, Timothy and Silas remain in Berea, and Paul goes to Athens alone; Timothy and Silas then rejoin Paul in Corinth (Acts 18:5). In 1 Thessalonians, Timothy (at least) accompanies Paul to Athens and then is sent back to Thessalonica to encourage the believers and report on their condition to Paul in Corinth. In such cases it is probably better to rely on Paul's firsthand account of the events rather than Luke's second-hand, later and often incomplete account.

THE CHRISTIANS PAUL LEFT BEHIND

Paul describes the Thessalonian believers' situation as "distress" or "tribulation" (Greek, *thlipsis*; 1 Thess 1:6; 3:3-4; 2 Thess 1:4, 6) and speaks of the believers as "suffering" (1 Thess 2:14; 2 Thess 1:5). On the one hand, converts to a new religion, particularly one that involved a complete reevaluation of everything once held sacred (like the piety and worldview now rejected as idolatrous), would certainly experience internal distress.[13] Lucian of Samosata describes the fictive experience of one such convert (to a philosophical school) thus:

> [The philosopher-preacher] went on to praise philosophy and the freedom it gives, and to ridicule the things that are popularly considered blessings—wealth and reputation, dominion and honor, yes and purple and gold—things accounted very desirable by most men, and till then by me also. I took it all in with eager, wide-open soul, and at the moment I couldn't imagine what had come over me; I was all confused. At first I felt hurt because he had criticized what was dearest to me—wealth and money and reputation—and I all but cried over their downfall. (*Nigrinus* 3-5)

Undoubtedly there would be much "distress" mingled with "joy" (1 Thess 1:6; the NRSV rendering of *thlipsis* as "persecution" is possible but also unduly limiting) as a convert left behind his or her former way of life, throwing away as worthless what a few weeks or months before had been of great worth and importance, and entered this new way of life called Christianity.

---

[9]Malherbe, *Paul and the Thessalonians,* pp. 17-20.

[10]Richard, *First and Second Thessalonians,* pp. 5-6; Jewett, *Thessalonian Correspondence,* p. 117.

[11]Brown, *Introduction to the New Testament,* p. 457.

[12]Ibid., pp. 458-59.

[13]Malherbe, *Letters to the Thessalonians,* p. 128.

In addition to this internal distress and sense of dislocation, the converts' non-Christian neighbors certainly added to the grief by expressing their disapproval of the converts' new ideology and actions. As solid citizens of Thessalonica began to withdraw from all contact with the gods whose favor cradled society and ensured the common good, and as they began to meet in unaccustomed places with people of like mind to await the coming of a new order that would replace Roman rule, their family, friends and associates would try to amend their deviant ways. Pressure of all kinds—reproach, shunning, economic distress—would be applied to "help" the converts decide to return to a suitable way of life.

Not all such pressure would be so benign in intention. As awareness of this "atheistic" and "exclusivistic" movement grew, local resentment and hostility would also grow. We need to remember that Christianity would have been seen as a political and social threat in this context. The proclamation of Jesus, the Messiah crucified by the Romans, as the coming Ruler and Judge was a proclamation that threatened Roman order and the security posited in the ideology of "Eternal Rome," the city which ensured the Thessalonians' enjoyment of peace. It was, moreover, a proclamation that moved formerly reliable citizens of Thessalonica to withdraw from cultic displays of gratitude toward the city's most important benefactors and cultic displays of loyalty and dedication to the welfare of the city.[14] The group gave all the warning signs of becoming a source of disunity, a cancer in the social body requiring treatment. Paul strategically praises the Thessalonians and connects their eternal honor in God's sight with that act that cost them the respect and support of their neighbors—turning "to God from idols, to serve a living and true God, and to wait for his Son from heaven" (1 Thess 1:9-10 NRSV).

Officially sanctioned persecution of the church was extremely rare in the first century, and we should not imagine martyrdoms to occur in Thessalonica at this time. (The reference to believers who died in 1 Thessalonians 4:13 presupposes the natural deaths of believers, since martyrdom would have invited very different topics of consolation.) Nevertheless, even unofficial persecution would be difficult to bear and would invite precisely the kinds of pastoral responses and strategies we find in 1-2 Thessalonians.

TIMOTHY'S VISIT

Paul's first response was not to write a letter but to send Timothy back to the sisters and brothers in Thessalonica to encourage them in person, and to find out for Paul how they were faring. Indeed, Paul longs to make this visit in person and ascribes the thwarting of his plans to Satan himself (1 Thess 2:17-20). Timothy is sent to encourage them in the midst of their afflictions, to do whatever he could to offset the influence of the dominant culture on the new community. Reflecting on his motives for sending Timothy, Paul shows special concern that the believers not succumb to the pressures they faced as a result of their conversion and turn back from the path of discipleship (1 Thess 3:1-5). He did not want the believers to be "shaken" (1 Thess 3:3) in their convictions or to doubt the rightness of the choice they made on account of society's disapproval and resistance. Indeed, as he reflects on his concern for the believers, Paul invites them to regard the outside world as the agent of the tempter, Satan, the enemy of the divine order. Their neighbors' attempts to "reform" them become instead a demonic "temptation" (1 Thess 3:5) that could lure them away from the path leading to safety.

---

[14]See the discussions of suspicion towards such self-separating groups in R. A. Markus, *Christianity in the Roman World* (London: Thames & Hudson, 1974), pp. 24-47.

Such an interpretation of their distress will help insulate the believers against yielding to those social pressures—they are not benign but malevolent.

Timothy carried back to Paul a positive report about the believers' steadfastness and their ongoing devotion to Paul and his teaching (1 Thess 3:6). The result is that Paul is now encouraged in the midst of his own hardships, just as he seeks to encourage the Thessalonian Christians in the midst of theirs (1 Thess 3:7). Throughout the letter Paul gives expression to the mutuality in their relationship that is characteristic of friends and partners. Nevertheless, Paul still prays "night and day . . . most earnestly that we may see you face to face and restore whatever is lacking in your faith" (1 Thess 3:10 NRSV). Timothy's work was only the first step in the ongoing pastoral task of maintaining the group's cohesion. What Paul prays to do "face to face" he will accomplish through the letter itself, the epistolary replacement for the apostle's presence. Moreover, he learned (no doubt from Timothy) of concerns that the believers had, which left gaps in their certainty and security in their newfound faith. First Thessalonians responds to both needs and serves to cement further the community's commitment in the face of society's hostility.

EXEGETICAL SKILL
Epistolary Analysis

In order to intervene in the affairs of his congregations from whom he was separated by distance, Paul made use of letters, familiar devices of communication in the ancient world. Paul built on well-established conventions, both in terms of the form that should structure a letter and in terms of the kinds of goals and topics deemed appropriate for letters. We can gain valuable insights into Paul's goals for and strategies employed in his letters as we grow in our knowledge of those conventions and become more familiar with common topics and their evocations in ancient letters. This provides a necessary complement to rhetorical analysis of Paul's letters.[a]

We employ conventions in our own letter-writing. For example, we begin a letter by addressing the recipient as "Dear So-and-so," even if the person is not especially "dear" to us, and we tend to close with "Sincerely," as though to provide a closing assurance of our honesty. If we were to modify this formula, the fact that there is a recognizable formula to be modified would make those changes meaningful for our reader. Thus to begin "My dear So-and-so," or "Precious So-and-so," or simply "So-and-So" all convey some added meaning because of the departure from convention.

In the ancient world a letter began with a salutation ("X to Y, Greetings"), followed by a thanksgiving or a "wish prayer" concerning the recipient, the letter body (disclosing its main purpose) and a brief closing that expressed

[a]Although many scholars still persist in an either-or mentality with regard to epistolary and rhetorical analysis, the most fruitful and richly nuanced studies recognize the usefulness of and employ both modes of analysis. See the excellent discussions in K. P. Donfried and J. Beutler, *The Thessalonians Debate: Methodological Discord or Methodological Synthesis?* (Grand Rapids: Eerdmans, 2000), pp. 179-339.

a wish for the recipient's well-being.[b] Paul followed this basic format but expands it at several points. Thus he begins with the usual "Sender to Recipient" formula, but he might significantly expand his self-description or the description of the recipients. These expansions sometimes signal matters of concern to him that will be developed at length in the letter. Moreover, Paul modified the standard "Greeting" *(chairein)* to "Grace *[charis]* and peace to you," a clever and potent reminder to the hearers that they have left behind the world of "business as usual" and entered the sphere of God's favor and calling. Paul's expressions of thanksgiving and prayers on behalf of the hearers are also much richer and longer than the stereotyped and often perfunctory expressions found in standard letters, and these opening sections also tend to provide the recipients with a preview of topics that will be important for the letter as a whole.

For an exercise, compare 1 Thessalonians 1:1, Philippians 1:1, Philemon 1-3, Galatians 1:1-5 and Romans 1:1-7. How does Paul expand the standard letter opening ("Paul to Philemon, greetings")? The last three show significant expansions. How might these expansion provide relevant signals or preparations in letters that would go on to (1) ask for a big favor (Philemon), (2) seek to restore the apostle's authority where rival teachers have weakened commitment to Paul's gospel (Galatians), and (3) seek to secure a church's support for a missionary they had not yet met (Romans)?

Ancient letters also tended to belong to one (or more) of a limited number of types of letter, classified according to the purpose or effect the letter was meant to have. We are familiar with a number of letter types. We write "letters of recommendation" for students or colleagues. We receive "letters of solicitation" every day, offering some product or service. We use "letters of friendship" to keep in touch with family or friends who live at a distance, and these are often also "letters of information," newsy letters keeping us abreast of developments in the lives of people important to us. Ancient teachers of the art of letter-writing highlighted the following types:

- The "friendly" letter expresses mutual concern, partnership and sharing of resources. It often includes the topics of separation "in body only," remembrances of the other and of shared experiences, concern for the other, and acting in the other's interest during the separation.

- The "commendatory" letter recommends some person as honorable and reliable, offering testimony of the writer's own experience of the person's faithfulness.

---

[b]Ben Witherington III, *Friendship and Finances in Philippi* (Valley Forge, Penn.: Trinity Press International, 1994), p. 8.

- The "consoling" letter expresses sympathy toward those who have suffered unpleasant things and seeks to make the hardship easier to bear.

- The "admonishing" letter identifies inappropriate behavior on the part of the recipient and prescribes a remedy.

- The "threatening" letter seeks to make the recipient afraid of past or potential future misdeeds, often using the topics of accountability and consequences.

- The "censuring" letter makes the recipient ashamed of some past action.

- The "praising" letter commends the recipient for past actions or commends and encourages him or her in proposed actions.

- The "encouraging" letter making the recipient bold in pursuit of some course of action.

- The "advisory" letter recommends one course of action or character trait over another, or seeks to dissuade the recipient from a course of action.

- The "supplicatory" letter makes requests of the recipient.

- The "inquiring" letter seeks to learn some information from the recipient.

- The "responding" letter responds to a previous inquiry made by the addressee.

- The "figurative" or "allegorical" letter uses cryptic language to prevent a third party from understanding the substance of the letter.

- The "accounting" letter allows the sender to explain why he or she has not, or will not, be able to do something expected of him or her.

- The "accusing" letter accosts the recipient with claims of improper behavior, attitude or associations.

- The "apologetic" letter seeks to defuse charges made against the sender (by the recipient or by a third party in the ears of the recipient), often offering evidence that the charges could not be true, transferring blame to other persons or causes, and using other strategies common to "judicial" defense speeches.

- The "congratulatory" letter expressing joy at honors or good things that have come to the recipient, often including some pious expression attributing the success to the gods.

- The "thankful" letter expresses gratitude toward the recipient for past kindnesses, often speaking of being indebted to the recipient, owing a return of the favor.

- The "moral" letter instructs the recipient on virtuous behavior.

- The "prayerful" letter shares the content of prayers offered on behalf of the recipient.

- The "reporting" letter updates the recipient on events known to the sender.

- The "didactic" letter teaches the recipient about some topic.

- The "mixed" letter combines two or more of the above types.[c]

We can readily see from this catalog of epistolary types how skill in argumentation and style (i.e., the art of rhetoric) would have served letter writers well. For example, deliberative strategies would enhance the encouraging and advisory letters, forensic strategies the accusatory and apologetic letters, and epideictic topics the praising, congratulatory and censuring letters, to state the most obvious.

Paul's letters are longer than most ancient letters, and they always fall into the category of the "mixed" type—the letter that seeks to accomplish several goals in a single communication. Nevertheless, each smaller section of a Pauline letter could be heard as representing a single letter type, and it is often a helpful guide to interpretation to think about how each paragraph would have been heard by Paul's readers, given the topics he invokes (e.g., as accomplishing the goals of a "letter of friendship," or "letter of commendation" or "letter of reproach").

To begin thinking about epistolary analysis, try the following exercises:

1. Read 2 John, 3 John, Philemon and Jude. These brief New Testament letters very closely resemble the typical Greco-Roman letter. As you read each letter, note where the author seems to address particular topics listed above in the description of epistolary types. How would an ancient reader "hear" the letter (what type or, in the case of the "mixed" letter, types would the hearer encounter in the letter)? How does this help clarify the purpose behind each letter? (On 2-3 John, see the section on "genre" in the chapter on the Johannine Epistles as a means of checking your findings).

2. Read through 1 or 2 Thessalonians paragraph by paragraph and ask yourself: How would the recipients have heard this paragraph? What would they have understood Paul's goal to be in that segment of the letter? Is there a particular type that keeps returning, that you might view as the primary type? What would be the ancillary letter types?

[c]The list is excerpted and analysis derived from the handbooks on letter writing by Pseudo-Demetrius and Pseudo-Libanius, collected and translated in Abraham J. Malherbe, "Ancient Epistolary Theorists," *Ohio Journal of Religious Studies* 5 (1977): 3-77.

1 THESSALONIANS

Renewing the bond of friendship. One important purpose served by 1 Thessalonians is the renewal of the friendship between Paul and the believers. This is not to say that the relationship had gone bad or was in danger of dying, but merely to acknowledge that all friendships need to be continually nurtured to be kept vibrant and strong. Friends in the ancient world, when they could not renew their friendship in person, had the form of the "friendly letter" ready at hand for the task. Letters aimed at this purpose would tend to touch on widely used "topics" expressive of friendship, including discussion of the nature and extent of separation, desires to or means of overcoming distance (for example, keeping the friend ever in mind), recollections of past shared experiences and interactions, expressions of concern for the other and indications of how one has worked for the friend's well-being even at a distance, expressions of confidence in the friend's similar commitment to the friendship and mutual aid.[15]

We can readily see how Paul has woven all these topics into 1 Thessalonians, especially the first three chapters of the letter. Paul and his team overcome distance in their friendship with the converts through remaining mindful of them, primarily in prayer (1 Thess 1:2), but also as they encounter praiseworthy reports of their friends even in remote places (1 Thess 1:8-9). Connections are reaffirmed by reminding the converts of their time together, the warm welcome, the displays of love and devotion, the deep, open sharing of good things (1 Thess 1:5, 9; 2:1-12). Paul also speaks of praying on their behalf all throughout their separation (1 Thess 1:2; 2:13; 3:10) and sends Timothy for a visit (1 Thess 3:1-2). He speaks of his longing to visit them, making plans to that effect but being thwarted by a cosmic enemy, and praying that God would yet make a way (1 Thess 2:17-18; 3:10). He recalls from Timothy's report that the Thessalonian believers feel the same way about the separation and maintain their positive feelings toward Paul (1 Thess 3:6). Paul speaks effusively about the importance of these friends, who are kept close to his heart as his encouragement, joy and pride now and in the future (2:19-20; 3:2, 7-8).

The attention Paul gives to these topics, and thus to the task of reaffirming and renewing the friendship, is quite appropriate to the needs of the situation. He needs to reassure the converts that they were not abandoned by their teacher, left alone to fend for themselves against the unsupportive society. When Paul left town he did not leave the Thessalonian Christians behind along with his troubles in that city—rather, he carried them with him daily in his heart and took thought for their well-being constantly. As other networks of support crumble around the converts, Paul seeks to reassure them that he and his team still maintain their friendship and support for them.

Reinforcing commitment to an unpopular way of life. Our earlier discussion of the social value of honor and our exploration of how Matthew used honor language to reinforce Christian commitment and the pursuit of discipleship prepares us to examine Paul's use of similar strategies in 1 Thessalonians. Even as their neighbors seek to shame the Christians into a return to their former way of life, Paul seeks to insulate them against the effects of their neighbors' shaming. Moreover, Paul reassures the believers that, far from losing honor, they have gained incomparable honor—and will attain yet greater honor as a result of their commitment to the way of Jesus.

How does Paul insulate the Christians

---

[15]See the example of a friendly letter in Pseudo-Demetrius *Epistolary Types* 1, conveniently provided in Malherbe, *Letters to the Thessalonians*, p. 181.

against the considerable pressure that could be mounted against them? We have already seen how Paul reinterprets this pressure as an assault orchestrated by "the tempter" (1 Thess 3:5), such that yielding to those pressures would mean defeat at the hands of God's arch-enemy, not a peaceful return to the bosom of unbelieving friends and family. Paul spends considerably more space, however, suggesting that these unbelieving neighbors actually act shamefully and stand in a position of disprivilege and dishonor compared to the Christians. The logic is this: if contemptible people shame you for being honorable and favored, are you going to make yourself contemptible in order to be well regarded by the moral and eschatological "losers"?

Paul censures non-Christian Gentiles as people given over to shameful lust and ignorance of God (a familiar pair in Hellenistic Jewish anti-Gentile polemic: see Wis 13:1-9; 14:22-27). When Paul tells the believers not to act "in the passion of desire like the Gentiles who do not know God" (1 Thess 4:5), Paul's contrast of lifestyle between the (Gentile) believers and the (unbelieving) Gentiles assumes that the unbelievers' values are incompatible with and inferior to the enlightened ethos of the Christian group. The Christians, therefore, should not be swayed by the unbelievers' evaluation of them, since the latter cannot evaluate honorable behavior properly and have no knowledge of what is ultimately honorable in God's sight.

Paul's introduction of "sanctification" in this context (1 Thess 4:3), which entails being "set apart" from the ordinary mass of humanity for a special connection with God, further underscores the boundary between the Christian community and the unbelieving world. Since this boundary is determined by God's own purposes, Paul assures the believers that their new group loyalties are absolutely legitimate, and that any resistance to their Christian commitment is resistance against the will of God himself.[16]

In 1 Thessalonians 5:3-8 Paul creates an even more elaborate contrast between the believers and unbelievers, each point showing the believers to occupy the more advantageous position. Non-Christians speak of "peace and security" (an ironic reference to the Roman peace, or *pax Romana*),[17] but they will be utterly surprised and overturned on the "day of wrath" when God visits the world in judgment. The believers are as different from outsiders as day is from night, light from darkness, wakefulness from sleeping, sobriety from drunkenness. In a similar way, when facing "last" or "ultimate things," believers are privileged to be able to face death with hope, unlike non-Christians, who grieve as those without hope (1 Thess 4:13). The unbelievers' perception of reality crumbles in the face of death and cannot adequately answer this threatening phenomenon. Their neighbors may pressure them to return to their old ways, but Paul depicts this in strokes that suggest returning to sleep and drunkenness when a crisis is at hand, to moral looseness when God's holiness beckons, to darkness when the bright light of God's "Day" is already dawning.

At the same time that Paul helps believers set aside society's negative opinion of them, he also reminds his friends about the body of people whose evaluation of them has real

---

[16]See O. L. Yarbrough on the boundary-maintaining function of 1 Thessalonians 4:3-8 (*Not Like the Gentiles: Marriage Rules in the Letters of Paul*, SBLDS 80 [Atlanta: Scholars Press, 1984], p. 87). Malherbe incorrectly claims that Paul cannot wish to separate Christians from Gentiles by means of such injunctions as 1 Thessalonians 4:3-8 *and* at the same time orient them toward seeking to make a good impression on outsiders (*Paul and the Thessalonians*, p. 239). This is exactly what conversionist groups do. They must reaffirm the difference between "us" and "them" even as they seek to invite the outsiders to cross over the boundary and join the group.

[17]For more on this, see K. Wengst, *Pax Romana and the Peace of Christ* (Fortress: Philadelphia: 1987), p. 73-78.

bearing on their worth and honor. While they are not to act with regard to their neighbors' disapproval, they must focus first and foremost on God's approval. Paul's thanksgiving sections teach this basic fact: by giving thanks to God and remembering the believers before God, Christians are reminded of this One in whose sight they live and in whose presence they seek remembrance, recognition and reward (1 Thess 1:2-3). Paul and his team underscore this point in their personal example. Paul seeks to please God rather than win the praise of human beings (1 Thess 2:4, 6), and this stands as part of the example the believers have imitated (1 Thess 1:6) and are called to imitate further in order also to please God (1 Thess 4:1). God's evaluation counts far more than society's, for on the day of the Lord the eternal effects of God's evaluation will be made manifest. It is always with a view to that "court" that believers seek to live in the present, preferring temporary danger and loss from human courts of opinion to the eternal danger and loss from God's court (1 Thess 1:5; 2:19-20; 3:13; 5:9).

As they seek God's approval, the Christians also enjoy the approval of fellow believers. Other Christians, especially those locally present in Thessalonica, become the people whose approval will come to matter most to the individual convert. As Christians live out Paul's injunctions to "exhort one another" (1 Thess 5:11; cf. 5:14), "build one another up" (1 Thess 5:11), "love one another" more and more (1 Thess 4:9-10),[18] and "comfort one another" (1 Thess 4:18), their relationships will also grow closer. Feelings of attachment and experiences of encouragement within the group will outweigh feelings of disconnected-

ness from society and experiences of discouragement at the hands of outsiders. Care for and being cared for by the brothers and sisters will lead to an increased desire to conform to the values of the group, and to be held in esteem by those who are important to a Christian's daily life.[19]

The local body of Christians, however, is but one cell in the body of Christ. Paul reminds the Thessalonian converts of the community of believers around the Mediterranean and draws attention to the way their honor has been enhanced in the eyes of all these people by their bold commitment to Jesus in the face of opposition. The loss of esteem they suffered in society's eyes receives ample compensation in the honor they now enjoy throughout the circles of Christians in Macedonia, Achaia and beyond (1 Thess 1:7-9). Significantly, the very acts that led them into dishonor in their neighbors' eyes—their turning away from all gods except the God made known by Jesus, and their commitment to live with a view to Jesus' return—have brought them honor in the eyes of a wider audience (1 Thess 1:9-10). Paul himself honors them for their "work of faithfulness and labor of love and constancy of hope" (1 Thess 1:3) and for their reception of the gospel in the face of society's opposition (1 Thess 1:6; 2:13-14). The fact that Paul gives thanks to God for these manifestations in the believers' lives also assumes God's approval. He speaks of the believers as specially "chosen" by God to be a part of this new community, which is now a mark of God's favor and approval (1 Thess 1:4; 2:12).

Paul gives considerable space to convincing the converts, moreover, that such hostility was "normal," only to be expected from the unbe-

---

[18]Paul actually uses *philadelphia*, a term meaning "sibling love," rather than *philanthrōpia*, "love for humanity" and beneficence in general. This is not because Paul is uninterested in acts of love and benevolence that reach beyond the group (cf. 1 Thess 3:12; 5:13), but because he seeks to promote first that level and kind of mutual affection and investment that will enhance the solidarity of the group, as well as convey to the individual member that these relationships are the most significant in his or her life.

[19]This is also a probable effect of Paul's own use of affective language in 1 Thess 2:7-12; 2:17—3:1, 6-10.

lieving world. This was part of Paul's team's own experience and example (1 Thess 2:2, 15-16), a topic addressed in Paul's preparation of the converts (1 Thess 3:3-4), the experience of Judean Christians at the hands of their compatriots (1 Thess 2:14), and now the Thessalonian Christians have fallen into the same pattern. Paul's emphasis on normalcy is important because the society is trying to get the believers to see themselves as deviant and in need of change. As Paul inverts this, society's opposition actually assures the believers that they are right where they should be, and not "out of line" with the norm. Encountering resistance from the outside world is part of the normal course of making progress toward the honor God has in store for the faithful.

Finally, Paul consistently urges his sisters and brothers to live with a view to attaining the honor and security that Jesus will provide for his faithful followers on the Day of the Lord. The opinion of outsiders during these days of struggle is inconsequential compared to the opinion God forms of the believers on that day of visitation. In light of their awareness of that coming day the believers have a great advantage over their detractors, who will be put to shame on that day as the converts are vindicated by God (1 Thess 5:4) and delivered from God's condemnation (1 Thess 1:10). Paul's repeated reminders of that day serve to focus the converts on the importance of being blameless in God's sight, no matter how their neighbors may respond to them as they walk in obedience to the coming Judge (see 1 Thess 3:12-13; 5:9, 23).

Despite the need to insulate Christians from the pull of an unsupportive society, Paul does not suggest that his converts cocoon entirely and shut out unbelievers, a response that was made by some isolationist groups like the Qumran community. Instead, he advises the Christians to reach out not only to fellow believers but also to all people (1 Thess 3:12; 5:15). The Christians should look for opportunities to benefit outsiders to dispel, to some extent, society's suspicion of them and perhaps even begin to regain respect. While society's opinion of them is not allowed to mute their witness to Jesus or compromise their exclusive commitment to the one God, they should seek to dispel prejudice by showing the virtues that devotion to this one God manifests in their lives, especially to the benefit of the whole society.

Addressing new questions in the community. Several other pastoral concerns occupy Paul as he writes 1 Thessalonians, and Timothy seems the most probable source of information. Along with the good report of the converts' perseverance in the faith and continued good will toward Paul, Timothy brought news of two situations that troubled the believers. First, some of the believers in Thessalonica have died, perhaps while Paul was still present or more likely after Paul's departure from the city. There are no signs that these unnamed brothers or sisters met a violent death (as in martyrdom) since Paul utilizes none of the typical topics we would expect to find in a "letter of consolation" where persecution and martyrdom were the cause of death. For example, he does not speak of God's vindication of the dead, who have suffered an unjust sentence from humans, nor of God's pleasure with and certain rewarding of those who showed steadfastness to the extreme limits of endurance. Rather, these believers suffered natural deaths. Given the susceptibility of people, especially people of limited means, to disease in the ancient world, it should not surprise us that this could have become a problem in the short space of a few months.

The surviving believers, having heard Paul's enthusiastic proclamation of the return of Christ, may have expected Christ's return to occur in a very short while. Indeed, Paul appears to expect himself to be among the "we" who will be alive at the time of Jesus' coming (1 Thess 4:15, 17). At this point in his career Paul does not seem to have had any concern about dying before that day came, and he may not have prepared his converts for that eventuality in their own midst. The community was taken aback when death intervened in the lives of some, and it was left wondering whether or not the dead brothers and sisters had been cut off from the hope of the community. Paul assures the believers that those who have died are not beyond the reach of God's protection, promise and patronage. Just as God triumphed over death in raising Jesus from the grave, so God is able to fulfill God's promises to those who have trusted in God and fallen "asleep." The living believers will be reunited with their dead sisters and brothers at the coming of Jesus, and all will experience the final triumph of God together. Separation of the living and dead will be overcome at that very moment that is also the culmination of the Christian hope.

Even within this topic, however, Paul continues to draw distinctions between Christians and non-Christians, showing the latter to be in a disadvantaged position. Because of their hope Christians can grieve in a manner distinctive from "those who have no hope," who are finally at a loss when faced with the death of a loved one. In the face of the ultimate experience of marginalization—death—the believer has a philosophy that will equip him or her to maintain balance of spirit, while the unbeliever, who may deride the believer now while all is well, is left unequipped at that critical juncture.

A second challenge facing the community appears to have been the presence of some believers who have ceased to work, living off the charitable support of the Christian community. This is certainly reflected in 1 Thessalonians 5:14 and will become a more pressing problem to be addressed more explicitly and forcefully in 2 Thessalonians 3:6-15. The ambience of a community dedicated to sharing possessions and mutual support, combined perhaps with a hyper-accentuated sense of the nearness of the end, may have tempted these people to avoid the mundane and trivial business of the world. Perhaps they were motivated by noble ambitions, like devoting themselves to prayer or a ministry of teaching believers and nonbelievers about the faith. Perhaps more selfish motivations lay behind their decision to refrain from working. Either way, Paul refused to countenance such behavior. His own model was one of showing love for fellow believers by working with his own hands so as not to be a burden. His converts were to do no less (1 Thess 4:12; 5:14). Indeed, the Thessalonians may have asked how far their "love for the brothers and sisters" should be taxed (1 Thess 4:9), with Paul subtly providing the instruction that all should contribute insofar as they were able to work, both for the good of the Christian community and for the reputation of the group in the eyes of outsiders (1 Thess 4:9-12).[20]

2 THESSALONIANS

The situation behind 2 Thessalonians. While we can readily situate 1 Thessalonians in the context of the life and work of Paul, and develop a clear picture of the situation addressed by Paul, matters become more complicated when we turn to 2 Thessalonians. The complications arise as noteworthy scholars raise serious doubts concerning the authorship of this letter, arguing that it was written not by Paul but in Paul's name.[21] Pseudepigraphy—the attribution of a work to a person who is not its actual author—was common in the centuries

---

[20]Malherbe, *Letters to the Thessalonians*, pp. 255-60.

[21]For a fuller discussion of these complex issues, see especially I. Howard Marshall, *1 & 2 Thessalonians*, NCBC (Grand Rapids: Eerdmans, 1983), pp. 28-45; Wanamaker, *Epistles to the Thessalonians*, pp. 17-28; Malherbe, *Letters to the Thessalonians*, pp. 366-74; J. A. Bailey, "Who Wrote II Thessalonians?" *NTS* 25 (1978): 131-45.

1 Thessalonians 2:1-12

IS PAUL DEFENDING HIMSELF?

Scholars debate whether or not we should read 1 Thessalonians 2:1-12 as Paul's self-defense against slanderous accusations being made against him in Thessalonica or whether some other purpose shapes the framing of these paragraphs.[a] The question has some bearing on what we understand to be the situation in Thessalonica and what Paul's driving point is in this section.

Paul met opposition, particularly assaults on his own character and authority, at many points during his ministry. The Jewish Christian missionaries seeking to bring Galatian Christianity closer to Jewish practice may have impugned his authority (Gal 1:1, 15-16; 5:11; 6:17). The rival teachers that followed him to Corinth certainly criticized his authority, his pastoral strategies, his abilities and his motives (2 Cor 10:10; 11:5-6; 12:11, 15-17). Paul is aware of people who misrepresent him as he writes to the Christians in Rome (Rom 3:8). The ample evidence that Paul had to defend or explain himself elsewhere no doubt predisposes scholars to expect that he would encounter similar opposition in Thessalonica. In 1 Thessalonians 2:1-12, we encounter a strongly antithetical style. He is consistently pointing out what he did *not* do (affirming instead that he did something else) or what motives did *not* motivate him (offering alternative motives for his actions). This could easily be interpreted to signify that someone in Thessalonica was attributing to Paul certain untoward actions or unflattering motives. Paul would then be negating what somebody in Thessalonica had been saying about him, even formally defending himself by calling forward "witnesses" to his behavior—first God and then the Thessalonian Christians themselves (1 Thess 2:5, 10).

Those who read 1 Thessalonians 2:1-12 as Paul's defense against charges do not agree on the source of the slanders. Perhaps rival Christian teachers came to Thessalonica, as elsewhere, and sought to undermine Paul's credibility. Perhaps members of the congregation themselves raised questions about Paul's motives. Perhaps their non-Christian neighbors slandered Paul as part of their attempt to draw the Christians away from their newfound faith, saying things like "I can't believe you were taken in by that old charlatan, peddling his superstition like the hucksters in the marketplace." Of all these possibilities the last one makes the most sense. Paul nowhere else gives any hint of rival teachers intruding on his ministry in Thessalonica, and Galatians and 2 Corinthians would lead us to expect much more explicit treatment of this problem by Paul if he faced it here. Nor does he give any hints elsewhere in this letter that his own converts mistrust him or challenge him. Paul's defense, then, would constitute part of his attempt to insulate his converts against the pressures of outsiders, reminding them that his ministry and their relationship was genuine, a true manifestation of mutual friendship and love in the Spirit of God. Therefore, they could continue to trust that relationship and the message Paul brought them, despite the slanders of outsiders.

---

[a]See Donfried and Beutler, *Thessalonians Debate,* pp. 31-134; Malherbe, *Letters to the Thessalonians,* pp. 153-56.

But is Paul really defending himself at all? Many scholars think not, rightly cautioning us not to assume that Paul's character was constantly under attack in every city. They also caution us not to read every denial Paul makes as a sign that someone else was making a claim, or every claim Paul makes as a sign that someone else was voicing a denial. Malherbe, for example, draws attention to the fact that many speakers in the first century would use antitheses in order to distinguish themselves from other speakers or philosophers, often in order to assert positively their own reliability and genuineness.[b]

Paul simply may seek to remind his converts that they could continue trusting him and his team, leaning on this relationship even as relationships with nonbelievers crumbled and turned sour. It may serve the goals of the rhetorical "appeal to ethos," establishing the credibility of the speaker, just as Paul's interpretation of society's pressure to desist from following Jesus as a manifestation of the "tempter" would undermine the credibility the converts gave to their non-Christian neighbors and friends. Just as the advice of the latter could not be trusted, stemming ultimately from Satan, so the advice of Paul could be trusted, since he had always proven himself a genuine, reliable friend with the converts' best interests at heart.

Paul's lengthy reflection on his own ministerial style, strategy and heart provides a more detailed reminder of the "model" or "example" that he had left for the Thessalonians, and that they had begun to imitate at their conversion (1 Thess 1:6). Paul's purpose may not be apologetic at all but rather ethical, as the reminiscences of his own example resonate so well with the needs of the situation. For example, just as Paul had shown courage in the face of persecution for the gospel's sake (1 Thess 2:2), so the believers must continue to show courage. Just as Paul worked with his hands in order not to burden the converts, whom he loved (1 Thess 2:5, 9), so the Thessalonians are to work with their hands and contribute to the common good (rather than unnecessarily tax the charity of the community). Just as Paul and his team conducted themselves in a "pure, upright and blameless" manner (1 Thess 2:10), so the converts are to be "blameless" before God (1 Thess 3:13; 5:23). Reading the passage simply as Paul's self-defense, we miss the rich resonances of this passage with the rest of the letter and the specific ways Paul's example is to be replicated in the lives of the disciples, then and now.

---

[b]Malherbe, *Letters to the Thessalonians*, pp. 154-55.

---

around the turn of the era. Most Jewish apocalypses were written in the name of some deeply respected figure like Enoch, Abraham, Moses or the twelve sons of Jacob. Many early Christian writings from the second and third centuries are attributed to Paul, Peter, Andrew or Thomas, but they surely were not written by these apostles. Such a practice would strike us a deceptive, a kind of reverse plagiarism. The real authors, however, probably chose pseudonymity as a means to mark their interest in and loyalty to a particular stream of tradition within the larger community, and by which that author could attach his or her work to the ongoing interpretation of the life and teachings of a venerable ancient figure.[22]

Scholars marshal several different kinds of evidence in the case against Pauline authorship. First, they note that the tone of 2 Thessalonians is somewhat more formal and less emotionally effusive than 1 Thessalonians. Second, they point to the similarities in structure (the letter opening, the doubling of thanksgivings and benedictions, which is peculiar to these two letters), suggesting that an unknown author used 1 Thessalonians as a rather rigid model for creating a sequel. Third, some deem the eschatology of the two letters, one stressing the imminence of the "Day" and the other stressing the events that have yet to occur before the arrival of the Day, to be incompatible.[23]

Despite the apparent weight of these observations, each can be accounted for within a theory of Pauline authorship. The differences in vocabulary, style and tone could point to a greater degree of participation in the writing of the letter by one of Paul's colleagues. We tend to overlook the claims made to collegial authorship in most Pauline letters, and many superficial differences between one letter and another could reflect the contributions of Timothy or Silvanus to the framing and writing of the letter. Moreover, a subtle shift in the composition of the addressees could account for the difference in tone. Malherbe has recently made the cogent suggestion that Paul writes 2 Thessalonians to a different house church in Thessalonica than the one to whom he sent 1 Thessalonians.[24] If indeed Paul's converts themselves engaged in evangelism in their city,[25] Paul may have had little or no acquaintance with a sizeable portion of the overall Christian community in Thessalonica. First Thessalonians would reflect the warmth and self-disclosure of personal acquaintance and friendship; 2 Thessalonians the ever-so-slightly more formal posture taken toward a group including a number of members the writer has not met face-to-face.

The alleged difference in eschatology, moreover, is simply overdrawn. In 2 Thessalonians the authors continue to anchor their exhortations to the community and the very boundaries of the group in the firm expectation of a forthcoming reversal (e.g., 2 Thess 1:6-10). This letter, however, demonstrates a concern to maintain the futurity as well as the certainty of the return of Christ. The collapse of the "Day of the Lord" into the present day, an error into which some Thessalonian believers appear to have fallen (2 Thess 2:2), threatens to shake this pillar of the Christian world construction, and Paul reasserts the futurity of the Day of the Lord through the use of the "man of lawlessness" tradition, an apocalyptic topic well-known from Daniel. Indeed, the imminence remains undiminished by the discussion of the "man of lawlessness,"[26] since his coming may itself be imminent given the presence of the warning signs of the deception that

---

[22]This is not to say that first-century readers would always "see through" the pseudonym. The author of Jude clearly does not with regard to *1 Enoch*, which he quotes as if the words indeed came from Enoch (see Jude 14-15; *1 Enoch* 1.9). See further "Excursus on Pseudepigraphy."

[23]See, for example, Earl Richard, *First and Second Thessalonians*, p. 25, who considers 2 Thessalonians to adopt an "anti-apocalyptic strategy"; F. W. Hughes, *Early Christian Rhetoric and 2 Thessalonians* (Sheffield, U.K.: JSOT Press, 1989), pp. 81-83. A hint of this appears in Gaventa, *First and Second Thessalonians*, p. 92.

[24]Malherbe, *Letters to the Thessalonians*, p. 355.

[25]As 1 Thessalonians 1:8 suggests; see Malherbe, *Letters to the Thessalonians*, p. 208.

[26]Some argue that the "man of lawlessness" motif depends on the myth of *Nero redivivus*, the return of the dead Nero at the head of a foreign army, but this is patently not the case. The activity of Antiochus IV (especially as interpreted by Daniel) and, in times recent for Paul, Caligula would have provided Jewish Christians with all the necessary materials to develop this end-time image.

has overtaken unbelievers.[27] The eschatological perspectives of the two letters, moreover, stand side-by-side elsewhere in the New Testament. Mark 13, for example, presents Jesus' teaching on signs that would precede his return in glory together with the warning that this coming would be sudden and unexpected. The juxtaposition of Mark 13:28-31 and 13:32-37 is especially striking, the first asserting that by careful observation of these signs the disciples will know that the Son of Man is near, the second cautioning them that "about that day or hour no one knows" but the Father. Objections that the eschatology of 2 Thessalonians is incompatible with that of 1 Thessalonians, then, fail to appreciate the many currents and eddies active within the stream of apocalyptic thought.

In the likely event, then, that Paul and his team composed 2 Thessalonians, this letter would have been written a fairly short time after 1 Thessalonians, for Timothy and Silvanus were only together for a brief period of time after the writing of 1 Thessalonians.[28] Second Thessalonians addresses several of the same topics found in its prequel. The believers had made some positive progress in the direction that 1 Thessalonians has urged them, as Paul affirms their growing mutual love (cf. 1 Thess 4:9-10 with 2 Thess 1:3) and the steadfastness of their faith (cf. 1 Thess 3:10 with 2 Thess 1:3). Relationships within the community are sufficiently strong and have become sufficiently primary for most members that Paul believes the Christians can now use shaming and shunning within the group to reinforce certain behaviors (2 Thess 3:14-15). Nevertheless, the pressures from outside the group continue to demand Paul's attention—he continues to en-courage the Christians to resist that pressure (2 Thess 1:4-12).

A second issue revolves around a misunderstanding of Christian eschatology, thinking that "the Day of the Lord has arrived" (2 Thess 2:2). Indeed, it is possible that such a misunderstanding arose from the discussion of 1 Thessalonians 5:1-11 and perhaps from some glossing of the copy or copies of that letter circulating among the other house churches in Thessalonica.[29] Finally, the "idle" or "disorderly" (*ataktoi*) of 1 Thessalonians 5:14 (cf. 1 Thess 4:11) emerge here as a more evident problem requiring the believers' direct intervention (2 Thess 3:6-15).

Continued efforts at insulating the believers from society's shaming. The thanksgiving section of 2 Thessalonians brings together a series of topics that continue Paul's pastoral work of subverting society's attempts to shame the Christians back into conformity with their former lifestyle. Indeed, the heightened emphasis on the fate of those who afflict the converts suggests that social pressure has become more burdensome in the intervening months. We should recognize this as an important facet of the pastoral situation being addressed by this letter, and not limit our focus to the doctrinal issues (chap. 2) or the problem of the idle (chap. 3).

As in 1 Thessalonians the opening paragraph immediately reminds the believers of those in whose eyes they have gained honor by virtue of their perseverance in their Christian commitments, namely, God and the network of Christians across the province and beyond (2 Thess 1:3-4). God's evaluation of people matters above all else because it will be manifest at the day of reversal and it alone has eternal value. Paul praises the believers for

---

[27]For a contemporary example, we need only to note how Hal Lindsey's endless talk about the events that must yet take place before Christ's coming in triumph has heightened rather than diminished apocalyptic anticipation.

[28]Malherbe, *Letters to the Thessalonians,* pp. 349-50.

[29]Ibid., p. 355.

their fidelity to Jesus and their new way of life (understanding *pistis,* 2 Thess 1:3, not merely as "belief" but as firmness and faithfulness toward God), and for their ongoing investment in one another (their "love," 2 Thess 1:3). What society maligns becomes a source of honor in God's sight. The believers' endurance is transformed once more into a source of honor among Christians throughout the world: "Therefore we ourselves boast of you among the churches of God for your steadfastness and faith during all your persecutions and the afflictions that you are enduring" (2 Thess 1:4 NRSV).

The hostility, insults and rejection experienced by the Christians are also interpreted as a sign of God's approval and acceptance of these people. The affliction does not reflect their deviance or lack of honor (as society would have it understood) but rather qualifies them for eternal honor before God: "This is evidence of the righteous judgment of God, and is intended to make you worthy of the kingdom of God, for which you are also suffering" (2 Thess 1:5 NRSV). Paul introduces a strategy learned from Hellenistic Jewish literature, turning the negative experiences of members of the minority culture into a positive experience that, however painful, qualifies them for God's reward by exercising their fidelity to God.[30] The first-century text Wisdom of Solomon, for example, turns the shameful treatment of the loyal Jew at the hands of apostate Jews into a form of educative suffering, exercising the pious one in those traits (such as faith/faithfulness) that are necessary to please God: "having been disciplined a little, they will receive great good, because God tested them and found them worthy of himself" (Wis 3:5 NRSV). This technique is also used in Hebrews 12:5-11 and 1 Peter 1:6-7. The focus of the righteous sufferers is also strategically shifted. No longer are they

concerned with their lost honor in the world's eyes but rather with proving themselves worthy of a greater honor ("worthy of God's kingdom," 2 Thess 1:5; "worthy of God's call," 1 Thess 1:11). In this way, any temporal ambitions are defused and the human trait of ambition is itself harnessed to help believers persevere for eternal honor.

Enduring the slings and arrows of the ungodly not only educates or trains the believers in the virtues of fidelity and hope that qualify them for their eternal inheritance, but also provides an assurance (a "sign") of God's forthcoming judgment on the ungodly. These hardships are a "sign of God's righteous judgment" not because God judged the converts worthy of punishment, such that they had to pass through the purgatory of persecution before being worthy of the kingdom. Rather, as the logic of 2 Thessalonians 1:6-7 makes clear, the believers' suffering is really a sign or proof of God's imminent vindication (positive judgment) of the believers and punishment (negative judgment) of those who afflict the innocent righteous. This too was a familiar topic in Jewish literature on suffering for righteousness or God's law (see 4 Macc 9:8-9, 24, 31-32; 10:10, 21; 11:22-23; 12:11-14). Because God is just—and this is the assumed premise for the argument—the unjust affliction of the converts is evidence that God's judgment will soon break in to set matters right. On the day of judgment a great reversal will take place, and the believers' honor and security will be manifest and actualized while the unrepentant members of the host society will suffer punishment and exclusion from the promised rest. The lasting disgrace will cling to the unbeliever, not the believer. In the end Christ will show forth his own honor through his clients, and the believers' honor will be made known in Christ (2 Thess 1:11-12; 2:14).

---

[30]See Jouette M. Bassler, "The Enigmatic Sign: 2 Thessalonians 1:5," *CBQ* 46 (1984): 496-510.

Paul's strategic reinterpretation of society's opposition to the gospel and those who follow the Way emerges once more in Paul's own request for prayer for deliverance from hostile non-Christians: "pray for us . . . that we may be rescued from wicked and evil people; for not all have faith" (3:1-2 NRSV). Paul censures those who have not aligned themselves with the new community (who have not come to "faith") as "deviant [*atopoi*] and dishonorable people" (1 Thess 3:2). Their character defi-

Christian eschatology. Paul does not pinpoint the source of this misunderstanding. He names prophetic utterance and a letter purporting to come from himself as possibilities. The second could indicate the presence of pseudonymous letters already circulating during Paul's lifetime, but it could also refer to a corrupted copy or presentation of 1 Thessalonians, in which some well-meaning recipient in the first house church attempted to clarify Paul's end-time teaching.[31] But Paul's words

Figure 13.1. A denarius showing the head of the emperor Caligula on the obverse and the crowned head of the deified Augustus flanked by two stars on the reverse. Caligula sought to make the Jerusalem temple a center of imperial cult by the erection of his statue in the temple precincts. (Photo courtesy of the Thessaloniki Archaeological Museum and Todd Bolen [BiblePlaces.com])

ciencies explain their hostility to the gospel and its followers. The choice of *atopos* to describe those who do not have faith is particularly strategic, turning society's claim that the Christians are "deviant" or "out of place" back on its own head.

The collapse of the future hope. In the second chapter Paul and his team begin to respond to a second concern, namely, the correction of a potential misunderstanding of

may also be merely prophylactic.

It is also not clear what threat this collapse of the future "Day of the Lord" into the present posed to the community beyond the error itself. If its promoters meant to say that the Judgment was passed and that the believers were raised already with Christ, then it could easily degenerate into the sort of moral license we find in Corinth and in some early Gnostic sects. If they meant to say that the end of his-

---

[31]See Malherbe, *Letters to the Thessalonians*, p. 355.

The Development of the "Man of Lawlessness"

The figure of a man of lawlessness, who would establish the false worship of himself in the Jerusalem temple and enjoy wide success in deceiving the ungodly, is assigned a prominent role in several eschatological dramas. Prototypes for this figure may be found in the king of Babylon whose fall is announced in Isaiah 14:12-15 and the prince of Tyre whose arrogance and unrighteousness brings about his downfall in Ezekiel 28, but the mold was fully set by Antiochus IV, who set aside the religious observances in the Jerusalem temple in favor of a pagan cult. Antiochus IV was also well known for his presentation of himself as the "Deity revealed," an inscription that regularly appears on the reverses of his coinage (see figure 2.1). This ruler is demonized throughout Daniel (7:7-8, 19-27; 8:9-14, 23-25; 9:26-27; 11:21-45), and the language used there to characterize Antiochus IV provides the primary materials from which the end-time "man of lawlessness" could be forged.

Antiochus's profanation of the Jerusalem temple, called the "abomination of desolation" by the authors of Daniel 11 and 1 Maccabees 1, comes to be projected into the end time (as in Mk 13:14). In the climate of the emperor cult the element of proclaiming self-worship by a ruler becomes a more important part of the tradition. This element was no doubt driven forward by Caligula, who tried to do the Jews a favor by giving them an image of their invisible God to worship—a statue of Caligula himself! This attempt had repercussions among Jews as far away as Antioch and Alexandria, and only the wise delays of the governor of Syria and the timely assassination of the emperor prevented tragedy. Paul's "man of lawlessness," then, stands in this long stream of the development of the persona of an eschatological antagonist.

---

tory had already arrived and all bets were off, it could easily promote social unrest as believers left their work, broke off whatever social relations might have been left to them, or just worked themselves into a frenzy, which would degrade them even further in the eyes of the host society. Although Paul himself makes no such connection explicit, many scholars connect the overzealous anticipation of the end with the problem of believers giving up their work and relying on community support for those last weeks or months of life in this present evil age.

Whatever the source of or larger threat posed by this distortion, Paul wants to clarify that the Day of the Lord had not yet arrived (2 Thess 2:1-2), even though it may be very near. While never speaking against the imminence of the Day, the authors revisit a basic end-time schedule of events that they share, to a large extent, with other Jewish apocalyptic groups. Before the end there will be a widespread revolt against God's order and standards, and a figure will emerge in whom the human and demonic revolt against God comes to its fullest and final expression—the "man of lawlessness" (2 Thess 2:3). Paul provides this information not as data for a timetable for further speculation about the end but as a clear sign that the announcement of the end at Thessalonica was premature.

In the present time, Paul writes, the "mystery of lawlessness" was already at work, seen especially in the rejection of the gospel and the persecution of the believers. These are signs both of Satan's success in deceiving the nations and of the approach of the "lawless one" (2 Thess 2:9-10). An unnamed "restraining force" or "restrainer" (2 Thess 2:6-7) holds him back for now but will be removed at the appropriate time. The lawless one will rise up, however, only to fall under God's condemnation, and he will perish together with those who have been deceived by Satan, when Christ appears (2 Thess 2:8, 11-12).

This passage introduces a number of unknowns. While we can trace the sources of the concept of a man of lawlessness, naming him is another matter. Indeed, the figure appears mainly to be a personification of all those forces that work against God's good purposes for the world, that are ubiquitous and elusive at the same time. These coalesce in one monumental but convenient enemy, who can then be disposed of once and for all. That which "restrains," referred to both as an impersonal force and a personal agent in this passage, is even less clear. A persistent suggestion is that Paul had in mind the rule of law personified by the Roman emperor who, for all his faults, still maintained order and prevented lawlessness from running amok during Paul's ministry.[32] But Paul may also have been referring to some angelic power, since these are often depicted as exercising a restraining role in apocalypses (for example, holding back the elements of judgment or controlling the gate of the abyss, as in Rev 7:1-3; 9:1-3; 20:1-3). Perhaps these matters were clearer to Paul's addressees; perhaps they were as shrouded in mystery as they are for us. Either way, Paul places the converts in the midst of the "beginning of sorrows" (Mk 13:8), the opening act of the end times (rather than at the denouement or even the curtain call, as the erroneous teaching suggested).

Second Thessalonians 2:1-12 is not merely about eschatological information, however. It plays a strategic part in shaping the outlook of the converts who heard it. It has a rhetorical function and social effect that we could easily overlook. Apocalypses and the invocation of apocalyptic topics often have as their goal the clarification of the cosmic significance of the choices and alliances people make in the here and now. While speaking of future and other-worldly realities, these apocalypses also shape the hearer's perception of present, this-worldly realities.

What the man of lawlessness will openly bring out in full force in the future is already at work behind the scenes, namely, the "mystery of lawlessness." At the same time, Satan is at work trying to block people from seeing the truth and from embracing the salvation that God has announced. Those who are liable to this deception (or have already succumbed to deception) are the converts' non-Christian neighbors—the very people trying to harass and shame them from continuing in their Christian walk. The persecutors, while seeking to act as the guardians of traditional values, are actually ensnared in Satan's delusion and rush headlong to the abyss without even realizing their danger and doom. Paul does not present them merely as victims, however, but as those who have chosen to reject God's truth and have clung to disobedience as their preferred lifestyle (2 Thess 2:12). Therefore, God consigns them wholly to that delusion and its consequences.

The believers, however, occupy a privileged position, even at the same time that they are being persecuted. They have received the necessary information to avoid

[32]See the discussion in Richard, *First and Second Thessalonians*, pp. 337-40. Peter Stuhlmacher accepts the view that Paul understood himself and his mission to the Gentiles to be the restraining force (*Revisiting Paul's Doctrine of Justification*, [Downers Grove, Ill.: InterVarsity Press, 2001], p. 51).

After Paul Wrote 2 Thessalonians

The records of Paul's subsequent relationship with his sisters and brothers in Thessalonica are sparse. It is likely that he visited them when he passed through Macedonia to encourage the churches there (1 Cor 16:5) and yet again in connection with the relief efforts Paul was coordinating on behalf of the poor in Judea (2 Cor 2:13; 7:5; Acts 19:21-22; 20:1-6). This was a mission of great significance to Paul, the "apostle to the Gentiles," since it represented the unity of the largely Gentile churches he had founded with the parent church in Judea, and it was a symbolic fulfillment of the prophecy that the wealth of the nations would stream into Jerusalem during the age of the Messiah. The Macedonian Christians contributed generously to this effort despite their own poverty (2 Cor 8:1-5), making them an example to other Christians (notably those in Corinth). Indeed, Paul anticipated that some of them might accompany him on his way from Macedonia to Corinth (and beyond?) as an escort, providing protection for him as he traveled with a substantial sum of money (2 Cor 9:2-4). Paul's relationship with the Macedonian Christians (including the church in Philippi) remained, therefore, the most consistently positive and supportive for the apostle.

falling prey to Satan's deceptions (2 Thess 2:3, 15). Standing firm in the face of societal pressure and holding on to the authentic message of Paul and his team emerges as the course of action that keeps them safe from falling prey to this global deception (2 Thess 2:9-12) and that leads to deliverance and the fulfillment of God's good purposes for the converts. If they do, they obtain a share in the honor that Jesus himself enjoys (2 Thess 2:13-14). The section that began at 2 Thessalonians 2:1 does not end until verse 15, which returns to the words "by word" and "by our letter" (cf. 2 Thess 2:2 and 2:15). Paul has used the literary device called *inclusio*, signaling that the thanksgiving in 2 Thessalonians 2:13 does not begin a new section but completes the current section, highlighting once again the contrast between the converts (2 Thess 2:13-15) and those outside the church (2 Thess 2:9-12) so that those inside will not be tempted to revert to the lifestyle and worldview of those outside.

The problem of the "idle" or the "unruly." The third pastoral challenge concerns the report that apparently reached Paul that some converts are "living in idleness" (2 Thess 3:6). The Greek adverb translated "in idleness" may also be rendered "in an unruly or undisciplined manner" (*ataktōs*). The word is a military metaphor for soldiers who are not lined up properly, not following orders. Paul paints them not just as lazy but as a potentially disruptive element within the noble life of the Christian community.

We do not really know why these believers were not engaged in fruitful labor. They might have been unemployed persons who were attracted to the gospel but who then continued to live off the charity of the community. They may have been employed, but after their conversion they came to believe that the closeness of the "end" meant that the ordinary business and rules of life no longer mattered, so they stopped working. They might have been people specially endowed with charismatic gifts who thought that they were thereby freed of the normal requirements of ungifted people, and who expected the church to support them as a return for their contribution to the community. The *Didache,* an early Christian manual of theology and church discipline, attests to this sort of possibility and offers regulations to cut down on the abuses of local church support by wandering spiritualists. They might have been the self-appointed spiritual directors of the community who gave up their mundane occupations to devote themselves full time to regulating the lives (i.e., meddling, being busybodies) of their less spiritual sisters and brothers. Or perhaps these idlers were seeking to avoid society's hostility, shrinking back, withdrawing from those places where they would expose themselves to insult, disapproving glares or worse. It may have been desirable for some not to show their faces in public anymore, but rather withdraw and wait for Christ's speedy return (which would hopefully occur before the food ran out).

Whatever the motivation for not working, Paul's response is clear enough. Part of the "tradition" the converts received from Paul was not just instruction from his lips but instruction from his example. This is in keeping with the tradition of Greco-Roman philosophers who taught how to live a life of virtue not only by word but also by example.[33] Paul's example taught that it was noble to work to support oneself and one's God-given mission (2 Thess 3:7-8; see 1 Thess 2:9-10). His explicit instruction also reinforced that it was necessary (2 Thess 3:10). Paul and his team would be the first to encourage charity toward those who were unable to support themselves or whose circumstances had forced them into need (as in his collection for the poor in Judea). But to abuse charity to support an ignoble and idle lifestyle went beyond the pale, dishonoring charity itself. The authors assert that they worked with their own hands even though they had the authority as apostles to receive community support (2 Thess 3:9; see 1 Cor 9:1-18), so important was it to them that their example should encourage all to persevere in profitable labor.

Paul calls on the local congregation to support his admonitions concerning these idlers, to exercise pressure of their own on the *ataktoi* to return to an orderly life and a productive occupation. Idlers, as potential sources of social disturbance within the group, would not help the group coexist with the outside world.[34] They did not need internal confirmation of society's anxieties about potential subversive elements among Christians. The idlers are called to go into the workplace, to earn money for their own support and as the means of doing good to others, and to endure society's hostility while bearing witness that the suspicions and fears regarding Christians are unfounded. The group is now strong enough to exercise internally the same sort of social control that the society had been attempting, however unsuccessfully, in its effort to call believers back to conformity with the dominant culture's norms. The strategy of shaming becomes a tool for promoting adherence to the values of the group and to Paul's directions in particular (2 Thess 3:6, 14-15). The goal of such pressure is, of course, to reincorporate the deviants back into the group—the very goal that the unbelievers no doubt had for their shaming of their Christian neighbors.

---

[33]Wanamaker, *Epistles to the Thessalonians,* p. 283.
[34]Ibid., pp. 282, 286.

THE THESSALONIAN CORRESPONDENCE
AND MINISTRY FORMATION

Paul's words to the young churches in Thessalonica continue to provide rich resources for shaping ministry and vital congregations in this age. One of the special resources provided by 1 Thessalonians is the firsthand testimony of Paul to the mode of life and heart he adopted in an effort to make Jesus present to his converts and to give them an example to follow (1 Thess 2:1-12). Such a practice was entirely in keeping with the expectations of all teachers of a philosophy or way of life. Paul often speaks of his converts becoming "imitators" of him, particularly as he himself seeks to imitate Jesus (1 Thess 1:6; 2 Thess 3:7-9; see 1 Cor 4:16; 11:1; Phil 3:17). He desires that every Christian learn not only from his words but also his personal example, but this is all the more relevant for Christian leaders who, like Paul, are entrusted with the formation of communities of disciples.

Paul presents himself as a model of integrity in Christian leadership. *Integrity* connotes "wholeness," "oneness," not going in two directions at the same time. Paul's integrity springs from a desire to serve God faithfully above all else, indeed from a refusal even to desire anything besides being found faithful to God. In a Christian leader's choices and actions, we should be able to observe a person who seeks to please God rather than desiring the approval of humans (1 Thess 2:4, 6). We misuse our ministry and abuse the gospel when we make it a means to enhance our reputation or standing in the eyes of humans, and in fact we become slaves to public opinion rather than slaves of Christ. Such a person would disobey Christ's call when summoned to lead in an unpopular direction or to challenge the sacred cows of congregation and country. Paul's team had the courage to bear witness to the truth of God in the face of a hostile society (1 Thess 2:2), and such courage derives from an adequate appreciation of the importance of God's approval over human approval.

In addition to prestige or respectability, Christian ministry could be construed as a source of material gain. Paul lays heavy emphasis on his working with his own hands to support himself and his team during their ministry as proof of his sincerity (1 Thess 2:9). He does not want anyone to be able to challenge his sincerity or integrity by suggesting that he is peddling Jesus or that he is only in it for the money. The ministry of several prominent individuals has suffered discredit on the basis of the luxurious lifestyle and extravagances funded by the contributions of the flock. Far from making money off the gospel, Paul believed so strongly in the message that he spent his own earnings to make it available (1 Thess 2:5, 9)!

The church has developed a professional clergy whose services are compensated with money and housing. Most clergy, myself included, prefer to live by the maxim "the laborer is worthy of his or her hire" (1 Tim 5:18) than by Paul's example. Nevertheless, it is imperative that we not allow desire for material goods, for wealth, for nice things to rob us of our integrity, our single-hearted commitment to serve the God who summoned us to the ministry. As long as we engage every task of ministry out of a desire to be found "worthy of the God who calls us into God's own kingdom and glory" (1 Thess 2:12) and not any lesser reward, we will also reflect Paul's integrity. All ministers of the church—which means all baptized Christians—are challenged to model this integrity, however, since Paul addresses not merely leaders but all Christians. All Christians are invited into this integrity of life and heart as they pour themselves out in service to God, and not for pride of place in, or the satisfaction of influence over, the congregation.

Finally, a Christian leader following in Paul's example will show gentleness, a commitment to nurturing the community of faith, a giving of himself or herself for the building up of others in the church (1 Thess 2:7-8, 11-12). The images of nurse and father are important here, for the authority of the leader must always be enacted with the selfless love of the nurturing parent. As Paul recalls with highly personal language the emotional bonds and nurturing relationships that he formed with the believers, he reminds us of the love for each individual in our charge that must permeate and energize our ministry.

These two letters speak to several other timely issues as well. Paul wrote to a church that was moving against the current of its society and that was increasingly buffeted by the waves of that current. Many of our sisters and brothers in the faith face far greater harassment and persecution than did the Thessalonian Christians, but Paul provides some hints as to how we can encourage them. Paul believed it important for the Thessalonian believers to know that their story had been heard outside of their locale and that it had won them the admiration of those who shared their faith. He encouraged them to continue facing the pressure by reminding them of God's special selection of them for God's kingdom and for high honors and safety on the day of Judgment. He encouraged them through the visit of an emissary and through writing of letters. He held them up before God and informed them of this partnership in prayer—a partnership they participated in by praying for him and his team as well.

All these signs point to ways that we can help our sisters and brothers persevere in their contests for the faith, making the good confession and retaining their grasp on their inheritance. The information age can work to our mutual advantage, as we dedicate ourselves and involve our congregations in learning about specific Christian communities facing persecution, as we tell their stories in the public hearing, and as we make contact with them by e-mail, letter or even personal visit. Through such personal contact we can provide encouragement, we can learn how to pray specifically for our Christian family, we can learn of other needs that we can meet from our resources. In all these ways we can stand beside our sisters and brothers, affirming their value and worth in the face of deprecation and abuse. We can let them know that the family and community they have joined is as caring and supportive as the family and community they left behind in order to respond to God's call. This is not charity work. Rather, it is our chance to participate in their victory and share in their honor.

Paul also speaks quite frankly about sexuality in the church. He links our call to holiness—to be a people fit for God's indwelling presence—to our sexuality, urging us to live out and enflesh our sanctification in our physical bodies. Paul called the Christians to be countercultural in this regard. Rather than allow the urges and compulsions of their animal selves to direct their use of their bodies, Paul challenges them to prefer nobility and sanctity. In particular, he shows an awareness of the devastating results of one Christian injuring another through sexual impropriety. Anyone who has witnessed the effects of adultery within the church on the whole congregation's morale, fellowship and effectiveness can attest to the wisdom of Paul's injunctions. The modern climate speaks of sexuality in terms of personal fulfillment, by which it means self-gratification, and it considers any restriction on consensual sex a vestige of a Victorian morality. Christian sexual ethics, however, are not predicated on the premise that the body is bad or dirty, but that it belongs to the Lord. It is not our own to use or abuse for our own pleasure, but to please the God who ransomed us, body, mind and spirit. Because God desires our sanctification as whole beings, it is necessary for God's ministers to model—and, less comfortably, teach—a sexual ethic that has honoring God as its primary compass point.

The impact of our apocalyptic hope on our lives in this world is another important resource for ministry, particularly for discipleship. In this age, most people are asleep to the knowledge of God and the reality of God's judgment. They live their lives in a drunken stupor, chasing phantoms that seem real only to the inebriate. "Sleeping" is an apt image for keeping from one's consciousness the coming visitation of God in judgment. "Drunkenness" is a similarly apt image for dulling one's spiritual alertness through indulging the passions of the flesh, losing one's focus on the eternal race through temporal distractions and having one's perception distorted through drinking in the values and ideology of the dominant, unbelieving culture. It is easy to become intoxicated with the pursuit of money, reputation or advancement, with the ethos of materialism and consumerism, or with the gratification of one's pride (for example, in family or church fights), appetites or lusts. From all such intoxicants the Christian is to abstain so that he or she may be undistracted and unimpeded from preparing for the coming of the Lord, and unembarrassed about his or her past behavior when that day arrives. This brings us back to the issue of integrity—living for God's approval in all things rather than living for the phantoms the worldly minded and distracted chase after.

Finally, Paul assumes and encourages a high level of communal involvement in the spiritual formation of each disciple. That is, each believer is called on to participate in the encouragement, consolation and admonition of every other believer. One of the most unfortunate side effects of a professional clergy class is that the "unremunerated" ministers of the church—the laity—abdicate their responsibility toward one another and deprive the community of believers of their personal ministry. This greatly impoverishes the whole church and falls far short of the level of mutual interaction and responsibility that enabled the church to grow in its first centuries. In Paul's model for the church, each believer encourages and builds up the other in times of challenge (1 Thess 5:11), each consoles the other in times of loss (1 Thess 4:18), each prays for the other (1 Thess 5:17). This communal partnership in ministry, moreover, unites leaders and congregation in mutual support. Christian leaders need the pastoral care of other Christians at all of life's difficult junctures, specifically the care of the communities that they serve. One important manifestation of this care for leaders is prayer on their behalf (1 Thess 5:25; 2 Thess 3:1-2).

Where this communal pastoral responsibility surfaces, two specific issues arise demanding Paul's attention. The first concerns the issue of grieving, a situation faced routinely in the life of any congregation. We are uncomfortable with death and prefer to leave it to the "professionals." In vital churches, however, we do not merely find the pastor but also lay sisters and brothers surrounding and loving those who grieve—for the family that grieves is not merely the deceased's natural relations but the whole church he or she was a part of. Paul also gives some good advice concerning how to comfort the grieving. Presence is, of course, more important than words, and many words that are spoken (like "it was God's will") negate any good that quiet presence would have provided! When Christians grieve, however (and grieve they must), they can grieve as people of hope. Our sisters and brothers can help remind us of that hope—can make that hope more real to us when we need it most—in times of heavy loss. There will be a time of reunion; Christ has overcome death *and* the separations that death inflicts on us in this age. That separation will always be painful to experience and to bear day by day, but we can bear it with hope and even witness to that hope in the midst of grief.

The second issue raises the question of communal involvement in correcting deviant behavior. Paul expects the "ordinary" sisters and brothers to take a direct and constructive role in the rehabilitation of those Christians whose walk is contrary to the ways learned from Christ and Paul. Rather than grumble to each other *about* the idle people, the believers are told to admonish them directly (1 Thess 5:14). When the idle refuse to yield to admonition from leaders and fellow believers alike, the community is called on to back their admonitions by withholding the deeper level of fellowship from them until shame brings them around to a better way (2 Thess 3:6-15). Again, putting this into practice today would be a countercultural move. The response of a fellow Christian to our admonition about an affair she is having, or about the abuse he is inflicting on his family, or about some other blemish is likely to be "what business is that of yours?" In Paul's letters (and the letters of other early Christian leaders) however, we learn that we do have a deep and abiding responsibility to one another, to help each other overcome obstacles to deeper discipleship and to persevere in our faithfulness to God. Indeed, without one another's admonition and correction, we will almost surely succumb to the pressures of the world, the flesh and the devil. Done in a spirit of love—as to a "brother or sister" and not an "enemy" (2 Thess 3:15)—such intervention saves many from making a shipwreck of their faith.

FOR FURTHER READING

Best, Ernest. *A Commentary on the First and Second Epistles to the Thessalonians.* BNTC. London: Black, 1972.

Bruce, F. F. *1 & 2 Thessalonians.* WBC. Waco, Tex.: Word, 1982.

deSilva, David A. *The Hope of Glory: Honor Discourse and New Testament Interpretation,* chap. 4. Collegeville, Minn.: Liturgical Press, 1999.

————. *Paul and the Macedonians.* Nashville: Abingdon, 2001.

Donfried, Karl P., and Johannes Beutler. *The Thessalonians Debate: Methodological Discord or Methodological Synthesis?* Grand Rapids: Eerdmans, 2000.

Jewett, Robert. *The Thessalonian Correspondence: Pauline Rhetoric and Millenarian Piety.* Philadelphia: Fortress, 1986.

Malherbe, Abraham J. *Paul and the Thessalonians: The Philosophic Tradition of Pastoral Care.* Philadelphia: Fortress, 1987.

————. *The Letters to the Thessalonians.* AB 32B. Garden City, N.Y.: Doubleday, 2000.

Marshall, I. Howard. *1 & 2 Thessalonians.* NCB. Grand Rapids: Eerdmans, 1983.

Menken, M. J. J. *2 Thessalonians.* London: Routledge, 1994.

Morris, Leon. *The First and Second Epistles to the Thessalonians.* NICNT. Grand Rapids: Eerdmans, 1991.

Richard, Earl J. *First and Second Thessalonians.* Sacra Pagina 11. Collegeville, Minn.: Liturgical Press, 1995.

Wanamaker, Charles A. *The Epistles to the Thessalonians: A Commentary on the Greek Text.* NIGTC. Grand Rapids: Eerdmans, 1990.

14

THE CORINTHIAN CORRESPONDENCE

Valuing Oneself and Others in the Lord

The Corinthian letters provide us with our most extended window into the ongoing relationship of Paul with a group of churches. As it happens, this relationship appears to have been particularly difficult, which makes these letters all the more valuable to those of us who minister within Christian communities and thus encounter many of the same kinds of issues. What makes a minister a credible and legitimate representative of God? Is the church properly another arena for self-promotion and politicking for a particular agenda? Is Christian culture compatible with a culture that insists on the exercise of individual rights and on the values of self-gratification and self-fulfillment? Paul's answers to the issues raised in Corinth assist us in discovering a more genuinely Christ-centered vision for life together in Christian community, for life in the body and for leadership in the church.

HISTORICAL SETTING

The city of Corinth. Corinth[1] enjoyed a long history as a Greek city-state until Roman forces destroyed it in 146 B.C.E. After a century of lying desolate and minimally inhabited, Julius Caesar ordered its resettlement in 44 B.C.E. He reorganized Corinth as a Roman colony, with a new local government modeled after the administration of the city of Rome itself. Corinth became the seat of the Roman proconsul, who was sent by the Senate to govern the whole province of Achaea. Lucius Junius Gallio (Acts 18:12-17), the brother of the philosopher Lucius Annaeus Seneca, was one such governor. The city was settled largely by freed slaves (*libertini*) from Rome and elsewhere in the empire (Syrians, Egyptians, Jews). This elicited disparaging remarks from orators, seen, for example, in the following excerpt from Crinagoras:

> What inhabitants, O luckless city, have you received—and in place of whom?! Alas for the great calamity to Greece! Would, Corinth, that you did lie lower than the ground and more desert than the Libyan sands, rather than be wholly abandoned to such a crowd of scoundrelly slaves![2]

---

[1]On the city of Corinth and its inhabitants, see further Jerome M. O'Connor, "Corinth," *Anchor Bible Dictionary,* ed. David N. Freedman (Garden City, N.Y.: Doubleday, 1992), 1.1134-39; *Saint Paul's Corinth: Texts and Archaeology* (Wilmington, Del.: Michael Glazier, 1983); Gordon D. Fee, *First Epistle to the Corinthians,* NICNT (Grand Rapids: Eerdmans, 1987), pp. 1-4; Victor P. Furnish, *II Corinthians,* AB (Garden City, N.Y.: Doubleday, 1984), pp. 4-22; B. W. Winter, *After Paul Left Corinth* (Grand Rapids: Eerdmans, 2001), pp. 7-22; Ben Witherington III, *Conflict and Community in Corinth* (Grand Rapids: Eerdmans, 1995), pp. 5-35.

[2]Crinagoras *Greek Anthology* 9.284. See also Strabo *Geog.* 8.6.23.

When Paul, therefore, speaks of the "not many" who are wise, powerful and rich (1 Cor 1:26), even those who *are* may well have very humble origins and be stung by Paul's remark.

Corinth was a politically important center of the province of Achaia (probably the capital city). It soon became a bustling center for trade, with two ports (Cenchreae to the east, own officers, parties and burial obligations, organized around devotion to a patron deity (and often patronized by a member of the local elite). Excavations of Corinth suggest that the central forum was lined with numerous small shops on three of its four sides, bearing silent testimony to the bustling productivity and commerce that filled the colony.

Figure 14.1. Ruins of Corinth, with the ancient Temple of Apollo in the background. (Photo courtesy of Todd Bolen [BiblePlaces.com])

which also had a Christian congregation after Paul's mission, and Lechaeum to the north). It was well placed to profit from trade between the eastern and western halves of the empire. Artisans flocked to Corinth to set up shop, whether they worked in bronze, pottery, glass or leather (like Paul and Aquila). Local artisans of like craft grouped together in *collegia*, which were rather like social fraternities with their

Corinth was a growing city of the nouveau riche. The elites and semi-elites there were not all "old money" but rather third-generation veterans and freed slaves turned entrepreneurs, social climbers and people of local political prominence. This contributed to making Corinth a highly competitive environment, with people vying in business, politics and claims to status. A host of inscriptions testify to the self-promoting mentality of the inhabitants there, who had many opportunities to rise along various social and political ladders. As a new city there was always the opportunity for would-be benefactors of the city to construct a public building or pave a courtyard and publicize his or her munificence with an inscription.

One celebrated example is the Erastus inscription (figure 14.4), whose subject may have been a member of the Corinthian church (see Rom 16:23): "Erastus laid this pavement at his own expense in exchange for the aedileship."[3] This thirst for honor and the desire for public recognition attested by these inscriptions provide an important background for the topic of "boasting" that runs throughout the Corinthian correspondence. The prominence of erecting new buildings "at one's own expense" as a public benefaction (and thus a source of honor in the community) also provides the background for Paul's description of apostolic activity through the metaphor of erecting a public building in 1 Corinthians 3:10-16. Paul can rightly claim to be the patron or benefactor of this congregation through the work he has done among them "at his own expense" (cf. *sui pecunia,* ["with his/her own money"] in the Erastus inscription and Paul's frequent discussion of his refusal to accept support from the Corinthian church).

Such a city of increasing prosperity and obvious wealth attracted artists and sophists seeking patronage. The northwest and south stoa (covered colonnades or porticoes) that bracketed the main agora and the north stoa that intersected with the north market would have afforded such sophists a venue for their self-promotion, as would the market places themselves. In this environment display was as important as substance in public speaking.

Even classical rhetorical theorists stressed the importance of delivery, posture, voice and stage presence. In the popular eye these became even more crucial to the evaluation and acclamation of the orator. Lucian, for example, writes a satirical speech in "A Professor of Public Speaking," highlighting (and no doubt exaggerating) this emphasis on externals over substance and careful preparation of argument.

Reflecting on his visit to Corinth, Dio Chrysostom, the philosopher and statesman, recalls that rivalries between sophists and declaimers in Corinth were rather fierce. He also paints a picture of the intense divisions that could arise between followers of different orators concerning whose favorite was the best. Dio describes the season of the famous Isthmian games, which were under Corinth's jurisdiction (and, incidentally, brought a huge influx of tourists into the city every two years),[4] as "the time when one could hear crowds of wretched sophists around Poseidon's temple shouting and reviling one another, and their disciples, as they were called, fighting with one another" (Dio Chrysostom *Or.* 8.9). Seneca the Elder's *Controversies* also provide eyewitness testimony to the activities of and rivalries between sophists. Orators would ridicule one another and compete for prestige before the crowds, who cheered their favorites like modern Americans cheer their favorite ball teams:

> Such competition in *sophoi logoi* sometimes became quite divisive. . . . One philosopher and another or one rhetor and another were often strenuous competitors. The group following a particular teacher could be so strong that they could be described as a *secta,* a "sect" or "party." This is the word Seneca the Elder uses to describe the followers of Apollodorus versus Theodorus, rival

---

[3]D. W. J. Gill, "Erastus the Aedile," *TynB* 40 (1989): 293-301.
[4]Witherington, *Conflict and Community,* p. 12.

rhetoricians in Rome in the first century BCE (see Seneca the Elder *Controversies* 10.15 and *passim*). [5]

These speakers found many new elites in Corinth quite willing to enhance their own reputation by collecting client-dependents. For these elites it became a source of pride and prestige to have the more able and gifted clients. This cultural backdrop provides important insights into the kinds of divisions that arose in Corinth after Paul left and other Christian missionaries arrived (see 1 Cor 1—4).

The arts also enjoyed a prominent place in Corinth. Just off to the northwest of the forum stands a large theater for dramatic productions and a smaller odeion for music and poetry recitals, each with the customary semicircular seating arrangement. These complexes no doubt brought a constant flow of the Greek and Latin classics as well as new literary compositions to the people of Corinth and its visitors. These in turn would put a wealth of maxims and other sayings within the reach of artisan-preachers like Paul (who quotes the poet Menander in at least one place in 1 Cor 15:33).

As in any major city in the first-century Greco-Roman world, the traditional Greco-Roman gods were well represented in religious sites and activities. The "many gods and many lords" to which Paul refers (1 Cor 8:5) are very visible in the city. There was no distinction between religion and secular life, no separation of church and state, as it were. Traditional Greco-Roman religion undergirded most aspects of society. The gods stood behind earthly rulers and authority, through whom they manifested their favor; each divinity was held to watch over the city, the guild and the family especially devoted to its providential care. Proper reverence toward the gods, namely, the

worship that acknowledged their gifts, was regarded as essential to continued political stability, economic prosperity and civil order. Civic festivals, the Isthmian games, meetings and dinners of the *collegia,* and private dinner parties all included some acknowledgment of one or another of these "many gods," and acts of reverence toward these gods (whether heartfelt or not) surrounded, indeed cradled, most of life.

In his travelogue of Greece, the second-century C.E. traveler Pausanias lists twenty-six sacred places (temples, courtyards, freestanding altars) in the Corinth of his day—truly an impressive number of sites. The prominent placement of many of these temples and other sites in the center of town gave visible expression to their importance in the life of the city. The dedication of large amounts of public space to such cult centers shows the symbolic importance of the cults to the Greco-Roman world. The cults of Aphrodite and Athena, and the Egyptian cults of Isis and Sarapis, are attested in Corinth and Cenchreae (for the latter, see Apuleius *Metamorphoses*, chap. 17-18). The imperial cult was prominently represented in downtown temples and at the greater Isthmian games (held every four years), which is only sensible given the city's close connections with Rome and its gratitude toward its founder, Julius Caesar. The oldest temple in Corinth was linked with Apollo, the patron deity of mantic wisdom and the arts. This cult's activity may shed some light on the issue of women speaking in the church (1 Cor 14:34-35). It is possible that some women, accustomed formerly to asking questions of the priests of Apollo (the god of prophecy and fortune telling), misunderstood the different nature of Christian prophecy and were making a disturbance in the church's worship time. [6] Corinth also had a temple of Hera (the

---

[5] S. M. Pogoloff, *Logos and Sophia*, SBLDS 134 (Atlanta: Scholars Press, 1992), p. 175.

[6] See Witherington, *Conflict and Community*, p. 287; Winter, *After Paul Left Corinth*, p. 211.

goddess presiding over marriage), at which devotees could be ritually wed to a deity. It has been suggested that this would have been a point of resonance for the believers when Paul spoke of presenting Corinthians as "a pure virgin" to Christ (2 Cor 11:2-3). There was also a temple of Tyche (good fortune, destiny; cf. *Fortuna Augusti* and *Fortuna Romae*). Coins and statues show this figure with the *corona muralis,* "the crown of the wall," on her head. The *corona muralis* was the award given to the soldier who in a siege was the first to scale the wall of the besieged city. Some have noted this as a possible ironic background to Paul's "boast" in 2 Corinthians 11:30-33, that he was let down the wall of a city in a basket to escape a ruler's anger.

Corinth also boasted a temple of Demeter and Kore, which had several private dining rooms, and an Asklepion (a cultic site of Asklepios, the god of healing; see figure 14.2) about one-half mile north of downtown. At the Asklepion was a temple, an *abaton* (place for sleeping to receive dream-visions), a bath house for purifications, an exercise area and dining facilities. These two temples offered private rooms for dinner parties, and invitations would be issued to the guests to "dine at the god's table." It is possible, though not certain, that Paul has such a setting in view when he proscribes eating at "the table of demons." Even at a private dinner in the home of a pa-

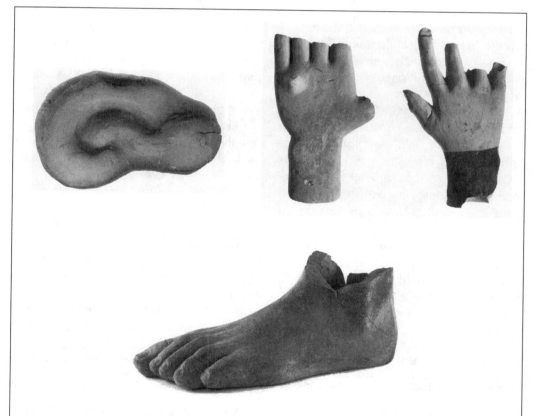

Figure 14.2. Votive offerings of hands, ear and foot left at the Sanctuary of Asklepios in Corinth as testimonies to healings experienced there. (Photo courtesy of the American School of Classical Studies, Corinth Excavations and Todd Bolen [BiblePlaces.com])

gan host, however, patron deities would be invoked and libations (sacrifices of poured wine) offered. Paul's strong warnings against participating in any form of idolatrous feast or ritual in 1 Corinthians 10:14-22 and his cautions about eating, in a nonworship setting, food that had previously been sacrificed to idols (cf. 1 Cor 8:1-13; 10:23-33) could cover a wide range of the believers' participation in the life of their city, their business associates, and their personal friends who had not converted. The avoidance of idolatry and scrupulousness about the source of meat (i.e., whether or not the meat came from an animal that had been sacrificed to a Greco-Roman deity) would have been a major factor in constructing boundaries between the Christian group and the outside world.

Paul in Corinth. The author of Acts records that after evangelizing Philippi and Thessalonica, Paul turned south into Greece.[7] After moderately successful stays in Berea and Athens, Paul went to Corinth (Acts 18:1), where he first encountered Priscilla and Aquila. A common trade—not a common commitment to the gospel—brought these leatherworkers together as Paul began his evangelistic efforts in Corinth, though the couple are certainly believers by the time they leave Corinth with Paul (see Acts 18:24-26; 1 Cor 16:19). Another point of contact between Acts and 1 Corinthians is the mention of Crispus, a synagogue official who is converted along with his household (Acts 18:8) and who is among the few believers that Paul personally baptized (1 Cor 1:14).[8] As is ever the pattern in Acts, very modest success in and hostility from the

synagogue leads to a more direct effort at converting Gentiles (Acts 18:4-8).

Acts locates Paul in Corinth for a full eighteen months, the latter part of which coincides with Lucius Annaeus Gallio's term as proconsul (see figure 14.3). This slender detail provides scholars with their only firm date for developing a chronology of Paul's life.[9] Gallio was sent out as proconsul in the spring of 51 C.E., and he returned to Rome with a fever before finishing his two-year term. It would appear that Paul arrived in Corinth sometime before Gallio's term began (Acts 18:12 introduces Gallio's proconsulship as a recently changed circumstance), giving a judicious estimate of late 50 through early 52 as the period of Paul's initial stay in Corinth. It is also highly probable that 1-2 Thessalonians were written from Corinth, that being the city where Timothy finally caught up with Paul with his confirming news about the Thessalonian converts' commitment (1 Thess 3:1-6; Acts 18:5)—notably another detail where the Acts account agrees with Paul's own. After Gallio's important ruling that Paul's mission was an inner-Jewish matter (and thus not a cause for Roman judicial intervention), Paul stayed on in Corinth "for a considerable time" (Acts 18:18), apparently not being rushed from this city as he was from Philippi and Thessalonica.

Paul reflects on the character of his own preaching and presence in Corinth at some length in both 1-2 Corinthians. Throughout, he shows a concern for the convergence of the message he preached (the power of God revealed in a crucified Messiah) and the form of presentation he used (relying on God's power

---

[7]See Winter, *After Paul Left Corinth*, p. xiv for an appropriate response from a historian to the tendency of many New Testament scholars to neglect Acts entirely as they reconstruct Paul's story from the epistles alone.

[8]The name may indeed be common, but since the Christian community in Corinth is so small the chances remain very high that this is one and the same Crispus.

[9]See the discussions of this datum in J. Becker, *Paul: Apostle to the Gentiles* (Louisville, Ky.: Westminster John Knox, 1993), pp. 30-31; Ben Witherington III, *New Testament History* (Grand Rapids: Baker, 2001), p. 272. Scholars have to work back from this date and forward from estimated dates for the crucifixion to reconstruct the chronology of Paul's early period. The trials before Felix and Festus provide other fixed points of reference, since the terms of their service in Judea are known.

Figure 14.3. The administrative building of Corinth with the *bema*, or judgment seat, where Gallio dismissed the local charges brought against Paul (Acts 18:12-17). (Photo courtesy of Todd Bolen [BiblePlaces.com])

rather than rhetorical flair for persuasion). Paul refused to play into the cultural norms of popular Hellenistic society. He did not go about using impressiveness of voice, gesture and vocabulary to win over his audience: "Christ sent me . . . to preach the gospel, and not with cleverness in the use of words, lest the cross of Christ be emptied of its power" (1 Cor 1:17). The proclamation must serve the message, not the tastes of the people and the reputation of the orator.

The apostle understood that using the world's means of gaining conviction would undermine the transformation that God sought to achieve in people's lives by confronting them not with beautiful speech but with the cross of a crucified Christ. Moreover, Paul explains that he was intent on having his converts' faith rooted in an experience of God and God's power, not in the persuasive artistry of a mere human being (1 Cor 2:1-5). This is not to say that Paul did not give a thought to rhetoric.

Even the claim to avoid using the flashiness of presentation to awe an audience, focusing instead on the content of the message, appears to have been a rhetorical device that was also used by the great orator Dio Chrysostom:

> My purpose is . . . neither to elate you nor to range myself beside those who habitually sing such strains, whether orators or poets. For they are clever persons, mighty sophists, wonder-workers; but I am quite ordinary and prosaic in my utterance, though not ordinary in my theme. For though the words I speak are not great in themselves, they treat of topics of the greatest possible importance. (*Or.* 32.39 LCL)

Nevertheless, Paul underscores the ultimate importance of experiencing the transcendent power of God as revealed in the crucified Christ. If the Corinthians were to be won to the gospel, it must be by the power of God

561

and the convicting power of God's Holy Spirit. Their trust needed to rest in God's transforming power rather than in any manifestation of human skill or fleshly excellence.

Paul decides therefore not to play to the cultural expectations of sophists and orators, those same expectations that lead to the "jealousy and strife" that characterized the adherents of one particular sophist over against another. Such was the business of "carnal" and "ordinary people" (1 Cor 3:3). In so doing he hoped to overthrow the values that focused on externals and performance, and to reveal the wisdom of God that turned the world's wisdom on its head (1 Cor 1:18-29), a wisdom reflected both in the executed Messiah and in the kinds of people God has gifted with adoption into God's family and with the indwelling of the Holy Spirit.

The congregation Paul left behind. The Corinthian church was really a collection of house churches, patronized by several wealthy converts who owned homes large enough to accommodate the smaller cells of the church. This is the pattern throughout Pauline Christianity. Aquila and Priscilla had opened up their house to such a "cell group" in Ephesus (1 Cor 16:19). In Laodicea and Colossae, Philemon and Nympha opened up their homes to host the meetings of their fellow Christians (Philem 1-2; Col 4:15). Stephanus, a householder whose people "have devoted themselves to the service of the saints" (1 Cor 16:15) is likely such a host in Corinth (as would have been Crispus and perhaps Chloe). These cell groups then came together as a whole assembly from time to time at the house of Gaius, "host . . . to the whole church" (Rom 16:23). The whole community of believers might not have numbered above fifty and, in-

deed, even if Gaius had one of the larger houses in Corinth it would be difficult to imagine any number larger than this gathering there. It is a charismatic community, where believers are vividly aware of the Spirit's presence in their midst and of the potential of being endowed with spiritual gifts.

This congregation has especially been the subject of extensive sociological study since Paul provides so much information about the people there either in the Corinthian letters or the closing chapter of Romans (written from Corinth during Paul's third visit).[10] Gerd Theissen and Wayne Meeks have subjected this information to close scrutiny with a view to determining the social level of Christians in Corinth.[11] Theissen examines statements made about the community as a whole (e.g., 1 Cor 1:26-31) and then statements made about individuals with a view to determining status and resources. He is particularly interested in references to offices held, services rendered, travel and property. He looks also at the statements about divisions in Corinth, noting how many of them appear to align with social divisions (most notably the abuses surrounding the Lord's Supper in 1 Cor 11:17-34). Meeks considers the contribution to an individual's status that would be made by his or her ethnic origins, liberty (whether free, freed person or slave), offices held, occupation, wealth and gender.

Both conclude that people were drawn into the church from a wide variety of social levels. When Paul says that "not many were powerful, not many were of noble birth" (1 Cor 1:26 NRSV), this should not mask the fact that some were indeed powerful and enjoyed privileged status. There were people of considerable means, such as Gaius, whose house was suffi-

---

[10]Research on the social level of early Christians in general is well surveyed and critiqued in Bengt Holmberg, *Sociology and the New Testament* (Minneapolis: Fortress, 1990), pp. 21-76.

[11]Gerd Theissen, *The Social Setting of Pauline Christianity* (Philadelphia: Fortress, 1982), pp. 69-119, see also pp. 121-74; Wayne A. Meeks, *The First Urban Christians* (New Haven, Conn.: Yale University Press, 1983).

ciently large to provide a meeting place for all the Christians in Corinth; Erastus, who was on the rise from "steward of the city" (Rom 16:23) to aedile (the occasion of his public benefaction of laying a pavement; see figure 14.4); Crispus, the "synagogue ruler" and householder; and Stephanus and Chloe, each of whom had houses and could finance travel for

were not represented, as well as the lowest—the peasant farmers and field workers, since Paul's work in Corinth was an urban phenomenon. This picture represents quite a shift from the late-nineteenth-century view, heavily influenced by Marxist historians, that Christianity was a movement of the lower classes.

It was also a congregation with a mixed

Figure 14.4. An inscription in Corinth bearing witness to the generosity of one Erastus in return for public office. The full inscription reads "ERASTVS PRO AEDILITATE S. P. STRAVIT," "Erastus laid this sidewalk at his own expense for the aedileship." (Photo courtesy of Todd Bolen [BiblePlaces.com])

themselves or their representatives to Ephesus, where Paul was staying when he wrote 1 Corinthians. There were also artisans and tradespeople of more modest means, and finally those who were of humble means, both free and slave, who appear to have been in the majority (1 Cor 1:26; 7:20-24; 12:12). Meeks argues that only the uppermost levels of society

ethnic constituency. There was a Jewish presence in Corinth, and at least one Jewish synagogue (probably at least two, since both Crispus and Sosthenes hold the title of "president of the synagogue," Acts 18:8, 17) to which Aquila and Priscilla, for example, would have attached themselves after their expulsion from Rome by Claudius (together with a large segment of the Jewish population, expelled for fomenting riots over one "Chrestus"). Some Jews appear to have joined the congregation, including the household of Crispus, but Paul's letter presumes a predominantly Gentile audience. Several passages presume that the converts were formerly engaged in idolatrous worship (1 Cor 6:9-11; 8:7; 12:2), while the issues of continuing to eat meat that had been sacrificed to idols and whether or not marriage was sinful reflect concerns more appropriate for non-Jews.

At some point between the founding of the Corinthian congregation and the writing of Romans, the Gospel spread to the neighboring seaport of Cenchreae as well. Prominent among that congregation is Phoebe, who bears Paul's letter from Corinth to Rome (Rom 16:1-2), and who serves as a "deacon" and "benefactor" to the Christians in Cenchreae.

Developments precipitating Paul's intervention. Whatever positive growth may have occurred in Corinth after Paul's departure, Paul encapsulates the problems as "divisions" and "quarrels" (1 Cor 1:10-11). The first area of strife centers on the various Christian teachers the Corinthians have encountered.[12] After Paul left Corinth, Apollos, a convert from Alexandria, visited the city and preached there. Here again is a point where Acts and Paul's own letters are in strong agreement, down to the high quality of Apollos's performance as a public speaker, which would surely play into the tastes of the believers there (Acts 18:24, 28; 19:1; 1 Cor 1:12; 3:5-6). Paul and Apollos do not appear to have regarded each other as a rival or to have been on bad terms with one another (1 Cor 16:12). The Corinthian Christians, however, fell into their learned behavior of measuring one against the other, arguing over their respective merits and forming factions around their fa-

vorite preacher (which may have included Cephas, or Peter, by the time 1 Corinthians was written). Attachment to Paul or to Apollos even provided an opportunity to "boast," to make a claim to honor and precedence over those who are attached to the "inferior" teacher. Thus they became "puffed up in favor of one against another" (1 Cor 4:6 NRSV).

These divisions were fueled further as the householders of the Christian community sought to enhance their own prestige through claiming the more illustrious Christian orator as their partner or even client. Most itinerant teachers would be glad to accept their patronage and, indeed, would depend on it (1 Cor 9:4, 6, 11-12, 14). Paul's refusal to accept patronage (and thus enhance the honor of any of the elites within the congregation) would also become a stumbling block in their relationship.[13] The partisanship in 1 Corinthians 1—4 therefore belongs to the cultural competition for honor, pursued here by collecting illustrious clients and then comparing one's own "sophist" with the "sophists" of rival households in an effort to assert precedence. This practice continued, leading to the problems underlying 2 Corinthians, where Paul is being compared unfavorably with other preachers, with whom he cannot (or will not) compete in terms of flashy style, speech and boasting about spiritual revelations—something certain itinerant preachers will exploit to the full.

This divisive competition for honor within the community extended itself to several other facets of church life. First, an argument about eating meat from animals that had been sacrificed to idols created lines of division between the "strong" toward the "weak" (1 Cor 8)—labels invented, no doubt, by those who claimed to be strong. This debate suggests that some were laying a claim to greater spiritual knowledge and power, and hence honor (in

---

[12]See, further, Pogoloff, *Logos and Sophia,* pp. 173-96, 237-71; Winter, *After Paul Left Corinth,* pp. 31-43.
[13]Witherington, *Conflict and Community,* p. 341.

Paul's words, being "puffed up," 1 Cor 8:1). Those who had achieved this status were challenging the honor and progress made by those who still labored as slaves to their scruples. Second, divisions along social lines marred the celebration of the Lord's Supper, where the differences in secular social status among the various Christians were being replicated at the communal meals of the Christian group.[14] These meals become an occasion to remind many believers of their low status and the social ladder of precedence on which they occupy merely the lower rungs (1 Cor 11:22). Third, even the spiritual endowments provided by God for the edification of the whole community had become the raw material for competition and precedence-seeking. The converts have been valuing more highly the more exotic signs of divine giftedness—ecstatic speech (speaking in tongues), for example. In this context Paul identifies a core problem in the church: in multiple areas of church life the Christians have not "given the greater honor" to the "less noble members" (1 Cor 12:23-26) to promote unity. Instead they have been acting in accordance with the cultural norms of competition for honor, promoting division through establishing precedence.

Even this list, however, does not exhaust the difficulties that developed. Some in the congregation had taken factiousness to the next level by going to court against one another, using the secular law to win settlements against a Christian sister or brother (and not always with just cause, hence Paul's use of the term "defrauding" and "injuring" in 1 Cor 6:7-8). Moreover, some believers insisted on making room for extramarital sexual indulgences in their lives, most likely in the context of the pagan banquets they attended in the homes of their non-Christian associates. At the "better" banquets, the host provided for all the appetites of the guests—eating extensively, drinking excessively and, after dinner, enjoying the companionship of members of the opposite sex.[15] Frequently, these companions were hired, hence prostitutes (1 Cor 6:15-16). Such indulgences were not moral lapses but rather the right of citizens of Corinth who, Christian or not, were simply living out their cultural mores.

The issue of immorality in the Corinthian church, at least, had come up before. Paul had written a previous letter (referred to explicitly in 1 Cor 5:9-11) that dealt with the church's response to people who claimed to be Christian but still lived the life of the unsanctified.[16] Paul clarifies and restates his earlier position in 1 Corinthians (which is thus the second letter that Paul *actually* wrote to the Corinthian congregation), but it is noteworthy that he has had to address this topic already.

Paul has received firsthand, though not unbiased, information about the developments in the Corinthian church. The fact that this information comes through two separate delegations is no doubt a symptom of the factiousness of the congregation. On the one hand, members of Chloe's household have brought an oral report to Paul (1 Cor 1:11). The contents of the oral report appear to have included the following:

- Divisions in the church based on weighing one apostle against another. Specific criticisms of Paul that appear to have been voiced, and to which Paul responds, include (1) Paul's refusal of support, unlike other Jewish Christian preachers (1 Cor 9), (2) Paul's inferior rhetorical skill and presentation (1 Cor 1:17; 2:1-5), (3) Paul's teaching being unspiritual, worldly, not sufficiently lofty (1 Cor 2:6—3:3).

---

[14]See further the important essay by Theissen (*Social Setting,* pp. 145-74), whose findings have been finely nuanced by Winter (*After Paul Left Corinth,* pp. 142-58).

[15]See Winter, *After Paul Left Corinth,* pp. 76-109.

[16]Indeed, the letter might have discussed other matters, but 1 Corinthians 5:9-11 is the only clue Paul gives about that previous letter's contents.

- Consternation about the church's response to the immoral brother (1 Cor 5:1-13; Paul speaks of this topic as something "heard" or "reported among you" in 1 Cor 5:1), and quite possibly the other topics of lawsuits among Christians and lack of sexual restraint (chap. 6) that follow.

- Concern about the social divisions manifested at the Lord's Supper (1 Cor 11:17-34; Paul, again, "hears" the report about this in 1 Cor 11:18).

On the other hand, Stephanus, Fortunatus and Achaicus (the latter two quite possibly being slaves in Stephanus's household) brought a letter from the congregation to Paul raising several other questions or issues (1 Cor 16:17-18). Some of these might reflect responses to or further questions about Paul's previous letter mentioned in 1 Corinthians 5:9-11. Paul specifically refers to "the matters about which you wrote" (1 Cor 7:1) and uses the formula "and concerning" (*peri de*) to introduce the topics in that letter that he takes up in 1 Corinthians. These topics include

- assertions or questions concerning existing and new marriages and the sexual expression of conjugal love (1 Cor 7)

- an assertion of freedom with regard to idol feasts and meats on basis of "knowledge" about the meaningless of idols and the religion they represent (1 Cor 8—10)

- assertions or questions about the possession of spiritual gifts, revealing a certain overzealousness with regard to the more ecstatic, "spiritual" gifts (1 Cor 12—14)

- the administration of the collection for the poor in Judea (1 Cor 16:1-4).

Two other matters might have been raised in either report—the denial of bodily resurrection (perhaps as basis for the lack of concern regarding fornication or eating food offered to idols, since the body's end is destruction) and the proper headdress for men and women in Christian worship.

Paul writes 1 Corinthians to address this plethora of concerns, seeking to transform the way the Corinthian Christians have been viewing one another and their life in this body and in this world. Competition and strife must yield to cooperation and unity; social and spiritual divisions must yield to the oneness of all believers united in Christ; boasting must yield to humble gratitude for God's gifting for service; self-indulgence must yield to the sanctification of the whole person.

THE MESSAGE OF 1 CORINTHIANS

The church: A culture of factious competition or familial cooperation? Prominent among the problems facing the Corinthian Christians are the divisions within the church. These are largely the result of individuals or groups claiming superiority in some regard at the expense of others in the church, or living out the norms and expectations of their social status (and thus flaunting this status in the eyes of other believers). In many respects these divisions reflect the age-old problem of "looking out for number one" rather than looking out for the interests of fellow believers. The effects of this mindset were far-reaching. Not only did it create rivalry between Christians on the basis of the teacher to whom they were most closely attached (1 Cor 1:11-13; 3:5, 21-23). It also manifested itself in Christians using the law courts to win honor and "damages" at the expense of other Christians (1 Cor 6:1-8). It led to the competitive measuring of spiritual gifts and the use of a charismatic endowment as a boast or claim to status in the community (1 Cor 12—14). It led to the replication of the hierarchy of social status at the celebration of the Lord's Supper as the rich provided fine fare for themselves and their guests of equal rank in addition to the bread and wine that was distributed to the "masses" (1 Cor 11:17-31). It led to contempt for the Christian who still had scruples about eating meat from animals sacrificed to idols—those who had "knowledge" that freed them from such superstitious taboos would not deny themselves their rights and the social networking that accepting invitations to the dinners of their non-Christian friends provided (1 Cor 8:1-13; 10:1—11:1).

Paul turned this way of thinking, evaluating and competing on its head by focusing on the mystery of the cross and on the abundance of God's generosity. Conventional wisdom and notions of power and status crumble before the mystery of the cross. There, the nature of God's wisdom and power makes itself known by commending as Lord of glory the One who died in disgrace and weakness for the sake of others (1 Cor 1:18-25). Such a revelation must overturn human ideas about what constitutes genuine honor and advantage. Lowering yourself in the world's eyes to serve others and assist them on their journey of discipleship emerges as the path to lasting honor and advantage, not claiming honor for yourself or insisting on the enjoyment of your prerogatives.

This affects the Corinthian situation at a number of points. First, it must affect the way the congregation celebrates the Lord's Supper. The rich are well within their rights and privileges to gorge themselves on fine food and indulge in drinking wine before the day-laborers arrive and on into the evening. They are well within their rights to reserve the finer foods for themselves, for they would already be seen as generous in supplying bread and wine for the whole congregation. This was quite in keeping with the way private dinners were served in the first century, especially in Roman contexts.[17] The quality of the food served should match the status of the person dining.

Paul roundly criticizes the importation of this practice into the new community of the new creation. By replicating within the church the social status that each person had outside the church, the rich were "show[ing] contempt for the church of God and humiliat[ing] those who had nothing" (1 Cor 11:22 NRSV).

At the Lord's Table there are no distinctions. All are sons and daughters of God; all enjoy equal status. If it is to be truly the Lord's Supper, the meal must reflect the new status of all believers in God's sight. The rich therefore should content themselves with the same fare as the poor—the bread and the wine—or else provide the same for all to enjoy together. By forgoing their right to better fare, the rich would voice a strong message of unity and solidarity with the rest of the church; by putting the feelings and sensitivities of the poorer members first, they would affirm the worth of their poorer sisters and brothers in their eyes and do what makes for harmony.

Second, Christ's example of serving the good of his sisters and brothers rather than himself must alter the way the "strong" respond to the scruples of the "weak." In Corinth this centers on the issue of meat previously sacrificed to idols. A fair portion of the meat available for sale in an ancient city came from a sacrifice at some temple or other. For the poorer citizens a civic festival or the meeting of a trade guild (always involving cultic acts and sacrifices devoted to one or other of the "many gods and many lords") would be the only occasions for tasting meat at all. Eating meat could be tied to idolatrous rites, therefore, in a number of ways exhibiting varying degrees of contact with the idols:

- Meat from sacrificed animals was doled out at free public dinners on festal occasions.
- Meat from sacrificed animals was served at private dinners held in dining rooms in temple precincts (the ancient equivalent of fellowship halls).
- Such meat could be served in private homes after having been purchased in the market.

With regard to the issue at hand, Paul was clear that a Christian could not take part in any ceremony honoring a false god (1 Cor 10:14-22). Beyond that, however, food was

---

[17]See the extensive and excellent essay in Theissen, *Social Setting,* pp. 145-74.

food (1 Cor 10:25-27), and it was not actually tainted by having been sacrificed to an idol at some point in the past.

Danger arises, however, if by eating food that had been sacrificed to idols, an "enlightened" believer provided an example that encouraged scrupulous believers to eat such meat. The latter would be unsure whether or not they committed a sin and would feel that kind of guilt that would hinder their communion with God. Paul teaches the "strong" that they have a responsibility to safeguard the consciences of their more scrupulous sisters and brothers. In the end the "strong" could only have one reason for eating meat that had been sacrificed to idols—their own pleasure or advantage. Everyone enjoys a good meal, to be sure, and in first-century Corinth a good meal also provided the all-important context for renewing friendships and partnerships with well-placed neighbors, and for enhancing one's social, business and political connections. Paul's rule for the church is clear, however: "Do not seek your own advantage, but that of the other" (1 Cor 10:24 NRSV). This might cost the more privileged in the church quite a lot in terms of their continued social climbing, or even the maintenance of their status in Corinthian society, but there can be no true advantage where a fellow Christian is injured.

Paul appears to digress from the topic of idols and foods in chapter 9, where he speaks of his right to receive support from his converts for his proclamation of the gospel, but this is really quite integral to the subject. Paul's chief point in this chapter is to present himself as an example of setting aside your own rights and prerogatives to safeguard or advance the well-being of your neighbor. In order to make the gospel more accessible (and less susceptible to being seen as yet another "philosophy for sale"), Paul does not expect money from those he is evangelizing and teaching. Rather than affirm his self-importance by exercising his privileges, his new boast—one quite up-side-down in the estimation of worldly wisdom—involves giving up his privileges for the benefit of others (1 Cor 9:15-18). The Corinthian Christians are challenged to do likewise, boasting no longer in the freedom that their knowledge gives them or their "rights," but seeking their ground for boasting in how fully they set aside their own rights to serve their sisters and brothers.

Turning to focus on God's generosity, Paul points out that the Corinthians have been joined to Christ by God's gift, and not through any claims to honor or worth that they could have made on the basis of the standard areas of "boasting" (power, wealth, wisdom; see 1 Cor 1:26). The only boast of any value that the Christians have is thus their "boasting in the Lord" (1 Cor 1:31; 2 Cor 10:17), the "claim to honor" God bestowed on each Christian by God's choice and inclusion of that person in the new creation. This is a boast shared by all believers, uniting them rather than dividing them. Moreover, the preachers of the gospel were God's gift to the community, a sign of God's patronage of the new community, and not a ground for the human patrons to promote their own honor. Neither could a believer's allegiance to a particular apostle provide a ground for boasting (and therefore rivalry and partisanship) because the apostles are God's gifts given to *all* the believers, not just to some who claim to be special devotees (1 Cor 4:7).

Spiritual endowments similarly appear to have become a source of rivalry and ranking. This is suggested by Paul's admonitions that just as one body part cannot call another body part unimportant or dispensable, so one member of Christ's body cannot claim precedence or put down another member on the basis of the endowments given to each. It is also suggested by the fact that the more clearly charismatic or ecstatic gifts were more valued and sought after, whereas the less visibly charismatic gifts were undervalued and the diversity

Paul's Use of the Old Testament in 1 Corinthians

In Galatians, Paul speaks without reservation about the limited duration of Torah as a binding law on the people of God. Nevertheless, the Old Testament as a whole remained the authoritative body of texts within Pauline Christianity (as it was in the early church). Although not binding as law now that the Christian was led by the Holy Spirit, the Torah in particular and the Old Testament in general still provided authoritative information about God's character, purposes and desire for God's people. In 1 Corinthians alone we find Paul putting Old Testament texts to the following uses:

- The stories of the exodus generation provide historical examples of the consequences that follow certain behaviors, showing God's desires to be clearly against such practices (1 Cor 10:1-13). The Old Testament contains paradigmatic stories from which moral instruction is to be derived (1 Cor 10:11).
- Paul interprets the law about not muzzling an ox while it treads the grain (Deut 25:4; 1 Cor 9:8-10) symbolically as revealing a moral principle concerning the rights of those who work for the gospel to share in the material resources of those they benefit. As with the narrative portions, so the legal portions of Torah invite discernment of the moral instruction contained therein.
- The Old Testament Scriptures continue to disclose the purposes of God. From this resource Paul finds confirmation about God's design to confound the wisdom of the world (1 Cor 1:19; 3:19-20) as well as God's provision for victory over death and the grave, and other lavish benefits for God's faithful people (1 Cor 2:9; 15:54-55).
- The Old Testament bears witness to Jesus and his work, not only during his earthly ministry but also beyond. For example, Paul finds in Psalm 8 a psalm traditionally read as a poem concerning the lofty status of human beings among God's creation, a witness to God's ongoing subjection of all things to Jesus as the consummation draws ever closer (1 Cor 15:25-28).

By no means, therefore, do Paul's radical statements about the limited duration of Torah as law mean that the Old Testament Scriptures, which always remain reliable oracles of God for Paul, lose their authority or force within the church.

---

of God's provision thus unappreciated. God's generosity—his giving of all things to all the believers—vitiates any attempts to claim honor or precedence on the basis of having some of these gifts while others lack them. Spiritual endowments are not given for the sake of the possessor (perhaps "vessel" would be a better term) but for the sake of the whole church (1 Cor 12:7). The gift any person exhibits is, in God's economy, a resource belonging to all. To make allegiance to a particular preacher or the possession of particular gifts into a ground for self-promotion in a setting of competition and rivalry is a dangerous perversion of God's generous intent, showing the worldly mind of the contenders (1 Cor 4:7).

For this reason Paul sets an encomium on love at the heart of his discussion of spiritual gifts. Our loving attitude toward our neighbor represents the greatest spiritual endowment we can receive from God—and it is precisely one in which a believer will not boast, nor one that a believer will use to claim precedence or foster competition! The gift of prophetic utterance, being a gift given not to elevate the speaker but to edify the congregation, is also brought to the fore as a primary spiritual gift, again because it is other-centered, benefiting the whole family of God rather than puffing up its possessor. Only insofar as spiritual gifts are exercised in an attitude of love will they be of any value to the possessor; if they are exercised to establish precedence in the community or any other self-serving purpose, they are "nothing."

Paul sets out a second rule for his converts, one that is even more countercultural. Christians are to be characterized by bestowing honor on their sisters and brothers, not competing for honor or claiming precedence at the expense of fellow believers. In particular, those who possess the more obvious gifts are all the more to honor the "weaker" or "less presentable" members rather than competing for precedence and maintaining hierarchies of status and prestige (1 Cor 12:22-26). Paul's vision for the church as a community of sisters and brothers again emerges here. It was proper for siblings to avoid competition against each other,[18] to make concessions rather than insist on their own way, to make each other share in the honor or good fortune that befell any one of them singly, and to take great care, where the status of siblings was unequal, to hide those differences in status wherever and however possible.[19] By such means, unity and co-operation, which benefited the whole family, would be assured.

The physical body in God's redemptive purposes. Another set of issues arise in 1 Corinthians surrounding the topic of sexuality and the venues for sexual expression. Some of the converts understood that they had the freedom to indulge their body's appetites. We have already seen how this was so in the matter of foods, with Paul agreeing in principal that food restrictions (like avoiding the purchase or consumption of meats previously sacrificed to idols) did not have binding force since foods all belong to this world that is passing away (see 1 Cor 6:13a, which appears to have been a slogan among these converts). Nevertheless, just as Paul restricted the applicability of that principle to those occasions when it would do no harm to a Christian sister or brother, so he refuses to allow that principle to be applied to matters of sexuality ("the body for sex and sex for the body," cf. 1 Cor 6:13b). Whether these converts made room for fornication (*porneia* being a broad term for sexual expressions beyond the limits imposed by God) out of a philosophical conviction that nature had provided for the body's pleasure during an individual's life[20] or out of a misunderstanding of the nature of Christian freedom, Paul advances a very different understanding of life in the body rooted in the scope of God's redemptive purposes for humanity.

God does not just save souls. God also sanctifies bodies. Paul looks back on the ex-

---

[18]The lawsuits between believers are thus especially odious to Paul (1 Cor 6:1-8). This pushes far beyond "competition" between family members, as far as intentional infliction of injuries against family members (1 Cor 6:8)—what the ancients would have called a "Cadmean victory" (recalling the civil war "won" by Eteocles against Polyneices, his brother, at the cost of their mutual slaughter). Among strangers and non-kin, it would be disgraceful to be taken advantage of; among kin, however, it would be more honorable to hide another's wrongdoing than exact public restitution for it.

[19]See Plutarch "On Fraternal Affection" discussed in David A. deSilva, *Honor, Patronage, Kinship, and Purity* (Downers Grove, Ill.: InterVarsity Press, 2000), pp. 166-69, 217-23.

[20]Winter advances a fine case that "fornication" was philosophically defended among the elite, whose banquets would have provided an occasion for bringing together meats from sacrificial animals and the enjoyment of sexual companions after dinner, making the issue of fornication another instance of the importation of the social norms of people of status into the church (*After Paul Left Corinth*, pp. 76-85).

perience of conversion and baptism as an occasion on which God separated the converts from their unsanctified past, that way of life that included idolatry, a variety of sexual indulgences and greed (1 Cor 6:9-11). Such behaviors are incompatible with the life of the kingdom of God, which is why God had to redeem human beings in the first place (1 Cor 6:20). That redemption extends to the whole person—the Christian belongs to God in toto, having been "bought with a price." Moreover, the Christian has been joined with Christ himself, having been made part of that mystery of the body of Christ (1 Cor 6:15). Sanctified by God, the believer is now a "temple of the Holy Spirit within you" (1 Cor 6:19), a reference to the pouring out of the Holy Spirit into the believers that was so central a feature of the early church (especially as Acts and the Pauline letters attest) as a sign of God's acceptance of the convert.

Paul is frequently painted as a repressed and repressive individual who devalues the flesh, but where he speaks of the "flesh" he speaks of the passions that drive a person toward sin (interpersonal as well as physical sin) or of the mindset that characterizes the wisdom of the world (e.g., Gal 5:16-21; 2 Cor 10:2-4). Paul is seen here, however, to have a very high view of the physical body in light of God's acts on its behalf and the privileges accorded the Christian as he or she lives in this body. God's investment in the whole person is so great that the only fitting response is for us to live for the Lord with the whole person (1 Cor 6:13b), to bring honor to God in the way we use our body (1 Cor 6:20). To reinforce this, Paul reminds the believers of God's ultimate ownership of the believer's body, with the result that the Christian is to use the body as God wishes, not as he or she might wish (i.e.,

to indulge its desires; 1 Cor 6:19; cf. Gal 5:13, 24). Thus, how we use our body provides us with a wide array of opportunities to honor God, bearing witness to God's redemption of our body from sin and to enhance our connection with Christ.

The value of the body also emerges as Paul defends the belief in the resurrection of the dead, the enjoyment of eternal life in a resurrected body. A common view of the afterlife was that it was enjoyed by a disembodied soul, freed from the prison or house of the body. Paul does not share the view of a disembodied afterlife, however, since God's redemptive purposes extend to all of God's creation, including the human body (cf. Rom 8:20-23). The body is not abandoned to death, for God will not allow death or the grave to have even that measure of victory (1 Cor 15:53-57). The physical body will be transformed and will "put on immortality." As a seed is related to the tree it will become, so the physical body is related to the resurrection body (1 Cor 15:42-49).[21]

This is not merely a facet of eschatology for Paul: it has direct bearing on how we live our life. Paul brings the resurrection into his discussion of ethics (1 Cor 6:14) and ethics into his discussion of resurrection (1 Cor 15:30-34, 58). What we do in the body is of eternal significance, with the result that the sanctification God provides for the whole person (1 Cor 6:9-11) is to be preserved and pursued with single-hearted focus. "Christians are commanded to bring one small piece of creation—their own bodies—into obedience to the healing love of God in Christ" as a foretaste and sign of God's redemption of the whole of creation.[22] Conversely, it is the hope of the resurrected body that gives the Christian boldness to use his or her body so boldly for a witness to the good news of Christ, facing dangers and

---

[21] Paul will continue to reflect on this mystery in 2 Corinthians 4:16—5:10, where he uses the image of garments, with the resurrection body being "fully" or "further" clothed, not unclothed, i.e., disembodied.

[22] N. T. Wright, *What Saint Paul Really Said* (Grand Rapids: Eerdmans, 1997), p. 164.

hardships rather than avoiding conflict for the sake of continued enjoyment of pleasure (1 Cor 15:30-32).

Therefore, although the strengths and graces of the physical body cannot provide the basis for validating or invalidating ourselves or others as bearers of the gospel or favored people of God, the physical body is integrally connected with that "body of glory" that we believers will "put on" at the resurrection of the dead. Its properties cannot now be overvalued or used to measure one person against another, but on the other hand, it cannot be abandoned to sin or rejected as valueless or as something that belongs only to this passing world. Rather, it is to be sanctified as we use life's opportunities for bearing witness to our connection to Jesus and God's Spirit (1 Cor 6:15-20) and our hope in the resurrection from the dead (1 Cor 6:14; 15:20-34, 50-58).

EXEGETICAL SKILL
Rhetorical Criticism (3)—The Analysis of Topics

Ancient rhetorical handbooks are brimming with topics for creating a case and decimating the arguments of rival speakers, whether the case has to do with a decision about the course of action to be pursued, a verdict about someone's behavior or the praise or censure of an individual or group. Awareness of these general topics helps a person understand how an author is framing an argument—what angles he or she is taking to persuade the hearers.

For example, if someone wants to persuade people to adopt a certain course of action or behavior, he or she could promote it by using any number of special, deliberative topics showing that it is

- virtuous, embodying *justice* (i.e., it renders to some other party what is his or her due, like gratitude to benefactors; loyalty to friends, family, guests and homeland; honor to parents; and the like), *courage* (preferring hardship to disgrace, choosing to face danger and pain rather than abandon duty), *wisdom* (weighing advantages and disadvantages with a view to achieving happiness, however that is defined by a group), or *temperance* (moderating desires for money, sex or food for the sake of some higher good)

- expedient, that is, it preserves existing goods, secures other goods or avoids loss

- honorable and praiseworthy, resulting in maintaining or increasing a person's reputation in a particular circle

- lawful

- necessary

- feasible

- productive of security and the safe enjoyment of a person's goods

- or leads to good consequences

If the speaker seeks to dissuade people from a course of action or behavior, he or she would argue the opposite. Very often, a speaker is urging one course over another, so he or she is engaged in persuasion and dissuasion at the same time, or weighing the relative merits of the various courses of action facing the hearers.

Another set of topics would assist a person seeking to confirm or refute the validity of a position. For example, a thesis could be refuted by pointing out its

- inconsistencies (it cannot be reconciled to known facts)
- implausibility or impossibility (there are inherent flaws in the position)
- impropriety (e.g., it asks us to believe things unworthy of the gods or people)
- its inexpediency (if it were true, disadvantageous circumstances would follow)

Confirmation of a position would, of course, invite the use of the opposite topics. Still another set of topics provided a speaker with a checklist for praising a person (as in a eulogy) or for invective (denouncing a person).

- external circumstances: (1) descent/lineage (e.g., prestige and virtue of parents and ancestors), (2) education, (3) wealth/resources, (4) offices/public service, (5) friendships, (6) native city and its reputation, (7) manner of death
- physical attributes: (1) health, (2) beauty, (3) strength
- moral character (how have the foregoing qualities been put to use?): (1) virtues exhibited (justice, courage, wisdom, temperance, etc.), (2) actions exhibiting moral character, (3) objectives: (undertaken in the interest of others rather than oneself; done in accordance with virtue rather than pleasure or utility), (4) circumstances (timely, first person to achieve such deeds; performed alone or with little help; efficient, at great cost to the doer)

These same topics provide starting points for a "comparison" of two people, such as Plutarch attempts throughout his *Lives* or as Paul attempts in his tirade against the rival teachers in 2 Corinthians 10—13.

Other topics could contribute fuel for argumentation across the spectrum of deliberative, judicial and epideictic oratory. These are called common topics because they provide ammunition for all kinds of speeches. They include:

- The possible and the impossible. This can be used in judicial cases to demonstrate, for example, an alternative explanation of potentially damaging evidence, or in deliberative cases to show, for example, that certain circumstances requiring a response can or cannot arise, or that the course of action urged can or cannot be accomplished. There are many ways of using this basic topic, including the following arguments: (1) if the harder of two like things is possible, the easier is also possible, (2) if the whole is possible, so is the part; if the specific instance is possible, so is the general application, (3) if the result is possible or has occurred, then the cause is also possible or has already occurred

- arguments from contraries (if X produced this state of affairs, the opposite of X will produce, or has produced, the opposite state of affairs)
- arguments from similar cases (we know such and such to have happened in a previous case under similar circumstances and dynamics; given the same circumstances and dynamics, it is plausible and probable that the same would happen in a new case)
- arguments from the greater case to the lesser case or vice versa (e.g., if the greater person could not achieve this, the lesser person cannot, or if the lesser person can achieve this, the greater person can do this and more)
- arguments from consideration of timing (e.g., if we received help from the city before we were citizens, we will certainly receive help now that we are citizens)
- arguments from the definition of a word or thing, or the meaning of a name
- arguments from induction (e.g., considering multiple cases and deriving a conclusion)
- arguments from a previous judgment rendered in a similar case or decision made in a similar situation
- arguments from the consequences
- arguments from analogy
- arguments from incentives or disincentives to some action

As beginning exercises, try the following:

1. Read Matthew 6:1—7:11. What common *and* deliberative topics does Jesus use as he promotes the pursuit or avoidance of certain behaviors? Do any particular topics stand out as more prominent and frequent than others?

2. The Gospels have been called "encomiastic biographies." That means that scholars have seen them not merely as records of Jesus' life but as attempts to demonstrate the virtue and praiseworthy character of Jesus using the topics of praise. How, for example, might the genealogy in Matthew 1 function "encomiastically" to promote Jesus' nobility? What topics of moral character are employed by John as he presents Jesus looking ahead to and enduring his crucifixion?

3. The same exercise could be profitably performed reading Hebrews.

Compare the statements about Jesus' person and achievements in Hebrews (including the comparisons made with angels, Moses and the Levitical priests) with the topics of praise and blame. What does the author have to say about Jesus' external and physical attributes, and moral excellence?

4. First Corinthians 15 seeks, among other goals, to refute the view that there will be no resurrection of the dead for believers. What refutative strategies does Paul use in 1 Corinthians 15:12-19, 29-34 (i.e., what topics of refutation can you discern)? What common topics are also at work supporting his refutation (and thus his confirmation of the position that there will indeed be a bodily resurrection for believers)?

5. Hebrews, one of the most rhetorically crafted texts in the New Testament, offers many examples of common and specific topics at work. Consider how the topic of "the lesser to the greater" is used in Hebrews 2:1-4; 10:26-29. How are topics of justice and expediency used throughout the sermon to dissuade the believers from breaking faith with Jesus? How might Hebrews 10:32-39 be understood to employ topics of the "feasible" to promote continued endurance?

Clearly, it will take some time to become familiar with how these topics work in real contexts. Nevertheless, becoming competent in recognizing and analyzing the topics used by authors will help you understand better how they intended the specific content to function as well as the logical steps they expected the audience to be able to make on their own for the argument to work. Such study is of value because it takes us beyond a surface reading of the text toward a slower, more probing analysis of the logic of the text.[a]

---

[a]The next step beyond these exercises is to move to a careful reading of the primary resources (Aristotle *Rhet.* 1.4-16; 2.18-26; Pseudo-Cicero *Rhet. ad Her.* 3.3-15; Pseudo-Aristotle *Rhet. ad Alex.* 1421b18-1423a11; Theon *Progymnasmata*; Aphthonius *Progymnasmata*). The last of these are now readily accessible in G. A. Kennedy, *Progymnasmata: Greek Textbooks of Prose Composition and Rhetoric* (Atlanta: Society of Biblical Literature, 2003). Thereafter you might move on to the continued reading of selections of New Testament discourse (speeches, sayings and letters) with a view to using this material as a heuristic device for unpacking the argumentation in the text.

READING BETWEEN THE LETTERS

The story of Paul's relationship with the Corinthian churches is still just beginning with the writing of 1 Corinthians. Second Corinthians bears witness to the ongoing saga of the apostle's dealings with this more difficult group of believers. A prerequisite to reconstructing these next phases of the relationship, however, is determining whether or not 2 Corinthians as we have it represents a single missive or several shorter letters that Paul had written over time, later blended into a single document by an unknown (and rather inept) editor. Many commentaries on 2 Corinthians, as well as reconstructions of this part of Paul's life, argue that 2 Corinthians contains as many as six letters or letter fragments. Such a view would greatly complicate our reconstruction. Because this view is fairly common among scholars, we would do well to consider it in some detail.

Second Corinthians: A composite letter. Scholars have detected a number of jumps or abrupt transitions as they read 2 Corinthians. The best explanation, in their opinion, is that 2 Corinthians is a composite document pieced together from several shorter letters. The content and order of these can be reconstructed by careful examination.[23] The primary indicators supporters of a "partition theory" point to include the following:

- Paul's narration of his travels breaks off abruptly in 2 Corinthians 2:13, where he leaves Troas for Macedonia, then resumes in 2 Corinthians 7:5 with Paul finding Titus in Macedonia.

- The tone of 2 Corinthians 1:1—2:13 plus 7:5-16 is markedly different from that of 2 Corinthians 2:14—7:4, with the former being conciliatory and the latter being argumentative, even polemic.

- The subject matter of 2 Corinthians 1:1—2:13 plus 7:5-16 also has little or nothing to do with that of 2 Corinthians 2:14—7:4. How are we prepared for the middle section by the beginning section?

- The various parts of 2 Corinthians 1—7 seem to presuppose different situations: 2 Corinthians 1:1—2:13 plus 7:5-16 seems to speak of reconciliation as accomplished and confidence restored, whereas 2 Corinthians 2:14—7:4 appears to be calling for reconciliation.

On the basis of these observations many scholars would form two letters from these opening chapters: 2 Corinthians 1:1—2:13 plus 7:5-16 becomes the "Letter of Reconciliation," while 2 Corinthians 2:14—7:4, which is missing at least an epistolary opening and closing, becomes a fragment of another, perhaps earlier, letter.

The observations of seams and irreconcilable differences then continues:

- 2 Corinthians 6:14—7:1 interrupts the appeal by Paul to the Corinthians to open up their hearts to him (2 Cor 6:11-13 and 7:2-4) with an appeal to disassociate themselves from some other group whose identity is debated. These verses also show a concentration of vocabulary atypical of Paul. This segment is usually excised, therefore, as a fragment of another letter, possibly the "previous letter" mentioned in 1 Corinthians 5:9-11.

- Chapters 8-9 are often separated from the rest of the letter because of the difference in topic (the collection rather than the relationship of the apostle and congregation). Chapters 8 and 9 are further separated from each other as redundant appeals, resulting in two separate and independent fundraising letters.[24]

- Even in the most conservative partition theories, chapters 10-13 are set apart as an independent letter because of the suddenness of the change of topic and tone, and because the invective of these chapters goes far beyond that of the earlier chapters. There is then further debate as to whether or not 2 Corinthians 10—13 was written prior to 2 Corinthians 1—7 (thus making it

---

[23]See further, Dieter Georgi, *The Opponents of Paul in Second Corinthians* (Philadelphia: Fortress, 1964), pp. 12-14; N. H. Taylor, "The Composition and Chronology of Second Corinthians," *JSNT* 44 (1991): 67-87. Excellent discussions of both positions can be found in V. P. Furnish, *II Corinthians*, pp. 30-34; Margaret E. Thrall, *A Critical and Exegetical Commentary on the Second Epistle to the Corinthians 1-7*, ICC (Edinburgh: T & T Clark, 1994), pp. 3-49; Paul Barnett, *The Second Epistle to the Corinthians* (Grand Rapids: Eerdmans, 1997), pp. 15-25; R. P. Martin, *2 Corinthians*, WBC (Waco, Tex.: Word, 1986), pp. xxxviii-lii.

[24]See, in particular, Hans Dieter Betz, *2 Corinthians 8 and 9*, Hermeneia (Philadelphia: Fortress, 1985).

the "tearful letter" mentioned in 2 Cor 2:4) or possibly joined to 2 Corinthians 2:14—7:1 as part of the "tearful letter" or written after the various other letters, marking a further deterioration of the relationship.

Second Corinthians might therefore represent four or five separate letters and fragments of letters, though the extent and order of these remains debated. We must also consider the purposes and methods of the editor or editors responsible. Why did they break up the original letters, discard parts (at least openings and closings, but in the case of 2 Corinthians 6:14—7:1 considerably more) and then rearrange the pieces into the letter's canonical shape? A plausible suggestion for the *occasion* for such a compilation has been found in the later problems the Corinthian church had with its leaders (reflected in *1 Clement*)—an appropriate time for a church to revisit Paul's words on the issue of authority in ministry—but not for why the particular editing it has received would have been necessitated by or better served that situation.

Second Corinthians: A unified whole. As is the way in scholarship, every argument advanced by a supporter of a partition theory has been countered plausibly by a supporter of a more unified view of 2 Corinthians (whether it is taken as a single whole or as two major letter fragments: 2 Cor 1—9 and 2 Cor 10—13). Additionally, the reconstructed letters are themselves open to criticism in terms of rough transitions and incongruities in vocabulary.

- Joining 2 Corinthians 2:13 directly to 7:5 makes the "for even" that begins the latter verse awkward (it should have been "but even") and the shift from "I" to "we" abrupt and inexplicable.

- The difference in tone between 2 Corinthians 1:1—2:13 and 2:14—7:3 is overstated since Paul is quite on the defensive in both sections (note especially 2 Cor 1:15—2:4).

- Second Corinthians 7:4 flows integrally from 2 Corinthians 7:2-3, but it reflects the vocabulary and tone of the alleged "letter of reconciliation." If it is detached from 2 Corinthians 2:13—7:3 and joined to the "letter of reconciliation," the "travel narrative" of 2 Corinthians 2:13 and 2 Corinthians 7:5 would still be interrupted (this was a major reason for excising 2 Cor 2:14—7:4). On the other hand, if it is left as part of 2 Corinthians 2:14—7:4, the arguments for separating that "fragment" on the basis of vocabulary and tone are substantially weakened.

Similar objections are raised down the line to every argument for detaching some part of 2 Corinthians as a separate communication.

On the one hand, making cases for dividing a New Testament letter into several reconstructed letters might seem like a scholarly fad or armchair exercise. On the other hand, by drawing attention to these rough transitions, differences in tone and the like, scholars do a valuable service to all readers of 2 Corinthians, who are led to read the text more closely as they attempt to make sense of these data. If the solution is not to be found in a partition theory, these observations push us to consider more carefully the complexities of the situation Paul addresses, and thus the complexity and strategy of his careful response.[25] Taken as a unified whole 2 Corinthians (or even just the first nine chapters) is certainly a complex letter. However, a complicated situation compounded both by lin-

---

[25]I have attempted to do so using the heuristic tools of rhetorical criticism in a series of articles: David A. deSilva, "Measuring Penultimate Against Ultimate Reality: An Investigation of the Integrity and Argumentation of 2 Corinthians," *JSNT* 52 (1993): 41-70; "Recasting the Moment of Decision: 2 Corinthians 6:14-7:1 In Its Literary Context," *Andrews University Seminary Studies* 31 (1993): 3-16; "Meeting the Exigency of a Complex Rhetorical Situation: Paul's Strategy in 2 Corinthians 1 Through 7," *AUSS* 34 (1996): 5-22. See also the compelling critique of partition theories and the rhetorical flow of canonical 2 Corinthians in Witherington, *Conflict and Community*, pp. 328-39.

gering prejudices against Paul and by lingering misunderstandings about the marks of a genuine apostle and minister would require a complex and carefully marshaled series of arguments as a response. The exploration of this strategy begins in the context of a discussion of yet another way that rhetorical criticism can assist us in the task of exegesis.

EXEGETICAL SKILL
Rhetorical Criticism (4)—
The Functions of Parts of an Oration

Greco-Roman orations, whether deliberative or judicial, tended to follow a certain pattern of development. The speech would begin with an exordium, or introduction, the purposes of which were to (1) provide the hearers with "a sample of the subject, in order that the hearers may know beforehand what [the speech] is about, and that the mind may not be kept in suspense" (Aristotle *Rhet.* 3.14.6), and (2) secure the good will of the hearers, since a hostile or unreceptive audience would not be moved by any amount of argumentation. It is critical for a speaker to remove any prejudice against him or her at the beginning of the speech (Aristotle *Rhet.* 3.14.6-7). This would be followed, especially in judicial speeches, by a "narration," or a statement of the facts of a case. The purpose of this section was to put the known facts into an interpretive narrative framework that would support the case one was trying to make. This would lead up to a "proposition," the main point to be proven, followed by the body of "proofs" that could be marshaled, usually the longest part of an oration (and often including a refutation of the opposing speaker's case). An orator would close with a "peroration" or conclusion, in which he would seek to (1) summarize the main points of the case, (2) arouse prejudice against opposing speakers and their arguments, and (3) reinforce the audience's favorable disposition to the speaker.[a]

New Testament letters rarely follow this pattern exactly, nor should they be expected to do so. A speech deals with a single issue; a letter such as 1 Corinthians or 1 Thessalonians may deal with multiple issues. Many attempts to force a New Testament letter into the mold of exordium-narration-proposition-proof-peroration have been rightly and roundly criticized. Overzealous application of this model unfortunately has soured some scholars against rhetorical criticism altogether (an example of throwing out the baby with the bath water). However, an awareness of what the various parts of an oration sought to accomplish can help us heuristically by suggesting what we might look for in the opening and closing sections or of the major sections of a letter, or how we might understand the function of narratives in

---

[a]See the full discussions in Aristotle *Rhet.* 3.13-19; Pseudo-Cicero *Rhet. ad Her.* 1.4, with the remainder of book 1 being given to specific discussions of each part.

Pauline letters. (For example, is Paul just sharing "news" or his "faith journey," or is he setting the record straight and establishing the facts?)

As we turn to 2 Corinthians, how might an understanding of the functions of the parts of a speech—particularly here the exordium, or introduction—help us rethink the relationship of 2 Corinthians 1:1—2:13 to the "middle" section, 2 Corinthians 2:14—7:4?

If 2 Corinthians 1:1—2:13 truly provides the opening of a letter that has 2 Corinthians 2:14—7:4 as its middle, we would expect there to be a sampling of themes introduced in the former that will be developed in the latter. We find one such sampling in 2 Corinthians 1:8-9, where Paul explains that the afflictions he and his team endured in Asia Minor, in which he despaired of life itself and felt like he was under a death sentence, happened "to make us rely not on ourselves but on God who raises the dead." That Paul should be made to rely on God and not himself announces the major theme of 2 Corinthians 2:14—7:4 (and, as it happens, chapters 10-13), namely, that the true apostle, who bears the true gospel, is the one who considers his or her legitimation (or "credentials" for ministry) to come not from fleshly or worldly strengths but from God, and who therefore allows God to pierce the veil of his or her flesh and manifest God's transforming power:

> Not that we are competent of ourselves to claim anything as coming from us; our competence is from God. (2 Cor 3:5 NRSV)

> But we have this treasure in earthen vessels, to show that the transcendent power belongs to God and not to us. (2 Cor 4:7)

Paul regards this as an essential mark of his own ministry, one that leads the Corinthians to place their faith in God, and not in human displays of strength or impressiveness.

A second sampling of the main argument emerges when Paul discusses his own hardships as the way that divine benefits come to the Corinthian believers. Paul's suffering of affliction might discredit him before a worldly minded audience—an audience looking for beauty, power and poise. Paul shows, however, that his affliction provides encouragement for the believers (2 Cor 1:3-7). This theme is taken up again in 2 Corinthians 4:3-15 (esp. visible in 4:10-15), where Paul's bearing the death of Jesus in his body actually works to the believers' advantage: that Jesus' life may be at work in them and that they might have a share in the world to come. His hardships are thematic throughout the body of the letter (2 Cor 4:7-18; 6:3-10; 11:21—12:10).

Second Corinthians 1:3-11, then, fulfills the first function of an exordium. An orator's success, however, rests on his ability to secure the good will of the hearers and to convey an impression of complete reliability, that is, establish the right ethos. It follows that an orator whose ethos, whose character, was called into question could not present his case effectively until those doubts about his behavior or motives were cleared up. Prior to writing 2 Corinthians, Paul faces a challenging rhetorical problem. His character has been called into question. He appears to have acted inconsistently, changing his travel plans and not keeping his promise to visit them on the way back from Macedonia as he announced previously. Rather, he appears to have acted in a cowardly fashion (or at least not in a friendly fashion), writing a nasty letter rather than visiting the Corinthians in person.

Before Paul can present his case developing the points he introduces in 2 Corinthians 1:3-11, he must carefully sweep away the prejudice that has accumulated against him. Pseudo-Cicero calls this the "subtle approach," to be used when significant prejudice exists against the speaker or his case (*Rhet. ad Her.* 1.9-10). The whole of 2 Corinthians 1:3—2:11 then may be understood as fulfilling this essential function of an exordium. Because the situation is complex, the exordium is similarly complex, providing a full-scale defense of Paul's behavior and motives before launching into the arguments of 2 Corinthians 2:14—7:4.

Paul begins this process in 2 Corinthians 1:3-11, reaffirming his own costly commitment to the congregation's well-being and growth (2 Cor 1:6), his favorable disposition toward them (2 Cor 1:7), and their partnership with him in prayer (2 Cor 1:11). Paul goes on, however, to address at some length the prejudices against him and, in particular, to explain his motives for causing pain by means of a harsh letter rather than making another visit in person. In this explanation he uses several topics reflecting the rhetorical tradition of defense speeches. When a defendant had to admit to some wrongful act, he or she could set forward a defense by "comparison with the alternative course," that is, "when we declare that it was necessary for us to do one or the other of two things, and that the one we did was better," or by rejecting responsibility, when we "transfer [responsibility for the action] to another person or attribute it to some circumstance" (Pseudo-Cicero *Rhet. ad Her.* 1.24-25). Additionally, "one may also substitute one motive for another, and say that one did not mean to injure, but to do something else . . . and that the wrongdoing was accidental" (Aristotle *Rhet.* 3.15.3).

In 2 Corinthians 1:15—2:11 Paul uses these topics to explain his decision not to come to them in another visit (2 Cor 1:23, 2:1, 2:9). The circumstances of the painful confrontation with the "offender" and the church's failure to stand up for their apostle at that occasion are responsible for Paul's decision not to make another visit and thus to break his word. He refrained from coming again to Corinth (1) to spare the congregation, (2) to avoid another painful encounter, and (3) to test their obedience. He urges that the alternative course he took, namely, writing to them (even if the letter was painful), was the more beneficial for both parties (2 Cor 2:3). He declares that he had the church's best interests at heart as well as his own, that is, that they should know the depth of his love for them (2 Cor 2:4) and not have grief from him (2 Cor 2:2) so that they might have joy from one another (2 Cor 2:2-3). Additionally, Paul offers an oath (2 Cor 1:18) by the faithfulness of God that his word is reliable and calls God as a witness for the defense (2 Cor 1:23), oaths and witnesses being among the strongest proofs advanced in judicial cases.

Such an elaborate defense, together with the passion of Paul's identification of the reliability of his word with the reliability of the promises of God (2 Cor 1:18-20), indicates that reconciliation has not been completely effected, even if steps have been taken in that direction with regard to the "offender" (2 Cor 2:5-11), whom the congregation is now to reinstate. Paul uses the language of reconciliation accomplished and confidence restored throughout these sections precisely in order to consolidate the reconciliation that has been accomplished through the tearful letter, and to facilitate the full restoration of confidence he calls for in this letter. Only after clearing away the prejudice that exists against him can Paul move into the main topics of his letter with the assurance that he will now receive an attentive and amicable hearing.

The following exercises will provide additional practice reflecting on how the functions of the various parts of an oration can open up the functions of segments of New Testament speeches and letters:

1. Analyze the defense speeches in Acts 22, 24 and 26 as samples of judicial speeches. Do certain verses line up with the functions of the various parts of an oration? Does considering the functions of narrative in judicial speeches as a strategic framing of a "statement of facts," for example, illumine the purpose and strategy of that part of the speech?

2. Analyze Galatians 1:1-10 in terms of the functions of an exordium, Galatians 1:11—2:14 in terms of the function of a "statement of facts," and Galatians 6:11-18 in terms of the functions of a peroration. Can you identify the proofs introduced in Galatians 3:1—4:31? What are the functions of Galatians 5:1—6:10 (e.g., where is Paul drawing conclusions from the proof section, summing up his fundamental advice or amplifying his advice)?

3. Analyze 1 Corinthians 15 as an approximation of a complete oration. This is somewhat artificial, since the opening would not need to accomplish all the functions of an exordium. Nevertheless, how might the opening verses enhance Paul's credibility and the audience's receptivity to his argument? Does Paul provide a "statement of facts" in the form of a narrative of some kind? What would you identify as the proposition of the chapter? How does Paul marshal proofs to demonstrate this proposition? Are there "digressions" from the main topic (i.e., treatments of secondary topics)?

FOR FURTHER READING

Kennedy, George. *New Testament Interpretation Through Rhetorical Criticism.* Chapel Hill: University of North Carolina Press, 1984.

Mack, Burton L. *Rhetoric and the New Testament.* Minneapolis: Fortress, 1990.

Watson, Duane F. *Invention, Arrangement, and Style: Rhetorical Criticism of Jude and 2 Peter,* pp. 1-28. SBLDS 104. Atlanta: Scholars Press, 1988. (See especially pp. 20-21 and the extensive references to the ancient rhetorical resources given in the notes.)

By means of a close rhetorical analysis we can see how 2 Corinthians 1:1—7:16 could function as a unified response to a moderately hostile situation. What then about the alleged interpolation of 2 Corinthians 6:14—7:1? And how would the "collection letters" (chaps. 8 and 9) and the rather more heated attack of chapters 10-13 function as part of the same piece of communication as chapters 1 through 7?

The objections against reading 2 Corinthians 6:14—7:1 as an integral part of its context are readily refuted:

- The atypical words found in this passage can be explained on the basis of the Old Testament quotations that Paul uses (the atypical words being part of a quotation) and of the rhetorical device of the multiple antitheses with which Paul opens the passage, a device that sends authors reaching for unusual synonyms and antonyms.

- The dualism reflected in the passage is quite at home in 2 Corinthians, which is pervaded by dualistic antitheses ("those who are perishing" versus "those who are being saved," 2 Cor 2:15-16; "that which is seen" versus "that which is unseen," and the "temporary" versus the "eternal," 2 Cor 4:16-18; see also 2 Cor 3:1-11).

- The Scriptural quotations do not reflect the saving value of Torah[26] but provide an argument from written authority concerning the importance of separating ourselves from the influences that keep us bound to this ungodly age so that we may receive the promised gifts of God.

- The argument that language of purification and uncleanness is out of place in Paul's letters is patently false: the apostle frequently uses these cultural values to draw or reinforce the boundaries of the Christian community.

Rather than interrupt an appeal for reconciliation between Paul and the believers, then, 2 Corinthians 6:14—7:1 can be understood as a further extension of that appeal: reconciliation with Paul means dissociation from others who have not understood the implications of the faith, who are still in effect siding with the present evil age. Paul has spoken throughout the letter of rival Christian sophists who have made their way to Corinth, who bolster their credibility with letters of recommendation from other churches (2 Cor 3:1), promote themselves by means of their appearance and performance rather than their heart (2 Cor 5:12), and whom Paul accuses of ped-

---

[26]The most novel suggestion regarding 2 Corinthians 6:14—7:1 was made by Hans Dieter Betz, who regarded it as an *anti*-Pauline text written by Paul's Judaizing opponents that somehow got pasted into a Pauline letter ("2 Cor 6:14—7:1: An Anti-Pauline Fragment?" *JBL* 92 [1973]: 88-108).

dling the gospel for food, shelter and gifts (2 Cor 2:17). These itinerant teachers, here grouped with the "unfaithful," will be attacked even more directly in 2 Corinthians 10—13 as "ministers of Satan."

With regard to chapters 8 and 9 it is clear that Paul is very concerned about the relief collection for the poor in the Judean churches. It is not unusual that he should include some instructions about this in a letter (see 1 Cor 16:1-4; Rom 15:25-29), especially since Paul hopes to complete the task and take his offering to Jerusalem in the near future. Since a letter, unlike the typical oration, could address numerous topics and concerns (1 Corinthians, for example, certainly runs the gamut of diverse topics), the introduction of a new topic at 2 Corinthians 8:1 should hardly surprise the reader.[27] Chapter 8 in particular shares a number of key words with the first seven chapters, including the very characteristic "encouragement/comfort" (*paraklēsis*), "trial" (*thlipsis*) and "boast" (*kauchēsis*). The Macedonian Christians, who serve as a paradigm of generosity for the Corinthians to emulate, first rededicated themselves to Christ and to Paul before completing their contributions (2 Cor 8:1-5). Paul exhorts the Corinthians directly to this same series of actions in 2 Corinthians 5:20, 6:11-13 and 8:7, suggesting a strong thematic connection between the first seven chapters and the praiseworthy example of the Macedonians in chapter 8.

The connection of chapters 8 and 9 has been ably argued by S. K. Stowers, who has shown that the opening words of 2 Corinthians 9:1 announce not a new topic (and thus something that would be out of place following chapter 8), but an explanation for the previous material.[28] Indeed, 2 Corinthians 9:1-5 depends on information in 2 Corinthians 8:16-24 to be fully intelligible, and so it can-

not be a separate communication. Moreover, the strategies of praising the Macedonian Christians' generosity to the Corinthians (2 Cor 8:1-5) and challenging the Corinthians not to disprove Paul's previous boasting of their generosity to the Macedonians (2 Cor 9:1-5) are entirely complementary. The Corinthians would lose face indeed if they had turned out not to be the generous exemplars that the Macedonians believed them to be—all the more as the Macedonians were spurred on to greater generosity by that example.

The collection material fits, therefore, quite well at the close of 2 Corinthians 1—7. After he has dealt with the problems in his relationship with the Corinthians and hopefully brought them back into line with his apostolate and message, Paul can now ask them to move ahead with the collection project. Indeed, their renewed participation in this endeavor would give them an opportunity to invest themselves in Paul's mission and in their restored relationship with him, acting again as his partners (2 Cor 1:7). It will also provide them with an opportunity to maintain their honor, which we saw the Corinthians so deeply concerned about throughout 1 Corinthians, in a manner that will benefit the global church (rather than merely serve the pretensions of individual honor-seekers).

Finally, we come to the question of chapters 10-13. It must be admitted that Paul employs a different rhetorical strategy in these chapters than in chapter 1-9. In the first part he moves delicately past the prejudices that alienate him from his hearers and subtly toward the issues that trouble him about the Corinthian believers' own grasp of the gospel. In the second part he declares open war on the rival itinerant preachers and is much more openly critical of the Corinthian Christians themselves. Given the stunning escalation of directness and criti-

---

[27]See Taylor, "Compositions and Chronology," p. 83.
[28]S. K. Stowers, "*Peri Men Gar* and the Integrity of 2 Cor. 8 and 9," *NovT* 32 (1990): 340-49.

cism in the last four chapters, a partition theory is most easily defended at this point on the ground that Paul's earlier attempts at rooting out the problems had not met with success, and that in response to further distressing reports Paul cast subtlety to the four winds and laid the issues on the line for his converts. The editor's activity would be limited to omitting the epistolary conclusion to the first letter and the epistolary prescript to the second letter.

If these chapters represent a separate letter, we must at least leave them chronologically in place as subsequent to the letter that contained 2 Corinthians 1—9. That is, they do not constitute the "tearful letter" written before chapters 1-9 (mentioned by Paul in 2 Cor 2:1-4; 7:8-12).[29] Chapters 10-13 never address the problem of an "offender" within the Corinthian congregation (whereas the punishment of this "offender" is the primary result of the "tearful letter," one that Paul regards as in keeping with the primary aims of that letter), but rather the problem of the influence of rival teachers on the congregation as a whole.

A number of scholars would argue, however, that even this modest partition theory should be disregarded. Apart from the complete lack of evidence in the ancient manuscripts that 2 Corinthians 1—9 ever circulated independently from chapters 10-13, they make the following observations:

- An intervening visit by Titus (one of the arguments put forward for the partition) need not have been made between 2 Corinthians 8:6 and 12:18 if the latter refers to the visit Titus made when he delivered the "tearful letter."[30]
- The objection that the abrupt shift in tone signals a change in situation (and therefore two separate letters) founders when

we encounter similar shifts of tone in texts such as Demosthenes' *Second Epistle,* the literary integrity of which has not been held suspect.[31]

- The shift in tone, the more direct attack on the integrity of the opponents as bearers of God's word and Paul's stepping forward as the sole author of chapters 10-13 (2 Cor 1—9 is written from the standpoint of co-authorship; cf. 2 Cor 1:1 with 10:1), can be explained as the result of Paul's decision to close this letter with the rhetorical form of *synkrisis,* a "comparison" of himself with his opponents, in which he pulls out all the rhetorical stops (including the devices of vituperation, irony, sarcasm and strong appeals to the emotions) in an attempt to fully win over the Corinthian believers.[32]

We may conclude that 2 Corinthians 1—9 and 10—13 address very closely related situations and quite possibly the same situation. The points at issue in both parts of the letter are substantially the same, indicated in the use of the same significant terms and topics in both. These issues all focus on "boasting," on the criteria by which we commend ourselves as servants of God, on the appropriate foundation of our confidence. The rival teachers commend themselves and criticize Paul based on appearances and quality of performance; Paul places his confidence solely in God, whose power is shown most completely where human strength fails (for example, in hardships), and insists that his converts cease evaluating their leaders from a worldly point of view. Only in this way will their own focus be detached from the temporary strengths of this present age and fixed on the power of God that alone suffices to bring us to the age to come.

---

[29]A position argued by Francis Watson, "2 Cor. X-XIII and Paul's Painful Letter to the Corinthians," *JTS* NS 35 (1984): 324-46, and adopted in Taylor, "Composition and Chronology," pp. 71-72.

[30]Witherington, *Conflict and Community,* pp. 332-33.

[31]Frances Young and David Ford, *Meaning and Truth in 2 Corinthians* (Grand Rapids: Eerdmans, 1987), pp. 36-40.

[32]Witherington, *Conflict and Community,* p. 338.

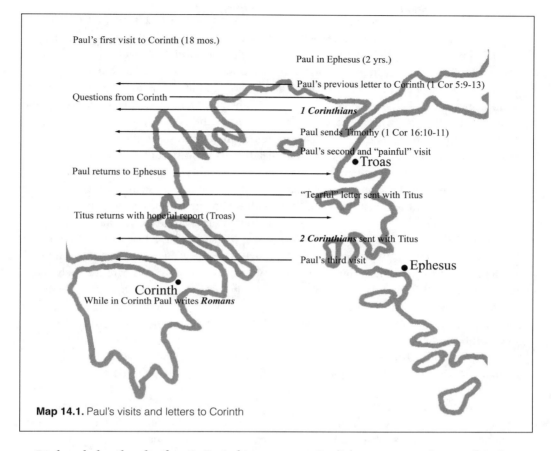

Paul's first visit to Corinth (18 mos.)

Paul in Ephesus (2 yrs.)

Paul's previous letter to Corinth (1 Cor 5:9-13)

Questions from Corinth

1 Corinthians

Paul sends Timothy (1 Cor 16:10-11)

Paul's second and "painful" visit

●Troas

Paul returns to Ephesus

"Tearful" letter sent with Titus

Titus returns with hopeful report (Troas)

2 Corinthians sent with Titus

Paul's third visit

●Ephesus

Corinth
While in Corinth Paul writes *Romans*

Map 14.1. Paul's visits and letters to Corinth

Paul and the church after 1 Corinthians. Based on the evidence in 2 Corinthians and Romans, Paul's relationship with the Corinthian Christians after the writing of the "previous letter" and 1 Corinthians unfolded as follows:

• After sending 1 Corinthians (and perhaps receiving word back from his emissary concerning how the letter was received), Paul makes a second visit, en route to Macedonia. This marks a departure from his originally stated plan to visit them on the way back from Macedonia (compare 1 Cor 16:5 with 2 Cor 1:15-17), and it is possible that his early arrival took them off guard. On this visit Paul has an unpleasant confrontation with a member of the congregation (the offender of 2 Cor 2:5-11; 7:11-12), making this the "painful" visit. It seems likely that the confrontation again centered

on Paul's legitimacy as a bearer of God's revelation, given the issues which dominate the remaining correspondence.

• Having left Corinth without resolution, Paul sends his third letter, the tearful letter, in place of a return visit from Macedonia. This letter (dispatched with Titus) together with Titus's personal presence and intervention, effect repentance on the part of the congregation for not taking action when the offender attacked Paul so openly. They respond now by punishing the offender in some way (probably exclusion). During this period Paul was in Ephesus facing some unspecified hardships (2 Cor 1:8-9), possibly including one of his frequent imprisonments.

• Titus returns to Paul with an encouraging report. Reconciliation seems possible, al-

585

though there are still some very trouble-some issues to address. The offender acted, it would appear, on behalf of outsiders who had come into Paul's field of missionary work to undermine his authority and assert theirs. Once more the issue of "who is the legitimate apostle" or "who is the superior bearer of revelation" emerges. From Paul's point of view they should rather have asked "who is the bearer of the superior revela-tion," that is, who makes the power of God more clearly present and genuine transfor-mation more accessible.

- Paul writes 2 Corinthians 1—13 (possibly all at once, possibly in two stages) to deal with these issues, to cement his relation-ship with the Corinthian believers and to promote renewed commitment to the col-lection project. He consolidates the ground that has been gained in their relationship due to their willingness to punish the of-fender. He calls them to complete their conversion from the worldly way of think-ing that focuses on appearances, or qualifi-cations pertaining to the flesh, in favor of looking away to the eternal realities and evaluating apostles on the basis of how transparent they are to God, who causes this age and all its values to pass away and brings forth a new age. He calls them to complete the collection project, which pro-vides an opportunity for them both to reaf-firm their bond with Paul and, through him, with the Jerusalem church.
- Titus and the "brothers" are dispatched to deliver the letter and oversee the collection.
- Paul visits Corinth a third time (as he antic-ipated in 2 Cor 13:1). Reconciliation ap-pears to have been achieved—the churches of Achaia come through with their contri-bution to the collection (Rom 15:25-27). Paul writes Romans from Corinth (Rom 15:25-28; 16:23) and sets out with the re-lief funds for Jerusalem, where the most trying phase of his career begins.

THE MESSAGE OF 2 CORINTHIANS

Human prowess or God's power: What makes an effective minister? Paul writes 2 Corin-thians in large measure to counter the influ-ence of certain traveling Jewish Christian preachers who have deeply impressed some portion of the congregation. Paul takes issue not with their explicit theological teachings, leading us to suspect that they are not Judaiz-ers comparable to the rival teachers we en-counter in Galatians. Paul takes issue instead with the manner these teachers play up to the cultural norms and expectations of their audi-ence, particularly in terms of the criteria they used to promote their own ministerial author-ity, as it were, and to compare themselves (fa-vorably) with Paul at his expense. They had a fundamentally different answer than Paul to the question, What makes a person a worthy Christian leader?—one that was much more in keeping with the values of the worldly mind than the values Paul believed were intrinsic to the gospel of the crucified Messiah. For Paul this was a serious matter, comparable in weight, though different in form, to the threat to the gospel in Galatia.

The rivals' self-understanding and the val-ues they embodied and promoted amounted to presenting "a different Jesus," preaching "a different gospel," and imparting "a different spirit" in the Corinthian congregation (2 Cor 11:4). In many respects they reinforced pre-cisely that ethos (competition, comparing one person against another, boasting in gifts and achievements as a means of asserting prece-dence) that Paul had sought to overturn in 1 Corinthians. An ancient orator and instruc-tor of orators wrote: "the greatest defect in a person is to show his or her humanness, for then a person ceases to be held divine." Paul's opponents embodied such worldly thinking. In building themselves up on the strength of their appearance and credentials, however, and asking that their followers evaluate them on this basis, they do not allow God's presence to shine through. Rather, they remain opaque to God's power, revealing no new basis for trust and confidence but mirroring and reaffirming the values of the world. Indeed, they empty the cross of its power to reveal the wholly other and greater wisdom and strength of God (cf. 1 Cor 1:17).

The gospel preached by Paul declared that this present world was passing away and that all marks of value (whether positive or negative) within this present world were therefore not of lasting value (see, for example, 2 Cor 4:16-18). The heart of Paul's gospel, indeed, is conformity to Christ in his death and his self-giving obedience to the work of God in the world, so that one may also share in Christ's resurrection. The present body—even if graced by poise, beauty, dramatic presence and all manner of human achievement—is still mere "nakedness." It is not until the resurrection that we will be fully clothed with a body of glory. This flesh is penultimate, subject to death and decay, which looks forward to the day when what is mortal will be swallowed up by life (2 Cor 5:1-4). Indeed, this body and all that belongs to it is still "dishonor" and "weakness" when set alongside the resurrection body that God calls into existence (1 Cor 15:43). Only the latter body has genuine honor and strength.

What value then can fleshly strengths really have before God? Rhetorical ability, charismatic virtuosity and all that makes for a fine appearance in the flesh cannot make someone sufficient for the ministry of the gospel. These things, together with all human credentials, belong to the present age that is passing away, and they will prove valueless and impotent in the face of death. They carry nothing of the power of God that brings a person to the life of the age to come. They are like the fading glory of Moses' face and, like Moses, the rival teachers are masking the truth of the temporary and fading nature of all human strengths (2 Cor 3:7-14). Only God can legitimate a person for the work of proclaiming the Word that separates those who are perishing from those who are being saved (2 Cor 3:4-6).

Paul therefore allows his humanness, his vulnerability, his seeming inadequacies to remain visible, so that when people look at him they will see not another paradigm of the myth of self-justification, but rather the fire of God's favor and power glowing through the translucent walls of an ordinary clay vessel. Paul does not seek to adorn this poor vessel with external trappings, which would only distract from the One his converts must encounter and in whom they must place their confidence. In this way Paul truly presents no stumbling block to the gospel, as he claims (2 Cor 6:3). Paul's experiences of affliction, understanding of apostleship and presence in the world all point away from human strength and self-reliance toward the provision of God and reliance on the divine. For Paul there must be no mistaking his successes for human triumphs, but rather they must be seen as God's strength at work. Far from discrediting him, then, his hardships qualify him as an emissary of God, for in his weakness God's strength is known and made present and accessible to the churches (2 Cor 1:3-7; 4:10-12; 12:9-10). The representative of the genuine gospel must resist the temptation to make himself or herself look more divine than human, to make himself or herself the focus of trust and confidence. Only thus can the reality of God's power and promise shine through and reveal itself to people in need of God's transformation.

Paul's model of ministry, which also must be replicated in each disciple, is mandated first by Christ's example and the nature of his messiahship (cf. 1 Cor 1:17-25; 2:1-2; 2 Cor 4:7-18; 13:4). Viewed "according to the flesh" *(kata sarka)*, Jesus is "Christ crucified," an image of weakness and degradation; viewed by faith he is the "Lord Messiah" (1 Cor 12:3), the place where God's transforming power breaks into the perishing world. When we look

---

Paul's Lists of Hardships

Paul prominently features lists of the hardships he has endured in his service to Christ throughout 2 Corinthians (2 Cor 4:7-12; 6:3-10; 11:21-33). In so doing he introduces a frequent topic of Greco-Roman philosophical texts into his defense of his ministry. These hardship catalogs served several ends. Often they reinforced the core value of the Stoic philosophy, namely, imperturbability in the face of external circumstances (Seneca *Constant.* 10.4; 15.1-3; Epictetus *Diss.* 4.7.1-18). A Stoic is a person "who though sick is happy, though in danger is happy, though dying is happy, though condemned to exile is happy, though in disrepute is happy" (Epictetus *Diss.* 2.19.24). Hardships prove the worth of a person, the inner strength, the determination of the will, the moral fortitude (Dio *Orations* 8). The person whose moral character and determination remains steadfast in the face of any hardship is the praiseworthy person (Seneca *Ep. Mor.* 82.11-12), and hardships can be viewed as the means by which God trains a person in virtue and proves that person's worthiness (Seneca *Prov.* 6.1-4; Epictetus *Diss.* 1.24.1-2). Hellenistic Jewish literature shows a similar tendency to interpret hardships as opportunities to display virtue, here transformed from "imperturbability" to "endurance for the sake of Torah," for example (4 Maccabees 11:9-12).

One important point of connection between Paul and philosophical interpretations of enduring hardships is their probative value. Paul's endurance of hardships proves his fidelity to God's commissioning him as a servant (2 Cor 11:23-29) and gives evidence of his courage and sincerity.[a] The positive spin that Stoics and others gave to the endurance of hardships (many of which would have entailed disgrace among nonphilosophers) certainly helped Paul set forward his own considerable list as proof of his genuineness as a philosopher of the Christian way of life.

However, there are some notable points of difference, as Victor Furnish ably demonstrates.[b] Paul speaks candidly of the impact his hardships have had on him. He experiences their crushing weight quite fully (2 Cor 1:8-9). Moreover, his ability to endure hardships is not ultimately a proof of his own accomplishment in putting philosophy into practice (although he would make such a claim in Phil 4:11-12)[c] or his moral determination, but of the "surpassing power of God," the God who raises the dead and emboldens the afflicted (2 Cor 1:9; 4:7).

---

[a]J. T. Fitzgerald, *Cracks in an Earthen Vessel*, SBLDS 99 (Atlanta: Scholars Press, 1988), p. 206.
[b]Furnish, *II Corinthians*, pp. 280-83.
[c]Fitzgerald, *Cracks in an Earthen Vessel*, p. 205.

---

at Jesus with the eyes of the Spirit, a veil is removed—the veil that covers the temporary, passing value of appearances and worldly achievements with a veneer of ultimate importance and reliability. Jesus, the Messiah who died on a cross—stripped, despised, worthless in the world's eyes—proves the unreliability of appearances. He whom the world regarded as worthless God estimated as of supreme worth. In obedience to God's purposes, Jesus allowed himself to be deprived of all outward signs of acceptability and worth, valuing the approval of God rather than the approval of society. The resurrection of Jesus proves that God's approval is of infinitely more worth than the world's, and it is to be pursued even at the cost of being evaluated as of no account by worldly standards.

Understanding that God's approval matters more than society's affirmation of our respectability gives us true freedom to follow Jesus, which will often lead us away from what the world affirms and encourages. Society counsels us to secure our financial future through hoarding and investing: Jesus calls us to invest in the poor and hungry. Society advises us to network with people who can advance our careers; Jesus calls us to network with the outcast, the homeless and the sick to advance their good. Where the veil is removed, we see clearly how Jesus' way leads to a better approval.

The disciple, therefore, must be free from evaluating worth, including his or her own worth, according to the criteria used by the worldly person. Rather, all that counts now is "the new creation" coming into being as a person is transformed into the likeness of Jesus (2 Cor 5:16-17). There is no more room for "boasting in appearances" (2 Cor 5:12). This frees the disciples to "live no longer for themselves but for him who died for them and was raised again" (2 Cor 5:15). Jesus' death on our behalf changes the object and purpose of our lives. Rising up the ladder, gaining prestige, collecting wealth, making a name for yourself—these are no longer the goals of life, for they are no longer valid criteria for measuring a person's ultimate value. The gospel proclaims advancement as serving and preferring others over yourself, investing yourself not in your reputation or standing in the community but rather in advancing the well-being of the community, caring for the weak members of the community. Jesus' resurrection gives us the assurance that the new agenda will result in the experience of full and abundant life.

Paul's theology of stewardship. Paul's attempt to renew commitment to the collection for the poor in Judea (2 Cor 8—9) provides us with the fullest single exposition of Paul's theology of stewardship. The opportunity to give is a "favor" from God "granted" to churches (2 Cor 8:1). This is quite a reversal of the cultural understanding of beneficence, according to which giving becomes a claim to honor and recognition on the part of the human giver. Here the recognition is referred back to God, the prime mover of every good gift and generous act. It is also a demonstration of the "genuineness" of the believer's love (2 Cor 8:8; 9:13), particularly for Christ, who became poor to make us rich (2 Cor 8:9), but also for the family of God. Christian giving is thus both a privilege granted by God and a proof of our gratitude and love for the God who has enriched us to give.

Paul undergirds his collection project with a vision for the equal sharing of resources across the church, the perfect realization of the ideal of friendship. It would never be fitting among friends or kin for some to have (and to keep) an abundance while others lack what is necessary. Paul grounds this vision in the story of God's miraculous provision of manna in the wilderness (Ex 16; Ex 16:18 is recited in 2 Cor 8:15). In that story God provides the required food for his people each day. Paul calls attention here to an often unnoticed "miracle": those who gather more than they need end up with the same amount as those who were not able to gather enough for their need. There was neither excess nor want. Paul reads this story as a lesson about wealth and resources. God is the source of all the resources a person enjoys, and it is God's desire that every person have what is needed for living. Paul has emphasized the first of these points before in 1 Corinthians, where he reminded them that anything the believers had, they had "received" from God (1 Cor 4:7) and taught them that spiritual endowments (including leadership and beneficence) are given to each Christian "for the common good" (1 Cor 12:7), and not for the benefit of the possessor. In God's

Paul and the Conventions of Acceptable Self-Praise

In order to counter the influence of the Christian sophists and to point the Corinthians past the veneer of human strengths to the transforming power of God, Paul has to engage in a fair amount of "self-praise." Self-praise could be highly offensive then as now, so the speaker who engaged in it had to be careful to do so only when circumstances and purposes justified it, and only in an inoffensive manner. Plutarch devotes an essay to this topic *(On Inoffensive Self-Praise)* in which he outlines the following parameters for acceptable self-praise. It is acceptable when the speaker does it (1) to establish the quality of his character with the hearers (i.e., appeals to ethos), (2) to benefit the hearers, whether by arousing them to the emulation of his or her virtues or achievements by emboldening them to some action or the like, or (3) "where mistaken praise injures and corrupts by arousing emulation of evil and inducing the adoption of an unsound policy where important issues are at stake" *(Self-Praise* 17, *Mor.* 545 D). Self-praise is rendered inoffensive when (1) it is mixed with praise of the audience, (2) the causes for praise are attributed to the gods or to good fortune, (3) when it is blended with the admission of shortcomings, (4) when it is indirect.

How well has Paul followed this advice? First and foremost, he has taken to heart the necessity of attributing all his successes and achievements to God, since this is thematic throughout 2 Corinthians (see, for example, 2 Cor 1:8-9; 2:14; 3:4-6; 4:6-7, 15). Paul also mixed his boasts with admissions of shortcomings, particular in terms of his stage presence as a speaker (2 Cor 11:6; 12:7-8, 11). He engages in a comparison of himself with the rival sophists so that the Corinthian Christians will be moved to make the right decisions and avoid disadvantage (2 Cor 12:19-22; 13:10), and above all else so that the rival's self-commendation will not induce the Corinthian Christians to continue to think and act in line with their cultural values where these conflict so egregiously with the values of Jesus. The ironic nature of Paul's self-praise, however, falls beyond the scope of what Plutarch could ever envision. By boasting most extravagantly in the things that show Paul's weaknesses, he flouts all conventions of boasting and uses the form of self-praise to call attention to God (2 Cor 11:30—12:10).

---

economy, and thus among those who are obedient to God's vision for human community, there is neither excess nor want, but "a fair balance" as those who have abundance provide for those who have need (2 Cor 8:13-14).

A more extensive reflection on stewardship appears in 2 Corinthians 9:6-12, a text that, with its language of sowing in order to reap, could easily be used to promote the old pagan principle of *do ut des:* we give so that God will give to us. In Paul's understanding, however, God enriches people in order that "by always having enough," they might "share abundantly in every good work" (2 Cor 9:8 NRSV). From God's provision a person is to use what is sufficient for his or her needs and share the rest with those who lack sufficiency. The harvest envisioned in 2 Corinthians 9:6 is specified in 2 Corinthians 9:10: material resources always remain seed for sowing (i.e., through sharing and acts of kindness); the harvest we hope to gain is righteousness, not more money to be spent on our own pleasure (cf. Jas 4:3).

Paul concludes his reflections with an affirmation of the mutuality of those who give and those who receive. The recipients respond with love for and prayers on behalf of those who have given material benefits, with the result that benefits flow in both directions and community between the parties is established (2 Cor 9:14). The primary value for Paul, then, is not the accumulation of wealth but the establishment and actualization of Christian community (locally and globally) through the sharing of resources.

THE CORINTHIAN LETTERS AND MINISTRY FORMATION

Status and factions in the church: An antique problem? A challenge facing every Christian leader, whether ordained or lay, is nurturing a community wherein each individual places the good of the other, and of the whole, above self-assertion and private agendas. The reader will be familiar with the stereotypes of the donor who expects to buy influence in the church, the faction that refuses to sing the praise choruses (or the opposite party that folds its arms and yawns during traditional hymns), the families who fall into rivalry over whose daughter gets to sing the lead in the children's musical, the group who preferred the former pastor, and so on ad nauseam. The squabbles and posturing might focus on loftier issues as well, but the dynamics would be the same and just as harmful to the health of the body.

As Paul addresses these issues at length in 1 Corinthians, he provides an alternative vision in which the person of less obvious giftedness is especially affirmed in the church, the people of privilege look to the sensitivities and sensibilities of the less privileged, and all seek the welfare of the sister or brother above their own enjoyment of entitlements. By word and example (Paul having given us a good start in regard to both), the Christian leader is challenged to cooperate with the Holy Spirit in calling the whole community toward this vision until the world's rules of competition are turned upside-down and the example of Christ is lived out in the nitty-gritty of committee meetings, choir rehearsals, counseling sessions and car washes.

The vision for the body in 1 Corinthians, however, reaches beyond the life of a local congregation to the interaction of Christians throughout their own denomination and within a community of diverse churches. Perhaps nowhere more egregiously than general conferences and conventions does the mindset of the world trump the mind of Christ and the ethos of cooperation and other-centeredness that Paul strives to nurture in the church. Moreover, in the situation of ever-splintering denominationalism, in which each believer can say "I am of Peter," "I am of Luther," "I am of Calvin," "I am of Wesley," "I am of Christ" or devise other divisive slogans that justify scorning and competing against Christians of another stripe, Paul's vision for a global church at unity and harmony with itself becomes all the more urgent and desirable. Moving toward the vision for the local church articulated above (and enacted at the global and interdenominational level) will give the gospel new wings for the third millennium.

Decision-making in the church. Paul's deliberations in 1 Corinthians 8—10 have important implications for decision-making and discipline in the church. Personal freedom to indulge in a particular pursuit or lifestyle is secondary to the purity of the conscience of the whole congregation. Personal preferences and pleasures must be secondary to what promotes the perseverance and growth of the group. Even what we know to be right and ultimately good cannot be forced on those who do not have such knowledge in the community. As one example, consider the widespread debates in churches concerning the style of worship. I have too often seen church leaders ride roughshod over the sensibilities of one sector of their flock as they move the church from a traditional to a contemporary-style service. As a music minister I have been privy to church leaders sharing their attitude toward the older generation: "they'll just have to adjust" or "those who don't like it can leave, but we need to do this to grow." Much could be accomplished through education of the whole congregation concerning the potential benefits of change *and* how the forms of worship that have nourished the faith of some in the congregation for over fifty years will continue to be honored and used. To force change on the congregation before they are ready, before their concerns have been heard and respected, before they are prepared to get on board may represent more of an act of self-assertion on the part of the leadership than an attempt to benefit the people the leaders serve. It is not an enticement to sin per se, as eating food sacrificed to idols in Corinth threatened to be, but it could represent the "strong" deciding to act in line with their knowledge with no regard for the "weak."

Consider another example: a church is pursuing a renovation project in the midst of a poor, urban neighborhood. The "strong" have thought out very carefully the needs of the congregation and have designed a new education and office wing to accommodate the desires of various church groups and personnel. A more attractive sanctuary would also be appropriate, both as a draw to visitors and as a suitable monument to the beauty of God's holiness. But some people in the congregation are reluctant to give their support. It is not that they are unwilling to spend the money, but they have scruples about spending it on the building, which is still functional, if not perfect, when there are so many needs crying out around the church. Would it not be better to take these resources and develop outreach programs, child care and mentoring programs, perhaps even begin to offer some health care and career counseling? The plans are in the works, however, and the leadership moves ahead with the renovations, leaving the consciences of several people in the church defiled when worshiping in that space because the cry of the needy has been given second place.

Were the dissenters being scrupulous, weak and legalistic? Or were they being prophetic? How we listen to and honor one another's concerns about such matters may keep our churches from choosing self-indulgence over service, and it may keep us from creating division rather than seeking that consensus in the Spirit that will build up the whole body.

Christian life in the body and in the world. Paul's attitude toward sexuality is distinctly unmodern. Sexual self-expression, self-fulfillment and self-gratification, so central to modern understandings of personhood and relationships, were not highly valued by him at all. The body fulfills its purpose as it restrains itself from pleasure contrary to God's revealed design, not as it indulges its sexual drives. We have been taught that a person needs to be sexually active to be whole, fulfilled and accomplished. Paul taught that a person has been privileged to have direct communion with Father, Son and Holy Spirit, to have been redeemed from sinful passions so as to remain a holy habitation for God's own Spirit. The purpose of the body is to honor God and honor the union with Christ that God has effected in us, not fornication (1 Cor 6:13-20). As so often is the case, Paul completely reorients us to the issue. The question of whether or not I should be allowed to enjoy certain forms of sexual expression, or to have my right to certain behaviors validated by the church is ultimately a self-oriented question, namely, how can I enjoy what I want. Paul would turn the question around toward God: How can I best honor God with the body God has deigned to indwell? With what will I join and in what manner will I now treat the body of Christ? Paul challenges us to deal wisely with the strong cultural currents toward acceptance of all manner of alternative lifestyles, not merely to run counter to them but to discern the essential marks of Christian culture. This includes the mortification of the fleshly passions for the sake of being driven by the Holy Spirit, and not by a lesser master—surely an unpopular concept in our age of gratification.

In 1 Corinthians 7 we see Paul at his most practical and pastoral as he deals with the issue of sexual expression within marriage, the divorce of "mixed" couples, remarriage and betrothal. We who tend to view the single person as the incomplete or disprivileged are challenged by Paul. He cautions us, at the very least, to affirm singleness as a gift with its own distinctive opportunities for service to the Lord, not as a condition to be remedied (1 Cor 7:7, 32-35). For those who cannot exercise self-control, however, marriage or (for widows) remarriage is a perfectly acceptable choice (1 Cor 7:9, 36, 38). Marriage emerges for Paul as the only acceptable context for sexual expression, and in this context he even speaks of the mutual *obligation* of husband and wife, save for mutually agreed-on intervals for the sake of prayer (1 Cor 7:1-6).

It is clear from this chapter, however, that sexual expression is not a major preoccupation for Paul, as it is for present-day Western culture. Sexuality, like so many other enterprises that occupy our attention, belongs to this present life, and the "present form of this world is passing away" (1 Cor 7:31). Because of the transitory nature of this age, Paul advocates an "as if not" ethic for Christians living in the body and in the world.[a] He calls for a certain detachment from

---

[a]Even if Paul's advice to the betrothed and single not to marry "because of the present crisis" (1 Cor 7:26) refers to a grain shortage in Corinth, as Winter argues (*After Paul Left Corinth,* pp. 215-68), the larger issue of the end of the present age still stands behind his ethics in 1 Corinthians 7:29-31.

the affairs of this world, not getting absorbed by them and losing sight of their temporary and penultimate nature. Here Paul lights on a central challenge for all who are disciples themselves and entrusted with forming disciples, namely, keeping everyday affairs in the perspective of eternity. Jesus likewise challenged us as he spoke of those who, like saplings choked out by thorns and thistles, allowed their dealings and interests in this world to eclipse and eventually eliminate their growth in God. If we can lead ourselves and our charges into adopting Paul's stance—"those who deal with the world" are to be "as though they had no dealings with it," and those who engage in commerce are to be "as though they had no possessions" (1 Cor 7:31)—we will be the more likely to find ourselves and our communities of faith investing our attentions and energies well in the sight of God.

The credentials of a Christian minister. Second Corinthians merits close and careful attention because this letter, perhaps above all others, speaks so directly to the issues of identity, self-respect, authority and legitimacy for those who are or will be ministers in Jesus' name. While we study and practice to become effective communicators in our preaching classes, learn the art of pastoral counseling and build up our academic credentials for the work of ministry, we may be tempted to place our confidence in these credentials as if they demonstrated our legitimation by God. Paul invites us to consider that our strength in the pulpit, the numerical growth of our churches or the increase in annual giving must never become the basis of our confidence in ministry, nor can such things ever become the basis of confidence of our congregations.

When we need reaffirmation of our call or are pressed to defend our ministry to those who call it into question, Paul's own explanation of true apostleship offers us much meat for reflection. He calls us especially to avoid pointing to and relying on externals or encouraging others to put their confidence in us because of externals, and calls us to look instead for God showing God's power and love through us. The model of Paul calls us to be transparent, to draw attention not toward our own prowess or achievement but toward the God who calls us to reconciliation and to the transformation of our mind, and to regard ourselves and others not according to appearances but according to the sincere heart. When the viewer looks at a preacher or teacher, does he or she see a testimony to human achievement, finesse or giftedness, or a person who has had a transforming encounter with the living God, someone who makes it easier to connect with God's transforming power by not putting his or her own strengths and credentials and impressiveness in the way? Only if the latter is true is the minister making God present for those he or she serves.

According to this model, experiences of hardship become opportunities to experience God's comfort and encouragement, and thus a resource for extending comfort and encouragement to other believers (2 Cor 1:3-7). Here is one way God takes what others might intend for harm, or what might simply be hurtful in and of itself, and uses it for good, namely, the restoration of many who find themselves facing similarly hurtful situations.

Stewardship. Perhaps one of the more dreaded challenges facing Christian leaders is raising support for the ministry (whether this is in the context of a church, an outreach venture, a relief organization or so forth). A gifted pastor once told me that he was counting down to his retirement by the number of stewardship campaigns he still faced. Closely related to this is the difficulty many ministers have finding willing volunteers to exercise leadership and to invest their energies in the work of the kingdom.

Paul's perspective on ownership and volunteerism may help alert us to how far Christian leaders, in their embarrassment about asking for money and volunteers, have bought into the secular mindset concerning money and other resources. Any resource, skill or property we might have is a gift from God, given to us for building up the whole body of Christ. Christians are never asked to part with "their" money or to give of "their" time and talents, but they are invited to be faithful with God's gifts and to use them enthusiastically for building up their Christian family. Indeed, another of society's givens must fall by the wayside here as well, namely, where the line is drawn between family and not family. All who are united in Christ have become sisters and brothers, and believers are challenged by Paul to invest in one another at the level of siblings, not polite strangers.

Before leaving the topic of stewardship, Paul's dedication to the importance of financial integrity merits attention. Suspicion has always been directed toward those who handle money or make money in the name of religion. Paul was no exception, as can be seen from the vigor with which he defends himself and his ministry team (2 Cor 12:14-18) and from the precautions Paul takes to guarantee his integrity in the sight of his churches (2 Cor 8:16-21). Although there is ample warrant for receiving support for one's work as a minister, Paul made it clear that he should not be confused with hucksters who peddle the gospel for profit (2 Cor 2:17), but rather that he ministers out of sincerity and duty to the God who called him. Paul wanted first to be sure that those he served knew that his passion for God and for them drove his ministry, not any desire for financial gain. This, combined with his desire to prove his sincerity and distinguish himself from those who peddle philosophies, led him to work with his hands in a leather shop. This debased him further in the eyes of the community pillars; menial work was akin to servile status in the eyes of the rich. Believers need to be careful today not to look down on those who engage in tent-making ministries as if they were less legitimate than professional clergy, for, in point of fact, they have a clearer testimony to the sincerity of their heart and their obedience to God. (I say this as a member of the "professional" guild.)

Paul also wanted to be sure that no suspicion of "skimming" from the collection for the poor could alienate his converts or impede the progress of that relief effort, thus reducing the good it would accomplish among the poor. Today, some *have* betrayed the trust of those who have supported a particular ministry or relief effort, and thus all Christian leaders are under scrutiny where finances are concerned. For the sake of their own integrity and of the good they can accomplish for the kingdom, it is absolutely essential for them not only to refrain from any hint of wrongful appropriation of funds but to even protect themselves from the accusation of such appropriation. Independent Christian auditors and other agencies for financial accountability can serve the same role as the unnamed Christian brothers who accompanied Titus and Paul when they finally gathered and delivered the relief funds for Judea.

Church discipline. The Corinthian correspondence brings the uncomfortable and unpopular question of church discipline to the fore. Paul frequently speaks of his authority to punish those who remain disobedient to the gospel in 2 Corinthians 10—13 (see, e.g., 2 Cor 13:1-4, 10). He gives specific directions for the discipline of the sexually immoral Christian brother living with his stepmother, instructing the other Christians to exclude him from fellowship and prescribing this excommunication for all who call themselves Christian and yet give themselves over to greed, idolatry, sexual immorality, drunkenness and hostile speech (1 Cor 5:11). Particularly now in the twenty-first century, "judge not that you not be judged" has become the slogan for the church, but Paul would still ask us, using the same verb, "Is it not those who are inside [the church] that you are to judge?" (1 Cor 5:12).

Once again, abuses of a scriptural mandate have led to the quiet attempt to reverse, ignore or eliminate that mandate. The gross exclusion of many people from the healing reach of the church on account of some particular sin or other, the devaluing of such people, and the use of religious rhetoric to pillory them has made it far more difficult for Christians of good conscience and heart to obey the scriptural mandates to keep fellow Christians on track when they fall into or persist in some sin. Paul himself is motivated by his desire to "present the church to Christ as a pure bride," as an appropriate partner to Christ in all his holiness (2 Cor 11:2-3). Such a passion for the church and for the privilege of being united with Christ results in healthful discipline, beginning with ourselves and moving out toward our sisters and brothers.

Just as in Corinth the "offender" remained first and foremost a brother to be restored (2 Cor 2:5-11), just as the goal for the sexually immoral brother of 1 Corinthians 5:1-13 was his eventual deliverance, so all discipline within the church must have the benefit and reclamation of the erring sister or brother in view at all times. If discipline makes an individual or a group into an object of hate or contempt, it has failed its commission miserably. Sin, however, is a subtle and deceitful force, and the individual believer often needs the assistance of fellow Christians to recognize sin for what it is and to be encouraged to renounce the deceptive pleasures of sin and to return to those behaviors that advance his or her relationship with Christ and subsequent sanctification.

FOR FURTHER READING

Barnett, Paul. *The Second Epistle to the Corinthians*. Grand Rapids: Eerdmans, 1997.

Barrett, C. K. *The First Epistle to the Corinthians*. New York: Harper & Row, 1968.

————. *The Second Epistle to the Corinthians.* New York: Harper & Row, 1973.

Conzelmann, Hans. *1 Corinthians.* Hermeneia. Philadelphia: Fortress, 1975.

deSilva, David A. *The Credentials of An Apostle: Paul's Gospel in 2 Corinthians 1 through 7.* North Richland Hills, Tex.: BIBAL, 1998.

————. *The Hope of Glory: Honor Discourse and New Testament Interpretation,* pp. 118-43. Collegeville, Minn.: Liturgical Press, 1999.

Fee, Gordon D. *First Epistle to the Corinthians.* NICNT. Grand Rapids: Eerdmans, 1987.

Fitzgerald, John T. *Cracks in an Earthen Vessel: An Examination of the Catalogues of Hardships in the Corinthian Correspondence.* SBLDS 99. Atlanta: Scholars Press, 1988.

Furnish, Victor P. *II Corinthians.* AB. Garden City, N.Y.: Doubleday, 1984.

Martin, Ralph P. *2 Corinthians.* WBC. Waco, Tex.: Word, 1986.

Meeks, Wayne A. *The First Urban Christians: The Social World of the Apostle Paul.* New Haven, Conn.: Yale University Press, 1983.

Mitchell, Margaret M. *Paul and the Rhetoric of Reconciliation.* Louisville, Ky.: Westminster John Knox, 1991.

Pogoloff, Stephen M. *Logos and Sophia: The Rhetorical Situation of 1 Corinthians.* SBLDS 134. Atlanta: Scholars Press, 1992.

Savage, Timothy B. *Power Through Weakness: Paul's Understanding of the Christian Ministry in 2 Corinthians.* Cambridge: Cambridge University Press, 1996.

Theissen, Gerd. *The Social Setting of Pauline Christianity: Essays on Corinth.* Philadelphia: Fortress, 1982.

Thrall, Margaret E. *A Critical and Exegetical Commentary on the Second Epistle to the Corinthians.* ICC. 2 vols. Edinburgh: T & T Clark, 1994, 1997.

Winter, Bruce W. *After Paul Left Corinth: The Influence of Secular Ethics and Social Change.* Grand Rapids: Eerdmans, 2001.

Witherington, Ben, III. *Conflict and Community in Corinth: A Socio-Rhetorical Commentary on 1 and 2 Corinthians.* Grand Rapids: Eerdmans, 1995.

Young, Frances, and David Ford. *Meaning and Truth in 2 Corinthians.* Grand Rapids: Eerdmans, 1987.

15

THE EPISTLE TO THE ROMANS

The God of Jew and Gentile

Philip Melanchthon, one of the great theological minds of the Reformation, described Romans as "an outline and compendium of all Christian doctrine," and its interpretation has often been driven by theological interests and debates. Indeed, until recently Romans has been read primarily as an essay in propositional theology, and interpreters have often lost sight of the concrete and specific set of circumstances and interests that called this letter into existence. Attempting to abstract the timeless theology of Romans, Christians have repeatedly broken off fellowship with other Christians over the interpretation of minute aspects of this letter, for example, the question of predestination versus free will, the degree of human depravity, the nature of "saving" faith and so forth. A tragic irony emerges when we consider that in Romans, Paul provides his fullest treatment of the way God has brought together people of diverse heritage and practice into the one body of the church, and he also gives several chapters of practical advice for preserving unity in the midst of this diversity.

Since the reading of Romans has been framed more by theological inquiry and debate than by listening to the text, the reader may have to work harder to hear Romans itself over the cacophony. Many of us have been brought up in a certain tradition of what Romans *has* to mean; thus we are caught in the endless cycle of reading into Romans what we have been taught to find there, which confirms in the end that Romans means exactly what we thought all along. But the mystery of God is always more difficult to domesticate than our traditions tend to admit. After Paul has said all he has to say about the mystery of God's righteousness, even he can still only exclaim, "How unsearchable are [God's] judgments and how inscrutable [God's] ways! 'For who has known the mind of the Lord? Or who has been [God's] counselor?'" (Rom 11:33-34 NRSV). It is perhaps more appropriate to do as Paul advises and simply "stand in awe" (Rom 11:20) rather than presume to systematize and codify this mystery. For Paul, standing in humble awe of God will allow Jew and Gentile to worship together in the one body (Rom 15:7-13), whereas the propositional approach to Romans has contributed to the fracturing of this body.

THE SETTING AND PURPOSES OF ROMANS

Romans has long been regarded as a treatise, not an adjustment of the gospel to address the specific needs of a given situation in the church. It was viewed almost as the distilled essence of Paul's thought, as recently as Günther Bornkamm, who called it Paul's "last will and testament."[1] Presumed to be "Pauline" in its purest form, Romans became the key to

---

[1]Günther Bornkamm, "The Letter to the Romans as Paul's Last Will and Testament," *AusBR* 11 (1963-1964): 2-14 (reprinted in *The Romans Debate*, ed. Karl P. Donfried, rev. ed. [Peabody, Mass.: Hendrickson, 1991], pp. 16-28).

reading all his other letters. Several breakthroughs have significantly advanced our understanding of Romans. The first of these came when students of the letter began to see that Romans is not without some contingent purpose and occasion; it seeks to achieve certain goals like every other of Paul's letters. A second important breakthrough came when scholars began to recapture the *corporate* dimension of Romans, which had long been overlooked in the history of reading Romans as a treatise on how the *individual* "gets saved."[2] A third breakthrough came as Romans ceased to be privileged above all the other letters in the discussion of Pauline theology, with the result that the theological contributions of the Corinthian and Macedonian letters are now honored equally in recent attempts to ascertain "the theology of Paul."

The Christian communities in Rome. Rome had a large Jewish population (estimated at forty to fifty thousand),[3] in part because the city itself naturally drew people from the provinces, in part because Pompey the Great had brought many thousands of Jews to Rome as slaves after his conquest of Jerusalem in 63 B.C.E. Many of these were liberated thereafter, with the result that most Jews in Rome would have occupied the status of slaves or freed persons. They were not nearly so large nor so unified as the Jewish community in Alexandria, but they nevertheless provided an ample seed bed for the Christian congregations.

The origins of Roman Christianity remain largely unknown. Jews converted elsewhere to Christianity, perhaps returning from a pilgrimage to Jerusalem (like those present for Pentecost in Acts 2:10), perhaps moving to the "Big Olive" for business opportunities (like Aquila and Priscilla of Pontus), brought the gospel to Rome and began making disciples among Jews and Gentile proselytes (or Gentiles otherwise first attracted to Judaism).[4] Christianity in Rome thus probably had a strong Jewish character and a deep rootedness both in the Old Testament (LXX) traditions and the practice of Jewish customs. It took shape, as elsewhere, in the form of house churches (see Rom 16:5, 14-15).

Since they were so largely intertwined, one event in the life of the Jewish community of Rome no doubt had a great impact on the Christian community there. In 49 C.E. Claudius expelled some segment of the Jewish population from Rome on account of a disturbance in that community over a person whom Suetonius, a Roman historian of the early second century, calls "Chrestus" (*Life of Claudius* 25).[5] While it remains possible that someone named Chrestus, a name commonly given to a slave, was fomenting riot, it is quite probable that Suetonius has mistaken *Chrestus* for *Christos*, the Greek word for Messiah. Many Jews in Rome, as elsewhere, no doubt resisted the

---

[2]A groundbreaking essay in this regard is Krister Stendahl, "The Apostle Paul and the Introspective Conscience of the West," *HTR* 56 (1963): 199-215, which demonstrated how Western individualism and preoccupation with "internal" matters, such as the feelings of guilt and acceptance, has skewed the reading of Romans. Stendahl's conclusion that Romans was written to explain how two ethnic bodies come together in the new people of God—how Gentiles come in without disinheriting the Jews—has opened up new vistas into every aspect of Paul's theology and the exegesis of Romans and Galatians in particular. His insistence that Romans is *not* about how an individual gets saved, however, has been justly critiqued as another instance of a pendulum swinging back too far in the other direction. (See D. J. Moo, *Encountering the Book of Romans* [Grand Rapids: Baker, 2002], p. 28; and Peter Stuhlmacher, *Revisiting Paul's Doctrine of Justification* [Downers Grove, Ill.: InterVarsity Press, 2001], pp. 44-52). A reading that holds together Paul's interest in people both as individuals and as ethnic groups will achieve the best balance.

[3]H. J. Leon, *The Jews of Ancient Rome*, rev. ed. (Peabody, Mass.: Hendrickson, 1995), pp. 135-36.

[4]Brendan Byrne, *Romans*, Sacra Pagina 6 (Collegeville, Minn.: Liturgical Press, 1996), p. 10. Paul speaks of Junia and Andronicus as "apostles" (Rom 16:7), perhaps knowing of their role in evangelizing in Rome.

[5]See, further, J. D. G. Dunn, *Romans 1-8*, WBC 38A (Waco, Tex.: Word, 1988), p. liii; J. Fitzmyer, *Romans* (Garden City, N.Y.: Doubleday, 1993), pp. 31-32, 77.

proclamation of this figure as the promised Messiah of Israel, and the disruption of the peace led to strong measures from the emperor to quell the shameful breach of civic unity in the capital of the world. If the trouble within the Jewish community was brewing as a reaction to the initial proclamation of the gospel, this would point to the beginnings of the Roman Christian community in 47 or 48 C.E. If they were responding, however, to later trends in this movement—perhaps the erosion of support for the synagogue among proselytes and God-fearers, perhaps the rise of less law-observant strains of Christianity—then the beginnings of the Roman church could be pushed back as far as 35 C.E. The emperor's

judgment, moreover, provides additional evidence for Christianity being regarded as a wholly intra-Jewish phenomenon by Roman authorities prior to the mid-sixties.

The church was strong enough to survive the expulsion of leading Jewish-Christians from Rome (this is when Aquila and Priscilla, for example, have to leave Rome and relocate in Corinth, see Acts 18:2), and it continued to grow in their absence.

After Claudius's death the edict of exile was rescinded and returning Jewish Christians came home to a predominantly Gentile church. There may have been some tension between the returnees and the Christians they left behind (as well as the newer Gentile con-

Figure 15.1. Excavations of the Roman Forum, the center of the political life of Rome and her empire. The three columns in the back left are the remains of a Temple to Castor and Pollux; the paved ruins occupying the center of the picture are the remains of the Basilica Julia; the large columns on the right are the remains of the Temple of Saturn. (Photo courtesy of Todd Bolen [BiblePlaces.com])

verts made in their absence).[6] For five or more years the church continued to grow and evolve without their direct influence and leadership, possibly in directions that some Jewish Christians would oppose (e.g., level of commitment to Judaistic customs among newer Gentile converts). Both sides now had to adjust: the Jewish Christians to a church which was no longer under their direction, the Gentile Christians to a group of estranged sisters and brothers whose practices some found difficult to integrate and whose objections were difficult to understand or honor. Paul's word in Romans would indeed serve as a "word on target" to such tensions within the community.

The Roman congregations continued to grow. Nero's actions against the Christians in 64 C.E. (see Tacitus *Annals* 15.44) testify to the size and visibility of this movement in Rome, to the tendency now to view it as something distinct from Judaism, and to the growing animosity felt against this movement.[7] Paul writes Romans, therefore, at something of a point of transition for this community, and much of its argumentation can be understand as an attempt to preserve its unity and internal solidarity through this transition.

Paul's personal goals for Romans. That Romans was not written to be a "last will and testament," a closing argument distilling the essence of Paul's theology, is seen in the fact that Paul does not regard Romans as his swan song but rather as a hinge between one phase of his mission and the next.[8] Writing from Corinth or its port, Cenchreae, sometime between 55 and 58 C.E.,[9] Paul sees himself standing at a juncture in his missionary endeavors. Having successfully proclaimed the gospel from Jerusalem to Illyricum (the province northwest of Macedonia and Greece), Paul senses a completion to his work in the East (Rom 15:19) and now looks ahead to new fields for sowing the gospel, namely, westward from Italy through Gaul to Spain (Rom 15:20-24). Presumably Paul would then have desired to continue through North Africa, Cyrenaica and Egypt, closing the circle of the *oikoumenē*, the civilized world, returning to Jerusalem perhaps just in time for the parousia and the deliverance of Israel at the Last Day.

Paul therefore wishes to gain the support of the Roman Christians for the next phase of this mission (to "reap some harvest" among them, and to be "sent on" by them, Rom 1:13; 15:24).[10] The well-established Christian community at Rome would make an ideal base of support for beginning a new mission. Paul is therefore at pains to establish a relationship with this church he has not founded. We can see how Paul begins to construct a "prior relationship" with the Roman Christians in Romans 1:8-10, 13. Both in his prayers and his intentions, the Roman Christians have been very much a part of Paul's life, a very real presence to him. Thus he subtly begins to lay a foundation for their future partnership with each other. Paul intends to bring "some spiritual gift" to strengthen them, but he also looks forward to being encouraged by their faithfulness as well (Rom 1:11-12). This provides a

---

[6]Byrne, *Romans,* p. 12.

[7]For more detailed discussion of the early history of Roman Christianity, see Fitzmyer, *Romans,* pp. 25-39.

[8]Byrne, *Romans,* p. 9.

[9]Paul can be confidently located in Corinth/Cenchreae if chapter 16 is taken as integral to the letter. Gaius and Erastus, both known from Corinth, are able to send their greetings with Paul to Rome (Rom 16:23) and, moreover, it is Phoebe of Cenchreae who will be delivering the letter to the Christians in Rome, hence the word of commendation for her (Rom 16:1). There is a marked preference for a date between 56 and 58 C.E. See Dunn, *Romans 1-8,* p. xliii; C. E. B. Cranfield, *A Critical and Exegetical Commentary on the Epistle to the Romans,* ICC (Edinburgh: T & T Clark, 1975), 1:12-16; Byrne, *Romans,* p. 8; Fitzmyer, *Romans,* pp. 85-88.

[10]A. J. M. Wedderburn, *The Reasons for Romans* (Philadelphia: Fortress, 1991), p. 43; Dunn, *Romans 1-8,* p. lv; Byrne, *Romans,* p. 10.

politic hint of the reciprocity relationship Paul is initiating with the Romans.[11] They cannot contribute now to the collection, as did the other Gentile churches that Paul founded, but they can contribute to the spread of the gospel.

In order to enter into partnership with Paul, they need to know precisely what he stands for. This prompts him to present himself and his message to this congregation, not only to "remind" them of the gospel (now given its distinctive Pauline accent) that they accepted, but also to "set the record straight" about his own commitment to a transformed life, his law-free gospel having been subject to misrepresentation elsewhere (see Rom 3:8, the clearest evidence that Paul knows about prejudice against his message and mission).[12] Here is one indication that Romans is not a simple, detached presentation of Paul's gospel but one designed to overcome doubt about the virtue of that gospel so that the Roman Christians will accept him as a missionary worthy of full support. Since the doubts focus on issues like how the Christian is supposed to live a moral life without becoming Torah-observant, this takes Paul more into the topics that arose in the situations in Antioch and Galatia, hence the plethora of connections between Galatians and Romans. (Unfortunately, this has also tended to lead to the privileging of these issues as central Pauline concerns, to the detriment of the contributions of Paul's other letters to a fuller understanding of his "gospel").

A second purpose concerns Paul's more immediate travel plans, as he prepares to de-part for Jerusalem with the relief funds he has collected from his converts in Achaia and Macedonia (Rom 15:25-29).[13] This is an act of charity and kindness that also serves as a symbol for the reciprocity and partnership between the Jerusalem church and Pauline churches. In Romans 15:30-32, Paul expresses concern for how the collection will be received by the Jerusalem community.[14] This collection effort represents Paul's way of signaling the solidarity between the Diaspora-Gentile churches and the Judean churches. The funds he takes to Jerusalem are the first-fruits of the eschatological pouring in of the wealth of the nations to Jerusalem. The grateful acknowledgment and acceptance of this gift from Paul on the part of the Jerusalem and Judean churches would signify an affirmation of peace and unity between the churches he has founded and the churches that emerged as a result of the Jewish mission. In light of the conflicts in Antioch and Galatia, and in light of the growing hostility against Paul in Jewish *and* Jewish Christian circles (see Acts 21:20-22), Paul was understandably concerned that the unity of the church would be sealed through the acceptance of this offering. He therefore asks the Roman Christians, who have not had the opportunity to contribute to this collection, to begin to act as Paul's partners even before he visits by supporting him in prayer (Rom 15:30-32), which Paul believes to be truly effective, and not just a casual request in religious circles.

Paul's pastoral goals for Romans. Some scholars have argued that Romans is not con-

---

[11]Romans 1:12 is not a "diplomatic rephrasing of his relation to them," correcting 1:11 (Fitzmyer, *Romans*, p. 75). Far from being a step backward, it is a step forward—calling for a response of faithfulness within the relationship that Paul is initiating. Part of the problem is the persistence of mistranslation of this verse. It is not "to be mutually encouraged by each other's faith, both yours and mine," but "to be mutually encouraged by our faith in [or trust in, or faithfulness toward] one another." Faith (*pistis*) here would have more of its usual meaning of trust or reliability in a business partnership.

[12]Byrne, *Romans*, pp. 9, 18-19.

[13]These verses inform us that during his third visit to Corinth (see 2 Cor 13:1) Paul successfully resolved the remaining tensions between himself and his congregation, and that Paul's directions in 2 Corinthians 8—9 had in fact been carried out, since the Christians in Achaia have indeed contributed to the collection for the poor in Judea.

[14]Wedderburn, *Reasons for Romans*, pp. 37-41; Dunn, *Romans 1-8*, p. lvi.

nected with circumstances internal to Roman churches.[15] However, several scholars have argued persuasively that Romans is written to address situation-specific circumstances and achieve specific goals within those circumstances. We have already seen how this is the case with regard to the aspirations and anxieties of Paul; it is similarly true with regard to circumstances facing the Roman church.[16] How would Paul get such information about a church he has not yet visited? The list of greetings in Romans 16, if it is accepted as an original part of the letter, reveals that Paul was not unknown to the church in Rome. Through his own travels he had met quite a few members of the Roman congregation, either while they were living abroad (for example, Priscilla and Aquila) or before they came to settle at Rome. Paul was not the only person to travel or write letters in the ancient world, and his personal acquaintances in Rome might easily have provided him with firsthand information prior to his writing Romans.[17]

The aspect of the Roman Christians' situation most clearly in view is found in Romans 14—15, where Paul seeks to bring harmony among the "strong" and the "weak."[18] While it is true that Paul uses these terms to address a specific situation in Corinth, it does not follow that Paul adds this admonition here simply because it *might* be useful, even though he has no knowledge of a specific tension among Roman Christians, for the discussion concerns not only eating meat versus abstaining from all meats (as potential objects of pagan sacrifice) but also the observation of special days versus the nonobservance of a sacred calendar. The tension reflects the known facts about Roman Christianity, namely, (1) its strong beginnings within the orbit of the synagogue, and (2) with the expulsion of the Jews (and possibly the influx of less Judaistic forms of the Way), the relaxation of Jewish observances among some sector of the population. This is not to say that the "strong" are entirely and uniformly Gentile Christians as opposed to "weak" Jewish Christians, since Priscilla and Aquila would surely share Paul's mind with regard to meat and calendrical observances, whereas some Gentile Christian converts who had first been converts to Judaism, or been converted through a more Judaistic Christianity, could easily maintain scruples about foods sacrificed to idols and the need to observe the sabbath and other holy days.[19]

The "strong" might scorn the "weak" for their enslavement to their scruples (or perhaps "superstition"), while the "weak" could accuse the "strong" of neglecting piety and not living in line with true religion. Paul's exposition of the gospel in Romans 1—11 impinges directly on such a situation, as Romans 15:7-13, the scriptural celebration of the bringing together of Jew and Gentile in the one church, shows. Paul's carefully balanced efforts both to negate the

---

[15]See, for example, C. H. Dodd who calls it "a waste of time" to try to deduce internal conditions from this letter (*The Epistle of Paul to the Romans* [New York: Harper & Brothers, 1932], pp. xxviii, xxxi).

[16]Thus, rightly, Karl P. Donfried, "False Presuppositions in the Study of Romans" in *The Romans Debate*, ed. Karl P. Donfried, rev. ed. (Peabody, Mass.: Hendrickson, 1991), p. 103.

[17]Dunn, *Romans 1-8*, 1:xlv. Paul's advice about paying taxes in Romans 13:6-7, for example, is often read as an indication of such detailed information about current issues in Rome. About the time Romans was written, people in Rome were actively protesting the extortionate collection of "indirect" taxes by the *publicani,* such that the matter was brought before the emperor and senate, who eventually intervened to correct this abuse. Paul is thus counseling Christians to provide a model of orderliness and submissiveness to authorities in a situation of restlessness and turmoil. (See Tacitus *Annals* 13.50-51; Dunn, *Romans 1-8,* pp. xliii-xliv, liv; Fitzmyer, *Romans,* pp. 35-36, 78-79.)

[18]See, further, Wedderburn, *Reasons for Romans,* pp. 64-65; Fitzmyer, *Romans,* p. 33.

[19]Wedderburn, *Reasons for Romans,* p. 141; Raymond E. Brown, *Introduction to the New Testament* (Garden City, N.Y.: Doubleday, 1997), pp. 572-73.

Figure 15.2. The interior of the Roman Colosseum, constructed under Titus (79-81 C.E.). A floor was originally constructed over the maze of passageways now visible in the center, where gladiators, animals and other entertainments were prepared prior to their entrance into the arena. The arena could even be flooded for the re-enactment of naval battles. (Photo courtesy of Todd Bolen [BiblePlaces.com])

ethnic privileges of Jews and to exclude a boastful or superior attitude among Gentile converts come to bear here on nurturing an attitude of tolerance across the lines of "strong" and "weak," putting Christ's welcome of all ahead of personal judgments. Resolving these tensions is also ancillary to Paul's personal ambitions, for a unified and harmonious church—especially one that has been helped along to harmony by Paul's timely intervention—will make for a stronger and more committed base of support for his future missionary endeavors.

GENRE AND STRUCTURE

Romans falls naturally into the major category of "letter." It has the standard form for an epistolary opening ("X to Y, greetings"), but it is substantially expanded, as Paul was accustomed to do (Rom 1:1-7). The final chapters also include the normal topics covered in a letter closing—indication of travel plans, concluding greetings and postscript. Within this letter frame, the body of Romans incorporates several subgenres[20] within a framework commonly called a "diatribe." This form is com-

---

[20]For example, testimony lists (chains of Scripture quotations; see Romans 3:10-18; 9:25-29; 15:9-12), hymns and a miniletter of recommendation (Rom 16:1-2). See further, Fitzmyer, *Romans*, pp. 91-92.

mon in popular philosophical teaching in urban centers and is found especially in the *Discourses* or *Dissertations* of Epictetus.[21] The speaker would present his case in a vivid style, engaging the hearers through direct address, paradoxes, rhetorical questions, asking questions and then providing answers, and dialogues with imaginary third parties (straw adversaries or "straight men" whose objections are answered or counterpositions dismantled). This form was especially effective because it allowed the speaker to address likely objections to his argument and prevent the hearers from drawing false conclusions from the argument. An audience is only won over if the secret objections they harbor in their minds are defused. For this reason, an effective speaker will show an awareness of likely objections to what is being said or questions prompted by what is being proposed and answer them up front.

Romans contains a lengthy, coherent, unified argument concerning the relationship of Jew and Gentile to God and each other in the one body of Christ. Within this argument some seams or stages are easily discernible; in other places it is difficult to know where to draw the lines between discrete pieces of the argument. An overall sketch of the letter might resemble the following:

1. Epistolary prescript (Rom 1:1-7), announcing the theme of the letter: Paul preaches to bring about the "obedience of faith" among the Gentile nations (Rom 1:6).

2. Thanksgiving (Rom 1:8-15), developing Paul's past and future partnership with the Roman Christians.

3. Thesis, or proposition (Rom 1:16-17): The gospel brings God's saving power to life in all who trust, whether Jew or Greek, revealing God's righteousness "from faith/faithfulness to faith/faithfulness."

4. The solidarity of Jew and Gentile under sin (Rom 1:18—3:20).

5. The solidarity of Jew and Gentile under God's favor in Christ (Rom 3:21—4:25).

6. Conclusion and transition (Rom 5:1-21), celebrating God's initiative in bringing human beings back into a state of favor, closing off the theme of wrath introduced in Romans 1:18 with the assurance of future salvation from that wrath in Romans 5:9 on account of the reconciliation effected in Christ. Romans 5:12-21 reinforces the negation of the Jew-Gentile distinction before God by viewing all of humanity as either "in Adam" under sin or "in Christ" under righteousness.

7. Clarifications of possible questions (Rom 6:1—8:39)

   a. What are the ethical implications of this new life in Christ "under grace" and without "law" (Rom 6:1—7:6)? This section takes up the slanderous misrepresentations of Paul cited in Romans 3:5-8 that his gospel encourages sin.

   b. What is the role of the law in regard to sin (Rom 7:7-25)? This section address questions raised by his treatment of the law in Romans 3:20; 4:15; 5:13, 20; 6:14; 7:6.

   c. How does Paul's gospel uphold the law rather than overthrow it (Rom 8:1-39)? Chapter 8 looks forward now through the life in the Spirit of Christ to the redemption of all creation and the glorification of the believers in Christ, thus reversing the condition of wrath (and the promise of eschatological wrath) with which the argument began in Romans 1:18.

8. Treatment of the questions raised in Ro-

---

[21]See S. K. Stowers, *The Diatribe and Paul's Letter to the Romans*, SBLDS 57 (Chico, Calif.: Scholars Press, 1981); Thomas Schmeller, *Paulus und die "Diatribe": Eine vergleichende Stilinterpretation* (Münster: Aschendorff, 1987); Fitzmyer, *Romans*, p. 91.

mans 3:1-4 about the advantages of Israel, and, more importantly, whether their unfaithfulness nullifies God's faithfulness to God's promises (Rom 9—11).

9. General instructions regarding how to respond to God's gracious gift of acceptance, promoting the core values of Christian unity, mutual love and respect for authority (Rom 12—13).

10. Specific instructions promoting unity and cohesiveness among the Christians, reflecting Christ's acceptance rather than our judgment of the brother or sister on indifferent matters of observance of Jewish customs (Rom 14:1—15:13).

11. Paul's travel plans and the role the Roman Christians are asked to play (Rom 15:14-32).

12. Greetings and concluding doxology (Rom 16:1-27).

THE MESSAGE OF ROMANS

Although prompted by situational concerns and goals like any other letter, Romans does indeed provide a more coherent expression and more substantial development of many of the motifs that Paul had been developing over a longer period of time.[22] Here we find Paul's most mature reflections on the relationship of Jew and Gentile and Israel and the nations in the plan of God, the role of the Torah, and the life of obedience made possible by the Spirit.

Jews and Gentiles in the one body. The theme that neither Jew nor Gentile holds a privileged status in God's sight and the way these diverse ethnic bodies are brought together in a single, unified community gives coherence to the whole of Romans, especially chapters 1-11 and 14-15. As James Dunn observes, " 'All' is one of the really key words in Romans. . . . The 'all' consistently means Jew as well as Gentile, Gentile as well as Jew."[23] This was indeed an important theme for Paul to take up in this letter. The Jewish people had long regarded themselves as set apart from the Gentiles by God's own self, and they regarded their maintenance of this distinctiveness, this separation, as their duty to God. The mandate and means for maintaining this distinctiveness, moreover, were bound up in the Torah. The possession of Torah gave Israel a great privilege and advantage over the Gentiles, and the observance of Torah gave Israel the way to maintain its distinctiveness.[24] Many Jewish Christians continued to uphold these premises, even to the point of insisting that a Gentile would need to become part of the people of God by means of the rites prescribed by Torah (e.g., circumcision). For them there was a distinction between Jew and Gentile in God's sight, with a marked preference for the former! The "works of the law" that Paul attacks, therefore, represent the attempt by Jews and Jewish Christians to maintain the distinction between Jew and Gentile by observing Torah (with all of its boundary-marking laws like circumcision, sabbath observance and dietary regulations as well as its ethical laws, since

---

[22]See the impressive lists of connections between topics and themes in Romans with the other undisputed letters of Paul in Dodd, *Epistle of Paul to the Romans,* 1:xxix-xxx; Fitzmyer, *Romans,* pp. 71-73.

[23]James D. G. Dunn, *The Theology of Paul the Apostle* (Grand Rapids: Eerdmans, 1998), p. 372.

[24]Dunn, *Romans 1-8,* p. lxix. On Torah as a sign of Israel's distinctiveness, see *Epistle of Aristeas* 139, 142: "the legislator . . . surrounded us with unbroken palisades and iron walls to prevent our mixing with any of the other peoples in any matter. . . . So, to prevent our being perverted by contact with others or mixing with bad influences, he hedged us in on all sides with strict observances connected with meat and drink and touch and hearing and sight, after the manner of the Law" (cited in Dunn, *Romans 1-8,* p. lxix; see the more extensive discussion of this topic in David A. deSilva, *Honor, Patronage, Kinship and Purity* [Downers Grove, Ill.: InterVarsity Press, 2000], pp. 269-74, with reference particularly to purity and dietary regulations). On the Torah as a sign of privilege in God's sight over against all other people groups, see Sir 24:23; Bar 3:36-4:4). According to these ancient authors, the law is privileged information, a sign of God's special love for Israel, which God clearly does not possess toward other nations to whom God did *not* give the Law.

The Literary Integrity of Romans

The ending of Romans was not entirely uniform in the early history of its transmission. Most of the major witnesses, including Codex Sinaiticus and Codex Vaticanus, preserve Romans as we have it (with the exception of Rom 16:24, which is likely to have been a scribal interpolation). Marcion, the mid-second-century Gnostic Christian who was quite influential in Rome, however, used a truncated version of Romans that included only the first fourteen chapters. Several Old Latin and Vulgate manuscripts follow this tradition, ending at Romans 14:23 and followed by the doxology (Rom 16:25-27). Papyrus 46, a witness to the Pauline epistles from about 200 C.E., places the doxology after Romans 15:33, with Romans 16:1-23 following the doxology. Codex Alexandrinus duplicates the doxology, placing it both after Romans 14:23 and Romans 16:23!

This strange textual data gave rise to the hypothesis that chapter 16, in particular, might be a later addition to Romans. While its Pauline authorship is hardly questioned, its place in Romans is. As support for this hypothesis, scholars began to suggest connections between Romans 16 and the church in Ephesus, positing that it represented greetings added by Paul to a copy of Romans sent to the church in Ephesus or else the only surviving part of an otherwise lost letter. These scholars point out that Paul would hardly know so many people in a church he had never visited, but having stayed in Ephesus for three years, he would have known many people in that congregation.

However, Paul does not regularly send personal greetings to individuals within the churches he founded, singling them out. It would be quite odd therefore for Romans 16 to have originally been part of a letter to Ephesus, where he knew the congregation intimately. The only other place we find such a list of personal greetings is Colossians, a letter to another church Paul did not found, whose members were largely unknown to Paul and he to them. Personal greetings in Colossians and Romans would serve to connect Paul to a church he did not found, showing that he is quite well connected to the community there. He is not an unknown variable but a person to whom, and to whose reliability, several respected Roman Christians could bear witness.[a]

The only section that proves to be truly problematic from the viewpoint of textual history is the concluding doxology (Rom 16:25-27), which may have been composed to provide a suitable conclusion to the shorter text of Romans (e.g., the Marcionite Romans 1—14), and thence to other texts dependent on or copied with reference to texts following Marcion's delimitation. The presence of terminology in this doxology not otherwise developed in Romans (e.g., a "mystery . . . kept secret for long ages but now disclosed," which is reminiscent of Eph 1:9-10; 3:3-6) supports the view that it is a secondary addition.[b] Even so, the author of Romans 16:25-27 has captured the major themes of Romans in this liturgical summary.

---

[a]Dodd, *Romans*, 1:xix-xx; Wedderburn, *Reasons for Romans*, pp. 13-14.
[b]See H. Gamble Jr., *The Textual History of the Letter to the Romans* (Grand Rapids: Eerdmans, 1977).

these still belong to *Israel's* Law and mark the separation of Jews from Gentiles).[25] At the same time, Gentile Christians had been developing a theology of triumphalism: *they* replaced the Jews in God's economy and in light of this the observances of their Jewish Christian sisters and brothers seemed like superstitious taboos.

Paul, however, argues that both Jew and Gentile are delivered from wrath and brought into line with God's righteous standards in precisely the same way—a way that is neither Jewish nor Gentile. The strange shape of Jesus' cruciform messiahship and the pouring out of God's Holy Spirit on Jewish and Gentile Christian alike without distinction convinced Paul that the priority of the Jew in the plan of God was temporal only, and not ontological.

He begins to develop this argument by demonstrating the solidarity (the unholy unity, as it were) of Jew and Gentile in sin and dishonoring God. The sinfulness of Gentiles—indeed, the use of "Gentile" and "sinner" as nearly synonymous—is a commonplace of Hellenistic Jewish apologetics, and Paul shows a deep familiarity with this tradition, especially as it appears in Wisdom of Solomon 13:5-10; 14:22-27. Both authors move through the same progression of thought. Gentiles should have been able to come to a knowledge of the one God through contemplation of God's creation, and so are "without excuse" (Wis 13:1-9; Rom 1:19-20). Gentiles turn rather to the worship of created things, denying God the honor due him (Wis 13:2, 7; Rom 1:22-23).[26] Ignorance of God gives rise to every kind of vice (Wis 14:22-27; Rom 1:24, 26-31), and God

justly pronounces sentence on all who do such acts (Wis 14:30-31; Rom 1:32).

The Gentiles, then, provoked God by refusing to honor God or show gratitude as God deserves. This leads to God's diminishing of the ungrateful, causing them to forfeit their own honor as they are "handed over" to the darkened mind, the grip of "dishonorable passions" (Rom 1:24, 26), the multiplication of vice (envy, murder, slander, deceit, arrogance, faithlessness, etc.). Paul has here modified the viewpoint of Wisdom of Solomon, since the acts of wickedness committed by Gentiles are but symptoms of the root problem of failing to honor God and God's claim on their lives. Dishonoring God works unrighteousness in the lives of idolaters just as honoring God produces the fruit of righteousness in the lives of believers. Idolatry destroys the whole of life just as the worship of the one God reintegrates and restores life (Rom 12:1-2).[27]

But Paul does not go on as does the author of Wisdom of Solomon, who immediately contrasts the debased behavior of Gentiles, and their judgment at God's hands, with the covenant loyalty of Jews and their experience of mercy at God's hands. Jews have not fallen into the trap of idolatry; they know that they belong to God; they will not sin, since they know they are God's own; even if they do sin, they remain God's people (Wis 15:1-5). In an unexpected move, Paul turns against his intertextual resource and goes on to convict the Jew of being equally involved in sin alongside the Gentile and equally vulnerable to God's condemnation.[28]

This is the essential foundation of Paul's position as seen in Antioch and Galatia. Jew

---

[25]See Dunn, *Theology of Paul*, pp. 354-59.

[26]In a sense this is very much at the heart of Greco-Roman religion. The Gentiles did not merely worship carvings; rather, the Greco-Roman pantheon represented aspects of the human social enterprise—arts, agriculture, military power, political power, benefaction and the like. Gentile society became its own object of worship.

[27]N. T. Wright, *What Saint Paul Really Said* (Grand Rapids: Eerdmans, 1997), p. 143.

[28]See L. Gregory Bloomquist, "Paul's Inclusive Language: The Ideological Texture of Romans 1," in *The Fabrics of Discourse: Essays in Honor of Vernon K. Robbins*, ed. David B. Gowler, L. Gregory Bloomquist and Duane F. Watson (Harrisburg, Penn.: Trinity Press International, 2003), pp. 189-90.

and Gentile are equally in need of the expiation provided by Jesus and in need of the Spirit as the guide and empowerment for a life of righteousness. Rather than follow up his condemnation of the Gentiles with a celebration of the blessed state of Jews who have circumcision and Torah, who possess in the Torah the means of life, Paul affirms the failure of Jews also to do what is pleasing before God. The Jew has shared in the Gentile's failure to honor God as God: the Gentiles did so by bestowing on created things the honor due God alone; the Jews by not obeying the Law that God imposed on them in the covenant agreement (Rom 1:20-21, 25; 2:23-24). Indeed, whereas the Jewish people had been entrusted with being a light to the nations to bring them to the knowledge of the one God (Rom 3:2-3),[29] the Jews have in fact contributed to the Gentile's dishonoring God by their own disregard for the Law of this God (Rom 2:23-24, quoting Is 52:5 as proof for this stunning claim).

A basic premise about the justice of God, indeed about any judge who would be "just," is that judgment is without partiality (Rom 2:11). No one enjoys privilege before God's judgment seat. Despite their historic advantages, Jews have no special claim on God's favor, no "pull" with the judge, as it were. Mere possession of the Law does not distinguish the Jew from the Gentile in God's sight, but doing what is right gives distinctiveness (Rom 2:1-11). Possession of the Law is no unique privilege or ground for boasting, since it has not been accompanied by obedience. Paul concludes this subsection by redefining true Jewishness—the boundaries of that "Israel" which does stand in God's favor (cf. Gal 6:15; Phil 3:3). All those who obey God's law, whether through observance of Torah or submission to the law written on the heart, are circumcised in their inner being and are approved by God. In so arguing Paul builds on the stance of the prophet Jeremiah, who argued that circumcision of the heart was of greatest value to God (Jer 4:4; Rom 2:25-29).

Paul reaches the climax of his survey of human sinfulness in Romans 3:9-20. Both Jews and Gentiles, for all the attempts made by Jews to preserve the boundaries between them, are united under the power of sin. Paul uses a catena (chain) of Scriptures to prove the pervasiveness of sin (Rom 3:10-18). The Law itself, functioning as Scripture and witness, attests to the universal need for redemption.

The implication of this becomes the major point of the following section. As there is no distinction between Jew and Gentile in sin, so there is no distinction between Jew and Gentile in salvation. Both are justified on the basis of God's favor extended to humanity in Jesus (Rom 3:21-26). Here Paul begins to develop the theme that he announced as the central tenet of the gospel—the "righteousness of God" that is "revealed from faith to faith" (Rom 1:17; the NRSV reads "through faith for faith"). The phrase "righteousness of God" contains some grammatical ambiguity. Is this the righteousness that God displays or a quality that God imparts? (This second option tends to be invoked where an author wishes to make "imputed righteousness" the constant theme in Romans.)[30] Romans 3:25-26 makes it clear, however, that God is revealing his own righteousness: "he did this to show his righteousness . . . it was to prove at the present time that he himself is righteous and that he justifies the one who has faith in Jesus" (NRSV).

In what sense is God "righteous" here? Peter Stuhlmacher comes very close to the point when he observes that "God's righteousness" re-

---

[29]Ibid., p. 127.
[30]For a much fuller discussion of *all* the grammatical possibilities, which are legion, see Wright, *What Saint Paul Really Said,* pp. 100-110; more briefly, Dunn, *Theology of Paul,* p. 344.

Figure 15.3. A small statuette of a *lar*, an ancestral spirit worshiped as part of the domestic religion of Roman homes. (Photo courtesy of the Cleveland Museum of Art)

fers to God's acts of deliverance and provision of well-being throughout Israel's history and at the last judgment.[31] God has been faithful to the people to whom God had committed himself, whether or not they had been faithful to him. This is precisely the affirmation Paul makes in Romans 3:3-4: "What if some were unfaithful? Will their faithlessness nullify the faithfulness of God? By no means!" (NRSV). *Righteousness* (or *justice*) is not merely an abstract, forensic term in the ancient world but a highly relational concept. Justice is manifested where "faith" is "zealously kept," "alliances and friendships . . . scrupulously honoured," and "ties of hospitality, clientage, kinship, and relationship by marriage . . . inviolably cherished" (Pseudo-Cicero *Rhet.*

---

[31]Stuhlmacher, *Revisiting Paul's Doctrine of Justification,* p. 19.

ad Her. 3.3.4). "God's righteousness" therefore indicates God's covenant faithfulness, God's commitment to do the acts that covenant faithfulness implies—acting to deliver his people, to judge wickedness and to remain impartial.[32] And God has shown this faithfulness not merely to Israel, but to Abraham, the father of many nations, and indeed to Adam, making provision for all humanity to be reconciled to God and recover the image of God.

God's righteousness is thus revealed in God's commitment to act in accordance with God's own purpose to bring blessing to all nations through transforming the sinner, by passing over former transgressions and justifying the ungodly (Rom 3:25-26). This is also, quite poignantly, a revelation of God's generosity. Going beyond all expectations of human generosity and magnanimity, God acts most sacrificially and generously toward us when we were most alienated from him and unworthy of any such consideration—"while we were yet sinners" and "enemies" (Rom 5:6-11). Such is the nature of God's righteousness and the measure of God's virtue as a generous benefactor, calling us into "favor" and extending "favor," making us friends while we were still enemies.

The erasure of distinction between Jew and Gentile under sin means that this distinction will not be meaningful in God's provision for restoration. God justifies the ungodly on the basis of a gift, of favor, approaching both Jew and Gentile on the same basis (Rom 3:22-24). Paul returns in Romans 3:27-31 to the core creed of Judaism, the *Shema*: "The LORD our God, the LORD is One." God is not God of the Jews only, that God should insist on saving only Jews and Gentiles who become Jews. This paragraph helps clarify precisely what Paul means by "works prescribed by the law" (Rom 3:28). Paul assumes that if justification were

indeed to come through works of the law, then God would be the "God of the Jews only" and "not the God of the Gentiles also" (Rom 3:29). "Works of the law," then, are the works that Jews do *as* Jews in distinction from Gentiles (i.e., by focusing on fulfilling the Jewish Law, the Torah).[33] In Galatians certain of these works stood more to the fore of the debate than others (notably, circumcision), but even taken as a whole, the Torah still represents the separation of Jew from Gentile—and thus can no longer have force now that God is bringing Jew and Gentile into the one body of the church through the Spirit. The one God thus proves to be God of Gentiles as well, justifying both Jew and Gentile on the same basis, namely, "faith" (Rom 3:27-30). Indeed, the oneness of God emerges as a powerful warrant for a unified people of God that is neither characterized as Jewish as opposed to Gentile nor Gentile as opposed to Jewish.

Paul has also negated all grounds for boasting, for thinking one group has a special claim to approval before God that sets it apart from and above another group (a viewpoint that stood at the heart of divisions in the early church). The Jew cannot boast over the Gentile on the basis of ethnic privilege, for the Jew's circumcision proved to be uncircumcision. But just as surely the Gentile cannot boast over the Jew, for the Gentile was grafted into the chosen vine of Israel, and God is equally able to graft in the Jews who had stumbled (Rom 11:11-24). As the argument of Romans 1—11 draws to a close, Paul turns his attention to the Gentile Christians, vigorously negating any boasting or gloating that the Gentile Christian might entertain, particularly against non-Christian Jews. The Gentile Christian must not look on non-Christian Jews with "triumphant contempt, but humbly, in recognition of the implicit responsibility that comes

---

[32]Wright, *What Saint Paul Really Said,* p. 103; Dunn, *Theology of Paul,* p. 342.
[33]Wright, *What Saint Paul Really Said,* pp. 128-29.

Faith in Romans

WHOSE FAITH IS INVOLVED?

In Romans 3:21-31, Paul lays great emphasis on the role of "faith" *(pistis)* in effecting justification. There are, however, a number of questions about this faith. Whose faith is in view? What nuances of faith are in view, for the word itself holds together the connotations of "faith," "trust" and "faithfulness." In Romans 3:22 Paul speaks of the "faith of Jesus Christ," which is often translated as "faith in Jesus Christ" (e.g., NRSV and NIV). In Romans 3:25, he says that expiation is received "through faith in his blood," but does this mean "through our trusting that Jesus' blood is an efficacious sacrifice" or "through faith (and is this the faith that Christ showed, or the faith that the believer has, or both) by means of his blood"? Does God justify the person who "believes in Jesus" or "shares Jesus' faith/faithfulness" (Rom 3:26)? Does God justify the circumcised and uncircumcised by means of "*their* faith" (thus the RSV, although the pronoun is not in the Greek), or simply by means of "faith," whether God's faithfulness, or Jesus' trust, or Jesus' faithfulness to God's will, or the Christian's trust, or all of these working together?

Faith is clearly operating at several different levels in Paul's understanding of the revelation of God's righteousness. This emerges from the "thesis statement" of Romans 1:17, where God's righteousness is revealed "out of faith/faithfulness to faith/faithfulness." At least two levels of faith are indicated here. Paul's use of the word becomes clearer as we recall that faith, like grace, is a concept very much at home in the relationship of patrons and clients as well as friendships (recall the discussion of this on pp.133-34 and the exploration of how it illumines Luke's Gospel on pp. 334-37). *Faith* denotes the patron's reliability, the client's acknowledgment of that reliability and the client's loyalty or fidelity toward the patron as part of the client's response of gratitude. Throughout Romans Paul is concerned with the faithfulness of God to God's promises. God can be trusted to deliver because salvation is based on God's favor and does not rest on human reliability (Rom 4:16). The sinner has been justified "on the basis of faith" (Rom 5:1), but here Paul immediately goes on to speak of God's initiative in making a way of deliverance (Rom 5:6, 8, 10). God's initiating love as shown in Christ's death on behalf of God's enemies provides the strongest assurance for salvation from the wrath to come. Thus the faith that justifies is, in the first instance, the faithfulness of God to God's promise to Abraham.[a]

The Christian, however, must also possess faith, for the gift comes to "all who trust" (Rom 3:22). This verse, however, would be needlessly redundant (as would Gal 2:16 in its context), if Christ's faith were not also part of the equation. As mediator or broker of God's favor, Jesus is faithful to his clients and faithful to God. Jesus was obedient to God's will, even to the point of a shameful death, and also trusted God to vindicate him. Jesus therefore also displays covenant faithfulness, both to God and to humanity. As such, Paul presents Jesus as both the object of

---

[a]See Dunn, *Theology of Paul,* pp. 341-42; Wright, *What Saint Paul Really Said,* pp. 96-103.

our trust (we rely on Jesus' mediation for our standing in God's favor) and the model for our trust (we who have received the Spirit of Christ are being transformed into his image, which is none other than the trust and obedience he himself displayed).

If we keep this model of mutual faithfulness between patrons and clients before us, the varied statements Paul makes about faith (unfortunately obscured in almost every English translation) make greater sense, without having to be reduced to an undue emphasis on the Christian's faith or belief—which certainly skews Paul's more God-centered model—and without neglecting the role of the Christian's trust/loyalty in the relationship.

---

with their new privilege, as gentiles, of joining in the praise of Israel's one God as the one God of all the world."[34] The Gentile Christian owes his or her place among God's people solely to God's kindness, and that same kindness can again graft the natural branches of unbelieving Israel back into the root. God's kindness should not result in contempt or boasting but in the Gentile Christians' persisting humbly in God's goodness (Rom 11:22), continuing in faithfulness, producing the harvest of righteousness, if they hope to remain in the vine. There is no new privilege or license given to them, for God is still the impartial judge!

After being united in sin and united in God's redemption, Jew and Gentile are finally left united in humble awe at the "mystery of God's kindness," in which God allows (or destines, since Paul discovers this to be part of the preannounced plan of God in Scripture: see Rom 9:32-33; 10:16-21; 11:8-10) the majority of the Jews to reject the gospel so that the Gentiles might be grafted into the new people of God. The disbelief of Israel will persist until the full number of the Gentiles is completed, which will complete "all Israel." And if such good can come from the Jews' exclusion from the new people of God, what greater good will surely result from their ongoing inclusion (Rom 11:11-24)!

The oneness of humanity in Abraham, Adam and Christ. Paul develops his thesis further through the example of Abraham, who stands at the root and foundation of salvation history as the recipient of God's promise that all the nations would be blessed through him, and that he would become the father of many nations (Gen 12:3; 17:4, 7; 22:18). Paul regards Abraham as the prototype for both Jew and Gentile in the church (Rom 4:11-12), and for both *equally* on the basis of the response of trust toward God.

Most Jewish authors reflecting on Abraham would emphasize his obedience as the basis of his righteousness, especially as reflected in his willingness to sacrifice his son Isaac at God's command. Indeed, the language of "righteousness being reckoned" to someone has its roots in Jewish texts that promote doing the works of the Torah and showing zeal for the Torah and for the covenant as the means by which one would be "reckoned righteous" before God. Phinehas's act of zeal, maintaining the boundaries that separated Israel from the Canaanites, "has been reckoned to him as righteousness" (Ps 106:30-31). The zeal of Simeon and Levi, also notably to preserve the bloodline of Israel from pollution by Gentiles, was "righteousness for them and written down for them for righteousness" (*Jubilees* 30:17; *OTP* 2.113). Faithfulness in observing

---

[34]M. D. Nanos, *The Mystery of Romans* (Minneapolis: Fortress, 1996), pp. 161-62.

the specific ways of keeping the Law promoted by the author of 4QMMT will result in righteousness being reckoned to the individual (4QMMT 30-31).[35]

Paul, however, holds up Abraham's trust in God's promise while still a Gentile as the sole basis of his righteousness before God. Abraham was accounted righteous (indeed, here too the notion of righteousness as faithfulness within the context of a relationship comes to the fore) because he responded to God's promise with trust (Gen 15:6)—and this *specifically* before he was circumcised (Rom 4:9-12; Gen 17:1-14). Paul emphasizes that Abraham must become the father of *many* nations, not just Israel (Rom 4:17; see Gen 17:5). Therefore the inheritance cannot be restricted by Torah, the Jewish Law that had functioned to keep Israel separate from and privileged above the Gentiles.[36] Rather, it must be passed on by that which unites all of Abraham's offspring with the character of their forebear, whom they must resemble, namely, trust in God's promise and reliability, and faithfulness toward God in that trust. The parallel between Abraham's faith and Christian faith is made sharper by Paul's focus on the topic of God's bringing life out of death. For Abraham this meant offspring from two bodies that were "as good as dead" (Rom 4:19); for the Christian this means the bringing back of Christ from the dead (Rom 4:23-25).

At this point it might be fitting to ask why trust or faith should be ever so much more important to God than works of the Law. Here the existentialist interpretation of Paul, which brought the notion of dependence on God to the fore, offers great benefit to our theological understanding. Those who "work" depend ultimately on a covenant—something independent of both parties to which they are bound.

This is also a matter of trust insofar as the "worker" depends on both the reliability of the covenant and the trustworthiness of God to fulfill his covenant responsibilities. However, Abraham's faith was in nothing other than God's own self—in God's character as reliable to fulfill the promise, in God's ability to give life to the dead, in God's goodness and generosity as the one who will make even the ungodly righteous. Because, according to faith, everything depends on God (Rom 4:16), God can and will effect the transformation of the person who trusts, just as God did for Abraham in the matter of fathering children (Rom 4:20-22). Placing trust in God and following wherever God leads, then, leads to the fulfillment of God's good purposes for humankind in a way that commitment to a particular code cannot. Paul will return to these topics in Romans 8, where he explores the role of the Holy Spirit in justifying the believer, empowering him or her to fulfill the "just requirements of the law."

As Paul had also argued in Galatians 3:10-18, so here he affirms that the ministry of Jesus is an outworking of God's commitment to the promise given to Abraham to bring blessing to all the nations and to extend Abraham's family of faith. The blessing of justification begins with the forgiveness of sins (Rom 4:6-9), but it is extended to include the "hope of righteousness" (Gal 5:5), being brought in line with the just requirements of the Law (Rom 8:2-4).

Paul advances his argument in Romans 5:12-21 by pushing beyond Abraham as the common ancestor of the people of faith, whether Jew or Gentile, to Adam, in whom all people are quintessentially united since they all (ideologically speaking) are children of Adam, whether Jew or Gentile, and share Adam's prototypical condition. That is, they all

---

[35]Dunn, *Theology of Paul,* p. 376.
[36]Dunn, *Romans 1-8,* pp. lxxi-lxxii.

Grace and Justification in Jewish Sources

Until recent decades, readers of the New Testament assumed that Judaism was a dry, futile religion of works righteousness, salvation through human effort and empty observance of laws (legalism). In large measure these readers took the *polemical* statements in the New Testament as a reflection of the true character of the Judaism of the period. This view permeates older scholarly literature and has gone far and wide into popular Christian writing as well.

A balanced understanding of the religion that gave birth to Christianity, however, requires that we also take seriously the literature written by Jews of the Second Temple Period that give expression to their understanding of their religion. The author of 4 Maccabees, for example, regards Torah obedience and loyalty to God in a Gentile world as the grateful response of those who know God as Benefactor, for whom Torah-keeping is a meaningful path to life and virtue. Keeping the law is not the means to win grace, but the law itself is the gift of a gracious God, and obedience is fueled by gratitude for what God has already done for Israel. This is a viewpoint shared by Ben Sira and the author of Baruch.

Even more striking is the hymn that concludes the *Community Rule* from Qumran. In this hymn from the first century B.C.E. we find many of the essential themes of Romans, thought for so long to be a revolutionary proclamation:

> As for me, my justification is with God. In God's hand are perfection of my way and the uprightness of my heart. He will wipe away my transgression through his righteousness. . . . From the source of his righteousness is my justification, and from his marvelous mysteries is the light in my heart. . . . As for me, I belong to wicked humankind, to the company of ungodly flesh. . . . For humanity has no way, and humanity is unable to establish their steps since justification is with God and perfection of way is out of his hand. . . . As for me, if I stumble, the mercies of God shall be my eternal salvation. If I stagger because of the sin of flesh, my justification shall be by the righteousness of God which endures forever. . . . He will draw me near by his grace, and by his mercy he will bring my justification. . . . Through his righteousness he will cleanse me of the uncleanness of humankind and of the sins of humankind, that I may confess to God his righteousness, and his majesty to the Most High. (1QS XI)

Here are the themes of the sinfulness of all humankind, the righteousness of God expressing itself in the justification of the sinner, the impossibility of establishing our own righteousness before God, and the initiative of God's grace or favor in restoring the sinner. What is decisively new in Paul is, first, the attachment of this to the proclamation of Jesus as Messiah who gives the Holy Spirit so that God's righteousness can take shape within the human being, and, second, the application of these religious insights to the social body, so that God's justifying gift is seen to extend past Israel to all the world. Qumran was essentially a separatist community that had no intercourse with other Jews or any Gentiles. Despite the Qumran community's expressions of grace theology, the dividing walls of hostility were actually intensified—walls Paul casts down on the basis of his Christ-centered experience of God's generosity.

participate in sin and its consequence, death.[37] The solution to this plight is for people to be incorporated into Christ, who again unites all, whether Jew or Gentile, into one new humanity. "In Adam" versus "in Christ" thus comes to replace the lines drawn between Jew and Gentile.[38] A further factor, indeed the ultimate factor, that unites Jew and Gentile and erases all distinctions between them is the boundlessness of God's favor toward *all,* irrespective of their ethnicity, since *all* are sinners (Rom 5:6-8, 15-21; 10:10-13). God has chosen to lavish God's favor and gifts on Jew and Gentile without distinction. (The Holy Spirit and its endowments would be "exhibit A" of this for Paul; see Gal 3:1-5; Acts 11; 15.) God's own action in this regard and the scope of God's favor must be determinative for the question of the solidarity of Jew and Gentile in the church.

In this section the importance of Jesus' obedience comes forcefully to the fore. Thinking specifically about Jesus' obedience "to the point of death, even death on a cross" (Phil 2:8), Paul affirms that this "one man's act of righteousness" leads to "justification and life for all," that the "one man's obedience" will make many righteous (Rom 5:18-19 NRSV). This echoes Isaiah's words about the Suffering Servant, who would "make many righteous" (Is 53:11). "Jesus has offered God the obedience and faithfulness that should have characterized Israel but did not."[39] This act of obedience, like the act of obedience and faithfulness offered by the martyrs in 2 Maccabees (see 2 Macc 6:18—7:42; 4 Macc 5—18),[40] turned away God's wrath and restored favor and the promise of deliverance—now not only for Is-

rael but for all who shared in the plight inherited from Adam. This passage has direct relevance for the "faith of Jesus Christ" debate, the question concerning whether it is "faith in Jesus" or "the faith shown by Jesus" that is the means by which righteousness comes to humanity (Rom 3:22-26; Gal 2:15-16). At the least we must make ample room for Jesus' act of faithfulness to God in any equation as the prerequisite to human faith having any value before God.

Paul returns once again in Romans 15:7-13 to the theme of the unity of Jew and Gentile in the one body as the fulfillment of the prophetic vision for the people of God, thus an important way in which "Christ is the end of the law" (Rom 10:4), having brought to fulfillment this important component of the Old Testament's witness to God's purposes. The goal of the law is truly fulfilled for the first time in Christ's ministry, for as a result of Christ's work Gentile and Jew now glorify God together, whereas before Christ the Gentile did not honor God and the Jew contributed to that dishonor (Rom 1:21; 2:23-24). In the worshiping community of the one church, the plight of humanity alienated from God finds itself resolved and reversed—this, at least, is the ideal that stands at the core of Paul's gospel and ministry.

The obedience of faith. One regrettable legacy of Reformation-era polemics is the tendency among Protestant Christians to oppose faith and good works, deemphasizing the importance of the latter in the Christian life. Paul never took up polemics against good works. Rather, he consistently opposed pursuing the

---

[37]As Wright insightfully observes, Rome and Gentile armies were not the ultimate enemy, but sin and death were—and against these Jesus had won a decisive victory on behalf of all. This has weighty implications for the end of the bifurcation of humanity into Jew and Gentile: Jesus has freed "all" from the plight that had kept "all" captive (Wright, *What Saint Paul Really Said,* pp. 93, 141).

[38]Byrne, *Romans,* p. 25.

[39]Wright, *What Saint Paul Really Said,* p. 54.

[40]See David A. deSilva, *4 Maccabees,* Guides to the Apocrypha and Pseudepigrapha (Sheffield, U.K.: Sheffield Academic Press, 1998), pp. 137-41, 143-45; *Introducing the Apocrypha* (Grand Rapids: Baker, 2002), pp. 373-74.

Paul's Hermeneutics and the Pesharim of Qumran

Like other New Testament authors Paul finds the story of Jesus, the Christian community and even his own missionary efforts in the Jewish Scriptures, which are held to be fulfilled in the story of the new community, itself the heir and fulfillment of Israel's sacred history. The acceptance of the gospel by a small portion of Jews, the rejection of the message by the majority of Jews, the spread of the gospel among Gentiles—Paul can find all these facets of the Christian community's experience in the sacred writings (see Rom 9:25-26; 10:14-21; 11:8-10; and the Old Testament texts quoted therein).

This is very much like what is found in the *persharim* at Qumran. That community also regarded the Jewish Scriptures as bearing witness to the founding events of the community and the life and struggles of its Teacher of Righteousness, to the ongoing history of that community and to events in the general history of Judea during the first century B.C.E. Both groups shared a conviction about their experience and about the sacred Scriptures of Judaism: the latter contained the revelation of God's foreordained plan for God's people, and the community's experience manifested the fulfillment of God's working out of God's purposes. The hermeneutical center for their reading of the texts was their conviction about what God was doing in their own story. Paul announced this exegetical principle in 2 Corinthians 3:14-16—whenever one turns to the Lord, that is, to Jesus as Messiah, the veil over the understanding of the Hebrew Scriptures is removed. Paul thereafter read the Law and the Prophets in light of Christ because the risen Lord was the ultimate authority for him.

"works of the law" as the means of showing ourself faithful to and righteous before God. In this he specifically meant the Jewish Torah, whose role in keeping Jews separate from the nations was now at an end. Rather, for Paul faith and righteous deeds are inseparable, not opposed. The apostle consistently insists that "the person who does what is right" is "pleasing in God's sight" (Rom 2:6-11; see also 2 Cor 5:9-10; Gal; 5:19-21; 6:7-10), and that "God shows no partiality," whether to Jew over Greek or Christian over non-Christian.[41]

Another way to conceptualize this dilemma is seen in the traditional dispute concerning justification. Does justification mean that we are counted righteous, treated by God as though we were righteous even though we are not (*imputed* righteousness), or does it mean that we are made righteous, transformed into people who actually do the things that a righteous God requires (*effective* righteousness)? Peter Stuhlmacher holds that Paul would not force a choice between *imputed* and *effective* righteousness but rather would connect both together in his view of justification.[42] We are both accounted righteous and transformed into people who do what is right in God's sight (Rom 6:12-19; 1 Cor 7:19; Gal 5:16-24), as God joins us with his Son and fills us with his Spirit. Being forgiven and reconciled with God sets us on the process of becoming righteous, for all will still appear before God's judgment

---

[41]See chapter one of D. B. Garlington, *Faith, Obedience and Perseverance*, WUNT 79 (Tübingen: Mohr-Siebeck, 1994).
[42]Stuhlmacher, *Revisiting Paul's Doctrine of Justification*, p. 62.

seat to give an account for the deeds done in the body (Rom 14:10-12; 2 Cor 5:10),[43] and God remains the impartial and just God. Another leading Pauline theologian, James Dunn, agrees that the "blessings of justification" are not limited to acquittal but include reconciliation and a restored relationship with the God who transforms us by his Spirit into the image of his Son, and who gathers us together into a people that experiences wholeness and peace in community.[44] We may have too narrowly limited justification to speak of our reconciliation with God, the forgiveness of our sins and the like, and not given sufficient attention to the fuller scope of justification that Paul envisions for the Christian, possessed and transformed by the Holy Spirit.[45]

In Romans 6:1 Paul begins to correct misunderstandings of his gospel: "And why not say (as some people slander us by saying that we say), 'Let us do evil so that good may come'" (Rom 3:8 NRSV). Paul wants to be sure that none of the Roman Christians might harbor doubts about his gospel based on hearsay (although he also will have powerful advocates in the city, given the list in Romans 16). Paul's gospel does not encourage a relaxed attitude toward sin but rather demands a radical break with sin. Baptism signifies the death of the believer to sin—that person is joined to Christ in Christ's death and now lives to God in the hope of the resurrection. The goal of coming to faith is "walking in newness of life," using the body no longer to serve sin, obeying its passions, but rather to serve God as a tool of righteousness (Rom 6:1-14). The disciple has been freed from the power of sin and the law

in order that he or she might become "obedient from the heart," entering into the "obedience of faith" (Rom 1:5) that is the primary goal of Paul's mission and the life that God's gift ultimately enables.[46]

The connection between trust in Jesus and righteous living is clarified by the framework of the reciprocity relationship. No one gave a gift to God, thus initiating a reciprocal relationship (Rom 11:35). The initiating was done by God (Rom 5:6, 8, 10). All are recipients of God's initiating beneficence, and all are obligated to God: "to him are all things." (Rom 11:36). Paul segues quite naturally from this statement to his instructions concerning how to live to please God in response to God's kindness, beginning with Romans 12:1. Christians are to present the remainder of their lives to God as the reasonable return (see also 2 Cor 5:15). Having been forgiven so graciously, joined with Christ in baptism and given the gift of the Holy Spirit, the believer is both *free* to serve God in righteousness and *bound* (i.e., obligated) to live for God because of the immensity of God's gift (Rom 6:6-7, 12-14, 18-19, 22). There is no room to indulge the old life of Adam, when it cost God's Son so dearly to incorporate us into his new life. Rather, just as our life "in Adam" produced transgressions in the service of sin, so the new life "in Christ" must produce righteousness in the service of God. Our forgiveness and acceptance by God's initiating favor finds its full expression as we live out the "newness of life" that God has made possible, that is, as we yield our members as instruments of righteousness.

---

[43]Ibid., p. 63.

[44]Dunn, *Theology of Paul,* pp. 344, 385-88.

[45]Separating out such discussions under the heading of "sanctification" effectively rends asunder what Paul would have held together.

[46]Wright describes the "obedience of faith" as the response to the declaration of God's reign inaugurated in the death and resurrection of Jesus, much like the announcement (the ***euangelion***) of the emperor's accession was a summons to give obedience and allegiance to the new ruler (*What Saint Paul Really Said,* p. 45). This analogy is a most helpful means to see the connection between the announcement that "Jesus is Lord" and the implications this announcement must have for the whole of our lives.

The witness of Romans 2:1-11 is often dismissed as irrelevant to the Christian since Paul is speaking, as it were, to the Jew and Gentile before incorporation into Christ, with both standing condemned because it is impossible to "do" what God requires. Romans 2:1-11, 6:1-23, 7:4-5, and 8:10-13, however, all have the same message: sin leads to death and dishonor, while obedience leads to righteousness, sanctification and eternal life. In Romans 2 this unchanging fact is viewed from the standpoint of all people having fallen short, thus needing the redemption Christ provided, whether Jew or Gentile. In Romans 6 and 8, it is viewed from the standpoint of the new life of righteousness for which Christ redeemed people, which Christ made possible. The difference is not that the principle has changed for the Christian (see the affirmation of this principle in 1 Cor 7:19, also addressed to people *as* Christians), but rather that what was formerly impossible apart from Christ is now made possible by Christ, and specifically by the empowerment of the Holy Spirit (Rom 8:2-4). Insisting on the "obedience of faith" should not be confused with works righteousness or earning salvation, since the whole process is the result of God's gift of forgiveness and God's endowment of the Spirit of Christ poured out into our hearts. Our obedience is a response to God's gift of redemption in Jesus and is in fact enabled by God's gift of the Spirit.

The "just requirement of the law," then, is neither set aside by Christ nor a matter of indifference for Christians. Obedience remains an important response to God's grace under both the old and the new covenant, just as pursuing holiness of life is the means to honor the dwelling of the holy God in their midst under both covenants.[47] What is decisively new, however, is that the effective means for living out this righteous life has now been provided in Christ, namely, the Spirit (Rom 8:4), which does in us what the law could not do (Rom 8:3; cf. Gal 3:21-22). For this reason "there is now no condemnation for those who are in Christ Jesus." The just requirements of a just God can be—and are—lived out by those who are endowed with the Spirit, follow it and live as the adopted sons or daughters of God (Gal 4:6-7), rather than walking in the flesh or following the halakhic traditions of a particular sect. Paul is not "antinomian," even though he denies that the Christian is "under the law" (Rom 6:14). The Spirit, God's promised gift, is sufficient to guide the disciple into the paths that please the Giver. This for Paul is the fulfillment of the promise of the new covenant given in Jeremiah: "I will write my law on their hearts," the counterpart to the first half of justification, "I will remember their sins no more" (Jer 31:33-34).

God's faithfulness to Israel. Focusing on the salvation of the individual as the theme of Romans often left interpreters in a quandary when it came to explaining Romans 9—11. C. H. Dodd represents something of the extreme when he presents Romans 9—11 as a sermon Paul composed for another occasion, which Paul included here as a kind of digression, for no apparent reason other than to provide a sample of his preaching.[48] For Dodd, Romans 8:39 flowed quite naturally into Romans 12:1. Such interpretations clearly fail to do justice to Romans 9—11, which, quite properly, has now come to be valued as an integral, even climactic, part of Paul's argument.

Since a major theme of Romans 1—8 is the righteousness, or justice, of God—God's faithfulness to the covenant obligations God has undertaken and to the promises God has made

---

[47]Frank Thielman, *Paul and the Law* (Downers Grove, Ill.: InterVarsity Press, 1994), pp. 240-41.
[48]Dodd, *Epistle of Paul to the Romans,* pp. 161-63.

The Enigma of Romans 7:7-25

Does Romans 7:7-25 speak of the present life of the believer or the plight of the pre-Christian person? A great number of readers understand this section as a description of the current state of the believer between conversion and consummation. This is driven first by our own experience (we often do what we know not to be right) and then confirmed by the use of the present tense in Romans 7:14-25, which would seem to indicate that Paul *must* be talking about his current condition. This passage, then, becomes a source of great comfort; Paul is seen to back away from his earlier idealistic pronouncements in Romans 6:1—7:6 of the believer living beyond the reach of sin. Now it is merely the *struggle* against the domination of sin that is the sign that life is at work in the believer. It is this struggle that the gift of the Spirit has enabled and that assures us that there is now no condemnation for us, even though we continue to fall prey to sin's lures and wiles. Only in an eschatological future will the believer achieve victory—part of the groaning of the present is due to the lingering power of sin over the believer.[a]

Many other students, however, find this reading objectionable on several grounds. First, if Paul says *as a Christian believer* that he is still sold under sin (Rom 7:14), then exactly what did Paul mean when he said that Christian believers were "set free from sin" (Rom 6:22) and that we have "died to sin" and no longer to "live in it" (Rom 6:2)? What did Paul mean when he said "sin will have no dominion over you" (Rom 6:14) if the believer is still at the mercy of sin (Rom 7:17-18)? How can Paul at one point affirm that only the "doers of the law" will be justified (Rom 2:13) but later be content with the mere *desire* to do good? How can we "present our bodies to God as instruments of righteousness" (Rom 6:13) and "yield our members to righteousness unto sanctification" (Rom 6:19) if "I can will what is right but I cannot do it" (Rom 7:18)? Such a reading represents not Paul's modification of his earlier claims in Romans 6:1—7:6 but a complete recantation of the newness of the life Christ has provided.

These students find it more in keeping with the declarations in chapters 6 and 8 to read Romans 7:7-25 as an expression of life apart from Christ and, in particular, life under the law apart from Christ. Paul is using the rhetorical device known as *prosopopoiia,* where the speaker presents a vivid characterization of some figure or position through first-person speech. The key to this speech is found in Romans 7:7: Paul is wrestling with the question of the function of the law (introduced in Rom 7:5-6), and speaks from a particular vantage point in salvation history—the position of humanity convicted by the law but powerless to keep the law. This, then, provides a more vivid depiction of the plight from which Christ frees the human being through the gift of the Spirit (Rom 6:1—7:6; 8:1-17). The verdict of "no condemnation" is in effect because the "law of the Spirit of life" has in fact set the believer free from the "law of sin and death." The past tense of Romans 8:2 shows Romans 7:23 (and thus Rom 7:7-25 as a whole) to be describing a past state as well, even though it uses the present tense characteristic of *prosopopoiia*. God is to be thanked precisely because the gift of the Holy Spirit has made it possible to live beyond the dominion of the passions of the flesh, reversing the state of Romans 1:18-32. Now God's righteousness can take hold of the believer, and God's standards of righteousness take shape within the believer.

---

[a]See, e.g., chapter five of Garlington, *Faith, Obedience, and Perseverance.*

to Abraham and to Israel[49]—Paul must return at length to discuss the troubling questions he raised and answered all too briefly in Romans 3:1-8. Paul's triumphant declaration that nothing "will be able to separate us from the love of God" (Rom 8:38-39) brings him back to the question of God's faithfulness to Israel (Rom 3:1-4). Has Israel been separated from the love of God? How has God been faithful to Israel? How is God's justice demonstrated in God's dealings with his historic people?[50] Here in Romans 9—11 Paul agonizes over the deeply upsetting fact that the majority of Jews have rejected the gospel, both in Judea and throughout the Diaspora. Given the historic advantages that belonged to the Jew (Rom 9:4-5; cf. 3:1-2), the way in which God groomed them for redemption, as it were, Paul must wrestle with the strange way God's promised redemption has been playing itself out on the stage of apostolic history; he needs to discover, for himself and his readers, how in fact God's Word has not failed.

Another factor that necessitates Paul's treatment of the issues raised in Romans 9—11 is the situation of the Christians in Rome. Here, the situation is quite the opposite of what we observed in Antioch and Galatia, where Jewish Christians were making the Gentile Christians feel like second-class members of the family of God. It would appear from Romans 14:1—15:7 that in Rome the more numerous and ascendant Gentile Christians were looking down on the quaint practices of their Jewish Christian sisters and brothers. This might indeed have extended to their viewing Christianity now as an essentially Gentile movement that has entirely replaced Israel and non-Christian Jews in God's providential care.[51] Paul's response is meant both to affirm God's covenant faithfulness and to remind the largely Gentile church that it must both value the Jewish Christian remnant in their midst and continue to include non-Christian Jews in its mission—for "what would their inclusion mean but life from the dead?" (Rom 11:15).

1. God's pattern of election. Paul begins by considering the principle of God's choice, or election, in the definition of who belongs to Israel and who is to be numbered among the descendants of Abraham. The examples of God's choice of Isaac, but not Ishmael, and Jacob, but not Esau, show how God's faithfulness to God's promises has worked from the beginning—and, notably, with the firstborn being displaced in favor of the later seed. Ishmael is Abraham's son "according to the flesh," but not part of Israel, which will be counted through Isaac. Both Jacob and Esau are grandsons of Abraham, but Jacob is selected to become "Israel" while Esau is cut off. From these historical examples (with the force, therefore, of logical proofs), Paul deduces that membership in Israel does not come merely through physical birth, but it must occur by promise and divine choice (Rom 9:8, 11). The existence of Jews who have refused to believe in Jesus, therefore, is not a priori a mark against God's faithfulness.

This raises another problem, however. Does God indeed play favorites, after all? Is God unjust precisely through this process of election? Paul appeals to an argument already developed in Ben Sira 33:7-13. As Creator, God has absolute sovereignty and freedom with regard

---

[49]Dunn, *Theology of Paul,* pp. 341-42; N. T. Wright, *The Climax of the Covenant: Christ and the Law in Pauline Theology* (Minneapolis: Fortress, 1993), p. 234. Dunn is mistaken, however, to call this a "Hebrew" meaning of righteousness as opposed to a "Greek" meaning that implies measuring the individual or the action against some absolute ideal. That *justice,* or *righteousness,* was indeed a relational term is most evident from the examples of "topics of justice" in Pseudo-Cicero *Rhet. ad Her.* 3.3.4, where it also means keeping faith with friends; honoring covenants and alliances; fulfilling obligations to kin, gods and fatherland; and so forth.
[50]Thielman, *Paul and the Law,* pp. 203-4.
[51]Wright, *Climax of the Covenant,* pp. 234, 248.

Figure 15.4. Interior of several adjoining rooms from a wealthy house in Pompeii, ornately decorated with floor mosaics and the remains of murals. (Photo courtesy of William Krewson [BiblePlaces.com])

to created things, including people, just as a potter has absolute sovereignty over a lump of clay, to make of it whatever he or she desires, for whatever purpose. Just as it is "fair" or "just" for the potter to do as he or she pleased with the lump of clay, so it is fair or just for God to do whatever God pleases with God's own creations. God is therefore free to select from both Jews and Gentiles those who would be appointed for the honor of inclusion into

the new people of God (Rom 9:22-24), a claim authenticated by an appeal to ancient testimony (Hos 2:23; Rom 9:25-26).

As Paul continues to wrestle with the rejection of the gospel by the majority of Jews in light of God's sovereignty over human beings, a mystery begins to emerge. God has in some way determined that ethnic Israel would largely reject the gospel. Their rejection of the gospel, after all, is preannounced in the prophets (Rom 9:33; 10:16, 21), so it must it-self be part of God's unfolding plan for the rev-elation of God's faithfulness to all nations. This raises, in turn, the question of human respon-sibility. Why should God blame people for their doing what displeases him if he has ap-pointed them for this very end? Paul rules this question out of bounds on the grounds of the lack of rights of the created thing to question the Creator. We should note at this point that Paul has in mind *specifically* the hardening of Israel against the gospel of Christ, which serves the goal of Gentile inclusion. This is not, therefore, a statement about sin and hu-man responsibility in general, even though the text ends up being dragged into those debates.

2. Israel's misstep. Israel's rejection of Jesus remains a choice for which they bear responsi-bility and a sin from which Paul believes they need to be redeemed: "For God has impris-oned all in disobedience so that he may be merciful to all" (Rom 11:32 NRSV). Paul dis-cusses this misstep directly in Romans 10:2-4, where he speaks, as one who knows from ex-perience, of his fellow Jews' "zeal for God" that expresses itself in ignorance of what God has done in Jesus.

The many Jews who have heard the good news but rejected it find themselves opposing God for the time being. They have rejected God's righteousness, God's expression of cove-nant faithfulness in the provision of Jesus as the Messiah of Israel and the Gentiles (in ful-fillment of God's promises to Abraham). They seek rather to establish "their own righteous-ness" (Rom 10:3). What does "establish their

own righteousness" mean in this context? It is often taken in the sense of "achieved merit" through "good works," in keeping with the reading of Romans as a manifesto against all human "will and exertion" in the quest to achieve God's favor.[52] It would be more in keeping with Paul's own past as a blameless, zealous Pharisee to understand this as a refer-ence to Israel's zeal to show itself loyal to the Mosaic covenant. This was, after all, the goal of every pious Jew and a core value of each of the many forms of Judaism in the first century. Israel wanted to show itself true to God (or "righteous") through the keeping of Torah, the "works of the law" that set Israel apart from other nations. This was at one time a noble goal but had now become a misdirected one ("not according to knowledge," Rom 10:2) since the term of Torah has come to its ap-pointed end with the coming of Christ (Rom 10:4; cf. Gal 3:23—4:7).[53]

Israel "failed to fulfill [its] Law" (Rom 9:31-32) and thus became a transgressor, precisely in not recognizing the Law's goal and endpoint in Christ. Israel has refused to recognize God's manifestation of covenant faithfulness in Jesus' death and resurrection, a faithfulness to Jews and to Gentiles (a faithfulness, ultimately, to the promises God made to Abraham), and to submit to this righteousness of God. Instead, they found themselves resisting God's determi-nation to create a multiethnic family for Abra-ham on the basis of trust/faith rather than on adherence to an ethno-specific code of behav-ior. Insisting on adherence to Israel's special Law and rejecting the implications that Christ's

---

[52]Seyoon Kim makes the good point that Romans 9:11, 16 do indeed point to the irrelevance of all human "will and ex-ertion" in regard to God's election (*Paul and the New Perspective* [Grand Rapids: Eerdmans, 2001], p. 59). God's actions and choices are sovereign; they move in the direction of God's initiative, and are not bound in response to any human desire or action. It is difficult to see, however, how Kim's observation, which is good in itself, militates against the read-ing of Romans 10:2-4 advanced by Dunn and Wright. Would this not all the more relativize the attempts of non-Chris-tian Jews to define the way they will relate to and be righteous before God—after God has acted sovereignly to inaugu-rate the post-Torah phase of extending God's blessings to all people on the basis of faith in Jesus and obedience to the Spirit? Therefore, I do not find Kim's reading of Romans 9:11, 16 and the reading of Romans 10:2-4 adopted above in-compatible but complementary.
[53]Wright, *Climax of the Covenant,* p. 240.

death and resurrection hold for the term limit of Torah amounted to an attempt to keep God's favor for the Jews alone when God has willed to make Abraham the father of many nations, many people groups.[54] Maintaining their separation from the nations was creditable under Torah in the period before the Messiah; now, after the fullness of time had come, this expression of "righteousness" runs counter to God's activity.[55]

3. Jewish Christians and the faithfulness of God. Paul returns to the issue of how God has shown faithfulness toward the historic people he had originally selected to be his own. Granted that God's sovereignty is manifested in the Gentiles' acceptance of the gospel and the majority of the Jews' rejection of the same, where is God's faithfulness manifested? Here Paul points to the presence of a remnant of Israel among the community of the saved in Christ: God has remained faithful now just as in the days of Elijah, preserving a remnant for himself (Rom 11:1-6), of which Paul himself is a part. Why only a remnant? Why did the majority of ethnic Israel not respond? Paul perceives that this was necessary so that the gospel could go out to the Gentiles. The natural branches (Israel) had to be cut off to make room for the wild branches (Gentiles) to be grafted into the chosen root of Abraham (Rom 11:11-24).

We now come to one of the most mysterious and hotly debated passages in Romans. What is Paul talking about in Romans 11:25-27? Is he predicting an end-time conversion of the Jewish people after "the full number of the Gentiles has come in" ("and then all Israel will be saved," 11:26)?[56] Or is he affirming the manner in which "all Israel" is saved, namely, as Jews and Gentiles alike respond to the gospel throughout history ("in this manner, all Israel will be saved")?[57]

Our answer to this question is determined by what we perceive to be the main issue Paul is addressing in Romans 11:11-36. A prominent line of thought believes the main issue to be God's faithfulness to Israel as it is defined "according the flesh," that is, to ethnic Jews. According to this reading the fact that "the gifts and the calling of God are irrevocable" (Rom 11:29) must lead eventually to the inclusion of all Jews into the people of God. A doctrine of irresistible grace is subtly at work here. After the full number of the Gentiles has come in, Christ will return to deliver Israel as well: "The Deliverer will come from Zion; he will banish ungodliness from Jacob" (Rom 11:26).

This view is not without major theological problems, not the least of which is that Paul, after spending Romans 1:18—3:31 establishing that no ethnic group has a privileged status in the eyes of the impartial judge, and Romans 4:1—8:39 showing how God has shown covenant faithfulness to all Abraham's descendants on the same universal basis, trumps himself with a grand finale in which ethnic privilege has again the last word. An attractive alternative takes a different approach to the way in which the "natural branches" may be grafted in and bases this on the statement that started the entire discussion (Rom 11:13-16). Paul claims that in own his mission to the Gentiles, he has himself not proved disloyal to his people, for the conversion of the Jews is always in his mind: "I glorify my ministry in order to make my own people jealous, and thus save some of them" (Rom 11:13-14 NRSV). "As they see the fulfillment of the promises . . . taking place before their very eyes without their par-

---

[54]Dunn, *Theology of Paul*, pp. 354-66; Wright, *Climax of the Covenant*, p. 240.

[55]Wright, *What Saint Paul Really Said*, p. 108.

[56]See, for example, Stuhlmacher, *Revisiting Paul's Doctrine of Justification*, p. 71.

[57]See, for example, Wright, *Climax of the Covenant*, p. 249.

ticipation," Paul hopes that the Jews would experience a change of heart.[58]

Starting from this point, the issue Paul is addressing might look quite different. Paul is trying to explain that the fact that many Jews had rejected the message about Jesus when they first heard it does not mean that the Jews have "had their chance" and are now nothing more than a casualty of bad judgment. They did not "stumble" (a temporary problem) "so as to fall" (to be permanently disqualified, Rom 11:11). "The gifts and the calling of God are irrevocable," not insofar as all will arrive at the promised end (interpreting *irrevocable* more as "irresistible"), but insofar as the invitation to receive God's gifts and to respond faithfully always remains open. The door is not closed to unbelieving Jews. God has not *shut them out,* for he will not revoke his promises. Gentile Christians cannot therefore say, The gospel is for us; it is not for them; they had their chance. According to this reading, Paul is arguing against the same kind of anti-Jewish tendencies among the Gentile Christians in Rome as he will do again in Romans 14:1—15:13. He wants them to value their Jewish Christian sisters and brothers as the root of God's historic people for which the Gentile Christians have been joined. He wants them also to continue to keep non-Christian Jews firmly in view in their evangelistic efforts rather than writing them off.[59]

In this view "all Israel" in Romans 11:26 denotes the church, those who are part of spiritual Israel, the true circumcision. Paul had indeed used the term *Israel* to denote ethnic Israel in Romans 11:25, where he set it in opposition to the Gentiles. But Paul has prepared us for shifting meanings in the use of *Israel* by introducing the idea of two Israels in Romans 9:6: "not everyone who is of Israel constitutes Israel."[60] "All Israel" thus comes to be saved not merely at the end but throughout the process—as Jewish Christians take the word to Gentiles; as non-Christian Jews are made jealous, seeing the gifts and privileges of their inheritance going to Gentiles, and are invited to come to faith as well.

Deciding between these two readings is not an easy matter. In the end we have to decide which is less inconsistent with the theology of Paul as a whole. Both readings, however, capture a truly profound point expressed by Paul: the justification of the ungodly continues until the parousia. There is not a point when we can look at a nation or a people and say "it is too late for them; they are beyond salvation." The purposes of God for "all" always have to do with extending mercy (Rom 11:32), and God's faithful are called to walk in line with that purpose rather than in line with prejudice.

Life together in Christian community. The connecting word *therefore* (Rom 12:1) that introduces Paul's exhortations is not artificial. The life of obedience is entirely a grateful response to God's benefactions and entirely predicated on them. Morality is not to be detached from theology but is truly only meaningful, possible and desirable when the connection between God's gift and our response is made clear. The only fitting response to such selfless generosity on the part of God—the self-giving of the benefactor—is a like return from the recipients of God's beneficence: "I appeal to you, therefore, brothers and sisters, through the mercies of God, to present your bodies as living and holy sacrifices, acceptable to God" (Rom 12:1; see 6:13, 19; 7:4).

As Paul goes on to present the ideal ethos of the Christian community, he uses many topics and images familiar from his earlier letters. Thus we find again the image of the single

---

[58]Nanos, *Mystery of Romans*, p. 287.
[59]Wright, *Climax of the Covenant*, pp. 248-50.
[60]Ibid., p. 250 (referring also to Rom 2:25-29).

The Law: Catalyst for Sin or Divine Remedy?

Paul's view of the role of the Jewish Law, the Torah, in God's plan differs markedly from that of other Jewish authors from the centuries before and after the turn of the era (and from that of other Jewish Christians, e.g., his opponents in Galatia). Particularly striking and distinctive is his understanding of the Law as the occasion for sin to increase its stranglehold on humanity. For Paul, sin is a spiritual power that drives people like cattle, a disorderliness and rebelliousness against order that can only flourish in the face of an established order (*nomos*, law). Where there is order (or law) disorder (or rebelliousness against order) shows itself all the more clearly and flagrantly (Rom 7:7-13).

This view stands in stark contrast to the expressions of confidence in the Law in Ben Sira and Baruch. For these two authors the Torah is the "law of life" (Sir 17:11; 45:5; Bar 3:9), but Paul negates the validity of this claim: "the law that promised life proved to be death in me" (Rom 7:10). Even more striking is the contrast between Paul and the near contemporary author of 4 Maccabees. In the latter text the law is the reliable guide to virtue. It not only promises but actually enables domination over the passions of the flesh. Quite instructive are the different conclusions drawn concerning the commandment, "You shall not covet." For the author of 4 Maccabees, "since the law has told us not to covet," he can "prove all the more that reason [the moral faculty of the mind] is able to control desires" (4 Macc 2:6 NRSV). The author presumes that what the law commands is quite within the realm of possibility for human beings to perform. Paul, on the other hand, quotes this same commandment as the occasion for the power of sin to come to life, arousing the passions to all manner of covetousness (Rom 7:7-10). The law provided, in effect, a focal point for the cosmic forces rebelling against God to concentrate their energies and triumph over the human being.

The author who might have been most sympathetic to Paul's view was the author of *4 Ezra*, a Jewish apocalypse dating from 95-100 C.E.:

> You bent down the heavens and shook the earth . . . to give the law to the descendants of Jacob, and your commandment to the posterity of Israel. Yet you did not take away their evil heart from them, so that your law might produce fruit in them. For the first Adam, burdened with an evil heart, transgressed and was overcome, as were also all who were descended from him. Thus the disease became permanent; the law was in the hearts of the people along with the evil root; but what was good departed, and the evil remained. (*4 Ezra* 3:12-27; 7:92)

This lament is similar to Paul's in Romans 7: the individual is presented with the law of God promising fruits that lead to life, yet the same individual is bound by the evil inclination to produce fruit unto death. The author of *4 Ezra* never solves this dilemma but rather acknowledges the difficulty of the contest facing humanity. At the same time he affirms the necessity of successfully fighting against the evil inclination and keeping God's commands if one hopes to enjoy the life of the age to come (*4 Ezra* 7:92).

Paul's view of the role of the Law is profoundly influenced by his experience of the risen Jesus *and* the pouring out of God's Holy Spirit. In view of the glorious liberation from the power of sin that came with the Spirit and its ongoing leading and empowerment, Paul comes to a new view about the limited role of the Law. This "limit" is also established by God's endowing both Jews and Gentiles with the Spirit, whereas the Law largely served to keep Jews apart from Gentiles rather than extending God's righteousness to them as well. While the Law reveals God's just requirements, it falls to the Spirit to empower human beings to live out those requirements. Only the Spirit is sufficient to overcome the power of sin, against which the human being only had his or her own moral resources prior to the gift of the Spirit (hence *4 Ezra*'s pessimism about how many could be saved). It is noteworthy that those requirements, as Paul begins to discuss them in Romans 12—15, have nothing to do with those aspects of Torah that set Jews apart from Gentiles but rather with those aspects of Torah that Jew or Gentile could fulfill as Jew and Gentile.

FOR FURTHER READING

Dunn, James D. G. *Jesus, Paul, and the Law: Studies in Mark and Galatians.* Louisville, Ky.: Westminster John Knox, 1990.

Gaston, Lloyd. *Paul and the Torah.* Vancouver: University of British Columbia Press, 1987.

Hübner, Hans. *The Law in Paul's Thought.* Edinburgh: T & T Clark, 1984.

Sanders, E. P. *Paul and Palestinian Judaism: A Comparison of Patterns of Religion.* Philadelphia: Fortress, 1977.

———. *Paul, the Law, and the Jewish People.* Philadelphia: Fortress, 1983.

Thielman, Frank. *From Plight to Solution: A Jewish Framework for Understanding Paul's View of the Law in Galatians and Romans.* NovTSup 6. Leiden: Brill, 1989.

Westerholm, Stephen. *Israel's Law and the Church's Faith: Paul and His Recent Interpreters.* Grand Rapids: Eerdmans, 1988.

---

body or organism that Paul had used in Corinth to cultivate unity and appreciation for one another's contributions to the whole, unmarred by the discord and strife that inevitably attends self-conceit (Rom 12:3-8; 1 Cor 12:4-31). Similarly, we encounter again Paul's emphasis on love of neighbor as the fulfillment of the just requirement of the Law (Rom 13:8-10; Gal 5:6, 14) and his exclusion of revenge as a suitable Christian response (Rom 12:14-21; 1 Thess 5:15). As the disciples have been freed from their own evil impulse, so they are freed from responding to the hostility of others. The believer is to act in accordance with virtue and God's own model of overcoming evil with good.

Once again we find that the disciple is told that genuine Christianity results in networking with the lowly and hurting, contrary to the cultural wisdom of improving our position through well-positioned contacts; it consists in showing honor to our fellow believers rather than promoting our own precedence over others (Rom 12:10, 16; 1 Cor 12:22-25; Phil 2:3).

All of these instructions are grounded in an eschatological perspective in Romans 13:11-14, a passage strikingly reminiscent of 1 Thessalonians 5:1-9. With each passing day the coming of Christ to deliver his faithful ones draws closer. The believer is called to live in the light of that day, even while anticipating the dawning of that day, as a witness to it. There is no room for the works of darkness, or for gratifying the desires of the flesh: putting on Christ, the very thing done in baptism, is the remedy all believers are called to embrace.

Many students find in Romans 14:1— 15:13 a matter of special concern to the Christian communities in Rome, although this remains a debated issue (especially since the instructions are so closely reminiscent of 1 Cor 8; 10, though with some notable differences here). At the very least Paul suspected that in a community embracing both those of a stricter Jewish orientation and those who were not disposed to regard observance of the Jewish Law as a part of their Christian obligations, these instructions would be timely and appropriate. The issue concerns, first, the eating of meat versus abstaining from meats and eating only vegetables. This is presumably tied to concerns over the ritual purity of meats as reflected, for example, in the apostolic decree (see Acts 15:29)—whether the meat might come from an animal that had been sacrificed to an idol or from an animal that had been improperly slaughtered (e.g., strangled and therefore containing blood as well). The issue also concerns the observation of a liturgical calendar versus not setting certain days apart for these observances. This would also tend to point in the direction of Jewish observances like the sabbath and other special days prescribed for special observances in the Torah, since Paul would not have been indifferent about those days of the Gentile converts' former sacred calendars (since these were tied to pagan rites and observances).

Paul is not concerned to establish the position of the "strong" as correct and to undermine the position of the "weak," although his use of these terms and his own confession that "nothing is unclean in itself" (Rom 14:14) reveals that Paul himself would align with the "strong" in his own practice. Rather, Paul wants to preserve unity and mutual consideration in the one community. God acted to bring together a diverse body of Jews and Gentiles, with a diversity of ways to honor God's claim on their lives and actions on their behalf, to worship the one God together in unity. In the one body of people accepted by the one God, there is no room for condemnation on the one hand or contempt on the other. Rather than thinking of themselves as superior on account of their freedom from scruples, or being self-righteous about their discipline because they rigorously observe certain rules, Paul calls the believers in Rome to "welcome one another" (Rom 14:1; 15:7) and to resolve not "to put a stumbling block or hindrance in the way of another" (Rom 14:13 NRSV).

Paul calls for mutual toleration in the realization that there is a realm of practice that is "indifferent"—one can observe or not observe these things equally well to the honor of God. He does not call for homogeneity in practice but rather for taking care lest their boldness with regard to eating certain foods or not observing certain days lead their brothers or sisters to follow their example, but against their conscience. If I eat in faith, and my behavior (including, perhaps, my open contempt for the "weak" in faith) drives another to eat while doubting, that person's conscience is defiled. If I eat in faith and another refuses to eat because of her faith, then we may simply both "welcome one another" and accept one another's practices as performed "to the Lord." As always, however, deference is to be paid by the "strong" to the "weak" in the church (again, quite against the grain of Greco-Roman culture). Out of love and concern for the spiritual well-being of the sister or brother, the disciple is challenged to give up what his or her freedom would permit so that fellowship with the "weak" may remain harmonious. Neither our scruples nor our lack of scruples should become new Torahs by which we decide who is in and who is out of the church, nor should it be a cause for disunity within the one body.

EXEGETICAL SKILL
Social-Scientific Criticism (2)—The Analysis of Ritual

Social-scientific interpretation of New Testament texts often calls our attention to the realities of early Christian religion. It fights the tendency to regard these texts as compendia of ideas only, and views them as witnesses to the embodied experiences of real-life people whose faith profoundly affects the social dynamics they experience, and whose experience of social dynamics profoundly affects their faith. One facet of social-scientific interpretation invites us to probe the meaningfulness of the rituals and liturgies that characterized the Christian's religious experience. It also examines the ways these rites impinged on the Christian's sense of self, relation to the group and relation to the society at large.[a]

Perhaps the most prominent ritual in the early Christian church is its rite of initiation: baptism. How was this rite enacted? What did that rite mean for the initiates? Wayne Meeks first looks at the language Paul uses to describe the transition from noninitiate to disciple, using language like "buried with Christ" and "putting aside the old person" and "putting on the new person." Such language suggests a ritual process in which the initiate lays aside his or her clothing (as far as modesty would permit, most probably), steps into a pool of water or stream, is immersed and raised up again, and is given a white garment as he or she emerges from the water. An alternative image involves the pouring of water over the head of the initiate, where sufficient water for immersion is unavailable.[b]

The study of rituals by anthropologists provides us with a wealth of theoretical models through which we can enter into a deeper appreciation of the profound impact baptism would have had on the consciousness of those entering the waters, and repeatedly thereafter as they witnessed new baptisms or were reminded of their own experience of this initiation. Mary Douglas, for example, invites us to consider how a ritual like baptism would function both as a reflection of early Christian culture and as a factor that shaped early Christian culture.[c] Bringing even greater theoretical detail to bear on rituals of status transformation (like initiation rites), status reversal (like cleansings) and status elevation (like coronation or ordination), Victor Turner's analysis of the ritual process provides a helpful, detailed crosscultural perspective.[d] From his observation a ritual has several phases—separation, a transitional period and reincorporation.[e] In the

---

[a]See, for example, Wayne A. Meeks, *The First Urban Christians: The Social World of the Apostle Paul* (New Haven, Conn.: Yale University Press, 1983), pp. 140-63; H. C. Kee, *Knowing the Truth: A Sociological Approach to New Testament Interpretation* (Minneapolis: Fortress, 1989), p. 66.
[b]Ibid., pp. 150-51.
[c]Mary Douglas, *Natural Symbols* (London: Barrie & Jenkins, 1973), p. 42.
[d]Victor Turner, *The Ritual Process* (Ithaca, N.Y.: Cornell University Press, 1969), pp. 94-165.
[e]Ibid., p. 94.

separation phase the status and identity that a person had before the ritual began is broken down and abolished. He or she becomes "marginal" or "liminal" with regard to society, not fitting into any of that society's lines of classification. During the ritual a new status and identity is formed, often in the context of a strong, common bond with other initiates, and the person is reintegrated into society at the completion of the ritual with this new status or identity, together with a new sense of camaraderie and solidarity with the fellow initiates. Rites of passage from childhood to adulthood or from common status to chieftain fit this model very neatly.

Baptism also functions as a rite of passage separating the initiate from his or her past life and associations—symbolically enacting his or her death—as well as rebirth to a new life and set of associations. It possesses a quality of mortification: the baptized are purified of that part of their past that they no longer wish to own (cf. 1 Cor 6:11). It enacts symbolically the initiates' renunciation of former allegiances, affiliations and relations.[f] Whatever status or identity they had before the rite, the waters of baptism washed it away, thus the repeated affirmations that in Christ there is neither Jew nor Greek, slave nor free, male and female (e.g., Gal 3:28). As they emerged from the waters, they were joined to a new community, the "sanctified," who are "washed with pure water" (Heb 10:22). As Douglas explains, the ritual provides a way for the initiates to "die to their old life" and be "reborn to the new."[g] It facilitates the setting aside of the values, beliefs, ethics and social interactions developed in their "primary socialization" outside the Christian group, and the adoption of a new system of values, beliefs, ethics and relationships.

Indeed, a most notable difference from Turner's typical rite of passage is that the reintegration after baptism leaves the Christian marginal or liminal with regard to the larger society. Their new identity and status is within the sect, but not recognized by the society. The Christian baptizand has been separated from his or her former social group with its networks, allegiances and position, but incorporated into a different social group, the *ekklēsia*. The early Christian movement compels the converts "to inhabit the fringes and interstices of the social structure . . . and to keep them in a permanent liminal state, where . . . the optimal conditions inhere for the realization of *communitas*,"[h] Turner's term for those close, intimate, egalitarian friendships formed in the middle phase of an extended initiation rite. Baptism thus provided a symbolic expression for the social boundaries that distinguished Christian community from the society around it and gave initiates a symbolic act by which those boundaries, and their

---

[f]R. M. Kanter, *Commitment and Community* (Cambridge, Mass.: Harvard University Press, 1972), p. 73.
[g]Mary Douglas, *Purity and Danger* (London: Routledge & Kegan Paul, 1966), p. 96.
[h]Turner, *Ritual Process*, p. 145.

transition across that divide, were communicated to them. The act also provided a set of images that could be drawn on repeatedly and powerfully by Christian leaders to reinforce those boundaries, encourage the avoidance of particular behaviors or promote the solidarity and unity of those who had been baptized (see, for example, Rom 6:3-12; 1 Cor 6:9-11; Gal 3:26-29; Col 3:1-17).

As you encounter reflections of rituals in the texts—the celebration of the Lord's Supper would be the next most obvious, but also the Jewish rituals recorded or discussed, along with aspects of the liturgical practices of the early Christians reflected in the texts—you might probe questions such as the following:

- What did this rite look like in action, and what would it communicate to its participants?
- What social relations (internal relations, boundaries and the like) was this rite used to promote?
- If an author is referring to, interpreting or otherwise invoking this rite, what interpretation does he give it, and what group-related goals does he have for discussing it? (For example, if he is critiquing the way it is being performed, why? How is its current practice failing to achieve the goal the author believes to be central to the rite?)
- How does the Christian's participation in this rite shape or reinforce his or her experience of everyday life, worldview and priorities?

ROMANS AND MINISTRY FORMATION

The negation of pride and prejudice. Paul gives much space to establishing that both the Jew and the Gentile stand accepted before God in Christ only because God has made them acceptable by God's own outreaching love. Because the believers' hope and deliverance rest entirely on God's kindness toward them, there can be no room for arrogance with regard to their status among the people of God, nor is there room for contempt toward others in the family of God or those not yet "in Christ."

Transcending the premier "dividing wall of hostility" of the first century, Paul challenges us as we face so many dividing walls of hostility in our global setting. So often the confession that "we are Christians" has been turned into the presumption that "we are better than they." Put otherwise, the fact that others are not Christian has often been used to devalue them, after which it is an easy step to oppress, injure or eliminate them. Paul insists, quite to the contrary, that the confession that "we are Christians" must manifest itself in a profound awareness that

God's kindness, and not our merit, have made us what we are. Therefore, the label "Christian" can never become a claim to be better than another—just to be gifted with the knowledge of God's Son and solicitous to share this gift.

Within the church Paul would have the knowledge that all are accepted solely by God's kindness stand against every lingering prejudice in the church. Racial prejudice is far from resolved; socioeconomic level and education continue to provide opportunities for pride and contempt; denominational partisanship continues to lacerate the body of Christ. The church that will effectively bear witness to the favor and kindness of God in the twenty-first century will first shape humility within the hearts of its members with regard to these and all such distinctions, along with harmony among its members and a spirit of solidarity with *all* who call on the name of the Lord.

Homosexuality and the Christian life. It would be disingenuous to avoid inviting the reader to consider homosexuality in the context of Paul's thought. It presents one of the more visible and probing challenges facing the church at the outset of the third millennium, and Romans 1:18-32 is often in the forefront of the debate. As I understand it, this is the principal question: Is homosexual practice compatible with the Christian life?

At the outset we must observe that Romans 1:18-32 is not primarily or exclusively about homosexual practice, as if this were the sin par excellence. Homosexual acts are but one among many manifestations of the "dishonorable passions" to which humanity finds itself a constant prey, alongside "covetousness, malice, envy, murder, strife, deceit, craftiness" as well as gossip, slander, haughtiness and a host of other symptoms (Rom 1:28-32). The climax is the loss of all sense of a moral compass. It is worth remembering this larger grouping since, in many ways, it is the particular targeting and shaming of persons of homosexual orientation—and the concurrent winking at the sins of greed, heterosexual promiscuity, marital infidelity, unethical business practices and the like—that has robbed the church of its competence to speak about issues of discernment and discipline.

We should also observe that shallow applications of Romans 1 to homosexual activity, such as suggesting that AIDS is the "due penalty for their error" (Rom 1:27 NRSV), increases the likelihood that an authentic hearing of the scriptural witness—let alone a consensus about how the church should address this issue—will remain unattainable. A careful reading of the passage shows that being subject to the rule of the passions of the flesh is itself the penalty for the root problem, namely, not honoring God as Creator. Failing to fall in line with the created order, the order of human nature itself was overturned: just as human beings were not subject to God, so the human being's passions would not be subject to reason.

Those cautions noted, how does Paul's description of the plight of the Gentile sinner begin to connect with the question facing the church?[a] First, he might

---

[a]The attempt to write off Paul's words in Romans 1:18-32 as a mere replication of Hellenistic Jewish polemics against Gentiles such as found in Wisdom of Solomon appears to me to be quite perverse, as if the fact that the same sentiments appear in a Jewish source makes Paul's witness less signifi-

remind us, as we contemplate the significance of "genetic predisposition," that our natural inclinations are not a reflection of God's purposes for us but rather a reflection of our need for redemption. When Paul speaks of God's giving the idolaters over to the "debased mind" and "degrading passions," he speaks of the consequences of humanity (as a whole) refusing to take their proper place in the cosmic order, centered on and honoring the one God in their lives. Human nature, indeed all of creation (Rom 8:20-21), became defaced and corrupt. Rather than understand a natural predisposition to represent God's will for an individual or take natural inclinations as moral guideposts, Paul points us to the battle against these drives of the flesh that the Spirit wages and seeks to win in us if we will walk by the Spirit and not in the flesh (Rom 8:7-8, 12-14).

At this point, Paul would challenge us, especially those disciples who live in the United States, Canada, Western Europe and other such countries. He would ask whether or not we have imbibed too deeply and uncritically of our culture's gratification of all desires, whether of the mind (greed and ambition), the eyes (desiring to possess this or that luxury, this or that commodity), the belly (gluttony and gourmandizing while many live at subsistence level or die of starvation), and the groin. Western culture has redefined what it means to be a "whole person" or to have a fulfilling life in terms frequently antithetical to the teaching of the New Testament and the church. How deeply has our internalization of these values affected our contest with sin in our own lives? How have these values entered into the specific debate concerning the right of Christians of homosexual orientation to the expression and gratification of their sexuality? Paul would challenge disciples to seek rather the freedom from domination by the passions that is the promise of the gift of the Spirit, urging us to keep "putting to death whatever in us is earthly" (Col 3:5) or "crucifying the flesh with its passions and desires" (Gal 5:24). The Pauline ethic could not be more at odds with modern Western culture on this point.

An important impetus behind much of the debate is to establish a "welcome" for people actively engaged in the homosexual lifestyle (and not merely for persons of homosexual orientation, which is in itself not a morally culpable matter[b] but rather a symptom of the sinful bent that inclines each one of us, in one way or another, from fulfilling God's vision for humanity). How would Paul counsel churches on this subject? This is more difficult to answer since Paul might begin

---

cant or enduring (all the more as this particular Jewish source is regarded as authoritative by the majority of the world's Christians). It is as absurd as saying that Jesus' teaching that we must forgive one another if we hope for God's forgiveness is not to be taken seriously, since he is merely repeating traditional Jewish wisdom (Sir 28:2-4).

[b]It is important, I believe, to make this distinction. Scripture does not condemn us for our sinful inclinations but for yielding to them—whether in thought, word or deed. Persons of homosexual orientation should not be made to feel unholy or unclean on account of the orientation, or hate themselves for their inclinations and inability to change them (where God does not change them). Rather, these disciples are called to resist the passions of the flesh, just as each one of us must daily resist the lure of other sinful inclinations (whether implanted by a nature that has been subjected to futility, or inculcated behaviorally by a worldly minded society) by the empowering of the Holy Spirit that has sanctified us.

by addressing other egregious violations of the bond of love and unity in the church, or take us to task for the relaxed, even brazen, attitude we have about so many other sins and vices. Wouldn't the critical attention of the apostle, who was eager to remember the poor in the church, more quickly focus on our short-sightedness when it comes to relieving our sisters and brothers in need across the globe? When he was ready to answer our question, however, he would probably exclaim yes—all who seek redemption in Jesus are welcome, and it is the task of the community of faith to support one another, sinners all, on the path to recovery. Paul would include homosexual acts among the sins from which the sister or brother would need to be "restored in a spirit of gentleness" (Gal 6:1). But he would also remind us of the spectrum of sins that show the flesh rather than the Spirit to be at work, calling us to humility before all else since we all stand by God's kindness and mercy alone.

Evangelizing the Jewish people? One of the pressing questions of the late twentieth century, far from resolved at its close, is the question of whether or not Jews need to become Christians in order to fulfill God's purposes for them, or whether the covenant made at Sinai is still valid for Jews and a viable and sufficient way for them to relate to God.[c] Indeed, several major Christian denominations have moved increasingly closer to affirming a "two covenant" theology, according to which God continues to work with Israel through the Torah and the nations through Christ. In this view, missionary outreach to the Jewish people is unnecessary, even wrong-headed. The problem with such a view, of course, is that its "separate but equal" philosophy runs so baldly counter to a major thrust of Pauline Christianity, namely, God's desire to bring Jews and Gentiles together in one worshiping community (see, e.g., Rom 15:7-13; Eph 2:11-22).

The strongest Pauline support for not attempting to convert Jews to Christianity might be found in Romans 11:25-27, where end-time deliverance comes to Israel without any explicit statement about the conversion of the Jews (except, perhaps, insofar as they recognize the returning Jesus as their Messiah on that day of visitation). Yet such a position cannot ultimately be called Pauline. He clearly regards their current state apart from Christ as something so undesirable that he would think it worth being accursed himself if that would remedy their situation (Rom 9:1-3). If the Jewish Christian remnant is analogous for Paul to the remnant of Israel that had not bowed the knee to Baal in the days of Elijah, to whom would the majority of non-Christian Jews have proven analogous (Rom 11:1-5)? Would it not be, indeed, to those who, in Elijah's time, had failed in regard to the covenant? Indeed, Paul expects that his mission to the Gentiles will result in the jealousy and, therefore, conversion of at least *some* Jews, and he relishes this prospect (Rom 11:13-14). Thus the natural branches (the Jews) will

---

[c]This position is advanced quite forcefully by Hans Joachim Schoeps, *Paul: The Theology of the Apostle in Light of Jewish Religious History* (London: Lutterworth, 1961). See also Krister Stendahl, *Paul Among Jews and Gentiles* (Philadelphia: Fortress, 1976), p. 2; Lloyd Gaston, *Paul and the Torah* (Vancouver: University of British Columbia Press, 1987), pp. 148-50.

be grafted back in throughout the course of history "if they do not persist in unbelief" (Rom 11:23).[d] For Paul, such a response would be necessary if they are to be saved (Rom 10:1; 11:14). But the strongest indicators of Paul's answer to the question of the necessity of evangelizing the Jewish people are to be found in his "inclusion of *all* (Jews and Gentiles) in solidarities of sin and grace" that permeates the letter,[e] and the fact that he regards non-Christian Jews as persisting in "disobedience" irrespective of their Torah observance (see Rom 11:30-32). Paul's statement in Galatians 2:15-16 also provides evidence that Jewish Christians of different stripes (Pauline and non-Pauline) would have agreed on the necessity of trust in Jesus for deliverance (what they would have disagreed on is the ongoing role of Torah). Ultimately, Paul cannot be co-opted as an ally to those who would suspend missionary efforts among Jews.

However, Paul would have much to say to Christian anti-Semitism (the kind against which those who have steered away from evangelism and toward affirming the viability of the Jewish faith alongside the Christian faith have been reacting). Paul would not have countenanced the triumphalism that has marred the church's attitude toward the Jewish people for millennia, nor the presentation of Jewish faith as bankrupt and a mere matter of externals. He honored their zeal for God (Rom 10:2) and understood that, tragic though it was, their rejection of the gospel was—and remains—part of God's mystery for the inclusion of the full number of the Gentiles. Rather than scorn the Jewish way of life, the Christian community should rather have stood in awe of God's "generosity and severity," regarding Jews as, in effect, suffering temporary exclusion *on their behalf,* so that the Gentile Christians might be included.

All too often the Christian has ignored Paul's admonitions against boasting, against despising the Jewish person and puffing him- or herself up at the expense of the Jewish people. Whether in the Inquisition of the fourteenth and fifteenth centuries, in the Holocaust in the mid-twentieth century or still in the arrogant ranting of ethnic supremacist groups, people bearing the title of "Christian" violate Paul's heart and vision. For those who follow the apostle, neither writing off Jews as those whom salvation history has passed by nor withholding Christ as a superfluity are viable options. Rather, he invites Christians to join him in his agony for his sisters and brothers in the flesh, to honor the mystery of God at work in history, and to keep witnessing to God's vision for humanity accomplished in Christ—the joining of Jew and Gentile in one worshiping body on the basis of God's generosity alone.

The Christian and the state. Paul's instructions on submission to the state (Rom 13:1-7) have provided authoritarian states and monarchies with powerful ideological tools to legitimate their rule as if by divine right and to enforce obedience. Taken as the last word on the subject, these words have tended to absolutize political authorities and to make of the church a kind of civil religion, the task of which was

---

[d]Wright, *Climax of the Covenant,* pp. 248.
[e]Byrne, *Romans,* p. 30.

to support and legitimate the policies of those in power. Even in situations where the policies were marred by gross injustice, Romans 13:1-7 has been used to maintain the status quo, silence prophetic critique and stifle the impetus for reform.

Paul calls for submission to authority, but it is notable that he does not leave any room for the ideology of Rome or the emperors so prominent at the time. The authorities have no quasi-divine status: they have authority only as God's servants. They are legitimated by God only to the extent that they reinforce God's justice and advance God's purposes for human society. With regard to the authorities, then, Paul advises a demythologized submission. The believer is thereby distanced from national and political ideologies and self-legitimating propaganda, and invited to view the governing authorities from the viewpoint of how they serve God's purposes. Submission, however, does not rule out criticism and prophetic direction. Indeed, Paul's formulation of the relationship of human authority to God, to whom every authority is accountable, calls disciples to proclaim this relationship to those in authority. If the authority is to serve God's interests, he or she must be made aware of what those interests are in order to have the opportunity to act in line with God's justice, and not deceive itself.

Paul's words concerning the role of the Christian vis-à-vis the authorities, moreover, cannot be heard apart from their context. Paul wrote these instructions during the first five or six years of Nero's reign (Nero came to power in 54 C.E.), well before his administration moved to the excesses for which he is remembered. The early years were a period of moderation, stability and justice. Would Paul have written these same words after Nero's excesses, particularly after the unconscionable brutalities perpetrated on the Roman Christians in 64 C.E., when the authorities became a terror to those who did good? A sound philosophy for Christian response to human authority must take into account the spectrum of New Testament witnesses to this subject, including Revelation's potent critique of the regime that upholds values contrary to the justice of God. When authority opposes God's designs, punishes the good while rewarding the evil, inflicts misery on the innocent for the benefit of the privileged, and pressures people to participate in idolatry and unholiness, prophetic critique and nonviolent protest and nonparticipation would be the more appropriate Christian response.

Tolerance or new Torahs? The challenge posed to the church in Romans 14:1—15:13 is perhaps one of Paul's most difficult. Christians who believed firmly that the apostolic decree was to be scrupulously observed or that sabbaths were to be strictly honored were convinced that this was God's will for them and therefore all committed disciples. It required substantial sacrifice and personal investment on their part to follow their conscience in these matters. Nevertheless, they were instructed to refrain from condemning or thinking less of their fellow Christians who did not do likewise, even as they continued to follow their convictions. Similarly, those who regarded food taboos and sacred days as symptoms of a superstitious faith were warned not to look down on their sisters and brothers, and even to refrain from exercising the freedom their conscience gave them when it would be deleterious to their fellow Christian's spiritual well being or the harmony of the fellowship.

Human beings have a very difficult time tolerating difference. Our own certainty about the correctness or appropriateness of our behavior is challenged, even threatened, by the certainty of others about different behaviors. We want to establish clear rules or guidelines and enforce conformity, and this innate human characteristic leads us very quickly to turn things "indifferent" before God into things necessary for salvation itself. Thus they become occasions to break fellowship and even doubt the other's place in the family of God. Consider the following issues:

- the drinking of wine
- dancing
- infant baptism or waiting for the time of "decision"
- baptism by immersion (forward? backward?) or pouring or sprinkling
- highly formal worship or a more "relaxed" style of liturgy
- veneration of the saints
- the size of the canon (i.e., whether or not it includes the Old Testament Apocrypha)
- charismatic expressions of devotion in public worship (e.g., raising of hands, spontaneous praise, speaking/praying in tongues)
- worship on Saturday or Sunday
- observing the liturgical calendar of festivals
- the number of sacraments (and whether they should be called sacraments at all)
- background music during prayer (my own pet peeve!)

The list could be expanded indefinitely. Many of these issues have resulted in the breaking of fellowship and multiplication of denominations; still others are simply points of friction within a congregation or between members of different denominations with different points of view. I would argue that in and of themselves none of these issues is determinative for whether or not a person is "in Christ" or not. If the Jewish Torah actually given by God and the rite of circumcision instituted for Abraham and all his descendants are no longer binding on Christians, I fail to see how any human ruling on these issues can be more absolute.

Whatever our position on these and similar issues, we should bear in mind that disunity in the body is not an "indifferent" matter for Paul (or Jesus; recall the prayer of Jn 17). If we follow Paul's instructions, we will allow that God can be honored by a variety of behaviors. God can be honored in drinking wine; he can be honored in abstaining from wine. God can be honored by worship on Saturday; he can be honored by worship on Sunday. God can be honored through high liturgy; he can be honored by low liturgy. God can be honored through a presbyterian form of church polity; he can be honored through an episcopal form of church polity. God can even be honored with music playing in the background of prayer times. But God is certainly not honored when one Christian condemns another, refusing to honor the work of the Lord in another person on the basis of disagreement over such matters—or worse, when one sister or brother despises or even hates another on such a basis. Unity and cooperation among all who call on the name of the Lord can be enjoyed if we are willing to accept diversity in finer matters of faith and practice, and respect one another enough to believe that the other has thought through the matter and acts out of faith. Paul challenges us to continually subjugate our own tastes, prejudices and even convictions to the fact that God is not nearly so threatened by diversity as we humans are.

Paul knows that there are two dangers: the first is that we will approve what leads to condemnation before God; the other is that we will elevate an indifferent thing to the level of something necessary for salvation. But he has confidence that as people seek no longer to confirm themselves by condemning or despising their sisters and brothers, the Spirit of God will make these matters clear: for our Lord is able to make us stand (Rom 14:4). If we adopt this attitude, we will begin to see one another as people gifted by God, each contributing to the life, health and mission of the body (Rom 12:3-8). The gifts God gives each of us for one another will reward our decision to welcome one another.

Paul's apocalyptic vision. In each of Paul's letters the apocalyptic orientation shines through. This is no less true for Romans. For example, in Romans 8:18-25 the cosmic scope of God's redemption, extending to creation itself and not merely the individuals inhabiting creation, shines through. The apocalyptic vision reminds us ever that God's purposes for God's creation are broad and all-encompassing, and that they are still being worked out in the present and into the future. The believer's posture also involved longing and waiting. While we have been incorporated into Christ and have peace with God and the endowment of the Spirit, we still groan with creation as our bodies are subject to mortality—to disease, decay and death—as we wait for their redemption at the resurrection (Rom 8:17-25). We are still subject to the onslaught of hostile powers, both physical and spiritual; we are still exposed to tribulation, distress, persecution, famine, nakedness, peril and sword (Rom 8:35). We labor for justice, but it does not appear; we encourage, but people are still beaten down; we share with the poor, but hunger still reigns; we proclaim God's righteousness, but at the peril of being regarded as subversive. As believers witness to Christ and obey the call of God, they still encounter the resistance of a hostile world, and their bodies are subject to the slings and arrows of the powers that have not submitted to God. Nevertheless, Paul gives the assurance that no power is able to separate believers from God's love—no matter how much the world resists God, Christians are assured of victory through our Lord Jesus Christ. The apocalyptic vision thus continues to empower witness and obedience, even when it proves costly, as it indeed does for so many believers across the globe today.

Paul reminds us yet again that we are not a people of *today,* that we cannot live guided by the concerns of this present state of affairs. We are a people of *tomorrow,* awaiting the dawning of God's kingdom in its fullness and allowing his Spirit to bring our lives fully in line with that morrow even while many around us live "wisely" by today's standards, that is, for this life only. There is still an immediacy and urgency to Paul's exhortation: if it is not motivated by the imminence of Christ's return, it is at least then by the urgency of our need to wake up from and not succumb to the stupor that still possesses the world (Rom 13:11-14).

For Further Reading

Achtemeier, Paul J. *Romans.* Interpretation. Atlanta: John Knox Press, 1985.

Barrett, C. K. *A Commentary on the Epistle to the Romans.* BNTC. 2nd ed. Peabody, Mass.: Hendrickson, 1991.

Boers, Hendrikus. *The Justification of the Gentiles.* Peabody, Mass.: Hendrickson, 1994.

Byrne, Brendan. *Romans.* Sacra Pagina 6. Collegeville, Minn.: Liturgical Press, 1996.

Cranfield, C. E. B. *A Critical and Exegetical Commentary on the Epistle to the Romans.* 2 vols. ICC. Edinburgh: T & T Clark, 1975, 1979.

Dodd, C. H. *The Epistle of Paul to the Romans.* New York: Harper & Brothers, 1932.

Donfried, Karl P., ed. *The Romans Debate.* Rev. ed. Peabody, Mass.: Hendrickson, 1991.

Dunn, James D. G. *Romans.* 2 vols. WBC. Waco, Tex.: Word, 1988.

Fitzmyer, Joseph A. *Romans.* AB 33. Garden City, N.Y.: Doubleday, 1993.

Garlington, Don B. *Faith, Obedience, and Perseverance: Aspects of Paul's Letter to the Romans.* WUNT 79. Tübingen: Mohr-Siebeck, 1994.

Leon, Henry J. *The Jews of Ancient Rome.* Updated ed. Peabody, Mass.: Hendrickson, 1995.

Moo, Douglas. *The Epistle to the Romans.* NICNT. Grand Rapids: Eerdmans, 1996.

Moxnes, Halvor. "Honour and Righteousness in Romans." *JSNT* 32 (1988): 61-77.

Wedderburn, A. J. M. *The Reasons for Romans.* Philadelphia: Fortress, 1991.

Wright, N. T. *What Saint Paul Really Said.* Grand Rapids: Eerdmans, 1997.

16

THE EPISTLE TO THE PHILIPPIANS

Unity in the Face of Adversity

Galatians has been called Paul's charter for Christian liberty. Philippians would then constitute Paul's charter for Christian unity. Paul writes to believers that have been reliable partners for Paul in the faith and in mission, who face the hostility of their neighbors on the one hand, and who have been distracted from their high calling by internal competition, posturing and discord on the other. He writes to strengthen their resolve in the face of opposition, while also restoring a harmonious and cooperative spirit among the believers.

This letter contains some of the most celebrated passages in Pauline literature: the lofty expression of Christology known as the "Christ Hymn" (Phil 2:6-11); the summons to "rejoice in the Lord always" (Phil 4:4-7); the confident affirmation that "I can do all things through Christ who strengthens me (Phil 4:13). It also provides another glimpse of the heart and ambitions of the apostle, as he has turned away from everything that gave him status and confidence "in the flesh" in order to pursue the greater treasures to be found in Christ (Phil 3:5-16), calling his converts to do likewise. Philippians continues to challenge us to reflect mature discipleship and to build up strong, harmonious communities of faith that are able to support their members in the face

of an unbelieving world's attempts to erode commitment.

THE HISTORICAL SETTING OF PHILIPPIANS

The Roman colony of Philippi. Philip II of Macedon, the father of Alexander the Great, took over the agricultural settlement called Krenides in 356 B.C.E., renaming it Philippi. Macedonia came under Roman control in 168 B.C.E., but Philippi as Paul knew it really only took shape during the civil wars that rocked the Roman Republic in the second half of the first-century B.C.E. The final battle between Caesar's armies, led by Marc Antony and Octavian (later the emperor Augustus), and the armies of the assassins of Julius Caesar, Brutus and Cassius, took place near Philippi in 42 B.C.E. Antony and Octavian rewarded veterans with settlement in Philippi and generous grants of farmland in the hinterland of that city.[1] After the alliance between Antony and Octavian broke down, the second civil war was effectively ended with Antony's defeat near Actium in 31 B.C.E. Octavian settled many of Antony's soldiers in Philippi since they had forfeited their claims to land in Italy.[2] Philippi was refounded as a colony of Rome (Acts 16:12) and named after Augustus's daughter (*Colonia Iulia Augusta*

---

[1]Gordon D. Fee, *Paul's Letter to the Philippians* (Grand Rapids: Eerdmans, 1995), p. 25.
[2]Holland Hendrix, "Philippi," *Anchor Bible Dictionary,* ed. David N. Freedman (Garden City, N.Y.: Doubleday, 1992), 5:314.

Figure 16.1. The *Via Egnatia*, a Roman road that Paul followed as he traveled from Neapolis to Philippi and on to Thessalonica. (Photo courtesy of Todd Bolen [BiblePlaces.com])

Philippensis), whose citizens thus enjoyed the privilege of Roman citizenship. The city as a whole and many of its inhabitants as individuals thus came to owe Augustus the debt and obligations of clients to a patron.

The city was administered by Roman law, a Roman colony being an extension of Rome itself. In Acts 16:21 the citizens identify themselves as "Romans" first, a reflection of their civic pride as part of a colony. This background gives a certain poignancy to Paul's use of "political" and citizenship language in the letter. He encourages the Philippian Christians to live less like grateful Roman citizens (especially by not participating in the imperial cult as a display of loyalty and gratitude) and to place more stock in

their citizenship in the city of God, of which the Philippian church is a kind of colony (Phil 3:20). He calls them to conduct themselves appropriately as citizens (*politeuesthai,* Phil 1:27) through displaying the value of "civic" unity in their relationships with fellow Christians. This background also accounts for why the believers in Philippi should experience hostility from the other inhabitants of the city, since their new commitment to Jesus as "Lord" competed with their obligation to Rome and her "lord," the emperor.

Philippi was not a major city,[3] but it was strategically located along the Via Egnatia (see figure 16.1), which connected Philippi to the southeast with Neapolis (which served, in ef-

---

[3]Many translations of Acts 16:12 present Philippi as "the leading city of the district of Macedonia" (e.g., NRSV and NIV), but this should rather be rendered "a city of the first district of Macedonia" (referring to the four administrative districts). See Helmut Koester, "Paul and Philippi: Evidence from Early Christian Literature," in *Philippi at the Time of Paul and After His Death,* ed. C. Bakirtzis and H. Koester (Harrisburg, Penn.: Trinity Press International, 1998), p. 51; Markus Bockmuehl, *The Epistle to the Philippians,* BNTC (Peabody, Mass.: Hendrickson, 1998), p. 10.

fect, as Philippi's seaport),[4] and to the west with Thessalonica and eventually the western coast of Macedonia. From there it would be a short sea voyage to Brundisium in southern Italy, the beginning point of the Via Appia that led to Rome. It was a city of modest proportions, surrounded by vast farmlands (much of this reflecting the original land grants to the veterans of the Roman armies). The population was a blend of the privileged descendants of the veterans, Greeks (either descended from the inhabitants of the city before it was made a Roman colony or attracted to the city for its commercial potential), native Macedonians and foreigners.[5]

Although archaeologists have excavated much of Philippi, the extensive development of the city during the later Roman and early Byzantine periods have made it difficult to recover first-century Philippi.[6] The Via Egnatia bisects "downtown" Philippi, running northwest to southeast at this point. Adjacent to the Via Egnatia on the south side lies the forum, the city's center of commercial activity and government. The city's council chamber and several temples have been identified surrounding the forum (see figure 16.2).[7] Two bath complexes have been discovered on the south side of the Via Egnatia. The area to the north of the Forum appears to have been the religious district, though most of the finds so far postdate Paul's visit. The city's walls and an impressive theater to the east of the forum (and north of the Via Egnatia) date from the time of Philip and Alexander.[8]

A great mix of cultic practices coexisted in Philippi. The imperial cult was strong in this colony. Inscriptions mention priests of the deified Julius, Augustus and Claudius. The temples in the forum were probably dedicated to the emperors (specifically to Augustus, Livia and Claudius) and Rome.[9] The cult of the Roman emperors was not imposed on the people by the emperors, but rather promoted locally in the eastern provinces of the empire as a means of showing loyalty and gratitude to the family of Augustus. The emperors were responsible for maintaining peace (a particularly valued commodity after the devastation of the civil wars), for administering justice, for organizing relief in time of famine or other hardship. In short, they provided what was normally sought from the gods—hence showing them thanks in the form of worship was deemed entirely appropriate.

The traditional Greek gods (deities such as Zeus, Apollo, Dionysus and Artemis) enjoyed temples and cult sites. Philippians also welcomed cults imported from the East, like the Egyptian cult of Isis and Osiris or the Phrygian cult of the mother goddess Cybele, although it is unclear how popular the Eastern cults were prior to the second century C.E.[10] Although Paul would dismiss all these cults as idolatry, they were filled with meaning for the inhabitants of Philippi. Honoring the traditional gods secured their favor for the whole city's well being. The more exotic cults promised a more personal religious experience, involving the personal protection of the deity and the hope for a better afterlife. These more personal cults coexisted alongside traditional religion and imperial cult without

---

[4]Merrill F. Unger, *Archaeology and the New Testament* (Grand Rapids: Zondervan, 1962), p. 216.

[5]Hendrix, "Philippi," p. 315.

[6]Chaido Koukouli-Chrysantaki, "Colonia Julia Augusta Philippensis," in *Philippi at the Time of Paul and After His Death*, ed. C. Bakirtzis and H. Koester (Harrisburg, Penn.: Trinity Press International, 1998), pp. 14-15.

[7]Koukouli-Chrysantaki, "Colonia Julia Augusta Philippensis," pp. 15-17.

[8]Hendrix, "Philippi," pp. 315; Koukouli-Chrysantaki, "Colonia Julia Augusta Philippensis," p. 18.

[9]P. T. O'Brien, *Commentary on Philippians* (Grand Rapids: Eerdmans, 1991), p. 5; F. W. Beare, *The Epistle to the Philippians* (New York: Harper, 1959), p. 7; Koukouli-Chrysantaki, "Colonia Julia Augusta Philippensis," p. 25.

[10]O'Brien, *Commentary on Philippians*, p. 5.

tension or competition. Christianity, however, could admit of no divinity except the One revealed through Jesus. This led to high tension between the Christian community and the world it left behind.

Apart from Acts 16:13, which tells us of a *proseuchē,* a "place of prayer," outside one of the city gates by a nearby stream (presumably for ritual purification), there are no references to a Jewish community living in Philippi until

this same term. In Halicarnassus the "place of prayer" was also located by a stream. There might have been, then, a small structure for the local adherents of Judaism just outside the city. In either case, the number of Jews or Godfearers appears to have been quite small and composed largely if not entirely of female adherents.

Paul and the Philippians. Paul says very little about his founding of the Philippian

Figure 16.2. Ruins of the Forum in Philippi. (Photo courtesy of Todd Bolen [BiblePlaces.com])

the third century C.E.[11] The term may simply refer to a designated meeting place in the open air. Josephus (*Ant.* 14.10.23-24), however, records several decrees giving Jews in the Eastern Mediterranean the right to build edifices for their religious observances, using

church in his letter. Acts, however, presents a rather plausible account of that first visit.[12] With the Jerusalem Council and the resolution of the question of circumcising Gentile converts behind them, and the Pauline churches in Syria and Asia Minor settled on

---

[11]Koukouli-Chrysantaki, "Colonia Julia Augusta Philippensis," pp. 26-35.

[12]The Acts narrative appears especially reliable in the account of Paul's missionary work in Macedonia and Achaia. The basic outline of Paul's movements in Acts 16:11—18:21 is confirmed at every point in the Pauline letters themselves. See the favorable assessment of Luke's knowledge of local terminology and geography with regard to his account of the mission in Philippi (Acts 16) in Bockmuehl, *Epistle to the Philippians*, pp. 10-12, 16.

this point, Paul and Silas enter a new phase of evangelism as they leave Asia Minor and enter Macedonia, probably in late 49 or 50 C.E. They may be accompanied by Timothy (Acts 16:3; 17:14), even though he drops from view in the narrative.[13] The author of Acts continues to emphasize the divine guidance of the spread of the gospel in the narrative of the vision of the Macedonian man who begged Paul to come evangelize that region (Acts 16:6-10). They land in Neapolis, Philippi's port city, and proceed to Philippi along the Via Egnatia.

Their mission efforts begin among a group of Jewish or Gentile Godfearing women who meet for prayer just outside the city gate. Lydia, a resident foreigner from Thyatira, opens her house to Paul and his team, and provides hospitality for the fledgling church (Acts 16:14-15). Such hospitality was crucial for providing the missionaries with a base of operations and the newly converted with a place to meet for worship, prayer, teaching and mutual encouragement. Lydia's prominence in Acts reminds us how important women are in the ministry of Paul. In this church Syntyche and Euodia will also be recognized as two women who had "contended alongside Paul for the gospel" (Phil 4:3). As in several of the local cults in Philippi, the early church provided women with opportunities to exercise their gifts in leadership.[14]

Public attention and opposition arise after Paul exorcizes a demon from a mantic slave girl, leaving her owners without their source of profit. Practical economics can motivate opposition to the gospel as much as religious sensibilities. (See how these work together in Acts 19:21-31.) The slave owners do not accuse Paul of hurting their business but of foisting on the Philippians "customs that are not lawful for Roman citizens to adopt or observe" (Acts 16:21), a charge that is not entirely a lie. Christian missionaries persuaded Gentiles to turn "to God from idols" (1 Thess 1:9), which from the other side looked like abandoning traditional Greco-Roman piety and dishonoring the gods. The slave owners also play on anti-Jewish sentiments that, though not universal, are well attested in Greek and Latin authors. Jews especially aroused opposition when they openly proselytized among Gentiles (see Dio Cassius *Roman History* 57.18.5a; Josephus *Ant.* 18.81-84; Tacitus *Hist.* 5.5.1-2), and this appears to be the angle Paul's accusers took.

In response, Paul and Silas are publicly whipped and jailed without a trial (1 Thess 2:1-2 incidentally corroborates Acts in regard to the opposition to and suffering and affronts endured by Paul and his team in Philippi). This incarceration leads to the conversion of another household, that of the jailer (Acts 16:25-34), and to Paul using his Roman citizenship to advantage the next morning. It is curious that Paul did not play this trump card the day before to avoid a flogging, but wholly in keeping with the conviction Paul himself expresses in his letters that his sufferings serve to advance the gospel (e.g., Phil 1:12). The city's pride in its connections with Rome make the authorities' treatment of Paul, the Roman, all the more horrific, and they apologize. Paul leaves Philippi prematurely, but he does not leave dishonored—something that his converts would have valued. He and his team venture further west along the Via Egnatia to Thessalonica, where their evangelizing continued to bear fruit.

The Acts narrative does not seem to allow enough time for the intensely close bond of friendship to develop that we find in Philippi-

---

[13]The Philippian Christians appear to know Timothy (Phil 1:1; 2:19-24), although their acquaintance could stem from a later visit or even from Philippian emissaries meeting Timothy as they brought aid to Paul.

[14]Bockmuehl, *Epistle to the Philippians*, p. 8.

ans, but we must remember that Paul had at least two more opportunities to visit this congregation. Both 1 Corinthians 16:5 and 2 Corinthians 1:16 refer to another visit to the Macedonian churches, and Acts 20:1-6 speaks of Paul's spending a Passover in Philippi just prior to his return to Jerusalem in 58 C.E. Moreover, the Philippians had contact with Paul several times through their emissaries, all of which stemmed from and continued to nurture their friendship. By the time Paul writes Philippians, their friendship has had many years and much opportunity to grow.

Paul bears witness to the special place the Philippian church had in Paul's ministry and heart. There is a mutuality—the reciprocity that is the essence of friendship in antiquity—that characterizes this relationship as it does no other. In Paul's letters to Corinth or Thessalonica he characterizes his relationship with the congregation as that of a "father" with his children; in Philippians, he charac-terizes the relationship as "partnership" (Phil 1:5). Unlike other churches (like Corinth, where he staunchly refused support), Paul accepted money from the Philippian Christians in support of his ministry (see Phil 1:5; 4:10, 14-16, 18; 2 Cor 11:8-9) to supplement what he made at his craft of leatherworking. Indeed, they helped finance his evangelism of nearby Thessalonica (Phil 4:16), sending gifts twice to him there. Philippians is itself occasioned, in large measure, by the gift the Philippians sent to Paul in prison by means of Epaphroditus (Phil 2:25-30; 4:10-20). Despite their relative poverty, these Christians also contributed in an exemplary way to the collection Paul was taking up among his Gentile churches for the impoverished Christians in Jerusalem and Judea (2 Cor 8:1-4; 9:1-5). Polycarp, bishop of Smyrna, bears witness to the continuing health of the church in Philippi in a letter written to that community around 110 C.E.

Figure 16.3. The harbor of Caesarea Maritima. Some scholars speculate that Paul wrote Philippians during his two-year detention in this city. (Photo courtesy of Todd Bolen [BiblePlaces.com])

Paul's work in that city bore lasting fruit.

Paul's location. Paul clearly writes Philippians from prison, but he does not say where he is incarcerated (Phil 1:7, 17). Other than his overnight imprisonment in Philippi, Acts speaks only of his two-year detention in Caesarea Maritima in Palestine (58-60 C.E.) followed by another two years spent in house arrest in Rome awaiting trial (60-62 C.E.). Paul was, however, imprisoned on other occasions prior to 58 C.E., the specific locations of which are unknown (see 2 Cor 6:5; 11:23).

Evidence tends to favor Paul's Roman imprisonment, making Philippians one of Paul's latest letters.[15] Paul's triumphant declaration that his imprisonment for the sake of Christ "has become known in the whole Praetorium" (Phil 1:13) and his word of greetings from converts within "Caesar's household" (Phil 4:22) are most natural—and most impressive—in a Roman setting. Paul's imprisonment would be significantly advancing the gospel indeed if the gospel is making headway in the very heart of the empire, behind the closed doors of Nero's own palace! In Rome, Paul was "in chains" under house arrest and was specifically awaiting a verdict that would result in life or death (Phil 1:12-13, 19-26).

The objections to the setting of Paul's Roman imprisonment coalesce around two points. First, Paul planned to continue westward from Rome to evangelize Spain (Rom 15:23-24), but in Philippians he plans to go to Philippi if he is released (Phil 2:23-24). This apparent contradiction is easily resolved, however, when we consider that after a four-year ordeal such as Paul suffered in 58-62 C.E., Paul would certainly need to return to a friendly and healing environment. He would find such among his friends at Philippi, where he could go to find refreshment and restoration before any further work would be undertaken.[16]

Second, the distance from Philippi to Rome makes it unlikely that Paul and the Philippians would be in such frequent contact as the letter presupposes. The distance is indeed impressive, but not impossible, especially since the Philippian Christians appear to have been disposed to put themselves out for Paul. Two major roads (the Via Egnatia across Macedonia and the Via Appia through Italy) and a short sea passage link Philippi and Rome. Moreover, fewer trips are really required than the opponents of a Roman provenance assume. These scholars suggest that, all within the two years of Paul's incarceration, (1) news about Paul in Rome would have to be taken to Philippi, (2) Epaphroditus would be sent to Rome with a gift, (3) Epaphroditus would fall ill in Rome, and news of his illness would have to be taken from Rome to Philippi, (4) the Philippians would send word to Rome expressing their concern for Epaphroditus, and (5) Paul would finally send Epaphroditus home with the letter, to be followed by Timothy and Paul himself at later dates. This timeline could be greatly abbreviated and the number of trips cut in half, however, if Epaphroditus fell ill on the way and sent word back home, and if Paul can *assume* that the Philippians will be concerned about Paul without their getting explicit word to him about this.[17]

The first alternative, Caesarea, has in its

---

[15]See the more extensive discussions in Fee, *Paul's Letter to the Philippians,* pp. 34-37; O'Brien, *Commentary on Philippians,* pp. 19-26; Moisés Silva, *Philippians,* BECNT (Grand Rapids: Baker, 1992), pp. 5-8; Bockmuehl, *Epistle to the Philippians,* pp. 25-32. All of these scholars favor a Roman provenance. See also Gerald F. Hawthorne, *Philippians,* WBC 43 (Dallas: Word, 1983), pp. xli-xliv, one of the very few modern authors to prefer the Caesarean imprisonment, and G. S. Duncan, *Paul's Ephesian Ministry* (New York: Scribner, 1929).

[16]Fee, *Paul's Letter to the Philippians,* p. 36; O'Brien, *Commentary on Philippians,* pp. 25-26.

[17]Fee, *Paul's Letter to the Philippians,* pp. 36-37, and O'Brien, *Commentary on Philippians,* p. 25

favor the fact that the governor's palace was indeed also called a "praetorium" (Acts 23:35), Judea being an imperial and not a senatorial province. All Roman functionaries were part of "Caesar's household," in an extended sense, and Paul was on trial for his life there (although the appeal to Caesar would make the outcome of this trial less serious). Since everything in favor of a Caesarean provenance is more strongly in favor of a Roman provenance, this remains a less attractive option. The third alternative, Ephesus, has in its favor the fact that Paul certainly faced severe hardships there that led him "to despair even of life" (see 1 Cor 15:32; 2 Cor 1:8-10). These ordeals might have included imprisonment, perhaps even on a capital charge. It is also much more conveniently located for multiple trips to Philippi. But Ephesus has against it the fact that Asia was a senatorial province. The governor's administrative center would not be called a praetorium there, unless Paul was using the term very loosely.[18] This locale, if preferred, would put the writing of the letter closer to 55 or 56 C.E.,[19] in the same period as Philemon and shortly before 2 Corinthians (written after the troubles in Ephesus were resolved).

Integrity of the letter. Before reconstructing the situation behind Philippians, we need to give attention to the question of whether to read the letter as a single, unified whole or as a composite of several letters woven together by a later editor. Several scholars have thought they detected seams in Philippians that suggest that more than one letter has been joined together to form our canonical Philippians. Some separate Philippians 4:10-20 from the rest of the letter as an originally independent note of thanks sent off quickly in response to the Philippians gift of material aid.[20] These readers consider it inconceivable (and not a little rude) that Paul would have delayed to show his gratitude until the very end of a long letter like canonical Philippians. Other ancient letters responding to a gift, moreover, tend to put such acknowledgments toward the beginning. Furthermore, some regard Philippians 3:1b-21 (or 3:1b—4:3), together with its closing in Philippians 4:8-9, as a fragment of a third letter, dealing mainly with rival teachers who have now made their way to Philippi and are disrupting the congregation there.[21] These readers assert that the tone of the polemic and the "anxiety" of Paul over the state of the church are incompatible with the tone of confidence in the remainder of the letter. Moreover, the call to "rejoice" in Philippians 3:1 flows more naturally into Philippians 4:4 without this interpolated passage (gross redundancy notwithstanding), and the problem of the double use of "finally" in Philippians 3:1 and Philippians 4:8 is resolved by using each as the conclusion of a separate

---

[18]Fee, *Paul's Letter to the Philippians,* p. 35; Bruce, *Philippians,* p. xxii. Bockmuehl adds that the nature of Paul's imprisonment—a capital charge where he could be acquitted or executed—could not fit an Ephesian incarceration (*Epistle to the Philippians,* p. 27). As a Roman citizen he would have the right to appeal to Rome (as he used in Caesarea), and so he would not be in immediate danger of a death sentence.

[19]See Fee, *Paul's Letter to the Philippians,* pp. 34-37; O'Brien, *Commentary on Philippians,* pp. 19-26; Raymond E. Brown, *Introduction to the New Testament* (Garden City, N.Y.: Doubleday, 1997), pp. 493-96.

[20]J.-F. Collange, *L'Épître de Saint Paul aux Philipiens* (Neuchâtel: Delachaux & Niestlé, 1973), p. 23; W. Schenk, *Die Philipperbriefe des Paules* (Stuttgart: W. Kohlhammer, 1984), p. 250; W. Schmithals, *Paul and the Gnostics* (Nashville: Abingdon, 1972), pp. 75-77.

[21]See the sources listed in n. 20; also Helmut Koester, "The Purpose of the Polemic of a Pauline Fragment (Philippians III)," *NTS* 8 (1961/1962): 317-32. Often this line of argumentation is accompanied by assertions of inconsistencies, for example in Paul's attitudes toward his opponents in Philippians 1:15-18; 3:2-3. However, such arguments rest on the mistaken assumption that these opponents are the same people rather than different groups about whom Paul feels differently.

letter.[22] Polycarp, moreover, speaks of Paul's *letters* to the Philippians (*Phil.* 3.2), although this could just as easily refer to letters now lost or result from Polycarp's misinformation.

As with the arguments for the composite nature of 2 Corinthians, scholars can offer no explanation of the alleged redactor's method or logic. In most cases where ancient editorial activity has been detected, the editors have striven to make a document more readily comprehensible, not less. There is also no evidence in the manuscript tradition for these parts ever circulating independently of the whole.

On the other hand, there is a wealth of evidence that suggests we read Philippians as a unified text.[23] First, the distribution of certain key terms throughout every part of canonical Philippians gives a linguistic and thematic coherence to the letter:

- The frequent use of nouns and verbs compounded with the preposition *syn-* ("together with," Phil 1:7, 27; 2:2, 17, 18, 25; 3:10, 17, 21; 4:3 [4 times], 14), a prefix that enhances the feeling of mutuality, partnership and common destiny between Christ, Paul and the Philippian converts throughout the letter.
- Words related to the verb "to rejoice" (*chairō*) or the noun "joy" (*chara*), which appear in Philippians 1:18 (twice), 25; 2:2, 17 (twice), 18 (twice), 28, 29; 3:1; 4:1, 4 (twice), 10.

- Nouns and verbs related to "partnership" or "sharing" (*koinōnia*) in Philippians 1:5, 7; 2:1; 3:10; 4:14, 15, which both give lexical coherence to the whole and support the characterization of Philippians as a unified "letter of friendship."[24]
- Forms of the verb "to consider, regard, think" (*phronein*) appear frequently (Phil 1:7; 2:2 [twice], 5; 3:15 [twice], 19; 4:2, 10 [twice]) and in particularly high concentrations near the introduction of the Christ hymn, the conclusion of Paul's personal example, the appeal to Syntyche and Euodia (recalling specifically Phil 4:2) and the beginning of the postponed note of thanks. This verb thus serves to highlight the more important points Paul makes in the letter and, again, suggests the unity and coherence of the work.

A further observation to be drawn from the verbal and structural similarities between the "Christ Hymn" of Philippians 2:6-11 and Paul's discussion of his own religious posture in Philippians 3:2-21 is that Paul presents himself in Philippians 3:2-16 as a further exemplification of what it means to think with the mindset that belongs to the believer in Christ.[25] Paul connects his example with Christ's by reusing the root for "form" or "shape" (*morph-*, Phil 2:6, 7; 3:10) and the word "death" (*thanatos*, Phil 2:8, twice; 3:10). The pattern of Paul's rejection of claims before God parallels Christ's refusal to

---

[22]Loveday Alexander has specifically addressed the issue of whether or not Phil 3:1 marks the end of a letter, *to loipon* being read as "finally" and *chairete* being read as "farewell" ("Hellenistic Letter-Forms and the Structure of Philippians," *JSNT* 37 [1989]: 96-97). Alexander presents a number of examples from Hellenistic letters where the former phrase merely introduces a new, not a final, topic (not to mention uses of the phrase for this purpose in 1 Thess 4:1 and 2 Thess 3:1). The second word occurs often as an infinitive to mean "greetings," but never in any form to mean "farewell." Given the importance of the *chair-/char-* family of words throughout Philippians, the meaning "rejoice" is more natural.

[23]See O'Brien, *Philippians*, pp. 10-18; Hawthorne, *Philippians*, pp. xxix-xxxii; Silva, *Philippians*, pp. 14-16; Carolyn Osiek, *Philippians, Philemon*, ANTC (Nashville: Abingdon, 2000), pp. 16-19; Bockmuehl, *Epistle to the Philippians*, pp. 20-25.

[24]J. T. Fitzgerald, "Philippians, Epistle to the," *Anchor Bible Dictionary*, ed. David N. Freedman (New York: Doubleday, 1992), 6:320.

[25]W. J. Dalton, "The Integrity of Philippians," *Bib* 60 (1979): 100; D. E. Garland, "The Composition and Unity of Philippians: Some Neglected Literary Factors," *NovT* 27 (1985): 157-59.

cling to equality with God. Both reach or will reach their eventual exaltation by emptying themselves and by pursuing the goal of obedience to God without seeking to secure any claims on God's reward or holding onto status and claims to precedence over others. Thus it becomes even less likely that Philippians 3:2-21 is a fragment of a separate letter and more likely that it is a coherent continuation of the picture of what it means to have the mind of Christ.

An analysis of vocabulary also allows the conclusion that Philippians 1:27 and Philippians 4:1 form an inclusio, a common device used in ancient literature to mark the boundaries of shorter or longer sections using similar vocabulary at the beginning and end of each section. Here we can observe the following correspondences:

- The verb "conduct yourselves as citizens" (*politeuesthe*) in Philippians 1:27 is echoed in the noun "state, citizenship" (*politeuma*) in Philippians 3:20.
- The phrase "stand firm in one spirit" in Philippians 1:27 is echoed in the phrase "stand firm thus in the Lord" in Philippians 4:1.
- The verb "striving together" (*synathlein*) appears in Philippians 1:27 and 4:3, bringing the exhortation to Syntyche and Euodia into the orbit of the argumentation of Philippians 1:27—4:1.[26]

Scholars who wish to separate Philippians 3:20—4:1 (possibly as far as 4:3) from the remainder of Philippians, therefore, are violating this clear sign of intentional structuring. Further, those who excise only Philippians 3:1b-21 are left with the impossibility of 3:1a leading directly into 4:1, which leaves them with the same difficulties of a rough transition that gave rise to the hypothesis of composite letters in the first place.

It makes far better sense both in literary/linguistic and rhetorical terms to regard canonical Philippians as a unified composition rather than resorting to speculative and poorly founded hypotheses.[27] Every part of the letter, therefore, is appropriate and integral to the development of a letter between friends. Philippians 1:1-26 begins with reaffirmations of friendship and the sharing of news. Philippians 1:27 ("Only let us conduct ourselves in a manner worthy of the gospel of Christ") suggests itself as the proposition of the letter, calling his friends' attention to the common core of values that hold them together. Paul then expounds the meaning of this exhortation by appealing to the unity and cohesion of the group (Phil 2:1-4, 14-16; 4:2-4), the example of Christ (Phil 2:5-11), his own example (Phil 3:2-21), and the examples of those around Paul (Timothy and Epaphroditus in Phil 2:19-30; 3:17). The postponed expression of thanks in Philippians 4:10-20 continues to support the theme of friendship and partnership in a common venture, rounding off the themes sounded in Philippians 1:3-11; 2:1-2. The placement of Paul's thanksgiving near the end, moreover, leaves these tones of gratitude and partnership ringing in the Philippians' ears as the reading of the letter is ended.

---

[26]Garland, "Composition and Unity of Philippians," p. 160.

[27]Resources using rhetorical criticism to demonstrate the unity of Philippians include D. F. Watson, "A Rhetorical Analysis of Philippians and Its Implications for the Unity Question," *NovT* 30 (1988): 57-88; and L. G. Bloomquist, *The Function of Suffering in Philippians,* JSNTSS 78 (Sheffield, U.K.: Sheffield Academic Press, 1993), pp. 97-118. Watson, for example, identifies six words or phrases in Philippians 1:3-26 that have verbal parallels in Philippians 3:2-21, supporting the case that Philippians 1:3-26 forms an introduction to the whole letter, including the disputed section (Phil 3:2-21) ("Rhetorical Analysis," p. 64). Bockmuehl (*Epistle to the Philippians,* pp. 23, 39) and Fee (*Paul's Letter to the Philippians,* pp. 14-17), however, are less impressed with this approach, which they find to be used in too prescriptive and rigid a manner.

EXEGETICAL SKILL
Discerning the Situation Behind a Text ("Mirror Reading")

An essential skill in exegesis is reconstructing the situation that a particular letter envisions and addresses. The major challenge to such reconstruction is that the only witness to what was going on in that situation is usually the New Testament text in question. Thus the student is involved in a circular enterprise, first using a text to reconstruct a historical setting, then interpreting that text in light of his or her reconstruction.

It is notoriously difficult to reconstruct a complete telephone conversation from listening to only one side of it—all the more when we're hearing only one line in a conference call. In New Testament studies, unbridled "mirror reading" of New Testament texts has often bred wild theories about the teachings and practices of heterodox Christians floating through the first-century Greco-Roman world. This situation has led several authors to reflect critically on appropriate methods for mirror reading, particularly in a clearly polemical situation (i.e., where the author squares off with rival teachers and their influence in his congregations). While their methodological suggestions, then, deal primarily with identifying opponents whose positions are addressed in a particular New Testament text, their work can also help guide the more general task of reconstructing the situation envisioned in a text, whether or not rival teachers are part of that landscape.

John Barclay responds to four methodological missteps that he has observed in many scholarly attempts to reconstruct the situation behind a letter:

1. undue selectivity (basing a theory on a few choice statements, but failing to make sense of our reconstruction in light of the whole text)

2. overinterpretation (proceeding as if every positive statement is a response to an opponent's or the congregation's denial, or every denial a rebuttal of an opponent's claim; similarly treating every command as a sign that the hearers are doing something different and every prohibition as a sign that the hearers are engaged in the prohibited activity)

3. mishandling polemics (failing to account for the inevitable distortions that will occur when an author is trying to draw people away from following other voices, presenting them in the worst possible light, ascribing the worst possible motives)[a]

4. latching onto particular words as if these gave us direct access to the opponents' slogans and key terms (like "knowledge," *gnōsis,* or "spiritual," *pneumatikos*). Paul *could* choose to use his rivals' terminology in an attempt to redefine it, but we have to be very judicious in deciding when this is the case.

---

[a]This would not only apply to Christian opponents, e.g., Paul's rivals in Galatia. In a situation where the nonbelieving society poses the only serious opposition to the faithful believers, the author of 1 Peter certainly presents Gentile non-Christians in the most negative light possible. First Peter 4:3-4 is certainly not a balanced and judicious assessment of Gentile society *tout court.*

In an attempt to avoid such exegetical missteps, Barclay employs the following criteria when sifting through a letter looking for indications of the situation behind it or opposing positions addressed.

1. Consider the *type of utterance*. Assertions, denials, commands and prohibitions are all open to a wide range of mirror reading—an author giving a command might be reinforcing what the readers already know and do, or he might be correcting egregious violations of the group's values. Other criteria will help determine where along the spectrum the audience or situation lies.

2. *Tone.* Is the author's tone urgent or emphatic or casual?

3. *Frequency.* Does the author return frequently to this topic or mention it once in passing?

4. *Clarity.* Do we really understand the passage we are reading, or is it too unclear or ambiguous to be of real help in getting behind the situation?

5. *Unfamiliarity.* The presence of vocabulary or themes that are atypical for the author might signal a feature of the particular situation or position to which the author is responding. (This criterion works best for Paul, of course, the only New Testament author for whom we have an adequate sampling of writings to determine what is atypical.)

6. *Consistency.* Work with the assumption of a single front rather than multiply types of rival teachers in a single letter. All things being equal, the simplest solution is to be preferred.

7. *Historical plausibility.* Are the rival teachers we reconstruct known or seen anywhere else in contemporaneous literature? Is the situation we envision plausible? Have we introduced anachronisms (like Gnostic doctrines attested elsewhere only in second- and third-century texts)?

Based on these criteria, Barclay also calls for an honest assessment of the level of certainty for each bit of information we gather about the situation or opponents. Priority, of course, should be given to those data that emerge as "certain" or "probable" elements of the situation. Since the author is selective in what he includes and addresses, we also need to bear in mind that many aspects of the situation will remain unknown.

Jerry Sumney adds several helpful guidelines for our task. First, he emphasizes the importance of basing any theory about the situation or opponents envisioned in a text *on data from that text itself*. We should not impose our theoretical models of Judaizers or Gnostics, nor data from alleged parallels, on a letter and its situation. Rather we should let the nature of the situation emerge from the text. Moreover, each letter needs to be interpreted on its own terms. It does no good to import the polemics of Galatians into Corinth; we must determine on the basis of the Corinthian letters what was going on in Corinth.

Further, he provides a more nuanced way of thinking about the "type of utterance" made in a given passage and assessing its level of reliability for providing information about the situation or, more especially, opponents in that situation. First, he distinguishes between explicit statements about the situation or opposition, possible allusions to the same, and simple affirmations of the author's own position. These present decreasing levels of certainty of reference to the historical details of the situation. He also calls us to weigh these kinds of statements differently in terms of the context the statement is made in—whether that of attacking the other position or defending oneself or one's position, of instruction or exhortation, or of the conventional elements of a letter (like the opening formula, the thanksgiving, the closing elements). The more heated the context, the more likely it is that the author will not present the opposing point of view fairly. For example, explicit statements about opponents in polemics or exhortation will have a greater chance of being more biased than explicit statements about opponents in more neutral contexts.

As an exercise, try reading through a short New Testament letter (Philippians, Colossians, 1 John, 2 Peter) with Barclay's and Sumney's criteria in mind. Where do you detect explicit statements about the audience's situation or about other voices to which they might be listening? Where might there be allusions to the situation or to rival teachers? What issues keep recurring throughout the letter? What issues are mentioned infrequently or in passing? What issues or concerns does an author's heightened tone suggest are more pressing in that situation? Is the author presenting data about the situation or rival teachers fairly and dispassionately, or is he speaking in the heat of polemics or exhortation? In other words, can you begin to weigh the levels of *reliability* of different statements made about opponents in the text? As you work through the criteria listed above, begin to postulate which data concerning the situation are virtually certain (e.g., circumcision was an issue in Galatia) down the line through probable to possible to improbable.

Reflecting on the method you might reliably use to move from a text back into the situation that text purports to address will not only make you more adept at understanding the challenges facing the early churches and the ways the New Testament authors addressed these challenges, but it will also make you more critical and judicious readers of the many commentaries and articles you will read in the course of your study and ministry. You can begin to grow in this area by weighing my own claims about the situation behind a letter and any opposing positions engaged in a letter against the evidence from the text. Continue to use these criteria as you weigh the resources you read for exegetical papers, in sermon preparation and the like. Paul's words concerning prophecy are all the more appropriate for reading the works of biblical scholars: "Test everything; hold fast to what is good" (1 Thess 5:21 NRSV).

GENRE AND PURPOSES

Philippians is clearly a letter, more specifically an example of a "letter of friendship."[28] You were introduced in a preliminary manner to epistolary analysis in the chapter on the Thessalonian Correspondence. Here we will look more closely at one specific letter type. Pseudo-Demetrius (*Epistolary Types* 1) provides a sample of a "friendly type" letter:

> Even though I have been separated from you for a long time, I suffer this in body only. For I can never forget you or the impeccable way we were reared together from childhood up. Knowing that I myself am genuinely concerned about your affairs, and that I have worked unhesitatingly for what is most advantageous to you, I have assumed that you, too, have the same opinion of me, and will refuse me in nothing. You will do well, therefore, to give close attention to the members of my household lest they need anything, to assist them in whatever they might need, and to write us about whatever you choose.[29]

This sample letter invokes several topics: (1) the fact of absence and the means by which the writer has kept his or her friends in mind, "present," in effect; (2) the author's assurance of interest in the affairs of the readers, and af-firmations of the ways that the author has advanced their interests or sought their advantage; (3) expressions of confidence in the readers' interest in the affairs of the author, and in their disposition to advance the author's interests as well; (4) requests for assistance on the basis of this mutual friendship.

All of these topics can be found prominently displayed in Philippians:

1. Paul makes the reality of his absence plain throughout the letter (Phil 1:27; 2:12, 24) and affirms that he keeps the Philippians "present" with him by keeping them constantly in mind as he remembers them before God in prayer (Phil 1:3-4, 8-11). Further, in Philippians 2:17-18, he makes their mutual joy in one another a "present" reminder of how dear each party is to the other.

2. Paul shows himself most solicitous about the Philippians' circumstances, planning to send Timothy to procure news about "your affairs," "how things stand with you" (Phil 2:19). His concern for specific aspects of their current situation (e.g., the spat between Syntyche and Euodia, and the fact of opposition from their pagan neighbors), shows that he has been eager to learn the news about them from Epaphroditus and is praying that all should go well with them. Paul repeatedly conveys the impression that he seeks their advantage. He prays con-

---

[28]See the excellent discussion in Fee, *Paul's Letter to the Philippians,* pp. 2-6.
[29]Quoted in A. J. Malherbe, "Ancient Epistolary Theorists," *Ohio Journal of Religious Studies* 5 (1977): 31.

Paul's Strange "Thank You" Note

The subdued tenor of Paul's expression of thanks has often been noted. Paul seems to say that while he appreciates the thought, he really didn't need the money. It is doubtful, however, that Paul seeks to belittle the gift. Rather, he affirms that his friends and their concern for him were more important to him than the money (Phil 4:10, 17). Since Christ has also been at work supplying Paul's need, Paul must bear witness to the help he has received from his divine Benefactor, balancing this with the help he receives from his human friends. We should note that the Philippians' act of generosity toward Paul is also a gift to God, a "fragrant offering . . . acceptable and pleasing to God" (Phil 4:18 NRSV). Although Paul is not in a position to repay the favor, he fully anticipates that God will look with favor on the generous act of God's children and will remember their good character when they are themselves in need of God's help (Phil 4:19). Thus in God's economy no generous act goes unrewarded, even if the human recipients are unable to return a favor.

stantly for their growth in discipleship and their ultimate vindication on the Day of the Lord (Phil 1:9-11). He assumes that if he is acquitted, he will use his life to continue to work for their "progress and joy in the faith" (Phil 1:25-26). He welcomes his potential death as a contribution to the completeness of the Philippians' own offering of faithfulness to God (Phil 2:17). Although Paul can certainly use the company and help, he sends Epaphroditus back, being more concerned and anxious about their love for Epaphroditus than for his own needs (Phil 2:28). Even in the matter of gifts, Paul is more excited about the profit that will come to the Philippians from God (Phil 4:19) on account of their generosity toward him.

3. Paul speaks with assurance that the Philippians hold Paul "in their heart" (Phil 1:7), something quite evident in their sending of yet another gift through Epaphroditus (Phil 4:14). He assumes that the Philippians continue to pray for him (Phil 1:19) and affirms their ongoing concern, even when they cannot send aid (Phil 4:10). Paul speaks as if the Philippians are genuinely concerned about his affairs, "how things stand with him" (Phil 1:12-26).

4. Paul's request that the Philippians regain their harmony and unity (Phil 2:1-4) is motivated by a desire on Paul's part that the Philippians will want to "make his joy complete" (Phil 2:2). Paul asks for aid in looking after the affairs of his household (the family of God) in his absence, particularly in regard to the resolution of conflict between Euodia and Syntyche (Phil 4:2-3).

Of course, this does not account for all of Philippians, since much of the letter falls into the genre of "moral exhortation" (e.g., Phil 1:27—2:18; 3:1—4:1, 4-9). Moral exhortation, however, was quite at home in letters between friends, as can be seen in the letters of Seneca and Cicero to their friends. Although it is granted that these are far more literary and essay-like, many of them give evidence of being part of an actual two-way correspondence about ethical and philosophical topics. This is all the more natural as the most "perfect" friendship was based on a shared commitment to virtue rather than merely pleasure or utility (Aristotle *Eth. Nic.* 8.3.6-7 11 56b 8-24).

What goals does Paul have for writing this letter of friendship? Three of these purposes relate directly to the Philippians' partnership with him. First (last, in the order of writing), Paul wants to thank them for the material support they sent him through Epaphroditus during his confinement (Phil 4:10-20). Second, Paul wants to ease their concern over the well-being of Epaphroditus, their emissary of mercy, whom they heard fell ill on his mission (Phil 2:25-30). Third, Paul wants to provide them with an update on his own situation (Phil 1:12-26).

At the same time, Paul, having learned something of the Philippians' challenges from Epaphroditus, wants to address two pressing aspects of their situation. First, Paul seeks reconciliation between two leading figures in the life of the church, Euodia and Syntyche (Phil 4:2-3), whose divisive quarrel (the particulars are forever lost to us thanks to Paul's discretion) threatened primary values of the Christian family—harmony and unity (Phil 2:1-4). Paul is therefore concerned to calm any ripples of rivalry or division that may be moving out from these two leaders into the larger congregation.

This is all the more urgent in light of the second concern, namely, the Philippian Christians' continued strength and perseverance in the face of their neighbors' hostility (Phil 1:27-30). The believers encountered some level of rejection and hostility by their fellow citizens of the Roman colony. Paul speaks explicitly concerning their receiving a share of the suffering that befell him in his work for the gospel there:

> Live your life in a manner worthy of the gospel of Christ, so that, whether I come and see you or am absent and hear about you, I will know that you are standing firm in one spirit, striving side by side with one mind for the faith of the gospel, and are in no way intimidated by your opponents. For them this is evidence of their destruction, but of your salvation. And this is God's doing. For he has graciously granted you the privilege not only of believing in Christ, but of suffering for him as well—since you are having the same struggle that you saw I had and now hear that I still have. (Phil 1:27-30 NRSV)

The believers' new commitment to another Lord and Savior (both titles being applied also to the *Augusti*) now set them apart from the pro-Roman crowd in Philippi; indeed it seemed to set them in opposition to the common good and the unity of the city. As in Thessalonica this unofficial but nonetheless difficult opposition to Christian commitments arises out of the non-Christians' loyalty toward the household of Augustus. The want their erring neighbors, the Christians, to likewise demonstrate that gratitude and loyalty. Paul encourages his friends in Philippi to match the external society's hostility with internal unity, support, encouragement and aid. Were this to erode from within, the assaults from without stood a good chance of achieving their objective of wearing down the "deviants" and bringing them back in line with Roman Philippi's values and commitments.

PAUL'S STRATEGY FOR SUSTAINING CHRISTIAN UNITY

A large percentage of Philippians can be understood as part of Paul's attempts to nurture a spirit of harmony, unity and solidarity among his friends. Paul directly urges his friends to "stand firm in one spirit, with one mind, striving side by side for the faith of the gospel" (Phil 1:27). He desires them to be "of the same mind, having the same love, being in full accord and of one mind" (Phil 2:2 NRSV), to exhibit humility and to "regard one another as better than yourselves" (Phil 2:3), to invest themselves in protecting one another's interests rather than pushing their own (Phil 2:4). One particular disruption in the circle of friends needs special attention: "I urge Euodia and I urge Syntyche to agree [think the same thing] in the Lord" (Phil 4:2). Competition, rivalry, "looking out for number one," pushing our own agenda—these are all rather natural human responses, familiar from our own experience with churches and not merely a relic of the Philippian Christians' experience. What resources does Paul use to cultivate a different and, from a fleshly point of view, quite unnatural set of responses to one's fellow believers?

Opponents of Paul at Philippi?

Many prominent scholars insist that opponents or rival teachers of Paul have infiltrated the congregation in Philippi, reading Philippians 1:15-18, 28; 3:2-16, 18-19 as evidence for these teachers' agenda and message. Some see as many as five different groups of opponents, while others blend the references together to create an unholy hybrid, such as "Jewish-Christian Gnostic perfectionists." In its more modest form the suggestion of opponents actually present in Philippi has tended to focus on Judaizers, much like those Paul encountered in Galatia.[a]

Some scholars have become so accustomed to defining Paul by discovering his opponents that they read all of his letters in a polemical context and insist on finding some opponents present behind every letter. It is unlikely, however, that Paul believes his friends face such an immediate threat to the gospel in Philippi.[b]

1. The references to these alleged opponents are slight when set against the information about Paul's rivals in Corinth or Galatia. Moreover, Paul offers no thoroughgoing argumentation against an opposing position (or in support of his own) comparable to what we find in Galatians and 2 Corinthians, where we know opponents to be at work among Paul's churches.

2. There is also no indication of a breach between Paul and the church at Philippi occasioned by their reception of preachers of another gospel, and there is no rhetoric of reconciliation. Throughout the letter Paul remains on firm ground and treats the Philippians as if they too are firmly bound to him.

3. The exhortations most prominently underscored by Paul (e.g., through repetition: see Phil 1:27-30; 2:1-4, 14-15; 3:15; 4:2-3) concern the restoration of unity and harmony within the church, not resistance to a false gospel coming in from without. This unity, furthermore, is not a matter of doctrine but of interpersonal attitude and behavior.

Why, then, did Paul speak about those who "preach Christ out of envy" (Phil 1:15-18), the Judaizing missionaries whom he calls "dogs" (Phil 3:2), and those Christians who live as "enemies of the cross of Christ" (Phil 3:18-19)? The character of Philippians as a letter of friendship may help clarify Paul's purposes here. In the ancient mind friendship is directly related to enmity. "Constant attentiveness to friends automatically meant constant watchfulness of enemies."[c] Since their friendship is based on mutual commitment to shared values and ideals, the bond of friendship—not just between Paul and the church but among the Philippian Christians who have begun to experience internal conflict—can be strengthened by the awareness of others who do not share these values, who are in fact committed to contradictory values. History has repeat-

---

[a]Hawthorne, *Philippians,* pp. xliv-xlvii; Silva, *Philippians,* pp. 9-10; Chris Mearns, "The Identity of Paul's Opponents at Philippi," *NTS* 33 (1987): 194-204.

[b]Fee (*Paul's Letter to the Philippians,* pp. 7-9, 33) and Bockmuehl (*Epistle to the Philippians,* pp. 6, 9, 19) both rightly regard Philippians 3 as a warning, not an indication the opponents are actually present in Philippi. See also Garland, "Composition and Unity," p. 166.

[c]Stanley K. Stowers, "Friends and Enemies in the Politics of Heaven: Reading Theology in Philippians," in *Pauline Theology,* ed. J. M Bassler (Minneapolis: Fortress, 1991), 1:113; see, more extensively, Peter Marshall, *Enmity in Corinth,* WUNT 2/23 (Tübingen: Mohr, 1987), pp. 35-69.

edly shown that a group's internal cohesion and cooperation can be enhanced by drawing attention to the "real" enemies outside the group.

References to deviant Christian "dogs" and "evil workers" of Philippians 3:2 and the "enemies of the cross of Christ," then, remind the Philippian Christians of those who are truly unlike them, thus reminding them of their essential unity and commonality. They also provide useful foils for the positive presentations of virtuous behavior—the true Christian mindset—such as Paul displays (Phil 3:4-16) and to which he calls the Philippians as they continue to live out their friendship with the cross of Christ by their looking out for the interests of one another over and above self-interests. Similarly, the rival preachers who are making trouble for Paul in the city of his imprisonment (Phil 1:15-18) exemplify the vices of strife, rivalry and selfish ambition, the very things Paul rises above and calls his friends to rise above in their relationships with one another. The situation in Philippi, then, does not involve rival Christian teachers; rather, Paul makes frequent and brief references to "enemies" in order to build up unity and cooperation within the group.

Exhortations based on friendship and civic virtue. Even though competing for precedence and advancing self interest were quite in keeping with popular cultural values (then as now), Paul regards these as entirely out of place in a community of siblings, friends and fellow citizens of heaven. In such a community there is no room for "selfish ambition or conceit" (Phil 2:3), or for seeking what will be advantageous to self rather than to family and friends (Phil 2:4). The values that guide kin and friends, then, must replace competition and self-seeking. Paul therefore calls for increased attention to the honor due the other and diminished attention to self-promotion; he summons believers to consider how to advance the interests of their fellow Christians rather than their own self interest. The ideals promoted in the exhortations cited above are commonly applied to friendship, especially, in ancient ethical literature, for the specific friendship that exists between siblings (as Christians, in fact, construed themselves to be; see Phil 1:12, 14; 2:25; 3:1, 13, 17; 4:1, 8,

21).[30] Moreover, Paul urges that these ideals be restored among the congregation on the basis of the friendship—the reciprocity and partnership—that the Philippians enjoy with Paul. This is the way that they can "make [Paul's] joy complete," and continue to minister to the heart of their friend in prison (Phil 2:2).

Paul overlays this set of values, however, with well-known civic ideals as well, using political language to shape his friends' self-understanding, their relationship with the outside world and their life together as a colony of the "city of God," as it were. This displays Paul's ability to adapt appropriate metaphors for different settings, here for an audience that had been proud of their city's civic status as a colony of Rome. Paul, therefore, will instruct them on the proper way to "live as citizens" (*politeuesthe*, Phil 1:27; most English translations fail to capture the political nuance of this term).

The heavy emphasis on living at peace with fellow citizens, on preserving unity and avoiding all disruption and civil strife, is very much at home in discussions of civic virtue and vice

---

[30]See, further, David A. deSilva, *Honor, Patronage, Kinship and Purity* (Downers Grove, Ill.: InterVarsity Press, 2000), pp. 169-71, 213-23.

in the ancient world. Aristotle had described "political friendship" as "unanimity," a state in which people "have the same opinion about what is to their [collective] interest, and choose the same actions, and do what they have resolved in common" (*Eth. Nic.* 9.6.1 1167a26-28). Virtuous people would exhibit the civic virtue of being "of one mind" (*Eth. Nic.* 9.6.3 1167b6-7), but people of a base and vicious character tend instead toward factionalism because "they aim at getting more than their share of advantages. . . . Each man wishing for advantage to himself criticizes his neighbour and stands in his way" (*Eth. Nic.* 9.6.4 1167b10-15). Nearly five centuries later Dio Chrysostom echoes the same sentiments. He seeks to prevent his fellow citizens from using the arrival of a new governor to air their grievances with one another and thus display their divisiveness. Thus he argues against parading their shame:

> If a quarrel arises among yourselves and your enemies taunt you because you have wicked citizens and civil unrest, are you not put to shame? . . . It is truly a noble and profitable thing for one and all alike to have a city show itself *of one mind*, on terms of friendship with itself and *one in feeling, united* in conferring both censure and praise. . . . Is it not disgraceful that bees are *of one mind* and no one has ever seen a swarm that is factious and fights against itself, but, on the contrary, they both work and live together, providing food for one another and using it as well? . . . Is it not disgraceful, then, that human beings should be more unintelligent than wild creatures which are so tiny and unintelligent? (*Or.* 48, emphasis added)

Paul employs topics commonly used by orators and political ethicists to speak of the ideal behavior of a city. Its citizens are at peace, at unity among themselves, fomenting no divisions or unrest. Only thus could a city have a good reputation and sufficient strength to stand against its enemies. Disunity was a blemish, pollution within the body politic. Indeed, Paul calls his friends to avoid such pollution and to let their virtue shine out all the more against the backdrop of the non-Christian society by doing "all things without grumbling or questioning" (Phil 2:14). Then they will continue to bring honor to their own "city," the *politeuma* ("state" or "community" or "citizenship") belonging to the heavens (Phil 3:20).

Mutuality in joy and grief. An aspect of Paul's strategy closely related to the abundance of "friendship" topics is his use of associative language in this letter. Paul and the Philippians are bound together by their common experience of the gospel (Phil 1:5), God's favor (Phil 1:7), and the sufferings each encounters as a result of their witness to Christ (Phil 1:29-30). Each party is the other's cause for joy (2:17-18; 4:1). Paul displays the commonality of Christian believers as he speaks of Epaphroditus: the suffering of his friend is his own grief, and the relief shown his partner is relief shown him and the church as well (Phil 2:26-28).

Paul enhances this sense of mutuality with an unusual number of compound words formed with the preposition *syn-*, meaning "together," or "with." The whole Christian life becomes a joining together with one another and with Christ himself. They are Paul's "fellow sharers" (*syn-koinōnous*, Phil 1:7), who "shared with him" in his sufferings (*syn-koinōnēsantes*, Phil 4:14), who are called to "compete together" (*syn-athlountes*, Phil 1:27), and be "like-souled" (*syn-psychoi*, Phil 2:2). They are called to "rejoice together" with Paul even as he "rejoices together" with them (*syn-chairō, syn-chairete*, Phil 2:17-18). Epaphroditus is Paul's "fellow worker" and "fellow soldier" (*syn-ergon, syn-stratiōtēn*, Phil 2:25). Paul seeks to be "formed together" with Christ in Christ's death (*syn-morphizomenos*, Phil 3:10), even as he calls the believers to become "imitators together" of Paul's example (*syn-mimētai,* Phil 3:17), so that they all will be "formed together" into the likeness of Christ's resurrected body (*syn-morphon,* Phil 3:21). The use of this prepositional prefix climaxes in Philippians 4:3, where it appears four times: "I ask you also, true yokefellow (*syn-zyge*), join in helping (*syn-lambanou*) these women, for they are my fellow contenders (*synēthlēsan*) in the gospel along with Clement and the rest of my fellow workers (*syn-ergoi*), whose names are in the book of life." This uncommonly high use of *syn-* compounds (and Paul's intentionality here is clearly marked by his invention of several of these compounds) contributes to Paul's goals of restoring the believers' sense of cooperation, partnership and mutuality.

The overall effect of all this language is to underscore the way that the well-being of any one believer is interwoven with the well-being of every other believer. According to such a model no one can truly gain advantage by depriving another believer of joy: either all win or no one wins. This is a further impetus to "look after the interests of others," since our own joy or sorrow is, in Christ, inseparably linked with the joy or sorrow of our Christian family.

Praiseworthy examples of the Christian attitude. A third facet of Paul's pastoral strategy is to hold up a number of praiseworthy examples, each crafted to underscore the desirability of the specific attitudes and interpersonal dynamics Paul promotes. The topics of praise and blame, and the setting forth of positive and negative examples were commonly used to reaffirm a group's values, commitments and behaviors. Honoring those people who embodied these values showed that continued commitment to living out such values indeed resulted in honor, motivating the hearers to emulate those praised exemplars and to act in line with the virtues they displayed.

The most prominent and celebrated of these examples is Jesus Christ, introduced by means of a poetic passage commonly called the "Christ Hymn" (Phil 2:6-11) that celebrates Jesus' demonstration of love and generosity toward humanity. Christ is the supreme example of looking out for the interests of others over those of oneself. Jesus refused to use his exalted status as an opportunity to exploit for personal gain, but rather poured himself out completely for others in obedience to God. The pattern of Jesus who "emptied himself" is a necessary remedy for people who are too full of themselves. Jesus, who had the most legitimate claim to preeminence, did not press that claim, but rather put God's will for God's people ahead of any desire for recognition of his own status. How much more should those whom Jesus saved, then, rid themselves of attempts to be acknowledged first in the community, casting off all conceit and selfishness!

The example of Jesus also demonstrates that those who follow such a course of action will not find themselves at a loss. In our limited perception of zero-sum interactions, where another person wins only at my expense, or where my interests are served only at the expense of someone else's, Paul's exhortations in Philippians 2:3-4 might seem like an invitation to become a perpetual "loser" as we try to make our fellow believers "winners." The end of Jesus' story, however, shows up the shallowness and shortsightedness of this way of thinking. He who, in serving the interests of others, came out looking like a complete loser in the world's way of thinking ("death on a cross," Phil 2:8), was in fact elevated to the highest honor by God for his obedience unto death. Believers may thus be assured that no honor will be lost in honoring fellow believers above themselves, no advantage missed by putting fellow believers' interests above their own. This is part of the mystery of the "wisdom of God" revealed in the cross (1 Cor 1:18-25), now made quite practical by Paul in Philippians 2:3-4.

The "Christ Hymn" in Philippians 2:6-11

It has become commonplace in scholarship to speak of Philippians 2:6-11 as an early Christian hymn that Paul has incorporated into his letter. The lofty, rhythmic nature of this passage and the elegant balance of the movement within the passage (the movement down into humiliation and up to glorification) has led to a variety of attempts to discern the original form and outline the strophes (stanzas) of this "hymn," and to reconstruct its meaning and setting in early Christian worship. In the early second century Pliny the Younger learned that, at their meetings, Christians would "chant verses alternately amongst themselves in honor of Christ as if to a God" (*Ep.* 10.96). Philippians 2:6-11 would well suit such an antiphonal recitation.

Other scholars are more cautious about this identification. Markus Bockmuehl points out that (1) scholars cannot agree about the division of the stanzas, often resorting to rearranging or shortening the text to make a particular scheme work, and (2) there is no evidence for its usage in early Christian liturgy or its existence as an independent work (the "hymn" only shows up here in Philippians). It also troubles him that the passage begins with a relative clause, meaning that we do not have the beginning of the alleged hymn (making reconstruction of stanzas all the more problematic).[a] Gordon Fee adds that the form of the "hymn," however reconstructed, corresponds to no other Greek or Semitic hymn.[b] These scholars think it is more likely that Paul has written this passage using earlier creedal language (including Old Testament language, seen in the use of Is 45:23 in Phil 2:10-11) in a quasi-poetic style, comparable to Romans 11:33-36.[c]

Even if we decided that Paul has incorporated an earlier hymn, it would be fallacious to replace an interpretation of Paul's *use* of this material with an interpretation of the "hymn" in its pre-Pauline, independent form. Paul incorporates it here because it speaks *his* message and serves *his* goals for the hearers in this letter, and it is consonant with his own Christology. A more pressing question, then, has to do with the meaning and function of Philippians 2:6-11 in the context of the letter. Here, scholarship has been largely divided between two positions. The first is the "ethical" reading, according to which Paul uses Jesus as a moral example. Supporters of this view typically point to the parallels between the ethical instructions of Philippians 2:1-4 and the ethos displayed by Christ in Philippians 2:6-11. The second is the "kerygmatic" reading, which regards the passage mainly as proclamation of the Christ event.

Against the ethical reading (the one I adopt), Ralph Martin objects that (1) Paul does not regard the actions of Christ as a pattern for imitation, using himself and his team more as ethical examples, and that (2) Philippians 2:9-11 would have no relevance in an ethical application of the hymn since "there is nothing in the text which hints at the Church's glorification with her Lord."[d] Why speak of Christ's exaltation if this hymn is being used to set forth an ethical example?

---

[a]Bockmuehl, *Epistle to the Philippians,* pp. 116-17.
[b]Fee, *Paul's Letter to the Philippians,* p. 41.
[c]Ibid., pp. 39-46; Bockmuehl, *Epistle to the Philippians,* p. 117.
[d]Ralph P. Martin, *A Hymn of Christ* (Downers Grove, Ill.: InterVarsity Press, 1997), pp. 72, 88.

With regard to the first objection, Paul's own pattern is the product of imitating Christ's pattern (1 Cor 11:1), showing that he does, in fact, regard Christ's actions and attitudes as ethical norms, and he explicitly invokes this in Romans 15:2-3. With regard to the second objection, the glorification of Christ in Philippians 2:9-11 resonates poignantly with Paul's own hope of sharing in the resurrection of Jesus, having been "conformed" to the likeness of Jesus' death (Phil 3:10-11), and Paul's expression of the general hope of the Christians that their mortal bodies will be transformed into the form of Jesus' "body of glory" (Phil 3:20-21). Indeed, the language of form-transform-conform in Philippians 3:10-11, 20-21 directly echoes the use of the *morph-* and *schema-* words in the Christ Hymn, as does the assurance of "all things" being subjected to Christ in Philippians 3:21 (cf. Phil 2:9-11). Philippians 2:9-11, then, fuels assurances throughout Philippians of the honorable consequences of following Christ's example, of taking on his likeness rather than fighting for recognition and self interest now as if there were no overwhelmingly superior future reward.

FOR FURTHER READING

Martin, Ralph P. *A Hymn of Christ: Philippians 2:5-11 in Recent Interpretation and in the Setting of Early Christian Worship.* Downers Grove, Ill.: InterVarsity Press, 1997.

O'Brien, Peter T. *The Epistle to the Philippians,* pp. 186-202. NIGTC. Grand Rapids: Eerdmans, 1991.

Paul offers two further examples of this Christlike behavior in Timothy and Epaphroditus (Phil 2:19-30). In this section Paul has moved more into the mode of the "letter of recommendation," praising Epaphroditus (who is returning to his congregation in Philippi with this letter), commending Timothy (whom Paul hopes to send to the congregation also once the outcome of Paul's trial is known) and requesting that they be received in a manner suited to their service and honor. Each of these fellow workers, however, is commended specifically as a living example of what it looks like to have the mind of Christ. Timothy distinguishes himself by being "genuinely concerned about your interests" (Phil 2:20) in stark contrast with some unnamed, less noble Christian workers who "all look after their own interests, not those of Jesus Christ" (Phil 2:21). Timothy thus embodies the exhortation in Philippians 2:4, offering a living example of that principle in action. The example of Epaphroditus will be even more personal for the congregation since he is one of their own. He put the service of the congregation and of Paul, the "work of Christ," above his own health and welfare, with the result that he drew near "to the point of death" (*mechri thanatou,* Phil 2:30, a deliberate echo of Phil 2:8). It is people like Epaphroditus who embody the mind of Christ that are to be held in honor (Phil 2:29), not those who insist on recognition or having matters go their way. In the church, unlike the world, precedence and esteem cannot come because individuals have sought and fought for such recognition, but only because they have, ironically, put others first out of a sincere love.

Since Paul frequently exhorts his converts to learn the Christian way of life by imitating him (e.g., 1 Cor 11:1; Phil 3:17)—a strategy very much in keeping with Greco-Roman philosophers who taught not only by words but by example—it is not surprising that he also reflects at several points on how his example, in particular, can guide the Philippian Christians into a deeper harmony and solidarity with one another. In the midst of sharing news of his own circumstances, Paul pauses to reflect on the two kinds of Christian workers active in his locale during his detention—those who are sincerely disposed and those who are driven to partisanship by selfish ambition and envy (Phil 1:15-18). Paul's response to both kinds is the same. As long as Christ is proclaimed and the interests of Christ are advanced, Paul rejoices! Paul is not concerned that other teachers might gain a wider following or become more celebrated within the Christian community. His friends in Philippi, particularly those at the center of rivalry, are challenged to act in their own affairs as Paul does in his, rising above the petty concerns of "coming out on top" in competition between people and focusing wholly on what advances Christ's cause.

Paul turns once again, and more fully, to his personal example in Philippians 3:2-21.[31] The "dogs," "evil workers" and "mutilation" (Phil 3:2), no doubt a reference to the Judaizing movement that Paul had staunchly opposed from its inception, are introduced as a foil to Paul's example. They exhibit the path he did *not* choose. They cling to their fleshly credentials and claims to ethnic privilege rather than placing their confidence before God in Christ and Christ alone (Phil 3:3). Paul's example, on the other hand, conforms

quite closely to the pattern of Christ in Philippians 2:6-11.[32]

Like Christ, Paul has serious claims to recognition and preeminence in the estimation of his fellow Jews (Phil 3:5-6). Rather than exploit these credentials, he "emptied himself" of them, throwing them all away because attaining Jesus and the life Jesus confers are of immensely greater value than the name he was making for himself prior to encountering Jesus (Phil 3:7-8). Like Christ, then, he preferred the reward of obedience to clinging to his rights.

For Paul, as for all the believers (Phil 2:1-11), gaining Christ and the prize of a resurrected life entails "becoming conformed (*symmorphizomenos*) to the likeness of Christ's death" (Phil 3:10). Again Paul echoes the Christ hymn, where the root meaning "form" (*morph-*) featured prominently as Christ moved from "the form of God" to "the form of a slave" (Phil 2:6-7). Paul is conformed to Christ's death not only through the sufferings he endures out of loyalty and obedience to Jesus (as do the Philippians; see Phil 1:27-30) but also as he has relinquished his claims to preeminence in the eyes of humans and taken on the "form of a slave" (notably, the term he uses to introduce himself and Timothy in this letter rather than the title of "apostle"; Phil 1:1)[33] to those he seeks to convert and nurture.

Philippians 3:10-11 helps to explain the nature of the "righteousness . . . that comes through faith in Christ," the "righteousness from God based on faith" (Phil 3:9). This righteousness means conformity with the

---

[31]See, further, David A. deSilva, "No Confidence in the Flesh: The Meaning and Function of Phil 3:2-21," *Trinity Journal* 15NS (1994): 27-54.

[32]See, further, Garland, "Composition and Unity," pp. 157-59; William S. Kurz, "Kenotic Imitation of Paul and of Christ in Philippians 2 and 3," in *Discipleship in the New Testament,* ed. Fernando Segovia (Philadelphia: Fortress, 1985), pp. 103-26.

[33]Paul introduces himself (or, in the case of deutero-Pauline authorship, is presented) as an apostle in 1 Cor 1:1; 2 Cor 1:1; Gal 1:1; Eph 1:1; Col 1:1; 1 Tim 1:1; 2 Tim 1:1; with no title in 1 Thess 1:1; 2 Thess 1:1; as a "prisoner" in Philem 1; and as a "slave and apostle" in Rom 1:1; Tit 1:1.

mind of Christ as displayed in his death, the process of dying with Christ that we may live to God (and thus attain to the life of the resurrection). It is another indicator that justification is not merely a matter of being treated as if we were righteous, but that justification entails becoming righteous as Christ's character, mind and heart take shape in our lives. This righteousness comes through trust/faith since it involves trusting the Spirit, trusting the reality of God's promises, trusting that Jesus is God's revelation of righteousness, and trusting that the investment of our lives in seeking conformity with the mind of Christ will indeed result in benefit for eternity (rather than proving the loser both in this world and the next, 1 Cor 15:19, 32). What Paul "left behind" (Phil 3:4-8) shows just how great an investment—and how great an act of trust—that this entails.

Paul goes on to provide his friends with a model of "Christian maturity" (Phil 3:15), beginning with the analogy of the footrace, in which the runner must keep his or her focus on the next step, straining ever forward toward the finish line, with his or her heart set on the prize to be enjoyed beyond the finish line. Looking back at how far I have traveled, taking pride in having made it halfway or boasting that I am running better than other racers—these would all be imprudent and meaningless distractions. As Paul sits in prison near the end of his course, he puts behind him all of his astounding accomplishments in the service of Christ.

The apostle had seen in Corinth the dangers of using "spiritual" progress, attachment to particular Christian teachers, and service as claims to enjoying privileged status over other Christians in the community. The result was a church deeply divided along several different lines. Perhaps he perceives that "looking back" has contributed to the rift between Syntyche and Euodia. Each one had served the church in an exemplary fashion, and in light of her heavy investment in and sacrifice for the church, each could advance an impressive claim to the right to have a say in where the church should go from there. In setting forward his own mind, Paul provides a potent remedy for this kind of competitive, self-focused and ultimately divisive thinking. All the focus must be on Christ (Phil 3:8-11) and on the goal of the race, which is not winning petty power struggles on earth but rather being invited into the commonwealth of God in heaven (Phil 3:20). Moreover, God's own favor is behind all progress a believer makes from beginning to end (Phil 1:6; 2:12-13; 3:12). The believers' service and accomplishments must all, therefore, tend toward recognition of Jesus' faithfulness toward the church, not the status or power of any particular Christian.

Paul therefore urges the believers to imitate him and all who walk as he does (Phil 3:17), and to avoid the pattern of those who live as enemies of the cross—not because they do not claim its benefits but because they refuse its claim on their lives, because they work to promote their own glory and indulge their own pleasures rather than promote God's glory and serve his good pleasure.

PERSEVERING IN THE FACE OF OPPOSITION

Thus far our focus has been primarily on Paul's concern with the ripples disrupting the unity of the believers in Philippi. We have also seen, however, that he wants to empower them to persevere in their commitment to Jesus in the face of the disapproval and opposition of their non-Christian, pro-Roman neighbors. Of course, resolving internal conflicts and restoring the other-centered solidarity of the church is a significant contribution to this end. Paul adds several other considerations, however, to assist the Philippians in their contest.

Paul transforms suffering for the sake of

the Name into a triumphant experience rather than one of victimization or marginalization. The opposition of their neighbors allows the believers to display the confidence and boldness that are tokens of their own deliverance, and that serve as a witness to the fate of unbelievers. But Paul does not only seek to empower his friends in the face of hardship; he claims that suffering hostility for the sake of Christ is actually an example of God's "gracing" or "favoring" the Christians (*echaristhe,* Phil 1:29). Suffering was, however, commonly regarded as a sign of divine *dis*favor. What then could substantiate such a seemingly absurd claim? Here, Christ's role as paradigm (Phil 2:5-11) moves deeper into a mystical participation in Christ's suffering and death. Paul himself embraces suffering for the gospel, knowing that "sharing in Christ's sufferings" and "being conformed to the pattern of his death" are actually the path to "attaining the resurrection from the dead" and experiencing "the power of his resurrection" (Phil 3:10-11). Similarly, the believers, though their bodies are subjected to "humiliation" now, have been given the assurance of being "morphed into the body of Christ's glory" (Phil 3:21) at his return.

Because of his assurance that suffering for Christ will lead to glory with Christ, Paul, whose words have a ring of authenticity precisely because he is detained and facing a capital charge, approaches his own trials with confidence. He cannot be certain of release from trial or acquittal, nor does he seem to seek this in particular. Since his detention has served to advance God's purposes, Paul is content with enduring the privations of imprisonment. The only temporal assurance he requires is that Christ will be honored in him whether he continues living or is executed (Phil 1:19-20). Since this is all that matters to him, and since he knows that his death would mean enjoyment of eternal honors in God's court, he does not regard these hardships as a disgrace to him. His single-hearted focus on serving God's interests prevents him from becoming demoralized, and he hopes his friends in Philippi will experience the same in their own contest. Indeed, their shared experience of suffering for their faith serves to deepen the friendship and mutual connectedness of Paul and the Philippians: their sacrifices and offerings to God continue to complement one another's service and joy (Phil 2:16-17).

Finally, Paul knows that God does not leave God's faithful ones to face opposition alone. Paul testifies to the way that Christ has strengthened him and given him "sufficiency" in his many encounters with hardship, the four-year detention being the most trying of them all (Phil 4:11-13). Because of his own experience of Christ's supply, he can confidently assure his friends that "the Lord is near" to them in their trials (for Paul, both in terms of his proximity in spirit and the proximity of his return). They have no need to give place to anxiety, for God is ever approachable in prayer, and will certainly supply his peace to their hearts and sustain them as they stay their course (Phil 4:4-7).

PHILIPPIANS AND MINISTRY FORMATION

Praying for the congregation. When we read the opening of Philippians, and indeed almost all the Pauline letters, we cannot fail to notice that Paul presents himself (or, in the case of deutero-Pauline letters, is remembered) as constantly and faithfully remembering his congregations and his coworkers in prayer.[a] In several cases we catch a glimpse of the things Paul passionately sought from God for his congregations.[b] He prayed that his charges would overflow in love toward one another, grow in wisdom and discernment of what is best in God's sight, and ever augment the harvest of righteousness that would bring them honor on the last day (Phil 1:9-11). In Ephesians Paul is depicted as praying that the great hope and endless resources the believers have in God would become a reality for them, empowering their labor for the kingdom (Eph 1:17-19). In both Colossians and 2 Thessalonians he prays that God would lead them to live worthily of God and of God's kingdom (Col 1:9-10; 2 Thess 1:11-12).

The frequency, passion and mere fact of Paul's praying for his congregations impresses on us the importance of following his example in our own ministries, whatever form they take. As we hold up those whom we serve in prayer, seeking nothing less than the full transformation of their lives and the full empowerment for discipleship God has for them, we forge a deeper and more constant connection between ourselves, our charges and our partners in ministry. Our love and desires for them come to be shaped more and more by God's heart for them. Like Paul, we will also find ourselves refreshed and encouraged as we respond to God in gratitude for the good that God is bringing into being in the midst of those whom we serve.

Quarrels in the church. Philippians is clearly concerned with the reconciliation of two prominent leaders in the congregation, Euodia and Syntyche, who would no doubt have seen themselves in Paul's exhortations long before he mentioned them by name. The reader is probably familiar from firsthand experience, however, with the damage done when two leading figures in a congregation get into a disagreement about some issue that turns personal, quickly becoming an issue of ego and wounded pride compounded with a sense that one's tireless efforts for the church are unappreciated and unreciprocated. Such a situation is well worth the intervention of a timely word.

We have already seen how Philippians offers a wealth of resources to the Christian leader who encounters such a quarrel in a congregation. Some other aspects of Paul's pastoral strategy, however, should not go unnoticed. First, he enlists an anonymous "loyal companion" (Phil 4:3)—indeed, many in the congregation might reasonably see themselves "intended" here—to help steer Syntyche and Euodia toward reconciliation. Other believers are challenged not to take sides in a conflict

---

[a]Rom 1:9; 1 Cor 1:4-7; Eph 1:16; Phil 1:3-4; Col 1:3-5; 1 Thess 1:2-3; 2:13; 2 Thess 1:3; 2:13; 2 Tim 1:3; Philem 4.

[b]We can find windows into the topics of Paul's prayer life prior to writing the letter (not counting prayers and wishes included in the letter) in Eph 1:17-19; Phil 1:9-11; Col 1:9-10; 2 Thess 1:11-12; Philem 6.

between two of their fellow Christians but to guide them toward reconciliation and harmony. Second, Paul speaks of each woman as someone who has struggled alongside Paul for the sake of the gospel, and as someone whose name is inscribed in the book of life (Phil 4:3). Paul thus reminds Euodia of Syntyche's worth and Syntyche of Euodia's worth. Neither one of them should be competing against the other or involved in a such a dispute. They are partners in the advancement of the gospel and in eternity, and they need to regard one another in that light.

Both proactively and in direct intervention, Christian leaders must work to shape the mind of Christ in those they serve, beginning with themselves as they follow Paul's example in Philippians 1:15-18. When we look at other clergy and lay leaders within the congregation and parachurch groups, do we see rivals or partners? How well do we model putting the interest of others and God above our own? The mind of Christ must be formed in us in our day-to-day interactions with fellow believers—in the often trying, wearing circumstances of committee meetings, choir rehearsals, administrative hassles, seminars and lecture halls. God gives us ample opportunities here to exercise ourselves in growing toward Paul's ideal (Phil 2:3-4).

Recovering unity in the bond of love. The harmony and unity Paul seeks in the face-to-face life of one local church cannot be limited to the boundaries of a congregation or even a denomination. The vision for the church in Philippians challenges us to seek harmony and build a spirit of unity and cooperation throughout the global Christian family. The dissension, divisiveness and disrespect that have characterized denominationalism have hindered our witness to the world like no other single sin. Many Christians live as if Paul's exhortation to "be of the same mind" means "if you are willing to think and to worship as I do, then we can have fellowship and experience God together."

Paul, however, predicates Christian unity on what God has richly supplied to all who call on the name of Christ. Since we have received encouragement from Christ, since we have shared in the one Spirit of God, we are called to live in full accord with one another, being of one mind (Phil 2:1-4). On far more than "seventy times seven" occasions, disagreements and disputes over small matters of doctrine, practice or polity have violated the unity of the body. Paul keeps challenging us to put mutual love, peace and solidarity above our confidence in our ability to know all the answers and our lack of confidence in our Christian neighbor's ability to know the same. Indeed, no Christian has *all* the facts, as Paul plainly says in 1 Corinthians 13:12-13, a wonderful bit of medicine for a conceited race. Therefore our denominational disagreements are not of ultimate value.[c] Our basis for unity—our common experience of God through the Spirit—is

---

[c]Frank Thielman is correct to warn that unity not to be purchased at the expense of the essential contours of the gospel (*Philippians,* NIVAC [Grand Rapids: Zondervan, 1995], p. 25). Paul, after all, maintained the boundaries between genuine Christians and the Christian Judaizers lambasted in Philippians 3:2-5 or the "enemies of the cross of Christ" in Philippians 3:18-19. However, I would venture that the "essential contours of the gospel" are at risk in a very small percentage of denominational splits or sectarian births.

of far greater importance than our disagreement on finer points of theology, liturgical practice and governance. Our unity is founded on God's acts on our behalf, but our disharmony and divisions on our own minds and hearts. To place greater importance on the latter is an act of pride and a gross affront to God.

Joy in the Lord. We cannot leave the study of Philippians without reflecting on the attitude of "joy" that so completely pervades it. In the midst of suffering Paul has found that the joy he has in the Lord keeps him centered and enables him to stay the course, and so he commends this to his friends suffering opposition as well (Phil 1:18; 2:17-18; 3:1; 4:4). Rejoicing in the Lord is precisely what Paul does when he abandons his confidence in the flesh and the self-centered, competitive, divisive way of life that it entails, and he seeks life as God's gift in Christ. Abandoning himself, he focuses completely on Christ and the course God has laid out before him. Rejoicing in God focuses Paul on God and what God is doing, and attunes Paul to the character and will of God. He encourages all his friends in Philippi to do the same. If they are individually attuned to God through delighting in God, they are much more likely to stay in tune with each other and to live and serve together in the harmony of peace. Delight does not coexist in the heart with envy or rivalry, and delight *in God* does not coexist in the heart with selfish ambition or conceit. It simply leaves no room for these baser manifestations. Paul offers here perhaps one of his wisest prescriptions for centering our hearts and ordering our common life—rejoice in the Lord always!

For Further Reading

Bockmuehl, Markus. *The Epistle to the Philippians.* BNTC. Peabody, Mass.: Hendrickson, 1998.

Craddock, Fred. *Philippians.* Interpretation. Atlanta: John Knox Press, 1985.

Fee, Gordon D. *Philippians.* NICNT. Grand Rapids: Eerdmans, 1995.

Hawthorne, Gerald F. *Philippians.* WBC 43. Dallas: Word, 1983.

Martin, Ralph P. *A Hymn of Christ: Philippians 2:5-11 in Recent Interpretation and in the Setting of Early Christian Worship.* Downers Grove, Ill.: InterVarsity Press, 1997.

O'Brien, Peter T. *The Epistle to the Philippians.* NIGTC. Grand Rapids: Eerdmans, 1991.

Osiek, Carolyn. *Philippians, Philemon.* ANTC. Nashville: Abingdon, 2000.

Silva, Moises. *Philippians.* BECNT. Grand Rapids: Baker, 1992.

Thielman, Frank. *Philippians.* NIVAC. Grand Rapids: Zondervan, 1995.

Witherington, Ben, III. *Friendship and Finances at Philippi.* Valley Forge, Penn.: Trinity Press International, 1995.

17

THE EPISTLE TO PHILEMON

The Slave Is Our Brother

Philemon, the shortest and most personal of Paul's letters, might easily be overlooked in a survey of the New Testament. This letter is a valuable window into the life of an individual house church, into Paul's pastoral finesse and into the transformation of real life human relationships that coming to faith must effect. Philemon thus demands our full attention. As Paul brings an alienated slave and master together as brothers both "in the Lord" and "in the flesh," he provides a profound lesson in the real difference the gospel could make in the life of one person, and in the way people who have received God's favor are to extend that favor to one another.

HISTORICAL SETTING AND PASTORAL PURPOSE: THE STORY BEHIND PHILEMON

Paul's situation. Paul writes Philemon from prison. Twice he emphasizes his status as prisoner (Philem 1, 9), and once he refers to a fellow prisoner, Epaphras (Philem 23). As with his other Prison Epistles, there is considerable debate concerning which imprisonment Paul suffers as he writes Philemon. If this is a reference to his house arrest in Rome (which would place the letter between 61 and 63 C.E.), it would have meant a very long and expensive journey for Onesimus. This would

also render Paul's instructions to prepare a guest room rather odd. While it would certainly make sense for Paul to plan to visit his congregations to the East after his release from four years in various prisons and awaiting various trials, Philemon's house in Asia Minor would not be the logical first choice! Paul had been imprisoned in Caesarea prior to his journey to Rome (58-60 C.E.), but while this is closer to Asia Minor it is still not the preferred choice.[1]

Once again, an imprisonment in Ephesus emerges as a likely situation in the life of the apostle. This would certainly be the most appropriate location for the kinds of movement reflected in Philemon.[2] Acts is silent about such an imprisonment, but Acts, like all history, is selective in the story it tells. Paul refers to some ordeal in Ephesus (see 1 Cor 15:32; 2 Cor 1:8-9) and speaks of suffering imprisonments in the plural (even before his Caesarean and Roman imprisonments) in 2 Corinthians 6:5; 11:23. A run-in with the authorities in Ephesus resulting in a brief imprisonment is therefore a plausible scenario.

Philemon and his household. There are close correspondences between the characters named in Philemon and Colossians. Onesimus, the main subject of Philemon, and Tychichus are depicted as traveling back to Colossae

---

[1]Joseph A. Fitzmyer, *The Letter to Philemon* (New York: Doubleday, 2000), p. 10.
[2]Fitzmyer adds that the Marcionite prologue to Colossians already supposes an Ephesian imprisonment, perhaps bearing an early witness to knowledge of such an experience (*Philemon*, p. 10).

from Paul's place of imprisonment (Col 4:7-9). Archippus is mentioned in the closing greetings of Colossians (Col 4:17; Philem 2). The same circle of coworkers, with minor variations, surround Paul in both letters (Epaphras, Mark, Aristarchus, Demas and Luke; Col 4:10-14; Philem 23-24).[3] It is almost certain, therefore, that Philemon lived in Colossae and that his house church was part of the network of house churches in the three neighboring cities of Colossae, Laodicea and Hierapolis.[4]

Paul had not evangelized these cities himself (he was unknown by face to them; Col 2:1), and its seems likely that this was the sphere of Epaphras's evangelistic ministry (Col 4:12-13). Paul had personally converted Philemon, however, to whom he could say "you owe me your very self" (Philem 19) and from whom Paul could assume a great debt of gratitude and obligation (Philem 13). Paul must have encountered Philemon outside of Colossae, most likely during his lengthy stay in Ephesus. Paul speaks very warmly of their relationship as one of partnership, or friendship (Philem 17), and of Philemon as "beloved" and as a "colaborer" (Philem 1). Apphia and Archippus may be members of Philemon's family,[5] converted either by Paul or by Philemon on his return. In any case, Paul appears to have personal knowledge of them as well.

Philemon seems to be a private letter of mediation between two individuals on behalf of a third rather than an impassioned exposition of the gospel, refutation of false teachers or series of broad, ethical instructions. There are ample parallels to this situation in the private correspondence of other individuals, such as Pliny the Younger. By addressing not only Philemon but also Apphia, Archippus and the assembly of believers that meet in Philemon's house (Philem 2), however, Paul turns what appears to be a private matter into a household matter in the broader sense of the Christian family. The local community of faith will become a witness to Paul's request and thus also to Philemon's response. Philemon cannot act privately in the matter of Onesimus, who now is a part of the larger household of God and not merely Philemon's household.

Onesimus's story. Onesimus was a slave, a "living tool" (Aristotle *Pol.* 1.4 1253b31), in the household of Philemon. We do not have any hard facts about Onesimus's motives for leaving Philemon. Paul admits that Onesimus was useless to Philemon as a slave (Philem 11), but beyond that we have only ambiguous hints. Many have assumed that Onesimus stole from his master and then ran away to avoid punishment, but this suggestion rests on the slender evidence of verse 18 and on the common stereotype of the "crafty slave" in Greek and Roman comedies who steals from the master and eventually buys his freedom with his master's own money, or runs away with his loot before facing the consequences.[6]

---

[3]Luke Timothy Johnson understands these all to be in prison with Paul (*The Writings of the New Testament,* 2nd ed. [Minneapolis: Fortress, 1996], p. 350), but I would agree with Fitzmyer that this is not required by the text (*Philemon,* p. 125). Indeed, each letter specifies only one "fellow prisoner" (Aristarchus in Col 4:10; Epaphras in Philem 23), and these need not have been prisoners simultaneously.

[4]This does not depend on Pauline authorship of Colossians: even if Colossians is pseudonymous, the similarities betray the awareness on the part of the unknown author of Colossians of the connections between Philemon and that church. John Knox proposed that Philemon was the bishop of Laodicea, with the result that this letter is the lost "Letter to the Laodiceans" mentioned in Colossians 4:16 (*Philemon Among the Letters of Paul,* rev. ed. [Nashville: Abingdon, 1959]), but his convoluted reconstruction of the situation (according to which Archippus is really Onesimus's master and cannot be addressed directly by Paul) has not won a following.

[5]Arthur G. Patzia mentions this as an indemonstrable possibility ("Philemon, Letter to," in *Dictionary of Paul and His Letters,* ed. G. F. Hawthorne and R. P. Martin [Downers Grove, Ill.: InterVarsity Press, 1993], p. 703).

[6]This critique is rightly posed by A. D. Callahan, "Paul's Epistle to Philemon: Toward an Alternative *Argumentum,*" HTR 86 (1993): 361.

Other scenarios would be equally possible. For example, Onesimus simply may have been deeply discontented with the life of the slave. Onesimus might have been a young man, perhaps even a teenager, a person who had not yet resigned himself to the lot to which he was likely born. Perhaps the meaninglessness of his duties gnaws away at him. Perhaps he is drawn to some particular craft, some art form, even to philosophy, and wants Philemon to permit him to pursue that life while remaining Philemon's slave. Epictetus, for example, made a very bad slave but a magnificent philosopher, and his master finally gave him leave to study with Musonius Rufus, a Stoic, and eventually his freedom to pursue the life of philosophy. Or perhaps in the course of his duties (or even in moment of rebelliousness) he crossed his master in some serious way, or a number of less significant ways, and feared the repercussions. We could speculate endlessly about the motives, but the act is clear enough: Onesimus left home without Philemon's consent.

The most common understanding of Onesimus is that he is a runaway slave, a *fugitivus,* which put him in great peril. If caught, a runaway slave could be punished by his or her master with severe beatings or even execution. Such a person would often go "underground" in a large city or a distant country, often existing through criminal activity. Some runaway slaves would seek asylum at a temple or statue of the emperor, not in the hope of freedom but in order to be sold by the priests to a better master. According to this model, Paul has persuaded the *fugitivus* to return to his master, trusting Paul's influence with Philemon to procure reconciliation and save him from the consequences of his action.

As we come to understand more about how patronage systems work in the ancient world, however, a different picture comes into focus. Slaves who were experiencing difficulty in their masters' homes were known to leave the master in search of one of the master's "friends," who would be sought out as an advocate to plead the slave's case. The master's friend would act as a broker or mediator between slave and master, in the hope of the slave's returning to a more endurable situation. Such a slave was not legally considered a fugitive, but remained, in effect, within the master's household by fleeing to a friend of the master—making him disobedient, perhaps, but not a runaway.[7] Onesimus still exposed himself to grave danger by his departure from Philemon's house—he could be punished as a fugitive at any point in his journey to Paul. (How could he prove that his intent was to contact a friend of the master?) Only a fragile letter from Paul protected him on his return.[8]

Once Onesimus encounters Paul, he finds not only an advocate but a spiritual father. Paul brings Onesimus to the faith—surprisingly something that Philemon did not achieve, perhaps did not even try to achieve. Now Paul can speak on behalf of Onesimus, not only as a suppliant in need of mediation but as a child in the Lord, a brother in the Lord toward whom Philemon must now embody a response worthy of Christian brotherhood. Moreover, this conversion to Christ has marked a transformation in Onesimus's own life. Paul says that Onesimus was formerly useless to Philemon, but now, after his conversion, he has become profitable both to Philemon and to Paul (Philem 11).

Onesimus begins the story discontented,

---

[7]Legal judgments to this effect are attributed to Proculus, a first-century-C.E. jurist, in Justinian's *Digest* (21.1.17.4), and to Paulus, a second century jurist (*Digest* 21.1.43.1). See P. Lampe, "Keine 'Sklavenflucht' des Onesimus," *ZNW* 76 (1985): 135-37; Fitzmyer, *Philemon,* p. 20.

[8]Markus Barth and Helmut Blanke, *The Letter to Philemon,* ECC (Grand Rapids: Eerdmans, 2000), p. 228.

looking for some improvement in his life. He does not, therefore, function well where he is. He cannot make himself useful to Philemon, because, in short, it is not where God has called him to be. After his conversion and tutelage in the faith in the company of Paul, Onesimus finds his vocation. Whatever he may have sought by going to Paul, he now wants to remain with Paul to learn more of the way of Christ and to assist Paul in his work.[9] Having found himself in God, Onesimus can offer himself in service now, and be profitable to Paul (an old man needing assistance, even if he is only in his mid-fifties) in a way he could never have been profitable to Philemon. He can therefore be profitable to Philemon now as the expression of Philemon's support for Paul's ministry.

Paul's purposes in writing. Paul writes this brief letter first to move the relationship between Philemon and Onesimus to a new level, one in which they will relate to each other no longer as master and slave but as brothers in the Lord. This requires a great step of obedience and magnanimity on Philemon's part, who is being asked to give away his rights by the world's standards so that he can live out what is right in the new family God is engendering. Second, Paul is asking for Onesimus's release. He never uses the word *manumission,* but Paul's negation of the slave-master model of relating (Philem 15-16), replacing this with the familial and egalitarian language of siblings, strongly pushes in this direction. Onesimus would remain Philemon's "freedman" in the eyes of the law, and thus remain a part of his household, a loyal client for life, but he would also be free now to obey the leading of his new Master, Jesus. Finally, Paul asks for a simpler gift—that of hospitality, as he anticipates his release from his current incarceration (Philem 22).

PAUL'S PASTORAL STRATEGY IN PHILEMON

Paul's pastoral strategy is anchored in the friendship he has with Philemon. "Friendship" here is a form of patron-client relationship, a relationship that involves the exchange of favors in ongoing reciprocity. Genuine friendship is usually found between people of equal or like social status (even though patrons of superior status would still refer to their clients as friends out of sensitivity toward their feelings). To the eyes of the unbeliever, Paul and Philemon might not appear to be candidates for such an equal relationship. Paul is a social inferior. He lacks property, works with his hands at a craft and is far removed from his native city, where he had status in a local community (though his Roman citizenship does give him a universal claim to a recognizable legal status). Philemon, on the other hand, is a householder of sufficient means that he can host a local assembly of believers (meaning that his house must have been well above average) and engage in charitable endeavors toward Christians in need, and probably Paul in particular. This means that Philemon, unlike the majority of people, had a good deal of money to spare. He enjoys the reputation of being a generous person, having "refreshed the hearts of the saints," and is no doubt regarded as the patron of the assembly that meets in his house.

Paul, however, claims to be Philemon's patron on the basis of bringing Philemon the message of salvation. Completely contrary to appearances it is Philemon who is perpetually indebted to Paul for connecting him to the living Christ and the promises of God, and not Paul who is in some sense the inferior partner in this friendship. When Paul asks for a "bene-

---

[9] I am assuming that this request originated with Onesimus himself, even though Paul expresses it as his own request of Philemon (v. 13). Otherwise, Paul would be seeking, in effect, to borrow Onesimus, asking Philemon to condemn Onesimus to another form of servitude.

Slavery in the Greco-Roman World

The Greco-Roman slave population is estimated at about one-in-three to one-in-four people. A huge portion of the population, therefore, would have been slaves. Unlike Western slavery in the seventeenth through the nineteenth centuries C.E., slavery in the ancient world was based not on a presumption of ethnic inferiority but on the practicalities of conquest, criminal proceedings, birth into a slave family or defaulting on debts.

The slave was considered "living property" (Aristotle *Pol.* 1.4 1253b31), entirely under the authority and power of the master/owner. Many philosophers and moralists advocated the ethical treatment of slaves, advising the benefits of preserving one's own property (Aristotle *Pol.* 1.6 1255b9-13) or lauding the master who shows anxious care for the welfare of his or her dependents (Philo *Decalogue* 167; Ecclus, *On Justice* 78, 10-11). Nevertheless, the conditions of the slave were wholly dependent on the goodness, or lack thereof, of the master. The treatment of slaves could be grossly exploitative, and the punishment of slaves frightfully harsh indeed. Slaves might be trained for specialized duties in the household, in the management of businesses, even in the administration of provinces (in the case of slaves in the emperor's household). Slaves would be found maintaining the grounds of temples and other public buildings, working the fields of the rich landholders or in the most abject of conditions, working in the galleys or the mines.

The family life of the slave was precarious and completely under the master's control. The slave was completely cut off from his or her ancestral lineage, alienated from the sense of identity that defined all free persons (Patterson, *Slavery and Social Death,* p. 5; Byron, *Slavery Metaphors,* pp. 115-22). Slaves had no legal standing and therefore contracted no legal marriages (though slaves would "marry" each other and often remain life-long companions). Xenophon (*Oeconomicus* 9.5) shows a certain ambiguity about slaves and families: the loyal slave is rendered more stable if he has a family, but the rogue is only made worse. Xenophon is clear on one point, however: "breeding" is to happen only with the master's consent. The children born to a male slave were the property of that slave's master. Most often, those children would remain a part of the master's estate, to be passed on to the master's heirs. It was always a possibility, however, that a slave would suffer seeing his family broken up if the master decided to give away or sell any of them.

Whether employed as a foreman or field hand, a scribe or scrubber, this lack of autonomy made slavery an evil for those unfortunate enough to be born or fall into it. Slaves of private individuals, however, did have the hope of manumission. Theoretically, a slave could purchase his or her own freedom from money squirreled away in the course of doing business on the master's behalf; more often they were freed by the master in his or her will as a gift for decades of faithful service and as a sign of a generous spirit. Freedmen, however, were expected to remain loyal to the house of their master for the remainder of their lives, and remained, in some sense, still a servant of the master's house.

For Further Reading

Bartchy, S. Scott. *First-Century Slavery and 1 Corinthians 7:21.* SBLDS 11. Missoula, Mont.: Scholars Press, 1973.

Barth, Markus, and Helmut Blanke. *The Letter to Philemon,* pp. 3-103. ECC. Grand Rapids: Eerdmans, 2000.

Bradley, K. R. *Slavery and Society at Rome.* Cambridge: Cambridge University Press, 1994.

Byron, John. *Slavery Metaphors in Early Judaism and Pauline Christianity.* WUNT 2/162. Tübingen: Mohr Siebeck, 2003.

Combes, I. A. H. *The Metaphor of Slavery in the Writings of the Early Church.* JSNTSS 156. Sheffield, U.K.: Sheffield Academic Press, 1998.

Finley, Moses I., ed. *Classical Slavery.* London: Frank Cass, 1987.

Garnsey, Peter. *Ideas of Slavery from Aristotle to Augustine.* Cambridge: Cambridge University Press, 1996.

Glancy, Jennifer A. *Slaves in Early Christianity.* Oxford: Oxford University Press, 2002.

Harill, James Albert. *The Manumission of Slaves in Early Christianity.* Tübingen: J. C. B. Mohr, 1995.

Martin, Dale B. *Slavery as Salvation: The Metaphor of Slavery in Pauline Christianity.* New Haven, Conn.: Yale University Press, 1990.

Patterson, Orlando. *Slavery as Social Death: A Comparative Study.* Cambridge, Mass.: Harvard University Press, 1982.

Westermann, William L. *The Slave System of Greek and Roman Antiquity.* Philadelphia: American Philosophy Society, 1955.

---

fit" from Philemon, therefore, he does so as the partner in the stronger, superior position, making it clear that Philemon cannot refuse Paul and still act justly and faithfully in their reciprocal relationship. Paul gently reminds Philemon of the scope of his indebtedness to Paul toward the end of the letter ("*not to mention that* you owe me your own self," Philem 19), asking openly for a material benefit as a timely response to and return for this spiritual benefit (Philem 20). Though the gift is invisible, it is nonetheless real and even superior to gifts that can be seen. (This same idea of reciprocity—material benefits being shared with those who bestow spiritual benefits—also appears in Romans 15:25-27.)

Paul claims authority to command Philemon's obedience as Paul's client, a social inferior whose response of service may be commanded on the basis of Paul's benefaction of salvation (Philem 8, 14). He prefers, however, to entreat him as a friend, coworker and partner, and only actually makes his request on that basis, hoping now to benefit from Philemon's continued generosity toward the saints, which has earned him much honor in the community (Philem 4-7). In so doing he provides an example to Philemon, who is also being asked to set aside his rights and powers as a slaveholder. Just as Paul refuses to use the power that (he believes) belongs to him by virtue of his senior relationship, offering Philemon freedom to act on his own initiative, so Philemon is being asked to refuse to use his power as slaveholder over Onesimus, offering Onesimus the freedom to act on his own initiative in response to the call of God on his life. This is but one of the many practical ways that the mind of Christ, as defined in Philippians 2:3-11, is seen to work itself out in the Pauline churches.

The gift Paul seeks, however, is only partially for himself. Paul writes this letter on behalf of a third party, Onesimus, placing himself in the well-established role of the broker or mediator in this letter. He is trying to gain a benefit from his friend, Philemon, for his new client, Onesimus. Indeed, Onesimus became Paul's client (or "friend") the same way Philemon did, namely, through receiving the gospel from Paul. Paul expresses this relationship in the affectionate terms of father and child. Paul's mediation means that Philemon is not to treat Onesimus as (Philemon may believe) Onesimus deserves but as his friend, Paul, deserves.

Verse 18, which speaks in the most general terms of whatever injury or loss Philemon might have sustained as a result either of Onesimus's poor service in the household, the trouble caused by his furtive departure from the household, or perhaps the theft of a small sum of money that might have been necessary for Onesimus's journey to see Paul,[10] may be best understood against this background. Paul interposes himself and the enormous debt he considers Philemon to owe him for his conversion between Philemon and whatever trouble Onesimus might have caused him prior to this letter; this removes any obstacles to reconciliation between

Philemon and Onesimus. Any injury goes on Paul's account, which remains perpetually in the black, and Philemon is to show his friendship to Paul by welcoming Onesimus favorably, as if he were welcoming Paul himself (Philem 12, 17).

This kind of mediation was common in the Greco-Roman world.[11] Pliny's letters to the emperor Trajan, for instance, offer many examples. In one letter (*Ep.* 10.4), Pliny seeks from Trajan the grant of a senatorial office for Voconius Romanus. Pliny approaches Trajan clearly as a client addressing his patron and proceeds to ask a favor for Voconius. Pliny offers his character as a guarantee of Voconius's character, and Trajan's assessment of the secondhand client is inseparable from his assessment of Pliny. Indeed, Trajan's favorable judgment of Pliny, not Voconius, will be the basis for Trajan's granting of this favor.[12]

Addressing this seemingly personal matter to the attention not only of Philemon but to several other members of the household and to the whole group of Christians meeting in Philemon's house also serves Paul's goals rather strategically. Paul makes the assembly a witness to how Philemon will respond—a court of reputation that will decide anew about Philemon's reputation for generosity, his faithfulness toward his friend Paul (who makes strong claims on Philemon's gratitude), and his faithfulness in the new kinship relations of the Christian family that Onesimus has now joined. What will Philemon's standing in the church be if he refuses this request? Paul's afterthought, requesting a guest room in Philemon's house, also indicates to Philemon

---

[10]The latter is suggested by P. T. O'Brien, *Colossians, Philemon*, WBC (Waco, Tex.: Word, 1982), pp. 299-300.

[11]It is still implicit, although somewhat weakened, in our practice of writing letters of recommendation.

[12]These dynamics of mediation in the patron-client exchange have an obvious corollary in the church's Christology and soteriology, wherein God, the Patron, regards Christ's clients (i.e., the Christians) not as they merit (from the vantage point of their offense against God) but according to the merit of Christ (from the vantage point of his obedience to God). This is another piece of evidence for the formative influence of ancient practices of patronage on the formulation of the gospel (the role of Christ as mediator; the meaning of *grace*) and its continued explication over the first four centuries.

that Paul intends to visit whenever he is freed from prison. Paul will come himself to find out the effect of his letter, whether or not Philemon has acted as a good friend and partner to Paul in the reciprocal obligations they share as friends.

Paul has made a request that Philemon can hardly refuse. Paul has the strongest claim to Philemon's gratitude because, as Paul counts it, Philemon owes him his very self—the new life he has found in Christ came through Paul's agency. To refuse Paul when he asks for a gift in return would be disgracefully ungrateful, all the more as Paul presents himself in special need of help (as both a prisoner and an old man; Philem 9). Paul claims to have the authority to command Philemon's response, but Paul allows Philemon to act generously on his own. Only if Philemon responds positively will his generosity bring him any credit at all in the community. If he refuses and Paul must command what he now asks, Philemon will either have to break with Paul or lose Onesimus anyway without gaining any honor as a benefactor and reliable friend. If Philemon acquiesces, however, Onesimus's service to Paul will redound to Philemon's credit, since Onesimus has ministered to Paul as perhaps Philemon ought to have done (Philem 13) and will be able to continue to do if Philemon frees him to do so.

SIGNIFICANCE OF THE LETTER

Neither slave nor free? Many have contested the authenticity of Colossians and Ephesians precisely because these letters incorporate the "household codes" that seem to take a giant step back from Paul's declaration that in Christ "there is not a Jew nor a Gentile, not a slave and a free person, not male and female" (Gal 3:28). Why wouldn't Paul fight against the distinctions of slave and free, for example, with

the same verve that he opposed the validity of the Jew-Gentile distinction?

Philemon may shed some light on this question if it is Paul's desire to have individuals fulfill this ideal on their own initiative (with some prompting, of course) rather than by way of command. True reconciliation across these dividing lines occurs when the parties involved live out the truth of our unity in Christ from a full heart rather than under compulsion. While slaves and masters are given codes of conduct, then, and are told to fulfill their social obligations in light of their commitment to Christ (Eph 6:5-9; Col 3:22-25), in Philemon Paul expresses his hope that between believers the new kinship relationship will replace the old social distinctions and "dividing walls of hostility."

When pressed as an individual, there are no household codes Philemon may retreat behind. New relationships formed in the Lord cannot be restricted to a spiritual or religious sense, but must be lived out "in the flesh" (Philem 16). Onesimus cannot be Philemon's brother on Sunday only and his slave the rest of the week. The new model of relating must be enacted in everyday life together as well. Paul forces Philemon to decide whether he will act as a Christian brother toward Onesimus (thus confirming Philemon's own place in the Christian family), or whether he will act as an angry slave owner (thus disconfirming his place in the Christian family).[13] He challenges Philemon to live out the truth expressed in 2 Corinthians 5:16-17 and to relate to Onesimus as part of the "new creation" coming into being in Christ, the new family of God, and not on the basis of Onesimus's identity "from a worldly point of view" as Philemon's slave.

Faith effective in generosity. This letter is framed by the usual greeting and closing, both

---

[13]This is beautifully developed in Norman Petersen, *Rediscovering Paul: Philemon and the Sociology of Paul's Narrative World* (Philadelphia: Fortress, 1985), pp. 264-70.

of which express the wish for God's continued favor to rest on the house church (Philem 3, 25). This becomes especially poignant in this letter, where Paul is asking for a benefit from Philemon, an expression of Philemon's favor, which Paul considers a fitting response to Philemon's reception of God's favor through Paul. God's extension of favor toward believers must always provoke our extension of favor to one another. Philemon has formerly done this in keeping with his ability as a well-financed householder, providing hospitality to the brothers and sisters who meet in his house and lavishing financial assistance where needed. He is asked again to grant a favor that is well within his power.

This short letter provides a useful study on stewardship and responding to God, cutting through our embarrassment about mixing religion and financial concerns. According to Paul's model, believers respond to God's generosity by using whatever God has given to meet the needs of others in the body, just as God has lavished God's generosity on us in Christ and in supplying the Spirit, and God will continue to act favorably as the time of inheritance draws near. This is how, for Paul, faith becomes effective (Philem 6), meeting real needs within the community of the believers. Paul also removes a major obstacle to unbegrudging generosity, namely, the excuse that we may have been injured in some way by the person in need. Paul tells Philemon not to withhold kindness from Onesimus because of any loss he may have suffered on Onesimus's account, but rather to symbolically charge that to Paul's own account. Similarly, we are challenged to measure other people's "debts" to us against our debt to God, to forgive as freely as we have been forgiven, to share and help as generously as we have been helped and sustained.

The end of the story? As he traveled to his execution in Rome, Ignatius of Antioch was met by representatives of several churches who brought him refreshment and encouragement, and who took back letters from him to their churches. Among these visitors was Onesimus, the bishop of Ephesus, of whom Ignatius speaks most favorably throughout his letter to the Ephesian church. Although Onesimus was a fairly common slave name, very few other slaves named Onesimus would also have been as likely to rise to such a prominent leadership role in the church. It is quite possible (though only possible) that Onesimus, having returned from Colossae to Paul in prison in Ephesus, served him there and then continued in service to the church in Ephesus, eventually becoming their overseer in the faith. If Onesimus were a young teenager at the time he sought Paul's mediation, he would be in his seventies when he met Ignatius in 110 C.E. This would help account for the preservation of so personal, brief and contextual a document, if it were in fact the apostle's testimony to a later church leader. It would also provide a stunning testimony to the potential for ministry and leadership that is unleashed when God's call, and not the destiny imposed by society's caste system or other external and artificial labels, is supported and enabled by a Christian community daring to live out the implications of our full and equal sisterhood and brotherhood in Christ.

EXEGETICAL SKILL
Postcolonial Criticism and Cultural Studies

Particularly in the past two decades, biblical scholars have become increasingly interested in the ideologies at work in and political agendas served by biblical criticism. This impetus has largely, though not exclusively, come from biblical scholars who belong to a minority group within a Western culture or who live in a country not considered part of the dominant culture of the West, such as Asia, Africa or Latin America.[a]

A frequently encountered challenge to "traditional" biblical interpretation is that the enterprise of biblical studies has been Eurocentric.[b] Indeed, this charge can be borne out in many ways:

- There is a certain Eurocentrism in the New Testament itself. The collection as a whole is selectively occupied with the expansion of the church into Europe to the exclusion of the growth of the church eastward into Persia and southward into Egypt and Africa.
- Scholars have had a tendency to privilege Jewish and Greco-Roman sources as the principal background for studying early Christianity.
- There has been an uncanny collusion between the spread of the gospel and the spread of European imperialism throughout the world.
- Traditional biblical criticisms have tended to be used to answer questions of interest to white males who spoke from the vantage point of the dominant culture, and have only recently begun to be used to address questions of interest to the less-empowered (e.g., women, people of color, etc.).
- The traditional "history of interpretation" of the Bible focuses on the pursuits of German, French and English scholars (and their American followers).

These observations are important because, taken as a whole, they strongly suggest that biblical interpreters have hitherto been far too concerned with Europe, what comes out of Europe and what is of interest to Europeans. In many instances the message of Scripture may have been limited or even undermined and subverted because of the interests of Europeans and Euro-Americans; they have not been allowed to speak prophetically "from the margins" as well.

Postcolonial studies in biblical criticism are intended to free the study of Scripture from the limitations placed on it by Eurocentric interpretation

---

[a]Some starting places for further reading might include: R. S. Sugirtharajah, ed., *Voices from the Margins* (Maryknoll: Orbis, 1991); *The Postcolonial Bible* (Sheffield, U.K.: Sheffield Academic Press, 1998); J. R. Levison and P. Pope-Levison, *Jesus in Global Contexts* (Louisville, Ky.: Westminster John Knox, 1992); and J. S. Pobee, ed., *Exploring Afrocentric Christology* (New York: Peter Lang, 1992).

[b]See, for example, the discussion of Eurocentricism in biblical studies and its effects particularly on African American students of the Bible in W. H. Myers, "The Hermeneutical Dilemma of the African American Biblical Student," in *Stony the Road We Trod,* ed. C. H. Felder (Minneapolis: Fortress, 1991), pp. 41-50.

and interests. The term *postcolonialism* captures this essential thrust fairly well. It refers to "ideological reflection on the discourse and practice of imperialism and colonialism from the vantage point of a situation where imperialism and colonialism have come . . . to a formal end but remain very much at work in practice."[c] Postcolonial criticism is interested in discovering how the Bible has been used as a tool for domesticating and "civilizing" the indigenous peoples of countries conquered (in one form or another) by Europeans (even as a symbol of Europeans bringing culture, knowledge and morality to the "savages"),[d] and against lingering attempts by European schools of biblical interpretation to control the reading and use of the Bible even after colonialism is formerly dissolved. At the same time it seeks to reverse the devaluation of indigenous cultures that accompanies imperialism and construct an "alternative hermeneutics" that honors the culture, experience, and reading and interpretative strategies of the non-Western peoples.[e]

Postcolonial interpretation is "a mental attitude rather than a method, more a subversive stance toward the dominant knowledge than a school of thought."[f] Another useful metaphor is that of the "postcolonial optic," a lens used to take a new look at Scripture and the way it has been and can be interpreted and used in real-life political and social situations. The emphasis on *real-life political and social situations* cannot be overdone here. The myth of the scientific reader who is objective and disinterested has yielded largely to the model of the "real reader" who is very much invested in his or her particular interpretation, whose interpretation grows out of his or her context and has political and ideological import.[g]

Postcolonial interpretation engages three distinct levels of analysis:[h]

1. *The analysis of imperialism or colonialism in the Jewish and Christian Scriptures themselves.* How is "empire" visualized in the text? Does the text speak *for* empire, legitimating it (e.g., in the Old Testament conquest and monarchical narratives)? How are the colonized presented in the text? Does the text speak *from* the margins (e.g., in Revelation)? How does it speak about empire? This level calls for close study of the ideology in the

---

[c]Fernando Segovia, "Biblical Criticism and Postcolonial Studies: Toward a Postcolonial Optic," in *Postcolonial Bible,* p. 51 n. 3.

[d]R. S. Sugirtharajah, "Biblical Studies after the Empire," in *Postcolonial Bible,* pp. 14-15.

[e]Ibid., p. 16.

[f]R. S. Sugirtharajah, "A Postcolonial Exploration of Collusion and Construction in Biblical Interpretation," in *Postcolonial Bible,* p. 93.

[g]Segovia, "Postcolonial Optic," p. 52. Indeed, the "scientific" or "objective" study of the Bible (the "historical-critical method" often becomes the prime example) comes to be seen as a construct by which European or Euro-American scholars attempt to control the Bible and its use, marginalizing the approaches of those not schooled in these interpretive models. Here, I hope, we will see some headway toward integration of postcolonial criticism and the tools of traditional biblical criticism. The use of these tools can make them Eurocentric, but the tools are not inherently and irredeemably biased.

[h]Ibid., pp. 57-63.

text, particularly as it relates to power and politics.

2. *The analysis of past readings or interpretations of these Scriptures.* Every interpretive act can be studied as an ideological construct of the interpreter. How does a particular interpretation address (or fail to address) issues of empire and marginalization in the text? Does the interpretation serve the goals of restricting or gaining power over others? Does it legitimize political domination (for example, in the name of missions or evangelism)?[i]

3. *The analysis of readers/interpreters.* Particularly in the modern climate of multiculturalism, students are invited to analyze the ways that social and political location shape particular readers and their strategies for interpretation, both with regard to the dominant culture (traditional European and Euro-American scholarship) and with regard to the emerging voices from minority groups in the Western world and from non-Western cultures.

As this delineation of the basic tasks of postcolonial criticism makes clear, this skill is more a matter of asking questions about the ideology in the text, in the history of interpretation and in the interpreter than a method per se. A similar statement could be made about African American biblical interpretation,[j] which has become in many ways a subset of postcolonial criticism, sharing many of its concerns and yearnings. A prominent scholar in this field has distinguished four principal areas of research being done by African American biblical scholars:

1. demonstrating the presence of Africa and Africans in the biblical text, and analyzing what Africans are "doing in the text"

2. exposing racism in the history of interpretation

3. studying the tradition and history of biblical interpretation in the African and African American community

4. exploring how the African American story or experience can become a "strategy for reading" [k]

How would postcolonial interpretation in general and African American biblical interpretation in particular orient us toward Philemon? A number of larger issues reflect the imperialism that provides the backdrop for the drama in the text itself. The use of Greek by a Jew (Paul) is a constant reminder of the effective colonialism begun by Alexander the Great—what we commonly call Hellenization—and continued under all his successors, including the Romans. The institution of slavery predates these empires, but on the other hand both the rise of Greece and of Rome resulted in vast

---

[i]Sugirtharajah, for example, observes the correlation between the development of the "missionary journeys of Paul" with the rise of mercantilism and colonialism, suggesting that the opportunities for mission opened up by colonialism led to the reading back of Western missionary practice onto the travels of Paul the apostle ("Postcolonial Exploration of Collusion," pp. 100-107).

[j]A collection of foundational essays on this topic can be found in Cain Hope Felder, ed., *Stony the Road We Trod: African American Biblical Interpretation* (Minneapolis: Augsburg Fortress, 1991).

[k]R. C. Bailey, "The Danger of Ignoring One's Own Cultural Bias," in *Postcolonial Bible*, pp. 81-84.

increases in the slave population (through conquest), and the institution was regulated now by Roman and local law. We might want to consider the formation of the church, an alternative family and indeed an alternate kingdom (the "kingdom of God"), as a reaction against Roman imperialism, an attempt from the margins (i.e., from Palestine and the Roman provinces) to rewrite their own destiny. Paul's imprisonment is another reminder of imperialism, since the message he bears and the subversions of the social order he encourages meet with resistance from the local authorities (and ultimately the emperor himself).

Postcolonial interpreters find in Philemon an interesting case study in the use of a biblical text to legitimate one aspect of a modern-era domination system. I refer, of course, to slavery in America, one of the most oppressive fruits of seventeenth- and eighteenth-century colonialism. The assumption that Onesimus was a *fugitive* slave, and moreover that he has done something wrong and was fleeing *justice,* played into this use rather well. The "fugitive slave" model made Philemon especially useful in antebellum America as a scriptural mandate for returning runaway slaves to their masters—Paul had allegedly done no differently. It was common to link Philemon, then, with the household codes in Colossians and Ephesians regarding slave-master relationships (and their legitimation by Scripture).

Abolitionists, at the same time, attempted to negate Onesimus's slave status entirely, arguing that he was in fact Philemon's natural brother and not a slave at all (on the basis of a misreading of verse 16). This too can be understood fully on the basis of the ideological interests of the nineteenth-century *readers* rather than on the text itself. Abolitionists needed to undermine Philemon's contribution to the ideological arsenal of proslavery advocates. We can see very prominently how the interests of the dominant culture (white proslavery) were served by an interpretation of Philemon, then, such that abolitionists had to work hard to wrest the text from their adversaries' ideological arsenal.[l]

Lloyd Lewis frankly acknowledges the problems that Philemon poses to African American biblical interpreters on account of its failure to speak directly against slavery and, indeed, the ease with which it lent itself to proslavery readings and to the legitimation of slavery in America (as well as the mandate to return runaway slaves to their owners). However, Lewis observes that if Philemon is read in light of Galatians (i.e., Gal 3:28) rather than the household codes of Colossians, a very different reading of the text emerges (the one largely adopted in this chapter).[m] Philemon is con-

---

[l]See, further, A. D. Callahan, "Paul's Epistle to Philemon," pp. 357-65. Callahan's attempt to support the claim that Onesimus was not a slave at all but Philemon's natural brother is a wistful revival of these nineteenth-century abolitionist interpretations (pp. 368-72). His arguments concerning the reading of vv. 15-16, against any natural reading of the passage, are effectively refuted by Fitzmyer and the literature he cites (*Philemon*, pp. 18-19).

fronted with the impossibility of responding to the convert Onesimus as a "slave" since both are equally heirs of the promise in Christ and hence brothers. Although Paul has not mandated manumission, the implications of his gospel have. The choice of reading Philemon in light of Colossians 3:22—4:1 or Galatians 3:28, however, is clearly one that proceeds from our social and political interests—either way—which brings to the fore again a major tenet of this mode of analysis.

It is more difficult to prescribe practical exercises in postcolonial criticism or cultural studies than, say, for rhetorical criticism, since the full-blown pursuit of the questions raised in this section require detailed and critical interaction not only with a passage of Scripture but with the history of its interpretation and application. However, as a preliminary exercise, you might wish to explore the following passages from the perspective of the "postcolonial optic" outlined in the three levels of analysis above (pp. 678-79), focusing also on the specific questions added below:

1. Read Luke 1—2. How is the empire (Roman power and its influence) presented in these narratives? What responses toward empire are detected within these narratives, especially the songs of chapter 1 and the angelic pronouncements of chapter 2? Is Luke proclaiming a counter-empire? What is Luke's orientation to the empire, from whose margins he writes his Gospel?

2. Read Mark 12:13-17. Again, how is the empire represented in this story? How might different groups interpret Jesus' response, depending on their location in regard to empire (e.g., the priestly elite vs. the Zealots, the ruling class vs. the peasant class)? Knowing the inscriptions on denarii to include such titles as "son of the divine Augustus," "chief priest [of the gods]" and the like, is Jesus' response only to be heard as an innocuous reply, or might there be some teeth to it where Caesar is concerned?

3. Read Romans 13:1-7 and 1 Peter 2:11-17. Again, how is imperial power manifested in these texts? Does the description of its manifestation in these passages correlate with its actual manifestation in many cases? Or is there an implicit critique of the intrusion of or at least limitation on imperial governance and "justice" here? What is the effect of a colonial voice speaking of imperial power as subject to the one God, into whose divine family the author and readers have been adopted (both in Romans and 1 Peter)?

4. Read Revelation, thinking about how first-century Christians in Asia Minor would hear and think about the "beast," the "image of the beast," "Babylon" and the like. The chapter on Revelation in this book will help in this task. How does John depict and interpret the presence and effects of

---

[m]L. A. Lewis, "An African American Appraisal of the Philemon-Paul-Onesimus Triangle," in *Stony the Road*, pp. 232-46.

empire on the world of the provinces? What critiques does this colorful voice from the margins level?

Read the treatment of these texts, insofar as you are inclined, in standard commentaries written from a variety of perspectives (theologically conservative, theologically liberal; historical-critical, narrative, social-scientific; written by scholars of European descent and non-European descent). To what extent do the various resources you read give attention to questions of power, imperialism, colonialism and the like? To what extent are the various authors aware of the implications of the text and its interpretation for the construction of power relationships, the marginalization of particular groups or voices, or the legitimation or delegitimation of current power relations? What correlations do you detect between the methodological preferences, theological alignment or the ethnicity of the scholar and the degree to which he or she engages in ideological criticism (especially of the kind presented here)? Finally, turn your gaze on yourself and your own reading of the Bible. How would you analyze your own sensitivity to and engagement of these issues in your own social, political and geographical setting?

PHILEMON AND MINISTRY FORMATION

The principal challenge of Philemon is to embody the essential truth of the new family that God is begetting in Christ, that all who call on the name of Jesus are sisters and brothers first and foremost, whatever other roles and respective statuses are given them by the society. When you and the people in your care see a Christian who belongs to a different race, what do you see first—a person of a different ethnicity or a sister or brother in Christ? Do the limitations and barriers that still regulate interethnic relations constrain your relationship with that other, or do you embrace and interact with him or her fully as your brother or sister in Christ? The same question could be asked of employers and employees, of people of disparate economic standing, of liberals and conservatives, and of blood relations (many dysfunctions among natural kin who are in Christ could be moved toward resolution by regarding one another first with the dignity and love belonging to the children of God). The same question could be asked of the couple having an affair within the congregation, where non-Christian scripts are overriding the healthful and redemptive relationships we are called to nurture in Christ.

If all questions were referred back to this basic question—am I treating this fellow Christian as I would my own sister or brother?—the beneficial effects would be far reaching indeed. Wherever Christians are placed by God, whether in national defense, industry, commercial banking or education, Paul invites them to consider how they are affecting their local and global family in Christ in all their decisions and practices. The genuineness of our faith and the reality of our place in God's family must show forth here.

Paul also suggests that believers belong to the church family as a whole, and not to a particular household. This is why Paul can refer the matter of Onesimus to the whole congregation and summon Philemon to accountability before that court of opinion with regard to his treatment of Onesimus. Similarly, the church is not meddling but rather fulfilling its role as family of God when it acts to ensure that all members of its family are being treated with the love and dignity that belong to children of God. Domestic violence, alcoholism and its effects, child abuse—none of these are private matters to be excluded from the *redemptive* attention of the church family.

Paul's refusal to use his authority to command Philemon models sound pastoral leadership in several ways. First, he reminds us of the importance of modeling Christ-mindedness to facilitate the development of the mind of Christ in those we serve. Second, he shows the importance of having correct actions proceed from the hearts and minds of the doers if the transformation God seeks to effect in our congregations is to happen at the deeper levels that God desires. Conformity to the pressures of authority is not what God seeks, but conformity to the mind of Christ and to the new possibilities that our divine kinship opens up for human relationships. If a pastoral leader must use authority to coerce rather than facilitate transformation, he or she may win a minor victory at the expense of the larger campaign for Christlikeness.

FOR FURTHER READING

Barclay, John M. G. *Colossians and Philemon,* pp. 97-126. New Testament Guides. Sheffield, U.K.: Sheffield Academic Press, 1997.

———. "Paul, Philemon, and the Dilemma of Slave Ownership." *NTS* 37 (1991): 161-86.

Bartchy, S. Scott. *Mallon Chrēsai: First Century Slavery and the Interpretation of 1 Corinthians 7:21.* SBLDS 11. Missoula, Mont.: Scholars Press, 1973.

Barth, Markus, and Helmut Blanke. *The Letter to Philemon.* ECC. Grand Rapids: Eerdmans, 2000.

Bruce, F. F. *The Epistles to the Colossians, to Philemon, and to the Ephesians.* pp. 189-225. NICNT. Grand Rapids: Eerdmans, 1984.

Callahan, Allen D. "Paul's Epistle to Philemon: Toward an Alternative *Argumentum.*" *HTR* 86 (1993): 357-76.

deSilva, David A. *Honor, Patronage, Kinship and Purity,* pp. 190-92, 233-37. Downers Grove, Ill.: InterVarsity Press, 2000.

Dunn, James D. G. *The Epistles to the Colossians and to Philemon: A Commentary on the Greek Text,* pp. 291-349. NIGTC. Grand Rapids: Eerdmans, 1996.

Fitzmyer, Joseph A. *The Letter to Philemon.* AB. New York: Doubleday, 2000.

Garland, David E. *Colossians and Ephesians,* pp. 293-375. NIVAC. Grand Rapids: Zondervan, 1998.

Lohse, Eduard. *A Commentary on the Epistles to Colossians and to Philemon.* Hermeneia. Philadelphia: Fortress, 1971.

Martin, Ralph P. *Colossians and Philemon.* NCB. Grand Rapids: Eerdmans, 1981.

Nordling, J. G. "Onesimus Fugitivus: A Defense of the Runaway Slave Hypothesis in Philemon." *JSNT* 41 (1991): 97-119.

O'Brien, Peter T. *Colossians, Philemon.* WBC. Waco, Tex.: Word, 1982.

Patzia, Arthur G. *Ephesians, Colossians, Philemon,* pp. 103-17. NIBC. Peabody, Mass.: Hendrickson, 1990.

Petersen, Norman. *Rediscovering Paul: Philemon and the Sociology of Paul's Narrative World.* Philadelphia: Fortress, 1985.

Wall, Robert W. *Colossians and Philemon,* pp. 179-218. IVPNTC. Downers Grove, Ill.: InterVarsity Press, 1993.

EXCURSUS

Pseudepigraphy and the New Testament Canon

Pseudepigraphy refers to the practice of writing in the name of another person or ascribing one's own work to another. This was a common practice in Jewish and Greco-Roman antiquity. As a rule apocalypses and testaments do not bear the name of their actual author but the name of a noteworthy figure from Israel's sacred history to whom work is attributed. Thus we have the *Apocalypse of Abraham,* written in the first-person from the perspective of Abraham, and the *Testaments of the Twelve Patriarchs,* each written as if taken down in dictation from Reuben, Simeon, Levi and the rest. There are dozens of other works where the text gives the explicit impression of having been written by someone other than its real author (*1 Enoch, 2 Baruch, 4 Ezra,* to name but a few). The practice is also well-known to Greeks and Romans. Early Christians—certainly throughout the second through fourth centuries and beyond—produced a host of pseudepigraphical literature, written in the name of a known apostle (like the *Apocalypse of Paul,* the *Infancy Gospel of Thomas,* the *Apocryphon of John,* the *Correspondence of Paul and Seneca* and the like).

This practice naturally led to questioning whether or not some of the New Testament books were written pseudonymously. In current scholarship this usually involves 2 Thessalonians, Ephesians, Colossians, 1-2 Timothy, Titus, James, 1-2 Peter and Jude. This is a wholly different question from that of the authorship of the four Gospels, Acts, Hebrews and 1-3 John, all of which are actually anonymous. When presented with a letter claiming to be from Paul but reflecting a writing style or theology quite different from the style or theology reflected in other letters attributed to Paul (the cardinal four tend to be Romans, Galatians and 1-2 Corinthians), the possibility that the letter was written by someone else in Paul's name is often thought to resolve these inconsistencies. Or where the situation and issues in a letter seem to reflect a later period in the development of the Christian movement than would have been possible during the purported author's lifetime, the possibility of pseudepigraphy again emerges as an expedient explanation.

Other scholars, most of whom inhabit the more conservative theological circles, dispute the propriety of speaking of New Testament pseudepigraphy at all. Some would oppose it on ideological grounds, claiming that the concept of pseudepigraphy is incompatible with a doctrine of Scripture that teaches that claims to authorship in the texts need to be "received as truth from God," all the more as the apostolicity guarantees the inspiration and reliability of the individual books.[1] Most, however, are willing to grant that "the inspiration of the Scriptures is consistent with any kind of form of literary composition that was in keeping with the character and habits of the speaker or writer" (including pseudonymous compositions) if it

---

[1] J. I. Packer, *Fundamentalism and the Word of God* (Grand Rapids: Eerdmans, 1958), p. 184.

can be shown that these were in fact an established and accepted convention.[2] A greater number have ethical problems with an author who exhorts his readers to put away all falsehood and deceit and to speak the truth to fellow Christians while pretending to write as the apostle Paul or Peter. This is perhaps the major objection among conservative scholars, ruling pseudepigraphy out of court in principle.[3]

These scholars also cite the evidence from the first through the fourth century, suggesting that early Christians rejected pseudepigraphical writings in principle, allowing no known pseudepigraphon to function authoritatively in the church (and thus excluding them from the emerging canon). Paul himself (if not, most ironically, the pseudonymous author of 2 Thessalonians) warns the church against letters written in Paul's name but not bearing genuine apostolic teaching (2 Thess 2:2). The Muratorian Canon makes note of an *Epistle to the Laodiceans* and an *Epistle to the Alexandrians,* forged in Paul's name by supporters of Marcion, and it affirms the Great Church's rejection of these texts. *Third Corinthians,* accepted as authentic in some parts of the church, was written pseudonymously by a second-century bishop out of sincere motives and admiration for the apostle, but when he confessed the document's origins, he was deprived of his ecclesiastical position (Tertullian *On Baptism* 17).[4]

This raises a number of important ques-

tions about the practice of pseudepigraphy as it relates to New Testament texts.

What conclusions should we draw from the decisions made by the early church concerning documents known or discovered to be pseudepigraphic? In all of the first- through fourth-century discussions concerning authorship and the authority of particular texts, the contents were as much under scrutiny as the authorship, save for the case of 3 *Corinthians.* It is difficult to assess whether the first- and early second-century church would have found known pseudepigrapha to be problematic in and of themselves, or whether the practice of pseudepigraphy became contaminated in the minds of the leaders of the Great Church because of its frequent employment to propagate teachings deemed by them to be out of line with the apostolic gospel.[5] The evidence can be explained either way, but it is not as clear-cut as either side would have the unsuspecting reader believe.[6]

Did a pseudepigrapher seek to deceive his or her readers into thinking the text was actually written by somebody else (making it in fact unethical), or would ancient conventions of authorship make pseudepigraphy—in certain cases at least— a fully ethical practice? In a classic study Bruce Metzger examines the typical motivations for forgery among Greco-Roman authors.[7] In several cases deception was clearly integral to the purpose for the forgery: when an author (1) sought financial gain by selling "newly discov-

---

[2]See Bruce M. Metzger, "Literary Forgeries and Canonical Pseudepigrapha," *JBL* 91 (1972): 21-22.

[3]See Terry L. Wilder, "Pseudonymity and the New Testament," in *Interpreting the New Testament: Essays on Method and Issues,* ed. D. A. Black and D. S. Dockery (Nashville: Broadman & Holman, 2001), pp. 301, 303, 318.

[4]William D. Mounce, *Pastoral Epistles,* WBC (Nashville: Thomas Nelson, 2000), pp. ccxiv-cxxv; Wilder, "Pseudonymity," pp. 304-7.

[5]See Metzger, "Literary Forgeries and Canonical Pseudepigrapha," pp. 3-24, esp. 14-15.

[6]The reader always needs to be wary about how evidence is interpreted and whether it is used in a manner inconsistent with its original context. Terry Wilder, for example, stressing that the early church examined both authorship and content, weights the reading of the evidence far too much in favor of the position he advocates ("Pseudonymity and the New Testament," p. 308). This is especially evident when, for example, he interprets a statement of W. Schneemelcher (which clearly shows attribution of "apostolicity" to be a function of the acceptability of the "content") as a sign that the early church examined both criteria independently.

[7]Metzger, "Literary Forgeries," pp. 5-11.

ered" works of Aristotle, for example, to ancient libraries, or (2) sought to bring a rival into disfavor by attributing words to him that would be damaging to him, or (3) sought to secure greater credence for his or her thoughts by assigning it to a venerated authority. Such works were often recognized as forgeries and maligned under that name.[8]

In other cases, however, deception and fraud were clearly not envisioned. For example, schoolroom exercises frequently involved writing a speech in the style of a particular orator as a means of practicing composition and argumentation skills. In other cases an author would ascribe his or her work to another out of love and respect, and out of a sense of authorship or "proprietary ownership" that differs markedly from our modern notions. Iamblichus (*De vita Pythagorica* 158, 198), for example, records the policy of the disciples of Pythagoras, writing their own works under the name of Pythagoras. Since they attribute to him all that they have learned, they do not deem it proper to claim their writings as their own but, as it were, their teacher's. Porphyry appears to have accepted these texts as, in some sense, authentic, even though not actually written by Pythagoras or even authorized by him.[9]

In discussions of potential candidates for pseudepigrapha in the New Testament, some authors regard them more as deceptive works that use the name of a revered figure in order to make the content authoritative. Others, however, assert that the disciples of Paul acted in line with the disciples of Pythagoras, assiduously avoiding taking credit for the teaching of the master. Which of the two would be the case depends, of course, on the specific presentation made by the text. In the cases of 2 Timothy and Titus, for example, the decision

to include so many personal details and fabricate a plausible historical setting for the content makes it hard to avoid the conclusion that the author or authors intended for the letter to be seen as Paul's own and not as pseudepigraphic.[10] The general nature of Ephesians, however, would give it a better claim to be the benign work of a modest disciple, if it is indeed judged to be pseudonymous.

There is another related matter to consider here. A pseudepigraphon written shortly after Paul's death to those who knew Paul would stand a good chance of being recognized as a pseudonymous work by its first readers. Only as readers became further removed from its production and first appearance—as the text was passed around from place to place and down through a few generations—would the fact of pseudepigraphy be lost and its attribution to the apostle be taken at face value. The passing of a century could make a great difference in the readers' awareness of whether a text was pseudonymous or authentic. Since it was grouped with the Writings and not the Prophets, the first readers of Daniel apparently understood the work to be a recent composition and not a true prophecy from Daniel. But by the first century C.E. Daniel is spoken of as the author of that book without qualification. Thus a writing not intended or likely to deceive came to be "deceptive," but not in a way that could be deemed unethical.

Is pseudepigraphy the best solution to questions of authorship when internal data (e.g., style, vocabulary, theology, situation) conflict with what can be known about the purported author? This is, to me, the most important question. Many of the arguments advanced for pseudepigraphy presume that modern interpreters can know the probable limits of what Paul or another first-

---

[8]Ibid., pp. 11-12.

[9]Wilder, "Pseudonymity in the New Testament," p. 299.

[10]See L. R. Donelson, *Pseudepigraphy and Ethical Argument in the Pastoral Epistles* (Tübingen: Mohr/Siebeck, 1986), pp. 24, 55.

century apostle could have or could not have written or thought. Frequently, these interpreters can be rightly accused of placing undue limitations "on Paul's ability and versatility as a writer and theologian" and failing to account adequately for "the changed epistolary situation" in each disputed letter.[11] Which information should be privileged? Do the undisputed Pauline letters determine the scope and range of Paul's expression and thought, or do the disputed Pauline letters open up new windows into the Pauline mission and its complexities?

How broadly should the interpreter conceive of "authorship"? The answer to this will greatly affect how much force arguments for pseudepigraphy will carry. What contribution was made by those named as cosenders (see, e.g., Timothy, Silvanus or Titus)? Might a particular letter represent a fairly free framing of the author's thoughts by a trusted associate or secretary?[12] Might certain circumstances constrain Paul or Peter to communicate intended contents to a colleague, who would then write in the master's name?[13] If authenticity can cover all such circumstances, arguments based on vocabulary and style will have no force, and arguments based on perceived theological discrepancy will lose considerable force, except in cases where a contradiction with an author's previous work is clear and unmistakable.

Deutero-Pauline literature could be seen as a development of this collaborative process between Paul and his coworkers.[14] Yet it is not clear why an early Christian leader would feel compelled to write in another's name. Clement, Ignatius, Polycarp and Hermas, for example, all wrote in their own names. These authors use apostolic traditions to (1) lend authority to their message, and (2) explore the applicability of those traditions to a new situation. In their case there was no perceived need for pseudonymity as a tool to gain credence for their texts. There would be even less need if the author had been a known coworker of Paul (and thus an "heir" to his mantle). The interpreter, therefore, also needs to consider the motive for pseudonymity. What would be gained by writing in Peter's name rather than citing Petrine traditions as authority for what was written in the author's own name? In some cases there would be a gain (e.g., to develop a body of Petrine traditions that could become the basis for such appeals); in other cases, it is not clear what the real author could have gained.

As we consider the texts most commonly judged to be pseudonymous (Ephesians, Colossians, the Pastoral Epistles, James, Jude and 2 Peter), the student will not always be given fast and hard answers. The evidence, in several

---

[11] P. T. O'Brien, *Colossians, Philemon*, WBC (Waco, Tex.: Word, 1982), p. 46.

[12] The contribution of a secretary (whether a professional assistant or one of Paul's coworkers and associates) could indeed be considerable, both at the level of content and especially at the level of vocabulary and style. E. Randolph Richards has shown that ancient secretaries did not merely "take dictation," but often would take notes as the sender described what it is he or she wished to communicate, and then exercised considerable freedom in framing the letter (*The Secretary in the Letters of Paul*, WUNT 42 [Tübingen: J. C. B. Mohr, 1991]). The sender would then check over and correct the letter to make sure it correctly captured his or her meaning, thus authorizing it. It is certain that Paul used a writing assistant for several of his letters. Tertius emerges as the hand through which Paul wrote Romans (Rom 16:22). In many letters Paul calls attention to a change of handwriting that signifies his personal authentication of the contents (the "Pauline signature" in 1 Cor 16:21; Gal 6:11; Col 4:18; 2 Thess 3:17; Philem 19; see Richards, *Secretary in the Letters of Paul*, p. 190). Changes in secretary—or Paul's writing in his own idiom—could well account for the variations in style and diction that often lead scholars to posit deutero-Pauline authorship (see ibid., pp. 169-201).

[13] Metzger observes that Tertullian saw no problem with the last option as still falling within the scope of "authenticity" ("Literary Forgeries," p. 14). Richard Bauckham provides a similarly broad definition of authenticity, including a letter written by someone else but authorized by the named "author" ("Pseudo-Apostolic Letters," *JBL* 107 [1988]: 469-94, esp. 470-71). See also Wilder, "Pseudonymity and the New Testament," pp. 296-97. John Calvin would apparently also have endorsed as "authentic" a letter written by an apostle's associate but approved by the named author (ibid., p. 310).

[14] E.g., Margaret Y. MacDonald, *Colossians and Ephesians*, Sacra Pagina 17 (Collegeville, Minn.: Liturgical Press, 2000), p. 8.

cases, defies a clear ruling, and it would do injustice to a century of scholarship to pretend that probabilities really stack in favor of one side rather than the other. Instead, the student is invited to engage this multifaceted debate, weigh the evidence and explanations, consider the ramifications of each position, and make some initial hypotheses on her or his own. It is important to remember two points throughout: (1) people of profound intellect and deep faith commitments have held to positions on either side, and (2) neither side is free from the pressures of a certain "faith community" pushing them toward one position or the other, whether it is a scholarly community that now holds certain truths to be self-evident,[15] or a conservative circle that is ideologically predisposed to defend the claims made by a text at face value.

Ultimately, the question is of great importance for the reconstruction of the history of first-century Christianity. (It makes a great deal of difference if the Pastoral Epistles are taken as sources for Pauline Christianity in the 60s or the 90s, or if James and Jude are understood to reflect Judean Christianity in the 50s or 80s.) It is also important for the study of a particular figure's "theology." (Again, the reconstruction of Paul's theology will be dramatically different if we include Ephesians and Colossians in the research base for such a project.) The question is of less importance, however, for our appreciation of the meaning and contribution of these texts to discipleship and ministry in the modern context, for whether written by the named author or not, they stand in the New Testament canon and invite our full attention from that standpoint.[16]

---

[15]See Markus Barth and Helmut Blanke, *Colossians*, AB 34B (Garden City, N.Y.: Doubleday, 1994), p. 111; Luke Timothy Johnson, *The First and Second Letters to Timothy*, AB (Garden City, N.Y.: Doubleday, 2000), p. 55.

[16]On other hand, Barth has demonstrated the tendency to depreciate texts that are considered inauthentic and to regard them as examples of how not to do theology, of being taken over too much by the very religion one opposes (Barth and Blanke, *Colossians*, pp. 114-15). Debates about authorship have, in many circles, effectively relegated the deutero-Pauline epistles and other texts deemed pseudepigraphic to the margins of theological and ethical inquiry.

18

THE EPISTLES TO THE CHRISTIANS IN COLOSSAE AND EPHESUS

Walking in the Light of Christ's Victory

Colossians and Ephesians are often grouped together not only because they appear to have been written by Paul from the same time and place of imprisonment, but because they share distinctive emphases on the cosmic significance of Jesus' exaltation, the implications of Christ's enthronement above every spiritual power, and the ways the mystery of God transforms believers' lives and relationships, especially within the household. The similarities between the two letters are so striking that some explanation for them must be found; the differences between them and the rest of Paul's letters also demand explanation.

These two letters contribute especially to the development of early Christology, ecclesiology and ethics. Colossians offers a statement of Christ's relationship to God and his role in creation, reconciliation and consummation that is rivaled only by the prologue to John and Hebrews 1:1-4. Ephesians celebrates the emergence of the church that has, as a direct result of the Pauline mission, united Jews and Gentiles in one community, which serves as the revelation of the central mystery of God at work in history. Both give significant attention to how the intervention of God on behalf of the believers shapes their lives and interactions. In contrast with externalistic but empty religious regimens, Colossians challenges believers to discern what the genuine taboos and impera-

tives of the new life in Christ are. In Ephesians, believers are challenged to put away all behaviors inconsistent with the light of Christ or with the fact that they are now "members of one another." Thus Christians will never again be served by disadvantaging a sister or brother.

THE CITY OF COLOSSAE AND ITS CHRISTIAN COMMUNITY

Colossae sits in close proximity to two other cities of prominence in the early Christian landscape. Laodicea is eleven miles to the northwest and Hierapolis fifteen miles north-northwest. Colossae was the oldest of the three cities, having been founded and populated by native Phrygians before the advent of the power of Greece and Rome. Formerly the principal town in Phrygia, it came to be overshadowed by neighboring Laodicea. Colossae was noted for the processing of scarlet-dyed wool as well as the usual crops of figs, olives and grapes.

Excavation of Colossae lags behind that of other cities prominent in the New Testament, but we do have some suggestive literary and numismatic evidence providing a few windows into the life of the city. It was the home of a cult of Cybele, the mother goddess, whose worship involved fertility rites, but also ascetic practices and ritual mutilation. The Jewish practice of circumcision might find a natural resonance with Phrygian religion at this point.[1] The designs of coins struck in Colossae suggest the existence of cults of Isis, Sarapis, Mithras, Demeter, Helios (the sun), Selene (the moon), the Ephesian Artemis and Men, a native Phrygian divinity.[2] The worship of the astral bodies (Selene and Helios) and the four elements as divinities might shed some light on the role the "elemental spirits of the cosmos" were thought to play in the alternative philosophy.[3]

A sizable Jewish community lived in the Lycus valley, partly as a result of Antiochus III's relocation of several thousand Jews from Babylon and its environs to the Lycus valley around 200 B.C.E. (Josephus *Ant.* 12.147-153).[4] It is estimated that between eleven thousand and fourteen thousand adult male Jews lived in the administrative district centered in Laodicea (which included Colossae and Hierapolis) in the mid-first century B.C.E.[5] Several scholars suggest that the Jews settled here were fully Hellenized and often open to blending their practice with the cult of certain local divinities or, alternatively, that local pagan cults were quite open to incorporating Jewish customs. Hellenization referred not only to making non-Greeks more like Greeks but also making it easier for all manner of local customs and cultures to influence other local customs and cultures. In all likelihood, therefore, the influence flowed in both directions.[6]

A regional earthquake in 61 C.E. probably wrought havoc on the city. Laodicea and Hier-apolis were both known to have suffered extensive damage at this time (Tacitus *Ann.* 14.27), and it is likely that their neighbor, Colossae, did as well. Coins have been found in Hierapolis for each emperor from Augustus through Nero, but then not again until Trajan, some fifty years later, suggesting that Hierapolis took generations to recover.[7] Laodicea rebuilt quickly with the city's own funds. It is not known what the citizens of Colossae did for their city, but the population gradually resettled elsewhere.[8]

While Paul may have passed through Colossae during his travels, he does not take credit for evangelizing there. Instead, the congregation at Colossae was founded by a Pauline coworker, Epaphras (Col 1:7-8; 4:12-13). Paul may have converted Epaphras in Ephesus, Paul's focal point during his Asian ministry, a connection which would explain why Paul regards the congregation as falling within his apostolic purview as a sort of spiritual nephew or niece, if not son or daughter. Paul knows several people in Colossae personally, perhaps because they met elsewhere in Asia Minor (again, most probably in Ephesus, the major commercial center of that region). Acts 19:26 indirectly testifies to the gospel spreading throughout Asia Minor while Paul is resident in Ephesus, perhaps mainly through Paul's coworkers. The letter gives the impression that most of the readers are Gentiles, formerly "dead in trespasses and the uncircumcision of your flesh" (Col 2:13; see also 1:21, 27).[9]

---

[1]Ralph P. Martin, *Colossians and Philemon,* NCB (Grand Rapids: Eerdmans, 1981), p. 4.

[2]Sherman E. Johnson, "Laodicea and Its Neighbors," in *The Biblical Archaeologist Reader 2,* ed. D. N. Freedman and E. F. Campbell Jr. (Garden City, N.Y.: Doubleday, 1964), p. 357.

[3]Martin, *Colossians and Philemon,* p. 5; Markus Barth and Helmut Blanke, *Colossians,* AB 34B (Garden City, N.Y.: Doubleday, 1994), pp. 11-12.

[4]Arthur G. Patzia, *Colossians, Philemon, Ephesians* (San Francisco: Harper & Row, 1984), p. xiii.

[5] P. T. O'Brien, *Colossians, Philemon,* WBC 44 (Waco, Tex.: Word, 1982), p. xxvii; James D. G. Dunn, *The Epistles to the Colossians and Philemon,* NIGTC (Grand Rapids: Eerdmans, 1996), p. 21.

[6]Barth and Blanke, *Colossians,* p. 16.

[7]Johnson, "Laodicea and Its Neighbors," pp. 363-64.

[8]C. E. Arnold, "Colossae," *Anchor Bible Dictionary,* ed. David N. Freedman (Garden City, N.Y.: Doubleday, 1992), 1:1089; Martin, *Colossians and Philemon,* p. 3.

[9]C. F. D. Moule, *The Epistles of Paul the Apostle to the Colossians and to Philemon,* CGTC (Cambridge: Cambridge University Press, 1957), p. 26.

OPPOSITION

One particular feature of the Colossian landscape receives particular attention in the letter: the "philosophy" (Col 2:8) that presents itself as an alternative to or as an element that can be combined with faith in Christ. The attraction some of the recipients might have to this philosophy is not the sole focal point of the letter,[10] but the philosophy certainly provides the parameters for the content of Colossians, as it moves from the exalted reflections on Christology in chapter 1 (incorporating a well-chosen early Christian hymn in Col 1:15-20), through the direct rebuttal in chapter 2, to the exposition of the only kind of asceticism that truly matters for eternity in chapter 3 (in contrast to the asceticism promoted within the philosophy). The ethical exhortations found in Colossians 3:1—4:6 thus grow out of the challenges of answering the philosophy, but they also grow considerably past those challenges as well.

The author seems genuinely concerned about what might happen to the believers' faith if they took this philosophy seriously (Col 2:4, 8) and writes vividly as if some had already begun experimenting with it (Col 2:20-23). Many questions about this philosophy remain, however. It remains uncertain whether there were there teachers "who sought to make inroads into the community"[11] or whether the philosophy was just an available alternative to which some of the Colossian Christians were attracted.[12] Was it already a Christian movement, or did it represent a non-Christian Jewish or pagan system that the Colossian converts themselves would be wedding to Christian discipleship for the first time? Moreover, scholars have not produced a clear explanation of the philosophy. Or more to the point, individual scholars have produced over forty very clear but very different and irreconcilable pictures of the philosophy from the meager evidence in Colossians. John Barclay's cautions concerning mirror reading would be well applied to a fresh study of the situation behind Colossians (see pp. 650-53 in the chapter on Philippians).

The letter explicitly provides the following data concerning the philosophy opposed by the author:

- It involved regulations concerning food and drink, the observance of a ritual calendar including new moons, sabbaths and other festivals (Col 2:16; 21).
- Self-abasement and "worship of angels" were a constituent part, perhaps as a precursor to experiencing visions, perhaps as part of what was seen in visions (Col 2:18). The phrase "worship of angels" is particularly problematic since it can mean "angelic worship" or "the worship of angels [by human beings]."[13] The picture of the philosophy will be very different depending on which way we go.
- It involved other taboos, particularly against touching or handling certain things (Col 2:21), though the text leaves tantalizingly unspecified *what* was not supposed to be touched.

---

[10]I use this term in order to avoid naming the alternative movement a heresy, for it may not have been Christian, or "false teaching" at all. It may not have been vigorously promoted by its teachers in a manner akin to the Judaizing gospel in Galatia. *Philosophy* in the first century referred not only to a system of thought but also to a way of life, and it was frequently indistinguishable from what a modern person would label a religion.

[11]O'Brien, *Colossians, Philemon*, p. xl.

[12]Dunn, *Epistle to the Colossians*, pp. 25-26.

[13]See the discussion in Eduard Lohse, *A Commentary on the Epistles to Colossians and to Philemon*, Hermeneia (Philadelphia: Fortress, 1971), pp. 127-28; O'Brien, *Colossians, Philemon*, pp. xxxvi-xxxvii, 142; Dunn, *Epistle to the Colossians*, p. 28. Mystical participation in the angels' worship of God is attested at Qumran and certainly suggested by Revelation's visions of worship. However, I prefer the first option ("worshiping the angels," which is also suggested as real-life possibility in Rev 19:10; 22:9), since it is presented as a parallel to the act of self-abasement.

- In large part these regulations and taboos were understood to constitute a kind of asceticism, a rigorous limitation of bodily indulgences (abstinence from certain pleasures and other forms of self-denial) held to facilitate spiritual progress (Col 2:23; reflected indirectly in Col 3:5-11).

Indirectly, the letter further suggests that

- Spiritual entities like "the elemental spirits of the cosmos," "powers," "principalities" and the like played an important part in the theoretical or practical content of this philosophy (Col 1:16; 2:8-10, 15, 20).

- The philosophy *may* have promoted itself as inducting its devotees into the knowledge or mysteries known to the spiritual elite,[14] thus presenting itself as having something new and important to offer even those who had been inducted into the Christian philosophy (Col 1:9; 2:2-3, 9-10).

The data are widely agreed on, but not their interpretation, since scholars choose some very different backgrounds against which to flesh out these data. Indeed, it is likely that a philosophy that combines so many diverse elements has drawn from multiple backgrounds. On the one hand, the philosophy has some clearly Jewish elements. Sabbath observance is unambiguous in this regard. New moons were also important and regular landmarks on the Jewish calendar. The philosophy's restrictions on diet would certainly resonate with Jewish food laws, though these are not unique to Judaism by any means. At the same time, these Jewish elements have been combined with elements of other religious practices and systems of thought.

Here the emphasis on the "elemental spirits of the universe" (*stoicheia tou kosmou*) demands attention. The author is happy to cite these as the source of the philosophy since it allows him to delegitimize the philosophy as "worldly," or coming from a sub-divine realm, as opposed to Paul's gospel (compare how Paul uses this term in Gal 4:1-11, mainly as a means of undermining the Judaizers' position). Nevertheless, their prominence in this letter is most easily explained if the elemental spirits are also an integral part of the philosophy.

Diogenes Laertius (*Lives* 8.24-33) speaks of the Pythagorean teaching that the upper air contains the sun, moon and stars, which are spirits that control human destiny. The atmosphere is filled with spirit-powers that are to be venerated, and the soul must be kept purified (through ascetic practices, including ritual washings, abstaining from meat, avoiding pollution [perhaps in the form of sexual contact]) if it is to pass through the spheres to the divine regions after death.[15] (Here is a natural point of contact with Judaism, with its rigorous avoidance of certain foods and the like.) The *Testament of Solomon* (a Christian pseudepigraphon) similarly speaks of the *stoicheia* as astral powers that set themselves against humankind. Against this background many have surmised that the Colossian philosophy teaches that the *stoicheia* are the masters of human and cosmic destiny. They "exercise a mediating function between the heavenly and earthly spheres."[16] Revering them may be thought to lead to kindly dispensations from the rulers of fate. The Christians have yet to be delivered from these spir-

---

[14]Focusing (perhaps too exclusively) on the word *embateuōn* ("entering into") in Colossians 2:18, a word also used in mystery cults as the initiate enters the sanctuary to encounter the deity, Martin Dibelius went so far as to suggest that the Colossian philosophy took the form of a pre-Christian Gnostic mystery cult dedicated to the "elemental spirits of the universe." See his "The Isis Initiation in Apuleius and Related Initiatory Rites," in *Conflict at Colossae*, ed. F. O. Francis and W. A. Meeks, SBLSBS 4 (Missoula, Mont.: Scholars Press, 1975). pp. 61-121.

[15]See, further, Martin, *Colossians and Philemon*, pp. 10-12, 18.

[16]Barth and Blanke, *Colossians*, p. 25.

itual powers, and so they need to adopt the practices promoted by this "philosophy."[17]

At this point connections with proto-Gnostic tendencies might emerge. God's "fullness" emanates throughout a series of lesser spiritual beings (angels, the elemental spirits of the universe) who hold authority over the various spheres between earth and God's realm. These must be revered and placated for the soul to pass to the higher realms. Ascetic practices would prepare individuals for mystical visions of these beings and give evidence of their submission to these supernatural beings.[18] The role of these intermediate beings also provides a point at which pagan and Jewish elements could converge. In the intertestamental period angels were believed (1) to have delivered the Law to Moses and (2) to govern the channels that allowed people to communicate with God, receive revelations from God and the like. To revere them and to obey their regulations would be regarded as advantageous.[19]

The Colossian philosophy truly "remains an unsolved puzzle,"[20] but its major contours are fairly well defined. Human life below and access to the realms above lie under the authority of intermediate spiritual beings (variously called angels, elemental spirits, principalities and the like). Ascetic practices and rigorous self-discipline were required either in obedience to these beings or as the means to enter into visionary experiences of them. Positive interaction with these beings was probably regarded as, in some sense, necessary for human beings to move into the fullness of the divine realm or experience the fullness of God.

PURPOSE AND MESSAGE

Colossians is written to keep the Christians in that area on course in their growth in discipleship (Col 1:9-10, 23; 2:6-7). One particular obstacle that might throw them off course is their attraction to this philosophy, and so the letter especially seeks to counter this attraction and the temptation to make room for it in their Christian discipleship (Col 2:4, 8). While showing why that alternative philosophy is no advance for them at all, the author also reminds them of the central tenets and ethics of the "philosophy" to which they have committed themselves, namely, the Christian faith.[21]

The focal point for the author's response is the supremacy of Christ, both in its cosmic and ethical dimensions. The leitmotif of the whole letter is that "Christ is Lord over everything—over powers and principalities, but also over the Christian's daily life."[22] Believers need only to be concerned about their connec-

---

[17]Furnish, "Colossians, Epistle to the," *Anchor Bible Dictionary*, ed. David N. Freedman (Garden City, N.Y.: Doubleday, 1992), 1.1092; Lohse, *Colossians and Philemon*, p. 3.

[18]Martin, *Colossians and Philemon*, p. 9; Lohse, *Colossians and Philemon*, pp. 128-30.

[19]E. K. Simpson and F. F. Bruce, *Commentary on the Epistles to the Ephesians and the Colossians*, NICNT (Grand Rapids: Eerdmans, 1957), p. 167.

[20]Barth and Blanke, *Colossians*, p. 39.

[21]Most who take this letter to be pseudonymous would understand the purpose in similar terms, even if Colossae is not taken to be the real author's real audience. Margaret MacDonald draws on Weber's theory of the routinization of charisma to explain the purpose of the pseudonymous author (*Colossians and Ephesians*, Sacra Pagina 17 [Collegeville, Minn.: Liturgical Press, 2000], pp. 7-8). According to Weber, new religious movements tend to arise through the agency of a charismatic leader, one who is regarded as endowed with a special revelation or as a person specially in touch with the divine. This leader is the authority figure for the movement. As the group grows, and especially after the leader dies, authority has to be vested in other people, and it tends to become associated with particular "offices" that can then be occupied by a succession of people. MacDonald suggests that the author of Colossians is helping the Pauline mission recover after the death of its "charismatic leader," reinforcing "the authority of Paul's co-workers (especially Epaphras and Tychicus)." Unfortunately, while all could agree that Colossians *could* serve this end, MacDonald brings forward no evidence to persuade that it *does* serve this end. This is an example of how a sociological model, and not data from the text, can drive a scholar's conclusions.

[22]Lohse, *Colossians and Philemon*, p. 178.

Wisdom Christology in Colossians 1:15-20

Early Christian reflection on Jesus, especially on his preincarnate existence and activity, owes a great deal to Jewish reflection on the figure of Wisdom. Already in Proverbs, Wisdom takes on something of a personality, inviting devotees and revealing her origins in a first-person speech (Prov 8:4-36). Especially relevant are Wisdom's assertion to have been the first creation of the Almighty (Prov 8:22-26), and not merely as a created thing but as something "born" from God (Prov 8:25), her claim to have been a coworker with God in the creation (Prov 8:27-31), and her claim to bring favor from God to all who find her (Prov 8:35).

The Wisdom of Solomon, written in the first century B.C.E. or early in the first century C.E., greatly intensifies the praise of Wisdom. Wisdom is a

> reflection of eternal light,
> a spotless mirror of the working of God,
> and an image of his goodness. (Wis 7:26 NRSV).

She was present at creation (Wis 9:9) and remains the mediator who secures "friendship with God" (Wis 7:14), who makes people "friends of God" (Wis 7:27), who teaches them how to please God (Wis 9:9-12).

Such speculation about the relationship of Wisdom to God and Wisdom's role as mediator between God and creation, and between God and God's creatures, provided the raw materials for early Christian reflection on the career of the One sent from God. The face of Wisdom came to represent the face of the Son before he took on flesh. Thus in this hymn, we find all of these major Wisdom motifs applied to Jesus Christ: he is the "image of the invisible God" (Col 1:15), the first fruit of God's creative acts ("firstborn," Col 1:15; 17), God's agent in creation (Col 1:16, 17) and the mediator between human beings and God (Col 1:19-20).

The differences and developments are just as significant. Now one can speak of God's fullness dwelling in a human being, of mediation and the securing of divine favor happening in terms of a death on behalf of humanity, and of the "life" that is promised to those who follow this mediator in terms of life beyond death (Col 1:18). There is also an *ecclesiological* dimension absent from the earlier Wisdom speculation. Christ has formed—and continues to remain connected to—a community of followers (Col 1:18). There is also a *cosmic* dimension, in that Christ has not merely reconciled individual people with God but has set in motion a much larger, all-encompassing peace (Col 1:20).

tion with this Christ and walking in the new life Christ has opened up. Christ is the image of God, the agent and goal of creation, the repository of God's fullness exercises authority above any intermediary spiritual entity (Col 1:15-20; 2:9-10, 15). An early Christian hymn (Col 1:15-17) provides a lofty starting point from which the author's teaching about Christ grows, establishing that no lesser spiritual power has authority to demand worship or tokens of obedience such as the observance of certain regulations.[23]

---

[23]Ibid., p. 3.

The language of Colossians 1:12-14 is thought to reflect traditional material as well, leading to the possibility that the author uses statements reminiscent of the words spoken over the audience at baptism as a means of affirming the deliverance from the powers already effected by being joined with Christ. There is nothing left for intermediary beings to do. The mystery (Col 1:26, 27; 2:2; 4:3) of the gospel into which they have been initiated has opened up to them all the knowledge (*gnōsis*; Col 1:9; 2:2) needed for salvation, for entering the divine realm, experiencing the divine "fullness" (Col 1:9; 19; 2:2, 9, 10). No other philosophy can deepen the believer's appreciation of this mystery, especially one that moves them back toward subservience to beings that are not divine. To have Christ, the author avers, is to have deliverance, the fullness that God intends (Col 2:10, 19; 3:1-4). The believer is already connected with and rooted in God's kingdom, and transferred out of the realm of the evil powers' influence (Col 1:12-14).

Christ is Lord not only over the cosmic powers but also the believers' lives. To live the new life opened up by baptism, however, does not depend on empty asceticism, humanly devised taboos or receiving visions. Believers have received a spiritual circumcision in baptism and the divinely given power to enjoy deliverance from the sway of the carnal passions (Col 2:11-14). The only necessary and fruitful asceticism is the mortification of the carnal desires—not external or ritualistic signs of world rejection but the concerted rejection of worldly ethics and the indulgence of the flesh (Col 3:1-17). Far from being a rejection of the world, the Christian philosophy encourages ongoing engagement with the world, particularly within the relationships of the household.

AUTHORSHIP

Colossians presents itself to the reader as a letter from Paul, but its authenticity has been challenged on numerous grounds. Scholarship is fairly evenly divided on this question.

Vocabulary and word usage. Colossians contains a number of words that do not appear elsewhere in Paul's letters (or the New Testament, for that matter; these are called *hapax legomena,* "things uttered once"), but this is generally confessed to be insignificant even among advocates of pseudonymity. It has no more *hapax legomena* than Philippians,[24] and many of these unusual words occur either in the hymn of Colossians 1:15-20 (traditional material that would not be expected to reflect Paul's typical vocabulary) or in the treatment of the philosophy opposed (material that introduces the distinctive vocabulary of the rival teaching).[25] Scholars have also observed that although a word from Colossians may be used frequently in the undisputed Paulines, the author of Colossians may use it in a different sense. Thus *hope* is used in Colossians 1:5, 23 to denote "hoped-for benefits" rather than the "attitude of hope," the more typical Pauline usage. The significance of such data is often hard to assess because all authors typically use words in more than one way. Paul himself uses "hope" to mean "hoped-for benefits" at least in Roman 8:24; Galatians 5:5; and 1 Thessalonians 2:19. Because of the flexibility of language, the versatility of authors and the particularities of the situation addressed, arguments from vocabulary and usage tend to be given little weight in discussions of authorship.

Style. A somewhat more useful criterion is the style of a text—the distinctive features of how an author habitually makes sentences, uses certain connective words like conjunctions, and the like. In a careful study Walter Bujard concluded that conjunctions were used

---

[24]Lohse, *Colossians and Philemon,* pp. 86, 91.
[25]O'Brien, *Colossians, Philemon,* p. xliii; Barth and Blanke, *Colossians,* p. 64.

half as frequently in Colossians as in Paul's other letters, while participles and relative clauses were used more frequently.[26] At the same time O'Brien finds evidence of "peculiarities of Pauline style" in Colossians.[27] The letter as a whole includes more traditional material and relies less on direct and innovative argumentation (as in Galatians or 1 Corinthians). Had Paul merely adopted a different rhetorical strategy to address the situation in Colossae, this would in itself account for a number of the peculiarities of style. What are the limits of an author's style? How much would an author's style naturally vary from year to year, situation to situation?

Theology. Although a person's expression may vary greatly, it is less likely that his or her fundamental convictions are going to change that dramatically. This fact makes arguments from theological differences far more weighty than arguments from vocabulary and style.[28] We must always weigh the theological differences we discover, however, against the particular challenges addressed by the author. A difference in *emphasis* that could argue impressively against Pauline authorship when considered apart from its historical and pastoral context might, when weighed within that context, be seen more as the fruits of a versatile mind adapting the message about Christ to new questions or developing new insights in light of new and stimulating challenges.[29] Discussion of the differences between Colossians and the undisputed Pauline letters has focused on the following:

- *Christology.* The author of Colossians stresses Christ's triumph over the cosmic powers, while saying nothing about Christ's

victory over the law, sin and death. This letter goes beyond any undisputed Pauline text concerning the exaltation of Christ when it speaks of the "fullness of God" dwelling in Christ "in a bodily manner" (Col 2:9).[30] However, statements like these tend to obscure the fact that Colossians makes frequent reference to the ways that Christ's death dealt with sin (cf. Col 2:13-14 with Rom 5:12, 18), effected forgiveness and reconciliation (cf. Col 1:20, 22 with 2 Cor 5:18-19), and other such common Pauline themes about the person and work of Christ (cf. the language of redemption and transfer in Col 1:13-14 with Gal 1:4; the metaphor of stripping off and clothing oneself anew in Col 3:9-10, 12 with Rom 13:14 and Gal 3:27; the mortification of the carnal passions in Col 3:5-8 with Gal 5:16-25), just as Paul's statements about Christ's exaltation provide a foundation for the development seen in Colossians (see 1 Cor 8:6; Phil 2:10; Rom 8:29).

- *Eschatology.* The author of Colossians places less emphasis on the future hope of the Christian and more on the present deliverance of believers and the present authority of Christ. For the author "a spatially determined mode of thought replaces the expectation which eagerly longs for the future fulfillment of the promise."[31] It is indeed true that future eschatology moves more into the background in Colossians, but again we need to keep in mind the wonderful balance of Colossians 3:1-4, which remains thoroughly apocalyptic as it looks ahead to the future revelation of Jesus as well as the expectation of future wrath and reward (Col

---

[26]W. Bujard, *Stilanalytische Untersuchungen zum Kolosserbrief als Beitrag zur Methodik von Sprachvergleichen,* SUNT 11 (Göttingen: Vandenhoeck & Ruprecht, 1973), pp. 74-75.

[27]O'Brien, *Colossians, Philemon,* p. xlii.

[28]Lohse relied almost exclusively on this criterion as he argued for pseudonymity (*Colossians and Philemon,* pp. 177-83).

[29]Barth and Blanke, *Colossians,* p. 126.

[30]Lohse, *Colossians and Philemon,* p. 178.

[31]Lohse, *Colossians and Philemon,* p. 180.

3:6, 24). It is not as though the author has abandoned future eschatology in favor of "realized" eschatology, but a matter of which Pauline aspect is underscored. The "spatially determined mode of thought" in Colossians, moreover, emerges clearly in response to the spatial orientation of the philosophy and its teaching about orders of spiritual beings and human interaction with them. One conceptual problem in this debate is the opposition between spatial and temporal interests, both of which are equally important to the apocalyptic mind.[32] The author's emphasis here need not be set against the temporal expectations discussed more thoroughly elsewhere in the Pauline corpus, but it can be seen quite naturally and unforcedly as complementary.

A more serious concern is the emphasis in Colossians on having already been raised with Christ (Col 2:12; 3:1-2), whereas Paul habitually speaks of dying with Christ in the hope of being raised with him (e.g., Phil 3:9-11). The future hope in Colossians is expressed not as resurrection but as the manifestation of the believers' new life that they already enjoy (Col 3:1-4).[33] Could Paul indeed, who elsewhere speaks only of the future resurrection of the dead, talk about Christians as already "raised with Christ" in some sense? Does the mixture of the "already" and the "not yet" of this resurrected life in Col 3:1-4 provide sufficient safeguard against the dangers that Paul perceived when other teachers denied the futurity of the resurrection?[34]

The "cosmic Christology" and emphasis on "realized eschatology" are the major objections to Pauline authorship. These peculiar emphases are, however, the most readily explicable in terms of the challenges posed by a philosophy that stresses the authority of powers, angels and principalities over human life. By emphasizing Christ's exaltation above and lordship over the angels, powers and principalities, and then by emphasizing the believers' present connection with this exalted Jesus as the head of the body, in whom they themselves are already removed from the sphere of the authority of the powers of this age, the author has pursued the necessary strategy for undermining the appeal of the Colossian philosophy.[35] Precisely as in Galatians the alternative course is made to appear as a step backward in salvation history rather than a clever step forward.

- *Ecclesiology.* In Colossians, Christ is head of the body, the church, whereas in 1 Corinthians 12 the church is simply the body, with the head being treated like just another member (Rom 12:4-5 does not discuss the head in any way, and so remains neutral).[36] Is this a sign of a different author's use of a Pauline metaphor or a natural development that Paul himself could have made, particularly in light of the situation he contemplated in Colossae. By naming Christ as the head, the author effects that link between the believers and the exalted Christ that drives home the believers' freedom from the authority of the cosmic powers.

---

[32]See the important work in this regard by J. J. Collins, *The Apocalyptic Imagination* (New York: Crossroad, 1987), and "Apocalyptic Literature," in *Early Judaism and Its Modern Interpreters,* ed. R. A. Kraft and G. W. E. Nickelsburg (Philadelphia: Fortress, 1986), p. 346, advances to which Lohse did not have access.

[33]Lohse, *Colossians and Philemon,* p. 180.

[34]The emphatic denials of a present resurrection or the fact that the resurrection has already happened in some sense ironically appear only in other disputed letters, and not the undisputed Pauline epistles (see 2 Thess 2:2; 2 Tim 2:18).

[35]The fact that these differences in theological emphasis occur both in sections that "argue against the 'philosophy'" as well as "sections that are free of polemic" (Lohse, *Colossians and Philemon,* p. 180) has no real bearing on the case, for *all* sections of the letter address the situation in Colossae. That situation would shape the author's exposition of the implications of Christ in all parts of the letter.

[36]Lohse, *Colossians and Philemon,* p. 179.

- *Soteriology.* In Romans 6:6 Paul speaks of the believer dying with Christ to *sin;* in Colossians 2:20 the believer has died with Christ to the *elements of the universe.*[37] Once again, the way the statement is framed (to reflect the differences) obscures the fundamental correlation—in both cases the process of deliverance is understood to involve a death on the part of the believers to some aspect of this age. The modification provides a clear-cut example of how Paul can adapt his proclamation of the deliverance God effects in Christ to a variety of specific situational challenges.

- *Paul's understanding of suffering.* The author of Colossians describes Paul's sufferings as "making up what is lacking in Christ's sufferings for the sake of his body, that is, the church" (Col 1:24). This is often held to conflict with Paul's view elsewhere that he is merely manifesting Christ's sufferings in his own body, not "completing" them (see 2 Cor 4:7-12).[38] This verse, however, could be understood quite differently. Paul regards the sufferings of Christ to be the measure he must live up to (along the lines of Phil 3:8-11, joining with Christ in his sufferings) as he fulfills the work to which he was called. It is not *Christ's* sufferings that are lacking and being made up by Paul as he suffers, but the full measure of Paul's experience of Christ's sufferings *in Paul's flesh* that is lacking and being filled up. Which interpretation we follow depends wholly on where we place the prepositional phrase "in my flesh"—does it qualify the verb ("I am completing") or the verbal adjective ("the things that are lacking").

- *Missing topics.* The objection that topics emphasized in undisputed Pauline letters are absent from Colossians is less weighty. Justification by faith, for example, is neither present in the Corinthian or Thessalonian letters nor Philemon. These topics arise only insofar as they address the perceived challenges of the situation or the goals of Paul. Indeed, the tendency to reduce Pauline theology to "justification by faith" and its constellation of topics is a special danger in Protestantism, leaving no room for the theological contributions of Colossians and Ephesians as part of the Pauline gospel.[39]

The similarities between the theology of Colossians and that of the undisputed Pauline letters causes proponents of pseudepigraphy to admit that the author was thoroughly schooled in Paul's thought (usually thought of as a member of a Pauline "school"), showing that we have to account not only for differences but also for the similarities. The other position—that the similarities are due to Paul being the author while the differences are due to Paul's thoroughgoing adaptation of the essence of the gospel to the contingencies of a specific situation[40]—accounts for the evidence just as well in this case, making it very difficult for any consensus to be reached in the field on this point.

The image of Paul. It is sometimes alleged that the presentation of Paul's apostolic authority and the scope of his ministry as depicted in Colossians conflict with undisputed letters. That is, here he looks after churches already founded by someone else, whereas in 2 Corinthians 10:13-16 he speaks of avoiding interloping in another's area of work. This objection is one of the less astute, for it overlooks Paul's connection with Epaphras, who, for all

---

[37]Ibid., p. 180.

[38]See, for example, Furnish, "Colossians," 1:1094.

[39]Simpson and Bruce, *Ephesians and Colossians,* p. 169.

[40]See O'Brien, *Colossians, Philemon,* pp. xlviii-xlix; Barth and Blanke, *Colossians,* p. 121. "As novel issues turned up, they helped the apostle to rethink and formulate in new terms his message of Jesus Christ" (Barth and Blanke, *Colossians,* p. 126).

intents and purposes, functions as one of Paul's team and indeed may have asked Paul to intervene. In 2 Corinthians Paul contrasts himself with teachers who are clearly not aligned with Paul and who are trying to subvert Paul's work; in Colossians Paul allies himself with a fellow evangelist (Epaphras) and works to undergird his partner's work. Paul's intervention in Colossae does not contradict the policy found in 2 Corinthians 10; he is nurturing the work of others, not laying another foundation or usurping the prerogatives of others.

Some proponents of pseudonymity suggest that the self-presentation of Paul in Colossians 1:24-29 makes extravagant claims about Paul's authority that Paul could not have made during his lifetime, singling out Paul as the chief and, effectively, only apostle to the Gentiles. Moreover, it presents Paul as the patron apostle not only of the churches he founded during his lifetime but of all Gentile Christian churches. However, this claim overlooks the presence of the "we" in Colossians 1:28, where Paul brings in all those who are partners in his missionary efforts, and fails to do justice to Paul's rather clear idea of his key role in the plan of God (cf. Col 1:24—2:5 with Gal 1:12-15; 2 Cor 3:10-13).[41] Moreover, Colossians 2:1 would function quite naturally within Paul's lifetime to show that Paul is concerned not only about his own converts but for all believers. He is a "team player," not just looking after his own.

Further, some scholars observe that Colossians 1:6, 23, which claim that "every creature" has heard the gospel, must be a sign of post-Pauline composition, since at no point in Paul's lifetime could this claim be made. The claim, however, would be just as hyperbolic in the post-Pauline period (indeed, up to the present time) as during Paul's lifetime, so this kind of evidence is far from helpful.

Setting in Paul's life. Classifying Colossians as a deutero-Pauline letter was established as a scholarly dogma by F. C. Baur and his school, who argued that the heresy opposed was a post-Pauline development (indeed, it represented second-century Christian Gnosticism).[42] Assumptions that Colossians combats fully developed Gnosticism had fueled early theories of pseudonymity, but the error envisioned in Colossians hardly needs to be more than proto-Gnostic, a syncretistic form of Judaism (or a pagan movement that has incorporated Jewish beliefs and practices) that would be quite appropriate to the middle of the first century.

In another vein the connections with Philemon, taken by some as evidence of authenticity, have also been interpreted as indications of a pseudepigrapher's attempts to link Colossians into the known history of Paul, and thus making the ascription more believable. In this case pseudepigraphy is meant to deceive: the addition of such details would be calculated to hide its true origin in the post-Pauline period.

In the case of Colossians, then, the arguments against authenticity are ambiguous at best. Some of the "evidence" we encounter is simply weak. The more important objections are readily explicable in reference to the contingent circumstances in Colossae, and would be even easier to explain if we allowed a substantial contribution to the framing of the letter on the part of Timothy.[43] Indeed, if we take the explicated setting at face value—namely, that Paul has been informed by Epaphras about recent developments among the Colossian Christians and decides to address converts he does not know personally—the letter itself

---

[41]Barth and Blanke, *Colossians*, p. 121.
[42]See O'Brien, *Colossians, Philemon*, p. lxi.
[43]As does Dunn, *Epistle to the Colossians*, pp. 35, 38.

gives us exactly what we would expect from an astute pastoral leader:

- the reliance on shared traditions and traditional forms (hymns in Col 1:15-20, possibly in Col 2:13-15; vice lists in Col 3:5, 8; the tradition of "household management" reflected in the topics treated in Col 3:18—4:1) serves to build up common ground between Paul and the hearers.

- Paul's brief reflection on his own calling and role in God's purpose, and the nature of his relationship with the Christians in Colossae and Laodicea (Col 1:24—2:5), establish ethos, showing the speaker to be authoritative, credible and favorably disposed toward the addressees (the three elements of securing a receptive hearing). This is all the more essential since Paul is personally unknown to the large majority of the addressees.

- the prayer request, greetings, personal word to Archippus, notices of the travel plans of Tychicus and Onesimus and, above all, authenticating signature (Col 4:18)[44] are all perfectly intelligible in this setting; indeed, even some who favor pseudonymity observe that Colossians 4:7-18 as a whole supports authenticity since these verses are so personal and give such weighty evidence of having been written to a specific community.[45]

The peculiarities of the challenges facing the addressees account for the peculiarities of language and a good deal of the theological emphases of the letter. The serious engagement of the opposition's position is also reminiscent of Paul's well-known style. Thus the charge that the Pastoral Epistles merely dismiss rather than engage the opponents, distinguishing them from Paul's usual strategy, could not be leveled against Colossians. Faced with a philosophy that played up the authority and importance of intermediate spiritual beings, Paul develops the Christians' connection to and rootedness in the triumphant Christ, liberating them from thinking they might be in bondage or need to be subservient to lesser powers. This would naturally lead to the notion of Christ as the head of the body, the church (but would not necessitate that Paul drag this development into Romans, where he could again use the more neutral conception he formulated in 1 Corinthians). Emphasizing the deliverance they already enjoy, while downplaying the future realization of this deliverance (which, in this context, could contribute to their insecurity and thus their susceptibility to the opponents' "safety net" rituals), would also serve Paul's goal of eliminating the attractiveness of the rival philosophy. If the heresy contains elements of the Pythagorean cosmology sketched out by Martin, teaching that the believers are already in some sense raised to the divine realm because of their connection with Christ would be an appropriate counterclaim, all the more as this is balanced in Colossians 3:4 by the apocalyptic expectation (when their spiritual deliverance is manifested and consummated in reality), as well as by the typically Pauline connection of this indicative with the imperatives of Christian life (Col 3:1—4:6).

PROVENANCE

Paul writes to the Colossian Christians from a prison (Col 4:3, 10, 18), but which prison? Was it written during his incarceration in Caesarea (about 58-60 C.E.) or his detention in Rome (about 60-62 C.E.) or another imprisonment. We do not know all of the specifics of Paul's life, nor all the imprisonments he endured. Acts only speaks of Philippi (overnight), Caesarea and Rome, but in 2 Corin-

---

[44]Advocates of pseudonymity acknowledge the ethical problem of falsifying the authenticating signature. To resolve this, Petr Pokorný, for example, appeals to "the grace of God," by which "the legitimate apostolic intention succeeded, despite human failure and literary falsification" (Petr Pokorný, *Colossians* [Peabody, Mass.: Hendrickson, 1991], pp. 16-17).

[45]MacDonald, *Colossians and Ephesians*, p. 7.

thians Paul speaks of having suffered several imprisonments already before the Caesarean imprisonment. Where does Colossians fit into the life of Paul? The connections with Philemon are suggestive. Onesimus returns to Colossae from Paul's location in both texts, and greetings are sent from virtually the same group of people in Philemon 23 and Colossians 1:7; 4:12-19. Archippus, furthermore, is addressed in both letters. Was Colossians sent at the same time as Philemon? Or was Colossians sent some time after Philemon, and thus is a sign that Philemon had honored Paul's request to free Onesimus for Paul's service?[46] Although Paul is surrounded by the same circle of colleagues, Aristarchus is Paul's "fellow prisoner" in Colossians, whereas Epaphras has that distinction in Philemon 23; but Aristarchus is a "fellow worker" in Philem 23 and Epaphras appears to be free to work as a "fellow servant" in Colossians 1:7. It is possible, therefore, that some time has elapsed between the two letters (enough time for Epaphras to be freed and Aristarchus to get into trouble) and even that the letters come from two separate incidents of imprisonment. The relationship of Colossians to Philemon figures largely in discussions of Paul's location.

The Marcionite prologue to Colossians, perhaps the earliest testimony to its origins, claims that Paul wrote this letter from a prison in Ephesus.[47] Given the movement envisioned in the letter (Epaphras's visit to Paul; Tychichus and Onesimus traveling to Colossae with the letter), Ephesus would be a convenient place of detention indeed—all the more if Philemon were written and dispatched at the same time

(see p. 668). The main objection to an Ephesian imprisonment (other than the lack of explicit documentation for such an imprisonment within the New Testament itself) is the development of Pauline motifs in Colossians, which are presumed to have taken several years to develop. In particular, some find it unlikely that Paul would speak of the "body" without giving the "head" any distinction in 1 Corinthians 12 but develop the notion of Christ as the "head" of the "body" in Colossians, and then revert to language about the body without reference to Christ as the head in Romans 12.[48] However, Paul was always shaping his metaphors to best serve the pastoral needs he perceived in the community he addressed, so such a series of shifts cannot be ruled out of court entirely. The images are so similar as to be interchangeable, depending on which pastoral potential Paul wishes to unlock. Focusing simply on the "body" serves as a resource for fostering unity and valuing the diversity of contributions of all disciples; focusing on the "body" as connected with the "head" provides a resource for directing attention centripetally toward Christ and emphasizing connectedness with Christ and all the benefits that would carry.

Some would favor the Caesarean imprisonment. Caesarea is only 350 miles from Colossae, as opposed to the 900 miles that separates Colossae from Rome, and could be traversed by Epaphras, Onesimus and others much more quickly than the trip to Rome. In Caesarea, moreover, Paul experiences extended detention for the first time, which may be reflected in Philemon 9: "an old ambassador but *now* also a prisoner for Christ."[49] Co-

---

[46]Petr Pokorný is certain that Colossians postdates Philemon based on Colossians 4:9, where Onesimus appears "already a proven coworker of the apostle" (*Colossians*, p. 9). This is possible but hardly necessitated by Colossians 4:9, in which Paul might have been commending Onesimus for his service to Paul shortly after his conversion. Perhaps Paul is trying to help the congregation see Onesimus now in a new light (not as Philemon's slave, yet to be freed, but already as Paul's coworker).

[47]O'Brien, *Colossians, Philemon*, p. lii.

[48]Barth and Blanke, *Colossians*, p. 128.

[49]Ibid.

lossians, with its identical cast of characters, would probably be written from the same place. One of the major objections to this view is the sizeable circle of colleagues Paul has around him, something much more natural in the area of his actual mission work (somewhere between Antioch and Rome) than his detention in Palestine.

A slight majority of scholars who favor Pauline authorship also favor a Roman imprisonment as the setting for Colossians, and thus a date between 60-62 C.E. Aristarchus, mentioned in Colossians 4:10 as Paul's "fellow prisoner," is known from Acts 27:2 to have journeyed with Paul to Rome.[50] The celebra-

tion of the gospel's progress (Col 1:6, 23), exaggerated in any generation of church history, is most natural if Paul has arrived in Rome and looks back at the headway made everywhere from Rome back to Jerusalem.[51] In general, the content of Paul's thought in Colossians (and Ephesians) is more easily explained as a development or deepening of material present in the other letters, and so a later date tends to be favored (again making Rome the preferred candidate).[52] The major objections to a Roman imprisonment really reflect data in Philemon rather than Colossians, so they only pose a problem if Colossians and Philemon are held to have been sent at the same time.

EXEGETICAL SKILL
Word Studies and Lexical Analysis

Cautions and procedures. Word studies are perhaps the most common way ministers and other students of the Bible delve into the original languages. The focus of expository preaching on the meaning of the words of the text gave rise to the many "word study" books available on the market. The study of the meaning of words, however, has often proceeded in isolation from the science of language (linguistics), with the result that some basic fallacies have become endemic to the very word-study enterprise. Being aware of such missteps will assist you in making critical use of dictionaries and of authors that engage in word studies.

The most common mistake is to confuse a word study with a thematic or topical study. Words are not concepts, even though most word studies confuse the two.[a] Often what preachers and Christian educators are interested

---

[a]This was a recurrent theme of James Barr's *The Semantics of Biblical Language* (Oxford: Oxford University Press, 1961); see also Max Turner, "Modern Linguistics and the New Testament," in *Hearing the New Testament*, ed. J. B. Green, (Grand Rapids: Eerdmans, 1995), pp. 153-54.

---

[50]O'Brien, *Colossians, Philemon*, p. 1.

[51]Ibid.; Barth and Blanke, *Colossians*, pp. 133-34.

[52]Simpson and Bruce, *Ephesians and Colossians*, p. 165. Dunn regards Colossians as the transition point between Pauline and post-Pauline theology (*Epistle to the Colossians*, p. 39). Most who decide that Colossians is pseudonymous emphasize that it must have been written very shortly after Paul's death (Lohse, *Colossians and Philemon*, p. 166; Pokorny, *Colossians*, p. 4). Pokorny has suggested that the letter was intended for Laodicea all along, but it was written as if to Colossae with instructions that it eventually be passed along to Laodicea (Col 4:16; Pokorny, *Colossians*, pp. 20-21). In effect, it got lost in the mail and arrived in Laodicea only after the apostle died. This assumes that the congregation in Colossae was largely defunct after the earthquake of 61 C.E.

in is the concept, not the word, which requires a different kind of study! For example, the student interested in the early Christian idea of "love" will not find this through the study of the famous word *agapē* or its verbal form, *agapaō*. The New Testament—or even just the Johannine—concept of "love" comes to expression through the use of a wide range of words in a wide range of contexts as well as through discourses and stories that demonstrate love without ever using the vocabulary of love.[a]

On the one hand, a word study is too narrow to substitute for a thematic or conceptual study; on the other hand, individual words are routinely made to bear the weight of concepts that are generated not by the word (and hence are not "meanings" of the word) but by the discourse surrounding the word. In other words, many word studies—and thus many Greek-English dictionaries (called lexica, singular lexicon) fail to distinguish between "lexical concepts" (the actual range of meanings a native speaker would be expected to attach to a word) and "discourse concepts" (the meanings generated by the larger discourse that provides the context for a particular use of a word, and not vested in single words in isolation). For example, a student might conclude from John 1:1-4 that *ho logos* can mean "divine Word" and then offer it as a translational choice for *logos*. When this happens, specific content developed by John is dumped into the "lexical meaning" of *logos*, whereas in reality the concept of "divine Word" is not a function of the meaning of *logos*, but of John's prologue as he makes use of this word.[b] Many lexica available today lead the student into this trap on every page, presenting contextual meanings (meanings in fact added from the context where a word might appear in a particular text) as translational equivalents, leading to all kinds of innovative translations in biblical Greek I and II!

Another common fallacy pertains to the etymology and the "original" meaning of a word. An early meaning of a word will frequently be invoked as the real or core meaning, which is then imposed on the text. This logic fails to consider that languages evolve. Thus etymological studies can do far more harm than good.[c] To take an English example, it does not illumine the modern practice of leasing apartments or automobiles to look to early seventeenth-century usage of this word, when *leasing* referred to promiscuous behavior, and then impose this as the real meaning of the word on the exegesis of the sign, "Now Leasing. Call 555-RENT." Linguists also caution us against leaning too much on observations about word formation (the sum of the meaning of the constituent parts of a word) when investigating a word. Though often a good, rough guide to the meaning of unfa-

---

[a]Peter Cotterell and Max Turner, *Linguistics and Biblical Interpretation* (Downers Grove, Ill.: InterVarsity Press, 1989), pp. 119-20; Turner, "Modern Linguistics," p. 154.
[b]Cotterell and Turner, *Linguistics and Biblical Interpretation*, pp. 120-21.
[c]Barr, *Semantics of Biblical Language*, pp. 111-29; Cotterell and Turner, *Linguistics and Biblical Interpretation*, pp. 113-15.

miliar words, it is not always a reliable one (for example, "understand" is not made up of the sum of the meaning of the words *under* and *stand*).

Finally, students are encouraged to resist the temptation to look for the "basic, underlying sense" of a Greek word, or to attempt to synthesize such a "root meaning" out of common aspects of known meanings. A given word might have a number of distinctly different senses, not one, general, overarching sense. Consider the word *right,* which has at least three distinct and irreducible meanings, even though it is the "same" word. Linguists call this "homonymy," and they would in fact distinguish between three words—*right₁, right₂* and *right₃*—on the grounds that three discrete meanings can be expressed by means of the same string of sounds. Any one of the homonyms expressed by the sound ("right") will also have a variety of senses (called "polysemy"). Here again the attempt to get behind all the senses to a root meaning will be misleading when it comes to determining what the word means in a particular context, for in any particular context the word will carry not a hypothetical root meaning but one of the particular senses.[d] This is also, by the way, a primary reason why there can be no consistent one-word translational equivalent in English for Greek words, no matter how much beginning Greek students long for such a chimera.[e]

Linguists teach us that words have meaning only in relation to other words—those that surround them in a sentence and are available as replacements in a sentence. For example, the meaning of *right* in the sentences "You have the right to remain silent," "You will find the house on the right" or "You have chosen the right answer" is determined by the context. (If the word is used as a noun, usually followed by the word *to* and some action or thing, *right* is usually understood as a sphere of undeniable authority; if it is used in a context describing the location of some noun, it will be understood as denoting one side as opposed to the other; used as an adjective, it will either denote "correctness" or again "the thing on one side" as opposed to another, and so contextual markers will be need to be observed even more carefully.) The context, both local (in the sentence) and global (in the text as a whole), is crucial for determining the meaning of the word. The larger context of the word's contemporary or near-contemporary usage provides the larger pool of meanings an author would be drawing on in a particular utterance.

On the other hand, in these sentences the word *right* has its sense in relation to other available words that could be meaningfully substituted in

---

[d]Cotterell and Turner, *Linguistics and Biblical Interpretation,* pp. 135-39.
[e]"Professor, when I see *pistis* in the Greek text, I just want to know what English word to use in my translation." "Well, that will depend on the context," the instructor replied. *Why does he make it so difficult?* thought the student.

the sentences, whether partial synonyms or not: "You have the *ability/ choice/authority/need/audacity* to remain silent," or "You will find the house on the *left*," or "You have chosen the *wrong/easy/partial* answer." It is thus also important to look at words particularly in relation to synonyms and partial synonyms and their usage in order to determine what distinctive sense or connotations might be associated by native speakers with the word under investigation.[f]

With these basic principles and caveats in mind, what steps should the student take in order to investigate the nuances and meanings of particular words?[g]

1. The first step is to identify words that invite further study. These can be words that are frequently repeated in the passage or book as a whole, words that are unclear (the resolution of which will dramatically affect interpretation), words that are thematically or theologically important, like *faith, grace* or *justify* (and would benefit from closer study rather than from reading our theological understanding into those terms). Little words, however, can also make a big difference. Very often it is a preposition that most needs to be closely analyzed, since these can often carry tremendous theological weight.

2. Using the various tools suited to this enterprise (see following section), determine the range of meanings this word had in the Greco-Roman and Jewish literature of the late-Hellenistic/early-Roman period. It is important not merely to look here at definitions but to examine actual passages that use the word being studied. In what contexts does the word usually appear? Is it linked with any specific social institutions or relationships? What contextual indicators would lead a native hearer to choose one sense over another as *the* meaning of the word in each passage? This information will be of great value when you turn to the New Testament usage of the word. Then you can begin to hear its resonances beyond the "religious" sphere of Christian Scripture and more in connection with the real-life, everyday contexts in which the New Testament authors and audi-

---

[f]Turner, "Modern Linguistics," pp. 159-60; Cotterell and Turner, *Linguistics and Biblical Interpretation,* pp. 139-75, esp. pp. 154-75.

[g]For what follows, I am particularly indebted to Gordon Fee's *New Testament Exegesis,* 3rd ed. (Louisville, Ky.: Westminster John Knox, 2002), pp. 80-85. Rather than present a specific example here, I would refer the reader to pp. 104-18 of my *Honor, Patronage, Kinship and Purity* (Downers Grove, Ill.: InterVarsity Press, 2000) as an extended study of the multivalent word *charis,* "grace." On pp. 104-5, I examine the lexical meanings of the word as exhibited in classical, Hellenistic and New Testament texts, and I discuss at length the social contexts in which someone was likely to use or hear—and thus to associate—this language (pp. 95-104). This led to an investigation of the further resonances and associations of two of the senses of *charis* (as "favorable disposition" and as "gratitude"), which moves, however, beyond word study into a study of concepts. Then throughout chapter four I turn to numerous specific New Testament texts, in many of which I have had to make decisions about the specific meaning of *charis* (whether "favorable disposition," "gift" or "gratitude"). There, the importance of contextual indicators in each specific passage becomes clear.

ences would have used the language.[h]

3. Again with the help of the standard tools, determine what range of meanings are represented in the author being studied (e.g., Paul, the author of Matthew or John). The possibility that an author is giving a word a specialized sense makes it important to look at the usage in a single author at some stage rather than simply blending together all New Testament uses of the word.[i] Next, investigate how other early Christian authors are using this word.

4. After collecting all this data, it is important to return to the specific context of the word in the passage or passages being considered. What contextual indicators do you find within this passage that might help you determine what sense or meaning of the word is likely to be intended and heard here? How does the preceding discourse and closer context lead us to hear the word in this place? The danger is to lump all the findings of our study into the sentence, whereas in actuality authors intend and native hearers hear a single sense (or narrow range of resonances), the one nurtured and determined by the context.[j]

As part of practicing the art of word studies, additional reading is highly recommended (especially the appropriate chapters in Cotterell and Turner, *Linguistics and Biblical Interpretation* and Fee, *New Testament Exegesis*). Students are then invited to work through the steps outlined above (in conjunction with the tools discussed immediately below) with the significant words in a passage of their choice. Some passages especially rich in significant terms include Matthew 6:9-15; Romans 3:22-26; Galatians 2:14-21; 5:16-25; Ephesians 1:3-14; 2:1-10; 2 Peter 1:3-11.

Tools. The student who wishes to pursue word studies in earnest will need to have access to some essential research tools. These tools, it should be noted, are also invaluable resources for the study of New Testament *concepts* as well as *words*, since the study of concepts builds in part on the investigation of the use of each of the key terms commonly used to give expression to that concept. The best research tools assume that the user has learned biblical Greek. Students without facility in the language of the New Testament will be limited in how much they can derive from certain resources, but they are not excluded. Students should at the very least master the Greek alphabet using the introductory chapter or chapters of any Greek textbook. They can then find the passage and the word to be studied more closely in an interlinear New Testament (a

---

[h]Looking at classical and preclassical usage can be used to supplement senses attested in this later period, but it should not be used to supply meanings for the later period that the word would no longer have had. It is far more important to determine what meanings or senses a word had during the first century than to trace the meanings the word had from Homer on (Turner, "Modern Linguistics," p. 150).
[i]Cotterell and Turner, *Linguistics and Biblical Interpretation*, p. 166.
[j]Ibid., pp. 175-78.

text that provides Greek and English on alternating lines). The form used in the New Testament will be an inflected form, but the lexical form (that is, the dictionary entry form) can be retrieved with the help of an analytical lexicon. At this point students are ready to use most of the Greek-based tools.[k]

Perhaps the most basic tool for studying the usage of a particular word within the New Testament is a Greek concordance.[l] The standard is *A Concordance to the Greek Testament According to the Texts of Westcott and Hort, Tischendorf and the English Revisers.*[m] This is still the most useful, though the student would derive all the basic benefits from alternatives (for example, *The Exhaustive Concordance to the Greek New Testament*).[n] A concordance will allow the student to easily find all the uses of a particular word in the New Testament, thus enabling study of a particular author's use of the word as well as the range of uses within the emerging Christian culture.

The standard Greek-English dictionary for New Testament study is *A Greek-English Lexicon of the New Testament and Other Early Christian Literature.*[o] This lexicon surveys the meanings of each Greek word across the corpus of first- and second-century Christian literature, bringing an extensive sampling of classical and Hellenistic-Roman period texts into the discussion of each word to set the Christian usage in its larger and proper context. Meanings are still contextual, but the student who investigates the larger contexts of the passages cited or quoted will gain a sense of the kinds of contextual signals that would evoke certain meanings. The student should use all dictionaries and other resources critically since there

---

[k]Certain Bible software programs, especially the *Scholar's Library* of Logos Bible Software Series X, have gone far toward bridging the gap between English-only students and original-language word study.

[l]English concordances, though popular and suited for "popular" use, will not suffice for a word study. A particular Greek word (e.g., *charis*) will be translated by several different English words in different contexts (e.g., *gift, grace, favor, gratitude, charm*), and a particular English word *(gift)* can be used as a translational equivalent for several different Greek words (*charis, dōron, dōrēma, charisma,* etc.). Therefore, an English concordance will not reflect the usage of a Greek word in the New Testament. *Young's Analytical Concordance* is one English resource that tries to account for this problem, but it is extremely unwieldy to use. Here, Bible software systems can be of tremendous help (see pp. 710-13, "A Note About Software").

[m]W. F. Moulton and A. S. Geden, *A Concordance to the Greek Testament According to the Texts of Westcott and Hort, Tischendorf and the English Revisers,* ed. I. Howard Marshall, 6th ed (Edinburgh: T & T Clark, 2002).

[n]*The Exhaustive Concordance to the Greek New Testament,* ed. John Kohlenberger III et al. (Grand Rapids: Zondervan, 1995).

[o]Walter Bauer, *A Greek-English Lexicon of the New Testament and Other Early Christian Literature,* ed. F. W. Danker, 3rd ed. (Chicago: University of Chicago Press, 2000). This is commonly abbreviated as BDAG after the four scholars responsible for the work and its ongoing updating: W. Bauer, F. W. Danker, W. F. Arndt and F. W. Gingrich. The abbreviations BAG and BAGD refer to previous editions of this long-lived tool.

is always a lot of interpretation and decision-making involved in every resource (with the exception of concordances). For example, a reader might come to disagree with the decisions made in BDAG regarding which sense of a word is intended in a particular passage. Nevertheless, the amount of information collected therein makes it an indispensable resource.

A helpful companion lexicon is the *Greek-English Lexicon of the New Testament Based on Semantic Domains*.[p] Unlike most alphabetical lexica, this dictionary groups words according to their families of meaning (e.g., words for various plants, names for parts of the human entity, words related to each particular emotion, virtue, kind of behaviors, etc.). This unique organizing principle assists word study by providing the range of words that gives a particular word its meaning and distinctiveness. It also enables the study of particular concepts and fields by laying out the primary groups of words that give expression to that concept or field. Broader usage of a word in Greco-Roman literature is conveniently summarized in *A Greek-English Lexicon,* which is also available in abridged or intermediate versions.[q]

One of the more important environments that lend meanings and resonances to particular words is the Septuagint (LXX), the Greek translations of the Hebrew Bible commonly used among Greek-speaking Jews and Christians in the centuries before and following the turn of the era. If a New Testament word or phrase had "biblical resonances" or "overtones" to the early Christian readers, it would more often be in reference to this textual tradition of the Old Testament (rather than the Hebrew text). The standard critical edition of the Septuagint is Rahlfs' *Septuaginta*.[r] A word's usage in the Septuagint can be discovered with the use of *A Concordance to the Septuagint and the Other Greek Versions of the Old Testament*.[s] The new standard lexicon is *A Greek- English Lexicon of the Septuagint*.[t]

As students move out further to explore other early Jewish uses or Greco-Roman uses of a word, they could consult the standard concordances or individual authors like Philo, Josephus or Aristotle,[u] but this is rarely practical for people in ministry. Here, the appropriate word entries

---

[p] *Greek-English Lexicon of the New Testament Based on Semantic Domains,* ed. Johannes Louw and Eugene Nida, 2nd ed. (Minneapolis: Fortress, 1994).

[q] H. G. Liddell and R. Scott, *A Greek-English Lexicon,* rev. H. S. Jones and R. McKenzie, 9th ed. (Oxford: Clarendon, 1940).

[r] *Septuaginta,* ed. Alfred Rahlfs (New York: United Bible Societies, 1959).

[s] Edwin Hatch and H. A. Redpath, *A Concordance to the Septuagint and the Other Greek Versions of the Old Testament (Including the Apocryphal Books),* 2 vols. (Grand Rapids: Baker, 1983).

[t] *A Greek-English Lexicon of the Septuagint,* ed. J. Lust, E. Eynikel and K. Hauspie, 2 vols. (Stuttgart: Deutsche Bibelgesellschaft, 1992, 1996).

[u] A far more efficient venue is provided by the *Thesaurus Linguae Graece* (TLG) database or, somewhat more limited, by the Perseus Project's website <www.perseus.tufts.edu>. Both allow the user to search for occurrences of a particular string of characters throughout a vast body of ancient literature.

in the *Theological Dictionary of the New Testament* (TDNT) provide quick access to such usages, as its contributors regularly bring together discussions of the word's usage in Philo, Josephus, and classical and Hellenistic authors.[v] This is perhaps the greatest value of the TDNT, especially for the student who is sufficiently familiar with Greek to study the panoply of quotations from these authors using the word under examination. At this point it is necessary to mention James Barr's criticism of the TDNT, developed at length in his *Semantics of Biblical Language*. The contributors to the TDNT regularly mistake "discourse" concepts (the special directions in which a word's meaning is developed by the paragraph or book of which it is a part) for "lexical" concepts (word meanings), making single words bear the full weight of the theological meanings developed in specific passages (while ignoring the fact that the word, used elsewhere, could not possibly carry such meanings). It is a resource, therefore, to be mined for the ancient authors' uses of a particular word, but not necessarily taken at face value in the conclusions it draws about New Testament word meanings. The user must also remain wary of taking archaic or anachronistic senses into the first century literature.

A note about Bible software. Study of the Bible in its original languages has been greatly facilitated by the development and constant improvement of computer-assisted research tools (Bible software). The four programs with which I am acquainted are

- *BibleWorks: Software for Biblical Exegesis and Research* by BibleWorks of Norfolk, Va.
- *Scholar's Library* (series X) by Logos Research Systems of Bellingham, Wash.
- *Bible Windows* by Silver Mountain Software of Cedar Hills, Tex.
- *Gramcord for Windows* by GRAMCORD Institute of Vancouver, Wash.[w]

These powerful packages are economical in two ways. First, each of these packages costs far less than purchasing the print versions of the resources (even if you tallied up just those resources you are likely to use frequently). Second, these programs allow you to conduct basic or advanced searches, access lexica and compare texts with far greater time efficiency than the printed resources. The learning curve can be rather high on these programs, but BibleWorks and Logos Research Systems offer

---

[v] *Theological Dictionary of the New Testament,* ed. Gerhard Kittel and Gerhard Friedrich, 10 vols. (Grand Rapids: Eerdmans, 1964-1976). Another briefer resource of this type is *Exegetical Dictionary of the New Testament,* ed. H. Balz and G. Schneider, 3 vols. (Grand Rapids: Eerdmans, 1990-1992), often abbreviated *EDNT.*

[w] More information about the resources, uses and costs of these products can be obtained by visiting their respective websites: <www.bibleworks.com>, <www.logos.com>, <www.silvermnt.com> and <www.gramcord.org>. My brief comments here are not meant to be comprehensive surveys or evaluations of these products—merely an introduction to the use of computer-assisted research in the study of the Greek New Testament.

video tutorials to assist beginning users, and all have good in-program help features and friendly technical support.

Common to these four programs are the basic, original-language biblical texts you will need for careful study of the Scriptures: the Hebrew Bible (the critical text of the *Biblia Hebraica Stuttgartensia*), the Septuagint, the Greek New Testament, together with several English versions.[x] The text of the Latin Vulgate is also included in all programs, though this is of use primarily to text critics and students of the Latin church fathers. Each program allows the user to compile Hebrew or Greek concordances, rendering print editions superfluous. Each allows the user to open several different texts and link them for simultaneous scrolling, making comparative study quite convenient. Each includes several different Greek and Hebrew lexica.[y] The use of just the most basic tools provided by these software packages already accomplishes an important goal, namely, helping beginning students of biblical Hebrew and Greek read the Scriptures in the original languages in a time-efficient and user-friendly manner.[z]

The greatest advantage of these programs, however, is the way they allow the use of a panoply of research tools in a natural and integrated man-

---

[x]The programs differ significantly in the number of texts included. *BibleWorks* and *Scholar's Library*, for example, provide not only the current critical text of the Greek New Testament but also the older critical editions of Westcott and Hort, and of Tischendorf as well as several different editions of the Textus Receptus and the Majority Text. *Bible Windows* and *Gramcord* provide two Greek texts (the standard and the Textus Receptus). *BibleWorks* and *Scholar's Library* also contain far more modern translations of the Bible, both in English and, in the case of *BibleWorks* twenty-seven other modern languages. Admittedly, however, most users would not need many of these extras.

[y]There are substantial differences between programs in this regard, however, which the student must consider carefully. All four offer the Louw-Nida *Lexicon* and a shorter version of the Lidell-Scott *Lexicon*, with *Gramcord, Bible Windows* and *BibleWorks* offering also the basic *Greek-English Dictionary* (ed. Barclay Newman [London: United Bible Societies, 1971]). *Gramcord* adds the important Lust-Eynikel-Hauspie *Lexicon of the Septuagint* mentioned above, a resource that the others lack. *Scholar's Library*, on the other hand, includes the ten-volume *Theological Dictionary of the New Testament* (and they are working, at the time of this writing, on making the unabridged Liddell-Scott *Greek-English Lexicon* available); both *Scholar's Library* and *BibleWorks* also provide the full text of the BDAG for an additional unlock fee. Hebrew resources vary similarly, the primary advantage of *BibleWorks* and *Scholar's Library* being the inclusion of the complete Brown-Driver-Briggs *Hebrew-English Lexicon*, which includes the discussion of specific texts and comparisons with other Semitic languages, rather than an abridged version, and the availability of the five-volume *Hebrew/Aramaic Lexicon of the Old Testament* for an additional unlock fee.

[z]*Gramcord* and *Bible Works* have the especially winsome feature of allowing the user to open the Greek text, a parsing window and a number of lexica, after which the user can scroll through all three simultaneously with the use of a mouse (as the mouse is moved across the Greek text, the parsing of every word appears and the lexical entry pops up automatically). *Scholar's Library* also provides the parsing with the move of the mouse, but then it requires a click or two of the mouse button to access meanings of the root forms. However, from that point on the user has fluidly integrated access to numerous lexical aids, including the *Theological Dictionary of the New Testament* and all the standard Greek lexica. Such features encouraged beginning language students to persevere in their language studies and in trying to read the Scriptures in the original languages.

ner.[aa] As the student reads along in Ephesians, for example, he or she might want to study a term more closely, perhaps *mystērion* ("mystery"). A few clicks on the mouse or the toolbar menus, and a concordance can be compiled for all forms of *mystērion* in the New Testament and Septuagint. Scrolling through these results, the student can study the occurrence of the word in each context, moving back and forth between Greek and English as needed. Additionally, several lexica can be consulted at once, either on the main screen or with a few clicks on the word.[ab] All the time spent finding entries in one print resource or another is saved for actual reflection on the texts themselves. Moreover, these programs are capable of conducting complex lexical searches (for example, looking for a word like *dikaiosynē*, only in the context of another particular word, like *theos*) that would take an inordinate amount of time using print resources.[ac] The more advanced student can also perform grammatical searches, where the object may not be to research the use of a word so much as the ways in which a particular author uses participles, or dative-case nouns, or particular constructions (like *pistis* followed by a noun in the genitive). Such a search could take hours with print resources; a computer-assisted search would take but a minute or two.[ad]

[aa]The software systems differ greatly on this point, largely in proportion to their cost. *Scholar's Library* quite justifiably prides itself on its user-friendly interface and its integration of many resources. For example, it offers "passage guide," "exegetical guide" and "word study guide" interfaces that enable a user to begin to mine the riches of the software from the moment it is installed, just by entering a verse citation. Each package comes with default desktops/workplaces. The "desktop" displays of *Scholar's Library*, *BibleWorks* and *Gramcord* can be customized rather easily, tailoring the program to the particular research interests of the user. I should also point out here that the four software systems differ tremendously in terms of the English-based resources that are available. *Scholar's Library* has the most to offer in terms of Bible helps (e.g., Bible dictionaries, maps, devotional resources) and pastoral resources (books on preaching, counseling, working with youth, small group resources, etc.). Additional purchases would make it possible to integrate the *Anchor Bible Dictionary*, *Essential IVP Reference Collection* and *Word Biblical Commentary* into this software system. More information on this can be found of the respective websites of each software company.

[ab]*BibleWorks* is probably the easiest to use in this regard. In addition to the brief lexical entries in the "auto-information" parsing and dictionary window, the user can open a full-text lexicon like the BDAG or the *Liddell-Scott* and access the appropriate entry with two clicks of the mouse on the Greek word in the passage being studied. Additionally, all the words in a verse can be sent to the default lexicon and the lexical entries are accessed by clicking once on each word. *Scholar's Library* has similar features. A few more menus need to be navigated and some additional clicks of the mouse need to be performed, but then the information made accessible is multiplied in comparison with its competitors. *Gramcord* performs quite adequately in this regard for the needs of most users, but the further you get into study of the original language the more you might want to consider the larger packages.

[ac]When performing word searches, differences between programs are again keenly felt. I have found *BibleWorks* and *Scholar's Library* to be the most efficient and complete for conducting searches directly out of the Greek or interlinear text, making them the best choices for lexical analysis. *Bible Windows* is also rather easy to use in this regard, and *Gramcord* the most difficult. These latter two resources, of course, also lack the same finesse of integration and breadth of original-language study helps to be found in the former two software systems.

[ad]*BibleWorks* and *Scholar's Library* appear to me to be the most advanced in this regard.

Bible software can also provide access to work in the original languages for the student with limited familiarity with Greek. Following along in the English text, a student finds a word that might be significant. If the student wishes to explore this further on the basis of the original languages, one or two clicks of the mouse will bring up an interlinear Bible so he or she can quickly locate the Greek word.[ae] From there the student has access to the same information as the person with facility with Greek (though, of course, he or she may not be able to make as full use of this information).

FOR FURTHER READING

Barr, James. *The Semantics of Biblical Language*. Oxford: Oxford University Press, 1961.

Black, David A. *Linguistics for Students of New Testament Greek*. Grand Rapids: Eerdmans, 1988.

Cotterell, Peter, and Max Turner. *Linguistics and Biblical Interpretation*. Downers Grove, Ill.: InterVarsity Press, 1989.

Fee, Gordon D. *New Testament Exegesis,* pp. 79-95. 3rd ed. Louisville, Ky.: Westminster John Knox, 2002.

Louw, Johannes P. *Semantics of New Testament Greek*. Philadelphia: Fortress, 1982.

Louw, Johannes P., and Eugene A. Nida. *Greek-English Lexicon of the New Testament Based on Semantic Domains*. 2 vols. New York: United Bible Societies, 1988.

Nida, Eugene A., and Charles R. Taber. *The Theory and Practice of Translation*. Leiden: Brill, 1969.

Nida, Eugene A., and Johannes P. Louw. *Lexical Semantics of the Greek New Testament*. Atlanta: Scholars Press, 1992.

Porter, Stanley E. *Idioms of the Greek New Testament*. Sheffield, U.K.: JSOT Press, 1992.

Turner, Max. "Modern Linguistics and the New Testament," pp. 146-74. In *Hearing the New Testament*. Edited by Joel B. Green. Grand Rapids: Eerdmans, 1995.

[ae] *Scholar's Library* is actually very sophisticated in this regard, with its "Word Study Guide" interface. It appears to go the furthest toward making original-language word study resources available (and reliably so) for people studying the Scriptures based on a knowledge of English only.

THE CITY OF EPHESUS

The adage that location is the most important criterion of value for real estate was no less true in the classical than the modern world. Ephesus, set on a long-established, major road leading eastward into the heart of Asia and Syria, but also adjacent to the Mediterranean and sporting a number of harbors, was strategically well-placed to become the leading commercial center in Asia Minor.[53] It was a natural juncture for maritime and land trade. Ephesus was therefore a wealthy city and an obvious choice for the provincial capital of Roman Asia Minor.

Ephesus had a marvelous amphitheater (see figure 18.1), about five hundred feet in diameter, capable of seating twenty to twenty-five thousand people. As was typical throughout the Mediterranean, the amphitheater was semicircular and was built into the side of a large hill. An east-west street one-third of a mile in length led from the theater to the harbor and was lined with shops.[54] South of the theater was the agora, or central market, surrounded by covered porticoes (*stoai*). These porticoes were broad, formed by three-aisled colonnades, decorated with statues honoring Augustus, Livia and members of the imperial family.[55] North of the agora and the theater were the administrative buildings (the *palaestra*). A bath and gymnasium complex adjoined the *palaestra,* and a second gymnasium, together with a massive stadium for

games and races (probably erected during Nero's reign),[56] enlivened the far north side of the city. Ephesus also had a well-developed system of fountains and aqueducts for its water supply. An earthquake in 23 C.E. opened the door to vast civic improvements, at which time Ephesus's public spaces were rebuilt even more extravagantly.[57]

The landmark for which Ephesus enjoyed its fame in the ancient world, however, was the grand Temple of Artemis, one of the seven wonders of the world (see Pliny *Natural History* 36.96). The platform of the temple was about 240 by 420 feet, approached by a staircase of ten steps, then three further steps to the actual building, which was 340 by 164 feet. The center of the temple (an altar, 20 by 20 feet, and colossal cult statue in an open courtyard) was surrounded by extensive colonnades, with rows of pillars, the base of each being 6 feet in diameter. The white marble was ornately decorated with color and gold.[58] Artemis (or Diana) was worshiped in Ephesus as the Eastern mother-goddess rather than the chaste virgin huntress (the Artemis of Greek myth, as in Euripides' *Hippolytus*). The statues of this Asian Artemis (see figure 18.2), sporting multiple rows of breasts covering the region from the neck to the waist, suggest connections with fertility, fecundity and family. Her cult was practiced throughout the region.[59] The scene in Acts 19:23-41, where a guild of interested silversmiths (who thrive from the promotion of

---

[53]Strabo *Geog.* 14.1.24 (641-642); Aelius Aristides *Orations* 23.24; Clinton Arnold, "Ephesus," in *Dictionary of Paul and His Letters,* ed. Gerald F. Hawthorne and Ralph P. Martin (Downers Grove, Ill.: InterVarsity Press, 1993), p. 249; R. J. Oster, "Ephesus," *Anchor Bible Dictionary,* ed. David N. Freedman (Garden City, N.Y.: Doubleday, 1992), 2.543.

[54]Merrill M. Parvis, "Ephesus in the Early Christian Era," in *The Biblical Archaeologist Reader 2,* ed. D. N. Freedman and E. F. Campbell Jr. (Garden City, N.Y.: Doubleday, 1964), 339.

[55]Peter Scherrer, "The City of Ephesos from the Roman Period to Late Antiquity," in *Ephesos: Metropolis of Asia,* ed. Helmut Koester (Valley Forge, Penn.: Trinity Press International, 1995), p. 5.

[56]Arnold, "Ephesus," p. 250.

[57]Scherrer, "City of Ephesos," pp. 7-8.

[58]Parvis, "Ephesus in the Early Christian Era," p. 338.

[59]Filson claims no fewer than thirty sites to have been connected with Artemis worship. See F. V. Filson, "Ephesus and the New Testament," in *The Biblical Archaeologist Reader 2,* ed. D. N. Freedman and E. F. Campbell Jr. (Garden City, N.Y.: Doubleday, 1964), pp. 345-46.

Figure 18.1. The great theater in Ephesus, where many townspeople assembled at the instigation of Demetrius the Silversmith (Acts 19:23-41). (Photo courtesy of Todd Bolen [BiblePlaces.com])

the cult of Artemis) rouse the civic body against Paul for detracting attention from the city's pride and joy, is quite within the realm of plausibility and shows how economic, as well as social and religious, factors could contribute to the rejection of or hostility against bearers of the Christian witness.

Temples to other deities attest to the diversity of religious traditions honored in the city, but the other cult worthy of special attention in Ephesus is the imperial cult. A temple of Rome and Julius Caesar, dating from Augustus's reign, stood beside the main administrative building. A sanctuary of Augustus was situated within the complex of the Temple of Artemis, with another Temple of Augustus standing adjacent to the agora. Statues honoring members of the imperial household from Augustus to Claudius and Nero were placed

prominently in the public areas. Later in the first century the Ephesians would erect a temple of Domitian, featuring a colossal statue of the emperor (about twenty feet tall).[60] Ephesus enjoyed the title of *neokoros,* "temple warden" of the imperial cult, a title that gave it additional prestige and precedence over its civic neighbors. Civic festivals, such as the Artemesia in the early spring, the provincial games and the quadrennial Ephesian Games, linked the major cults of the city with the major social events of the province.[61]

Ephesus is remembered for magic both outside and within the New Testament.[62] Especially noteworthy is Acts 19:18-20, where a very expensive heap of magical books containing incantations and formulas for conjuring spirits was burned as a result of conversions to Christianity. Part of the triumph of the gospel,

---

[60]S. R. F. Price, *Rituals and Power* (Cambridge: Cambridge University Press, 1984), pp. 254-55.
[61]Arnold, "Ephesus," p. 250.
[62]See C. E. Arnold, *Ephesians: Power and Magic,* SNTSMS 63 (Cambridge: Cambridge University Press, 1989), pp. 22-24.

Figure 18.2. A gold stater minted in Ephesus around 87-85 B.C.E., showing the crowned head of Artemis on the obverse and the cult statue of Ephesian Artemis on the reverse. The Greek letters epsilon and phi, the first two letters of *Ephesus*, are clearly visible on the reverse as well. Coinage from Ephesus frequently featured some aspect of the worship of Artemis, a phenomenon that lay close to the heart of the city's pride and identity. (Courtesy of Edgar L. Owen Coin Company, www.edgarlowen.com)

for the author of Acts, was its triumph over magic. This may be reflected in Ephesians and Colossians as well in their celebration of Christ's triumph over all lesser spiritual powers, and Christ's liberation of his followers from their domination.[63]

Ephesus was home to a significant Jewish community from the time of the Hasmonean period and before. Josephus (*Ant.* 12.3.2; 14.10.11-12, 25; 16.6.1-8) records that the Jewish community regularly enjoyed permission to follow its ethnic customs, exemption from military service (particularly because army life would involve violation of sabbath and dietary regulations) and permission to send money to Jerusalem for support of the sacrificial system there. When these rights

were threatened, the community was strong enough to have them reestablished through well-placed petitions.

AUTHORSHIP

Ephesians appears to have been known to and used by Christian authors as early as Ignatius of Antioch in the first decade of the second century, possibly by Clement of Rome in the last decade of the first.[64] Pauline authorship went unchallenged for eighteen centuries. As with Colossians the authenticity of Ephesians has been subject to close scrutiny during the past century and a half. Some affirm Pauline authorship without reservation (like Barth and O'Brien).[65] Others seek a mediating position, ascribing the main work to a colleague of Paul

---

[63]Arnold, *Ephesians*, pp. 165-71.

[64]P. T. O'Brien, *The Letter to the Ephesians* (Grand Rapids: Eerdmans, 1999), p. 4; Ernest Best, *A Critical and Exegetical Commentary on the Epistle to the Ephesians*, ICC (Edinburgh: T & T Clark, 1998), pp. 115-17.

[65]Markus Barth, *Ephesians*, AB 34 (Garden City, N.Y.: Doubleday, 1974), 1.3-4.

who wrote shortly before or shortly after Paul's execution.[66] Still others ascribe it to a disciple of Paul who wrote Ephesians without consulting Paul at all, often in conjunction with the supposition that he used Colossians as a basis for a reinterpretation of Paul's message for a new situation.[67] The arguments tend to follow the same lines as Colossians, and consensus is far from being reached. However, on the whole the authenticity of Ephesians is affirmed by fewer scholars than the authenticity of Colossians.

Language and style. The language of Ephesians differs from the undisputed letters of Paul is minor ways: Ephesians speaks of the "devil" rather than using proper names for the adversary (though Paul also uses impersonal titles like "the god of this age" in 2 Cor 4:4). Paul does not elsewhere call Christ the "Beloved," and he customarily speaks of things "in the heavens" rather than "in the heavenlies." Despite these differences, however, we must keep in focus the way the vast majority of the language in Ephesians mirrors the undisputed letters.

It is sometimes argued that the language of Ephesians has more in common with the early church fathers, but this points more to the influence of Ephesians on their language. (It was known to have been used already by Ignatius of Antioch.) The author of Ephesians certainly indulges in a more redundant and otiose style than Paul does elsewhere, and uses long sentences more frequently. Is this the sign of a different author, or is this style the result of the liturgical character the author has given to the first half of the letter, not only by including hymns and doxologies but extending their cadences and tone to make one great "hymn" in celebration of the mystery of God?[68]

H. J. Cadbury put the matter of language and style well: "Which is more likely—that an imitator of Paul in the first century composed a writing ninety or ninety-five percent in accordance with Paul's style or that Paul himself wrote a letter diverging five or ten percent from his usual style?"[69]

Theology. As with Colossians, the concerns about the theology of Ephesians carry greater weight in the debate.[70] But as with Colossians again it is far from clear whether the differences in theological nuance necessitate non-Pauline authorship or reflect Paul's contextualization of the message of the cross and resurrection for the Christians in Asia Minor, who, after all, would have wrestled with some significantly different issues than those in Greece, Macedonia and Rome. Some of the more important arguments include the following:

Ephesians emphasizes the resurrection and exaltation of Christ rather than his death and the cross. Paul's undisputed letters encompass both, however, and which he emphasizes is directly related to the aspect of the gospel he is driving home to his converts. In Ephesians the exaltation of Christ "is central to the writer's intention of bringing home to his readers the significance of Christ's lordship over the spirit-powers."[71] Moreover, Ephesians does give attention to the death of Jesus and its effects (Eph 1:7; 2:13-14, 16; 5:2, 25).

- The broader vision of Paul's concept of a deliverance that is both "already" and "not yet" is collapsed into a "completed salvation" in Ephesians 2:7-10. This letter evi-

---

[66]Ralph P. Martin, *Ephesians, Colossians and Philemon* (Atlanta: John Knox Press, 1991), p. 4.

[67]A. T. Lincoln, *Ephesians,* WBC 42 (Dallas: Word, 1990), p. lxvii.

[68]O'Brien, *Ephesians,* pp. 6-7.

[69]H. J. Cadbury, "The Dilemma of Ephesians," *NTS* 5 (1958-1959): 101.

[70]Best, who is strikingly unimpressed with other arguments against authenticity, finds this line of argumentation determinative for pseudepigraphy. There are "no outside circumstances" (by which he must mean pressing problems or rival teachers rather than the everyday circumstances of Ephesian Christians) to which the theological variations from the undisputed Pauline letters can be attributed (*Ephesians,* p. 36).

[71]O'Brien, *Ephesians,* p. 22.

dences a realized eschatology rather than a clear expectation of the future resurrection of the dead and consummation, emphasizing the cosmic dimension of Christ's victory far more than seen in the undisputed letters (as in Colossians; see Eph 1:3-4, 9-10, 20-23; 2:6; 4:8-10).

The difference between Ephesians and the undisputed letters, however, is far from absolute. Future eschatology is by no means absent (see Eph 1:10, 14, 21; 2:7; 4:30; 5:6);[72] the struggle against cosmic enemies is far from over (Eph 6:10-20).[73] Would the challenges in Ephesus, perhaps not unlike those in Colossae, call for this different emphasis, and would Paul be sufficiently supple in his thinking to place such an emphasis? In order to proclaim the Christians' deliverance from the sway and authority of all hostile spiritual forces (remembering that Ephesus was especially noted for the practice of magic as well as the ubiquitous practice of astrology), Paul now stresses the implications of Christ's exaltation for believers in the manner that he had formerly stressed the implications of his death and resurrection.[74]

Once again, we need to remind ourselves that the spatial and temporal dimensions in Ephesians are both equally at home in an apocalyptic worldview, which holds Ephesians and the rest of the Pauline corpus together. Much of the attention to hostile spiritual forces and to Christ's exaltation "in the heavenly places" over those forces is just as at home in apocalypticism as discussions of future hope, and Paul was an *apocalyptic* thinker, not just an *eschatological* one. A spatial versus temporal emphasis, therefore, may be a false dichotomy.

- The church has become a translocal entity, with Christ as its head, whereas Paul had al-

ways spoken of the church in terms of specific, local communities of believers. Paul's use of body imagery, moreover, involved all Christians as members of one body, without specifying Christ as the head of that body. As we saw in regard to Colossians, however, such a natural development of the image could well have been made by Paul himself.

- The author of Ephesians looks back on the apostles and prophets (Eph 2:20), a sign of second generation Christianity.[75] Describing them as the "holy" apostles and prophets (Eph 3:5) implies a veneration of the apostles more appropriate for a second generation since Paul would surely not have thus designated himself and others like him. As the foundation, the apostles have now replaced Christ, whom Paul designated the foundation in 1 Corinthians 3:9-17.

The founding role of the apostles, however, need not be read as an arrogant statement but as a simple fact. Moreover, the fact that *all* Christians are "holy ones" (*hagioi,* "saints") would make the description of the apostles and prophets as "holy" far less problematic. It would be just as natural for Paul to use this term to merely denote their being "set apart" by God for some purpose (as in Rom 1:1-5) as it would be for a later generation to use this term as an indication of the special veneration accorded the founding figures.[76] That the apostles are the "foundation" of the building does in fact alter the image in 1 Corinthians 3:9-17, where Paul and Apollos lay the foundation, which is Christ. It is not the case, however, that the apostles have supplanted Christ's preeminent and root position, however, since Christ is now placed as the cornerstone of the whole building (Eph 2:20).[77]

---

[72]Lincoln, *Ephesians,* pp. lxxxix-xc.
[73]O'Brien, *Ephesians,* p. 33; Arnold, *Ephesians,* pp. 155-57.
[74]Arnold, *Ephesians,* pp. 147-50.
[75]MacDonald, *Colossians and Ephesians,* p. 16.
[76]Klyne Snodgrass, *Ephesians,* NIVAC (Grand Rapids: Zondervan, 1996), pp. 25-27.
[77]O'Brien, *Ephesians,* p. 28.

The Parallels Between Ephesians and Colossians

Ephesians	Colossians	
1:1-2	1:1-2	opening address
1:22-23	1:17-19	Christ the head of the body, the church
2:13-18	1:20-22	reconciliation with God through Jesus' death on the cross
4:16	2:19	connectedness of the body to and nourishment from Christ
5:19-20	3:16	singing psalms and spiritual songs, and giving thanks to God
5:22—6:9	3:18—4:1	instructions for behavior in the household
6:21-22	4:7-8	Tychicus's commendation and commission

- Ephesians does not mention justification by faith.

The absence of themes that dominate other letters, however, does not make nearly as strong a contribution to the argument for pseudepigraphy as does the demonstrable modification of Pauline theology. The absence of Judaizing rivals in Ephesus and the surrounding churches would explain the absence adequately. It is their presence that guides the use of this topic in Galatians; in Romans, Paul dwells on the theme because he must defend justification against the misrepresentations of his proclamation of a gospel without law.

Dependence on Colossians. The reader of both letters cannot fail to notice that much of the material in Colossians (about one-third) has parallel material in Ephesians.[78] A closer comparison of such passages would quickly confirm this impression.

Both letters also feature certain themes that are not common in other letters attributed to Paul. *Mystery* (Col 1:26, 27; 2:2; 4:3; Eph 1:9; 3:3, 4, 9) and *fullness* (and related forms: see Col 1:9, 19; 2:9, 10; Eph 1:23; 3:19; 4:10) figure prominently, and in connection with the central themes of each letter. A significant difference between the letters is that the "mystery" is Christ-centered in Colossians but more church-focused in Ephesians. In both letters Christ emerges as the "head" of the church. Both focus on God's act in Christ effecting reconciliation (cf. 2 Cor 5:19-20) and speak of the believers' resurrection with Christ as accomplished already in some sense.

A. T. Lincoln regards Ephesians' use of Colossians as the primary reason to reject Pauline authorship of the former.[79] As different scholars have evaluated these parallels in detail, however, they have come to surprisingly differ-

---

[78]See details in Victor P. Furnish, "Ephesians, Epistle to the," *Anchor Bible Dictionary,* ed. David N. Freedman (Garden City, N.Y.: Doubleday, 1992), 2.536.

[79]Lincoln, *Ephesians,* pp. xlvii-xlviii.

ent conclusions. Many hold, almost as an assumed starting point, that Ephesians is dependent on Colossians. Some argue that, on the contrary, Colossians is dependent on Ephesians, bringing its general contents to bear on a specific, polemical situation. Still others suggest that Ephesians is dependent on an earlier letter that also provided the basis for Colossians. Of course, it is also possible that there is no formal literary dependence between the two, the similarities being the result of the

lossians is prior and at still others that there is a stalemate.[81] Ephesians can be seen to have conflated different texts from Colossians into a single passage, but then the argument can be used in reverse for still other passages.[82]

Did Colossians serve as a resource for a disciple of Paul, or do the similarities rather result from Paul having written the two letters at about the same time to different audiences and with different but related purposes in view? The evidence is far from clear.

Figure 18.3. The main, column-lined street running through the city of Ephesus. (Photo courtesy of Todd Bolen [BiblePlaces.com])

same author writing both letters in close proximity to one another.[80] Markus Barth's representative analysis of parallel biographical, hymnic, doctrinal and parenetic passages in both letters reveals the genuine complexity of the situation. At some points it is more plausible to argue that Ephesians is prior, at others that Co-

In a related vein the parallels between Ephesians and other New Testament texts, like 1 Peter,[83] also can be used to support post-Pauline authorship, but are also amenable to other interpretations (e.g., reliance of Paul and other authors on common early Christian traditions).

---

[80]Barth and Blanke, *Colossians,* p. 114.

[81]Ibid., pp. 72-80.

[82]Ibid., p. 83; Best, *Ephesians,* pp. 22-25; O'Brien, *Ephesians,* pp. 8-21.

[83]Furnish invites the reader to compare Ephesians 1:20-22; 5:21-6:9 with 1 Pet 3:21-22; 2:18-3:7, respectively ("Ephesians," p. 537).

Autobiographical details and the picture of Paul in Ephesians. According to Acts 19, Paul spent at least two, and possibly three, years evangelizing and building up the church in Ephesus. Yet the author of Ephesians does not show any specific signs of familiarity with them. The letter has a rather impersonal tone, speaking, for example, of "hearing" about their faith as if he has no firsthand knowledge of it, and the author sends no specific greetings to anyone (see Eph 1:15; 3:1-4; 4:21; 6:23-24).

The impersonal tone could be explained by the likelihood that Ephesians represents a circular letter of some kind (see the "Destination" section below), whether for churches in and around Ephesus, some of which would have come into being after Paul's departure, or for churches around Asia Minor beginning with Ephesus. Paul would be addressing Christians the majority of whom perhaps, he had never met. That Paul has "heard" of their faith does not mean he played no part in evangelizing the city, nor that he had no firsthand experience of their faithfulness to Christ. Rather, Paul uses this expression to indicate that the Ephesian Christians enjoy a translocal reputation for their growth in discipleship (as in 1 Thess 1:8-10). The absence of personal greetings is in keeping with the nature of the letter as a circular letter intended for multiple congregations.[84]

As in Colossians the author of Ephesians requests prayer in his imprisonment (Eph 6:19-20) and indicates that Tychicus will be coming with the letter and with news about Paul (Eph 6:21-22). Such details have been used to suggest that the letter derives in fact from a real situation in Paul's life, but proponents of pseudonymity argue that these are part of the fiction that promotes the letter as Pauline.

In sum, Pauline authorship has been challenged on a number of fronts, though the case has not been made sufficiently well to convince a large minority of scholars. Either position faces serious obstacles, and it is best to conclude that there are no easy resolutions of this particular question (however much scholars on both sides might represent the solution as clear and indisputable!).

DESTINATION

Was Ephesians originally addressed "to the saints who are *in Ephesus* and also faithful in Christ" or was it addressed more generally "to the saints who are also faithful in Christ"? The prepositional phrase "in Ephesus" does not appear in P[46], Codex Sinaiticus or Codex Vaticanus, three important and early witnesses to the Pauline corpus. The committee that produced the standard critical text of the Greek New Testament was evenly split on this question, leaving the words in the main text on account of the vast number of good witnesses to it, but bracketing it on account of the quality of these three witnesses that do not include these words.[85] The words *in Ephesus* might have been eliminated by scribes to "universalize" the letter (which seems less situation-specific than the rest of the Pauline corpus), but it is equally possible that the originally unspecific address, appropriate for a circular letter, was filled in early in its history of transmission.

Marcion spoke of Ephesians as the letter to the Laodiceans (Col 4:16), an indication of some dispute concerning the proper historical setting for the letter in the second century. However, the fact that so many early manuscripts have the address as Ephesus, whether or not it was supplied by the author or an early scribe, and the fact that no manuscripts have an alternative destination (like Smyrna, Laodicea or Hierapolis, all of which had vibrant Christian communities in the late-first and early-sec-

---

[84]Simpson and Bruce, *Ephesians and the Colossians*, p. 18. Arnold also observes that Paul does not send personal greetings to churches he knows well, as in the Corinthian letters, Galatians or Philippians (Arnold, "Ephesus," p. 244).
[85]Bruce Metzger, *Textual Commentary on the Greek New Testament* (Stuttgart: United Bible Societies, 1971), p. 601.

ond centuries), strongly suggest that the letter was at least intended for Ephesus and, if circular, for churches in and around Ephesus.

With regard to the implied audience, the author of Ephesians refers to the Gentiles among them explicitly at several points (e.g., Eph 2:11-13), or speaks of their past conduct and conversion experience in ways appropriate to Gentile rather than Jewish converts. A Gentile Christian majority, at least, seems to be presupposed. This would not necessarily exclude some Jewish-

to Paul, Ephesians gives no sense of responding to a new, specific challenge in the life of the churches in and around that city. Its existence is due not to some interloping rival teachers (there is only one general reference to the dangers of false teachings, Eph 4:14), some infelicitous change in the community's faith or practice, or some local upheaval, but rather to the author's desire to edify and encourage them. It is more of a prophylactic medicine or nutritional supplement than a remedy for a known malady.

Figure 18.4. The main Roman road leading out of Ephesus, as seen from the Ephesus theater. (Photo courtesy of Todd Bolen [BiblePlaces.com])

Christian readership, of course, since parts of a letter could be addressed more specifically to a certain part of the audience (and expected to be "overheard" by other parts of the audience).

PURPOSE

Unlike every other letter written by or ascribed

Ephesians is a letter where cautions about mirror reading are well served. Does the celebration of the "mystery" of the inclusion of Gentiles in the spiritual heritage of Israel indicate a situation of tension between Jewish and Gentile Christians in Ephesus?[86] Or is this merely a celebration of a central achievement

---

[86]Arthur Patzia understands Ephesians as an attempt to reaffirm the unity of the church in the face either of Jewish exclusivism (the tendency to regard only Jews or full converts to Judaism as potential full members of the church, as in the Galatians controversy) or Gentile exclusivism (the tendency to divorce the church from the salvation history of the particular people, Israel; see *Ephesians, Colossians, Philemon,* NIBC [Peabody, Mass.: Hendrickson, 1990], pp. 1113-15).

of the Christian gospel in the Mediterranean world? The absence of explicit exhortations to the congregation such as found in Romans 14:1—15:7 and the lack of reflections of specific points of conflict tend strongly to suggest that there was no such problem. Does the exhortation to unity presuppose disunity? Or is this letter simply celebrating what the author deems to be the core truths of which he wishes congregations to remain mindful and what he deems to be the core values he wishes congregations to continue to enact for their ongoing growth in the faith?[87]

Most interpreters, whether they favor Pauline or deutero-Pauline authorship, agree that the purpose of Ephesians is to remind the Christians of some central and distinctive features of their identity, and to keep encouraging them to pursue the distinctive values and behaviors that characterize this group.[88] Those who advocate Pauline authorship tend to view the letter as a more general application and refinement of the thoughts Paul had developed in regard to the specific problems in Colossae.[89] Others tend to regard it as "the first interpretation of and guide to Pauline tradition in light of the disappearance of Paul."[90]

PROVENANCE

Ephesians is closely linked with Colossians in terms of content and of the specific actions of Tychicus, who will bear each letter and bring news of Paul's situation in prison (cf. Eph 6:21-22 with Col 4:7-9, the most extensive verbatim parallel between the two letters). The same visit by Tychicus must be in view, the absence of any mention of Onesimus in Ephesians being due to the fact that he is going directly to Colossae. If Ephesians is authored by Paul then this would tilt the balance in favor of Colossians and Ephesians both being sent from Rome (if Paul were in an Ephesian jail, Christians in Ephesus would hardly need Tychicus for news), and quite possibly Philemon as well, if it was written at the same time as Colossians.

If Ephesians was written by a disciple or colleague of Paul after the apostle's death, however, there is no way of knowing where it was written from. Indeed, it could have been written within Ephesus itself: the early church preserved traditions indicating that the Pauline influences (like Timothy) remained strong there. This might account for the possible omission of the reference to a place name (if the author were writing, in fact, to congregations locally).

THE MESSAGE OF EPHESIANS

The central theme of Ephesians is the celebration of the multidimensional "mystery" revealed in the gospel (Eph 1:9; 3:3, 4, 9; 5:32; 6:19). In its horizontal dimension this mystery concerns the inclusion of the Gentiles in the spiritual heritage of Israel (Eph 3:3-6), the achievement of reconciliation effected by Christ's death (Eph 2:11-22, esp. 2:13-16). The "dividing wall of hostility" (a revolutionary way to refer to the Torah; Eph 2:14) that separated Jew from Gentile is now regarded as a major problem in the history of humankind. This wall would be viewed very positively from within the Jewish worldview since it was ordained by God (see Lev 20:22-26), but it conflicts with another increasingly strong tradition, namely, the universalism of God. Paul had already affirmed the incongruity between

---

[87]O'Brien, correctly I believe, opts for the latter (*Ephesians*, pp. 51-53).

[88]J. P. Sampley speaks of Ephesians helpfully in terms of identity formation ("Ephesians," in *The Deutero-Pauline Letters* [Minneapolis: Fortress, 1993], p. 23).

[89]F. F. Bruce, *The Epistles to the Colossians, to Philemon, and to the Ephesians*, NICNT (Grand Rapids: Eerdmans, 1984), p. 241; O'Brien, *Ephesians*, pp. 56-57.

[90]MacDonald, *Colossians and Ephesians*, p. 16.

Ephesians and Qumran

One of the more important contributions of the study of the Dead Sea Scrolls to our knowledge of early Christianity is the amount of new background material these texts have provided, broadening our understanding of the range of Jewish thought in the first century C.E. Many terms that automatically suggested a particular Greco-Roman background for a text prior to the discovery of the Scrolls have now been found to be completely at home on Judean soil and in Jewish thinking as well. The use of the word *mystery* in Ephesians, for example, led scholars to investigate the field of the Hellenistic mystery religions as the religious environment in which to interpret Ephesians. The prominence of the term *mystery* or the contemplation of "mysteries" at Qumran now leads students to reconsider the Palestinian Jewish backgrounds of the term and its possible significance for the letter.[a] In the Qumran literature, as in Ephesians, we find phrases linking mystery, insight, wisdom, intelligence, knowledge and revelation. In both the "mysteries" are eschatologically oriented and were "hitherto hidden in God." The difference lies in the specific content of this eschatological mystery—the eschatological reign of Jesus and the fusing of Gentile and Jewish converts into a single community.[b]

The style of Ephesians also mirrors that of the *Community Rule* and *Damascus Document* in some striking ways, particularly in the series of genitives (e.g., "*of* the glory *of* the grace *of* him," Eph 1:6), the use of doublets (synonyms), and claims about "all" people or members of one group. Such details led Karl Kuhn to conclude that "the language of the Epistle to the Ephesians has been influenced specifically by *these* texts," referring to the Scrolls.[c]

Many of the images or topics found in Ephesians have parallels in the sectarian texts from Qumran. The grouping of fornication, impurity and greed in Ephesians 5:3 reflect the "three nets of Belial" in CD 4:15-16 (where *impurity* appears in its strictly ritual context of "defilement of the Holy Place"). Both the *Rule of the Community* and Ephesians proscribe frivolous speech and silliness in favor of thanksgiving and edifying speech (Eph 5:4; 1 QS 10:2-4). Both of these texts also distinguish sharply between the members of the community, who were formerly in the dark but now have come into the light (Eph 5:6-8) and the "sons of disobedience" (Eph 5:6) or "sons of darkness," "sons of perversity," or "company of the perverse" (1QS 3:20-21, 5:1, 10-11; 6:14-15).[d] Ephesians and the Qumran Hymns both speaks of the community's access to a place or station in the heavenly realm (Eph 2:5-6; 1QH 11:10-12; 3:19-22), a topic formerly interpreted

---

[a]P. Benoit, "Qumran and the New Testament," in *Paul and the Dead Sea Scrolls,* ed. J. Murphy-O'Connor and J. H. Charlesworth (New York: Crossroad, 1990), pp. 21-24; J. Fitzmyer, "The Dead Sea Scrolls and the New Testament After Thirty Years," *TD* 29 (1981): 351-67, 616; K. G. Kuhn, "The Epistle to the Ephesians in the light of the Qumran Texts," in *Paul and the Dead Sea Scrolls,* ed. J. Murphy-O'Connor and J. H. Charlesworth (New York, Crossroad,1990), p. 118.

[b]F. Mussner, "Contributions Made by Qumran to the Understanding of the Epistle to the Ephesians," in *Paul and the Dead Sea Scrolls,* ed. J. Murphy-O'Connor and J. H. Charlesworth (New York, Crossroad,1990), p. 163.

[c]Kuhn, "Epistle to the Ephesians," pp. 116-20.

[d]Ibid., pp. 120-24.

against a Gnostic background. The purpose of the establishment of unity or fellowship is "the praise of God's glory" both in Ephesians 1:6, 12, 14 and 1QH 3:23; 9:14. The image of the community as a temple and the specific imagery of the cornerstone and foundation appear in both Ephesians 2:20-22 and 1QS 8:4-10, with differences, of course, because now Christ is the cornerstone and the apostles and prophets the foundations.[e]

Such parallels continue to encourage students of any New Testament text to consider multiple streams of both Jewish and Greco-Roman traditions informing the author and the reading of the text, rather than privileging one such stream exclusively as *the* background.

FOR FURTHER READING

Kuhn, Karl G. "The Epistle to the Ephesians in the Light of the Qumran Texts," pp. 115-31. In *Paul and the Dead Sea Scrolls*. Edited by J. Murphy-O'Connor and J. H. Charlesworth. New York: Crossroad, 1990.

Mussner, Franz. "Contributions Made by Qumran to the Understanding of the Epistle to the Ephesians," pp. 159-78. In *Paul and the Dead Sea Scrolls*. Edited by J. Murphy-O'Connor and J. H. Charlesworth. New York: Crossroad, 1990.

Benoit, Pierre. "Qumran and the New Testament," pp. 1-30. In *Paul and the Dead Sea Scrolls*. Edited by J. Murphy-O'Connor and J. H. Charlesworth. New York: Crossroad, 1990.

Fitzmyer, Joseph A. "The Dead Sea Scrolls and the New Testament after Thirty Years." *TD* 29 (1981): 351-67.

---

[e]See, further, Mussner, "Contributions Made by Qumran," pp. 167-71.

---

the confession that "God is one" and the division of humanity into Jews who were properly associated with this God and Gentiles who were cut off from God (Rom 3:27-30). In Ephesians the Pauline gospel has actualized the universalist ideal, wedding humanity into one community mirroring the one God "from whom every family in heaven and on earth takes its name" (Eph 3:15 NRSV). Perhaps the most profound theological contribution of Ephesians, and the most challenging still to modern constructs of boundaries and identity, is found in this emphasis on God's breaking down of religious and ethnic barriers by means of the crucifixion of Jesus.

In its vertical dimension the mystery concerns the reconciliation and reunion of human beings with God. As people are reconciled and brought together with one another through incorporation into the one body, they are also joined to the Head of that body, which is Christ (Eph 1:10, 22-23; 5:32). The church, which remains in focus, is also the place where God's determination to reconcile and unify heavenly realities with earthly realities makes itself effective (Eph 1:10) as believers on earth are also brought into the heavenly sphere by their incorporation into Christ (e.g., Eph 2:6). The author of Ephesians places great emphasis on Christ's exaltation, since by that event he reenters heaven and gives the whole church a beachhead there. Nevertheless, the fundamental event that makes this reconciliation with God possible remains Christ's death (Eph 1:7, 14; 2:16).

The opening of Ephesians makes the increase and celebration of God's honor and favor a refrain (Eph 1:6, 12, 14). The "praise of God's glorious grace" and the "praise of his glory" emerge as the natural consequence of God's mighty acts on behalf of humanity. The author himself imitates and enfleshes this principle in his own hymnlike declaration of the mystery in the first three chapters of the letter, but more significantly he calls attention to the fact that the church itself is the main vehicle by which the proclamation of God's achievement must be made to the heavenly and earthly audiences (Eph 3:9-10). Just as Christ provides believers with a point of entry into heaven, so the believers provide God, as it were, with an ongoing point of entry into creation, making God's generosity and will for humanity known as they live out the consummation of God's mystery.

Of course, the author himself knows that the actual achievements of the church might lag behind its vocation, so in the last three chapters of the letter he turns to consider the life of the Christian community from another angle. How will its members incarnate the church's identity as the "reconciled people of God" (chaps. 1—3) in their interactions with one another and in their personal lives as part of that people (chaps. 4—6). The indicative and the imperative, the declaration of what the believers "are" in Christ and the ethical demands that this places on them, remain fundamentally linked in Ephesians, as they do in the undisputed Pauline letters.

As a reconciled people the church is to maintain unity above all else (Eph 2:13-16; 4:3-6). In particular the author seeks ways to bring the lofty theological principle that Christ has unified a people for God (Eph 2:11-21; 3:3-6) to bear on the day-to-day relationships and interactions between Christians. The touchstone for ethics in Ephesians is the fact that "we are members of each other" (Eph 4:25), and so we must treat the other as an extension of ourself. This applies to relationships between all Christians (Eph 4:1-6; 4:25-5:2) and is applied specifically to relationships between spouses (Eph 5:21-33).

Theology is always transformative in the New Testament and not merely speculative. In Ephesians this comes to expression particularly in the author's interest in how the believer should "walk" in light of the Christian group's ideology. Indeed, walk is a key word in the second half of the letter (Eph 4:1, 17; 5:2, 8, 15),[91] carried over from Ephesians 2:2, 10, which contrast the way the (largely Gentile) believers formerly "walked" and the life of good works that God has prepared for them to "walk" in. His attention to practical detail in this letter serves as an eloquent reminder to the church that the Christian confession is less a matter of lips and more a matter of legs.

Although triumphant in its outlook, Ephesians also bears witness to the ongoing struggle between hostile spiritual forces and the people of God (Eph 2:2; 3:10; 6:10-18). The author brings to focus the activity of the "spirit that is now at work among those who are disobedient," the ways and means of withstanding the assaults of the devil (Eph 6:10-18) and his defeat through the advance of the church toward maturity (Eph 3:10). The prevalence of magic in Ephesus, and the popular awareness and manipulation of spiritual forces that ancient magic entailed, might account for the prominence of this theme here, but the attention given to these topics throughout the New Testament suggests that the battle against demonic powers was part and parcel of the early Christians' understanding of their experience.

Rudolf Bultmann would demythologize this aspect of Ephesians: "now that the forces and the laws of nature have been discovered, we can no longer believe in spirits, whether good or

---

[91]O'Brien, *Ephesians*, p. 72.

evil."[92] The program of demythologizing, however, is blatantly a case of privileging one world construction (the post-Enlightenment, naturalistic one) over another (the supernaturalistic one that predominated in the pre-Enlightenment era and continues to dominate non-Eurocentric cultures). Who is to say which reflects reality more closely?[93] Artistic depictions of angels and demons may well be mythographic constructions, but part of the ongoing testimony of Paul and his followers is that we wrestle not merely with the forces of our own passions, nor with human beings, but also with powers beyond the human that manipulate human beings to a degree that challenges our myths of autonomy. To ignore the struggle at this level is to abdicate a very large battlefield to the powers and principalities from whose tyranny Christ seeks to liberate humanity.

In light of the tendencies of modern and postmodern scholars to boast of having finally achieved so firm a grasp on the real and the possible, it is appropriate that Ephesians also reminds us of how much of God remains mystery. The author prays in Ephesians 1:17-23; 3:14-21 that the congregations will discover the vast inheritance God has prepared for them, the power that God puts to work in them and the love that Christ has for them. In so doing he reminds Christians throughout the ages that the most valuable knowledge comes not through academic study but through the experience of the living God and openness to God's revelations of God's self.

EPHESIANS, COLOSSIANS AND MINISTRY FORMATION

The do's and don'ts of religious people. Colossians warns the church against humanmade regulations, self-imposed asceticism and all that makes for the appearance of being a rigorous devotee of religion but lacks genuine power to transform a person. Having already rejected the Torah as a binding code on the behavior of Christians, it would be utter foolishness to hem ourself in with any other body of regulations that is guaranteed to be inferior to the one already rejected. Moreover, as Paul had discovered in regard to the Torah (Rom 7:5; 8:3), so any other combination of rules and taboos was bound to fail to address the real problem of the human condition, namely, the power of the *flesh,* the sinful nature (not merely the body but the self-serving, self-centered nature—those many drives within us that are not submissive to God).

Christianity in the modern age has been no less susceptible than the Colossian Christians when it comes to devising and enforcing regulations: "Do not handle, Do not taste, Do not touch" (Col 2:21 NRSV). According to many "conservative" Christians, the transformation that the gospel would achieve in people's lives is to get them to stop consuming alcoholic beverages, smoking, dancing and perhaps going to movies *tout court.* To this could be added avoiding card playing, avoiding pants ("male" clothing) for women and rigorous observance of

---

[92]Rudolf Bultmann, "New Testament and Mythology," in *Kerygma and Myth,* ed. Hans Werner Bartsch; rev. Reginald H. Fuller (New York: Harper & Row, 1961), p. 4.

[93]See my detailed critique in "The Meaning of the New Testament and the *Skandalon* of World Constructions," *EvQ* 64 (1992): 3-20.

the sabbath (with the subdebate concerning whether this should be Saturday or Sunday). Reaching into my own tradition I might even throw in fasting on Friday, observance of the liturgical calendar and careful performance of ritual. These are regulations contrived by and imposed on human beings as a proper, rigorous observance of "Christian holiness." Yet often they only serve to promote pride, prejudice and division. They are certainly ineffective regimens for rooting out the desire to sin—and innumerable sins not covered by the code of conduct.

The focus on regulations like "do not drink, do not smoke, do not even dance" distracts us from the genuine and valuable "mortification" described in Colossians 3:5-11, which trains us to strip off not just certain socially unacceptable behaviors (in the eyes of a particular group) but to strip off our very selves in favor of the new self God wishes to birth in us through the Spirit. In the process of becoming this new person, we are challenged far more deeply than by any code of behavior designed to make us look "Christian." In opposition to the pale shadows of Christian life seen in the lifestyles that promote the "holier than thou" mentality stands the vision of Colossians 3:12-17, in which love, forgiveness and mutual encouragement toward growth characterizes every interaction between those who call themselves by Christ's name.

Christ, the fullness of God. Colossians proclaims not merely the centrality of Christ but Christ as the fullness of God's wisdom, redemption and God-directed growth. Ephesians, moreover, reminds us of the vastness of the riches of God in Christ, admonishing us that wherever we are in our discipleship, we are still just beginning to plumb the depths of God's wisdom, power and love in Christ. In light of this we must wonder about the motivation for supplementing the revelation of God in Christ with other streams of religious knowledge, or with other paraspiritual programs like psychic readings, astrology, Wicca and the like. As the Colossian philosophy would have led the Christians into a new bondage to the "elemental spirits of the cosmos," so many of these supplements threaten the Christian with the same. The voice of a psychic or astrologer (perhaps masking the voice of another kind of spirit) plants seeds and suggestions that replace those of the Holy Spirit; involvement with witchcraft invites other spiritual forces into one's life even more openly; long-standing and respected streams of religious tradition, though containing much that is wise and insightful, nevertheless do not share the central convictions of Christianity and so are certainly an inferior resource to becoming more like Christ than spending time in the presence of Christ himself.

Do Christians turn to these supplements because they have indeed exhausted what they can learn of God in Christ, or because they have not been shown the full, vast and sufficient wisdom that God makes known through his Son and through his Holy Spirit? Christian leaders have an enormous responsibility and opportunity to keep mining those depths so that those in their care can glimpse something of the full dimensions of the wisdom God provides to those who seek it in Christ.

Christian households. Colossians 3:18—4:1 and Ephesians 5:21—6:9 contain detailed prescriptions for the ways that Christians are to understand and fulfill their roles in the natural household. Common to all of these, and standing at the core of each, is *the imperative for Christians to allow our knowledge of and relationship with Christ to shape our relationships with those closest to us—to be mindful of Jesus in our household interactions.* Each author develops rationales and models for these relationships from Christian premises (or from models and resources available in the shared Jewish and Christian heritage). For example, the slave's and master's relationship to the divine Master provides the framework for each one's fulfillment of his or her role in the household (Col 3:22—4:1). The way that Christ relates to the church becomes the norm for husband-wife relations and provides a new frame of mind for each partner.

These sets of instructions have been taken to task of late on account of the way they uphold the hierarchical structures of the first-century household. Nevertheless, we must not lose sight of what these "household codes" achieve within that context. Relationships between husbands and wives now must model the relationship of Christ and church (Eph 5:21-33). In our context the words about the submissiveness of women prove a serious stumbling block and draw our attention, but in the first-century context a challenge was placed before the Christian husband to love and serve his wife in a manner that represented Christ's love for the church—a love that put the church before Christ's own good in every circumstance: that meant serving rather than being served! The author of Ephesians, though preserving the form of a hierarchical relationship, nevertheless confounds the dominant culture's understanding of the implications of hierarchy by introducing the model of the Lord who is Servant (Mk 10:41-45; Jn 13:1-17).[a] Similarly, the master-slave relationship is set in the light of God's lordship over all people. Ephesians 6:8-9 announces the conventional nature of the "slave" and the "master"; in God's sight these distinctions are unreal and all are simply people. The social institution is thus deabsolutized since the "way things are" in human society are no longer affirmed as "the way things are" in the eyes of God.

So much attention has been focused on the particulars of these codes, whether to reject or affirm them as a binding ethic, that the larger principle here falls by the wayside, namely, that Christ must shape our in-house, interpersonal relationships, just as Christ must shape our relationships with the larger family of God (Col 3:5-17) and with outsiders (Col 4:5-6). Before this principle can be meaningfully recontextualized, Christians need to ponder how the "traditional" family has changed due to the pressures and pushes of the modern era, and consider how we can continue to fulfill the basic challenge of these household codes—making Christ evident and enacting the truths of the new creation and the "kingdom of God's beloved Son" in our relationships—in light of the best fam-

---

[a]The author has also used an injunction to mutual submission (Eph 5:21) as the introduction to the household codes, which contributes greatly to the modification of the model of the husband as a dominant partner. The reader should be very suspicious of translations of the New Testament that insert a paragraph heading between Ephesians 5:21 and 5:22, since the two verses are part of one sentence, and since verse 22 depends on verse 21 to supply the verb "submit." This is an instance where editorial paragraph headings are blatantly ideologically motivated, all the more as it is grammatically insupportable.

ily ethics of our period. The early Christians sought to live up to and surpass the best ethics of household relations in their environment. In our environment marriage is conceived more as a partnership than a hierarchy of dominant and subaltern. In our culture master-slave relationships no longer exist, but employer-employee relationships do (and human community would be measurably improved if employees were thought of as part of the household rather than disposable labor). We have also been informed by centuries of study of the parent-child relationship. As with so many areas of New Testament interpretation, here also the essence of the challenge of these texts needs to be carefully discerned and detached from the contextual so they can be fruitfully recontextualized.

The unity of faith. The church is called to make known "the manifold wisdom of God . . . to the principalities and powers in the heavenly places" by being a community where the dividing walls of hostility imposed on humanity by the "powers and principalities," the forces beyond each individual that shape our social consciousness, are overcome in reconciliation, love and unity (Eph 2:11-21; 3:6, 10). How fully is the church universal embodying this principle? How fully is the church embodying it in your area? How are the dividing walls of ethnicity, language, socioeconomic status and mere "taste" being overcome in the church community, including your local congregation? What forces in or around your local Christian community resist the full embodiment of God's wisdom for all to see? What opportunities are presently before the local Christian community to enflesh this wisdom, to bear witness to "a different way of being human, a way characterized by self-giving love, by justice, by honesty, and by the breaking down of traditional barriers that reinforce the divisions which keep human beings separate from, and often at odds with, one another"?[b]

Unity among Christians reflects the oneness of God, from whom all the families of the earth are named (Eph 4:1-6). While the author of Ephesians addresses local congregations, Ephesians 4:4-6 invites broad application to the Christian family as a whole, to all who call on the one God through the one faith in the one Lord, sealed with the one Spirit in the one baptism in the name of Christ. Baptists and Brethren, United Methodists and United Church of Christ, Episcopalians and Evangelical Free—we are all joined in one body whether we like it or not, whether we affirm it or not. The question Ephesians poses is, Will we live out the apostolic vision for the one body and bear witness to Christ's victory over the power and principalities that carve up humanity between them?[c] Or will we continue to give the powers and principalities an occasion to laugh at our failure as we turn the church that was meant to proclaim God's reconciling and unifying wisdom to all creation into a case study in divisiveness, territorialism and exclusivism?

The ideal of unity need not entail the elimination of distinctive witnesses to the Christian faith, distinctive practices and distinctive polities. On the contrary, it should lead to valuing the multiplicity of forms in which the gospel has taken

[b]N. T. Wright, *What Saint Paul Really Said* (Grand Rapids: Eerdmans, 1997), p. 154.
[c]The image is taken from ibid., p. 146.

shape in the various limbs of the body of Christ. Each denomination has a distinctive understanding of the gospel and some part of the truth that is the mystery of God, and each can greatly enrich the others where we come together to learn from one another in humility and join together in ministry. Ephesians challenges members of any one Christian group to regard members of another Christian group not as competitors but as teammates; not in terms of the minor points of disagreement that separate them (and that tend to result from each group focusing one side of a issue that in Scripture, taken as a whole, is ambiguous) but in terms of the grand core of the Christian faith and hope that unify them; not as members of another religion but as members of our own family, dearly loved by God and bought with the blood of the Lamb.

The ministry of the saints. Ephesians 4:11-16 articulates a healthy model for ministry, one that needs to be universally grasped and enacted if the church hopes to keep up with the needs of the world. Those who occupy specialized church offices, who are therefore designated "clergy," are set apart by God to fulfill an equipping role, but the work of ministry belongs to *all* the saints. In the middle of its basic catechism, the Episcopal Church's *Book of Common Prayer* reads "Who are the ministers of the Church? The ministers of the Church are lay persons, bishops, priests, and deacons" (p. 855). This bold statement took deep root also in the theology of ministry of one of the Anglican Church's daughters, the United Methodist Church, which distinguishes between the "general ministry" to which all baptized Christians are called and the "representative ministry" carried out by the clergy. The representative ministry is a model and serves an equipping capacity for the general ministry. Many congregations need to be awakened to this truth and equipped to rise to their great calling and responsibility before God. Many pastors need to recover the focus of their work, moving away from the model of doing ministry on behalf of the congregation (a model many churches force their pastor to accept) to helping their parishioners discover and fulfill their own ministries.

Walking in newness of life. Both Ephesians and Colossians place great emphasis on living in accordance with the "new nature," which reflects God's likeness in righteousness and holiness. Indeed, imitation of God and Christ becomes an ethical touchstone (Eph 4:32—5:2), another way that Christians make God's character known. (The church collectively is the vehicle for making God's wisdom known.) Ephesians offers guidelines about behaviors that reflect the "old nature" that is "corrupted by deceitful lusts" (Eph 4:22) and therefore *not* a reliable guide to be followed, and about the behaviors that proceed from the "new nature." Because of their general nature, they cannot be mistaken for a new law but rather offer a resource that will help the self-examining disciple perceive which nature he or she is nurturing/cultivating (see also Gal 5:16—6:10). The guidelines help us discern what behaviors proceed from our new nature:

- not doing what fosters enmity and rifts in relationships but what fosters unity, harmony, solidarity
- not predatorial grasping but beneficence
- not harboring grudges but seeking reconciliation

- not lying, treating others as outsiders and nonfamily but speaking the truth
- not indulging in distractions but focusing on the work of building up the church, fulfilling the obligation of thanksgiving and searching out God's direction (Eph 4:25—5:20).

These epistles help keep before our eyes, and the eyes of those we serve, the truth that the gospel is transformative and that a Christianity that does not change a person's heart, mind and life is empty. They call for fortitude as we face the truth about the passions and values that drive us when Christ's model and God's desire are not in view, but they also encourage us with words about the light God shines on us so that at each step we may walk in his ways and delight in his will.

FOR FURTHER READING

Barth, Markus. *Ephesians*. 2 vols. AB 34, 34A. Garden City, N.Y.: Doubleday, 1974.

Barth, Markus, and Helmut Blanke. *Colossians: A New Translation and Commentary*. AB 34B. Garden City, N.Y.: Doubleday, 1994.

Best, Ernest. *A Critical and Exegetical Commentary on the Epistle to the Ephesians*. ICC. Edinburgh: T & T Clark, 1998.

Bruce, F. F. *The Epistles to the Colossians, to Philemon, and to the Ephesians*. NICNT. Grand Rapids: Eerdmans, 1984.

Caragounis, Chrys C. *The Ephesian Mysterion: Meaning and Context*. Lund: Gleerup, 1944.

Dunn, James D. G. *The Epistles to the Colossians and Philemon*. NIGTC. Grand Rapids: Eerdmans, 1996.

Francis, Fearghail O., and Wayne A. Meeks, eds. *Conflict at Colossae*. SBLSBS 4. Missoula, Mont.: Scholars Press, 1975.

Koester, Helmut, ed. *Ephesos: Metropolis of Asia*. Valley Forge, Penn.: Trinity Press International, 1995.

Lincoln, Andrew T. *Ephesians*. WBC 42. Dallas: Word, 1990.

Lohse, Eduard. *A Commentary on Colossians and Philemon*. Hermeneia. Philadelphia: Fortress, 1971.

MacDonald, Margaret Y. *Colossians and Ephesians*. Sacra Pagina 17. Collegeville, Minn.: Liturgical Press, 2000.

Martin, Ralph P. *Colossians and Philemon*. NCB. Grand Rapids: Eerdmans, 1981.

Mitton, C. Leslie. *The Epistle to the Ephesians*. Oxford: Clarendon, 1951.

Moule, C. F. D. *The Epistles of Paul the Apostle to the Colossians and to Philemon*. CGTC. Cambridge: Cambridge University Press, 1957.

O'Brien, Peter T. *Colossians, Philemon*. WBC 44. Waco, Tex.: Word, 1982.

Patzia, Arthur G. *Colossians, Philemon, Ephesians*. San Francisco: Harper & Row, 1984.

Pokorný, Petr. *Colossians: A Commentary*. Peabody, Mass.: Hendrickson, 1991.

Schnackenburg, Rudolf. *The Epistle to the Ephesians*. Edinburgh: T & T Clark, 1991.

Simpson, Edmund K., and F. F. Bruce. *Commentary on the Epistles to the Ephesians and the Colossians*. NICNT. Grand Rapids: Eerdmans, 1957.

Snodgrass, Klyne. *Ephesians*. NIVAC. Grand Rapids: Zondervan, 1996.

Van Roon, A. *The Authenticity of Ephesians*. Leiden: Brill, 1974.

19

THE LETTERS TO TIMOTHY AND TITUS

Trustworthy Management of God's Household

The letters to Timothy and Titus stand out among the letters attributed to Paul in that they are addressed not to churches but to Paul's coworkers and delegates. They are known collectively as the Pastoral Epistles because they are written to individuals entrusted with the oversight of specific congregations, and they directly concern the roles and responsibilities of the pastor. Though there is a marked tendency to treat all three letters as one corpus, we should not lose sight of the differences between them, especially in regard to 2 Timothy. This is the most personal of the letters attributed to Paul, written to prepare Timothy to carry on the work of ministry after Paul's impending death.

The Pauline authorship of these letters is widely rejected in favor of pseudonymity, although a respected minority still argues for their authenticity or for some mediating position. Whether we find the case for authenticity or pseudonymity more persuasive, the historical-critical questions do not begin to touch on the riches of these texts, which address issues of concern for ministry formation more directly and more openly than most of their canonical peers. The open question of their authorship and the problematic nature of some of their content (especially 1 Tim 2:8-15) must not eclipse the positive contribution these texts can offer our understanding of the roles and responsibilities of the Christian leader, and the advice they offer concerning the challenges of ministry.

THE HISTORICAL SETTING OF THE PASTORAL EPISTLES

The explicated setting. The first and second letters to Timothy purport to be written by Paul to his younger partner in missions, Timothy. Timothy stands out as perhaps the most prominent, trusted and longstanding of Paul's fellow workers. According to Acts, Paul encounters Timothy after he has already come to faith in Christ (Acts 16:1-2) and takes him along as a helper in the ministry (Acts 16:3). Although he is not specifically mentioned, Timothy is assumed to be present with Paul and Silas as they evangelize Philippi, Thessalonica and Berea. He and Silas remain in Macedonia while Paul travels on to Athens and then to Corinth, where Timothy and Silas join up with Paul again (Acts 17:14-15; 18:5). Timothy again appears to be with Paul in Corinth and Ephesus, and is sent by Paul from Ephesus to Macedonia to prepare for Paul's return to that region (Acts 19:21-22). Timothy is last seen in Acts accompanying Paul after the latter's return to encourage the churches in Macedonia and Greece, and finally staying with Paul at Troas (Acts 20:1-6).

The undisputed letters of Paul (together with some "less disputed" letters) provide a portrait that is consonant with the portrait in Acts. Paul frequently sends Timothy on missions as his delegate to strengthen the congregations in Paul's absence (as in Thessalonica; see 1 Thess 3:1-6), to keep a church on track by "reminding" them of Paul's teaching (1 Cor 4:17; 16:10-11) or to bear news about Paul and the church back and forth (Phil 2:19-24; 1 Thess 3:6).[1] Timothy is also named as the coauthor or cosender of several letters (2 Cor 1:1; Phil 1:1; Col 1:1; 1 Thess 1:1; 2 Thess 1:1; Philem 1), and he sends greetings to the church at Rome (Rom 16:21).

First Timothy presupposes that Timothy has been left in Ephesus by Paul while the latter made a brief visit to Macedonia. Paul is known to have made at least two such visits from Ephesus (Acts 20:1-3; 2 Cor 1:16; 2:12-13; 7:5-6), so this scenario is quite plausible.[2] Timothy has been entrusted with keeping the church in Ephesus on track in Paul's absence. Several issues need his attention. First, Timothy must address a few would-be teachers in Ephesus who promote "myths and endless genealogies" and other "speculations" (1 Tim 1:4), some form of Torah observance (1 Tim 1:7-8), and an ascetic lifestyle, forbidding marriage (no doubt including sexual intercourse) and teaching abstinence from certain foods (1 Tim 4:3). Second, Paul provides guidelines for selecting local leaders, perhaps because one or two believers have come forward desiring these responsibilities or nominating someone for a leadership role (1 Tim 3:1-13). Third, Paul gives practical directions for regulating the community's support of widows (1 Tim 5:3-16). In addition to these rather specific issues, Paul also advises Timothy on how to comport himself as a model leader for the Christians in Ephesus and requests that Timothy teach the Christians to show themselves model citizens, wives, slaves—in short, to live with a view to demonstrating that Christianity is far from socially subversive. Given Paul's experiences of being accused of subversion in Philippi, Corinth and Ephesus, this last agenda item is not so surprising or non-Pauline.

Second Timothy appears to come from a later period in Paul's ministry from a Roman prison, after the apostle has given up hope that his trial would result in acquittal (2 Tim 4:6-8), expecting only to be delivered "for his heavenly kingdom" (2 Tim 4:18). Timothy's whereabouts are uncertain: Paul mentions that he has sent Tychicus to Ephesus (2 Tim 4:12), but with no mention of Tychicus and Timothy meeting up with one another in that city Timothy appears not to be there any longer. Wherever he is, however, Timothy is expected to travel to see Paul (2 Tim 4:9, 21) and specifically to pass through Troas, where he will retrieve Paul's cloak, books and parchments from a certain Carpus (2 Tim 4:13).

In this letter Paul encourages and instructs his junior colleague concerning how to carry on the work of building up the churches now that the senior partner is passing from the scene and will no longer be available in person. Timothy will have to rely on his memory of Paul's teaching and example (2 Tim 1:13-14; 2:1-2; 3:10-17) as well as whatever wisdom Paul can pass along now in this letter (e.g., 2 Tim 2:4-7, 15-16, 20-26). Timothy faces new opponents, teachers like Hymenaeus and Philetus, who teach "that the resurrection has already taken place" (2 Tim 2:17-

---

[1] M. M. Mitchell, "NT Envoys in the Context of Greco-Roman Diplomatic and Epistolary Conventions: The Example of Timothy and Titus," *JBL* 111 (1992): 641-62; Luke Timothy Johnson, *The First and Second Letters to Timothy*, AB (Garden City, NY: Doubleday, 2000), pp. 135-36.

[2] Johnson, *First and Second Letters to Timothy*, p. 135.

18). Paul very rarely names his opponents, but the fact that this is a personal, not a public, letter could account for his freedom to do so here, all the more if he desires to put Timothy on guard against these two men specifically. The signs of living in the "last times" are already to be seen in the activity of false teachers who peddle heresy for material gain and for illicit encounters with "silly women" (2 Tim 3:1-9), but Paul assures Timothy that the opposition will amount to nothing.

The letter to Titus presents itself as a letter written by Paul to Titus, another coworker whose activity is well attested in other letters by Paul (see 2 Cor 2:13; 7:6-7, 13-14; 8:6, 16-17, 23; 12:18; Gal 2:1-3), though he is not mentioned at all in Acts. Titus accompanied Paul and Barnabas to Jerusalem as a kind of test case, to see whether or not the Jerusalem apostles would accept him as a convert without circumcision (Gal 2:1-3). Thereafter, he appears only in connection with Paul's dealings with the Corinthian congregations. Titus carried Paul's tearful letter to Corinth and brought back news of their repentance (2 Cor 2:12-13; 7:5-7); he was also entrusted with moving the collection project forward in Corinth (2 Cor 8:6, 16-17, 23; 12:18). Clearly, Titus was a coworker who could be trusted with some very delicate matters.

The letter to Titus presumes a mission to Crete by Paul and Titus that was not part of the visit to Crete on the way to trial in Rome, and that is otherwise unknown from early Christian literature. Paul may have spearheaded a mission to Crete after being released from the Roman imprisonment (or after a journey to Spain, if he made it that far),[3] but it seems equally possible to place it earlier in his lifetime since Acts does not relate all of Paul's movements and missionary endeavors, let alone those of his many coworkers.[4] Paul left Titus in Crete to encourage and help organize the congregations there (Tit 1:5).

This letter bears striking similarities to 1 Timothy. As with Timothy in Ephesus, Titus is also charged with rebuking "those of the circumcision" who seek to promote some form of speculative Judaism, combining interest in "Jewish myths" and "genealogies" with observance of some of the commandments of Torah (Tit 1:10-11, 14; 3:9). These are probably Jewish Christians, since Paul does not speak of the need to win them to the faith but to make them "sound in the faith" (Tit 1:13). Titus is also given a list of qualifications to identify potential "overseers" or "elders" (Tit 1:5-9) that overlaps considerably with the qualifications found in 1 Timothy 3:2-7. These letters also share an interest in promoting conduct that will show Christians to be supporters of a stable social order (Tit 2:3-10; 3:1-2).

A literary fiction? Beginning in earnest with Ferdinand Baur in the nineteenth century, scholars have sharply questioned whether this is truly the *historical* setting of these letters or merely the *literary* setting given to texts that were written after Paul's death in Paul's name. At the close of the twentieth century the position that the Pastoral Epistles are pseudonymous has reached the status of academic dogma—"one of those dogmas first learned in college and in no need of further examination."[5] The question remains open, however, despite the pressures within the guild to yield to the "social fact of consensus."

Before we review the arguments concerning authorship and setting in depth, it is well to

---

[3]Frank Thielman favors a post-62 mission of Paul and Titus to Crete as the setting (*Paul and the Law* [Downers Grove, Ill.: InterVarsity Press, 1994], p. 230).

[4]Johnson counts over forty people involved as part of the Pauline missionary team at one point or another, with Paul coordinating the movements and activity of a great many evangelists and workers (*First and Second Letters to Timothy*, p. 92).

[5]Ibid., p. 55.

consider some general principles that have marked and marred this discussion. The tendency to treat Titus, 1 Timothy and 2 Timothy as a single literary unit and then to compare this group to the "undisputed letters" taken as a group has been shown to obscure some very important differences between individual Pastoral Epistles and very striking similarities between single Pastoral Epistles and other Pauline letters taken one by one. That is to say, the results of most discussions have been skewed by this tendency to compare corpus with corpus rather than considering each of the Pastoral Epistles independently. Second Timothy, taken on its own, has an especially strong claim to authenticity, becoming pseudonymous mainly by association.[6] Moreover, many arguments against authenticity show a high degree of selectivity when presenting the evidence. As with the discussions of Colossians and Ephesians, similarities between the Pastoral Epistles and the undisputed Pauline letters are muted or passed over in silence, while the differences are amplified.

These debates, finally, can be highly ideologically charged. For example, the automatic equation of pseudonymous with unreliable (or deceptive or errant) often (though not always) drives arguments for authenticity.[7] Similarly, those who promote social conservatism (and unequal power relationships in the family) find it helpful to decide that these texts are indeed authentic, and thus have Paul's support for their position. On the other hand, the Paul of the Pastoral Epistles doesn't fit the egalitarian Paul that many scholars want to discover and promote. Consigning them to pseudonymity allows them to distance the authoritative Paul from the objectionable content and to deprive these texts of their authority for the church.[8] Common to both extremes is the presumption that pseudonymity relegates the text to a secondary level within the canon or even undermines its place in the canon entirely. The Pastorals, however, remain part of the body of literature the churches recognized as authoritative, preserving the "authentic" apostolic witness, already by the end of the second century. Inquiries into their authorship have no bearing on their status as sacred Scripture, for the church determined these *texts* to have been inspired.

The question of authorship. *1. Unusual vocabulary.* Titus, 1 Timothy and 2 Timothy share some characteristic language that is also distinctive when set against other literature attributed to Paul. Only in these letters do we find such a concentrated focus on "sound teaching" (1 Tim 1:10; 4:6; 2 Tim 1:13, 4:3; Tit 1:9; 2:1), "sound speech" (Tit 2:8) and being "sound in the faith" (Tit 1:13; 2:2). These letters are deeply interested in the "[good] conscience" and "sincere faith" (1 Tim 1:5, 19; 3:9; 2 Tim 1:3, 5). In all three we find the legitimating statement that "the saying is sure" (1 Tim 1:15; 3:1; 4:9; 2 Tim 2:11; Tit 3:8) or that "this testi-

---

[6]See Michael Prior, *Paul the Letter Writer and the Second Letter to Timothy,* JSNTMS 23 (Sheffield, U.K.: Sheffield Academic Press, 1989); J. Murphy O'Connor, "2 Timothy Contrasted with 1 Timothy and Titus," *RB* 98 (1991): 403-10; Alfred Plummer, *The Pastoral Epistles* (New York: A. C. Armstrong, 1889). p. 12.

[7]Seen, for example, in Terry L. Wilder, "Pseudonymity and the New Testament," in *Interpreting the New Testament: Essays on Method and Issues,* ed. D. A. Black and D. S. Dockery (Nashville: Broadman & Holman, 2001), p. 326. To offset this tendency, Marshall and Towner promote the use of the term *allonymity* as a less value-laden alternative to *pseudonymity,* helpfully replacing the prefix associated with "lying" and "falsehood," throughout the introduction of their commentary. See I. H. Marshall, with P. H. Towner, *A Critical and Exegetical Commentary on the Pastoral Epistles* (Edinburgh: T & T Clark, 1999).

[8]This is seen rather blatantly in Joanna Dewey, "1 Timothy," in *The Women's Bible Commentary,* ed. C. A. Newsome and S. H. Ringe (Louisville, Ky.: Westminster John Knox, 1992). Pseudonymity is taken as a hard fact, and the conclusion drawn: "Thus the command for silence in church is not a command from Paul valid for all time; rather, it is the view of one author (not Paul) or one Christian group on how they would like to see women behave" (Dewey, "1 Timothy," p. 355).

mony is true" (Tit 1:13), and the interest this shows in preserving reliable traditions from which theology and ethics can be drawn.

The distinctive language of these letters, observable by any careful reader, invited closer study of the vocabulary and style of the Pastorals vis-à-vis other Pauline letters. Scholars have noted that

- there is a disproportionately high occurrences of words unique to the New Testament *(hapax legomena)*, thirteen to sixteen per page as opposed to four to six per page in the undisputed Pauline letters. The distinctiveness of the vocabulary is reinforced when we add words that appear in the Pastorals and other New Testament books but not in the undisputed Pauline letters.[9]
- many particles and connecting words common in the undisputed Pauline letters are absent from the Pastorals (like *since, because, therefore, but now, is it not? with the result that*). The flow of these letters strikes the reader as quite different.
- the vocabulary has less in common with the Septuagint and more in common with other ethical compositions of Hellenistic Judaism (like 4 Maccabees and the *Testaments of the Twelve Patriarchs*).[10]
- the non-Pauline vocabulary seems to have more in common with early-second-century literature, suggesting composition well after Paul's death.

Such observations begin to suggest to many scholars that Paul himself did not write these letters, although the evidence is certainly open to other explanations. Most of the unusual vocabulary can be attributed, to a great extent, to

- the specifics of the historical situation (e.g., words uniquely related to the movements of Paul and his coworkers, actions to be

taken in Crete and Ephesus, mention of Timothy's grandmother, language about church leaders and their qualifications, and other such topics not typically discussed at such length in the other letters)
- the teaching and behavior of the opponents, and Paul's characterization of the same (including the use of vice lists)
- the use of earlier traditional material (early Christian hymns and creeds) and topics (household management, virtue and vice lists)
- the changed nature of the letter's target— not a congregation but well-known, familiar coworkers[11]

Paul simply could not have addressed the topics and issues he did with the vocabulary he used in his other letters to address very different topics and issues! An expanded range of topics requires an expanded vocabulary, and if Paul could use 2,177 different words in the other ten letters, why should he not add another 306 as he writes the Pastorals?[12]

Vocabulary counts, moreover, can be somewhat misleading. Conjunctions appropriate to argumentative development (*therefore, since, with the result that, but now* and the like) will be absent from these letters because of their nature and intent, and not because of who did or did not write them. These are letters instructing friends on what needs to be done, not letters persuading churches to do something (especially churches that have already been impressed with the arguments of other teachers, as in Galatians). Dialogical conjunctions and particles are common in Galatians and Romans, but not in Philippians or 1 Thessalonians. It would be more accurate to say that the Pastoral Epistles resemble the latter more than the former than to say

---

[9]C. K. Barrett, *The Pastoral Epistles in the New English Bible* (Oxford: Clarendon, 1963), p. 1.

[10]J. D. Quinn, *The Epistle to Titus,* AB (Garden City, N.Y.: Doubleday, 1990), p. 6.

[11]William D. Mounce, *Pastoral Epistles,* WBC (Nashville: Thomas Nelson, 2000), pp. xcix-cxvii.

[12]Ceslaus Spicq, *Saint Paul: Les Épîtres pastorales,* 4th ed. (Paris: Gabalda, 1969), 1:186.

this is a non-Pauline trait. Since Paul uses more quotations from the Septuagint (and hence Septuagintal vocabulary) in argumentative situations, we should not be surprised to find that the vocabulary of the Pastoral Epistles is less Septuagintal. Again, this could be said to make the Pastorals resemble Philippians and Philemon more than Galatians and Romans (rather than make them "un-Pauline").[13] If an interpreter is sufficiently selective, he or she could compile similar lists of words for an undisputed Pauline letter to marshal evidence that Philippians, for example, uses atypical vocabulary[14] or that Galatians shows an unusual style[15] when set against the rest of the Pauline corpus. Once again, then, there are serious methodological questions about what vocabulary counts can tell us about authorship.

An additional unknown factor regarding vocabulary and style is the influence of the particular scribe or secretary used, or even the absence of such an assistant. Most of Paul's letters include another name in the greeting (Sosthenes in 1 Cor 1:1; Timothy in 2 Cor 1:1; Phil 1:1; Col 1:1; Philem 1; Silvanus and Timothy in 1 Thess 1:1 and 2 Thess 1:1), suggesting some level of coauthorship. The opening of Romans makes mention only of Paul (Rom 1:1), but Tertius later emerges as the secretary who "wrote" the letter (Rom 16:22). Galatians and Ephesians make no mention of a cosender or secretary, although Galatians 6:11 is usually taken as evidence that a secretary has written Galatians 1:1—6:10. The differences observed with regard to the style and "voice" of the Pastoral Epistles could result from the influence of an uncredited coworker who helped Paul frame the letter, or from Paul writing solo without any mediating scribe.[16]

2. The Pastorals in the framework of Paul's life. The events presupposed by the Pastoral Epistles do not reflect events known from other sources about Paul's life. There is no mission to Crete mentioned in Acts or the undisputed letters, nor a deputation of Titus to minister in that locale. There is no independent witness to Timothy being left in charge of the work in Ephesus during an absence by Paul (and an absence of sufficient duration to merit the detailed instructions we find in 1 Timothy). Even 2 Timothy is called into question on this point, since Acts does not speak of a terminal imprisonment of Paul in Rome.

Acts, however, is a very selective "history" of the expansion of the early church. Its author does not seek to document every missionary endeavor or movement of Paul and his rather large number of associates, nor does the author tell of the events subsequent to Paul's imprisonment in Rome in 60-62 C.E.[17] Acts does not mention a mission in Illyricum (the territory west of Macedonia), but this is presumed in Romans 15:19. Paul speaks of having endured multiple imprisonments prior to his arrest in Jerusalem (2 Cor 11:23), but Acts reports only an overnight detention in Philippi (Acts 16:22-34). Acts make no mention of Paul's letters at all. So sketchy, in fact, is the account of Paul's ministry in Acts that "eight of the twelve years between 50 and 62 are dealt with by Acts in four lines."[18]

There is little warrant, therefore, for using Acts' lack of references to missionary work in Crete or the movements reflected in 1 Timothy as an argument against Pauline author-

---

[13]Johnson, *First and Second Letters to Timothy,* pp. 69-71.

[14]Mounce, *Pastoral Epistles,* p. cxiii.

[15]Plummer, *Pastoral Epistles,* p. 12.

[16]Michael Prior, *Paul the Letter-Writer and the Second Letter to Timothy,* JSNTS 23 (Sheffield, U.K.: JSOT Press, 1989), pp. 38-39; see also C. F. D. Moule, "The Problem of the Pastoral Epistles: A Reappraisal," *BJRL* 47 (1964-1965): 430-52.

[17]Plummer, *Pastoral Epistles,* p. 7; Wilder, "Pseudonymity," p. 326.

[18]Johnson, *First and Second Letters to Timothy,* pp. 61-62

ship.[19] On the contrary, since Acts and the other letters do not provide a full and adequate account of Paul's ministry, the movements and missions reflected in the Pastoral Epistles supplement our historical data for understanding the Pauline mission.[20] Even if it should be decided (on other grounds) that these letters are pseudonymous, they remain important evidence of an early tradition that Paul's ministry was more extensive than Acts allows. Whether the events reflected in Titus and 1 Timothy fit within the period prior to Paul's Caesarean imprisonment or after a release from the detention in Rome recounted in Acts 28 remains a matter of debate. That Paul's ministry eventually ended in Rome with an imprisonment and execution rests on strong early tradition, providing a suitable setting for 2 Timothy.[21]

Although the Pastorals do not fit into the framework of Acts, each does presuppose a strikingly detailed historical framework.[22] Most pseudonymous works display a lack of concrete setting. Where they attempt to "create" a historical setting, we find a superfluity of narrative setting the scene, a sign that the author does not presume the readers' familiarity with the situation, and thus a clear sign of pseudonymity.[23] The Pastoral Epistles relate to their setting much as Paul's undisputed letters do. Concrete references to specifics are present, but with no need to explain what can be presumed to be familiar for people involved in the situation firsthand.

The personal requests for a cloak and books and a visit before winter, and oblique indications of where various coworkers and ex-coworkers have gone, are exactly the sort of thing we would expect from an authentic personal letter (2 Tim 4:9-21).[24] Details on the movements of about fifteen other associates do not contradict what is known from other sources, save for the figure of Trophimus.[25] The announcements of travel plans, requests and greetings in Titus 3:12-15, moreover, with the figure of Apollos and the otherwise unknown Zenas the lawyer (presumably bearing the letter to Titus in Crete), also suggest authenticity. Although a pseudepigrapher could have reproduced the pattern from other letters, why should he not use a Tychicus, famous for carrying Paul's letters, rather than these obscure brothers?

3. Church order. The organization of the local congregations assumed in the Pastoral Epistles (specifically, in 1 Timothy and Titus) is often thought to reflect a post-Pauline stage in institutional development. The terms "overseer" (*episkopos*), or "elder" (*presbyteros*), and "deacon" (*diakonos*) seem to refer to well-defined, appointed offices held by individuals. There is a reference to a "council of elders" (*presbyterion*, 1 Tim 4:14) that was involved in laying hands on Timothy, an early reference to a kind of ordination. Moreover, a case can be made that a single "overseer" is now responsible for the overall care of a congregation, since the office is only referred to in the singular.[26]

---

[19]Would a forger, moreover, write letters that do not fit into the historical framework known from Acts or the authentic letters of Paul (see Mounce, *Pastoral Epistles*, p. cxxvii)?

[20]Johnson, *First and Second Letters to Timothy*, p. 67.

[21]Plummer, *Pastoral Epistes*, p. 14; see also 1 Clement 5.5-7 (a strong witness if people in Rome still had memory of Paul's specific fate); the Muratorian Canon; *Acts of Peter;* and Eusebius *Hist. eccl.* 2.22.2 (which adds that 2 Timothy was written during a second imprisonment).

[22]Gordon D. Fee, "Reflections on Church Order in the *Pastoral Epistles,* with Further Reflections on the Hermeneutics of Ad Hoc Documents," *JETS* 28 (1985): 141-51.

[23]Richard Bauckham, "Pseudo-Apostolic Letters," *JBL* 107 (1988): 490.

[24]J. N. D. Kelly, *A Commentary on the Pastoral Epistles,* HNTC (New York: Harper & Row, 1964), p. 33.

[25]Johnson, *First and Second Letters to Timothy*, p. 66.

[26]Eduard Lohse, *The Formation of the New Testament,* trans. M. E. Boring (Nashville: Abingdon, 1981), p. 104.

This suggests the rise of the office that would become known as the bishop. The attention given to these offices suggests that the well-being of the congregation is entrusted more and more to qualified people, and less and less to the direct operation of charismatic forces.[27] The church organization of the Pastoral Epistles is thus often compared with the organization reflected in the *Didache* (late first century C.E.) or the letters of Ignatius of Antioch (early second century C.E.).

But is it the case that the Pastoral Epistles assume a more advanced stage of institutionalization than the undisputed Paulines? Against the claim that "the Pastorals are concerned with offices that had not developed in Paul's time,"[28] Philippians already refers to *episkopoi* and *diakonoi* (Phil 1:1) in a manner that suggests an awareness of these terms as offices. Paul appointed elders from the beginning of his missionary work, at least according to Acts 14:23, and the term *overseer* is used interchangeably with *elder* in Titus 1:5-7. The overseer—envisioned here as a congregational leader entrusted with overseeing funds, providing hospitality and guarding the congregation against doubtful teachings—functions in a manner analogous to the "ruler of the synagogue," an office already available for duplication by the church before Paul began his ministry.

The kind of organization presumed by 1 Timothy and Titus was typical of synagogues and Greco-Roman clubs, or *collegia*. Even if the church in Ephesus had existed for only a few years at the time 1 Timothy was written, it would still be old enough to have developed the rudimentary structures we find in that letter, since models for organizing leadership were available in its immediate environment.[29] There is no discussion of the division of labor, jurisdiction or lines of accountability. The whole focus is on moral character and qualifications for leadership in the church. All this suggests the church order of the Pastorals is still quite rudimentary. There is no need to read into the Pastoral Epistles the monarchical bishop promoted by Ignatius of Antioch in the early second century.

The level of interest in these offices on the part of the author, moreover, is frequently overdrawn (e.g., in the description of the genre of 1 Timothy and Titus as transitional forms on the way to "church orders" in the guise of letters).[30] In Titus only five verses (Tit 1:5-9) are devoted to a topic of church order and, as in 1 Timothy, it only treats personal qualifications and not delineation of duties or sphere of authority. The difference between the Pastoral Epistles and the other letters is that, here, qualifications for church leadership become a topic for direct treatment. If Paul had reasonable cause to address this topic, would he have written to delegates entrusted with consolidating the formation of congregations? An affirmative answer would be defensible.

4. Argumentative strategy. The impression of non-Pauline authorship has been supported with observations about the rather different manner of engagement with opponents and opposing positions seen in the Pastoral Epistles. The rhetoric of Paul's authentic letters, sporting a rich diversity of persuasive strategies, "shows the lively presence of his partners in the dialogue." Paul engages his opposition; the author of the Pastoral Epistles merely "imposes doctrine and engages in monologue"[31] with a view to silencing the opposition. The

---

[27]Martin Dibelius and Hans Conzelman, *The Pastoral Epistles,* Hermeneia (Philadelphia: Fortress, 1972), p. 7.

[28]Dewey, "1 Timothy," p. 353.

[29]Elisabeth Schüssler Fiorenza, *In Memory of Her* (New York: Crossroad, 1983), p. 287; Johnson, *First and Second Letters to Timothy*, pp. 74-75.

[30]Dibelius and Conzelmann, *Pastoral Epistles*, pp. 5-7.

[31]J. C. Beker, *Heirs of Paul* (Minneapolis: Fortress, 1991), pp. 38-40; also Dibelius and Conzelmann, *Pastoral Epistles*, p. 2.

Pastoral Epistles rely on the acceptance of traditional information and its authority, seen for example in the frequent appeal to sayings that are "sure" or "trustworthy." The absence of "the controversy with Judaism—so prominent in Paul, Luke-Acts, Mark, Matthew, and John," is also taken as a sign of post-Pauline, post-apostolic composition.[32]

Some of these sweeping claims are betrayed by the evidence. For example, the deviant teaching in Titus, which explicitly refers to the source of the trouble as "those of the circumcision" (Tit 1:10), and probably 1 Timothy as well, still manifests the tensions between fidelity to and interest in Jewish traditions on the one hand, and the ethic of the new community on the other. Moreover, as Johnson points out, the author of the Pastoral Epistles does in fact engage the opposing position at some length in 1 Timothy 1:8-11; 4:3-5, 7-8; 6:5-10.[33]

Nevertheless, it is true that the Pastoral Epistles contain nothing like the extended argumentation addressing this deviant position such as one finds in Galatians 3—4 or 2 Corinthians 10—13. Is this a function of non-Pauline authorship or of the difference in audience envisioned in these letters? "Paul" writes to his colleagues and to their congregations only insofar as they need to understand the authority and commission of Titus and Timothy. He is not writing to the churches themselves, calling on them to reject a heretical perversion of the gospel, but to Titus and Timothy, calling them to oppose the rival teachers, and calling on the church to recognize their apostolic commission to do so. In other words, unlike Galatians, the Pastoral Epistles are not written directly to people who need to be *persuaded* to reject a deviant teaching, with the result that lengthy arguments against the deviant position would be superfluous ("preaching to the choir").

5. Theology of the Pastoral Epistles. There appears to be some significant distance between the theology of the Pastoral Epistles and the undisputed Pauline letters. For example, the Pastoral Epistles use the term "righteousness" (*dikaiosynē*) as an ethical quality rather than using it with "its Pauline meaning of God's redemptive intervention in Christ."[34] These letters emphasize "good works" and stress the moral obligations of the Christian. *Faith* is not only used to denote "trust" in God or Jesus but to describe the moral quality of reliability or fidelity. In other words, the Pastorals are often criticized as a mere moralistic shadow of Paul. The increased attention to moral behavior in the Pastorals is well established, but have scholars (largely influenced by the heritage of Protestantism) paid too little attention to the "moral" Paul of the undisputed letters, the Paul who is intensely concerned about forming virtue and ethical behavior in his converts (see, e.g., Gal 5:16—6:10; Rom 12:9—13:14; 1 Cor 6:9-20; Phil 4:8-9; 1 Thess 4:1-12; 5:14-15) and promoting good deeds (Rom 2:6-7; 13:2; 2 Cor 5:10; 9:8; Col 1:10)?[35]

The Pastoral Epistles use language that resonates more with Hellenistic religious terminology than we would expect if Paul wrote them, given the undisputed letters. For example, the language of epiphany is quite prominent in these letters but entirely absent from undisputed letters (2 Thess 2:8 is the only other Pauline text to use this terminology, and its authorship is disputed). The Pastorals speak of the "appearing" of Christ as "Savior" (2 Tim 1:10), of the time when "the goodness and beneficence of our Savior God appeared" (Tit 3:4) or when "grace appeared, bringing salvation"

---

[32]Beker, *Heirs of Paul,* p. 38.

[33]Johnson, *First and Second Letters to Timothy,* p. 73.

[34]Beker, *Heirs of Paul,* p. 42.

[35]Johnson, *First and Second Letters to Timothy,* pp. 92-93.

(Tit 2:11). The future coming of Christ is also styled an epiphany (1 Tim 6:14; 2 Tim 4:8; possibly in 2 Tim 4:1). Only Luke-Acts also uses this terminology. How are we to interpret such data? Is this a sign of a different author? Has Paul changed his terminology from *coming* to *appearing,* or is he equally happy with either mode? Is this the word choice of a coworker who helped Paul pen these letters (perhaps Luke, as some have suggested)?[36]

Some suggest that the Pastorals reflect an absence of eschatological expectations, and that instead the author now seeks a stable place in Roman society.[37] We have already seen, however, that the expectation of Christ's appearing in the future remains quite strong. Indeed, 1 Timothy 4:1-5 could be taken as evidence of a lively eschatological expectation, with the author understanding the rise of the heresies as a sign that the author and reader are in the last times (hence, that the outlook of the letter is consistent with an apocalyptic expectation).

As always, we must carefully notice commonalities while observing differences, lest our perspective on the issue be skewed. Several key Pauline themes, such as the mission to the Gentiles, the conviction that present suffering leads to glory, the belief that salvation comes by grace rather than merit and the use of the apostle as example, all connect the Pastoral Epistles with the undisputed letters.[38]

6. Nature of the heresy addressed. Scholars frequently speak of the deviant Christians who are infatuated with "myths and endless genealogies" (1 Tim 1:4; see Tit 3:9), involved in "quarrels about the law" (Tit 3:9), and appear to talk about their teaching as a kind of "knowledge" (*gnōsis,* 1 Tim 6:20) as promoting a kind of Gnosticism. In the nineteenth century this led to the theory that the Pastorals were written to combat second-century Gnosticism, with its elaborate genealogies of the divine powers and emanations, its creation myths, and the like. The information about the deviant Christians in the Pastoral Epistles is scant at best, and it is not even clear that we should assume that they all refer to the same opponents. Explicit statements about the opposition being Jewish or Jewish-Christian occur only in Titus, not 1 Timothy, though these two letter do appear to address similar strands of innovation. Deviants who claim that the resurrection has already occurred are mentioned only in 2 Timothy 2:17-18, and not in connection with asceticism or interest in the Jewish law, genealogies and myths.

The mere mention of the word *knowledge,* which is very common in the undisputed letters of Paul, always conjures up specters of Gnostics, but this tendency to find Gnostics under every verse has been rightly and roundly criticized as overzealous mirror reading. The genealogies and stories (myths) of the Old Testament could be of interest to early Christians in many ways, and not just the ways that second-century Gnostics pursued. Philo of Alexandria, for example, applies his allegorical exegesis to the genealogies of Genesis with the same rigor as to the narratives (see, for example, *Posterity and Exile of Cain* 33-124), using these passages as a means of inquiring into the faculties and foibles of the human mind. The deviant Christians might just as easily have been preoccupied with this line of inquiry as with the later Gnostic variety. In short, the author reveals too little about these innovators to identify them with later Gnosticism. What he does say remains quite consonant with the streams of thought available to Christians in the middle of the first century.[39]

---

[36]Quinn, *Epistle to Titus,* p. 21.

[37]Beker, *Heirs of Paul,* p. 44.

[38]Johnson, *First and Second Letters to Timothy,* p. 77.

[39]Spicq, *Saint Paul,* 1:lxxi; Dibelius and Conzelmann, *Pastoral Epistles,* p. 3.

7. Genre. The question of genre is usually independent of the question of authorship, but with the Pastoral Epistles the questions have some bearing on each other. Second Timothy has often been compared to a "testament," a genre of considerable popularity during the intertestamental period and subsequently (see, e.g., the *Testaments of the Twelve Patriarchs, Testament of Job, Testament of Moses, Testament of Abraham*). The "testament" is the deathbed speech of a patriarch, involving exactly the kinds of material found in 2 Timothy. The testator looks ahead to his own impending death, provides instructions for his gathered children and grandchildren (see the use of *child* in 2 Tim 1:2; 2:1), draws moral lessons from his own life experience, and predicts conditions after the testator's death, often involving eschatological predictions. All of these elements can be found in 2 Timothy, including two passages that predict conditions after the writer's death and instruct his "child" concerning how to respond to those eventualities (2 Tim 3:1-5; 4:3-4).[40] This is a standard technique for bridging the distance between the historical situation of the testator and the actual readers of the testament. This Pauline testament is framed as a letter, the typical mode of Pauline expression. Since testaments are, as a genre, pseudonymous, this identification of 2 Timothy as a kind of testament would tend to support the case for pseudonymity.

But what would someone write if, facing execution, he or she wished to prepare a dear friend and protégé to carry on in the ministry, knowing that the friend will no longer have the mentor's living voice to guide and encourage him? Wouldn't the mentor write precisely the kind of letter found in 2 Timothy? Luke Timothy Johnson therefore suggests the genre of the "personal paraenetic letter" as an alternative to viewing 2 Timothy as a testament.[41] The fact that the letter is full of specific details reflecting the situation facing Paul and Timothy (down to the request that Timothy bring the cloak and literature Paul had left in Troas) distances the text from testaments, which tend to be much more vague, and suggests that it arose from the concrete situation of Paul in prison. While it can be seen as comparable to the testament in some respects, it is also akin to the literature exemplified by the anonymous instructions given to Demonicus (attributed to Isocrates) to prepare him for life after the death of his father. There too we find the writer drawing the son's attention to what he learned and observed from his father, exhorting him to imitate the model of his father and teacher, and sharing maxims that would continue to guide him.[42] Second Timothy is, then, not so obviously a specimen of the testament that is *has* to be pseudonymous.

First Timothy and Titus are also clearly letters, but, as noted already, they are often seen as a transitional genre between the letter and the "church order," the handbook on church polity.[43] Such "church orders" certainly already existed in the intertestamental period, if the anachronism would be permitted. At Qumran, community life was regulated according to the *Community Rule* (1QS). Essene groups, spread throughout the towns of Judea and beyond, appear to have been regulated by the *Damascus Document* (CD). These anonymous texts provided detailed ethical instructions, rules of conduct in the community (complete with penalties for nonobservance), guidelines for the practice of community rituals, and delineation of the roles and responsibilities of community officers. By the end of the first or beginning of the second century, the church had produced its own "community rule," called the *Didache*.

---

[40]Bauckham, "Pseudo-Apostolic Letters," p. 493.

[41]Johnson, *First and Second Letters to Timothy,* p. 322.

[42]Ibid., p. 323.

[43]Dibelius and Conzelman, *Pastoral Epistles,* pp. 5-7.

The Didache

The earliest known adaptation of the genre of the "community rule" for Christian communities is the *Didache,* or the *Teaching of the Twelve Apostles to the Nations.* This text probably reached its final form in the mid-second century, although it appears to have evolved over a long period of time. Its earliest edition (which might also account for the majority of the book) may have come from the turn of the first century, making it contemporaneous with the later books of the New Testament. The church organization it envisions is certainly in keeping with what we encounter in the letters of Paul, with traveling evangelists and prophets moving from church to church, and local overseers and deacons providing leadership on a regular basis.

The *Didache* opens with a section on ethics using the motif of "the two ways," the Way of Life and the Way of Death, drawn from Deuteronomy 30:15, 19-20 (*Didache* 1—6). The Way of Life involves loving God and neighbor, and doing to others as one would have them do—in short, the summaries of the Law provided by Jesus in the Synoptic tradition. These commands are then amplified by means of more Jesus traditions drawn from the Sermon on the Mount, and then by ethical instructions couched in the language of the wisdom tradition or advice collections, in which the teacher addresses the student as "my son." After the Way of Death is more briefly elaborated, the *Didache* segues into a series of instructions on community rites, piety and organization:

- how to conduct baptism, offering both immersion and sprinkling as acceptable forms (*Didache* 7)
- days on which to fast (Wednesday and Friday, to distinguish the group from the Jewish community that fasts on Monday and Thursday, *Didache* 8.1)
- how, and how often, to pray (providing the text of the Lord's Prayer with the concluding doxology, *Didache* 8.2)
- how to celebrate the Eucharist (the "Thanksgiving," the early Christian name for the Lord's Supper, or Holy Communion), including a liturgy for the blessing of the cup and the bread, and a prayer of thanksgiving for after Communion (*Didache* 9—10); noteworthy here is the instruction concerning confession of sin and reconciliation of estranged Christians prior to partaking (*Didache* 14)
- How to receive traveling evangelists and prophets, and how to distinguish the genuine emissary of God from the charlatan who uses the gospel or the gifts of the Spirit as a means of profit (*Didache* 11—13; the amount of space given to this topic shows its importance for the early churches)
- The appointment of overseers and deacons, local leaders who carry out the ministry of the traveling leaders (evangelists and prophets) in a place on a regular basis (*Didache* 13, 15)

The text concludes with a chapter on eschatological expectations, showing close connections with Mark 13 // Matthew 24 and with the "Man of Lawlessness" tradition of 2 Thessalonians.

The *Didache* was held in high regard by Christian leaders in Egypt, being treated as Scripture by Clement of Alexandria and Origen. It fell into obscurity, however, and was only rediscovered in the nineteenth century.

First Timothy and Titus bear some resemblance to the *Didache* in terms of content. The former provide instructions about praying, the selection of officers (*episkopoi* and *diakonoi*), the care for widows in the community, almsgiving and various ethical instructions. The differences, however, are also quite notable. The Pastoral Epistles urge that prayers be offered, and in what spirit and to what end; the *Didache* provides actual forms for individual and corporate prayer (the Lord's Prayer and eucharistic prayers). The Pastoral Epistles provide ethical instructions in terms of household codes, with different sets of instruction pertaining to different groups within families (young men, young women, older women); the *Didache* provides universal ethical instruction without differentiation. Most significantly, the Pastoral Epistles still have particular challenges and situation-specific needs in view, while the *Didache* is intentionally general, written to have universal applicability. This difference is reflected in the difference in genre itself: the former are letters, which are situation-specific documents; the latter is a "rule," a community-specific document—however broadly that community is manifested in local congregations (the *Didache* is very similar to the *Damascus Document* in this regard).

FOR FURTHER READING

Draper, Jonathan A., ed. *The Didache in Modern Research.* Leiden: E. J. Brill, 1996.

Lightfoot, J. B., and John R. Harmer. *The Apostolic Fathers: Greek Texts and English Translations of Their Writings.* Edited and revised by Michael R. Holmes. 2nd ed. Grand Rapids: Baker, 1992.

Niederwimmer, Kurt. *The Didache: A Commentary.* Translated by L. M. Maloney. Hermeneia. Minneapolis: Fortress, 1998.

van de Sandt, Huub, and David Flusser. *The Didache: Its Jewish Sources and Its Place in Early Judaism and Christianity.* Assen: Royal Van Gorcum, 2002.

A comparison of 1 Timothy or Titus with these other texts, however, shows just how far away from a church manual these letters really are. None of them address a particular individual entrusted with the care of a community, as the Pastoral Epistles do, and therefore none have any of the direct exhortations and instructions regarding how this delegate is to conduct himself. The true "community rules" address a much broader array of topics and cases, while 1 Timothy and Titus retain their ad hoc, situational character, being more comparable to 1 Corinthians (and treating many of the same topics) than to "church orders."[44] The specific duties of specific officials receive comprehensive treatment in the Essene rules; 1 Timothy and Titus give very little hint as to what the actual functions of deacons and overseers were. The nature of the Pastoral Epistles is obscured rather than clarified by calling them "church orders," although the topics treated therein provide an important bridge in that direction, attesting also to the increasing attention to the institutionalization of the Christian movement shortly before or after the death of Paul.

As an alternative, 1 Timothy and Titus

---

[44]Johnson, *First and Second Letters to Timothy,* pp. 153-54. In both texts Paul is seen to be aware that his responsibility toward God's call includes the faithful ordering of God's house (1 Cor 9:17; 1 Tim 1:4).

could be seen as adaptations of royal correspondence, the *mandata principis,* the orders given by a superior to a delegate to be carried out in that delegate's sphere of authority (as when an emperor or king sent a governor to a province).[45] These were both private and public documents given to the delegate but also posted in a public space (often in the form of an inscription) as a means both of authorizing the delegate in the eyes of the provincials and keeping the delegate "in check" by making public his commission. These instructions to delegates gave attention not only to the particulars of what needed to be done but also to the demeanor the delegate was to have.

The genre of "instructions to a delegate" suits the content of 1 Timothy and Titus, where the act of giving such instructions actually becomes an explicit topic (1 Tim 1:18), and where the authorization of a delegate is explicitly in view (as in 1 Tim 1:3, which refers to a previous commissioning, retroactively legitimating Timothy's actions and jurisdiction since Paul's departure). Both Titus 1:4 and 1 Timothy 1:2 describe the delegate as "reliable," or "loyal," a descriptor not reproduced in the private letter in this group (2 Tim 1:2). Even such a subtle variation between the letters could be due to the mixed audience of Titus and 1 Timothy and the desire to affirm these delegates as reliable in the public ear in order to bolster their authority to work and act in Paul's name. The quasi-public nature of these letters to delegates also explains their displaying a more detached tone (e.g., in the abrupt ending of 1 Timothy, devoid of personal remarks) than the warm tone we would expect from a private letter to a friend.

The shape of 1 Timothy and Titus need not therefore be read as a clumsy attempt at imitating Paul's genuine letters, but as Paul's own use of a well-established literary form.[46]

8. Date and location. The date of composition is integrally related to the question of authorship. Unfortunately, neither the scant internal references to the deviant teachings involved nor the church order envisioned provide sufficient data for a precise dating.[47] However, literary relationships with other texts can at least set the upper limit for the date of composition. Polycarp, the overseer (*episkopos*) of the church in Smyrna, appears to have drawn extensively on the Pastoral Epistles as a resource for his letter to the Philippian Christians:

- Polycarp writes that "the love of money is the beginning of all evils. Knowing, therefore, that we brought nothing into the world, but neither do we have anything to carry out, let us make use of the tools of righteousness" (Pol. *Phil.* 4.1), obviously alluding to 1 Timothy 6:7, 10.
- Polycarp writes of the martyrs that "they did not love this present age" (Pol. *Phil.* 9.2), a contrast with Demas, who was "in love with this present world" (2 Tim 4:10).[48]

to which we could add:

- Attention is given in both to teaching women to raise their children in the faith (Pol. *Phil.* 4.2; cf. 1 Tim 2:15).
- Instructions are given to widows to pray constantly and avoid gossip (Pol. *Phil.* 4.3; cf. 1 Tim 5:5, 13).
- Both outline the character of deacons and presbyters (Pol. *Phil.* 5.2; 6.1; cf. 1 Tim 3:1-13).

---

[45]This genre is suggested and the connections laid out in Johnson, *First and Second Letters to Timothy,* pp. 97, 139-42.

[46]The somewhat overblown opening of Titus suggested to Jerome Quinn that these three letters are actually an example of the genre of the "letter collection," not just individual letters written at different times, and that Titus originally stood at the opening of the collection (Quinn, *Epistle to Titus,* p. 9; J. D. Quinn, "The Last Volume of Luke: The Relation of Luke-Acts to the Pastoral Epistles," in *Perspectives on Luke-Acts,* ed. C. H. Talbert [Danville, Va.: Association of Baptist Professors of Religion, 1978], pp. 63-64, 72). If these were semipublic "instructions to delegates," however, Paul's full self-identification in Titus 1:1-3 would be explicable as written for the sake of the Cretan Christians who would "overhear" this letter of commissioning.

[47]Barrett, *Pastoral Epistles,* pp. 18-19.

[48]Barrett, *Pastoral Epistles,* p. 1; Quinn, *Epistle to Titus,* p. 5.

- Both instruct the young males and females in the church, especially concerning the avoidance of the passions associated with youth (Pol. *Phil.* 5.3; cf. Tit 2:4-6).
- Both display a concern not to bring the faith into disrepute among nonbelievers (Pol. *Phil* 10.2-3; cf. 1 Tim 5:14; 6:1).

The Pastoral Epistles must have been written before 112-113 C.E. and probably at least some decades before.[49] (Polycarp writes this letter after Ignatius has moved on from Asia Minor on the way to execution at Rome but before receiving a report of the outcome.) Does the composition of Acts provide the earliest date? Second Timothy 3:11 seems, for example, to be a reflection of the itinerary in Acts 13—14 (the narrative of opposition in Antioch, Iconium and Lystra). It is still possible, however, that Acts 13—14 is written on the basis of accurate information about Paul's travels and thus reflects knowledge that Paul (as the author of 2 Timothy) would have had available as he wrote prior to Acts.

The Pastoral Epistles are used by Irenaeus and Tertullian as Pauline texts, and Eusebius records no dispute over the acceptance of this book in the early fourth century (*Hist. eccl.* 3.3.5).[50] If they were composed pseudonymously, these letters would still have had to be written very early—closer to Paul's death than to the turn of the century.[51]

Conclusion. Although several of the observations made by proponents of pseudepigraphy can be falsified, and many of their obser-

vations can be subjected to a different evaluation or interpretation, it still must be admitted that they have raised enough doubt to prevent us from blithely assuming Pauline authorship. On the other hand, the case against authenticity—especially when 2 Timothy is separated from the other—is not airtight. So it is presumptuous to discount the possibility that Paul did write these letters in some sense. Students of these letters should investigate the evidence more fully and weigh carefully the implications of the many positions offered as solutions to explain the data:

- The Pastoral Epistles are pseudonymous compositions of the late first century, the work of Christian leaders faithfully seeking to adapt Paul's message to the changing needs of the church. They seek to rescue Paul's authority from misuse by deviant believers; steering a course between works-righteousness and world-renouncing asceticism[52]; cultivating an ethos of "good citizenship"[53]; promoting structure, order and the maintenance of patriarchal society as a means to find a stable place in the world for the church; and providing in Timothy and Titus models for the continuing work of the Pauline apostolate in new generations.[54]
- The Pastoral Epistles represent expansions of fragments of short Pauline letters, the fragments containing mainly personal information about Paul and the movements of his coworkers.[55] Alternatively, 2 Timothy

---

[49] Some have suggested on the basis of these parallels, however, that Polycarp actually wrote the *Pastoral Epistles*, but this seems to be far too presumptuous a move for the humble and self-effacing bishop.

[50]Plummer, *Pastoral Epistles,* pp. 5-6

[51]Quinn, *Epistle to Titus,* p. 21.

[52]Dibelius and Conzelmann, *Pastoral Epistles,* p. 10.

[53]Ibid., p. 8.

[54]Quinn, *Epistle to Titus,* p. 17.

[55]P. N. Harrison sought to resolve the problem of (1) the detailed accounts of various people's movements and (2) the difficulty fitting the Pastorals into the known career of Paul by isolating the following passages as fragments of different, genuine letters: (a) Titus 3:12-15; (b) 2 Tim 4:13-15, 20-21a; (c) 2 Tim 4:16-18; (d) 2 Tim 4:9-12, 22b; (e) 2 Tim 1:16ff.; 3:10-11; 4:1, 2a, 5b; 4:6ff.; 4:18b, 19, 21b, 22a (Barrett, *Pastoral Epistles,* pp. 10-11). The hair-splitting in the last four of these five, however, makes the hypothesis highly suspect—why would the pseudepigrapher weave together four separate fragments so completely and without discernible strategy into 2 Timothy 4?

could be regarded as authentic, or based on an authentic last letter of Paul to Timothy and expanded and rewritten to continue the apostle's work in Ephesus shortly after his death, with 1 Timothy and Titus being patterned after 2 Timothy (a letter to a delegate), written by a close associate of Paul who wrote "as (they thought that) he would have done."[56]

- The Pastoral Epistles are authentic, highly situational letters of Paul, written to give specific instructions to Timothy and Titus as they faced particular challenges in their ministry. He may have written them himself, or perhaps more likely, had the help of a coworker or secretary, one that was not involved in the writing of the undisputed letters.

The debate over authorship, however, should not be regarded as a debate over authority and value, even though the results of the former debate are frequently brought to bear on the latter question. The church recognized these *texts* as authoritative and reflective of the apostolic witness and vision for the church. If Paul were discovered to have written more letters, they would not therefore become authoritative; nor should the value of the Pastorals be diminished should they be found decisively to be pseudonymous.

THE MESSAGE OF THE PASTORAL EPISTLES

"How one ought to behave in the household of God." First Timothy 3:15 provides something of a thematic statement for these letters, for each is concerned with laying out "how one ought to behave in the household of God, which is the church of the living God, the pillar and bulwark of the truth" (NRSV). The most prominent theme of these letters concerns "God's household management" (*oikonomian theou,* 1 Tim 1:4), which the author of 1 Timothy promotes as the fundamental concern of the genuine Christian teacher (as opposed to the speculative theology that occupies the deviant teachers in the Pastorals).

The specific instructions running especially throughout 1 Timothy and Titus reveal a concern that the Christians should present the best possible face to Greco-Roman society and live in the manner that most enhances the positive reputation of the Christian movement while not compromising on essential points (e.g., participating in idolatrous religion). The motive clauses used to promote certain kinds of behavior point strongly in this direction:

> "so as to give the opponent no occasion for slander" (1 Tim 5:14)

> "in order that God's name and the teaching might not be slandered" (1 Tim 6:1)

> "in order that the word of God might not be slandered" (Tit 2:5)

> "in order that the opponent might be put to shame, having nothing bad to say about us" (Tit 2:8)

> "in order that they might adorn the teaching of our Savior God in everything" (Tit 2:10)

The author promotes behaviors and attitudes that will reinforce an image of Christians as people who support and respect the social order, steering away from behaviors that might appear subversive, where subversion is nonessential. The Christian movement would always be seen to subvert traditional religion in its abhorrence of idolatry and the worship of any god save the God of Israel (though even on this point the apologists would later seek to present the Greco-Roman philosophers, who

---

[56]I. H. Marshall, with P. H. Towner, *A Critical and Exegetical Commentary on the Pastoral Epistles* (Edinburgh: T & T Clark, 1999), pp. 59-108. See especially pp. 84, 92.

also advocated monotheism and imageless religion, as their allies). The Christian group could, however, offset the tendency for their neighbors to view them as an enemy of the social order. This was an understandable tendency, since the Christian missionaries proclaimed the coming of some "kingdom of God" as the successor to the Roman Empire, hailed an executed disturber of the peace as the "Lord" and "Deliverer," and made good god-fearing people into atheists.

To this end the author of 1 Timothy wants Christians to see themselves as friends of the *pax Romana,* supporting that peace and its guarantors through their prayers and leading unobjectionable, indeed exemplary, lives (1 Tim 2:1-6). This, the author avers, is the preferred strategy for evangelism and expanding the kingdom. Far from being subversive of the social order, Christians will show themselves submissive to that order at every level. All believers are to show themselves obedient to the designated political authorities (Tit 3:1). They are also, however, to submit to the social order manifested in the traditional Greco-Roman household, in which the head of the household has authority over every other member, whether as father, husband or master.[57]

Christian leaders are summoned to instruct slaves to model the qualities of obedience and respect toward their masters, whether those masters are Christian or not (1 Tim 6:1-2; Tit 2:9-10). By such conduct they will clarify that Christianity is not a revolutionary movement that breeds revolt and threatens the fundamental bedrock of the Greco-Roman economy—slave labor. Older women are enjoined to teach the younger women how to embody the Greco-Roman ideal of the "virtuous wife," which combines submissiveness to the husband, modesty in dress and demeanor, silence ("invisibility") in public, and competent diligence in the management of domestic concerns (1 Tim 2:9-15; Tit 2:3-5).[58] Wives were also expected to adopt their husband's religion[59]—one point where the Christian wife of the non-Christian husband would necessarily transgress the Greco-Roman ideal.

First Timothy 2:11-15 is undoubtedly the most controversial passage in the Pastoral Epistles (though from the perspective of history, the remarks about slaves and masters would vie for this distinction). These verses grow organically out of 1 Timothy 2:9-10, developing further the author's vision of what "is proper for women who profess reverence for God" (1 Tim 2:10 NRSV), or more precisely, what the non-Christian society will affirm as proper, respectable conduct on the part of Christian women. Because the church assembles in households, the lines between public and private, domestic and ecclesial do not exist. For the sake of the group's reputation the author insists that women (almost all of whom would be wives) not cease to model the ideal of submissiveness and silence when the church gathers. Wherever non-Christians might observe Christians, the impression must be made that Christians embody traditional social and domestic values rather than overturning them. Even though the author presents theological warrants to support his in-

---

[57]See Aristotle *Pol.* 1.12-13; Xenophon *Oeconomicus;* Plutarch, "Advice on Marriage." These and other texts, and their contribution to illumining the New Testament, are discussed at length in David A. deSilva, *Honor, Patronage, Kinship and Purity* (Downers Grove, Ill.: InterVarsity Press, 2000), pp. 173-74, 178-93, 227-37.

[58]For a representative sampling, see Xenophon *Oeconomicus* 3.10-15; 7.16-41; Plutarch, "Advice on Marriage"; Sir 26:14-16; Josephus *Ag. Ap.* 2.199.

[59]"A married woman should therefore worship and recognize the gods whom her husband holds dear, and these alone. The door must be closed to strange cults and foreign superstition. No god takes pleasure in cult performed furtively and in secret by a woman" (Plutarch, "Advice on Marriage" 19; *Mor.* 140D).

structions (1 Tim 2:13-14), it is not the author's understanding of God's revealed will for husbands and wives (as derived from Genesis) that drives them.[60] Rather, these instructions and the theological rationales are driven by the larger agenda of building bridges between the Christian culture and the larger society that will in turn assist the church to win the battles that it deems essential.

Concern for the group's reputation also emerges as the author addresses the conduct of younger widows, who are advised to remarry, continue in the role of child-raising and manage their households well (1 Tim 5:14). By stepping back into such a role the Christian widow will again be intelligible to non-Christians as a virtuous woman. The householders, as well, "must be well thought of by outsiders" (1 Tim 3:7 NRSV) if they hope to be Christian leaders. Since local leaders (overseers) will provide the most public face for the community, it is essential they be off to a good start.

In addition to conforming Christian behavior to core political and domestic ideals of the Greco-Roman society, the Pastoral Epistles also seek to shape Christians who will embody the ethical ideals of that culture. Christians are to take care in their interactions with non-Christians in general "to be ready for every good work, . . . to be gentle, and to show every courtesy to everyone" (Tit 3:1-2 NRSV). In this way the Christians' winsome behavior will provide the witness of a virtuous life and kind disposition to the positive value of the Christian gospel, while maintaining the group's differing convictions about the nature of and loyalty to the one God made known in Christ. Especially through benevolent deeds ("every good work," Tit 3:1; devotion to "good works in order to meet urgent needs," Tit 3:14; also 3:8), the Christians will win the admiration

and gratitude of their non-Christian neighbors and enhance the honor of the group.

The author of Titus especially presents Christianity as a philosophy that trains people in the renunciation of "impiety and worldly passions," so they can "live lives that are self-controlled, upright, and godly" (Tit 2:12 NRSV). As the author lays out how local Christian leaders are to instruct various segments of their congregation, central virtues of Greco-Roman ethics emerge regularly. Christians are to model self-control and temperance (Tit 1:6-8; 2:1, 3, 6, 12), reverence (Tit 2:3, 12), prudence (Tit 1:8; 2:1), and fortitude (Tit 2:2). Most non-Christians would readily recognize and approve these virtues and goals, and the fruits of having joined the Christian movement should hopefully contribute to a positive (re-)assessment of the movement as a whole.

The Pastoral Epistles do not neglect behavior within the household of God, for much of what has already been reviewed plays itself out in the interaction of Christians with one another. The model of the household of God once again invites Christians to regard and treat one another as family (in the best sense). First Timothy 5:1-2 applies this particularly to Timothy, the leader, who is to approach senior Christians as fathers and mothers, and peers as brothers and sisters. By embedding pastoral authority in family relations the Christian leader is trained to act with respect and deference to those who are older (rather than be domineering), with camaraderie and cooperation toward same-sex peers, and with purity toward peers of the opposite sex. The fact that a young Christian woman is also a sister serves to provide an alternative model for how she should be viewed and interactions guided (one that is, moreover, bolstered by incest taboos).

The health of the household requires that individuals not indulge themselves in the kinds

---

[60]First Timothy 2:14 is especially problematic because Adam's sin was all the more culpable, being committed willfully and in full knowledge.

The Mastery of the Passions in Ethical Philosophy

The Pastoral Epistles repeatedly extol the virtue of rational judgment, moderation and self-control (shades of meaning of *sōphrosynē* and related words: see 1 Tim 2:9, 15; 3:2; 2 Tim 1:7; Tit 1:8; 2:2, 4, 5, 6, 12) along with other virtues such as justice, piety, self-discipline and the like. Similarly, they warn repeatedly against being carried away by the "desires" (*epithymiai:* see 1 Tim 6:9; 2 Tim 2:22; 3:6; 4:3; Tit 2:12; 3:3). In so doing, these texts intersect with an important complex of topics from Greco-Roman and Hellenistic Jewish ethical philosophy.

Ethical philosophers had long agreed that the major impediment to the life of virtue was the "passions" *(pathē pathēmata epithymiai).* The passions represent a complex range of human experiences from emotions (e.g., fear or anger) to desires (e.g., greed or lust) to sensations (e.g., pleasure and pain). If the person were to be ruled by the passions, he or she would inevitably run into vicious courses of action. If the person followed his or her rational faculty, against which the passions continually hurled themselves, that person would pursue virtue. Plato had taught that the wise person did not allow his or her soul to yield to the "feelings of the body" but rather opposed them. The rational faculty was to rule the feelings "like a tyrant" and keep them in check (*Phaedo* 93-94). Plutarch, a spokesperson for "popular philosophy" in the later first century, regarded moral virtue mainly to consist of the subjection of the emotions and desires to reason (*On Moral Virtue* 1 *Mor.* 440D). Philosophers debated whether or not the goal of the disciplined life was merely the mastery of the passions (some Stoics, Aristotelians and Platonists; see Plutarch *On Moral Virtue* 3 [*Mor.* 443D]) or the extirpation of the passions (more hardcore Stoics; see Cicero *Tusculan Disputations* 3.22; 4.57), but all agreed that these were the enemy of consistent virtuous living.

Jewish authors also recognized the importance of this topic and agreed with their Greek counterparts that the desires, emotions and sensations were the enemies of virtue. The author of the *Letter of Aristeas,* for example, presents the "highest rule" as "To rule oneself and not be carried away by passions" (*Aristeas* 221-22). Self-control rather than self-indulgence was the path to living nobly and justly (*Aristeas* 277). Fourth Maccabees takes the mastery of the passions by reason, as reason is trained and shaped by observance of the Jewish Law, as its theme (4 Macc 1:1). The Jewish way of life, regulated by the Torah, is presented as the divinely given remedy for the passions and desires of the flesh, providing steady training in self-control through the dietary laws and other regulations, and keeping the power of the passions in check (4 Macc 1:15—2:14; 5:22-26). The ability to master the passions, however, comes from following God and God's Law. This comes very close to the thought of Titus 2:11-13, where God is "training us to renounce impiety and worldly passions" and to "live lives that are self-controlled, upright, and godly" (NRSV). By following the Christian way of life, disciples are held to attain to the highest ethical ideals of Greco-Roman philosophy. As this becomes more and more clearly manifest to outsiders, the virtue of Christians should provide one more reason that outsiders should hold the group in high regard rather than slander the Way.

of controversies and arguments that do no good but only "injure those who are listening" (2 Tim 2:14, 23-26; Tit 3:9-11). The Pastorals thus call for self-control not only over the body and its cravings but also over the mind, its wanderings and its assertiveness about what it thinks to have discovered. Timothy and Titus are not to feed such controversies, and those who raise such controversies appear in these letters as negative foils to the proper behavior of the Christian teacher, who focuses on what promotes godliness throughout the community rather than prideful promotion of pet positions.

Finally, the formation of the household of God does not negate natural households and the individual's responsibilities to them. The Pastoral Epistles do not foster a cult mentality by which attachment to the group transcends and replaces participation in a natural family. In the discussion of widows, for example, their natural kin must continue to play the major role in providing support and care (1 Tim 5:3-4, 8, 16). Again, the Christian philosophy must *at least* have taught its members to be as virtuous and dutiful as Greco-Roman philosophical ethics!

The roles and responsibilities of Christian leaders. The Pastoral Epistles are distinctive among New Testament epistles for the amount of attention they give to the roles and responsibilities of Christian leaders. Whereas the majority of New Testament exhortations directly affect all believers, these letters are especially concerned with the local leaders and how they will shape the life and ethos of the believing community.

In the forefront of these instructions stands the example of the Christian leader, which forms the core of the leader's message, authority and legacy. Here is a point of strong conti-nuity with the undisputed Pauline letters, for Paul understands the importance of providing a living example of the message he preaches (see, for example, 1 Cor 11:1; Phil 3:17; 2 Cor 12:6). In 1 Timothy 1:12-17 Paul's life story provides the proof, as it were, of his proclamation of the extent of God's mercy and kindness,[61] and the fruit of that mercy was to make Paul a living example of the transformation effected by the gospel of Christ.

Like the apostle, delegated representatives of the gospel must also proclaim the transformative power of the gospel not only with their lips but in their lives. The Christian leader must take seriously the need to overcome challenges to personal integrity and to make his or her life congruent with the call of discipleship. Second Timothy 2:20-22, for example, introduces the image of various kinds of utensils, some for common uses and some for noble uses. Those who cleanse themselves from "youthful passions" and misguided teachings, and dedicate themselves to "righteousness, faith, love and peace" will find themselves in the latter category. The author appeals to the leader's desire for honor, assuring him or her that allowing God's call to holiness to shape his or her life will result in distinctive opportunities to serve.

First Timothy 4:12 emphasizes the importance of setting "an example in speech and conduct, in love, in faith, in purity" (NRSV). Unlike the deviant teachers described in this letter, whose message is soiled by their bad conduct, the genuine leader must adorn his or her teaching with a lifestyle in conformity with that teaching. This is ultimately the source of Timothy's authority, not his age or even his commission by Paul. It is expected that integrity of word and deed will gain Timothy the credibility and authority that his jun-

---

[61]The specific topic of God's mercy toward the greatest of sinners resonates so strongly with the prayer of Manasseh that one suspects familiarity with that text on the part of the author. See David A. deSilva, *Introducing the Apocrypha* (Grand Rapids: Baker, 2002), pp. 296-300.

ior age might not. (See also Titus 2:7-8, where upright conduct on the part of the leader protects the leader and the group from slander and disgrace.)

The author of 1 Timothy brings another specific example to the fore as he discusses the dangers of the desire for riches. Timothy is charged to avoid falling prey to these desires himself, setting his ambitions instead on progress in discipleship that will lead to eternal life (1 Tim 6:11-12). Not only will this preserve Timothy from making a shipwreck of his own faith (1 Tim 6:9-10), but it will also lend him the credibility needed to lead those who are rich in material goods to safety in their use of them and to a particularly "Christian" investment strategy (using their resources to do good and relieve need, 1 Tim 6:17-19). Walking in line with the gospel is absolutely essential for the Christian leader for this dual purpose—the leader's own salvation and that of the leader's congregation depend on it (1 Tim 4:15-16).

Although the Pastoral Epistles lack discussion of the division of responsibilities and lines of authority among leaders, they do display a great interest in the character of those people entrusted with local leadership. The directions specifically given to Titus and Timothy establish the importance of leaders being living examples of the fruit of Christian faith. There are also lists of qualifications for those who would serve as overseers (equated with elders in Tit 1:5, 7) and deacons. The terms *overseers* and *deacons* were already in use in the Pauline churches prior to the composition of the Pastoral Epistles (*diakonos*, Rom 16:1; Eph 6:21; Phil 1:1; Col 1:7; 4:7; *episkopos*, Phil 1:1), and the Pastoral Epistles seem to reflect a stage in the development of these offices that is still quite informal, certainly a far cry from the monarchical bishop whose authority and role is defined at length by Ignatius of Antioch (c. 110 C.E.).

These qualifications coalesce around several focal points. First, the overseers and deacons are to be masters of themselves, showing self-control and mastery of the passions (1 Tim 3:2-3, 8, 11; Tit 1:6-8). Under this heading fall the qualities of restraint where money, wine or violent temper are concerned. Second, these leaders are to be model heads of households, revealing an interesting assumption that leaders in the church would normally be leaders of natural households as well, especially showing evidence of having brought their natural children into the faith (Tit 1:6) and holding them to virtuous standards of behavior (1 Tim 3:4-5, 12). The management of the household becomes the proving ground for the management of the household of God. Moreover, hospitality will be required of the overseer, who will serve as host to visiting missionaries and teachers, and quite likely as host to the congregation for its meetings. Third, they are to be thoroughly grounded in the apostolic faith (1 Tim 3:9; Tit 1:9)

Those in leadership are entrusted with a number of important tasks. Prominent among these is the preservation of the Pauline gospel in the face of deviant innovators (1 Tim 1:3-5; 2 Tim 2:24-26; Tit 1:13-14) and of the disappearance of Paul's living voice (2 Tim 1:13-14; 2:1-2; 3:14). This latter set of instructions are often taken as a sign of the post-Pauline character of these letters, speaking in terms of a set body of religious traditions rather than speaking in dynamic interaction with ever new circumstances. They are, however, particularly appropriate admonitions, forming an appropriate shift in normal Pauline emphasis for a historical setting in which Paul himself contemplates his own execution. (Paul does not expect deliverance from the sword but from this age, and thus he will enter into the kingdom of God; 2 Tim 4:18.) What will Timothy have to guide him after Paul is dead? He will have "the standard of sound teaching" that he heard from Paul and that has now been entrusted to him (2 Tim 1:13-14). It is particularly informative that the author of 2 Timothy keeps the personal connection between the content of the faith and the living voice of the apostle alive: Timothy will hold to the former, always "knowing from whom [he] learned it" (2 Tim 3:14 NRSV).

Although the majority of directives reflecting this task are addressed to Timothy and Titus, overseers are certainly expected to share in this task through teaching *and* refuting (Tit 1:9), and as overseers became more and more the successors of the apostles, they would have read the charges to Paul's delegates as charges to themselves. The public reading of Scripture lays an essential foundation, providing the larger story into which the congregation now feeds and the ideological resources for shaping the group's identity and behavior. Teaching and exhorting are the activities by which this shaping takes place (1 Tim 4:13), and this remains a primary task of leaders in the church (2 Tim 4:2). The Christian leader must therefore be well grounded and fully skilled in these Scriptures.

Preservation of the Pauline gospel against innovations that betray its essence merges into the other major task facing leaders according to the Pastoral Epistles: church discipline. The leader must rebuke those spreading false teachings, but always with a view to reformation, bringing them back around to pure love, a good conscience and sincere faith (1 Tim 1:3-5; Tit 1:13). Nevertheless, even patient admonition has its limits. To avoid prolonging contentiousness within the group, the delegate is instructed to let one or two admonitions suffice, after which the contrary person is deemed "self-condemned" (Tit 3:9-11). Nothing is said here about shunning or excommunication, as in 2 Thessalonians 3:6-15 and 1 Corinthians 5:11-13, but this would appear to be the implication of Paul's actions with regard to Hymenaeus and Alexander in 1 Timothy 1:19-20. Those who willfully persist in teaching what is contrary to the Pauline gospel

and spread division and dissension in the body become personae non gratae. Even the radical-sounding action of turning these two men "over to Satan," however, may have their reformation and restoration in view (1 Tim 1:20). One important caveat introduced by the author of 1 Timothy is that overseers or other leaders cannot themselves be exempt from being held accountable to the group's beliefs and values (1 Tim 5:20-21). The author enjoins that discipline be conducted without partiality in the church, in accordance with the ideal that justice always be enacted impartially.

Fortitude in the face of suffering and shaming. A particular emphasis of 2 Timothy addresses the need to overcome shame in the eyes of the dominant culture if a person is to be a reliable partner to Christian missionaries and leaders, and a faithful leader and disciple. This provides an important counterpoint to the emphasis of 1 Timothy and Titus on deflecting unnecessary censure or criticism by embodying the ideal of the peaceful supporter of the social order. Ultimately, Christian commitment must remain independent of the opinion of non-Christians, all the more as no amount of virtue and upright living will ever free the Christian entirely from hostility, reproach and rejection by the unbelieving society. Their necessary commitment to one and only one God in a polytheistic society, and their proclamation of the forthcoming kingdom of God—ushered in by an executed criminal, no less—would assure them of some measure of perpetual tension with the host society.

Paul speaks candidly of the fact of suffering hardship and degrading circumstances for the sake of the gospel, imprisonment and chains being his lot as he writes (2 Tim 2:9) and persecution being the prognosis for all who devote themselves to "a godly life in Christ" (2 Tim 3:12). Even though pursuing virtue and genuine piety, the ideals that should lead to honor and respect, Christians will be treated as shameful deviants by the world around them.

In these circumstances Onesiphorus emerges as a stellar example of how the Christian community is to respond to the marginalized among them. Rather than being "ashamed" of Paul's chains, that is, afraid of how his own reputation might suffer were he to associate with one considered a "criminal" by the unbelieving society, Onesiphorus boldly comes alongside Paul and refreshes him in his imprisonment (2 Tim 1:16-18). It was critical to the success of the Christian movement that its members be ready to visibly support those whom society marginalized most dramatically.

In the face of such social pressure, whether prospective or already felt, Paul encourages Timothy: "Do not be ashamed, then, of the testimony about our Lord or of me his prisoner, but join with me in suffering for the gospel" (2 Tim 1:8 NRSV). Though society labels Paul as a deviant and the Christian way shameful, the Christian leader must keep faith with the message and with marginalized believers, and remain willing to accept society's deviancy-control measures for him- or herself as well. Paul's example again undergirds his exhortation, for he lived as a paradigm of endurance and faithfulness in spite of opposition (2 Tim 3:10-12).

In refusing to yield to society's shaming measures, the Christian is aided by several important rationales that turn apparently disadvantageous circumstances into the path to lasting honor. First, enduring hostility and censure for the sake of Jesus brings the believer into conformity with the example and experience of Christ, and fidelity to Christ leads to enjoyment of the promised rewards that Christ also experienced (2 Tim 2:11-13). Moreover, imprisonment or resistance does not truly defeat the Christian leader, for "the word of God is not chained" (2 Tim 2:9). Their work spreads and bears fruit whether they are free or incarcerated, building up the church

Ignatius of Antioch on Chains and Execution

Ignatius, bishop of Antioch, was caught up in a persecution of the church in Syria in 110 C.E. As he was taken to Rome for public execution in the arena (he anticipated being thrown to the beasts in the games), he wrote six letters to churches that sent representatives to him on the journey and a seventh letter to Polycarp, the bishop of Smyrna, who eventually faced martyrdom himself. In these letters Ignatius shows how deeply he has drank of Paul's (and other apostolic voices') attitude toward society's shaming techniques. He regarded his execution as an honor bestowed on him and as an opportunity to bring honor to God (Ign. *Eph.* 21.2). He speaks of the chains with which he is bound to his Roman guard as "most honorable" or "most worthy even of God" (Ign. *Smyrn.* 11.1). He commends the emissaries from the church in Smyrna in a manner quite similar to Paul's commendation of Onesiphorus: "My spirit and my chains, concerning which you never showed contempt or shame, are a ransom for you. Neither will the perfect faith, Jesus Christ, be ashamed of you" (Ign. *Smyrn*. 10.2).

Such confidence in the face of a shameful and brutal execution, and such a positive evaluation of the degradations of imprisonment and chained escort that led up to it, were rooted in the conviction that the disciple was called to walk in the way of the Master (Ign. *Magn.* 5.2; Ign. *Eph.* 10.3). Just as Jesus' suffering and death led to resurrection for eternity, Ignatius regarded suffering for the name of Christ as the refinement and perfection of his faith and commitment, which would lead to the same end.

and winning for them eternal honor (2 Tim 2:10). Such a conviction transforms victimization into victory. The assurance of this future vindication and honor is perhaps the strongest incentive to endure temporary loss of honor now (2 Tim 1:12; 16-18). The eschatological perspective, according to which the Last Judgment pronounces the only verdict that ultimately matters, makes the Christian's relationship with God primary and thus the opinion of humankind secondary. Believers are thereby freed from the power of the mob, the judge and the governor to follow their own convictions, to remain faithful to the God whom they encountered in Christ, and thus to maintain their freedom and self-respect. Timothy appears to have taken these counsels to heart, having himself accepted imprisonment as part of the cost of obedience to the gospel (Heb 13:23) and having remained undaunted by it as he continued to travel and minister to the churches after his release.

The gospel and God's creation. Titus and 1 Timothy address the question of the Christian's relationship with the creation. Does discipleship manifest itself through ascetic renunciation of certain parts and processes of the created order, like marriage (and thus sex and procreation) and abstention from certain foods? Or does discipleship invite a full engagement with the gifts of creation, provided that this engagement align with the intentions of the Giver? Titus and 1 Timothy affirm the goodness of creation: "For everything created by God is good, and nothing is to be rejected, provided it is received with thanksgiving, for it is sanctified by God's word and by prayer" (1 Tim 4:4-5 NRSV). Marriage, together with procreation, is part of God's created order and therefore to be received and affirmed by Chris-

tians.[62] And what makes food acceptable to God is not the kind of food itself (whether kosher or not, the obvious implication of bringing up distinctions of this kind in connection with Jewish Law) but whether it is received with mindfulness of the Creator and in thankfulness to God. Purity or sanctification is not established by external distinctions but by bringing externals into our relationship with God through prayer.

The author of Titus takes a somewhat different approach, but to the same end: "To the pure all things are pure, but to the corrupt and unbelieving nothing is pure" (Tit 1:15 NRSV). Purity is ultimately not a matter of food or objects to be touched or not, but of conscience and mind. Those who have been purified internally by God, transformed by God's Spirit, cannot be defiled by foods alleged to be unclean, while distinctions between clean and unclean make no difference for those who have not been so cleansed within by God. The Pastoral Epistles thus continue to push toward the complete transcendence of the purity regulations and holiness code in Torah (as it is conceived in terms of things "out there" in the world). This is indeed a very common thread running throughout the canonical representations of Christianity, seen also in the Gospels, for example (Mt 15:1-20; Mk 7:1-23).

A correlation between foods and people groups was firmly established in the Levitical holiness code:

I am the LORD your God; I have separated you from the peoples. You shall therefore make a distinction between the clean animal and the unclean, and between the unclean bird and the clean; you shall not bring abomination on

---

[62]This might also account for the increased attention to and affirmation of what is perceived as the natural order of human relationships, namely, the complementarity of husband-wife relationships perceived also by Xenophon and other Greco-Roman ethicists (Johnson, *First and Second Letters to Timothy*, p. 149; deSilva, *Honor, Patronage, Kinship and Purity*, pp. 178-83).

yourselves by animal or by bird or by anything . . . which I have set apart for you to hold unclean. You shall be holy to me; for I the LORD am holy, and I have separated you from the other peoples to be mine. (Lev 20:24-26 NRSV)

Avoiding certain foods as impure was a means by which the Jew could mirror and enact the distinction God had made between clean and unclean people groups.

Such a correlation is also found in Pauline literature, including the Pastorals. Specifically, the rejection of distinctions drawn between ethnic groups correlated with the rejection of distinctions between clean and unclean foods.

This manifests itself in the Pastorals in the universalistic statements such as Titus 2:11: "For the grace of God has appeared, bringing salvation to all" (NRSV). Jesus Christ gave himself as a ransom for "all" (1 Tim 2:6) even as God desires "all to be saved and to come to the knowledge of the truth" (1 Tim 2:4) and acts as Savior "of all, especially of those who believe" (1 Tim 4:10). The emphasis on *all* people as the objects of God's mercy and deliverance echoes Paul's emphasis on God's grace toward Jew and Gentile, God's determination to deliver both from their *human* predicament, which unifies both ethnic groups into a single "all" (as in Rom 3:23).

EXEGETICAL SKILL
Feminist Criticism

Feminist criticism is a kind of ideological criticism, sharing many of the principles already discussed in regard to postcolonial criticism and cultural studies in the chapter on Philemon (see pp. 677-82). Like the latter, it is more of a perspective or agenda than a method. It is intent on exposing the political nature of biblical texts and interpretation, this time in terms of power relations between genders. Though characterized by a great diversity, there are some common principles, aims and strategies that characterize the work of feminist critics.

Basic to feminist criticism is a rejection of patriarchy—an ideology in which men and the male agenda are privileged and empowered, while women and the female agenda are relegated to ancillary roles. Patriarchy is connected with a host of baneful results: sexism, classicism, racism, devaluation of the physical body, abuse of children and ecological rapine. Many of these result directly from the kinds of values and agendas promoted by societies where males exercise power without a balance of females in leadership positions. Feminist criticism serves the larger goal of feminist theology, which includes nothing less than "social transformation,"[a] the "liberation of women from male domination" (focusing on the political, social and economic rights of women),[b] and the corresponding liberating of

[a]Sandra M. Schneiders, "Feminist Hermeneutics," in *Hearing the New Testament*, ed. Joel B. Green (Grand Rapids: Eerdmans, 1995), p. 349; Anthony Thiselton, *New Horizons in Hermeneutics* (Grand Rapids: Zondervan, 1992), p. 434.
[b]Dana Nolan Fewell, "Reading the Bible Ideologically: Feminist Criticism," in *To Each Its Own Meaning*, ed. S. R. Haynes and S. L. McKenzie (Louisville, Ky.: Westminster John Knox, 1993), p. 238.

men from the roles and attitudes patriarchy forces on them, encouraging them to nurture both the strong and the gentle qualities within them.[c] Feminist critical readings of Scripture tend to promote this agenda.

Along with rejecting patriarchy, feminist critics tend to reject models of theological thinking that are grounded in patriarchal presuppositions. They tend to place a high value on women's experience as a critical principle. How do women's lives and experiences—not least of which would be the "experience of marginalization and 'inferiorization' imposed over generations by male-dominated societies"—connect with the text and the stories told in it?[d] This becomes an important starting point for theological reflection, countering the myth that objectivity is truly possible in theology or biblical interpretation. Indeed, claims to objectivity in biblical criticism are seen to reflect the scientific paradigm, itself a product of patriarchal thinking with its alienation of the thing observed from the observer and its suppression of the fact that social location and experience always and inevitably color, shape and limit what we can see.[e]

Feminist critics, like other ideological critics, approach the biblical texts with a "hermeneutic of suspicion." They do not view these texts as neutral, objective, "pure" pieces of communication, but rather as the literary products of real people (males) with real interests and agendas. Texts inscribe ideology just as much as interpreters use texts to undergird ideologies. In the Bible we see women as men picture and locate them, through the male ideology of the time.[f] Feminist criticism, then, invites readers to inquire into the unspoken dynamics of the story and its effects on women and men in their relation to one another, and to ask whose agenda and interests in the "real world" it is really serving.

Feminist critical interpretations expose the way that the Bible and the history of the interpretation of these texts (including critical scholarship) reflect the perspectives, ideologies and interests of the males or females that produced them.[g] It is just as central to the task of this discipline to critique misogynistic and oppressive acts of interpretation in the history of scholarship and application of the Bible.[h] At its best, feminist criticism strives to free the Scripture "from its own participation in the oppression of women, and finally the transformation of the church that continues to model, underwrite, and legitimate the oppression of women in family and society on the basis of the biblical text into the discipleship of equals

---

[c]S. J. Nortjé, "On the Road to Emmaus—A Woman's Experience," in *Test and Interpretation,* ed. P. J. Hartin and J. H. Petzer (Leiden: Brill, 1991), pp. 272-73.
[d]Thiselton, *New Horizons,* p. 433.
[e]Ibid., p. 431; Nortjé, "Road to Emmaus," p. 272.
[f]Schneiders, "Feminist Hermeneutics," p. 351; Thiselton, *New Horizons,* pp. 430, 432-33.
[g]Fewell, "Reading the Bible Ideologically," pp. 238-39.
[h]Scheniders, "Feminist Hermeneutics," pp. 352-55.

which it is called to be."[i] In this quest feminist critics face more of an upward climb than liberation theologians. The Old Testament prophets, the voice of Jesus and the writings of the apostles uniformly condemn economic and social oppression, calling for the improvement of the plight of the poor. Many of the stories and prescriptions of Scripture, however, actually model and perpetuate the inequality of women, with the result that feminist critics often find themselves wrestling against the text, questioning at a very fundamental level whether or not the text truly reveals the will of God or the will of men where women are concerned. However, feminist critics place the priority on real disciples and their wholeness and liberation rather than on the unassailable authority of the text.[j]

Another very important aspect of feminist criticism is the historical task of recovering the lost voices of women in the texts and in history after they have been "written over" or negated or neglected by the male writers.[k] Feminist critics are often drawn to the careful study of texts that highlight women and present them as positive models, finding this to be a helpful means to recover the Scripture's liberating face. They also are attentive to all the ways women are visible in the text and the implications of women's presence in those places (e.g., in the crowds following Jesus) This is one reason that the use of inclusive language where contextually appropriate (*people*, not *men; children*, not *sons*) becomes so important: it is a means that women's presence in certain texts can be affirmed and contemplated rather than hidden beneath the generic use of the male pronouns and the use of *man* to denote "man and woman."

After a text has been studied in light of its social location and ideology, the interests served by it and by its use in the history of interpretation, the feminist critic inquires into the text's authority and message for women and men today. Some choose to reject the Scripture as hopelessly entangled in the web of patriarchy. Others, however, seek to rehabilitate the text and recover its liberating potential.[l] Fundamental to this discipline is the conviction that the Scriptures do not have authority in and of themselves, but insofar as they advance egalitarian reform of family, church and world.

Feminist criticism does not pretend to "objectivity," but rather confronts ideological agenda with ideological agenda. Thus its fruits are often as ideologically colored as the history of interpretation it seeks to correct. Consider, for example, the following statement by Tina Pippin: "For two thousand years the dominant agenda in Christianity has been keeping

---

[i]Ibid., p. 350.
[j]Ibid., p. 367.
[k]Fewell, "Reading the Bible Ideologically," p. 239.
[l]See ibid., pp. 241-42; Schneiders, "Feminist Hermeneutics," pp. 251-52; Elisabeth Schüssler Fiorenza, *Bread Not Stone* (Boston: Beacon, 1984).

women submissive to men (and out of the priesthood), arguing that homosexuality is a sin, supporting the physical disciplining of children, accepting the death penalty, legitimizing warfare and Christian participation in it, and anticipating a violent end of the world."[m] Pippin creates an ideological construct of the "dominant agenda" of a monolithic and unfriendly Christianity. She suppresses mention of the many voices and currents within Christianity that had quite a different agenda, namely, making disciples, nurturing families, bringing aid to the hurting, clothing and feeding the poor, and the like. Were a careful, quantitative analysis performed on Christianity in the last two thousand years, it might prove that this was in fact the dominant agenda. But it serves Pippin's agenda to try to lead the reader to see Christianity in a particular, limited light—one that will make it easier to reject that monster in favor of the "new Christianity" that she wishes to see take shape. The reader needs to remain astute, approaching every such claim with a hermeneutic of suspicion, for ideological critics do not seek to eliminate ideologies from reading but rather to displace certain ideologies so as to make room for other ones.

The voice of feminist criticism can also be marred by excess, as in the creation of liturgical rituals to celebrate the beginning of menopause or union of a lesbian couple. In the words of one practitioner of this discipline, "Feminist theology has come to a crossroad. To be significant in the church, to women and to men, the 'movement' should be more trustworthy in its biblical interpretation, hermeneutical tools, church ceremonies and gender-free religion than it has been to the present."[n]

Anthony Thiselton raises another important caution as he distinguishes between "socio-critical" and "socio-pragmatic" methods in feminist criticism.[o] A socio-pragmatic approach excludes all interpretations that would hinder or retard progress forward on the journey or agenda to which the interpreter is already committed. Put more bluntly, it is a hermeneutic entirely in the service of an ideological and practical agenda. This approach rejects or avoids any scriptural texts, any possible explanations and often even conversation partners that might "put the brakes on" or raise critical questions about that agenda.

A socio-critical approach does not exclude commitment to ideological and practical agendas but includes the exploration of interpretations—and dialogue with conversation partners—that provide the opportunity for critical reflection on and potential correction of its own agenda and conclusions. This approach does not "foreclose certain possibilities before

---

[m]Tina Pippin, "Ideological Criticisms, Liberation Criticisms, and Womanist and Feminist Criticisms," in *Handbook to Exegesis of the New Testament,* ed. S. E. Porter (Leiden: Brill, 1997), p. 269.
[n]Nortjé, "Road to Emmaus," p. 275.
[o]Thiselton, *New Horizons,* pp. 439-52.

they are examined,"[p] even if those possibilities are not congenial to the direction in which the interpreter wishes to move. Obviously, Thiselton—and this writer as well—believe that the socio-critical approach is preferable and that the socio-pragmatic leads to serious problems. Not the least of these problems is the continued use of scriptural texts merely as the tools to legitimate a partisan, human agenda rather than tools that free us all to perceive and follow God's agenda.

Feminist criticism is difficult for many to engage calmly and meaningfully, since the discipline calls us to examine our own presuppositions and to accept the possibility that "the Bible shows us a broken world more often than it does an exemplary one."[q] Nevertheless, if patriarchy is indeed one of those "elemental spirits of the universe" that should not exercise power over the new creation of the church, we certainly cannot afford to neglect these prophetic voices calling us to such self-examination and criticism. This is a task for evangelicals and nonevangelicals alike, for women and men, for all who are engaged in discovering God's vision for the community of his sons and daughters.[r]

1 Timothy 2:8-15 and feminist criticism. Perhaps the most objectionable words about women found in the Protestant canon are found in 1 Timothy 2:8-15, which not only imposes sweeping limitations on the role for women in the church but also uses rationales derived from creation and soteriology to support those limitations. The bibliography on this passage is one of the most extensive for any single text of Scripture.[s] Many of those works are explicitly dedicated to promoting 1 Timothy 2:8-15 as a perpetually valid ordinance regarding the proper place of women in the church and the home. Many others argue that the text is a tragic concession to a patriarchal society, an attempt to make the early church blend in and support common social and cultural values where possible, and thus to avoid unnecessary hostility and slander. Both positions are highly ideological—that is, both serve the interests and agendas of real people in the real world—and it is most informative to consider how the ideological position adopted by the individual critic (in connection, significantly, with his or her community of significant others) carries with it its own logic and blinders in regard to dealing with the evidence.

At first glance the case that the complementary and subordinate role of

---

[p]Ibid., pp. 448.

[q]Fewell, "Reading the Bible Ideologically," p. 249.

[r]See, for example, Mary Evans, *Woman in the Bible* (Downers Grove, Ill.: InterVarsity Press, 1984); Elaine Storkey, *What's Right with Feminism* (London: SPCK, 1985); Elizabeth Achtemeier, "Female Language for God: Should the Church Adopt It?" in *The Hermeneutical Quest,* ed. D. G. Miller (Allison Park, Penn.: Pickwick Press, 1986); Catherine Clark Kroeger and Mary J. Evans, eds., *The IVP Women's Bible Commentary* (Downers Grove, Ill.: InterVarsity Press, 2001).

[s]See the extensive bibliography in William D. Mounce, *Pastoral Epistles,* WBC (Nashville: Thomas Nelson, 2000), pp. 95-102.

women reflects God's design for human relationships from creation to consummation seems quite unassailable. The passage explicitly and unambiguously forbids a woman from exercising authority over or teaching a man (v. 12). Rather, submission to the man and learning in silence constitute her appropriate role (v. 11). Is this not, after all, the lesson derived from creation itself? For Adam was formed first and Eve second (v. 13). The chronology of Genesis undergirds the hierarchy of 1 Timothy. Moreover, what do we learn from the next episode in Genesis? Adam was not deceived by the serpent, but Eve was, and she became a transgressor (v. 14). We surely learn from this story the danger of allowing a woman to teach, since she herself is more prone to deception.[t] However, there is hope—if the woman fulfills her God-given responsibilities in her own sphere, namely, begetting children and nurturing them in discipleship so that they "continue in faith and love and holiness," and if she guards that virtue most central to womanhood, modesty/chastity (1 Tim 2:15).[u]

The examples of women in ministry in the Pastoral Epistles do not contradict or provide an alternative to this prohibition, for nowhere does it say that those women are in a role of teaching males or exercising authority over them.[v] Rather, it is a case of women teaching women (Tit 2:3-5). If women indeed served as deacons (1 Tim 3:11), there is no indication that they performed a teaching ministry (unlike overseers, Tit 1:5-9). This position, moreover, has substantial support in the undisputed Pauline corpus.

---

[t]Much to his credit, Mounce contends that 1 Timothy 2:14 does not teach that a woman has an inferior intellect or an inferior ability to discern false teaching (*Pastoral Epistles*, p. 137). If that were the case, then women would not be allowed to teach other women and children. It is difficult, however, to understand the purpose of verse 14 if Mounce is correct. Are women barred from teaching simply because their prototype was led astray, even though the female mind is no less equipped to deflect deception than the man's? If this is so, the author is excluding women from certain roles in the church on account of a crime long past, and one in which his contemporary sisters were in no danger of becoming involved. A more reasonable, though less winsome, conclusion is that the author of 1 Timothy saw Eve's removal of herself from Adam's authority and inappropriate initiative as the root of the problem (as well as God's institution of the husband's "rule" over the wife as a consequence of her transgression; Gen 3:16). This would then explain how the allusion supports his rejection of giving a woman authority in the assembly.

[u]The soteriology of 1 Timothy 2:15 is an obvious problem. Paul nowhere advocates the view that women are "saved" on any basis different from men, just as Jew and Gentile are saved on the same basis. Moreover, the author makes the mother's salvation dependent, in effect, on how her children turn out! For this reason, those who advocate the ongoing validity of the passage's injunctions try to construe this verse differently to mean "she [i.e., woman] will be saved through childbirth, if they [i.e., the women] remain in faith," etc. (see, e.g., Mounce, *Pastoral Epistles*, p. 143). All he offers in support of his objection is that children "have no necessary effect on their mother's salvation" and so it would disrupt the thought to introduce "children" as the subject of this verb (Mounce, *Pastoral Epistles*, p. 147). However, the theological presupposition of Mounce (that children "have no necessary effect on their mother's salvation") may not be a presupposition shared by the author of 1 Timothy: that is what needs to be demonstrated here. Further, the shift from singular verbs to plural verbs certainly suggests a corresponding change of subject.

[v]Mounce, *Pastoral Epistles*, p. 124.

That the creation story teaches the priority and therefore authority of the man over the woman is affirmed also in 1 Corinthians 11:3, 7-10. That women should be silent and subordinate in the assembly is also prescribed in 1 Corinthians 14:34-35. Ephesians 5:22-24, moreover, affirms submissiveness on the part of wives to their husbands, as a means by which the church's submission to Christ is modeled to the world. What we read in 1 Timothy, therefore, could be read not as a step back from Pauline practice but merely as a continuing affirmation of Paul's own understanding of the proper and honorable roles for men and women to occupy.

Feminist criticism invites a closer examination of the "interests" served by 1 Timothy 2:8-15, the situation that it addresses and the intellectual value of the theological arguments used to promote the exclusion of women from roles of teaching and authority. It also calls for a full consideration of all potentially contradictory evidence in the New Testament and in the practice of the early church, which would in turn lead to the consideration of why this particular author has chosen to affirm one possible set of roles for women while other authors did not. Feminist criticism would also ask, however, that this passage be considered in light of the history of its use and the interests served by those who have appealed to it to exclude women from positions of authority in the church as well as in light of the experience of women who have sensed God's call to ministry *and* whose gifts and graces have borne much fruit for the kingdom in the capacity of preacher, teacher and minister.

What and whose interests are served then by this passage? We have already seen that the author is concerned throughout 1 Timothy to enhance the standing of the Christian group in the eyes of outsiders, and that a primary strategy to attain this end involves Christians showing themselves to be model supporters of the domestic, social and political order. Even if the gospel inherently pushes in egalitarian directions, seen for example in the recognition that slave and master are actually "brothers" in the Lord (Philem 15-16) and are equal in God's sight (Eph 6:9), the author of 1 Timothy (in concert with several other New Testament authors) does not consider these to reflect the essential agenda of the gospel. Rather than fight those battles, which would fuel society's suspicion against the group as subversive of the social order, he postpones those battles in favor of the larger interest of nurturing an environment in which the gospel can spread and every person come to a knowledge of God in Jesus Christ (1 Tim 2:4).[w] Directing women to be submissive to their husbands, exemplars of modesty and silent in public spaces serves those interests.

---

[w]Mounce criticizes the view that the author is making a concession here to the dominant culture to avoid giving outsiders a negative impression of the Christian movement (represented, for example, in Craig Keener, *Paul, Women, Wives: Marriage and Ministry in the Letters of Paul* [Peabody, Mass.: Hendrickson, 1992], p. 111), saying that, "to be consistent," Paul (the author of 1 Timothy) would

The author is also competing against voices in the church that forbid marriage (1 Tim 4:3), a policy that would surely make the Christian group appear radically subversive. The literature of the second and third centuries provides informative windows into this tendency, particularly in the *Acts of Paul and Thecla* and *Acts of Andrew.* Instructed by Paul on the virtues of celibacy, Thecla gains great freedom, authority and notoriety as a Christian teacher by virtue of her commitment to chastity and singleness. This commitment, however, gets Paul imprisoned after he is denounced as an enemy of the social order by Thecla's aggrieved fiancé. In the apocryphal *Acts of Andrew,* Andrew also advocates chastity for all who hope to share in the resurrection, winning over the proconsul's wife, Maximilla. Thenceforth, she refuses to share her husband's bed. Learning the source of this disruptive teaching, the proconsul orders Andrew to be crucified. These later, legendary stories reveal the important social dynamics behind advocating celibacy and the rejection of the connubial and childbearing responsibilities of women in Greco-Roman families. This struck at the heart of the household, the authority of the *paterfamilias* and the survival of the family. The strong reaffirmation of childbearing and childrearing as intrinsic to the woman's salvation/deliverance could be seen as an early attempt to eliminate these ascetic tendencies that would provoke hostile responses from the dominant culture.

Of course, there are other more pedestrian interests served by this passage, extending to the use of the passage in successive generations. Feminist critics have not been slow to point out that males in general might have an interest in keeping the female half of the population out of the competition for leadership roles in the church.[x] And who would reap the benefits of teaching wives to suppress their own interests in favor of serving the agenda of the male head of the household?

If "ideology is inscribed . . . in discourses, myths, presentations, and representations of the way 'things' are,"[y] 1 Timothy 2:13-15 affords a study of how the stories of creation and Fall in Genesis (fundamental "myths" of the Judeo-Christian heritage) feed particular gender ideologies in real-life communities in the first century C.E. But how intellectually viable are the arguments brought forward by the author? The author presents Adam's pri-

---

have had to take out the offense of the cross as well (*Pastoral Epistles*, p. 134). The author of 1 Timothy, however, like the author of 1 Peter (a text that shows this principle at work most clearly), could eliminate what he deemed to be *nonessential* points of conflict with the dominant culture, while accepting the tensions and negative assessments that might remain on account of *necessary* tensions (e.g., "the offense of the cross"). Indeed, making concessions elsewhere would make the critical points of Christian self-definition stand out all the more sharply.

[x]Schüssler Fiorenza discusses the developing trend in the early church whereby male heads of households became the premier candidates for leadership in the "household of God," a trend and interest clearly served by this passage (*In Memory of Her*, p. 235).

[y]Catherine Belsey, *Critical Practice* (London: Methuen, 1980), p. 42.

ority in creation as a warrant for the man's authority (a different kind of "priority") over the woman, but is that the lesson of Genesis 1 and 2? If earlier creation implies superiority, the animals should have authority over humanity, and not vice versa.[z] Indeed, it is the creation of woman that consummates creation, as partner (Gen 2:18) for Adam. We should be also cautious about understanding the word *helper* as "assistant," in the sense of a subordinate, since God is also frequently described as a "helper" throughout the Old Testament. The first indication of hierarchy enters this relationship only after the Fall (Gen 3:16). We also miss the fine nuancing of Adam's priority in creation found in Paul's discussion in 1 Corinthians 11:11-12 (notably, again in the context of a discussion of gender distinctions and how they should be manifested in the church). There, the mutuality of male and female was better preserved as Paul acknowledged that ever since Adam, every male has also depended on a woman for life, just as Woman (Eve) originally depended on Man (Adam).[aa]

The argument that Eve was deceived, not Adam, hardly speaks better for Adam, who emerges as a willful and knowing transgressor. What should we make of the author's sharp and exclusive focus on Eve's transgressions, when Adam was just as entangled in transgression (he was, after all, "with her" by the tree when he ate; Gen 3:6)? Indeed, Paul regularly refers to *Adam's* transgression, and not Eve's as somehow prior, independent or more egregious (see, e.g., Rom 5:12-21; 1 Cor 15:22). This argument, moreover, is offered as a warrant for excluding women from teaching, since the first time a woman taught a man things worked out badly, the woman having first believed a lie. All the doctrinal problems in 1-2 Timothy, however, seem to be caused by male teachers like Hymenaeus, Alexander and Philetus (1 Tim 1:19-20; 2 Tim 2:16-18). Gender is no guarantee of reliable teaching. On what solid basis, then, does the author of 1 Timothy prohibit the female gender from teaching the male gender? Again, we are faced with the possibility that what is driving this paragraph is the author's conviction that it would be vitally important for Christian women in the first-century Greco-Roman world to walk completely in line with the then-current ideal, so that the gospel would arouse less hostility on nonessential matters. Our examination of the problems with the logic of 1 Timothy 2:13-15, however, suggests that it should not be taken as binding on the church of all generations.

What other evidence might we need to consider before fixing on 1 Timothy 2:8-15 as a perpetually valid prescription and as an authoritative revelation of God's will for God's church? Ideological criticism calls interpreters to look not only at the evidence brought in to make a case but also the

---

[z]Paul K. Jewett, *Man as Male and Female* (Grand Rapids: Eerdmans, 1975), pp. 119-27.
[aa]Johnson, *First and Second Letters to Timothy,* pp. 206-7.

evidence *not* introduced. How might the following factor into a decision about this passage?

- the audible prayers and prophecies spoken by women in the assembly in Corinth (1 Cor 11:4-6), which might well have been "instructive" to the males around them
- the fact that women are indeed taking an active and vocal role in the assemblies of the early church, which is clear from the pains the author takes to change this behavior here (as well as from 1 Cor 14:34-35 [ab]
- Phoebe's role as deacon in the church at Cenchreae (Rom 16:1)
- Syntyche and Euodia's role as Paul's "fellow contenders for the gospel" (Phil 4:2-3)
- Priscilla's role, in conjunction with her husband Aquila, in instructing Apollos (Acts 18:24-26)
- the evangelistic role of the Samaritan woman (Jn 4:28-30, 39)

There are also other principles in Scripture that might be found to "override" the specific restrictions in 1 Timothy on women's roles in the church and the preservation of hierarchy in the home. Foremost among these would be the following:

- Galatians 3:28 presents a grand vision of the truth of who we are in Christ, in which the meaningfulness of distinctions of ethnicity, social status and gender in God's sight are swept away. This vision keeps raising the question, Should the community that the Holy Spirit is bringing into being reflect the vision of the old or the new creation?[ac]
- In the early church, particularly its first twenty or thirty years, the activity of the Holy Spirit establishes the norm. In Acts 10:44-48, for example, it is the movement of the Spirit on Gentiles that guides Peter to baptize them, and it becomes the primary warrant in that version of the debate for the acceptance of Gentiles into the church *as Gentiles.* In 1 Corinthians Paul may tell the women to be silent in the church (1 Cor 14:34-35), but if the Spirit prompts them to speak (e.g., in the exercise of the gift of prophecy), such speech cannot be silenced (1 Cor 11:4-6), although Paul can still require appropriate attire. Might not the absolute reaffirmation of silent and submissive as the "woman's place" be open to the criticism that it rejects, in fact, the normative significance of the Holy Spirit in the church?
- The Gospel traditions reveal a Jesus who rejected traditional hierarchies and named those who most serve others as, in fact, those who have the greatest precedence (Mk 10:41-45; Jn 13:1-17). The author of 1 Timothy unilaterally reaffirms hierarchy in domestic relationships (as opposed to the much more mutual service and submission envisioned in

---

[ab]Dewey, "1 Timothy," p. 355.
[ac]Johnson, *First and Second Letters to Timothy,* pp. 208-9; Dewey, "1 Timothy," p. 356.

Eph 5:21-33). While this might have been necessary for him to attain his own goals for the church vis-à-vis the dominant culture, does it not stand in conflict with a more fundamental value that is binding on all Christians in all settings?

The answers to these questions are not easy. We must be grateful, however, to the kind of interpretive strategy that bids us to raise them, since our response to Scripture's voice will be all the more careful and sound for the enterprise. If in fact we decide that the prescriptions given for women, like those given for slaves and for Christians as a whole in this letter, represent the author's agenda for removing every possible obstacle to the spread of the gospel in his setting, then that agenda (and not its particular enculturation in the first century) should have an ongoing claim on the church. We would have to discern anew what the expendable battles are and how best both to witness to the essence of our Christian calling and to facilitate the spread of the gospel in our contemporary setting. And just as the text was culturally conditioned, so we will need to keep allowing the text to challenge our own contemporary perceptions about the family, for neither a first-century nor a twenty-first-century model has absolute validity.[ad]

One important thing that feminist critics have brought prominently to attention is the pain that stands behind so much of women's experience—and the regrettable role the Bible has been made to play in sustaining and increasing that pain. Frances Young writes:

> As Scripture, the Pastorals have shaped a world in which women and others have been subordinated and devalued. . . . Such texts contained in a sacred authoritative canon cannot but becomes "texts of terror" in a democratic society which views the position of women, lay people, servants, slaves, etc., in a totally different light. . . . How can we be true to ourselves, to our deepest social and moral commitments, while remaining true to the Christian tradition?[ae]

William Mounce attempts to address such concerns by distinguishing role from worth, arguing that a limited role for women in no way implies inferior worth.[af] But the issue is not merely one of value, and we must weigh his "subordinate but equally valued" argument against the experience of actual women for whom "subordinate but equally valued" would ring hollow. Moreover, Mounce's treatment would be justly criticized from a feminist critical perspective insofar as he fails to encompass the *experience* of so many women who have sensed God's call to active participation in ministry, but who have been denied the opportunity to answer that call—or

---

[ad]Johnson, *First and Second Letters to Timothy*, p. 210.

[ae]Frances Young, *The Theology of the Pastoral Epistles* (Cambridge: Cambridge University Press, 1994), pp. 146-47.

[af]Mounce, *Pastoral Epistles*, pp. 148-49.

worse, had their very *experience* of call denied ("How could God give you such a call when his own word says . . ."). Woman's dilemma has been and, in many circles, continues to be whether to adopt an ancillary role to the agenda of the males around her, or to be directly available for God's agenda. Does her gender indeed limit the Holy Spirit's capacity to gift her and God's desire to use her, or are such suggestions merely the result of believing communities' unreflective misapplication of 1 Timothy 2:8-15? Another great contribution of feminist criticism is that our answers to such questions do not merely affect policy and are not merely functions of our view of Scripture; they affect real people in real relationship with God and their community of faith.

The application of feminist criticism involves a rather far-reaching hermeneutical perspective, rather than merely the application of a specific procedure, but some preliminary exercises might include the following:

1. Read several treatments of the question of the ordination of women or the question of the status of women within the Christian family from a number of different perspectives (e.g., theologically conservative and theologically liberal; egalitarian versus hierarchalist, etc.). What arguments are advanced by each author? To what sources of authority does each author appeal (e.g., Scripture, experience, science) and to what degree? What assumptions are being made by each author in the course of the discussion (even in the way the argument is framed)? How fully is the scriptural evidence treated (both those texts that would naturally tend to support and those that would naturally be seen to oppose the position being advocated by the author)? Are there blind spots where an author refuses to look, or places where contrary evidence is undervalued? What other kinds of evidence will one author consider but another author entirely overlook? What correlations can you make between the results of these various inquiries?

2. Read one of the four Gospels in its entirety, noting all the ways women are present in the story (Luke and John might yield the most fruit). What gender issues arise within the narrative itself? How does the Evangelist negotiate these issues? In what ways are the characters trying to reaffirm stereotyped female roles and status or trying to transform the same? Where does the author stand in regard to these questions? Insofar as you are able, read secondary sources (like commentaries) on the passages where women's issues come most to the fore. To what extent are the secondary sources engaged with these issues? What ideological perspective do they bring to the text? To what end?

3. Read through the three Pastoral Epistles. Where are women present in these texts? What female roles are depicted in these texts? What values are held up for females to embody? What patterns are held up for them not to embody? What would the result have been in terms of real, social relationships and the place of women in the Christian community and the household

if the author's advice was completely heeded? Are these directions in keeping with what you discovered in the Gospel(s)? Are they in keeping with other ideals in the New Testament (e.g., Gal 3:28)? What ideological commitments stand behind your own responses to these questions?

4. Read Revelation. What images of the female appear in that text? What female "types" are presented? What gender-related values, roles and stereotypes are associated with these images? How do you think such images have affected the perception and treatment of women in Western society?

FOR FURTHER READING

Achtemeier, Elizabeth. "Female Language for God: Should the Church Adopt It?" pp. 97-114. In *The Hermeneutical Quest: Essays in Honor of James Luther Mays*. Edited by D. G. Miller. Allison Park, Penn.: Pickwick Press, 1986.

Collins, Adela Yarbro, ed. *Feminist Perspectives on Biblical Scholarship.* (Chico, Calif.: Scholars Press, 1985).

Dewey, Joanna. "1 Timothy," pp. 353-58. In *The Women's Bible Commentary.* Edited by Carol A. Newsome and Sharon H. Ringe. Louisville, Ky.: Westminster John Knox, 1992.

Evans, Mary. *Woman in the Bible: An Overview of All the Crucial Passages on Women's Roles.* Downers Grove, Ill.: InterVarsity Press, 1984.

Fewell, Dana Nolan. "Reading the Bible Ideologically: Feminist Criticism," pp. 237-51. In *To Each Its Own Meaning: An Introduction to Biblical Criticisms and their Application.* Edited by Stephen R. Haynes and Steven L. McKenzie. Louisville, Ky.: Westminster John Knox, 1993.

Kroeger, Catherine Clark, and Mary J. Evans, eds. *The IVP Women's Bible Commentary.* Downers Grove, Ill.: InterVarsity Press, 2001.

Martin, Clarice. "The Haustafeln (Household Codes) in African American Biblical Interpretation: 'Free Slaves' and 'Subordinate Women,'" pp. 206-31. In *Stony the Road We Trod: African American Biblical Interpretation.* Edited by Caom H. Felder. Minneapolis: Fortress, 1991.

Newsome, Carol A., and Sharon H. Ringe, eds. *The Women's Bible Commentary.* Louisville, Ky.: Westminster John Knox, 1992.

Nortjé, S. J. "On the Road to Emmaus—A Woman's Experience," pp. 271-80. In *Text and Interpretation: New Approaches in the Criticism of the New Testament.* Edited by P. J. Hartin and J. H. Petzer. Leiden: Brill, 1991.

Osiek, Carolyn. *Beyond Anger: On Being a Feminist in the Church.* New York: Paulist, 1986.

Pippin, Tina. "Ideological Criticisms, Liberation Criticisms, and Womanist and Feminist Criticisms." In *Handbook to Exegesis of the New Testament.* Edited by Stanley E. Porter. Leiden: Brill, 1997.

Russell, Letty M., ed. *Feminist Interpretation of the Bible.* Philadelphia: Westminster Press, 1985.

Sakenfeld, Katherine D. "Feminist Perspectives on Bible and Theology: An Introduction to Selected Issues and Literature." *Interpretation* 42 (1988): 5-18.

Schüssler Fiorenza, Elisabeth. *Bread Not Stone: The Challenge of Feminist Biblical Interpretation.* Boston: Beacon, 1984.

———. *In Memory of Her: A Feminist Theological Reconstruction of Christian Origins.* New York: Crossroad, 1983.

Schneiders, Sandra M. "Feminist Hermeneutics," pp. 349-69. In *Hearing the New Testament: Strategies for Interpretation.* Edited by Joel B. Green. Grand Rapids: Eerdmans, 1995.

Storkey, Elaine. *What's Right with Feminism.* London: SPCK, 1985.

Thiselton, Anthony. *New Horizons in Hermeneutics.* Grand Rapids: Zondervan, 1992. See especially pp. 430-70.

THE PASTORAL EPISTLES AND MINISTRY FORMATION

Perhaps more than any other New Testament text, these letters directly address issues of "practical theology." The primary goal of the Pastorals is, indeed, ministry formation. Because of this, our investigation of the message of these letters has already brought to the fore some important ways that these texts contribute to our reflection on the identity and task of the Christian leader. That discussion, however, may be beneficially extended.

The character of Christian leaders. Authenticity is foundational to effective ministry. The Pastoral Epistles repeatedly challenge the Christian leader to seek to make his or her walk congruent with the message the leader proclaims (1 Tim 4:12-16; 2 Tim 2:20-22; Tit 2:7-8). Such integrity provides the leader with the most genuine form of authority, and it gives the sisters and brothers around the leader a living example of the Christian life to encourage them in their own attempts to take up the challenge of discipleship. Ultimately, however, the Christian leader must embody his or her faith consistently in thought, word and action for the sake of the health of his or her own soul. Even if it could be successfully hidden, the divided heart and double life erodes self-respect, prevents a person from discovering the power of God at work in his or her own life, and undermines the hope and confidence that empower courageous ministry. What, in the end, would it profit a leader to save the whole world but forfeit his or her own soul?

Scholars often slight the Pastoral Epistles on the ground that "faith" is less of a vibrant trust in Jesus and more of an ethical quality, denoting reliability, faithfulness, firmness. I would regard this, however, as a positive achievement and a much-needed word for denominations that have a surfeit of "trusting Jesus" and a famine of faithfulness to the way of life taught by Jesus.

Selection of local leadership. The pastor might be surprised to see the lists of qualifications provided for those who would function as "overseers" or "deacons" in each local congregation. Very often, pastors feel relieved just to have found warm bodies to occupy the leadership offices of the congregation! The author of 1 Timothy reminds us that leadership in the church is a noble task that requires people of noble mind, virtuous conduct and proven character so that the church and the gospel will not be disgraced (1 Tim 3:1-13). Leadership selection could become merely a matter of filling spaces, or it could be seen as a way to encourage people to refine their character, develop their gifts and reliably discharge their service to the community.

Exercising discipline in the church. This is an inescapable topic in a body of texts that gives such attention to the need not only to teach but also to correct, not only to equip but also to excommunicate (2 Tim 2:14; 4:2; 1 Tim 1:3, 19-20; Tit 1:13-14; 2:1-15; Tit 3:8-11). The practice of church discipline, however, makes many Christian leaders uneasy because it is often either overdone, turning the church into a grossly restrictive and authoritarian environment, or neglected completely, providing no guard rails whatsoever for individual or corporate discipleship.

The Christian movement has always had a plurality of voices, each trying to promote its version of sound doctrine and proper practice. The Pastoral Epistles speak to such a situation as though the parameters of sound doctrine and behavior were absolutely clear, commissioning Christian leaders to rebuke or correct those who deviate from these norms. Christian leaders today, however, cannot pretend that rulings on every complex issue are clear, and so merely seek to silence or expel dissenting voices in a totalitarian manner. Nevertheless, we abandon an essential facet of our life together as a Christian community if we do not try to help one another remain faithful to the call of God.

Church discipline calls for both courage and humility, therefore, on the part of the people involved. We need to boldly broach uncomfortable subjects with our sisters and brothers when we see them living or speaking in ways that contradict the Scriptures and tradition of the church. We need to be humble, however, knowing how limited our own grasp of the truth is, and allowing that the sister or brother we approach might have thought a great deal about the consonance of his or her actions with the gospel. The goal of all such intervention must always remain the good of the sister or brother (and the whole body). It should never be a morbid desire to meddle or to shame. It rests on the premise that each of us has the ability to be led astray from the truth by our own wandering minds, unholy desires and influences external to ourselves, and that we each need the help of our sisters and brothers to stay centered on Christ, to avoid deception, and to live an authentic Christian life. As long as it remains a process of discernment, healing and restoration, the task of church discipline provides an essential component to ministry as the New Testament authors conceive of ministry.

Courage in witness to God's truth. Second Timothy provides yet another witness to the fact that suffering will befall all those who speak God's truth to people rather than avoid challenging the practices, prejudices and presuppositions of worldly people (2 Tim 1:6, 8; 1:17-18; 2:3, 10-11, 13; 3:12). Yet it is incumbent on the Christian leader to be committed to speaking God's truth and pouring him- or herself into effecting the change God desires—or at least calling Christians out of collusion with systems that resist God's desires for creation and all people. The leader must therefore keep insulating him- or herself from the power of shame and the terror of suffering for the sake of boldness for the gospel, or else become a mere puppet for the powers that be.

Controversial topics and the focus of faithful ministry. Second Timothy and Titus caution Christian leaders against "wrangling over words, which does no good but only ruins those who are listening" (2 Tim 2:14 NRSV). There may be a time and place for refined theological arguments, but leaders especially need to put the building up of the faith of the hearers above indulging in arguments. Reading through these injunctions I am reminded of a spirited discussion I (as a United Methodist) had with a brother from the Church of Christ regarding whether or not it was necessary for a person to be baptized as a believer to be saved. As we sparred, countering claim with claim and Scripture with Scripture, a listener remarked that such arguments were precisely why she had walked away from the church years before and was glad she was no longer a Christian. Immediately, the gulf between my Church of Christ brother and myself disappeared: we understood that, baptized as an adult or not, we both had Christ and sought to live out the vision of the Scriptures, but this woman did not have or want Christ. While we indulged in wrangling over some theological nicety, the Spirit would rather have had us bear a united witness to this woman and be occupied with bringing her to faith.

Differences of opinion about theology, ethics and practice will continue among Christians until the second coming of Christ. The work of the kingdom, however, must be given priority over trying to prove our position right. The spiritual health of our sisters and brothers, and the ministry of Christ to the lost, must come first. That spiritual health is not advanced by "stupid and senseless controversies" that only "breed quarrels" (2 Tim 2:23 NRSV; cf. Tit 3:9) but by the unity of the Spirit in humility toward one another and in submission to the Spirit's leading.

This continues to present a great challenge to ministers and disciples today, all the more in our cultural environment that thrives on controversy. From the *Jerry Springer Show* to the general conference of a denomination, we can witness the energy that comes from digging into a hot issue. Pushing these to the fore, however, saps vital strength from the real work of the kingdom—ministries to the sick and homeless, outreaches to the refugees and victims of abuse, relief trips to churches facing persecution or villages facing starvation. In controversies, heated emotions fuel and augment divisions, obscuring the vast areas of fundamental agreement and unity. It may prove that those hot issues where committed conservatives and liberals both invest themselves fully and take their stand most vehemently are the most clever stratagem yet devised by the enemy for hobbling the church.

The Pastoral Epistles challenge us to confront hot issues responsibly for the sake of our charges but not indulge our desire for controversy and argument, getting distracted from the real work of the kingdom. Indeed, they would prefer that we always put our focus on God's agenda rather than the agenda imposed by some controversial topic. As we keep calling our sisters and brothers into the presence of God, laying the foundation of sound teaching and equipping them for the acts of service that God desires, the real battle is being won.

Wealth and discipleship. 1 Timothy concludes with a lengthy reflection about the nature and potential of material wealth (1 Tim 6:5b-19), joining that chorus of New Testament and other early Christian voices that chant a tune quite different from the anthems of capitalist and materialist societies (e.g., Mt 6:24). This text strongly cautions against the deadly dangers of craving money, of making the acquisition of material wealth our primary value. The pursuit of wealth is a driving force of Western society, the key to what many people regard as the path to "life," to the fullness of what life has to offer. The author warns us that, in the end, it does not deliver what it promises.

> Those who want to be rich fall into temptation and are trapped by many senseless and harmful desires that plunge people into ruin and destruction. . . . [I]n their eagerness to be rich some have wandered away from the faith and pierced themselves with many pains. (1 Tim 6:9-10 NRSV)

To attain financial goals, as they are often called, both husband and wife often work, or one of them must work obscenely long hours. Those who are now young children suffer more and more from a lack of parenting. Is amassing wealth worth such piercing of hearts? The amount of time and energy invested in attaining our financial objectives, if these are set on wealth, often leaves very little time for the discovery and exercise of those gifts that God has given each one of us for the nurture of the church and the care of others. The drive for acquiring more money means that seeking God and putting ourself at God's service recedes. We serve a new master. That lifestyle is a path of pain—the pain of never acquiring enough to fill the void inside (because only God and meaningful investment in other people can do that), the pain of throwing away our life for things that cannot give life, the pain of regret at the end of life, when our 20/20 hindsight will be our friend or our accuser.

Instead, the author urges Christian leaders especially to model the pursuit of the life that really is life. One of the great countercultural statements Christians can make is to flee from the craving for wealth, living out a life that shows instead the value of family, service and knowing God, putting the needs of others ahead of material goods and their display. This is the kind of life that results in being rich toward God, in finding that we have invested wisely and laid up quite an endowment against the Day of Visitation, when Christ will return. Those who are graced with wealth must be taught to invest it wisely, not in the volatile and uncertain stock market but in places where it will bear certain good now and eternal dividends later. Wealth is to be measured by generosity, the use of these material resources not to make ourself look upscale but to relieve the members of the family of God in any kind of need or distress (Mt 6:19-21; Lk 12:33-34; 1 Tim 6:17-19). As always, the Christian leader is challenged to lead by example in this difficult area (1 Tim 6:11-12).

Responsible mobilization of relief. In its discussion of how the community is to respond to the needs of widows in their midst (1 Tim 5:3-16), 1 Timothy provides a veritable case study for contemplating how to provide relief effectively and responsibly with limited resources. The practical side of these letters appears nowhere more plainly than here, challenging Christian leaders today to give careful thought at the same time to the ideals that give us vision and to their practical implementation. Since there is never enough money in a church budget to relieve all the needs that come to the congregation's attention, the author's considerations remain timely and helpful:

- Are other forms of support available, and how can these be mobilized? The primary means of support for those who have living family is the natural kinship group, where the virtue of charity must be promoted (1 Tim 5:4, 8). Failure to care for kin in need is regarded as a disgrace, whether inside or outside of the church.
- Is the community aid enabling destructive or distracting behavior rather than supporting continued growth in virtue (1 Tim 5:6, 13, 15)? This is an uncomfortable question, but it needs to be examined if the relief systems are ultimately going to aid the recipients rather than participate in their demise.
- Do some *merit* support more than others? If so, support for them must come first and not be lacking (1 Tim 5:10). The author insists that consideration be given to those who have spent themselves and their resources on the life of the community of faith. That they have the first claim to the generosity of that community in their time of need is basic to the code of reciprocity.

The author does not present any hard and fast guidelines that will make every relief program a success and a positive contribution, but the questions he poses will help move the church in that direction. Most important, the kinds of questions he poses force the church to regard relief not just as throwing money at another problem but as one way it is involved in the lives of real people, to whom they are responsible not only to give but to give well.

For Further Reading

Barrett, C. K. *The Pastoral Epistles in the New English Bible.* Oxford: Clarendon, 1963.

Beker, J. Christiaan. *Heirs of Paul: Paul's Legacy in the New Testament and in the Church Today.* Minneapolis: Fortress, 1991.

Dibelius, Martin, and Hans Conzelman. *The Pastoral Epistles.* Hermeneia. Philadelphia: Fortress, 1972.

Johnson, Luke Timothy. *The First and Second Letters to Timothy.* AB. Garden City, N.Y.: Doubleday, 2000.

Knight, George. *The Pastoral Epistles.* NIGTC. Grand Rapids: Eerdmans, 1992.

Marshall, I. Howard. *A Critical and Exegetical Commentary on the Pastoral Epistles.* ICC. Edinburgh: T & T Clark, 1999.

Mounce, William D. *Pastoral Epistles.* WBC. Nashville: Thomas Nelson, 2000.

Plummer, Alfred. *The Pastoral Epistles.* New York: A. C. Armstrong, 1889.

Quinn, Jerome D. *The Epistle to Titus.* AB. Garden City, N.Y.: Doubleday, 1990.

Quinn, Jerome D., and William C. Wacker. *The First and Second Letters to Timothy.* ECC. Grand Rapids: Eerdmans, 2000.

Verner, David C. *The Household of God: The Social World of the Pastoral Epistles.* SBLDS 71. Chico, Calif.: Scholars Press, 1983.

Young, Frances. *The Theology of the Pastoral Epistles.* Cambridge: Cambridge University Press, 1994.

20

THE EPISTLE TO THE "HEBREWS"

Living in Trust and Gratitude Toward God

The anonymous letter to the "Hebrews" provides the interpreter with neither the identity of the author nor that of the recipients. We do not know when it was written, and the location of both author and recipients remains unclear. Nevertheless, its message remains clear and pertinent: God's favor and benefits are worth the cost of keeping faith with him, no matter how great the pressure society places on the disciples to mute their witness and compromise their obedient response to God's generosity. The cost paid by the Son to bring the disciples into God's favor, moreover, necessitates their perseverance in fidelity to that relationship.

The argument of this letter often seems remote, dealing with priesthood, rituals and purification—topics that appear to be of arcane interest only. To the careful reader, however, Hebrews unfolds rich resources for reflection on the person of Jesus and the meaning of his death and exaltation, and it shows how a deeper awareness of Jesus' achievement on our behalf can empower a deeper commitment to discipleship in unsupportive surroundings. Hebrews also challenges us, somewhat ironically, not to take God's grace for granted but rather to respond to God in a way that always honors the Giver,

to testify openly to the value of God's favor, and to show in our faithfulness and obedience how much we value the relationship Jesus has opened up for us.

THE SITUATION BEHIND HEBREWS

Who were the "Hebrews"? Many modern readers share with the scribes who first titled this text "To the Hebrews" the assumption that the recipients were Jews (most likely, Jewish Christians). These readers point to the author's extensive use of Old Testament texts, the interest in the Jewish cult and the use of rabbinic methods of exegesis as "proof" of this claim, supposing that a Gentile readership would not be as interested in or likely to follow such arguments.[1] Moreover, these readers find that any proof of the obsolescence of the Old Covenant would be important for Jewish rather than Gentile Christians. According to this line of thinking, Hebrews is written to dissuade Jewish Christians from reverting to non-Christian Judaism to avoid ongoing tension with their non-Christian Jewish families and neighbors.

Against this tendency, consider the following:
- The title "To the Hebrews" is a second-century conjecture about the original audience based on the same kinds of observations

---

[1]See, e.g., Paul Ellingworth, *Commentary on Hebrews,* NIGTC (Grand Rapids: Eerdmans, 1993), p. 25.

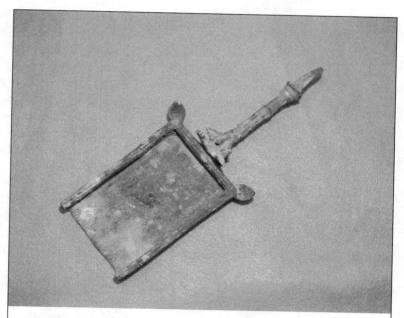

Figure 20.1. A metal shovel for burning incense, probably used in connection with domestic rituals in a Jewish home. The incense was placed in the small rosettes at the upper corners of the shovel, with glowing coals from a fire placed on the shovel. The heat from the coals activated the incense. (Photo: Sam Renfroe; courtesy of Ashland Theological Seminary)

concerning its content noted above.[2] Moreover, second-century Christians might have viewed this letter as addressing Jews precisely because they needed some kind of canonical "response" to the parent religion that had rejected them, a manifesto of supersessionism that legitimated the Christian movement and delegitimated the parent body.

- Texts like Galatians and 1 Peter, both of which are clearly addressed to Gentile Christians (no doubt with some number of Jewish Christians in their midst) show us how well-versed Christian authors assumed their Gen-

tile readers to be in the Old Testament, and how interested they were expected to be in arguments based on those texts. Gentile Christians received the Jewish Scriptures as the "oracles of God" (indeed, as their inheritance by virtue of being joined to the "true Israel") and would have received a thorough introduction to a Christ-centered interpretation of the Old Testament in the course of their conversion, early instruction in the faith, and ongoing participation in the worship life of the church.[3]

- Hebrews rather directly addresses the scan-

[2]Ibid., p. 21; Thomas Long boldly but correctly suggests that the person "who attached a title to this document . . . was probably just speculating about its original recipients and was as much in the dark as we are" (*Hebrews*, Interpretation [Louisville, Ky.: John Knox Press, 1997], p. 1).

[3]See James Moffatt, *A Critical and Exegetical Commentary on the Epistle to the Hebrews*, ICC (Edinburgh: T & T Clark, 1924), pp. xvi-xvii, who cites Tatian's declaration (*Ad Graecos* 29) to have been converted to Christianity by reading the Old Testament (similarly, Justin *Dial.* 8); also P. M. Eisenbaum, *The Jewish Heroes of Christian History*, SBLDS 156 (Atlanta: Scholars Press, 1997), pp. 8-9.

dal of the Old Testament for Gentile Christian: the particular challenge of how to read the Old Testament as a record of divine revelation while rejecting the sacrificial system and cultic regulations commanded therein.

- The rules of exegesis employed in Hebrews are not strictly rabbinic: the "lesser to greater" argument was also a staple of Greco-Roman rhetoric, and the interpretation of one text through the use of a second text that contained the same key word (*gezera shawa*) became a staple of early Christian exegesis.

- The lengthy argument concerning the Levitical cult does not presuppose a return to temple worship as the pressing problem among the addressees. Rather, it serves the positive goal of affirming all Christians that they stand in the more privileged position in the history of God's experience with humanity, which will, in turn, sustain commitment to Christ and forestall apostasy (whether toward pagan religion or non-Christian Jewish practice).

- The use of the Old Testament and the methods employed by the author to apply the sacred texts tell us more about the author and his background than about the recipients.

We should therefore consider the letter to the "Hebrews" actually to address Christians of mixed ethnic backgrounds, and not merely Jewish Christians.[4] Reading Hebrews as if it addressed a primarily Jewish Christian audience, moreover, has tended to prevent readers from perceiving how the sustained comparison of Jesus with the mediators of access to God under the Torah and Levitical cult contributed positively to the formation of Christian identity, rather than merely serving as a series of polemics against an alleged "reversion" to Judaism. Taking a broader view of the audience will allow us to see more clearly the connections between the exposition and exhortation sections that intentionally alternate throughout this word of exhortation.

The experience of the addressees. At several points the author provides us with glimpses of the community's earlier history. These are strategically selected, of course, because remembering these experiences is meant to move the audience closer to the author's goal for them. Nevertheless, we can use them to draw a sketch of the community.

The birth of the community in response to the preaching of the gospel by the witnesses of Jesus is remembered in Hebrews 2:1-4. The fact that the author includes himself among those who thus came to faith is perhaps the strongest argument against Pauline authorship, for Paul adamantly insists that he came to faith through a direct intervention by Jesus and *not* through any human being's words (see 1 Cor 15:3-10; Gal 1:11-17). God confirmed the testimony of the preachers with "signs and wonders and various miracles, and by gifts of the Holy Spirit, distributed according to his will" (Heb 2:4 NRSV), making the account very similar to Paul's reminiscences of his preaching in Galatia and Corinth (1 Cor 2:1-5; Gal 3:2-5), where he himself notes the activity of God confirming the validity of the message. The congregation was thus born in the midst of a deep awareness of God's presence and power, which assures, and should continue to assure, the believers of the legitimacy of the gospel.

These converts are likely to have come from all social levels in the city where they lived. The literate vocabulary and style of Hebrews itself suggests an audience capable of attending meaningfully to such language and syntax, unless the author was simply a bad preacher who

---

[4]See, further, H. W. Attridge, *Hebrews*, Hermeneia (Philadelphia: Fortress, 1989), pp. 10-13; A. H. Trotter Jr., *Interpreting the Epistle to the Hebrews* (Grand Rapids: Baker, 1997), pp. 28-31; David A. deSilva, *Perseverance in Gratitude: A Socio-Rhetorical Commentary on the Epistle "to the Hebrews"* (Grand Rapids: Eerdmans, 2000), pp. 2-7.

spoke over the heads of his congregation.[5] The letter tells us also that a number of the community members also possessed property worth confiscating (Heb 10:32-34), and that they were capable of charitable activity and hospitality (Heb 10:33-34; 13:2, 16), and even needed warnings against over-ambition (Heb 13:5, 14). The gospel had not appealed, therefore, only to the poor and lower social levels.

After their conversion the new disciples had received extensive instruction in the basics of the Jewish-Christian worldview and the Christian message (Heb 6:1-2). They were taught the meaning of "the oracles of God" (Heb 5:12; cf. Rom 3:2), namely, the Jewish Scriptures, thus being indoctrinated into the Christian and christological reading of these texts that the author will himself apply extensively. They were also taught about "repentance from dead works and faith toward God, instruction about baptisms, laying on of hands, resurrection of the dead, and eternal judgment" (Heb 6:1-2 NRSV). The first of these pairs is the familiar renunciation of the way of life learned from the converts' pagan past (or for Jewish Christians, sins against the Torah) and their turning to God in trust and loyalty. The last of these pairs introduced the converts to the cornerstone of the Christian apocalyptic worldview, according to which ultimate importance is not attached to enjoying the comforts of this life but living to please God and receiving life beyond death. This simple shift of focus from this life to the next stands behind the majority of the exhortations of Hebrews.

The middle pair (baptism and laying on of hands) speaks of rituals with which the addressees would have been familiar. Whatever else might have been included under "baptisms," the addressees would at least have recalled that in baptism they died to their old life and self, and rose up out of the waters to a new identity, a new life, a new family and a new inheritance. The closely linked "laying on of hands" invokes rites whereby the human touch imparts divine power. Given the connections that Hebrews shows elsewhere with the Pauline mission and its interest in the availability of the Holy Spirit for believers (e.g., Heb 2:4; 6:4), this may refer to the early Christian experience of the baptism of the Holy Spirit, a new access to the power of God and experience of the gifts of the Spirit that became an existential reminder of their new closeness to God and God's favor.

In a third phase remembered by the author, the believers were the victims of society's attempts to bring them back in line with its values (Heb 10:32-34). The non-Christians around them regarded the Christians' witness to the one God as a threat, a subversion of proper piety and hence a danger to the continued well-being of the society. For it was the traditional gods who upheld the social order, secured political stability and provided good crops. Formerly good citizens were now pulling back from participation in the traditional religion, withdrawing from social, civic and business duties where the gods were celebrated. The society, therefore, acted to deter any further defections to this group and to bring the believers to their senses, if possible.

During this time the converts came under heavy fire from the associates and neighbors they left behind. The author recalls no martyrdoms (see Heb 12:4) but paints a picture of "a severe contest of sufferings" (Heb 10:32), including insult, physical assaults, public disgrace, imprisonment and confiscation of goods. The latter two could be accomplished with trumped-up charges, manipulating the courts against an increasingly unpopular segment of society; the plundering of property could result from either a court ruling or from

---

[5]See the review of the question of the social level of early Christians in Bengt Holmberg, *Sociology and the New Testament: An Appraisal* (Minneapolis: Fortress, 1990).

looting and pillaging while the owners were in prison, exiled or otherwise occupied. Public disgrace was used by the society to dissuade the afflicted from continuing in (and others from joining) the Christian minority culture. Shaming and reviling were society's ways of neutralizing the threat Christians posed to the accepted worldview and values, and of motivating the deviants into returning to their former obligations to their neighbors and ancestral way of life.

The believers, however, did not at first succumb to these pressures: they remained intensely loyal to Christ and to one another, willingly suffering the loss of their place in society. So great was their commitment that even those who had not come directly under fire showed open and public solidarity with those who were subjected to public humiliation, caring for those who had been imprisoned.[6] In this way Christians even invited reproach from their neighbors rather than fail to show one another support in times of need. Sustaining one another through mutual assistance and caring ("love and good works," Heb 6:9-10), the Christians continued to resist society's attempts to discourage them in their new hope. Their loss of reputation, and no doubt the loss of much economic security as their property was taken and their networks with non-Christian patrons and partners eroded, did not cause them to lose sight of the goal of the journey that they had begun.

The pastoral situation addressed by Hebrews. The impression given by this text is that the earlier fervor of those Christians had cooled. We do not know how long ago "those earlier days" were (Heb 10:32), but enough time has passed for the converts reasonably to have been expected to become mature in the faith (Heb 5:11-14). During that time the ongoing pressures applied by society—perhaps far less intense than those described in Hebrews 10:32-34 but more effective over a long period of time—are beginning to take their toll. Some have already begun to dissociate themselves from the Christian group (Heb 10:25), precisely what their non-Christian neighbors have been after. Others have not lived up to what is expected from mature believers (Heb 5:12), mainly in not being proactive in keeping the faltering on track.

The author speaks as if some among the congregation are in danger of drifting away (Heb 2:1) from the message that they received, of "turning away from the living God" (Heb 3:12), of neglecting the message spoken by Jesus and attested by God (Heb 2:3), of failing to attain the promised rest (Heb 4:1), of falling through unbelief in the same way as the wilderness generation (Heb 4:11), of growing weary and losing heart (Heb 12:3). In the more heated moments the author speaks of the dangers of falling away (Heb 6:6) and of "trampling underfoot the Son of God, regarding as profane the blood by which you are sanctified, and affronting the Spirit of grace" (Heb 10:29). In general, the author sees the possibility of a faltering commitment (Heb 10:35-36; 12:12).

How did the congregation go from the bold, committed stance described in Hebrews 10:32-34 to a place of such danger?[7] While some readers find in the "not yet" of Hebrews 12:4 ("you have *not yet* resisted to the point of

---

[6]Lucian of Samosata, a second-century C.E. writer of satirical prose, provides a moving (if somewhat mocking) description of the resources a Christian group would mobilize for one of its own when he or she was imprisoned (*On the Death of Peregrinus* 12-13). See also the ministry of Epaphroditus to Paul in prison (Phil 2:25).

[7]Obviously, not all in the congregation are faltering in their commitment. We need to guard against reading a text as if *all* the addressees are in the same place spiritually or equally touched by the challenges and issues raised by the author. Some of these Christians are in danger, but some—perhaps many—remain firm in their faith. Indeed, the author seems to count on a firm core of solid disciples as he calls the audience to look out for the wavering and to encourage those who are about to exchange an eternal inheritance for temporary ease.

shedding your blood") an implication of growing persecution, this is not likely. First, the major examples invoked throughout the letter have to do with internal faltering or commitment, not with bloody persecution. We should expect far more to have been made of Daniel, the young men in the furnace and the Maccabean-era martyrs were this the case. Others stress that the addressees are considering a massive conversion or reversion to Judaism, which enjoyed a measure of toleration within the empire. Still others focus on new heresies, rebutted in the lengthy exposition sections of Hebrews (such as an "angelic Christology," allegedly refuted in Heb 1:1-13).[8]

When trying to determine what the believers must *endure* in order to attain the goal, we are struck by the failure to mention new, dramatic developments or any strong foreshadowing of increasing hostility (such as we find in the Revelation of John, for example). Rather, it appears that the danger of falling away stems from the lingering effects of the believers' loss of status and esteem in their neighbors' eyes, and their inability to regain approval by any means that would allow them to remain rigidly faithful to Jesus and the one

God. The believers have experienced the loss of property and status in the host society without yet receiving the promised rewards, and so they are losing hope in the promise that God would overturn their disgrace. As time passes without improvement, they begin to feel the inward pressure for their neighbors' affirmation and approval. The fervor and certainty of their earlier life in Christ has cooled with their prolonged exposure to non-Christian neighbors, who no doubt continued to disparage the believers and treat them as subversive and shameful. They have begun to be concerned for their societal reputation. Though they were able to resist it at the outset, the machinery of social control is in the long run wearing down their resistance. Living with their loss has proven difficult. Some of the addressees, feeling too strongly the loss of their honor and place in the dominant culture, are motivated to renounce their connections with Jesus and the Christian community.[9] In the eyes of society and perhaps increasingly in the eyes of some believers, renouncing that "confession" that had first alienated them from the dominant culture might be accepted as a step toward "recovery."

EXEGETICAL SKILL
Rhetorical Criticism (5)—Appeals to the Emotions

Ancient rhetoricians knew that persuasion required three components. First, the hearers had to know that they could trust the speaker (and, often, that they should not trust the speaker's opponents). Second, rational proofs—the substance of the speech—needed to be presented, often using both inductive and deductive forms of argumentation. Third, the hearers themselves had to be put in a certain frame of mind that would make them

---

[8]Such reconstructions reveal more the tendency in some circles to privilege doctrinal disputes and ignore more mundane social pressures. They also fail to perceive the ways that the exposition sections are consistently used to fuel the exhortations to perseverance throughout Hebrews.

[9]This need not have been an open, public renunciation of Christ. It would suffice to stop being seen with other Christians and start to be seen in the places formerly avoided (e.g., the idol temples, for Gentile Christians).

more likely to act in the way, or to decide in the direction, that the speaker was guiding them.[a]

The study of how to put an audience in a particular, strategically chosen emotional state was an essential component of the art of rhetoric. Indeed, it continues to be so to this day (especially in courtroom rhetoric). Aristotle recognized correctly that people are prone to make different decisions depending on the emotional state they are in at the time of decision. They are more likely to take action against a person, group or state when they feel anger than when they feel calm. They are more likely to take certain precautions or pursue a certain remedy when they are afraid than when they feel secure or complacent. They are more like to acquit a defendant when they feel more pity for than indignation against that defendant. Arousing emotions to move the hearers closer to taking the action or making the decision the speaker is promoting is always part of a strategy of persuasion.

To arouse a particular emotion, like anger, the orator needs to know the kind of people listening, their frame of mind and the circumstances that will produce the emotion in them. He or she would then make those circumstances and that frame of mind come alive in the audience. Aristotle provided a rather thorough catalog of ways that speakers could arouse twelve basic emotions appropriate to civic debate and to courtroom rhetoric (*Rhet.* 2.1-11). Studying his discussion provides us with an important window not only into how a speaker might arouse an emotion (our main interest here), but incidentally into classical psychology and the kinds of social relationships and expectations then prevalent between people.

- *Anger.* Anger is defined as a combination of pleasure and pain—pain at having suffered a slight from someone (or having a dependent slighted by someone) and pleasure at the prospect of revenge. Anger can be aroused wherever it can be shown that someone has belittled or slighted the hearer, whether through failing to return gratitude for favors done, failing to acknowledge the honor due the hearer, showing disregard for the things that are valuable for the hearer, impeding the hearer's progress toward his or her goals, and the like.
- *Calm.* Calm is simply defined as the mollification of anger. When anger has been provoked, calm can be restored if the offender is shown to have provoked the hearer unwillingly, unknowingly or, having done it intentionally, to be remorseful and contrite, confessing the misdeed and seeking to make reparations.
- *Friendship.* Aristotle defines the feeling of friendship as wishing good for another person (for that person's own sake and not for our own ben-

---

[a]We considered the first two at length in the discussion of appeals to *ethos* and *logos*. See pp. 508-10, 572-75 respectively). Appeals to *logos* will be considered further on pp. 858-61.

efit) and helping that good come about insofar as we are able. Friendship entails the feeling of another's pain and joy, the sharing of values, the sharing of friends and enemies (shared friends establishes feelings of friendship between people; common enemies reinforce feelings of partnership and friendship), silence about another's faults and the tendency to speak well of his or her achievements, mutual encouragement, and seeking the good of the other.

- *Enmity.* Enmity is the opposite of friendship, and the feeling of enmity is aroused by acts contrary to those listed under friendship.
- *Fear.* Feeling fear results from the impression of impending harm, and Aristotle especially underscores the importance that this danger should be seen as close at hand rather than far off. People are afraid when someone they have offended is shown to have power and inclination to seek satisfaction, or when they face some danger without assurances of assistance and the like.
- *Confidence.* As the opposite of fear, confidence is the sense that safety and well-being are near at hand, or that the means of deliverance are close by and available. Confidence is felt when danger or anxiety-producing things are distant and remote, and when we have many friends, allies and other means of support in the face of danger. People who have often faced danger and escaped it are more likely to feel confident; so are those who are secure in their own virtue and know that the gods are favorably disposed toward them.
- *Shame.* Ancients did not speak of shame in the sense of a debilitating emotion such as it has become in popular psychological parlance. Rather, this was a feeling of pain or discomfort at the thought that one was held in disrepute. It would be applied as a means of promoting avoidance of some course or action, or the cessation of some particular connection or direction that was shown to bring disrepute (and thus the feeling of shame). Shame is felt when our deeds or associations are shown to exhibit some vice (like injustice, cowardice, intemperance or foolishness), when we are helped by someone inferior to us, when we are unable to achieve the good things or bravely endure the bad things that our peers and inferiors are able to achieve or endure, when we do not enjoy the good things that people generally enjoy—all the more if we are deprived of these things through our own fault. We feel shame before virtuous people, our peers and superiors, and those whose opinion we value, but not before people more vicious than ourself or whose opinion is not a matter of concern.
- *Favor.* The backbone of patronage, friendship and reciprocity, favor *(charis)* is a feeling of being well-disposed toward someone such that we wish to benefit him or her. It is also the feeling of gratitude toward those who have done something to benefit us. We feel gratitude in proportion

to the need that was met, the generosity and sacrifice of the giver, the timeliness of the gift, the uniqueness of the gift. Any feeling of gratitude can be undone if a speaker shows that the "benefactor" was really acting in his or her own self-interest rather than for the good of the recipient, or did the deed under compulsion or by chance rather than voluntarily and intentionally.

- *Pity.* Pity is an experience of pain at the undeserved suffering of another person, usually a person who is like us. (We pity that which might otherwise have befallen us.)
- *Indignation.* This feeling is a counterpart to pity—an experience of pain at the good fortune of those who do not deserve to enjoy it, either because those who enjoy it are unworthy or have acquired good things unjustly. It is also felt when a virtuous person does not receive the recognition or rewards that are due him or her.
- *Envy.* An emotion not characteristic of virtuous people, envy is a feeling of pain at others' enjoyment of some good and a desire to deprive them of that good. New Testament authors will not attempt to arouse envy, but Aristotle's descriptions of situations in which it is aroused can be helpful for understanding certain passages. For example, the parable of the laborers in the vineyard (Mt 20:1-16) employs a standard topic of envy: those who have worked much to get what they enjoy see those who have worked little or easily enjoying the same rewards and are pained.
- *Emulation.* An emotion characteristic of virtuous people and a kind of counterpart to envy, emulation is the desire to acquire (by virtuous means) those goods enjoyed by other people who are like us (while not therefore aiming at depriving others of what they justly enjoy). In rhetoric, emulation is aroused as the hearers listen to other people being praised for their achievements, insofar as they believe themselves capable of similar achievement and desire the same praise.

Aristotle does not cover every possible emotion that a speaker might wish to arouse in his or her audience (e.g., disgust, admiration), but provides a starting point for further reflection. He is particularly lacking in any treatment of emotions specifically associated with religious experience (e.g., holy awe, regret, joy), though some of the emotions he treats are no strangers to religious settings. His discussion alerts us, however, to the importance of thinking through what emotional responses an author might be trying to trigger in a passage, and *to what end* the author would seek to arouse this response.

Appeals to pathos in Hebrews. The author of Hebrews shows a high level of interest in putting his audience in a particular emotional frame of mind. Indeed, in the course of his "sermon," he moves them through a great variety of emotional responses, each one calculated to support the decisions and actions he is promoting. Consider the following sample passages:

- Read Hebrews 4:14-16. After warning the hearers not to follow the pattern of the wilderness generation, who provoked God's anger through their fear and disobedience, the author writes a passage that will make them feel confident. As the audience faces their own contest with hostile sinners, they have assurance that help is near at hand—and from no less a source than God's own self, secured through Jesus' mediation. The hearers have access to God's "throne of favor," where they can receive the "timely help" they need to meet any challenge. This passage combines several topics to produce confidence (the proximity of aid and the assurance of divine favor) and encourage the hearers to persevere in their Christian commitment, against the pressures of their neighbors.

- Read Hebrews 5:11-14. The author seeks to recapture the hearers' attention and their investment in listening to the sermon by shaming them.[b] He speaks as though the audience ought to have achieved more by this point in their Christian journey, to have "measured up" better and taken more responsibility for keeping one another on track rather than waiting for the author's instruction and motivation. He uses "milk" and "solid food," familiar topics of preliminary and advanced education, to shame the audience for performing at the former level when they ought to have reached the latter level. This arousal of shame should motivate the audience to acquit themselves of being immature in their grasp of their responsibilities toward one another and in their grounding in the values and wisdom of the Christian culture. Then they will be prepared to accept the author's call to take more seriously their response to God and obligation to look after one another (Heb 6:1-12).

- Read Hebrews 10:26-31. The language of this passage is calculated to arouse fear (*fearful* is twice used to describe these circumstances; Heb 10:27, 31). In this passage we quite plainly find the topics of imminent harm (the "eager fire that is about to devour the adversaries," Heb 10:27), the anger of One who is quite capable of inflicting harm (Heb 10:30-31), and "outraged" virtue seeking satisfaction against those who have responded to beneficence with insult (Heb 10:29).

  Aristotle had underscored the importance of impressing on the hearers' minds the proximity of the danger if the orator was to arouse fear successfully. The author of Hebrews has attended to the topic of imminence. In Hebrews 10:25 he speaks of the hearers' seeing "the Day drawing nearer," by which he means the day of Christ's return to vindicate the faithful and judge the adversaries (as in Heb 10:26-27). Similarly, in Hebrews 10:37-39 the author has used a quotation from Habakkuk to stress the nearness of "the coming one" who "will come and

---

[b]This is one reason among several not to take this passage as an accurate reading of the hearers' spiritual pulse.

not delay," even going so far as to add three words (in Greek) from Isaiah 26:20: "in a very little while." This citation of ancient authority, with its focus on the nearness of Christ's return, enhances both the appeal to fear in Hebrews 10:26-31 and the appeal to confidence in Hebrews 10:32-36. The purpose, of course, is to make the hearers dread the consequences of one course of action (withdrawing from the community, which would have looked advantageous from a worldly point of view) and feel confident about their security as they continue to pursue the opposite course (persevering in faith).

- Read Hebrews 11:1—12:3. The author's encomium (praise) of the examples of faith aims at arousing emulation among the hearers. One of the direct purposes of the funeral eulogy was to reaffirm the commitment of the living to the values exemplified by the deceased.[c] The hearers would go through a mental process of comparing the accomplishments of the deceased with their own achievements and would be roused to emulate the deceased so they would secure a praiseworthy remembrance as well. The author of Hebrews praises the heroes of the Jewish Scriptures and intertestamental period writings for their demonstration of faith. This was a means both of defining how faith "operates" in this world and of rousing the hearers to run their own race with excellence, having all these successful runners as spectators.

For further practice in identifying and analyzing appeals to the emotions of the audience, and reflecting on the rhetorical goals such appeals would serve, consider the following passages (which move from the more simple to the more complex):

1. Read Philippians 1:3-11. How do the topics Paul invokes create (reinforce) a feeling of friendship and favor toward Paul among the hearers?

2. Read Galatians 4:12-20. What emotional responses does Paul seek to arouse (e.g., through remembrance of the past quality of relationship he enjoyed with the Galatians) toward himself and the rival teachers in this paragraph? How might this provide an important balance to the emotional strategy pursued at the outset of Galatians (read 1:6-10)?

3. Read Matthew 23. What emotional response does Jesus' invective against the scribes and Pharisees produce among the readers/hearers of this text in the early Christian community? Why would Matthew want to invoke this response (e.g., by preserving and including this series of pronouncements about and against their leadership)?

4. Read the speeches for the prosecution and defense in Acts 24. What emotions does Tertullus seek to arouse in Felix, both toward himself and against Paul? How does Paul's defense potentially counteract negative

---

[c]See David A. deSilva, *Despising Shame: Honor Discourse and Community Maintenance in the Epistle to the Hebrews,* SBLDS 152 (Atlanta: Scholars Press, 1995), pp. 47-50.

emotions aroused against himself by Tertullus and redirect Felix's positive dispositions toward himself and negative feelings against a third party?

5. Read Galatians 1:6-10; 5:2-4, 7-12; 6:11-18. What feelings about themselves, about their position (i.e., if they accept circumcision), about Paul and the rival teachers does Paul appear to arouse in these passages, and how would feeling such emotional responses at these points in the letter help dispose the Galatians to follow Paul's advice?

6. Read Revelation 6:9-11; 16:5-7; 18:1-24. What negative emotions toward the Roman order (the enemies of the church) does John try to arouse in these passages? How (e.g., through depicting the satisfaction of the very emotions John seeks simultaneously to arouse) and to what end? Ask, for example, Does Rome deserve the fortune it currently enjoys in the late first century C.E.? What actions of Rome's does John highlight, and what should be the hearers' emotional response to considering these actions?

Who wrote Hebrews? While the author omitted his name, readers since the second century have been quick to supply one, based primarily on the passing mention of Timothy in the closing greetings (Heb 13:23). By the second century some scribes attributed the work to Paul, but the style of Hebrews is so different from the known Pauline letters that scholars such as Origen, Clement of Alexandria and Tertullian had to attribute the letter to one of Paul's associates (whether Apollos or Barnabas).[10] Only after Jerome and Augustine championed the cause of Pauline authorship did this view take deep roots.

While the identity of the author cannot be known, Paul, at least, can be ruled out. The evidence of the early church fathers actually favors non-Pauline authorship. The internal evidence, however, is even more certain:

- Paul vociferously insists that he came to faith by a direct, divine intervention in his life, and not by hearing someone preach (1 Cor 15:3-10; Gal 1:11-17) whereas the author of Hebrews admits to coming to faith by virtue of the apostolic witnesses (Heb 2:3-4).

- None of Paul's other writings come close to the rhetorical finesse and stylistic polish of Hebrews. Indeed, Paul's own philosophy of preaching runs completely counter to what we encounters in Hebrews. Paul refused to rely on well-crafted rhetoric ("the loftiness of words or wisdom," 1 Cor 2:1), insisting that the response of his audience be based on their encounter with God's power through the message; the author of Hebrews uses every rhetorical ornament in the handbooks and shows an astounding array of argumentative techniques.[11]

---

[10]Some attempt to save Pauline authorship by saying Paul wrote the letter in Hebrew and one of his associates translated it into Greek. But this flies in the face of the fact that the author's argument turns at several points on the Greek version of the Old Testament, precisely where the Greek version departs significantly from the Hebrew text. A Hebrew author would be unlikely to retranslate the LXX back into Hebrew, and a Hebrew audience would be unlikely to overlook the significant points of difference.

[11]Suggesting that Paul was simply writing in a different style, as if preaching in a synagogue, is a desperate attempt to hold on to Pauline authorship, and as we have seen, it does not account for the author's use of the Septuagint version of Old Testament passages rather than following the readings in the Hebrew text.

- Although Hebrews shares important topics with Pauline letters (e.g., the Torah, the use of Abraham and Jesus as models for Christians to imitate), the author of Hebrews develops these topics distinctively.

- The thickness of Platonic concepts, interest in cult and exposition of Jesus' work in terms of priesthood make this letter stand out from the Pauline corpus.

Once Paul is ruled out, little further can be said. Both Barnabas and Apollos have been and remain viable candidates (especially the latter, given his reputation for his rhetorical ability and his skill in handling the Old Testament; see Acts 18:24, 28). Scholars have also proposed Priscilla, Luke, Silas, Epaphras and Aristion. No convincing case can be made for any candidate, however,[12] and Origen's final statement on the question of authorship remains the wisest of all—"But who wrote the epistle? God knows the truth" (quoted in Eusebius *Hist. Eccl.* 6.25.14).

The unnamed author does not present himself as a witness to the Lord Jesus but rather as one who has himself been evangelized by the apostolic founders (Heb 2:3). He is not a leader from within the community he addresses, for he always refers to the community leaders in the third person (Heb 13:7, 17, 24). He has visited the community before, since he hopes to be "restored" to them (Heb 13:19). He appears to be part of a "we" group distinct from the audience, a circle of leaders including Timothy (Heb 13:23). The author, like Timothy or Titus, was part of the staff of an apostolic founder (in this case, Paul), evangelized by the apostle and now carrying on the mission of the departed apostle (whether he moved on to new mission grounds or died). The connection with Timothy, as well as the clear points of contact with known Pauline letters,[13] confirms that the author comes from that circle within early Christianity. The team exercises authority over the apostle's former mission field and seeks to preserve his work. Although the author often associates himself with the audience as a "we" or "us," he also has sufficient authority to rebuke the audience where necessary and to expect that they will honor his instructions. The author does not rely on charismatic authority but on his ability to connect his exhortations with the authoritative traditions of the community (chiefly the Old Testament and the proclamation of Jesus). His rhetorical ability,[14] which distinguishes him above his canonical peers, no doubt also contributed greatly to his authority: eloquence and the ability to persuade were highly admired.

Date and location. Clement of Rome appears to have been influenced by Hebrews 1, which would mean that Hebrews had been written sometime prior to 96 C.E. Internal evidence, though slight, tends to favor a date before 70 C.E. Although the author focuses on the desert tabernacle rather than the Jerusalem temple, the rhetorical question "would they [the sacrifices prescribed by Leviticus] not have ceased being offered?" (Heb 10:2 NRSV) suggests that, in fact, these sacrifices are still being offered somewhere, an ongoing "yearly reminder of sins" (10:3). Although arguments based on what the author does *not* say are weak, the absence of any mention of the destruction of the temple, which the author

---

[12]The author's use of a masculine ending for the self-referential participle "telling" (*diegoumenon,* Heb 11:32) rules out Priscilla or another female author. The author of Hebrews would not make such a mistake, and there would be no reason for a female teacher to hide her gender, given the openness to female leadership in the early church. Moreover, the author assumes that the readers will know who he is (Heb 13:18-24).

[13]Ben Witherington III has conducted a close examination of the points of contact between Galatians and Hebrews, demonstrating how Pauline thought provides a primary formative matrix for the theology, OT interpretation and even choice of diction of the author of Hebrews ("The Influence of Galatians on Hebrews," NTS 37 [1991]: 146-52).

[14]See deSilva, *Perseverance in Gratitude,* pp. 35-39, 46-58.

could have used to demonstrate the obsolescence or final rejection of the Levitical cult, tentatively suggests a pre-70 date as well.[15]

The author addresses a particular Christian community whose circumstances are personally known to him,[16] and whom he plans to visit in person when his own circumstances permit. But the solution of the mystery of the location of author or addressees rests completely on the greetings sent by "those from Italy" (Heb 13:24), and secondarily on the early reception of the letter in Rome by Clement. While this does anchor Hebrews in Italy in some way, it is not clear how.

- Does the author write "from Italy" to Christians elsewhere, a pattern seen also in 1 Peter and *1 Clement,* sending the greetings of Italian Christians to their sisters and brothers across the Mediterranean (again, compare 1 Pet 5:13)?[17] Several scribal additions to the superscription of the letter support this reading.
- Does the author write to Christians in Italy, sending along greetings of other Italian Christians currently with the author?[18]
- Does the author write from outside Italy to Christians also outside Italy, passing along the greetings of the expatriate Italian Christians who are with him along (thus placing neither audience or author in Italy)?

Some connection with Roman Christianity remains likely (though perhaps on the part of the author rather than the recipients), and the early use of Hebrews by Clement would tend to support this.

GENRE AND STRUCTURE

Although we have referred to Hebrews as a letter, based on the closing greetings, instructions and other recognizable letter-closing ingredients in Hebrews 13:18-25, it has more in common with a speech than a written document. Hebrews does not open with any signals of being a letter, but with an ornate, beautifully phrased, carefully balanced sentence that does precisely what the exordium of a speech (or in this context, a sermon) was expected to do—catch the hearers' attention, establish the speaker's credibility and give some hints of the topics to be developed. It is thus probably truer to the author's intentions to hear Hebrews as a sermon (a "word of encouragement," Heb 13:22; see Acts 13:15 for an indication that this was the name of the early Christian equivalent for the homily, or sermon) addressing the congregation and thus to analyze the text more in terms of rhetoric than epistolary categories.

The sermon alternates between exposition and exhortation, the former largely providing the grounds and motivations for the latter. It may be outlined as follows.

I. Appeal to heed properly the word of God in the Son (1:1—2:18)

- Thesis and confirmation: God's final and complete word has been spoken through the Son, who has greater honor even than the angels (1:1-14)
- Exhortation, drawing "lesser-to-greater" inference from 1:1-13 (2:1-4)
- Argument in support of the exhortation: Attachment to Jesus is the path to a share in his honor as well as the path of gratitude for past benefits and Jesus' ongoing mediation (2:5-18)

II. Appeal to honor God's word through trust and perseverance (3:1—4:13)

- Argument: Jesus, as Son over God's house, has greater honor than Moses, the servant in God's house (3:1-6)

---

[15]Ellingworth, *Commentary on Hebrews,* p. 32.

[16]Thus, rightly, ibid., p. 26, if by "part of a wider Christian community" he means the church as a whole.

[17]Attridge provides an impressive list of places where the expression is used idiomatically to indicate place of origin rather than to indicate separation from their home (*Hebrews,* p. 410 n. 79).

[18]Thus W. L. Lane, *Hebrews 1-8,* WBC 47A (Dallas: Word, 1991), p. lviii; V. C. Pfitzner, *Hebrews,* ACNT (Nashville: Abingdon, 1997), p. 30.

- Exhortation: do not imitate those who rejected God's patronage under the servant, Moses, for we would find ourselves similarly subject to judgment; rather, let us strive to enter the "rest" that remains open to us (3:7—4:13)

III. Central exposition—the "long and difficult word" (4:14—10:18)

- Exhortation: take advantage of the access to God Jesus provides (4:14-16)
- Argument: Jesus' appointment to high priesthood (5:1-10)
- Digression (a second *captatio benevolentiae*) (5:11—6:20)
  Interruption and appeal for attentive and responsive hearing (5:11-14)
  Exhortation to move forward in Christian journey (6:1-3)
  Argument in support of exhortation (6:4-8)
  Palliation: topics of confidence (6:9-12)
  Argument confirming cause for confidence (6:13-20)
- Argument resumed: Christians' superior access to God, thanks to Jesus (7:1—10:18)
  Jesus' superior qualifications for priesthood (7:1-28)
  Jesus' location in a better sanctuary, mediating a better covenant (8:1-13)
  Jesus' unique achievement: preparing all the people to enter God's real presence (9:1—10:18)

IV. Climactic exhortation to persevere in gratitude for the benefactions bestowed by Jesus and God (10:19—13:25)

- Exhortation based on this new access (10:19-25)
- Rationale for accepting exhortation based on consideration of the contrary (10:26-31)
- Exhortation: imitate your former endurance and remain constant (show "faith") (10:32-39)
- Encomium on faith, developing the portrait of this virtue in action (11:1—12:3)
- Encouragement to endure opposition (12:4-17)

- Exhortation to confidence and gratitude (12:18-29)
- Specific exhortations: living out gratitude in everyday life (13:1-21)
- Epistolary postscript (13:22-25)

THE PASTORAL STRATEGY OF HEBREWS

Helping people commit to an unpopular way of life—one that has already cost them a great deal—is a challenge for even the most skilled of orators. The author of Hebrews, however, rose to this challenge by means of a cohesive, multipronged attack on the forces that were eroding the commitment of the Christians.

- He helps them rediscover their priorities in light of their Christian confession, as opposed to the priorities that would emerge from contemplating their disprivileged place in society.
- He reminds them of the value of the gifts they have received from God, the value of Jesus as their mediator with God and the value of the ultimate benefit of an eternal homeland that they are yet to enter, so that they will be reluctant to violate their bond with God through Jesus and exchange God's favor for God's wrath.
- Since sensitivity to their neighbors' negative opinion of them was a pressing factor, he encourages them to continue to "despise shame," as Abraham, Moses and Jesus did, with a view to attaining the promised reward.
- He insulates them from the effects of being devalued and marginalized by their neighbors, turning their endurance of such hostility into an opportunity for honor in God's sight.
- He mobilizes the community members to support one another, to keep watch for signs of straying or succumbing to society's pressures, and to show such love for and solidarity with one another that each member finds the strength to press on.

- Finally, he replaces any self-image the believers might have formed on account of their neighbors' censure and rejection with a powerful picture of their place in God's plan: they have been cleansed by their baptism and participation in the death of Jesus and consecrated to move out from this world into the "holy places" in the eternal realm, to have direct access to the holy God. It is a journey from being at home in this world, out to the marginal places and into the lasting realm where they will come into their true honor and home.

Cosmology, eschatology and setting the priorities of a congregation. At the foundation of the author's rhetorical strategy is his understanding of the nature and destiny of the cosmos. This worldview becomes the touchstone for the deliberations he lays before the congregation, leading them to invest in what abides forever, even if that means loss in terms of temporary pleasures and security. The author distinguishes between the visible, material realm of everyday experience and the eternal realm. The visible realm comprises earth and the "heavens," the plural consistently referring to the sky and stars that are part of the changing, temporary creation (cf. Heb 1:10-12). This earth and these heavens will eventually be shaken and removed (Heb 12:26-28). Beyond these stands a superior, eternal realm—"heaven itself," in the author's language (Heb 9:24). This is the realm where God's full presence is enjoyed by the angelic hosts and the glorified Christ. Like other Jewish authors, he conceives of this realm in terms of the architecture of the tabernacle, which was presumed to be a model of God's realm.[19] This realm existed before the creation of the visible world and will last beyond "the end." From the perspective of human beings it is the "coming realm" (Heb 2:5), not in the sense that it does not already exist but that it has yet to be revealed to human beings. Because God's realm alone lasts, all that belongs to it is labeled "better," superior to the things that belong to this realm. There the believers will find their "better and lasting possessions" (Heb 10:34), their "better" because it is "heavenly homeland" (Heb 11:16) and the "unshakable kingdom" (Heb 12:28) in which is their "abiding city" (Heb 13:14). As the addressees are invited to reaffirm their commitment to this worldview throughout Hebrews, they will come to agree with the author that though their association with Jesus may have lost them possessions in this realm, it has gained for them better and lasting possessions. With Abraham, they can disregard being "at home" in this realm and look forward to their "better homeland, that is, a heavenly one" (Heb 11:16).

Promoting this worldview undergirds the author's deliberative cause at every point, primarily in making perseverance in faith advantageous and expedient. The honor, wealth and sense of having a home in this world, all of which was lost by the addressees, pale in comparison with the honor, possessions and enfranchisement that the believers who persevere will receive in the realm beyond (Heb 2:10; 10:34; 13:14). The addressees will therefore be urged to invest only in the eternal possessions (Heb 10:34; 11:13-16; 12:26-28; 13:13-14) and to consider worldly goods and security to be a bad and foolish investments (Heb 11:24-26; 12:16-17). Ongoing commitment to Christ and the church, though it means deprivation of this world's goods, security and honor, becomes preferable on the basis of the belief that the visible world is of secondary value to the invisible world, in which the believers are to set their hopes and ambitions.

One of the major pastoral strategies pursued by the author, therefore, is to keep the addressees' eyes fixed on those shared truths and their ambitions fixed on those pursuits

---

[19]See *1 Enoch* 90:28-29; *Testament of Levi* 5.

and prizes that will enable perseverance in the face of hostility and loss. With regard to those who have already pulled back from the assembly (Heb 10:25) and those who might be considering such a leave of absence, their focus had moved from their hope and their relationship with God to the hostility and disapproval of their unbelieving neighbors. An essential element in the author's strategy is not to focus on the same phenomena but to address the situation in a way that would reorient those wavering Christians. For this cause, the author repeatedly calls their attention to the Son and the significance of their response to this Son. The main question is, How will they respond to the Son, and how will they encounter him at his appearing? In this sermon they will see God's wrath at the ungrateful and their loss of place in the eternal realm as the real dangers facing them (see especially Heb 2:1-4; 4:1-13; 6:4-8; 10:26-31; 12:16-17, 25), not the ongoing loss of temporal prestige and goods.

Honoring the divine Patron. The central thread of the author's strategy is to keep the disciples focused on the incredible benefits that have come to them by virtue of their connection with Jesus and, through him, with God. The expository sections of Hebrews revolve around the question of mediation between God and human beings. Who can effectively bring human beings into God's favor? Who can establish and sustain a lasting relationship between God and humanity? The author's answer is, of course, Jesus and *only* Jesus. These topics take us deep into the roles, obligations and dynamics of patron-client relationships (presented at length in chapter three on pp. 130-37), with Jesus emerging as the mediator, or broker (Heb 8:6; 9:15; 12:24), whose main gift is access to the favor of another patron, in this case, God's own self.

The expository sections lay out the superior worth or honor of Jesus by discussing his divine sonship, his exaltation to the high priesthood of the better sanctuary and his session at the "right hand of the God." All these attributes are grounded in the author's Christ-centered reading of Psalms 2 and 110. On the one hand, Jesus' exalted honor magnifies the danger of abusing that honor through disloyalty to or devaluing of connection with Jesus (e.g., through apostasy, whether quiet or open). On the other hand, Jesus' remarkable proximity to God (genealogically, as Son, and spatially, as one who stands in God's real presence in the divine realm) makes him the most effective person to connect people to God—more effective than all other mediators known in the history of Jewish tradition (e.g., angels, Moses and the Levitical priests). There is danger, therefore, in denying or minimizing our connection with Jesus; there is limitless advantage, however, in continuing to claim this connection and to respond to Jesus with loyalty and gratitude, no matter what the cost in this world. Within the argument of Hebrews, we either honor and obey God at the risk of dishonoring and provoking the world, or we honor and conform to society at the risk of dishonoring and provoking God. Stated another way, we either seek to gain security through friendship with the representatives of the unbelieving society, or we attach ourselves to God and enjoy the benefits gained through Christ.

Jesus helps the descendants of Abraham (Heb 2:16) and comes "to the aid of those who are tempted" (Heb 2:18). He is thus the one to whom Christians are to look to supply what is wanting in their own resources. Through his death on behalf of all (Heb 2:9) he brought the greatest gifts to humankind, freeing them from the slavery of the fear of death (Heb 2:14-15) and opening up access to God through his death, ascension and exaltation (conceived of cumulatively as Jesus' appointment as "high priest after the order of Melchizedek"). This access to God involves not only God's generous and timely provision of all that believers need now to endure in their obedience and bold confession (Heb

4:14-16) but also the consecration of body and conscience that authorizes Christ's followers to go where Christ has gone as a "forerunner for us" (Heb 6:19-20), namely, into the invisible, lasting realm of heaven itself (Heb 9:24), the unshakable kingdom and city that God has prepared for the people of faith (Heb 11:14; 12:26-28; 13:13-14).

The author develops an extended comparison of Jesus with the Levitical priests (Heb 7:1—10:18) precisely to underscore the immense and incomparable value of the benefits Jesus has provided, so that the believers will not throw these away on account of temporary hardships. While the Levitical priests, the only other priests authorized by God, could not even broaden access to all the people with regard to the earthly tabernacle, a mere copy of the real place of God's dwelling in the eternal realm, Jesus' death and ministry on the people's behalf has opened up access not merely to the copy but to the real holy of holies in heaven. This is because Jesus' death was the first and only sacrifice that could reach beyond the surface of defilement and cleanse the heart of the worshiper and the memory of God from the stains of sin that kept humanity and God at a distance. The breach in the divine-human relationship is sealed, divine favor is restored, and the final fulfillment of the promise that God would dwell in the midst of God's people is made possible at last.

In light of such great benefits, and especially in light of the tremendous cost undertaken by Jesus to provide these benefits, the necessary response is to make full use of and attest to the value of what Jesus has provided. This is, again, a culture where reciprocity—receiving gifts well and returning gratitude in an appropriate manner—is a core value not to be neglected. In cases where a person could not repay the favor, gratitude manifests itself in open testimony to the generosity and virtue of the giver (an incentive to Christian witness, or evangelism), loyalty to the giver, and service to the giver in whatever ways are deemed appropriate. Thus the author will urge the believers to make use of the access to God that is theirs, and to strain eagerly forward to that final entry into God's realm for which they have been prepared by Jesus' sacrifice and priestly intervention (e.g., Heb 4:14-16; 10:19-25; 12:28).

Any response that shows disregard for the giver and the gifts is to be avoided at all costs, yet this is the perceived danger facing some in the community. Because some are wavering in their commitment to the divine Patron on account of the opposition they encounter, Hebrews is full of parallel warning passages that call attention to the dire consequences of valuing Jesus' gifts and God's favor so lightly that Christians would exchange these for society's gifts of affirmation and acceptance (Heb 2:1-4; 3:7—4:11; 6:4-8; 10:26-31; 12:25-29).

As a historical precedent and example of the dangers of failing to trust God's promises, the author deals at length with the story of the wilderness generation (the people who left Egypt with Moses; Heb 3:7—4:11). He opens by quoting Psalm 95 from the LXX, in which the Hebrew place names "Massah" and "Meribah" (which would otherwise invoke Ex 17:1-7 and Num 20:2-13) are translated as the nouns "provocation" and "testing." The focus of the Greek version of the psalm, therefore, rests completely on the story of Numbers 14, where the people finally refuse to take possession of the promised land because they fear the inhabitants of that land.

This is a tragic turning point in the story. Although they have God's promise that he will give them the land of Canaan, the spies' report concerning the strength of Canaan's inhabitants makes them falter. Abandoning their confidence in God, they accuse him of leading them out to the desert to die, refuse the command to invade Canaan and start formulating a plan to return to Egypt (Num 14:1-4). God receives all this as a flagrant denial of his reliability and ability to provide, a reliability that should have been beyond doubt, given all the earlier occasions where God came through for them. This denial is an affront to God's goodness, and their disobedience a flouting of the right and authority of the Patron to command obedience. Those whom God desired to benefit returned insult for favor, slighting God through their distrust of God's good will and ability. God responds with wrath, or anger (Heb 3:10) toward those who have been disobedient, who have trampled the promise and faltered in their trust. The result of God's wrath is the people's irrevocable loss of access to the promised benefit: "As I swore in my wrath, 'They shall not enter my rest' " (Heb 3:11).

In this example the addressees encounter a group brought to the very border of their promised inheritance, who at the last moment panic and withdraw their trust from God. They fear and respect the people over whom God had promised to give them victory, rather than fear and respect the God who promised them a lasting inheritance. The audience is invited to see the dangers of their own situation reflected in this story. Having endured a period of "wandering" in which they experienced the world's rejection and still held onto God's promise (Heb 10:32-34), some of the believers are wavering in their commitment at the very time when they are closer than ever to attaining what was promised. Some stand in danger of falling into distrust, of disobeying God by not continuing to assemble together to worship (Heb 10:25) and by dissociating from those in need (Heb 13:3), and of regarding the opinion and hostility of society more than the God who promises them an unshakable kingdom.

The author heightens the addressees' awareness of the danger through a number of stern warnings designed to arouse fear and dread—fear of the consequences of pursuing any course that would provoke their Patron. Perhaps one of the most troublesome passages in the history of theological interpretation is Hebrews 6:4-8, where the author warns that those who have enjoyed God's gifts and then bring open contempt on Jesus by returning to the bosom of society will have no opportunity to return to favor. First and foremost we need to recognize that by again arousing fear of the dread consequences of falling away, the author helps assure that the faltering among the congregation will find the resources to persevere. The author claims, however, no more than what was assumed by the ethics of reciprocity. Dio Chrysostom, for example, warned others in danger of showing ingratitude that "those who insult their benefactors will by nobody be esteemed to deserve a favour" (*Orat.* 31.65). This presupposition lies behind this passage, the even stronger warning in Hebrews 10:26-31 and the example of Esau in Hebrews 12:16-17, who similarly exchanged an eternal good for a very temporary relief of hardship.

The believers have enjoyed many gifts from God that are full of promise for the future perfection of these gifts. Having tasted God's goodness, their return to the bosom of the society would make a public witness that God's gifts are not worth what they cost to keep, and would thus bring dishonor on God's name. The agricultural maxim that follows this warning is quite apt and further reinforces the "naturalness" of the consequences the author forsees. Rain is regarded as a benefaction of God (cf. Mt 5:45), which looks for a proper return in fruitful soil. God's gifts should bring forth gratitude and loyalty toward God as well as useful fruits for the fellow believers (e.g., the acts of service and love commended and recommended in Heb 6:10). Such a response will lead to the consummation of blessing. The improper response of breaking with the benefactor, indeed, bringing dishonor to the name of the benefactor, leads to the curse and fire, that is, exclusion from the promise and exposure to the anger of the Judge. The warning in Hebrews 10:26-31 will heighten the addressees' awareness both of the significance of dissociating from the congregation (in terms of what such an act does to Jesus) as well as of the frightful consequences of choosing to encounter God as Judge rather than to remain within God's favor.

It would be inappropriate to derive from these texts a "doctrine of the impossibility of a return for the apostate" for a number of reasons.[20] First, the texts clearly appeal to the emotions; specifically they attempt to arouse fear strategically in the service of the author's goal of *preventing* apostasy or any other inappropriate response to God's favor. Second, Greco-Roman texts especially bear witness to a kind of "double standard" in patron-client relations. On the one hand, recipients of gifts were to keep in mind certain facts, including the necessity of returning a favor and the exclusion from favor of those who showed themselves ungrateful. On the other hand, givers were to keep in mind other facts, like the importance of giving with no thought of a return and the nobility of extending favor even to those who have proven themselves ungrateful. If human patrons could extend grace to the ungrateful, how much more does this remain a possibility for God? Nevertheless, such thoughts ought never to enter our minds as a prelude to presuming on God's favor. As clients ourselves, we are to keep in mind the first set of facts and, along with the first recipients of Hebrews, let them guide us to take the course of action that shows respect, loyalty and gratitude toward God and Jesus.

Despising shame. As we survey Hebrews for factors that could cool the believers' fervor or cause them to lose sight of the great benefits of being connected to God through Jesus, the experience of disapproval, censure and loss of honor comes to the fore. This is most evident as the author recalls the "former time" of their neighbors' open censure and abuse of their new commitments (see especially Heb 10:32-

34), but it also shines through the author's pastoral response as he selects and shapes the biblical examples that show faith in action and as he helps them come to terms with living through difficult circumstances.

The author sees it as vital, then, to insulate the Christians against internalizing their neighbors' censure and disapproval. Only if they can "despise shame" will they press forward in confident faith rather than "shrink back" in the face of society's pressures (Heb 10:36-39). One important strategy the author pursues is the praising of respected figures from the past who have faced similar challenges and made precisely the same choices that the audience has. The primary examples the author holds up as worthy of imitation in Hebrews 10:32—12:3—the community itself, Abraham, Moses, the martyrs and Jesus—all share a common feature. They have chosen to embrace a lower status in society's eyes in order to pursue the greater and lasting honor to be won through obedience to God. Renouncing the honor and approval that accompany success and integration into the unbelieving society, they have all borne witness to a hope for the greater, lasting rewards promised by God. In their loyal obedience to this hope, they have accepted marginality with regard to human networks of honor and status.

The climax of the encomium on faith is the example of Jesus (Heb 12:1-3), "the pioneer and perfecter of faith." In Jesus, faith finds its most complete expression. Jesus shows this faith by "enduring a cross, despising shame" (Heb 12:2); this same faith led to the honor that followed when "he sat down at the right hand of God" (Heb 12:2). The phrase "despising shame" brings us to the heart of one of the author's main goals, to detach his audience from valuing society's approval or disapproval. Such concern for reputation in the eyes of nongroup members, as we have seen, would

---

[20]For a much fuller exploration of this issue, see deSilva, *Perseverance in Gratitude,* pp. 234-36, 240-44.

pull believers away from the group and its values, and lead them to assimilate back into the dominant culture.

For the author of Hebrews, Jesus' humiliation begins with the incarnation (Heb 2:5-9, applying Ps 8:4-6 to the ministry of Christ) and climaxes in the crucifixion, a pattern familiar from the Christ hymn of Philippians 2:6-11. In order to achieve the great purpose of bringing human beings to God, he had to "despise shame." That is, he placed no weight at all on the negative opinion society formed of him. He did not yield to the internal desire for society's approval and affirmation because he knew greater benefits would result from his steadfastness. Jesus' example thus teaches the hearers that faith looks only to God's approval, seeks honor only as recognized by God's court. Faith therefore remains steadfast in the face of society's attempts to pressure the believer into conforming to its values. Jesus' exaltation, moreover, proves the rule by exemplifying the extreme: the most revolting and degrading death in the world's eyes leads to the most exalted status in God's eyes.

Jesus' example brings into sharper focus the examples that precede his in Hebrews 10:32—11:40. The faith of Abraham, Isaac and Jacob (Heb 11:8-22) is summarized in their confession to be "foreigners and sojourners upon the earth." Leaving behind the higher status of citizens in their native land, they voluntarily embrace the lower status of foreigner and sojourner while awaiting the promise. This marginal status, however, became a witness to their hope for a "better, heavenly homeland." Refusing to be at home in this world becomes evidence of the believer's commitment to the better homeland. The author concludes his letter by reminding the hearers of their citizenship in heaven and calling them to continue in their procession out of the entanglements of this world's cities in order to attain that homeland (Heb 13:13-14).

The second prominent example, Moses, begins life as an honored member of Pharaoh's household (Heb 11:24, 26). Faith expresses itself, however, not in maintaining honor in society's eyes but in achieving honor in God's eyes. In light of God's promises, voluntarily identifying with the "reproach of the Anointed" was of greater value than the wealth of Egypt, and the person of faith will evaluate the society's promise correctly in the light of God's reward, as did Moses (Heb 11:26). Moses is remembered and honored across the centuries precisely because he chose ill-treatment in the company of God's people rather than temporary enjoyment of safety and security in the unbelieving society (Heb 11:25). Moses' pattern of faith had already been reproduced in the community's past, when they became "partners" with those who had been imprisoned or shamefully treated for their confession (Heb 10:33-34). The author keeps calling them to walk in this pattern in the future, as he exhorts them to "remember those who are imprisoned, as if imprisoned with them; those who are being mistreated, as though you yourselves were in their skins" (Heb 13:3).

Another group of low-status examples appears in Hebrews 11:35-38. The list begins with the Maccabean-era martyrs who were tortured to death "in order to attain a better resurrection" (see 2 Macc 6—7), who came to be honored by God and the community of faith because they endured torture rather than yield to the pressure to conform to the Gentile way of life. These are followed with a remembrance of the prophets and other devoted followers of God who were pushed to the margins of society (living in caves rather than homes and clad with skins rather than cloth garments), degraded and abused on account of their obedience to God. By society's standards this constitutes a list of sorry examples, a parade of those who were utterly disgraced and had no honor. The author of Hebrews, however, introduces an ironic evaluation. Of such people, "the world was not worthy" (Heb

11:38). So with the Christians addressed here, their neighbors' response is not an evaluation of the believers' true worth but of the unbelievers' ignorance of God.

The first praiseworthy example in this closing block of exhortation, however, is the community's own past conduct (Heb 10:32-34). Using a group's own successful past is a powerful source of encouragement to repeat the desired behavior. This is seen often in speeches on the threshold of a decisive battle. The way the Christians formerly responded to loss of esteem and security on account of their faith provides them with their own best model for imitation.

Sensing the addressees' reawakening ambition to regain their lost status in their neighbors' eyes, the author uses these positive examples to direct their attention back toward the alternate arena of honor where so many have successfully competed and attained a lasting and praiseworthy remembrance before God. Like Abraham, they have left behind the esteem of their native land and chosen to become outsiders for the sake of finding a better homeland. Like Moses, they have chosen to connect themselves with God through God's people, though it has cost them dearly in terms of their reputation. Like the martyrs, they are challenged not to escape the tension and pressure through yielding to the demands of the unbelievers. Their continued rejection of the quest for society's honor will free them to pursue and achieve honor in the sight of God and of the believing community, and thus to attain the "reward" (Heb 10:35).

Reinterpreting experiences of disgrace. To empower Christians to maintain their commitments to one another and to Christ in an unsupportive environment the author re-interprets the believers' experience of disgrace at the hands of the dominant culture. From the perspective of God's purposes and rewards, the experience of deprivation and disapproval takes on positive significance. By so doing, he not only undermines the force of society's attempts at social control (i.e., by shaming the "deviants" back into conformity) but even makes these same experiences an occasion for strengthening commitment to Christ by turning the experiences of disgrace into tokens of honor and promises of greater reward.

First, the author recasts the believers' experiences of ridicule, trial, loss of status and property, and endurance of continued reproach, as the training or discipline by God of God's adopted children.[21] The community's endurance of society's rejection and censure turns out to be the token of God's acceptance and discipline (Heb 12:5-11), whereby the addressees are fitted to receive their birthright and to enjoy the honor to which God leads them (Heb 2:10). The believers' struggle to hold onto their confession in the face of society's hostility and censure is their endurance in *paideia,* the often-painful education all parents use to mold the character of their children. What society intends as an experience of disgrace aimed at bringing the deviant back into line with the values of the dominant culture, the author transforms into the proof of the believers' adoption into God's family and a powerful encouragement to persevere. Only those who have shared in discipline (Heb 12:8) will also share the rewards as "partners of Christ" (Heb 3:14) and "partners in a heavenly calling" (Heb 3:1). The believers may even cherish their marginalization and censure by society as a process by which their character is tried and

---

[21]It is of critical importance to observe that the passage identifies suffering encountered as a result of commitment and obedience to Jesus, but not other forms of suffering (such as political-economic oppression, domestic abuse, disease and the like). See N. C. Croy, *Endurance in Suffering*, SNTSMS (Cambridge: Cambridge University Press, 1998), pp. 222-24 for an excellent discussion of the application of this passage to the lives of believers. The remainder of his book supports these pastoral conclusions admirably.

proven, and which guarantees their future honor and vindication.

Second, the author uses the image of the contest *(agōn)* to speak of the traumatic experience of public disgrace and social and economic disenfranchisement suffered by the believers (Heb 10:32-34). The author sums up this experience as a competition, the rhetorical force of which was to set their endurance of hardships in the context of competition for an honorable victory. A more extended use of this imagery appears in the exhortation built around the example of Jesus in Hebrews 12:1-4. The heroes of faith are not only witnesses to God and the promised reward: the image of the encircling "cloud of witnesses" also evokes the image of the spectators of competitions or games from whom the competitors seek honor and esteem. Like those who compete in races, the believers are to "lay aside" everything that might impede their running. They are to set aside "sin" as if it were a clinging garment restricting their movement toward the prize. Sin—the temptation to yield to society's pressures—is their antagonist (Heb 12:4) in this race. According to this image, ironically, yielding to society's pressures would actually signify a disgraceful defeat (rather than an honorable rehabilitation), while resisting remains the path to honor. Finally, just as runners clear their minds of all distractions and set their eyes wholly toward the goal, so the believers are to fix their gaze on Jesus, who has run ahead to the victory in which all may share (Heb 12:2).

In an honor culture like the Greco-Roman world, athletic competitions held a great appeal, affording the victors in the various events an opportunity for achieving fame. It quickly became a realm of metaphors minority cultures used to reinterpret the disgrace and abuse suffered by their adherents (which parallel the rigors of athletic training) as an opportunity for victory and honor. We find this frequently in the writings of philosophers such as Epictetus and Dio, as well as in Jewish mi-

nority cultural literature, such as 4 Maccabees and Philo. The author of Hebrews thus applies a firmly established tradition to the needs of his audience. Moreover, interpreting the addressees' experience as a contest allows Hebrews' author to harness the widely praised virtue of courage and to define it as perseverance or "endurance" in Christian community and activity.

The community's experience of disgrace and rejection at the hands of the unbelieving society, far from being a sign of their lack of honor and their deviance, becomes a source of assurance of their worth and future reward. Their perseverance in the face of society's social control methods (e.g., dishonor and rejection) is in fact a noble contest in which believers compete for a heavenly prize, a sign of their adoption by God and the training by which they are fitted to be God's children. It is the path to honor pursued by Abraham, Moses, the martyrs and Jesus himself—those who walk such a path should fear no disgrace, for their honor is assured by God and God's Son.

Nurturing a supportive faith community. While insulating believers against the erosive pressures from outside, the author also seeks to strengthen interaction and mutual reinforcement within the group. He calls the believers "partners of Christ" (Heb 3:14) and "partners in a heavenly calling" (Heb 3:1), and challenges them to look after one another as partners, struggling forward together. He alerts them to look out for the straying, who are on the verge of succumbing to society's pressure to conform (Heb 3:12-13). He adjures them to "see to it that no one fails to obtain the grace of God" (Heb 12:15 NRSV), making each believer aware that he or she must take some responsibility for keeping his or her fellow believers on track. In the face of unbelievers' encouragements to join in the life and values of the Greco-Roman society, the Christians are to double their efforts with encouragements of their own, calling back the wavering, reinforcing the values of the group and the rewards of perseverance and loyalty. It is necessary for all members of the sect to continue to teach one another through reminder, exhortation and censure, and thus to reinforce the meaningfulness and plausability of their commitment to Jesus in a society unsupportive of the Christian enterprise (Heb 5:11-14).

The author wants encounters between believers to be frequent and meaningful in order to offset the impact of outsiders and reinforce behaviors that support the community as honorable and praiseworthy. Thus they are to "consider how to provoke one another to love and good deeds," and to continue "meeting together" and "encouraging one another, and all the more as you see the Day approaching" (Heb 10:24-25 NRSV). The author himself acts as part of this alternate court of opinion, censuring the addressees for their waning fervor and lack of zeal (Heb 5:11-14), praising them for their displays of love and service (Heb 6:9-10) and for their former demonstration of commitment even at great cost (Heb 10:32-34). The community leaders will also function as an important part of this alternate court, ascribing honor to the obedient and committed, and rebuking the half-hearted.

Further, this encouragement is to extend to material support and acts of service, so that believers help fellow Christians feel their losses less. The apparently unrelated exhortations of chapter 13 continue the author's interests in maintaining a strong group culture. He urges that "sibling love" (*philadelphia*, Heb 13:1) continue so that members of the community will continue to regard fellow believers as kin. As family, fellow believers will also be the primary source of a Christian's identity and honor, and the primary group to whom he or she owes first duty and allegiance. The exhortation to provide hospitality for traveling fellow believers (Heb 13:2) links the local Christian community to the broader Christian minority culture. The author also urges solidarity with those whom society has targeted as deviants (Heb 13:3; cf. 10:32-34; 11:25), because only the group that is willing to support its members under such conditions can maintain the loyalty and trust of its adherents, and show that society's court is not, after all, the final adjudicator of worth. Their loyalty to and confession of Christ is thus joined, in the concluding exhortations, to loyalty and support for one another:

> Through [Jesus] then, let us continually offer up a sacrifice of praise to God, that is, the fruit of lips that confess his name. Do not neglect to do good and to share what you have, for such sacrifices are pleasing to God. (Heb 13:15-16 NRSV)

The believers themselves are thus invited to exercise a sort of priestly service appropriate to the access they have to enter the holy of holies itself, before the very throne of God. This priestly service includes liturgy (praising the Patron through the Mediator) and liturgical service, but now in the everyday activity of loving, encouraging and helping one another.

Where believers take an active part in reinforcing the convictions, values and promises of the group, and where believers look to one another and to their leaders for approval rather than to the unbelieving society (Heb 13:17), it will be easier for Christians to disregard the many and forceful voices calling them back to a life that supports the existing society's values and structure. The believers will thus affirm one another's worth and honor as children of God, partners with Christ, full citizens of the city of God, and heirs of the better and lasting possessions. They may assure one another of the firm basis for their hope in the better covenant that Jesus has established between God and human beings. They will spur one another on to endure the contest and discipline that, though painful for a time, lead to eternal honor and approval before God.

EXEGETICAL SKILL
The Analysis of Intertexture (1)

Authors frequently weave the words of older, existing texts (whether those texts are written or passed on orally, ancient or contemporary) into the new texts they create. This is called "intertexture." Authors create intertexture in a variety of ways, with varying degrees of self-consciousness about introducing words from an existing text into their new text (e.g., from an indication of quotation ("as it is written . . .") to the reuse of a phrase or line without any indication that another text is being brought in) and with varying degrees of exactness. The astute hearer may recognize many of these incorporations of other texts, even if the author is not drawing attention to the fact that he is quoting. The connections made between the new text and the traditions it incorporates, moreover, will have direct bearing on how the new text is understood, what effect it will have and even how it acts back on the hearer's understanding of the older tradition.

Analysis of intertexture gives us a window into how an author is shaping and interpreting existing traditions as he addresses and shapes a new situation. This kind of analysis also provides windows into what the author hoped to accomplish by introducing these other voices into his own text, or what impact the text might have had on the hearers/readers who connected the new text with the older texts. Intertextual analysis asks the following kinds of basic questions of the text:

1. What intertextual resources is the author incorporating (or potentially using) in the new text? These resources can include the Old Testament, early Christian traditions (like Jesus sayings), and Jewish apocryphal and pseudepigraphical texts. They can also include Greco-Roman literature and the "texts" available to readers of inscriptions, coins and monuments. A rich analysis of a New Testament passage cannot afford to neglect resonances with Greco-Roman traditions and texts, or with "nonliterary" texts.[a]

2. In what way are those intertextual resources brought into the new text? Is there an explicit indication of quotation? With what degree of exactness are words from the older text brought into the newer text? What might account for the alterations?

3. How do the intertextual resources enhance the hearers' experience of the new text? How do they contribute to the topics being developed? What would be lost if the quotation, reference or allusion was not there? What

---

[a]For example, knowledge of a certain minting of a coin during the reign of Domitian, namely, the emperor's deceased son reaching out to seven stars, would obviously illumine the presentation of Jesus, God's deceased and resurrected Son, holding seven stars. Knowledge of Greek and Roman texts about the emperor and the "idea" of Rome would be essential to understand John's transfiguration of those images in Revelation. For an excellent discussion of the neglect of Greco-Roman resonances in favor of Jewish resonances, see Vernon K. Robbins, *The Tapestry of Early Christian Discourse* (London: Routledge, 1996), pp. 232-35.

specific rhetorical goals are advanced by the introduction of these resources and by the author's shaping of them?

Much of the data collecting (the goal of the first question) has already been done and the results can be found in critical commentaries (e.g., those recommended at the end of each chapter). The student will need to consult several different commentaries, however, since different commentators tend to have different areas of focus. For example, one commentator may have extensive experience with (or at least interest in) inscriptions and numismatics, and another is more in touch with Greco-Roman philosophical texts. A third follows the more traditional path of focusing mainly on the use of Old Testament texts. Of course, there is nothing like immersing yourself in the literature of a former age, and no student of mine has regretted poring over the Apocrypha, the more important pseudepigrapha, and an array of major Greco-Roman authors. If such is part of your education as well, you will be able to add to the collective scholarship in regard to intertexture.

With regard to the second question, we can be rather precise. The first thing to observe is whether or not the author is drawing direct attention to the fact that he is quoting another person or text. This carries a directness and claims a level of accuracy that demands attention from the hearer and the interpreter. This kind of intertexture is called "recitation." Recitation can be exact or inexact. If it is inexact, you should examine what the author has done to the original text that he now re-presents in inexact form. More importantly, you will want to be able to account for the alterations made to the quotation. Did the author leave out a potentially problematic word or phrase? Did he simply abbreviate the text to present the salient points more concisely? Did he substantially alter the content to make the text serve his ends better? Did he simply know a different textual tradition from the ones to which we have access?

It often happens that a New Testament author will incorporate a long string of words that are clearly a quotation from the Old Testament or some other source without giving the ancient equivalents of quotation marks. In this case the old text has been woven seamlessly into the new without the hearer having any explicit indication that a voice other than the author's has intruded into the text. These are called "recontextualizations." It is, however, often probable that the hearer would "get it" and would engage in a mutually interpretative interplay between the older tradition and the new text (see the use of Ps 22 in Mk 15). Even where the hearer might not have perceived the intertextual conversation, observing these recontextualizations gives us a window into how the author was interpreting the older traditions and strategically incorporating them.

Sometimes an author will reconfigure the older text or story as he writes the new one. John does this with the exodus story as he writes Revelation, and Mark appears to do this with Psalm 22 as he narrates the crucifixion. The dynamics and content of the older story or text shine through the new text and inform it, but the relationship is broader and looser than recitation and recontextualization.

It also happens that an author may allude to or echo another text without drawing direct attention to it or even incorporating exact words from the text. For example, in John 3:14 Jesus alludes to the lifting up of the bronze serpent by Moses. The actual words of Numbers 21:9 are not used or quoted, but it is still an unmistakable allusion to that event. Some are often harder to pin down, and a New Testament phrase or verse might be thought to reverberate with several older texts without there being enough evidence to choose one text over another. In this case the goal is not to pin down a definite reference (like trying to insert a footnote) but to analyze the impact of the several possibilities. "Echoes" are the most mercurial of intertextual conversations, and it is often difficult to know whether the author intended an echo, whether the first audience would have heard the echo or whether it is just a connection being made by the interpreter. Is the provision of manna in the wilderness to be heard behind the stories of the feeding of the five thousand? In Matthew this is a possible resonance, but one left completely unexploited by him; in John the connection is made explicit.

It is in answering the kinds of questions grouped together under number three, above, that the real rewards of this kind of analysis will come. The gathering and analyzing of the data just provides the raw materials. Now the interpreter must examine closely how the resource is used and to what end. The older resource may provide information, motivate action, legitimate a position, suggest a precedent and serve any of a thousand other rhetorical purposes. Even if your own exposure to rhetoric is limited, however, pausing long enough to ponder how the author has introduced the older resource and what he expects to gain by doing so will greatly enrich your reading of any New Testament passage.

EXAMPLE

The Use of the Jewish Scriptures in Hebrews 10:26-31

Because Hebrews is especially noted for its use of the Jewish Scriptures, we will focus on this body of resources in this example of intertextual analysis at work.[b] As we work through the passage, we will attend to each of the three steps outlined above.

---

[b]For much fuller discussions and examples of intertextual analysis, see Robbins, *Tapestry,* pp. 96-143; David A. deSilva, "A Sociorhetorical Interpretation of Revelation 14:6-13," *BBR* 9 (1999): 65-117, especially pp. 85-103; and deSilva, *Perseverance in Gratitude.*

In Hebrews 10:26 the assertion that no sacrifice can be effective for willfully *(hekousiōs)* committed sins echoes Numbers 15:22-31, where Moses distinguishes between sins committed "unintentionally" *(akousiōs)*, for which there are prescribed sacrifices, and those committed arrogantly ("with a high hand"), for which there is only punishment. The allusion substantiates the claim being made by the author that there are no remedies for willful disloyalty and disobedience in the addressees' context, a claim that is meant to remove one strong incentive to doing wrong (namely, that it can always be made right later).

In the next verse the author warns that only the "expectation of a jealous fire on the verge of eating the adversaries" (Heb 10:27) remains for those who willfully break faith with God. This is a recontextualization of Isaiah 26:11, "jealousy will take an uneducated people and now fire will eat the adversaries." The author of Hebrews condensed the Isaiah text by describing the fire as "jealous," leaving out the remainder of that first clause, and heightened the imminence of God's judgment (imminence being crucial to the arousal of the emotion of fear) by changing the future tense of the verb ("fire will eat") to a verb expressive of forthcoming action *(mellō:* "a fire about to eat"). Using Isaiah at once lends legitimacy and imminence to the threat the author invokes and thus contributes to turning the wavering among the congregation away from apostasy.

In Hebrews 10:28 the author first refers to the prescriptions of the death penalty for certain offenses against God, and then he moves to recontextualization at the end of the verse, where he reproduces Deuteronomy 17:6 verbatim ("upon the testimony of two or three witnesses"). The author has not altered the words but has certainly altered the meaning by generalizing Deuteronomy 17:6 to include all infractions against "the law of Moses" rather than the specific transgression of idolatry. Deuteronomy 17:6 is used to provide the lesser case in a lesser-to-greater argument (if offending against Torah brought these consequences, how much worse will befall the one who offends the Son?). It thus contributes materially to the development of the argument against a particular course of action (namely, violating the covenant with Jesus through shrinking back from open association with the Christian group).

Two recitations from the Song of Moses follow in Hebrews 10:30. This verse begins with a recitation of Deuteronomy 32:35: "for we know the one who said, 'Vengeance belongs to me; I will repay.' " The quotation given by the author represents a conflation of the Masoretic Text ("Vengeance is mine, and retribution") and Septuagint version ("In the day of vengeance I will repay"). The words are essentially the same, but the new context has given those words a new meaning and impact. This was originally a promise by God to vindicate his own people after they were trodden upon by their enemies. Here it becomes a warning directed toward God's own people (supporting the author's dissuasion from apostasy).

The author then recites Deuteronomy 32:36 as a second quotation ("and again, 'The Lord will judge his people'"). In the Masoretic text this verse looks forward to God's vindicating the people: "The LORD will vindicate his people, and will have compassion on his servants." The Septuagint translation, while carrying essentially the same meaning, opens up a new possibility when it renders "vindicate" as "judge." The author exploits this ambiguity, reciting the verse as a warning of God's forthcoming judgment *of* the people (rather than *on behalf of* the people). The terse, forceful statements from the Song of Moses concerning God's judgment are now brought to bear on the potential apostate, who must be reminded that "to fall into the hands of the living God is a fearful thing" (Heb 10:31). This conclusion continues to resonate with the Song of Moses, as God declares in Deuteronomy 32:39 that "there is none who shall deliver out of my hands." The ultimate danger any human being could face is to encounter God, the Judge of all, as an enemy.

The author adduces these texts to emphasize his point that God avenges violations of his honor, which is the topic of the whole Song of Moses. The addressees are reminded that there is one to fear, namely, the One with power to inflict the punishment that is greater than death: the friendship of this One is worth maintaining even in the face of the hostility of "those who can kill the body but cannot kill the soul" (Mt 10:28).

EXAMPLE

Complications in the Use of Scripture: Hebrews 10:37-39

A close and careful study of intertexture in Hebrews 10:37-39 yields some surprising but important results. The text reads:

> "For yet a little while, the coming one will arrive and will not delay: but my righteous one will live by trust, and if he or she shrinks back my soul takes no pleasure in him or her." But we are not characterized by shrinking back unto destruction but rather by trust unto the preservation of life.

The author does not introduce the quotation as the introduction of an older text into the newer one but rather weaves it directly into the fabric of the exhortation. It is technically a recontextualization, but the hearer remains very much aware, nevertheless, that the author is no longer speaking in his own voice but rather in God's ("*my* righteous one . . . *my* soul takes no pleasure"), returning to his own voice with the "we" in Hebrews 10:39.

Moreover, the author combines two different texts without giving any indication to the hearers of this blending. The author introduces a quotation from Habakkuk with a few strategic words from Isaiah 26:20: "yet a little while." In its original context this phrase spoke of the length of time that God's people are instructed to hide away in their chambers, until God's punishment of the inhabitants of the earth runs its course. In this new context, however, it emphasizes the proximity of the visitation of God or of Christ (the subject now of Hab 2:3). This serves a double rhetorical goal. Negatively, it reinforces the sense of the imminence of judgment, which will arouse fear among those who have contemplated a return to society's bosom. Positively, it provides a scriptural proof for the claim made in Hebrews 10:36, namely, that the reward is very near, thus facilitating endurance.

The author works mainly from the LXX version of Habakkuk 2:3-4 rather than the Masoretic Text (which begins to account for the differences anyone would note comparing Heb 10:37-38 with Hab 2:3-4 in the English Bible). The Masoretic Text of Habakkuk 2:3 speaks of "a vision for the appointed time; it speaks of the end, and it does not lie. If it seems to tarry, wait for it; it will surely come, it will not delay." The LXX version of Habakkuk 2:3 shifts the focus from the "vision" that will "come and not delay" to the "coming one": "there is yet a vision for the end and it will come to light at last, and not in vain: if it/he tarries, wait for it/him, for the coming one will arrive and will not delay." The ambiguity of the pronoun and pronominal suffix in Habakkuk 2:3b already invites a personal reading, which is then made explicit by the introduction of "the coming one." A second significant difference emerges in Habakkuk 2:4. The Masoretic Text reads: "Look at the proud! Their spirit is not right in them, but the righteous one lives by faith." This is transformed by the LXX translators into "if he shrinks back, my soul has no pleasure in him, but the righteous one will live by faith." The censure of the proud turns into a statement about the "coming one," namely, that if he shows cowardice he will not be pleasing to God.

The author of Hebrews *further* transforms the meaning of this text by transposing the order of LXX Habakkuk 2:4a and 4b. The phrase "if he shrinks back" applies no longer to the "coming one" but to those who wait for God's deliverance. Those who await it in trust and firmness will live, while those whose hearts fail will not please God. The way this transformation serves the author's pastoral goal is evident. The Habakkuk text can now be made to outline two courses of action—that of trusting and remaining firm, and that of shrinking back. The former explicitly leads to "life," while the one who shrinks back (an image that recalls rather sharply the affront of the wilderness generation) is censured by God—God takes no pleasure in that person. This is perhaps the most any New Testament author will "rewrite" Scripture to find support. He is excused, perhaps, by the fact that he did not present this as a quotation, instead using and reordering the language of Habakkuk to make his point.

Hebrews 10:39 provides a conclusion for this section, recontextualizing two key terms of Habakkuk 2:4: "shrinking back" and "faith/trust." The affirmation that the hearers are people "exhibiting trust" rather than "shrinking back" seeks to bring into existence the very commitment to "trust" that it affirms. The author's transposition of the clauses in Habakkuk 2:4 allows him now to distinguish between two groups—those who show trust and firmness, who preserve their lives, and those who show cowardice and distrust, who fall into destruction. Some intermediate exegetical steps are presupposed. "Living" in Habakkuk 2:4 is interpreted by the author as eschatological salvation, and failing to please God is taken to signify eschatological destruction. Reading both Isaiah 26:20 and Habakkuk 2:3-4 as oracles of end-time deliverance has made these moves possible. The hearers are thus explicitly led to identify with the group that is marked by "trust" rather than by "shrinking back," and the consequences of both courses of action are again expressed to reinforce the hearers' desire to identify with "faithfulness/trust."

Virtually any passage of the New Testament offers opportunities for the exploration of intertexture. You might wish to begin by posing the three sets of questions outlined above to one or more of the following passages: Matthew 21:33-44; Luke 4:16-30; Romans 9:1-33; Hebrews 1:1-13; 1 Peter 2:1-10; Revelation 14:1—15:4.

CONTRIBUTIONS OF HEBREWS TO EARLY CHRISTOLOGY

In the course of motivating Christians to remain connected with the Son and the people called in Jesus' name, the author of Hebrews offers some of the richest reflections on the person and work of Jesus in the entire New Testament. In particular, he focuses on the activity of the Son not only in this realm but also in the divine realm, both before his incarnation and after his ascension. Where does he find witnesses for these phases in the Son's career? There were many witnesses to Jesus' comings and goings "beginning from John's baptism up until the time he was taken up from us" (Acts 1:22), but where are the witness to the times prior and subsequent to these events?

The author of Hebrews finds these witnesses in the Old Testament Scriptures and in other intertestamental Jewish resources like the Wisdom of Solomon. Of course he read the Old Testament as a source of ethical guidance for the community of faith. This is evident in his homiletical application of the story of the wilderness generation to the situation of the Christian audience in Hebrews 3:7—4:11, his use of Esau as a pattern for nonimitation, and his extensive survey of Old Testament and intertestamental figures as patterns for imitation and emulation in Hebrews 11. Even more extensively, however, the author finds the meaning of the Old Testament and the cumulative Jewish heritage in their testimony to the achievement and significance of Jesus. Since Jesus is the self-expression of the Father that brings together all God's former partial revelations (Heb 1:1-2), the author uses Jesus as a reference point from which these older oracles take their meaning. Thus he will interpret texts from the Psalms or Isaiah as if they speak *to* Jesus, speak *about* Jesus or are even *spoken by* Jesus. All of these interpretive techniques are displayed in Hebrews 1:5—2:13. The

Scriptures can also be read typologically, that is, as proto*types* of what God would later do through Jesus or what Jesus would himself do. Thus the author can reconstruct the work of Jesus in the divine realm based on his convic-

tion that the Old Testament description of the Levitical cult provides the shadow of Jesus' more effective priestly service.

In the opening rhapsodies on the person of the Son, the author draws heavily on the "royal

---

Which Old Testament Did the Author of Hebrews Use?

The Old Testament in our English Bibles follows what is known as the Masoretic Text, the Hebrew text of the Jewish Scriptures as preserved and edited by fifth-century C.E. Jewish scholars. This substantially preserves the Hebrew text of earlier centuries, although the biblical manuscripts discovered at Qumran have shown that variations within the Hebrew text tradition certainly existed. Alongside the Hebrew text, however, stood the Greek versions of the Old Testament, translations made for the benefit of Greek-speaking Jews. Translations of the Torah began in the third-century B.C.E., and shortly after the Prophets and Writings were translated. They usually are lumped together under the title "Septuagint." This usage of the term *Septuagint* is somewhat misleading since it is anachronistic (our edited versions of the Septuagint are based primarily on fourth- and fifth-century C.E. codices) and since it tends to obscure the variations that have been found between Greek translations known to exist in the first century.

Although the quotations found in the letter to the "Hebrews" sometimes agree with the readings we know from the Hebrew text tradition, at several significant points these quotations disagree with that tradition in favor of the Greek text type. If we were to compare the citation of Psalm 40 in Hebrews 10:5-7 with Psalm 40:6-8 in the Old Testament of most printed Bibles, we would be immediately struck by the differences. The Masoretic Text (standing behind the English Bible) of Psalm 40:6 reads "sacrifice and offering you have not desired, but ears you have dug for me," whereas Hebrews (following the Septuagint text type) reads "sacrifice and offering you did not desire, but you prepared a body for me" (Heb 10:5; Ps 39:7 LXX).[a] The Hebrew text clearly speaks of "ears" to emphasize "hearing" the Torah and doing it as the work that pleases God (rather than ritual acts for sins against Torah and the like). The Greek translator probably understood the Psalm in the same way, but found the expression about "digging out ears" to be distasteful, and so substituted "a body" to live out the requirements of Torah. The Septuagint version, however, opens up the Psalm to a christological interpretation that would be impossible based on the Masoretic Text. Now Christ becomes the speaker of the Psalm and receives a body from God to effect the perfect sacrifice that replaces all the ineffective rituals of the Levitical cult. Thus what is arguably the climax of Hebrews' interpretation of Jesus' death does not rest on what we consider to be our Old Testament version but on a reading from a Greek translation of the Old Testament current in the first century C.E.

---

[a] Because the LXX joins Psalms 9 and 10 into a single hymn, the numbering of the rest of the book is off until Psalm 148 (Ps 147 being split into two hymns in the LXX).

Psalms" (Psalms 2 and 110 in particular). These psalms were originally sung at events like the coronation of the new king in ancient Judah and its annual commemoration, but they came to be applied to the eschatological heir to the throne of David—the Messiah. Promises once given to David and his heirs are now applied to Jesus, who is "Son" to God and "heir of all things" (see Ps 2:7-8), who, after his ascension, took his seat at God's right hand (an inference drawn from applying Ps 110:1 to Jesus).

The author also draws on Jewish reflection on the figure of Wisdom, who appears personified as Lady Wisdom as early as Proverbs 8. All the attributes formerly ascribed to Wisdom are now ascribed to the Son, who gives Wisdom a new face, as it were. Wisdom was seen as an active agent in creation (Prov 8:22-31; Wis 7:22; 9:9) and was thought to be involved in the ongoing governance and preservation of the created realm (Wis 7:27; 8:1). Wisdom was also lauded as the "reflection of eternal light" and "the image of God's goodness" (Wis 7:26). Such reflections on Wisdom provide the author of Hebrews with resources to understand the activity of the preincarnate Son. Thus he ascribes to the Son the roles of partner in creation and in the preservation of the created order (Heb 1:2, 3), and he affirms that the Son manifests the "radiance" and is "the exact representation" of God's nature (1:3).

The author of Hebrews read beyond the first verse of Psalm 110, which speaks of the exaltation of God's anointed to God's right hand (see Heb 1:4, 13; 8:1; 10:12), to the declaration by God that the same "you" addressed as Son in Psalm 2:7 should also serve as "priest forever in the order of Melchizedek" (Ps 110:4; see Heb 5:5-6). The thoroughgoing interpretation of Jesus' death and ascension/exaltation in terms

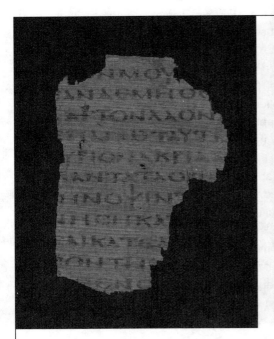
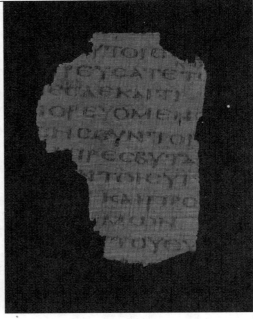

Figure 20.2. A small papyrus fragment of Exodus from the Septuagint, the Greek translation of the Old Testament. The script and spacing resembles the handwriting found in the important uncial Sinaiticus, and may indeed date to the fourth century C.E. (Courtesy of Ashland Theological Seminary)

of priestly and sacrificial categories is probably the most distinctive contribution of Hebrews to early Christology and soteriology. The Old Testament sacrificial rites, the tabernacle and the work of the Levitical priests provides him with a means of talking about the significance of Jesus' crucifixion. We should not read Hebrews 9:1—10:18 as if this is a report of some actual service that took place in the realm beyond, as if Jesus really carried a basin of his own blood into the invisible, immaterial realm and splashed it on some altar there. The Old Testament rites, especially the covenant-inauguration ceremony of Exodus 24:1-8 and the Day of Atonement liturgy of Leviticus 16, are read as prototypes of what the eschatological high priest would accomplish through his obedient death and his return to the divine realm as advocate for his followers.

Jesus' death provides the necessary prerequisite for the ratification of the new covenant spoken of by Jeremiah (Jer 31:31-34; see Heb 8:1-13), which promised the decisive removal of sins from God's memory and God's people. The defilement of sin had always kept human beings at a distance from God. This was, for the author, the lesson to be drawn from the earthly tabernacle and the limitations placed on access to its outer and inner holy places (Heb 9:1-10), and from the fact that huge numbers of animal sacrifices never transformed this arrangement so that the people could draw any closer to God (Heb 10:1-4). Jesus' procession to Calvary becomes a ritual journey "outside the camp" to the place where the bodies of the sin offerings from Yom Kippur were burned (Lev 16:27), and his death the means by which the defilement of sin is finally removed from our consciences. His journey from the grave to "heaven itself" surpasses the journey of the Levitical high priest into the holy place in the earthly tabernacle and provides assurance that the defilement of those sins has also been removed

from God's presence. Thus, in Christ, nothing stands between a cleansed and consecrated people and a holy God.

The author's Christology becomes an essential part of his development of discipleship and the ideology he hopes to implant in his audience as they continue to live in this world. Those who have become "partners of Christ" (Heb 3:14), then, have been prepared for a ritual journey of their own, following Jesus on his trajectory. The concept of perfection in Hebrews, a term that has engendered extensive scholarly discussion, is largely to be understood in terms of this journey. It speaks of the qualification of Jesus as high priest and of his entry into his final state, and of the consecration of believers for direct access to God and the completion of their own journey from this penultimate reality to their divinely appointed destiny in "heaven itself."[22]

Where there is temptation to move backward, back toward acceptance by the families, associates and neighbors who are alienated by the confession of Jesus, the author of Hebrews repeatedly reminds the believers that their destiny lies forward, further along the path that Jesus has pioneered (Heb 2:9-10; 6:19-20; 10:19-23; 13:12-14). This path takes disciples from the places of acceptance in the cities of this world to places that are "unclean" and yet where God is encountered (the ambiguous resonances of being "outside the camp," as seen in Ex 33:1-7 on the one hand, and Lev 13:45-46; Num 5:2-4; 12:14-15 on the other). As they leave behind their emotional, material and social rootedness in their earthly homeland, they come to the threshold of the "better country, that is, the heavenly one" (Heb 11:16 NRSV). Following their forerunner, and thus prepared to go into God's full presence, they are challenged to keep their forward-looking orientation until the way into those heavenly places is revealed at the last day (Heb 12:26-28).

---

[22]See, further, deSilva, *Perseverance in Gratitude*, pp. 194-204 and the literature cited there.

HEBREWS AND MINISTRY FORMATION

Seen by many as uninviting on account of the denseness of the argumentation, Hebrews nevertheless offers a wealth of resources for and timely words concerning the formation of committed disciples and vital communities of faith.[a] A sermon of the highest quality, Hebrews continues to proclaim its challenge forcefully across the millennia.

Throughout the sermon the author challenges us on the most basic question of our values and priorities. Perhaps at the root of this sermon is the challenge, *Do not lose sight of life's top priority!* How we define our first priority has a profound effect on the choices and investments we make, and, conversely, the activities and ambitions we invest ourselves in most fully reveal our first priority. The author of Hebrews would have our first priority be responding to the Word that God speaks. God's Word and our response runs as a refrain throughout the sermon. We can find this theme reflected in Hebrews 1:1-4; 2:1-4; 3:7—4:13; 5:11; 6:4-6, 13-20; 10:29-30; 11:7, 8; 12:5-6, 25-29. How we respond to the message spoken by the Son—whether or not we harden our heart when hearing God's voice, whether or not the "good word of God" has produced a suitable response—is a matter of life and death, of eternal judgment and deliverance for eternity for this author.

There are many ways that disciples can be distracted from making their response to God's Word the top priority in their lives. The addressees' situation connects very directly with the situation of many Christians throughout the world, whose contest, indeed, has been and threatens to be "to the point of blood" (Heb 12:4). Through insult, abuse, economic deprivation, intimidation, torture and even execution (whether overt or implicit, as in the starvation of entire populations), many societies pressure disciples to displace their response to God with the desire to hold onto freedom, family and life itself. Although persecution is not an issue for many disciples in the Western world, these believers might also be tempted to sell their birthright for a single meal (Heb 12:16) as they are led to give their first and best efforts to "laying up treasures on earth." How much time, energy and resources are siphoned off from growing in our relationship with God, investing ourselves in meaningful service in God's name, and discipling younger believers (including our own natural children) for the sake of acquiring better and higher-status products to gain the quality of life promoted by media and reinforced by worldly minded neighbors and friends, or for the sake of a promotion at work?

Hebrews reminds us at every turn that all such goods belong to the temporary realm, to a world that is not lasting but is destined to be "shaken" along with all who have invested in it. Instead, the author challenges us to act with a wisdom far greater than Esau's, investing in all that fits us for the world to come and for "better and lasting" possessions, and in what assists our sisters and brothers

---

[a]See, further, deSilva, *Perseverance in Gratitude,* pp. 75-82, 125-30, 175-78, 205-8, 254-60, 289-90, 328-32, 371-76, 440-44, 479-82, 518-27. Because I have written on the intersection of Hebrews with practical theology at such length there, I will keep my reflections here rather brief.

along that journey as well. This is, in effect, what it means to live by faith in Hebrews. *Faith* here is not merely about beliefs; it is also about making important decisions in our daily lives based on a broader perspective that looks to invisible and future realities as the compass points for all our deliberations. Faith acts as if all of God's promises are true and reliable. Faith orders life always with a view to pleasing God and straining forward to the inheritance that God has promised rather than settling for the shallow wages the world offers to its devotees.

To facilitate faithfulness and to remind disciples in every age why a loyal and obedient response to God remains the most rewarding course of action, the author would issue a second challenge: *Don't lose sight of what God has given you!* The experience of God's Spirit, adoption into the family of God, the promise of eternal deliverance (which, in light of the experience of so many other gifts, can be trusted), the availability of help in the face of all life's trials and temptations—if these good and enjoyable things are allowed to have their full effect in the disciples' lives, they constitute a greater catalog of benefits than the world can offer or take away!

The author brings his discussion of the good gifts that Jesus has secured for his followers to a climax with the open access to God that Jesus has won through his effective death for all who follow him. No longer is there graded access to God, with the laypeople able to approach only so near and the professionals privileged to stand between the people and the holy God. The vision of Hebrews is endangered when Christian ministers place themselves in the role of the Levitical priests or allow their congregations to elevate them to the role of mediators of divine favor. Christ did not die to limit or restrict access to God. Following the lead of the author, Christian leaders will direct believers toward prayer as the means to effectively encounter the God whose favor supplies timely help for all Christians. Prayer will assist them in their journey toward their eternal inheritance, and through it none need fall by the wayside (Heb 4:14-16). Ministry shaped by this vision will arouse in believers a fuller appreciation of the access to God opened up to them and the way their lives are now sanctified for service to God through witness, worship, acts of love and sharing (Heb 13:15-16). Such investment now brings the greatest assurance concerning our ultimate access to God, an access enjoyed as we pass from this transitory world to the abiding realm.

Closely connected with this second challenge are the author's words about God's generosity, Christ's costly favor toward us and the absolute necessity of making an appropriate return. The grave danger facing some members of the congregation is that they will not value God's gifts and favor appropriately, and thus they will choose friendship with the world over friendship with God. To such menaces the author shouts: *Don't lose sight of the honor and gratitude due God and God's Son!* As we become more aware (and help our fellow believers become more aware) of the astounding generosity that God has lavished on us in Christ, our awareness of the gravity of properly valuing and responding to that generosity also increases. Theology and ethics, belief and response, creed and Christian life are held together and mutually energized by the author's words about (1) the grace relationship initiated by Christ, and (2) the disciples' obligation to value this relationship enough to do whatever it takes, to pay whatever price it involves, in order to remain loyal and obedient to God in Christ. Half-hearted attention to this relationship, while we pour our lives into temporary pleasures and goods, is as much an affront to our great Benefactor as open apostasy, and thus it is as dangerous to us.

A current that has run through many New Testament texts, and that also flows through Hebrews, is the importance of vital Christian community for individual disciples to progress to maturity in the faith and arrive at God's goal. Throughout this sermon we have observed the author calling out to his congregation: *Don't lose sight of one another!* The author challenges Christian leaders in every age to nurture a supportive faith community in which fellow believers invest themselves in each other's lives and into making sure everyone attains God's gift. This mutual investment is to occur at a level more appropriate for natural kin than for members of a voluntary organization, since in Jesus we truly become sisters and brothers, and we are given as gifts and resources for one another in our journey as a family.

To offset the effects of the non-Christian society's witness to what is valuable, praiseworthy and important, believers need to gather frequently with one another, both in the formal settings of worship and informally for support and encouragement. Disciples are challenged to provide for one another's needs so that the grace of God will indeed prove sufficient for the journey. Those most targeted by the unbelieving world for reclamation or marginalization must be all the more completely supported with sibling love, sharing of resources, prayer and all those things that will assist them to bear the cost of their commitment to Jesus (Heb 10:32-34; 13:3). This challenge takes on new urgency and meaning as Western churches become aware of the needs of sisters and brothers worldwide, especially in countries where Christianity is a restricted religion, and as the means to help increase. As we grow to think globally in so many areas, our definitions of church and the family of God need to keep step. The author of Hebrews models many strategies for empowering costly witness and costly obedience: (1) the assurance that bearing the price of such witness and obedience marks a disciple as another example of faith, (2) the assurance that through the endurance of hardship in the name of Christ God is shaping the believer for his or her destiny as God's child, and (3) the challenge to compete nobly and victoriously against sin, the ultimate adversary behind the onslaughts of unbelievers. Even in relatively "free" countries, these strategies can be employed to encourage disciples to bear the considerably milder costs of witness and obedience.

FOR FURTHER READING

Attridge, Harold W. *The Epistle to the Hebrews.* Philadelphia: Fortress, 1989.

Croy, N. Clayton. *Endurance in Suffering: Hebrews 12:1-13 in Its Rhetorical, Religious, and Philosophical Contexts.* SNTSMS. Cambridge: Cambridge University Press, 1998.

deSilva, David A. *Perseverance in Gratitude: A Socio-Rhetorical Commentary on the Epistle "to the Hebrews."* Grand Rapids: Eerdmans, 2000.

Eisenbaum, Pamela M. *The Jewish Heroes of Christian History: Hebrews 11 in Literary Context.* SBLDS 156. Atlanta: Scholars Press, 1997.

Ellingworth, Paul. *The Epistle to the Hebrews.* NIGTC. Grand Rapids: Eerdmans, 1993.

Filson, Floyd V. *"Yesterday": A Study of Hebrews in the Light of Chapter 13.* London: SCM Press, 1967.

Guthrie, George H. *The Structure of Hebrews: A Text-Linguistic Analysis.* Leiden: Brill, 1994.

Hurst, Lincoln D. *The Epistle to the Hebrews: Its Background of Thought.* SNTSMS 65. Cambridge: Cambridge University, 1990.

Koester, Craig. *The Epistle to the Hebrews.* AB. Garden City, N.Y.: Doubleday, 2001.

Lane, William Lane. *Hebrews 1-8.* WBC 47A. Dallas: Word, 1991.

———. *Hebrews 9-13.* WBC 47B. Dallas: Word, 1991.

Long, Thomas. *Hebrews.* Interpretation. Louisville, Ky.: Westminster John Knox, 1997.

Pfitzner, Victor C. *Hebrews.* ACNT. Nashville: Abingdon, 1997.

21

THE EPISTLE OF JAMES

Promoting Consistency of Belief and Behavior

After reading the letters of Paul and other members of the Pauline circle, some wonder what to make of James. Here is no explicit reflection on Christology, no development of doctrines, no obvious situation requiring remedy. Indeed, so striking is the lack of attention to reflection on Jesus in this letter that Martin Luther held the letter in lowest esteem, calling it an "epistle of straw."

Contrary to this shallow estimation, James serves an essential role within the New Testament. From beginning to end James promotes the disciple's integrity, the "wholeness" or "completeness" that comes from walking straight in line with our convictions and beliefs. James urges disciples to let what they have learned about God and from God to move like leaven throughout their whole person—mind, heart, speech and action. The opposite of integrity is "double-mindedness," living now according to God's wisdom and later according to what the world deems wise, setting our heart now on God and later on our own desires. Throughout his presentation of his "wisdom," James challenges the disciples who would think one thing with their mind but then fail to allow that conviction to shape their

behavior in real-life situations, falling in line with earthly wisdom instead. Rather than set forward more doctrine, James calls believers to deepen their grasp of what they have already learned so that their whole persons may be transformed by the "implanted word that has the power to save your souls" (Jas 1:21 NRSV).

"JAMES" AND HIS READERS

Who wrote "James"? The author identifies himself merely as "Jacob" (Greek, *Iakōbos*), a "slave of God and of the Lord Jesus Christ" (Jas 1:1). Who is this "Jacob," or "James"? Several disciples in leadership roles were named James: James the son of Zebedee and brother of John, one of the inner circle of Jesus' disciples; James the son of Alphaeus, another of the Twelve; James "the lesser" or "younger"; and James, the half-brother of Jesus (Mk 6:3). Of these four, most scholars believe only the last to have sufficient authority and visibility (not to mention longevity) to be seriously considered as the James named at the head of this letter.[1] James became a disciple after encountering the risen Jesus (see 1 Cor 15:7; Gal 1:19) and eventually the leader of the church in Jerusalem (in Acts, at least, the acknowledged leader of the Chris-

---

[1] E.g., R. J. Bauckham, *James*, New Testament Readings (London: Routledge, 1999), p. 16; Luke Timothy Johnson, *The Letter of James*, AB (Garden City, N.Y.: Doubleday, 1995), p. 92. It is, however, still possible that the author was an otherwise unknown Christian teacher (Jas 3:1) with the common name "Jacob" (see Todd C. Penner, *The Epistle of James and Eschatology*, JSNTSup 121 [Sheffield, U.K.: Sheffield Academic Press, 1996], pp. 263-64).

tian movement). He was so well known that Jude found it best to identify himself simply as "the brother of James" (Jude 1:1).

Many scholars have disputed the traditional ascription of this letter to James of Jerusalem or, for that matter, to any James raised in Palestine and operative during the first generation of Christianity. Among the more important objections are the following.

The letter shows extensive connections with Greco-Roman ethical topics and with the form of the Stoic "diatribe." These are odd features for a text coming out of Jerusalem. The diatribe was a common way Greco-Roman philosophers presented their ethics and dismantled opposing positions. The diatribe frequently addresses its hearers directly, advances a case by posing question and answer, carries on dialogues with imaginary conversation partners, uses "speech in character" to articulate positions being dismantled by the author, and employs standard formulas like "what is the benefit?" or "show me, then."[2] James indeed shares these formal features and treats many of the same ethical problems that Greco-Roman ethicists took on. But Cynics and Stoics were known to be active especially in Galilee, and Jerusalem itself was a cosmopolitan city. James would have had ample opportunities throughout his life there to hear Stoics and Cynics expound their ethics via the diatribe.

Since James attacks Paul in James 2:14-26, especially positions Paul develops in Galatians and Romans, James would have to write after those letters were written, but still before his death in 62 C.E. Moreover, James's lack of clarity about the debate (speaking as if Paul opposed faith to "good works" rather than to "works of the Law" like circumcision and other distinctively Jewish aspects of Torah) *shows that James writes long after the real debate was forgotten.* This is a more complicated objection, but at its heart it is the assumption that James 2:14-26 is a direct attack on Paul's position and, moreover, that it is dependent on knowledge of Paul's letters rather than on information gathered orally from those who heard Paul, or even from Paul himself (e.g., at one of the face-to-face meetings of James with Paul). The question of James's "anti-Pauline" position will be taken up below.

The author of James has an exceptional grasp of Greek, even to the point of attending to rhetorical ornamentation and devices throughout. It strains credulity to think the son of a Galilean artisan family capable of this level of fluency in a second language.[3] It is certainly true that the Greek of James is of a high quality and that the author is well-skilled in the use of puns, word plays and other rhetorical ornaments characteristic of the period.[4] The objection rests, however, on the outdated presupposition that literary proficiency in Greek was beyond the reach of James. J. N. Sevenster devoted a monograph to examining this question with particular reference to the letter of James, concluding that this particular sacred cow should be put out to pasture.[5]

The objection, moreover, does not take adequate account of James's life experience. The author of this letter is not the Galilean craftsperson of 32 C.E., but the head of the

---

[2]See, further, Johnson, *Letter of James,* pp. 8-10; D. F. Watson, "James 2 in Light of Greco-Roman Schemes of Argumentation," *NTS* 39 (1993): 118-19.

[3]Eduard Lohse, *The Formation of the New Testament,* trans. M. E. Boring (Nashville: Abingdon, 1981), pp. 208-9; Martin Dibelius, *James,* Hermeneia (Philadelphia: Fortress, 1975), p. 17.

[4]On the quality of the language, see Johnson, *James,* pp. 8-10; for excellent analyses of the argumentation and ornamentation of James 2:1—3:13, see D. F. Watson, "James 2," pp. 94-121; and his "The Rhetoric of James 3:1-12 and a Classical Pattern of Argumentation," *NovT* 35 (1993): 48-64.

[5]J. N. Sevenster, *Do You Know Greek? How Much Greek Could the First Jewish Christians Have Known?* (Leiden: Brill, 1968), pp. 4-21, 190-91; also J. P. Meier, *A Marginal Jew* (Garden City, N.Y.: Doubleday, 1991), 1:255-68; Penner, *Epistle of James and Eschatology,* pp. 35-47.

Christian movement in the cosmopolitan city of Jerusalem as late as 61 C.E. A person can grow in many ways and learn much in the course of thirty years spent in a very different venue and occupation. Richard Bauckham underscores the importance of the Jerusalem church in the evangelization and instruction of not only the residents of Jerusalem (10 to 20 percent of whom had Greek as their native language)[6] but also Jewish pilgrims from the Diaspora. Those charged with this task, especially the leaders of the movement, would have to grow in Greek fluency and even begin to use the Greek translation of the Jewish Scriptures for the equipping of new converts who would eventually return to their homelands to spread the word and form communities of faith.[7] The language of James could be read as evidence, in other words, for the linguistic legerdemain possible in Palestine rather than as an a priori objection to authorship by a religious leader in Palestine.

If the author of James is from Galilee or Judea, it is surely strange that he knows so well, and depends so fully on the Greek translation of the Jewish Scriptures throughout this letter. It is true in most instances that the language of James resonates with the LXX rather than the known Hebrew texts (e.g., the quotation of Prov 3:34 at Jas 4:6 and the recontextualization of Is 5:9 at Jas 5:4), though not in every case (e.g., "slow to anger" in Jas 1:19 represents better the Hebrew idiom used in the Hebrew version of Prov 14:29; 15:18 than the LXX, which uses *makrothymos*; see also the quotation of Prov 10:12 in Jas 5:20, which resembles a fresh translation from the Hebrew, where "love covers all sins" rather than a reading from the LXX, where "love covers those not loving strife").

This objection, however, has already been answered above. As the leader of a movement involved in converting and instructing Greek-speaking Jews from across the Diaspora, James would have grown in his knowledge and use of the LXX version of the Jewish Scriptures. His use of LXX readings is all the more appropriate as he formulates his wisdom for an audience who reads this version, and not the Hebrew text, as its Scripture.

Although it remains possible that James is a pseudonymous document written after the execution of Jesus' brother in 62 C.E., or by an otherwise unknown James at any point in the first century, a strong case can be made that we find in this letter the tradition passed on by the James who otherwise figures so prominently in early church history. Some incidental observations that favor Jacobean authorship and an early (pre-62 C.E.) date are:

- The simple self-designation and lack of attempts to link the letter more obviously to James of Jerusalem by self-referential speech and "memoirs" (as in 2 Peter) favors authenticity rather than pseudonymity.
- The letter's close connection with the Jesus tradition, especially in a form that cannot simply be identified as literary dependence on one or more of the Gospels.[8]
- The absence of the emphasis on church order, the waning eschatological expectation and the concern over identifying and resisting heresies that are generally supposed to indicate postapostolic date.

The absolute *terminus ante quem* is set by the use of James by the *Shepherd of Hermas* (early- to mid-second century C.E.) and most probably by *1 Clement*, hence a date prior to 96 C.E.[9] The early reception of James in and its

---

[6]Martin Hengel, *The "Hellenization" of Judaea in the First Century After Christ* (Philadelphia: Trinity Press International, 1989), p. 10.

[7]Bauckham, *James*, pp. 18, 24.

[8]See Johnson, *Letter of James*, p. 119; P. J. Hartin, *James and the Q Sayings of Jesus* (Sheffield, U.K.: JSOT Press, 1991).

[9]Johnson provides a thorough discussion of the points of the possible and probable influence of James on these two documents (*Letter of James*, pp. 72-80).

How Christian Is James?

Because James contains little that is distinctively Christian, it has been suggested that it was originally a Jewish manual of instruction given a mere veneer of Christianity by means of the references to Jesus in James 1:1; 2:1. But even though James does not reflect on the death and resurrection of Jesus or develop any other distinctively Christian theology, the author's prominent and broad use of Jesus traditions argues for an author and readers who regard Jesus' teachings as authoritative and normative, hence it is "Christian." Compare the following passages in James with the corresponding passages in the Gospels (remembering that James is more probably dependent on oral traditions rather than one or more of the written Gospels for access to Jesus' teachings):

- James 1:4; Matthew 5:48 ("maturity/completeness" as the goal of discipleship)
- James 1:5; Matthew 7:7 (assurance that God gives generously to those who ask: "ask . . . and it will be given to you")
- James 1:22; Matthew 7:24-27 (the importance of doing, not merely hearing, the "word")
- James 2:5; Luke 6:20 (the poor will be heirs of the kingdom of God)
- James 2:13; Matthew 5:7 (the merciful will be shown mercy)
- James 2:14; Matthew 7:21 (doing the will of God [the "works" that spring from faith] is what matters)
- James 3:12; Matthew 7:16 (the fruits show the kind and quality of the tree)
- James 4:4; Matthew 6:24; John 15:18-19 (one cannot be a friend both to God and the world [or its treasures])
- James 4:10; Matthew 23:12; Luke 14:11 (those who humble themselves will be exalted by God)
- James 4:11-12; 5:9; Matthew 7:1 (against condemning one's neighbor, for fear of God's judgment)
- James 5:2-3; Matthew 6:19-21 (laying up treasures on earth where rust and moth destroy, and the consequences of laying up treasure rather than dealing justly with others)
- James 5:12; Matthew 5:34-37 (against swearing "either by heaven or by earth")

Many of these traditions spoken by Jesus also have parallels in contemporary or previous Jewish literature. Nevertheless, the accumulation of so many parallels between James and Jesus suggests that Jesus' teachings—both Jesus' passing along of available tradition and innovation within that tradition—were highly formative for James and so, James expected, for the lives of his audiences.

---

authoritative use by the Roman church (where Clement and Hermas originated) accord with the importance of the Jewish-Christian community there and the explicit claim in James 1:1 that this was a communication to Jewish-Christian communities in the Diaspora.

Who read James? James addresses the twelve tribes in the Diaspora. Whatever we make of this way of describing the readers, the author seems to address a very broad audience whose circumstances will vary widely from place to place. Students need to be cautious

Figure 21.1. A fragmentary, late third-century papyrus found at Oxyrhynchus, Egypt, source of many literary and nonliterary papyrus discoveries. This page contains James 2:26—3:9 (*P.Oxy. IX 1171*). (Photo courtesy of Department of Rare Books and Special Collections, Princeton University Library)

when mirror reading this text, since it addresses, ostensibly, Christians around the known world. Unlike Paul's letter, James is not occasioned by some specific problems to be inferred from the contents. Rather, it is wisdom instruction concerning what James would have considered typical conditions and challenges facing Christians in a great variety of locales.[10] James assumes a number of things about his readers. For example, he expects them to assemble together and to have "teachers" and "elders" as leaders in the group (Jas 2:2; 3:1; 5:14) performing special ministries (though "elders" might not refer to an office so much as a group of senior Christians; see p. 862 on 1 Pet 5:1-4). He expects oppression by the rich non-Christians to be a sufficiently familiar reality (Jas 2:6-7).[11] From decades of teaching and leadership James may have learned the most common and important issues in Christian community needing to be addressed, but the general and typical nature of his letter prevents us from drawing up any real profile of the addressees.

Most scholars agree that it would be most natural to regard the intended readership as Jewish Christians. These scholars point out that "twelve tribes" was a designation for the totality of ethnic Jews, while "Diaspora" referred to the alien residence of Jews everywhere outside Palestine (and, arguably, even in Palestine while under Gentile domination). But the early church, comprising Jews and Gentiles, took over the labels used by ethnic Israel as it developed its identity. *Diaspora* is used in 1 Peter 1:1 clearly as a designation for the life of Gentile Christians in the world.[12] We cannot

---

[10]Bauckham, *James*, pp. 26-28.

[11]James 2:6 probably refers not to religious persecution but to the kind of oppression that can also make use of legal means to achieve its ends, manipulating the courts and perverting justice for the sake of gain (Sophie Laws, "James, Epistle of," *Anchor Bible Dictionary*, ed. David N. Freedman [Garden City, N.Y.: Doubleday, 1992]: 3.623). Brown mistakenly regards the oppressors as rich Christians, but they blaspheme the name invoked over the "you" of the addressees, not over "themselves" (see Raymond E. Brown, *Introduction to the New Testament* [Garden City, N.Y.: Doubleday, 1997], p. 730 n. 13).

[12]It is not so unsuitable as a reference to Gentile Christians as Bauckham senses (*James*, p. 14). So prominent an exception may suggest a wider practice.

be certain, then, about the ethnic composition of the addressees based on James 1:1. More telling is James's silence with regard to typically Gentile vices requiring correction; this has been taken as an argument for a Jewish Christian audience.[13] There is no mention of idolatry or the sexual vices assumed to characterize the Gentile world, topics that are frequent in Paul's letters to predominantly Gentile Christian congregations (even those that weren't "misbehaving") and in 1 Peter.

COMPOSITION AND STRUCTURE

Compared to the tightly knit, thematically consistent arguments advanced by Paul and the author of Hebrews, James comes across as a disjointed collection of good advice that lacks an overarching theme or logical development. So great was this impression on Martin Dibelius that he concluded that James has no real structure at all, being just a collection of wise sayings arranged by catchwords and the like.[14] James resembles a collection similar to the Sermon on the Mount or other extended blocks of independent sayings that have been arranged to give the appearance of coherence by a later editor. Another suggestion is that the letter represents a compendium of James's wisdom, comparable in structure to what we find in Ben Sira.[15] Both are thoughtfully compiled and arranged (by the sage himself), but do not seek logical development from beginning to end.

We must be careful not to impose order and connections between paragraphs where none exist. Duane Watson, however, used rhetorical criticism to demonstrate the argumentative coherence of large blocks of James, at least at the level of the extended paragraph (e.g., Jas 2:1-26; 3:1-13).[16] His work shows that if parts of James are capable of such careful composition and development, other parts that appear disjointed (like Jas 1:2-21) may also have an inner coherence and logical development,[17] and the whole may enjoy more than haphazard organization.

Beyond a series of individual, discernible "essays" on particular moral themes (see preceding outline), does anything more give the work thematic and logical coherence? A particular question here concerns the coherence and function of James 1:1-27. Some read this as an *epitome,* a summary, of the contents of the whole,[18] giving a preview of themes to be treated at greater length later. Thus the theme of patient endurance announced in James 1:2-4 reemerges in James 5:7-11; the theme of the rich and the humble (or poor) announced in James 1:9-11 is visited again in James 2:1-13; 4:16—5:6;[19] the theme of being lured into sin by our own desires receives further attention in James 4:1-10.

We can detect the development of a single topic through a variety of angles. The simple instruction to be "quick to hear" (Jas 1:19) leads to an exhortation to put what is heard into practice (Jas 1:22-25), followed by two specific examples of how this must be done. First we must hear Jesus' choice of the poor as

---

[13]Brown, *Introduction to the New Testament,* p. 728. Brown also regards the use of the term *synagogē* (Jas 2:2) to refer to the gathering of believers as pointing in a Jewish direction, but the use of *ekklēsia* in James 5:14 mitigates the force of this observation.

[14]Dibelius, *James,* p. 11.

[15]Bauckham, *James,* pp. 108-11.

[16]Watson, "James 2"; "The Rhetoric of James 3:1-12."

[17]An attempt at exposing this inner coherence of James 1:2-21 follows in the section "The Message of James" (see pp. 823-30).

[18]For example, see Johnson, *Letter of James,* pp. 14-15.

[19]The terms for "poor" or "humble" in James 1:9 and "rich" in James 1:10 emerge again in James 4:6 (with humility becoming a major theme through the end of the chapter) and James 5:1 (with the wrongful accumulation and use of wealth becoming topical through Jas 5:6).

An Outline of James

Epistolary greeting (1:1)

The joyful results of enduring temptations (1:2-4)

Receiving wisdom from God (perhaps specifically as a resource for enduring temptation?) (1:5-8)

Transvaluation of poverty and wealth (1:9-11)

The source of temptation and the source of all good gifts (1:12-18)

Listening and humility preferred to speech and anger (1:19-21)

Doing the Law versus hearing only (1:22-25)

Against partiality (2:1-13)

The importance of putting faith into action (2:14-26)

The challenge of controlling the tongue (3:1-12)

The results of worldly wisdom contrasted with the wisdom from above (3:13—4:10)

Humility in evaluating our neighbor (4:11-12)

Humility in remembering our dependence on God (4:13-17)

Denunciation of those who grow rich unjustly (5:1-6)

Exhortation to patient endurance (5:7-11)

Prohibition against oaths, in favor of absolute honesty in all speech (5:12)

Restoring the sick and sinful (5:13-20)

heirs of the kingdom of God and allow this to shape our interaction with people (Jas 2:1-13); second, the author insists that faith is not just a matter of knowing, the result of hearing, but of living out God's love in care for those in need (Jas 2:14-26). The second part of the aphorism in Jas 1:19, "let everyone be . . . slow to speak," leads to a number of teachings about the difficulty of controlling our speech and using it only in ways that are consistent with our confession about God (e.g., that people are created in God's image, Jas 3:9; that all human purposes are subordinate to God's, Jas 4:13-15; that all stand equally under God's judgment, not one another's judgment, Jas 4:11-12). The instruction to be "slow to anger" (and the corresponding importance of "gentleness," Jas 1:21) is developed in the discussion of the worldly wisdom that produces strife and

enmity as opposed to the wisdom from above that results in peace and a humble heart (3:13—4:10). Such obvious thematic connections help to give James's instruction an overall coherence.

There are, however, indications of even more conscious organization of the book following the first chapter, with James 1:26-27 providing a sort of thesis statement that will be expounded on throughout the remainder of the book. James 1:26 cites two flaws that render religion empty—failure to control speech, and the tendency to indulge one's own heart,[20] two topics that dominate James 3:1—4:10. James 1:27 then provides the thesis statement for James 2:1-26: the teaching against partiality in James 2:1-13 provides one concrete example of how the Christian community is to remain "unstained by the world," here the world's pref-

---

[20]Reading *apatan* as "to indulge" rather than "to deceive" (see Johnson, *Letter of James*, pp. 210-11).

James and the Jewish Wisdom Tradition

Compare the following passages in James with the earlier Jewish wisdom texts listed below:

James 1:13; Sirach 15:11-13 (God is not the source of temptation and sin.)

James 1:19; Sirach 5:11 (on being "quick to listen")

James 1:19; Sirach 5:11—6:1 (also Sir 22:27—23:1; 23:7-8 on being "slow to speak")

James 1:19; Proverbs 14:29; 15:18; Ecclesiastes 7:9; Sirach 28:8-12 (on being "slow to anger")

James 2:6; Proverbs 14:21 (on the proper treatment of the poor)

James 3:6; Proverbs 16:27 (on speech being like a fire)

James 3:9-12; Sirach 28:12 (the anomaly of the mouth as the source of opposite substances and effects)

James 4:6; Proverbs 3:34; Sirach 2:17-20 ("God opposes the proud, but shows favor to the humble")

James 4:13-14; Proverbs 27:1 (on not boasting about tomorrow since tomorrow is beyond human control)

James 5:12; Sirach 23:9-11 (against swearing oaths)

James 5:20; Proverbs 10:12 (on covering over offenses with love/restoration of the sinner)

James seldom quotes another wisdom text, but these parallels show that James treats many of the same topics in much the same way as the earlier Jewish wisdom tradition, adding to the collective wisdom of that tradition.

---

erence for the rich and powerful, and contempt for the poor and powerless; James 2:14-26 develops the claim that "real" religion results in acts of charity toward those in need.

This is not to suggest that James should be read as a linear, logically coherent progression of thought in the same way that Romans, Galatians, 1 Peter or Hebrews are. But there is also far more thematic connection and logical development of ideas than Dibelius allowed. Part of the appeal of James has been its invitation to meditate on its seemingly disconnected instructions and to synthesize from them that deeper coherence which stands at the root of James's vision for discipleship and Christian community.

GENRE AND PURPOSE

Based on the epistolary opening of James 1:1 this text falls under the category of "letter," even though it lacks all the closing epistolary con-

ventions. Unlike most letters, it lacks the kind of situation-specific occasion that we come to expect from letters after studying the other nineteen canonical letters (even 1 Peter). It most resembles the paraenetic letter, the kind of letter that gives ethical advice that is generally assumed to be true and irrefutable, holding up core values of the culture in which it is written.

Beyond this epistolary framework (if one verse can be called a framework), James finds its closest counterparts in the exhortations of the Greco-Roman ethical philosophers like Epictetus, who use the form of the diatribe to promote a particular set of behaviors and attitudes while calling contrary behaviors and attitudes into question, and in the collections of advice attributed to Pseudo-Isocrates, in which instructions for a wide variety of typical circumstances are authoritatively laid out. If differs from these pagan counterparts in that it engages in this enterprise within the context of the Jewish Christian wisdom and ethical traditions, and within the context of Christian community life rather than individual success or attainment of virtue (though the degree of overlap with Greco-Roman ethics is truly striking and worthy of attention).

Outside of the blocks of Jesus sayings preserved in the Synoptic Gospels, James comes the closest of all New Testament texts to reflecting the Jewish wisdom tradition and, indeed, having a claim to belong to that tradition.

In addition to the extensive intertexture with Proverbs, Ben Sira and other Jewish wisdom literature (including Jesus), wisdom itself is topical in a manner rarely seen in the New Testament. Like the contrast between Wisdom and Folly in Proverbs, James also contrasts two kinds of thinking—the wisdom "from above" and the "earthly" wisdom (Jas 3:13—4:4). Even his interest in law (Jas 1:22-25; 2:8-11; etc) goes hand in hand with his interest in Wisdom, since the latter came more and more to include the study and doing of the former.[21] James differs from collections of wisdom sayings in his focus strictly on morality rather than social conventions like fostering friendships, behavior at dinner parties, management of the household and the like.[22] James's interest in the practical issues that face disciples in Christian community, treating topics that have many parallel treatments in wisdom literature, further suggests that James be read as a Christian development of that genre.

James also shares a great number of ethical ideals and admonitions with the broader body of Jewish ethical writings from the Second Temple Period (including the wisdom of Jesus), to say nothing of the Greco-Roman philosophers.[23] Even when James resonates with apocalyptic texts, like 1 Enoch,[24] it is with passages in which instruction is being given, behaviors being commended or censured and the like (thus with those parts of the texts that themselves resonate most fully with wisdom discourse and apocalyptic discourse).

James writes "Christian wisdom"—wisdom now profoundly shaped by the addition of Jesus as the authoritative teacher of Wisdom. Since no particularly new crisis or situation can be discerned from the general and typical instructions brought together in this letter, the main purpose for its composition may be nothing other than James's desire (or the desire of Jewish Christian disciples who urged him to this task) to preserve and disseminate the "wisdom" he had gathered to the wider (Jewish) Christian community. It would have served the ancillary goal of refreshing the sense of connectedness between Jewish Christian communities abroad and the center of the movement in Jerusalem.

JAMES AND PAUL

A common presupposition about James's purposes in writing is that he seeks to counter Pauline influence. In the history of biblical interpretation James and Paul have frequently been depicted as bitter adversaries, each representing an opposing gospel. James would have taken the church in the direction of remaining a sect of Judaism; Paul led the church in a more universalist direction. The controversy in Galatia is read, according to this model, as a

---

[21]See David A. deSilva, *Introducing the Apocrypha* (Grand Rapids: Baker, 2002), pp. 176-78.

[22]Such attention to "manners" is especially prominent in Ben Sira. See deSilva, *Introducing the Apocrypha*, pp. 178-81; Johnson, *Letter of James*, p. 81.

[23]See Johnson, *Letter of James*, pp. 27-29, 34-48 for a thorough review of points of contact between James and extrabiblical texts.

[24]Compare, for example, James 5:1-6 with *1 Enoch* 97:1-10, where we find shared motifs of the cries of the righteous and the oppressed rising up to God and bringing down judgment on the rich who have established their wealth unjustly, the futility of riches unjustly gained in the light of God's judgment, and encouragement to the righteous to take heart in light of this fact (see Jas 5:7-8; *1 Enoch* 96:1; 97:1)

direct attack on the Pauline mission by emissaries sent from James specifically to subvert Paul's message and bring it more in line with the mother church in Jerusalem.

According to this anti-Pauline reading of James, James 2:14-26 seeks to set the record straight about the alleged opposition of faith and works, about what is truly required for justification and about the real import of Abraham's example (invoking Gen 15:6, as does Paul). The similarities in language and content between James and Paul is often taken to suggest that James is responding to Paul in Paul's own idiom. James 2:24, in particular, sounds like a corrective to such statements as are found in Romans 3:28 or Galatians 2:16. However, at the same time, James misunderstands Paul, even as he opposes him. Paul was quite clear that faith stood against the ethnic privilege of Jews (hence, against "works of the law"), not against "good works," as in James 2:14-26. In the end this line of reasoning becomes an argument in favor of a late date and pseudonymous authorship because the real James would not have misunderstood his rival thus.

Even if we grant that the shared language and concepts point, in some sense, to James's dependence on Paul's language rather than mutual dependence on a common tradition,[25] the question remains concerning the nature of James's response. When James insists that genuine faith—faith worth anything—must reveal itself through the doing of acts of charity and other manifestations of obedience to God, is James actually opposing Paul? When Paul himself speaks of works, he does so in the same way as James—as the necessary fruits of a living faith. Romans 2:13 compares quite favorably with James 1:22; 2:24, where "being justified" happens as a result of doing what is good

in God's sight (whether this is expressed as "works," as in Jas 2:14-26, or "doing the law," as in Rom 2:13). Paul is similarly committed to the doing of the commandments of God (1 Cor 7:19), or to the fulfilling of the "just requirement of the law" (Rom 8:4), by Christians empowered by the Spirit to this end.

James, moreover, does not oppose faith, which is operative in all works that lead to righteousness (Jas 2:22) and which is assumed to characterize all participants in the debate in James 2:14-26. The issue for James is not "faith versus works" but "what kind of faith justifies." When Paul opposes faith to works, it is always "works of Torah" in the sense of those rites and observances that give the Jew a ground for "boasting" over the Gentile, thus threatening the unity of the new people being formed in Christ.

The opposition between James and Paul is thus apparent, not real. The problem has come as scholars, rightly noting the similarity in language between, for example, Galatians 2:15-16 or Romans 3:21-28 and James 2:14-26, have assumed that these passages are addressing the same question. In fact, the two authors are addressing different questions in these places: where they address the same question (should faith in Christ result in the doing of good works?) the two authors are in agreement. If James has in fact taken up Pauline language, it is not to oppose Paul's position. Rather, it is to advance James's own exhortation to his readers to be "doers of the word and not hearers only" (Jas 1:22, 25).

THE MESSAGE OF JAMES

Temptation. James opens with advice concerning "testing" or "temptation" and the results of a successful encounter with it (Jas 1:2-4, 12-15).[26] The necessity of encountering tests on

---

[25]This position is advanced quite cogently in Penner, *Epistle of James and Eschatology,* pp. 47-74 (in the context of a thorough review of the question of anti-Paulinism in James); see also Johnson, *Letter of James,* pp. 58-65; 111-16.

[26]Many English translations tend to use different words to translate the Greek *peirasmoi* in James 1, obscuring an important connection that would have been apparent to the Greek readers. The "trials" discussed in James 1:2-3 are the same as the "temptations" discussed in James 1:12-15, and so they should be interpreted as developing the same topic.

the path to gaining wisdom and to being approved or proven in God's sight, and of persevering in the face of testing with singleness of mind and conduct, had long been acknowledged (Sir 2:1-4, 12-14; Wis 3:4-5). James differs from Wisdom 3:4-5 on an essential point, however, stressing that God is not the source of these "tests," which are rather posed by "one's own desire," which lures and entices the individual (Jas 1:13-14). On this point Ben Sira's position undergirds James's own: "Do not say 'It was [God] who led me astray'; for God has no need of the sinful" (Sir 15:12).

James's primary focus is on the testing of a person's faithfulness from within rather than from without. His focus is not on external pressures and persecution (unlike 1 Pet 1:6-7, where these are the trials that prove the genuineness of faith) so much as the challenges of being lured away from obedience by the duplicity of our own desires. The contest of faith for him is not against powers external to ourselves, but against our internal vulnerability to the desires that derail faith by dividing our focus between God and this world. Even if James does include the experience of persecution under the heading "trials," his focus remains on the importance of the internal battle. The real battle in the "trial" or "temptation" for the persecuted Christian would be against cowardice, or against the desire for comfort and security, either of which would lure the disciple away from the path of steadfastness.

James places testing, or temptation, at the front of his letter because it is the quintessential situation in which our single-mindedness (integrity) or double-mindedness manifests itself. When tempted to sin we have an opportunity to experience joy as we struggle to walk in line with faith, to grow in the quality of steadfast endurance and finally to achieve that integrity of heart and life that marks the "perfect" disciple. The question remains, however, whether the disciple will act in line with "faith" (Jas 1:3, 6) or with the desires that introduce other goals

and concerns alongside of and contrary to obeying God and honoring him (Jas 1:14).

When a situation is recognized as a "trial" that can prove faith, the disciple's goal is to be steadfast, the ultimate goal of which is completeness (Jas 1:2-4). The next paragraph speaks of the ready availability of God-given wisdom as a resource for persevering through a test, for discerning the way of remaining faithful through the test. When seeking God's gift of wisdom, however, the believer needs to ask "in faith, wavering with regard to nothing" (Jas 1:6). The real enemy to receiving God's wisdom is not doubting whether or not God will give this wisdom but wavering in our commitment (faith, firmness) to discover and do what is wise before God in that situation. This wavering comes from the "double mind" that threatens to destroy integrity by looking now to God's desire in the trial and then to what would gratify our own desires in that situation (Jas 1:14). It leaves the disciple without an anchor in the midst of a troubled sea, at the mercy of conflicting desires and goals. Only those committed to walk in line with faith can expect God's help in temptation and the joy of growing in endurance.

The apparent interruption of James 1:9-11 may serve to develop the topic of double-mindedness. In the Jesus tradition double-mindedness emerges when a person tries to serve two masters, God and money (Mt 6:24). Wealth thus emerges quite directly as a challenge to single-mindedness. Laying up treasure on earth binds the heart to the earth, keeping it from God (Mt 6:19-21). The rich person failed to respond to Jesus' call (and to his desire to follow Jesus) because his heart was divided between discipleship and possessions (Mt 19:16-22). But, as James points out, the end of self-gratifying material pursuits is to fade away like the grass of the field when it is scorched by the sun (Jas 1:10-11). Dwelling on these consequences is meant to reinforce commitment to that single-minded desire that navi-

Figure 21.2. Golden crown with oak leaves, such as was used to crown victors in athletic and other competitions. (Photo courtesy of the Archaeological Museum of Amphipolis and Todd Bolen [BiblePlaces.com])

gates trials in line with the demands of a faithful response to God. The result of such fidelity is a "crown of life" (Jas 1:12). Since victors' crowns were normally made of sprigs and fronds of plants, this would be heard as a striking contrast to the grass that withers away (see figure 21.2).

James 1:12-15 and 16-18 provide a balanced counterpoint to one another. In the first passage James denies God's involvement in testing the believers, pointing instead to the duplicitous desires of the heart. An unholy lineage follows: desire breeds sin and sin breeds death. God, however, who bred[27] us instead to be God's own possession among creation, gives every good gift. James offers these sayings, then, as a further antidote to the divided heart. As we single-mindedly attend to God and God's resources when facing a temptation or trial of faith, we are assured of life; if we yield in the trial to those desires that speak of self-gratification, we participate in our own demise.

The remainder of James can be seen, in many ways, to address a wide array of specific trials and temptations faced by believers, in which the genuineness of their faith can be demonstrated or belied:

- When the rich person and the poor person enter my congregation, I face a "trial"—will I live out my faith that claims God to be free from partiality, that knows Jesus to have favored the poor and that commands me to "love the neighbor," both poor and rich, "as myself," or will I yield to the worldly mind that is attracted to wealth and fancy adornment, while contemptuous of the homeless and poor (Jas 2:1-13)?
- When I encounter a sister or brother in need, will I content myself to mumble religious platitudes to assuage my conscience while I keep my goods for my own pleasures, or will I invest myself in them as if

---

[27]Note the double use of *apokyeō*, "to bear," in James 1:15, 18, underscoring the contrast.

they were my own family (Jas 2:14-26)?

- When I speak, will I live out my conviction that all people are created in God's image and thus to be blessed rather than cursed with my mouth, or will I indulge the passions of anger, frustration and contempt, and so use my mouth to tear down the other person (Jas 3:1-12; 4:11-12)?
- Will I seek what makes for harmony and peace in human community at the cost of indulging my own desires, or will I seek self-gratification, with the result that competitiveness, envy and conflict will continue to characterize my attitude toward and relations with others (Jas 3:13—4:12)?
- Will I live mindful of my utter dependence on God and God's pleasure, or will I make plans and set goals for my life as if I were my own master (Jas 4:13-17)?
- Will I bring my financial practices in line with my confession of a returning Christ who judges those who have laid up treasures and withheld life-giving aid, or will I indulge my desire to seek security in amassing wealth by any means (Jas 5:1-6)?

These situations are "trials" in that they each ask the disciple to give up something of him- or herself and to endure some kind of loss. When encountered thus, however, each situation becomes an opportunity for moving closer to wholeness, to that integrity that James so greatly yearns for Christians to possess, and to that transformation of life that leads to a positive verdict when we come to be judged by the "law of freedom" (Jas 2:12).

Consistency of faith and action. If James should be reduced to any single message, it would be that discipleship and faith are real when they are lived out (Jas 1:22-27; 2:12-13;

3:13). If the "word of truth" gave us new birth (Jas 1:18), it follows that we must do this word and allow our whole lives to be shaped by and given consistency through this word that was the starting point for our new existence in God (Jas 1:22-25). The image of the person who looks in the mirror and forgets what he or she looks like is quite apt here: looking into God's Word, like a mirror, tells the disciples what kind of people they are and must remain throughout the day. To fail to *do* what we *see* in the Word is to forget who we have become in God.

When James urges the doing of the law of the God we confess, what does he have in mind? Those who see James as the champion of Jewish Christianity *over against* Paul would assume that he means the whole Torah in all its particulars (including circumcision, sabbath observance, observance of dietary regulations, purity codes and cultic law). Against this reading James never mentions the laws that distinguish Jew from Gentile.[28] Instead, he elevates the Decalogue (Jas 2:11), commandments that have to do with just dealings between people (rather than cultic and dietary observances), such as Leviticus 19:13, 15, 18 (see Jas 5:4; 2:2-4, 8, respectively), and principles learned from the wisdom tradition deduced from the "moral" law. Where James applies the language of purity and pollution, he does so in much the same way as other Christian leaders (including Paul), as a means to promote moral integrity, shape healthful community relations and maintain ideological boundaries between assembly and society.[29] Undoubtedly, the "word," the "royal law," and the "law of freedom" include the teachings of Jesus—indeed, they include the Torah, prophets and writings especially as the light of these traditions passes

---

[28]Johnson, *Letter of James,* pp. 30-32.

[29]Thus rightly John H. Elliott: "James employs notions of purity and pollution to undergird an ethic of holy non-conformity. The restoration and maintenance of integrity, cohesion, commitment, and justice, according to James, requires rejection of alien values and behavior as corrupting sources of pollution and fidelity to God and the royal law of love as the means toward holiness and wholeness" ("The Epistle of James in Rhetorical and Social-Scientific Perspective: Holiness-Wholeness and Patterns of Replication," *BTB* 23 (1993): 79).

through the lens of Jesus' teaching.

James 2 provides two concrete examples of how the "word" is to be done rather than heard only. The first focuses on the virtue of impartiality, the refusal to assign positive value to someone on account of his or her wealthy appearance and to withhold positive value from someone on account of his or her poverty. After urging Christians to "remain uncontaminated by the world," the tendency to be partial toward the wealthy and those of fine appearance provides a prime example of worldly values contaminating the Christian community. Christians know well that it is God's character not to regard the appearance of things but to evaluate people on the basis of what is in the heart (1 Sam 16:7; Rom 2:11). How then can the Christian who is called to reflect God's character give preferential treatment toward the rich visitor while dishonoring the poor by treating them with less dignity?[30]

James 1:9-11 already begins to speak against the practice of evaluating ourselves or others in terms of wealth. That passage provides a stern reminder of the transitory value and nature of riches, and the ironic reality of any boast in temporal wealth. Now in James 2:5, however, the disciple is challenged to take very seriously Jesus' reevaluation of people, according to which it is the poor who are "favored" or "honored" to be heirs of the "kingdom of God" (Lk 6:20) and the rich are the disprivileged ones (Lk 6:24). James insists that these reevaluations "heard" from Jesus now shape interactions in the community of faith. A second "word" that pertains to this situation is Leviticus 19:18, the command to "love your neighbor as yourself." Treating people differently on the basis of appearance is a violation of this part of the "royal law" (Jas 2:8-9). Leviticus 19:18 is elevated alongside commands from the Decalogue in both Matthew 19:18-19 (Jesus' response to the rich man) and here in James 2:8-11. In the former context the rich man's refusal to spend his wealth on his poor neighbors belies his commitment to doing the commandments of God; here, the Christian's refusal to value another human being as he or she would wish to be valued makes the Christian a transgressor of the law, a mere "hearer" who does not allow an understanding of the law to shape his or her response in each new situation.

In James 5:1-6 we see how a wealthy person might look from God's perspective, if the wealth has been attained by unjust means (e.g., by withholding wages from the workers) and if this wealth is simply left to accumulate until the day of judgment rather than used to save those in need (as in Jas 2:14-16). The world treats such people preferentially, but how might they look from God's perspective, and which perspective should believers embody?

A second example of bringing action in line with faith is provided in James 2:14-26, namely, putting our money where our prayers are—investing ourselves, our resources and our energies in caring for the orphan and widow, the representatives of the weak, the poor, those dependent on others for support and enfranchisement. James joins the chorus raised by John and Paul as he calls for living out our faith in works of kindness (cf. Jas 2:14-16 with Gal 5:6 and 1 Jn 3:16-17).

---

[30]Some scholars understand James 2:2-3 to reflect the setting of ecclesiastical courts, such as Paul envisions in 1 Corinthians 6:1-6 (e.g., Watson, "James 2," p. 99; Pedrito Maynard-Reid, *Poverty and Wealth in James* [Maryknoll, N.Y.: Orbis, 1987], pp. 56-58). The use of the term *judges* in James 2:4, and the familiarity of the warning against partiality in the law court (see Lev 19:15; Sir 4:22, 27) could be seen to point in this direction. However, James could also be using the language of law courts, rich with intertexture on partiality toward the wealthy and against the poor, to put the broader phenomenon of preferential treatment of the rich in a different, more sinister light by comparing it to the injustice where rich non-Christians take advantage of the judges' partiality to the Christians' disadvantage (Jas 2:6). Linking the experiences and settings thus, the Christians might be disinclined to continue to inflict injustice in the form of preferential treatment for others in their community life.

James 2:15-16 ultimately serves as an example for the thesis of James 2:14, however, and not as an independent instruction. Just as it would do no good to wish a naked and hungry sister or brother to be clothed and fed without actually taking steps to bring that wish into reality, so it does no good to have faith without following that up with obedience. Christians ultimately must have a different level of faith than the demons, who also know all about God and God's promises (Jas 2:19). The lesson James takes from the example of Abraham (quoting Gen 15:6, but really working from Gen 22, especially Gen 22:12, 15-18) and Rahab is that genuine faith results in action that grows out of that faith. Rahab is often overlooked here. Because she believed that God would overthrow Jericho, she acted hospitably toward the Hebrew spies, making herself a friend of God and enemy of her native land. The same clear relationship between actions and belief (our behaviors flowing from and grounded in what we know about God and God's just expectations), and the same unmistakable allegiance to God rather than the world, will mark the faith that is able to save (Jas 2:14).

Consistency in speech. Like Proverbs and Ben Sira, James gives considerable space to the topic of controlling our speech. The topic is announced in James 1:19, 26, and is seen to be of sufficient importance that the lack of control of our tongue renders our religion "empty." Speech becomes thus another trial or test by which the genuineness of faith is manifested or disproved.

James takes Jesus' words about the seriousness of speech to heart (see, for example, Mt 12:36-37), expecting that God will judge our speech as well as our actions (Jas 3:1). He laments the difficulty—indeed, the impossibility—of keeping ourselves from sinning in our speech, and the dangers that the tongue poses to the whole body. The images of the bit in the horse's mouth or the rudder of a ship as similes for the tongue appear inappropriate at first, since the bit and the rudder control the larger horse or ship, whereas the challenge for people is to control the tongue (Jas 3:3-5). Nevertheless, James is aware that, in a very real sense, the tongue can steer the whole body, leading a person into trouble, disgrace or a compromising position. The second-century B.C.E. sage, Ben Sira, spoke with even greater trepidation concerning his fear lest his speech lead him to ruin (Sir 22:27—23:3, 7-8).

The specific compromising position that James introduces, however, has nothing to do with revealing state secrets or alienating a ruler. Rather, he holds up the unnatural irony of using the tongue both to bless God and to curse and slander human beings made in the image of God (Jas 3:9-12). This actually provides a third example of bringing action in line with our faith convictions (see previous section), for the faith conviction that God created humanity in God's own image ought to lead the disciple to honor both God and the creatures that bear God's reflected image. If we really believed the former, we would not curse the latter. James's illustrations (Jas 3:10-12) are reminiscent of Ben Sira's similar words about the irony of opposite effects coming forth from the same mouth (extinguishing or fanning a flame by means of spitting or blowing, Sir 28:12), and the Jesus tradition (see Mt 7:16-17, which, though using the same imagery, does not deal with the same topic). Integrity of life must extend, therefore, to the ephemeral words that escape our lips, particularly with regard to our sisters and brothers within the church (see Jas 4:11-12), where speech can be used to nurture unity and encourage growth or to foment strife and tear down a fellow believer.

James's brief pronouncement concerning oaths (Jas 5:12) also springs from a concern for consistency of faith and life. *Oaths* here refer not to "swear words" in the vernacular sense but to calling God to witness or invoking God's honor as a means of affirming the truth of something spoken. Ben Sira spoke at some length (Sir 23:9-11) about the danger of oaths, since they invite divine scrutiny and since it is so easy to fail to live up to a sworn oaths. Jesus had gone further, forbidding the use of oaths at all (see Mt 5:34-37), and this is the position James advances as well. The oath served to establish true speech in a culture in which speaking truth or deceit were both acceptable strategies for dealing with people outside one's kinship group. Jesus and James call instead for a setting aside of all duplicity in speech. Rather than use oaths to reinforce some part of their speech, disciples are to prove reliable in all speech, yet another facet of the integrity of those who have had the "word of truth" implanted in their own hearts and sowed at the start of their new life (Jas 1:18, 21).

Wholeness in community. The integrity or wholeness that James has been promoting in the conduct of individual believers also must manifest itself in the corporate life of the Christian community. Not only must each life be lived in accordance with the truth we profess, but also our collective life needs to be brought in line with that truth. The integrity of the individual is jeopardized as he or she is pulled in different directions by conflicting desires; similarly, the integrity of the community is threatened with rupture and disintegration where it is pulled in different directions by conflicting members and their conflicting desires. Wisdom shows itself in noble conduct and "in the gentleness of wisdom" rather than in jealousy and strife (Jas 3:13-14). Clever speech that wins arguments and clever stratagems that gain ground in disputes do not give any cause for boasting if strife and envy motivate the heart, for then the soundness of the church is in danger and the disciples are walking against (indeed, "lying against") the truth of God.

Again the topic of desires emerges, now as "the pleasures waging war among your members" (Jas 4:1, 3). Self-gratification—catering to our own desires—was seen to be the source

of temptation (Jas 1:14) and the cause of the "divided mind" (Jas 1:8) that prevents us from walking in line with our faith with complete integrity. Now these forces reemerge as the source of a lack of integrity in the Christian community. Relationships and church unity rupture and disintegrate as each sister or brother brings that divided mind into the church, looking out for her or his own pleasure rather than solely for God's pleasure (Jas 4:1-4, 8). Self-gratification and competition with others whose own selfish desires jeopardize our self-gratification stand at the root of "worldly" wisdom (Jas 3:15-16). The result is a community that is no different from the world around it, save that it murmurs platitudes about God and religion. This is far from the vision for the church that James promotes!

James calls believers to embody God's wisdom (the "wisdom from above," Jas 3:17-18) in our actions, interactions and handling of our speech and desires rather than the world's wisdom and the world's character. The language of friendship in James 4:4 is especially apt here, since one basic component of friendship in Greco-Roman and Jewish ethics was the sharing of common traits, interests and values. Double-minded people who know God's values but still try to gratify their worldly desires and allow worldly values to shape their interactions with others remain "friends" of the world. They are friendly to the world's way of doing things and the world's goals for human society. But this is an act of faithlessness (hence "adulteresses" in Jas 4:4) toward God and ultimately makes one an enemy of God. Again, walking in line with the convictions and values we have learned from God is seen to be essential for salvation itself; and in this way we will not be found to be God's "enemy" on the day of judgment (Jas 2:12-13; 5:20).

Again James calls the hearers to purify themselves from the contamination of the world (see Jas 1:27), no longer allowing selfish goals and desires to disrupt the soundness and strength of the church. This calls for humility (*tapeinos;* see the use of this word in Jas 1:9), laying down our own desires and giving up what would please ourself in community life to please God, and enjoying the gifts and exaltation that God promises to such people (Jas 1:9; 4:6, 10). Our agenda for engaging Christian community is not about pleasing ourselves but serving the ill sister and going after the wayward brother, putting ourselves at the disposal of our fellow Christians in these areas of need (Jas 5:13-20). Our agenda for prayer refrains from asking God for things that satisfy our own desires and pleasures, but uses the great privilege of prayer instead to seek the reconciliation of the penitent and the healing of the sick (Jas 4:2-3; 5:14-16). Prayer is not a means to tap into God's generosity to serve worldly ends; it is a means for seeking God's resources for the restoration of the community and each of its members to wholeness.

The humble person and the rich. Being "humble" (*tapeinos*) depicts the fundamental posture of the disciple (Jas 1:9; 4:6-10). For James humility has a positive value—it results in exaltation by God. James develops this topic with two examples in which the humble course of action is contrasted with the arrogant posture (the opposite of humility in Jas 4:6; Prov 3:34). The first example challenges our right to speak ill of or pronounce judgment on another person (Jas 4:11-12). In so doing, we exchange our proper role with regard to the law (namely, a doer who is equally under the law as the neighbor slandered) and usurps God's unique role as judge. The humble person, by contrast, refuses to arrogate this privilege, being content to keep focused on his or her own faltering obedience. The second example challenges the delusions about our own self-sufficiency and autonomy that lead to boastful speech about our plans for our lives, our businesses, our future—our projections concerning what we will accomplish. By contrast, the humble person remembers and acknowledges in all such planning and speaking his or her utter dependence on God for life itself. In reality, all human plans are subordinate to God's plans (cf. Jas 4:14 and Prov 27:1).

The foil for the humble person is once again the "rich" (as in Jas 1:9-11). The main points of James's bitter attack in James 5:1-6 are threefold: (1) these riches have been amassed through economic injustice (withholding wages from the actual workers; see Lev 19:13) and violence (Jas 5:4, 6); (2) they have been hoarded rather than used according to the Lord's directives (from Deuteronomy to the Prophets to Jesus this is consistently in the direction of sharing with those in need; cf. Jas 5:2-3 and Mt 6:19-21 and, especially, Lk 12:33); (3) where they have been used, it was for self-gratification (Jas 5:5). James thus continues Jesus' challenging teaching about the proper investment of wealth in redeeming people in distress rather than laying it up for the future. According to worldly wisdom a large nest egg is the fruit of a successful career, but what would it say about our lives, our priorities and our choices to have the Judge return to find these resources squirreled away with so many people dying today for a lack of bread?

The denunciation of rich oppressors leads naturally to the exhortation to patience "until the appearing of the Lord," when all would be set right (Jas 5:7-11). James had assumed that his readers, or at least a great number of them, would be familiar with being oppressed by rich unbelievers (see Jas 2:6-7), and so these verses become a source of encouragement to persevere. But the warning to the rich oppressors in James 5:1-6 becomes also a warning to the rich Christians to be sure that their handling of wealth is in line with their confession of Jesus as Lord, for "look! the Judge stands at the door" (Jas 5:9), and he shows no partiality.

EXEGETICAL SKILL
Social-Scientific Criticism (3)—
Analyzing Worldview and Ethos

Serious advances in New Testament studies occur when we learn to answer old questions better (for example, when new data are made available, as in the Dead Sea Scrolls) or when we learn and ask whole new sets of questions. These bring to life neglected aspects of these texts and the situations and communities that produced and sought to have an effect on them. A great deal of the energy of social-scientific analysis of biblical texts comes from listening to what sociologists and anthropologists have been doing with the contemporary study of cultures and religion. Through this, New Testament scholars are learning new and appropriate questions to ask of these texts. These questions can orient us toward the texts in new ways, inviting us to observe a foreign culture or social phenomenon, collect data from our native informants and produce an analytical synthesis of this data. The difference, of course, is that the New Testament scholar works with a world that is available only through artifacts and texts.

Leaders in the field of social-scientific analysis of the New Testament focus our attention on the kinds of questions that they have learned to ask the texts. John H. Elliott and Howard Clark Kee have produced readily accessible and very helpful collections of such questions that can lead us deeper into social-scientific analysis.[a] These questions invite us to explore group boundaries and their maintenance, distinctions of status and role within a group, the location of authority and how it is maintained, the social function of rituals, the social dynamics within and between groups, and the symbolic world embraced by the group. All such questions (and, in many cases, the methodological tools for answering them) inevitably derive from the work of people in the fields of sociology and anthropology, who are themselves (often) far removed from biblical studies departments. The student of the New Testament is particularly concerned to discern what impact a given text has on the community of readers in regard to each of these questions.[b]

---

[a]Howard Clark Kee, *Knowing the Truth: A Sociological Approach to New Testament Interpretation* (Minneapolis: Fortress, 1989), pp. 65-69; John H. Elliott, *What Is Social-Scientific Criticism?* (Minneapolis: Fortress, 1993), pp. 72-74; see also the "data inventories" for synchronic and diachronic analysis on pp. 110-23.

[b]Many biblical scholars shy away from and even vehemently oppose social-scientific analysis because sociology of religion tends to be reductionistic in its approach to religion. That is to say sociologists "bracket out" divine causes and study religion as a purely human, social phenomenon. Nevertheless, social-scientific analysis does not need to subscribe to this ideology of the study of religion. Social-scientific questions and models can be used to elicit new information from the text and to study the interaction between religious symbols and real-life motivations and actions, all of which is just as useful and appropriate to a theistic interpretation of early Christianity *and* a purposeful application of those insights in a community of faith.

As an example of how reading the work of an anthropologist can stimulate our digging deeper into a New Testament text, we might turn to the work of Clifford Geertz, whose interest in the meaning and effects of symbols and symbolic systems makes him a natural ally for those who study religion. Geertz defines a religion as "(1) a system of symbols which acts to (2) establish powerful, pervasive, and long-lasting moods and motivations in men [and women] by (3) formulating conceptions of a general order of existence and (4) clothing these conceptions with such an aura of factuality that (5) the moods and motivations seem uniquely realistic."[c] What this definition says (in the first three phrases) is that a religion expresses a view of reality largely though the use of symbols and symbolic language, and this view of reality directly affects a devotee's feelings, desires and behaviors. Moreover, participating in a religion leads to experiencing this view of reality as somehow real, a reliable impression of the way things *really* are, so that the emotions and motivations that are derived from that view of reality have real and lasting force in the everyday life of the devotee (the last two phrases of the definition).[d]

These insights derived from extensive fieldwork in the anthropology of indigenous cultures (e.g., tribes in Java and Bali) give the New Testament interpreter a series of questions with which to interrogate the culture of early Christianity.

1. What are the symbols invoked within the text? How are they coordinated into a framework of meaning? What is the relationship of these symbols (and the whole symbolic construct) to the symbols and symbolic universes of other groups or of other realms of life?

2. How does this symbolic world interpret the everyday world? How does the world of the symbolic universe "complete" or "correct" perception of aspects of everyday reality?[e] How is this interpretation different from or similar to other such interpretations of the everyday reality?

3. Since symbols provide both patterns of culture and patterns for culture, how does the symbolic world of the text mirror social relations, values and behaviors? How does it try to change these? How does the symbolic world of the text interrupt other available symbolic worlds as these mirror and influence society?

4. What attitudes and motivations does an author seek to arouse by means of a particular presentation of some part of this symbolic world? How does he or she attempt to reinforce or correct the ethos of the group?

5. What does the author do to reinforce the plausibility of the worldview

---

[c]Clifford Geertz, *The Interpretation of Cultures* (New York: Basic Books, 1973), pp. 90-91.
[d]Geertz pursues the coherence of the "worldview" and "ethos" propounded in a religion and the kinds of behavior that grow out of that view of reality. See "Ethos, World View, and the Analysis of Sacred Symbols," *Interpretation of Culture*, pp. 126-41.
[e]Geertz, *Interpretation of Culture*, p. 122.

he or she invokes and the moods and motivations he or she arouses? What factors might be brought to bear on this within the context from which the text is read by the audience (e.g., a worship setting)?

These questions provide a set of lenses for examining James, or a set of sieves for sifting out data and observations that can complement the insights caught by the sieves provided by historical-critical, rhetorical and literary approaches to the Bible.

Turning to James we can begin by interrogating the text concerning its view of the world, the "symbolic universe," the basic convictions about the cosmos that James articulates and assumes his audience will accept as obvious facts about reality. We will be especially interested in those elements assumed to be real even though they are not open to direct, empirical confirmation. These elements are especially important as part of the interpretative framework that the worldview provides for everyday reality.[f]

First, James assumes the reality of God, who is constant and unchanging (Jas 1:17), and thus a secure center and foundation for the symbolic world of the early Christians. God is believed to provide needed resources for the community freely and reliably, whether wisdom for the advantageous navigation of trials (Jas 1:5), forgiveness for the sinner or healing for the sick (Jas 5:15). "Every good gift" comes from this God (Jas 1:17). The audience's past experiences of gifts that they consider good will implicitly reinforce the reality of God and the author's claims about God's character and will to interact beneficently with God's obedient devotees. The acts of prayer and anointing with oil become windows of invitation for God to break into a situation with whatever is needed. As they participate in expectant prayer for one another in each others' company, the devotees reinforce for each other the reality and effectiveness of speech directed toward God, of the God who is really there to hear, and the character of God as generous and reliable Provider. To help reinforce this point even further, James offers historical proof of the efficacy of prayer and the reality of the God who listens to prayer by referring to the Elijah story (Jas 5:17-18).

God has a purpose for specific, individual human lives, as exemplified by the story of Job (Jas 5:11), and seen in God's use of James as God's "servant" (Jas 1:1) and others as "prophets" to speak God's word in the world (Jas 5:10). God also has a more general purpose for human beings, seen especially in the new birth that God gives those who join the Christian group. God's action is behind conversion itself, so that being a part of the group is in accordance with God's wishes (Jas 1:18). This implanted word, the seed of the new birth, shapes all of this new life (Jas

---

[f]A fuller application of the questions raised by Geertz's definition of a "religion" to a biblical text can be found in my article, "The Construction and Social Function of a Counter-Cosmos in the Revelation of John," *Forum* 9:1-2 (1993): 47-61.

1:18-25).[9] It is akin to if not identical with the "wisdom from above," a gift from the heavenly realm that has direct impact on human behavior as the latter is conformed to the former (i.e., as the individual lives out the ethos prized by the group, embodying the values of purity, peacefulness, gentleness, restraint of self-assertion and so forth; Jas 3:13, 17-18).

God's interaction with the world is manifested in some way in the "lordship" of the man Jesus (Jas 1:1; 2:1), whose story is presupposed by James (clearly, at least, his exaltation to God's realm, where he exercises this lordship). Because of this, Jesus' teachings are normative for the group. (His place in the symbolic world sustains the place of his teaching as formative for the ethos of the group.)

The proper response to God is submission (Jas 4:7, 10), a response facilitated by the belief that God has the ultimate authority to order all things, to limit our lives or allow our activities (Jas 4:15). Submissiveness to God is presented as positive (Jas 4:7), reasonable and necessary (4:13-15), and advantageous (Jas 4:10). Valuing submission facilitates a passive reception of the positive values upheld by the group's worldview, paralleling acquiescence to the ethos of the group. As we drive further and harder toward congruity of life in the visible world with the values formed by the symbolic world, we come into a closer orbit around the center of meaningfulness for this worldview: we "draw near to God" (Jas 4:8).

But God and Jesus are not the only forces in the unseen realm. James gives expression to a dualistic worldview in which opposing and incompatible forces are understood to be at work (Jas 4:4). This introduces, then, a dualistic ethos, according to which the person who is faithful with regard to the larger worldview (the symbolic universe) will seek to participate wholly in God's valued behaviors and abstain wholly from that which is influenced by the world, the flesh and the devil, the three main symbols for the forces of destruction in life. In a cosmos at war, the believer *must* choose one side or the other rather than live a "double-minded" or "two-

---

[9]Another aspect of this exercise would invite us to look at how James shaped the identity of the group members. All humans are the reflection of God's image and are to be valued as such (Jas 3:9), but those who have come under Jesus' lordship have been given this new birth by God, have had God's word and wisdom implanted in their beings like a gene that will remap their entire being (if I might be permitted so modern an analogy), and have been brought together into a new family where all are siblings (see the frequent use of "brothers and sisters" throughout James). James calls them the "twelve tribes," which gives them a specific identity and ideological location among the peoples of the world (i.e., as "Israel," the people selected by God to be a special people for God), and connects them as an extended family that is distinct from all the other families of the world. *Diaspora* implies a view of history according to which this particular people had been scattered and would one day be gathered together again (now, the day of judgment). The way the author constructs the group's identity is directly informative for the ethos promoted. Here the ideology of identity directly reinforces the ethos of distinctiveness and separation from what characterizes the behavior of the world (of nongroup members), the mutual commitments of believers, and the impetus to yield oneself more and more to the embodiment of group values and expectations as the realization of the growth of that "implanted word" (Jas 1:21).

souled" life (Jas 1:8; 4:8). James's concern for the "integration" of the believer's whole life into the ethos of the group is thus an outgrowth of this aspect of the Christian worldview.

The character of the devil is not developed in any way but is assumed to be familiar as an enemy of God and a power to be resisted (Jas 4:7). He is not alone, for James also mentions demons (Jas 2:19). Just as God's power is expected to break into everyday experience, so demonic power breaks into this visible reality, for example, through the misuse of the tongue (Jas 3:6). The posture of resistance urged by James encourages the active filtering out and avoidance of all that is "worldly, unspiritual, demonic" (Jas 3:15).

More immediate than the devil is the "world"—not conceived here as nature, which still reveals God's wisdom and provides paradigms for Christian behavior (Jas 3:10-12). The worldview of the Jewish wisdom tradition, according to which God's creation encodes God's values, survives in James. The world, on the other hand, is a spiritual power that is in league with the devil (Jas 3:15). Identifying the world as a source of defilement reinforces abstention from whatever can be said to belong to the sphere of the world (Jas 1:27), such as the attitudes labeled and marginalized as "worldly wisdom" (Jas 3:14-15).[h]

The most immediate source of danger is our own desires (Jas 1:14; 4:1, 3), which promote death for those who gratify those desires (Jas 1:14-15)[i] and is a source of disruption into the community. The unseen, spiritual powers of the devil and the world impinge most directly on the individual believer. As a believer becomes more attuned to the movements of the prohibited desires and hears more about the unseen spiritual forces that move in the same directions (and may even stand behind those desires), those unseen realities become real, familiar and even felt. Because they are believed to alienate us from God and lead to death, all attitudes or ambitions derived from the flesh, the world or the devil are identified as "trials" to be courageously endured, but not indulged (Jas 1:2-4, 13-15).

The worldview expressed by James has not only a cosmic dimension but a temporal dimension as well, which strongly reinforces the moods and motivations aroused by the spatial or cosmic dimensions. But the visible reality is ephemeral (Jas 1:9-11), since the absolute value of people cannot be determined by reference to it. Like most early Christian leaders, James looks firmly ahead to the end not only of each individual's life in

---

[h]Note the use of purity language, another fruitful venture into worldview since purity language has to do primarily with "ordering" reality into clean and unclean, sacred and ordinary, and so on. See, further, chapters seven and eight of my *Honor, Patronage, Kinship, and Purity* (Downers Grove, Ill.: InterVarsity Press, 2000).

[i]James 5:19-20 also speaks of death as the result of wandering away from the ethos promoted by the group, if one is not brought back to a way of life in line with the group's values.

this world (Jas 4:13-14), but the end of this world's story as we know it on the day of judgment. God is a just Being, who hears the cries of the victims of injustice (Jas 5:4) and who established laws for the human race to live by. Because God is just, at some point in the future God will enact judgment on the basis of this law (Jas 2:12-13; 4:12). This conviction strongly supports the group's understanding of God's requirements as the norm for behavior. References to the coming judgment abound:

- James 3:1 uses it to underscore the seriousness of the call to be a teacher.
- James 3:18 uses the images of sowing and harvest to reinforce the eschatological component of the worldview. The believer holds to the group values *now* for the sake of a *later* reward.
- James 5:3 speaks of "testimony" or "evidence" against the oppressive rich, a judicial image that has meaning in reference to the final judgment.
- James 5:7-8 refers twice to the "coming of the Lord" (the parousia), using the harvest image again. This fosters patient expectation that in turn builds a firm commitment to walk in line with the group values now.
- James 5:9 refers to the imminent judgment, arousing fear[j] in order to discourage grumbling against fellow Christians and taking oaths (Jas 5:12). The goal is to always speak the truth.

In addition James uses subtle reminders of God's evaluation of human beings to help believers conform their attitudes and actions to the gospel worldview (Jas 1:27).

Connected with judgment are God promises of future rewards ("life" is promised for the future; Jas 1:12) for those who embody the requisite values, and future punishment for those who fail to embody these values. James 5:1 speaks of coming "miseries" for the unjust rich and of the "day of slaughter" for the fattened rich (Jas 5:5), causing rich *Christians* to fear and to be motivated to use their wealth in line with the group's values and priorities. The temporal dimension of this worldview, at least as invoked by James, affirms the ultimate importance of living according to the values of the Christian group. Acting contrary to these values may seem to be advantageous. But God's judgment acts powerfully to relativize these advantages as merely temporary, purchased at the cost of much more lasting harm. Eschatology in James, recently so well underscored by Todd Penner,[k] is an important incentive to pursue integrity and to set aside the competing temporal goals and desires that lead to the paralysis of the "double mind."

James provides a serendipitous witness to the truth of Geertz's claim

---

[j]An emotion aroused by the perception of imminent danger; see Aristotle *Rhet.* 2.5.1.
[k]See Penner, *Epistle of James and Eschatology,* pp. 121-213.

that "between ethos and world view, between the approved style of life and the assumed structure of reality, there is conceived to be a simple and fundamental congruence."[1] James himself quite directly connects ethos with worldview, calling for the conformity of attitudes and actions with that worldview. Thus an unrestrained tongue and orientation to self-gratification (failure at the level of embodying the group's ethos) threaten the value of a person's whole "religion" (Jas 1:26). Actions and attitudes are expected to be completely congruent. James's most celebrated passage (Jas 2:14-26) argues that the reality of our commitment ("faith") to the symbolic world of the group is only shown through acting ("works") in line with the values supported by that symbolic world. This paragraph also points to a mode of legitimation—as Christians see other Christians doing works that faith should generate, their own conviction about the reality of that faith will be solidified, and thus their willingness to commit their time, resources and lives to living out the group's ethos will grow. If a particular course of action is incompatible with the convictions (worldview) of the group, that course of action must be altered. Thus partiality is not censured because it is unjust or inimical to the maintenance of group solidarity, but because it is incongruent with the confessed lordship of Jesus (Jas 2:1).

Once the interpreter works through the text, outlining the worldview assumed and invoked by the text and noting the connections between this symbolic world and the attitudes and actions that have become normative for the group, he or she is in a position to understand how this wider view of reality is being brought to bear on specific phenomena of real life and to ask:

- How does James put these phenomena in perspective by invoking aspects of the Christian worldview?
- How will the larger picture of unseen realities (God; future judgment; the power of the devil, the world and the desires) offer a more complete and correct perspective on these phenomena than we might glean just from considering them in light of everyday experience or from the perspective of temporal advantages and gains?
- How will this perspective shape the believer's orientation toward these realities, changing the hearer of James's discourse and encouraging attitudes and actions that advance the maintenance of the group (e.g., by preserving the distinctiveness of its values and thus its identity, or by facilitating smoother and more congenial interactions within the group)?

These are the kinds of questions that Christian leaders must always ask as they seek to are to bring their own and their congregations' actions, interactions and attitudes ever more fully in line with the God they worship

---

[1]Geertz, *Interpretation of Culture*, p. 129.

and the Lord they proclaim. As we grow in our analysis of New Testament texts, we will also become more adept in discerning how Christian convictions about the nature of the cosmos and its destiny could or should form a congregation's obedience to the gospel in the face of new challenges to faith and life.

To begin exploring ways that a text reveals a worldview and strategically uses it to shape its hearers' responses, select another brief New Testament text (e.g., Philippians, Titus, 1 Peter, 2 Peter or 1 John) and investigate it with the questions derived from Clifford Geertz's definition of a religious system and from the questions posed at the conclusion of the sample analysis of James above. Another approach is to select a specific issue treated in a longer text (e.g., the consumption of food offered to idols and participation at the idol's table in 1 Cor 8 and 10, the issue of the weak and strong in Rom 14:1—15:13, or the possibility of withdrawal from the Christian community in Hebrews) and investigate how the worldview of the whole text is brought to bear on shaping a particular response to those particular challenges.

This is but one example of the kind of analysis that social-scientific models can provide for enriching our reading of Scripture. The reader is encouraged to look to the works listed below to get a sense of the broader kinds of questions being asked of the New Testament, and fruitfully answered, from this interdisciplinary perspective.

FOR FURTHER READING

Berger, Peter L. *The Sacred Canopy.* New York: Doubleday, 1967.

deSilva David A. "Embodying the Word: Social-Scientific Interpretation of the New Testament." In *The Face of New Testament Studies,* ed. Scot McKnight and Grant Osborne. Grand Rapids: Baker, 2004.

———. "The Revelation to John: A Case Study in Apocalyptic Propaganda and the Maintenance of Sectarian Identity." *Sociological Analysis* 53 (1992): 375-95.

Elliott, John H. *What Is Social-Scientific Criticism?* Minneapolis: Fortress, 1993.

Harrington, Daniel J. "Second Testament Exegesis and the Social Sciences: A Bibliography." *BTB* 18 (1988): 77-85.

Holmberg, Bengt. *Sociology and the New Testament: An Appraisal.* Minneapolis: Fortress, 1990.

Theissen, Gerd. *The Social Setting of Early Palestinian Christianity.* Philadelphia: Fortress, 1978.

———. *The Social Setting of Pauline Christianity: Essays on Corinth.* Philadelphia: Fortress, 1982.

JAMES AND MINISTRY FORMATION

Because James is so focused on the practical living out of faith in the context of Christian community, writing about situations still so frequently encountered in churches, little more needs to be added here. The church that receives James's word and takes it to heart will be characterized by the following traits:

- In all seriousness, church leaders and members will attempt to discover how knowledge about God's character and desires, and how the law of God expressed through both Testaments, should shape all of life. Making speech, action and ambition consistent with the knowledge of God and teaching of Jesus will be a primary goal of individual members and of the church as a whole (Jas 1:2-8, 22-25).

- The witness of this church will flow from the consistency its members have attained individually and collectively in living out its understanding of the gospel. It will, in effect, show its faith by means of its works. This includes works of kindness and charity, the speech and spirit of its members in their interactions with one another and in the world, and in the degree to which their life choices reflect obedience to God's values rather than worldly wisdom (Jas 2:14-26).

- This church will resist the tendency to value people according to wealth, appearance, beauty and all the other temporary and temporal characteristics that are inconsistent with the ways God values people. The poor person in filthy rags receives as loving a welcome and as respectful a reception as the richest donor; the wisdom communicated by God's Spirit through the least of the community is weighed as carefully as the wishes of the head of the largest and wealthiest family (Jas 2:1-13).

- This church's members will help quarreling disciples evaluate whether God's purposes or human desires and wishes are being served by their altercation. If the strife results from the infiltration of worldly impulses into the community, the congregation will work to restore unity of spirit and a God-centered perspective (Jas 3:13—4:6).

- The use of wealth and resources by the church and its individual members will reflect God's priorities rather than secular financial "wisdom." This becomes a most eloquent witness to the priority of loving your neighbor as yourself (Jas 2:8, 14-16) and to the certainty of judgment by One who has commanded his followers to care for human needs now if they hope to be rich toward God, and who will measure wealth in terms of the relief offered or not (Jas 5:1-3, 5).

- The church will attend meaningfully to the restoration not only of the ill (which, with their emphases on pastoral care, many churches tend to do well) but also the reclamation of the sinner (which many churches are reluctant to do). Rather than watch a wayward youth continue to move further into the drug scene, or allow the less well-liked partner in a divorce to fade into oblivion, or quietly alienate and drive away the accused sex offender, all believers have the responsibility to invest themselves in bringing erring family members back to the safe and sure ways of God. Perhaps the advice in James 5:16 is a necessary prerequisite for the greater challenge of James 5:19-20. As we seek to make the church a hospital for sinners—beginning with ourselves—and learn to support one another's recovery with honesty, love and integrity, we will become more comfortable with and better equipped for those more extreme cases where the danger to the wayward is more apparent, though no more deadly.

FOR FURTHER READING

Bauckham, Richard J. *James*. New Testament Readings. London: Routledge, 1999.

Cranfield, C. E. B. "The Message of James." *SJT* 18 (1965): 182-93, 338-45.

Davids, Peter H. *Commentary on James*. NIGTC. Grand Rapids: Eerdmans, 1982.

Dibelius, Martin. *James*. Hermeneia. Philadelphia: Fortress, 1975.

Elliott, John H. "The Epistle of James in Rhetorical and Social-Scientific Perspective: Holiness-Wholeness and Patterns of Replication." *BTB* 23 (1993): 71-81.

Hartin, Patrick J. *James and the Q Sayings of Jesus*. JSNTSup 47. Sheffield, U.K.: JSOT, 1991.

Johnson, Luke Timothy. *The Letter of James*. AB. Garden City, N.Y.: Doubleday, 1995.

Laws, Sophie. *A Commentary on the Epistle of James*. Harper New Testament Commentaries. New York: Harper & Row, 1980.

Martin, Ralph P. *James*. WBC. Waco, Tex.: Word, 1988.

Maynard-Reid, Pedrito U. *Poverty and Wealth in James*. Maryknoll, N.Y.: Orbis, 1987.

Penner, Todd C. *The Epistle of James and Eschatology*. JSNTSup 121. Sheffield, U.K.: Sheffield Academic Press, 1996.

Wall, Robert W. *The Community of the Wise: The Book of James*. New Testament in Context. Harrisburg, Penn.: Trinity, 1997.

Watson, Duane F. "James 2 in Light of Greco-Roman Schemes of Argumentation." *NTS* 39 (1993): 94-121.

———. "The Rhetoric of James 3:1-12 and a Classical Pattern of Argumentation." *NovT* 35 (1993): 48-64.

22

THE FIRST LETTER OF PETER

An Ethic for Resident Aliens Awaiting Their Inheritance

Association with the name of Jesus and the group spreading across the Mediterranean in his name did not make an individual popular with his or her neighbors. On the contrary, being dedicated to one and only one God, choosing a new primary reference group (namely, the church), and being committed to live out the ethical values of this God in community with fellow believers made the convert appear antisocial and even subversive. In almost every region, Christians appear to have faced their neighbors' attempts to rehabilitate them, to cajole and pressure them back into a more acceptable way of life.

The first letter of Peter seeks to counteract these pressures, motivating ongoing commitment to Christ and his people by reminding them of the great honor and privilege they have in Christ, and of the advantage their obedience to Christ gives them in light of God's judgment. At the same time the author wants to shape their behavior in such a way as to overcome prejudice against them. This includes a respectful attitude, beneficent actions and living out their new "family" obligations of love and support one for another.

THE ADDRESSEES OF 1 PETER

Like James, 1 Peter addresses people of the Diaspora, but now localized to the five Roman provinces that comprise most of modern Turkey—Pontus, Galatia, Cappadocia, Asia and

Bithynia. New Testament literature features the provinces of Asia and Galatia most prominently. Within Asia we find the congregations in Ephesus and Colossae addressed by letters attributed to Paul. We also find the seven churches addressed by John in Revelation. Paul spent significant time in Ephesus (see Acts 19—20), and John the Evangelist came to be associated with the city in early church tradition. Epaphras, an associate of Paul, founded the congregation in Colossae (Col 1:7). The province of Galatia contains the cities Antioch, Iconium, Lystra and Derbe, the major focal points of Paul and Barnabas in Acts 13—14. Whether addressed to churches in north or south Galatia, one of Paul's cardinal letters was addressed to Christians in this province at a critical juncture in Christianity's self-definition as a movement (i.e., whether or not it would define itself as a group within Judaism). Thus Asia and Galatia have a long history of association with Pauline missionary efforts and traditions.

The New Testament texts offer very little information, however, about the growth of Christianity in Bithynia-Pontus and Cappadocia. No stories are told of apostles visiting these regions—in fact, Paul and his team are said to have been prevented from missionary work in Bithynia, being sent to Macedonia instead (Acts 16:7). The one New Testament tradition that might account for the spread of

Christianity to these regions is the story of Pentecost in Acts 2. Jewish pilgrims from many different regions, including specifically Pontus, Cappadocia and Asia (Acts 2:9), were present in Jerusalem for the festival of Pentecost, and they are remembered to have been profoundly affected by Peter's proclamation of Jesus. While the author of Acts records the exponential growth of the Christian group in Jerusalem it is likely that many if not most of these converts returned to their own countries at some point. These converts no doubt would have engaged in evangelism there, founding assemblies of Christians across the Mediterranean.[1]

In contrast to the areas where Paul was active, Cappadocia, northern Galatia and Bithynia-Pontus (except for its coastal areas) were far less Hellenized and less urbanized provinces.[2] An important witness to early-second-century Christianity in Bithynia-Pontus is a letter from Pliny the Younger, governor of that province in 112-113 C.E., written to seek the advice of the emperor Trajan concerning those denounced as Christians. In this letter Pliny observes that "many persons of every age, every rank, and also of both sexes" are associated with Christianity and that "the contagion of this superstition has spread not only to the cities but also to the villages and farms" (*Ep.* 10.96). As in the Pauline mission the Christian movement spans the various strata of society; unlike the Pauline mission it encompasses the smaller villages and rural areas as well.

The ethnic background of these Christians must likewise be assumed to be diverse. The use of the term *Diaspora,* the extensive use of the Jewish Scriptures throughout the letter, and the application of labels like "holy nation" and "royal priesthood" to the readers have mistakenly led many to assume that 1 Peter addresses Jewish Christians.[3] This reflects, however, the author's use of traditional titles of privilege and identity to bolster Christian identity and the Christian's sense of privilege as the heir to this great heritage. It reflects the Christian appropriation of Jewish titles, not the actual ethnicity of the addressees.[4] Further support is thought to come from Peter's understanding of his mission as evangelizing the circumcised (Gal 2:7-9). While Jewish Christians are no doubt present among the congregations addressed, the letter itself presupposes that Gentile Christians make up the more visible and dominant part of the audience.

First, Peter is remembered to have been God's first agent for evangelizing the Gentiles in the person of Cornelius and his household (Acts 10; 15:7), while Paul is remembered to have begun his work in each new city by preaching in the synagogue. Granted that the author of Acts may minimize differences and

---

[1]John H. Elliott, *1 Peter,* AB 37B (Garden City, N.Y.: Doubleday, 2000), pp. 87-89. Of course, the festival in Acts 2 does not represent the only occasion when Jewish pilgrims would have come into meaningful contact with the Jerusalem church. Three times each year crowds of Diaspora Jews came to the holy city, and so three times each year new, unnamed missionaries might have returned to their cities and towns with the fire of the gospel.

[2]Ibid., p. 90.

[3]See the review of scholarship in J. Ramsey Michaels, *1 Peter,* WBC 49 (Waco, Tex.: Word, 1988), pp. xlv-xlvi. Michaels himself, though, recognizes that they are largely Gentile Christians.

[4]The absence of any mention of non-Christian Jews, in fact, strikes some scholars as noteworthy. Michaels, for example, sees here a certain pro-Jewishness that aligns Christians with Jews against the hostility of pagans (ibid., p. liv) and evidence that the author did not subscribe to a "displacement" theory whereby the Christians took the place of Israel in God's plan (ibid., p. 1). The author's complete silence with regard to non-Christian Jews, however, may admit of less positive interpretations as well. Indeed, it could be the most extreme form of a displacement theory, in which the displaced body disappears, rather than a pro-Jewish avoidance of such a theory. While Michaels regards 1 Peter as a more moderate voice between Judaizers, on the one hand, and advocates of displacement, on the other, I read it as far less moderate than Paul, who at least still wrestled openly with the place of non-Christian Jews in God's covenant.

disagreements among the apostles, his presentation is not likely to have been fabricated in this regard; this makes it less than clear what that agreement in Galatians 2:7-9 really meant and to what degree Peter would have felt restricted by it. Moreover, the letter is not concerned with evangelizing but with strengthening disciples, so the agreement mentioned in Galatians 2:7-9 hardly applies at all to the question of audience.[5]

More important, the way the author refers to the addressees' past way of life makes it clear that he has Gentile Christians in view.[6] The Jewish heritage could hardly be described as "the futile way of life inherited from your ancestors" (1 Pet 1:18) or as an "ignorance" that failed to check the passions of the flesh (1 Pet 1:14). Even Paul, who is most sweeping in his claims that no one can be justified apart from Christ, holds Jews to have an enviable lot (see Rom 3:1-2; 9:4-5). The Jews' *heritage* is sound, which makes the mystery of their failure to respond to the gospel in droves all the more astounding to Paul. Moreover, the Torah was well recognized for its power to instruct people in virtue and even to train people in the mastery of the passions (see, e.g., 4 Maccabees and the *Letter of Aristeas*). "Ignorance" and "a futile way of life" distinguish Gentiles in this world of thought. Moreover, the past conduct of the addressees as described in 1 Peter 4:1-4 clearly marks them as Gentiles. Jewish scruples about sexual indulgence and excess in drinking alone make it unlikely that this could refer to Jews, but the inclusion of "abominable idolatries" clinches the case.[7]

THE PASTORAL PROBLEM ADDRESSED BY 1 PETER

Although he addresses a great variety of Christians, the author focuses on one central pastoral problem—helping these Christians endure in the face of their neighbors' negative reactions to their obstinate perseverance in the Christian faith. The author describes the audience's condition as one of great privilege (e.g., 1 Pet 1:3-5, 9-12; 1:13—2:10) and substantial distress (e.g., 1 Pet 1:6-7; 2:11-12, 15, 18-20; 3:13—4:6; 4:12-19; 5:8-9). The author presents these in such a way that the privilege is the more prominent and weighty, but this is part of his strategy for encouraging those who feel distressed to a greater degree.

A major cause of distress is the disrepute into which the believers have fallen in the eyes of their neighbors. Insult, slander and other forms of verbal abuse are prominent in this letter (1 Pet 2:12, 15; 3:16; 4:4, 14). The Christians find themselves maligned as though they were deviant and vice-ridden, unworthy elements of society. They have fallen victim to their society's social-control techniques of shaming, labeling and marginalizing, all reflective of their neighbors' attempts to cajole them back into conformity with the local customs and values (see especially 1 Pet 4:1-4). In some cases, however, this response extends to inflicting physical affronts where the law permits, as in the case of Christian slaves of unbelieving masters (1 Pet 2:18-21).[8]

In the eyes of their neighbors the Christian are seen to snub their former friends and as-

---

[5]See Peter H. Davids, *The First Epistle of Peter,* NICNT (Grand Rapids: Eerdmans, 1990), pp. 8-9.

[6]See Davids, *First Epistle of Peter,* p. 8; Michaels, *1 Peter,* p. xlvi; Elliott, *1 Peter,* pp. 96-97.

[7]The author's use of the term *Gentile* (e.g., 1 Pet 2:11-12) to denote unbelievers should not obscure this. He uses the term strategically to set the Gentile Christian readers apart from and over against their unbelieving compatriots. It is a boundary-marking term, not an ethnic one.

[8]It is important to continue to distinguish this from official, imperially enacted persecution, such as found localized in Rome under Nero and perhaps not again until Pliny was confronted with denunciations of Christians by the local population in Asia Minor (see Elliott, *1 Peter,* pp. 99-101). The persecution faced by the recipients of 1 Peter, as elsewhere, was the fruit of local resentment against and suspicion toward the converts to this seemingly subversive sect.

sociates (again, reflected in 1 Pet 4:1-4), pulling away from social gatherings, civic festivals and anything that involved even a hint of idolatry. This is clearly mandated by the apostolic gospel (see 1 Cor 10:14-21; 2 Cor 6:14—7:1; 1 Thess 1:9-10). This necessary withdrawal from all idolatrous religion and from settings where vice was all too prevalent made the Christians appear first as atheistic and second as antisocial in their new way of life (see the testimony of Tacitus *Ann.* 15.44; Minucius Felix *Octavius* 12). Denying the gods their due, Christians would have appeared impious and therefore dangerous because they might provoke the gods' disfavor. Their withdrawal from many associations with their neighbors would have made them appear factious, possibly subversive.

This would be complicated by the behavior of Christian slaves, wives or children in the household of an unbelieving master/husband/father, who would see Christianity as promoting disobedience in slaves (who would refuse to participate in domestic religious rites) and upsetting families (as wives or children withdrew from the religious activities of the household and embarrassed the husband/father in public settings). Good people show solidarity with their neighbors and pursue what makes for unity in a city or rural community. The converts no longer seemed to do either. The hostility, therefore, was primarily directed at shaming the Christians into returning to a more "respectable" way of life, one that affirmed the traditional gods, the traditional values of the region and the order of household and society, and secondarily to dissuading new conversions.

In such circumstances a believer might easily come to question the value of his or her faith, and whether or not its promises were sufficiently real to merit all the very real abuse suffered and insults endured. After a while,

conforming to the expectations of their neighbors, whether in small ways (making room for a few idols) or large (all-out defection), might seem sensible. First Peter seeks to counter this pressure. The author helps the believers to disallow their neighbors' disparaging remarks and other affronts. He underscores the great value of their faith in Christ and the advantages it brings over their former way of life (1 Pet 1:3-5, 10-12, 14, 17-19, 23; 2:4-10; 4:17-19), explains the experience of harassment in a way that renders it more endurable and its avoidance through apostasy disadvantageous (1 Pet 1:6-7; 2:21-25; 3:18-22; 4:1-6, 12-19; 5:8-10), and directs the Christians to such a winsome manner of life that their neighbors cannot help but be impressed with the virtue of Christianity (1 Pet 2:11-20; 3:1-16). In a sense 1 Peter really sets the agenda for the next two centuries of Christian history as Christians continue to struggle to demonstrate that their way of life is virtuous and worthy of imitation, not persecution. Though the "fiery trials" were destined to last many generations (indeed, they continue today in so many non-Western countries), the author's confidence that blameless conduct would eventually overcome suspicion and hostility proved correct.

WHO WROTE 1 PETER, AND WHEN?

Although scholars are fairly well agreed on the nature and situation of the audience, the authorship is a matter of dispute. Early Christian leaders accepted the letter's claim to come from Peter, the most prominent of the twelve apostles, with no serious dispute (see, e.g., Irenaeus *Adv. Haer.* 4.9.2; 4.16.5; 5.7.2; and Eusebius *Hist. eccl.* 2.15.2).[9] The same cannot be said of 2 Peter (see, e.g., the opinion of Origen on both letters cited in Eusebius *Hist. eccl.* 6.25.8), which speaks well of the early church's ability to face the difficult issues of authenticity with some de-

---

[9]These references are given in Michaels, *1 Peter,* pp. xxxii-xxxiii.

gree of critical acumen and a high degree of seriousness.[10]

Several hints from the letter might support the traditional view. For example, the author shows a broad awareness of Jesus sayings that are preserved especially in the Synoptic Gospels (but also John), especially the ethical teachings that are collected in the Sermon on the Mount.[11] In particular the notion of God's impartial assessment of human beings (1 Pet 1:17; cf. Acts 10:34), discipleship as conformity to the example of Christ in his sufferings (1 Pet 2:21-24; cf. Mk 8:27-38) and shepherding as an apt metaphor for leadership in the church (1 Pet 5:2-4; cf. Jn 21:15-17) resonate with traditions in which Peter plays a prominent role.[12] Some aspects of the letter take on a special irony if Peter is presumed to be the author, as for example the focus on "stones" gathering around Jesus, the foundational "stone," in 1 Peter 2:4-8, since Peter was the "rock" that Jesus himself found a "stumbling block" (Mt 16:23),[13] but this hardly contributes to an argument for Petrine authorship. An intelligent pseudonymous author might have taken more delight in such echoes than Peter himself.

During the past two centuries the letter's authorship has come into serious question. Prominent in these discussions are the following observations:

- Peter is described in Acts (admittedly by the opposition) as an "uneducated and untrained" person (Acts 4:13), and is remembered as needing Mark as an "interpreter" in Rome (but for the purpose of translating Greek, or Latin?), while the author of 1 Peter handles Greek masterfully.

- The author tends to quote the Jewish Scriptures according to the Septuagint text type rather than known Hebrew or Aramaic texts, which is held to be at odds with Peter's Galilean upbringing.

- The absence of any personal reminiscences of Jesus is striking: the author reveals a knowledge about Jesus that any reader of the Gospels would also have.

- The letter shows deep affinities with Pauline letters, suggesting a later author who was influenced by both Peter and Paul.

- The author refers to Rome as "Babylon," a practice otherwise seen only in literature written after 70 C.E. (e.g., *4 Ezra, 2 Baruch* and *Revelation*), when Rome destroyed the Jerusalem temple as historic Babylon had done 657 years before (see 2 Kings 24—25). If Peter died under Nero, his use of the eponym *Babylon* to refer to Rome would be strikingly ahead of its time.

- The situation presupposed by the letter is thought to reflect the conditions of Christians in Asia Minor later in the first century, even into the early second century, based largely on a comparison with Pliny's famous correspondence with Trajan (*Ep.* 10.96-97).[14]

These arguments collectively suggest to many scholars that 1 Peter was written by Peter's surviving associates in the Roman church (including Mark and Silvanus). Aware of their profound debt to Peter for their own formation, and believing that they could accurately convey the apostle's teaching, mind, and pastoral concern for the benefit of Christians in distant lands[15] (even as they would continue

---

[10]J. N. D. Kelly's observation that 1 Peter does not show any of "the telltale pointers to pseudonymity," such as too much attention to the personality and life experience of the alleged author or clear assumptions about the apostolic age being past, is also quite apt here, distinguishing 1 Peter from 2 Peter rather clearly (*The Epistles of Peter and Jude*, HNTC [New York: Harper & Row, 1969], p. 30).

[11]A fine resource for tracing these out is found in Davids, *First Epistle of Peter*, pp. 26-27.

[12]Elliott, *1 Peter*, p. 119.

[13]Michaels, *1 Peter*, p. lxi.

[14]See, further, Michaels, *1 Peter*, pp. lxxii-lxvi; Elliott, *1 Peter*, pp. 120-30.

[15]Elliott, *1 Peter*, p. 130.

to do in Rome *viva voce*), they ascribed the ultimate authorship of the letter to their deceased leader. The letter would still contain authentic Petrine traditions and teachings, mediated through the apostle's junior partners.[16]

As might be suspected, scholars favoring the traditional view have little trouble proposing counterarguments. With regard to style and literary quality, some allow that Peter grew in his facility in Greek expression over the thirty years of his work as a preacher and teacher, while others suggest that Peter had help from coworkers, gifted disciples or professional scribes.[17] During these decades, in which his ministry took him more and more into Greek-speaking areas, Peter would have become increasingly familiar with the Greek versions of the Old Testament and would begin to draw on them more than the Hebrew-text tradition remembered from his earlier years in Galilee and Judea. Affinities with Paul's letters reflect not Pauline influence so much as the common stock of early Christian tradition on which both Peter and Paul drew.[18] Finally, Peter may have called Rome "Babylon" on the basis of its Babylon-like character in other regards, such as its mastery of the world through power and violence, its self-glorification and its luxury, all of which are also prominent in the prophetic denunciations of Babylon (e.g., Jer 51). Even John, who wrote after the destruction of Jerusalem, does not tie that event in with his denunciation of Rome as Babylon (see Rev 17—18), underscoring rather the traits mentioned

above. It is not certain then that Babylon has to signal a post-70 C.E. date or that the destruction of Jerusalem is an essential prerequisite to applying this label to Rome.

The discussion about the nature of the claim to authorship made in 1 Peter 1:1 is far from resolved, but some guidelines for interpretation can be suggested. If, on the one hand, we decide that Peter was primarily responsible for writing the letter, we must recognize that Peter does so as a Christian teacher on the basis of shared Christian tradition thirty years after the resurrection. There is no warrant for introducing speculation about the connection between events in the life of Peter or what he may have learned privately from Jesus into the interpretation of the text.[19] If, on the other hand, Peter is not the author in the modern, conventional sense, he is the author according to more ancient notions of authorship—faithful disciples could be said to make the master speak afresh in new settings, addressing new challenges and questions. That is to say the letter can still preserve the authentic apostolic witness of Peter, adding his voice to the conversation within the canon, even without having been penned personally by him. Pseudonymity does not automatically preclude apostolicity.[20]

The letter was sent to the churches of the five provinces "through Silvanus" (*dia Silouanou*), a common way of designating not the coauthor but the bearer of a letter.[21] Silvanus, if he is to be identified with the Silas of Acts,

---

[16]Michaels, though favoring Petrine authorship, still admits this to be a possibility (*1 Peter,* p. lxvi).

[17]Davids attributes the style (and the points of contact with Paul) to Silvanus's hand in composing the letter (*First Epistle of Peter,* p. 7). But weighty arguments have been advanced for reading the formula "through Silvanus" as an indicator that Silvanus was the bearer of the letter, not the scribal agent (see Elliott, *1 Peter,* pp. 123-24; 872-74; and Michaels, *1 Peter,* pp. lxii, 306-7).

[18]See the extensive review of this question in Elliott, *1 Peter,* pp. 20-30, 37-40 (though he favors pseudonymity on other grounds).

[19]All the more if Davids is correct in his understanding of Silvanus's major role in the composition of 1 Peter (*First Epistle of Peter,* pp. 6-7).

[20]As it would be in the case of the many texts falsely attributed to apostles for the purpose of stealing credibility for non-apostolic notions.

[21]Michaels, *1 Peter,* pp. 306-7; Elliott, *1 Peter,* pp. 872-74.

acted as an emissary before (Acts 15:22-32). Such a ministry should not be regarded as that of an errand boy, but as an honored representative of the senders. The sequence of the names of the provinces (1 Pet 1:1) may indicate the route taken by Silvanus as he delivered this letter to various centers within each province for dissemination to the other Christians in the smaller cities and rural areas of the province.

Mark was first associated with Peter in Jerusalem (Acts 12:12), and after working alongside Paul Mark was remembered by Papias as Peter's "interpreter" in Rome and as the author of Peter's memoirs, in the form of Mark's Gospel. The mention of Mark here (1 Pet 5:13) is therefore quite appropriate for a letter ascribed to Peter. In both the Gospel and this letter he provides a link with the authentic voice of Peter in the memory of the early church.

The question of date is usually intertwined with that of authorship. If Peter substantially wrote the letter, and if the tradition of his martyrdom under Nero in 65-66 C.E. is correct, a date before that would be required.[22] The situation of the addressees would suit a pre-65 date since the kind of harassment they endured marked unbelievers' responses from the beginning.[23] If the letter was written in Peter's name by his coworkers after his death, a date between 70 and 96 C.E. would be most likely.[24]

1 PETER'S PASTORAL RESPONSE AND RHETORICAL STRATEGY

Peter's overall pastoral strategy consists of several complementary tactics. First, in stark contrast to their unbelieving neighbors' attempts to make them feel disgraced on account of their connections with Jesus, Peter reminds the hearers of the greater (and eternal!) honor and privileges that they enjoy as a result of those connections. He thus encourages them to remain committed to that distinctive confession and way of life that has brought them into disrepute in their neighbors' eyes. Second, he addresses head-on their experience of society's insult and abuse, reinterpreting these experiences as meaningful and even positive and honorable in light of their faith convictions. Third, he redefines what should be the primary focus and agenda for the Christians, namely, attaining God's promised benefits at the appearing of Christ. Finally, he prescribes a code of conduct for the believers in their relations with unbelievers and one another. Their interactions with outsiders are to be geared toward removing unnecessary prejudice against the Christian movement, while their interactions within the Christian community are to enhance mutual support and commitment to Jesus and to each other.

In support of these goals Peter offers a letter that builds extensively on recognizable Christian traditions. Recognizing what could be

---

[22]The validity of this tradition, of course, is open to serious question. Michaels, for example, maintains that the counter-tradition, namely, that Peter remained in Rome a long time and eventually had contact with Clement, to whom he passed the episcopal oversight, has just as much credibility (*1 Peter*, pp. lvii-lxi). However, Davids rightly counters that the tradition that Peter's long stay takes him past 68 C.E. is developed to serve the obvious agenda of linking Peter with Clement and ensuring apostolic succession. Peter may have both exercised a lengthy ministry in Rome *and* have been martyred in or around 64 C.E. (Davids, *First Epistle of Peter*, p. 10 n. 12).

[23]Jesus warned the disciples about the harassment they would experience (e.g., Mt 10:24-25), and Paul encouraged numerous congregations facing similar kinds of verbal abuse and unofficial pressure, as the Thessalonian letters and Philippians attest, all three of which predate 62 C.E. Hebrews, which probably predates 70 C.E., addresses a situation similar to and in some respects worse than that presupposed by 1 Peter.

[24]First Peter clearly informs Polycarp's *Letter to the Philippians*, written shortly after Ignatius passed through Asia Minor in 110-111 C.E. (see especially the echoes of 1 Peter in Pol. *Phil.* 1.3; 2.1-2; 8.1-2; 10.2-3), necessitating composition before 110 C.E. and probably before the turn of the century. *First Clement* shares many affinities with 1 Peter, so if dependence on 1 Peter can be established (see Elliott, *1 Peter*, pp. 138-40 for an impressive array of proofs in this regard), the latest possible date would be pushed back before 96 C.E.

snatches of early Christian hymns, references to the rite of baptism and its significance, and echoes of credal statements and other liturgical forms, scholars have long debated whether or not 1 Peter is really a "baptismal homily" or "baptismal liturgy" of some kind that has been given the veneer of epistolary form with the addition of such passages as 1 Peter 1:1-2 and 5:12-14.[25] Good observations about the resources Peter uses to support Christian commitment have often grown into imaginative theories about the "original setting" for the bulk of 1 Peter, in large measure obscuring how the letter was framed as a word on target for the congregations in the five provinces addressed. Most recent commentators, having a better view of the terrain of the text and less enamored with the speculative source theories that occupied earlier generations, recognize these theories to be dead ends. Rather, Peter roots his response widely and deeply in the Jewish Scriptures, in early Christian confessions about Jesus, in the important ritual experiences of his readers (like baptism), in Jesus' sayings, and in other familiar traditions so that the audience, recognizing the resources to be familiar and true, will more readily take to heart Peter's admonitions. His message will come to them with the force of their collective experience of Scripture and liturgy, of word and sacrament, which is the most effective way to affirm what is "the genuine gift of God" (1 Pet 5:12) for which he encourages them to persevere.

Reaffirming the honor and identity of the disgraced. Peter begins by addressing the Christians as "chosen exiles" (or better, "resident aliens"; 1 Pet 1:1), a striking oxymoron lost in nearly every English translation. The juxtaposition is critically important, however, since it defines quite precisely the paradox of Christian identity and experience in this life. On the one hand, they are no longer at home in their society. Like resident aliens, they no longer have a place participating in the central currents of their society (if they ever enjoyed this), but they find themselves pushed to the margins.[26] They are vulnerable, unprotected and exposed to the vicissitudes of strangers in a strange land. Using the label *Diaspora* to describe further the believers' experience invites them to understand that they cannot expect to be "at home" in their society—they have joined a new people whose home is elsewhere ("kept in heaven" rather than localized in Palestine, 1 Pet 1:4). On the other hand, and at the same time, they are specially "chosen," selected by God for a special destiny unlike that which awaits those who insult and cajole them. The first section of 1 Peter (1:1-2:10), although touching on the theme of suffering, focuses mainly on developing the implications of this chosenness for the honor and destiny of the believers.

The focal metaphor for their identity is their new birth into a new household with a new heritage and a new destiny.[27] Their posi-

---

[25]For an excellent review of such discussions, see Elliott, *1 Peter,* pp. 7-11; and Davids, *First Epistle of Peter,* pp. 11-13.

[26]Whether or not "resident aliens" (*parepidemoi*) should be taken literally as a reference to the addressees' legal status or metaphorically as an image defining what their relationship to society should be has been a matter of considerable debate. Elliott correctly points out that "resident alien" was an actual legal classification, and that the sense of displacement experienced by the believers lined up with the vulnerability of the resident alien living in the midst of a land not his or her own (*1 Peter,* pp. 101, 312-13). While there must have been many resident aliens who became Christians, perhaps attracted to the group on account of their need for a better-defined community and the support it afforded, there were also citizens (both of the local city and perhaps even those accorded Roman citizenship) and peasants as well. Thus the debate between literal and metaphorical sense becomes moot—what would be true literally of some comes to be applied metaphorically to all. Even the full-fledged citizens in the Christian community must come to view their lives in this world as that of "resident aliens." Elliott himself, in the final analysis, must admit this (*1 Peter,* p. 102).

[27]Thus, correctly, T. W. Martin, *Metaphor and Composition in 1 Peter,* SBLDS 131 (Atlanta: Scholars Press, 1992), p. 161-87; John H. Elliott, *A Home for the Homeless,* 2nd ed. (Minneapolis: Fortress, 1990).

tive response to Jesus has meant, first, a "new birth" (1 Pet 1:3) that differs markedly from their natural birth. The birth of their bodies destined them for the way of all flesh, namely, death and decay, but their new birth by reception of the word of God has destined them for an eternal life (1 Pet 1:23-25, using Is 40:6-8 as authoritative proof for this claim). Their old way of life was marred by "the futile ways inherited from [their] ancestors" (1 Pet 1:18 NRSV), ways of life marked by conformity to "the desires you had in ignorance" (1 Pet 1:14), exemplified in sexual excess, wild parties and idolatry (1 Pet 4:3-4). The believers have been ransomed from the paths of dishonor that end in God's judgment, and now look forward to deliverance from judgment (1 Pet 1:5, 9) and an eternal, pure and noble inheritance (1 Pet 1:4). In all these comparisons of their new and former identities, Peter stacks everything in favor of maintaining the new identity. Accepting his descriptions, the believers would be inclined to continue to resist attempts to get them to resume their former way of life. What would be gained by getting sucked back into that dead-end path? And great, lasting advantages would be lost!

One important subtheme introduced here is "holiness." Because they are now children of God, the Christians are called to reflect God's character (since children are held to reflect their parents). Peter invokes the heart of the Levitical holiness code—"Be holy, for I am holy" (Lev 11:44-45; 19:2)—as the warrant for this. In Israel this command manifested itself as the people did what they saw God doing—resting on the sabbath day, making distinctions between clean and unclean, and the like. The intense commitment to distinguishing between the clean and the unclean was a direct reflection of God's setting Israel apart (thus making it "clean") from the other nations

(see Lev 20:22-26). Jewish purity and dietary regulations, therefore, mirrored this ideology of election. They served to limit Jewish intercourse (in the broad sense) with Gentiles and to mark the Jewish people off as a distinctive and separate people wherever they lived.[28]

Early Christian leaders did not fail to make use of this important aspect of holiness. Christians will live out holiness by keeping themselves separate from those acts and settings that formerly characterized their way of life (1 Pet 1:14, 18) and that still characterize their non-Christian neighbors (1 Pet 4:3-4). The strategic value of this concept for the pastoral challenge Peter addresses cannot be missed. The danger is that their neighbors' pressure will wear down the believers' commitment to their visibly distinctive way of life. In response they must elevate the positive value of holiness and use this to bolster commitment to that same way of life. By doing so the believers reflect God's good character and show themselves to be God's children.

The theme of holiness continues to inform the rhapsodic description of the believers' new honor and privilege in 1 Peter 2:4-10. Peter first summons the believers to move forward toward their divinely appointed destiny—being joined together into a new temple of living bodies that serves as God's abode. The Christians are invited to become both temple and priesthood, a possibility opened up by the fact that God's Spirit now dwells in purified hearts (as in 1 Cor 3:16; 6:19) by virtue of the Christians' connection with Jesus Christ, the pivotal stone (1 Pet 2:4-5). The privilege of being God's house and priesthood draws the hearers in the centripetal direction Peter desires—toward Christ and one another, committed to Christian community—and offsets the centrifugal forces of society's pressures.

The Old Testament resources subtly em-

---

[28]For a more detailed analysis of purity and pollution, review the discussion of this cultural background earlier in this volume, and see David A. deSilva, *Honor, Patronage, Kinship and Purity* (Downers Grove, Ill.: InterVarsity Press, 2000), chaps. 7, 8.

bedded in 1 Peter 2:4-5 (i.e., Is 28:16 and Ps 118:22) are then openly recited in 1 Peter 2:6-8, with the addition of Isaiah 8:14-15. Peter brings these texts to the fore to establish the consequences both of belonging to Christ and of failing to recognize Jesus' honor and place in God's design. Though shamed now by their neighbors, the Christians are assured by Scripture that they "will not be put to shame" ultimately (1 Pet 2:6; LXX Is 28:16). Peter interprets this as a promise: "Honor, then, belongs to you believers!" (1 Pet 2:7).[29] This stands in stark contrast with the shameful consequences of their unbelieving neighbors' failure to obey God's word in Christ (1 Pet 2:8).

The section concludes with an accumulation of titles and labels attached to Israel in their original Old Testament context (mainly drawn from Ex 19:5-6; Is 43:20-21; Hos 1:6, 9; 2:23). Each one of these labels had been used to distinguish ethnic Israel from all other people groups: *chosen,* as opposed to not selected by God; a collective *priesthood,* thus set apart for a special level of interaction with the deity; a *holy nation,* as opposed to the profane nations that had not been so privileged; a *special possession* for God among the nations. Now they are applied to the Christian body of Jews and Gentiles to the same end, emphasizing their difference from the people around them and making that difference something to value positively and to preserve. Again Peter characterizes their past existence (to which their neighbors would draw them back) most negatively: *darkness* (which lines up well with "ignorance" in 1 Pet 1:14), *not a people* (lack of identity) and *excluded from mercy.* Having moved into the positive counterpart of all

these categories, why would they allow anything to draw them back? In all of this the authority of the Old Testament, from which the language and labels are drawn, undergirds Peter's appeal to the believers to maintain their new identity at all costs.

Reinterpreting the experience of suffering.
While reminding the Christians of the greater honor they have attained and will attain by virtue of their association with Jesus, Peter also enables perseverance in the face of their neighbors' disapproval and censure by interpreting that perseverance positively. The hostility of the unbelievers is not thereby excused, but it becomes the arena in which positive good can accrue to the steadfast believer.

At the outset Peter prominently speaks of the believers' "various trials" as the proving ground of the genuineness of their trust and commitment to God (1 Pet 1:6-7). He draws on the well-established philosophical tradition of the "probative" value of suffering, according to which God uses hardships to test and prove the worth of the righteous or the wise. Their neighbors' censure and hostility is thus no longer an actual assault on their honor, but an opportunity for the believers to attain greater "praise and glory and honor" in God's sight when Christ comes in glory. This strategically reorients them to the opposition—resistance to the pressures around them becomes the path to honor, whereas society taught that yielding was the road to recovery.

Peter also makes the astounding claim that suffering for the sake of the "name" (i.e., for Christ) is actually a "gift" or a sign of "favor" (*charis,* 1 Pet 2:19-20) before God. He declares that the one who thus suffers is

---

[29]This verse has been mistranslated in nearly every English version of the New Testament. Under the influence of translating the adjective *entimos* in 1 Peter 2:4, 6 as "precious," the KJV translators provided the same translation for the noun *timē* in 1 Peter 2:7, and they have been followed by generations of translators. First Peter 2:7, however, does not make an affirmation about the value of Jesus in the perception of believers (contrasted with the lack of value ascribed to Jesus in the perception of unbelievers, which is the topic in 1 Pet 2:4), but an affirmation about the destiny of those who have made such a positive evaluation of Jesus. Believers will receive honor, not shame, at the last, whereas unbelievers will "stumble" and "fall" into disgrace under God's judgment.

Suffering as "Proving Ground"

Both Jewish and Greco-Roman philosophers frequently interpret the experience of suffering in terms of its probative value. That is, by enduring sufferings, honorable people prove the reality of their virtue. The author of Wisdom of Solomon, for example, writes of the pious Jews who held firm in the face of the persecution of the ungodly:

> Though in the sight of others they were punished,
> their hope is full of immortality.
> Having been disciplined a little, they will receive great good,
> because God tested them and found them worthy of himself;
> like gold in the furnace he tried them,
> and like a sacrificial burnt offering he accepted them. (Wis 3:4-6)

The attempts of the ungodly to humiliate and hurt the righteous (detailed in Wis 2:12-20) become the means God uses to test and prove the commitment and value of the pious. The end result of perseverance is to enjoy rewards in God's presence. In a similar way the author of 4 Maccabees depicts Antiochus IV's torturous attempts to compel pious Jews to transgress the Torah as an opportunity for these Jews to be tested and proven. The first of seven brothers approaches the tortures as an opportunity to demonstrate that the "children of the Hebrews alone are invincible where virtue is concerned" (4 Macc 9:18 NRSV). The fifth brother gives ironic thanks to the tyrant for providing them with "an opportunity to demonstrate [their] endurance for the law" (4 Macc 11:12 NRSV), proving their commitment in deeds. Such a view of suffering is a natural development of the Jewish wisdom tradition, where we regularly find the metaphor of refining and proving precious metals applied to the work of the Lord in testing human beings and proving their worth (see Prov 17:3; Sir 2:5).

Peter's words (1 Pet 1:6-7) would also resonate with the Stoic tradition. Seneca, for example, writes that the wise person "counts even injury profitable, for through it he finds a means of putting himself to the proof and makes trial of his virtue" (*Constant.* 9.3). In another book that has striking connections with Hebrews and 1 Peter in terms of the educative and probative value of suffering, Seneca writes that "fire tests gold, misfortune [tests] brave men" (*Prov.* 5.10). Peter incorporates this tradition in order to assure the Christians that greater honor and acceptance comes not from yielding to their neighbors' pressure and thus recovering face in their eyes, but from resisting it to the end and gaining honor in God's sight. For a rich introduction to Jewish and Greco-Roman traditions about suffering, see N. C. Croy, *Endurance in Suffering*, SNTSMS 98 (Cambridge: Cambridge University Press, 1998), pp. 77-162.

"blessed" or "favored" or "honored" (*makarios*, 1 Pet 4:14). This clearly contravenes conventional wisdom, according to which suffering of any kind is seen precisely as a lack of divine favor, the absence of divine help. The taunt "Where is your God now?" familiar from the lament Psalms, bears witness to the popular conviction that God is not "with" those who suffer and are not immediately rescued. Indeed, their neighbors may even have used this taunt on them! Peter emphasizes, however, that God's favor is real and present for Christians in the midst of their trials; God is near to hear and help (see 1 Pet 3:12; 5:7).

Plato argued that it was better to suffer injustice than to inflict injustice (see *Gorg.* 469 C, for example), but Peter goes well beyond this philosophical commonplace, grounding his claims repeatedly in Christ's own example (1 Pet 1:11; 2:21-25; 3:18—4:2; 4:13).[30] Suffering for Christ is a favor or token of honor specifically because sharing in Christ's sufferings is prerequisite to sharing in his glory (1 Pet 4:13; see also Rom 8:17; Phil 3:10-11; 2 Tim 2:11-12). As the Christians conform to the pattern of Jesus' life in this world (a pattern that includes persevering in obedience to God in the face of great opposition), they can be assured that the honorable end to his story will be theirs as well. The Christians' identification with Christ, where that association now brings hardship and abuse, becomes their assurance of identification with Christ when God comes "to judge the living and the dead" (1 Pet 4:5). Suffering of this kind becomes a positive good, where Christians can keep the hope of vindication with Christ in the forefront of their mind.

As a third strategy for enabling believers to cope with the experience of censure and opposition, Peter calls into question the ability of the unbelievers to form a reliable opinion about what is honorable or shameful. After all, they are mired in sensuality and ignorance about the true God (1 Pet 4:1-3), and the main source of their opposition is their feeling of being alienated from their former associates who have turned to a better way of life (1 Pet 4:4). Peter also subtly reminds them of the difference between human opinion and God's opinion, notably as enacted toward Jesus. Human opinion is severely flawed and unreliable. What does the crucifixion say about Jesus' estimation in the eyes of human beings? But God showed them to be so wrong in this rejection of the cornerstone (1 Pet 2:4-8)! If they were wrong about Jesus, they are wrong now in their estimation of Jesus' followers. Their censure is "slander" (1 Pet 4:4), the "ignorance of the foolish" (1 Pet 2:15). And if God vindicated Jesus' honor in the resurrection (1 Pet 1:21), God will do same for Jesus' followers as well (1 Pet 4:4-5, 13; 5:10).

Those who interpret the word must remember that what 1 Peter says about suffering is specifically about suffering hostility and censure for the sake of being associated with Christ. Our text only affirms this kind of suffering as "in accordance with God's will," since it is brought on by obedience to God's commands and out of duty toward God. It does not speak about disease, domestic abuse, systemic oppression, violent crime, grief or deprivations brought on for some other reason. It would be dangerous to use 1 Peter to hallow forms of suffering not specifically addressed therein. God's word to people under such conditions must be sought elsewhere in Scripture.[31] Nevertheless, 1 Peter provides valuable resources for encouraging one another—especially those who face far worse opposition for their faith than 1 Peter's audience—to chose loyalty to God's ways above a peaceful conformity to the will of unbelievers.

Redefining the real challenge. Time and again we observe how a New Testament author helps the audience live up to the challenge of a faithful witness and walk by redefining what the real challenge is in their situation. By reorienting their perspective on their situation, the authors give believers the ideological edge they

---

[30]First Peter 2:21-25, incidentally, contains one of the earliest testimonies to early Christian interpretation of the Suffering Servant Song (Is 52:13—53:12) as a prophetic text illuminating the meaning of Jesus' death.

[31]See, further, David A. deSilva, "1 Peter: Strategies for Counseling Individuals on the Way to a New Heritage," *Ashland Theological Journal* 32 (2000): 33-54.

need to remain on track and not lose sight of the unseen goal. In 1 Peter this happens primarily as Peter reminds the addressees that their top priority is the successful acquisition of the gift of God to be manifested at Christ's coming (1 Pet 1:13; 5:13).[32] Because it has eternal consequences, this priority is raised far above any temporal concern, and it can assist those believers whose commitment to God's promises has been eroded by the waves of many years of censure and hardship for their faith.

Another place this strategy emerges is 1 Peter 5:8-9, where Peter sets the addressees' experience of opposition within the larger framework of the spiritual war over their lives. The slander and signs of rejection offered by their neighbors are the manifestations of the greater enemy, who seeks to defeat them—indeed, to swallow them up—by subverting their commitment to Christ. With such a vision Peter has transformed yielding to society's pressures (which might appear as a neutral act) into conceding victory to the devil (which could never appear positive to those who had once converted).

Finally, Peter repeatedly brings the imminence of the end to view (e.g., 1 Pet 1:5; 4:7, 17-19), making readiness for the judgment, and specifically being proved faithful at the judgment, a heightened priority for the addressees. Indeed, the very hardships imposed on Christians by their unbelieving neighbors are interpreted by Peter as a sign that God's judgment has in fact begun with God's own family. Jeremiah had similarly interpreted the devastation that would befall Jerusalem (Jer 25:29), taking it as a sign that the judgment of the non-Jews would follow quickly (see also *Testament of Benjamin* 10:8-9). For Peter, however, this in-house "judgment" is not punishment (as it will be for their detractors) but God's proving the sincerity of the Christians' commitment.[33]

So we see how Peter demonstrates that what appears to be the disadvantageous path (censure and scorn in this life) emerges as the truly advantageous path (honor and safety at the judgment and in the life to come).

Shaping Christian response to a hostile, suspicious society. By addressing the Christian readers and hearers as "chosen exiles" (1 Pet 1:1) and as "sojourners and resident aliens" (1 Pet 2:11), Peter encourages them to embrace the marginal status they occupy vis-à-vis the larger society. If they were marginal to that society before they became Christian, that marginality now takes on a positive meaning. If they were full-fledged citizens before their new lifestyle alienated them from their networks of associates and friends, their newfound marginality is not a loss to them. What is "alien" to them now, in fact, is the lifestyle they left behind, a lifestyle marred by ignorance of God and slavery to the passions. Peter urges them to embrace their marginality as an opportunity to consider their former life as "foreign" to them and to make greater progress in their life of virtue (1 Pet 2:11-12).

Despite being marginalized by their neighbors the Christians are instructed to behave respectfully in every situation (beginning with 1 Pet 2:13-17). Christ's example and teachings provide powerful sanctions against indulging in the same kind of insulting speech and behavior as they suffer:

> When [Christ] was abused, he did not return abuse; when he suffered, he did not threaten; but he entrusted himself to the one who judges justly. (1 Pet 2:23 NRSV)

---

[32]An observation well made in Martin, *Metaphor and Composition,* p. 269, 274.

[33]The quotation of Proverbs 11:31 in 1 Peter 4:18 provides another opportunity to observe the differences between the Hebrew Bible and the Septuagint text type. Compare the verse in Proverbs in the English Old Testament, which follows the Hebrew text, with the quotation here in 1 Peter, which follows the Septuagint. What is different about these renditions of the proverb? How does the LXX version serve Peter's point, where the Hebrew original doesn't?

Preaching to the Spirits in Prison

One of the more difficult passages in this letter is 1 Peter 3:19-22, where we read that Christ "made a proclamation to the spirits in prison" (1 Pet 3:19 NRSV). Who are these spirits, and what was the nature of Christ's proclamation to them? Two principal lines of thought emerge from the history of interpretation.

The first interpretation reads this passage as evidence that Jesus proclaimed the gospel to the departed souls in Hades (whether merely to those of the pre-flood age or to all those who died prior to his coming). Such a tradition finds ample support in early Christian literature. The second-century apocryphal *Gospel of Peter* says that as Jesus and two other men came forth from the grave, followed by the cross, the soldiers "heard a voice from heaven, saying, 'Have you preached to those that sleep?' " to which a voice from the cross responded "Yes!" (*Gospel of Peter* 10). Ignatius of Antioch also wrote that "he, whom [the prophets] were rightly awaiting, came to visit them, and raised them from the dead" (Ign. *Magn.* 9.2). The purpose of such proclamation either would be to offer salvation to these souls or perhaps to bring deliverance to the righteous dead who had waited for Christ's appearing. The latter stands behind the "Harrowing of Hell" traditions, in which Jesus leads a host of captives out from hell.

The second, and more probable, interpretation looks to the story of the "Watchers" for the background (see also 2 Pet 2:4-5 and Jude 5-7, two canonical texts that refer to this story explicitly). This story has its roots in the odd tale of Genesis 6:1-4, but it was expanded into a rich saga by the time of Jesus. The complete story can be found in *1 Enoch* 6—36, a very popular text from the second-century B.C.E. The Watchers are those angels who left their proper place to mate with human females, beget the giants and teach forbidden arts and practices to humanity. These are shut away in a prison by God, awaiting their final judgment and punishment (see *1 Enoch* 10.11-15; 18.13-16; 21.1-6). The location of this prison is not clear: it might be within the caverns of the earth (*1 Enoch* 10.4, 12-13; 14.5) or at the extreme reaches of earth and heaven (beyond the range of human travel; *1 Enoch* 18.1—19.2). *Second Enoch* 7 locates the prison in one of the lower heavens. This story has an intimate connection with Noah and the flood (as here in 1 Pet 3:18-22). The flood is God's "clean-up" operation after all the havoc and ungodliness wrought on the earth by the Watchers and their evil offspring (the giants), through whom they had infected humankind. Both Genesis 6:1-5 and *Jubilees* 5.1-5 also suggest a link between the Watchers, the giants and the flood.

In this interpretation 1 Peter 3:19 and 22 refer to the same reality (the subjection of the rebellious orders of angels to Christ) and same movement on Jesus' part (his ascent after his resurrection), not his activity among the dead between his own death and resurrection, which would then be out of sequence with 1 Peter 3:18. Enoch, whom *1 Enoch* presents as having been commissioned by God to proclaim to the Watchers their fate and the fate of their offspring (*1 Enoch* 12.4—13.3), becomes a type for Christ, just as Noah (saved through water) becomes a type for believers (saved through the waters of baptism). Christ's declaration of victory over the fallen angels would then assure the believers of their victory over the hostile forces and the demonic power ultimately behind those forces (see 1 Pet 5:8-9).

First Peter 4:6 raises many of the same questions as 1 Peter 3:19, speaking of "the dead" to whom "good news was proclaimed." Would this provide another indication that Christ took the gospel to the dead who had not had the opportunity to hear during their lifetimes? Again, second-century Christian texts bear witness to precisely this kind of expectation. Justin Martyr quotes the following as a verse omitted from Jeremiah: "The Lord God remembered His dead people of Israel and who lay in the graves; and He descended to preach *(euangelisasthai)* to them His own salvation" *(Dial. 72).*

The parallelism between 1 Peter 3:18 and 4:6, however, suggests a different solution. Christ was executed "in the flesh" and made alive "in the spirit," and these "dead" are "judged" in the flesh and thereafter live "in the spirit." The "dead," then, were Christians converted prior to their death. Like Christ, they died under the world's disapproval ("judged as men" would be better translated "condemned by human standards"), but are assured of a glorious future in the presence of God. Other churches had also wrestled with the problem of sisters and brothers who died before Christ's return (see 1 Thess 4:13-18). The judgment pronounced on their lives in the flesh was negative "in the sight of human beings," but they will yet live "in God's sight" as does the One they followed in life.

Do not repay evil for evil or abuse for abuse; but, on the contrary, repay with a blessing. (1 Pet 3:9 NRSV; cf. Lk 6:27-28)

Christians are to defend their honor in a much more constructive way than returning like for like. Throughout this letter Peter strategically seeks to shape the behavior of Christian wives of unbelieving partners (1 Pet 3:1-6), slaves of unbelieving masters (1 Pet 2:18-25), and Christians in general (1 Pet 2:12-17; 3:9-12, 16) so that the only "reproach" can be against their association with Jesus, not legitimately censurable conduct. Although feeling no shame at their neighbors' reproaches for being Christian, the believers are nevertheless challenged to show that these reproaches are groundless by their "honorable deeds" (1 Pet 2:12; cf. Mt 5:16).

Peter joins several other New Testament voices in calling believers to dispel the prejudice against them through moral, virtuous living (see also 1 Thess 4:11-12; 1 Tim 3:7; 6:1;

Tit 2:5, 8). This includes, in large measure, making every possible concession to the norms of the non-Christian society in order to show that Christians can fit in with conventional morality (save for specific points of conflict, like idolatry) and thus avoid conflict over matters nonessential to the Christian confession. This should lead us to take great care in our application of New Testament codes of conduct for slaves, wives, the governed and so on, lest we take what was a concession to first-century culture and read it as a mandate for twenty-first-century Christianity.

Converted slaves and wives would come into unavoidable conflict in the domestic sphere if the master or husband had not also become a Christian. Those within the household were expected to follow the religion of the head of the household (usually, but not always a male) as part of their recognition of the respect due the head.[34] The Christian's avoidance of idolatry would automatically bring

---

[34]Concerning wives, at least, Plutarch writes: "A married woman should therefore worship and recognize the gods whom her husband holds dear, and these alone. The door must be closed to strange cults and foreign superstition. No god takes pleasure in cult performed furtively and in secret by a woman" (Plutarch "Advice on Marriage" 19; *Mor.* 140D).

tension as the wife or slave refused to participate in the domestic rites that involved invocations of the household gods. For the slave it might also entail refusing commands that would compromise morality (for, indeed, slaves could also become the sexual playthings of the masters and mistresses of the household). Peter wants to ensure that if a slave must suffer in the household, it will not be for any perception of laziness or disrespect, but only for the sake of his or her commitment to Christ and the way of life Christ enjoins (1 Pet 2:18-25). Similarly, the Christian wife will so embody the cultural "ideal" of submissiveness, modesty and quietness that this will outweigh any displeasure incurred on account of her unwillingness to yield in matters religious (1 Pet 3:1-6).[35] The instructions given to Christian slaves become the advice given to Christians in general (cf. 1 Pet 2:18-25 with 3:13-22; 4:12-16). The expectation throughout is that Christians can overcome the prejudice against them by showing that discipleship does not make people subversive of the social order. In fact, it makes them better subjects (in every sphere, both public and domestic).

Once they are divorced from their original context, it is easy to see how these texts could become manifestos for maintaining the status quo, even under oppressive and unjust conditions. Such uses, however, lose sight of the author's goal for giving these instructions (as well as the arenas in which he calls for "civil disobedience") and make the prophetic Spirit a cipher for domination systems. Peter tells

slaves to be the best slaves they can in this situation; a few decades later John denounces the domination system—the great whore—built on the backs of slaves (Rev 18:11-13). We need great discernment to know how God would have us speak at any specific time and in any specific situation.

Shaping relations within the church. In order to withstand the loss of meaningful relationships with unbelievers and the reduction of emotional and material support from those connections, the early Christians had to surround one another with a love that equaled the love of kin. Indeed, since all Christians have been born anew by the same Father (see 1 Pet 1:23-24), it is appropriate that they assume the responsibilities and attitudes of siblings toward one another:

> Having purified your hearts . . . for an unfeigned brotherly and sisterly love, love one another constantly from the heart. (1 Pet 1:22)[36]

> Let all be of one mind, sympathetic, characterized by sibling love, compassionate, humble. (1 Pet 3:8)

The kind of relationships that siblings should manifest was well defined in the ancient world, and it is precisely to this level of support, mutual commitment, unity of mind and spirit, and humility in dealings with one another that Peter enjoins his addressees (1 Pet 3:8; 4:8-11; 5:5-6).[37] They are to be "family" for one another in the best sense of that word, which will give to each the inner and

---

[35]For more information on slavery and marriage in the first century, see deSilva, *Honor, Patronage, Kinship, and Purity*, pp. 178-93, 229-37, and the literature cited there.

[36]This is my translation. Translations like the NRSV that laudably aim for inclusive language where human referents are concerned unfortunately make bad choices when it comes to the language that evokes the all-important values of siblinghood and sibling love within the Christian community. Thus the NRSV renders "brotherly and sisterly love" in 1 Peter 1:22 as "genuine mutual love," and frequently replaces "brothers" with "believers" or "friends" rather than the more cumbersome but necessary "brothers and sisters." This drastically reduces the readers' awareness of the importance for early Christians of the conception of the church as a collection of people who lived out the obligations of siblings one to another.

[37]See, further, pp. 137-43, 436-38, and deSilva, *Honor, Patronage, Kinship and Purity*, 165-73, 212-26 and the literature cited there.

Hospitality and the Early Church

Hospitality, such as 1 Peter urges on its addressees (1 Pet 4:9), was regarded as a sacred obligation and sacred trust in both the Greco-Roman and Jewish cultures. The Greeks considered it an attribute of Zeus, seen for example in the epithet *Zeus Xenios,* "Zeus, friend of strangers." Dio Chrysostom refers to this title for Zeus and draws from it the moral that "it is the very beginning of friendship not to be unmindful of strangers or to regard any human being as an alien" (*Or.* 1.41).

In the early Jewish tradition, Abraham and Lot emerge as exemplars of hospitality (Gen 18—19). Lot shows the extreme value placed on the safety of guests, setting it above the virginity of his own daughters when the residents of Sodom came to call on him, demanding that Lot violate the duty of a host and turn his guests over to them. Wisdom of Solomon 19:13-17 censures the ancient Egyptians as inhospitable, interpreting the enslavement of the Hebrews as a violation both of the codes of hospitality and of the proper treatment of those who benefit a nation (recalling Joseph as the savior of Egypt).

Hospitality was of central importance to the early church, without which it would hardly have flourished as it did. The gathered community of disciples, together with those who were still inquiring into the movement, met most regularly in the houses of its wealthier members (see, e.g., Acts 18:7-8; 20:20; Rom 16:5, 23; 1 Cor 16:19; Col 4:15; Philem 2). Itinerant evangelists and teachers depended on hospitality as they spread the gospel and built up the church from place to place (Mt 10:11-15; Lk 9:4-5; 10:5-12; 24:28-31; Acts 9:43; 10:5-6; 17:5-7; 18:7; 20:20; 21:8-10, 15-16; 28:7; 2 Jn 1:10-11). It was critical, therefore, to keep reinforcing this value for the early church (see also Rom 12:13; 1 Tim 3:2; 5:10; Tit 1:8; Heb 13:2; 3 Jn 5-11).

---

external resources needed for perseverance.

All "ugly" behavior among siblings (such as the vices listed in 1 Pet 2:1) must be banished from the new family. The saying "love covers a multitude of sins" (1 Pet 4:8) should probably be heard in the context of the kinship ethic as well. In the *Testament of Joseph,* we find a comparable saying "love one another and in patient endurance conceal one another's shortcomings" (*T. Jos.* 17.2). The author of this text draws the lesson from his expansive retelling of the Joseph story that a brother or sister ought to hide the faults and disgraceful acts of his or her siblings rather than expose them to public view. Out of "brotherly love," many injuries are overlooked or covered over to save a sibling from falling into disgrace. Peter is thus not laying out some mystical teaching about removing sins but giving very practical advice for Christian community. It would be easy to focus on slights and errors, provoking feelings of enmity and arousing ill feelings, but the obligation to love one another as family calls us to eliminate rather than foster discord.

We also need to focus on the instructions given to Christian husbands (of Christian wives, Peter assumes, since whole households tended to convert when the head of the household did). It was a commonplace that women were "weaker" in the sense of having a more vulnerable constitution, and this observation about their nature was frequently used to justify their relegation to the private, indoor spaces, while men took up the work that would take them outside and into the more strenuous, public arenas (see Xenophon *Oeco-*

nomicus 7.22-28). Peter agrees with other Greco-Roman ethicists that the woman's "weakness" called for consideration, not domination. He goes beyond them, however, when he insists that Christian husbands honor their wives as "fellow heirs of the grace of life" (1 Pet 3:7; recall 1:4). Within the Christian home it is their relationship as sister and brother that ultimately governs the relationship, which stands in considerable tension with the hierarchical model of husband and wife taught in the culture. The model of "fellow heirs," hence sibling relations, makes cooperation as partners the dominant mode in the household rather than the female's submission to the male.

EXEGETICAL SKILL
Exploring Argumentative Texture

Most New Testament passages you encounter will have some dimension of "argumentative texture." The passage will be part of an attempt to demonstrate some thesis, motivate some action, uphold some value—in short, it will have some persuasive goal and thus use persuasive strategies. We have looked at various aspects of rhetorical criticism throughout this book, including recognizing and analyzing appeals to the emotions, to the reliability of the speaker and to various kinds of rational argument. Following a New Testament author's argument depends on our ability to answer questions such as: How do sections of the document cohere as persuasive demonstrations? Can we discern how the whole coheres as a "logical" demonstration? How are exhortations "explained" by rationales or grounded in discussions of theology or ecclesiology? What premises are shared by the author and recipients, but not explicitly expressed in the discourse? Close analysis of the argumentative steps an author takes is an essential part of exegesis, and 1 Peter openly invites further exploration of this aspect of interpretation.

Arguments come in many different kinds and forms, but one pattern of argumentation that many aspiring orators learned early in their education merits close attention. This is not because Peter was formally trained in rhetoric, but because the more basic a rhetorical concept is, the more likely it is that a sharp speaker would be exposed to it and be able to imitate and employ it him- or herself. The "elaboration" pattern (also called "descanting on a theme") was a staple of *Progymnasmata,* the elementary exercises in rhetoric that came rather early in the curriculum. The pattern establishes a variety of different approaches a speaker might take to demonstrate a claim or thesis of some kind, or to elaborate on a principle. The elaboration generally proceeded as follows:
1. the statement to be defended or elaborated
2. a rationale in support of the statement
3. a confirmation of that rationale
4. a restatement of the claim in the contrary form (e.g., if the original

claim was expressed positively, this restatement would be in the negative)

5. an appeal to an acknowledged written authority in the culture of the speaker (e.g., a line from Homer or, in the case of Jews and Christians, the Old Testament)

6. a historical example where the statement proved true

7. an argument from analogy (a general observation about nature, society or the like that supported the statement)

8. a conclusion to wrap up the demonstration

First Peter comes very close to this pattern at two points (1 Pet 2:18-25 and 4:12-19), with the result that knowledge of the pattern can help us discern and explain how Peter's argument unfolds.

1 PETER 2:18-25

Thesis in the form of a command: "Servants, be submissive to your masters with all respect, not only to the kind and gentle but also to the overbearing."

Rationale: "For one is approved if, mindful of God, he endures pain while suffering unjustly."

Argument from the contrary (confirming the rationale): "For what credit is it if when you do wrong and are beaten for it, you take it patiently?"

Restatement of the rationale: "But if you endure patiently when you suffer for doing right, you have God's approval."

Argument from historical example (repositioning the argument): Halfway through the hearer is made to focus on his or her indebtedness to Christ, which gives impetus to submitting to Christ's example. "For to this you have been called because Christ also suffered for you, leaving you an example that you should follow in his steps. He committed no sin; no guile was found on his lips. When he was reviled, he did not revile in return; when he suffered, he did not threaten; but he trusted him who judges justly. He himself bore our sins in his body on the tree that we might die to sin and live to righteousness. By his wounds you have been healed."

Conclusion (based on repositioned argument): In this case, the conclusion is based on our relationship to Christ, including an embedded appeal to the analogy of shepherding. "For you were straying like sheep but have now returned to the Shepherd and Guardian of your souls."

1 PETER 4:12-19

Thesis in the form of a command (stated in the negative): "Beloved, do not be surprised at the fiery ordeal which comes upon you to prove you, as though something strange were happening to you."

Restatement of the thesis in the form of a command (positively) with a rationale: "But rejoice in so far as you share Christ's sufferings, that you may also rejoice and be glad when his glory is revealed."

Confirmation of the rationale: "If you are reproached for the name of Christ, you are blessed, because the spirit of glory and of God rests on you."

Contrary: "But let none of you suffer as a murderer or a thief or a wrong-doer or a mischief-maker."

Restatement of the thesis: "Yet if one suffers as a Christian, let him not be ashamed, but under that name let him glorify God."

Second rationale: "For the time has come for judgment to begin with the household of God; and if it begins with us, what will be the end of those who do not obey the gospel of God?"

Argument from written authority: "And 'If the righteous person is scarcely saved, where will the impious and sinner appear?'"

Conclusion: "Therefore let those who suffer according to God's will do right and entrust their souls to a faithful Creator."

Such an analysis does not seek to merely attach labels to the parts of an argument, but to provide a framework that can help us discern more carefully and precisely how each new sentence advances the case that the author is making.

Not all arguments follow this "elaboration" pattern, but within it we see many of the basic building blocks of ancient argumentation. It leads us to look further in 1 Peter, not for the whole pattern but for places where a point is being defended by an appeal to a written authority (i.e., the Jewish Scriptures) or an authoritative example (e.g., the life of Jesus), or where a point is being argued by considering its opposite (an argument from the contrary). It also leads us to look closely at the rationales used to support claims made by the author, for these are places where we can reconstruct that world of presuppositions and beliefs shared by author and recipients. This happens not only where we see a claim followed by a clause giving a reason ("Pursue X because Y"). Where we find "if . . . then . . ." clauses, we can also inquire further into the hidden premise that makes the "then" clause follow logically from the "if" clause. Where commands or exhortations have a rationale, we may discover a hidden premise that lets us into the implicit logic of the document (located in the world of meanings shared by author and recipient).

We may consider 1 Peter 4:1-2, for example. The exhortation to "arm yourselves" to suffer in the body is grounded in the rational "since Christ suffered in the flesh." This works "logically" only if the author and recipients share the presupposition that the disciple is to imitate Christ or somehow replicate Christ's experience in his or her own life (cf. Jn 15:20). As we examine the use of Christ's example throughout the letter, we find that the disciple's solidarity with Jesus' experience is indeed a major foundational premise for much of 1 Peter.

This kind of analysis also makes us carefully consider exactly what exhortations or statements a rationale is meant to support. For example, a rationale is embedded within 1 Peter 2:11-17, namely in verse 15. Does the rationale relate only to verses 13-14, or to the whole? Or in 1 Peter 2:1-3, the fact that we "have tasted the kindness of the Lord" is brought in as a rationale to support the exhortation to "put away all malice and all guile and insincerity and envy and all slander" and to "long for the pure spiritual milk, that by it you may grow up to salvation." Is the rationale "working" to support 1 Peter 2:1-2 by saying "since you have tasted God's kindness you are obliged to let that kindness appear in all your dealings with one another and the world"?

As a further exercise you are invited to work through the two extended passages given above, inquiring into hidden presuppositions as well as why the author would reposition the first argument from a discussion of the merits of suffering unjustly to a discussion of our return to obedience to Christ. You might then practice further by analyzing the argumentative texture of the following passages in terms of categories selected from the full pattern of elaboration explored above: Matthew 6:25-34; 1 Corinthians 9:1-12; 15:12-22, 29-34 (vv. 23-28 is a digression); Hebrews 6:1-8; 12:3-11. Inquire into the logic of each step in the argumentation. What makes the argument "work"? What convictions must the audience and author share? Are there leaps in logic, and how might the audience overcome these?

The elaboration and other patterns of argumentation and very helpful lists of specific topics and strategies employed in argumentation and refutation can be found in such texts as Theon of Alexandria's *Progymnasmata* (available in G. A. Kennedy, *Progymnasmata: Greek Textbooks of Prose Composition and Rhetoric* [Atlanta: Society of Biblical Literature, 2003]) and Aristotle's *Art of Rhetoric*. (See also "Exegetical Skill: The Analysis of Topics," pp. 572-75). These and other ancient textbooks on logic and rhetoric are indispensable aids to helping us unpack the argument of a New Testament text and to enter into the thought world of the early Christians that made these arguments "logical" and "convincing."

1 PETER AND MINISTRY FORMATION

Our discussion of Peter's pastoral response to the pressures faced by his audience feeds directly into the pastor's ongoing challenge of nurturing a distinctive, Christian identity that encourages believers to distance themselves ideologically from the expectations of their society. We do this so they will be free to pursue the actions and embody the values God sets before them. In many settings, notably those where Christianity is a restricted or proscribed religion (such that our fellow believers face far worse now than Peter's addressees), Peter's strategies can be adopted without substantial modification as resources for empowering costly obedience and ongoing witness. At the same time, however, Christian sisters and brothers in free countries are responsible to their family under repressive circumstances, both to aid them directly through prayer, emotional connections and material support, and to lobby for an end to the repressive policies and practices through raising public awareness and using the machines of politics and foreign policy.

In lands where Christianity has been a long-established, tolerated religion, 1 Peter can assist in recovering a distinctive sense of Christian identity and in challenging believers thoroughly at home in their society. Is their comfort level due to their having lost sight of the call to holiness (1 Pet 1:13-16)? Have they hallowed the "futile ways inherited from the ancestors" (1 Pet 1:18) and thus failed to surprise their non-Christian neighbors by living out a different set of values (1 Pet 4:3-4). What priorities should we be striving for? What idolatries and passions should we be abstaining from? First Peter provides rich resources for helping comfortable Christians recover their vision and step out boldly from collusion with all that is not of God in society—and then endure when neighbors and colleagues begin to question and even censure.

This letter also reminds us that individuals will progress in faith and witness only as much as the community of believers supports them. Running throughout the New Testament are clarion calls to the church to be "family" to one another, to contravene biological conceptions of the boundaries of family and invest ourselves in Christians we know and those we don't know—as if we were born of the same Parent.

Peter also provides important reflections on leadership in the church in his advice to elders (1 Pet 5:1-4). We must take care not to read back our denominational policies of ordination or the meaning of the terms *elder* and *deacon* into the early church's setting. A clear, hierarchical polity was slow in forming. *Elder* refers in the first instance to those who were "senior" in age and experienced in the faith, and it was most natural for leadership responsibilities to fall to the senior members of a congregation. It does not refer to "paid staff," although such leaders would be included in the admonitions; it refers to all who exercise leadership in the local congregation. This might include pastoral care, orchestrating relief within the local church, presiding over assemblies and sharing in the teaching.

Many churches, where members look to the "paid staff" to do the work of ministry and avoid responsibility themselves, suffer from a lack of indigenous, natural leadership. In other churches the opposite problem emerges, where a few elders attempt to control the congregation. First Peter calls for leadership that is both healthy and strong, challenging the elders in churches at both ends of this spectrum.

Peter urges those who are called on for service (whether teaching the senior high youth, organizing a missions trip or giving direction to a stewardship program) to do so "not under compulsion," but understanding this as an invitation to work with God to strengthen and build the church, and thus to give specific expression to the general obligation to show love for their sisters and brothers. Moreover, God equips and strengthens those whom God calls out in such ways (1 Pet 4:11).

We do not labor in the church, however, for temporal profit, whether in the form of material gain (which could be as subtle as using our "service" in the church as a means of promoting our local business) or personal influence. Leaders need especially to be free of the love of money (1 Tim 3:8; Tit 1:7), and indeed this distinguishes the sincere minister from those who "peddle the word of God" (2 Cor 2:17; see *Didache* 11—13). The salaried staff of the church must also model what it means to labor for an imperishable reward, namely, unfading honor in Christ's kingdom. On the one hand, this does not mean denying the legitimate needs of self and family where a church has set an inappropriately low compensation; on the other hand, we need to recognize how much is truly "enough" and to model the very noncapitalist value of contentment with what we have. The pastor and other ministry staff should resist the pressure to compare their compensation with those in other fields, modeling confidence in the promise that, "when the chief shepherd appears, you will receive the unfading crown of honor" (1 Pet 5:4).

Using ministry (whether lay or clergy) as a means to power or influence is also entirely out of keeping with the model of Jesus, who "came not to be served but to serve" (Mk 10:45), and the model of the apostles (see 2 Cor 1:24). It is their example that the Christian leader is called to model in his or her leadership, thus contravening the popular values of enjoying precedence and dominance. An elder in a local church might regard his recompense for good and faithful service to be the unspoken right to have things go his way, both within and beyond his sphere of immediate involvement. A pastor or counselor might forget the healing arts as she seeks to dominate the "patient" in her role as the expert in a theological disagreement. Whatever the scenario, good shepherding requires the dismissal of every inner drive to dominate. The hierarchy described by the author of 1 Peter is helpful in this regard: there is one chief Shepherd. To all other shepherds belong neither the flock nor the turf, but only the opportunity and obligation to tend what is Another's.

FOR FURTHER READING

Achtemeier, Paul J. *1 Peter.* Hermeneia. Minneapolis: Fortress, 1996.

Balch, David L. *Let Wives Be Submissive: The Domestic Code in 1 Peter.* SBLMS 26. Chico, Calif.: Scholars Press, 1981.

Campbell, Barth. *Honor, Shame, and the Rhetoric of 1 Peter.* SBLDS 160. Atlanta: Scholars Press, 1998.

Chester, Andrew, and Ralph P. Martin. *The Theology of the Letters of James, Peter, and Jude.* Cambridge: Cambridge University Press, 1994.

Davids, Peter H. *The First Epistle of Peter.* NICNT. Grand Rapids: Eerdmans, 1990.

deSilva, David A. "1 Peter: Strategies for Counseling Individuals on the Way to a New Heritage." *Ashland Theological Journal* 32 (2000): 33-52.

Elliott, John H. *A Home for the Homeless: A Social-Scientific Criticism of 1 Peter, Its Situation and Strategy.* 2nd ed. Minneapolis: Fortress, 1990.

————. *1 Peter.* AB 37B. Garden City, N.Y.: Doubleday, 2000.

Goppelt, Leonhard. *A Commentary on 1 Peter.* Grand Rapids: Eerdmans, 1993.

Kelly, J. N. D. *The Epistles of Peter and Jude.* HNTC. New York: Harper & Row, 1969.

Marshall, I. Howard. *1 Peter.* IVPNTC. Downers Grove, Ill.: InterVarsity Press, 1991.

Martin, Troy W. *Metaphor and Composition in 1 Peter.* SBLDS 131. Atlanta: Scholars Press, 1992.

McKnight, Scot. *1 Peter.* NIVAC. Grand Rapids: Zondervan, 1996.

Michaels, J. Ramsey. *1 Peter.* WBC 49. Waco, Tex.: Word, 1988.

Reicke, Bo. *The Epistles of James, Peter, and Jude.* AB 37. Garden City, N.Y.: Doubleday, 1964.

Talbert, Charles H., ed. *Perspectives on First Peter.* National Association of Baptist Professors of Religion Special Studies Series 9. Macon, Ga.: Mercer University Press, 1986.

23

JUDE AND 2 PETER

The Dangers of Deviant Disciples

These two short letters, full of obscure allusions, full of the spirit of polemic and addressing murky situations, are perhaps appropriately nestled toward the back of the New Testament, where they can be revered and conveniently forgotten. Indeed, they make no substantial appearances in Sunday lectionaries, are rarely the subject of "book studies" in churches and do not readily invite appropriation in personal times of devotion.

Nevertheless, these texts speak to two issues of great relevance for the contemporary church, namely, the location of authority in the church (Jude) and the challenges of maintaining an apocalyptic hope for rational people (2 Peter). They also preserve important witnesses to the diversity of the early church, which is often too easily lost to view in the shadow of Paul and Paul's greatest promoter, the author of Acts. Here, a younger half-brother of Jesus reminds the churches of its deep roots in the Jewish Scriptures and Palestinian Jewish traditions, and an unknown author, who apparently does not find Paul's writings all that helpful given their potential for misuse (2 Pet 3:15-16), provides a model for an "enlightened" Christianity that does not lose its apostolic moorings.

THE LETTER OF JUDE

Authorship and date. This letter presents itself as the product of "Jude, a servant of Jesus Christ and brother of James" (v. 1 NRSV). The hearer thus encounters the voice of one of Jesus' younger half-brothers (see Mt 13:55; Mk 6:3) who, together with "James the Just," exercised a leadership role in Jewish Christianity. Western Christianity has tended to focus on the great missionary apostles Peter and Paul, with their connections to the great Gentile centers of Christianity like Rome, Ephesus, Corinth and the like, forgetting the important role played in Palestine by the blood relations of Jesus, particularly by James (see Acts 15; 21). According to the traditions of the early church, leadership stayed in the family. During the reign of Domitian we find Jesus' "grand nephews," the grandsons of Jude, stepping forward to take the helm of the Jerusalem church and guiding it into the reign of Trajan (see Eusebius *Hist. eccl.* 3.19.1-3.20.8).

But did Jude truly write this letter, or was it written in his name by someone claiming his authority and speaking, as it were, on his behalf to a situation after Jude's death? Some arguments against authenticity are weak indeed, particularly the argument that the letter reflects an "early Catholic" (i.e., early second century) perspective as the author speaks about "the faith that was once for all entrusted to the saints" (v. 3).[1] *Faith* is understood here to denote a deposit of doctrines that must be

---

[1]Thus Eduard Lohse, *The Formation of the New Testament,* trans. M. E. Boring (Nashville: Abingdon, 1981), p. 216; J. N. D. Kelly, *The Epistles of Peter and Jude,* BNTC (London: Adam & Charles Black, 1969), pp. 233-34.

defended against heresy, a use appropriate to the second-century disputes against Gnostics and other heretics, rather than the more dynamic sense of Jesus' faithfulness toward believers or believers' toward Jesus (as in Paul).

Granted that Jude does not use *faith* in a manner typical for Paul, it does not follow that the use is *later* than Paul. Indeed, Paul himself bears witness to such use when he recites the words of amazement spoken by those reporting on his postconversion preaching: "The one who formerly was persecuting us is now proclaiming the faith he once tried to destroy" (Gal 1:23 NRSV). Here too *faith* is used to denote the whole set of commitments and way of life that flows from accepting the gospel, and it is an undeniably early use. Paul will even use the word himself with this meaning (Phil 1:27), again in the context of opposition and defense (as in Gal 1:23; Jude 3).[2] Moreover, Jude manifests none of the other marks of "early Catholicism," namely, the waning of apocalypticism and assumption of a well-developed church hierarchy. Jude is thoroughly apocalyptic and steeped in the apocalyptic traditions of early Judaism (see vv. 14-15, 21, 24),[3] and makes no appeal to church leaders to deal with the problem of the false teachers.

A more cogent challenge to authenticity focuses on the command of the Greek language, both with regard to a varied vocabulary and consistent style. Many find this to be inconsistent with authorship by a junior son in a Galilean artisan family.[4] Although Galilean craftspersons could be expected to know enough Greek to do business with non-Jews living in the cities of that region, especially the Roman occupying force, it is highly improbable that such a background would have equipped Jude to write so fine a letter. However, this argument assumes that Jude could not have acquired proficiency in Greek composition during the decades of his work in Jerusalem and his missionary endeavors (see 1 Cor 9:5, where Paul refers to the "brothers of the Lord" being accompanied by their wives on their missionary work). The cogency of the argument from style and diction, therefore, is proportional to the limits we place on Jude's ability to learn the skills of a bilingual communicator in his new life as a leader of a religious movement.[5]

Alongside such considerations we must also ponder the letter's deep roots in Palestinian Jewish traditions. First, the author uses the Jewish Scriptures from a text type more reflective of the Hebrew than the Septuagint. For example, Jude 12 echoes an image from the Hebrew Proverbs 25:14 "clouds and wind without rain" that is not conveyed in the Septuagint ("like winds and clouds and rains"); Jude 13 speaks of "wild waves . . . casting up the foam of their shame," borrowing an image from the Hebrew Isaiah 57:20 ("the tossing sea" whose "waters toss up mire and mud") absent from the Septuagint version of this verse.[6] Second, the author shows a broad familiarity with works like *1 Enoch* and extrabiblical traditions about Cain, Balaam and Moses that are otherwise mainly attested in Palestine (see, e.g., *1 Enoch*'s popularity at Qumran). The author shares with the Qumran community the hermeneutical principle that the Hebrew Scriptures speak about the last days, which are being fulfilled in the particulars of the life of the sect and its leaders and opponents.

Arguments for a later date also appeal to

---

[2]A similar use can be observed side-by-side with the more relational use of the term throughout Acts (see Acts 6:7; 13:8; 14:22; 16:5), Ephesians (Eph 4:5, 13) and Colossians (Col 1:23; 2:7), none of which need be late documents.

[3]See R. L. Webb, "The Eschatology of the Epistle of Jude and Its Rhetorical and Social Functions," *BBR* 6 (1996): 139-51.

[4]For example, Kelly, *Epistles of Peter and Jude*, p. 233.

[5]Richard J. Bauckham discusses the quality of style and language at some length, also favoring Jude's ability to grow into new skills and facilities (*Jude, 2 Peter*, WBC 50 [Waco, Tex.: Word, 1983], pp. 6-7, 15-16).

[6]Bauckham, *Jude, 2 Peter*, p. 7.

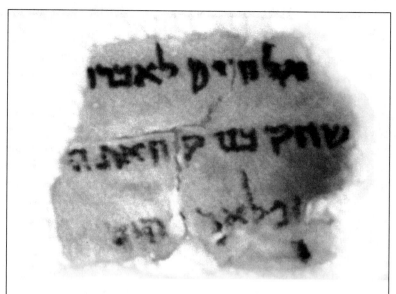

Figure 23.1. An unpublished fragment of a commentary, or *pesher*, on Genesis 22. This is one of a myriad of such fragments from the Dead Sea Scrolls. (Courtesy of a private collector)

Jude 17-18, which are taken to reflect a situation after the deaths of the apostles (and hence a period after 70 or 80 C.E.). The author, however, is only asking the audience to remember the "words" spoken to them by the apostles (i.e., those apostles who founded and nurtured these particular communities) at some time in the past, and he presupposes that the same audience who heard those apostles now hears the letter of Jude being read to them. That is to say, the apostles' converts are Jude's audience, and not a later generation of believers.[7]

The cumulative evidence of the foregoing suggests that the letter may very well have been written by Jude himself, and may be contemporaneous with the letters of Paul or, at least, date from a period not later than 80 C.E. This short letter becomes, then, not another stage in the monolithic, linear development of early Christianity, but a witness to the vibrant diversity of traditions and voices that contributed to early Christian discourse in its first generation.

Purpose and strategy. Although commonly classified as a "general" epistle, meaning a letter written broadly to Christians in many locations and facing a variety of challenges, Jude addresses a very specific problem posed by the emergence of a very particular group of teachers. It is not, like James, a collection of good advice for churches in any locale (and, in effect, any time), but a letter written as a pastoral response to address a particular challenge facing the readership. Indeed, Jude has turned aside from writing a letter of a different kind— a letter concerning "the salvation we share"— to address this new exigency.

The congregation or congregations addressed have encountered itinerant Christian teachers bearing a message that Jude considers incompatible with the apostolic gospel. Itinerant teachers claiming revelations received from God as their authority and legitimation (by

---

[7]Bauckham, *Jude, 2 Peter,* p. 13.

The Pesharim of Qumran

The community at Qumran was intensely interested in not only the preservation of texts (evidenced by the massive cache of scrolls found in the eleven caves around or near their settlement) but also the interpretation of texts. One focal point for such interpretative activity was the proper way to live out the Torah and to perfect holiness in the land. Another focal point was the meaning of the prophetic books (including the Psalms, which were treated not only as hymns but also as prophetic oracles). Several biblical commentaries, called *pesharim*, were found among the Dead Sea Scrolls. These all have a similar form. A brief passage of Scripture is recited, and then its interpretation is given (hence the name, from the Hebrew *peshro*, "its interpretation is . . .").

Perhaps the most celebrated of these is the *Commentary on Habakkuk* . In this *pesher*, passages from Habakkuk are interpreted as being fulfilled in the early history of the sect, with the rise of the Teacher of Righteousness, the ongoing opposition of the Wicked Priest (probably the high priest Jonathan, one of the brothers of Judas Maccabeus and the first Hasmonean to have the title of high priest) and his allies, the growing power of the Roman Empire, the community of the faithful at Qumran, the continued rejection of their teaching by the majority of Israel, and events yet to come in the story of the sect and God's judgment of Israel and the nations. The commentaries on Isaiah, Nahum and the Psalms also make explicit connections between the Scriptures and the fulfillment of their prophecies in the ongoing history and future expectations of the Qumran community.

Of great importance to New Testament study is the parallel mode of interpretation: the Scriptures foretold and legitimate the founder of this group and their way of living out "righteousness" before God; the opposition to the group and its leader is not disconfirming but was foretold long ago; the eschatological prophecies have to do specifically with the future of the sect and the way God will vindicate their way of life and their covenant loyalty at the end of days. For further investigation, see G. Vermes, *The Complete Dead Sea Scrolls in English* (New York: Penguin, 1997), pp. 466-504; Larry R. Helyer, *Exploring Jewish Literature of the Second Temple Period* (Downers Grove, Ill.: InterVarsity Press, 2002), pp. 226-53 (also an excellent point of departure into current scholarship on this literature and on the question of its relevance for New Testament study).

dreaming, v. 8) were a familiar phenomenon in the early church. The reawakening of the prophetic voice and the belief that God would reveal truth and insights directly to believers through the Holy Spirit prominently characterized early Christianity. Paul, for example, expects such manifestations to be part of the life of every congregation (see 1 Cor 12:1-11, 27-31; 14:26-33). It should not surprise us, then, to find Christians taking these gifts "on the road," sometimes for the edification of other churches, sometimes for the false prophet's own enrichment and enjoyment of esteem and influence. Discerning the true from the false charismatist therefore became a pressing need (see the injunctions and advice given in Mt 7:15-20; Col 2:18-19; 1 Jn 4:1-3; *Didache* 11—12).

Jude intervenes in this discernment process on behalf of his addressees. Very little is known about the teachers' doctrine, although it has been popular (and highly speculative) to label them as Gnostics.[8] Jude, rather, observes

---

[8]See, for example, Kelly, *Peter and Jude*, p. 231.

Figure 23.2. The interior and exterior of one of the caves (Cave 4) in the area surrounding the Qumran settlement, where many of the Dead Sea Scrolls were found. (Photos courtesy of Todd Bolen [Bible-Places.com])

the fruits of their message in their own life and perceives their distance from God on that basis. The main problem appears to be their disregard for the ethical norms upheld in both Jewish and Christian tradition, perverting "the grace of God into licentiousness" (v. 4; see also vv. 6-7, 8, 16, 18). Paul himself had been accused of this very thing, since the grace of God meant setting aside Torah as binding law (Rom 3:8; 6:1), and he had to defend himself by showing how this grace really led to the ability to live a self-controlled, moral life that was entirely in agreement with the moral standards of God's law (Rom 6:1—8:11). Others, however, would indeed use grace as an opportunity for the flesh and the gospel as an opportunity to set aside conventional morality. This interpretation of grace manifested itself in the sexual indiscretions of Corinthian Christians (see 1 Cor 5—6) and in the freer association with idolatry among some Christians in Asia Minor (Rev 2:14-16, 20-25). Moreover, the flouting of authority (so prominent a part of Jude's characterization of these teachers—vv. 4, 8,

10, 18), by which is meant the traditional legitimation behind the ethical norms of the early church, would be the necessary precursor to promoting far different ethical norms based on a new authority.

Clearly, Jude seeks to present these teachers in the most negative light possible, but behind his charges and innuendos lies something more than the standard picture of the self-serving peddler of a philosophy or religion. On the one hand, Jude uses topics that are standard fare for accusing sophists of insincerity—using flattery to gain their ends (v. 16), eager to make a profit from religion (vv. 11-12), indulging the belly and the loins (vv. 4, 12, 16, 18). On the other hand, the gospel was, and continued to be, exploited as a tool to make room for those very powerful forces within the human being that morality and religion traditionally restrain. Their message, which offered assurances about being favored by God while actually unleashing the appetites, would have been as popular then as it is today.

1 Enoch

First Enoch is the title given to a highly influential apocalyptic text that took shape between the early second century B.C.E. and the first century C.E. As a man who was taken up alive into the heavenly realm, Enoch became a natural focal point for Jews interested in revelations from the realm beyond ordinary experience. What did Enoch see when he was taken up? What mysteries did he learn? Why did God take him up at all? Was there some task for him to perform? Some revelation to pass on to his children?

The original kernel of the apocalypse was written prior to the success of the Maccabean revolt and included the Apocalypse of Weeks (*1 Enoch* 91:12-17; 93:1-10) and large parts of the Book of the Watchers (*1 Enoch* 6—36). The story of the latter section, a creative expansion of Genesis 6:1-4, is of most interest to students of the New Testament. A large number of the angels left their natural abode in order to copulate with human females, begetting by them the race of the giants. These angels taught humanity the forbidden arts of warfare and weaponry, sorcery, jewelry and cosmetics, the casting of spells, astrology and the like, while their unnatural offspring wrought havoc on the earth. God punishes the angels by binding them and casting them into a pit at which point Enoch is commissioned by God to proclaim to the angels God's judgments against them. The angels ask Enoch to intercede for them, but God will not hear their entreaties. The angels are to remain chained in dark prisons until the judgment; their evil offspring are to be killed (giving rise to the proliferation of evil spirits, their "ghosts"). Enoch is then shown the places of reward and punishment, among other mysteries. This story stands in the background of Jude, 2 Peter and 1 Peter, resonating deeply with Revelation as well.

Other major additions to *1 Enoch* include the Book of Heavenly Luminaries (*1 Enoch* 72—82), the Book of Dream Visions (*1 Enoch* 83—90), the Letter of Enoch (*1 Enoch* 91—107, incorporating the Apocalypse of Weeks) and the Parables of Enoch (*1 Enoch* 37—71). The Book of Heavenly Luminaries prescribes a solar year (364 days) rather than a lunar year (365-1/4 days) for the calculation of sabbaths and religious festivals. The lunar calendar was followed in the Jerusalem temple, but the solar calendar was observed at Qumran, where *1 Enoch* was cited as an authority. The community at Qumran bitterly critiqued their fellow Jews for not observing the sabbath and other festivals, having "changed the days" by adopting the wrong calendar. This difference in calendars accounts for the fact that the soldiers of the "Wicked Priest" (one of the Hasmonean high priests in Jerusalem) could attack the Qumran community on its sabbath (calculated according to the solar year) without themselves violating the sabbath (calculated according to the lunar year).

The Parables of Enoch are of great interest due to the attention they give to the figure of the "Son of Man" and his role in the end-time judgment and deliverance of the elect. Since copies of this section of *1 Enoch* were not found among the Dead Sea Scrolls, it is more difficult to ascertain the date of these visions. It remains likely, however, that they predate the Gospels and, thus, shed valuable light on the use of the title "Son of Man" by Jesus and his disciples.

First Enoch was an influential book in Jewish circles for whom apocalypticism was a defining mark, as at Qumran and throughout the early church. Its citation by Jude as an authoritative text caused many to challenge the inclusion of Jude in the Christian canon, yet it also led Tertullian to argue that *1 Enoch* should be included in the canon. *First Enoch* was in fact read as canonical in the Ethiopic church, with the result that Ethiopic translations of the book have become principal witnesses to the text of *1 Enoch*.

Jude's rhetorical strategy first reminds the congregations of the certainty of judgment by God according to the standards of godliness and ungodliness already revealed in the Jewish Scriptures, standards that never grow old or outmoded. He proves this thesis first from example (vv. 5-7, 11) and then from a citation of ancient authority (vv. 14-15), surprising the modern reader by quoting *1 Enoch* as an authoritative and reliable witness to the acts of God. Second, Jude depicts the character and aims of these teachers in such a way as to create the greatest distance between them and the addressees. He reminds the congregations of the resources they had already received from the apostolic missionaries, and through these resources they could evaluate the new teachers' message and con-

duct (vv. 17-18) as yet another round of false prophets condemned by God (vv. 4, 11). Relying on the addressees' agreement that self-indulgence is contrary to the Spirit-led life, he shows how the teachers' claim to inspiration by the Spirit must be found false (v. 19). He uses the language of holiness and pollution to emphasize the incompatibility of the teachers and their influence with the special calling of the addressees (vv. 8, 20, 23-24). The dreamers "defile the flesh," whereas God seeks to make the believers stand "blameless" in God's holy presence (vv. 8, 24). Therefore, the addressees are only secure as they build themselves up in their "holy faith" in direct contrast to the influence of the teachers (vv. 19-20) and seek to reclaim any who have been "defiled" by their influence (v. 23).

EXEGETICAL SKILL
The Analysis of Intertexture (2)

The distance the modern reader feels when reading Jude is compounded by the density of Jude's allusions to unfamiliar religious traditions. It is a text where intertextual analysis is critical to an appreciation of its meaning and significance. Intertextual analysis begins with the study of recitations, recontextualizations and reconfigurations of older texts (see "Exegetical Skill: The Analysis of Intertexture" on pp. 800-806). Jude provides a lengthy recitation of a text from *1 Enoch,* one of the most influential books of the intertestamental period. In verses 14-15, Jude quotes *1 Enoch* 1.9 as an authoritative word concerning the certainty of God's judgment on ungodliness and disrespectful speech concerning God, two areas where, Jude avers, the itinerant teachers have excelled.[a] He also recontextualizes the words "The LORD rebuke you" from Zechariah 3:2 (original context: a dispute between God and Satan concerning the high priest Joshua), using them now in the context of a different dispute. Finally, he recites an apostolic tradition (v. 18) otherwise unattested in these exact words, though similar content is reflected elsewhere (e.g., Acts 20:29-31; 1 Tim 4:1-5).

But Jude works even more at the level of allusion, reference and sum-

[a]The fact that Jude quotes a noncanonical work as authoritative convinced Tertullian (*De cult. fem.* 1.3) that the church should regard *1 Enoch* as Scripture, although this argument had also worked the other way in attempts to exclude Jude from the New Testament.

mary, expecting that the addressees share enough information about the stories to which he refers to follow the references and supply any significant, but unexplained, material. In verses 5 and 7, the references to the wilderness generation (Num 14) and Sodom (Gen 19) are straightforward enough, but the reference to the angels in verse 6 is more elusive. This reference points to Genesis 6:1-4, the brief story of the angels who left heaven to mate with human females, which became the focus of much expansion in the intertestamental period (*1 Enoch* 6—36 is the most dramatic example; see also *Jubilees* 5.1-14). Even more oblique is the reference to the dispute between Michael and Satan over the rights to the body of Moses (v. 9), which was developed as storytellers expanded on the narrative of the mysterious death and burial of Moses in Deuteronomy 34:5-6. All extant texts containing this story postdate Jude, and so it is difficult to know the exact contours of the story as it was known prior to Jude. In addition, there are brief allusions to Cain, Balaam and Korah in verse 11. While the full story of Korah is found in Numbers 16, the force of the other allusions will only be perceived by readers aware of extrabiblical legends about Cain that depicted him as a teacher of immorality who denied God's

Figure 23.3. A modern shepherd keeping his flock. (Photo courtesy of Todd Bolen [Bible-Places.com])

judgment and future rewards and punishments (see Josephus *Ant.* 1.2.2) and the tendency to connect Balaam with the seduction of the Israelites at Baal-Peor (Num 25:1-3; 31:16; a connection made in Rev 2:14-15, for example). Finally, the description of the teachers as "feeding themselves" alludes to the false shepherds of Ezekiel 34:1-10, who preyed on God's sheep and would be judged by God.

Discerning the meaning and rhetorical impact of Jude, therefore, hinges on a fuller understanding of the older texts, traditions and legends to which it refers. This also has bearing on the profile of the audience, for the degree of familiarity with extracanonical texts and traditions on their part presupposed by Jude is quite pronounced. Review the Old Testament stories unearthed for you here and, if possible, also review the extracanonical texts that will illumine Jude. Then ask the more significant follow-up questions for the analysis of intertexture given in the earlier introduction to this skill: How does each intertextual resource enhance the hearers' experience of the new text? How does each contribute to the topic being developed? What would be lost if the quotation, reference or allusion were not there? What specific rhetorical goals are advanced by the introduction of each of these resources and by the author's shaping of them (e.g., in the depiction of the character of the itinerant teachers, for the discernment of the threat they pose to the community and for the shaping of community response to them)?

JUDE AND MINISTRY FORMATION

Is Raymond Brown correct to conclude that "today most would not appreciate or find germane" Jude's argumentation from Jewish traditions, or that "its applicability to ordinary life remains a formidable difficulty"?[a] Granted that its argumentation is indeed obscure (see "Intertextual Analysis of Jude" above), Jude nevertheless raises the issue of the location of authority, which is germane to many debates affecting the church. The charismatic prophets emerge as authorities unto themselves, using claims to new divine revelations to legitimate their innovations. Such self-legitimation is indeed difficult to counter, as those who feared for the well-being of (and now grieve the loss of) their relatives in Jim Jones's "People's Temple" in Guyana, David Koresh's "Branch Davidians" in Texas and Marshall Applewhite's "Heaven's Gate" in California can attest. Once authority becomes located in the teacher's alleged access to the divine, it is quite diffi-

---

[a]Raymond E. Brown, *Introduction to the New Testament* (Garden City, N.Y.: Doubleday, 1997), pp. 759-60.

cult to bring external, objective standards to bear on evaluating their claims.

Jude returns to the revelations of God in Scripture and the apostolic teaching as the means to show that these people who claim to follow the Spirit are in fact "devoid of the Spirit" (v. 19). He assumes that any new revelation from God must be consonant with former revelations from God, and only those addressees who share this conviction can be reclaimed. With their contempt for traditional bases of authority, we would not expect these itinerant teachers to honor Jude's critique, but Jude is less concerned for them than for the churches they trouble. In the face of the teachers' deviations from traditional morality, particularly in the area of sexual ethics (making this case study extremely relevant for the church today), Jude's response is essentially a conservative one: he urges his audience to "contend for the faith that was once for all entrusted to the saints [or holy ones]" (v. 3 NRSV) against the advances of these promoters of their own dreams. The message of the teachers now redirects the "grace of God." What formerly was the source of the gift of the Holy Spirit, meant to free the believer from the tyranny and determination of carnal drives and passions for a life of virtue and holiness (see Gal 5:16-25), has become a legitimation for sexual license and other forms of self-serving indulgence. Based on this deviation from the former revelations of God, Jude dares to call their message a "perversion" of God's good intentions for the believing community.

Although he does not shy away from polemic—indeed, he is as willing to engage in vituperation as any prosecutor in a Greek or Roman law court—Jude would prefer to focus on "the salvation we share" (v. 3). This is central to the heart of the effective minister who leads the church toward unity and harmony, toward a healthy focus on the essential calling of Christ. He does not prefer to find points of contention, highlight them and focus all his energies on them. A ministry that focuses mainly on what the Christian faith is not may provide an effective outlet for our innate suspicion and even hatred of difference, but it will not build up mature disciples for Jesus who reach out to all with the boundary-leaping love of Jesus.

Nevertheless, within a ministry focused more healthfully on "the salvation we share," it will become necessary to "contend for the faith" where that faith is being subverted. The reality of God's justice and judgment must never be lost to view as we consider God's love, favor and capacity to forgive ("grace"). Grace will not be trampled on with impunity; grace will not be perverted into license without consequences (vv 4, 5-7, 14-15). In such situations Jude especially urges all those entrusted with oversight within the church to a courageous love—*love,* because it seeks to restore God's best purposes for each individual and for human community; *courageous,* because it often goes against the tide of a pluralistic society where "authority" rests more in the individual than in God.

Ultimately, we will use the words of the apostles and prophets to evaluate new teachers, or we will allow the teachers to replace the apostles and prophets (vv. 17-18). The labels used by Jude ("scoffers," "worldly people" and the like) can be applied carelessly and dishonestly to those with whom we simply disagree, in which case we are mere rhetoricians defending our turf rather than contending for the faith. But there are instances where they can be applied with integrity, prophetically calling teachers to account on the pavement of the apostolic foundation. Do they develop a theology that makes room for and renders "legitimate" the passions of the flesh that wage war against the soul? Do they teach innovations that cast off the yoke of the apostolic teaching as "outdated" or "uninformed" and foments new divisions and disruptions of unity in the church? Jude's example impels us to timely discernment through prayer and study done in a spirit of humility before the God who alone has the full truth but who also gives wisdom to those who ask. To this discernment Jude would add the naming of clear and present dangers to the "faith that was once for all entrusted to the saints," a trust for which we will be accountable when God comes in visitation on the world.

Jude's final words of advice to churches confronting innovators who seek to detach the disciples from their mooring in the apostolic harbor remain poignant. He directs the congregation (not just its leaders) toward a program of restoration. Not condemnation and exclusion but mercy and rescue are to be the agenda for the strong in Christ. Jude will not have believers idly watch others be seduced by deceptive teaching or overtaken by the passions of the flesh. Instead, they are entrusted with reclaiming their sisters and brothers in Christian mercy, with the love that manifests itself in the investment of time that dialogue requires, in the boldness that dares to go into uncomfortable areas, and in the wary caution that keeps a vigilant watch over our own passions and weaknesses (so we will not be enticed ourself).

THE SECOND LETTER OF PETER

Occasion and purpose. The emergence of innovative teachers is the occasion for 2 Peter, just as it was for Jude. The teachers opposed by 2 Peter, however, are of a different sort. They question the idea that God will decisively intervene in human affairs through judgment and the destruction of the cosmos (2 Pet 3:3-7). The credibility of the Christian hope has often been held to falter on the grounds that Jesus' words that at least some of those who walked with him during his earthly ministry would "see that the kingdom of God has come with power" (Mk 9:1; see Mk 13:30). The fact that the first Christian generation did indeed "pass away" without seeing Jesus' words fulfilled has often been used to urge sensible Christians to abandon the apocalyptic hope. The teachers opposed in 2 Peter appear to have been among the first to pose this argument (see 2 Pet 3:3-4). In their eyes the failure of this promise casts further doubt on the reliability of both the apostles' witness and the Old Testament prophecies used to speak of a final judgment (hence the defense in 2 Pet 1:17-21).

These teachers are trying to "liberate" Christianity from a number of elements that might be considered unenlightened in a Gentile milieu. The Jewish apocalyptic notions of a returning Messiah and a God who disrupts the course of history and nature could be viewed as backward or superstitious elements detracting from the purer contributions Christianity could make in the Greco-Roman world. This would especially be true from the vantage point of Epicureanism, with which the skepticism of these teachers has much in

Epicureanism and the Teachers Opposed in 2 Peter

Epicurus was the founder of one of the more influential schools of thought in the Greco-Roman world, Epicureanism taking third place to Platonism and Stoicism. Epicurus taught that "undisturbedness" *(ataraxia)* was the highest good. By definition the gods possess the highest good, so they cannot be disturbed and distraught over what human beings do. The gods, therefore, are free from the feelings of anger and the desire for vengeance. "A blessed and eternal being has no trouble himself and brings no trouble upon any other being; hence he is exempt from movements of anger or partiality" (Diogenes Laertius *Lives* 10.139). A clear sign that the gods do not intervene to sort out human affairs is "the delay and procrastination of the Deity in punishing the wicked." The gods' "slowness destroys belief in providence" (Plutarch "On the Delays of Divine Punishment 2, 3" *Mor.* 548D, 549B). The fact that a criminal can escape detection and live for decades without mishap supports the claim that the gods do not watch over human affairs or hold human beings accountable.

Epicurus sought to free people from religion's tyranny of fear (see 2 Pet 2:19) and thus eliminate one source of anxiety (see Cicero *On the Nature of the Gods* 1.117; Lucretius *On the Nature of Things* 5.1194-97). An unfortunate side effect of this "freedom" was a tendency to indulge the appetites and desires in ways that Epicurus would never have approved, and it would appear that the teachers opposed by 2 Peter added such license to their liberty (see 2 Pet 2:18).

common.[9] Unlike the teachers in Jude, who claimed direct access to divine revelation as the authority for their teaching, these teachers relied on rationalism as they sought to create a more palatable gospel.

2 Peter attempts to answer the objections raised by these teachers, setting the future hope of Christ's return as Lord and Judge on firm footing among the addressees once more. Alongside this, the letter must vindicate the authority and reliability of the apostolic tradition and Old Testament oracles, and it must counter the libertine tendencies that the rival teachers embody and arouse in their hearers, promoting instead an agenda of virtue and godliness. In so doing the au-

thor has created a stunningly acute model for Christian life between the passion and the parousia.

Authorship and date. Although the authenticity of 2 Peter continues to have its defenders,[10] it is the New Testament text for which a theory of pseudonymous authorship has the most to commend itself. The book presents itself to modern readers straightforwardly as a letter written by the apostle Peter, shortly before his own death in 64 C.E. (2 Pet 1:1, 14-15). But would first-century readers have been as inclined to take the book at face value, or could it be that an alternative would have been culturally acceptable? A popular literary genre of the intertestamental

---

[9]See the especially important article by J. H. Neyrey, "The Form and Background of the Polemic in 2 Peter," *JBL* 99 (1980): 407-31, esp. 407-22.

[10]E.g., Donald Guthrie, *New Testament Introduction* (Downers Grove, Ill.: InterVarsity Press, 1970), pp. 814-48, still one of the most remarkably balanced and detailed assessments of all the evidence for and against. See also E. M. B. Green, *2 Peter Reconsidered* (London: Tyndale Press, 1961).

period was the "testament," a deathbed speech placed on the lips of an important figure from antiquity. Pseudonymity—pretending to write as if a figure from the revered past—was thus a necessary and consistent feature of this genre. The genre was inspired by deathbed scenes such as Genesis 49, in which Jacob blesses his twelve sons and predicts their own and their tribes' futures. It became a popular genre for passing on ethical instruction and promoting a particular eschatology: the speaker would first instruct his children and then (since death was deemed a mystical experience that gave one unique access to heavenly mysteries) foretell the future, usually focusing on God's decisive intervention on behalf of God's people.

In a testament, the implied author shows an awareness of his impending death, includes personal reminiscences of his life and draws moral lessons from it, gives ethical instructions to his gathered descendants, and often looks ahead to the future condition of those descendants and God's intervention in their story. Second Peter exhibits all these traits, with the sole modification that the testament is couched as a letter—the typical form of apostolic communication—rather than a speech.[11] Peter is aware of his impending death (2 Pet 1:13-15) and expresses his desire to provide moral instruction (2 Pet 1:12-13) that will serve as ongoing guidance and influence after his "departure" (2 Pet 1:15). He gives ethical instructions to his spiritual children (see 2 Pet 1:3-11; 3:14-15, 17-18) and predicts future events pertinent both to the challenges that his "children" will face (2 Pet 2:1-3; 3:1-4) and to the ultimate intervention of God (2 Pet 3:8-

13). The audience of 2 Peter, especially those of Jewish heritage, might have been expected to recognize these generic signals and assume that the letter was in fact pseudonymous.[12]

This accords well with the likely timing for the emergence of radical skepticism regarding the parousia and the apocalyptic dawning of the kingdom of God, namely, after the well-known sayings about the apostles' generation living to see this event proved false. Peter's own death is thus presupposed. Another clue that this is indeed the case is the shift in verb tenses throughout the letter. "Peter's" predictions are cast in the future tense (2 Pet 2:1-3; 3:1-4), but are followed immediately by the author's application of the prophecy to his audience's circumstances in the present tense (2 Pet 2:10-22; 3:5-7). Rather than indicating Petrine authorship, this shift of tenses appears to be a later author's way of asserting that apostolic predictions and admonitions from decades ago were now being fulfilled as the false teachers carry on their work of calling the apostolic foundations in doubt and crafting a more enlightened Christianity.

In our setting pseudonymity looks very much like forgery, a specific kind of deceptive and often criminal activity. During the second and third centuries heretics would indeed use pseudonymity as a means to promote deviant beliefs as the "secret" teaching of the apostles. Second Peter, however, exhibits a more "genuine pseudonymity," falling more in line with the Jewish use of pseudonymity as an act of respect and as an attempt to present the author's work as standing in an established tradition rather than stealing the authority of a dead

---

[11]Bauckham, *Jude, 2 Peter,* p. 133.

[12]Bauckham very plausibly suggests that 2 Peter came to be regarded as a genuine Petrine letter as the church became increasingly composed of Gentiles, and thus increasingly alienated from its Jewish heritage and traditions (including the cultural knowledge that testaments were pseudonymous compositions). Additionally, with the prominence of apostolicity among the criteria for establishing a text's authority and canonicity, the acceptance of 2 Peter depended on making claims to Petrine authorship, regardless of the generic features of testamentary literature (ibid., p. 162).

Testamentary Literature in Second Temple Judaism

The two centuries before the turn of the era saw the rise of the genre known as the "testament," a deathbed speech placed on the lips of an ancient worthy as he addressed parting reflections, instructions, and even revelations to his family. Early testaments appear in *1 Enoch* 91—105, in which Enoch summons his whole family to hear him reveal the future epochs of history and encourage them to pursue righteousness at all times to avoid God's judgment. The second-century B.C.E. expansion of Genesis 1 through Exodus 14 known as *Jubilees* also contains several testaments. Particularly noteworthy are the testaments ascribed to Abraham (*Jub.* 20—22) and Isaac (*Jub.* 36). In the former, Abraham enjoins all of his sons and their families to avoid idols and keep God's commandments, and then he gives Isaac special instructions about how sacrifices are to be performed. In the latter, Isaac enjoins the worship of the one God and the maintenance of brotherly love and assistance between Jacob and Esau.

The first-century B.C.E. *Testaments of the Twelve Patriarchs* (the twelve sons of Jacob) provides a more fully developed example of this genre. This collection provides the testaments of each of the twelve sons of Jacob, each with the distinctive features of (1) recalling salient features of his life story, (2) drawing ethical lessons from his own successes or failures for the benefit of his children, and often (3) addressing future events and interventions of God in the history of God's people. Reuben, for example, emphasizes the importance of avoiding lust and fornication. Simeon warns against envy (because of which he had acted against his own brother Joseph). Judah uses his own failures to teach his children to avoid lust, intemperate drinking and greed. Joseph becomes a model of self-control (in regard to the advances of Potiphar's wife) and of honorably hiding the shame of one's kin (in regard to not making his brothers' mischief against him known). This work remained influential in Christian circles, sometimes being edited and emended to make the text more explicitly Christian. A great deal of attention has been given by scholars to reconstructing the original Jewish form of the text. Other important examples include the turn-of-the-era *Testaments of the Three Patriarchs* (Abraham, Isaac and Jacob), *Testament of Job* and *Testament of Moses* .

For further introduction to this genre and literature, see J. J. Collins, "Testaments," in *Jewish Writings of the Second Temple Period,* ed. M. E. Stone, CRINT 2.2 (Philadelphia: Fortress, 1984). The most convenient collection of testaments is J. H. Charlesworth, ed., *The Old Testament Pseudepigrapha,* vol 1, *Apocalyptic Literature and Testaments* (New York: Doubleday, 1983).

---

person worthy for ideas and teachings unworthy of his or her name. In 2 Peter an anonymous Christian leader has sought to preserve and defend the apostolic message for a new generation.[13] In the voice of Peter, this author defends the apostolic teaching he has received against rival teachers who promote their own innovations and threaten the churches' hold on the heritage that Peter and his peers bequeathed to them.

---

[13]Ibid., 160-61.

EXEGETICAL SKILL
Redaction Analysis in Epistolary Literature

Redaction criticism is an essential tool not only for the study of the Gospels but also for the study of other literature in which a literary relationship is demonstrable. Second Peter and Jude are commonly held to stand in such a relationship. Although it is possible that Jude condensed 2 Peter or that the two depend on a common source, most scholars now agree that it is more likely that the author of 2 Peter expanded and adapted Jude, using especially Jude 4-18 as a resource for meeting the challenges of a new and different situation. A close comparison of the letters can therefore shed light on the interests and goals of the author of 2 Peter. Space prevents a complete analysis here, but a few salient observations can be made as a starting point for your own analysis.

Jude 4//2 Peter 2:1-3. Both texts discuss the teachers' secretive introduction of themselves or their message, licentiousness and denial of Christ as a summary of their stance, and the fact that they are marked out for judgment. Second Peter 2:1-3, however, doubles the emphasis on the teachers' impending condemnation, introduces the topics of greed and false speech (which Jude will only introduce later in v. 16), thus concentrating the negative portrayal of these teachers, and posits that the teachers pose a danger to the reputation of the Christian group, given the fruits of their teaching. The last point, wholly absent from Jude, falls in line with 2 Peter's interest in crafting a statement of Christianity that is both true to its apostolic foundations and enlightened in its points of contact with the highest expressions of religious aspirations among Greeks and Romans (especially apparent in 1:3-11).

Jude 5-7//2 Peter 2:4-9. Peter omits the reference to the wilderness generation (Jude 5) but expands the references to the fallen angels of Genesis 6:1-4 and to Sodom by presenting their positive counterparts as well, namely, Noah (the flood was generally seen as a response to the mayhem introduced among human beings by the fallen angels and their offspring) and Lot. To Jude's lesson that God's judgment is assured, 2 Peter adds the complement—God also knows how to rescue the godly at the time of judgment. The double emphasis here reflects the author's interest in not only condemning the teachers (especially chap. 2) but also promoting the pious and just response to God's grace that leads to surviving the judgment (see 2 Pet 1:3-11; 3:11-18).

Jude 8-16//2 Peter 2:10-22. Most of the motifs introduced by Jude are taken up by the author of 2 Peter in sequence, but with a great deal of freedom. Most striking in this regard are the allusions to Old Testament and intertestamental traditions. Jude's specific reference to the dispute over Moses' body (v. 9) is omitted in favor of a general contrast between the arrogance of the teachers toward the "glories" (frequently understood as a reference to fallen angels) and the (good) angels' forbearance in this regard. Similarly, where Jude recites *1 Enoch* 1:9, the author of 2 Peter departs from Jude and uses resources from the Gospel tradition (cf. Mt 12:45 and 2 Pet 2:20-21) and from traditional wisdom material (Prov 26:11 and *Ahiqar* 8.18). This may reveal a lesser familiarity with or regard for apocryphal apocalyptic traditions on the part of the author or his audience.

Moreover, the author of 2 Peter omits the references in Jude 11 to Cain and Korah, focusing instead on Balaam alone—and on a part of the Balaam story that was likely not intended by Jude, namely, his being rebuked by his own donkey (2 Pet 2:15-16; see Num 22:15-35). Also 2 Peter 2:19 introduces the contrast between the "freedom" the teachers promise and their actual enslavement to the passions of the flesh. These modifications reflect the new situation faced by the author, in particular the teachers' alignment with Epicurean reforms of traditional views about the gods, which involved freedom from the superstitious fear of divine punishment and their failure, like Balaam, to see the clear danger in front of them on the road.

Jude 17-18//2 Peter 3:1-4. What Jude presents as a recitation of apostolic tradition, the author of 2 Peter appropriately frames as a statement out of the mouth of Peter himself (2 Pet 3:3-4). This statement, however, becomes the major focus of the author's refutation (2 Pet 3:5-10), since the denial of the parousia is a major feature of the rival teachers' message, at which point the author leaves Jude behind.

Wrestling with the prolonged interim. In his response to the enlightened teachers the author shows himself equally thoughtful and dedicated to a rationally credible Christianity. As he begins the letter with an exordium that is both learned in its vocabulary and ornate in its rhetoric (2 Pet 1:3-11), he describes salvation in terms that would appeal to the philosophically minded. He speaks of sharing in "the divine nature" (2 Pet 1:4), meaning immortality (as in Wis 2:23; 4 Macc 18:3), moral perfection and completeness. Salvation entails the escape from the decay inherent in this physical world, a decay due to the effects of "desire," another common topic in philosophical discourse, on the world and its inhabitants.

In his response to the objections raised by the rival teachers to the belief in a coming intervention of God, the author relies not on mere dogmatic assertions but offers a series of logical proofs—topics that contribute to the refutation of the opponents' position. First, he affirms the historical basis for the Christian hope, finding this in the transfiguration narrative (see Mk 9:2-8), an appropriate selection given Peter's prominence in that story. The author affirms that "eyewitness" testimony stands behind this narrative (2 Pet 1:16, 18), making it a strong, authentic proof that offers a solid basis for refuting the teachers' claims.[14]

---

[14]According to Aristotle the strongest proofs in an argument, especially in a courtroom, were those that the orator did not have to invent, such as eyewitness testimony, oaths, written documents, evidence extracted under torture and the like (*Rhet.* 1.15).

The author understands the transfiguration story to signal God's investment of Jesus with a special "honor and glory" (2 Pet 1:17), a phrase that suggests the author has connected the transfiguration with Psalm 8:5-6: "You . . . crown him with glory and majesty [honor]. . . . You have put all things under his feet." Although the psalm originally expressed God's privileging of human beings over creation, early Christians read its words about "the son of man" as a testimony about Jesus, *the* Son of Man (as in Heb 2:5-9). God's pronouncement at this event that Jesus was God's Son, moreover, connects the event with Psalm 2:7. Originally a "royal psalm" expressing the divine favor enjoyed by the Davidic king, Psalm 2 came to be read as an oracle about the ultimate Davidic monarch, the Messiah. As Son, Jesus would inherit the nations and "break" them "with a rod of iron" (Ps 2:8-9)—an oracle pointing forward to the return of Christ to usher in his kingdom. The transfiguration event, therefore, becomes historical proof of the fact that Christ would return as ruler and judge.

To refute the contention that God does not intervene to judge and punish, the author produces a string of historical precedents demonstrating that God does in fact intervene both to punish the ungodly and to rescue the just. Aristotle advised the use of historical examples in deliberative oratory because "as a rule the future resembles the past" (Aristotle *Rhet.* 2.20.8) and because "it is by examination of the past that we divine and judge the future" (*Rhet.* 1.9.40). The fact, then, that God intervened in the past to destroy the primeval world by means of the flood and the cities of the plain (e.g., Sodom) by means of fire (2 Pet 2:4-10; 3:5-7) at once refutes the premise that "God does not concern himself with punishing people" and sets up a series of precedents that make credible the expectation that God will continue to intervene, both in particular cases and in the general case of a global assize.

Nevertheless, the rival teachers have raised an important challenge that merits an answer, and so the author attempts to explain the "delay" of divine vengeance using topics also employed by other authors addressing this dilemma, though in different religious contexts (see Plutarch "On the Delays of Divine Punishment" 5-9, and Wis 12:8-10, 18). The first topic the author raises is the difference between the divine and human experience of time, using Psalm 90:4 to underscore the difference in perspective: "a thousand years in your sight are like yesterday when it is past" (NRSV). If God seems to delay, it is only because our time is so short but God's time is without end. Second, he invokes God's mercy, patience and forbearance toward those who are not yet prepared for judgment (2 Pet 3:9). Plutarch had also used this topic in his own refutation of Epicureanism: "God . . . reserves his penalties for the future and awaits the lapse of time" out of "gentleness and magnanimity." He does this to "make room for repentance," the delay of punishment being "a period of grace" ("On the Delays" 5-6; see also Wis 12:10, 18; Rom 2:4). The delay in final judgment, then, is a necessary outworking of the character of the God who is "slow to anger, and abounding in steadfast love" (Ex 34:6-7 NRSV).

2 PETER AND MINISTRY FORMATION

One of the main contributions of this letter is its construction of a map for the successful navigation of the Christian life. The reader is located in the world between the two compass points of Jesus' redemptive death and Jesus' return as Judge at the dissolution of the material cosmos. These are two compass points that cannot be lost to view (note the dangers of forgetting the first in 2 Pet 1:9 and ignoring the facts that undergird the second in 3:5, 8), for if they are, the disciples will lose their way as surely as did the teachers refuted in this text.

The author echoes the standard topics and even the language of inscriptions engraved or official decrees announced to honor public benefactors (2 Pet 1:3-11). These include the mention of the gift, the virtues of the giver manifested in that gift (reflecting his or her "glory and goodness"), and the resolution passed by the local assembly as a response of gratitude to honor the giver. Here, the way to honor the gift of having received "everything needful" for eternal life and the "cleansing of past sins" is not the erection of stone monuments but the building of a virtuous life, living in such a way as pleases the Giver and makes full use of God's gifts to fulfill the purpose for which God gave them. The failure to nurture these virtues, however, reflects the recipient's forgetfulness of the gifts, a grave insult to the Giver (especially when they had been provided at such great cost as the life of the Son).[a]

Such failure would be "nearsighted" (2 Pet 1:9) as well, for it is the way the disciple prepares to encounter the second landmark on the map, the parousia. For this author there is an intimate connection between eschatology and ethics. The rival teachers' failure to maintain the apocalyptic expectations of the apostolic teaching directly results in their tendency toward the indulgence of the passions and satisfaction of other base desires, such as greed. Losing sight of the eternal reward for godliness, they settle for more temporary and available rewards. Where we maintain our expectation of God's judgment of the ungodly and rescue of the righteous for an eternal inheritance, however, our internal deliberations are empowered so that we will choose what makes for eternal advantage.

What many Christian denominations recite as the "mystery of faith," therefore—"Christ has died; Christ is risen; Christ will come again"—is not merely a matter of the mind and mental assent to doctrines. It sets the parameters of our conceptual world in such a way that, mindful of Christ's death for us and his coming again as Lord and Judge, a life of progress in virtue, justice and holiness is the most natural outgrowth. A principal task of Christian leaders is to help believers understand the connection between beliefs and the choices and ambitions

---

[a]Cicero and Seneca may be taken to represent the general odium of "forgetfulness of benefits": "all people hate forgetfulness of benefactions, thinking it to be an injury against themselves since it discourages generosity and thinking the ingrate to be the common enemy of the needy" (Cicero *De officc.* 2.63); "the most ungrateful of all is the person who had forgotten a benefit. . . . Who is so ungrateful as the person who has so completely excluded and cast from his mind the benefit that ought to have been kept uppermost in his thoughts and always before him?" (Seneca *Ben.* 3.1.3-3.2.1).

that drive real life so they may be brought to that point of integration and wholeness where their walk reflects, rather than contradicts, the creed they embrace. Second Peter also offers something of a corrective where eschatological topics receive obsessive fixation. The "signs of the times" are not a matter of interest for their own sake but the handmaid to empowering an ethical response to the God who washed away our sins.

Second Peter also reminds us of the nature of Christian freedom (2 Pet 2:19-22). As in Paul (Gal 5:13), so here it is impressed on us that our freedom *from* the law is not freedom *for* self-indulgence. It is freedom for a deeper level of self-giving and commitment to holiness from the heart than the Law could empower on its own. Christ did not die to make room in our lives for greed, pride or sexual lust; wherever the gospel is used to make room for these things, teachers and their followers are deceiving themselves, forging again the chains of bondage to the passions of the flesh.

Finally, 2 Peter, like Jude, raises the issue of the location of authority. Traditional centers of authority—the Old Testament and the apostolic witness—were being challenged from the vantage point of popular philosophy. The author's response models integrity for all Christian leaders facing such a challenge:

- He identifies and refuses to abandon principal pillars of the apostolic tradition.
- Rather than blindly affirming these pillars, he seeks out the rational and defensible foundation for them.
- He fully engages the challenges posed by the rival teachers, treating their argument seriously by offering a thoughtful and careful refutation.
- Sympathizing with the need to present a faith that appeals nonetheless to the philosophically minded, he translates key ideas like "salvation" in terms that resonate with the rich resources of Greek religious thought—that is, he refuses to allow Christianity to remain in a Jewish apocalyptic ghetto, helping it to take on flesh in new ways that reach out to a Greek religious mindset as well.
- He insists that any interpretation of the gospel enflesh itself in a manner of life that honors God and fulfills God's purposes for human beings and human community. This is what he finds lacking in the rival teachers and what contributes to the disqualification of their message. It is also what he insists his readers embody themselves so as not to bring the faith into disrepute.

FOR FURTHER READING

Bauckham, Richard J. *Jude, 2 Peter.* WBC 50. Waco, Tex.: Word, 1983.

Charles, J. D. "Jude's Use of Pseudepigraphical Source Material as Part of a Literary Strategy." *NTS* 37 (1991): 130-45.

———. " 'Those' and 'These': The Use of the Old Testament in the Epistle of Jude." *JSNT* 38 (1990): 109-24.

Deshardins, M. "The Portrayal of the Dissidents in 2 Peter and Jude." *JSNT* 30 (1987): 89-102.

Dunnett, W. M. "The Hermeneutics of Jude and 2 Peter: The Use of Ancient Jewish Traditions." *JETS* 31 (1988): 287-92.

Eybers, I. E. "Aspects of the Background of the Letter of Jude." *Neotestamentica* 9 (1975).

Fornberg, T. *An Early Church in a Pluralistic Society: A Study of 2 Peter.* Coniectanea Biblica 9. Lund: Gleerup, 1977.

Joubert, S. J. "Language, Ideology, and the Social Context of the Letter of Jude." *Neotestamentica* 24 (1990): 335-49.

Kelly, J. N. D. *The Epistles of Peter and Jude.* BNTC. London: Adam & Charles Black, 1969.

Knight, Jonathan. *2 Peter and Jude.* Sheffield, U.K.: Sheffield Academic Press, 1995.

Neyrey, Jerome H. "The Apologetic Use of the Transfiguration in 2 Peter 1:16-21." *CBQ* 42 (1980): 504-19.

————. "The Form and Background of the Polemic in 2 Peter." *JBL* 99 (1980): 407-31.

————. *2 Peter, Jude.* AB. Garden City, N.Y.: Doubleday, 1993.

Rowston, D. J. "The Most Neglected Book in the New Testament." *NTS* 21 (1975): 554-63.

Watson, D. F. *Invention, Arrangement, and Style: Rhetorical Criticism of Jude and 2 Peter.* SBLDS 104. Atlanta: Scholars Press, 1988.

Webb, R. L. "The Eschatology of the Epistle of Jude and Its Rhetorical and Social Functions." *BBR* 6 (1996): 139-51.

Wolthius, T. R. "Jude and Jewish Traditions." *CTJ* 22 (1987): 21-41.

24

THE REVELATION OF JOHN

Living in the Light of God's Triumph

Many popular interpreters of Revelation try to make sense of its visions by looking to the future, decoding its images in terms of contemporary politics and forecasting how our history will unfold. In so doing they ignore the basic principle of exegesis that a text is written to make sense to its original audience. John's wild and fantastic images invite Christians living in the Roman province of Asia Minor during the last decade of the first century to perceive the true character of the realities that face them everyday, and to respond to them in a way that will allow them to share in the triumph of the Lamb rather than in the punishment of Babylon. Revelation liberates first-century Christians from the myth of the emperor and Rome, from the tainted prosperity that beguiled the peoples of the Mediterranean, from witnessing violence and calling it "rule of law." It frees them to live out their lives in witness to the one God, to the demands of God's justice and to God's beneficent vision for human community and wholeness, and thus in critique of the pretensions and injustice of the dominant culture and its order.

The persistent challenge of Revelation is not to discern the fulfillment of its predictions in contemporary history or to map out the "seven last years," but to discern the true nature of the society around us in the light of God and the Lamb, and in light of the inevitable "day of their wrath." Understanding John's critique of the Roman Empire (and of all quiet

and profitable compromise with that system) provides a paradigm for lifting the veil that every power system dons to hide its true nature and to win unquestioning support from the undiscerning.

READING REVELATION: THE QUESTION OF GENRE

I first read Revelation when I was thirteen years old. It seemed, on face value, to speak to *me* about horrific events yet to come in *my* future. This was confirmed for me as I heard about Revelation on religious television shows and as I read the literature of such authors as Jack van Impe, Hal Lindsey and other prophecy "experts." Their interpretation of Revelation tried to decode its visions with regard to events happening in the present time, and from this to extrapolate what would occur in international politics and domestic policy in the coming years. It did not seem to matter that they had to revise their story every few years as their interpretations and projections failed one after another.

While all this is very exciting, and it is easy to understand how it captivates the curious mind, this mode of interpretation ignores some of the most basic principles of reading a text correctly, beginning with the determination of the *genre* of the text. We make decisions about genre daily, and these decisions affect how we experience the texts we read (or, in the case of television, see). We recognize instinctively the genre of the newspaper article, the commercial, the joke, the letter, the exegesis paper, the test, the shopping list, the sitcom, the bedtime story. Understanding the genre gives us clues regarding the form, expectations and purpose of the "text" and is essential to a proper reading of each of these texts.

How would the readers in the seven churches understand Revelation? What clues are there in the text that would help them make these decisions about its form, features and purpose? Revelation can be seen to combine several genres, and each one contributes significantly to a less sensationalist but far more probing and penetrating interpretation of this powerful text.

Revelation as letter. Revelation 1:4 begins the work like any other New Testament letter's beginning: "John to the seven churches that are in Asia: Grace to you and peace." The epistolary formula of "Sender to addressees, greeting" is clearly present. And just as Paul introduces the important themes of his letters in the introduction, so Revelation 1:4-8 announces several themes of importance for understanding the whole text. The first generic feature to underscore is the fact that Revelation is a letter addressed to seven very real communities of Christians spread throughout the Roman province of Asia in western Turkey.

Some interpreters take these churches to be representative of seven eras in church history, with our generation falling in the seventh and last (surprise!). While this strategy enables the prophecy "expert" to make the two-millennia leap, it also has the following weaknesses:

- It fails to do justice to the fact that John addressed his work to seven real communities, and he intended it to be understood by *them,* shaping *their* perceptions of *their* everyday realities, and motivating a particular response to *their* very real circumstances.
- It grossly caricatures the periods of church history it purports to describe, as if the essence of the global church in any era could

be sketched out on a seven-verse canvas.
- More insidiously, it presumes that God, in revealing this information, is really only concerned with the Western church up through the Reformation and, thereafter, with the Protestant churches, largely in America. If God gave the oracle to Laodicea to characterize the church of our contemporary period, God would be giving no notice to the millions of faithful Christians in the developing world whose fidelity to God under great pressure and whose enthusiasm for evangelism far more closely resemble the conditions in Smyrna and Philadelphia than Laodicea.
- There are absolutely no indications in the text that the seven churches should stand for successive epochs in church history. This interpretation is necessitated, rather, by the presuppositions of the prophecy "expert" that the meat of Revelation (chaps. 4-22) all have to do with still future events.

The fact that the number seven is so pervasive in Revelation does indeed suggest that the seven churches are, in some way, symbolic. Since, however, the diversity of the churches of Revelation could probably be found in every era, it would be more prudent to regard all of them together as typical of the church in every age. Nevertheless, even while they typify the achievements and challenges facing churches across the Mediterranean in the first century (and across the globe now), these seven churches are seven very real churches whose difficulties and situations were very particular, and whose response to their world John wanted to affect profoundly. A grounded and responsible reading of Revelation begins, therefore, where it does for every other New Testament epistle—with an understanding of the historical situation of these seven churches and the problems besetting them, and the ways that Revelation interacts with and reorients the first-century addressees toward that situation. This will provide a secure place from which to hear the challenge of Revelation for the churches today.

Revelation as early Christian prophecy. John also identifies his work as a "prophecy" (Rev 1:3; 22:7, 10, 18, 19). We tend to think of *prophecy* as synonymous with *prediction*. While this element was certainly included in the sphere of prophecy, Jewish and early Christian prophecy was also, and in fact was primarily, a declaration of what God is doing in the present, that is, a declaration of God's perspective on the present life of God's people. Where a prophet speaks of the future, he or she usually limits the prediction to the imminently forthcoming future, not the distant future. John remains within these limits, as seen from his emphasis on the imminence of the confrontations and events he narrates (Rev 1:3, 19; 22:6, 7, 10, 12, 20).

Prophecy is a "word of the Lord" breaking into the situation of the Lord's people who need guidance or encouragement or a call to repentance and recommitment. In Revelation the seven letters to the seven churches are a prime example of early Christian prophecy. They might be better labeled the seven oracles to the seven churches, for they each begin in a manner reflecting the prophetic "Thus says the Lord" (e.g., "These are the words of the Son of God," Rev 2:18). The risen and glorified Lord speaks a word to the churches through the prophet John, affirming their strengths, diagnosing their weaknesses, calling them to faithful action, threatening judgment on the recalcitrant and promising favor for the penitent and faithful. In short, they do precisely what so much of the prophetic corpus of the Old Testament sought to do for the communities of Israel and Judah. The visions of Revelation continue this prophetic word, providing the picture of reality and the interpretation of the believers' world (particularly Rome, its agencies and its politico-economic system) that will motivate and legitimate the response of faithful witness and protest.

One basic tenet of the prophecy expert is that every biblical forecast of some future event must be fulfilled at some point. If the "predictions" of Revelation were not fulfilled literally during the first or second century, they must be fulfilled at some later point. Such a tenet, however, largely ignores the purpose of prophecy, which is not necessarily to give a hard and fast statement about an unchangeable future. Jonah proclaimed that "forty days more, and Nineveh shall be overthrown" (Jon 3:4 NRSV). In response to this vision of the future, the city's inhabitants repented and turned to God, with the result that God spared the city (Jon 3:10). Jonah, like the prophecy expert, was still watching, however, "to see what would become of the city" (Jon 4:5) and remained disappointed that the prophecy was not to be fulfilled. God's purposes for the prophetic word, however, were fulfilled—it provoked the repentance of an entire population. The divine purpose in prophecy is mainly to stimulate faithful response *in the present,* not to provide an absolute blueprint for an uncertain future.

Revelation as apocalypse. The major genre of Revelation, however, is "apocalypse," the designation that first greets the reader in Revelation 1:1 (*apokalypsis Iēsou Christou,* "the apocalypse/revelation of Jesus Christ"). The word *apokalypsis* strictly translated would mean an "unveiling," a "lifting off of a veil." But precisely what is unveiled by this strange book? Revelation has perhaps been misread because for many people it is a unique book, with no basis for comparative analysis except Daniel in the Hebrew Scriptures. In fact, however, there are scores of similar documents from the second century B.C.E. through the first century C.E. that should inform our reading of Revelation. These include, in whole or in part, *1 Enoch, 2 Enoch, 2 Baruch, 4 Ezra,*[1]

---

[1]See David A. deSilva, *Introducing the Apocrypha* (Grand Rapids: Baker, 2002), chap. 17.

Apocalypse of Abraham, the *Testament of Levi,* the *Sibylline Oracles* and many others.

Recognizing the similarities between these works, a number of scholars worked to clarify the features and expectations on which these "apocalypses" played. The basic features common to this literature include the portraying of revelation as coming through visions or appearances of some divine or angelic mediator and through conversations with such figures; "otherworldly journeys," allowing the reader to see into the invisible regions that surround the everyday world and the beings that inhabit them (such as the seven spheres, the throne of God, the Abyss and their occupants); narrations of the "history" that brackets normal history (such as creation and primeval events or judgment and consummation). As a result of compiling these common features, J. J. Collins provided this comprehensive definition of the genre apocalypse:

> "Apocalypse" is a genre of revelatory literature with a narrative framework, in which a revelation is mediated by an otherworldly being to a human recipient, disclosing a transcendent reality which is both temporal, insofar as it envisages eschatological salvation, and spatial, insofar as it envisages another, supernatural world.[2]

Apocalypses paint the cosmic backdrop of the everyday realities of the audience, placing those realities under the interpretive light of that cosmic backdrop. The seer places the audience's time in the context of a sacred history of God's activity and carefully defined plan; the seer places the audience's location on earth within the context of the invisible world and interprets the human situation against that larger context.

An apocalypse is therefore a medium of communication that puts an everyday situation in perspective by looking at the larger context (the cosmos of faith) that should interpret that situation. From this an apocalypse derives its power to comfort those who are discouraged or marginalized in their situation, admonish those whose responses to everyday reality are not in line with the values of the faith, and provide the necessary motivation to take whatever action the prophet recommends. The function of the genre is to allow the recipients to examine their behavior (whether "to continue to pursue, or if necessary to modify" it) in light of "a transcendent, usually eschatological, perspective on human experiences and values."[3] The genre allows for the legitimation of its message, or the values it seeks to impart, by inviting the recipients into an experience of the transcendent realities that message is grounded in. In effect, the recipients are allowed to see the otherworldly and converse with supernatural beings through the mediation of the apocalypse.[4]

Revelation shares much in common with other texts identified as apocalypses. The book presents its message in the form of visionary experiences: the author sees into the invisible realm and witnesses the proceedings there. He hears what is spoken and even engages in conversation with a number of heavenly beings. It contains an otherworldly journey: John finds himself a spectator of the throne of God as well as the Abyss, the lake of fire and the New Jerusalem. It focuses on time and history beyond the present. While it may not look back to the events of prehistory, such as creation, life in Eden, the giants and so on, it does look back to cosmic conflict between the dragon and God's angels and forward to the judgment

---

[2]J. J. Collins, ed., *Apocalypse: The Morphology of a Genre,* Semeia 14 (Missoula, Mont.: Scholars Press, 1979), p. 9.
[3]David E. Aune, *Revelation 1-5,* WBC 52A (Dallas: Word, 1997), p. lxxxii.
[4]Ibid., p. lxxxii.

and renewal of all things. It shares in the dualistic view of humanity and envisages the eschatological judgment that will sort the wheat from the chaff, and it ends with a vision of cosmic transformation, the new heavens and new earth which will replace the current cosmos. In all of this it shares a basic grammar with the other apocalypses of the period.

One notable difference is the lack of a pseudonym. Most other apocalypses, both Jewish and Christian, claim to come from the hand of a venerable figure from the past (like Enoch or Ezra). The name John, however, most likely represents the real name of a person known personally to the first audiences. This is in keeping with the Christian conviction that the gift of prophecy, conferred by the Spirit that was poured out on believers, was again available and actively manifesting itself in the Christian communities (see Acts 2:14-21; 1 Cor 12:4-11; 14:1-33). Such a conviction stands in stark contrast with the common perception within Judaism that the prophetic voice had ceased (see 1 Macc 4:46; 14:41; Pr Azar 1:15), though notably the expectation that prophecy would revive is also attested.

Conclusion. Having identified John's Revelation as an apocalypse addressed to seven specific churches (as a "letter") and serving the aims of Christian prophecy, how do these genre labels orient us to understanding the meaning of the book?

- As a *letter* Revelation is anchored firmly in the historical situation of the churches in Asia Minor that it addresses. Just as we read Galatians with reference to the specific situation and challenges of Gentile Christians in the Roman province of Galatia, and just as we seek to understand how it reshapes their perspective on and response to that situation, so it is to be with Revelation.
- As *prophecy* Revelation purports to bring "a word from the Lord" into a specific situation, for specific people. It would be expected to reveal God's perspective on the hearers, their behaviors and the challenges around them, alerting them to the course of action they must take to remain in or return to favor with God, and to avoid judgment.
- As an *apocalypse* Revelation accomplishes its goals by spreading before the eyes of the Christians in Asia Minor that larger canopy of space and time that puts this mundane reality in its proper perspective. It puts their everyday situations, choices and challenges in perspective by looking at their larger context. The world of those Christians will look different when seen in the light of the endless worship that surrounds God's throne, the reality and ferocity of God's judgments on idolaters, the rewards of faithfulness. More than needing to *be interpreted,* Revelation *interprets* the reality of the audience, showing them the *true* character of the emperor, the ruler cult and the city that has enslaved the world, the *true* struggle behind the scenes of the visible world, the *true* stakes of the choices believers make, the *true* nature of the character and message of other prophets in the communities John addresses.

John lifts the veil under which everyday realities in our visible world parade as all-important and ultimate, showing them all to be of secondary importance to the call of God. Thus he enables the Christians in Asia Minor to reconsider how they will act in the world. He frees them from responding to the demands of a political and economic system as if these were the ultimate powers to be reckoned with and enables them to respond instead to God, who, although invisible to the world, is nevertheless the only ultimate power. While Revelation appears to lift the veil from future events, its ultimate goal is to lift the veil from contemporary actors, events and options.

Does Revelation Stem from a Genuine Visionary Experience?

There are two popular models for how John composed Revelation. The one probably held by most readers is that John experienced his visions and conversations with heavenly beings, and wrote things down as he went along. The other, held by most critically trained scholars, is that Revelation is a literary product of the author's creativity and interpretive interaction with the Old Testament, other apocalypses and early Christian traditions about the return of Christ. Turn to any apocalypse (like *1 Enoch*, *4 Ezra* or *2 Baruch*), and you will find a narrator who sees heavenly and infernal scenes, who looks and beholds past and future events, who hears supernatural conversation partners. We could say, then, that the trappings of visionary experience belong to the generic features of apocalypses rather than providing a real indication of the source of the content.

Neither view seems to this reader to do justice to John's self-designation as a prophet on the one hand, or to the clear signs of extensive reflection and shaping that is found in Revelation on the other. It is too easy for rationalists to dismiss the importance of "altered states of consciousness" for most religious traditions. Early Christianity appears to have thrived on direct experience of the otherworldly. The Holy Spirit of God was poured out on all believers, equipping them with a variety of spiritual gifts, some of which, like the "word of knowledge" or the "revelation," presume some communication from the supernatural world. Moreover, Christians had visionary experiences. Paul encountered the glorified Christ at his conversion and undertook an otherworldly journey into heaven (recounted in 2 Cor 12:1-7). Peter's dream-vision stands at the heart of Acts and the inclusion of the Gentiles in the church.

As he sought God's word for the congregations to whom he ministered, John, as one gifted with prophetic utterance, would have been a prime candidate for having auditory and visionary experiences during his times of prayer and meditation. A vision of God's throne, a clear impression of the true character of the emperor and the ruler cult he witnessed in all of these cities, a word from God about Rome's essence in God's sight, scenes of judgment—all of these would be very much in keeping with mystical experiences.

Nevertheless, a word from the Lord has to have a framework to take shape for the prophet, and the prophet has to shape that word to be meaningful for and have the desired effect on his hearers. Any visionary or mystical experience John might have had would be shaped by his own immersion in the conceptual world of the Hebrew Scriptures and early Christian tradition (including intertestamental Jewish traditions). Moreover, a vision has to be put into words to be communicated. In Revelation John may combine visionary experiences from decades of prophetic work. Between the prayerful trance or ecstatic experience and the writing down of a message for the churches, there is the opportunity for careful reflection, for meditation on the vision in light of Scripture, for using Old Testament language and resonances to give just the right interpretive cast both to the visions and to the situation facing the congregations.

The literary character of Revelation in the context of early Christian prophecy and ecstatic experience, then, might call for a much more nuanced view of the formation of this amazing text. This view would take into account the complex interplay between experiences received in an altered state of consciousness, the conceptual world (especially reflected in known texts and traditions) that provides the framework and raw materials for such experiences in the first place, and the interpretive process by which a prophet turns impressions, visions, and "words from the Lord" into a literary work of art. Such a work is energized just as much by claims to seeing and hearing the unseen world as it is by evidence of reading and interpreting and applying the textual world of Scripture to the life and realities of the seven congregations.

The structure of Revelation. Revelation unfolds in an orderly progression, containing many divergent indicators that give a sense of structure to the whole.

• *Series of sevens.* Perhaps the most pervasive structuring device is the enumeration of sevens. The book opens with oracles written to seven churches. After the scene in heaven there are seven seals, and the effects of opening each are recounted. The seventh seal gives way to seven trumpets, and the effects of each are then recounted. The final trumpet gives way to seven bowls of wrath. Interspersed in these series of sevens are other visions, sometimes interrupting the series (i.e., before the seventh seal and before the seventh trumpet), sometimes not. The series of sevens, however, still give an overall sense of order to the whole.

• *Recapitulation.* One challenge to determining a linear structure for Revelation is the author's penchant for recapitulation—bringing the hearers to the same point repeatedly, revisiting the same event from a number of different angles. For example, the sixth seal already brings us to the "great day of wrath" (Rev 6:16) when the cosmos is overturned (Rev 6:12-14), but John then drops back and spends the rest of the book revisiting the events leading up to that climax. The sixth and seventh bowls, likewise, bring the reader to the "battle on the great day of God the Almighty" (Rev 16:14 NRSV) and the judgment of Babylon (Rev 16:19), topics that are then taken up again in greater detail in Revelation 17—19.

• *Paired visions.* Another important aspect of the book's structure involves the presentation of complementary visions, for example the worship and activity surrounding God and the Lamb (chaps. 4-5), and the activity and worship surrounding the dragon and the beast (chaps. 12-13), or the description and judgment of the city Babylon (17:1—19:8) and the description and praise of the heavenly city, New Jerusalem (chaps. 21-22).

• *References to the scroll.* Another touchstone for the reader are the scenes that present the sealed scroll (which is then opened) in chapter 5 and the opened scroll that is given to John in chapter 10 as the fuel for the remainder of his prophetic ministry. The structure of Revelation could thus be seen as the story of the reading (or representation) of this heavenly scroll.

• *Liturgical scenes.* Revelation is punctuated with scenes of worship and celebration in heaven, many of which come at critical junctures in the structure. For example, the scene that sets the whole in motion (chaps. 4-5) is largely the narration of a heavenly liturgy. The scene that interrupts the seven seals is a liturgy of "sealing" followed by worship that joins people on earth with the angels around God's throne (chap. 7). The series of trumpets closes with a hymn celebrating God's triumph (Rev 11:15-18). The last seven plagues are inaugurated with a hymn (Rev 15:1-4). The fall of Babylon is greeted with a heavenly antiphon (Rev 19:1-8), which also serves to introduce the next scene of the triumphant Christ's return. John has used these scenes to highlight important moments and transitions in the whole.

Ironically, then, Revelation gives the reader the impression of careful ordering and progression, yet defies attempts to nail down a completely acceptable outline on account of the variety of structuring devices John employs.

Sources Behind and Stages in the Composition of Revelation

Source criticism, the attempt to look beyond the available form of a text to discern earlier texts that have contributed to it, is nowhere more alive than in the history of interpretation of Revelation. Particularly in the late-nineteenth and early-twentieth centuries, scholars devoted great energy and imagination to recreating the literary history of Revelation by reconstructing its sources.[a]

What makes a scholar suspect a source? Compositions written "from scratch," as it were, tend to be coherent and fluid. It is unlikely, though not impossible, that we would find abrupt transitions or contradictions within an essay composed afresh over a brief period of time. When different texts by different authors, or written at different times, are joined (or where one or more older texts are woven together with new material), seams and contradictions inevitably remain. David Aune therefore lists the following as primary criteria for discerning sources:

1. abrupt transitions, parenthetical statements, and other "seams" in the fabric of the text
2. inconsistencies or discrepancies within the text
3. superfluous repetition
4. peculiarities in the use of the definite article ("the")[b]
5. repetitions that function as resumptions after an editorial insertion
6. concentrated use in a single passage of a certain term or terms that are rare or nonexistent elsewhere in the text
7. interpolations that serve as attempts to link blocks of material together (references to something being mentioned earlier or later)
8. interpolations introducing theological consistency between sections of a text where such consistency was originally absent
9. distinctively Christian statements made in an otherwise non-Christian (or, not distinctively Christian) passage[c]

Source criticism seems especially appropriate for apocalypses because many examples of this genre give clear signs of having been expanded, adapted and updated over time.[d] *First Enoch*, for example, grew to its present size of 108 chapters over two centuries, as readily discernible blocks of material were added and joined. The *Testaments of the Twelve Patriarchs*, written by Jewish authors before the turn of the era, were "Christianized" and kept alive by the church. *The Shepherd of Hermas* contains a core that dates back to the end of the first century, but it continued to be expanded with new material through the mid-second century. The more

---

[a]See, e.g., R. H. Charles, *A Critical and Exegetical Commentary on the Revelation of St. John*, 2 vols. ICC (Edinburgh: T & T Clark, 1920) and Wilhelm Bousset, *Die Offenbarung Johannes*, KEK 16 (Göttingen: Vandenhoeck & Ruprecht, 1906). An excellent review of source-critical theories concerning Revelation can be found in Aune, *Revelation 1-5*, pp. cv-cxvii.

[b]For example, a definite article may be used with a noun when it is first introduced, as if it is already known to the readers, and then not used with that same noun afterward, as if the noun is being introduced for the first time. The beast is thus introduced with a definite article in Revelation 11:7, as if this character were already familiar, while "a beast" is introduced, as if for the first time, in Revelation 13:1.

[c]These nine points are found in Aune, *Revelation 1-5*, p. cxix.

[d]Ibid., p. cvii.

extravagant and speculative attempts at source criticism of Revelation (with scholars confidently reconstructing three, four or five "original" apocalypses woven together by the "author" of Revelation) have given place to far more modest and sober attempts to address the kinds of literary problems that first gave rise to source theories.

David Aune offers an example of a modest and balanced application. He begins by taking into consideration the studies of the language and style of Revelation, the consistency of which argues strongly for a single author but says nothing about the manner or time of composition. Aune then uses source criticism to identify discrete units authored by John at various points and in different settings, and then he seeks to understand how these have been woven together into a single and integrated whole.[e] Based on the criteria identified above, Aune first draws attention to blocks of self-contained material, like Revelation 7:1-17; 10:1-11; 11:1-13. He notes the lack of continuity in the "cast of characters" from episode to episode (save for a central few), the lack of literary links connecting these sections together (like continuity and development of plot), and the diversity of genres represented by these various text blocks. These blocks of material represent shorter revelatory visions composed by John at an earlier stage in his prophetic ministry.[f] Aune suggests that several of these stem from an earlier time of activity in Palestine, since some closely reflect the First Jewish Revolt.

At the end of his analysis Aune concludes that there were two editions of Revelation. The first edition combined these smaller blocks with new material into a unified whole, consisting mainly of Rev 1:7-12a; 4:1—22:5. In a second edition John adds the title (Rev 1:1-3), the seven "letters" and their introduction (Rev 1:12b—3:22), and an epilogue (Rev 22:6-21) as well as several interpolations throughout of a more prophetic or parenetic nature, bringing his collected visions to bear on a particular set of historical circumstances. Such a source-critical analysis helps resolve some nagging questions concerning the book, such as the ongoing debate concerning the date and circumstances of composition, as will be seen below, as well as providing direction for the interpretation of such passages as chapter 11. If John originally wrote all or part of this chapter prior to the destruction of Jerusalem and then incorporated it into the larger text to make a new point for a new setting, many difficulties disappear.

---

[e]Ibid., p. cxviii.
[f]Ibid., pp. cxix-cxx.

THE SETTING OF REVELATION

The author. The author of Revelation identifies himself as John. From the mid-second century on the tendency has been to identify this John with John the apostle, the son of Zebedee and brother of James, who is also commonly named as the author of the Fourth Gospel and the Epistles of John.[5] Of the numerous well-known Johns of the first century (John the Baptist, John Mark, the apostle John, John the Elder) and the many other Johns whose names are not recorded elsewhere in Scripture, what led to this connection with the apostle John? On the one hand, it might reflect direct

---

[5]Justin *Dial.* 81.4 is the earliest such attribution.

knowledge of the identity of this John passed on in the Christian culture. On the other hand, in light of the tendency to attribute all valued early Christian writings to an apostle or someone closely connected with an apostle, it might have served as a means of promoting the authority and normative use of the book. Such a position results not from an intent to deceive but from a different logic: if a book had the ring of the apostolic witness, it would follow that it is attributable to an apostle. This would work in both directions. Gaius, for example, believing Revelation to advance heretical views, argued that it could not have been written by an apostle. Instead, he suggests that the late-first-century heretic Cerinthus wrote it, attributing it to the apostle John to advance his heretical program.[6] Many notable scholars continue to follow the traditional attribution of Revelation to the apostle John,[7] but the way that attribution of authorship has been so closely tied to the ideological agenda of proponents and antagonists of the book suggests that the question of authorship is really a cipher for the question of the role and authority a book should have in the church, not a matter of historical inquiry.

Internal evidence tends to carry more weight than traditional ascriptions where questions of authorship are concerned. Noteworthy in this regard is the critique of the traditional view by the third-century scholar Dionysius of Alexandria. His careful analysis of the language and style of Revelation vis-à-vis the Fourth Gospel led him to conclude that the same author could not have written both (see Eusebius *Hist. eccl.* 7.25). Dionysus's mode of inquiry anticipated the rise of critical investigation.

What profile of the author emerges from the text itself? John does not appear to be pseudepigraphic, a fact that separates John from every other known apocalypse except for *Shepherd of Hermas*. If "John" were a pseudonym, we should expect more hints from the apocalypse concerning the life setting of the vision in the activity of a famous John. Rather, John makes no special claims about himself with the exception that he is a "slave of God" (Rev 1:1), a "brother" to those whom he addresses (Rev 1:9) and, indirectly, a prophet (Rev 22:9). The first of these also described some of the great Old Testament worthies, most frequently Moses, and New Testament leaders such as Paul. While denoting absolute submissiveness to God, it is also an honorary title. He does not make any explicit or implicit claims to have known Jesus in the flesh or to have been one of the Twelve; in fact he looks on the circle of the apostles from the outside (Rev 21:14). His "brothers" are the "prophets" (Rev 22:9), not the apostles.

John was probably from Palestine. His work resonates with both the Hebrew and the Greek text traditions of the Old Testament.[8] The genre of apocalypse itself is most at home in Palestine. He appears to be familiar with the Jerusalem temple and its accouterments. He writes Greek in a manner that suggests that Aramaic or Hebrew is his native language and Greek a secondary acquisition. Given the Judean focus of some of his visions and the possibility that a number of them were originally linked with the First Jewish Revolt (like Rev 11:1-13; 17:1-18), John might have carried on his visionary ministry first in Palestine and then emigrated to Asia Minor in the tumult preceding or following the Jewish War, a time when so many Jews left Palestine. From then on he exercised a prophetic ministry to

---

[6]See Eusebius *Hist. eccl.* 3.28.1-2. Gaius incidentally displays an awareness as early as the third century C.E. that pseudepigraphy was being used for deceptive ends.

[7]Robert H. Mounce, *The Book of Revelation,* rev. ed., NICNT (Grand Rapids: Eerdmans, 1998), p. 31; S. S. Smalley, *Thunder and Love* (Milton Keynes, U.K.: Word, 1994), pp. 37-40.

[8]Aune, *Revelation 1-5,* p. l.

the churches in that province. Indeed, he appears to have known these churches well prior to writing, given the number of local references to realities in the seven cities or the local culture and knowledge of each place, which speak of significant prior contact.[9]

Revelation is addressed to churches resident in seven known cities of the Roman province of Asia, the westernmost province in what is now called Turkey. These cities—Ephesus, Smyrna, Pergamum, Thyatira, Sardis, Philadelphia and Laodicea—form a horseshoe-shaped circuit, each one or two days' walking distance from the next. This arrangement would suit well the ministry of an itinerant prophet. Such itinerant prophets, whose authority derived mainly from their claim to mediate knowledge from the divine realm and to enjoy charismatic endowments, are a well-attested phenomenon in early Christianity. Paul's troubles in the Corinthian church, particularly the later stages as attested in 2 Corinthians 10—13, were occasioned by such traveling charismatists.

The late-first- or early-second-century manual of church order called the *Didache* also bears witness to a body of prophets within the larger church communities. This manual gives detailed instructions about how to both treat genuine prophets and discern false prophets. Itinerant prophets must have been a familiar experience to command the attention of and take so much space in so brief a manual. These charismatic prophets moved from church to church; they were to receive up to three days' provisions and move on. If a prophet were to stay longer, that one was to be regarded as a fraud. While there were several tests prescribed for these itinerant charismatics, to determine whether or not they were true or false, there was considerable

latitude given to them while speaking in a trance. As long as they neither asked for food or money while in the Spirit, the community was "on no account to subject such a one to any tests or verifications," for "every sin shall be forgiven, but this sin shall not be forgiven" (*Didache* 11). John, who grounds his message entirely in the presentation of supernatural communications (rather than speaking directly and on his own authority, like Paul, Peter, James, Jude and John the Elder), may be such a Christian prophet. Moreover, there were rival teachers on the move through these churches: "prophets" were gaining a hearing in Pergamum and Thyatira but were rebuffed at Ephesus, together with a "prophetess," also in Thyatira, who seems to be in league with them. So in Revelation we find a competition between Christian prophets for the right to determine faithful response to the gospel in their situation.

At some point John moves from the mainland to the island of Patmos, west of Miletus. Eusebius records the tradition that John was exiled to Patmos during the reign of Domitian as a result of his activity in the churches, but he later returned and continued his work into Trajan's reign (*Hist. eccl.* 2.20). This would be the most natural reading for being on Patmos "*on account of* the word of God and the testimony of Jesus" (Rev 1:9).[10] The way John embeds a particularly trenchant critique of Gentile religion in general and the ideology of the emperor and Rome in particular in his presentation of the "testimony of Jesus" makes his deportation to Patmos as a political dissident a likely enough scenario. Contrary to popular illustrations showing Patmos as a barren rock, the island supported a military garrison, an Artemis cult and two gymnasia.[11] There is no

---

[9]C. J. Hemer, *The Letters to the Seven Churches of Asia in their Local Setting* (1986; reprint, Grand Rapids: Eerdmans, 2001), p. 29.

[10]The preposition used (*dia,* followed by a noun in the accusative) indicates the cause or reason for some action, not the purpose for some action (see A. Y. Collins, *Crisis and Catharsis* [Philadelphia: Westminster Press, 1984], p. 55).

[11]L. L. Thompson, *The Book of Revelation* (New York: Oxford, 1990), p. 173; see also H. D. Saffrey, "Relire l'Apocalypse à Patmos," *RB* 82 (1975), pp. 386-90.

Figure 24.1. A denarius of Nero, featuring a portrait of the emperor on the obverse and the Temple of Vesta in Rome on the reverse. (Photo courtesy of Classical Numismatic Group, Inc., www.CNG-coins.com)

evidence of a penal colony per se, but Patmos would still be an appropriate location to which to remove a troublesome agitator, placing him under the supervision of a military garrison.

On Patmos John had time to pray, meditate, enter into visionary experiences and reflect on their meaning and the ways to communicate their import for the congregations he served. Many scholars will say that Revelation was written *from* Patmos, but in fact, John only says that he had visionary experiences there. Revelation 1:9 says nothing about the *present* location of the author, just where he *was* when this experience came to him. While he may have finished Revelation there and dispatched it from that island, John might also have returned to the mainland prior to writing or dispatching Revelation.

Date. Revelation is usually dated either to the end of Domitian's reign (thus 95-96 C.E.) or to the "Year of the Four Emperors" (68-69 C.E.). Proponents of both dates have strong arguments. The following points are often advanced in favor of an early date:

• The reference to the temple in Revelation 11:1-2 and the prediction of the extent of the Gentiles' trampling (the outer courts only) shows that it must have been written before 70 C.E., when Titus's armies invaded the holy of holies itself and burned the whole edifice.

• The enumeration of the number of the beast as 666 clearly indicates Nero as the intended "man" spoken of in Revelation 13:18. The Hebrew letters in the name "Nero Caesar" (Heb, *nrwn qsr,* נרון קסר) add up to 666; if the final "n" (נ) is dropped from נרו, following the Latin spelling, the number 616 emerges, which is a significant textual variant here. Thus Revelation is written during Nero's reign, pointing to him as the Beast.

• The enumeration of the seven kings in Revelation 17:9-10 makes Nero the fifth or sixth, Galba the sixth or seventh and Otho the seventh or eighth (all depending on whether we start with Julius or Augustus), suggesting a date shortly after Nero's death but before the Roman civil wars of 68-69 are settled. Indeed, this would have been a

Figure 24.2. A bronze sesterce featuring Vespasian's image and titles on the obverse. On the reverse, Vespasian advances to take the hand of Roma and raise her up to a standing position again, with the inscription "Rome Resurgent." The issue commemorates the restoration of peace and health to the empire after the civil wars of 68/69 C.E. and the ideology of the Flavian house as the restorers of Rome. (Photo courtesy of Edward Waddell [www.coin.com])

time in which an anti-Roman provincial like John might have expected the beast (here, the claimants to the imperial power carrying on a self-destructive civil war) to have devoured the whore (i.e., Rome).

Thus there are a number of passages that might be taken most naturally to derive from the troubled interregnum between Nero and Vespasian, and before the Jewish War had concluded. In favor of a late-first-century date, scholars point out the following:

- Irenaeus locates the writing of Revelation toward the end of Domitian's reign (*Adv. Haer.* 5.30.3), a tradition that was accepted by the majority of early church fathers, and which Eusebius regarded as authoritative (*Hist. eccl.* 3.18.3; 5.30.3).

- The "healing of the death blow" dealt to the beast must point to the accession of Vespasian, since the reigns of Galba, Otho and Vitellius were a period of civil war when Rome was shaken at the very foundations (see *4 Ezra* 12:17-18). Healing came only with the establishment of the new dynasty

(see figure 24.2).

- This observation suggests that the "head count" in Revelation 17:9-10 might not include the "interregnum emperors," who were more a part of the wound than part of the healing: the count could thus extend to Domitian.

- The spread of Christianity to the seven cities addressed by Revelation, five congregations of which are not mentioned elsewhere in the New Testament (especially Paul and Acts), presupposes a period of growth well past the death of Paul.

- Naming Rome "Babylon" best suits a post-70 date, after it has repeated the atrocity of its predecessor in destroying the Jerusalem temple, though this is by no means necessary (see 1 Peter).

- The situation described in the seven oracles to the seven churches and reflected in the vision—a heightened interest in imperial cult, the growing impatience of martyrs who need to wait still longer for their vindication (Nero's single act of persecution in

Rome being the likely cause of the majority of martyrs in the first century), the separation and antagonism of synagogue and church, and the growing sense of forthcoming persecution centered on the imperial cult—points to conditions known during the later first century.

This debate is considerably eased if we consider that the final form of Revelation may incorporate earlier materials written by John during the First Jewish Revolt.[12] The few specific passages that reflect conditions in Judea or the empire at large prior to the conclusion of the First Jewish Revolt had been written by John earlier, perhaps indeed for Jewish Christians in Judea. These were then woven into a larger work (Revelation) and would have been interpreted quite differently now by its Christian audience in Asia Minor. References to the temple in chapter 11 would now be understood as a promise of protection for the Christian people; the number of Nero's name remains a reminder of the empire's true potential for evil and opposition to God's people; the "head count" can be read to assure these believers that they are now close to seeing the end of the beast and its ungodly rider.

The addressees and their situation. Many study Bibles have a one-page introduction to Revelation that includes a statement like this: "Revelation was addressed to comfort Christians undergoing persecution in Asia Minor, encouraging them to endure by providing a picture of God's ultimate victory over their persecutors." In reality, however, such a summary only tells a small part of the story.[13] John writes to *seven* churches, many of which experience widely divergent challenges: indeed, within a single church, different groups face different challenges. The Christians in Ephesus have had to "bear up patiently" (Rev 2:3), probably in the face of harassment; Christians in Smyrna have experienced the "slander" of the synagogue (Rev 2:9; see also 3:9) and can expect imprisonment for a time (Rev 2:10); one Christian, Antipas, has died for his faith in Pergamum, and those Christians are commended for enduring during that time (Rev 2:13). There are also commendations for some Christians in Thyatira and all in Philadelphia for "patient endurance" (Rev 2:19; 3:10) and for not denying the name (Rev 3:8). However, Laodicean Christians appear to have experienced no loss for their faith. On the contrary, they prosper (Rev 3:17). A movement toward assimilation is gaining strength in Pergamum and Thyatira (Rev 2:14-16, 20-23). A number of Christians in Sardis similarly have "soiled their clothes," probably through too close a partnership with the society around them (Rev 3:2, 4). That is to say, Revelation is *as much* a challenge to the comfortable within their society as it is comfort for those whose pure commitment has brought them into tension with the host society. Revelation is as much challenge and protest as it is comfort and encouragement.

Roman rule and its manifestations. An essential background for reading Revelation is the scope and ideology of Roman rule. Popular prophecy experts keep looking to the future for a beast and his one-world empire because they are insufficiently familiar with the perception of the Roman Empire held by most of its

---

[12]Aune, *Revelation 1-5*, pp. cxx-cxxii.

[13]The impression probably also results from a misreading of the visions of Revelation 4—22. Persecution is a common topic of these visions, but it belongs either to the past (the martyrs in Rev 6:9-11 calling out for justice, which is forthcoming) or to the imminent future, as the conflict over who is worthy of worship escalates. Indeed, Revelation could be said to equip believers to accept persecution rather than (continue to) compromise their loyalty and obedience to God and the Lamb. On the question of persecution of Christians under Domitian, see David A. deSilva, "The 'Image of the Beast' and the Christians in Asia Minor: Escalation of Sectarian Tension in Revelation 13," *TrinJ* 12NS (1991): 185-208, especially pp. 197-201 and the literature cited there.

Figure 24.3. A bronze sesterce of Nero minted in 65 C.E. The reverse features the personification of the city of Rome, seated, dressed in military attire, and holding the icon for victory in her outstretched arm. (Photo courtesy of Superior Galleries, Beverly Hills)

inhabitants and purposefully promoted by imperial propaganda. Virgil's *Aeneid*, the court epic of the Augustan age, celebrates the promise of Zeus that the Romans would "rule the sea and all the lands about it" (1.236-37), a reference to the *orbis terrarum*, the "circle of the lands" about the Mediterranean that was considered the civilized world. Virgil also has Zeus summarize Aeneas's mission and the destiny of Rome thus: to "bring the whole world under law's dominion" (*Aeneid* 4.232). Indeed, as the wings of the Roman eagle overshadowed more and more of the Mediterranean basin, it exercised "authority over every tribe and people and language and nation" (Rev 13:7 NRSV). Minucius Felix, a second-century Christian, would write of the Romans that "their power and authority has occupied the circuit of the whole world [again, the concept of the *orbis terrarum*]: thus it has propagated its empire beyond the paths of the sun, and the bounds of the ocean itself" (*Octavius* 6). Rome was thus indeed seen as "the great city that rules over the kings of the earth" (Rev 17:18 NRSV). If it is objected that Rome did not

rule over *every* other nation, it should also be noted that the political landscape of Revelation also allows for foreign powers from the East, especially, to threaten the order of the West (Rev 16:12-16).

Roman power was represented in the seven cities named by John in many ways, but perhaps the most prominent and enduring was the imperial cult. The cult was not imposed by Augustus on the provinces. Rather, it was a natural response on the part of provincials to the tremendous power of the emperor, which was perceived as truly godlike, and to the benefits that the rule of the emperor brought to the provinces. The imperial cult especially focused attention on the emperor as the patron of the world. Since his gifts matched those of the deities, it was deemed only fitting that the expressions of gratitude and loyalty should take on the forms used to communicate with the patron deities themselves. Nicolaus of Damascus thus explained the phenomenon in the opening of his *Life of Augustus:* "all people address him [as Augustus] in accordance with their estimation of his honor, revering him with temples and sacrifices across islands and continents, organized in cities and provinces, matching the greatness of his virtue and repaying his benefactions toward them."

The "Peace of Augustus" (*pax Augusti*) following the tumultuous civil wars that ended the Republic was viewed as relief of divine proportions, and the return of thanks had to be equal to the gift. Ongoing loyalty to the emperor and his household, of which the imperial cult was a visible manifestation, ensured both that the empire would remain strong (hence averting the disasters of civil war and foreign invasion, and ensuring continued peace and prosperity) and that the emperor would remain well-disposed toward the province when it was in need of imperial aid. It was a most politic decision that the province's ambassadors to the emperor should also be those elites who held priesthoods in the imperial cult.

The imperial cult was embedded in the cults of the traditional deities. Frequently, the statues of the emperor and traditional deities shared the same sacred space, emphasizing their connectedness. The emperor was not simply a god but the vessel by which the traditional gods established order and showered their gifts on humanity. As the chief priest of the Roman world (*Pontifex Maximus*), he stood as mediator between the gods and the human race. Many coins minted during the first century provide a graphic depiction of this: on the front (obverse), a portrait of the emperor with his titles (including *divi filius*, "son of the deified," and *Pontifex Maximus*); on the reverse, a portrait of some deity, showing that his rule was grounded in the rule of the gods (or of "Fortune," or destiny). He ruled by divine right, and his achievements were signs of divine favor.

The emperor was often worshiped in tandem with the goddess Roma, or Roma Aeterna, the personified and deified representation of Rome (see figures 24.3 and 24.4). Smyrna established a temple to Rome as early as 195 B.C.E. Augustus refused to allow any temple to be consecrated to himself, unless Roma were also included. In 29 B.C.E. Pergamum erected such a temple to Augus-

Figure 24.4. A silver tetradrachm minted in the province of Asia Minor *(COM ASI)* during the reign of Claudius. The reverse shows the Temple to *Roma et Augusti*, with a statue of Augustus being crowned with a wreath by the goddess Roma. (Photo courtesy of www.CNGcoins.com)

tus and Roma. In the same year, Ephesus re-dedicated part of its famous temple of Artemis to the deified Julius and Roma. The imperial cult thus also reinforced the belief that Rome was chosen by the gods to rule the world, to subdue all nations and to lead them into a golden age of lasting peace and well-being, united under its banner.

The cult was not imposed on the provinces from above by the emperor or his staff. Rather, it was initiated from below and from the periphery as a means of connecting with the emperor and, especially, gaining the favors and status that could be bestowed by the emperor. Local provincial elites fostered active cults, enjoying the opportunities that holding priesthoods in these cults brought for advancing their prestige and ambitions for higher offices in the emperor's administration. At the same time, the fear of the return of civil disorder and the ever-present threat of invasion from foreign kingdoms like Parthia made the strength of Rome a welcome bulwark for those under its protection. Rome's power meant order and security, and the cult of the *Augusti et Roma* became an important expression of loyalty to that sheltering power.

The imperial cult was extremely active in the province of Asia Minor, as archaeological evidence from each of the seven cities abundantly attests.[14] Ephesus and Pergamum were rivals for the title of *neokoros*, "temple warden," of the provincial imperial cult, a title that gave the city preeminence in the province. Ephesus and Pergamum were each honored as "twice *neokoros*" by the end of Trajan's reign (117 C.E.). During Domitian's reign, when the provinces had experienced a surge of prosperity (as well as benefiting from Domitian's interest in protecting them from corrupt governors), a massive new temple

was erected to Domitian, with a cult statue that stood twenty feet high. As they went about their daily business, Christians in these seven cities passed temples, shrines and free-standing altars and statues representative of the imperial cult, and they witnessed the festivities marking the emperor's birthday and the birthdays of his family members and other civic festivals. The Gentile Christians among them would have faced strong pressures to participate lest they arouse the ill will of their neighbors and local elites.

John thus addresses a situation in which Christians stand in tension with their neighbors in ways similar to those encountered in Philippi and Thessalonica. The imperative to avoid all forms of idolatry and worship of other gods would have meant conspicuous avoidance of participation in the ubiquitous imperial cult or in *any* rite that focused attention on another god beside the God of Israel. This would severely limit a Christian's social, economic and political participation since some pious rite adorned most gatherings, and almost every occasion involving a common meal included acknowledging the patron deity "presiding" at the meal. It would mean a voluntary resignation of access to the economic advantages of full participation in the trade guilds. It would reduce the number of non-Christian friends, not just in the social sense but also in the sense of business associates who could increase Christians' access to prosperity and patrons who could provide protection and aid in time of need. In addition suspicion increased concerning the goals of this "atheistic" and "antisocial" group growing in the midst of the city. Some voices in the churches sought to minimize and reduce these tensions; John seeks to escalate these tensions.

---

[14]Landmark studies on this subject include S. R. F. Price, *Rituals and Power: The Roman Imperial Cult in Asia Minor* (Cambridge: Cambridge University, 1984); S. J. Friesen, *Twice Neokoros: Ephesus, Asia and the Cult of the Flavian Imperial Family* (Leiden: Brill, 1993).

The Other Side of Revelation 13?

Pliny the Younger, the imperial envoy to (or governor of) the provinces of Bithynia and Pontus in 112-113 C.E., wrote a letter to the emperor Trajan that sheds considerable light on the situation envisioned in Revelation 13:11-17. In this letter we find Pliny asking advice from the emperor Trajan concerning how to proceed with the prosecution of those brought up on charges of being Christian. Pliny had a great regard for precedents, and although he had perhaps heard of trials of Christians and assumed that there were customary penalties, he had no precedents available.[a] Perhaps he was setting some. Nevertheless, it was self-evident to him that being a Christian was a punishable offense, particularly because it involved the refusal to sacrifice to the emperor and gods of the empire. It is a matter-of-fact account that depicts the very sort of encounter for which John prepares his congregations in his apocalypse.

> The method I have observed toward those who have been brought before me as Christians is this: I asked them whether they were Christians; if they admitted it, I repeated the question twice, and threatened them with punishment; if they persisted, I ordered them to be at once punished: for I was persuaded, whatever the nature of their opinions might be, a contumacious and inflexible obstinacy certainly deserved correction. [Those who denied ever being Christians] repeated after me an invocation to the gods, and offered religious rites with wine and incense before your statue (which for that purpose I had ordered to be brought, together with those of the gods), and even reviled the name of Christ. [Those who admitted they were once Christians, but now recanted] worshiped your statue and the images of the gods, uttering imprecations at the same time against the name of Christ.[b]

Pliny urges Trajan that the last group, though they were formerly Christians, should be pardoned, and closes by expressing his hopes of reclaiming great numbers of people who have strayed and reviving attention to traditional religious rites.

This is our oldest surviving account of legal prosecutions (as opposed to Nero's persecution, which did not involve trials) of Christians on the charge of simply professing Christianity. A simple act, the offering of a little incense and wine, combined with two little words *("Anathema Christos")* could get one off the hook. John, however, insists that the testimony of Jesus be maintained to the end, that the Christian not deny the name of Christ. Compromise would result in the death of the testimony of Jesus—the liberating word contained in the cross and resurrection—even if the church survived in a new form, as another religion contributing to the legitimation of Rome and the status quo. It is a great testimony to John that the clash between the confession of Christ and loyalty to the emperor that he foresaw became reality only fifteen years after writing Revelation.

---

[a]F. G. Downing, "Pliny's Prosecutions of Christians," *JSNT* 34 (1988): 105-23.
[b]My translation.

Tensions with the synagogue. The oracles to the seven churches reveal other important tensions being negotiated by the Christians addressed. The oracles to the Christians in Smyrna and Philadelphia highlight the tension with the synagogue, the non-Christian Jewish population, in those cities. First, there is the familiar conflict over which group—the synagogue or the church—has the right to call themselves "Jews," or to claim the heritage of being the genuine "Israel" (see, e.g., Gal 3:29; 6:16; Phil 3:5-6). Second, there is the clear indication of a hostile response toward Christians on the part of the synagogue, summed up as "slander" (*blasphēmia* among human beings would denote "slander" or even "denunciation").

Throughout the New Testament we encounter resistance toward and even hostility against the Christian sect on the part of segments of non-Christian Judaism. Christianity, especially as practiced by Pauline Christians, was a radical challenge to the traditional understanding of what it meant to be a Jew and to keep covenant with God. Paul attributes to his Judaizing rivals in Galatia the desire to avoid persecution, meaning persecution from non-Christian Jews who would accept a Christianity that made Gentiles full proselytes, but not a Christianity that made Jews violate *kashrut* by eating with Gentile sinners.

This tension increased markedly, however, after the destruction of the Jerusalem temple in 70 C.E. and the consolidation of Judaism around Torah. There was even less room for toleration after a major pillar of Judaism had been demolished, especially toleration of a sect that claimed to be the genuine heir of Israel. Toward the end of the first century, we find the "benediction against heretics" (*Birkhat ha-Minim*) spreading in its use, marking a new commitment to distinguish "true Jews" from deviant derivations. Indeed, purging itself of impure representations of Judaism (like Christianity) would have been a timely and cathartic move for synagogues seeking the survival of their way of life after the disasters in Jerusalem.

Slander, on the one hand, could simply indicate the verbal assaults of non-Christian Jews with regard to the Christians not being genuine heirs of Abraham but only law-breaking deviants. On the other hand, there may be a causal link between the "slander" by the synagogue and the imprisonment, suffering and testing John predicts for the congregation in Smyrna. Reading *slander* as "denunciation," John may be referring to attempts made by some Jews to bring official and public attention to the Christian movement, and specifically to the fact that Christians (whether Gentile or Jewish) do not belong to the Jewish group, nor should they enjoy the benefits that pertain to the synagogue.[15] Christians would have only begun to be endangered from official powers after it was made clear that these were no longer Jews. The Jewish people had received the favor of Augustus in the establishment of Judaism as a *religio licita* in the empire, which allowed them to practice their religion freely and to be exempted from the civic and imperial cults. This did not always make it safe to be a Jew, but at least made anti-Jewish actions more the exception than the rule. When the shelter of Judaism is removed from the Christian movement, however, so is the relative safety Christians enjoyed.

Prophets of compromise. The oracles to Ephesus, Pergamum and Thyatira give considerable attention to the presence of teachers whose message John does not affirm (to put it mildly). John describes these alternative voices as "false apostles" (Rev 2:2), "Nicolaitans" (Rev 2:6, 15), who are also followers of Balaam (Rev

---

[15]See, for example, Hemer, *Letters to the Seven Churches,* pp. 8-10. A similar situation is attested in Acts 18:12-17. Aune collects an impressive array of evidence from first- through third-century Christian authors attesting to the role of non-Christian Jews in arousing local opposition to Christians (*Revelation 1-5,* pp. 162-63).

2:14),[16] and "Jezebel, who calls herself a prophet" (Rev 2:20). Nothing meaningful can be deduced concerning the first group, but the latter three designations represent what John understands to be a (functionally) uniform group advocating a more tolerant and accommodating stance toward the non-Christian society and its expectations. This group has already surfaced in three of the seven congregations and has at least gained a foothold in Pergamum and Thyatira. John is engaged in a struggle with other prophets over the right and authority to define what constitutes a "faithful" response to the gospel, particularly as this comes to bear on interaction with non-Christians.

These prophets, John says, advocate eating food sacrificed to idols and committing fornication (Rev 2:14; 2:20), and no doubt they have developed a theological legitimation for this activity. What their message was, however, must be reconstructed through an analysis of the Old Testament precedents that John is invoking with his labels ("Balaam" and "Jezebel") and with this strange accusation about eating foods sacrificed to idols and committing fornication.

Although Balaam blessed Israel when Balak called him to curse the people, it was the short and obscure reference in Number 31:16 that remained his epitaph. There, Balaam is blamed for the apostasy of Israel at Peor (Num 25:1-3), when the Israelites "began to play the harlot with the daughters of Moab," with the consequence that they accepted the Moabites' invitation to bow down to their gods and eat of their sacrifices. Balaam became a figure for apostasy, the false teacher accused of devising this clever stratagem for destroying Israel's distinctiveness and dissolving their identity, blending them into the nations around them. The loss of this distinctiveness, however, would also mean the loss of the blessing and promise of the holy God who called them to be distinct and absolute in their loyalty to one God.

When John attacks the Nicolaitans as "disciples of Balaam," highlighting "eating food sacrificed to idols," the main issue appears to be whether or not Christians can participate in the religious life of the Greco-Roman society. There are obvious advantages for doing so. It eliminates all the tension between the church and society if Christians can again go out in public and show themselves pious and reliable through participation in the cults of the traditional gods and emperors. It keeps important economic channels open through membership in the trade guilds. Christians in Corinth had already asserted that "an idol is nothing" (1 Cor 8:4, 7). Jesus himself had taught that the ingestion of food does not carry any spiritual value (see, e.g., Mk 7:15, 18-19). Why then should Christians offend their neighbors unnecessarily? What harm would there be in keeping up old business ties, enjoying social occasions that also reaffirm networks of alliances with our neighbors?

Just as Paul, however, would not tolerate the compromise of the Christians' witness to the one and only God (1 Cor 10:14-21), so John will not advocate compromise on so essential a matter as idolatry. In this context, despite the fact that sexual entertainments would often accompany a trade guild party or private dinner, it is better to read the second charge —"committing fornication"—metaphorically. Adopting the Nicolaitans' compromising position amounts to forsaking a faithful relationship to Jesus. Indeed, the symbols of the virgin and harlot in Revelation are best understood in these terms rather than being reduced to a glorification of celibacy and asceticism. John

---

[16]The Nicolaitans are held by John to teach the same thing as the disciples of Balaam and Jezebel (cf. Rev 2:14-15, 20); moreover the name Nicholas is the Greek equivalent for "Balaam" (the etymology of *Nico-laos*, the first root referring to conquering, the second meaning "people," is a rough Greek equivalent for *bl' 'm*, "he wears out the people").

wants the church's critique of society and its dedication to self-worship to remain pure and without compromise.

A metaphorical use of sexual language also emerges in John's denunciation of the "fornication" of Jezebel and of "those who have committed adultery with her" (Rev 2:21-22). The label "Jezebel" forces the Christians to connect this prophetess in their midst with the wicked wife of King Ahab, who materially supported the prophets of Baal in Israel and endorsed their cause vocally and socially. This Thyatiran woman, herself claiming the prophetic gift, may also serve in some way as a principal supporter of the Nicolaitan movement, supporting their itinerant teachers in the same way others supported John in his itinerant ministry. "Adultery" with this woman signals compliance with her way of thinking. The compromise with pagan religion advocated by this "Jezebel" and the Nicolaitans came at a dangerous time for the community, a time when the social pressures were mounting in a way that they may not have seen, which could result in total absorption of the Christian community into the pagan environment if the boundaries were not fortified and the lines clearly drawn.

The lure of prosperity. The prosperity promised by Rome, and the possibility of sharing in this prosperity, is a particularly important aspect of the situation of these congregations. No doubt the hope for economic prosperity provided the main motivation for developing a theology that could accommodate "eating food sacrificed to idols." The lure of wealth has sunk its hooks deepest, however, into the mouths of Laodicean Christians. John addresses them mainly on the basis of their civic identity, as if to say that the church and society shared everything in common and that he could not address the church in terms that the whole society would not share. The appeal to images of the lukewarm and nauseating water forming their water supply, the medical achievements of the school in the city, and the civic sense of pride in their riches and need for nothing, an allusion to the city's ability to rebuild itself only thirty years earlier without imperial aid,[17] all depict the Laodicean Christians first as Laodicean citizens. From this posture they are called to trade in their civic identity for a renewed Christian identity, and it is mainly their pride in their wealth that John attacks as the source of their spiritual malaise.

Such wealth really makes Christians "poor" and "wretched" (Rev 3:17), whereas the Christians in Smyrna are truly "rich" despite their "poverty." The road to riches is the way of accommodation and compromise. Wealth gained through compromise is tainted because Babylon was already drunk with the blood of the saints who held up an alternative definition of life, and material prosperity had been purchased at the cost of maintaining "the testimony of Jesus." John foresees even greater economic embargoes being leveled against Christians in the near future (the boycott on buying and selling without the mark of the beast, for example), and so he seeks to negate the society's definition of what constitutes desirable wealth.

The purpose and effects of Revelation. John's purposes for Revelation are as diverse as the audiences addressed and the particular challenges facing them. Nevertheless, the common denominator in John's pastoral response to these diverse situations is the desire to reveal for his congregations the true nature of the realities they encounter, the real crisis facing them, and the real significance of the choices they might make. The author's use of apocalypse as the dominant genre already suggests this. As an "unveiling," its primary purpose is to *open the eyes* of the Christians to the spiritual dimension of the world around them.

---

[17]Robert H. Mounce, *The Book of Revelation*, rev. ed., NICNT (Grand Rapids: Eerdmans, 1998), p. 98.

John's more specific purposes can be clarified by considering the alternative agendas among the seven churches and their neighbors. "Jezebel" and the "Nicolaitans" are trying to reduce the tension between the Christian group and the society around them by making room for Christians to have fellowship with their neighbors in settings where idolatrous rites are performed. They seek to erase those boundaries that threaten the group's peaceful coexistence with society and that impede its members' ongoing prosperity within that society. While the Christians would still know that "an idol is nothing," their neighbors would no longer think of them as atheists or as antisocial and therefore potentially subversive. In the course of this movement, however, the Christian group's distinctive ethos and witness would be lost. Christians would no longer confront their neighbors with the reality of one God and the exclusive honors due that God; they would no longer witness against the empty pretensions of Roman imperial ideology, especially as enshrined in the cult of Augustus and Roma.

Against this trend John calls for the maintenance of the group's distinctiveness, even its heightened separation from all those situations and entanglements where its loyalty and obedience to the one God might be compromised. John writes to strengthen boundaries and Christians' commitments to those boundaries, so that the distinctive message and witness of the group will not be muted but will continue to trumpet the call of the one God in the midst of the world. John not only predicts heightened tension between the Christians and society, he ensures that this tension will be heightened and that the conflict will escalate in his near future.

THE RHETORIC OF REVELATION
Before analyzing the particulars of John's message, the strange nature of Revelation's rhetoric invites some discussion concerning how Revelation "persuades." After all, the stakes are very

high for its addressees and for those who would take its message seriously in any age. When prosperity, reputation and even life itself are on the line, why would a Christian take this message seriously and submit, in effect, to its interpretation of reality? What makes *this* prophet's message and vision plausible and thus worthy of being taken seriously?

First, the genre of apocalypse itself contributes immensely to the authority of John's words (what the rhetorician would call ethos), mainly because they are not presented as John's words at all. Rather, John draws the hearers into a visionary experience, allowing them also to see the bigger picture in terms of space and time and to hear the words of supremely trustworthy narrators like God, Christ, angels, elders and the Spirit, who is seen as the ultimate source of the visionary experiences John crafts. In Galatians, Paul speaks on his own authority in his own voice; in Revelation, John's voice is merely the means by which the hearers are brought into "direct" contact with those otherworldly realities and voices whose authority is beyond question.

John's saturation of Revelation with the language of the Old Testament—phrases, lines or whole sentences of which are woven into nearly every verse—also works to his advantage. By weaving the words of authoritative Scriptures so fully into his new work, John causes them to lend their authority to his own words. If the words of the prophets and psalms were inspired in their original contexts, they remain recognizable as inspired in their new context, helping that new word to be accepted as authentic revelation from God to the extent that it is infused directly with older revelations from God. Moreover, the widespread use of formulas and phrases known from Daniel or other prophetic and apocalyptic texts enhances the hearers' impression that they are hearing another authoritative prophecy—another species of the same genus.

Second, the genre of apocalypse allows

John to do what a speech or sermon cannot begin to do as persuasively, that is, narrate future events. Aristotle had declared this impossible (*Rhet.* 3.16.11), with the result that narrative was rarely used in deliberations. John, however, can use narrative directly and extensively to support his attempts to dissuade the hearers from collusion with the dominant culture and to persuade them to take up an even more radical stance of exclusive commitment to God and God's values. As revelation, the Spirit of God can make the future unfold before John's eyes and thus before the hearers' eyes, allowing them to see the consequences of following the various courses of action and the ultimate advantage or disadvantage that attends these courses. John's suppression of his own voice, not issuing warnings about the consequences but rather allowing the hearers to see these for themselves, enhances the plausibility of this future he narrates.

Here again the use of the Old Testament throughout Revelation lends considerable support to John's depiction of the future. The plagues to be poured out on the whole inhabited world in response to the trumpets and vials thoroughly recall the plagues poured out on the Egyptians before the exodus. The final battle takes place at a site that has witnessed many terrible battles, including the battle between the priests of Baal and Elijah. The contemporary world power, Rome, is labeled "Babylon," and the words of the prophets describing Babylon's sins and projecting historical Babylon's fate are now applied to Rome. In each of these cases the recontextualizing of Old Testament language allows John to connect the foreseen future with the historical past. Rhetoricians noted the importance of historical examples and precedents when predicting the consequences of a course of action since, "as a rule, the future resembles the past" (Aristotle *Rhet.* 2.20.8). The future John foresees, however fantastic, is merely a broadening of what God already has done to God's ene-

mies and on behalf of God's people.

The appeals to the mind (what the rhetorician would call *logos*) work mainly in these areas of presentation of the consequences, explanation of causes (as in the depiction of the activity of Satan behind the emperor and his cult), and evocation of Old Testament intertexture to support what the visions say about God's character and interventions in history. John persuades in more conventional ways as well. For example, when a command is issued, it is often supported with rationales (implicit or explicit) providing the grounding for that command. The injunction to "fear God and give God glory . . . and worship him" in Revelation 14:6-7, for example, is supported first by the rationale, "for the hour of God's judgment came," an argument from the consequences that reminds the hearers of the importance of acting now to be acquitted then. Second, it is supported by an implicit rationale as God is identified as the one who "made the heavens and the earth, the seas and springs of water." As Creator, God and God alone is worthy of the worship and obedience of God's creatures, an implicit appeal to the topic of "justice."

Finally, it cannot be denied that John seeks to persuade by arousing emotional responses in his hearers (what rhetoricians call pathos). Putting an audience in a certain emotional state was considered an integral part of the art of persuasion: people make different decisions when they are afraid than when they are confident, when they feel indignation than when they feel friendship. John rouses the feelings of enmity and indignation toward Rome, who continues to profit despite its arrogance, violence and consumption of the world's goods, and toward those who represent an accommodating approach to the dominant culture (like "Jezebel" and the "Nicolaitans"). Here again Old Testament intertexture contributes to the rhetorical power of Revelation, for the revulsion and hostility felt toward Babylon, Jezebel or Balaam (with whom John connects the so-called Nicolaitans) are harnessed and redirected toward contemporary realities. These feelings dispose the hearers to break ties with such figures. As God's judgments and anger are graphically portrayed, John rouses fear among those who have already lived a compromised walk, motivating them to repent; the same visions arouse confidence in those whose single-hearted obedience has already begun to cost them more dearly.

EXEGETICAL SKILL
Identifying and Analyzing Repetitive Texture

One of the more basic exercises in exploring the "inner texture" of a passage is noting repetitions of words and even phrases occurring within that passage and then running throughout the whole book. Ideally, this exercise would be done using the Greek text. Translations can easily mask repetitions that would be evident in the Greek as well as introduce repetitions by using one English word to translate two different Greek words. The New Testament texts were composed for oral delivery and aural reception, and listeners are especially attuned to repetitions of words or phrases. All we need to do is listen carefully to how a gifted preacher might use repetition of key words or longer phrases. The speaker might use repetitions to

- keep the topic or theme firmly in the forefront of the hearers' minds
- stimulate the hearers to make connections or contrasts within the message
- emphasize the attitude or action he or she most wants to implant in the hearers
- mark off the beginning and end points of a section
- simply decorate the sermon

Speakers in the first century would often use repetitions of significant words or phrases to the same ends.

This exegetical procedure is rather simple, calling for a close reading of the passage in light of the whole text, noting any repetitions that might be significant for getting at the meaning, structure or persuasive strategy of the passage within the larger work. Many repetitions might be accidental, ornamental or insignificant for some other reason, and we should take care not to overanalyze. However, as this exercise is practiced alongside all the others introduced in this book or taught in any well-crafted class on exegesis, it can lead to some surprising insights into the ways that something as simple as verbal repetition contributes to the larger rhetorical and ideological goals of the author.

EXAMPLE

Revelation 14:6-13

The language of Revelation is highly repetitive, so much so that John is clearly and deliberately setting up aural echoes and cross-references throughout his work. These aural/oral echoes remind the audience of other parts of the vision, creating an environment for mutual reinforcement and interpretation. We will look only at the more important contributions to repetitive texture here. What we discover consistently in Revelation is that John uses repetitions of words and phrases (1) to help guide his audiences to "see" and "partition" the world around them in such a way that they are faced with incompatible alternatives, and (2) to reinforce the negative consequences of participation in idolatrous cults and the prosperity of Rome, and the positive consequences of adopting his stance toward Roman society.

Working through Revelation 14:6-13 (both by close reading and through concordance work), we might note the following repetitions:

1. "worship" (vv. 7, 9, 11; the latter two adding "the beast and its image")
2. "rest" (vv. 11, 13)
3. "of the wine of the passion [or wrath]" (vv. 8, 10)
4. receiving the "mark" associated with the beast (vv. 9, 11)

Turning then to consider repetitions that might connect pieces of Revelation 14:6-13 with other passages for the hearers, we might note the following:

5. "every nation and tribe and language and people" (v. 6; see Rev 5:9; 7:9; 10:11; 11:9; 13:7; 17:15)
6. "fear God and give him glory" (v. 7; see Rev 4:9; 11:13; 15:4; 16:9; 19:5, 7)
7. "worship" (vv. 7, 9, 11; see Rev 3:9; 4:10; 5:14; 7:11; 9:20; 11:1, 16; 13:4, 8, 12, 15; 15:4; 16:2; 19:4, 10, 20; 20:4; 22:8, 9)
8. "Babylon the Great" (v. 8; see Rev 16:19; 17:5; 18:2, 10, 21)
9. causing the nations to "drink from the wine of the passion of her fornication" (v. 8; see Rev 17:2; 18:3)
10. "her fornication" (connecting v. 8 with Rev 2:21; 17:4; 19:2)
11. drinking "from the cup of the wrath of God" (linking v. 10 with Rev 16:19)
12. "the smoke of their torment goes up for ever and ever" (linking v. 11 with Rev 19:3)
13. the ingredients of torment including "fire and sulfur" (connecting v. 10 with Rev 19:20; 20:10
14. "not having rest by day and by night" (connecting v. 11 with Rev 4:8 (and also, partially, with 20:10).

The list could be extended further.

After gathering such data, the next step would involve thinking carefully about the contexts of these repetitions and what kinds of connections or contrasts—if any—the author would have the hearer make, and how the repetitions in the discourse might serve to reinforce the rhetorical strategy and ideological agenda of the whole.

One of the more notable repetitions running through Revelation, intersecting with Revelation 14:6-13, is the listing of humanity as "nation and tribe and tongue and people," recurring some seven times with minor variations. What the hearer of Revelation discovers through this web of echoes is an environment of competition. The beast exercises authority "over every tribe and people and language and nation" (Rev 13:7), and the whore is enthroned on "peoples and crowds and nations and languages" (Rev 17:15). Nevertheless, they are not allowed to claim all of humanity. The Lamb has "ransomed for God" people "from every tribe and language and people and nation" (Rev 5:9), gathering an innumerable crowd "out from every nation and tribes and peoples and languages" (Rev 7:9). Repetition of this phrase exhibits the ideology of the text, insisting that the Lamb and the beast are in competition for people from every group (that is, there can be no cooperation between followers of the Lamb and supporters of the beast). Through skillful use of repetition, John is creating divisions and positing incompatible alternatives where other voices in the seven churches do not see such stark separations.

The pervasive use of the verb "to worship" *(proskyneō)* invites closer examination in this regard. The objects of worship are God and the Lamb (Rev 4:10; 5:14; 7:11; 11:16; 19:4, 10; 22:8-9) on the one hand, and the dragon, idols or "the beast and its image" on the other hand (Rev 9:20; 13:4, 8, 12, 15; 14:9, 11; 16:2; 19:20). God and the Lamb stand diametrically opposed to the dragon, the beast and all idols, however. Moreover, as John develops the visions, "those who worship the beast" or the dragon or idols always find themselves opposed to God and the Lamb, and ultimately suffering their wrath, whereas those who refuse such worship emerge triumphant in God's presence (Rev 15:2; 20:4). By characterizing people consistently in terms of their objects of worship, John subtly reinforces one of his major contentions: the worship of God and the Lamb is incompatible with the worship of any other, contrary to the position being argued by the Nicolaitans and Jezebel. Even at the level of repetitive patterns in the text, John is rending asunder what Jezebel would join together.

The first angel's message calls the inhabitants of the earth to "fear God and give him glory" (Rev 14:7), which is only proper considering God's status as Creator and Judge. The angelic beings that surround God's throne "give glory . . . to the one seated on the throne" (Rev 4:9), as do all those invited to the marriage feast of the Lamb (Rev 19:5, 7), who are notably described as those who fear God (Rev 19:5). The combination of fearing God and giving God glory appears twice more in Revelation. Those who witness the martyrdom and resurrection of the two witnesses "became afraid and gave glory to the God of heaven" (Rev 11:13). Finally, those who "overcome the beast and its image" sing a song that resonates with the first angel's message at three key points (fearing God, glorifying God and worshiping God):

> Lord, who will not fear
> and glorify your name? . . .
> All nations will come
> and worship before you,
> for your judgments have been revealed. (Rev 15:4 NRSV)

The song of the conquerors, however, is answered contrary to all expectation in Revelation 16:9, where the worshipers of the beast face the judgments of God, but they "did not repent, so as to give glory to him [God]" (Rev 16:9). John displays the activity of superhuman beings as "giving God glory," and he sets up the expectation that all people will "fear and glorify God." Those who fail to do so, namely, those outside the Christian community (and more specifically those who are not Christian as John defines "Christian"), are set up by these repetitions to be viewed as all the more deviant and base for their failure. Repetitive texture thus reinforces the impression John wishes his congregations to have of their idolatrous neighbors: all who fail to "give God glory" are the deviant ones, no matter how great a majority they may seem to be.

Many of the other repetitions we have noted focus on the fate of those who join themselves to Rome and the emperor cult, buying temporal security at the cost of exclusive obedience to God:

- The worshipers of the beast and its image "do not have rest by day and by night" from their torments (Rev 14:11), just as the beasts and the dragon will eventually be tormented "by day and by night" (Rev 20:10), whereas those whose loyalty to the exclusive worship of God extends even to death "rest from their labors" (Rev 14:13). The former is itself a parody of the four living creatures, who also "do not have rest by day or by night" from worshiping God (Rev 4:8), again setting up the stark alternatives that John wishes the hearers to internalize: worship God without lapse or be punished without lapse.
- Those who drink "of the wine of the violent passion of her [i.e., Babylon's] fornication" (Rev 14:8; cf. also Rev 17:2; 18:3) also drink "of the wine of the violent passion of God (Rev 14:10). The effect of this repetition seems to suggest that if Christians "drink in" the ideology of Rome as benefactress of the world and engage in the cultic expressions of gratitude to that benefactress and her representatives, the emperors, they will also "drink in" the wrath of God as a sort of chaser. Babylon herself, however, is also doomed to drink the cup "of the wine of the violent passion of [God's] anger" (Rev 16:19), being judged for "her fornication" (Rev 19:2). The second angel's message (Rev 14:8), in fact, appears verbatim again at Revelation 18:2, doubly emphasizing the true destiny of "Roma

Aeterna." Those who participate in Babylon's self-deluded orgy, therefore, also join themselves to her punishment, the verbal repetitions enacting what John declares explicitly in Revelation 18:4. The emphasis on Babylon's "fornication" will undoubtedly also affect the way the hearers remember Jezebel's "fornication" (Rev 2:21), this verbal cue serving to paint the prophetess even more insidiously as the mouthpiece for the Great Harlot itself.

- In a similar vein "the smoke of the torment" of the idolater "goes up into the ages of ages" (Rev 14:11), just as the smoke of Babylon's burning will ("the smoke of her goes up into the ages of ages," Rev 19:3).

- The same can be said of the beast: those who wish to be seen as grateful clients of the beast and make themselves idolaters will be seen by God as enemies to be punished along with Satan, the beast and the false prophet. The fate of all these figures is linked by the verbal repetition of "torment" with the specific elements of "fire and sulfur" (see Rev 14:10; 19:20; 20:10; 21:8).

Not every excursion into repetitive texture will produce this level of correspondence between verbal repetitions, rhetorical strategy and ideological agenda, but John's extreme and carefully crafted use of repetition alerts us to the *possibilities* of such an inventory and analysis in the context of a fuller exegesis of a passage.

While almost every passage would bear some fruit in analyzing repetitive texture, you might begin with one or more of the following passages: Matthew 4:1-11; 6:1-18; Luke 6:20-49; John 3:1-21; 4:1-42; 6:22-71; Romans 1:18-32; 5:12-21; 6:1-23; 1 Corinthians 15; Hebrews 3:7—4:11; 1 John 2:28—3:10. Pursue this exercises based on the Greek text if you are at all able. Map out the repetitions of words/word groups (e.g., all the words formed from the *dikai*- root, pertaining to "justice" or "righteousness") in the passage. Inquire into the effects these repetitions have on the hearers: Are they of no effect? Do they provide structure? Do they signal comparisons and contrasts? Do they create connections and correlations in meaningful ways? Check your findings against what you know of the pastoral goals of the author.

THE MESSAGE OF REVELATION: REDRAWING REALITY

The real crisis facing believers. The first audience of Revelation faced a myriad of challenges in their situations. We have already considered the hostility of non-Christian Jewish groups and the pressures on Gentile Christians to conform again to the way of life they

left behind. Beyond these, there would have been the everyday concerns of providing for their families, dealing with disappointment, dealing with doubt concerning the choices they had made and a host of other challenges. John immediately confronts his readers, however, with the one critical challenge that must be given attention before all else—the forthcoming visitation of God and God's Messiah.

God is described not only as the "one who is and was" but also as "the one who is coming" (Rev 1:4, 8), whose intervention in human affairs is imminent. At the outset John paints a dramatic portrait of this crisis, amplifying its scope:

> Look! He is coming with the clouds;
>   every eye will see him,
>   even those who pierced him;
>   and on his account all the tribes of the
>   earth will wail. (Rev 1:7 NRSV)

The proximity of this "coming" is repeatedly emphasized (Rev 3:11; 14:6-7; 16:15; 22:7, 12), each time linked with some key to preparing for and surviving the coming crisis. The greatest threats to the hearers, since they carry the most lasting disadvantages, are connected with not being prepared to encounter God at his coming, thus being exposed to the threat of the "second death" (Rev 2:11) or being written out of the "book of life" (Rev 3:5).

The visions will continue to amplify the great dangers of facing the "day of the wrath" of God and the Lamb (Rev 6:12-17). In Revelation 14:14-20 John weaves together many Old Testament and traditional Jewish images of judgment (see Is 63:2-6; Dan 7:13; Joel 3:13; *1 Enoch* 100:3-4) as a means of reminding the hearers of God's commitment to judge the world, treading down all who have acted as God's enemies. John expands these images in order to impress all the more on the hearers the danger and horror of that judgment, and thus the paramount importance of living now to meet that challenge safely and be found a loyal servant of God. The primary impending crisis—the real crisis facing each audience—is God's judgment. What is most needed is a strategy to encounter and survive that crisis rather than the less threatening crises of temporary hardship or deprivation.

John thus strongly imposes one particular crisis on the attention of the hearers, replacing many alternative challenges they might otherwise choose to focus on and for which they might be concerned to find a solution. As long as they focus on their neighbors' pressure or on remaining on firm economical footing, or any other of the everyday-life challenges that they face because of the name of Jesus, they will most likely move toward accommodating to the society around them, since that would generally resolve these challenges. John trumps all these rival foci, in effect, by placing before them the ultimate crisis. The danger of the "second death" relativizes the pains of the first death (Rev 2:10-11); the danger of encountering God as enemy relativizes the losses incurred by making an enemy of society, no matter how terrible those losses might become.

John does not only call Christians to be ready to encounter Christ at his future coming; even more urgently he summons them to prepare to encounter Christ as the one who walks in the midst of his churches. The image of Christ—now invested with the awesome glory of his place at the right hand of God—walking "among the seven gold lampstands" that represent the churches (Rev 1:20; 2:1) presents an even more immediate threat to congregations that have not kept faith with him. Unless they act swiftly to fall in line with his righteous demands (recovering their former love and their former commitment to avoid every semblance of participating in the lies of idolatrous worship), Christ's immediacy threatens swift judgment:

> I will come to you and remove your lampstand from its place, unless you repent. (Rev 2:5 NRSV)

> Repent then. If not, I will come to you soon and war against them with the sword of my mouth. (Rev 2:16; see figure 24.5)

> I am throwing her on a bed, and those who commit adultery with her I am

throwing into great distress, unless they repent of her doings; and I will strike her children dead. And all the churches will know that I am the one who searches minds and hearts, and I will give to each of you as your works deserve. (Rev 2:22-23)

At the same time, however, if someone is disposed to opening up to Jesus' summons and submitting to them, Jesus' presence in the midst of the churches also signifies promise of immediate fellowship and nurture (Rev 3:20). Whether for judgment or strengthening, then, Christians must come to terms at once with the glorified Christ who stands at the door.

Redrawing the center: The honor due God and the Lamb. The basic question behind Revelation is "who is worthy of honor and worship?" Much of Revelation demonstrates what John knows to be the correct answer, and it also displays the consequences both of giving God the honor that is exclusively God's due

and of violating God's honor by bestowing it on another (violations that are rampant in the world of the seven churches). As Christians refuse to share the honor of God or God's Anointed with any other at any cost, their own honor in God's sight and God's kingdom is assured. Failure to reserve divine honors for God and the Lamb might result in temporary advantages, but ultimately it will lead to greater and more lasting loss and disgrace.

John's visions begin at the center of John's universe, at the very throne of God (Rev 4:2). The way John unfolds his vision of the cosmos is rhetorically significant. Many modern readers jump to the dragon and beasts as the focal point of interest: for John the key figures in this drama are not the "bad guys." God and the Lamb, not the beast, occupy center stage. This is in itself an attack on Roman imperial ideology, which depicts the emperor (and the gods which give him his power) at the center of the conceptual universe.

In this opening scene the various orders of

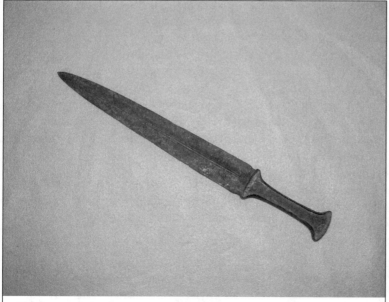

Figure 24.5. The Roman short sword, or dagger, part of the standard equipment of the legionnaire. (Photo: Sam Renfroe; courtesy of Ashland Theological Seminary)

angels render to God and to the Lamb the honor they deserve, and their hymns remind John's audience of the grounds for such worship and thanksgiving. God sits on the throne, the symbol of God's rule and authority, surrounded by concentric circles of worshiping beings: the four living creatures (reminiscent of the seraphim of Is 6), the seven spirits (corresponding to the seven archangels or angels of the presence in other Jewish texts, cf. *T. Levi* 3; Tob 12:15), and the twenty-four elders on their thrones (perhaps corresponding to the angelic order known as "thrones" in Col 1:16; again see *T. Levi* 3). Myriads upon myriads of angels join the liturgy (Rev 5:11), and finally the orders of angels are joined by "every creature in heaven and on earth and under the earth and in the sea" (Rev 5:13 NRSV), all united in worshiping God and the Lamb for their mighty acts of creation and redemption.

Revelation thus opens with a vision of perfect order, with all created beings in concentric spheres looking in toward the true center of the cosmos, worshiping God and the Lamb as they deserve. The hymns of the cosmic liturgy rehearse the reasons that God and the Lamb merit this level of attention and devotion. God has created all things for no other reason than God's own desire, with the result that all creatures owe God their very being, a debt that can never be repaid but must always be acknowledged in worship (Rev 4:11). The Lamb, uniquely invested with the authority of bringing about the "end" and the new beginning (Rev 5:1-5), purchased back for God a holy people "from every tribe and language and people and nation" to be "a kingdom and priests" for God (Rev 5:9-10 NRSV). This great act of redemption was achieved at a great price—the death of the Lamb—and so it demands all the more fervent a response of gratitude. Other hymns and acclamations will add to this repertoire, focusing on God's authority to judge the world as a cause for rendering to God now the honor and obedience that is

God's due (Rev 11:15-18; 15:3-4), and especially to avoid the breach of the first commandment, to have no other gods before the One (Ex 20:3). The other face of this judgment is the deliverance from this world's hostility that God and the Lamb bring to their loyal servants, celebrated by the "innumerable multitude" in Revelation 7:9-12 and described in beautiful images by the elder in Revelation 7:14-17.

Revelation thus loudly proclaims the lordship of God and God's Messiah, the "ruler of the kings of the earth" (Rev 1:5; cf. 11:15), the center of the cosmos, whose honor is rightfully lauded by creatures celestial and terrestrial. Christians have been made a part of God's kingdom (Rev 1:6; 5:9-10), and they express their first allegiance honorably as they too offer exclusive worship to God and the Lamb without lapse, even as the heavenly beings worship without rest (Rev 4:8). The lordship of God and the Lamb relativizes all other claims to power or progress. All institutions must be measured in light of faithfulness to God's rule and what God's rule brings: creation, redemption, bestowal of dignity, formation of community out of great diversity, reconciliation out of division, truth, justice, holiness.

As the visions continue to unfold, however, it becomes clear that not all acknowledge God's just claim to honor. Indeed, there are significant pockets of resistance to and even rebellion against the divine order. After several episodes of divine judgment in chapters 8 and 9, John introduces those who gather around rival centers of worship:

> The rest of humankind, who were not killed by these plagues, did not repent of the works of their hands or give up worshiping demons and idols of gold and silver and bronze and stone and wood, which cannot see or hear or walk. And they did not repent of their murders or

their sorceries or their fornication or their thefts. (Rev 9:20-21)

The dominant majority surrounding the Christians were engaged in idolatrous religion, which John, like Paul before him, links with the worship of demons (see 1 Cor 10:19-20) and even with the archenemy of God (Rev 13:4). The Christians who, together with Jews, opposed the worship of idols, formed a distinct minority in the empire. As John has remapped the cosmos, however, it is the idolater who is deviant and in the minority. "Every creature in heaven and on earth and below the earth" know where worship and adoration are properly directed. Contrary to what the dominant cultural ideology about the nature of the gods and the virtue of piety posits as true, the worship of the Greco-Roman divinities does not bring an individual in line with the cosmic order. Such worship points away from the center, such that the person is no longer acting in accord with the hosts of heaven or the rest of creation.

John's message to his congregations is clear: the non-Christians are trying to make you feel like deviants who have departed from the true paths of piety, and their sheer numbers might even make you begin to doubt yourself, but it is this seemingly powerful majority who are the deviants and who will be shown to be powerless when faced with the wrath of God and the Lamb (Rev 6:15-17). John's remapping of the larger cosmos, therefore, helps the Christian minority get the necessary perspective on their situation in order to persevere in their commitment, assured of their conformity with the "way things are" in the heavenly realm and the "way things ought to be" in the visible sphere.

Deconstructing Roman imperial ideology.
Alongside reinforcing the Judeo-Christian

view of reality, John engages in a thoroughgoing dismantling of the dominant culture's view of reality, particularly its view of Roman rule. Roman power was represented by two primary symbols—the emperors (the *Augusti*) and Rome. Augustus's rule and power were greeted as evidence of the beneficent rule of the gods,[18] and this benign dogma was applied to his successors as well. The practical benefits of peace, stability of government and the mobilization of relief in times of regional need won the emperors the undying gratitude of the provinces. Beyond this, however, they were regarded as the pious mediators of divine favor, often portrayed on coins or stone reliefs piously performing some religious rite, adorned with titles that emphasized their place in linking gods and people. What John found blasphemous—the claiming for a human the titles "lord" and "God"—was for most of Asia Minor a matter of gratitude and welcome security.

John completely rewrites this ideology of the head of the empire in chapters 12 and 13. The very use of the term *beast* hides the humanness of the emperor and negates any legitimate claims he might have to the gratitude or loyalty of the audiences. As John begins to give the beast his full attention, he first displays that the beast's origins are not what the public discourse about the emperor claims. Chapter 12 provides the cosmic backdrop behind current events and against which everyday life in Asia Minor was playing itself out. Using rich mythological imagery, John recalls Satan's revolt against God, in which Satan, the source of chaos and disorder, upsets the cosmic order, causes the fall of a great number of angels (recalling the tradition of *1 Enoch* 6—36) and is eventually defeated. The beast's rise to power, the worship of the beast and the dragon, and

---

[18]See, for example, the inscription at Priene celebrating the birth of Augustus as Providence's provision for the "highest good" of the people, a ruler whom Providence "filled with excellence for the benefit of humanity" (F. W. Danker, *Benefactor* [St. Louis, Mo.: Clayton, 1982], p. 217).

Figure 24.6. A silver denarius minted by the emperor Domitian to commemorate the death of his infant son. His wife, Domitia, appears on the obverse. On the reverse, the defied child sits on the globe and reaches out with his hands to seven stars, representing the sun and the then-known planets. The inscription on the reverse reads, "The Divine Caesar, Son of the Emperor Domitian." John's depiction of the One who grasps the seven stars in his right hand (Rev 1:16, 20; 2:1; 3:1) presents Jesus as the genuine Son of God, of whom Domitian's son is one of many imperial counterfeits. (Photo courtesy of www.CNGcoins.com)

the enforcement of the worship of the beast's cult image are all part of Satan's last attempt to deceive people and lead them astray from God's truth (after Satan is already defeated and awaiting final punishment). The power of the beast and the fervor of his cult actually becomes a sign of Christ's triumph over Satan (Rev 12:10-12), since Satan's focus is now the earth rather than heaven. It is also a sign of the "short time" (Rev 12:12) that God's enemy has left, the very fierceness of the campaign a token of the death throes of the enemies of God.

Not a benign providence but Satan, the source of chaos, gives power to the beast from the sea (Rev 13:2). The emperor is not a pious mediator of divine favor but a fount of blasphemy against God (Rev 13:1, 5, 6). His divine titles (including "son of the divine," *divi filius*)

are illegitimate, the "names of blasphemy" that offend the Most High.[19] In a parody of Christ's legitimate bringing together of a people for God from every "tribe and language and people and nation" (Rev 5:9), the beast from the sea seeks to exercise rule over the members of every "tribe and people and language and nation" (Rev 13:7), and indeed the imperial cult was an essential unifying feature of the many different groups brought under the aegis of Rome.

The second beast is presented as the organizer of religious cult for the first beast, making the worship of the beast a requirement for continued economic and physical well-being. Again, this is a reversal of the majority view of the imperial cult, understood as a pious response of gratitude to a great benefactor. John sees it as an imposition, not a voluntary cult,

---

[19]Indeed, many of the titles ascribed to God and the Lamb throughout Revelation are, in effect, "stolen back" by John from the emperor for the true God. The title "lord of lords" was ascribed to the emperor; the acclamations of Christ as "worthy" in chapter 5 echo the sorts of acclamations with which citizens greeted their emperor. Zeus was lauded with the formula "Zeus was, Zeus is, Zeus will be, O great Zeus!" which is now taken over by John and transformed for the one God, "who was, and is, and is coming."

giving poignant expression to the pressures Christians felt and would soon feel all the more. Once again, the ultimate recipient of such cult practice is not a benign deity but the enemy of God, whose worship is linked to that of the beast (Rev 13:4), even as the cults of the traditional gods were frequently linked to the imperial cult. Ultimately, it is not the Christians who, in opposition to Roman imperial ideology, act seditiously, but the supporters of Rome who rebel against the rule of the Most High and his Anointed.

Figure 24.7. The head from a colossal statue of the emperor Domitian, erected in the Temple of Domitian in Ephesus. In recognition of the honors it bestowed on the emperor, Ephesus was awarded the title of *Neokoros*, a "Temple Warden," of the imperial cult in Asia Minor. (Photo courtesy of the Ephesus Museum, the Turkish Ministry of Art and Culture, and Todd Bolsen [BiblePlaces.com])

As he traveled from city to city, John would have frequently found the cult of the goddess Roma Aeterna, "Eternal Rome," yoked to the cult of the emperor. Plutarch celebrated the rise of Rome, uniting the Mediterranean region, thus: "Rome developed and grew strong, and attached to herself not only nations and peoples but foreign kingdoms beyond the sea; and then at last the world found stability and security, when the controlling power entered into a single, unwavering cycle and world order of peace" ("On the Fortune of the Romans" 2 [*Mor.* 317]). Virgil, a poet in Augustus's court, identified the Romans' "art" to be "to pacify, to impose the rule of law, to spare the conquered, battle down the proud" (*Aeneid* 6.851-3). The goddess Roma was the visible representation of the "order," the "rule of law," the "peace" and "stability" that the dominant cultural order brought, and her cult was the ultimate legitimation of Roman power and the means by which it operated.

When John calls the famous city set upon seven hills "Babylon" and unveils her as a debauched harlot, he strikes hard and deep at the heart of the public ideology. He will not allow the words *peace* or *stability* to mask the violence with which that "peace" has been forged and continues to be maintained. The "mother of whores" is "drunk with the blood of the saints and the blood of the witnesses to Jesus" (Rev 17:6 NRSV). She is responsible for "the blood of prophets and of saints, and of all who have been slaughtered on earth" (Rev 18:24 NRSV), and this very fact necessitates divine vengeance on Rome, just as it did on historic Babylon (Rev 18:20; cf. Rev 6:9-11; 16:5-7).[20] Rome claimed honor (Rev 18:7) beyond what it rightly should have claimed, and the cult of Roma would have been an especially egregious offense. Rome unjustly spent on itself wealth that did not rightly

---

[20]John does not raise the only voice against Roman rule. Tacitus, though a devout supporter of Rome, places a similar critique on the lips of the British chieftain Calgacus, probably reflecting known criticisms leveled by discontented victims of the Roman peace: "Robbery, savagery, and rape they call 'government'; they make a wasteland and call it 'peace'" (*Agr.* 30).

belong to it (what John calls "luxury," Rev 18:3, 7). If Rome brings prosperity, it does so only to the merchants and shipmasters and others who profit (or profiteer) as they direct the world's wealth to its ravenous maw; rather than enrich the world, it devours the wealth of the lands under its power. The arrogant forecast of Rome's destiny to rule forever (Rev 18:7) flies in the face of God's power to allot kingdoms their periods and their ends (see Dan 2:21; 4:26; 5:21), and God will shortly assert that power. The "eternal city" stands under God's imminent judgment, sentenced already to destruction for its crimes against "apostles, saints, and prophets." To enter into partnership with Rome is to fall victim to its deceit (Rev 18:23), which intoxicates the ignorant (Rev 17:2). Those who are Rome's partners have been "taken in" by the agents of Satan. Moreover, connection with Rome is labeled "fornication" and pollution (Rev 17:2, 4; 18:3; 19:2), bringing defilement rather than opening the door to the acquisition of honorable things.

This alternative view would not be self-evident to every Christian. The church in Laodicea appears to be in especially grave danger of having had the wool pulled over its collective eyes. Christians, like non-Christians, may drink in the dominant cultural ideology, and they need to reexamine their society and their participation in it from the perspective of God's claims on humanity and God's desires for all people. If John's revelation about the real character of Rome and her emperors is accepted, it will dramatically reinforce his summons to remain aloof from all activities and speech that legitimate their rule and radically undermine the agenda of Jezebel and the Nicolaitans. The virtuous, pious and advantageous path will be clear: continue to bear witness to God's truth, and avoid kneeling before God's rivals or participating in the sins of a doomed empire.

God's commitment to justice. One of the more haunting visions in Revelation involves the souls of those who had been unjustly slain for speaking the truth about God, crying out for justice and vindication against those who had brutalized them (Rev 6:9-11). Their earnest expectation that God will act on their behalf, the only question being *when,* points to a core truth underscored by Revelation, namely, that God administers certain justice, rewarding those who have kept faith with God and God's values, punishing those who have acted faithlessly against other human beings and against the earth itself (Rev 11:18). The response given the martyrs chillingly predicts that more injustice is yet to come, but it also assures them of vindication when injustice reaches its set limit.

Many of the hymns sung or spoken in Revelation address the topic of God's justice rather directly, especially Revelation 15:3-4 and 16:5-7. These hymns, composed almost completely from passages from the Psalms and other Old Testament texts,[21] reinforce primary convictions concerning God's justice. The old songs about God's power, justice and truth manifesting themselves in judicial actions on behalf of God's people and against God's adversaries will be renewed in the future. Just as divine justice resulted in judgments on behalf of God's people against God's enemies in the past, God's justice necessitates such interventions in the forthcoming future. All nations will come to recognize the constant truth in the cosmos that they currently suppress in their idolatries, violence, economic rapine and false ideologies. This will result in the faithful being vindicated in the sight of those who do not heed the decrees of the one God.

As the visions of God's forthcoming interventions unfold, the slaughtered witnesses under the altar speak a second time (see Rev 6:10

---

[21]Compare Revelation 15:3-4, for example, with Psalm 86:9-10, Deuteronomy 32:4, *Prayer of Azariah* 4 and Jeremiah 10:7.

for the first), this time to affirm that God has avenged their blood: "Yes, Lord God Almighty, true and just are your judgments" (Rev 16:7). In John's vision of the future, the victims of injustice themselves speak as witnesses (almost in a forensic sense here) to God's unfailing commitment to bring justice, acknowledging the appropriateness of God's judgments in the form of the seven last plagues.

John's narration of the victory of God over Babylon, the pouring out of the plagues on the beast and his kingdom and the celebration of the conquerors in heaven all provide a narrative confirmation of the truth of these basic Jewish and Christian convictions about God's power, God's justice and God's manifestation of these attributes to the unbelievers (Rev 18:21-24; 19:2). This unfaltering truth lends impetus to the summons of Revelation 18:4. At the same time that it assures those who suffer injustice because they have united themselves to God's truth, the character of God also provides a strong incentive to not participate in a tainted system but to live as a witness to God's justice, and not to enable ongoing injustice or its legitimation.

An alternative vision for human community. John moves beyond critiquing the society in which he lives to a vision for human community that reflects God's desires for people. It is a vision as different from his world as a pure bride is different from a depraved harlot. The contrast of two cities, depicted as women from such different "walks of life" and of such different character, could not be more striking.

God's goal for humanity begins with an inclusive vision in which people from every ethnic group, every nation, every tribe and every language are joined into one humanity, divided no longer by the barriers observed and erected by the fallen mind. In this new kingdom the dignity of priesthood—of access to God—is bestowed on all. The distinction between priest and layperson was fundamental to the hierarchy in Israel and Judea, and it was

one important marker of status in the Greco-Roman world as well. In God's kingdom there is the absence of hierarchy, of haves and have-nots, of castes and divisions (Rev 1:5-6; 5:9-10). All are elevated to privileged status.

The new Jerusalem is clothed with the righteous acts of God's holy ones (Rev 19:8), quite a different wardrobe from Babylon's. Justice, mercy, keeping God's commandments, keeping the testimony of Jesus—these adorn the alternative society. It is entered through the historic people of God that, for all its failings, still kept the witness to one God alive in a world populated with idols and false ideas about the divine, and from which the church was born (Rev 21:12). It is built on the foundations of the apostles (Rev 21:14), not on the foundations of violence or greed but on the gospel of the truth of God. God's presence fills this community (Rev 21:3, 22; 22:3-5), and people walk by God's light (Rev 21:23) rather than stumble in the darkness of Satan's deceit. The great distance between humanity and God is closed proportionally as righteousness and peace-making flourish. The city exists to bring peace and healing for the nations (Rev 22:2) rather than to establish "peace" by controlling, dominating and subduing. The city faces no threat (the gates are never shut, Rev 21:25), since Satan's ways of violence, deceit and self-indulgence have been eliminated, along with all those who remained committed to those ways of forging and maintaining society.

John knows, however, that New Jerusalem is a costly alternative. One cannot be a citizen of Babylon, profiting by her partnership and violence, and expect a welcome in the New Jerusalem (Rev 21:8, 27). Refusing to participate in those activities and pursuits that legitimate Babylon's rule, however, will bring hardship. Throngs of faithful ones pass through great tribulation to arrive at the New Jerusalem, but God's consolation after a hard struggle with the powers of this world that resist such a vision is assured (Rev 21:4; see also

7:13-17). This is *not,* moreover, a mere "pie in the sky in the sweet by-and-by" compensator. As John uses this vision (and thus as we must use it), New Jerusalem is a proclamation of God's purpose for creation, and in light of this all human purposes and societies are judged, critiqued, weighed in the balance and found wanting. Christians are challenged not only to *wait* but to *witness,* to proclaim and protest, to encourage and direct, in light of God's vision. Our society's failure to enact God's righteousness, however this failure manifests itself, cannot be legitimated either by our participation or our silence.

John's shaping of the Christian's response. John wants his hearers to see their world in terms of stark alternatives rather than possible compromises, so that the boundaries of the church and the distinctiveness of its "testimony" will not become blurred. John coordinates many images that create this sense of incompatible alternatives, one of the more striking being the images of the seal of God and the mark of the beast. Both suggest ownership, and in the context of the competition of the Lamb and the beast over the "peoples, nations, tribes and languages" it is clear that we cannot belong to both. As the visions devolve, it is the "seal of God" that proves the advantageous stamp. Even though lacking the mark of the beast would mean considerable temporal disadvantages (Rev 13:11-18), accepting that mark would invite far greater and more lasting disadvantages (Rev 14:9-11) while refusing it would bring eternal privilege (Rev 15:2; 20:4).

On their own, then, these images orient the Christians toward their society with great reservation. Since they belong to God and must maintain their single-minded allegiance, they will be cautious about the manner and extent of their participation in the society controlled by the beast. They will look on their world not as if it were a neutral field that could be enjoyed to a far greater extent (as Jezebel and the Nicolaitans would urge), but as a field of deceit and corruption that could entangle and disqualify the believer from the eternal prize.

These images function in concert, however, with many other images. One set of images works together to create the pattern of a new exodus. The sealing of God's own (Rev 7:1-8) recalls the blood of the Passover lamb that protected the Hebrews from the tenth plague, and indeed their exemption from all the plagues that befell Egypt (see Ex 8:22-24; 9:4-7, 26; 10:21-23; 11:4-7). The plagues falling on the unsealed, on those marked with the beast's number (Rev 8:6—9:21; 16:1-21) are interwoven with language from the plagues of Exodus, deliberately correlating those judgments. The lack of repentance on the part of the non-Christians, the beast and his minions (Rev 9:20-21; 16:9, 11) re-presents in grander scale the stiffness of the heart of Pharaoh and his forces. The new song of deliverance by a sea, specifically mentioning the Song of Moses (Rev 15:1-4), recalls the song sung by the Red Sea after the first exodus. Those who "overcome" the beast and its image by virtue of enduring the cost of nonparticipation in the cult now celebrate the Lord's deliverance of the faithful ones as a second and grander exodus.

The paradigm of a "new exodus" cannot help but shape the Christians' perception of their world and their place in it. The surrounding society is cast in the role of oppressor, a power from which to be delivered, not in which to participate and prosper. The yearnings of the believer are directed away from making one's way in that society to making one's way out from that society. Their neighbors stand under God's judgment for their disobedience to God's commands (notably in their idolatries but also in their profiting by a system whose wheels are greased with the blood of its victims) and for their hostility toward those who bear witness to Jesus. It is an image that sustains and even escalates the sense of mutual hostility and antagonism, and thus also the boundaries of the group.

The Christian is called to "conquer," or "overcome," repeatedly throughout Revelation, starting with the seven oracles (Rev 2:7, 11, 17, 26-28; 3:5, 12, 21). This orients hearers toward certain imposing realities in their world in an antagonistic way, as if to do battle. It promotes a posture that is thus not conducive to compromise since assimilation would mean defeat, and the loss of the privileges that will be awarded to those who overcome. It also empowers those who, being in full agreement with John, already suffer deprivation and face increasing hardship: they are not victims of society but contestants actively engaging the darker forces in the dominant culture.

How does John lay out the path to overcoming? The first model of overcoming is the "Lion of the tribe of Judah" (Rev 5:5). Witness to God and obedient death constitute victory and lead to acclamations of his worthiness (Rev 5:9-10), opening up a path for his followers to pursue as well. Just as Jesus conquered through complete obedience to God, even unto death, so believers conquer wherever they hold fast to their witness to Jesus and God's Word (e.g., wherever they call for justice, peace, holiness, reconciliation and whatever else God desires and works toward), "not loving their lives even unto death" (Rev 12:11). Such a death is not defeat at the hands of Satan and his cronies but a participation in the defeat of the dragon.

The witnesses in Revelation 11:3-13 provide a further model for how the battle or contest unfolds and how victory is acquired. The witnesses oppose the powers that be and work wonders by the power of God, but they still must consummate their testimony by their deaths. Nevertheless, God vindicates God's witnesses in the sight of their enemies through resurrection, giving them the final victory over the world that opposed them. The hearers must be struck by the importance of witness to the testimony of Jesus throughout Revelation. John's visions underscore the value of keeping our mouth from being defiled by falsehood, by acquiescing to the lies spoken by the members of the dominant culture about the gods and the political order of the day (Rev 14:5; 21:8; 22:15). The Christians are thus motivated to a lifestyle of continued witness to the testimony of Jesus and Word of God. The role of the martyrs, those who die for the sake of their Christian confession, is accorded the highest value in Revelation. Only those who have been motivated to accept this role are truly free to encounter the larger society in a prophetic, critical role and bear witness to an alternative way of ordering society.

The pattern of overcoming is further nuanced in Revelation 15:2, where "those who had conquered the beast and its image and the number of its name" (NRSV) gather before the throne of God to celebrate God's justice and their deliverance. Conquering the beast and its image, however, means resisting the considerable pressures to worship the beast (Rev 13:15-17), even if that entails accepting execution (see Rev 20:4-5). The way to overcome, and thus to enjoy the promises extended to the "one who overcomes," means separation from the dominant culture and resistance to its efforts to "reform" the Christians. It involves obedience to the summons to believers to "come out from her" (Rev 18:4), to enact a radical separation from what is ungodly, what is incompatible with living a faithful and obedient response to the God and to the Lamb. Whatever temporal benefits might be gained by playing along with a system founded in blood, greed and self-delusion, the eternal costs and the defilement of our own soul are too great a price to pay.

The movement out from Babylon, moreover, is matched by the movement of believers toward the throne of God and of the Lamb in unbroken worship, joining the circles of heavenly beings in the celebration of God's past, present and forthcoming deeds, living out their redemption by the Lamb, and withholding these honors from any rival god established by human beings (at the unseen prompting of the enemy). David Barr draws an informative parallel from the letter of the martyr Ignatius to the Ephesians: "Seek, then, to come together more frequently to give thanks and glory to God. For when you gather together frequently the powers of Satan are destroyed, and his mischief is brought to nothing, by the concord of your faith."[22] Worship is similarly effective in Revelation, declaring God's triumph over Satan (Rev 12:10-12) and over the kingdoms of the world that set themselves against God (Rev 11:16-18). Moreover, it is from the vision of the worship of the one God that believers are empowered to take the testimony of Jesus into the world and to faithfully keep the commandments of this God, thus keeping their prophetic witness—and the call of God—alive in Asia Minor.

REVELATION, THE FUTURE AND THE END

We have reflected at length on Revelation as an unveiling not of a series of events still in our future but as an unveiling of the true nature of the realities faced daily by the Christians in the seven churches addressed by John the Seer. Revelation also reveals the significance of the choices and associations open to those Christians when seen from the perspective of God's claims on humanity, God's standards for human community and God's expectations of response to God's gifts.

Does Revelation, then, have nothing to say about *our* future? Finding the answer to this question is not so much a task of culling out still-unfulfilled prophecies here and there in Revelation, as if we have been advancing a "preterist" perspective on the book.[23] Rather, this task calls us to look at Revelation as an *apocalypse* and from the perspective of how apocalypticists come to understand the future. The task calls us to examine the spatial and temporal realities of John's worldview to discern the eschatological horizon that, for him, put his world and his congregations' situations in their proper perspective. This takes us to those very affirmations about God's decisive, final interventions that John shares with other New Testament voices. It also calls us to look at how John reconfigured and reapplied Old Testament Scriptures and patterns to what he expected God to do in his hearers' situations. John learned from those texts about the challenges that the faithful would encounter, the evils that human beings would perpetrate and the ways that God's just character would lead God to intervene in human affairs. Recovering this sort of information, we begin to see more clearly how Revelation speaks about the future in the many situations Christians continue to find themselves in.

As John reflects on the revelation of the fate

---

[22]D. L. Barr, "The Apocalypse as Symbolic Transformation of the World," *Interpretation* 38 (1984): 47.

[23]The history of interpretation of Revelation is often surveyed in terms of four kinds of approach to the prophecy of the book (as in Steve Gregg, ed., *Revelation: Four Views* [Nashville: Thomas Nelson, 1997]). *Preterists* consider most of the prophecies to have been fulfilled during the first three centuries of the church, with a great gap between the fulfilled prophecies and the yet-to-be-fulfilled prophecies. *Historicists* consider the prophecies to be fulfilled over the long course of church history. *Futurists* regard the prophecies of chapters 4-22 to refer to future events (aside from the flashback in Rev 12:1-9). *Idealists* do not read these as literal prophecies but as the medium for communicating unchanging spiritual truths. None of these, strictly speaking, represents the approach advocated by contemporary scholarship, which seeks to understand Revelation as an apocalypse, not as a forecast of the hearers' future (*prophecy,* in one sense of that word). Preterists, historicists and futurists agree on the basic premise that Revelation is to be read as a prophetic forecast, disagreeing only on the timing and manner of fulfillment. The idealist reading, though a bit closer to understanding what an apocalypse seeks to accomplish, tends to be divorced from the historical and social context of John and his audiences, searching for general and universal spiritual truths in the visions. Therefore, none of these four classical approaches really captures the orientation to Revelation followed by scholars such as Adela Yarbro Collins, Leonard L. Thompson, Elisabeth Schüssler Fiorenza and advanced in this volume as well.

Revelation and the Millennium

One of the more controverted topics in the interpretation of Revelation, and in eschatology in general, is the "millennium," the reign of certain saints with Christ prior to the last judgment and new creation (Rev 20:4-6). The debate is usually defined in terms of three basic positions:

- *Premillennialism* affirms a literal one-thousand-year reign of the saints *after* Christ returns and establishes the kingdom.

- *Postmillennialism* looks for a one-thousand-year reign of the saints *prior* to Christ's return, a result of the successful evangelization of the nations and establishment of Christian government.

- *Amillennialism* does not affirm a literal one-thousand-year reign; rather, the binding of Satan was accomplished by Jesus on the cross, and the age of the church (the span between Christ's first and second comings) is the time when Christians are "more than conquerors" and are seated "with Christ in the heavenly places" (Rom 8:37; Eph 2:6).

There is more at stake here for both pre- and postmillennialists than the interpretation of Revelation 20:4-6. The Hebrew prophets, especially Isaiah, promise a Jerusalem-based kingdom under the reign of the Davidic Messiah, an era of justice, peace and prosperity. Would these promises not have some kind of literal fulfillment?

Similar concerns, indeed, seem to have driven not only modern interpreters but ancient apocalypticists as well. *Fourth Ezra* 7:26-36, written perhaps a few years after Revelation, speaks of a four-hundred-year messianic kingdom, at the end of which the Messiah and all who are with him die. The cosmos reverts to "primeval silence for seven days" (as at the beginning of this cosmos), after which the resurrection, judgment and eternal recompense follow. The connection—indeed, the typology—between creation and end time is unmistakable. *Second Baruch* 29, contemporaneous with *4 Ezra* and Revelation, speaks of a messianic age of great fecundity, with each grape and each wheat stalk yielding enough wine and bread to satisfy many people, prior to the resurrection and judgment. Such a vision is often criticized as a fantasy of worldly indulgence and gratification, but perhaps it would be an appropriate and suitable hope for those who have always known need to seek a kingdom where there is finally enough to go around, in which all people are at last *satisfied*.

The idea of an interim messianic kingdom seems to emerge, then, as an apocalyptic survival of the prophetic hope of a restored kingdom of Israel under a descendant of David. This messianic kingdom was originally supposed to be "an everlasting one" (Is 11:2-6; Dan 7:14, 27),[a] but apocalypticism could not accommodate the perpetual survival of this present age in any form. So John, like other apocalypticists, preserves the hope for God's triumph over the nations and establishing of God's rule, including the rule of God's saints, *in this present world* (see Rev 5:9-10 as well as the order of events in chapter 20) prior to the last judgment and the end of the history of this world.

---

[a]See also Mounce, *Revelation*, pp. 357

As for the length of time, *4 Ezra* could envisage a four-hundred-year kingdom, while others might leave the length of time unspecified. The *Epistle of Barnabas* looks to the "week" of creation for a template of the age as a whole. Just as God labored for six days to create the world, so the world would last for six thousand years (for, with God, a day is as a thousand years; Ps 90:4). The seventh day of creation prefigures a period of rest "when His Son comes and destroys the season of the lawless one" (*Epistle of Barnabas* 15.5; the idea that this creation would endure for seven thousand years is also found in *2 Enoch* 33:1-2). *Barnabas* does not go on to speak of this "rest" as a thousand-year period so much as an end to the disorder of unredeemed humanity prior to the "eighth day, which is the beginning of another cosmos" (*Barnabas* 15.8). John's anticipation of a thousand-year period at the end of creation, then, is quite in keeping with current views of the periodization of history and the use of the seven days of creation as a template for the whole age.

John's vision for this interim rule, however, is quite different. In neither *4 Ezra* nor *2 Baruch* do the righteous dead come to life to enjoy this period, whereas John specifically names the martyrs for the privilege of sharing this reign. John does not speak of the temporal benefits of the period (e.g., food in abundance), but of a just rule by those who serve as priests to God and God's Messiah (Rev 20:5-6). What is at stake for John? First and foremost, he seeks to affirm—in the visual and spatial terms of apocalypses—the vindication specifically of the martyrs and others who kept faith with Jesus rather than courting Roman imperialism and participating in the public worship of the emperor as rightful lord and patron of the world. Second, John affirms the lordship of God over this age, this world. It cannot be completely abandoned to Satan and his minions but must first be reclaimed for God, God's Messiah and God's saints before it gives way to the new creation. Jesus' work of redemption involves not only individual souls but the world itself, over which the redeemed will exercise just governance (Rev 5:10). The new heavens and new earth cannot, then, be taken as a sign of God's *inability* to assert himself over this creation and bring all things in line with his will! The "message" of Revelation 20:4-6 could come to fruition in many ways, only one of which might involve some literal fulfillment.

FOR FURTHER READING

Gregg, Steve, ed. *Revelation: Four Views. A Parallel Commentary.* Nashville: Thomas Nelson, 1997.

Hill, Craig C. *In God's Time: The Bible and the Future.* Grand Rapids: Eerdmans, 2002.

Wainwright, Arthur W. *Mysterious Apocalypse: Interpreting the Book of Revelation.* Nashville: Abingdon, 1993.

of historic Babylon, Tyre and other oppressive centers of empire in the Hebrew Scriptures, he learns what will also be the fate of their embodiment in Rome. The cumulative witness of all such texts is that self-glorifying, self-legitimating nations that build their power, peace and privilege through violence, suppression and economic rapine will not endure. Wherever new Babylon-like and bestial powers arise, their destiny will be determined not by their own propaganda but by God's thirst for justice in human community. Revelation continues to pronounce a word of warning to any nation that derives its foreign, economic and domestic policies ultimately from Babylon, telling us how it stands under God's judgment and calling to us to "come out and be separate" from its injustices.

John reveals that witness will continue to be costly. Those who keep faith with Jesus will continue to do so by walking in the way of Jesus—the way of obedience unto death. The accuracy of such a word is proven daily in the lives of sisters and brothers in restricted nations across the globe. Even though John's word about their immediate future is grim, he also assures them that they will yet be vindicated in the future and that their faithfulness, though costly here, will prove ultimately advantageous.[24] God remains constant, and his commitment to bring justice to his faithful ones, who have honored God with their lives and preserved their own integrity at great cost, remains undiminished.

The opening of the seals by God's Messiah and the measured progress of the trumpets and bowls tell us to look to the future with the expectation that God's sovereign control over this age will be clearly manifested, bringing it to its end. John's heavy reuse of images from the first exodus and other episodes of deliverance from Israel's sacred history provides another affirmation that God's character remains unchanging and can be counted on for the future. The end, like the beginning, is in God's hands and the hands of God's Son, not ours. Moreover, John leads us to expect God to keep judging "little by little" (cf. Wis 12:10)—the

partial devastations of the trumpets precede the utter devastation of the bowls, calling on people to repent even to the end (Rev 9:20-21; 14:7; 16:9, 11 imply that this is a goal of God throughout). Just as in the first exodus, so in the greater exodus God will distinguish between the faithful and his opponents: the plagues are for the latter, but they also work toward the deliverance of the former.

The "last things" that ultimately shape John's proclamation are those to which (almost) every New Testament author bears witness—Christ's return to enforce God's claims on creation, holding God's enemies to account and vindicating the faithful; the resurrection of the dead and the judgment of all people before the throne of God and the Lamb; the destruction of all that has opposed God's rule; God's provision of a cosmos where righteousness is at home, where God and God's order are fully and perfectly experienced. On the firm conviction of these events rests everything else in Revelation, especially the deliberations that John asks his congregations to engage. All will be held accountable before God and to God's standards and just demands of his creatures. God and God's Messiah have the power to crush all opposition and to bring their loyal followers to the promised blessings. In light of such convictions about the future, the values we are to embody and choices we are to make become crystal clear—as soon as we discern our situation correctly from the larger perspective to which Revelation opens us up. Seeking more detail than this, moreover, adds nothing to our commitment and may even prove a dis-

---

[24]There is therefore no place in Revelation for the "rapture." (First Thess 4:13-18, moreover, has to be read in conjunction with the events in Revelation 20 if harmonizing—the main strategy of dispensationalism—is to be pursued at all, for Revelation 20:4-6 speaks of the "first" of two resurrections, and so the resurrection of the saints in 1 Thess 4:16 cannot be prior to that and cannot refer to a "pretribulation rapture.") John calls Christians to arm themselves to die out of faithfulness to Jesus, and indeed the so-called tribulation descends on his hearers in earnest in but a few short decades. We also have to reckon with the peculiarity that Western Christians (especially from the United Kingdom and the United States), who invented the idea of a rapture, should be the only ones never to taste tribulation for their Lord. Even now, sisters and brothers across the globe face marginalization, privation and death for their testimony—but *we* will be spared any such tests of our faithfulness! For a timely treatment of the subject, see C. C. Hill, *In God's Time* (Grand Rapids: Eerdmans, 2002), pp. 199-209.

traction from prayer and discernment. We engage in these to see clearly the challenges before us as we seek to live in this world while remaining loyal citizens of the next. What we need to know is not the details of how God's judgments will unfold but how we are still participating in and profiting from that which stands under God's judgment.

REVELATION AND MINISTRY FORMATION

Revelation pushed those early Christians who would "keep the words of this prophecy" to look critically at the empire that dominated the world and the systems that legitimated its rule. It evaluates the world in light of what the God of Israel and of Jesus stands for. It showed them that its prosperity was a tainted one, its peace a lie, its piety a blasphemy. It called them to maintain a stance of critical distance, to refuse to buy into the dominant ideology, to keep alive the Christian vision of a just and life-affirming world and to give their wholehearted allegiance to *that* world. John did not hesitate to arouse anger and indignation against the crimes perpetrated in the name of peace and the preservation of order. Rather, he empowered a minority of visionaries committed to God's values to stand up in the face of a majority who had pointedly different aspirations. The challenge for us is, of course, to consider how this powerful vision may be brought to bear on twenty-first-century realities.

John looked into the mysteries of God much as a person looks off toward the horizon. A person can see a fair distance and pretty much establish what objects are in front of other objects, but it is very difficult if not impossible to judge the distance between objects that stand in front of one another. So John saw much that was near on the temporal horizon, and saw these circumstances against the backdrop and in the context of what was far away on the horizon—things that are still in front of us and that provide the interpretive and evaluative context for the realities we face every day.

Revelation still interprets, and calls us to interpret, the social, political, religious and economic realities of our everyday experience—not on the principle of *identity* but on the principle of *analogy*. We cannot justifiably attach labels from Revelation's visions to persons or institutions in our experience and claim that this is the definitive meaning of John's visions. We are only playing endless games when we say such-and-such an earthquake fulfills such-and-such a sign, or that so-and-so is the beast or the third horseman, and so forth. Too many voices already engage in endless attempts to play "pin the tail on the antichrist." Rather, as we probe Revelation to discover what John was after in his own setting, to determine his rationales for opposing this figure or that activity, we can then move to our setting and see where an analogous situation might exist. In such a way Revelation continues to move believers beyond the interpretation of the status quo *our* dominant cultures impose on us to see things in the light of God and the demands of God's justice.

We see in Revelation a God who seeks justice and opposes all injustice. This challenges us to examine our society and our own participation in that society to see where injustice marks and mars our world. In Revelation we see a God who affirms the dignity of human beings by calling them to be God's priests and God's own people. This moves us to be on guard against the violation of human dignity that appears to be so rampant in our world, whether in the form of violent crime, racial prejudice and institutionalized discrimination or homelessness. We see in Revelation a God who seeks the nurture and fulfillment of all humanity, and who resists the concentration of resources and opportunities in the hands of an elite few. This again challenges us to critique domination systems that currently ensure the poverty of billions.

Revelation moves us to think beyond our national borders and consider the global community, those "from every race, tribe, language, and people," as John repeatedly reminds us. Revelation opens up our minds to the possibility of thinking beyond national borders—boundaries that the dominant ideologies of this world have engraved deeply into our hearts. Military conquest, international strife and struggles for maintaining a balance of power are done away with in the vision of the New Jerusalem. Such a vision compels us to consider the possibility of a world at peace and the benefits of a cooperative global community where resources are expended no longer in futile wars and power struggles but rather for the well-being of all. Where an ideology stands in the way of perfecting God's vision of a world at peace, whose inhabitants all have access to the gifts that God intended for all and whose inhabitants accord one another the full respect due to children of God, Revelation calls us to unveil that ideology for what it is: yet another aspect of the dragon's activity in leading people astray from God's truth.

Such a broader vision forces us to look at Western economies differently. Consumer-driven economies could look a lot like Babylon to many developing countries struggling with plague and starvation. What is our responsibility to such people? Is a world where all are fed and free to pursue the fullness of joy in family, friends and work worth giving up the present order? Is there something Babylon-like to be protested in the current distribution and consumption of this world's resources and wealth? As long as the hungry die for lack of food while millions of others amass superfluous commodities, God's priorities are certainly not being honored.

Revelation poses questions about the use of power and use of force. Where one part of society or nation dominates another, where power and force are used for the securing of endless resources for the use of a privileged few, the "whore" is back in business and all her partners stand under God's impending judgment. But Revelation also sets clear limits on the use of force to protest such harlotry. In a world where a Lamb conquers by dying and the dragon is defeated by believers who lay down their lives rather than collude with an idolatrous system, the path for resistance is clear. We are called to protest, to bear witness to what society *could* be if God were allowed to break in and reign, but we are not to defile ourselves with blood as God's enemies have done.

Revelation, indeed, speaks much of pollution, defilement, washing, cleansing and preserving cleanness. Just as John used purity language metaphorically in order to identify specific threats to Christian commitment and faithfulness, so we too are invited to name the deeds, the attitudes and the words that defile and pollute, and call our fellow disciples to wash their robes in the blood of the Lamb, to put away the defilements of racism, hard-heartedness toward the needy, grudges, petty factionalism and so forth.

Revelation offers us a new perspective on the power of congregational worship to transform perceptions, to instill motivations and holy desires, to make a lasting impact on those who participate. Revelation itself is full of liturgies (ritual acts and hymns; see Rev 4:1—5:4; 7:1-12; 19:1-8) and free-standing hymns (see Rev 11:15-18; 12:10-12; 15:2-4), and much of its drama emerges out of solemn rituals in the heavenly tabernacle (as in Rev 8:1-5; 15:5-8). Moreover, Revelation was intended to be read aloud to the gathered Christian community in a given place (Rev 1:3 makes the most sense in such a setting). The celestial hymns and liturgies recounted in Revelation then would be heard in the context of the gathered worshiping community on earth and would, in fact, complement the worship of the Christian group on earth.

John invited his congregations into an experience of liturgies that reoriented their minds and ambitions toward the realities of this world, that reminded them of the larger realities that surrounded this world and its history, and that made the unseen realm present and palpable to them and in light of which they were to navigate their daily life. It reminded the participants about the order of the world, who is important in it and for what reasons, and what their duties were to these central characters.[a] If we, like John, can embrace the realities of Monday through Saturday in our worship service, we'll have a much fuller impact on the lives of our parishioners. All aspects of life are brought under the lordship of Christ in Revelation, which provides a model for the worship team's task on Sunday morning. Liturgy informed by Revelation will celebrate God's acts of creation (Rev 4:8, 11), the Lamb's redemption (Rev 5:9-13) and the coming consummation (Rev 11:15-18; 15:3-4; 19:1-8), and it will set all of human experience between those two coordinates.

Revelation still speaks about the future, and makes us look at the present in light of that future. The "mystery of God" is not yet fulfilled, the kingdoms of this world have not yet surrendered to God and God's Christ. The marriage of the bride and the Lamb has not yet been celebrated, and death, sorrow, and the curse still weigh on our hearts. Revelation is thus also a book of longing, of desire, of hope—a longing that echoes through our churches in the season of Advent, which, traditionally, not only remembers Christ's first coming but also calls Christians to prepare for his coming again. The hymns of the church point us to our great need of God's redemption and for the mystery of God to be fulfilled. As John prays, "Come, Lord Jesus," so we pray, "O come, O come,

---

[a]Peter L. Berger, *The Sacred Canopy* (New York: Doubleday, 1967), p. 40.

Emmanuel." As John shows us the destiny to which God leads us, we sing with great longing: "Make safe the way that leads on high, and close the path to misery . . . bid thou our sad divisions cease, and be thyself our King of Peace." And just as Revelation arouses those longings, it assures the pilgrims of the satisfaction of those desires in the plan and sovereignty of the God of history: "Rejoice! Rejoice! Emmanuel *shall* come to thee, O Israel!"

Revelation is a visionary text. Often deliberately elusive, it resists being pegged down absolutely to any concrete setting. This is why many do the text an injustice when they use it as a grid on which to label their political or religious enemies, to build up barriers rather than tear them down. Indeed, we are perhaps most true to it when we too engage in constructing visions true to the ideals represented by God. When I first saw the bumper sticker that reads "Visualize world peace," I thought, *That's a rather insipid response to the realities of violence and hatred!* But the more I thought about it, the more I was convinced that something profound was being displayed on a car bumper. Those who are able to dream—to visualize a state of affairs where war, violence, prejudice and poverty are no more—can never again devote their gifts and services to anything but bringing that vision into reality. Perhaps this is why the prophet Joel linked dreaming dreams and seeing visions to the activity of God's Holy Spirit—what else could possibly stand behind an activity that could change the world! Revelation closes our scriptural canon, but not without first opening us up to the task of the seer, the visionary. We are called to continue to dream: to search out through the study of literature, history, philosophy, religion and the social sciences the virtues and ideals lacking in our societies and nations; to envision a society where each person's dignity is respected, the value and potential of each human life affirmed; to share and refine that vision with one another. Once the vision is in place, nothing can prevent our working together toward its realization.

Revelation, for all its strange images and for all the diversity of interpretations available, remains a revelation *of Jesus Christ,* and it should leave us ultimately focused on Jesus Christ, who is not merely the *source* of this message but also its object and content. Speaking in his own idiom, John is nevertheless singing in concert with many other New Testament voices as he too "gives us Jesus." The primary image for Jesus is that of the "Lamb," and since that Lamb was slaughtered it is an image of redemption and of exodus (Rev 5:9-10), with Jesus both leading and enabling our pilgrimage from a land of oppression (where God's values and vision fail to be honored) toward the land of promise (where God's reign is fully known). Like the Evangelists and Paul, John presents us with Jesus' cruciform triumph over the powers of sin and Satan (Rev 5:5-7), and calls us to follow in that pattern as well, assured that death and deprivation for the cause of God is not defeat, but victory (Rev 12:10-12).

Unlike other authors, John shows us Jesus in all his radiance now and calls us to consider the authority and power Jesus now has as the glorified Lord of the churches (Rev 1:9-20), the coming judge of the world (Rev 19:11-20), and the one who holds the keys to death and hell (Rev 1:18; 3:7). Jesus is not as he was when he walked the roads of Palestine, but he has entered into a transformed existence beyond all mortal experience. While the continuity between the two is critical to maintain, so is the distance, so that we might know the awesome majesty of the One whom we worship and in whose name we go forth to serve as priests (Rev 1:6; 5:10). As we prepare to meet him at his coming, we find him already standing in the midst of his churches affirming our works of faith, confronting our compromise and encouraging our renewed devotion. When we call people to respond to the good news, confront evil and oppression in families, businesses and governments, and relieve the needs of the suffering, we do so not in fear of the overshadowing powers of the enemy, but in confidence in the triumph of the Christ who sits at God's right hand, invested with God's power, and who is coming to bring justice to "every tribe, language, people and nation"—he who is the beginning and the ending, and who will always have the last word over all who oppose God's righteous reign. In that confidence John dismisses us, sending us back to face the challenges in such a way that our choices, allegiances, investments and acts all bear witness to that undying hope: "even so, come, Lord Jesus!"

FOR FURTHER READING

Aune, David E. *Revelation 1-5*. WBC. Dallas: Word, 1997.

———. *Revelation 6-16*. WBC. Dallas: Word, 1998.

———. *Revelation 17-21*. WBC. Dallas: Word, 1998.

Bauckham, Richard J. *The Climax of Prophecy: Studies in the Book of Revelation*. Edinburgh: T & T Clark, 1993.

———. *The Theology of the Book of Revelation*. Cambridge: Cambridge University Press, 1993.

Beale, Gregory K. *Revelation*. NIGTC. Grand Rapids: Eerdmans, 1998.

Brook-Howard, Wes, and Anthony Gwyther. *Unveiling Empire: Reading Revelation Then and Now*. New York: Orbis, 1999.

Caird, George B. *The Revelation of St. John*. London: Black, 1966.

Collins, Adela Y. *Crisis and Catharsis: The Power of the Apocalypse*. Philadelphia: Westminster Press, 1984.

deSilva, David A. "The Construction and Social Function of a Counter-Cosmos in the Revelation of John." *Forum* 9, nos. 1-2 (1993).

———. "Honor Discourse and the Rhetorical Strategy of the Apocalypse of John." *JSNT* 71 (1998).

———. "The Image of the Beast and the Christians in Asia Minor." *Trinity Journal* 12NS (1991).

———. "The Social Setting of the Apocalypse of John: Conflicts Within, Fears Without." *Westminster Theological Journal* 54 (1992).

———. "A Socio-Rhetorical Interpretation of Revelation 14:6-13: A Call to Act Justly Toward the Just and Judging God." *BBR* 9 (1999).

Harrington, Wilfrid J. *Revelation*. Sacra Pagina. Collegeville, Minn.: Michael Glazier, 1993.

Hemer, Colin J. *The Letters to the Seven Churches of Asia in their Local Setting*. Grand Rapids: Eerdmans, 2001.

Koester, Craig. *Revelation and the End of All Things*. Grand Rapids: Eerdmans, 2001.

Mounce, Robert H. *The Book of Revelation*. Rev. ed. NICNT. Grand Rapids: Eerdmans, 1998.

Ramsey, William M. *The Letters to the Seven Churches in Asia*. Rev. ed. Peabody, Mass.: Hendrickson, 1994.

Roloff, Jürgen. *The Revelation of John*. Minneapolis: Fortress, 1993.

Schüssler Fiorenza, Elisabeth. *The Book of Revelation: Justice and Judgment*. Philadelphia: Fortress, 1985.

Smalley, Stephen S. *Thunder and Love: John's Revelation and John's Community*. Milton Keynes, U.K.: Word, 1994.

Talbert, Charles. *The Apocalypse of John: A Reading*. Louisville, Ky.: Westminster John Knox, 1994.

Thompson, Leonard L. *The Book of Revelation: Apocalypse and Empire*. New York: Oxford, 1990.

Wainwright, Arthur W. *Mysterious Apocalypse: Interpreting the Book of Revelation*. Nashville: Abingdon, 1993.

Author Index

Subject Index

abomination of desolation 45, 308, 546

Abraham 38, 74, 80-81, 101, 110, 135, 137-38, 143, 147, 214, 248-49, 257, 262-63, 317-19, 322, 362, 389, 425, 437, 480, 483, 485, 493, 502-7, 513-17, 528, 534, 541, 554, 611-14, 621, 623-24, 637, 685, 788, 790-92, 795-98, 828, 857, 878, 888, 903

Actium, battle of 57, 527, 640

Acts of Paul and Thecla 32, 33, 764

Acts of Paul 32, 33, 35, 379, 794

Acts of Andrew 33, 764

Acts of Peter 232, 739

Acts of the Apostles
and ancient historiography 348-51, 354
apostles as bearers of God's authority 357-61
apostolic preaching 352-53, 354, 367
character of the church 362, 386-89
the church and Roman law 355, 367-69
the church in the Jewish Scriptures 362-65
the church in the plan of God 354, 362-67
and the historical Paul 375-80, 475-80, 486-91, 493-96
Holy Spirit in the church 359
Gentiles in the people of God 364-67
historicity 350-51, 369, 373-79
Jesus and the Jewish Scriptures 361-62
purposes 354-56
redefinition of the

people of God 354-55
speeches in 351, 354, 382-85
structure 356-57, 358

Aelius Aristides 91, 714

African American biblical interpretation 679-81

Ahiqar 880

Akiba, Rabbi 54, 514

Alexander the Great 39, 40, 42, 45, 47, 52, 89, 101, 183, 640, 642, 679, 754

Alexandria 33-34, 37, 42-44, 54, 59, 61, 101-4, 147, 277, 301, 394, 412, 415, 546, 564, 599, 742, 744, 861, 894

ambition 30, 56, 75, 108, 202, 277, 347, 461, 524, 539, 604, 633, 640, 657, 662, 667, 753, 779, 791, 810, 839, 882, 901, 929

angel, angels 50, 51, 74, 83-85, 88, 129, 207, 243, 249, 283, 316, 318, 327, 332, 366, 418, 421, 575, 692, 694, 698, 789, 792, 854-55, 870, 872, 879-80, 888, 891, 906

Annas (high priest) 55, 68, 83, 409

Antigonus 47, 63

Antiochus III 43, 45, 52, 100, 691

Antiochus IV 43-47, 52, 89, 542, 546, 851

Antipater 52, 63, 67

Aphthonius 575

Apocalypse of Abraham 110, 685, 888

Apocalypse of Paul 685

Apocalypse of Peter 33, 34, 35

apocalypticism 38-39, 45, 50-52, 66, 72, 85, 110, 153, 172, 181-82, 200, 212, 221, 226, 232-33, 239, 248, 276, 329, 333, 415, 453, 455, 467, 472-73, 479, 482-83, 497, 527, 542-

43, 546-47, 552, 638, 697-98, 701, 718, 742, 779, 822, 865-66, 870, 875, 877-78, 880, 882-83, 887-89, 906, 923-24

Apocrypha (Old Testament) 33, 48-49, 82, 86, 105, 109-10, 270, 637, 800, 854

Apocryphon of John 685

Apollos 332, 489, 564, 718, 739, 766, 787-88

apostates, Christian 504-5, 507, 780-81, 793-95, 802-6, 902-5

apostates, Jewish 44, 46-47, 103-4, 479, 490, 501-2

appearances 83, 149, 179, 184, 224-25, 291, 293-94, 311, 315, 405, 427, 460, 584, 586, 588-89, 594, 671, 865

Apuleius 558, 693

Aquila 61, 332, 489, 556, 560, 562, 599-600, 603, 766

Aramaic Testament of Levi (4Q213-214) 86

Aramaic 48, 161, 196, 235, 313, 354, 845

Archelaus 65, 67-68

Aristobulus II 52, 63

Aristotle 97, 108, 126, 130, 132-33, 137, 139, 141-42, 222, 270, 327, 362, 381-83, 385, 427, 508-9, 575, 578, 580, 654, 658, 669, 672, 687, 709, 749, 782-85, 836, 861, 880-81, 907

Artemis, cult of 93-94, 365, 642, 691, 714-16, 895, 901

artisan 40, 209, 437, 529, 556, 558, 563-64, 815, 866

Asia Minor 32, 39, 42, 52, 62, 94, 100, 150, 176, 236, 309, 365, 401, 403, 454, 579, 643-44, 668, 681, 691, 714, 717, 721, 843, 845, 847, 885, 889, 894, 898, 900-901,

916, 923, 931

Assyria 38, 100, 250

Athanasius' Easter Letter 34

Athens 93, 99, 373, 376-77, 488, 529, 733

Augustine 156, 157, 160, 162, 177, 184, 184, 241, 301, 339, 341, 370, 787

Augustus 55, 57-59, 63-66, 69, 76, 109, 127, 275, 329, 335, 344, 368, 379, 528, 545, 640-42, 681, 691, 714-15, 896, 899, 900, 903, 906, 916, 918

autarkeia 97-98

Babylon 39, 45, 78, 89, 100, 203, 211, 248, 253, 546, 681, 845-46, 885, 891, 897, 905, 907, 909, 911-12, 918, 920, 922, 925-26, 928

Babylonian Talmud 381

baptism 95, 153, 164, 167, 174, 185, 207, 257, 291, 306, 345, 428-29, 459, 482, 513, 571, 618, 628-30, 637, 686, 696, 730, 744, 779, 806, 848, 854

Barnabas 35, 299, 327, 331, 358, 364, 366, 368, 376-77, 379, 477, 487-88, 495-96, 498, 511-12, 735, 787-88, 841, 925

Baruch 48, 82, 615, 626

2 Baruch 51, 72, 109, 415, 685, 845, 887, 890, 925

Beloved Disciple 392-94, 401, 403-4, 406-9, 417, 432, 453-54

bios. See Gospels, genre of

birkhat ha-minim 80, 81, 239, 403, 903

blessing 50-52, 54, 75, 80, 87, 114, 133, 170, 205, 217, 257, 268, 334, 363, 387, 500, 503, 513-14, 516-17, 529, 611, 614, 618, 623, 744, 794, 855, 904, 926

Index of Ancient Texts

Scripture Index

James
1, *822, 823*
1:1, *814, 817, 819, 821,*
833, 834
1:1-27, *819*
1:2-3, *823*
1:2-4, *819, 823, 824, 835*
1:2-8, *839*
1:2-21, *819*
1:3, *824*
1:4, *817*
1:5, *817, 833*
1:6, *824*
1:8, *829, 835*
1:9, *819, 830*
1:9-11, *819, 824, 827,*
830, 835
1:10, *819*
1:10-11, *824*
1:12, *825, 836*
1:12-15, *823, 825*
1:13, *821*
1:13-14, *824*
1:13-15, *835*
1:14, *824, 829, 835*
1:14-15, *98, 520, 835*
1:15, *825*
1:17, *833*
1:18, *825, 826, 829, 833*
1:19, *816, 819, 820, 821,*
828
1:21, *814, 820, 829, 834*
1:22, *817, 823*
1:22-25, *819, 822, 826,*
839
1:22-27, *826*
1:25, *823*
1:26, *820, 828, 837*
1:26-27, *820*
1:27, *291, 820, 829, 835,*
836
2, *815, 819, 827, 840*
2:1, *817, 834, 837*
2:1-13, *819, 820, 825, 839*
2:1-26, *819, 820*
2:1—3:13, *815*
2:2, *818, 819*
2:2-3, *827*
2:2-4, *826*
2:4, *827*
2:5, *817, 827*
2:6, *818, 821, 827*
2:6-7, *818, 830*
2:8, *826, 839*
2:8-9, *827*
2:8-11, *822, 827*
2:11, *826*
2:12, *826*

2:12-13, *826, 829, 836*
2:13, *817*
2:14, *817, 828*
2:14-16, *827, 839*
2:14-26, *815, 820, 821,*
823, 826, 827, 837, 839
2:15-16, *828*
2:19, *828, 835*
2:22, *823*
2:24, *823*
2:26—3:9, *818*
3:1, *814, 818, 828, 836*
3:1-12, *815, 819, 826, 840*
3:1-13, *819*
3:1—4:10, *820*
3:3-5, *828*
3:6, *821, 835*
3:9, *820, 834*
3:9-12, *821, 828*
3:10-12, *828, 835*
3:12, *817*
3:13, *826, 834*
3:13-14, *829*
3:13—4:4, *822*
3:13—4:6, *839*
3:13—4:12, *826*
3:14-15, *835*
3:15, *835*
3:15-16, *829*
3:17-18, *829, 834*
3:18, *836*
4:1, *829, 835*
4:1-4, *829*
4:1-10, *819*
4:2-3, *830*
4:3, *590, 829, 835*
4:4, *817, 829, 834*
4:6, *816, 819, 821, 830*
4:6-10, *830*
4:7, *834, 835*
4:8, *829, 834, 835*
4:10, *817, 830, 834*
4:11-12, *817, 820, 826,*
828, 830
4:12, *836*
4:13-14, *821, 836*
4:13-15, *820*
4:13-17, *826*
4:14, *830*
4:15, *834*
4:16—5:6, *819*
5:1, *819, 836*
5:1-3, *839*
5:1-6, *822, 826, 827, 830*
5:2-3, *817, 830*
5:3, *836*
5:4, *816, 826, 830, 836*
5:5, *830, 836, 839*

5:6, *819, 830*
5:7-8, *822, 836*
5:7-11, *819, 830*
5:9, *817, 830, 836*
5:10, *833*
5:11, *833*
5:12, *817, 821, 828, 836*
5:13-18, *442*
5:13-20, *830*
5:14, *818, 819*
5:14-16, *830*
5:15, *833*
5:16, *839*
5:17-18, *833*
5:19-20, *296, 835, 840*
5:20, *816, 821, 829*

1 Peter
1:1, *818, 846, 847, 848,*
853
1:1-2, *848*
1:2, *229*
1:3, *849*
1:3-5, *843, 844*
1:4, *848, 849*
1:5, *849, 853*
1:6-7, *544, 824, 843, 844,*
850, 851
1:9, *849*
1:9-12, *843*
1:10-12, *844*
1:11, *852*
1:13, *853*
1:13-16, *229, 862*
1:13—2:10, *843*
1:14, *843, 844, 849, 850*
1:17, *845*
1:17-19, *844*
1:18, *843, 849, 862*
1:21, *852*
1:22, *856*
1:23, *844*
1:23-24, *856*
1:23-25, *849*
2:1, *857*
2:1-2, *861*
2:1-3, *861*
2:1-10, *806*
2:4, *850*
2:4-5, *849, 850*
2:4-8, *845, 852*
2:4-10, *844, 849*
2:6, *850*
2:6-8, *850*
2:7, *850*
2:8, *850*
2:9-11, *229*
2:11, *98, 853*

2:11-12, *843, 853*
2:11-17, *681, 861*
2:11-20, *844*
2:12, *843, 855*
2:12-17, *855*
2:13-17, *69, 853*
2:15, *843, 852*
2:15-17, *136*
2:18-20, *843*
2:18-21, *843*
2:18-25, *855, 856, 859*
2:18—3:7, *143, 720*
2:19-20, *850*
2:21-24, *845*
2:21-25, *844, 852*
2:23, *853*
3:1-6, *855, 856*
3:1-16, *844*
3:7, *858*
3:8, *856*
3:9, *855*
3:9-12, *855*
3:12, *852*
3:13—4:6, *843*
3:16, *843, 855*
3:17, *97*
3:18, *854, 855*
3:18-22, *844, 854*
3:18—4:2, *852*
3:19, *854, 855*
3:19-22, *854*
3:21-22, *720*
4:1-2, *860*
4:1-3, *98, 852*
4:1-4, *843, 844*
4:1-6, *844*
4:3-4, *849, 862*
4:4, *843, 852*
4:4-5, *852*
4:5, *852*
4:7, *853*
4:8, *857*
4:8-11, *856*
4:9, *857*
4:11, *863*
4:12-19, *105, 843, 844*
4:13, *852*
4:14, *843, 851*
4:14-16, *97, 107*
4:17-19, *844, 853*
4:18, *853*
5:1-4, *818, 862*
5:2-4, *845*
5:4, *863*
5:5-6, *856*
5:7, *852*
5:8-9, *843, 853, 854*
5:8-10, *844*